The Sporting News
PRO FOOTBALL REGISTER

2002 EDITION

Editors/Pro Football Register
JEFF PAUR
DAVID WALTON

CONTENTS

Veteran players 3
This section includes all veteran NFL players who appeared in at least one NFL game during the 2000 season and many who have previous game experience in the NFL, USFL, NFL Europe or CFL and were listed on an NFL roster as of June 8, 2002.

2002 draft picks 431
This section lists college statistics for all players selected in the 2002 NFL draft.

Head coaches 480

EXPLANATION OF ABBREVIATIONS AND TERMS

LEAGUES: AFL: American Football League. **Ar.FL., Arena Football:** Arena Football League. **CFL:** Canadian Football League. **CoFL:** Continental Football League. **NFL:** National Football League. **NFLE:** NFL Europe League. **USFL:** United States Football League. **WFL:** World Football League. **W.L.:** World League. **WLAF:** World League of American Football.

TEAMS: Birm.: Birmingham. **Jack., Jax.:** Jacksonville. **L.A. Raiders:** Los Angeles Raiders. **L.A. Rams:** Los Angeles Rams. **New Eng.:** New England. **N.Y. Giants:** New York Giants. **N.Y. Jets:** New York Jets. **N.Y./N.J.:** New York/New Jersey. **San Ant.:** San Antonio. **San Fran.:** San Francisco. **Sask.:** Saskatchewan. **StL.:** St. Louis.

STATISTICS: Att.: Attempts. **Avg.:** Average. **Blk.:** Blocked punts. **Cmp.:** Completions. **FGA:** Field goals attempted. **FGM:** Field goals made. **50+:** Field goals of 50 yards or longer. **F., Fum.:** Fumbles. **G:** Games. **In. 20:** Punts inside 20-yard line. **Int.:** Interceptions. **Lg.:** Longest made field goal. **L:** Lost. **Net avg.:** Net punting average. **No.:** Number. **Rat.:** Passer rating. **Pct.:** Percentage. **Pts.:** Points scored. **T:** Tied. **TD:** Touchdowns. **2-pt.:** Two-point conversions. **W:** Won. **XPA:** Extra points attempted. **XPM:** Extra points made. **Yds.:** Yards.

POSITIONS: C: Center. **CB:** Cornerback. **DB:** Defensive back. **DE:** Defensive end. **DT:** Defensive tackle. **FB:** Fullback. **G:** Guard. **K:** Kicker. **LB:** Linebacker. **OL:** Offensive lineman. **OT:** Offensive tackle. **P:** Punter. **QB:** Quarterback. **RB:** Running back. **S:** Safety. **TE:** Tight end. **WR:** Wide receiver.

SINGLE GAME HIGHS (regular season): If a player reached a single game high on numerous occasions—had one rushing touchdown in a game, for example—the most recent occurrence is listed.

EXPLANATION OF AWARDS

AWARDS: Butkus Award: Nation's top college linebacker. **Chuck Bednarik Award:** Nation's top defensive player. **Davey O'Brien Award:** Nation's top college quarterback. **Doak Walker Award:** Nation's top college junior or senior running back. **Fred Biletnikoff Award:** Nation's top college wide receiver. **Harlon Hill Trophy:** Nation's top college Division II player. **Heisman Trophy:** Nation's top college player. **Jim Thorpe Award:** Nation's top college defensive back. **Lombardi Award:** Nation's top college lineman. **Lou Groza Award:** Nation's top college kicker. **Maxwell Award:** Nation's top college player. **Outland Trophy:** Nation's top college interior lineman. **Walter Payton Award:** Nation's top college Division I-AA player.

ON THE COVER: Kurt Warner. (Large photo by Albert Dickson/THE SPORTING NEWS; small photo by Robert Seale/THE SPORTING NEWS.)

NFL statistics compiled by STATS, Inc., a News Corporation company; 8130 Lehigh Avenue, Morton Grove, IL 60053. STATS is a trademark of Sports Team Analysis and Tracking Systems, Inc.

Copyright © 2002 by The Sporting News, a division of Vulcan Sports Media; 10176 Corporate Square Dr., Suite 200, St. Louis, MO 63132. All rights reserved. Printed in the U.S.A.

No part of the Pro Football Register may be reproduced or transmitted in any form or by any means, electronic or mechanical, including photocopy, recording or any information storage and retrieval system now known or to be invented, without permission in writing from the publisher, except by a reviewer who wishes to quote brief passages in connection with a review written for inclusion in a magazine, newspaper or broadcast.

ISBN: 0-89204-673-2   10 9 8 7 6 5 4 3 2 1

VETERAN PLAYERS

Please note for statistical comparisons: In 1982, only nine of 16 games were played due to the cancellation of games because of a player's strike. In 1987, only 15 of 16 games were played due to the cancellation of games in the third week because of a player's strike. Most NFL players also missed games scheduled in the fourth, fifth and sixth weeks.
Sacks became an official NFL statistic in 1982.
Two-point conversions became an official NFL statistic in 1994.

- * Indicates league leader.
- ‡ Indicates NFC leader.
- ∞ Indicates tied for NFC lead.
- † Indicates tied for league lead.
- § Indicates AFC leader.
- ▲ Indicates tied for AFC lead.
- ... Statistics unavailable, unofficial, or mathematically impossible to calculate.

ABDULLAH, RABIH — RB — BEARS

PERSONAL: Born April 27, 1975, in Martinsville, Va. ... 6-0/227. ... Full name: Rabih Fard Abdullah. ... Name pronounced RAH-bee ab-DUE-lah.
HIGH SCHOOL: Barham Clark (Roselle, N.J.).
COLLEGE: Lehigh.
TRANSACTIONS/CAREER NOTES: Signed as non-drafted free agent by Tampa Bay Buccaneers (April 20, 1998). ... Inactive for all 16 games (1998). ... On injured reserve with thumb injury (December 28, 1999-remainder of season). ... Granted free agency (March 2, 2001). ... Re-signed by Buccaneers (March 2, 2001). ... Granted unconditional free agency (March 1, 2002). ... Signed by Chicago Bears (March 6, 2002).
PRO STATISTICS: 2000—Returned one kickoff for 16 yards. 2001—Returned five kickoffs for 92 yards and recovered one fumble.
SINGLE GAME HIGHS (regular season): Attempts—10 (December 3, 2000, vs. Dallas); yards—38 (December 3, 2000, vs. Dallas); and rushing touchdowns—0.

			RUSHING				RECEIVING				TOTALS		
Year Team	G	GS	Att.	Yds.	Avg.	TD	No.	Yds.	Avg.	TD	TD	2pt.	Pts.	Fum.
1999—Tampa Bay NFL	15	1	5	12	2.4	0	2	11	5.5	0	0	0	0	0
2000—Tampa Bay NFL	12	0	16	70	4.4	0	2	14	7.0	0	0	0	0	0
2001—Tampa Bay NFL	16	0	11	40	3.6	0	2	26	13.0	0	0	0	0	0
Pro totals (3 years)	43	1	32	122	3.8	0	6	51	8.5	0	0	0	0	0

ABRAHAM, DONNIE — CB — JETS

PERSONAL: Born October 8, 1973, in Orangeburg, S.C. ... 5-10/192. ... Full name: Nathaniel Donnell Abraham.
HIGH SCHOOL: Orangeburg-Wilkinson (Orangeburg, S.C.).
COLLEGE: East Tennessee State (degree in business management, 1995).
TRANSACTIONS/CAREER NOTES: Selected by Tampa Bay Buccaneers in third round (71st pick overall) of 1996 NFL draft. ... Signed by Buccaneers (July 13, 1996). ... Released by Buccaneers (March 14, 2002). ... Signed by New York Jets (April 22, 2002).
CHAMPIONSHIP GAME EXPERIENCE: Played in NFC championship game (1999 season).
HONORS: Played in Pro Bowl (2000 season).
PRO STATISTICS: 1996—Recovered two fumbles for three yards. 1997—Recovered one fumble for two yards. 1998—Recovered two fumbles. 1999—Credited with two sacks. 2000—Returned blocked field goal for 53 yards and a touchdown. 2001—Recovered one fumble.
MISCELLANEOUS: Holds Tampa Bay Buccaneers all-time record for most interceptions (31).

			INTERCEPTIONS			
Year Team	G	GS	No.	Yds.	Avg.	TD
1996—Tampa Bay NFL	16	12	5	27	5.4	0
1997—Tampa Bay NFL	16	16	5	16	3.2	0
1998—Tampa Bay NFL	13	13	1	3	3.0	0
1999—Tampa Bay NFL	16	16	†7	115	16.4	†2
2000—Tampa Bay NFL	16	16	7	82	11.7	0
2001—Tampa Bay NFL	15	5	6	98	16.3	0
Pro totals (6 years)	92	78	31	341	11.0	2

ABRAHAM, JOHN — LB — JETS

PERSONAL: Born May 6, 1978, in Timmonsville, S.C. ... 6-4/256.
HIGH SCHOOL: Lamar (Timmonsville, S.C.).
COLLEGE: South Carolina.
TRANSACTIONS/CAREER NOTES: Selected by New York Jets in first round (13th pick overall) of 2000 NFL draft. ... Signed by Jets (July 10, 2000). ... On injured reserve with hernia (November 17, 2000-remainder of season).
HONORS: Named defensive end on THE SPORTING NEWS NFL All-Pro team (2001).
PRO STATISTICS: 2001—Recovered three fumbles for seven yards and one touchdown.

Year Team	G	GS	SACKS
2000—New York Jets NFL	6	0	4.5
2001—New York Jets NFL	16	15	13.0
Pro totals (2 years)	22	15	17.5

ACKERMAN, TOM — G — RAIDERS

PERSONAL: Born September 6, 1972, in Bellingham, Wash. ... 6-3/296. ... Full name: Thomas Michael Ackerman.
HIGH SCHOOL: Nooksack (Wash.) Valley.
COLLEGE: Eastern Washington.
TRANSACTIONS/CAREER NOTES: Selected by New Orleans Saints in fifth round (145th pick overall) of 1996 NFL draft. ... Signed by Saints (July 14, 1996). ... Granted free agency (February 12, 1999). ... Re-signed by Saints (April 14, 1999). ... Granted unconditional free agency

(February 11, 2000). ... Re-signed by Saints (February 15, 2000). ... Released by Saints (March 12, 2002). ... Signed by Oakland Raiders (May 22, 2002).
PLAYING EXPERIENCE: New Orleans NFL, 1996-2001. ... Games/Games started: 1996 (2/0), 1997 (14/0), 1998 (15/10), 1999 (16/8), 2000 (15/0), 2001 (16/0). Total: 78/18.
PRO STATISTICS: 2001—Returned two kickoffs for 11 yards and fumbled once.

ADAMS, FLOZELL — OT — COWBOYS

PERSONAL: Born May 18, 1975, in Chicago. ... 6-7/335. ... Full name: Flozell Jootin Adams. ... Cousin of Hersey Hawkins, guard, with five NBA teams (1988-89 through 2000-01).
HIGH SCHOOL: Proviso West (Hillside, Ill.).
COLLEGE: Michigan State.
TRANSACTIONS/CAREER NOTES: Selected by Dallas Cowboys in second round (38th pick overall) of 1998 NFL draft. ... Signed by Cowboys (July 17, 1998). ... Granted free agency (March 1, 2002).
PLAYING EXPERIENCE: Dallas NFL, 1998-2001. ... Games/Games started: 1998 (16/12), 1999 (16/16), 2000 (16/16), 2001 (16/16). Total: 64/60.
HONORS: Named offensive tackle on THE SPORTING NEWS college All-America third team (1997).
PRO STATISTICS: 1998—Recovered one fumble. 1999—Recovered one fumble. 2001—Recovered one fumble.

ADAMS, KEITH — LB — COWBOYS

PERSONAL: Born November 22, 1979, in College Park, Ga. ... 5-11/223.
HIGH SCHOOL: Westlake (Atlanta).
COLLEGE: Clemson.
TRANSACTIONS/CAREER NOTES: Selected after junior season by Tennessee Titans in seventh round (232nd pick overall) of 2001 NFL draft. ... Signed by Titans (July 13, 2001). ... Released by Titans (August 31, 2001). ... Signed by Dallas Cowboys to practice squad (November 8, 2001). ... Activated (November 21, 2001).
HONORS: Named linebacker on THE SPORTING NEWS college All-America third team (1999). ... Named linebacker on THE SPORTING NEWS college All-America first team (2000).

Year Team	G	GS	SACKS
2001—Dallas NFL	4	0	0.0

ADAMS, SAM — DT

PERSONAL: Born June 13, 1973, in Houston. ... 6-3/330. ... Full name: Sam Aaron Adams. ... Son of Sam Adams Sr., guard with New England Patriots (1972-80) and New Orleans Saints (1981).
HIGH SCHOOL: Cypress Creek (Houston).
COLLEGE: Texas A&M.
TRANSACTIONS/CAREER NOTES: Selected after junior season by Seattle Seahawks in first round (eighth pick overall) of 1994 NFL draft. ... Signed by Seahawks (July 30, 1994). ... Granted unconditional free agency (February 11, 2000). ... Signed by Baltimore Ravens (April 17, 2000). ... Released by Ravens (March 1, 2002).
CHAMPIONSHIP GAME EXPERIENCE: Played in AFC championship game (2000 season). ... Member of Super Bowl championship team (2000 season).
HONORS: Named defensive lineman on THE SPORTING NEWS college All-America first team (1993). ... Played in Pro Bowl (2000 season).
PRO STATISTICS: 1996—Recovered one fumble for two yards. 1998—Intercepted one pass for 25 yards and a touchdown and recovered one fumble. 1999—Recovered one fumble. 2000—Recovered one fumble.

Year Team	G	GS	SACKS
1994—Seattle NFL	12	7	4.0
1995—Seattle NFL	16	5	3.5
1996—Seattle NFL	16	15	5.5
1997—Seattle NFL	16	16	7.0
1998—Seattle NFL	16	11	2.0
1999—Seattle NFL	13	13	1.0
2000—Baltimore NFL	16	16	2.0
2001—Baltimore NFL	14	14	2.0
Pro totals (8 years)	119	97	27.0

AHANOTU, CHIDI — DE

PERSONAL: Born October 11, 1970, in Modesto, Calif. ... 6-2/285. ... Full name: Chidi Obioma Ahanotu. ... Name pronounced CHEE-dee a-HA-noe-too.
HIGH SCHOOL: Berkeley (Calif.).
COLLEGE: California (degree in physical education).
TRANSACTIONS/CAREER NOTES: Selected by Tampa Bay Buccaneers in sixth round (145th pick overall) of 1993 NFL draft. ... Signed by Buccaneers (July 9, 1993). ... Granted free agency (February 16, 1996). ... Re-signed by Buccaneers (February 20, 1996). ... On injured reserve with shoulder injury (October 27, 1998-remainder of season). ... Designated by Buccaneers as franchise player (February 12, 1999). ... Re-signed by Buccaneers (July 30, 1999). ... Released by Buccaneers (April 20, 2001). ... Signed by St. Louis Rams (August 20, 2001). ... Granted unconditional free agency (March 1, 2002).
CHAMPIONSHIP GAME EXPERIENCE: Played in NFC championship game (1999 and 2001 seasons). ... Played in Super Bowl XXXVI (2001 season).
PRO STATISTICS: 1996—Recovered one fumble. 1997—Recovered two fumbles. 2000—Recovered one fumble. 2001—Recovered one fumble.

Year Team	G	GS	SACKS
1993—Tampa Bay NFL	16	10	1.5
1994—Tampa Bay NFL	16	16	1.0
1995—Tampa Bay NFL	16	15	3.0
1996—Tampa Bay NFL	13	13	5.5
1997—Tampa Bay NFL	16	15	10.0
1998—Tampa Bay NFL	4	4	0.0
1999—Tampa Bay NFL	16	15	6.5
2000—Tampa Bay NFL	16	16	3.5
2001—St. Louis NFL	16	16	2.0
Pro totals (9 years)	**129**	**120**	**33.0**

AKBAR, HAKIM — S — TEXANS

PERSONAL: Born August 11, 1980, in Riverside, Calif. ... 6-0/212.
HIGH SCHOOL: Polytechnic (Riverside, Calif.).
COLLEGE: Washington.
TRANSACTIONS/CAREER NOTES: Selected after junior season by New England Patriots in fifth round (163rd pick overall) of 2001 NFL draft. ... Signed by Patriots (June 15, 2001). ... On non-football injury list with multiple injuries (November 16, 2001-remainder of season). ... Claimed on waivers by Houston Texans (March 26, 2002).
PLAYING EXPERIENCE: New England NFL, 2001. ... Games/Games started: 2001 (6/0).

AKERS, DAVID — K — EAGLES

PERSONAL: Born December 9, 1974, in Lexington, Ky. ... 5-10/200. ... Full name: David Roy Akers. ... Name pronounced A-kers.
HIGH SCHOOL: Tates Creek (Lexington, Ky.).
COLLEGE: Louisville.
TRANSACTIONS/CAREER NOTES: Signed as non-drafted free agent by Carolina Panthers (April 19, 1997). ... Released by Panthers (August 17, 1997). ... Signed by Atlanta Falcons (April 28, 1998). ... Released by Falcons (July 7, 1998). ... Re-signed by Falcons (July 21, 1998). ... Released by Falcons (August 24, 1998). ... Signed by Washington Redskins to practice squad (September 1, 1998). ... Activated (September 15, 1998). ... Released by Redskins (September 22, 1998). ... Signed by Philadelphia Eagles (January 11, 1999). ... Assigned by Eagles to Berlin Thunder in 1999 NFL Europe enhancement allocation program (February 22, 1999).
CHAMPIONSHIP GAME EXPERIENCE: Played in NFC championship game (2001 season).
HONORS: Named kicker on THE SPORTING NEWS NFL All-Pro team (2001).
PRO STATISTICS: 2000—Rushed once for 15 yards.

					KICKING			
Year Team	G	XPM	XPA	FGM	FGA	Lg.	50+	Pts.
1998—Washington NFL	1	2	2	0	2	0	0-0	2
1999—Berlin NFLE	...	3	3	10	15	0	2-5	33
—Philadelphia NFL	16	2	2	3	6	∞53	1-3	11
2000—Philadelphia NFL	16	34	36	29	33	51	1-1	121
2001—Philadelphia NFL	16	37	38	26	31	50	2-3	115
NFL Europe totals (1 year)	...	3	3	10	15	0	2-5	33
NFL totals (4 years)	49	75	78	58	72	53	4-7	249
Pro totals (5 years)	...	78	81	68	87	53	6-0	282

AKINS, CHRIS — DB — BROWNS

PERSONAL: Born November 29, 1976, in Little Rock, Ark. ... 5-11/195. ... Full name: Christopher Drew Akins. ... Second cousin of Jackie Harris, tight end with four NFL teams (1990-2001). ... Name pronounced A-kenz.
HIGH SCHOOL: Little Rock (Ark.) Hall.
COLLEGE: Arkansas, then Arkansas-Pine Bluff.
TRANSACTIONS/CAREER NOTES: Selected by Green Bay Packers in seventh round (212th pick overall) of 1999 NFL draft. ... Signed by Packers (June 1, 1999). ... Released by Packers (September 5, 1999). ... Re-signed by Packers to practice squad (September 14, 1999). ... Signed by Dallas Cowboys off Packers practice squad (October 27, 1999). ... Assigned by Cowboys to Rhein Fire in 2000 NFL Europe enhancement allocation program (February 18, 2000). ... Claimed on waivers by Packers (November 2, 2000). ... Claimed on waivers by Cleveland Browns (December 11, 2001). ... Granted free agency (March 1, 2002).
PLAYING EXPERIENCE: Dallas NFL, 1999; Rhein NFLE, 2000; Dallas (8)-Green Bay (2) NFL, 2000; Green Bay (11)-Cleveland (4) NFL, 2001. ... Games/Games started: 1999 (9/0), NFLE 2000 (games played unavailable), 2000 (Dal.-8; G.B.-2; Total: 10/0), 2001 (G.B.-11/0; Cleve.-4/0; Total: 15/0). Total NFL: 34/0.
PRO STATISTICS: NFLE: 2000—Intercepted one pass for 13 yards. 2001—Returned one kickoff for no yards and fumbled once.

ALBRIGHT, ETHAN — OL — REDSKINS

PERSONAL: Born May 1, 1971, in Greensboro, N.C. ... 6-5/268. ... Full name: Lawrence Ethan Albright.
HIGH SCHOOL: Grimsley (Greensboro, N.C.).
COLLEGE: North Carolina.
TRANSACTIONS/CAREER NOTES: Signed as non-drafted free agent by Miami Dolphins (April 28, 1994). ... Released by Dolphins (August 22, 1994). ... Re-signed by Dolphins to practice squad (August 29, 1994). ... Released by Dolphins (September 14, 1994). ... Re-signed by Dolphins to practice squad (September 28, 1994). ... Released by Dolphins (November 2, 1994). ... Re-signed by Dolphins (February 16, 1995). ... On injured reserve with knee injury (November 15, 1995-remainder of season). ... Released by Dolphins (August 20, 1996). ... Signed by Buffalo Bills (August 26, 1996). ... Granted free agency (February 13, 1998). ... Re-signed by Bills (April 15, 1998). ... Granted unconditional free agency (February 12, 1999). ... Re-signed by Bills (April 1, 1999). ... Released by Bills (March 1, 2001). ... Signed by Washington Redskins (March 9, 2001).
PLAYING EXPERIENCE: Miami NFL, 1995; Buffalo NFL, 1996-2000; Washington NFL, 2001. ... Games/Games started: 1995 (10/0), 1996 (16/0), 1997 (16/0), 1998 (16/0), 1999 (16/0), 2000 (16/0), 2001 (16/0). Total: 106/0.
PRO STATISTICS: 1998—Recovered one fumble. 1999—Fumbled once for minus eight yards. 2000—Recovered one fumble for 19 yards.

ALDRIDGE, ALLEN — LB — TEXANS

PERSONAL: Born May 30, 1972, in Houston. ... 6-1/254. ... Full name: Allen Ray Aldridge. ... Son of Allen Aldridge, defensive end with Houston Oilers (1971-72) and Cleveland Browns (1974).
HIGH SCHOOL: Willowridge (Sugar Land, Texas).
COLLEGE: Houston.
TRANSACTIONS/CAREER NOTES: Selected by Denver Broncos in second round (51st pick overall) of 1994 NFL draft. ... Signed by Broncos (July 12, 1994). ... Granted free agency (February 14, 1997). ... Re-signed by Broncos (April 15, 1997). ... Granted unconditional free agency (February 13, 1998). ... Signed by Detroit Lions (February 14, 1998). ... Granted unconditional free agency (March 1, 2002). ... Signed by Houston Texans (May 9, 2002).
CHAMPIONSHIP GAME EXPERIENCE: Played in AFC championship game (1997 season). ... Member of Super Bowl championship team (1997 season).
PRO STATISTICS: 1995—Recovered one fumble. 1998—Recovered one fumble. 1999—Fumbled once and recovered one fumble for eight yards and a touchdown. 2000—Intercepted one pass for four yards and recovered one fumble.

Year Team	G	GS	SACKS
1994—Denver NFL	16	2	0.0
1995—Denver NFL	16	12	1.5
1996—Denver NFL	16	16	0.0
1997—Denver NFL	16	15	0.0
1998—Detroit NFL	16	15	3.0
1999—Detroit NFL	16	14	3.0
2000—Detroit NFL	16	14	2.0
2001—Detroit NFL	16	16	1.0
Pro totals (8 years)	128	104	10.5

ALEXANDER, BRENT — S — STEELERS

PERSONAL: Born July 10, 1971, in Detroit. ... 5-11/200. ... Full name: Ronald Brent Alexander.
HIGH SCHOOL: Gallatin (Tenn.).
COLLEGE: Tennessee State.
TRANSACTIONS/CAREER NOTES: Signed as non-drafted free agent by Arizona Cardinals (April 28, 1994). ... Granted unconditional free agency (February 13, 1998). ... Signed by Carolina Panthers (March 20, 1998). ... Released by Panthers (April 18, 2000). ... Signed by Pittsburgh Steelers (May 30, 2000).
CHAMPIONSHIP GAME EXPERIENCE: Played in AFC championship game (2001 season).
PRO STATISTICS: 1995—Credited with 1/2 sack and recovered one fumble. 1998—Recovered one fumble for 12 yards. 2000—Credited with 1 1/2 sacks and recovered one fumble. 2001—Credited with two sacks.

			INTERCEPTIONS			
Year Team	G	GS	No.	Yds.	Avg.	TD
1994—Arizona NFL	16	7	0	0	0.0	0
1995—Arizona NFL	16	13	2	14	7.0	0
1996—Arizona NFL	16	15	2	3	1.5	0
1997—Arizona NFL	16	15	0	0	0.0	0
1998—Carolina NFL	16	16	0	0	0.0	0
1999—Carolina NFL	16	16	2	18	9.0	0
2000—Pittsburgh NFL	16	16	3	31	10.3	0
2001—Pittsburgh NFL	16	16	4	39	9.8	0
Pro totals (8 years)	128	114	13	105	8.1	0

ALEXANDER, DAN — RB/FB — TITANS

PERSONAL: Born March 17, 1978, in Wentzville, Mo. ... 6-0/252.
HIGH SCHOOL: Wentzville (Mo.).
COLLEGE: Nebraska.
TRANSACTIONS/CAREER NOTES: Selected by Tennessee Titans in sixth round (192nd pick overall) of 2001 NFL draft. ... Signed by Titans (July 10, 2001). ... Released by Titans (September 6, 2001). ... Re-signed by Titans to practice squad (September 8, 2001). ... Activated (November 21, 2001).
PLAYING EXPERIENCE: Tennessee NFL, 2001. ... Games/Games started: 2001 (7/0).

ALEXANDER, DERRICK — WR

PERSONAL: Born November 6, 1971, in Detroit. ... 6-2/206. ... Full name: Derrick Scott Alexander.
HIGH SCHOOL: Benedictine (Detroit).
COLLEGE: Michigan (degree in sports management).
TRANSACTIONS/CAREER NOTES: Selected by Cleveland Browns in first round (29th pick overall) of 1994 NFL draft. ... Signed by Browns (August 3, 1994). ... Browns franchise moved to Baltimore and renamed Ravens for 1996 season (March 11, 1996). ... Granted unconditional free agency (February 13, 1998). ... Signed by Kansas City Chiefs (March 2, 1998). ... Released by Chiefs (June 3, 2002).
PRO STATISTICS: 1995—Fumbled twice. 1997—Fumbled once.
SINGLE GAME HIGHS (regular season): Receptions—9 (November 5, 2000, vs. Oakland); yards—198 (December 1, 1996, vs. Pittsburgh); and touchdown receptions—2 (November 5, 2000, vs. Oakland).
STATISTICAL PLATEAUS: 100-yard receiving games: 1994 (3), 1996 (3), 1997 (3), 1998 (2), 1999 (4), 2000 (6). Total: 21.
MISCELLANEOUS: Shares Baltimore Ravens all-time records for most touchdowns (18) and touchdown receptions (18).

Year	Team	G	GS	RUSHING Att.	Yds.	Avg.	TD	RECEIVING No.	Yds.	Avg.	TD	PUNT RETURNS No.	Yds.	Avg.	TD	KICKOFF RETURNS No.	Yds.	Avg.	TD	TOTALS TD	2pt.	Pts.
1994	Cleveland NFL	14	12	4	38	9.5	0	48	828	17.3	2	0	0	0.0	0	0	0	0.0	0	2	1	14
1995	Cleveland NFL	14	2	1	29	29.0	0	15	216	14.4	0	9	122	13.6	†1	21	419	20.0	0	1	0	6
1996	Baltimore NFL	15	14	3	0	0.0	0	62	1099	17.7	9	1	15	15.0	0	1	13	13.0	0	9	1	56
1997	Baltimore NFL	15	13	1	0	0.0	0	65	1009	15.5	9	1	34	34.0	0	0	0	0.0	0	9	0	54
1998	Kansas City NFL	15	14	0	0	0.0	0	54	992	18.4	4	0	0	0.0	0	0	0	0.0	0	4	0	24
1999	Kansas City NFL	16	15	2	82	41.0	1	54	832	15.4	2	0	0	0.0	0	0	0	0.0	0	3	0	18
2000	Kansas City NFL	16	16	3	45	15.0	0	78	1391	§17.8	10	0	0	0.0	0	0	0	0.0	0	10	0	60
2001	Kansas City NFL	13	11	2	16	8.0	0	27	470	17.4	3	0	0	0.0	0	0	0	0.0	0	3	0	18
Pro totals (8 years)		118	97	16	210	13.1	1	403	6837	17.0	39	11	171	15.5	1	22	432	19.6	0	41	2	250

ALEXANDER, ELIJAH   LB

PERSONAL: Born August 2, 1970, in Fort Worth, Texas. ... 6-2/235. ... Full name: Elijah Alfred Alexander III.
HIGH SCHOOL: Dunbar Senior (Fort Worth, Texas).
COLLEGE: Kansas State (degree in accounting).
TRANSACTIONS/CAREER NOTES: Selected by Tampa Bay Buccaneers in 10th round (254th pick overall) of 1992 NFL draft. ... Signed by Buccaneers (June 3, 1992). ... Released by Buccaneers (August 31, 1992). ... Re-signed by Buccaneers (September 1, 1992). ... Released by Buccaneers (October 16, 1992). ... Re-signed by Buccaneers to practice squad (October 22, 1992). ... Activated (November 10, 1992). ... Claimed on waivers by Denver Broncos (August 31, 1993). ... On injured reserve with shoulder injury (November 22, 1995-remainder of season). ... Granted unconditional free agency (February 16, 1996). ... Signed by Indianapolis Colts (August 6, 1996). ... Selected by Cleveland Browns from Colts in NFL expansion draft (February 9, 1999). ... Released by Browns (June 1, 1999). ... Signed by Oakland Raiders (March 14, 2000). ... Released by Raiders (March 6, 2002).
CHAMPIONSHIP GAME EXPERIENCE: Played in AFC championship game (2000 season).
PRO STATISTICS: 1994—Recovered one fumble for nine yards. 1998—Recovered two fumbles.

Year	Team	G	GS	INTERCEPTIONS No.	Yds.	Avg.	TD	SACKS No.
1992	Tampa Bay NFL	12	0	0	0	0.0	0	0.0
1993	Denver NFL	16	0	0	0	0.0	0	0.0
1994	Denver NFL	16	16	1	2	2.0	0	1.0
1995	Denver NFL	9	8	2	5	2.5	0	0.5
1996	Indianapolis NFL	14	3	0	0	0.0	0	1.0
1997	Indianapolis NFL	13	11	1	43	43.0	1	1.0
1998	Indianapolis NFL	13	9	1	12	12.0	0	0.0
1999	—					Did not play.		
2000	Oakland NFL	16	16	0	0	0.0	0	2.0
2001	Oakland NFL	14	13	0	0	0.0	0	1.0
Pro totals (9 years)		123	76	5	62	12.4	1	6.5

ALEXANDER, SHAUN   RB   SEAHAWKS

PERSONAL: Born August 30, 1977, in Florence, Ky. ... 5-11/220.
HIGH SCHOOL: Boone County (Ky.).
COLLEGE: Alabama (degree in marketing, 1999).
TRANSACTIONS/CAREER NOTES: Selected by Seattle Seahawks in first round (19th pick overall) of 2000 NFL draft. ... Signed by Seahawks (July 20, 2000).
HONORS: Named running back on THE SPORTING NEWS college All-America second team (1999).
PRO STATISTICS: 2001—Recovered three fumbles for eight yards.
SINGLE GAME HIGHS (regular season): Attempts—35 (November 11, 2001, vs. Oakland); yards—266 (November 11, 2001, vs. Oakland); and rushing touchdowns—3 (November 11, 2001).
STATISTICAL PLATEAUS: 100-yard rushing games: 2001 (4).

Year	Team	G	GS	RUSHING Att.	Yds.	Avg.	TD	RECEIVING No.	Yds.	Avg.	TD	TOTALS TD	2pt.	Pts.	Fum.
2000	Seattle NFL	16	1	64	313	4.9	2	5	41	8.2	0	2	0	12	2
2001	Seattle NFL	16	12	309	1318	4.3	*14	44	343	7.8	2	§16	0	96	4
Pro totals (2 years)		32	13	373	1631	4.4	16	49	384	7.8	2	18	0	108	6

ALEXANDER, STEPHEN   TE   CHARGERS

PERSONAL: Born November 7, 1975, in Chickasha, Okla. ... 6-4/246.
HIGH SCHOOL: Chickasha (Okla.).
COLLEGE: Oklahoma.
TRANSACTIONS/CAREER NOTES: Selected by Washington Redskins in second round (48th pick overall) of 1998 NFL draft. ... Signed by Redskins (July 13, 1998). ... On injured reserve with ankle injury (December 26, 2001-remainder of season). ... Granted unconditional free agency (March 1, 2002). ... Signed by San Diego Chargers (March 21, 2002).
HONORS: Played in Pro Bowl (2000 season).
SINGLE GAME HIGHS (regular season): Receptions—7 (December 13, 1998, vs. Carolina); yards—86 (September 19, 1999, vs. New York Giants); and touchdown receptions—2 (September 19, 1999, vs. New York Giants).

Year	Team	G	GS	RECEIVING No.	Yds.	Avg.	TD	TOTALS TD	2pt.	Pts.	Fum.
1998	Washington NFL	15	5	37	383	10.4	4	4	0	24	2
1999	Washington NFL	15	15	29	324	11.2	3	3	0	18	0
2000	Washington NFL	16	16	47	510	10.9	2	2	0	12	2
2001	Washington NFL	7	5	9	85	9.4	0	0	0	0	0
Pro totals (4 years)		53	41	122	1302	10.7	9	9	0	54	4

ALFORD, DARNELL   OT   CHIEFS

PERSONAL: Born June 11, 1977, in Fredricksburg, Va. ... 6-4/328. ... Full name: Darnell LaShawn Alford.
HIGH SCHOOL: Chancellor (Fredricksburg, Va.).
COLLEGE: Boston College.
TRANSACTIONS/CAREER NOTES: Selected by Kansas City Chiefs in sixth round (188th pick overall) of 2000 NFL draft. ... Signed by Chiefs (July 20, 2000).
PLAYING EXPERIENCE: Kansas City NFL, 2000 and 2001. ... Games/Games started: 2000 (1/0), 2001 (2/0). Total: 3/0.

ALLEN, BRIAN   LB

PERSONAL: Born April 1, 1978, in Lake City, Fla. ... 6-0/232. ... Cousin of Reinard Wilson, defensive end, Cincinnati Bengals.
HIGH SCHOOL: Columbia (Lake City, Fla.).
COLLEGE: Florida State.
TRANSACTIONS/CAREER NOTES: Selected by St. Louis Rams in third round (83rd pick overall) of 2001 NFL draft. ... Signed by Rams (June 5, 2001). ... Selected by Houston Texans from Rams in NFL expansion draft (February 18, 2002). ... Released by Texans (May 20, 2002).
PLAYING EXPERIENCE: St. Louis NFL, 2001. ... Games/Games started: 2001 (3/0).
CHAMPIONSHIP GAME EXPERIENCE: Member of Rams for NFC championship game (2001 season); inactive. ... Member of Rams for Super Bowl XXXVI (2001 season); inactive.

ALLEN, ERIC   DB   RAIDERS

PERSONAL: Born November 22, 1965, in San Diego. ... 5-10/185. ... Full name: Eric Andre Allen.
HIGH SCHOOL: Point Loma (San Diego).
COLLEGE: Arizona State (degree in broadcasting, 1988).
TRANSACTIONS/CAREER NOTES: Selected by Philadelphia Eagles in second round (30th pick overall) of 1988 NFL draft. ... Signed by Eagles (July 19, 1988). ... Granted free agency (February 1, 1992). ... Re-signed by Eagles (September 2, 1992). ... Granted roster exemption (September 2-4, 1992). ... Designated by Eagles as transition player (February 25, 1993). ... Tendered offer sheet by New Orleans Saints (March 20, 1995). ... Eagles declined to match offer (March 27, 1995). ... Traded by Saints to Oakland Raiders for fourth-round pick (DB Fred Weary) in 1998 draft (March 5, 1998). ... On injured reserve with knee injury (November 18, 1998-remainder of season).
CHAMPIONSHIP GAME EXPERIENCE: Played in AFC championship game (2000 season).
HONORS: Played in Pro Bowl (1989 and 1991-1995 seasons).
RECORDS: Shares NFL single-season record for most touchdowns by interception—4 (1993). ... Shares NFL single-game record for most touchdowns by interception—2 (December 26, 1993, vs. New Orleans).
PRO STATISTICS: 1989—Fumbled once for seven yards. 1990—Returned one kickoff for two yards and recovered one fumble. 1991—Recovered one fumble. 1992—Recovered two fumbles. 1993—Credited with two sacks. 1994—Recovered one fumble for 30 yards. 1999—Recovered one fumble. 2000—Credited with one sack. 2001—Recovered one fumble for 26 yards and a touchdown.
MISCELLANEOUS: Shares Philadelphia Eagles all-time record for most interceptions (34).

			INTERCEPTIONS			
Year Team	G	GS	No.	Yds.	Avg.	TD
1988—Philadelphia NFL	16	16	5	76	15.2	0
1989—Philadelphia NFL	15	15	‡8	38	4.8	0
1990—Philadelphia NFL	16	15	3	37	12.3	1
1991—Philadelphia NFL	16	16	5	20	4.0	0
1992—Philadelphia NFL	16	16	4	49	12.3	0
1993—Philadelphia NFL	16	16	6	*201	33.5	*4
1994—Philadelphia NFL	16	16	3	61	20.3	0
1995—New Orleans NFL	16	16	2	28	14.0	0
1996—New Orleans NFL	16	16	1	33	33.0	0
1997—New Orleans NFL	16	16	2	27	13.5	0
1998—Oakland NFL	10	10	5	59	11.8	0
1999—Oakland NFL	16	16	3	33	11.0	0
2000—Oakland NFL	16	15	6	145	24.2	*3
2001—Oakland NFL	16	15	1	19	19.0	0
Pro totals (14 years)	217	214	54	826	15.3	8

ALLEN, JAMES   RB   TEXANS

PERSONAL: Born March 28, 1975, in Wynnewood, Okla. ... 5-10/215.
HIGH SCHOOL: Wynnewood (Okla.).
COLLEGE: Oklahoma.
TRANSACTIONS/CAREER NOTES: Signed as non-drafted free agent by Tennessee Oilers (May 14, 1997). ... Released by Oilers (August 20, 1997). ... Signed by Philadelphia Eagles to practice squad (August 27, 1997). ... Released by Eagles (September 2, 1997). ... Re-signed by Eagles to practice squad (September 10, 1997). ... Signed by Chicago Bears off Eagles practice squad (December 9, 1997). ... Inactive for two games (1997). ... Released by Bears (August 25, 1998). ... Re-signed by Bears to practice squad (August 31, 1998). ... Activated (October 13, 1998). ... Granted free agency (March 2, 2001). ... Re-signed by Bears (April 24, 2001). ... Granted unconditional free agency (March 1, 2002). ... Signed by Houston Texans (March 15, 2002).
PRO STATISTICS: 1998—Recovered two fumbles.
SINGLE GAME HIGHS (regular season): Attempts—37 (December 10, 2000, vs. New England); yards—163 (December 20, 1998, vs. Baltimore); and rushing touchdowns—1 (October 14, 2001, vs. Arizona).
STATISTICAL PLATEAUS: 100-yard rushing games: 1998 (1), 2000 (1), 2001 (1). Total: 3.

Year Team	G	GS	Att.	Yds.	Avg.	TD	No.	Yds.	Avg.	TD	TD	2pt.	Pts.	Fum.
1997—Chicago NFL							Did not play.							
1998—Chicago NFL	6	2	58	270	4.7	1	8	77	9.6	1	2	0	12	1
1999—Chicago NFL	12	3	32	119	3.7	0	9	91	10.1	0	0	0	0	0
2000—Chicago NFL	16	15	290	1120	3.9	2	39	291	7.5	1	3	0	18	5
2001—Chicago NFL	16	7	135	469	3.5	1	30	203	6.8	1	2	0	12	1
Pro totals (4 years)	50	27	515	1978	3.8	4	86	662	7.7	3	7	0	42	7

ALLEN, LARRY — G — COWBOYS

PERSONAL: Born November 27, 1971, in Los Angeles. ... 6-3/326. ... Full name: Larry Christopher Allen.
HIGH SCHOOL: Centennial (Compton, Calif.), then Vintage (Napa, Calif.).
JUNIOR COLLEGE: Butte College (Calif.).
COLLEGE: Sonoma State (Calif.).
TRANSACTIONS/CAREER NOTES: Selected by Dallas Cowboys in second round (46th pick overall) of 1994 NFL draft. ... Signed by Cowboys (July 16, 1994).
PLAYING EXPERIENCE: Dallas NFL, 1994-2001. ... Games/Games started: 1994 (16/10), 1995 (16/16), 1996 (16/16), 1997 (16/16), 1998 (16/16), 1999 (11/11), 2000 (16/16), 2001 (16/16). Total: 123/117.
CHAMPIONSHIP GAME EXPERIENCE: Played in NFC championship game (1994 and 1995 seasons). ... Member of Super Bowl championship team (1995 season).
HONORS: Named guard on THE SPORTING NEWS NFL All-Pro team (1995-97 and 1999). ... Played in Pro Bowl (1995-1998 and 2000 seasons). ... Named to play in Pro Bowl (1999 season); replaced by Adam Timmerman due to injury. ... Named offensive tackle on THE SPORTING NEWS NFL All-Pro team (1998). ... Named guard on THE SPORTING NEWS NFL All-Pro team (2000 and 2001).
PRO STATISTICS: 1995—Recovered one fumble. 2000—Recovered two fumbles.

ALLEN, TAJE — CB — CHIEFS

PERSONAL: Born November 6, 1973, in Fairburn, Ga. ... 5-11/185. ... Full name: Taje LaQuane Allen.
HIGH SCHOOL: Estacado (Lubbock, Texas).
COLLEGE: Texas.
TRANSACTIONS/CAREER NOTES: Selected by St. Louis Rams in fifth round (158th pick overall) of 1997 NFL draft. ... Signed by Rams (July 3, 1997). ... Granted free agency (February 11, 2000). ... Re-signed by Rams (June 2, 2000). ... Granted unconditional free agency (March 2, 2001). ... Signed by Kansas City Chiefs (April 17, 2001).
PLAYING EXPERIENCE: St. Louis NFL, 1997-2000; Kansas City NFL, 2001. ... Games/Games started: 1997 (14/1), 1998 (16/0), 1999 (16/2), 2000 (11/1), 2001 (16/0). Total: 73/4.
CHAMPIONSHIP GAME EXPERIENCE: Played in NFC championship game (1999 season). ... Member of Super Bowl championship team (1999 season); did not play.
PRO STATISTICS: 1999—Intercepted two passes for 76 yards and credited with $1/2$ sack.

ALLEN, TERRY — RB

PERSONAL: Born February 21, 1968, in Commerce, Ga. ... 5-10/208. ... Full name: Terry Thomas Allen Jr.
HIGH SCHOOL: Banks County (Homer, Ga.).
COLLEGE: Clemson.
TRANSACTIONS/CAREER NOTES: Selected after junior season by Minnesota Vikings in ninth round (241st pick overall) of 1990 NFL draft. ... Signed by Vikings (July 2, 1990). ... On injured reserve with knee injury (August 28, 1990-entire season). ... On injured reserve with knee injury (August 23, 1993-entire season). ... Released by Vikings (May 8, 1995). ... Signed by Washington Redskins (June 15, 1995). ... Granted free agency (February 16, 1996). ... Re-signed by Redskins (July 17, 1996). ... Granted unconditional free agency (February 14, 1997). ... Re-signed by Redskins (February 26, 1997). ... Released by Redskins (April 19, 1999). ... Signed by New England Patriots (August 27, 1999). ... Released by Patriots (February 14, 2000). ... Signed by New Orleans Saints (November 14, 2000). ... Granted unconditional free agency (March 2, 2001). ... Signed by Baltimore Ravens (August 11, 2001). ... Granted unconditional free agency (March 1, 2002).
HONORS: Played in Pro Bowl (1996 season).
PRO STATISTICS: 1991—Returned one kickoff for 14 yards and recovered one fumble. 1992—Recovered two fumbles. 1994—Recovered two fumbles for four yards. 1995—Recovered one fumble. 1997—Recovered one fumble. 1998—Recovered one fumble. 1999—Recovered one fumble. 2000—Ran six yards with lateral from kickoff return.
SINGLE GAME HIGHS (regular season): Attempts—36 (September 28, 1997, vs. Jacksonville); yards—172 (December 20, 1992, vs. Pittsburgh); and rushing touchdowns—3 (December 22, 1996, vs. Dallas).
STATISTICAL PLATEAUS: 100-yard rushing games: 1991 (1), 1992 (3), 1994 (3), 1995 (4), 1996 (5), 1997 (3), 1999 (2), 2001 (2). Total: 23. ... 100-yard receiving games: 1992 (1).

Year Team	G	GS	Att.	Yds.	Avg.	TD	No.	Yds.	Avg.	TD	TD	2pt.	Pts.	Fum.
1990—Minnesota NFL							Did not play.							
1991—Minnesota NFL	15	6	120	563	‡4.7	2	6	49	8.2	1	3	0	18	4
1992—Minnesota NFL	16	16	266	1201	4.5	13	49	478	9.8	2	15	0	90	9
1993—Minnesota NFL							Did not play.							
1994—Minnesota NFL	16	16	255	1031	4.0	8	17	148	8.7	0	8	1	50	3
1995—Washington NFL	16	16	338	1309	3.9	10	31	232	7.5	1	11	0	66	6
1996—Washington NFL	16	16	347	1353	3.9	*21	32	194	6.1	0	*21	0	126	4
1997—Washington NFL	10	10	210	724	3.4	4	20	172	8.6	1	5	0	30	2
1998—Washington NFL	10	10	148	700	4.7	2	17	128	7.5	0	2	0	12	4
1999—New England NFL	16	13	254	896	3.5	8	14	125	8.9	1	9	0	54	8
2000—New Orleans NFL	4	3	46	179	3.9	2	1	7	7.0	0	2	1	14	0
2001—Baltimore NFL	11	8	168	658	3.9	3	17	68	4.0	0	3	0	18	1
Pro totals (10 years)	130	114	2152	8614	4.0	73	204	1601	7.8	6	79	2	478	41

ALLEN, WILL — CB — GIANTS

PERSONAL: Born August 5, 1978, in Syracuse, N.Y. ... 5-10/192. ... Full name: Will D. Allen.
HIGH SCHOOL: Corcoran (Syracuse, N.Y.).
COLLEGE: Syracuse.
TRANSACTIONS/CAREER NOTES: Selected by New York Giants in first round (22nd pick overall) of 2001 NFL draft. ... Signed by Giants (July 26, 2001).
HONORS: Named cornerback to THE SPORTING NEWS college All-America third team (2000).
PRO STATISTICS: 2001—Recovered one fumble.

				INTERCEPTIONS		
Year Team	G	GS	No.	Yds.	Avg.	TD
2001—New York Giants NFL	13	12	4	27	6.8	0

ALSTOTT, MIKE — FB — BUCCANEERS

PERSONAL: Born December 21, 1973, in Joliet, Ill. ... 6-1/248. ... Full name: Michael Joseph Alstott.
HIGH SCHOOL: Joliet (Ill.) Catholic.
COLLEGE: Purdue (degree in business, 1995).
TRANSACTIONS/CAREER NOTES: Selected by Tampa Bay Buccaneers in second round (35th pick overall) of 1996 NFL draft. ... Signed by Buccaneers (July 21, 1996).
CHAMPIONSHIP GAME EXPERIENCE: Played in NFC championship game (1999 season).
HONORS: Played in Pro Bowl (1997-2000 seasons).
PRO STATISTICS: 1996—Returned one kickoff for 14 yards. 1997—Returned one kickoff for no yards. 1998—Attempted one pass without a completion and returned one kickoff for eight yards. 1999—Returned one kickoff for 19 yards. 2000—Attempted one pass without a completion and recovered one fumble.
SINGLE GAME HIGHS (regular season): Attempts—28 (October 28, 2001, vs. Minnesota); yards—131 (September 26, 1999, vs. Denver); and rushing touchdowns—3 (October 28, 2001, vs. Minnesota).
STATISTICAL PLATEAUS: 100-yard rushing games: 1998 (2), 1999 (2), 2001 (2). Total: 6.
MISCELLANEOUS: Holds Tampa Bay Buccaneers all-time records for most rushing touchdowns (40) and most touchdowns (50).

			RUSHING				RECEIVING				TOTALS		
Year Team	G	GS	Att.	Yds.	Avg.	TD	No.	Yds.	Avg.	TD	TD	2pt.	Pts.	Fum.
1996—Tampa Bay NFL	16	16	96	377	3.9	3	65	557	8.6	3	6	0	36	4
1997—Tampa Bay NFL	15	15	176	665	3.8	7	23	178	7.7	3	10	0	60	5
1998—Tampa Bay NFL	16	16	215	846	3.9	8	22	152	6.9	1	9	0	54	5
1999—Tampa Bay NFL	16	16	242	949	3.9	7	27	239	8.9	2	9	0	54	6
2000—Tampa Bay NFL	13	13	131	465	3.5	5	13	93	7.2	0	5	0	30	3
2001—Tampa Bay NFL	16	16	165	680	4.1	10	35	231	6.6	1	11	†2	70	2
Pro totals (6 years)	92	92	1025	3982	3.9	40	185	1450	7.8	10	50	2	304	25

AMBROSE, ASHLEY — CB — FALCONS

PERSONAL: Born September 17, 1970, in New Orleans. ... 5-10/187. ... Full name: Ashley Avery Ambrose.
HIGH SCHOOL: Alcee Fortier (New Orleans).
COLLEGE: Mississippi Valley State (degree in industrial technology).
TRANSACTIONS/CAREER NOTES: Selected by Indianapolis Colts in second round (29th pick overall) of 1992 NFL draft. ... Signed by Colts (August 11, 1992). ... On injured reserve with leg injury (September 14-October 29, 1992); on practice squad (October 21-29, 1992). ... Granted free agency (February 17, 1995). ... Re-signed by Colts (April 29, 1995). ... Granted unconditional free agency (February 16, 1996). ... Signed by Cincinnati Bengals (February 25, 1996). ... Granted unconditional free agency (February 12, 1999). ... Signed by New Orleans Saints (July 13, 1999). ... Granted unconditional free agency (February 11, 2000). ... Signed by Atlanta Falcons (February 12, 2000).
CHAMPIONSHIP GAME EXPERIENCE: Played in AFC championship game (1995 season).
HONORS: Played in Pro Bowl (1996 season).
PRO STATISTICS: 1992—Returned eight kickoffs for 126 yards. 1994—Recovered one fumble. 1997—Credited with one sack and recovered two fumbles. 1999—Recovered two fumbles for 29 yards. 2001—Recovered two fumbles.

				INTERCEPTIONS		
Year Team	G	GS	No.	Yds.	Avg.	TD
1992—Indianapolis NFL	10	2	0	0	0.0	0
1993—Indianapolis NFL	14	6	0	0	0.0	0
1994—Indianapolis NFL	16	4	2	50	25.0	0
1995—Indianapolis NFL	16	0	3	12	4.0	0
1996—Cincinnati NFL	16	16	8	63	7.9	1
1997—Cincinnati NFL	16	16	3	56	18.7	0
1998—Cincinnati NFL	15	15	2	0	0.0	0
1999—New Orleans NFL	16	16	6	27	4.5	0
2000—Atlanta NFL	16	16	4	‡139	34.8	1
2001—Atlanta NFL	16	16	5	43	8.6	0
Pro totals (10 years)	151	107	33	390	11.8	2

ANDERSEN, MORTEN — K — CHIEFS

PERSONAL: Born August 19, 1960, in Copenhagen, Denmark. ... 6-2/205.
HIGH SCHOOL: Ben Davis (Indianapolis).
COLLEGE: Michigan State (degrees in communications and German).
TRANSACTIONS/CAREER NOTES: Selected by New Orleans Saints in fourth round (86th pick overall) of 1982 NFL draft. ... On injured reserve with sprained ankle (September 15-November 20, 1982). ... Designated by Saints as transition player (February 25, 1993). ... Released by

Saints (July 19, 1995). ... Signed by Atlanta Falcons (July 21, 1995). ... Granted unconditional free agency (March 2, 2001). ... Signed by New York Giants (August 29, 2001). ... Granted unconditional free agency (March 1, 2002). ... Signed by Kansas City Chiefs (March 25, 2002).
CHAMPIONSHIP GAME EXPERIENCE: Played in NFC championship game (1998 season). ... Played in Super Bowl XXXIII (1998 season).
HONORS: Named kicker on THE SPORTING NEWS college All-America first team (1981). ... Named kicker on THE SPORTING NEWS NFL All-Pro team (1985-1987 and 1995). ... Played in Pro Bowl (1985-1988, 1990, 1992 and 1995 seasons).
RECORDS: Holds NFL career records for most consecutive games scoring—286 (December 11, 1983-present); and for most made field goals of 50 or more yards—39. ... Holds NFL single-season record for most made field goals of 50 or more yards—8 (1995). ... Holds NFL single-game record for most made field goals of 50 or more yards—3 (December 11, 1983, at Philadelphia).

					KICKING				
Year	Team	G	XPM	XPA	FGM	FGA	Lg.	50+	Pts.
1982	New Orleans NFL	8	6	6	2	5	45	0-1	12
1983	New Orleans NFL	16	37	38	18	24	52	3-4	91
1984	New Orleans NFL	16	34	34	20	27	53	2-3	94
1985	New Orleans NFL	16	27	29	31	35	§55	3-4	120
1986	New Orleans NFL	16	30	30	26	30	53	2-5	108
1987	New Orleans NFL	12	37	37	*28	*36	52	2-6	121
1988	New Orleans NFL	16	32	33	26	36	51	1-4	110
1989	New Orleans NFL	16	44	45	20	29	49	0-4	104
1990	New Orleans NFL	16	29	29	21	27	52	3-4	92
1991	New Orleans NFL	16	38	38	25	32	*60	2-4	113
1992	New Orleans NFL	16	33	34	29	34	52	3-3	∞120
1993	New Orleans NFL	16	33	33	28	35	56	1-5	117
1994	New Orleans NFL	16	32	32	28	†39	48	0-6	116
1995	Atlanta NFL	16	29	30	‡31	37	*59	8-9	122
1996	Atlanta NFL	16	31	31	22	29	∞54	1-5	97
1997	Atlanta NFL	16	35	35	23	27	∞55	2-3	104
1998	Atlanta NFL	16	51	52	23	28	53	2-2	120
1999	Atlanta NFL	16	34	34	15	21	49	0-1	79
2000	Atlanta NFL	16	23	23	25	31	51	2-3	98
2001	New York Giants NFL	16	29	30	23	28	51	2-5	98
Pro totals (20 years)		308	644	653	464	590	60	39-81	2036

ANDERSON, BENNIE   G   RAVENS

PERSONAL: Born February 17, 1977, in St. Louis. ... 6-5/305. ... Full name: Tyrone Lamar Anderson.
HIGH SCHOOL: Cleveland Junior Naval Academy (St. Louis).
COLLEGE: Tennessee State.
TRANSACTIONS/CAREER NOTES: Signed as non-drafted free agent by St. Louis Rams (May 3, 2000). ... Released by Rams (July 19, 2000). ... Signed by Baltimore Ravens (June 14, 2001).
PLAYING EXPERIENCE: Baltimore NFL, 2001. ... Games/Games started: 2001 (16/13).
PRO STATISTICS: 2001—Recovered one fumble.

ANDERSON, GARY   K

PERSONAL: Born July 16, 1959, in Parys, Orange Free State, South Africa. ... 5-11/193. ... Full name: Gary Allan Anderson. ... Son of Rev. Douglas Anderson, former professional soccer player in England.
HIGH SCHOOL: Brettonwood (Durban, South Africa).
COLLEGE: Syracuse (degree in management and accounting, 1982).
TRANSACTIONS/CAREER NOTES: Selected by Buffalo Bills in seventh round (171st pick overall) of 1982 NFL draft. ... Signed by Bills for 1982 season. ... Claimed on waivers by Pittsburgh Steelers (September 7, 1982). ... Designated by Steelers as transition player (February 15, 1994). ... On reserve/did not report list (August 23-25, 1994). ... Free agency status changed by Steelers from transition to unconditional (February 17, 1995). ... Signed by Philadelphia Eagles (July 23, 1995). ... Released by Eagles (April 22, 1997). ... Signed by San Francisco 49ers (June 11, 1997). ... Granted unconditional free agency (February 13, 1998). ... Signed by Minnesota Vikings (February 20, 1998). ... Granted unconditional free agency (March 1, 2002).
CHAMPIONSHIP GAME EXPERIENCE: Played in AFC championship game (1984 and 1994 seasons). ... Played in NFC championship game (1997 and 1998 seasons). ... Member of Vikings for NFC Championship game (2000 season); did not play.
HONORS: Played in Pro Bowl (1983, 1985, 1993 and 1998 seasons). ... Named kicker on THE SPORTING NEWS NFL All-Pro team (1998).
RECORDS: Holds NFL career record for most points—2,133; most seasons with 100 or more points—13 (1982-2001); most field goals made—476; and most consecutive field goals made—40. ... Holds NFL single-season records for most PATs made without a miss—59 (1998); and most points scored without a touchdown—164 (1998). ... Shares NFL single-season record for highest field-goal percentage—100.0 (1998).
POST SEASON RECORDS: Holds NFL postseason career record for most made field goals—26. ... Holds NFL postseason record for most consecutive made field goals—16 (1989-95).
PRO STATISTICS: 1994—Rushed once for three yards.

					KICKING				
Year	Team	G	XPM	XPA	FGM	FGA	Lg.	50+	Pts.
1982	Pittsburgh NFL	9	22	22	10	12	48	0-1	52
1983	Pittsburgh NFL	16	38	39	27	31	49	0-0	§119
1984	Pittsburgh NFL	16	45	45	▲24	32	55	2-3	§117
1985	Pittsburgh NFL	16	40	40	*33	*42	52	1-4	§139
1986	Pittsburgh NFL	16	32	32	21	32	45	0-3	95
1987	Pittsburgh NFL	12	21	21	22	27	52	2-2	87
1988	Pittsburgh NFL	16	34	35	28	36	52	1-2	118
1989	Pittsburgh NFL	16	28	28	21	30	49	0-0	91
1990	Pittsburgh NFL	16	32	32	20	25	48	0-2	92
1991	Pittsburgh NFL	16	31	31	23	33	54	1-6	100
1992	Pittsburgh NFL	16	29	31	28	36	49	0-2	113
1993	Pittsburgh NFL	16	32	32	28	30	46	0-0	*116

Year Team	G	KICKING						
		XPM	XPA	FGM	FGA	Lg.	50+	Pts.
1994—Pittsburgh NFL	16	32	32	24	29	50	1-2	104
1995—Philadelphia NFL	16	32	33	22	30	43	0-3	98
1996—Philadelphia NFL	16	40	40	25	29	46	0-0	115
1997—San Francisco NFL	16	38	38	29	36	51	1-3	125
1998—Minnesota NFL	16	*59	*59	‡35	∞35	53	2-2	*164
1999—Minnesota NFL	16	46	46	19	30	44	0-2	103
2000—Minnesota NFL	16	‡45	‡45	22	23	49	0-1	111
2001—Minnesota NFL	16	29	30	15	18	44	0-0	74
Pro totals (20 years)	309	705	711	476	596	55	11-38	2133

ANDERSON, JAMAL   RB

PERSONAL: Born September 30, 1972, in Newark, N.J. ... 5-11/237. ... Full name: Jamal Sharif Anderson.
HIGH SCHOOL: El Camino Real (Woodland Hills, Calif.).
JUNIOR COLLEGE: Moorpark (Calif.) Junior College.
COLLEGE: Utah.
TRANSACTIONS/CAREER NOTES: Selected by Atlanta Falcons in seventh round (201st pick overall) of 1994 NFL draft. ... Signed by Falcons (June 21, 1994). ... On injured reserve with knee injury (September 22, 1999-remainder of season). ... On injured reserve with knee injury (October 2, 2001-remainder of season). ... Released by Falcons (June 3, 2002).
CHAMPIONSHIP GAME EXPERIENCE: Played in NFC championship game (1998 season). ... Played in Super Bowl XXXIII (1998 season).
HONORS: Named running back on THE SPORTING NEWS NFL All-Pro team (1998). ... Played in Pro Bowl (1998 season).
RECORDS: Holds NFL single-season record for most rushing attempts—410 (1998).
PRO STATISTICS: 1996—Recovered one fumble. 1997—Attempted four passes with one completion for 27 yards and one touchdown and a interception and recovered one fumble. 1998—Attempted two passes without a completion and recovered one fumble. 2000—Recovered one fumble.
SINGLE GAME HIGHS (regular season): Attempts—33 (December 21, 1997, vs. Arizona); yards—188 (November 29, 1998, vs. St. Louis); and rushing touchdowns—3 (October 6, 1996, vs. Detroit).
STATISTICAL PLATEAUS: 100-yard rushing games: 1996 (3), 1997 (2), 1998 (12), 2000 (2). Total: 19.

			RUSHING				RECEIVING				KICKOFF RETURNS				TOTALS			
Year Team	G	GS	Att.	Yds.	Avg.	TD	No.	Yds.	Avg.	TD	No.	Yds.	Avg.	TD	TD	2pt.	Pts.	Fum.
1994—Atlanta NFL	3	0	2	-1	-0.5	0	0	0	0.0	0	1	11	11.0	0	0	0	0	0
1995—Atlanta NFL	16	0	39	161	4.1	1	4	42	10.5	0	24	541	22.5	0	1	0	6	0
1996—Atlanta NFL	16	12	232	1055	4.5	5	49	473	9.7	1	4	80	20.0	0	6	0	36	4
1997—Atlanta NFL	16	15	290	1002	3.5	7	29	284	9.8	3	0	0	0.0	0	10	0	60	4
1998—Atlanta NFL	16	16	*410	‡1846	4.5	‡14	27	319	11.8	2	0	0	0.0	0	16	1	98	5
1999—Atlanta NFL	2	2	19	59	3.1	0	2	34	17.0	0	0	0	0.0	0	0	0	0	0
2000—Atlanta NFL	16	16	282	1024	3.6	6	42	382	9.1	0	0	0	0.0	0	6	1	38	6
2001—Atlanta NFL	3	3	55	190	3.5	1	3	111	37.0	1	0	0	0.0	0	2	0	12	1
Pro totals (8 years)	88	64	1329	5336	4.0	34	156	1645	10.5	7	29	632	21.8	0	41	2	250	20

ANDERSON, MIKE   RB   BRONCOS

PERSONAL: Born September 21, 1973, in Winnsboro, S.C. ... 6-0/230. ... Full name: Michael Moschello Anderson.
HIGH SCHOOL: Fairfield (S.C.).
JUNIOR COLLEGE: Mount San Jacinto Community College (Calif.).
COLLEGE: Utah.
TRANSACTIONS/CAREER NOTES: Selected by Denver Broncos in sixth round (189th pick overall) of 2000 NFL draft. ... Signed by Broncos (July 14, 2000).
SINGLE GAME HIGHS (regular season): Attempts—37 (December 3, 2000, vs. New Orleans); yards—251 (December 3, 2000, vs. New Orleans); and rushing touchdowns—4 (December 3, 2000, vs. New Orleans).
STATISTICAL PLATEAUS: 100-yard rushing games: 2000 (6), 2001 (2). Total: 8.

			RUSHING				RECEIVING				TOTALS			
Year Team	G	GS	Att.	Yds.	Avg.	TD	No.	Yds.	Avg.	TD	TD	2pt.	Pts.	Fum.
2000—Denver NFL	16	12	297	1487	§5.0	§15	23	169	7.3	0	15	1	92	4
2001—Denver NFL	16	7	175	678	3.9	4	8	46	5.8	0	4	▲1	26	1
Pro totals (2 years)	32	19	472	2165	4.6	19	31	215	6.9	0	19	2	118	5

ANDERSON, RASHARD   CB   PANTHERS

PERSONAL: Born June 14, 1977, in Forest, Miss. ... 6-2/204.
HIGH SCHOOL: Forest (Miss.).
COLLEGE: Jackson State.
TRANSACTIONS/CAREER NOTES: Selected by Carolina Panthers in first round (23rd pick overall) of 2000 NFL draft. ... Signed by Panthers (July 17, 2000). ... On suspended list for violating league substance abuse policy (May 23, 2002-present).
PRO STATISTICS: 2001—Recovered three fumbles for 97 yards and one touchdown.

			INTERCEPTIONS			
Year Team	G	GS	No.	Yds.	Avg.	TD
2000—Carolina NFL	12	0	0	0	0.0	0
2001—Carolina NFL	15	9	1	0	0.0	0
Pro totals (2 years)	27	9	1	0	0.0	0

ANDERSON, RICHIE   FB   JETS

PERSONAL: Born September 13, 1971, in Sandy Spring, Md. ... 6-2/230. ... Full name: Richard Darnoll Anderson II.
HIGH SCHOOL: Sherwood (Sandy Spring, Md.).
COLLEGE: Penn State.
TRANSACTIONS/CAREER NOTES: Selected after junior season by New York Jets in sixth round (144th pick overall) of 1993 NFL draft. ... Signed by Jets (June 10, 1993). ... On injured reserve with ankle injury (December 31, 1993-remainder of season). ... On injured reserve with ankle injury (November 30, 1995-remainder of season).
CHAMPIONSHIP GAME EXPERIENCE: Member of Jets for AFC championship game (1998 season); did not play.
HONORS: Played in Pro Bowl (2000 season).
PRO STATISTICS: 1993—Recovered one fumble. 1994—Recovered one fumble. 1995—Attempted one pass without a completion. 1996—Recovered one fumble. 1997—Recovered one fumble.
SINGLE GAME HIGHS (regular season): Attempts—9 (November 13, 1994, vs. Green Bay); yards—74 (November 13, 1994, vs. Green Bay); and rushing touchdowns—1 (October 27, 1996, vs. Arizona).
STATISTICAL PLATEAUS: 100-yard receiving games: 2000 (3).

			RUSHING				RECEIVING				KICKOFF RETURNS				TOTALS		
Year Team	G	GS	Att.	Yds.	Avg.	TD	No.	Yds.	Avg.	TD	No.	Yds.	Avg.	TD	TD	2pt.	Pts.	Fum.
1993—New York Jets NFL......	7	0	0	0	0.0	0	0	0	0.0	0	4	66	16.5	0	0	0	0	1
1994—New York Jets NFL......	13	5	43	207	4.8	1	25	212	8.5	1	3	43	14.3	0	2	0	12	1
1995—New York Jets NFL......	10	0	5	17	3.4	0	5	26	5.2	0	0	0	0.0	0	0	0	0	2
1996—New York Jets NFL......	16	13	47	150	3.2	1	44	385	8.8	0	0	0	0.0	0	1	0	6	0
1997—New York Jets NFL......	16	3	21	70	3.3	0	26	150	5.8	1	0	0	0.0	0	1	0	6	2
1998—New York Jets NFL......	8	2	1	2	2.0	0	3	12	4.0	0	0	0	0.0	0	0	0	0	0
1999—New York Jets NFL......	16	9	16	84	5.3	0	29	302	10.4	3	0	0	0.0	0	3	0	18	0
2000—New York Jets NFL......	16	10	27	63	2.3	0	88	853	9.7	2	0	0	0.0	0	2	0	12	2
2001—New York Jets NFL......	16	15	26	102	3.9	0	40	252	6.3	2	0	0	0.0	0	2	0	12	1
Pro totals (9 years)............	118	57	186	695	3.7	2	260	2192	8.4	9	7	109	15.6	0	11	0	66	9

ANDERSON, SCOTTY   WR   LIONS

PERSONAL: Born November 24, 1979, in Jonesboro, La. ... 6-2/184. ... Brother of Stevie Anderson, wide receiver with New York Jets (1994) and Arizona Cardinals (1995 and 1996); and brother of Anthony Anderson, defensive back with San Diego Chargers (1987).
HIGH SCHOOL: Jonesboro-Hodge (Jonesboro, La.).
COLLEGE: Grambling State.
TRANSACTIONS/CAREER NOTES: Selected by Detroit Lions in fifth round (148th pick overall) of 2001 NFL draft. ... Signed by Lions (July 16, 2001).
SINGLE GAME HIGHS (regular season): Receptions—3 (November 22, 2001, vs. Green Bay); yards—69 (December 16, 2001, vs. Minnesota); and touchdown receptions—1 (November 22, 2001, vs. Green Bay).

				RECEIVING			
Year Team	G	GS	No.	Yds.	Avg.	TD
2001—Detroit NFL...	9	4	12	211	17.6	1

ANDERSON, WILLIE   OT   BENGALS

PERSONAL: Born July 11, 1975, in Mobile, Ala. ... 6-5/340. ... Full name: Willie Aaron Anderson.
HIGH SCHOOL: Vigor (Prichard, Ala.).
COLLEGE: Auburn.
TRANSACTIONS/CAREER NOTES: Selected after junior season by Cincinnati Bengals in first round (10th pick overall) of 1996 NFL draft. ... Signed by Bengals (August 5, 1996).
PLAYING EXPERIENCE: Cincinnati NFL, 1996-2001. ... Games/Games started: 1996 (16/10), 1997 (16/16), 1998 (16/16), 1999 (14/14), 2000 (16/16), 2001 (16/16). Total: 94/88.
PRO STATISTICS: 1998—Recovered one fumble. 1999—Recovered one fumble. 2000—Recovered one fumble.

ANDREW, TROY   C   DOLPHINS

PERSONAL: Born December 12, 1977, in Tamuning, Ohio. ... 6-4/305. ... Full name: Troy Warden Andrew.
HIGH SCHOOL: Klein (Texas).
COLLEGE: Duke.
TRANSACTIONS/CAREER NOTES: Signed as non-drafted free agent by Miami Dolphins (April 26, 2001).
PLAYING EXPERIENCE: Miami NFL, 2001. ... Games/Games started: 2001 (8/0).

ANDRUZZI, JOE   G   PATRIOTS

PERSONAL: Born August 23, 1975, in Staten Island, N.Y. ... 6-3/315. ... Full name: Joseph Dominick Andruzzi. ... Name pronounced ann-DROOZ-ee.
HIGH SCHOOL: Tottenville (Staten Island, N.Y.).
COLLEGE: Southern Connecticut State.
TRANSACTIONS/CAREER NOTES: Signed as non-drafted free agent by Green Bay Packers (April 25, 1997). ... Inactive for all 16 games (1997). ... Assigned by Packers to Scottish Claymores in 1998 NFL Europe enhancement allocations program (February 18, 1998). ... On injured reserve with knee injury (November 23, 1999-remainder of season). ... Released by Packers (August 27, 2000). ... Signed by New England Patriots (September 9, 2000). ... On injured reserve with knee injury (December 7, 2000-remainder of season).
PLAYING EXPERIENCE: Scottish NFLE, 1998; Green Bay NFL, 1998 and 1999; New England NFL, 2000 and 2001. ... Games/Games started: NFLE 1998 (10/10), NFL 1998 (15/1), 1999 (8/3), 2000 (11/11), 2001 (16/16). Total NFLE: 10/10. Total NFL: 50/31. Total Pro: 60/40.
CHAMPIONSHIP GAME EXPERIENCE: Member of Packers for NFC championship game (1997 season); inactive. ... Member of Packers for Super Bowl XXXII (1997 season); inactive. ... Played in AFC championship game (2001 season). ... Member of Super Bowl championship team (2001 season).
PRO STATISTICS: 1998—Recovered one fumble. 2000—Recovered one fumble for two yards. 2001—Recovered one fumble.

ANTHONY, REIDEL   WR   REDSKINS

PERSONAL: Born October 20, 1976, in Pahokee, Fla. ... 5-11/180. ... Full name: Reidel Clarence Anthony. ... Name pronounced REE-dell.
HIGH SCHOOL: Glades Central (Belle Glade, Fla.).
COLLEGE: Florida.
TRANSACTIONS/CAREER NOTES: Selected after junior season by Tampa Bay Buccaneers in first round (16th pick overall) of 1997 NFL draft. ... Signed by Buccaneers (July 20, 1997). ... Granted unconditional free agency (March 1, 2002). ... Signed by Washington Redskins (March 1, 2002).
CHAMPIONSHIP GAME EXPERIENCE: Member of Buccaneers for NFC championship game (1999 season); inactive.
HONORS: Named wide receiver on THE SPORTING NEWS college All-America first team (1996).
PRO STATISTICS: 1998—Recovered one fumble. 2001—Returned three punts for 12 yards and recovered one fumble.
SINGLE GAME HIGHS (regular season): Receptions—7 (October 3, 1999, vs. Minnesota); yards—126 (November 15, 1998, vs. Jacksonville); and touchdown receptions—2 (November 15, 1998, vs. Jacksonville).
STATISTICAL PLATEAUS: 100-yard receiving games: 1998 (1).

			RUSHING				RECEIVING				KICKOFF RETURNS				TOTALS		
Year Team	G	GS	Att.	Yds.	Avg.	TD	No.	Yds.	Avg.	TD	No.	Yds.	Avg.	TD	TD	2pt.	Pts.	Fum.
1997—Tampa Bay NFL	16	12	5	84	16.8	0	35	448	12.8	4	25	592	23.7	0	4	0	24	0
1998—Tampa Bay NFL	15	13	4	43	10.8	0	51	708	13.9	4	46	1118	24.3	0	7	1	44	0
1999—Tampa Bay NFL	13	7	1	2	2.0	0	30	296	9.9	1	21	434	20.7	0	1	0	6	1
2000—Tampa Bay NFL	16	1	0	0	0.0	0	15	232	15.5	4	3	88	29.3	0	4	0	24	0
2001—Tampa Bay NFL	13	4	3	22	7.3	0	13	162	12.5	0	0	0	0.0	0	0	0	0	1
Pro totals (5 years)	73	37	13	151	11.6	0	144	1846	12.8	16	95	2232	23.5	0	16	1	98	2

ARAGUZ, LEO   P

PERSONAL: Born January 18, 1970, in Pharr, Texas. ... 5-11/190. ... Full name: Leobardo Jaime Araguz. ... Name pronounced ara-GOOSE.
HIGH SCHOOL: Harlingen (Texas).
COLLEGE: Stephen F. Austin State.
TRANSACTIONS/CAREER NOTES: Signed as non-drafted free agent by Miami Dolphins (March 28, 1994). ... Released by Dolphins prior to 1994 season. ... Signed by San Diego Chargers (1995). ... Released by Chargers prior to 1995 season. ... Signed by Rhein Fire of the World League for 1996 season. ... Signed by Oakland Raiders (December 4, 1996). ... Released by Raiders (August 27, 2000). ... Signed by St. Louis Rams (June 14, 2001). ... Released by Rams (August 27, 2001). ... Signed by Detroit Lions (November 27, 2001). ... Released by Lions (December 18, 2001).
RECORDS: Holds NFL single-game record for most punts—16 (October 11, 1998, vs. San Diego).
PRO STATISTICS: 1996—Rushed once for no yards and recovered one fumble. 1997—Rushed once for no yards, fumbled once and recovered one fumble for minus 21 yards. 1998—Rushed once for minus 12 yards and completed only pass attempt for minus one yard.

		PUNTING					
Year Team	G	No.	Yds.	Avg.	Net avg.	In. 20	Blk.
1996—Rhein W.L.	...	41	1735	42.3	37.8	17	0
—Oakland NFL	3	13	534	41.1	34.5	4	0
1997—Oakland NFL	16	§93	§4189	‡45.0	*39.1	▲28	0
1998—Oakland NFL	16	§98	§4256	43.4	33.4	29	0
1999—Oakland NFL	16	76	3045	40.1	32.3	25	1
2000—				Did not play.			
2001—Detroit NFL	3	17	713	41.9	34.0	6	0
W.L. totals (1 year)	...	41	1735	42.3	37.8	17	0
NFL totals (5 years)	54	297	12737	42.9	35.0	92	1
Pro totals (6 years)	...	338	14472	42.8	35.3	109	1

ARCHULETA, ADAM   S   RAMS

PERSONAL: Born November 27, 1977, in Chandler, Ariz. ... 5-11/209. ... Full name: Adam J. Archuleta.
HIGH SCHOOL: Chandler (Ariz.).
COLLEGE: Arizona State.
TRANSACTIONS/CAREER NOTES: Selected by St. Louis Rams in first round (20th pick overall) of 2001 NFL draft. ... Signed by Rams (July 29, 2001).
CHAMPIONSHIP GAME EXPERIENCE: Played in NFC championship game (2001 season). ... Played in Super Bowl XXXVI (2001 season).
PRO STATISTICS: 2001—Returned one kickoff for no yards, fumbled twice and recovered one fumble for 24 yards.

			INTERCEPTIONS				SACKS
Year Team	G	GS	No.	Yds.	Avg.	TD	No.
2001—St. Louis NFL	13	12	0	0	0.0	0	2.0

ARIANS, JAKE   K

PERSONAL: Born January 26, 1978, in Blacksburg, Va. ... 5-11/200. ... Full name: Jacob Bruce Arians.
HIGH SCHOOL: Starkville (Va.).
COLLEGE: Alabama Birmingham.
TRANSACTIONS/CAREER NOTES: Signed as non-drafted free agent by Atlanta Falcons (April 28, 2000). ... Released by Falcons (August 27, 2000). ... Re-signed by Falcons to practice squad (October 30, 2000). ... Released by Falcons (September 1, 2001). ... Signed by Buffalo Bills to practice squad (September 6, 2001). ... Activated (September 8, 2001). ... Released by Bills (November 26, 2001).

		KICKING						
Year Team	G	XPM	XPA	FGM	FGA	Lg.	50+	Pts.
2001—Buffalo NFL	10	16	17	12	21	49	0-0	52

ARMOUR, JoJUAN   S   BENGALS

PERSONAL: Born July 10, 1976, in Toledo, Ohio. ... 5-11/220. ... Name pronounced JOE-wan.
HIGH SCHOOL: Central Catholic (Cleveland).
COLLEGE: Miami of Ohio.
TRANSACTIONS/CAREER NOTES: Selected by Oakland Raiders in seventh round (224th pick overall) of 1999 NFL draft. ... Signed by Raiders (July 24, 1999). ... Claimed on waivers by Jacksonville Jaguars (September 7, 1999). ... Inactive for two games with Jaguars (1999). ... Claimed on waivers by Cincinnati Bengals (September 21, 1999). ... Released by Bengals (October 15, 1999). ... Re-signed by Bengals to practice squad (October 16, 1999). ... Activated (December 16, 1999). ... Released by Bengals (August 27, 2000). ... Re-signed by Bengals to practice squad (August 28, 2000). ... Activated (October 2, 2000). ... Assigned by Bengals to Barcelona Dragons in 2001 NFL Europe enhancement allocation program (February 19, 2001). ... Granted free agency (March 1, 2002). ... Re-signed by Bengals (April 23, 2002).
PLAYING EXPERIENCE: Cincinnati NFL, 1999-2001; Barcelona NFLE, 2001. ... Games/Games started: 1999 (2/0), 2000 (4/0), NFLE 2001 (games played unavailable), NFL 2001 (16/11). Total: 22/11.
HONORS: Named outside linebacker on THE SPORTING NEWS college All-America second team (1997).

ARMSTEAD, JESSIE   LB   REDSKINS

PERSONAL: Born October 26, 1970, in Dallas. ... 6-1/240. ... Full name: Jessie W. Armstead.
HIGH SCHOOL: David W. Carter (Dallas).
COLLEGE: Miami (Fla.) (degree in criminal justice, 1992).
TRANSACTIONS/CAREER NOTES: Selected by New York Giants in eighth round (207th pick overall) of 1993 NFL draft. ... Signed by Giants (July 19, 1993). ... Released by Giants (February 28, 2002). ... Signed by Washington Redskins (March 1, 2002).
CHAMPIONSHIP GAME EXPERIENCE: Played in NFC championship game (2000 season). ... Played in Super Bowl XXXV (2000 season).
HONORS: Named outside linebacker on THE SPORTING NEWS NFL All-Pro team (1997). ... Played in Pro Bowl (1997-2000 seasons).
PRO STATISTICS: 1995—Recovered one fumble. 1996—Fumbled once and recovered two fumbles. 1997—Recovered one fumble. 2000—Recovered one fumble.

				INTERCEPTIONS				SACKS
Year Team		G	GS	No.	Yds.	Avg.	TD	No.
1993—New York Giants NFL		16	0	1	0	0.0	0	0.0
1994—New York Giants NFL		16	0	1	0	0.0	0	3.0
1995—New York Giants NFL		16	2	1	58	58.0	0	0.5
1996—New York Giants NFL		16	16	2	23	11.5	0	3.0
1997—New York Giants NFL		16	16	2	57	28.5	1	3.5
1998—New York Giants NFL		16	16	2	4	2.0	0	5.0
1999—New York Giants NFL		16	16	2	35	17.5	0	9.0
2000—New York Giants NFL		16	16	1	-2	-2.0	0	5.0
2001—New York Giants NFL		16	16	0	0	0.0	0	1.5
Pro totals (9 years)		144	98	12	175	14.6	2	30.5

ARMSTRONG, TRACE   DE   RAIDERS

PERSONAL: Born October 5, 1965, in Bethesda, Md. ... 6-4/275. ... Full name: Raymond Lester Armstrong.
HIGH SCHOOL: John Carroll (Birmingham, Ala.).
COLLEGE: Arizona State, then Florida (degree in psychology, 1989).
TRANSACTIONS/CAREER NOTES: Selected by Chicago Bears in first round (12th pick overall) of 1989 NFL draft. ... Signed by Bears (August 18, 1989). ... On injured reserve with knee injury (September 24-November 3, 1991). ... Granted free agency (March 1, 1993). ... Re-signed by Bears (March 14, 1993). ... Traded by Bears to Miami Dolphins for second- (P Todd Sauerbrun) and third-round (G Evan Pilgrim) picks in 1995 draft (April 4, 1995). ... Granted unconditional free agency (March 2, 2001). ... Signed by Oakland Raiders (March 5, 2001). ... On injured reserve with Achilles' tendon injury (October 2, 2001-remainder of season).
HONORS: Named defensive lineman on THE SPORTING NEWS college All-America first team (1988). ... Played in Pro Bowl (2000 season).
PRO STATISTICS: 1989—Recovered one fumble. 1990—Recovered two fumbles. 1992—Recovered one fumble. 1993—Recovered three fumbles for three yards. 1995—Recovered one fumble. 1996—Recovered two fumbles. 1997—Recovered three fumbles. 1998—Recovered one fumble for two yards.

Year Team	G	GS	SACKS
1989—Chicago NFL	15	14	5.0
1990—Chicago NFL	16	16	10.0
1991—Chicago NFL	12	12	1.5
1992—Chicago NFL	14	14	6.5
1993—Chicago NFL	16	16	11.5
1994—Chicago NFL	15	15	7.5
1995—Miami NFL	15	0	4.5
1996—Miami NFL	16	9	12.0
1997—Miami NFL	16	16	5.5
1998—Miami NFL	16	0	10.5
1999—Miami NFL	16	2	7.5
2000—Miami NFL	16	0	§16.5
2001—Oakland NFL	3	0	0.5
Pro totals (13 years)	186	114	99.0

ARRINGTON, LaVAR   LB   REDSKINS

PERSONAL: Born June 20, 1978, in Pittsburgh. ... 6-3/250. ... Full name: LaVar RaShad Arrington.
HIGH SCHOOL: North Hills (Pittsburgh).
COLLEGE: Penn State.
TRANSACTIONS/CAREER NOTES: Selected after junior season by Washington Redskins in first round (second pick overall) of 2000 NFL draft. ... Signed by Redskins (July 22, 2000).

HONORS: Named linebacker on THE SPORTING NEWS college All-America first team (1998 and 1999). ... Butkus Award winner (1999). ... Chuck Bednarik Award winner (1999).
PRO STATISTICS: 2000—Returned one kickoff for 39 yards. 2001—Recovered two fumbles.

Year Team	G	GS	INTERCEPTIONS No.	Yds.	Avg.	TD	SACKS No.
2000—Washington NFL	16	11	0	0	0.0	0	4.0
2001—Washington NFL	14	14	3	120	40.0	1	0.5
Pro totals (2 years)	30	25	3	120	40.0	1	4.5

ASHMORE, DARRYL — G/OT — RAIDERS

PERSONAL: Born November 1, 1969, in Peoria, Ill. ... 6-7/310. ... Full name: Darryl Allan Ashmore.
HIGH SCHOOL: Peoria (Ill.) Central.
COLLEGE: Northwestern (degree in business).
TRANSACTIONS/CAREER NOTES: Selected by Los Angeles Rams in seventh round (171st pick overall) of 1992 NFL draft. ... Signed by Rams (July 13, 1992). ... On injured reserve with knee injury (September 3-October 7, 1992). ... On practice squad (October 7, 1992-remainder of season). ... Granted free agency (February 17, 1995). ... Rams franchise moved to St. Louis (April 12, 1995). ... Re-signed by Rams (July 20, 1995). ... Released by Rams (October 14, 1996). ... Signed by Washington Redskins (October 26, 1996). ... Granted unconditional free agency (February 14, 1997). ... Re-signed by Redskins (May 9, 1997). ... Granted unconditional free agency (February 13, 1998). ... Signed by Oakland Raiders (April 25, 1998). ... Granted unconditional free agency (February 11, 2000). ... Re-signed by Raiders (February 22, 2000). ... Granted unconditional free agency (March 1, 2002). ... Re-signed by Raiders (March 22, 2002).
PLAYING EXPERIENCE: Los Angeles Rams NFL, 1993 and 1994; St. Louis NFL, 1995; St. Louis (6)-Washington (5) NFL, 1996; Washington NFL, 1997; Oakland NFL, 1998-2001. ... Games/Games started: 1993 (9/7), 1994 (11/3), 1995 (16/15), 1996 (St.L-6/0; Wash.-5/0; Total: 11/0), 1997 (11/2), 1998 (15/4), 1999 (16/2), 2000 (16/0), 2001 (14/1). Total: 119/34.
CHAMPIONSHIP GAME EXPERIENCE: Played in AFC championship game (2000 season).
PRO STATISTICS: 1998—Recovered one fumble for one yard and a touchdown. 1999—Returned one kickoff for no yards.

ATKINS, LARRY — LB — CHIEFS

PERSONAL: Born July 21, 1975, in Santa Monica, Calif. ... 6-3/243. ... Full name: Larry Tabay Atkins III.
HIGH SCHOOL: Venice (Los Angeles).
COLLEGE: UCLA.
TRANSACTIONS/CAREER NOTES: Selected by Kansas City Chiefs in third round (84th pick overall) of 1999 NFL draft. ... Signed by Chiefs (July 15, 1999). ... Granted free agency (March 1, 2002).
PLAYING EXPERIENCE: Kansas City NFL, 1999-2001. ... Games/Games started: 1999 (9/0), 2000 (15/0), 2001 (12/0). Total: 36/0.
HONORS: Named free safety on THE SPORTING NEWS college All-America second team (1998).
PRO STATISTICS: 2000—Recovered one fumble. 2001—Returned one kickoff for no yards.

AUSTIN, REGGIE — CB — BEARS

PERSONAL: Born January 21, 1977, in Atlanta. ... 5-9/178.
HIGH SCHOOL: Harper (Atlanta).
COLLEGE: Wake Forest.
TRANSACTIONS/CAREER NOTES: Selected by Chicago Bears in fourth round (125th pick overall) of 2000 NFL draft. ... Signed by Bears (June 8, 2000). ... On injured reserve with heel injury (August 23, 2000-entire season).

Year Team	G	GS	INTERCEPTIONS No.	Yds.	Avg.	TD
2000—Chicago NFL			Did not play			
2001—Chicago NFL	9	0	0	0	0.0	0

AYANBADEJO, OBAFEMI — FB

PERSONAL: Born March 5, 1975, in Chicago. ... 6-2/235. ... Name pronounced oh-BUH-fem-me eye-an-buh-DAY-ho.
HIGH SCHOOL: Santa Cruz (Calif.).
JUNIOR COLLEGE: Cabrillo College (Calif.).
COLLEGE: San Diego State.
TRANSACTIONS/CAREER NOTES: Signed as non-drafted free agent by Minnesota Vikings (April 25, 1997). ... Released by Vikings (August 18, 1997). ... Re-signed by Vikings (February 6, 1998). ... Assigned by Vikings to England Monarchs in 1998 NFL Europe enhancement allocation program (February 17, 1998). ... Released by Vikings (August 24, 1998). ... Re-signed by Vikings to practice squad (August 31, 1998). ... Activated (December 1, 1998). ... Released by Vikings (December 23, 1998). ... Re-signed by Vikings to practice squad (December 24, 1998). ... Released by Vikings (September 21, 1999). ... Signed by Baltimore Ravens (September 27, 1999). ... On injured reserve with toe injury (November 28, 2000-remainder of season). ... Granted free agency (March 1, 2002).
PRO STATISTICS: 2001—Recovered two fumbles.
SINGLE GAME HIGHS (regular season): Attempts—9 (October 21, 2001, vs. Cleveland); yards—48 (October 21, 2001, vs. Cleveland); and rushing touchdowns—1 (December 2, 2001, vs. Indianapolis).

Year Team	G	GS	RUSHING Att.	Yds.	Avg.	TD	RECEIVING No.	Yds.	Avg.	TD	TOTALS TD	2pt.	Pts.	Fum.
1998—England NFLE	...	...	0	0	0.0	0	2	28	14.0	0	0	0	0	0
—Minnesota NFL	1	0	0	0	0.0	0	0	0	0.0	0	0	0	0	0
1999—Minnesota NFL	2	0	0	0	0.0	0	0	0	0.0	0	0	0	0	0
—Baltimore NFL	12	0	0	0	0.0	0	1	2	2.0	0	0	0	0	0
2000—Baltimore NFL	8	4	15	37	2.5	1	23	168	7.3	1	2	0	12	0
2001—Baltimore NFL	16	5	46	173	3.8	1	24	121	5.0	1	2	0	12	1
NFL Europe totals (1 year)	...	...	0	0	0.0	0	2	28	14.0	0	0	0	0	0
NFL totals (4 years)	39	9	61	210	3.4	2	48	291	6.1	2	4	0	24	1
Pro totals (5 years)	...	...	61	210	3.4	2	50	319	6.4	2	4	0	24	1

AYI, KOLE — LB — PATRIOTS

PERSONAL: Born September 27, 1978, in Ann Arbor, Mich. ... 6-1/231. ... Full name: Bamikole Richard Ayi.
HIGH SCHOOL: Nashua (N.H.).
COLLEGE: Massachusetts.
TRANSACTIONS/CAREER NOTES: Signed as non-drafted free agent by St. Louis Rams (May 3, 2001). ... Released by Rams (October 23, 2001). ... Re-signed by Rams to practice squad (October 24, 2001). ... Signed by New York Giants off Rams practice squad (October 25, 2001); did not play. ... Claimed on waivers by New England Patriots (November 15, 2001). ... On injured reserve with leg injury (November 28, 2001-remainder of season).
PLAYING EXPERIENCE: St. Louis (6)-New England (1) NFL, 2001. ... Games/Games started: 2001 (St.L.-6/0; N.E.-1/0; Total: 7/0).

AZUMAH, JERRY — CB — BEARS

PERSONAL: Born September 1, 1977, in Worcester, Mass. ... 5-10/189. ... Name pronounced ah-ZOO-muh.
HIGH SCHOOL: St. Peter-Marian (Worcester, Mass.).
COLLEGE: New Hampshire.
TRANSACTIONS/CAREER NOTES: Selected by Chicago Bears in fifth round (147th pick overall) of 1999 NFL draft. ... Signed by Bears (June 8, 1999).
HONORS: Walter Payton Award winner (1998).
PRO STATISTICS: 2001—Ran 16 yards with lateral from punt return, returned four kickoffs for 65 yards, credited with two sacks and recovered one fumble.

				INTERCEPTIONS		
Year Team	G	GS	No.	Yds.	Avg.	TD
1999—Chicago NFL	16	2	0	0	0.0	0
2000—Chicago NFL	14	4	1	2	2.0	0
2001—Chicago NFL	16	5	1	14	14.0	0
Pro totals (3 years)	46	11	2	16	8.0	0

BABER, BILLY — TE — CHIEFS

PERSONAL: Born January 17, 1979, in Charlottesville, Va. ... 6-3/258. ... Full name: William Franklin Baber.
HIGH SCHOOL: Western Albermarle (Va.).
COLLEGE: Virginia.
TRANSACTIONS/CAREER NOTES: Selected by Kansas City Chiefs in fifth round (141st pick overall) of 2001 NFL draft. ... Signed by Chiefs (May 24, 2001). ... Released by Chiefs (September 2, 2001). ... Re-signed by Chiefs to practice squad (September 3, 2001). ... Activated (December 3, 2001).

				RECEIVING		
Year Team	G	GS	No.	Yds.	Avg.	TD
2001—Kansas City NFL	1	0	0	0	0.0	0

BACKUS, JEFF — OT — LIONS

PERSONAL: Born September 21, 1977, in Midland, Mich. ... 6-5/308. ... Full name: Jeffrey Carl Backus.
HIGH SCHOOL: Norcross (Ga.).
COLLEGE: Michigan.
TRANSACTIONS/CAREER NOTES: Selected by Detroit Lions in first round (18th pick overall) of 2001 NFL draft. ... Signed by Lions (July 23, 2001).
PLAYING EXPERIENCE: Detroit NFL, 2001. ... Games/Games started: 2001 (16/16).

BADGER, BRAD — OT — RAIDERS

PERSONAL: Born January 11, 1975, in Corvallis, Ore. ... 6-4/319.
HIGH SCHOOL: Corvallis (Ore.).
COLLEGE: Stanford.
TRANSACTIONS/CAREER NOTES: Selected by Washington Redskins in fifth round (162nd pick overall) of 1997 NFL draft. ... Signed by Redskins (May 5, 1997). ... Granted free agency (February 11, 2000). ... Tendered offer sheet by Minnesota Vikings (April 10, 2000). ... Redskins declined to match offer (April 11, 2000). ... Released by Vikings (March 12, 2002). ... Signed by Oakland Raiders (April 12, 2002).
PLAYING EXPERIENCE: Washington NFL, 1997-1999; Minnesota NFL, 2000 and 2001. ... Games/Games started: 1997 (12/2), 1998 (16/16), 1999 (14/4), 2000 (16/0), 2001 (13/12). Total: 71/34.
CHAMPIONSHIP GAME EXPERIENCE: Member of Vikings for NFC Championship game (2000 season); did not play.
PRO STATISTICS: 2000—Recovered one fumble. 2001—Recovered one fumble.

BAILEY, CHAMP — CB — REDSKINS

PERSONAL: Born June 22, 1978 ... 6-1/188. ... Full name: Roland Champ Bailey.
HIGH SCHOOL: Charlton County (Folkson, Ga.).
COLLEGE: Georgia.
TRANSACTIONS/CAREER NOTES: Selected after junior season by Washington Redskins in first round (seventh pick overall) of 1999 NFL draft. ... Signed by Redskins (July 24, 1999).
HONORS: Named cornerback on THE SPORTING NEWS college All-America second team (1998). ... Played in Pro Bowl (2000 season).

PRO STATISTICS: 2000—Rushed once for seven yards and one touchdown, caught three passes for 78 yards and returned one punt for 65 yards. 2001—Recovered one fumble.

Year Team	G	GS	INTERCEPTIONS No.	Yds.	Avg.	TD	SACKS No.
1999—Washington NFL	16	16	5	55	11.0	1	1.0
2000—Washington NFL	16	16	5	48	9.6	0	0.0
2001—Washington NFL	16	16	3	17	5.7	0	0.0
Pro totals (3 years)	48	48	13	120	9.2	1	1.0

BAILEY, ROBERT   CB

PERSONAL: Born September 3, 1968, in Barbados. ... 5-10/182. ... Full name: Robert Martin Luther Bailey.
HIGH SCHOOL: Miami Southridge Senior.
COLLEGE: Miami (Fla.) (degree in science).
TRANSACTIONS/CAREER NOTES: Selected by Los Angeles Rams in fourth round (107th pick overall) of 1991 NFL draft. ... Signed by Rams (July 17, 1991). ... On injured reserve with broken hand (August 27-October 11, 1991). ... On injured reserve with finger injury (November 19, 1991-remainder of season). ... On injured reserve with knee injury (December 11, 1993-remainder of season). ... Granted free agency (February 17, 1994). ... Re-signed by Rams (June 10, 1994). ... Released by Rams (August 22, 1995). ... Signed by Washington Redskins (September 11, 1995). ... Released by Redskins (October 17, 1995). ... Signed by Dallas Cowboys (October 19, 1995). ... Granted unconditional free agency (February 16, 1996). ... Signed by Miami Dolphins (March 7, 1996). ... Released by Dolphins (March 20, 1997). ... Signed by Detroit Lions (April 24, 1997). ... Released by Lions (June 20, 1997). ... Re-signed by Lions (July 22, 1997). ... Granted unconditional free agency (February 13, 1998). ... Re-signed by Lions (March 6, 1998). ... Granted unconditional free agency (February 11, 2000). ... Signed by Baltimore Ravens (March 16, 2000). ... Released by Ravens (March 13, 2001). ... Signed by Lions (May 17, 2001). ... On injured reserve with neck injury (December 4-12, 2001). ... Announced retirement (December 12, 2001).
CHAMPIONSHIP GAME EXPERIENCE: Played in NFC championship game (1995 season). ... Member of Super Bowl championship team (1995 season). ... Played in AFC championship game (2000 season). ... Member of Super Bowl championship team (2000 season).
RECORDS: Holds NFL record for longest punt return—103 yards, touchdown (October 23, 1994, at New Orleans).
PRO STATISTICS: 1994—Returned one punt for 103 yards and a touchdown and recovered one fumble. 1996—Credited with one sack. 1997—Credited with two sacks. 1999—Credited with two sacks. 2000—Recovered two fumbles for 27 yards.

Year Team	G	GS	INTERCEPTIONS No.	Yds.	Avg.	TD
1991—Los Angeles Rams NFL	6	0	0	0	0.0	0
1992—Los Angeles Rams NFL	16	6	3	61	20.3	1
1993—Los Angeles Rams NFL	9	3	2	41	20.5	0
1994—Los Angeles Rams NFL	16	2	0	0	0.0	0
1995—Washington NFL	4	0	0	0	0.0	0
—Dallas NFL	9	0	0	0	0.0	0
1996—Miami NFL	14	0	0	0	0.0	0
1997—Detroit NFL	15	0	1	0	0.0	0
1998—Detroit NFL	16	0	0	0	0.0	0
1999—Detroit NFL	16	11	2	39	19.5	0
2000—Baltimore NFL	16	0	0	0	0.0	0
2001—Detroit NFL	9	0	2	74	37.0	1
Pro totals (11 years)	146	22	10	215	21.5	2

BAILEY, RODNEY   DE   STEELERS

PERSONAL: Born October 7, 1979, in Cleveland. ... 6-3/300. ... Full name: Rodney Dwayne Bailey.
HIGH SCHOOL: St. Edwards (Cleveland).
COLLEGE: Ohio State.
TRANSACTIONS/CAREER NOTES: Selected by Pittsburgh Steelers in sixth round (181st pick overall) of 2001 NFL draft. ... Signed by Steelers (June 6, 2001).
CHAMPIONSHIP GAME EXPERIENCE: Played in AFC championship game (2001 season).

Year Team	G	GS	SACKS
2001—Pittsburgh NFL	16	1	2.0

BAKER, JASON   P   49ERS

PERSONAL: Born May 17, 1978, in Fort Wayne, Ind. ... 6-1/195.
HIGH SCHOOL: Wayne (Ind.).
COLLEGE: Iowa.
TRANSACTIONS/CAREER NOTES: Signed as non-drafted free agent by Philadelphia Eagles (April 23, 2001). ... Released by Eagles (August 28, 2001). ... Signed by San Francisco 49ers (August 29, 2001).
PRO STATISTICS: 2001—Rushed once for no yards.

Year Team	G	No.	Yds.	PUNTING Avg.	Net avg.	In. 20	Blk.
2001—San Francisco NFL	16	69	2813	40.8	35.4	21	0

BAKER, JOHN   P   TEXANS

PERSONAL: Born April 22, 1977, in Brenham, Texas. ... 6-3/223.
HIGH SCHOOL: Brenham (Texas).
JUNIOR COLLEGE: Blinn Junior College.
COLLEGE: North Texas State.

TRANSACTIONS/CAREER NOTES: Signed as non-drafted free agent by Indianapolis Colts (April 16, 2000). ... Traded by Colts to St. Louis Rams for undisclosed draft pick (August 22, 2000). ... Claimed on waivers by Houston Texans (April 23, 2002).
CHAMPIONSHIP GAME EXPERIENCE: Played in NFC championship game (2001 season). ... Played in Super Bowl XXXVI (2001 season).
PRO STATISTICS: 2001—Rushed once for no yards and fumbled once for minus nine yards.

		PUNTING					
Year Team	G	No.	Yds.	Avg.	Net avg.	In. 20	Blk.
2000—St. Louis NFL	15	43	1736	40.4	34.2	13	1
2001—St. Louis NFL	16	43	1809	42.1	34.9	9	0
Pro totals (2 years)	31	86	3545	41.2	34.6	22	1

BAKER, TIM   WR   PANTHERS

PERSONAL: Born October 23, 1977, in Amarillo, Texas. ... 6-4/208. ... Full name: Timothy Charles Baker.
HIGH SCHOOL: Borger (Amarillo, Texas).
COLLEGE: Texas Tech.
TRANSACTIONS/CAREER NOTES: Signed as non-drafted free agent by Pittsburgh Steelers (April 23, 2001). ... Released by Steelers (August 31, 2001). ... Re-signed by Steelers to practice squad (September 3, 2001). ... Activated (September 12, 2001). ... Released by Steelers (October 15, 2001). ... Re-signed by Steelers to practice squad (October 16, 2001). ... Released by Steelers (October 23, 2001). ... Re-signed by Steelers to practice squad (November 7, 2001). ... Granted free agency after 2001 season. ... Signed by Carolina Panthers (March 13, 2002).
PLAYING EXPERIENCE: Pittsburgh NFL, 2001. ... Games/Games started: 2001 (3/0).

BANKS, TONY   QB

PERSONAL: Born April 5, 1973, in San Diego. ... 6-4/230. ... Full name: Anthony Lamar Banks. ... Cousin of Chip Banks, linebacker with Cleveland Browns (1982-86), San Diego Chargers (1987) and Indianapolis Colts (1989-92).
HIGH SCHOOL: Herbert Hoover (San Diego).
JUNIOR COLLEGE: San Diego Mesa College.
COLLEGE: Michigan State.
TRANSACTIONS/CAREER NOTES: Selected by St. Louis Rams in second round (42nd pick overall) of 1996 NFL draft. ... Signed by Rams (July 15, 1996). ... On injured reserve list with knee injury (December 14, 1998-remainder of season). ... Granted free agency (February 12, 1999). ... Re-signed by Rams (April 17, 1999). ... Traded by Rams to Baltimore Ravens for fifth-round pick (G Cameron Spikes) in 1999 draft and seventh-round pick (traded to Chicago) in 2000 draft (April 17, 1999). ... Granted unconditional free agency (February 11, 2000). ... Re-signed by Ravens (February 17, 2000). ... Released by Ravens (March 1, 2001). ... Signed by Dallas Cowboys (March 28, 2001). ... Released by Cowboys (August 14, 2001). ... Signed by Washington Redskins (August 16, 2001). ... Granted unconditional free agency (March 1, 2002).
CHAMPIONSHIP GAME EXPERIENCE: Member of Ravens for AFC championship game (2000 season); did not play. ... Member of Super Bowl championship team (2000 season).
PRO STATISTICS: 1996—Led league with 21 fumbles and recovered four fumbles for minus 17 yards. 1997—Tied for NFC lead with 15 fumbles and recovered three fumbles for minus 27 yards. 1998—Fumbled 10 times and recovered eight fumbles for minus 23 yards. 1999—Fumbled 11 times and recovered two fumbles. 2000—Fumbled five times and recovered two fumbles for minus two yards. 2001—Fumbled 10 times and recovered one fumble for minus 22 yards.
SINGLE GAME HIGHS (regular season): Attempts—49 (September 28, 1997, vs. Oakland); completions—29 (September 6, 1998, vs. New Orleans); yards—401 (November 2, 1997, vs. Atlanta); and touchdown passes—5 (September 10, 2000, vs. Jacksonville).
STATISTICAL PLATEAUS: 300-yard passing games: 1996 (2), 1997 (1), 1999 (1), 2001 (1). Total: 5.
MISCELLANEOUS: Regular-season record as starting NFL quarterback: 33-42 (.440).

				PASSING							RUSHING			TOTALS		
Year Team	G	GS	Att.	Cmp.	Pct.	Yds.	TD	Int.	Avg.	Rat.	Att.	Yds.	Avg.	TD	TD	2pt.	Pts.
1996—St. Louis NFL	14	13	368	192	52.2	2544	15	15	6.91	71.0	61	212	3.5	0	0	1	2
1997—St. Louis NFL	16	16	487	252	51.7	3254	14	13	6.68	71.5	47	186	4.0	1	1	0	6
1998—St. Louis NFL	14	14	408	241	59.1	2535	7	14	6.21	68.6	40	156	3.9	3	3	1	20
1999—Baltimore NFL	12	10	320	169	52.8	2136	17	8	6.68	81.2	24	93	3.9	0	0	0	0
2000—Baltimore NFL	11	8	274	150	54.7	1578	8	8	5.76	69.3	19	57	3.0	0	0	0	0
2001—Washington NFL	15	14	370	198	53.5	2386	10	10	6.45	71.3	47	152	3.2	2	2	0	12
Pro totals (6 years)	82	75	2227	1202	54.0	14433	71	68	6.48	72.0	238	856	3.6	6	6	2	40

RECORD AS BASEBALL PLAYER

TRANSACTIONS/CAREER NOTES: Threw right, batted right. ... Selected by Minnesota Twins organization in 10th round of free-agent draft (June 3, 1991).

					BATTING							FIELDING		
Year Team (League)	Pos.	G	AB	R	H	2B	3B	HR	RBI	Avg.	BB	SO	SB	PO	A	E	Avg.
1991—GC Twins (GCL)	DH	17	57	7	13	3	0	0	1	.228	4	16	2	...	...	...	...

BANNISTER, ALEX   WR   SEAHAWKS

PERSONAL: Born April 23, 1979, in Cincinnati. ... 6-5/201.
HIGH SCHOOL: Hughes Center (Cincinnati).
COLLEGE: Eastern Kentucky.
TRANSACTIONS/CAREER NOTES: Selected by Seattle Seahawks in fifth round (140th pick overall) of 2001 NFL draft. ... Signed by Seahawks (July 9, 2001).
PRO STATISTICS: 2001—Returned blocked punt for nine yards and a touchdown and recovered one fumble.
SINGLE GAME HIGHS (regular season): Receptions—1 (December 23, 2001, vs. New York Giants); yards—17 (December 2, 2001, vs. San Diego); and touchdown receptions—0.

			RECEIVING			
Year Team	G	GS	No.	Yds.	Avg.	TD
2001—Seattle NFL	16	0	4	50	12.5	0

BANTA, BRADFORD TE LIONS

PERSONAL: Born December 14, 1970, in Baton Rouge, La. ... 6-6/255. ... Full name: Dennis Bradford Banta.
HIGH SCHOOL: University (Baton Rouge, La.).
COLLEGE: Southern California.
TRANSACTIONS/CAREER NOTES: Selected by Indianapolis Colts in fourth round (106th pick overall) of 1994 NFL draft. ... Signed by Colts (July 22, 1994). ... Granted free agency (February 14, 1997). ... Re-signed by Colts (May 14, 1997). ... Granted unconditional free agency (February 11, 2000). ... Re-signed by Colts (March 9, 2000). ... Released by Colts (August 27, 2000). ... Signed by New York Jets (August 29, 2000). ... Granted unconditional free agency (March 2, 2001). ... Signed by Detroit Lions (April 19, 2001).
PLAYING EXPERIENCE: Indianapolis NFL, 1994-1999; New York Jets NFL, 2000; Detroit NFL, 2001. ... Games/Games started: 1994 (16/0), 1995 (16/2), 1996 (13/0), 1997 (15/0), 1998 (16/0), 1999 (16/0), 2000 (16/0), 2001 (16/0). Total: 124/2.
CHAMPIONSHIP GAME EXPERIENCE: Played in AFC championship game (1995 season).
PRO STATISTICS: 1995—Caught one pass for six yards. 1998—Caught one pass for seven yards and recovered one fumble. 2001—Fumbled once for minus six yards.
SINGLE GAME HIGHS (regular season): Receptions—1 (November 1, 1998, vs. New England); yards—7 (November 1, 1998, vs. New England); and touchdown receptions—0.

BARBER, RONDE CB BUCCANEERS

PERSONAL: Born April 7, 1975, in Montgomery County, Va. ... 5-10/184. ... Full name: Jamael Oronde Barber. ... Twin brother of Tiki Barber, running back, New York Giants. ... Name pronounced RON-day.
HIGH SCHOOL: Cave Spring (Roanoke, Va.).
COLLEGE: Virginia (degree in commerce, 1996).
TRANSACTIONS/CAREER NOTES: Selected after junior season by Tampa Bay Buccaneers in third round (66th pick overall) of 1997 NFL draft. ... Signed by Buccaneers (July 18, 1997). ... Granted free agency (February 11, 2000). ... Re-signed by Buccaneers (June 13, 2000). ... Granted unconditional free agency (March 2, 2001). ... Re-signed by Buccaneers (April 10, 2001).
CHAMPIONSHIP GAME EXPERIENCE: Played in NFC championship game (1999 season).
PRO STATISTICS: 1998—Returned one punt for 23 yards and a touchdown. 2000—Recovered one fumble for 24 yards and a touchdown. 2001—Recovered two fumbles.

			INTERCEPTIONS				SACKS
Year Team	G	GS	No.	Yds.	Avg.	TD	No.
1997—Tampa Bay NFL	1	0	0	0	0.0	0	0.0
1998—Tampa Bay NFL	16	9	2	67	33.5	0	3.0
1999—Tampa Bay NFL	16	15	2	60	30.0	0	1.0
2000—Tampa Bay NFL	16	16	2	46	23.0	1	5.5
2001—Tampa Bay NFL	16	16	†10	86	8.6	1	1.0
Pro totals (5 years)	65	56	16	259	16.2	2	10.5

BARBER, SHAWN LB EAGLES

PERSONAL: Born January 14, 1975, in Richmond, Va. ... 6-2/237.
HIGH SCHOOL: Hermitage (Richmond, Va.).
COLLEGE: Richmond.
TRANSACTIONS/CAREER NOTES: Selected by Washington Redskins in fourth round (113th pick overall) of 1998 NFL draft. ... Signed by Redskins (May 13, 1998). ... Granted free agency (March 2, 2001). ... Re-signed by Redskins (June 1, 2001). ... On injured reserve with knee injury (October 2, 2001-remainder of season). ... Granted unconditional free agency (March 1, 2002). ... Signed by Philadelphia Eagles (March 15, 2002).
PRO STATISTICS: 1999—Credited with one sack. 2000—Credited with two sacks and recovered three fumbles.

			INTERCEPTIONS			
Year Team	G	GS	No.	Yds.	Avg.	TD
1998—Washington NFL	16	1	1	0	0.0	0
1999—Washington NFL	16	16	2	70	35.0	1
2000—Washington NFL	14	14	0	0	0.0	0
2001—Washington NFL	3	3	0	0	0.0	0
Pro totals (4 years)	49	34	3	70	23.3	1

BARBER, TIKI RB GIANTS

PERSONAL: Born April 7, 1975, in Roanoke, Va. ... 5-10/200. ... Full name: Atiim Kiambu Barber. ... Twin brother of Ronde Barber, cornerback, Tampa Bay Buccaneers. ... Name pronounced TEE-kee.
HIGH SCHOOL: Cave Spring (Roanoke, Va.).
COLLEGE: Virginia.
TRANSACTIONS/CAREER NOTES: Selected by New York Giants in second round (36th pick overall) of 1997 NFL draft. ... Signed by Giants for 1997 season. ... Granted free agency (February 11, 2000). ... Re-signed by Giants (June 8, 2000). ... Granted unconditional free agency (March 2, 2001). ... Re-signed by Giants (March 8, 2001).
CHAMPIONSHIP GAME EXPERIENCE: Played in NFC championship game (2000 season). ... Played in Super Bowl XXXV (2000 season).
PRO STATISTICS: 1997—Fumbled three times. 1998—Fumbled once. 1999—Fumbled five times and recovered five fumbles. 2000—Fumbled nine times and recovered five fumbles. 2001—Fumbled eight times and recovered six fumbles for two yards.
SINGLE GAME HIGHS (regular season): Attempts—24 (December 23, 2000, vs. Jacksonville); yards—144 (September 3, 2000, vs. Arizona); and rushing touchdowns—2 (September 3, 2000, vs. Arizona).
STATISTICAL PLATEAUS: 100-yard rushing games: 1997 (1), 2000 (1), 2001 (3). Total: 5. ... 100-yard receiving games: 1999 (1).

				RUSHING				RECEIVING			PUNT RETURNS			KICKOFF RETURNS				TOTALS	
Year Team	G	GS	Att.	Yds.	Avg.	TD	No.	Yds.	Avg.	TD	No. Yds. Avg. TD			No.	Yds.	Avg.	TD	TD	2pt.	Pts.
1997—NY Giants NFL....	12	6	136	511	3.8	3	34	299	8.8	1	0 0 0.0 0			0	0	0.0	0	4	1	26
1998—NY Giants NFL	16	4	52	166	3.2	0	42	348	8.3	3	0 0 0.0 0			14	250	17.9	0	3	0	18
1999—NY Giants NFL	16	1	62	258	4.2	0	66	609	9.2	2	∞44 ‡506 11.5 ∞1			12	266	22.2	0	3	0	18
2000—NY Giants NFL	16	12	213	1006	4.7	8	70	719	10.3	1	‡39 332 8.5 0			1	28	28.0	0	9	0	54
2001—NY Giants NFL	14	9	166	865	5.2	4	72	577	8.0	0	38 338 8.9 0			0	0	0.0	0	4	1	26
Pro totals (5 years)	74	32	629	2806	4.5	15	284	2552	9.0	7	121 1176 9.7 1			27	544	20.1	0	23	2	142

BARKER, BRYAN — P — REDSKINS

PERSONAL: Born June 28, 1964, in Jacksonville Beach, Fla. ... 6-2/200. ... Full name: Bryan Christopher Barker.
HIGH SCHOOL: Miramonte (Orinda, Calif.).
COLLEGE: Santa Clara (degree in economics).
TRANSACTIONS/CAREER NOTES: Signed as non-drafted free agent by Denver Broncos (May 1988). ... Released by Broncos (July 19, 1988). ... Signed by Seattle Seahawks (1989). ... Released by Seahawks (August 30, 1989). ... Signed by Kansas City Chiefs (May 1, 1990). ... Released by Chiefs (August 28, 1990). ... Re-signed by Chiefs (September 26, 1990). ... Granted unconditional free agency (February 1-April 1, 1991). ... Re-signed by Chiefs for 1991 season. ... Granted unconditional free agency (February 1-April 1, 1992). ... Re-signed by Chiefs for 1992 season. ... Released by Chiefs (1994). ... Signed by Minnesota Vikings (May 18, 1994). ... Released by Vikings (August 30, 1994). ... Signed by Philadelphia Eagles (October 11, 1994). ... Granted unconditional free agency (February 17, 1995). ... Signed by Jacksonville Jaguars (March 7, 1995). ... Granted unconditional free agency (March 2, 2001). ... Signed by Washington Redskins (April 12, 2001).
CHAMPIONSHIP GAME EXPERIENCE: Played in AFC championship game (1993, 1996 and 1999 seasons).
HONORS: Played in Pro Bowl (1997 season).
PRO STATISTICS: 1997—Rushed once for no yards, attempted one pass with a completion for 22 yards and fumbled once for minus 19 yards. 1999—Rushed once for six yards.

					PUNTING		
Year Team	G	No.	Yds.	Avg.	Net avg.	In. 20	Blk.
1990—Kansas City NFL............	13	64	2479	38.7	33.3	16	0
1991—Kansas City NFL............	16	57	2303	40.4	35.0	11	0
1992—Kansas City NFL............	15	75	3245	43.3	35.2	16	1
1993—Kansas City NFL............	16	76	3240	42.6	35.3	19	1
1994—Philadelphia NFL............	11	66	2696	40.8	‡36.2	20	0
1995—Jacksonville NFL............	16	82	3591	43.8	*38.6	19	0
1996—Jacksonville NFL............	16	69	3016	43.7	35.6	16	0
1997—Jacksonville NFL............	16	66	2964	44.9	38.8	27	0
1998—Jacksonville NFL............	16	85	3824	45.0	38.5	28	0
1999—Jacksonville NFL............	16	78	3260	41.8	36.9	32	0
2000—Jacksonville NFL............	16	76	3194	42.0	34.4	29	0
2001—Washington NFL.............	16	90	3747	41.6	34.8	27	0
Pro totals (12 years)	183	884	37559	42.5	36.1	260	2

BARLOW, KEVAN — RB — 49ERS

PERSONAL: Born January 7, 1979, in Pittsburgh. ... 6-1/238. ... Full name: Kevan C. Barlow.
HIGH SCHOOL: Peabody (Pittsburgh).
COLLEGE: Pittsburgh.
TRANSACTIONS/CAREER NOTES: Selected by San Francisco 49ers in third round (80th pick overall) of 2001 NFL draft. ... Signed by 49ers (July 25, 2001).
SINGLE GAME HIGHS (regular season): Attempts—16 (January 6, 2002, vs. New Orleans); yards—83 (October 1, 2002, vs. New York Jets); and rushing touchdowns—2 (December 16, 2001, vs. Miami).

			RUSHING				RECEIVING				TOTALS			
Year Team	G	GS	Att.	Yds.	Avg.	TD	No.	Yds.	Avg.	TD	TD	2pt.	Pts.	Fum.
2001—San Francisco NFL................	15	0	125	512	4.1	4	22	247	11.2	1	5	0	30	1

BARLOW, REGGIE — WR/PR/KR — RAIDERS

PERSONAL: Born January 22, 1973, in Montgomery, Ala. ... 6-0/190. ... Full name: Reggie Devon Barlow.
HIGH SCHOOL: Lanier (Montgomery, Ala.).
COLLEGE: Alabama State.
TRANSACTIONS/CAREER NOTES: Selected by Jacksonville Jaguars in fourth round (110th pick overall) of 1996 NFL draft. ... Signed by Jaguars (May 28, 1996). ... Granted free agency (February 12, 1999). ... Re-signed by Jaguars (March 23, 1999). ... Released by Jaguars (February 27. 2001). ... Signed by Oakland Raiders (March 21, 2001). ... On injured reserve with foot injury (August 28, 2001-entire season).
CHAMPIONSHIP GAME EXPERIENCE: Played in AFC championship game (1996 and 1999 seasons).
PRO STATISTICS: 1997—Recovered one fumble. 1998—Recovered one fumble. 1999—Recovered one fumble.
SINGLE GAME HIGHS (regular season): Receptions—4 (December 2, 1999, vs. Pittsburgh); yards—50 (October 12, 1998, vs. Miami); and touchdown receptions—0.

			RECEIVING				PUNT RETURNS				KICKOFF RETURNS				TOTALS		
Year Team	G	GS	No.	Yds.	Avg.	TD	No.	Yds.	Avg.	TD	No.	Yds.	Avg.	TD	TD	2pt.	Pts.	Fum.
1996—Jacksonville NFL	7	0	0	0	0.0	0	0	0	0.0	0	0	0	0.0	0	0	0	0	0
1997—Jacksonville NFL	16	0	5	74	14.8	0	36	412	11.4	0	10	267	26.7 ▲1		2	0	12	2
1998—Jacksonville NFL	16	2	11	168	15.3	0	43	*555	§12.9	2	30	747	24.9	0	1	0	6	1
1999—Jacksonville NFL	14	2	16	202	12.6	0	38	414	10.9	1	19	396	20.8	0	1	0	6	4
2000—Jacksonville NFL	16	0	1	28	28.0	0	29	200	6.9	0	11	224	20.4	0	0	0	0	0
2001—Oakland NFL.................								Did not play.										
Pro totals (5 years)	69	4	33	472	14.3	0	146	1581	10.8	2	70	1634	23.3	1	4	0	24	7

BARNDT, TOM — DT

PERSONAL: Born March 14, 1972, in Mentor, Ohio. ... 6-3/300. ... Full name: Thomas Allen Barndt.
HIGH SCHOOL: Mentor (Ohio).
COLLEGE: Pittsburgh.
TRANSACTIONS/CAREER NOTES: Selected by Kansas City Chiefs in sixth round (207th pick overall) of 1995 NFL draft. ... Signed by Chiefs for the 1995 season. ... Released by Chiefs (August 27, 1995). ... Re-signed by Chiefs to practice squad (August 29, 1995). ... Assigned by Chiefs to Scottish Claymores in 1996 World League enhancement allocation program (February 19, 1996). ... Granted free agency (February 12, 1999). ... Re-signed by Chiefs (June 16, 1999). ... Granted unconditional free agency (February 11, 2000). ... Signed by Cincinnati Bengals (February 18, 2000). ... Released by Bengals (September 4, 2001). ... Signed by New York Jets (September 11, 2001). ... Released by Jets (November 6, 2001).
PRO STATISTICS: 1998—Recovered two fumbles. 1999—Recovered one fumble. 2000—Recovered one fumble. 2001—Recovered one fumble.

Year Team	G	GS	SACKS
1995—Kansas City NFL		Did not play.	
1996—Scottish W.L.	...	...	0.0
—Kansas City NFL	13	0	0.0
1997—Kansas City NFL	16	1	2.0
1998—Kansas City NFL	16	16	3.5
1999—Kansas City NFL	16	13	2.5
2000—Cincinnati NFL	14	5	0.0
2001—New York Jets NFL	6	1	0.0
W.L. totals (1 year)	...	...	0.0
NFL totals (5 years)	81	36	8.0
Pro totals (6 years)	...	...	8.0

BARNES, LIONEL — DE

PERSONAL: Born April 19, 1976, in New Orleans. ... 6-5/274. ... Full name: Lionel Barnes Jr.
HIGH SCHOOL: Lakenheath American (Suffolk, England).
JUNIOR COLLEGE: Barton County Community College, Kan. (did not play football).
COLLEGE: Northeast Louisiana.
TRANSACTIONS/CAREER NOTES: Selected by St. Louis Rams in sixth round (176th pick overall) of 1999 NFL draft. ... Signed by Rams (July 19, 1999). ... Claimed on waivers by Indianapolis Colts (October 12, 2000). ... Released by Colts (November 17, 2001). ... Re-signed by Colts (November 21, 2001). ... Granted free agency (March 1, 2002).
PLAYING EXPERIENCE: St. Louis NFL, 1999; St. Louis (1) and Indianapolis (1) NFL, 2000; Indianapolis NFL, 2001. ... Games/Games started: 1999 (3/0), 2000 (St.L-1/0; Ind.-1/0; Total: 2/0), 2001 (6/0). Total: 11/0.
CHAMPIONSHIP GAME EXPERIENCE: Member of Rams for NFC championship game (1999 season); inactive. ... Member of Super Bowl championship team (1999 season); inactive.

BARRETT, DAVID — CB — CARDINALS

PERSONAL: Born December 22, 1977, in Osceola, Ark. ... 5-10/195.
HIGH SCHOOL: Osceola (Ark.).
COLLEGE: Arkansas.
TRANSACTIONS/CAREER NOTES: Selected by Arizona Cardinals in fourth round (102nd pick overall) of 2000 NFL draft. ... Signed by Cardinals (June 15, 2000).
PLAYING EXPERIENCE: Arizona NFL, 2000 and 2001. ... Games/Games started: 2000 (16/0), 2001 (16/9). Total: 32/9.
PRO STATISTICS: 2000—Recovered one fumble and ran 46 yards with lateral from kickoff return. 2001—Intercepted two passes for 30 yards.

BARROW, MIKE — LB — GIANTS

PERSONAL: Born April 19, 1970, in Homestead, Fla. ... 6-2/240. ... Full name: Micheal Colvin Barrow.
HIGH SCHOOL: Homestead (Fla.) Senior.
COLLEGE: Miami (Fla.) (degree in accounting, 1992).
TRANSACTIONS/CAREER NOTES: Selected by Houston Oilers in second round (47th pick overall) of 1993 NFL draft. ... Signed by Oilers (July 30, 1993). ... Granted free agency (February 16, 1996). ... Re-signed by Oilers (August 9, 1996). ... Granted unconditional free agency (February 14, 1997). ... Signed by Carolina Panthers (February 20, 1997). ... Released by Panthers (February 22, 2000). ... Signed by New York Giants (March 2, 2000).
CHAMPIONSHIP GAME EXPERIENCE: Played in NFC championship game (2000 season). ... Played in Super Bowl XXXV (2000 season).
HONORS: Named linebacker on THE SPORTING NEWS college All-America first team (1992).
PRO STATISTICS: 1995—Recovered one fumble. 1996—Recovered one fumble. 1997—Recovered two fumbles. 1998—Intercepted one pass for 10 yards and recovered two fumbles. 1999—Recovered one fumble. 2000—Intercepted one pass for seven yards and recovered one fumble. 2001—Recovered two fumbles for 13 yards.

Year Team	G	GS	SACKS
1993—Houston NFL	16	0	1.0
1994—Houston NFL	16	16	2.5
1995—Houston NFL	13	12	3.0
1996—Houston NFL	16	16	6.0
1997—Carolina NFL	16	16	8.5
1998—Carolina NFL	16	16	4.0
1999—Carolina NFL	16	16	4.0
2000—New York Giants NFL	15	15	3.5
2001—New York Giants NFL	16	16	6.0
Pro totals (9 years)	140	123	38.5

BARTEE, WILLIAM   CB   CHIEFS

PERSONAL: Born June 25, 1977, in Daytona Beach, Fla. ... 6-1/196.
HIGH SCHOOL: Atlantic (Daytona Beach, Fla.).
JUNIOR COLLEGE: Butler County Community College (Kan.).
COLLEGE: Oklahoma.
TRANSACTIONS/CAREER NOTES: Selected by Kansas City Chiefs in second round (54th pick overall) of 2000 NFL draft. ... Signed by Chiefs (July 21, 2000).

Year — Team	G	GS	SACKS
2000—Kansas City NFL	16	3	1.0
2001—Kansas City NFL	16	5	1.0
Pro totals (2 years)	32	8	2.0

BARTON, ERIC   LB   RAIDERS

PERSONAL: Born September 29, 1977, in Alexandria, Va. ... 6-2/240.
HIGH SCHOOL: Thomas A. Edison (Alexandria, Va.).
COLLEGE: Maryland.
TRANSACTIONS/CAREER NOTES: Selected by Oakland Raiders in fifth round (146th pick overall) of 1999 NFL draft. ... Signed by Raiders for 1999 season.
CHAMPIONSHIP GAME EXPERIENCE: Member of Raiders for AFC Championship game (2000 season); inactive.

Year — Team	G	GS	SACKS
1999—Oakland NFL	16	3	3.0
2000—Oakland NFL	4	0	0.0
2001—Oakland NFL	16	1	0.0
Pro totals (3 years)	36	4	3.0

BARTRUM, MIKE   TE   EAGLES

PERSONAL: Born June 23, 1970, in Gallipolis, Ohio. ... 6-4/245. ... Full name: Michael Weldon Bartrum.
HIGH SCHOOL: Meigs (Pomeroy, Ohio).
COLLEGE: Marshall (degree in education).
TRANSACTIONS/CAREER NOTES: Signed as non-drafted free agent by Kansas City Chiefs (May 5, 1993). ... Released by Chiefs (August 30, 1993). ... Re-signed by Chiefs to practice squad (August 31, 1993). ... Activated (October 27, 1993). ... Released by Chiefs (August 23, 1994). ... Signed by Green Bay Packers (January 20, 1995). ... On injured reserve with broken arm (October 11, 1995-remainder of season). ... Traded by Packers with DE Walter Scott to New England Patriots for past considerations (August 25, 1996). ... On injured reserve with forearm injury (November 12, 1997-remainder of season). ... Granted unconditional free agency (February 13, 1998). ... Re-signed by Patriots (April 7, 1998). ... Released by Patriots (April 10, 2000). ... Signed by Philadelphia Eagles (April 17, 2000). ... Granted unconditional free agency (March 1, 2002). ... Re-signed by Eagles (March 8, 2002).
PLAYING EXPERIENCE: Kansas City NFL, 1993; Green Bay NFL, 1995; New England NFL, 1996-1999; Philadelphia NFL, 2000 and 2001. ... Games/Games started: 1993 (3/0), 1995 (4/0), 1996 (16/0), 1997 (16/0), 1998 (16/0), 1999 (16/0), 2000 (16/0), 2001 (16/0). Total: 96/0.
CHAMPIONSHIP GAME EXPERIENCE: Member of Chiefs for AFC championship game (1993 season); inactive. ... Played in AFC championship game (1996 season). ... Played in Super Bowl XXXI (1996 season). ... Played in NFC championship game (2001 season).
PRO STATISTICS: 1996—Caught one pass for one yard and a touchdown. 1999—Caught one pass for one yard and a touchdown and fumbled once for minus seven yards. 2000—Recovered one fumble. 2001—Caught one pass for four yards and a touchdown.
SINGLE GAME HIGHS (regular season): Receptions—1 (November 11, 2001, vs. Minnesota); yards—4 (November 11, 2001, vs. Minnesota); and touchdown receptions—1 (November 11, 2001, vs. Minnesota).

BASHIR, IDREES   DB   COLTS

PERSONAL: Born December 7, 1978, in Decatur, Ga. ... 6-2/198.
HIGH SCHOOL: Dunwoody (Calif.).
COLLEGE: Memphis.
TRANSACTIONS/CAREER NOTES: Selected by Indianapolis Colts in second round (37th pick overall) of 2001 NFL draft. ... Signed by Colts (July 25, 2001).

			INTERCEPTIONS		
Year — Team	G	GS	No.	Yds.	Avg.	TD
2001—Indianapolis NFL	15	15	1	0	0.0	0

BATCH, CHARLIE   QB

PERSONAL: Born December 5, 1974, in Homestead, Pa. ... 6-2/220. ... Full name: Charles D'Donte Batch.
HIGH SCHOOL: Steel Valley (Munhall, Pa.).
COLLEGE: Eastern Michigan (degree in business, 1997).
TRANSACTIONS/CAREER NOTES: Selected by Detroit Lions in second round (60th pick overall) of 1998 NFL draft. ... Signed by Lions (July 19, 1998). ... On injured reserve with back injury (December 24, 1998-remainder of season). ... On injured reserve with shoulder injury (December 5, 2001-remainder of season). ... Released by Lions (June 3, 2002).
RECORDS: Holds NFL rookie-season record for lowest interception percentage—1.98.
PRO STATISTICS: 1998—Fumbled twice. 1999—Fumbled four times. 2000—Fumbled six times and recovered one fumbled for minus five yards. 2001—Fumbled six times and recovered two fumbles.
SINGLE GAME HIGHS (regular season): Attempts—62 (November 18, 2001, vs. Arizona); completions—36 (November 18, 2001, vs. Arizona); yards—436 (November 18, 2001, vs. Arizona); and touchdown passes—3 (November 18, 2001, vs. Arizona).
STATISTICAL PLATEAUS: 300-yard passing games: 2001 (3).

MISCELLANEOUS: Regular-season record as starting NFL quarterback: 19-27 (.413).

				PASSING						RUSHING				TOTALS		
Year Team	G	GS	Att.	Cmp.	Pct.	Yds.	TD	Int.	Avg.	Rat.	Att.	Yds.	Avg.	TD	TD	2pt.	Pts.
1998—Detroit NFL	12	12	303	173	57.1	2178	11	6	7.19	83.5	41	229	5.6	1	1	0	6
1999—Detroit NFL	11	10	270	151	55.9	1957	13	7	7.25	84.1	28	87	3.1	2	2	0	12
2000—Detroit NFL	15	15	412	221	53.6	2489	13	15	6.04	67.3	44	199	4.5	2	2	0	12
2001—Detroit NFL	10	9	341	198	58.1	2392	12	12	7.01	76.8	12	45	3.8	0	0	0	0
Pro totals (4 years)	48	46	1326	743	56.0	9016	49	40	6.80	76.9	125	560	4.5	5	5	0	30

BATES, D'WAYNE — WR — VIKINGS

PERSONAL: Born December 4, 1975, in Aiken, S.C. ... 6-2/215. ... Full name: D'Wayne Lavoris Bates.
HIGH SCHOOL: Silver Bluff (Aiken, S.C.).
COLLEGE: Northwestern.
TRANSACTIONS/CAREER NOTES: Selected by Chicago Bears in third round (71st pick overall) of 1999 NFL draft. ... Signed by Bears (July 22, 1999). ... Granted free agency (March 1, 2002). ... Tendered offer sheet by Minnesota Vikings (March 27, 2002). ... Offer matched by Bears (April 3, 2002). ... Claimed on waivers by Vikings (April 9, 2002).
PLAYING EXPERIENCE: Chicago NFL, 1999-2001. ... Games/Games started: 1999 (7/1), 2000 (5/0), 2001 (11/1). Total: 23/2.
PRO STATISTICS: 1999—Caught two passes for 19 yards. 2000—Rushed once for minus two yards and caught four passes for 42 yards. 2001—Caught nine passes for 160 yards and a touchdown.
SINGLE GAME HIGHS (regular season): Receptions—4 (January 6, 2002, vs. Jacksonville); yards—107 (December 30, 2001, vs. Detroit); and touchdown receptions—1 (December 30, 2001, vs. Detroit).
STATISTICAL PLATEAUS: 100-yard receiving games: 2001 (1).
MISCELLANEOUS: Selected by Toronto Blue Jays organization in 53rd round of free-agent draft (June 2, 1994); did not sign.

BATES, MICHAEL — RB/KR — PANTHERS

PERSONAL: Born December 19, 1969, in Tucson, Ariz. ... 5-10/189. ... Full name: Michael Dion Bates. ... Brother of Mario Bates, running back, with New Orleans Saints (1994-97), Arizona Cardinals (1998-99) and Detroit Lions (2000).
HIGH SCHOOL: Amphitheater (Tucson, Ariz.).
COLLEGE: Arizona.
TRANSACTIONS/CAREER NOTES: Selected after sophomore season by Seattle Seahawks in sixth round (151st pick overall) of 1992 NFL draft. ... Missed 1992 season due to contract dispute. ... Signed by Seahawks (March 7, 1993). ... Claimed on waivers by Carolina Panthers (August 28, 1995). ... Traded by Panthers to Cleveland Browns for LB Travis Hill (August 29, 1995). ... Granted unconditional free agency (February 16, 1996). ... Signed by Panthers (March 12, 1996). ... Granted unconditional free agency (February 13, 1998). ... Re-signed by Panthers (March 4, 1998). ... Granted unconditional free agency (March 2, 2001). ... Signed by Washington Redskins (July 10, 2001). ... Released by Redskins (March 12, 2002). ... Signed by Panthers (March 25, 2002).
CHAMPIONSHIP GAME EXPERIENCE: Played in NFC championship game (1996 season).
HONORS: Named kick returner on THE SPORTING NEWS NFL All-Pro team (1996 and 1997). ... Played in Pro Bowl (1996-2000 seasons).
PRO STATISTICS: 1993—Rushed twice for 12 yards and recovered two fumbles for three yards. 1994—Rushed twice for minus four yards. 1997—Returned one punt for eight yards and recovered two fumbles. 1999—Rushed three times for 12 yards. 2000—Rushed five times for 13 yards, returned seven punts for 31 yards and recovered one fumble. 2001—Returned two punts for five yards and recovered two fumbles.
SINGLE GAME HIGHS (regular season): Attempts—2 (December 3, 2000, vs. St. Louis); yards—14 (November 7, 1999, vs. Philadelphia); and rushing touchdowns—0.
MISCELLANEOUS: Won bronze medal in 200-meter dash in 1992 Summer Olympics.

			RECEIVING				KICKOFF RETURNS				TOTALS			
Year Team	G	GS	No.	Yds.	Avg.	TD	No.	Yds.	Avg.	TD	TD	2pt.	Pts.	Fum.
1992—Seattle NFL							Did not play.							
1993—Seattle NFL	16	1	1	6	6.0	0	30	603	20.1	0	0	0	0	1
1994—Seattle NFL	15	0	5	112	22.4	1	26	508	19.5	0	1	0	6	3
1995—Cleveland NFL	13	0	0	0	0.0	0	9	176	19.6	0	0	0	0	0
1996—Carolina NFL	14	0	0	0	0.0	0	33	998	*30.2	1	1	0	6	2
1997—Carolina NFL	16	0	0	0	0.0	0	47	1281	*27.3	0	0	0	0	4
1998—Carolina NFL	14	0	0	0	0.0	0	59	1480	25.1	1	1	0	6	1
1999—Carolina NFL	16	0	1	2	2.0	0	52	1287	24.8	†2	2	0	12	1
2000—Carolina NFL	16	0	5	38	7.6	0	42	941	22.4	1	1	0	6	4
2001—Washington NFL	16	0	0	0	0.0	0	49	1150	23.5	0	0	0	0	4
Pro totals (9 years)	136	1	12	158	13.2	1	347	8424	24.3	5	6	0	36	20

BATTAGLIA, MARCO — TE — BUCCANEERS

PERSONAL: Born January 25, 1973, in Howard Beach, N.Y. ... 6-3/248. ... Name pronounced buh-TAG-lee-uh.
HIGH SCHOOL: St. Francis (Fresh Meadows, N.Y.).
COLLEGE: Rutgers.
TRANSACTIONS/CAREER NOTES: Selected by Cincinnati Bengals in second round (39th pick overall) of 1996 NFL draft. ... Signed by Bengals (July 15, 1996). ... Granted free agency (February 12, 1999). ... Re-signed by Bengals (May 25, 1999). ... On non-football illness list with appendectomy (November 17-December 10, 2001). ... Claimed on waivers by Washington Redskins (December 11, 2001). ... Granted unconditional free agency (March 1, 2002). ... Signed by Tampa Bay Buccaneers (March 19, 2002).
HONORS: Named tight end on THE SPORTING NEWS college All-America first team (1995).
PRO STATISTICS: 1996—Returned one kickoff for eight yards and recovered one fumble. 1997—Recovered two fumbles. 1998—Returned one kickoff for five yards and recovered three fumbles.
SINGLE GAME HIGHS (regular season): Receptions—4 (November 11, 2001, vs. Jacksonville); yards—57 (October 21, 2001, vs. Chicago); and touchdown receptions—1 (November 1, 1998, vs. Denver).

				RECEIVING				TOTALS		
Year Team	G	GS	No.	Yds.	Avg.	TD	TD	2pt.	Pts.	Fum.
1996—Cincinnati NFL	16	0	8	79	9.9	0	0	0	0	0
1997—Cincinnati NFL	16	0	12	149	12.4	1	1	0	6	2
1998—Cincinnati NFL	16	0	10	47	4.7	1	1	0	6	1
1999—Cincinnati NFL	16	0	14	153	10.9	0	0	0	0	0
2000—Cincinnati NFL	16	10	13	105	8.1	0	0	0	0	0
2001—Cincinnati NFL	8	1	13	118	9.1	0	0	0	0	1
—Washington NFL	3	0	1	9	9.0	0	0	0	0	0
Pro totals (6 years)	91	11	71	660	9.3	2	2	0	12	4

BATTEAUX, PATRICK   WR   CHARGERS

PERSONAL: Born April 18, 1978, in Houston. ... 6-0/195.
HIGH SCHOOL: Elkins (Sugar Land, Texas).
COLLEGE: Texas Christian.
TRANSACTIONS/CAREER NOTES: Signed as non-drafted free agent by San Diego Chargers (February 21, 2001). ... Assigned by Chargers to Rhein Fire in 2001 NFL Europe enhancement allocation program (February 21, 2001). ... Released by Chargers (September 2, 2001). ... Re-signed by Chargers to practice squad (September 4, 2001). ... Activated (November 14, 2001). ... Released by Chargers (December 4, 2001). ... Re-signed by Chargers to practice squad (December 6, 2001). ... Activated (December 14, 2001).
SINGLE GAME HIGHS (regular season): Receptions—2 (December 30, 2001, vs. Seattle); yards—19 (December 30, 2001, vs. Seattle); and touchdown receptions—0.

				RECEIVING		
Year Team	G	GS	No.	Yds.	Avg.	TD
2001—Rhein NFLE	...	...	0	0	0.0	0
—San Diego NFL	5	0	3	25	8.3	0
NFL Europe totals (1 year)	...	...	0	0	0.0	0
NFL totals (1 year)	5	0	3	25	8.3	0
Pro totals (2 years)	5	0	3	25	8.3	0

BATTLES, AINSLEY   S   JAGUARS

PERSONAL: Born November 6, 1978, in Lilburn, Ga. ... 5-10/200.
HIGH SCHOOL: Parkview (Lilburn, Ga.).
COLLEGE: Vanderbilt.
TRANSACTIONS/CAREER NOTES: Signed as non-drafted free agent by Pittsburgh Steelers (April 21, 2000). ... Claimed on waivers by Jacksonville Jaguars (September 3, 2001).
PRO STATISTICS: 2000—Fumbled once and recovered two fumbles for minus one yard. 2001—Recovered two fumbles for 60 yards and a touchdown.

			INTERCEPTIONS				SACKS
Year Team	G	GS	No.	Yds.	Avg.	TD	No.
2000—Pittsburgh NFL	16	1	0	0	0.0	0	1.0
2001—Jacksonville NFL	13	11	2	26	13.0	0	1.0
Pro totals (2 years)	29	12	2	26	13.0	0	2.0

BAXTER, FRED   TE   BEARS

PERSONAL: Born June 14, 1971, in Brundidge, Ala. ... 6-3/252. ... Full name: Frederick Denard Baxter.
HIGH SCHOOL: Pike County (Brundidge, Ala.).
COLLEGE: Auburn.
TRANSACTIONS/CAREER NOTES: Selected by New York Jets in fifth round (115th pick overall) of 1993 NFL draft. ... Signed by Jets (July 13, 1993). ... On injured reserve with broken hand (November 21, 2000-remainder of season). ... Released by Jets (December 23, 2000). ... Signed by Chicago Bears (February 27, 2001).
CHAMPIONSHIP GAME EXPERIENCE: Played in AFC championship game (1998 season).
PRO STATISTICS: 1994—Returned one kickoff for 20 yards and recovered one fumble. 1995—Returned six kickoffs for 36 yards and recovered two fumbles for eight yards. 1997—Returned one kickoff for no yards. 1998—Returned one kickoff for eight yards and recovered one fumble. 1999—Recovered one fumble. 2000—Returned one kickoff for 15 yards and recovered one fumble. 2001—Recovered one fumble.
SINGLE GAME HIGHS (regular season): Receptions—6 (September 17, 1995, vs. Jacksonville); yards—99 (September 17, 1995, vs. Jacksonville); and touchdown receptions—1 (December 16, 2001, vs. Tampa Bay).

				RECEIVING				TOTALS		
Year Team	G	GS	No.	Yds.	Avg.	TD	TD	2pt.	Pts.	Fum.
1993—New York Jets NFL	7	0	3	48	16.0	1	1	0	6	0
1994—New York Jets NFL	11	1	3	11	3.7	1	1	0	6	0
1995—New York Jets NFL	15	3	18	222	12.3	1	1	0	6	1
1996—New York Jets NFL	16	4	7	114	16.3	0	0	0	0	1
1997—New York Jets NFL	16	9	27	276	10.2	3	3	0	18	0
1998—New York Jets NFL	14	1	3	50	16.7	0	0	0	0	0
1999—New York Jets NFL	14	8	8	66	8.3	2	2	0	12	0
2000—New York Jets NFL	9	6	4	22	5.5	2	2	0	12	0
2001—Chicago NFL	14	14	22	148	6.7	2	2	0	12	0
Pro totals (9 years)	116	46	95	957	10.1	12	12	0	72	3

BAXTER, GARY   CB   RAVENS

PERSONAL: Born November 24, 1978, in Tyler, Texas. ... 6-2/204. ... Full name: Gary Wayne Baxter.
HIGH SCHOOL: John Tyler (Tyler, Texas).
COLLEGE: Baylor.
TRANSACTIONS/CAREER NOTES: Selected by Baltimore Ravens in second round (62nd pick overall) of 2001 NFL draft. ... Signed by Ravens (July 20, 2001).
PLAYING EXPERIENCE: Baltimore NFL, 2001. ... Games/Games started: 2001 (6/0).

BEAN, ROBERT　　　CB　　　BENGALS

PERSONAL: Born January 6, 1978, in Atlanta. ... 5-11/178. ... Full name: Robert D. Bean Jr.
HIGH SCHOOL: Lakeside (Atlanta).
JUNIOR COLLEGE: Georgia Military College.
COLLEGE: Mississippi State.
TRANSACTIONS/CAREER NOTES: Selected by Cincinnati Bengals in fifth round (133rd pick overall) of 2000 NFL draft. ... Signed by Bengals (June 16, 2000).
PRO STATISTICS: 2001—Recovered one fumble for 10 yards.

			INTERCEPTIONS		
Year Team	G	GS	No.	Yds.	Avg.	TD
2000—Cincinnati NFL	12	4	1	0	0.0	0
2001—Cincinnati NFL	15	4	0	0	0.0	0
Pro totals (2 years)	27	8	1	0	0.0	0

BEASLEY, AARON　　　CB　　　JETS

PERSONAL: Born July 7, 1973, in Pottstown, Pa. ... 6-0/205. ... Full name: Aaron Bruce Beasley.
HIGH SCHOOL: Pottstown (Pa.), then Valley Forge Military Academy (Wayne, Pa.).
COLLEGE: West Virginia.
TRANSACTIONS/CAREER NOTES: Selected by Jacksonville Jaguars in third round (63rd pick overall) of 1996 NFL draft. ... Signed by Jaguars (May 24, 1996). ... Granted free agency (February 12, 1999). ... Re-signed by Jaguars (March 3, 1999). ... Granted unconditional free agency (February 11, 2000). ... Re-signed by Jaguars (February 11, 2000). ... On injured reserve with shoulder injury (December 21, 2001-remainder of season). ... Released by Jaguars (February 28, 2002). ... Signed by New York Jets (March 8, 2002).
CHAMPIONSHIP GAME EXPERIENCE: Played in AFC championship game (1996 and 1999 seasons).
PRO STATISTICS: 1998—Recovered one fumble for 90 yards and a touchdown and ran 30 yards on a lateral from punt return. 2000—Recovered one fumble. 2001—Recovered one fumble for 40 yards and a touchdown.
MISCELLANEOUS: Holds Jacksonville Jaguars all-time record for most interceptions (15).

			INTERCEPTIONS				SACKS
Year Team	G	GS	No.	Yds.	Avg.	TD	No.
1996—Jacksonville NFL	9	7	1	0	0.0	0	1.0
1997—Jacksonville NFL	9	7	1	5	5.0	0	0.0
1998—Jacksonville NFL	16	15	3	35	11.7	0	0.0
1999—Jacksonville NFL	16	16	6	*200	§33.3	†2	1.5
2000—Jacksonville NFL	14	14	1	39	39.0	0	5.0
2001—Jacksonville NFL	12	12	3	0	0.0	0	0.0
Pro totals (6 years)	76	71	15	279	18.6	2	7.5

BEASLEY, FRED　　　FB　　　49ERS

PERSONAL: Born September 18, 1974, in Montgomery, Ala. ... 6-0/246. ... Full name: Frederick Jerome Beasley.
HIGH SCHOOL: Robert E. Lee (Montgomery, Ala.).
COLLEGE: Auburn.
TRANSACTIONS/CAREER NOTES: Selected by San Francisco 49ers in sixth round (180th pick overall) of 1998 NFL draft. ... Signed by 49ers (July 18, 1998). ... Granted free agency (March 2, 2001). ... Re-signed by 49ers (March 2, 2001). ... Granted unconditional free agency (March 1, 2002). ... Re-signed by 49ers (March 8, 2002).
PRO STATISTICS: 1999—Recovered two fumbles.
SINGLE GAME HIGHS (regular season): Attempts—12 (December 26, 1999, vs. Washington); yards—65 (December 26, 1999, vs. Washington); and rushing touchdowns—2 (December 12, 1999, vs. Atlanta).

			RUSHING				RECEIVING				TOTALS			
Year Team	G	GS	Att.	Yds.	Avg.	TD	No.	Yds.	Avg.	TD	TD	2pt.	Pts.	Fum.
1998—San Francisco NFL	16	0	0	0	0.0	0	1	11	11.0	0	0	0	0	0
1999—San Francisco NFL	13	11	58	276	4.8	4	32	282	8.8	0	4	0	24	2
2000—San Francisco NFL	15	15	50	147	2.9	3	31	233	7.5	3	6	0	36	0
2001—San Francisco NFL	15	12	23	73	3.2	1	16	99	6.2	0	1	0	6	1
Pro totals (4 years)	59	38	131	496	3.8	8	80	625	7.8	3	11	0	66	3

BECHT, ANTHONY　　　TE　　　JETS

PERSONAL: Born August 8, 1977, in Media, Pa. ... 6-5/272.
HIGH SCHOOL: Monsignor Bonner (Drexel Hill, Pa.).
COLLEGE: West Virginia (degree in business, 1999).
TRANSACTIONS/CAREER NOTES: Selected by New York Jets in first round (27th pick overall) of 2000 NFL draft. ... Signed by Jets (May 26, 2000).
PRO STATISTICS: 2000—Fumbled once and returned two kickoffs for no yards.
SINGLE GAME HIGHS (regular season): Receptions—5 (October 21, 2001, vs. St. Louis); yards—58 (September 9, 2001, vs. Indianapolis); and touchdown receptions—2 (October 21, 2001, vs. St. Louis).

			RECEIVING		
Year Team	G	GS	No.	Yds.	Avg.	TD
2000—New York Jets NFL	14	10	16	144	9.0	2
2001—New York Jets NFL	16	15	36	321	8.9	5
Pro totals (2 years)	30	25	52	465	8.9	7

BECKETT, ROGERS — S — CHARGERS

PERSONAL: Born January 31, 1977, in Apopka, Fla. ... 6-3/205.
HIGH SCHOOL: Apopka (Fla.).
COLLEGE: Marshall (degree in political science).
TRANSACTIONS/CAREER NOTES: Selected by San Diego Chargers in second round (43rd pick overall) of 2000 NFL draft. ... Signed by Chargers (July 24, 2000).
HONORS: Named free safety on THE SPORTING NEWS college All-America third team (1999).
PRO STATISTICS: 2001—Recovered one fumble for one yard.

Year Team	G	GS	INTERCEPTIONS No.	Yds.	Avg.	TD	SACKS No.
2000—San Diego NFL	16	3	1	7	7.0	0	1.0
2001—San Diego NFL	16	16	1	8	8.0	0	0.0
Pro totals (2 years)	32	19	2	15	7.5	0	1.0

BEDELL, BRAD — OL — BROWNS

PERSONAL: Born February 12, 1977, in Arcadia, Calif. ... 6-4/299.
HIGH SCHOOL: Arcadia (Calif.).
JUNIOR COLLEGE: Mount San Antonio College (Calif.).
COLLEGE: Colorado.
TRANSACTIONS/CAREER NOTES: Selected by Cleveland Browns in sixth round (206th pick overall) of 2000 NFL draft. ... Signed by Browns (July 10, 2000).
PLAYING EXPERIENCE: Cleveland NFL, 2000 and 2001. ... Games/Games started: 2000 (12/0), 2001 (15/4). Total: 27/4.

BEISEL, MONTY — LB — CHIEFS

PERSONAL: Born August 20, 1978, in Douglass, Kan. ... 6-3/267.
HIGH SCHOOL: Douglass (Kan.).
COLLEGE: Kansas State.
TRANSACTIONS/CAREER NOTES: Selected by Kansas City Chiefs in fourth round (107th pick overall) of 2001 NFL draft. ... Signed by Chiefs (July 23, 2001).

Year Team	G	GS	SACKS
2001—Kansas City NFL	16	0	0.0

BELL, JASON — CB — COWBOYS

PERSONAL: Born April 1, 1978, in Long Beach, Calif. ... 6-0/182. ... Full name: Jason Dewande Bell.
HIGH SCHOOL: Millikan (Calif.).
COLLEGE: UCLA.
TRANSACTIONS/CAREER NOTES: Signed as non-drafted free agent by Dallas Cowboys (April 27, 2001).
PLAYING EXPERIENCE: Dallas NFL, 2001. ... Games/Games started: 2001 (16/0).

BELL, KENDRELL — LB — STEELERS

PERSONAL: Born July 17, 1980, in Augusta, Ga. ... 6-1/254.
HIGH SCHOOL: Laney (August, Ga.).
JUNIOR COLLEGE: Middle Georgia College.
COLLEGE: Georgia.
TRANSACTIONS/CAREER NOTES: Selected by Pittsburgh Steelers in second round (39th pick overall) of 2001 NFL draft. ... Signed by Steelers (June 11, 2001).
CHAMPIONSHIP GAME EXPERIENCE: Played in AFC championship game (2001 season).
HONORS: Named NFL Rookie of the Year by THE SPORTING NEWS (2001).

Year Team	G	GS	SACKS
2001—Pittsburgh NFL	16	16	9.0

BELL, MARCUS — LB — SEAHAWKS

PERSONAL: Born July 19, 1977, in St. John's, Ariz. ... 6-1/240. ... Full name: Marcus Udall Bell.
HIGH SCHOOL: St. John's (Ariz.).
COLLEGE: Arizona.
TRANSACTIONS/CAREER NOTES: Selected by Seattle Seahawks in fourth round (116th pick overall) of 2000 NFL draft. ... Signed by Seahawks (June 13, 2000).
PRO STATISTICS: 2001—Credited with one sack.

Year Team	G	GS	INTERCEPTIONS No.	Yds.	Avg.	TD
2000—Seattle NFL	16	0	1	30	30.0	0
2001—Seattle NFL	13	0	0	0	0.0	0
Pro totals (2 years)	29	0	1	30	30.0	0

BELL, MARCUS — DT — CARDINALS

PERSONAL: Born June 1, 1979, in Memphis, Tenn. ... 6-2/323.
HIGH SCHOOL: Kingsbury (Tenn.).
COLLEGE: Memphis.
TRANSACTIONS/CAREER NOTES: Selected by Arizona Cardinals in fourth round (123rd pick overall) of 2001 NFL draft. ... Signed by Cardinals (June 4, 2001).

Year Team	G	GS	SACKS
2001—Arizona NFL	13	0	0.5

BELL, MYRON — S

PERSONAL: Born September 15, 1971, in Toledo, Ohio. ... 5-11/212. ... Full name: Myron Corey Bell.
HIGH SCHOOL: Macomber-Whitney (Toledo, Ohio).
COLLEGE: Michigan State.
TRANSACTIONS/CAREER NOTES: Selected by Pittsburgh Steelers in fifth round (140th pick overall) of 1994 NFL draft. ... Signed by Steelers (July 18, 1994). ... Granted free agency (February 14, 1997). ... Re-signed by Steelers (April 15, 1997). ... Granted unconditional free agency (February 13, 1998). ... Signed by Cincinnati Bengals (June 26, 1998). ... Granted unconditional free agency (February 11, 2000). ... Signed by Steelers (December 20, 2000). ... Granted unconditional free agency (March 1, 2002).
CHAMPIONSHIP GAME EXPERIENCE: Played in AFC championship game (1994, 1995, 1997 and 2001 seasons). ... Played in Super Bowl XXX (1995 season).
PRO STATISTICS: 1995—Recovered one fumble. 1996—Recovered two fumbles. 1997—Recovered one fumble. 2001—Recovered one fumble.

			INTERCEPTIONS				SACKS
Year Team	G	GS	No.	Yds.	Avg.	TD	No.
1994—Pittsburgh NFL	15	0	0	0	0.0	0	0.0
1995—Pittsburgh NFL	16	9	2	4	2.0	0	0.0
1996—Pittsburgh NFL	16	4	0	0	0.0	0	2.0
1997—Pittsburgh NFL	16	8	1	10	10.0	0	1.5
1998—Cincinnati NFL	16	2	0	0	0.0	0	1.0
1999—Cincinnati NFL	16	16	1	5	5.0	0	2.0
2000—Pittsburgh NFL	1	0	0	0	0.0	0	0.0
2001—Pittsburgh NFL	16	1	0	0	0.0	0	0.0
Pro totals (8 years)	112	40	4	19	4.8	0	6.5

BELLAMY, JAY — S — SAINTS

PERSONAL: Born July 8, 1972, in Perth Amboy, N.J. ... 5-11/200. ... Full name: John Jay Bellamy. ... Name pronounced BELL-a-me.
HIGH SCHOOL: Matawan Regional (Aberdeen, N.J.).
COLLEGE: Rutgers.
TRANSACTIONS/CAREER NOTES: Signed as non-drafted free agent by Seattle Seahawks (April 27, 1994). ... On injured reserve with shoulder injury (November 11, 1994-remainder of season). ... Granted unconditional free agency (March 2, 2001). ... Signed by New Orleans Saints (April 4, 2001).
PRO STATISTICS: 1997—Credited with two sacks. 1998—Credited with one sack and recovered two fumbles. 1999—Recovered one fumble. 2000—Credited with two sacks. 2001—Credited with two sacks.

			INTERCEPTIONS			
Year Team	G	GS	No.	Yds.	Avg.	TD
1994—Seattle NFL	3	0	0	0	0.0	0
1995—Seattle NFL	15	0	0	0	0.0	0
1996—Seattle NFL	16	0	3	18	6.0	0
1997—Seattle NFL	16	7	1	13	13.0	0
1998—Seattle NFL	16	16	3	40	13.3	0
1999—Seattle NFL	16	16	4	4	1.0	0
2000—Seattle NFL	16	16	4	132	33.0	1
2001—New Orleans NFL	16	16	3	21	7.0	0
Pro totals (8 years)	114	71	18	228	12.7	1

BELSER, JASON — DB — CHIEFS

PERSONAL: Born May 28, 1970, in Kansas City, Mo. ... 5-10/191. ... Full name: Jason Daks Belser. ... Son of Caeser Belser, defensive back with Kansas City Chiefs (1968-71) and linebacker with San Francisco 49ers (1974). ... Name pronounced BELL-sir.
HIGH SCHOOL: Raytown (Mo.) South.
COLLEGE: Oklahoma.
TRANSACTIONS/CAREER NOTES: Selected by Indianapolis Colts in eighth round (197th pick overall) of 1992 NFL draft. ... Signed by Colts (July 22, 1992). ... Granted free agency (February 17, 1995). ... Tendered offer sheet by Carolina Panthers (April 17, 1995). ... Offer matched by Colts (April 19, 1995). ... Granted unconditional free agency (March 2, 2001). ... Signed by Kansas City Chiefs (June 12, 2001).
CHAMPIONSHIP GAME EXPERIENCE: Played in AFC championship game (1995 season).
PRO STATISTICS: 1992—Fumbled once and recovered two fumbles. 1993—Recovered three fumbles. 1995—Returned one kickoff for 15 yards and recovered two fumbles. 1996—Recovered one fumble. 1998—Returned one punt for 53 yards and recovered one fumble. 2000—Recovered one fumble. 2001—Returned three kickoffs for 58 yards.

			INTERCEPTIONS				SACKS
Year Team	G	GS	No.	Yds.	Avg.	TD	No.
1992—Indianapolis NFL	16	2	3	27	9.0	0	0.0
1993—Indianapolis NFL	16	16	1	14	14.0	0	0.0
1994—Indianapolis NFL	13	12	1	31	31.0	0	0.0
1995—Indianapolis NFL	16	16	1	0	0.0	0	0.0

				INTERCEPTIONS				SACKS
Year Team	G	GS	No.	Yds.	Avg.	TD		No.
1996—Indianapolis NFL	16	16	4	81	20.3	†2		1.0
1997—Indianapolis NFL	16	16	2	121	60.5	1		1.0
1998—Indianapolis NFL	16	16	1	19	19.0	0		1.0
1999—Indianapolis NFL	16	16	0	0	0.0	0		1.0
2000—Indianapolis NFL	16	16	0	0	0.0	0		5.0
2001—Kansas City NFL	16	0	0	0	0.0	0		0.0
Pro totals (10 years)	157	126	13	293	22.5	3		9.0

BENJAMIN, RYAN   C   PATRIOTS

PERSONAL: Born November 17, 1977, in Greenfield, Mass. ... 6-1/260. ... Full name: Ryan Arthur Benjamin.
HIGH SCHOOL: River Ridge (New Port Richey, Fla.).
COLLEGE: South Florida.
TRANSACTIONS/CAREER NOTES: Signed as non-drafted free agent by Tampa Bay Buccaneers (April 23, 2001). ... Released by Buccaneers (June 7, 2001). ... Signed by New England Patriots (August 13, 2001). ... Released by Patriots (August 26, 2001). ... Signed by Chicago Bears (October 13, 2001). ... Released by Bears (October 16, 2001). ... Signed by Patriots (February 11, 2002).
PLAYING EXPERIENCE: Chicago NFL, 2001. ... Games/Games started: 2001 (1/0).

BENNETT, BRANDON   RB   BENGALS

PERSONAL: Born February 3, 1973, in Taylors, S.C. ... 5-11/220.
HIGH SCHOOL: Riverside (Greer, S.C.).
COLLEGE: South Carolina.
TRANSACTIONS/CAREER NOTES: Signed as non-drafted free agent by Cleveland Browns (July 25, 1995). ... Released by Browns (August 18, 1995). ... Signed by Chicago Bears to practice squad (December 6, 1995). ... Released by Bears (August 19, 1996). ... Re-signed by Bears to practice squad (September 24, 1996). ... Released by Bears (November 1, 1996). ... Signed by Miami Dolphins to practice squad (November 5, 1996). ... Activated (December 17, 1996); did not play. ... Released by Dolphins (August 12, 1997). ... Signed by Cincinnati Bengals (April 20, 1997). ... Released by Bengals (August 30, 1998). ... Re-signed by Bengals (September 7, 1998). ... Released by Bengals (June 3, 1999). ... Re-signed by Bengals (March 2, 2001).
PRO STATISTICS: 1998—Recovered one fumble. 2000—Recovered one fumble.
SINGLE GAME HIGHS (regular season): Attempts—25 (December 20, 1998, vs. Pittsburgh); yards—87 (December 13, 1998, vs. Indianapolis); and rushing touchdowns—1 (December 3, 2000, vs. Arizona).
STATISTICAL PLATEAUS: 100-yard receiving games: 1998 (1).

			RUSHING				RECEIVING				KICKOFF RETURNS				TOTALS		
Year Team	G	GS	Att.	Yds.	Avg.	TD	No.	Yds.	Avg.	TD	No.	Yds.	Avg.	TD	TD	2pt.	Pts.	Fum.
1995—Chicago NFL								Did not play.										
1996—Miami NFL								Did not play.										
1997—								Did not play.										
1998—Cincinnati NFL	14	1	77	243	3.2	2	8	153	19.1	0	3	61	20.3	0	2	0	12	1
1999—								Did not play.										
2000—Cincinnati NFL	16	0	90	324	3.6	3	19	168	8.8	0	0	0	0.0	0	3	0	18	2
2001—Cincinnati NFL	16	1	50	232	4.6	0	20	150	7.5	0	4	60	15.0	0	0	0	0	1
Pro totals (3 years)	46	2	217	799	3.7	5	47	471	10.0	0	7	121	17.3	0	5	0	30	4

BENNETT, DARREN   P   CHARGERS

PERSONAL: Born January 9, 1965, in Sydney, Australia. ... 6-5/235. ... Full name: Darren Leslie Bennett.
HIGH SCHOOL: Applecross (Perth, Western Australia).
COLLEGE: None.
TRANSACTIONS/CAREER NOTES: Played Australian Rules Football (1987-1993). ... Signed as non-drafted free agent by San Diego Chargers (April 14, 1994). ... Released by Chargers (August 28, 1994). ... Re-signed by Chargers to practice squad (August 29, 1994). ... Assigned by Chargers to Amsterdam Admirals in 1995 World League enhancement allocation program (February 20, 1995). ... Granted unconditional free agency (February 11, 2000). ... Re-signed by Chargers (March 7, 2000).
HONORS: Named punter on THE SPORTING NEWS NFL All-Pro team (1995). ... Played in Pro Bowl (1995 and 2000 seasons).
PRO STATISTICS: 1998—Fumbled once and recovered one fumble.

				PUNTING			
Year Team	G	No.	Yds.	Avg.	Net avg.	In. 20	Blk.
1994—San Diego NFL				Did not play.			
1995—Amsterdam W.L.	10	60	2296	38.3	35.1	24	1
—San Diego NFL	16	72	3221	44.7	36.6	28	0
1996—San Diego NFL	16	87	3967	45.6	37.2	23	0
1997—San Diego NFL	16	89	3972	44.6	37.7	26	1
1998—San Diego NFL	16	95	4174	43.9	36.8	27	0
1999—San Diego NFL	16	89	3910	43.9	*38.7	32	0
2000—San Diego NFL	16	92	4248	*46.2	36.2	23	0
2001—San Diego NFL	16	78	3308	42.4	36.9	25	0
W.L. totals (1 year)	10	60	2296	38.3	35.1	24	1
NFL totals (6 years)	112	602	26800	44.5	37.2	184	1
Pro totals (7 years)	122	662	29096	44.0	37.0	208	2

BENNETT, DONNELL — FB

PERSONAL: Born September 14, 1972, in Fort Lauderdale, Fla. ... 6-0/245.
HIGH SCHOOL: Cardinal Gibbons (Fort Lauderdale, Fla.).
COLLEGE: Miami (Fla.).
TRANSACTIONS/CAREER NOTES: Selected after junior season by Kansas City Chiefs in second round (58th pick overall) of 1994 NFL draft. ... Signed by Chiefs (May 6, 1994). ... On injured reserve with knee injury (December 20, 1994-remainder of season). ... On physically unable to perform list with knee injury (August 22-October 31, 1995). ... Granted free agency (February 14, 1997). ... Re-signed by Chiefs (April 22, 1997). ... Granted unconditional free agency (March 2, 2001). ... Signed by Washington Redskins (May 9, 2001). ... Granted unconditional free agency (March 1, 2002).
PRO STATISTICS: 1994—Returned one kickoff for 12 yards and recovered one fumble. 1999—Returned three kickoffs for 51 yards. 2001—Recovered one fumble.
SINGLE GAME HIGHS (regular season): Attempts—30 (September 20, 1998, vs. San Deigo); yards—115 (September 6, 1998, vs, Oakland); and rushing touchdowns—3 (September 27, 1998, vs. Philadelphia).
STATISTICAL PLATEAUS: 100-yard rushing games: 1998 (1).

				RUSHING				RECEIVING				TOTALS		
Year Team	G	GS	Att.	Yds.	Avg.	TD	No.	Yds.	Avg.	TD	TD	2pt.	Pts.	Fum.
1994—Kansas City NFL	15	0	46	178	3.9	2	7	53	7.6	0	2	0	12	2
1995—Kansas City NFL	3	1	7	11	1.6	0	1	12	12.0	0	0	0	0	0
1996—Kansas City NFL	16	0	36	166	4.6	0	8	21	2.6	0	0	0	0	0
1997—Kansas City NFL	14	1	94	369	3.9	1	7	5	0.7	0	1	0	6	0
1998—Kansas City NFL	16	10	148	527	3.6	5	16	91	5.7	1	6	0	36	4
1999—Kansas City NFL	15	1	161	627	3.9	8	10	41	4.1	0	8	0	48	1
2000—Kansas City NFL	7	2	27	24	0.9	1	2	17	8.5	0	1	0	6	0
2001—Washington NFL	16	14	10	39	3.9	0	15	112	7.5	0	0	1	2	1
Pro totals (8 years)	102	29	529	1941	3.7	17	66	352	5.3	1	18	1	110	8

BENNETT, DREW — WR — TITANS

PERSONAL: Born August 26, 1978, in Berkeley, Calif. ... 6-5/203. ... Full name: Andrew Russell Bennett.
HIGH SCHOOL: Miramonte (Calif.).
COLLEGE: UCLA.
TRANSACTIONS/CAREER NOTES: Signed as non-drafted free agent by Tennessee Titans (April 22, 2001).
SINGLE GAME HIGHS (regular season): Receptions—4 (December 9, 2001, vs. Minnesota); yards—87 (December 9, 2001, vs. Minnesota); and touchdown receptions—1 (December 2, 2001, vs. Cleveland).

			RECEIVING				TOTALS		
Year Team	G	GS	No.	Yds.	Avg.	TD	TD	2pt.	Pts.	Fum.
2001—Tennessee NFL	14	1	24	329	13.7	1	1	▲1	8	0

BENNETT, MICHAEL — RB — VIKINGS

PERSONAL: Born August 13, 1978, in Milwaukee. ... 5-9/211.
HIGH SCHOOL: Milwaukee Tech.
COLLEGE: Wisconsin.
TRANSACTIONS/CAREER NOTES: Selected after junior season by Minnesota Vikings in first round (27th pick overall) of 2001 NFL draft. ... Signed by Vikings (July 30, 2001).
PRO STATISTICS: 2001—Recovered one fumble.
SINGLE GAME HIGHS (regular season): Attempts—25 (December 30, 2001, vs. Green Bay); yards—113 (December 9, 2001, vs. Tennessee); and rushing touchdowns—2 (December 9, 2001, vs. Tennessee).
STATISTICAL PLATEAUS: 100-yard rushing games: 2001 (2).

			RUSHING				RECEIVING				TOTALS		
Year Team	G	GS	Att.	Yds.	Avg.	TD	No.	Yds.	Avg.	TD	TD	2pt.	Pts.	Fum.
2001—Minnesota NFL	13	13	172	682	4.0	2	29	226	7.8	1	3	0	18	0

BENNETT, TOMMY — S

PERSONAL: Born February 19, 1973, in Las Vegas, Nev. ... 6-2/212.
HIGH SCHOOL: Samuel F.B. Morse (San Diego).
COLLEGE: UCLA.
TRANSACTIONS/CAREER NOTES: Signed as a non-drafted free agent by Arizona Cardinals (April 23, 1996). ... Granted free agency (February 12, 1999). ... Re-signed by Cardinals (June 16, 1999). ... Granted unconditional free agency (February 11, 2000). ... Re-signed by Cardinals (July 21, 2000). ... Granted unconditional free agency (March 2, 2001). ... Re-signed by Cardinals (June 1, 2001). ... Released by Cardinals (August 16, 2001). ... Signed by Detroit Lions (August 29, 2001). ... On suspended list for violating league substance abuse policy (December 10-January 6, 2002). ... Released by Lions (February 22, 2002).
PRO STATISTICS: 1997—Recovered blocked punt in end zone for a touchdown. 1999—Recovered one fumble. 2000—Returned one kickoff for 17 yards.

			INTERCEPTIONS				TOTALS		
Year Team	G	GS	No.	Yds.	Avg.	TD	TD	2pt.	Pts.	Fum.
1996—Arizona NFL	16	1	0	0	0.0	0	0	0	0	0
1997—Arizona NFL	13	7	1	0	0.0	0	1	0	6	0
1998—Arizona NFL	16	16	2	100	50.0	1	1	0	6	0
1999—Arizona NFL	15	15	1	13	13.0	0	0	0	0	0
2000—Arizona NFL	11	0	0	0	0.0	0	0	0	0	0
2001—Detroit NFL	8	1	0	0	0.0	0	0	0	0	0
Pro totals (6 years)	79	40	4	113	28.3	1	2	0	12	0

BERGER, MITCH — P — RAMS

PERSONAL: Born June 24, 1972, in Kamloops, B.C. ... 6-4/228.
HIGH SCHOOL: North Delta (Vancouver).
JUNIOR COLLEGE: Tyler (Texas) Junior College.
COLLEGE: Colorado.
TRANSACTIONS/CAREER NOTES: Selected by Philadelphia Eagles in sixth round (193rd pick overall) of 1994 NFL draft. ... Signed by Eagles (July 11, 1994). ... Released by Eagles (October 10, 1994). ... Signed by Cincinnati Bengals to practice squad (October 13, 1994). ... Released by Bengals (November 30, 1994). ... Signed by Chicago Bears (March 7, 1995). ... Released by Bears (May 4, 1995). ... Signed by Indianapolis Colts (May 16, 1995). ... Claimed on waivers by Green Bay Packers (August 24, 1995). ... Released by Packers (August 27, 1995). ... Signed by Bears (November 7, 1995). ... Released by Bears (November 13, 1995). ... Signed by Minnesota Vikings (April 19, 1996). ... Granted unconditional free agency (February 11, 2000). ... Re-signed by Vikings (February 21, 2000). ... On injured reserve with knee injury (December 18, 2001-remainder of season). ... Released by Vikings (February 22, 2002). ... Signed by St. Louis Rams (April 17, 2002).
CHAMPIONSHIP GAME EXPERIENCE: Played in NFC championship game (1998 and 2000 seasons).
HONORS: Named punter on THE SPORTING NEWS NFL All-Pro team (1999). ... Played in Pro Bowl (1999 season).
PRO STATISTICS: 1997—Rushed once for no yards and fumbled once for minus nine yards. 1999—Recovered one fumble. 2000—Had only pass attempt intercepted. 2001—Attempted one pass without a completion.

				PUNTING			
Year Team	G	No.	Yds.	Avg.	Net avg.	In. 20	Blk.
1994—Philadelphia NFL	5	25	951	38.0	31.3	8	0
1995—				Did not play.			
1996—Minnesota NFL	16	88	3616	41.1	32.3	26	2
1997—Minnesota NFL	14	73	3133	42.9	34.1	22	0
1998—Minnesota NFL	16	55	2458	44.7	37.0	17	0
1999—Minnesota NFL	16	61	2769	‡45.4	‡38.4	18	0
2000—Minnesota NFL	16	62	2773	‡44.7	36.2	16	0
2001—Minnesota NFL	12	47	2046	43.5	32.9	10	0
Pro totals (7 years)	95	411	17746	43.2	34.8	117	2

BERLIN, EDDIE — WR — TITANS

PERSONAL: Born January 14, 1978, in Urbandale, Iowa. ... 5-11/194.
HIGH SCHOOL: Urbandale (Iowa).
COLLEGE: Northern Iowa.
TRANSACTIONS/CAREER NOTES: Selected by Tennessee Titans in fifth round (159th pick overall) of 2001 NFL draft. ... Signed by Titans (July 9, 2001).
SINGLE GAME HIGHS (regular season): Receptions—2 (September 23, 2001, vs. Jacksonville); yards—28 (September 23, 2001, vs. Jacksonville); and touchdown receptions—0.

			RECEIVING			KICKOFF RETURNS			TOTALS			
Year Team	G	GS	No.	Yds.	Avg.	TD	No.	Yds.	Avg.	TD	TD	2pt.	Pts.	Fum.
2001—Tennessee NFL	11	0	2	28	14.0	0	13	253	19.5	0	0	0	0	0

BERRY, BERT — DE — BRONCOS

PERSONAL: Born August 15, 1975, in Houston. ... 6-3/250. ... Full name: Bertrand Demond Berry.
HIGH SCHOOL: Humble (Texas).
COLLEGE: Notre Dame.
TRANSACTIONS/CAREER NOTES: Selected by Indianapolis Colts in third round (86th pick overall) of 1997 NFL draft. ... Signed by Colts (July 9, 1997). ... Granted free agency (February 11, 2000). ... Signed by St. Louis Rams (July 20, 2000). ... Released by Rams (August 20, 2000). ... Signed by Denver Broncos (January 3, 2001).
PRO STATISTICS: 2001—Recovered two fumbles for one yard.

Year Team	G	GS	SACKS
1997—Indianapolis NFL	10	1	0.0
1998—Indianapolis NFL	16	12	4.0
1999—Indianapolis NFL	16	0	1.0
2000—		Did not play.	
2001—Denver NFL	14	0	2.0
Pro totals (4 years)	56	13	7.0

BETTIS, JEROME — RB — STEELERS

PERSONAL: Born February 16, 1972, in Detroit. ... 5-11/255. ... Full name: Jerome Abram Bettis. ... Nickname: The Bus.
HIGH SCHOOL: Mackenzie (Detroit).
COLLEGE: Notre Dame.
TRANSACTIONS/CAREER NOTES: Selected after junior season by Los Angeles Rams in first round (10th pick overall) of 1993 NFL draft. ... Signed by Rams (July 22, 1993). ... Rams franchise moved to St. Louis (April 12, 1995). ... Traded by Rams with third-round pick (LB Steven Conley) in 1996 draft to Pittsburgh Steelers for second-round pick (TE Ernie Conwell) in 1996 draft and fourth-round pick (traded to Miami) in 1997 draft (April 20, 1996). ... Granted unconditional free agency (February 14, 1997). ... Re-signed by Steelers (February 17, 1997). ... Granted unconditional free agency (March 2, 2001). ... Re-signed by Steelers (March 2, 2001).
CHAMPIONSHIP GAME EXPERIENCE: Played in AFC championship game (1997 and 2001 seasons).
HONORS: Named NFL Rookie of the Year by THE SPORTING NEWS (1993). ... Played in Pro Bowl (1993, 1994, 1996 and 1997 seasons).
PRO STATISTICS: 1994—Recovered three fumbles. 1995—Recovered two fumbles. 1996—Recovered two fumbles. 1997—Recovered one fumble. 1999—Completed only pass attempt for 21 yards and a touchdown and recovered three fumbles for one yard. 2000—Attempted two passes without a completion and one interception and recovered one fumble. 2001—Attempted two passes with one completion for 32 yards and one touchdown and recovered two fumbles.

SINGLE GAME HIGHS (regular season): Attempts—39 (January 2, 1994, vs. Chicago); yards—212 (December 12, 1993, vs. New Orleans); and rushing touchdowns—3 (November 30, 1997, vs. Arizona).
STATISTICAL PLATEAUS: 100-yard rushing games: 1993 (7), 1994 (4), 1996 (10), 1997 (10), 1998 (6), 1999 (2), 2000 (7), 2001 (5). Total: 51.

				RUSHING				RECEIVING				TOTALS		
Year	Team	G	GS	Att.	Yds.	Avg.	TD	No.	Yds.	Avg.	TD	TD	2pt.	Pts.	Fum.
1993—Los Angeles Rams NFL		16	12	‡294	1429	4.9	7	26	244	9.4	0	7	0	42	4
1994—Los Angeles Rams NFL		16	16	319	1025	3.2	3	31	293	9.5	1	4	∞2	28	5
1995—St. Louis NFL		15	13	183	637	3.5	3	18	106	5.9	0	3	0	18	4
1996—Pittsburgh NFL		16	12	320	1431	4.5	11	22	122	5.5	0	11	0	66	7
1997—Pittsburgh NFL		15	15	*375	1665	4.4	7	15	110	7.3	2	9	0	54	6
1998—Pittsburgh NFL		15	15	316	1185	3.8	3	16	90	5.6	0	3	0	18	2
1999—Pittsburgh NFL		16	16	299	1091	3.6	7	21	110	5.2	0	7	0	42	2
2000—Pittsburgh NFL		16	16	355	1341	3.8	8	13	97	7.5	0	8	0	48	1
2001—Pittsburgh NFL		11	11	225	1072	§4.8	4	8	48	6.0	0	4	0	24	3
Pro totals (9 years)		136	126	2686	10876	4.0	53	170	1220	7.2	3	56	2	340	34

BEUERLEIN, STEVE   QB   BRONCOS

PERSONAL: Born March 7, 1965, in Hollywood, Calif. ... 6-3/220. ... Full name: Stephen Taylor Beuerlein. ... Name pronounced BURR-line.
HIGH SCHOOL: Servite (Anaheim, Calif.).
COLLEGE: Notre Dame (degree in American studies, 1987).
TRANSACTIONS/CAREER NOTES: Selected by Los Angeles Raiders in fourth round (110th pick overall) of 1987 NFL draft. ... Signed by Raiders (July 24, 1987). ... On injured reserve with elbow and shoulder injuries (September 7, 1987-entire season). ... Granted free agency (February 1, 1990). ... Re-signed by Raiders (September 3, 1990). ... Granted roster exemption (September 3-16, 1990). ... Inactive for all 16 games (1990). ... Granted free agency (February 1, 1991). ... Re-signed by Raiders (July 8, 1991). ... Traded by Raiders to Dallas Cowboys for fourth-round pick (traded to Indianapolis) in 1992 draft (August 25, 1991). ... Granted unconditional free agency (March 1, 1993). ... Signed by Phoenix Cardinals (April 21, 1993). ... Cardinals franchise renamed Arizona Cardinals for 1994 season. ... Selected by Jacksonville Jaguars from Cardinals in NFL expansion draft (February 15, 1995). ... Granted free agency (February 16, 1996). ... Signed by Carolina Panthers (April 10, 1996). ... Released by Panthers (March 19, 2001). ... Signed by Denver Broncos (May 30, 2001). ... On injured reserve with elbow injury (October 5, 2001-remainder of season).
CHAMPIONSHIP GAME EXPERIENCE: Member of Raiders for AFC championship game (1990 season); inactive. ... Played in NFC championship game (1992 season). ... Member of Super Bowl championship team (1992 season). ... Member of Panthers for NFC championship game (1996 season); did not play.
HONORS: Played in Pro Bowl (1999 season).
PRO STATISTICS: 1988—Caught one pass for 21 yards, fumbled six times and recovered two fumbles for minus one yard. 1989—Fumbled six times and recovered three fumbles for minus eight yards. 1993—Fumbled eight times and recovered two fumbles. 1994—Fumbled eight times and recovered three fumbles for minus 13 yards. 1995—Fumbled three times. 1996—Fumbled nine times and recovered two fumbles for minus seven yards. 1997—Fumbled once. 1998—Fumbled 13 times and recovered five fumbles for minus 19 yards. 1999—Tied for NFC lead with 12 fumbles for minus four yards. 2000—Fumbled nine times for minus five yards.
SINGLE GAME HIGHS (regular season): Attempts—53 (December 19, 1993, vs. Seattle); completions—34 (December 19, 1993, vs. Seattle); yards—431 (December 19, 1993, vs. Seattle); and touchdown passes—5 (January 2, 2000, vs. New Orleans).
STATISTICAL PLATEAUS: 300-yard passing games: 1988 (1), 1993 (2), 1999 (5), 2000 (3). Total: 11.
MISCELLANEOUS: Regular-season record as starting NFL quarterback: 45-54 (.455). ... Postseason record as starting NFL quarterback: 1-1 (.500). ... Holds Carolina Panthers all-time records for most passing yards (12,690) and touchdown passes (86).

					PASSING						RUSHING			TOTALS		
Year	Team	G	GS	Att.	Cmp.	Pct.	Yds.	TD	Int.	Avg.	Rat.	Att.	Yds.	Avg.	TD	TD	2pt.	Pts.
1987—L.A. Raiders NFL								Did not play.										
1988—L.A. Raiders NFL		10	8	238	105	44.1	1643	8	7	6.90	66.6	30	35	1.2	0	0	0	0
1989—L.A. Raiders NFL		10	7	217	108	49.8	1677	13	9	7.73	78.4	16	39	2.4	0	0	0	0
1990—L.A. Raiders NFL								Did not play.										
1991—Dallas NFL		8	4	137	68	49.6	909	5	2	6.64	77.2	7	-14	-2.0	0	0	0	0
1992—Dallas NFL		16	0	18	12	66.7	152	0	1	8.44	69.7	4	-7	-1.8	0	0	0	0
1993—Phoenix NFL		16	14	418	258	61.7	3164	18	17	7.57	82.5	22	45	2.0	0	0	0	0
1994—Arizona NFL		9	7	255	130	51.0	1545	5	9	6.06	61.6	22	39	1.8	1	1	0	6
1995—Jacksonville NFL		7	6	142	71	50.0	952	4	7	6.70	60.5	5	32	6.4	0	0	0	0
1996—Carolina NFL		8	4	123	69	56.1	879	8	2	7.15	93.5	12	17	1.4	0	0	0	0
1997—Carolina NFL		7	3	153	89	58.2	1032	6	3	6.75	83.6	4	32	8.0	0	0	0	0
1998—Carolina NFL		12	12	343	216	63.0	2613	17	12	7.62	88.2	22	26	1.2	0	0	0	0
1999—Carolina NFL		16	16	571	*343	60.1	*4436	36	15	7.77	94.6	27	124	4.6	2	2	0	12
2000—Carolina NFL		16	16	533	324	60.8	3730	19	18	7.00	79.7	44	106	2.4	1	1	1	8
2001—Denver NFL								Did not play.										
Pro totals (12 years)		135	97	3148	1793	57.0	22732	139	102	7.22	80.7	215	474	2.2	4	4	1	26

BEVERLY, ERIC   C   LIONS

PERSONAL: Born March 28, 1974, in Cleveland. ... 6-3/294. ... Full name: Eric Raymonde Beverly.
HIGH SCHOOL: Bedford Heights (Ohio).
COLLEGE: Miami of Ohio.
TRANSACTIONS/CAREER NOTES: Signed as non-drafted free agent by Detroit Lions (April 24, 1997). ... Released by Lions (August 24, 1997). ... Re-signed by Lions to practice squad (August 26, 1997). ... Activated (December 20, 1997). ... Active for one game (1997); did not play. ... Granted free agency (March 2, 2001). ... Tendered offer sheet by Miami Dolphins (March 8, 2001). ... Offer matched by Lions (March 15, 2001).
PLAYING EXPERIENCE: Detroit NFL, 1998-2001. ... Games/Games started: 1998 (16/0), 1999 (16/2), 2000 (16/7), 2001 (16/16). Total: 64/25.
PRO STATISTICS: 2000—Returned one kickoff for no yards. 2001—Fumbled twice for minus 21 yards.

BIAKABUTUKA, TSHIMANGA RB

PERSONAL: Born January 24, 1974, in Kinsasha, Zaire. ... 6-0/215. ... Name pronounced tee-MON-guh bee-ock-a-ba-TWO-kah. ... Nickname: Tim.
HIGH SCHOOL: John Jacques Rosseau (Longueuil, Que.), then Vanier College (Montreal).
COLLEGE: Michigan.
TRANSACTIONS/CAREER NOTES: Selected after junior season by Carolina Panthers in first round (eighth pick overall) of 1996 NFL draft. ... Signed by Panthers (August 16, 1996). ... On injured reserve with knee injury (October 1, 1996-remainder of season). ... On injured reserve with broken foot (October 23, 2001-remainder of season). ... Released by Panthers (February 22, 2002).
PRO STATISTICS: 2001—Recovered one fumble for two yards.
SINGLE GAME HIGHS (regular season): Attempts—31 (November 28, 1999, vs. Atlanta); yards—142 (October 3, 1999, vs. Washington); and rushing touchdowns—3 (October 3, 1999, vs. Washington).
STATISTICAL PLATEAUS: 100-yard rushing games: 1997 (1), 1998 (2), 1999 (2), 2000 (1), 2001 (1). Total: 7.
MISCELLANEOUS: Holds Carolina Panthers all-time record for most yards rushing (2,530) and most rushing touchdowns (14).

				RUSHING				RECEIVING			TOTALS			
Year Team	G	GS	Att.	Yds.	Avg.	TD	No.	Yds.	Avg.	TD	TD	2pt.	Pts.	Fum.
1996—Carolina NFL	4	4	71	229	3.2	0	0	0	0.0	0	0	0	0	0
1997—Carolina NFL	8	2	75	299	4.0	2	0	0	0.0	0	2	0	12	1
1998—Carolina NFL	10	3	101	427	4.2	3	8	138	17.3	1	4	0	24	1
1999—Carolina NFL	11	11	138	718	5.2	6	23	189	8.2	0	6	0	36	3
2000—Carolina NFL	12	11	173	627	3.6	2	34	341	10.0	2	4	0	24	4
2001—Carolina NFL	5	4	53	230	4.3	1	12	121	10.1	0	1	0	6	3
Pro totals (6 years)	50	35	611	2530	4.1	14	77	789	10.2	3	17	0	102	12

BIDWELL, JOSH P PACKERS

PERSONAL: Born March 13, 1976, in Roseburg, Ore. ... 6-3/220. ... Full name: Joshua John Bidwell.
HIGH SCHOOL: Douglas (Winston, Ore.).
COLLEGE: Oregon (degree in English).
TRANSACTIONS/CAREER NOTES: Selected by Green Bay Packers in fourth round (133rd pick overall) of 1999 NFL draft. ... Signed by Packers (July 27, 1999). ... On non-football illness list with cancer (September 5, 1999-entire season).
HONORS: Named punter on THE SPORTING NEWS college All-America second team (1998).
PRO STATISTICS: 2000—Fumbled once and recovered one fumble.

			PUNTING				
Year Team	G	No.	Yds.	Avg.	Net avg.	In. 20	Blk.
1999—Green Bay NFL			Did not play.				
2000—Green Bay NFL	16	78	3003	38.5	34.6	22	0
2001—Green Bay NFL	16	82	3485	42.5	36.5	21	0
Pro totals (2 years)	32	160	6488	40.6	35.6	43	0

BIEKERT, GREG LB RAIDERS

PERSONAL: Born March 14, 1969, in Iowa City, Iowa. ... 6-2/255. ... Name pronounced BEEK-ert.
HIGH SCHOOL: Longmont (Colo.).
COLLEGE: Colorado (degree in marketing, 1992).
TRANSACTIONS/CAREER NOTES: Selected by Los Angeles Raiders in seventh round (181st pick overall) of 1993 NFL draft. ... Signed by Raiders (July 13, 1993). ... Raiders franchise moved to Oakland (July 21, 1995).
CHAMPIONSHIP GAME EXPERIENCE: Played in AFC championship game (2000 season).
PRO STATISTICS: 1994—Intercepted one pass for 11 yards. 1996—Recovered one fumble. 1997—Returned one kickoff for 16 yards. 1998—Recovered one fumble. 1999—Intercepted two passes for 57 yards. 2000—Recovered two fumbles. 2001—Recovered one fumble.

Year Team	G	GS	SACKS
1993—Los Angeles Raiders NFL	16	0	0.0
1994—Los Angeles Raiders NFL	16	14	1.5
1995—Oakland NFL	16	14	1.0
1996—Oakland NFL	16	15	0.0
1997—Oakland NFL	16	16	2.5
1998—Oakland NFL	16	16	3.0
1999—Oakland NFL	16	16	2.0
2000—Oakland NFL	16	16	2.0
2001—Oakland NFL	16	16	3.0
Pro totals (9 years)	144	123	15.0

BINN, DAVID C CHARGERS

PERSONAL: Born February 6, 1972, in San Mateo, Calif. ... 6-3/245. ... Full name: David Aaron Binn.
HIGH SCHOOL: San Mateo (Calif.).
COLLEGE: California (degree in ecology and the social system, 1993).
TRANSACTIONS/CAREER NOTES: Signed as non-drafted free agent by San Diego Chargers (April 28, 1994). ... Granted unconditional free agency (February 13, 1998). ... Re-signed by Chargers (February 25, 1998). ... Granted unconditional free agency (February 11, 2000). ... Re-signed by Chargers (February 11, 2000). ... Granted unconditional free agency (March 1, 2002). ... Re-signed by Chargers (March 5, 2002).
PLAYING EXPERIENCE: San Diego NFL, 1994-2001. ... Games/Games started: 1994 (16/0), 1995 (16/0), 1996 (16/0), 1997 (16/0), 1998 (15/0), 1999 (16/0), 2000 (16/0), 2001 (16/0). Total: 127/0.
CHAMPIONSHIP GAME EXPERIENCE: Played in AFC championship game (1994 season). ... Played in Super Bowl XXIX (1994 season).
PRO STATISTICS: 1999—Fumbled once for minus 36 yards.

BIRD, CORY — DB — COLTS

PERSONAL: Born August 10, 1978, in Atlantic City, N.J. ... 5-10/216. ... Full name: Cory James Bird.
HIGH SCHOOL: Oakcrest (Mays Landing, N.J.).
COLLEGE: Virginia Tech.
TRANSACTIONS/CAREER NOTES: Selected by Indianapolis Colts in third round (91st pick overall) of 2001 NFL draft. ... Signed by Colts (July 25, 2001).

Year Team	G	GS	SACKS
2001—Indianapolis NFL	14	0	0.5

BIRK, MATT — C — VIKINGS

PERSONAL: Born July 23, 1976, in St. Paul, Minn. ... 6-4/308. ... Full name: Matthew Robert Birk.
HIGH SCHOOL: Cretin-Derham Hall (St. Paul, Minn.).
COLLEGE: Harvard (degree in economics, 1998).
TRANSACTIONS/CAREER NOTES: Selected by Minnesota Vikings in sixth round (173rd pick overall) of 1998 NFL draft. ... Signed by Vikings (June 24, 1998). ... Granted free agency (March 2, 2001). ... Re-signed by Vikings (March 6, 2001).
PLAYING EXPERIENCE: Minnesota NFL, 1998-2001. ... Games/Games started: 1998 (7/0), 1999 (15/0), 2000 (16/16), 2001 (16/16). Total: 54/32.
CHAMPIONSHIP GAME EXPERIENCE: Member of Vikings for NFC championship game (1998 season); did not play. ... Played in NFC championship game (2000 season).
HONORS: Played in Pro Bowl (2000 season).
PRO STATISTICS: 2000—Fumbled once.

BISHOP, BLAINE — S — EAGLES

PERSONAL: Born July 24, 1970, in Indianapolis. ... 5-9/203. ... Full name: Blaine Elwood Bishop.
HIGH SCHOOL: Cathedral (Indianapolis).
COLLEGE: Saint Joseph's College (Ind.), then Ball State (degree in insurance, 1993).
TRANSACTIONS/CAREER NOTES: Selected by Houston Oilers in eighth round (214th pick overall) of 1993 NFL draft. ... Signed by Oilers (July 16, 1993). ... Granted free agency (February 16, 1996). ... Re-signed by Oilers (June 17, 1996). ... Designated by Oilers as franchise player (February 14, 1997). ... Oilers franchise moved to Tennessee for 1997 season. ... Re-signed by Oilers (August 27, 1997). ... Oilers franchise renamed Tennessee Titans for 1999 season (December 26, 1998). ... On injured reserve with foot injury (December 22, 2001-remainder of season). ... Released by Titans (February 28, 2002). ... Signed by Philadelphia Eagles (March 14, 2002).
CHAMPIONSHIP GAME EXPERIENCE: Played in AFC championship game (1999 season). ... Played in Super Bowl XXXIV (1999 season).
HONORS: Played in Pro Bowl (1995, 1997 and 2000 seasons). ... Named to play in Pro Bowl (1996 season); replaced by Tyrone Braxton due to injury.
PRO STATISTICS: 1993—Fumbled once and recovered one fumble. 1994—Returned two kickoffs for 18 yards and recovered one fumble. 1995—Recovered four fumbles for six yards. 1997—Recovered two fumbles. 1998—Recovered one fumble. 1999—Recovered two fumbles.

			INTERCEPTIONS			SACKS
Year Team	G	GS	No.	Yds.	Avg. TD	No.
1993—Houston NFL	16	2	1	1	1.0 0	1.0
1994—Houston NFL	16	13	1	21	21.0 0	1.5
1995—Houston NFL	16	16	1	62	62.0 ▲1	1.5
1996—Houston NFL	15	15	1	6	6.0 0	0.0
1997—Tennessee NFL	14	14	0	0	0.0 0	1.5
1998—Tennessee NFL	13	13	1	13	13.0 0	3.0
1999—Tennessee NFL	15	15	0	0	0.0 0	2.5
2000—Tennessee NFL	16	16	0	0	0.0 0	2.5
2001—Tennessee NFL	5	4	0	0	0.0 0	0.0
Pro totals (9 years)	126	108	5	103	20.6 1	13.5

BLACK, AVION — WR — TEXANS

PERSONAL: Born April 24, 1977, in Nashville. ... 5-11/185. ... Full name: Avion Carlos Black.
HIGH SCHOOL: Maplewood (Nashville).
COLLEGE: Tennessee State.
TRANSACTIONS/CAREER NOTES: Selected by Buffalo Bills in fourth round (121st pick overall) of 2000 NFL draft. ... Signed by Bills (July 10, 2000). ... Selected by Houston Texans from Bills in NFL expansion draft (February 18, 2002).
PRO STATISTICS: 2001—Returned one punt for 34 yards and recovered one fumble.
SINGLE GAME HIGHS (regular season): Receptions—2 (September 30, 2001, vs. Pittsburgh); yards—25 (October 18, 2001, vs. Jacksonville); and touchdown receptions—0.

			RECEIVING				KICKOFF RETURNS			TOTALS		
Year Team	G	GS	No.	Yds.	Avg.	TD	No.	Yds.	Avg. TD	TD	2pt.	Pts. Fum.
2000—Buffalo NFL	2	0	0	0	0.0	0	9	165	18.3 0	0	0	0 0
2001—Buffalo NFL	14	0	8	90	11.3	0	25	498	19.9 0	0	0	0 0
Pro totals (2 years)	16	0	8	90	11.3	0	34	663	19.5 0	0	0	0 0

BLACKMON, HAROLD — CB — SEAHAWKS

PERSONAL: Born May 20, 1978, in Chicago. ... 5-11/208. ... Full name: Harold Gene Blackmon.
HIGH SCHOOL: Leo (Chicago).
COLLEGE: Northwestern.

TRANSACTIONS/CAREER NOTES: Selected by Seattle Seahawks in seventh round (210th pick overall) of 2001 NFL draft. ... Signed by Seahawks (July 12, 2001). ... Released by Seahawks (October 2, 2001). ... Re-signed by Seahawks to practice squad (October 3, 2001). ... Activated (January 4, 2001).
PLAYING EXPERIENCE: Seattle NFL, 2001. ... Games/Games started: 2001 (2/0).

BLACKWELL, WILL   WR

PERSONAL: Born July 9, 1975, in Texarkana, Texas. ... 6-0/196. ... Full name: William Herman Blackwell Jr.
HIGH SCHOOL: Skyline (Oakland).
COLLEGE: San Diego State.
TRANSACTIONS/CAREER NOTES: Selected after junior season by Pittsburgh Steelers in second round (53rd pick overall) of 1997 NFL draft. ... Signed by Steelers (July 15, 1997). ... On injured reserve with foot injury (December 6, 1999-remainder of season). ... Granted free agency (February 11, 2000). ... Re-signed by Steelers (March 17, 2000). ... On physically unable to perform list with knee injury (August 21-November 20, 2000). ... Granted unconditional free agency (March 2, 2001). ... Re-signed by Steelers (May 7, 2001). ... On injured reserve with knee injury (September 12, 2001-remainder of season). ... Granted unconditional free agency (March 1, 2002).
CHAMPIONSHIP GAME EXPERIENCE: Played in AFC championship game (1997 season).
PRO STATISTICS: 1997—Recovered two fumbles.
SINGLE GAME HIGHS (regular season): Receptions—4 (November 21, 1999, vs. Tennessee); yards—68 (September 28, 1997, vs. Tennessee); and touchdown receptions—1 (November 26, 1998, vs. Detroit).

			RECEIVING				PUNT RETURNS				KICKOFF RETURNS				TOTALS			
Year Team	G	GS	No.	Yds.	Avg.	TD	No.	Yds.	Avg.	TD	No.	Yds.	Avg.	TD	TD	2pt.	Pts.	Fum.
1997—Pittsburgh NFL............	14	0	12	168	14.0	1	23	149	6.5	0	32	791	24.7	▲1	2	0	12	3
1998—Pittsburgh NFL............	16	2	32	297	9.3	1	4	22	5.5	0	20	382	19.1	0	1	1	8	1
1999—Pittsburgh NFL............	11	1	20	186	9.3	0	1	39	39.0	0	14	282	20.1	0	0	0	0	0
2000—Pittsburgh NFL............	5	0	2	23	11.5	0	0	0	0.0	0	10	281	28.1	▲1	1	0	6	0
2001—Pittsburgh NFL............	1	0	1	8	8.0	0	0	0	0.0	0	2	36	18.0	0	0	0	0	0
Pro totals (5 years)............	47	3	67	682	10.2	2	28	210	7.5	0	78	1772	22.7	2	4	1	26	5

BLAISE, KERLIN   G   LIONS

PERSONAL: Born December 25, 1974, in Orlando, Fla. ... 6-5/323.
HIGH SCHOOL: Maynard Evans (Orlando, Fla.).
COLLEGE: Miami (Fla.).
TRANSACTIONS/CAREER NOTES: Signed as non-drafted free agent by Detroit Lions (April 24, 1998). ... Released by Lions (August 30, 1998). ... Re-signed by Lions to practice squad (September 1, 1998). ... Activated (October 27, 1998); did not play. ... On injured reserve with knee injury (December 1, 1998-remainder of season). ... Granted free agency (March 2, 2001). ... Re-signed by Lions (April 26, 2001). ... Granted unconditional free agency (March 1, 2002). ... Re-signed by Lions (April 2, 2002).
PLAYING EXPERIENCE: Detroit NFL, 1999-2001. ... Games/Games started: 1999 (16/4), 2000 (12/0), 2001 (6/0). Total: 34/4.

BLAKE, JEFF   QB   RAVENS

PERSONAL: Born December 4, 1970, in Daytona Beach, Fla. ... 6-0/210. ... Son of Emory Blake, running back with Toronto Argonauts of CFL (1974).
HIGH SCHOOL: Seminole (Sanford, Fla.).
COLLEGE: East Carolina.
TRANSACTIONS/CAREER NOTES: Selected by New York Jets in sixth round (166th pick overall) of 1992 NFL draft. ... Signed by Jets (July 14, 1992). ... Inactive for all 16 games (1993). ... Claimed on waivers by Cincinnati Bengals (August 29, 1994). ... Granted free agency (February 17, 1995). ... Re-signed by Bengals (May 8, 1995). ... On injured reserve with wrist injury (December 24, 1998-remainder of season). ... Granted unconditional free agency (February 11, 2000). ... Signed by New Orleans Saints (February 11, 2000). ... On injured reserve with broken foot (November 20, 2000-remainder of season). ... Released by Saints (March 1, 2002). ... Signed by Baltimore Ravens (April 24, 2002).
HONORS: Played in Pro Bowl (1995 season).
PRO STATISTICS: 1992—Fumbled once. 1994—Fumbled six times. 1995—Fumbled 10 times for minus seven yards. 1996—Fumbled seven times and recovered one fumble for minus five yards. 1997—Fumbled seven times. 1998—Fumbled once. 1999—Fumbled 12 times and recovered seven fumbles for minus 28 yards. 2000—Fumbled seven times and recovered three fumbles for minus two yards.
SINGLE GAME HIGHS (regular season): Attempts—46 (September 10, 2000, vs. San Diego); completions—33 (September 10, 2000, vs. San Diego); yards—387 (November 6, 1994, vs. Seattle); and touchdown passes—4 (December 5, 1999, vs. San Francisco).
STATISTICAL PLATEAUS: 300-yard passing games: 1994 (2), 1995 (1), 1996 (2), 1997 (1), 1998 (1), 1999 (1). Total: 8.
MISCELLANEOUS: Regular-season record as starting NFL quarterback: 33-45 (.423).

			PASSING							RUSHING				TOTALS		
Year Team	G	GS	Att.	Cmp.	Pct.	Yds.	TD	Int.	Avg.	Rat.	Att.	Yds.	Avg.	TD	TD	2pt.	Pts.
1992—New York Jets NFL......	3	0	9	4	44.4	40	0	1	4.44	18.1	2	-2	-1.0	0	0	0	0
1993—New York Jets NFL......							Did not play.										
1994—Cincinnati NFL............	10	9	306	156	51.0	2154	14	9	7.04	76.9	37	204	5.5	1	1	1	8
1995—Cincinnati NFL............	16	16	567	§326	57.5	3822	§28	17	6.74	82.1	53	309	5.8	2	2	1	14
1996—Cincinnati NFL............	16	16	549	308	56.1	3624	24	14	6.60	80.3	72	317	4.4	2	2	0	12
1997—Cincinnati NFL............	11	11	317	184	58.0	2125	8	7	6.70	77.6	45	234	5.2	3	3	0	18
1998—Cincinnati NFL............	8	2	93	51	54.8	739	3	3	7.95	78.2	15	103	6.9	0	0	0	0
1999—Cincinnati NFL............	14	12	389	215	55.3	2670	16	12	6.86	77.6	63	332	5.3	2	2	0	12
2000—New Orleans NFL........	11	11	302	184	60.9	2025	13	9	6.71	82.7	57	243	4.3	1	1	0	6
2001—New Orleans NFL........	1	0	1	0	0.0	0	0	0	0.0	39.6	1	-1	-1.0	0	0	0	0
Pro totals (9 years)............	90	77	2533	1428	56.4	17199	106	72	6.79	79.5	345	1739	5.0	11	11	2	70

BLEDSOE, DREW QB BILLS

PERSONAL: Born February 14, 1972, in Ellensburg, Wash. ... 6-5/240.
HIGH SCHOOL: Walla Walla (Wash.).
COLLEGE: Washington State.
TRANSACTIONS/CAREER NOTES: Selected after junior season by New England Patriots in first round (first pick overall) of 1993 NFL draft. ... Signed by Patriots (July 6, 1993). ... Traded by Patriots to Buffalo Bills for first-round pick in 2003 draft (April 21, 2002).
CHAMPIONSHIP GAME EXPERIENCE: Played in AFC championship game (1996 and 2001 seasons). ... Played in Super Bowl XXXI (1996 season). ... Member of Super Bowl championship team (2001 season); did not play.
HONORS: Played in Pro Bowl (1994, 1996 and 1997 seasons).
RECORDS: Holds NFL single-season record for most passes attempted—691 (1994). ... Holds NFL single-game records for most passes completed—45; most passes attempted—70; and most passes attempted without an interception—70 (November 13, 1994, vs. Minnesota).
POST SEASON RECORDS: Shares Super Bowl single-game record for most passes intercepted—4 (January 26, 1997, vs. Green Bay).
PRO STATISTICS: 1993—Fumbled eight times and recovered five fumbles for minus 23 yards. 1994—Fumbled nine times and recovered three fumbles for minus five yards. 1995—Caught one pass for minus nine yards, fumbled 11 times and recovered one fumble for minus eight yards. 1996—Fumbled nine times and recovered one fumble for minus two yards. 1997—Fumbled four times and recovered three fumbles for minus four yards. 1998—Fumbled nine times and recovered four fumbles for minus 10 yards. 1999—Fumbled eight times and recovered six fumbles for minus 13 yards. 2000—Fumbled nine times and recovered three fumbles for minus 20 yards. 2001—Fumbled once and recovered one fumble.
SINGLE GAME HIGHS (regular season): Attempts—70 (November 13, 1994, vs. Minnesota); completions—45 (November 13, 1994, vs. Minnesota); yards—426 (November 13, 1994, vs. Minnesota); and touchdown passes—4 (October 1, 2000, vs. Denver).
STATISTICAL PLATEAUS: 300-yard passing games: 1993 (1), 1994 (6), 1995 (2), 1996 (4), 1997 (3), 1998 (4), 1999 (5), 2000 (1). Total: 26.
MISCELLANEOUS: Regular-season record as starting NFL quarterback: 63-60 (.512). ... Postseason record as starting NFL quarterback: 3-3 (.500). ... Holds New England Patriots all-time record for most yards passing (29,657).

				PASSING						RUSHING				TOTALS		
Year Team	G	GS	Att.	Cmp.	Pct.	Yds.	TD	Int.	Avg.	Rat.	Att.	Yds.	Avg.	TD	TD	2pt.	Pts.
1993—New England NFL........	13	12	429	214	49.9	2494	15	15	5.81	65.0	32	82	2.6	0	0	0	0
1994—New England NFL........	16	16	*691	*400	57.9	*4555	25	*27	6.59	73.6	44	40	0.9	0	0	0	0
1995—New England NFL........	15	15	*636	323	50.8	3507	13	16	5.51	63.7	20	28	1.4	0	0	0	0
1996—New England NFL........	16	16	*623	*373	59.9	4086	27	15	6.56	83.7	24	27	1.1	0	0	0	0
1997—New England NFL........	16	16	522	314	60.2	3706	28	15	7.10	87.7	28	55	2.0	0	0	0	0
1998—New England NFL........	14	14	481	263	54.7	3633	20	14	7.55	80.9	28	44	1.6	0	0	0	0
1999—New England NFL........	16	16	§539	305	56.6	3985	19	§21	7.39	75.6	42	101	2.4	0	0	0	0
2000—New England NFL........	16	16	531	312	58.8	3291	17	13	6.20	77.3	47	158	3.4	2	2	0	12
2001—New England NFL........	2	2	66	40	60.6	400	2	2	6.06	75.3	5	18	3.6	0	0	0	0
Pro totals (9 years)...............	124	123	4518	2544	56.3	29657	166	138	6.56	75.9	270	553	2.0	2	2	0	12

BLY, DRE' CB RAMS

PERSONAL: Born May 22, 1977, in Chesapeake, Va. ... 5-9/190. ... Full name: Donald Andre Bly.
HIGH SCHOOL: Western Branch (Chesapeake, Va.).
COLLEGE: North Carolina (degree in exercise and sports science).
TRANSACTIONS/CAREER NOTES: Selected after junior season by St. Louis Rams in second round (41st pick overall) of 1999 NFL draft. ... Signed by Rams (July 16, 1999).
CHAMPIONSHIP GAME EXPERIENCE: Played in NFC championship game (1999 and 2001 seasons). ... Member of Super Bowl championship team (1999 season). ... Played in Super Bowl XXXVI (2001 season).
HONORS: Named cornerback on THE SPORTING NEWS college All-America first team (1996). ... Named cornerback on THE SPORTING NEWS college All-America third team (1997).
PRO STATISTICS: 2000—Credited with one sack and recovered one fumble. 2001—Recovered one fumble for 15 yards.

			INTERCEPTIONS				PUNT RETURNS				KICKOFF RETURNS				TOTALS		
Year Team	G	GS	No.	Yds.	Avg.	TD	No.	Yds.	Avg.	TD	No.	Yds.	Avg.	TD	TD	2pt.	Pts. Fum.
1999—St. Louis NFL	16	2	3	53	17.7	1	0	0	0.0	0	1	1	1.0	0	1	0	6 0
2000—St. Louis NFL	16	3	3	44	14.7	0	0	0	0.0	0	9	163	18.1	0	0	0	0 1
2001—St. Louis NFL	16	4	6	150	25.0	†2	7	71	10.1	0	6	128	21.3	0	2	0	12 1
Pro totals (3 years)...............	48	9	12	247	20.6	3	7	71	10.1	0	16	292	18.3	0	3	0	18 2

BOBER, CHRIS OT GIANTS

PERSONAL: Born December 24, 1976, in Omaha, Neb. ... 6-5/305.
HIGH SCHOOL: South (Omaha, Neb.).
COLLEGE: Nebraska-Omaha.
TRANSACTIONS/CAREER NOTES: Signed as non-drafted free agent by New York Giants (April 20, 2000). ... Released by Giants (August 27, 2000). ... Re-signed by Giants to practice squad (August 29, 2000). ... Activated (November 6, 2000); did not play.
PLAYING EXPERIENCE: New York Giants NFL, 2001. ... Games/Games started: 2001 (16/0).

BOBO, ORLANDO G

PERSONAL: Born February 9, 1974, in Westpoint, Miss. ... 6-3/320.
HIGH SCHOOL: Westpoint (Miss.).
JUNIOR COLLEGE: East Mississippi Community College.
COLLEGE: Northeast Louisiana.
TRANSACTIONS/CAREER NOTES: Signed as non-drafted free agent by Minnesota Vikings (April 26, 1996). ... Released by Vikings (August 20, 1996). ... Re-signed by Vikings to practice squad (August 26, 1996). ... Released by Vikings (August 27, 1997). ... Re-signed by Vikings to practice squad (August 29, 1997). ... Activated (September 12, 1997). ... On injured reserve with leg injury (October 27, 1998-remainder

of season). ... Selected by Cleveland Browns from Vikings in NFL expansion draft (February 9, 1999). ... Granted free agency (February 11, 2000). ... Signed by Baltimore Ravens (April 7, 2000). ... Granted unconditional free agency (March 2, 2001). ... Re-signed by Ravens (March 5, 2001). ... Released by Ravens (September 5, 2001). ... Re-signed by Ravens (September 10, 2001). ... Granted unconditional free agency (March 1, 2002).
PLAYING EXPERIENCE: Minnesota NFL, 1997 and 1998; Cleveland NFL, 1999; Baltimore NFL, 2000 and 2001. ... Games/Games started: 1997 (5/0), 1998 (4/0), 1999 (9/1), 2000 (7/0), 2001 (12/0). Total: 37/1.
CHAMPIONSHIP GAME EXPERIENCE: Member of Ravens for AFC Championship game (2000 season); inactive. ... Member of Super Bowl championship team (2000 season); inactive.
PRO STATISTICS: 1999—Caught one pass for three yards. 2001—Fumbled once and returned one kickoff for 11 yards.

BOOKER, MARTY WR BEARS

PERSONAL: Born July 31, 1976, in Marrero, La. ... 6-0/209. ... Full name: Marty Montez Booker.
HIGH SCHOOL: Jonesboro-Hodge (Jonesboro, La.).
COLLEGE: Northeastern Louisiana.
TRANSACTIONS/CAREER NOTES: Selected by Chicago Bears in third round (78th pick overall) of 1999 NFL draft. ... Signed by Bears (July 22, 1999). ... Granted free agency (March 1, 2002).
PRO STATISTICS: 1999—Rushed once for eight yards. 2000—Rushed twice for minus one yard and recovered one fumble. 2001—Rushed four times for eight yards and attempted two passes with one completion for 34 yards and one touchdown.
SINGLE GAME HIGHS (regular season): Receptions—9 (December 30, 2001, vs. Detroit); yards—165 (November 18, 2001, vs. Tampa Bay); and touchdown receptions—3 (November 18, 2001, vs. Tampa Bay).
STATISTICAL PLATEAUS: 100-yard receiving games: 1999 (1), 2001 (2). Total: 3.

			RECEIVING				TOTALS			
Year Team	G	GS	No.	Yds.	Avg.	TD	TD	2pt.	Pts.	Fum.
1999—Chicago NFL	9	4	19	219	11.5	3	3	0	18	0
2000—Chicago NFL	15	7	47	490	10.4	2	2	0	12	2
2001—Chicago NFL	16	16	100	1071	10.7	8	8	0	48	2
Pro totals (3 years)	40	27	166	1780	10.7	13	13	0	78	4

BOOKER, MICHAEL CB

PERSONAL: Born April 27, 1975, in Oceanside, Calif. ... 6-2/200. ... Full name: Michael Allen Booker.
HIGH SCHOOL: El Camino (Calif.).
COLLEGE: Nebraska.
TRANSACTIONS/CAREER NOTES: Selected by Atlanta Falcons in first round (11th pick overall) of 1997 NFL draft. ... Signed by Falcons (July 16, 1997). ... Released by Falcons (August 27, 2000). ... Signed by Tennessee Titans (August 30, 2000). ... Granted unconditional free agency (March 2, 2001). ... Re-signed by Titans (July 2, 2001). ... Released by Titans (February 27, 2002).
CHAMPIONSHIP GAME EXPERIENCE: Played in NFC championship game (1998 season). ... Played in Super Bowl XXXIII (1998 season).
PRO STATISTICS: 1998—Fumbled once and recovered one fumble for five yards.

			INTERCEPTIONS		
Year Team	G	GS	No.	Yds.	Avg.	TD
1997—Atlanta NFL	15	2	3	16	5.3	0
1998—Atlanta NFL	14	6	1	27	27.0	0
1999—Atlanta NFL	13	1	2	10	5.0	0
2000—Tennessee NFL	15	1	1	2	2.0	0
2001—Tennessee NFL	16	0	1	0	0.0	0
Pro totals (5 years)	73	10	8	55	6.9	0

BOOKER, VAUGHN DE BENGALS

PERSONAL: Born February 24, 1968, in Cincinnati. ... 6-5/300. ... Full name: Vaughn Jamel Booker.
HIGH SCHOOL: Taft (Cincinnati).
COLLEGE: Cincinnati.
TRANSACTIONS/CAREER NOTES: Signed by Winnipeg Blue Bombers of CFL (June 1992). ... Granted free agency after 1993 season. ... Signed as non-drafted free agent by Kansas City Chiefs (May 2, 1994). ... Traded by Chiefs to Green Bay Packers for DT Darius Holland (May 13, 1998). ... Granted unconditional free agency (February 11, 2000). ... Signed by Cincinnati Bengals (February 16, 2000). ... On injured reserve with knee injury (December 7, 2000-remainder of season).
PRO STATISTICS: CFL: 1992—Recovered four fumbles and returned one kickoff for three yards. NFL: 1994—Recovered two fumbles for six yards and returned two kickoffs for 10 yards. 1995—Recovered one fumble for 14 yards and a touchdown. 1996—Recovered one fumble. 1997—Recovered one fumble.
MISCELLANEOUS: Served in U.S. Army (1988-90).

Year Team	G	GS	SACKS
1992—Winnipeg CFL	15	...	2.0
1993—Winnipeg CFL	9	...	4.0
1994—Kansas City NFL	13	0	0.0
1995—Kansas City NFL	16	10	1.5
1996—Kansas City NFL	14	12	1.0
1997—Kansas City NFL	13	13	4.0
1998—Green Bay NFL	16	4	3.0
1999—Green Bay NFL	14	14	3.5
2000—Cincinnati NFL	9	9	0.0
2001—Cincinnati NFL	14	13	1.5
CFL totals (2 years)	24	...	6.0
NFL totals (8 years)	109	75	14.5
Pro totals (10 years)	133	...	20.5

— 37 —

BOONE, ALFONSO — DT — BEARS

PERSONAL: Born January 11, 1976, in Saginaw, Mich. ... 6-4/325.
HIGH SCHOOL: Arthur Hill (Saginaw, Mich.).
JUNIOR COLLEGE: Mount San Antonio College (Calif.).
COLLEGE: Central State (did not play football).
TRANSACTIONS/CAREER NOTES: Selected after sophomore season by Detroit Lions in seventh round (253rd pick overall) of 2000 NFL draft. ... Signed by Lions (July 16, 2000). ... Released by Lions (August 27, 2000). ... Re-signed by Lions to practice squad (August 29, 2000). ... Signed by Chicago Bears off Lions practice squad (November 21, 2000). ... Inactive for five games (2000).
PRO STATISTICS: 2001—Recovered one fumble for six yards.

Year Team	G	GS	SACKS
2001—Chicago NFL	11	0	2.0

BOOSE, DORIAN — DE — TEXANS

PERSONAL: Born January 29, 1974, in Frankfurt, West Germany. ... 6-5/292. ... Full name: Dorian Alexander Boose.
HIGH SCHOOL: Henry Foss (Tacoma, Wash.).
JUNIOR COLLEGE: Walla Walla (Wash.) Community College.
COLLEGE: Washington State.
TRANSACTIONS/CAREER NOTES: Selected by New York Jets in second round (56th pick overall) of 1998 NFL draft. ... Signed by Jets (July 8, 1998). ... Released by Jets (May 18, 2001). ... Signed by Washington Redskins (August 6, 2001). ... Released by Redskins (December 26, 2001). ... Signed by Houston Texans (February 12, 2002).
PLAYING EXPERIENCE: New York Jets NFL, 1998-2000; Washington NFL, 2001. ... Games/Games started: 1998 (9/0), 1999 (12/0), 2000 (9/0), 2001 (10/0). Total: 40/0.
CHAMPIONSHIP GAME EXPERIENCE: Member of Jets for AFC championship game (1998 season); inactive.
PRO STATISTICS: 1999—Recovered one fumble.

BORUM, JARVIS — OT — CARDINALS

PERSONAL: Born September 16, 1978, in Columbia, S.C. ... 6-7/324.
HIGH SCHOOL: Keenan (Columbia, S.C.).
COLLEGE: North Carolina State.
TRANSACTIONS/CAREER NOTES: Signed as non-drafted free agent by Arizona Cardinals (April 23, 2001).
PLAYING EXPERIENCE: Arizona NFL, 2001. ... Games/Games started: 2001 (1/1).

BOSELLI, TONY — OT — TEXANS

PERSONAL: Born April 17, 1972, in Boulder, Colo. ... 6-7/322. ... Full name: Don Anthony Boselli Jr.
HIGH SCHOOL: Fairview (Boulder, Colo.).
COLLEGE: Southern California (degree in business administration, 1995).
TRANSACTIONS/CAREER NOTES: Selected by Jacksonville Jaguars in first round (second pick overall) of 1995 NFL draft. ... Signed by Jaguars (June 1, 1995). ... On injured reserve with knee injury (January 4, 2000-remainder of playoffs). ... On injured reserve with shoulder injury (October 22, 2001-remainder of season). ... Selected by Houston Texans from Jaguars in NFL expansion draft (February 18, 2002).
PLAYING EXPERIENCE: Jacksonville NFL, 1995-2001. ... Games/Games started: 1995 (13/12), 1996 (16/16), 1997 (12/12), 1998 (15/15), 1999 (16/16), 2000 (16/16), 2001 (3/3). Total: 91/90.
CHAMPIONSHIP GAME EXPERIENCE: Played in AFC championship game (1996 season).
HONORS: Named offensive lineman on THE SPORTING NEWS college All-America first team (1994). ... Played in Pro Bowl (1996-1998 seasons). ... Named offensive tackle on THE SPORTING NEWS NFL All-Pro team (1997-99). ... Named to play in Pro Bowl (1999 season); replaced by Walter Jones due to injury. ... Named to play in Pro Bowl (2000 season); replaced by Lincoln Kennedy due to injury.
PRO STATISTICS: 1996—Recovered one fumble. 1998—Recovered one fumble for two yards. 1999—Recovrd three fumbles.

BOSTON, DAVID — WR — CARDINALS

PERSONAL: Born August 19, 1978, in Humble, Texas. ... 6-2/222.
HIGH SCHOOL: Humble (Texas).
COLLEGE: Ohio State.
TRANSACTIONS/CAREER NOTES: Selected after junior season by Arizona Cardinals in first round (eighth pick overall) of 1999 NFL draft. ... Signed by Cardinals (August 2, 1999).
HONORS: Named wide receiver on THE SPORTING NEWS college All-America second team (1998). ... Named wide receiver on THE SPORTING NEWS NFL All-Pro team (2001).
PRO STATISTICS: 1999—Recovered one fumble. 2000—Recovered one fumble.
SINGLE GAME HIGHS (regular season): Receptions—9 (November 11, 2001, vs. New York Giants); yards—184 (December 3, 2000, vs. Cincinnati); and touchdown receptions—2 (December 30, 2001, vs. Carolina).
STATISTICAL PLATEAUS: 100-yard receiving games: 1999 (1), 2000 (4), 2001 (9). Total: 14.

			RUSHING				RECEIVING				PUNT RETURNS				TOTALS		
Year Team	G	GS	Att.	Yds.	Avg.	TD	No.	Yds.	Avg.	TD	No.	Yds.	Avg.	TD	TD	2pt.	Pts.	Fum.
1999—Arizona NFL	16	8	5	0	0.0	0	40	473	11.8	2	7	62	8.9	0	2	0	12	2
2000—Arizona NFL	16	16	3	9	3.0	0	71	1156	16.3	7	0	0	0.0	0	7	0	42	2
2001—Arizona NFL	16	15	5	35	7.0	0	98	*1598	16.3	8	0	0	0.0	0	8	0	48	1
Pro totals (3 years)	48	39	13	44	3.4	0	209	3227	15.4	17	7	62	8.9	0	17	0	102	5

BOULWARE, PETER   LB   RAVENS

PERSONAL: Born December 18, 1974, in Columbia, S.C. ... 6-4/255. ... Full name: Peter Nicholas Boulware. ... Name pronounced BOWL-ware.
HIGH SCHOOL: Spring Valley (Columbia, S.C.).
COLLEGE: Florida State (degree in management information systems, 1997).
TRANSACTIONS/CAREER NOTES: Selected after junior season by Baltimore Ravens in first round (fourth pick overall) of 1997 NFL draft. ... Signed by Ravens (August 16, 1997).
CHAMPIONSHIP GAME EXPERIENCE: Played in AFC championship game (2000 season). ... Member of Super Bowl championship team (2000 season).
HONORS: Named defensive end on THE SPORTING NEWS college All-America first team (1996). ... Played in Pro Bowl (1998 and 1999 seasons).
PRO STATISTICS: 1998—Recovered one fumble. 2001—Recovered one fumble.
MISCELLANEOUS: Holds Baltimore Ravens all-time record for most sacks (52).

Year—Team	G	GS	SACKS
1997—Baltimore NFL	16	16	11.5
1998—Baltimore NFL	16	16	8.5
1999—Baltimore NFL	16	11	10.0
2000—Baltimore NFL	16	15	7.0
2001—Baltimore NFL	16	14	§15.0
Pro totals (5 years)	80	72	52.0

BOUMAN, TODD   QB   VIKINGS

PERSONAL: Born August 1, 1972, in Ruthton, Minn. ... 6-2/229. ... Name pronounced Bow-man.
HIGH SCHOOL: Ruthton (Minn.).
COLLEGE: South Dakota State, then St. Cloud State.
TRANSACTIONS/CAREER NOTES: Signed as non-drafted free agent by Minnesota Vikings (April 25, 1997). ... Released by Vikings (August 23, 1997). ... Re-signed by Vikings to practice squad (August 25, 1997). ... Activated (December 5, 1997). ... Inactive for all 16 games (1999). ... Assigned by Vikings to Barcelona Dragons in 1999 NFL Europe enhancement allocation program (February 22, 1999). ... Inactive for all 16 games (2000).
CHAMPIONSHIP GAME EXPERIENCE: Member of Vikings for NFC championship game (1998 and 2000 seasons); inactive.
SINGLE GAME HIGHS (regular season): Attempts—38 (December 16, 2001, vs. Detroit); completions—21 (December 9, 2001, vs. Tennessee); yards—348 (December 9, 2001, vs. Tennessee); and touchdown passes—4 (December 9, 2001, vs. Tennessee).
STATISTICAL PLATEAUS: 300-yard passing games: 2001 (1).
MISCELLANEOUS: Regular-season record as starting NFL quarterback: 1-2 (.333).

				PASSING						RUSHING				TOTALS		
Year—Team	G	GS	Att.	Cmp.	Pct.	Yds.	TD	Int.	Avg.	Rat.	Att.	Yds.	Avg.	TD	TD	2pt.	Pts.
1999—Barcelona W.L.	...	...	324	170	52.5	2296	16	11	7.09	77.6	47	213	4.5	2	2	0	12
2000—Minnesota NFL	...	...					Did not play.										
2001—Minnesota NFL	5	3	89	51	57.3	795	8	4	8.93	98.3	9	61	6.8	0	0	0	0
W.L. totals (1 year)	...	...	324	170	52.5	2296	16	11	7.09	77.6	47	213	4.5	2	2	0	12
NFL totals (1 year)	5	3	89	51	57.3	795	8	4	8.93	98.3	9	61	6.8	0	0	0	0
Pro totals (2 years)	5	3	413	221	53.5	3091	24	15	7.48	82.1	56	274	4.9	2	2	0	12

BOWEN, MATT   S   PACKERS

PERSONAL: Born November 12, 1976, in Glen Ellyn, Ill. ... 6-1/208.
HIGH SCHOOL: Glenbard West (Glen Ellyn, Ill.).
COLLEGE: Iowa.
TRANSACTIONS/CAREER NOTES: Selected by St. Louis Rams in sixth round (198th pick overall) of 2000 NFL draft. ... Signed by Rams (July 7, 2000). ... On injured reserve with broken foot (October 3-November 6, 2001). ... Released by Rams (November 6, 2001). ... Signed by Green Bay Packers (November 30, 2001).
PLAYING EXPERIENCE: St. Louis NFL, 2000; St. Louis (1)-Green Bay (1) NFL, 2001. ... Games/Games started: 2000 (16/2), 2001 (St.L.-1/0; G.B.- 5/0; Total: 6/0). Total: 22/2.

BOWENS, DAVID   DE   DOLPHINS

PERSONAL: Born July 3, 1977, in Denver. ... 6-3/260. ... Full name: David Walter Bowens.
HIGH SCHOOL: St. Mary's (Orchard Lake, Mich.).
COLLEGE: Michigan, then Western Illinois.
TRANSACTIONS/CAREER NOTES: Selected after junior season by Denver Broncos in fifth round (158th pick overall) of 1999 NFL draft. ... Signed by Broncos (July 22, 1999). ... Traded by Broncos to Green Bay Packers for fourth-round pick (C Ben Hamilton) in 2001 draft (February 24, 2000). ... Traded by Packers to Buffalo Bills for TE Bobby Collins (August 7, 2001). ... Claimed on waivers by Washington Redskins (September 3, 2001). ... Released by Redskins (September 26, 2001). ... Signed by Miami Dolphins (October 22, 2001).
PRO STATISTICS: 1999—Recovered one fumble. 2000—Returned one kickoff for 12 yards and recovered one fumble.

Year—Team	G	GS	SACKS
1999—Denver NFL	16	0	1.0
2000—Green Bay NFL	14	0	3.5
2001—Miami NFL	8	0	1.0
Pro totals (3 years)	38	0	5.5

BOWENS, TIM — DT — DOLPHINS

PERSONAL: Born February 7, 1973, in Okolona, Miss. ... 6-4/320. ... Full name: Timothy L. Bowens.
HIGH SCHOOL: Okolona (Miss.).
JUNIOR COLLEGE: Itawamba Community College (Miss.).
COLLEGE: Mississippi.
TRANSACTIONS/CAREER NOTES: Selected after junior season by Miami Dolphins in first round (20th pick overall) of 1994 NFL draft. ... Signed by Dolphins (June 2, 1994). ... Designated by Dolphins as franchise player (February 13, 1998). ... Re-signed by Dolphins (August 21, 1998). ... On injured reserve with torn biceps muscle (January 3, 1999-remainder of playoffs). ... Released by Dolphins (February 28, 2002). ... Re-signed by Dolphins (February 28, 2002).
HONORS: Named to play in Pro Bowl (1998 season); replaced by Cortez Kennedy due to injury.
PRO STATISTICS: 1994—Recovered one fumble. 1995—Recovered two fumbles. 1996—Recovered one fumble. 1997—Recovered one fumble in end zone for a touchdown. 2000—Intercepted one pass for no yards.

Year Team	G	GS	SACKS
1994—Miami NFL	16	15	3.0
1995—Miami NFL	16	16	2.0
1996—Miami NFL	16	16	3.0
1997—Miami NFL	16	16	5.0
1998—Miami NFL	16	16	0.0
1999—Miami NFL	16	15	1.5
2000—Miami NFL	15	15	2.5
2001—Miami NFL	15	15	3.0
Pro totals (8 years)	126	124	20.0

BOWERS, ANDY — DE — CARDINALS

PERSONAL: Born February 22, 1976, in Salt Lake City, Utah. ... 6-5/283.
HIGH SCHOOL: Hillcrest (Utah).
COLLEGE: Utah.
TRANSACTIONS/CAREER NOTES: Signed as non-drafted free agent by Arizona Cardinals (April 23, 2001). ... Released by Cardinals (September 2, 2001). ... Re-signed by Cardinals to practice squad (September 3, 2001). ... Activated (October 25, 2001).
PLAYING EXPERIENCE: Arizona NFL, 2001. ... Games/Games started: 2001 (1/1).

BOWERS, R.J. — FB — STEELERS

PERSONAL: Born February 10, 1974, in Honolulu, Hawaii. ... 6-0/245. ... Full name: Raymond Keith Bowers Jr.
HIGH SCHOOL: West Middlesex (Pa.).
COLLEGE: Grove City (Pa.).
TRANSACTIONS/CAREER NOTES: Signed as non-drafted free agent by Carolina Panthers (April 23, 2001). ... Released by Panthers (August 28, 2001). ... Signed by Pittsburgh Steelers to practice squad (September 3, 2001). ... Activated (December 21, 2001).
CHAMPIONSHIP GAME EXPERIENCE: Member of Steelers for AFC championship game (2001 season); inactive.
SINGLE GAME HIGHS (regular season): Attempts—11 (January 6, 2002, vs. Cleveland); yards—67 (January 6, 2002, vs. Cleveland); and rushing touchdowns—1 (January 6, 2002, vs. Cleveland).

			RUSHING				RECEIVING				TOTALS		
Year Team	G	GS	Att.	Yds.	Avg.	TD	No.	Yds.	Avg.	TD	TD	2pt.	Pts.	Fum.
2001—Pittsburgh NFL	3	0	18	84	4.7	1	1	0	0.0	0	1	0	6	0

BOWNES, FABIEN — WR — SEAHAWKS

PERSONAL: Born February 29, 1972, in Aurora, Ill. ... 5-11/189. ... Name pronounced FAY-bee-en BOW-ens.
HIGH SCHOOL: Waubonsie Valley (Aurora, Ill.).
COLLEGE: Western Illinois.
TRANSACTIONS/CAREER NOTES: Signed as non-drafted free agent by Chicago Bears (April 27, 1995). ... Released by Bears (August 27, 1995). ... Re-signed by Bears to practice squad (August 29, 1995). ... Activated (December 14, 1995). ... Released by Bears (August 19, 1996). ... Re-signed by Bears to practice squad (October 15, 1996). ... Claimed on waivers by Seattle Seahawks (September 6, 1999). ... Granted free agency (February 11, 2000). ... Re-signed by Seahawks (May 1, 2000). ... Granted unconditional free agency (March 2, 2001). ... Re-signed by Seahawks (April 19, 2001).
PRO STATISTICS: 1997—Recovered one fumble. 1999—Rushed once for minus 14 yards.
SINGLE GAME HIGHS (regular season): Receptions—4 (November 2, 1997, vs. Washington); yards—56 (September 27, 1998, vs. Minnesota); and touchdown receptions—1 (September 19, 1999, vs. Chicago).

			RECEIVING				KICKOFF RETURNS				TOTALS			
Year Team	G	GS	No.	Yds.	Avg.	TD	No.	Yds.	Avg.	TD	TD	2pt.	Pts.	Fum.
1995—Chicago NFL	1	0	0	0	0.0	0	0	0	0.0	0	0	0	0	0
1996—Chicago NFL							Did not play.							
1997—Chicago NFL	16	0	12	146	12.2	0	19	396	20.8	0	0	0	0	0
1998—Chicago NFL	16	0	5	69	13.8	1	1	19	19.0	0	1	0	6	0
1999—Seattle NFL	15	0	4	68	17.0	1	2	40	20.0	0	1	0	6	0
2000—Seattle NFL	16	0	0	0	0.0	0	3	83	27.7	0	0	0	0	0
2001—Seattle NFL	16	0	0	0	0.0	0	0	0	0.0	0	0	0	0	0
Pro totals (6 years)	80	0	21	283	13.5	2	25	538	21.5	0	2	0	12	0

BOYD, JAMES — S — JAGUARS

PERSONAL: Born October 17, 1977, in Norfolk, Va. ... 5-11/208. ... Full name: James Aaron Boyd.
HIGH SCHOOL: Indian River (Chesapeake, Va.).
COLLEGE: Penn State.
TRANSACTIONS/CAREER NOTES: Selected by Jacksonville Jaguars in third round (94th pick overall) of 2001 NFL draft. ... Signed by Jaguars (June 14, 2001).
PLAYING EXPERIENCE: Jacksonville NFL, 2001. ... Games/Games started: 2001 (16/0).
HONORS: Named strong safety on THE SPORTING NEWS college All-America third team (2000).
PRO STATISTICS: 2001—Returned one kickoff for no yards and recovered one fumble for 47 yards.

BOYD, STEPHEN — LB

PERSONAL: Born August 22, 1972, in Valley Stream, N.Y. ... 6-0/242. ... Full name: Stephen Gerard Boyd.
HIGH SCHOOL: Valley Stream (N.Y.).
COLLEGE: Boston College (degree in human development).
TRANSACTIONS/CAREER NOTES: Selected by Detroit Lions in fifth round (141st pick overall) of 1995 NFL draft. ... Signed by Lions (July 19, 1995). ... Granted free agency (February 13, 1998). ... Re-signed by Lions (April 17, 1998). ... On injured reserve with shoulder injury (December 23, 1998-remainder of season). ... Granted unconditional free agency (February 12, 1999). ... Re-signed by Lions (February 23, 1999). ... On injured reserve with back injury (November 19, 2001-remainder of season). ... Released by Lions (February 27, 2002).
PLAYING EXPERIENCE: Detroit NFL, 1995-2000. ... Games/Games started: 1995 (16/0), 1996 (8/5), 1997 (16/16), 1998 (13/13), 1999 (14/14), 2000 (15/15), 2001 (4/4). Total: 86/67.
HONORS: Named linebacker on THE SPORTING NEWS college All-America first team (1994). ... Played in Pro Bowl (1999 season). ... Named to play in Pro Bowl (2000 season); replaced by Brian Urlacher due to injury.
RECORDS: Shares NFL single-game record for most opponents' fumbles recovered—3 (October 4, 1998, vs. Chicago).
PRO STATISTICS: 1995—Credited with one sack. 1997—Intercepted one pass for four yards and recovered one fumble for 42 yards and a touchdown. 1998—Credited with four sacks and recovered four fumbles for one yard. 1999—Intercepted one pass for 18 yards. 2000—Intercepted one pass for no yards, credited with 1/2 sack and recovered one fumble. 2001—Credited with one sack.

BOYER, BRANT — LB — BROWNS

PERSONAL: Born June 27, 1971, in Ogden, Utah. ... 6-1/230. ... Full name: Brant T. Boyer.
HIGH SCHOOL: North Summit (Coalville, Utah).
JUNIOR COLLEGE: Snow College (Utah).
COLLEGE: Arizona.
TRANSACTIONS/CAREER NOTES: Selected by Miami Dolphins in sixth round (177th pick overall) of 1994 NFL draft. ... Signed by Dolphins (July 11, 1994). ... Released by Dolphins (September 21, 1994). ... Re-signed by Dolphins to practice squad (September 22, 1994). ... Activated (October 5, 1994). ... Selected by Jacksonville Jaguars from Dolphins in NFL expansion draft (February 15, 1995). ... Released by Jaguars (August 27, 1995). ... Re-signed by Jaguars (September 13, 1995). ... Released by Jaguars (August 25, 1996). ... Re-signed by Jaguars (September 24, 1996). ... Released by Jaguars (September 25, 1996). ... Re-signed by Jaguars (September 27, 1996). ... Granted free agency (February 13, 1998). ... Re-signed by Jaguars (March 18, 1998). ... On injured reserve with neck injury (December 2, 1998-remainder of season). ... Granted unconditional free agency (February 12, 1999). ... Re-signed by Jaguars (March 15, 1999). ... Released by Jaguars (March 1, 2001). ... Signed by Cleveland Browns (March 12, 2001).
PLAYING EXPERIENCE: Miami NFL, 1994; Jacksonville NFL, 1995-2000; Cleveland NFL, 2001. ... Games/Games started: 1994 (14/0), 1995 (2/0), 1996 (12/0), 1997 (16/2), 1998 (11/0), 1999 (15/0), 2000 (12/5), 2001 (16/2). Total: 98/9.
CHAMPIONSHIP GAME EXPERIENCE: Played in AFC championship game (1996 and 1999 seasons).
PRO STATISTICS: 1997—Credited with 1 1/2 sacks. 1998—Credited with one sack. 1999—Intercepted one pass for five yards and credited with four sacks. 2000—Intercepted one pass for 12 yards and credited with 3 1/2 sacks. 2001—Intercepted two passes for 12 yards.

BRACKENS, TONY — DE — JAGUARS

PERSONAL: Born December 26, 1974, in Fairfield, Texas. ... 6-4/265. ... Full name: Tony Lynn Brackens Jr.
HIGH SCHOOL: Fairfield (Texas).
COLLEGE: Texas.
TRANSACTIONS/CAREER NOTES: Selected after junior season by Jacksonville Jaguars in second round (33rd pick overall) of 1996 NFL draft. ... Signed by Jaguars (May 28, 1996). ... Designated by Jaguars as franchise player (February 11, 2000).
CHAMPIONSHIP GAME EXPERIENCE: Played in AFC championship game (1996 and 1999 seasons).
HONORS: Named defensive lineman on THE SPORTING NEWS college All-America first team (1995). ... Played in Pro Bowl (1999 season).
PRO STATISTICS: 1996—Intercepted one pass for 27 yards and recovered three fumbles. 1997—Recovered one fumble. 1998—Recovered three fumbles for eight yards. 1999—Intercepted two passes for 16 yards and one touchdown and recovered two fumbles for six yards. 2000—Intercepted one pass for seven yards and recovered two fumbles for 15 yards. 2001—Recovered one fumble for one yard and credited with one safety.
MISCELLANEOUS: Holds Jacksonville Jaguars all-time record for most sacks (48).

Year Team	G	GS	SACKS
1996—Jacksonville NFL	16	1	7.0
1997—Jacksonville NFL	15	3	7.0
1998—Jacksonville NFL	12	8	3.5
1999—Jacksonville NFL	16	15	12.0
2000—Jacksonville NFL	16	16	7.5
2001—Jacksonville NFL	12	12	11.0
Pro totals (6 years)	**87**	**55**	**48.0**

BRADFORD, COREY — WR — TEXANS

PERSONAL: Born December 8, 1975, in Baton Rouge, La. ... 6-1/197. ... Full name: Corey Lamon Bradford.
HIGH SCHOOL: Clinton (La.).
JUNIOR COLLEGE: Hinds Community College (Miss.).
COLLEGE: Jackson State.
TRANSACTIONS/CAREER NOTES: Selected by Green Bay Packers in fifth round (150th pick overall) of 1998 NFL draft. ... Signed by Packers (July 17, 1998). ... Granted free agency (March 2, 2001). ... Re-signed by Packers (March 20, 2001). ... Granted unconditional free agency (March 1, 2002). ... Signed by Houston Texans (March 11, 2002).
PRO STATISTICS: 1998—Returned two kickoffs for 33 yards.
SINGLE GAME HIGHS (regular season): Receptions—6 (November 21, 1999, vs. Detroit); yards—117 (November 18, 2001, vs. Atlanta); and touchdown receptions—1 (January 6, 2002, vs. New York Giants).
STATISTICAL PLATEAUS: 100-yard receiving games: 1999 (1), 2001 (2). Total: 3.

			RECEIVING				TOTALS			
Year Team	G	GS	No.	Yds.	Avg.	TD	TD	2pt.	Pts.	Fum.
1998—Green Bay NFL	8	0	3	27	9.0	0	0	0	0	1
1999—Green Bay NFL	16	2	37	637	17.2	5	5	1	32	1
2000—Green Bay NFL	2	2	0	0	0.0	0	0	0	0	0
2001—Green Bay NFL	16	6	31	526	17.0	2	2	0	12	1
Pro totals (4 years)	42	10	71	1190	16.8	7	7	1	44	3

BRADFORD, RONNIE — CB — VIKINGS

PERSONAL: Born October 1, 1970, in Minot, N.D. ... 5-10/198. ... Full name: Ronald L. Bradford.
HIGH SCHOOL: Adams City (Commerce City, Colo.).
COLLEGE: Colorado.
TRANSACTIONS/CAREER NOTES: Selected by Miami Dolphins in fourth round (105th pick overall) of 1993 NFL draft. ... Signed by Dolphins (July 14, 1993). ... Released by Dolphins (August 24, 1993). ... Signed by Denver Broncos to practice squad (September 1, 1993). ... Activated (October 12, 1993). ... On injured reserve with knee injury (September 28, 1995-remainder of season). ... Released by Broncos (August 25, 1996). ... Signed by Arizona Cardinals (August 27, 1996). ... Granted unconditional free agency (February 14, 1997). ... Signed by Atlanta Falcons (April 11, 1997). ... Granted unconditional free agency (February 12, 1999). ... Re-signed by Falcons (March 11, 1999). ... Released by Falcons (February 25, 2002). ... Signed by Minnesota Vikings (May 15, 2002).
CHAMPIONSHIP GAME EXPERIENCE: Played in NFC championship game (1998 season). ... Played in Super Bowl XXXIII (1998 season).
PRO STATISTICS: 1993—Returned one punt for no yards and fumbled once. 1994—Credited with one sack and recovered two fumbles. 1996—Recovered one fumble. 1998—Credited with a safety and recovered one fumble. 2001—Credited with one sack.

			INTERCEPTIONS				TOTALS			
Year Team	G	GS	No.	Yds.	Avg.	TD	TD	2pt.	Pts.	Fum.
1993—Denver NFL	10	3	1	0	0.0	0	0	0	0	1
1994—Denver NFL	12	0	0	0	0.0	0	0	0	0	0
1995—Denver NFL	4	0	0	0	0.0	0	0	0	0	0
1996—Arizona NFL	15	11	1	0	0.0	0	0	0	0	0
1997—Atlanta NFL	16	15	4	9	2.3	0	0	0	0	0
1998—Atlanta NFL	14	10	3	11	3.7	1	1	0	8	0
1999—Atlanta NFL	16	16	0	0	0.0	0	0	0	0	0
2000—Atlanta NFL	16	15	3	25	8.3	0	0	0	0	0
2001—Atlanta NFL	14	14	0	0	0.0	0	0	0	0	0
Pro totals (9 years)	117	84	12	45	3.8	1	1	0	8	1

BRADY, KYLE — TE — JAGUARS

PERSONAL: Born January 14, 1972, in New Cumberland, Pa. ... 6-6/277. ... Full name: Kyle James Brady.
HIGH SCHOOL: Cedar Cliff (Camp Hill, Pa.).
COLLEGE: Penn State.
TRANSACTIONS/CAREER NOTES: Selected by New York Jets in first round (ninth pick overall) of 1995 NFL draft. ... Signed by Jets (July 17, 1995). ... Designated by Jets as transition player (February 12, 1999). ... Tendered offer sheet by Jacksonville Jaguars (February 16, 1999). ... Jets declined to match offer (February 18, 1999).
CHAMPIONSHIP GAME EXPERIENCE: Played in AFC championship game (1998 and 1999 seasons).
HONORS: Named tight end on THE SPORTING NEWS college All-America second team (1994).
PRO STATISTICS: 1995—Returned two kickoffs for 25 yards. 1996—Returned two kickoffs for 26 yards. 1998—Returned one kickoff for 20 yards.
SINGLE GAME HIGHS (regular season): Receptions—10 (October 29, 2000, vs. Dallas); yards—138 (October 29, 2000, vs. Dallas); and touchdown receptions—2 (October 19, 1998, vs. New England).
STATISTICAL PLATEAUS: 100-yard receiving games: 2000 (2).

			RECEIVING				TOTALS			
Year Team	G	GS	No.	Yds.	Avg.	TD	TD	2pt.	Pts.	Fum.
1995—New York Jets NFL	15	11	26	252	9.7	2	2	0	12	0
1996—New York Jets NFL	16	16	15	144	9.6	1	1	1	8	0
1997—New York Jets NFL	16	14	22	238	10.8	2	2	0	12	1
1998—New York Jets NFL	16	16	30	315	10.5	5	5	0	30	0
1999—Jacksonville NFL	13	12	32	346	10.8	1	1	1	8	0
2000—Jacksonville NFL	16	16	64	729	11.4	3	3	1	20	0
2001—Jacksonville NFL	16	16	36	386	10.7	2	2	0	12	2
Pro totals (7 years)	108	100	225	2410	10.7	16	16	3	102	3

BRADY, TOM — QB — PATRIOTS

PERSONAL: Born August 3, 1977, in San Mateo, Calif. ... 6-4/220. ... Full name: Thomas Brady.
HIGH SCHOOL: Serra (San Mateo, Calif.).
COLLEGE: Michigan.
TRANSACTIONS/CAREER NOTES: Selected by New England Patriots in sixth round (199th pick overall) of 2000 NFL draft. ... Signed by Patriots (July 14, 2000).
CHAMPIONSHIP GAME EXPERIENCE: Played in AFC championship game (2001 season). ... Member of Super Bowl championship team (2001 season).
HONORS: Named Most Valuable Player of Super Bowl XXXVI (2001 season).
PRO STATISTICS: 2001—Fumbled 12 times, recovered four fumbles for minus 18 yards and caught one pass for 23 yards.
SINGLE GAME HIGHS (regular season): Attempts—54 (October 14, 2001, vs. San Diego); completions—33 (October 14, 2001, vs. San Diego); yards—364 (October 14, 2001, vs. San Diego); and touchdown passes—4 (November 25, 2001, vs. New Orleans).
STATISTICAL PLATEAUS: 300-yard passing games: 2001 (1).
MISCELLANEOUS: Selected by Montreal Expos organization in 18th round of free-agent draft (June 1, 1995); did not sign. ... Regular-season record as starting NFL quarterback: 11-3 (.786). ... Postseason record as starting NFL quarterback: 3-0.

				PASSING						RUSHING				TOTALS		
Year Team	G	GS	Att.	Cmp.	Pct.	Yds.	TD	Int.	Avg.	Rat.	Att.	Yds.	Avg.	TD	TD	2pt.	Pts.
2000—New England NFL........	1	0	3	1	33.3	6	0	0	2.00	42.4	0	0	0.0	0	0	0	0
2001—New England NFL........	15	14	413	264	63.9	2843	18	12	6.88	86.5	36	43	1.2	0	0	0	0
Pro totals (2 years)...............	16	14	416	265	63.7	2849	18	12	6.85	86.1	36	43	1.2	0	0	0	0

BRAHAM, RICH — C — BENGALS

PERSONAL: Born November 6, 1970, in Morgantown, W.Va. ... 6-4/309. ... Name pronounced BRAY-um.
HIGH SCHOOL: University (Morgantown, W.Va.).
COLLEGE: West Virginia (degree in finance).
TRANSACTIONS/CAREER NOTES: Selected by Arizona Cardinals in third round (76th pick overall) of 1994 NFL draft. ... Signed by Cardinals (July 30, 1994). ... Claimed on waivers by Cincinnati Bengals (November 18, 1994). ... On injured reserve with ankle injury (August 29, 1995-entire season). ... Granted free agency (February 14, 1997). ... Tendered offer sheet by New England Patriots (April 8, 1997). ... Offer matched by Bengals (April 15, 1997). ... On injured reserve with knee injury (December 3, 1998-remainder of season). ... Granted unconditional free agency (March 2, 2001). ... Re-signed by Bengals (March 12, 2001).
PLAYING EXPERIENCE: Cincinnati NFL, 1994 and 1996-2001. ... Games/Games started: 1994 (3/0), 1996 (16/16), 1997 (16/16), 1998 (12/12), 1999 (16/16), 2000 (9/9), 2001 (16/16). Total: 88/85.
HONORS: Named offensive lineman on THE SPORTING NEWS college All-America second team (1993).
PRO STATISTICS: 1999—Recovered one fumble. 2000—Fumbled once for minus 16 yards. 2001—Fumbled once for minus 22 yards.

BRANDT, DAVID — C — REDSKINS

PERSONAL: Born September 25, 1977, in Jenison, Mich. ... 6-4/309.
HIGH SCHOOL: Jenison (Mich.).
COLLEGE: Michigan.
TRANSACTIONS/CAREER NOTES: Signed as non-drafted free agent by Washington Redskins (April 25, 2002).
PLAYING EXPERIENCE: Washington NFL, 2001. ... Games/Games started: 2001 (13/1).

BRATZKE, CHAD — DE — COLTS

PERSONAL: Born September 15, 1971, in Waukegan, Ill. ... 6-5/272. ... Full name: Chad Allen Bratzke. ... Name pronounced BRAT-ski.
HIGH SCHOOL: Bloomingdale (Valrico, Fla.).
COLLEGE: Eastern Kentucky.
TRANSACTIONS/CAREER NOTES: Selected by New York Giants in fifth round (155th pick overall) of 1994 NFL draft. ... Signed by Giants (July 17, 1994). ... On injured reserve with knee injury (November 12, 1997-remainder of season). ... Granted unconditional free agency (February 12, 1999). ... Signed by Indianapolis Colts (March 1, 1999).
PRO STATISTICS: 1996—Recovered two fumbles. 1997—Recovered two fumbles. 1998—Recovered one fumble. 1999—Fumbled once and recovered one fumble for three yards. 2000—Credited with one safety and recovered one fumble. 2001—Recovered one fumble.

Year Team	G	GS	SACKS
1994—New York Giants NFL............	2	0	0.0
1995—New York Giants NFL............	6	0	0.0
1996—New York Giants NFL............	16	16	5.0
1997—New York Giants NFL............	10	10	3.5
1998—New York Giants NFL............	16	16	11.0
1999—Indianapolis NFL.................	16	16	12.0
2000—Indianapolis NFL.................	16	16	7.5
2001—Indianapolis NFL.................	15	14	8.5
Pro totals (8 years)....................	97	88	47.5

BREES, DREW — QB — CHARGERS

PERSONAL: Born January 15, 1979, in Austin, Texas. ... 6-0/221. ... Full name: Drew Christopher Brees.
HIGH SCHOOL: Westlake (Austin, Texas).
COLLEGE: Purdue.
TRANSACTIONS/CAREER NOTES: Selected by San Diego Chargers in second round (32nd pick overall) of 2001 NFL draft. ... Signed by Chargers (August 7, 2001).

HONORS: Named quarterback to THE SPORTING NEWS college All-America third team (2000). ... Maxwell Award winner (2000).
PRO STATISTICS: 2001—Fumbled twice and recovered one fumble.
SINGLE GAME HIGHS (regular season): Attempts—27 (November 4, 2001, vs. Kansas City); completions—15 (November 4, 2001, vs. Kansas City); yards—221 (November 4, 2001, vs. Kansas City); and touchdown passes—1 (November 4, 2001, vs. Kansas City).

				PASSING							RUSHING			TOTALS		
Year Team	G	GS	Att.	Cmp.	Pct.	Yds.	TD	Int.	Avg.	Rat.	Att.	Yds.	Avg.	TD	TD	2pt.	Pts.
2001—San Diego NFL	1	0	27	15	55.6	221	1	0	8.19	94.8	2	18	9.0	0	0	0	0

BREWER, SEAN — TE — BENGALS

PERSONAL: Born October 5, 1977, in Riverside, Calif. ... 6-4/255.
HIGH SCHOOL: Polytechnic (Riverside, Calif.).
JUNIOR COLLEGE: Riverside.
COLLEGE: San Jose State.
TRANSACTIONS/CAREER NOTES: Selected by Cincinnati Bengals in third round (66th pick overall) of 2001 NFL draft. ... Signed by Bengals (July 18, 2001). ... On injured reserve with leg injury (September 1, 2001-entire season).

			RECEIVING		
Year Team	G	GS	No.	Yds.	Avg.	TD
2001—Cincinnati NFL				Did not play.		

BRIEN, DOUG — K — VIKINGS

PERSONAL: Born November 24, 1970, in Bloomfield, N.J. ... 6-0/180. ... Full name: Douglas Robert Zachariah Brien.
HIGH SCHOOL: De La Salle Catholic (Concord, Calif.).
COLLEGE: California (degree in political economies).
TRANSACTIONS/CAREER NOTES: Selected by San Francisco 49ers in third round (85th pick overall) of 1994 NFL draft. ... Signed by 49ers (July 27, 1994). ... Released by 49ers (October 16, 1995). ... Signed by New Orleans Saints (October 31, 1995). ... Granted free agency (February 14, 1997). ... Re-signed by Saints (July 17, 1997). ... Released by Saints (March 1, 2001). ... Signed by Indianapolis Colts (December 5, 2001). ... Released by Colts (December 15, 2001). ... Signed by Tampa Bay Buccaneers (December 27, 2001). ... Granted unconditional free agency (March 1, 2002). ... Signed by Minnesota Vikings (April 29, 2002).
CHAMPIONSHIP GAME EXPERIENCE: Played in NFC championship game (1994 season). ... Member of Super Bowl championship team (1994 season).
POST SEASON RECORDS: Shares Super Bowl single-game record for most extra points—7 (January 29, 1995, vs. San Diego).
PRO STATISTICS: 1998—Punted twice for 72 yards. 1999—Punted once for 20 yards.

		KICKING						
Year Team	G	XPM	XPA	FGM	FGA	Lg.	50+	Pts.
1994—San Francisco NFL	16	*60	*62	15	20	48	0-1	105
1995—San Francisco NFL	6	19	19	7	12	51	1-1	40
—New Orleans NFL	8	16	16	12	17	47	0-1	52
1996—New Orleans NFL	16	18	18	21	25	‡54	3-4	81
1997—New Orleans NFL	16	22	22	23	27	53	4-5	91
1998—New Orleans NFL	16	31	31	20	22	56	4-6	91
1999—New Orleans NFL	16	20	21	24	29	52	2-2	92
2000—New Orleans NFL	16	37	37	23	29	48	0-2	106
2001—Indianapolis NFL	1	0	0	0	0	0	0-0	0
—Tampa Bay NFL	2	2	2	5	6	42	0-0	17
Pro totals (8 years)	113	225	228	150	187	56	14-22	675

BRIGANCE, O.J. — LB

PERSONAL: Born September 29, 1969, in Houston. ... 6-0/236. ... Full name: Orenthial James Brigance.
HIGH SCHOOL: Willowridge (Sugar Land, Texas).
COLLEGE: Rice (degree in managerial studies).
TRANSACTIONS/CAREER NOTES: Signed by B.C. Lions of CFL (May 1991). ... Granted free agency (February 1994). ... Signed by Baltimore Stallions of CFL (April 1994). ... Granted free agency (February 16, 1996). ... Signed as non-drafted free agent by Miami Dolphins (May 17, 1996). ... Re-signed by Dolphins (February 12, 1999). ... Re-signed by Dolphins (May 20, 1999). ... On physically unable to perform list with back injury (July 30-August 25, 1999). ... Granted unconditional free agency (February 11, 2000). ... Signed by Baltimore Ravens (June 15, 2000). ... Granted unconditional free agency (March 2, 2001). ... Signed by St. Louis Rams (June 1, 2001). ... Released by Rams (August 20, 2001). ... Re-signed by St. Louis Rams (November 12, 2001). ... Granted unconditional free agency (March 1, 2002).
CHAMPIONSHIP GAME EXPERIENCE: Played in AFC championship game (2000 season). ... Member of Super Bowl championship team (2000 season). ... Played in NFC championship game (2001 season). ... Played in Super Bowl XXXVI (2001 season).
PRO STATISTICS: CFL: 1991—Intercepted one pass for seven yards. 1992—Returned five kickoffs for 40 yards and recovered three fumbles. 1993—Recovered one fumble for 27 yards. 1994—Recovered two fumbles. 1995—Intercepted one pass for 13 yards and recovered three fumbles for 10 yards. NFL: 1997—Recovered one fumble. 2000—Recovered one fumble.

Year Team	G	GS	SACKS
1991—British Columbia CFL	18	...	2.0
1992—British Columbia CFL	18	...	0.0
1993—British Columbia CFL	18	...	20.0
1994—Baltimore CFL	18	...	6.0
1995—Baltimore CFL	18	...	7.0
1996—Miami NFL	12	0	0.0
1997—Miami NFL	16	0	0.0
1998—Miami NFL	16	0	0.0
1999—Miami NFL	16	0	0.0
2000—Baltimore NFL	16	0	0.0
2001—St. Louis NFL	8	0	0.0
CFL totals (5 years)	90	...	35.0
NFL totals (6 years)	84	0	0.0
Pro totals (11 years)	174	...	35.0

BRIGHAM, JEREMY TE RAIDERS

PERSONAL: Born March 22, 1975, in Boston. ... 6-6/250.
HIGH SCHOOL: Saguaro (Scottsdale, Ariz.).
COLLEGE: Washington.
TRANSACTIONS/CAREER NOTES: Selected by Oakland Raiders in fifth round (127th pick overall) of 1998 NFL draft. ... Signed by Raiders (July 18, 1998).
PLAYING EXPERIENCE: Oakland NFL, 1998-2001. ... Games/Games started: 1998 (2/0), 1999 (16/2), 2000 (15/3), 2001 (14/3). Total: 47/8.
CHAMPIONSHIP GAME EXPERIENCE: Played in AFC championship game (2000 season).
PRO STATISTICS: 1999—Caught eight passes for 108 yards. 2000—Caught 13 passes for 107 yards and two touchdowns. 2001—Caught 12 passes for 85 yards and one touchdown.
SINGLE GAME HIGHS (regular season): Receptions—3 (December 30, 2001, vs. Denver); yards—39 (September 19, 1999, vs. Minnesota); and touchdown receptions—2 (December 24, 2000, vs. Carolina).

BROCKERMEYER, BLAKE OT

PERSONAL: Born April 11, 1973, in Fort Worth, Texas. ... 6-4/300. ... Full name: Blake Weeks Brockermeyer.
HIGH SCHOOL: Arlington Heights (Texas).
COLLEGE: Texas.
TRANSACTIONS/CAREER NOTES: Selected after junior season by Carolina Panthers in first round (29th pick overall) of 1995 NFL draft. ... Signed by Panthers (July 14, 1995). ... Granted unconditional free agency (February 12, 1999). ... Signed by Chicago Bears (February 27, 1999). ... Released by Bears (April 5, 2002).
PLAYING EXPERIENCE: Carolina NFL, 1995-1998; Chicago NFL, 1999-2001. ... Games/Games started: 1995 (16/16), 1996 (12/12), 1997 (16/13), 1998 (14/14), 1999 (15/15), 2000 (15/14), 2001 (16/16). Total: 104/100.
CHAMPIONSHIP GAME EXPERIENCE: Played in NFC championship game (1996 season).
HONORS: Named offensive lineman on THE SPORTING NEWS college All-America first team (1994).
PRO STATISTICS: 1998—Recovered two fumbles. 2001—Recovered two fumbles.

BROMELL, LORENZO DE VIKINGS

PERSONAL: Born September 23, 1975, in Georgetown, S.C. ... 6-6/268. ... Full name: Lorenzo Alexis Bromell.
HIGH SCHOOL: Choppee (Georgetown, S.C.).
JUNIOR COLLEGE: Georgia Military College.
COLLEGE: Clemson.
TRANSACTIONS/CAREER NOTES: Selected by Miami Dolphins in fourth round (102nd pick overall) of 1998 draft. ... Signed by Dolphins (July 10, 1998). ... Granted free agency (March 2, 2001). ... Re-signed by Dolphins (April 19, 2001). ... Granted unconditional free agency (March 1, 2002). ... Signed by Minnesota Vikings (April 9, 2002).
PRO STATISTICS: 1998—Recovered one fumble.

Year Team	G	GS	SACKS
1998—Miami NFL	14	0	8.0
1999—Miami NFL	15	1	5.0
2000—Miami NFL	8	0	2.0
2001—Miami NFL	16	1	6.5
Pro totals (4 years)	53	2	21.5

BRONSON, ZACK S 49ERS

PERSONAL: Born January 28, 1974, in Jasper, Texas. ... 6-1/201. ... Full name: Robert Zack Bronson.
HIGH SCHOOL: Jasper (Texas).
COLLEGE: McNeese State.
TRANSACTIONS/CAREER NOTES: Signed as non-drafted free agent by San Francisco 49ers (May 2, 1997). ... On injured reserve with foot injury (December 29, 1999-remainder of season). ... Granted free agency (February 11, 2000). ... Re-signed by 49ers (June 15, 2000). ... Granted unconditional free agency (March 2, 2001). ... Re-signed by 49ers (May 15, 2001).
CHAMPIONSHIP GAME EXPERIENCE: Played in NFC championship game (1997 season).
PRO STATISTICS: 1997—Recovered one fumble for three yards. 2001—Fumbled once and recovered one fumble.

			INTERCEPTIONS			
Year Team	G	GS	No.	Yds.	Avg.	TD
1997—San Francisco NFL	16	0	1	22	22.0	0
1998—San Francisco NFL	11	0	4	34	8.5	0
1999—San Francisco NFL	15	2	0	0	0.0	0
2000—San Francisco NFL	9	7	3	75	25.0	0
2001—San Francisco NFL	16	16	7	‡165	23.6	†2
Pro totals (5 years)	67	25	15	296	19.7	2

BROOKING, KEITH LB FALCONS

PERSONAL: Born October 30, 1975, in Senoia, Ga. ... 6-2/245. ... Full name: Keith Howard Brooking.
HIGH SCHOOL: East Coweta (Sharpsburg, Ga.).
COLLEGE: Georgia Tech.
TRANSACTIONS/CAREER NOTES: Selected by Atlanta Falcons in first round (12th pick overall) of 1998 NFL draft. ... Signed by Falcons (June 29, 1998). ... On injured reserve with foot injury (November 1, 2000-remainder of season).
PLAYING EXPERIENCE: Atlanta NFL, 1998-2001. ... Games/Games started: 1998 (15/0), 1999 (13/13), 2000 (5/5), 2001 (16/16). Total: 49/34.
CHAMPIONSHIP GAME EXPERIENCE: Played in NFC championship game (1998 season). ... Played in Super Bowl XXXIII (1998 season).
PRO STATISTICS: 1998—Intercepted one pass for 12 yards. 1999—Credited with two sacks. 2000—Credited with one sack. 2001—Intercepted two passes for 17 yards, credited with 3$\frac{1}{2}$ sacks and recovered two fumbles for minus six yards.

– 45 –

BROOKINS, JASON — RB — PACKERS

PERSONAL: Born January 5, 1976, in Mexico, Mo. ... 6-0/235. ... Full name: Jason Arnaz Brookins.
HIGH SCHOOL: Mexico (Mo.).
JUNIOR COLLEGE: Kemper Military School and College (Mo.).
COLLEGE: Lane.
TRANSACTIONS/CAREER NOTES: Signed as non-drafted free agent by Baltimore Ravens (April 21, 2000). ... Released by Ravens (August 26, 2000). ... Re-signed by Ravens to practice squad (August 27, 2000). ... Released by Ravens (October 3, 2000). ... Signed by Oakland Raiders to practice squad (October 4, 2000). ... Released by Raiders (November 8, 2000). ... Signed by Jacksonville Jaguars to practice squad (November 9, 2000). ... Released by Jaguars (December 24, 2000). ... Signed by Ravens (February 12, 2001). ... Assigned by Ravens to Rhein Fire in 2001 NFL Europe enhancement allocation program (February 18, 2001). ... Released by Ravens (May 20, 2002). ... Signed by Green Bay Packers (May 31, 2002).
PRO STATISTICS: NFL: 2001—Returned one kickoff for 23 yards and recovered two fumbles.
SINGLE GAME HIGHS (regular season): Attempts—32 (November 25, 2001, vs. Jacksonville); yards—89 (November 18, 2001, vs. Cleveland); and rushing touchdowns—2 (November 25, 2001, vs. Jacksonville).

			RUSHING				RECEIVING				TOTALS		
Year Team	G	GS	Att.	Yds.	Avg.	TD	No.	Yds.	Avg.	TD	TD	2pt.	Pts.	Fum.
2001—Rhein NFLE	...	...	34	115	3.4	1	7	104	14.9	0	1	0	6	0
—Baltimore NFL	12	3	151	551	3.6	5	6	45	7.5	0	5	0	30	3
NFL Europe totals (1 year)	...	...	34	115	3.4	1	7	104	14.9	0	1	0	6	0
NFL totals (1 year)	12	3	151	551	3.6	5	6	45	7.5	0	5	0	30	3
Pro totals (2 years)	...	...	185	666	3.6	6	13	149	11.5	0	6	0	36	3

BROOKS, AARON — QB — SAINTS

PERSONAL: Born March 24, 1976, in Newport News, Va. ... 6-4/210. ... Full name: Aaron Lafette Brooks.
HIGH SCHOOL: Homer L. Ferguson (Newport News, Va.).
COLLEGE: Virginia (degree in anthropology).
TRANSACTIONS/CAREER NOTES: Selected by Green Bay Packers in fourth round (131st pick overall) of 1999 NFL draft. ... Signed by Packers (July 27, 1999). ... Traded by Packers with TE Lamont Hall to New Orleans Saints for LB K.D. Williams and third-round pick (traded to San Francisco) in 2001 draft (July 31, 2000).
PRO STATISTICS: 2000—Fumbled four times for minus four yards. 2001—Fumbled 13 times and recovered six fumbles for minus 50 yards.
SINGLE GAME HIGHS (regular season): Attempts—54 (September 30, 2001, vs. New York Giants); completions—30 (December 3, 2000, vs. Denver); yards—441 (December 3, 2000, vs. Denver); and touchdown passes—3 (December 23, 2001, vs. Tampa Bay).
STATISTICAL PLATEAUS: 300-yard passing games: 2000 (1), 2001 (3). Total: 4. ... 100-yard rushing games: 2000 (1).
MISCELLANEOUS: Regular-season record as starting NFL quarterback: 10-11 (.476). ... Postseason record as starting NFL quarterback: 1-1 (.500).

			PASSING							RUSHING			TOTALS		
Year Team	G	GS	Att.	Cmp.	Pct.	Yds.	TD	Int.	Avg.	Rat.	Att.	Yds.	Avg.	TD	TD	2pt.	Pts.
1999—Green Bay NFL							Did not play.										
2000—New Orleans NFL	8	5	194	113	58.2	1514	9	6	7.80	85.7	41	170	4.1	2	2	0	12
2001—New Orleans NFL	16	16	558	312	55.9	3832	26	∞22	6.87	76.4	80	358	4.5	1	1	0	6
Pro totals (2 years)	24	21	752	425	56.5	5346	35	28	7.11	78.8	121	528	4.4	3	3	0	18

BROOKS, BOBBY — LB — RAIDERS

PERSONAL: Born March 3, 1976, in Vallejo, Calif. ... 6-2/240.
HIGH SCHOOL: Hogan (Vallejo, Calif.).
COLLEGE: Fresno State.
TRANSACTIONS/CAREER NOTES: Signed as non-drafted free agent by Oakland Raiders (April 1999). ... Released by Raiders (September 5, 1999). ... Re-signed by Raiders to practice squad (October 20, 1999). ... Activated (December 1999).
PLAYING EXPERIENCE: Oakland NFL, 1999-2001. ... Games/Games started: 1999 (1/0), 2000 (16/0), 2001 (16/0). Total: 33/0.
CHAMPIONSHIP GAME EXPERIENCE: Played in AFC championship game (2000 season).

BROOKS, DERRICK — LB — BUCCANEERS

PERSONAL: Born April 18, 1973, in Pensacola, Fla. ... 6-0/235. ... Full name: Derrick Dewan Brooks.
HIGH SCHOOL: Booker T. Washington (Pensacola, Fla.).
COLLEGE: Florida State (degree in communications, 1994).
TRANSACTIONS/CAREER NOTES: Selected by Tampa Bay Buccaneers in first round (28th pick overall) of 1995 NFL draft. ... Signed by Buccaneers (May 3, 1995).
CHAMPIONSHIP GAME EXPERIENCE: Played in NFC championship game (1999 season).
HONORS: Named linebacker on THE SPORTING NEWS college All-America first team (1993 and 1994). ... Played in Pro Bowl (1997-2000 seasons). ... Named linebacker on THE SPORTING NEWS NFL All-Pro team (1999 and 2000).
PRO STATISTICS: 1997—Fumbled once and recovered one fumble. 1999—Recovered two fumbles for four yards.

			INTERCEPTIONS				SACKS
Year Team	G	GS	No.	Yds.	Avg.	TD	No.
1995—Tampa Bay NFL	16	13	0	0	0.0	0	1.0
1996—Tampa Bay NFL	16	16	1	6	6.0	0	0.0
1997—Tampa Bay NFL	16	16	2	13	6.5	0	1.5
1998—Tampa Bay NFL	16	16	1	25	25.0	0	0.0
1999—Tampa Bay NFL	16	16	4	61	15.3	0	2.0
2000—Tampa Bay NFL	16	16	1	34	34.0	1	1.0
2001—Tampa Bay NFL	16	16	3	65	21.7	0	0.0
Pro totals (7 years)	112	109	12	204	17.0	1	5.5

BROOKS, JAMAL — LB — COWBOYS

PERSONAL: Born November 9, 1976, in Los Angeles. ... 6-2/240.
HIGH SCHOOL: Grenada Hills (Calif.).
JUNIOR COLLEGE: Pasadena City College.
COLLEGE: Hampton.
TRANSACTIONS/CAREER NOTES: Signed as non-drafted free agent by New Orleans Saints (April 27, 2000). ... Released by Saints (August 22, 2000). ... Selected by Scottish Claymores in 2001 NFL Europe draft (February 18, 2001). ... Signed by Dallas Cowboys (July 10, 2001).
PLAYING EXPERIENCE: Scottish NFLE, 2001; Dallas NFL, 2001. ... Games/Games started: NFLE 2001 (games played unavailable), NFL 2001 (16/1).
PRO STATISTICS: NFLE: 2001—Intercepted one pass for no yards and credited with 1½ sacks.

BROOKS, RODREGIS — CB — COLTS

PERSONAL: Born August 30, 1978, in Alexander City, Ala. ... 5-9/184. ... Full name: Rodregis A. Brooks.
HIGH SCHOOL: Dadeville (Ala.).
COLLEGE: Alabama-Birmingham.
TRANSACTIONS/CAREER NOTES: Selected after junior season by Indianapolis Colts in seventh round (238th pick overall) of 2000 NFL draft. ... Signed by Colts (June 28, 2000). ... On injured reserve with neck injury (August 17, 2000-entire season).
PLAYING EXPERIENCE: Indianapolis NFL, 2001. ... Games/Games started: 2001 (5/0).

BROUGHTON, LUTHER — TE — BEARS

PERSONAL: Born November 30, 1974, in Charleston, S.C. ... 6-0/248. ... Full name: Luther Rashard Broughton Jr.
HIGH SCHOOL: Cainhoy (Huger, S.C.).
COLLEGE: Furman.
TRANSACTIONS/CAREER NOTES: Selected by Philadelphia Eagles in fifth round (155th pick overall) of 1997 NFL draft. ... Signed by Eagles (July 15, 1997). ... Active for one game with Eagles (1997); did not play. ... Released by Eagles (November 5, 1997). ... Re-signed by Eagles to practice squad (November 5, 1997). ... Signed by Carolina Panthers from Eagles practice squad (December 15, 1997). ... Inactive for one game with Panthers (1997). ... Traded by Carolina Panthers to Philadelphia Eagles for seventh-round pick (TE Mike Roberg) in 2001 draft (September 5, 1999). ... Granted free agency (February 11, 2000). ... Re-signed by Eagles (April 10, 2000). ... Granted unconditional free agency (March 2, 2001). ... Signed by Panthers (May 8, 2001). ... Granted unconditional free agency (March 1, 2002). ... Signed by Chicago Bears (March 6, 2002).
PRO STATISTICS: 1998—Recovered one fumble. 1999—Returned one kickoff for five yards and recovered one fumble. 2000—Returned one kickoff for 20 yards. 2001—Returned three kickoffs for 46 yards.
SINGLE GAME HIGHS (regular season): Receptions—4 (November 21, 1999, vs. Indianapolis); yards—78 (December 20, 1998, vs. St. Louis); and touchdown receptions—2 (November 28, 1999, vs. Washington).

			RECEIVING				TOTALS			
Year Team	G	GS	No.	Yds.	Avg.	TD	TD	2pt.	Pts.	Fum.
1997—Philadelphia NFL						Did not play.				
1998—Carolina NFL	16	4	6	142	23.7	1	1	0	6	1
1999—Philadelphia NFL	16	3	26	295	11.3	4	4	0	24	0
2000—Philadelphia NFL	15	1	12	104	8.7	0	0	0	0	1
2001—Carolina NFL	15	0	2	22	11.0	0	0	0	0	0
Pro totals (4 years)	62	8	46	563	12.2	5	5	0	30	2

BROWN, CHAD — LB — SEAHAWKS

PERSONAL: Born July 12, 1970, in Altadena, Calif. ... 6-2/240. ... Full name: Chadwick Everett Brown.
HIGH SCHOOL: John Muir (Pasadena, Calif.).
COLLEGE: Colorado (degree in marketing, 1992).
TRANSACTIONS/CAREER NOTES: Selected by Pittsburgh Steelers in second round (44th pick overall) of 1993 NFL draft. ... Signed by Steelers (July 26, 1993). ... Granted unconditional free agency (February 14, 1997). ... Signed by Seattle Seahawks (February 15, 1997).
CHAMPIONSHIP GAME EXPERIENCE: Played in AFC championship game (1994 and 1995 seasons). ... Played in Super Bowl XXX (1995 season).
HONORS: Named linebacker on THE SPORTING NEWS NFL All-Pro team (1996 and 1998). ... Played in Pro Bowl (1996, 1998 and 1999 seasons).
PRO STATISTICS: 1996—Fumbled once and recovered two fumbles. 1997—Recovered four fumbles for 68 yards and two touchdowns. 1998—Recovered one fumble. 1999—Recovered one fumble. 2000—Recovered three fumbles for 16 yards. 2001—Recovered one fumble for three yards.

			INTERCEPTIONS				SACKS
Year Team	G	GS	No.	Yds.	Avg.	TD	No.
1993—Pittsburgh NFL	16	9	0	0	0.0	0	3.0
1994—Pittsburgh NFL	16	16	1	9	9.0	0	8.5
1995—Pittsburgh NFL	10	10	0	0	0.0	0	5.5
1996—Pittsburgh NFL	14	14	2	20	10.0	0	13.0
1997—Seattle NFL	15	15	0	0	0.0	0	6.5
1998—Seattle NFL	16	16	1	11	11.0	0	7.5
1999—Seattle NFL	15	15	0	0	0.0	0	5.5
2000—Seattle NFL	16	16	1	0	0.0	0	6.0
2001—Seattle NFL	16	16	0	0	0.0	0	8.5
Pro totals (9 years)	134	127	5	40	8.0	0	64.0

BROWN, COURTNEY — DE — BROWNS

PERSONAL: Born February 14, 1978, in Charleston, S.C. ... 6-4/266. ... Full name: Courtney Lanair Brown.
HIGH SCHOOL: Macedonia (Alvin, S.C.).
COLLEGE: Penn State (degree in integrative arts, 1999).
TRANSACTIONS/CAREER NOTES: Selected by Cleveland Browns in first round (first pick overall) of 2000 NFL draft. ... Signed by Browns (May 10, 2000). ... On injured reserve with ankle injury (January 2, 2002-remainder of season).
HONORS: Named defensive end on THE SPORTING NEWS college All-America first team (1999).
PRO STATISTICS: 2000—Recovered one fumble. 2001—Recovered two fumbles for 25 yards and one touchdown.

Year Team	G	GS	SACKS
2000—Cleveland NFL	16	16	4.5
2001—Cleveland NFL	5	5	4.5
Pro totals (2 years)	21	21	9.0

BROWN, DAVE — QB

PERSONAL: Born February 25, 1970, in Summit, N.J. ... 6-6/230. ... Full name: David Michael Brown.
HIGH SCHOOL: Westfield (N.J.).
COLLEGE: Duke (degrees in history and political science, 1992).
TRANSACTIONS/CAREER NOTES: Selected by New York Giants in first round of 1992 NFL supplemental draft. ... Signed by Giants (August 12, 1992). ... On injured reserve with thumb injury (December 18, 1992-remainder of season). ... Granted unconditional free agency (February 16, 1996). ... Re-signed by Giants (May 3, 1996). ... Released by Giants (February 20, 1998). ... Signed by Arizona Cardinals (April 29, 1998). ... Granted unconditional free agency (February 11, 2000). ... Re-signed by Cardinals (February 23, 2000). ... Granted unconditional free agency (March 1, 2002).
PRO STATISTICS: 1994—Punted twice for 57 yards, fumbled 11 times and recovered four fumbles for minus 15 yards. 1995—Punted once for 15 yards, fumbled 10 times and recovered two fumbles for minus eight yards. 1996—Fumbled nine times and recovered one fumble for minus three yards. 1997—Fumbled once. 1999—Fumbled four times and recovered one fumble. 2000—Fumbled twice for minus three yards.
SINGLE GAME HIGHS (regular season): Attempts—50 (September 17, 1995, vs. Green Bay); completions—28 (September 14, 1997, vs. Baltimore); yards—299 (November 5, 1995, vs. Seattle); and touchdown passes—2 (September 28, 1997, vs. New Orleans).
MISCELLANEOUS: Regular-season record as starting NFL quarterback: 26-34 (.433).

					PASSING						RUSHING				TOTALS		
Year Team	G	GS	Att.	Cmp.	Pct.	Yds.	TD	Int.	Avg.	Rat.	Att.	Yds.	Avg.	TD	TD	2pt.	Pts.
1992—N.Y. Giants NFL	2	0	7	4	57.1	21	0	0	3.00	62.2	2	-1	-0.5	0	0	0	0
1993—N.Y. Giants NFL	1	0	0	0	0.0	0	0	0	0.0	...	3	-4	-1.3	0	0	0	0
1994—N.Y. Giants NFL	15	15	350	201	57.4	2536	12	16	7.25	72.5	60	196	3.3	2	2	0	12
1995—N.Y. Giants NFL	16	16	456	254	55.7	2814	11	10	6.17	73.1	45	228	5.1	4	4	0	24
1996—N.Y. Giants NFL	16	16	398	214	53.8	2412	12	20	6.06	61.3	50	170	3.4	0	0	0	0
1997—N.Y. Giants NFL	7	6	180	93	51.7	1023	5	3	5.68	71.1	17	29	1.7	1	1	0	6
1998—Arizona NFL	1	0	5	2	40.0	31	0	0	6.20	61.3	1	2	2.0	0	0	0	0
1999—Arizona NFL	8	5	169	84	49.7	944	2	6	5.59	55.9	13	49	3.8	0	0	0	0
2000—Arizona NFL	6	2	69	40	58.0	467	2	3	6.77	70.1	1	0	0.0	0	0	0	0
2001—Arizona NFL	1	0	0	0	0.0	0	0	0	0.0	...	0	0	0.0	0	0	0	0
Pro totals (10 years)	73	60	1634	892	54.6	10248	44	58	6.27	67.9	192	669	3.5	7	7	0	42

BROWN, DELVIN — S — DOLPHINS

PERSONAL: Born September 17, 1979, in Miami. ... 6-0/205. ... Full name: Delvin Jaquin Brown.
HIGH SCHOOL: Carol City (Miami).
COLLEGE: Miami (Fla.).
TRANSACTIONS/CAREER NOTES: Signed as non-drafted free agent by Jacksonville Jaguars (April 23, 2001). ... Released by Jaguars (September 4, 2001). ... Re-signed by Jaguars (September 12, 2001). ... Released by Jaguars (November 7, 2001). ... Signed by Miami Dolphins (January 15, 2002).
PLAYING EXPERIENCE: Jacksonville NFL, 2001. ... Games/Games started: 2001 (5/0).

BROWN, ERIC — S

PERSONAL: Born March 20, 1975, in San Antonio. ... 6-0/210. ... Full name: Eric Jon Brown.
HIGH SCHOOL: Judson (Converse, Texas).
JUNIOR COLLEGE: Blinn College (Texas).
COLLEGE: Mississippi State.
TRANSACTIONS/CAREER NOTES: Selected by Denver Broncos in second round (61st pick overall) of 1998 NFL draft. ... Signed by Broncos (July 16, 1998). ... On injured reserve with knee injury (November 18, 1999-remainder of season). ... Granted unconditional free agency (March 1, 2002).
CHAMPIONSHIP GAME EXPERIENCE: Member of Broncos for AFC championship game (1998 season); inactive. ... Member of Super Bowl championship team (1998 season); inactive.
PRO STATISTICS: 1998—Recovered one fumble. 1999—Fumbled twice and recovered one fumble. 2000—Recovered three fumbles for eight yards. 2001—Recovered one fumble.

			INTERCEPTIONS				SACKS
Year Team	G	GS	No.	Yds.	Avg.	TD	No.
1998—Denver NFL	11	10	0	0	0.0	0	0.0
1999—Denver NFL	10	10	1	13	13.0	0	1.5
2000—Denver NFL	16	16	3	9	3.0	0	1.0
2001—Denver NFL	16	16	2	0	0.0	0	3.0
Pro totals (4 years)	53	52	6	22	3.7	0	5.5

BROWN, GILBERT — DT — PACKERS

PERSONAL: Born February 22, 1971, in Detroit. ... 6-2/339. ... Full name: Gilbert Jesse Brown.
HIGH SCHOOL: Mackenzie (Detroit).
COLLEGE: Kansas.
TRANSACTIONS/CAREER NOTES: Selected by Minnesota Vikings in third round (79th pick overall) of 1993 NFL draft. ... Signed by Vikings (July 16, 1993). ... Claimed on waivers by Green Bay Packers (August 31, 1993). ... On injured reserve with knee injury (December 6, 1994-remainder of season). ... Granted unconditional free agency (February 14, 1997). ... Re-signed by Packers (February 18, 1997). ... Granted unconditional free agency (February 11, 2000). ... Re-signed by Packers (March 23, 2001). ... Granted unconditional free agency (March 1, 2002). ... Re-signed by Packers (April 23, 2002).
CHAMPIONSHIP GAME EXPERIENCE: Played in NFC championship game (1995-97 seasons). ... Member of Super Bowl championship team (1996 season). ... Played in Super Bowl XXXII (1997 season).

Year — Team	G	GS	SACKS
1993—Green Bay NFL	2	0	0.0
1994—Green Bay NFL	13	1	3.0
1995—Green Bay NFL	13	7	0.0
1996—Green Bay NFL	16	16	1.0
1997—Green Bay NFL	12	12	3.0
1998—Green Bay NFL	16	16	0.0
1999—Green Bay NFL	16	15	0.0
2000—	Did not play.		
2001—Green Bay NFL	11	11	0.0
Pro totals (8 years)	**99**	**78**	**7.0**

BROWN, JOE — DT — SEAHAWKS

PERSONAL: Born March 5, 1977, in Columbus, Ohio. ... 6-6/288.
HIGH SCHOOL: Catalina (Tucson, Ariz.).
COLLEGE: Ohio State.
TRANSACTIONS/CAREER NOTES: Signed as non-drafted free agent by Seattle Seahawks (April 27, 2001). ... Released by Seahawks (September 1, 2001). ... Re-signed by Seahawks to practice squad (September 3, 2001). ... Activated (December 19, 2001).
PLAYING EXPERIENCE: Seattle NFL, 2001. ... Games/Games started: 2001 (2/0).

BROWN, JONATHON — DE — RAMS

PERSONAL: Born November 28, 1975, in Chickasha, Okla. ... 6-3/270. ... Full name: Jonathon Bernard Brown.
HIGH SCHOOL: Booker T. Washington (Tulsa, Okla.).
COLLEGE: Tennessee.
TRANSACTIONS/CAREER NOTES: Selected by Green Bay Packers in third round (90th pick overall) of 1998 NFL draft. ... Signed by Packers (June 12, 1998). ... Released by Packers (August 31, 1999). ... Signed by Denver Broncos to practice squad (December 8, 1999). ... Released by Broncos (December 21, 1999). ... Selected by Berlin Thunder in 2000 NFL Europe draft (February 22, 2000). ... Signed by San Diego Chargers (June 27, 2000). ... Released by Chargers (August 27, 2000). ... Signed by St. Louis Rams to practice squad (November 28, 2000). ... Released by Rams (September 2, 2001). ... Re-signed by Rams to practice squad (September 4, 2001). ... Activated (October 23, 2001). ... Released by Rams (November 16, 2001). ... Re-signed by Rams (November 20, 2001). ... Released by Rams (December 7, 2001). ... Re-signed by Rams to practice squad (December 11, 2001).
PLAYING EXPERIENCE: Green Bay NFL, 1998; Berlin NFLE, 2000; St. Louis NFL, 2001. ... Games/Games started: 1998 (4/0); NFLE 2000 (games played unavailable), NFL 2001 (3/0). Total: 7/0.
PRO STATISTICS: NFLE: 2000—Credited with 10 sacks.

BROWN, KRIS — K — TEXANS

PERSONAL: Born December 23, 1976, in Southlake, Texas. ... 5-11/206.
HIGH SCHOOL: Carroll (Southlake, Texas).
COLLEGE: Nebraska.
TRANSACTIONS/CAREER NOTES: Selected by Pittsburgh Steelers in seventh round (228th pick overall) of 1999 NFL draft. ... Signed by Steelers (June 29, 1999). ... Granted free agency (March 1, 2002). ... Signed by Houston Texans (March 25, 2002).
CHAMPIONSHIP GAME EXPERIENCE: Played in AFC championship game (2001 season).
PRO STATISTICS: 2001—Rushed once for six yards, fumbled once and recovered one fumble.

				KICKING				
Year — Team	G	XPM	XPA	FGM	FGA	Lg.	50+	Pts.
1999—Pittsburgh NFL	16	30	31	25	29	51	1-1	105
2000—Pittsburgh NFL	16	32	33	25	30	52	1-2	107
2001—Pittsburgh NFL	16	34	37	30	*44	*55	2-2	124
Pro totals (3 years)	**48**	**96**	**101**	**80**	**103**	**55**	**4-5**	**336**

BROWN, LANCE — DB

PERSONAL: Born February 2, 1972, in Jacksonville. ... 6-2/203.
HIGH SCHOOL: Terry Parker (Jacksonville).
COLLEGE: Indiana.
TRANSACTIONS/CAREER NOTES: Selected by Pittsburgh Steelers in fifth round (161st pick overall) of 1995 NFL draft. ... Signed by Steelers (July 18, 1995). ... Claimed on waivers by Arizona Cardinals (September 25, 1995). ... Released by Cardinals (September 10, 1996). ... Signed by New York Jets to practice squad (November 19, 1996). ... Released by Jets (August 7, 1997). ... Signed by Steelers (February 13, 1998).

... Granted unconditional free agency (February 11, 2000). ... Re-signed by Steelers (April 10, 2000). ... Released by Steelers (August 27, 2000). ... Signed by Buffalo Bills (March 13, 2001). ... Granted unconditional free agency (March 1, 2002).
PLAYING EXPERIENCE: Arizona NFL, 1995 and 1996; Pittsburgh NFL, 1998 and 1999; Buffalo NFL, 2001. ... Games/Games started: 1995 (11/5), 1996 (1/0), 1998 (16/0), 1999 (16/0), 2001 (14/1). Total: 58/6.
PRO STATISTICS: 1995—Recovered one fumble. 1998—Recovered two fumbles for one yard. 1999—Credited with one sack.

BROWN, LOMAS   OT

PERSONAL: Born March 30, 1963, in Miami. ... 6-4/280. ... Full name: Lomas Brown Jr. ... Cousin of Joe Taylor, defensive back with Chicago Bears (1967-74); cousin of Guy McIntyre, guard with San Francisco 49ers (1984-93), Green Bay Packers (1994) and Philadelphia Eagles (1995 and 1996); and cousin of Eric Curry, defensive end, with Tampa Bay Buccaneers (1993-97) and Jacksonville Jaguars (1998-99).
HIGH SCHOOL: Miami Springs Senior.
COLLEGE: Florida (degree in public recreation, 1996).
TRANSACTIONS/CAREER NOTES: Selected by Orlando Renegades in second round (18th pick overall) of 1985 USFL draft. ... Selected by Detroit Lions in first round (sixth pick overall) of 1985 NFL draft. ... Signed by Lions (August 9, 1985). ... Designated by Lions as franchise player (February 25, 1993). ... Granted roster exemption (September 1-3, 1993). ... Designated by Lions as franchise player (February 15, 1995). ... Re-signed by Lions (September 7, 1995). ... Granted unconditional free agency (February 16, 1996). ... Signed by Arizona Cardinals (February 28, 1996). ... Granted unconditional free agency (February 12, 1999). ... Signed by Cleveland Browns (March 9, 1999). ... On injured reserve with knee injury (December 14, 1999-remainder of season). ... Released by Browns (February 8, 2000). ... Signed by New York Giants (February 2, 2000). ... Released by Giants (February 28, 2002).
PLAYING EXPERIENCE: Detroit NFL, 1985-1995; Arizona NFL, 1996-1998; Cleveland NFL, 1999; New York Giants NFL, 2000 and 2001. ... Games/Games started: 1985 (16/16), 1986 (16/16), 1987 (11/11), 1988 (16/16), 1989 (16/16), 1990 (16/16), 1991 (15/15), 1992 (16/16), 1993 (11/11), 1994 (16/16), 1995 (15/14), 1996 (16/16), 1997 (14/14), 1998 (16/16), 1999 (10/10), 2000 (16/16), 2001 (16/16). Total: 252/251.
CHAMPIONSHIP GAME EXPERIENCE: Played in NFC championship game (1991 and 2000 season). ... Played in Super Bowl XXXV (2000 season).
HONORS: Named tackle on THE SPORTING NEWS college All-America first team (1984). ... Played in Pro Bowl (1990-1996 seasons). ... Named offensive tackle on THE SPORTING NEWS NFL All-Pro team (1992).
PRO STATISTICS: 1989—Rushed once for three yards and recovered one fumble. 1991—Recovered one fumble. 2000—Recovered one fumble.

BROWN, MIKE   S   BEARS

PERSONAL: Born February 13, 1978, in Scottsdale, Ariz. ... 5-10/203.
HIGH SCHOOL: Saguaro (Scottsdale, Ariz.).
COLLEGE: Nebraska.
TRANSACTIONS/CAREER NOTES: Selected by Chicago Bears in second round (39th pick overall) of 2000 NFL draft. ... Signed by Bears (July 23, 2000).
PRO STATISTICS: 2000—Recovered one fumble for 12 yards. 2001—Credited with three sacks and recovered one fumble for five yards.

			INTERCEPTIONS		
Year Team	G	GS	No.	Yds.	Avg.	TD
2000—Chicago NFL	16	16	1	35	35.0	1
2001—Chicago NFL	16	16	5	81	16.2	†2
Pro totals (2 years)	32	32	6	116	19.3	3

BROWN, NA   WR   EAGLES

PERSONAL: Born February 22, 1977, in Reidsville, N.C. ... 6-0/196. ... Full name: Na Orlando Brown. ... Name pronounced NAY.
HIGH SCHOOL: Reidsville (N.C.).
COLLEGE: North Carolina.
TRANSACTIONS/CAREER NOTES: Selected by Philadelphia Eagles in fourth round (130th pick overall) of 1999 NFL draft. ... Signed by Eagles (July 28, 1999). ... Granted free agency (March 1, 2002). ... Re-signed by Eagles (April 26, 2002).
CHAMPIONSHIP GAME EXPERIENCE: Played in NFC championship game (2001 season).
PRO STATISTICS: 2001—Returned five punts for 30 yards.
SINGLE GAME HIGHS (regular season): Receptions—4 (December 5, 1999, vs. Arizona); yards—60 (December 19, 1999, vs. New England); and touchdown receptions—1 (December 8, 2000, vs. Washington).

			RECEIVING				TOTALS			
Year Team	G	GS	No.	Yds.	Avg.	TD	TD	2pt.	Pts.	Fum.
1999—Philadelphia NFL	12	5	18	188	10.4	1	1	0	6	0
2000—Philadelphia NFL	14	2	9	80	8.9	1	1	0	6	0
2001—Philadelphia NFL	16	2	7	95	13.6	0	0	0	0	0
Pro totals (3 years)	42	9	34	363	10.7	2	2	0	12	0

BROWN, RALPH   CB   GIANTS

PERSONAL: Born September 9, 1978, in Hacienda Heights, Calif. ... 5-10/185. ... Full name: Ralph Brown II.
HIGH SCHOOL: Bishop Amat (La Puente, Calif.).
COLLEGE: Nebraska.
TRANSACTIONS/CAREER NOTES: Selected by New York Giants in fifth round (140th pick overall) of 2000 NFL draft. ... Signed by Giants (July 18, 2000). ... On injured reserve with kidney injury (October 3, 2000-remainder of season).
PLAYING EXPERIENCE: New York Giants NFL, 2001. ... Games/Games started: 2000 (2/0), 2001 (8/0). Total: 10/0.
HONORS: Named cornerback on THE SPORTING NEWS college All-America first team (1999).

BROWN, RAY — G

PERSONAL: Born December 12, 1962, in Marion, Ark. ... 6-5/318. ... Full name: Leonard Ray Brown Jr.
HIGH SCHOOL: Marion (Ark.).
COLLEGE: Memphis State, then Arizona State, then Arkansas State.
TRANSACTIONS/CAREER NOTES: Selected by St. Louis Cardinals in eighth round (201st pick overall) of 1986 NFL draft. ... Signed by Cardinals (July 14, 1986). ... On injured reserve with knee injury (October 17-November 21, 1986). ... Released by Cardinals (September 7, 1987). ... Re-signed by Cardinals as replacement player (September 25, 1987). ... On injured reserve with finger injury (November 12-December 12, 1987). ... Cardinals franchise moved to Phoenix (March 15, 1988). ... Granted unconditional free agency (February 1, 1989). ... Signed by Washington Redskins (March 10, 1989). ... On injured reserve with knee injury (September 5-November 4, 1989). ... On injured reserve with knee injury (September 4, 1990-January 4, 1991). ... Granted unconditional free agency (February 1-April 1, 1991). ... Re-signed by Redskins for 1991 season. ... On injured reserve with elbow injury (August 27, 1991-entire season). ... Granted unconditional free agency (February 16, 1996). ... Signed by San Francisco 49ers (March 1, 1996). ... Released by 49ers (June 3, 2002).
PLAYING EXPERIENCE: St. Louis NFL, 1986 and 1987; Phoenix NFL, 1988; Washington NFL, 1989, 1992-1995; San Francisco NFL, 1996-2001. ... Games/Games started: 1986 (11/4), 1987 (7/3), 1988 (15/1), 1989 (7/0), 1992 (16/8), 1993 (16/14), 1994 (16/16), 1995 (16/16), 1996 (16/16), 1997 (15/15), 1998 (16/16), 1999 (16/16), 2000 (16/16), 2001 (16/16). Total: 199/157.
CHAMPIONSHIP GAME EXPERIENCE: Played in NFC championship game (1997 season).
PRO STATISTICS: 1999—Recovered two fumbles. 2000—Recovered one fumble.

BROWN, RUBEN — G — BILLS

PERSONAL: Born February 13, 1972, in Englewood, N.J. ... 6-3/304. ... Full name: Ruben Pernell Brown. ... Brother of Cornell Brown, linebacker, with Baltimore Ravens (1997-2000).
HIGH SCHOOL: E.C. Glass (Lynchburg, Va.).
COLLEGE: Pittsburgh.
TRANSACTIONS/CAREER NOTES: Selected by Buffalo Bills in first round (14th pick overall) of 1995 NFL draft. ... Signed by Bills (June 20, 1995). ... Granted unconditional free agency (February 11, 2000). ... Re-signed by Bills (March 31, 2000).
PLAYING EXPERIENCE: Buffalo NFL, 1995-2001. ... Games/Games started: 1995 (16/16), 1996 (14/14), 1997 (16/16), 1998 (13/13), 1999 (14/14), 2000 (16/16), 2001 (16/16). Total: 105/105.
HONORS: Named offensive lineman on THE SPORTING NEWS college All-America second team (1994). ... Played in Pro Bowl (1996-2000 seasons).
PRO STATISTICS: 1997—Recovered one fumble.

BROWN, TIM — WR — RAIDERS

PERSONAL: Born July 22, 1966, in Dallas. ... 6-0/195. ... Full name: Timothy Donell Brown.
HIGH SCHOOL: Woodrow Wilson (Dallas).
COLLEGE: Notre Dame (degree in sociology).
TRANSACTIONS/CAREER NOTES: Selected by Los Angeles Raiders in first round (sixth pick overall) of 1988 NFL draft. ... Signed by Raiders (July 14, 1988). ... On injured reserve with knee injury (September 12, 1989-remainder of season). ... Granted free agency (February 1, 1992). ... Re-signed by Raiders (August 13, 1992). ... Designated by Raiders as transition player (February 25, 1993). ... Tendered offer sheet by Denver Broncos (March 11, 1994). ... Offer matched by Raiders (March 16, 1994). ... Raiders franchise moved to Oakland (July 21, 1995).
CHAMPIONSHIP GAME EXPERIENCE: Played in AFC championship game (1990 and 2000 seasons).
HONORS: Named wide receiver on THE SPORTING NEWS college All-America first team (1986 and 1987). ... Heisman Trophy winner (1987). ... Named College Football Player of the Year by THE SPORTING NEWS (1987). ... Named kick returner on THE SPORTING NEWS NFL All-Pro team (1988). ... Played in Pro Bowl (1988, 1991 and 1993-1997 seasons). ... Named wide receiver on THE SPORTING NEWS NFL All-Pro team (1997). ... Named to play in Pro Bowl (1999 season); replaced by Terry Glenn due to injury.
RECORDS: Holds NFL rookie-season record for most combined yards gained—2,317 (1988).
PRO STATISTICS: 1988—Fumbled five times and recovered seven fumbles. 1989—Fumbled once. 1990—Fumbled three times. 1991—Fumbled once. 1992—Fumbled six times and recovered one fumble. 1993—Fumbled once. 1994—Fumbled three times. 1995—Recovered one fumble for three yards. 1996—Fumbled three times and recovered one fumble. 1997—Fumbled once. 1998—Fumbled three times and recovered two fumbles. 2001—Fumbled once.
SINGLE GAME HIGHS (regular season): Receptions—14 (December 21, 1997, vs. Jacksonville); yards—190 (October 24, 1999, vs. New York Jets); and touchdown receptions—3 (August 31, 1997, vs. Tennessee).
STATISTICAL PLATEAUS: 100-yard receiving games: 1988 (1), 1991 (1), 1992 (1), 1993 (4), 1994 (4), 1995 (6), 1996 (2), 1997 (7), 1998 (3), 1999 (6), 2000 (2), 2001 (4). Total: 41.
MISCELLANEOUS: Holds Raiders franchise all-time record for most receptions (937), most yards receiving (13,237), most touchdowns (100) and most receiving touchdowns (95).

			RUSHING				RECEIVING				PUNT RETURNS				KICKOFF RETURNS				TOTALS		
Year Team	G	GS	Att.	Yds.	Avg.	TD	No.	Yds.	Avg.	TD	No.	Yds.	Avg.	TD	No.	Yds.	Avg.	TD	TD	2pt.	Pts.
1988—LA Raiders NFL...	16	9	14	50	3.6	1	43	725	16.9	5	§49	§444	9.1	0	†41	*1098	*26.8	†1	7	0	42
1989—LA Raiders NFL...	1	1	0	0	0.0	0	1	8	8.0	0	4	43	10.8	0	3	63	21.0	0	0	0	0
1990—LA Raiders NFL...	16	0	0	0	0.0	0	18	265	14.7	3	34	295	8.7	0	0	0	0.0	0	3	0	18
1991—LA Raiders NFL...	16	1	5	16	3.2	0	36	554	15.4	5	29	§330	11.4	▲1	1	29	29.0	0	6	0	36
1992—LA Raiders NFL...	15	12	3	-4	-1.3	0	49	693	14.1	7	37	383	10.4	0	2	14	7.0	0	7	0	42
1993—LA Raiders NFL...	16	16	2	7	3.5	0	80	§1180	14.8	7	40	§465	11.6	1	0	0	0.0	0	8	0	48
1994—LA Raiders NFL...	16	16	0	0	0.0	0	89	§1309	14.7	9	40	*487	12.2	0	0	0	0.0	0	9	0	54
1995—Oakland NFL......	16	16	0	0	0.0	0	89	§1342	15.1	10	36	364	10.1	0	0	0	0.0	0	10	0	60
1996—Oakland NFL......	16	16	6	35	5.8	0	90	1104	12.3	9	32	272	8.5	0	1	24	24.0	0	9	0	54
1997—Oakland NFL......	16	16	5	19	3.8	0	†104	§1408	13.5	5	0	0	0.0	0	1	7	7.0	0	5	1	32
1998—Oakland NFL......	16	16	1	-7	-7.0	0	81	1012	12.5	9	3	23	7.7	0	0	0	0.0	0	9	0	54
1999—Oakland NFL......	16	16	1	4	4.0	0	90	1344	14.9	6	0	0	0.0	0	0	0	0.0	0	6	0	36
2000—Oakland NFL......	16	16	3	12	4.0	0	76	1128	14.8	11	0	0	0.0	0	0	0	0.0	0	11	0	66
2001—Oakland NFL......	16	16	4	39	9.8	0	91	1165	12.8	9	6	111	18.5	1	0	0	0.0	0	10	0	60
Pro totals (14 years)......	208	167	44	171	3.9	1	937	13237	14.1	95	310	3217	10.4	3	49	1235	25.2	1	100	1	602

BROWN, TRAVIS — QB — BILLS

PERSONAL: Born July 17, 1977, in Phoenix. ... 6-3/212.
HIGH SCHOOL: Moon Valley (Phoenix).
COLLEGE: Northern Arizona.
TRANSACTIONS/CAREER NOTES: Signed as non-drafted free agent by Philadelphia Eagles (April 19, 2000). ... Released by Eagles (August 27, 2000). ... Signed by Seattle Seahawks to practice squad (August 30, 2000). ... Activated (November 21, 2000). ... Released by Seahawks (August 21, 2001). ... Signed by Buffalo Bills (August 22, 2001).
PRO STATISTICS: 2001—Fumbled once.
SINGLE GAME HIGHS (regular season): Attempts—33 (January 6, 2002, vs. Miami); completions—15 (January 6, 2002, vs. Miami); yards—201 (January 6, 2002, vs. Miami); and touchdown passes—1 (January 6, 2002, vs. Miami).

				PASSING						RUSHING				TOTALS		
Year Team	G	GS	Att.	Cmp.	Pct.	Yds.	TD	Int.	Avg.	Rat.	Att.	Yds.	Avg.	TD	TD	2pt.	Pts.
2000—Seattle NFL	1	0	1	0	0.0	0	0	0	0.0	39.6	0	0	0.0	0	0	0	0
2001—Buffalo NFL	1	0	33	15	45.5	201	1	2	6.09	50.2	1	10	10.0	0	0	0	0
Pro totals (2 years)	2	0	34	15	44.1	201	1	2	5.91	48.8	1	10	10.0	0	0	0	0

BROWN, TROY — WR — PATRIOTS

PERSONAL: Born July 2, 1971, in Barnwell, S.C. ... 5-10/193. ... Full name: Troy Fitzgerald Brown.
HIGH SCHOOL: Blackville (S.C.)-Hilda.
JUNIOR COLLEGE: Lees-McRae College (N.C.).
COLLEGE: Marshall.
TRANSACTIONS/CAREER NOTES: Selected by New England Patriots in eighth round (198th pick overall) of 1993 NFL draft. ... Signed by Patriots (July 16, 1993). ... On injured reserve with quadriceps injury (December 31, 1993-remainder of season). ... Released by Patriots (August 28, 1994). ... Re-signed by Patriots (October 19, 1994). ... Granted unconditional free agency (February 14, 1997). ... Re-signed by Patriots (March 10, 1997). ... Granted unconditional free agency (February 11, 2000). ... Re-signed by Patriots (February 26, 2000).
CHAMPIONSHIP GAME EXPERIENCE: Played in AFC championship game (1996 and 2001 seasons). ... Member of Patriots for Super Bowl XXXI (1996 season); inactive. ... Member of Super Bowl championship team (2001 season).
PRO STATISTICS: 1993—Recovered a fumble. 1994—Recovered two fumbles. 1995—Recovered one fumble for 75 yards and a touchdown. 1997—Rushed once for minus 18 yards. 1999—Attempted one pass without a completion and recovered two fumbles. 2000—Rushed six times for 46 yards. 2001—Rushed 11 times for 91 yards and recovered one fumble.
SINGLE GAME HIGHS (regular season): Receptions—12 (December 4, 2000, vs. Kansas City); yards—125 (October 19, 1997, vs. New York Jets); and touchdown receptions—2 (October 1, 2000, vs. Denver).
STATISTICAL PLATEAUS: 100-yard receiving games: 1997 (2), 1999 (1), 2000 (4), 2001 (3). Total: 10.

			RECEIVING				PUNT RETURNS				KICKOFF RETURNS				TOTALS		
Year Team	G	GS	No.	Yds.	Avg.	TD	No.	Yds.	Avg.	TD	No.	Yds.	Avg.	TD	TD	2pt.	Pts.	Fum.
1993—New England NFL	12	0	2	22	11.0	0	25	224	9.0	0	15	243	16.2	0	0	0	0	2
1994—New England NFL	9	0	0	0	0.0	0	24	202	8.4	0	1	14	14.0	0	0	0	0	2
1995—New England NFL	16	0	14	159	11.4	0	0	0	0.0	0	31	672	21.7	0	1	0	6	1
1996—New England NFL	16	0	21	222	10.6	0	0	0	0.0	0	29	634	21.9	0	0	0	0	0
1997—New England NFL	16	6	41	607	14.8	6	0	0	0.0	0	0	0	0.0	0	6	0	36	0
1998—New England NFL	10	0	23	346	15.0	1	17	225	13.2	0	0	0	0.0	0	1	0	6	0
1999—New England NFL	13	1	36	471	13.1	1	38	405	10.7	0	8	271	33.9	0	1	0	6	1
2000—New England NFL	16	15	83	944	11.4	4	39	504	12.9	1	2	15	7.5	0	5	0	30	2
2001—New England NFL	16	12	101	1199	11.9	5	29	413	*14.2	*2	1	13	13.0	0	7	0	42	2
Pro totals (9 years)	124	34	321	3970	12.4	17	172	1973	11.5	3	87	1862	21.4	0	21	0	126	10

BROWNING, JOHN — DT — CHIEFS

PERSONAL: Born September 30, 1973, in Miami. ... 6-4/293.
HIGH SCHOOL: North Miami (Fla.).
COLLEGE: West Virginia.
TRANSACTIONS/CAREER NOTES: Selected by Kansas City Chiefs in third round (68th pick overall) of 1996 NFL draft. ... Signed by Chiefs (July 24, 1996). ... On injured reserve with Achilles' tendon injury (September 1, 1999-entire season). ... Granted unconditional free agency (February 11, 2000). ... Re-signed by Chiefs (February 11, 2000). ... On injured reserve with shoulder injury (October 25, 2001-remainder of season).
PRO STATISTICS: 1997—Recovered one fumble. 2000—Intercepted one pass for no yards and recovered one fumble.

Year Team	G	GS	SACKS
1996—Kansas City NFL	13	2	2.0
1997—Kansas City NFL	14	13	4.0
1998—Kansas City NFL	8	8	0.0
1999—Kansas City NFL	Did not play.		
2000—Kansas City NFL	16	16	6.0
2001—Kansas City NFL	6	6	1.5
Pro totals (5 years)	57	45	13.5

BRUCE, ISAAC — WR — RAMS

PERSONAL: Born November 10, 1972, in Fort Lauderdale, Fla. ... 6-0/188. ... Full name: Isaac Isidore Bruce. ... Cousin of Derrick Moore, running back with Detroit Lions (1993 and 1994) and Carolina Panthers (1995).
HIGH SCHOOL: Dillard (Fort Lauderdale, Fla.).
JUNIOR COLLEGE: West Los Angeles Junior College, then Santa Monica (Calif.) Junior College.
COLLEGE: Memphis State.
TRANSACTIONS/CAREER NOTES: Selected by Los Angeles Rams in second round (33rd pick overall) of 1994 NFL draft. ... Signed by Rams (July 13, 1994). ... On injured reserve with sprained right knee (December 9, 1994-remainder of season). ... Rams franchise moved to St. Louis (April 12, 1995). ... On injured reserve with hamstring injury (December 9, 1998-remainder of season).

CHAMPIONSHIP GAME EXPERIENCE: Played in NFC championship game (1999 and 2001 seasons). ... Member of Super Bowl championship team (1999 season). ... Played in Super Bowl XXXVI (2001 season).
HONORS: Named wide receiver on THE SPORTING NEWS NFL All-Pro team (1999). ... Played in Pro Bowl (1996 and 1999 season). ... Named to play in Pro Bowl (2000 season); replaced by Torry Holt due to injury.
PRO STATISTICS: 1995—Ran 52 yards with lateral from punt return and recovered one fumble. 1996—Attempted two passes with one completion for 15 yards and one interception.
SINGLE GAME HIGHS (regular season): Receptions—15 (December 24, 1995, vs. Miami); yards—233 (November 2, 1997, vs. Atlanta); and touchdown receptions—4 (October 10, 1999, vs. San Francisco).
STATISTICAL PLATEAUS: 100-yard receiving games: 1995 (9), 1996 (4), 1997 (2), 1998 (2), 1999 (4), 2000 (4), 2001 (3). Total: 28.
MISCELLANEOUS: Holds St. Louis Rams all-time record for most receiving touchdowns (56).

				RUSHING				RECEIVING				TOTALS		
Year Team	G	GS	Att.	Yds.	Avg.	TD	No.	Yds.	Avg.	TD	TD	2pt.	Pts.	Fum.
1994—Los Angeles Rams NFL	12	0	1	2	2.0	0	21	272	13.0	3	3	0	18	0
1995—St. Louis NFL	16	16	3	17	5.7	0	119	1781	15.0	13	13	1	80	2
1996—St. Louis NFL	16	16	1	4	4.0	0	84	*1338	15.9	7	7	0	42	1
1997—St. Louis NFL	12	12	0	0	0.0	0	56	815	14.6	5	5	0	30	1
1998—St. Louis NFL	5	5	1	30	30.0	0	32	457	14.3	1	1	0	6	0
1999—St. Louis NFL	16	16	5	32	6.4	0	77	1165	15.1	12	12	1	74	0
2000—St. Louis NFL	16	16	1	11	11.0	0	87	1471	16.9	9	9	0	54	1
2001—St. Louis NFL	16	16	4	23	5.8	0	64	1106	17.3	6	6	0	36	4
Pro totals (8 years)	109	97	16	119	7.4	0	540	8405	15.6	56	56	2	340	9

BRUENER, MARK   TE   STEELERS

PERSONAL: Born September 16, 1972, in Olympia, Wash. ... 6-4/261. ... Full name: Mark Frederick Bruener. ... Name pronounced BREW-ner.
HIGH SCHOOL: Aberdeen (Wash.).
COLLEGE: Washington (degree in economics).
TRANSACTIONS/CAREER NOTES: Selected by Pittsburgh Steelers in first round (27th pick overall) of 1995 NFL draft. ... Signed by Steelers (July 25, 1995). ... On injured reserve with knee injury (November 29, 1996-remainder of season). ... On injured reserve with shoulder injury (November 21, 2001-remainder of season).
CHAMPIONSHIP GAME EXPERIENCE: Played in AFC championship game (1995 and 1997 seasons). ... Played in Super Bowl XXX (1995 season).
PRO STATISTICS: 1995—Returned two kickoffs for 19 yards. 1998—Lost seven yards with lateral from kickoff return. 1999—Recovered two fumbles for four yards. 2001—Recovered one fumble.
SINGLE GAME HIGHS (regular season): Receptions—5 (December 13, 1997, vs. New England); yards—51 (November 28, 1999, vs. Cincinnati); and touchdown receptions—1 (December 3, 2000, vs. Oakland).

			RECEIVING				TOTALS			
Year Team	G	GS	No.	Yds.	Avg.	TD	TD	2pt.	Pts.	Fum.
1995—Pittsburgh NFL	16	13	26	238	9.2	3	3	0	18	0
1996—Pittsburgh NFL	12	12	12	141	11.8	0	0	1	2	0
1997—Pittsburgh NFL	16	16	18	117	6.5	6	6	0	36	1
1998—Pittsburgh NFL	16	16	19	157	8.3	2	2	0	12	0
1999—Pittsburgh NFL	14	14	18	176	9.8	0	0	0	0	0
2000—Pittsburgh NFL	16	16	17	192	11.3	3	3	0	18	0
2001—Pittsburgh NFL	9	9	12	98	8.2	0	0	0	0	0
Pro totals (7 years)	99	96	122	1119	9.2	14	14	1	86	1

BRUNELL, MARK   QB   JAGUARS

PERSONAL: Born September 17, 1970, in Los Angeles. ... 6-1/217. ... Full name: Mark Allen Brunell.
HIGH SCHOOL: St. Joseph (Santa Maria, Calif.).
COLLEGE: Washington (degree in history).
TRANSACTIONS/CAREER NOTES: Selected by Green Bay Packers in fifth round (118th pick overall) of 1993 NFL draft. ... Signed by Packers (July 1, 1993). ... Traded by Packers to Jacksonville Jaguars for third- (FB William Henderson) and fifth-round (RB Travis Jervey) picks in 1995 draft (April 21, 1995).
CHAMPIONSHIP GAME EXPERIENCE: Played in AFC championship game (1996 and 1999 seasons).
HONORS: Played in Pro Bowl (1996, 1997 and 1999 seasons). ... Named Outstanding Player of Pro Bowl (1996 season).
PRO STATISTICS: 1994—Fumbled once. 1995—Fumbled five times and recovered three fumbles. 1996—Led AFC with 14 fumbles and recovered five fumbles for minus 14 yards. 1997—Fumbled four times and recovered two fumbles for minus five yards. 1998—Fumbled three times and recovered two fumbles for minus one yard. 1999—Fumbled six times and recovered three fumbles for minus two yards. 2000—Fumbled seven times and recovered three fumbles for minus two yards. 2001—Fumbled eight times and recovered two fumbles for minus eight yards.
SINGLE GAME HIGHS (regular season): Attempts—52 (October 20, 1996, vs. St. Louis); completions—37 (October 20, 1996, vs. St. Louis); yards—432 (September 22, 1996, vs. New England); and touchdown passes—4 (November 29, 1998, vs. Cincinnati).
STATISTICAL PLATEAUS: 300-yard passing games: 1995 (2), 1996 (6), 1997 (3), 1998 (2), 1999 (3), 2000 (3), 2001 (2). Total: 21.
MISCELLANEOUS: Regular-season record as starting NFL quarterback: 57-42 (.576). ... Postseason record as starting NFL quarterback: 4-4 (.500). ... Holds Jacksonville Jaguars all-time record for most yards passing (22,426) and most touchdown passes (125).

			PASSING								RUSHING			TOTALS		
Year Team	G	GS	Att.	Cmp.	Pct.	Yds.	TD	Int.	Avg.	Rat.	Att.	Yds.	Avg.	TD	TD	2pt.	Pts.
1993—Green Bay NFL						Did not play.											
1994—Green Bay NFL	2	0	27	12	44.4	95	0	0	3.52	53.8	6	7	1.2	1	1	0	6
1995—Jacksonville NFL	13	10	346	201	58.1	2168	15	7	6.27	82.6	67	480	7.2	4	4	0	24
1996—Jacksonville NFL	16	16	557	353	§63.4	*4367	19	§20	*7.84	84.0	80	396	5.0	3	3	2	22
1997—Jacksonville NFL	14	14	435	264	60.7	3281	18	7	§7.54	§91.2	48	257	5.4	2	2	0	12
1998—Jacksonville NFL	13	13	354	208	58.8	2601	20	9	7.35	89.9	49	192	3.9	0	0	0	0
1999—Jacksonville NFL	15	15	441	259	58.7	3060	14	9	6.94	82.0	47	208	4.4	1	1	†1	8
2000—Jacksonville NFL	16	16	512	311	60.7	3640	20	14	7.11	84.0	48	236	4.9	2	2	0	12
2001—Jacksonville NFL	15	15	473	289	61.1	3309	19	13	7.00	84.1	39	224	5.7	1	1	0	6
Pro totals (8 years)	104	99	3145	1897	60.3	22521	125	79	7.16	85.0	384	2000	5.2	14	14	3	90

BRUSCHI, TEDY   LB   PATRIOTS

PERSONAL: Born June 9, 1973, in San Francisco. ... 6-1/245. ... Full name: Tedy Lacap Bruschi. ... Stepson of Ronald Sandys, former professional tennis player. ... Name pronounced BREW-ski.
HIGH SCHOOL: Roseville (Calif.).
COLLEGE: Arizona (degree in communications).
TRANSACTIONS/CAREER NOTES: Selected by New England Patriots in third round (86th pick overall) of 1996 NFL draft. ... Signed by Patriots (July 17, 1996). ... Granted free agency (February 12, 1999). ... Re-signed by Patriots (June 1, 1999). ... Granted unconditional free agency (February 11, 2000). ... Re-signed by Patriots (March 22, 2000).
CHAMPIONSHIP GAME EXPERIENCE: Played in AFC championship game (1996 and 2001 seasons). ... Played in Super Bowl XXXI (1996 season). ... Member of Super Bowl championship team (2001 season).
HONORS: Named defensive lineman on THE SPORTING NEWS college All-America first team (1994 and 1995).
PRO STATISTICS: 1996—Returned blocked punt four yards for a touchdown. 1997—Recovered two fumbles. 1998—Returned one kickoff for four yards. 1999—Intercepted one pass for one yard and recovered one fumble. 2000—Returned two kickoffs for 13 yards. 2001—Intercepted two passes for seven yards, returned one kickoff for 10 yards, fumbled once and recovered one fumble.

Year Team	G	GS	SACKS
1996—New England NFL	16	0	4.0
1997—New England NFL	16	1	4.0
1998—New England NFL	16	7	2.0
1999—New England NFL	14	14	2.0
2000—New England NFL	16	16	1.0
2001—New England NFL	15	9	2.0
Pro totals (6 years)	93	47	15.0

BRYANT, FERNANDO   CB   JAGUARS

PERSONAL: Born March 26, 1977, in Albany, Ga. ... 5-10/180. ... Full name: Fernando Antoneiyo Bryant. ... Nephew of Don Griffin, cornerback with San Francisco 49ers (1986-93), Cleveland Browns (1994 and 1995) and Philadelphia Eagles (1996); and nephew of James Griffin, defensive back with Cincinnati Bengals (1983-85) and Detroit Lions (1986-89).
HIGH SCHOOL: Riverdale (Murfreesboro, Tenn.).
COLLEGE: Alabama.
TRANSACTIONS/CAREER NOTES: Selected by Jacksonville Jaguars in first round (26th pick overall) of 1999 NFL draft. ... Signed by Jaguars (August 9, 1999). ... On injured reserve with foot injury (January 1, 2002-remainder of season).
CHAMPIONSHIP GAME EXPERIENCE: Played in AFC championship game (1999 season).
PRO STATISTICS: 1999—Recovered three fumbles for 27 yards. 2000—Recovered one fumble for five yards.

			INTERCEPTIONS		
Year Team	G	GS	No.	Yds.	Avg.	TD
1999—Jacksonville NFL	16	16	2	0	0.0	0
2000—Jacksonville NFL	14	14	1	0	0.0	0
2001—Jacksonville NFL	10	9	0	0	0.0	0
Pro totals (3 years)	40	39	3	0	0.0	0

BRYANT, TONY   DE   RAIDERS

PERSONAL: Born September 3, 1976, in Marathon, Fla. ... 6-6/280.
HIGH SCHOOL: Marathon (Fla.).
JUNIOR COLLEGE: Copiah-Lincoln Junior College (Miss.).
COLLEGE: Florida State.
TRANSACTIONS/CAREER NOTES: Selected by Oakland Raiders in second round (40th pick overall) of 1999 NFL draft. ... Signed by Raiders (July 22, 1999).
CHAMPIONSHIP GAME EXPERIENCE: Played in AFC championship game (2000 season).
PRO STATISTICS: 2000—Recovered one fumble for three yards.

Year Team	G	GS	SACKS
1999—Oakland NFL	10	0	4.5
2000—Oakland NFL	16	16	5.5
2001—Oakland NFL	16	16	5.0
Pro totals (3 years)	42	32	15.0

BRYSON, SHAWN   RB   BILLS

PERSONAL: Born November 30, 1976, in Franklin, N.C. ... 6-1/228. ... Full name: Adrian Shawn Bryson.
HIGH SCHOOL: Franklin (N.C.).
COLLEGE: Tennessee.
TRANSACTIONS/CAREER NOTES: Selected by Buffalo Bills in third round (86th pick overall) of 1999 NFL draft. ... Signed by Bills (July 27, 1999). ... On injured reserve with knee injury (August 30, 1999-entire season). ... Granted free agency (March 1, 2002).
SINGLE GAME HIGHS (regular season): Attempts—28 (December 30, 2001, vs. New York Jets); yards—130 (December 23, 2001, vs. Atlanta); and rushing touchdowns—2 (December 23, 2001, vs. Atlanta).
STATISTICAL PLATEAUS: 100-yard rushing games: 2001 (2).

			RUSHING				RECEIVING				KICKOFF RETURNS				TOTALS		
Year Team	G	GS	Att.	Yds.	Avg.	TD	No.	Yds.	Avg.	TD	No.	Yds.	Avg.	TD	TD 2pt.	Pts.	Fum.
1999—Buffalo NFL							Did not play.										
2000—Buffalo NFL	16	7	161	591	3.7	0	32	271	8.5	2	8	122	15.3	0	2 1	14	1
2001—Buffalo NFL	15	3	80	341	4.3	2	9	59	6.6	0	16	299	18.7	0	2 0	12	0
Pro totals (2 years)	31	10	241	932	3.9	2	41	330	8.0	2	24	421	17.5	0	4 1	26	1

BRZEZINSKI, DOUG G EAGLES

PERSONAL: Born March 11, 1976, in Livonia, Mich. ... 6-4/305. ... Full name: Douglas Gregory Brzezinski. ... Name pronounced bruh-ZHIN-skee.
HIGH SCHOOL: Detroit Catholic Central.
COLLEGE: Boston College.
TRANSACTIONS/CAREER NOTES: Selected by Philadelphia Eagles in third round (64th pick overall) of 1999 NFL draft. ... Signed by Eagles (July 28, 1999). ... Granted free agency (March 1, 2002). ... Re-signed by Eagles (March 28, 2002).
PLAYING EXPERIENCE: Philadelphia NFL, 1999-2001. ... Games/Games started: 1999 (16/16), 2000 (16/0), 2001 (16/1). Total: 48/17.
CHAMPIONSHIP GAME EXPERIENCE: Played in NFC championship game (2001 season).
HONORS: Named offensive guard on THE SPORTING NEWS college All-America first team (1998).

BUCHANAN, RAY CB FALCONS

PERSONAL: Born September 29, 1971, in Chicago. ... 5-9/186. ... Full name: Raymond Louis Buchanan.
HIGH SCHOOL: Proviso East (Maywood, Ill.).
COLLEGE: Louisville.
TRANSACTIONS/CAREER NOTES: Selected by Indianapolis Colts in third round (65th pick overall) of 1993 NFL draft. ... Signed by Colts (July 26, 1993). ... Designated by Colts as transition player (February 13, 1997). ... Tendered offer sheet by Atlanta Falcons (February 25, 1997). ... Colts declined to match offer (March 3, 1997). ... Granted unconditional free agency (February 21, 2001). ... Re-signed by Falcons (February 21, 2001).
CHAMPIONSHIP GAME EXPERIENCE: Played in AFC championship game (1995 season). ... Played in NFC championship game (1998 season). ... Played in Super Bowl XXXIII (1998 season).
HONORS: Played in Pro Bowl (1998 season).
PRO STATISTICS: 1994 —Credited with one sack and recovered one fumble. 1995—Returned one kickoff for 22 yards, credited with one sack and recovered two fumbles. 1996—Returned one kickoff for 20 yards. 1997—Ran 37 yards with lateral from punt return. 1999—Credited with one sack. 2000—Recovered two fumbles for one yard. 2001—Recovered one fumble.

			INTERCEPTIONS				PUNT RETURNS				TOTALS		
Year Team	G	GS	No.	Yds.	Avg.	TD	No.	Yds.	Avg.	TD	TD	2pt.	Pts.	Fum.
1993—Indianapolis NFL	16	5	4	45	11.3	0	0	0	0.0	0	0	0	0	0
1994—Indianapolis NFL	16	16	8	221	27.6	†3	0	0	0.0	0	3	0	18	0
1995—Indianapolis NFL	16	16	2	60	30.0	0	16	113	7.1	0	0	0	0	1
1996—Indianapolis NFL	13	13	2	32	16.0	0	12	201	16.8	0	0	0	0	0
1997—Atlanta NFL	16	16	5	49	9.8	0	0	37	0.0	0	0	0	0	0
1998—Atlanta NFL	16	16	7	102	14.6	0	1	4	4.0	0	0	0	0	0
1999—Atlanta NFL	16	16	4	81	20.3	1	0	0	0.0	0	1	0	6	0
2000—Atlanta NFL	16	16	6	114	19.0	0	0	0	0.0	0	0	0	0	0
2001—Atlanta NFL	16	16	5	85	17.0	0	0	0	0.0	0	0	0	0	0
Pro totals (9 years)	141	130	43	789	18.3	4	29	355	12.2	0	4	0	24	1

BUCKHALTER, CORRELL RB EAGLES

PERSONAL: Born October 6, 1978, in Collins, Miss. ... 6-0/222.
HIGH SCHOOL: Collins (Miss.).
COLLEGE: Nebraska.
TRANSACTIONS/CAREER NOTES: Selected by Philadelphia Eagles in fourth round (121st pick overall) of 2001 NFL draft. ... Signed by Eagles (May 24, 2001).
CHAMPIONSHIP GAME EXPERIENCE: Played in NFC championship game (2001 season).
PRO STATISTICS: 2001—Returned one kickoff for 28 yards and recovered two fumbles.
SINGLE GAME HIGHS (regular season): Attempts—21 (October 7, 2001, vs. Arizona); yards—134 (October 7, 2001, vs. Arizona); and rushing touchdowns—1 (November 11, 2001, vs. Minnesota).
STATISTICAL PLATEAUS: 100-yard rushing games: 2001 (1).

			RUSHING				RECEIVING				TOTALS		
Year Team	G	GS	Att.	Yds.	Avg.	TD	No.	Yds.	Avg.	TD	TD	2pt.	Pts.	Fum.
2001—Philadelphia NFL	15	6	129	586	4.5	2	13	130	10.0	0	2	0	12	2

BUCKLEY, TERRELL CB

PERSONAL: Born June 7, 1971, in Pascagoula, Miss. ... 5-10/180. ... Full name: Douglas Terrell Buckley.
HIGH SCHOOL: Pascagoula (Miss.).
COLLEGE: Florida State.
TRANSACTIONS/CAREER NOTES: Selected after junior season by Green Bay Packers in first round (fifth pick overall) of 1992 NFL draft. ... Signed by Packers (September 11, 1992). ... Granted roster exemption for one game (September 1992). ... Traded by Packers to Miami Dolphins for past considerations (April 3, 1995). ... Granted unconditional free agency (February 11, 2000). ... Signed by Denver Broncos (July 20, 2000). ... Granted unconditional free agency (March 2, 2001). ... Signed by New England Patriots (July 13, 2001). ... Granted unconditional free agency (March 1, 2002).
CHAMPIONSHIP GAME EXPERIENCE: Played in AFC championship game (2001 season). ... Member of Super Bowl championship team (2001 season).
HONORS: Named defensive back on THE SPORTING NEWS college All-America second team (1990). ... Jim Thorpe Award winner (1991). ... Named defensive back on THE SPORTING NEWS college All-America first team (1991).
PRO STATISTICS: 1992—Recovered four fumbles. 1994—Recovered one fumble. 1995—Returned one kickoff for 16 yards. 1996—Returned one kickoff for 48 yards and recovered two fumbles. 1997—Recovered two fumbles for 23 yards and one touchdown. 1998—Recovered two fumbles. 1999—Credited with one sack. 2001—Credited with one sack.

Year Team	G	GS	INTERCEPTIONS				PUNT RETURNS				TOTALS		
			No.	Yds.	Avg.	TD	No.	Yds.	Avg.	TD	TD	2pt.	Pts.	Fum.
1992—Green Bay NFL	14	12	3	33	11.0	1	21	211	10.0	1	2	0	12	7
1993—Green Bay NFL	16	16	2	31	15.5	0	11	76	6.9	0	0	0	0	1
1994—Green Bay NFL	16	16	5	38	7.6	0	0	0	0.0	0	0	0	0	0
1995—Miami NFL	16	4	1	0	0.0	0	0	0	0.0	0	0	0	0	0
1996—Miami NFL	16	16	6	*164	27.3	1	3	24	8.0	0	1	0	6	1
1997—Miami NFL	16	16	4	26	6.5	0	4	58	14.5	0	1	0	6	0
1998—Miami NFL	16	16	8	157	19.6	1	29	354	12.2	0	1	0	6	1
1999—Miami NFL	16	11	3	3	1.0	0	8	13	1.6	0	0	0	0	1
2000—Denver NFL	16	16	6	110	18.3	1	2	10	5.0	0	1	0	6	0
2001—New England NFL	15	1	3	76	25.3	1	0	0	0.0	0	1	0	6	0
Pro totals (10 years)	157	124	41	638	15.6	5	78	746	9.6	1	7	0	42	11

BUCKNER, BRENTSON   DT   PANTHERS

PERSONAL: Born September 30, 1971, in Columbus, Ga. ... 6-2/305. ... Full name: Brentson Andre Buckner. ... Name pronounced BRENT-son.
HIGH SCHOOL: Carver (Columbus, Ga.).
COLLEGE: Clemson (degree in English, 1993).
TRANSACTIONS/CAREER NOTES: Selected by Pittsburgh Steelers in second round (50th pick overall) of 1994 NFL Draft. ... Signed by Steelers (July 23, 1994). ... Traded by Steelers to Kansas City Chiefs for seventh-round pick (traded to San Diego) in 1997 draft (April 4, 1997). ... Claimed on waivers by Cincinnati Bengals (August 25, 1997). ... Granted unconditional free agency (February 13, 1998). ... Signed by San Francisco 49ers (May 26, 1998). ... On physically unable to perform list with pulled quadricep muscle (July 17-August 15, 1998). ... Granted unconditional free agency (February 12, 1999). ... Re-signed by 49ers (April 7, 1999). ... Granted unconditional free agency (February 11, 2000). ... Re-signed by 49ers (August 8, 2000). ... Granted unconditional free agency (March 2, 2001). ... Signed by Carolina Panthers (April 21, 2001).
CHAMPIONSHIP GAME EXPERIENCE: Played in AFC championship game (1994 and 1995 seasons). ... Played in Super Bowl XXX (1995 season).
PRO STATISTICS: 1994—Recovered one fumble. 1995—Recovered one fumble for 46 yards and a touchdown. 1996—Fumbled once and recovered one fumble for 13 yards. 1998—Recovered one fumble. 2001—Intercepted one pass for 29 yards, fumbled once and recovered one fumble.

Year Team	G	GS	SACKS
1994—Pittsburgh NFL	13	5	2.0
1995—Pittsburgh NFL	16	16	3.0
1996—Pittsburgh NFL	15	14	3.0
1997—Cincinnati NFL	14	5	0.0
1998—San Francisco NFL	13	0	0.5
1999—San Francisco NFL	16	5	1.0
2000—San Francisco NFL	16	16	7.0
2001—Carolina NFL	16	10	4.5
Pro totals (8 years)	119	71	21.0

BULLUCK, KEITH   LB   TITANS

PERSONAL: Born April 4, 1977, in Suffern, N.Y. ... 6-3/232. ... Full name: Keith J. Bulluck.
HIGH SCHOOL: Clarkstown (New City, N.Y.).
COLLEGE: Syracuse.
TRANSACTIONS/CAREER NOTES: Selected by Tennessee Titans in first round (30th pick overall) of 2000 NFL draft. ... Signed by Titans (July 19, 2000).
PRO STATISTICS: 2001—Recovered two fumbles.

Year Team	G	GS	INTERCEPTIONS				SACKS
			No.	Yds.	Avg.	TD	No.
2000—Tennessee NFL	16	1	1	8	8.0	1	0.0
2001—Tennessee NFL	15	2	2	21	10.5	0	1.0
Pro totals (2 years)	31	3	3	29	9.7	1	1.0

BURGESS, DERRICK   LB/DE   EAGLES

PERSONAL: Born August 12, 1978, in Riverdale, Md. ... 6-2/266.
HIGH SCHOOL: Eleanor Roosevelt (Greenbelt, Md.).
COLLEGE: Mississippi.
TRANSACTIONS/CAREER NOTES: Selected by Philadelphia Eagles in third round (63rd pick overall) of 2001 NFL draft. ... Signed by Eagles (July 26, 2001).
CHAMPIONSHIP GAME EXPERIENCE: Played in NFC championship game (2001 season).
PRO STATISTICS: 2001—Recovered one fumble.

Year Team	G	GS	SACKS
2001—Philadelphia NFL	16	4	6.0

BURKE, THOMAS   DE   CARDINALS

PERSONAL: Born October 12, 1976, in Poplar, Wis. ... 6-3/271.
HIGH SCHOOL: Northwestern (Poplar, Wis.).
COLLEGE: Wisconsin.
TRANSACTIONS/CAREER NOTES: Selected by Arizona Cardinals in third round (83rd pick overall) of 1999 NFL draft. ... Signed by Cardinals (June 18, 1999). ... On injured reserve with abdominal injury (December 15, 2000-remainder of season). ... Granted free agency (March 1, 2002).

HONORS: Named defensive end on THE SPORTING NEWS college All-America first team (1998).
PRO STATISTICS: 2001—Returned one kickoff for 15 yards and recovered one fumble.

Year Team	G	GS	SACKS
1999—Arizona NFL	16	3	2.5
2000—Arizona NFL	3	0	0.0
2001—Arizona NFL	12	9	2.0
Pro totals (3 years)	31	12	4.5

BURNETT, ROB   DE

PERSONAL: Born August 27, 1967, in East Orange, N.J. ... 6-4/270. ... Full name: Robert Barry Burnett.
HIGH SCHOOL: Newfield (Selden, N.Y.).
COLLEGE: Syracuse (degree in economics).
TRANSACTIONS/CAREER NOTES: Selected by Cleveland Browns in fifth round (129th pick overall) of 1990 NFL draft. ... Signed by Browns (July 22, 1990). ... Granted free agency (March 1, 1993). ... Re-signed by Browns (June 11, 1993). ... Browns franchise moved to Baltimore and renamed Ravens for 1996 season (March 11, 1996). ... Granted unconditional free agency (February 11, 2000). ... Re-signed by Ravens (February 17, 2000). ... Released by Ravens (March 1, 2002).
CHAMPIONSHIP GAME EXPERIENCE: Played in AFC championship game (2000 season). ... Member of Super Bowl championship team (2000 season).
HONORS: Played in Pro Bowl (1994 season).
PRO STATISTICS: 1991—Recovered one fumble for nine yards. 1992—Recovered two fumbles. 1993—Recovered two fumbles. 1994—Recovered one fumble. 1995—Recovered one fumble. 1997—Recovered one fumble. 1998—Credited with a safety and recovered one fumble. 2000—Intercepted one pass for three yards and recovered five fumbles. 2001—Recovered one fumble.

Year Team	G	GS	SACKS
1990—Cleveland NFL	16	6	2.0
1991—Cleveland NFL	13	8	3.0
1992—Cleveland NFL	16	16	9.0
1993—Cleveland NFL	16	16	9.0
1994—Cleveland NFL	16	16	10.0
1995—Cleveland NFL	16	16	7.5
1996—Baltimore NFL	6	6	3.0
1997—Baltimore NFL	15	15	4.0
1998—Baltimore NFL	16	16	2.5
1999—Baltimore NFL	16	16	6.5
2000—Baltimore NFL	16	16	10.5
2001—Baltimore NFL	13	13	0.0
Pro totals (12 years)	175	160	67.0

BURNS, KEITH   LB   BRONCOS

PERSONAL: Born May 16, 1972, in Greelyville, S.C. ... 6-2/235. ... Full name: Keith Bernard Burns.
HIGH SCHOOL: T. C. Williams (Alexandria, Va.).
JUNIOR COLLEGE: Navarro College (Texas).
COLLEGE: Oklahoma State.
TRANSACTIONS/CAREER NOTES: Selected by Denver Broncos in seventh round (210th pick overall) of 1994 NFL draft. ... Signed by Broncos (July 12, 1994). ... Granted free agency (February 14, 1997). ... Re-signed by Broncos (June 30, 1997). ... Granted unconditional free agency (February 12, 1999). ... Signed by Chicago Bears (April 6, 1999). ... Released by Bears (August 27, 2000). ... Signed by Broncos (September 19, 2000). ... Granted unconditional free agency (March 2, 2001). ... Re-signed by Broncos (April 6, 2001).
PLAYING EXPERIENCE: Denver NFL, 1994-1998, 2000 and 2001; Chicago NFL, 1999. ... Games/Games started: 1994 (11/1), 1995 (16/0), 1996 (16/0), 1997 (16/0), 1998 (16/0), 1999 (15/0), 2000 (13/0), 2001 (16/0). Total: 119/1.
CHAMPIONSHIP GAME EXPERIENCE: Played in AFC championship game (1997 and 1998 seasons). ... Member of Super Bowl championship team (1997 and 1998 seasons).
PRO STATISTICS: 1995—Credited with 1$\frac{1}{2}$ sacks, returned one kickoff for five yards and recovered two fumbles. 1997—Returned four kickoffs for 45 yards. 1998—Returned two kickoffs for 17 yards, fumbled once and recovered one fumble. 1999—Intercepted one pass for 15 yards and recovered one fumble. 2000—Recovered one fumble. 2001—Recovered two fumbles.

BURRESS, PLAXICO   WR   STEELERS

PERSONAL: Born August 12, 1977, in Norfolk, Va. ... 6-5/229.
HIGH SCHOOL: Green Run (Virginia Beach, Va.).
COLLEGE: Michigan State.
TRANSACTIONS/CAREER NOTES: Selected after junior season by Pittsburgh Steelers in first round (eighth pick overall) of 2000 NFL draft. ... Signed by Steelers (July 20, 2000). ... On injured reserve with wrist injury (December 1, 2000-remainder of season).
CHAMPIONSHIP GAME EXPERIENCE: Played in AFC championship game (2001 season).
PRO STATISTICS: 2000—Fumbled once. 2001—Fumbled once.
SINGLE GAME HIGHS (regular season): Receptions—8 (December 16, 2001, vs. Baltimore); yards—164 (December 16, 2001, vs. Baltimore); and touchdown receptions—2 (December 30, 2001, vs. Cincinnati).
STATISTICAL PLATEAUS: 100-yard receiving games: 2001 (4).

			RECEIVING			
Year Team	G	GS	No.	Yds.	Avg.	TD
2000—Pittsburgh NFL	12	9	22	273	12.4	0
2001—Pittsburgh NFL	16	16	66	1008	15.3	6
Pro totals (2 years)	28	25	88	1281	14.6	6

BURRIS, JEFF — CB — BENGALS

PERSONAL: Born June 7, 1972, in Rock Hill, S.C. ... 6-0/190. ... Full name: Jeffrey Lamar Burris.
HIGH SCHOOL: Northwestern (Rock Hill, S.C.).
COLLEGE: Notre Dame.
TRANSACTIONS/CAREER NOTES: Selected by Buffalo Bills in first round (27th pick overall) of 1994 NFL draft. ... Signed by Bills (July 18, 1994). ... On injured reserve with knee injury (November 20, 1995-remainder of season). ... Granted unconditional free agency (February 13, 1998). ... Signed by Indianapolis Colts (February 18, 1998). ... Released by Colts (February 21, 2002). ... Signed by Cincinnati Bengals (March 26, 2002).
HONORS: Named defensive back on THE SPORTING NEWS college All-America second team (1993).
PRO STATISTICS: 1994—Recovered one fumble. 1996—Recovered one fumble. 1997—Returned one kickoff for 10 yards and recovered one fumble. 1999—Credited with two sacks. 2000—Credited with three sacks.

			INTERCEPTIONS			PUNT RETURNS			TOTALS			
Year Team	G	GS	No.	Yds.	Avg.	TD	No.	Yds.	Avg.	TD	TD	2pt.	Pts.	Fum.
1994—Buffalo NFL	16	0	2	24	12.0	0	32	332	10.4	0	0	0	0	2
1995—Buffalo NFL	9	9	1	19	19.0	0	20	229	11.5	0	0	0	0	0
1996—Buffalo NFL	15	15	1	28	28.0	0	27	286	10.6	0	0	0	0	1
1997—Buffalo NFL	14	14	2	19	9.5	0	21	198	9.4	0	0	0	0	3
1998—Indianapolis NFL	14	14	1	0	0.0	0	0	0	0.0	0	0	0	0	0
1999—Indianapolis NFL	16	16	2	83	41.5	0	0	0	0.0	0	0	0	0	0
2000—Indianapolis NFL	16	16	4	38	9.5	1	0	0	0.0	0	1	0	6	0
2001—Indianapolis NFL	15	15	3	69	23.0	1	0	0	0.0	0	1	0	6	0
Pro totals (8 years)	115	99	16	280	17.5	2	100	1045	10.5	0	2	0	12	6

BURTON, SHANE — DL — PANTHERS

PERSONAL: Born January 18, 1974, in Logan, W.Va. ... 6-6/305. ... Full name: Franklin Shane Burton.
HIGH SCHOOL: Bandys (Catawba, N.C.).
COLLEGE: Tennessee.
TRANSACTIONS/CAREER NOTES: Selected by Miami Dolphins in fifth round (150th pick overall) of 1996 NFL draft. ... Signed by Dolphins (June 18, 1996). ... Granted free agency (February 12, 1999). ... Re-signed by Dolphins (April 13, 1999). ... Claimed on waivers by Chicago Bears (August 24, 1999). ... Granted unconditional free agency (February 11, 2000). ... Signed by New York Jets (March 20, 2000). ... Released by Jets (February 26, 2002). ... Signed by Carolina Panthers (March 27, 2002).
PRO STATISTICS: 1996—Recovered one fumble. 1997—Recovered one fumble. 1998—Recovered one fumble. 1999—Intercepted one pass for 37 yards. 2000—Recovered one fumble for four yards. 2001—Intercepted one pass for no yards.

Year Team	G	GS	SACKS
1996—Miami NFL	16	8	3.0
1997—Miami NFL	16	4	4.0
1998—Miami NFL	15	0	2.0
1999—Chicago NFL	15	0	3.0
2000—New York Jets NFL	16	16	1.0
2001—New York Jets NFL	15	13	2.0
Pro totals (6 years)	93	41	15.0

BUSH, DEVIN — S — BROWNS

PERSONAL: Born July 3, 1973, in Miami. ... 6-0/210. ... Full name: Devin Marquese Bush.
HIGH SCHOOL: Hialeah (Fla.) Miami Lakes.
COLLEGE: Florida State.
TRANSACTIONS/CAREER NOTES: Selected after junior season by Atlanta Falcons in first round (26th pick overall) of 1995 NFL draft. ... Signed by Falcons (August 8, 1995). ... Granted unconditional free agency (February 12, 1999). ... Signed by St. Louis Rams (February 18, 1999). ... Released by Rams (September 2, 2001). ... Signed by Cleveland Browns (September 3, 2001).
CHAMPIONSHIP GAME EXPERIENCE: Member of Falcons for NFC championship game (1998 season); inactive. ... Played in Super Bowl XXXI-II (1998 season). ... Played in NFC championship game (1999 season). ... Member of Super Bowl championship team (1999 season).
PRO STATISTICS: 1995—Recovered one fumble. 1996—Recovered one fumble. 1997—Recovered one fumble. 1999—Recovered two fumbles for 31 yards. 2000—Credited with one sack and recovered one fumble for 15 yards and a touchdown. 2001—Recovered one fumble.

			INTERCEPTIONS			
Year Team	G	GS	No.	Yds.	Avg.	TD
1995—Atlanta NFL	11	5	1	0	0.0	0
1996—Atlanta NFL	16	15	1	2	2.0	0
1997—Atlanta NFL	16	16	1	4	4.0	0
1998—Atlanta NFL	13	0	0	0	0.0	0
1999—St. Louis NFL	16	7	2	45	22.5	1
2000—St. Louis NFL	13	12	0	0	0.0	0
2001—Cleveland NFL	16	7	2	62	31.0	1
Pro totals (7 years)	101	62	7	113	16.1	2

BUSH, LEW — LB — CHIEFS

PERSONAL: Born December 2, 1969, in Atlanta. ... 6-2/247. ... Full name: Lewis Fitzgerald Bush.
HIGH SCHOOL: Washington (Tacoma, Wash.).
COLLEGE: Washington State.
TRANSACTIONS/CAREER NOTES: Selected by San Diego Chargers in fourth round (99th pick overall) of 1993 NFL draft. ... Signed by Chargers (July 9, 1993). ... Granted free agency (February 16, 1996). ... Re-signed by Chargers (June 14, 1996). ... Granted unconditional free agency

(February 14, 1997). ... Re-signed by Chargers (May 13, 1997). ... On injured reserve with knee injury (December 26, 1998-remainder of season). ... Released by Chargers (March 1, 2000). ... Signed by Kansas City Chiefs (March 4, 2000).
PLAYING EXPERIENCE: San Diego NFL, 1993-1999; Kansas City NFL, 2000 and 2001. ... Games/Games started: 1993 (16/0), 1994 (16/0), 1995 (16/15), 1996 (16/16), 1997 (14/13), 1998 (10/10), 1999 (16/14), 2000 (16/8), 2001 (12/11). Total: 132/87.
CHAMPIONSHIP GAME EXPERIENCE: Played in AFC championship game (1994 season). ... Played in Super Bowl XXIX (1994 season).
PRO STATISTICS: 1994—Recovered one fumble. 1995—Intercepted one pass and recovered two fumbles. 1996—Credited with one sack and recovered two fumbles. 1998—Credited with one sack. 1999—Credited with one sack and recovered one fumble. 2000—Credited with one sack, intercepted one pass for 33 yards and recovered one fumble.

BUSH, STEVE   TE/FB   CARDINALS

PERSONAL: Born July 4, 1974, in Phoenix. ... 6-3/258. ... Full name: Steven Jack Bush.
HIGH SCHOOL: Paradise Valley (Phoenix).
COLLEGE: Arizona State.
TRANSACTIONS/CAREER NOTES: Signed as non-drafted free agent by Cincinnati Bengals (April 25, 1997). ... Granted free agency (February 11, 2000). ... Re-signed by Bengals (April 25, 2000). ... Granted unconditional free agency (March 2, 2001). ... Signed by St. Louis Rams (July 20, 2001). ... Released by Rams (August 27, 2001). ... Signed by Arizona Cardinals (November 6, 2001).
PLAYING EXPERIENCE: Cincinnati NFL, 1997-2000; Arizona NFL, 2001. ... Games/Games started: 1997 (16/0), 1998 (12/2), 1999 (13/0), 2000 (16/0), 2001 (9/6). Total: 66/8.
PRO STATISTICS: 1998—Caught four passes for 39 yards. 1999—Caught one pass for four yards. 2000—Caught three passes for 39 yards and returned three kickoffs for 18 yards. 2001—Caught eight passes for 80 yards and returned one kickoff for nine yards.
SINGLE GAME HIGHS (regular season): Receptions—3 (January 6, 2002, vs. Washington); yards—31 (December 24, 2000, vs. Philadelphia); and touchdown receptions—0.

BUTLER, JERAMETRIUS   CB   RAMS

PERSONAL: Born November 28, 1978, in Dallas. ... 5-10/181.
HIGH SCHOOL: Carter (Dallas).
COLLEGE: Kansas State.
TRANSACTIONS/CAREER NOTES: Selected after junior season by St. Louis Rams in fifth round (145th pick overall) of 2001 NFL draft. ... Signed by Rams (June 27, 2001).
PLAYING EXPERIENCE: St. Louis NFL, 2001. ... Games/Games started: 2001 (16/0).
CHAMPIONSHIP GAME EXPERIENCE: Played in NFC championship game (2001 season). ... Played in Super Bowl XXXVI (2001 season).
PRO STATISTICS: 2001—Ran minus one yard with lateral from punt return.

BUTLER, LeROY   S   PACKERS

PERSONAL: Born July 19, 1968, in Jacksonville. ... 6-0/203. ... Full name: LeRoy Butler III. ... Name pronounced luh-ROY.
HIGH SCHOOL: Robert E. Lee Senior (Jacksonville).
COLLEGE: Florida State.
TRANSACTIONS/CAREER NOTES: Selected by Green Bay Packers in second round (48th pick overall) of 1990 NFL draft. ... Signed by Packers (July 25, 1990). ... On suspended list (December 9, 1992). ... Designated by Packers as transition player (February 15, 1994). ... On injured reserve with shoulder injury (November 19, 2001-remainder of season).
CHAMPIONSHIP GAME EXPERIENCE: Played in NFC championship game (1995-1997 seasons). ... Member of Super Bowl championship team (1996 season). ... Played in Super Bowl XXXII (1997 season).
HONORS: Named strong safety on THE SPORTING NEWS NFL All-Pro team (1993 and 1996-1998). ... Played in Pro Bowl (1993 and 1996-1998 seasons).
PRO STATISTICS: 1991—Recovered one fumble. 1992—Recovered one fumble for 17 yards. 1993—Ran 25 yards with lateral from fumble recovery for a touchdown. 1996—Recovered two fumbles for two yards. 1997—Recovered one fumble. 1998—Recovered two fumbles for 32 yards and one touchdown. 1999—Recovered one fumble. 2000—Recovered one fumble.

			INTERCEPTIONS				SACKS
Year Team	G	GS	No.	Yds.	Avg.	TD	No.
1990—Green Bay NFL	16	0	3	42	14.0	0	0.0
1991—Green Bay NFL	16	16	3	6	2.0	0	0.0
1992—Green Bay NFL	15	15	1	0	0.0	0	0.0
1993—Green Bay NFL	16	16	6	131	21.8	0	1.0
1994—Green Bay NFL	13	13	3	68	22.7	0	1.0
1995—Green Bay NFL	16	16	5	105	21.0	0	1.0
1996—Green Bay NFL	16	16	5	149	29.8	1	6.5
1997—Green Bay NFL	16	16	5	4	0.8	0	3.0
1998—Green Bay NFL	16	16	3	3	1.0	0	4.0
1999—Green Bay NFL	16	16	2	0	0.0	0	1.0
2000—Green Bay NFL	16	16	2	25	12.5	0	2.0
2001—Green Bay NFL	9	9	0	0	0.0	0	1.0
Pro totals (12 years)	181	165	38	533	14.0	1	20.5

BYRD, ISAAC   WR   PANTHERS

PERSONAL: Born November 16, 1974, in St. Louis. ... 6-1/188. ... Full name: Isaac Byrd III. ... Brother of Israel Byrd, defensive back with New Orleans Saints (1994-95).
HIGH SCHOOL: Parkway Central (Chesterfield, Mo.).
COLLEGE: Kansas.
TRANSACTIONS/CAREER NOTES: Selected by Kansas City Chiefs in sixth round (195th pick overall) of 1997 NFL draft. ... Signed by Chiefs (May 6, 1997). ... Released by Chiefs (August 23, 1997). ... Re-signed by Chiefs to practice squad (August 25, 1997). ... Signed by Tennessee

Oilers off Chiefs practice squad (November 7, 1997). ... Oilers franchise renamed Tennessee Titans for 1999 season (December 26, 1998). ... Granted free agency (February 11, 2000). ... Re-signed by Titans (June 6, 2000). ... Claimed on waivers by Carolina Panthers (August 29, 2000).
CHAMPIONSHIP GAME EXPERIENCE: Played in AFC championship game (1999 season). ... Played in Super Bowl XXXIV (1999 season).
PRO STATISTICS: 1998—Recovered one fumble. 1999—Returned two punts for eight yards and returned two kickoffs for 16 yards. 2000—Returned one punt for 10 yards, returned nine kickoffs for 172 yards and recovered one fumble. 2001—Rushed once for minus two yards, returned five punts for 56 yards and returned 10 kickoffs for 225 yards.
SINGLE GAME HIGHS (regular season): Receptions—7 (December 30, 2001, vs. Arizona); yards—84 (December 19, 1999, vs. Atlanta); and touchdown receptions—1 (December 23, 2001, vs. St. Louis).

			RECEIVING				TOTALS			
Year Team	G	GS	No.	Yds.	Avg.	TD	TD	2pt.	Pts.	Fum.
1997—Tennessee NFL	2	0	0	0	0.0	0	0	0	0	0
1998—Tennessee NFL	4	3	6	71	11.8	0	0	0	0	0
1999—Tennessee NFL	12	6	14	261	18.6	2	2	0	12	1
2000—Carolina NFL	15	4	22	241	11.0	2	2	0	12	0
2001—Carolina NFL	15	5	37	492	13.3	1	1	0	6	0
Pro totals (5 years)	48	18	79	1065	13.5	5	5	0	30	1

RECORD AS BASEBALL PLAYER
TRANSACTIONS/CAREER NOTES: Batted right, threw right. ... Selected by San Diego Padres organization in 24th round of free-agent draft (June 3, 1993); did not sign. ... Selected by St. Louis Cardinals organization in 11th round of free agent draft (June 2, 1996).

					BATTING							FIELDING			
Year Team (League)	Pos.	G	AB	R	H	2B	3B	HR	RBI	Avg.	BB	SO	SB	PO	A	E	Avg.
1996—Johnson City (Appal.)	OF	24	94	16	26	6	1	2	15	.277	8	19	5	37	1	1	.974

CADREZ, GLENN — LB — CHIEFS

PERSONAL: Born January 2, 1970, in El Centro, Calif. ... 6-2/240. ... Full name: Glenn E. Cadrez. ... Name pronounced ku-DREZ.
HIGH SCHOOL: El Centro Central Union (El Centro, Calif.).
JUNIOR COLLEGE: Chaffey College (Calif.).
COLLEGE: Houston.
TRANSACTIONS/CAREER NOTES: Selected by New York Jets in sixth round (154th pick overall) of 1992 NFL draft. ... Signed by Jets (July 13, 1992). ... Released by Jets (September 19, 1995). ... Signed by Denver Broncos (September 27, 1995). ... Released by Broncos (May 2, 2001). ... Signed by Kansas City Chiefs (June 6, 2001). ... Granted unconditional free agency (March 1, 2002). ... Re-signed by Chiefs (March 13, 2002).
CHAMPIONSHIP GAME EXPERIENCE: Played in AFC championship game (1997 and 1998 seasons). ... Member of Super Bowl championship team (1997 and 1998 seasons).
PRO STATISTICS: 1992—Recovered one fumble. 1994—Returned one kickoff for 10 yards and recovered one fumble. 1995—Recovered one fumble. 1996—Recovered one fumble. 1998—Intercepted two passes for 11 yards. 1999—Recovered four fumbles for 74 yards and one touchdown. 2001—Intercepted one pass for no yards and recovered one fumble for 20 yards.

Year Team	G	GS	SACKS
1992—New York Jets NFL	16	0	0.0
1993—New York Jets NFL	16	0	0.0
1994—New York Jets NFL	16	0	0.0
1995—New York Jets NFL	1	0	0.0
—Denver NFL	10	7	2.0
1996—Denver NFL	16	0	0.0
1997—Denver NFL	16	0	0.0
1998—Denver NFL	16	15	4.0
1999—Denver NFL	16	15	7.0
2000—Denver NFL	16	3	0.0
2001—Kansas City NFL	16	5	1.5
Pro totals (10 years)	155	45	14.5

CALDWELL, MIKE — LB — BEARS

PERSONAL: Born August 31, 1971, in Oak Ridge, Tenn. ... 6-2/237. ... Full name: Mike Isiah Caldwell. ... Nickname: Zeke.
HIGH SCHOOL: Oak Ridge (Tenn.).
COLLEGE: Middle Tennessee State (degree in business administration, 1996).
TRANSACTIONS/CAREER NOTES: Selected by Cleveland Browns in third round (83rd pick overall) of 1993 NFL draft. ... Signed by Browns (July 14, 1993). ... Granted free agency (February 16, 1996). ... Browns franchise moved to Baltimore and renamed Ravens for 1996 season (March 11, 1996). ... Re-signed by Ravens for 1996 season. ... Granted unconditional free agency (February 14, 1997). ... Signed by Arizona Cardinals (July 16, 1997). ... Granted unconditional free agency (February 13, 1998). ... Signed by Philadelphia Eagles (April 9, 1998). ... Granted unconditional free agency (March 1, 2002). ... Signed by Chicago Bears (March 15, 2002).
CHAMPIONSHIP GAME EXPERIENCE: Played in NFC championship game (2001 season).
PRO STATISTICS: 1993—Recovered one fumble. 1994—Returned one punt for two yards. 1999—Recovered one fumble.

			INTERCEPTIONS				SACKS
Year Team	G	GS	No.	Yds.	Avg.	TD	No.
1993—Cleveland NFL	15	1	0	0	0.0	0	0.0
1994—Cleveland NFL	16	1	1	0	0.0	0	0.0
1995—Cleveland NFL	16	6	2	24	12.0	▲1	0.0
1996—Baltimore NFL	9	9	1	45	45.0	1	4.5
1997—Arizona NFL	16	0	1	5	5.0	0	2.0
1998—Philadelphia NFL	16	8	1	33	33.0	0	1.0
1999—Philadelphia NFL	14	2	1	12	12.0	0	1.0
2000—Philadelphia NFL	16	3	1	26	26.0	1	0.0
2001—Philadelphia NFL	16	16	0	0	0.0	0	3.0
Pro totals (9 years)	134	46	8	145	18.1	3	11.5

CAMPBELL, DAN   TE   GIANTS

PERSONAL: Born April 13, 1976, in Glen Rose, Texas. ... 6-5/260. ... Full name: Daniel Allen Campbell.
HIGH SCHOOL: Glen Rose (Texas).
COLLEGE: Texas A&M.
TRANSACTIONS/CAREER NOTES: Selected by New York Giants in third round (79th pick overall) of 1999 NFL draft. ... Signed by Giants (July 29, 1999). ... Granted free agency (March 1, 2002).
PLAYING EXPERIENCE: New York Giants NFL, 1999-2001. ... Games/Games started: 1999 (12/1), 2000 (16/5), 2001 (16/12). Total: 44/18.
CHAMPIONSHIP GAME EXPERIENCE: Played in NFC championship game (2000 season). ... Played in Super Bowl XXXV (2000 season).
PRO STATISTICS: 2000—Caught eight passes for 46 yards and three touchdowns and fumbled once. 2001—Caught 13 passes fo 148 yards and one touchdown and returned two kickoffs for eight yards.
SINGLE GAME HIGHS (regular season): Receptions—2 (December 30, 2001, vs. Philadelphia); yards—31 (December 30, 2001, vs. Philadelphia); and touchdown receptions—1 (October 7, 2001, vs. Washington).

CAMPBELL, LAMAR   CB   LIONS

PERSONAL: Born August 29, 1976, in Chester, Pa. ... 5-11/183.
HIGH SCHOOL: Strath Haven (Wallingford, Pa.).
COLLEGE: Wisconsin.
TRANSACTIONS/CAREER NOTES: Signed as non-drafted free agent by Detroit Lions (April 24, 1998). ... Granted free agency (March 2, 2001). ... Re-signed by Lions (April 19, 2001). ... Granted unconditional free agency (March 1, 2002). ... Re-signed by Lions (March 14, 2002).
PLAYING EXPERIENCE: Detroit NFL, 1998-2001. ... Games/Games started: 1998 (12/0), 1999 (15/2), 2000 (16/2), 2001 (12/12). Total: 55/16.
PRO STATISTICS: 2000—Intercepted one pass for 42 yards and a touchdown. 2001—Credited with one sack and recovered one fumble.

CAMPBELL, MATT   G/OT

PERSONAL: Born July 14, 1972, in North Augusta, S.C. ... 6-4/300. ... Full name: Mathew Thomas Campbell.
HIGH SCHOOL: North Augusta (S.C.).
COLLEGE: South Carolina.
TRANSACTIONS/CAREER NOTES: Signed as non-drafted free agent by New Orleans Saints (April 28, 1994). ... Released by Saints (August 23, 1994). ... Re-signed by Saints to practice squad (August 30, 1994). ... Released by Saints (September 20, 1994). ... Signed by Carolina Panthers (December 15, 1994). ... Granted free agency (February 13, 1998). ... Tendered offer sheet by Miami Dolphins (February 20, 1998). ... Offer matched by Panthers (February 27, 1998). ... Granted unconditional free agency (March 2, 2001). ... Signed by Washington Redskins (May 8, 2001). ... Selected by Houston Texans from Redskins in NFL expansion draft (February 18, 2002). ... Released by Texans (May 28, 2002).
PLAYING EXPERIENCE: Carolina NFL, 1995-2000; Washington NFL, 2001. ... Games/Games started: 1995 (10/1), 1996 (9/8), 1997 (16/14), 1998 (10/10), 1999 (10/10), 2000 (14/14), 2001 (11/5). Total: 80/52.
CHAMPIONSHIP GAME EXPERIENCE: Played in NFC championship game (1996 season).
PRO STATISTICS: 1995—Caught three passes for 32 yards and fumbled once.
MISCELLANEOUS: Played tight end during 1995 season.

CANIDATE, TRUNG   RB   RAMS

PERSONAL: Born March 3, 1977, in Phoenix. ... 5-11/205. ... Full name: Trung Jered Canidate.
HIGH SCHOOL: Central (Phoenix).
COLLEGE: Arizona.
TRANSACTIONS/CAREER NOTES: Selected by St. Louis Rams in first round (31st pick overall) of 2000 NFL draft. ... Signed by Rams (July 20, 2000). ... On injured reserve with wrist injury (November 13, 2000-remainder of season).
CHAMPIONSHIP GAME EXPERIENCE: Played in NFC championship game (2001 season). ... Played in Super Bowl XXXVI (2001 season).
PRO STATISTICS: 2001—Recovered two fumbles.
SINGLE GAME HIGHS (regular season): Attempts—23 (October 21, 2001, vs. New York Jets); yards—195 (October 21, 2001, vs. New York Jets); and rushing touchdowns—2 (October 21, 2001, vs. New York Jets).
STATISTICAL PLATEAUS: 100-yard rushing games: 2001 (2). ... 100-yard receiving games: 2001 (1).

			RUSHING				RECEIVING				KICKOFF RETURNS				TOTALS		
Year Team	G	GS	Att.	Yds.	Avg.	TD	No.	Yds.	Avg.	TD	No.	Yds.	Avg.	TD	TD	2pt.	Pts. Fum.
2000—St. Louis NFL	3	0	3	6	2.0	0	1	4	4.0	0	0	0	0.0	0	0	0	0 0
2001—St. Louis NFL	16	2	78	441	5.7	6	17	154	9.1	0	36	748	20.8	0	6	0	36 3
Pro totals (2 years)	19	2	81	447	5.5	6	18	158	8.8	0	36	748	20.8	0	6	0	36 3

CANNIDA, JAMES   DT   COLTS

PERSONAL: Born January 3, 1975, in Savannah, Ga. ... 6-2/305. ... Full name: James Thomas Cannida II.
HIGH SCHOOL: American (Fremont, Calif.).
COLLEGE: Nevada-Reno.
TRANSACTIONS/CAREER NOTES: Selected by Tampa Bay Buccaneers in sixth round (175th pick overall) of 1998 NFL draft. ... Signed by Buccaneers (June 4, 1998). ... Granted free agency (March 2, 2001). ... Re-signed by Buccaneers (March 2, 2001). ... Granted unconditional free agency (March 1, 2002). ... Signed by Indianapolis Colts (April 20, 2002).
PLAYING EXPERIENCE: Tampa Bay NFL, 1998-2001. ... Games/Games started: 1998 (10/0), 1999 (2/1), 2000 (16/0), 2001 (12/2). Total: 40/3.
CHAMPIONSHIP GAME EXPERIENCE: Member of Buccaneers for NFC championship game (1999 season); inactive.
PRO STATISTICS: 2000—Credited with two sacks.

CARLISLE, COOPER   OT   BRONCOS

PERSONAL: Born August 11, 1977, in Greenville, Miss. ... 6-5/295. ... Full name: Cooper Morrison Carlisle.
HIGH SCHOOL: McComb (Miss.).
COLLEGE: Florida.
TRANSACTIONS/CAREER NOTES: Selected by Denver Broncos in fourth round (112th pick overall) of 2000 NFL draft. ... Signed by Broncos (July 19, 2000).
PLAYING EXPERIENCE: Denver NFL, 2000 and 2001. ... Games/Games started: 2000 (13/0), 2001 (16/0). Total: 29/0.

CARMAN, JON   OT   BILLS

PERSONAL: Born January 14, 1976, in Herndon, Va. ... 6-7/329. ... Full name: Jonathon Daniel Carman.
HIGH SCHOOL: Herndon (Va.).
COLLEGE: Georgia Tech.
TRANSACTIONS/CAREER NOTES: Signed as non-drafted free agent by Buffalo Bills (April 22, 2000). ... Released by Bills (September 2, 2001). ... Re-signed by Bills to practice squad (September 4, 2001). ... Activated (September 29, 2001).
PLAYING EXPERIENCE: Buffalo NFL, 2000 and 2001. ... Games/Games started: 2000 (3/0), 2001 (9/2). Total: 12/2.
HONORS: Named offensive tackle on THE SPORTING NEWS college All-America second team (1999).

CARNEY, JOHN   K   SAINTS

PERSONAL: Born April 20, 1964, in Hartford, Conn. ... 5-11/180. ... Full name: John Michael Carney.
HIGH SCHOOL: Cardinal Newman (West Palm Beach, Fla.).
COLLEGE: Notre Dame (degree in marketing, 1987).
TRANSACTIONS/CAREER NOTES: Signed as non-drafted free agent by Cincinnati Bengals (May 1, 1987). ... Released by Bengals (August 10, 1987). ... Signed as replacement player by Tampa Bay Buccaneers (September 24, 1987). ... Released by Buccaneers (October 14, 1987). ... Re-signed by Buccaneers (April 5, 1988). ... Released by Buccaneers (August 23, 1988). ... Re-signed by Buccaneers (November 22, 1988). ... Granted unconditional free agency (February 1-April 1, 1989). ... Re-signed by Buccaneers (April 13, 1989). ... Released by Buccaneers (September 5, 1989). ... Re-signed by Buccaneers (December 13, 1989). ... Granted unconditional free agency (February 1, 1990). ... Signed by San Diego Chargers (April 1, 1990). ... Released by Chargers (August 28, 1990). ... Signed by Los Angeles Rams (September 21, 1990). ... Released by Rams (September 26, 1990). ... Signed by Chargers (October 3, 1990). ... Granted free agency (February 1, 1992). ... Re-signed by Chargers (July 27, 1992). ... Granted free agency (March 1, 1993). ... Re-signed by Chargers (June 9, 1993). ... Granted unconditional free agency (February 17, 1994). ... Re-signed by Chargers (April 6, 1994). ... On injured reserve with knee injury (November 15, 1997-remainder of season). ... Granted unconditional free agency (March 2, 2001). ... Signed by New Orleans Saints (August 5, 2001). ... Granted unconditional free agency (March 1, 2002). ... Re-signed by Saints (March 12, 2002).
CHAMPIONSHIP GAME EXPERIENCE: Played in AFC championship game (1994 season). ... Played in Super Bowl XXIX (1994 season).
HONORS: Named kicker on THE SPORTING NEWS NFL All-Pro team (1994). ... Played in Pro Bowl (1994 season).
PRO STATISTICS: 1993—Punted four times for 155 yards. 1999—Recovered one fumble. 2001—Rushed once for minus one yard.

				KICKING				
Year Team	G	XPM	XPA	FGM	FGA	Lg.	50+	Pts.
1988—Tampa Bay NFL	4	6	6	2	5	29	0-0	12
1989—Tampa Bay NFL	1	0	0	0	0	0	0-0	0
1990—Los Angeles Rams NFL	1	0	0	0	0	0	0-0	0
—San Diego NFL	12	27	28	19	21	43	0-1	84
1991—San Diego NFL	16	31	31	19	29	54	2-4	88
1992—San Diego NFL	16	35	35	26	32	50	1-3	113
1993—San Diego NFL	16	31	33	31	40	51	2-3	124
1994—San Diego NFL	16	33	33	†34	§38	50	2-2	*135
1995—San Diego NFL	16	32	33	21	26	45	0-2	95
1996—San Diego NFL	16	31	31	29	36	53	3-3	118
1997—San Diego NFL	4	5	5	7	7	41	0-0	26
1998—San Diego NFL	16	19	19	26	30	54	2-3	97
1999—San Diego NFL	16	22	23	31	36	50	1-1	115
2000—San Diego NFL	16	27	27	18	25	▲54	2-4	81
2001—New Orleans NFL	15	32	32	27	31	50	1-1	113
Pro totals (14 years)	181	331	336	290	356	54	16-27	1201

CARPENTER, KEION   S   FALCONS

PERSONAL: Born October 31, 1977, in Baltimore. ... 5-11/205. ... Full name: Keion Eric Carpenter.
HIGH SCHOOL: Woodlawn (Baltimore).
COLLEGE: Virginia Tech.
TRANSACTIONS/CAREER NOTES: Signed as non-drafted free agent by Buffalo Bills (April 19, 1999). ... Granted free agency (March 1, 2002). ... Signed by Atlanta Falcons (March 6, 2002).
PLAYING EXPERIENCE: Buffalo NFL, 1999-2001. ... Games/Games started: 1999 (10/0), 2000 (12/12), 2001 (15/10). Total: 37/22.
PRO STATISTICS: 2000—Intercepted five passes for 63 yards.

CARSON, LEONARDO   DT   CHARGERS

PERSONAL: Born February 11, 1977, in Mobile, Ala. ... 6-2/285. ... Full name: Leonardo Tremayne Carson.
HIGH SCHOOL: Shaw (Mobile, Ala.).
COLLEGE: Auburn.
TRANSACTIONS/CAREER NOTES: Selected by San Diego Chargers in fourth round (113th pick overall) of 2000 NFL draft. ... Signed by Chargers (July 20, 2000). ... On injured reserve with shoulder injury (November 17, 2000-remainder of season).
PLAYING EXPERIENCE: San Diego NFL, 2000 and 2001. ... Games/Games started: 2000 (4/0), 2001 (16/13). Total: 20/13.
PRO STATISTICS: 2001—Returned one kickoff for 10 yards, credited with three sacks and recovered two fumbles.

CARSWELL, DWAYNE   TE   BRONCOS

PERSONAL: Born January 18, 1972, in Jacksonville. ... 6-3/260.
HIGH SCHOOL: University Christian (Jacksonville).
COLLEGE: Liberty (Va.).
TRANSACTIONS/CAREER NOTES: Signed as non-drafted free agent by Denver Broncos (May 2, 1994). ... Released by Broncos (August 26, 1994). ... Re-signed by Broncos to practice squad (August 30, 1994). ... Activated (November 25, 1994).
CHAMPIONSHIP GAME EXPERIENCE: Played in AFC championship game (1997 and 1998 seasons). ... Member of Super Bowl championship team (1997 and 1998 seasons).
PRO STATISTICS: 1994—Returned one kickoff for no yards and recovered one fumble. 1997—Recovered one fumble. 2000—Returned one kickoff for no yards. 2001—Recovered one fumble.
SINGLE GAME HIGHS (regular season): Receptions—6 (December 25, 1999, vs. Detroit); yards—68 (October 22, 2000, vs. Cincinnati); and touchdown receptions—1 (November 22, 2001, vs. Dallas).

				RECEIVING				TOTALS		
Year Team	G	GS	No.	Yds.	Avg.	TD	TD	2pt.	Pts.	Fum.
1994—Denver NFL	4	0	0	0	0.0	0	0	0	0	0
1995—Denver NFL	9	2	3	37	12.3	0	0	0	0	0
1996—Denver NFL	16	2	15	85	5.7	0	0	0	0	0
1997—Denver NFL	16	3	12	96	8.0	1	1	0	6	0
1998—Denver NFL	16	1	4	51	12.8	0	0	0	0	0
1999—Denver NFL	16	11	24	201	8.4	2	2	0	12	0
2000—Denver NFL	16	16	49	495	10.1	3	3	0	18	0
2001—Denver NFL	16	16	34	299	8.8	4	4	▲1	26	0
Pro totals (8 years)	109	51	141	1264	9.0	10	10	1	62	0

CARSWELL, ROBERT   S   CHARGERS

PERSONAL: Born October 26, 1978, in Gary, Ind. ... 5-11/215. ... Full name: Robert Lee Carswell.
HIGH SCHOOL: Stone Mountain (Ga.).
COLLEGE: Clemson.
TRANSACTIONS/CAREER NOTES: Selected by San Diego Chargers in seventh round (244th pick overall) of 2001 NFL draft. ... Signed by Chargers (June 20, 2001).
PLAYING EXPERIENCE: San Diego NFL, 2001. ... Games/Games started: 2001 (16/0).
HONORS: Named free safety on THE SPORTING NEWS college All-America third team (2000).
PRO STATISTICS: 2001—Recovered one fumble.

CARTER, ANDRE   DE   49ERS

PERSONAL: Born May 12, 1979, in Denver, Colo. ... 6-4/265.
HIGH SCHOOL: Oak Grove (San Jose, Calif.).
COLLEGE: California.
TRANSACTIONS/CAREER NOTES: Selected by San Francisco 49ers in first round (seventh pick overall) of 2001 NFL draft. ... Signed by 49ers (July 26, 2001).
HONORS: Named defensive end on THE SPORTING NEWS college All-America first team (2000).
PRO STATISTICS: 2001—Recovered one fumble for one yard.

Year Team	G	GS	SACKS
2001—San Francisco NFL	15	15	6.5

CARTER, CHRIS   S   TEXANS

PERSONAL: Born September 27, 1974, in Tyler, Texas. ... 6-2/212. ... Full name: Christopher Cary Carter. ... Cousin of Joe Carter, first baseman/outfielder with five major league baseball teams (1984-98).
HIGH SCHOOL: John Tyler (Tyler, Texas).
COLLEGE: Texas.
TRANSACTIONS/CAREER NOTES: Selected by New England Patriots in third round (89th pick overall) of 1997 NFL draft. ... Signed by Patriots (July 15, 1997). ... Granted free agency (February 11, 2000). ... Re-signed by Patriots (July 14, 2000). ... Claimed on waivers by Cincinnati Bengals (August 28, 2000). ... Granted unconditional free agency (March 1, 2002). ... Signed by Houston Texans (April 5, 2002).
PLAYING EXPERIENCE: New England NFL, 1997-1999; Cincinnati NFL, 2000 and 2001. ... Games/Games started: 1997 (16/0), 1998 (16/0), 1999 (15/15), 2000 (16/10), 2001 (16/4). Total: 79/29.
PRO STATISTICS: 1998—Credited with one sack. 1999—Intercepted three passes for 13 yards, credited with one sack and recovered two fumbles. 2000—Intercepted one pass for six yards, credited with one sack and recovered one fumble. 2001—Intercepted one pass for 10 yards and recovered two fumbles for 12 yards.

CARTER, CRIS   WR

PERSONAL: Born November 25, 1965, in Troy, Ohio. ... 6-3/208. ... Full name: Christopher D. Carter. ... Brother of Butch Carter, head coach with Toronto Raptors (February 13, 1998-99).
HIGH SCHOOL: Middletown (Ohio).
COLLEGE: Ohio State.
TRANSACTIONS/CAREER NOTES: Selected by Philadelphia Eagles in fourth round of 1987 NFL supplemental draft (September 4, 1987). ... Signed by Eagles (September 17, 1987). ... Granted roster exemption (September 17-October 26, 1987). ... Claimed on waivers by Minnesota Vikings (September 4, 1990). ... Granted free agency (February 1, 1991). ... Re-signed by Vikings (July 9, 1991). ... Granted free agency

(February 1, 1992). ... Re-signed by Vikings (July 26, 1992). ... On injured reserve with broken collarbone (December 4-30, 1992). ... Granted unconditional free agency (March 1, 2002). ... Announced retirement (May 21, 2002).
CHAMPIONSHIP GAME EXPERIENCE: Played in NFC championship game (1998 and 2000 seasons).
HONORS: Played in Pro Bowl (1993-2000 seasons). ... Named wide receiver on THE SPORTING NEWS NFL All-Pro team (1994).
PRO STATISTICS: 1987—Attempted one pass without a completion and returned 12 kickoffs for 241 yards. 1988—Recovered one fumble in end zone for a touchdown. 1989—Recovered one fumble. 1993—Recovered one fumble. 1996—Returned one kickoff for three yards and recovered one fumble. 2000—Recovered two fumbles.
SINGLE GAME HIGHS (regular season): Receptions—14 (October 2, 1994, vs. Arizona); yards—168 (September 10, 2000, vs. Miami); and touchdown receptions—3 (November 14, 1999, vs. Chicago).
STATISTICAL PLATEAUS: 100-yard receiving games: 1988 (1), 1989 (1), 1990 (2), 1991 (4), 1992 (1), 1993 (3), 1994 (5), 1995 (5), 1996 (1), 1997 (4), 1998 (3), 1999 (5), 2000 (6), 2001 (1). Total: 42.
MISCELLANEOUS: Holds Minnesota Vikings all-time records for most receptions (1,004), most yards receiving (12,383), most touchdowns (110) and most touchdown receptions (110).

				RUSHING				RECEIVING				TOTALS		
Year	Team	G	GS	Att.	Yds.	Avg.	TD	No.	Yds.	Avg.	TD	TD	2pt.	Pts.	Fum.
1987—Philadelphia NFL		9	0	0	0	0.0	0	5	84	16.8	2	2	0	12	0
1988—Philadelphia NFL		16	16	1	1	1.0	0	39	761	19.5	6	7	0	42	0
1989—Philadelphia NFL		16	15	2	16	8.0	0	45	605	13.4	11	11	0	66	1
1990—Minnesota NFL		16	5	2	6	3.0	0	27	413	15.3	3	3	0	18	0
1991—Minnesota NFL		16	16	0	0	0.0	0	72	962	13.4	5	5	0	30	1
1992—Minnesota NFL		12	12	5	15	3.0	0	53	681	12.8	6	6	0	36	1
1993—Minnesota NFL		16	16	0	0	0.0	0	86	1071	12.5	9	9	0	54	0
1994—Minnesota NFL		16	16	0	0	0.0	0	*122	1256	10.3	7	7	2	46	4
1995—Minnesota NFL		16	16	1	0	0.0	0	122	1371	11.2	†17	17	0	102	0
1996—Minnesota NFL		16	16	0	0	0.0	0	96	1163	12.1	10	10	0	60	1
1997—Minnesota NFL		16	16	0	0	0.0	0	89	1069	12.0	*13	13	3	84	3
1998—Minnesota NFL		16	16	1	-1	-1.0	0	78	1011	13.0	12	12	0	72	0
1999—Minnesota NFL		16	16	0	0	0.0	0	90	1241	13.8	*13	13	0	78	0
2000—Minnesota NFL		16	16	0	0	0.0	0	96	1274	13.3	9	9	0	54	3
2001—Minnesota NFL		16	16	1	4	4.0	0	73	871	11.9	6	6	0	36	2
Pro totals (15 years)		229	208	13	41	3.2	0	1093	13833	12.7	129	130	5	790	16

CARTER, DALE CB SAINTS

PERSONAL: Born November 28, 1969, in Covington, Ga. ... 6-1/194. ... Full name: Dale Lavelle Carter. ... Brother of Jake Reed, wide receiver, New Orleans Saints.
HIGH SCHOOL: Newton County (Covington, Ga.).
JUNIOR COLLEGE: Ellsworth (Iowa) Community College.
COLLEGE: Tennessee.
TRANSACTIONS/CAREER NOTES: Selected by Kansas City Chiefs in first round (20th pick overall) of 1992 NFL draft. ... Signed by Chiefs (June 2, 1992). ... Designated by Chiefs as transition player (February 25, 1993). ... On injured reserve with broken arm (January 7, 1994-remainder of 1993 playoffs). ... Tendered offer sheet by Minnesota Vikings (July 12, 1996). ... Offer matched by Chiefs (July 19, 1996). ... Granted unconditional free agency (February 12, 1999). ... Signed by Denver Broncos (February 19, 1999). ... Suspended by NFL for violating league substance abuse policy (April 25, 2000-November 6, 2001). ... Released by Broncos (November 6, 2001). ... Signed by Minnesota Vikings (November 6, 2001). ... Granted unconditional free agency (March 1, 2002). ... Signed by New Orleans Saints (March 12, 2002).
HONORS: Named kick returner on THE SPORTING NEWS college All-America first team (1990). ... Named defensive back on THE SPORTING NEWS college All-America first team (1991). ... Played in Pro Bowl (1994, 1995 and 1997 seasons). ... Named cornerback on THE SPORTING NEWS NFL All-Pro team (1996). ... Named to play in Pro Bowl (1996 season); replaced by Terry McDaniel due to injury.
PRO STATISTICS: 1992—Recovered two fumbles. 1993—Rushed once for two yards and recovered two fumbles. 1994—Recovered one fumble. 1995—Recovered two fumbles. 1996—Rushed once for three yards, caught six passes for 89 yards and a touchdown and recovered two fumbles for seven yards.

				INTERCEPTIONS				PUNT RETURNS				KICKOFF RETURNS				TOTALS		
Year	Team	G	GS	No.	Yds.	Avg.	TD	No.	Yds.	Avg.	TD	No.	Yds.	Avg.	TD	TD	2pt.	Pts.	Fum.
1992—Kansas City NFL		16	9	7	65	9.3	1	38	398	10.5	†2	11	190	17.3	0	3	0	18	7
1993—Kansas City NFL		15	11	1	0	0.0	0	27	247	9.1	0	0	0	0.0	0	0	0	0	4
1994—Kansas City NFL		16	16	2	24	12.0	0	16	124	7.8	0	0	0	0.0	0	0	0	0	1
1995—Kansas City NFL		16	14	4	45	11.3	0	0	0	0.0	0	0	0	0.0	0	0	0	0	0
1996—Kansas City NFL		14	14	3	17	5.7	0	2	18	9.0	0	0	0	0.0	0	1	0	6	1
1997—Kansas City NFL		16	15	2	9	4.5	0	0	0	0.0	0	0	0	0.0	0	0	0	0	0
1998—Kansas City NFL		11	9	2	23	11.5	0	0	0	0.0	0	0	0	0.0	0	0	0	0	0
1999—Denver NFL		14	14	2	48	24.0	0	0	0	0.0	0	0	0	0.0	0	0	0	0	0
2000—Denver NFL										Did not play.									
2001—Minnesota NFL		8	8	0	0	0.0	0	0	0	0.0	0	0	0	0.0	0	0	0	0	0
Pro totals (9 years)		126	110	23	231	10.0	1	83	787	9.5	2	11	190	17.3	0	4	0	24	13

CARTER, DYSHOD DB BROWNS

PERSONAL: Born June 18, 1978, in Denver. ... 5-10/197. ... Full name: Dyshod Vontae Carter.
HIGH SCHOOL: Thomas Jefferson (Denver).
COLLEGE: Kansas State.
TRANSACTIONS/CAREER NOTES: Signed as non-drafted free agent by Kansas City Chiefs (April 26, 2001). ... Released by Chiefs (August 28, 2001). ... Signed by Cleveland Browns to practice squad (October 9, 2001). ... Activated (October 24, 2001). ... Released by Browns (November 7, 2001). ... Re-signed by Browns to practice squad (November 9, 2001). ... Activated (November 29, 2001).
PLAYING EXPERIENCE: Cleveland NFL, 2001. ... Games/Games started: 2001 (5/0).

CARTER, JONATHAN WR GIANTS

PERSONAL: Born March 20, 1979, in Anniston, Ala. ... 5-11/173.
HIGH SCHOOL: Lineville (Ala.).
COLLEGE: Troy State.
TRANSACTIONS/CAREER NOTES: Selected by New York Giants in fifth round (162nd pick overall) of 2001 NFL draft. ... Signed by Giants (July 26, 2001). ... Released by Giants (September 2, 2001). ... Re-signed by Giants to practice squad (September 3, 2001). ... Activated (December 29, 2001).
PLAYING EXPERIENCE: New York Giants NFL, 2001. ... Games/Games started: (2/0).
PRO STATISTICS: 2001—Returned eight kickoffs for 155 yards.

CARTER, KEVIN DE TITANS

PERSONAL: Born September 21, 1973, in Miami. ... 6-5/280. ... Full name: Kevin Louis Carter. ... Brother of Bernard Carter, linebacker with Jacksonville Jaguars (1995).
HIGH SCHOOL: Lincoln (Tallahassee, Fla.).
COLLEGE: Florida.
TRANSACTIONS/CAREER NOTES: Selected by St. Louis Rams in first round (sixth pick overall) of 1995 NFL draft. ... Signed by Rams (July 17, 1995). ... Designated by Rams as franchise player (February 22, 2001). ... Traded by Rams to Tennessee Titans for first-round pick (DT Ryan Pickett) in 2001 draft (March 28, 2001).
CHAMPIONSHIP GAME EXPERIENCE: Played in NFC championship game (1999 season). ... Member of Super Bowl championship team (1999 season).
HONORS: Named defensive lineman on THE SPORTING NEWS college All-America first team (1994). ... Named defensive end on THE SPORTING NEWS NFL All-Pro team (1999). ... Played in Pro Bowl (1999 season).
PRO STATISTICS: 1995—Credited with one safety. 1996—Recovered two fumbles. 1997—Recovered two fumbles for five yards. 1999—Recovered two fumbles. 2000—Fumbled once and recovered one fumble.

Year Team	G	GS	SACKS
1995—St. Louis NFL	16	16	6.0
1996—St. Louis NFL	16	16	9.5
1997—St. Louis NFL	16	16	7.5
1998—St. Louis NFL	16	16	12.0
1999—St. Louis NFL	16	16	*17.0
2000—St. Louis NFL	16	13	10.5
2001—Tennessee NFL	16	16	2.0
Pro totals (7 years)	**112**	**109**	**64.5**

CARTER, KI-JANA RB

PERSONAL: Born September 12, 1973, in Westerville, Ohio. ... 5-10/222. ... Full name: Kenneth Leonard Carter. ... Name pronounced KEE-john-uh.
HIGH SCHOOL: Westerville (Ohio) North.
COLLEGE: Penn State.
TRANSACTIONS/CAREER NOTES: Selected after junior season by Cincinnati Bengals in first round (first pick overall) of 1995 NFL draft. ... Signed by Bengals (July 19, 1995). ... On injured reserve with knee injury (August 22, 1995-entire season). ... On injured reserve with wrist injury (September 7, 1998-remainder of season). ... On injured reserve with knee injury (September 29, 1999-remainder of season). ... Released by Bengals (June 1, 2000). ... Signed by Washington Redskins (July 31, 2001). ... Granted unconditional free agency (March 1, 2002).
HONORS: Named running back on THE SPORTING NEWS college All-America first team (1994).
PRO STATISTICS: 1996—Recovered two fumbles for minus eight yards. 1997—Attempted one pass without a completion, returned one kickoff for nine yards and recovered two fumbles. 2001—Returned eight kickoffs for 111 yards and recovered two fumbles.
SINGLE GAME HIGHS (regular season): Attempts—19 (August 31, 1997, vs. Arizona); yards—104 (September 21, 1997, vs. Denver); and rushing touchdowns—2 (December 30, 2001, vs. New Orleans).
STATISTICAL PLATEAUS: 100-yard rushing games: 1997 (1).

			RUSHING				RECEIVING				TOTALS		
Year Team	G	GS	Att.	Yds.	Avg.	TD	No.	Yds.	Avg.	TD	TD	2pt.	Pts.	Fum.
1995—Cincinnati NFL							Did not play.							
1996—Cincinnati NFL	16	4	91	264	2.9	8	22	169	7.7	1	9	0	54	2
1997—Cincinnati NFL	15	10	128	464	3.6	7	21	157	7.5	0	7	0	42	3
1998—Cincinnati NFL	1	0	2	4	2.0	0	6	25	4.2	0	0	0	0	0
1999—Cincinnati NFL	3	0	6	15	2.5	1	3	24	8.0	0	1	0	6	0
2000—							Did not play.							
2001—Washington NFL	14	0	63	308	4.9	3	13	83	6.4	0	3	0	18	1
Pro totals (5 years)	**49**	**14**	**290**	**1055**	**3.6**	**19**	**65**	**458**	**7.0**	**1**	**20**	**0**	**120**	**6**

CARTER, MARTY S

PERSONAL: Born December 17, 1969, in La Grange, Ga. ... 6-1/213. ... Full name: Marty LaVincent Carter.
HIGH SCHOOL: La Grange (Ga.).
COLLEGE: Middle Tennessee State.
TRANSACTIONS/CAREER NOTES: Selected by Tampa Bay Buccaneers in eighth round (207th pick overall) of 1991 NFL draft. ... Signed by Buccaneers (July 19, 1991). ... Granted unconditional free agency (February 17, 1995). ... Signed by Chicago Bears (March 3, 1995). ... Granted unconditional free agency (February 12, 1999). ... Signed by Atlanta Falcons (March 12, 1999). ... On injured reserve with knee injury (November 30, 1999-remainder of season). ... Released by Falcons (October 16, 2001). ... Signed by Detroit Lions (December 11, 2001). ... Granted unconditional free agency (March 1, 2002).

PRO STATISTICS: 1993—Recovered two fumbles. 1994—Caught one pass for 21 yards and returned one kickoff for no yards. 1995—Recovered one fumble. 1998—Recovered two fumbles. 1999—Recovered one fumble. 2000—Recovered two fumbles.

				INTERCEPTIONS				SACKS
Year Team		G	GS	No.	Yds.	Avg.	TD	No.
1991—Tampa Bay NFL		14	11	1	5	5.0	0	0.0
1992—Tampa Bay NFL		16	16	3	1	0.3	0	2.0
1993—Tampa Bay NFL		16	14	1	0	0.0	0	0.0
1994—Tampa Bay NFL		16	14	0	0	0.0	0	1.0
1995—Chicago NFL		16	16	2	20	10.0	0	0.0
1996—Chicago NFL		16	16	3	34	11.3	0	0.0
1997—Chicago NFL		15	15	1	14	14.0	0	1.0
1998—Chicago NFL		16	16	0	0	0.0	0	0.0
1999—Atlanta NFL		11	11	1	4	4.0	0	0.0
2000—Atlanta NFL		16	16	0	0	0.0	0	2.0
2001—Atlanta NFL		5	5	0	0	0.0	0	0.0
—Detroit NFL		4	1	1	0	0.0	0	0.0
Pro totals (11 years)		161	151	13	78	6.0	0	6.0

CARTER, QUINCY — QB — COWBOYS

PERSONAL: Born October 13, 1977, in Decatur, Ga. ... 6-2/231.
HIGH SCHOOL: Southwest DeKalb (Decatur, Ga.).
COLLEGE: Georgia.
TRANSACTIONS/CAREER NOTES: Selected after junior season by Dallas Cowboys in second round (53rd pick overall) of 2001 NFL draft. ... Signed by Cowboys (July 19, 2001).
HONORS: Named College Football Player of the Year by THE SPORTING NEWS (1998).
PRO STATISTICS: 2001—Fumbled five times and recovered two fumbles for minus four yards.
SINGLE GAME HIGHS (regular season): Attempts—33 (December 16, 2001, vs. Seattle); completions—17 (December 9, 2001, vs. New York Giants); yards—241 (December 30, 2001, vs. San Francisco); and touchdown passes—2 (December 30, 2001, vs. San Francisco).
MISCELLANEOUS: Regular-season record as starting NFL quarterback: 3-5 (.375).

				PASSING						RUSHING				TOTALS		
Year Team	G	GS	Att.	Cmp.	Pct.	Yds.	TD	Int.	Avg.	Rat.	Att.	Yds.	Avg.	TD	TD	2pt.	Pts.
2001—Dallas NFL	8	8	176	90	51.1	1072	5	7	6.09	63.0	45	150	3.3	1	1	0	6

CARTER, TIM — CB — SAINTS

PERSONAL: Born July 15, 1978, in Tallahassee, Fla. ... 6-0/183. ... Full name: Timothy Jerome Carter.
HIGH SCHOOL: Rickards (Tallahassee, Fla.).
COLLEGE: Tulane.
TRANSACTIONS/CAREER NOTES: Signed as non-drafted free agent by New Orleans Saints (April 26, 2001). ... Released by Saints (August 28, 2001). ... Signed by Buffalo Bills (September 5, 2001). ... Released by Bills (November 14, 2001). ... Signed by Saints (December 29, 2001).
PLAYING EXPERIENCE: New Orleans NFL, 2001. ... Games/Games started: 2001 (2/0).

CARTER, TOM — CB

PERSONAL: Born September 5, 1972, in St. Petersburg, Fla. ... 6-0/190. ... Full name: Thomas Carter III.
HIGH SCHOOL: Lakewood (Fla.).
COLLEGE: Notre Dame (degree in finance, 1996).
TRANSACTIONS/CAREER NOTES: Selected after junior season by Washington Redskins in first round (17th pick overall) of 1993 NFL draft. ... Signed by Redskins for 1993 season. ... Designated by Redskins as transition player (February 15, 1994). ... Designated by Redskins as transition player (February 12, 1997). ... Tendered offer sheet by Chicago Bears (March 31, 1997). ... Redskins declined to match offer (April 7, 1997). ... On injured reserve with broken collarbone (September 30, 1998-remainder of season). ... Claimed on waivers by Cincinnati Bengals (December 14, 1999). ... Released by Bengals (March 1, 2001). ... Re-signed by Bengals (April 9, 2001). ... On injured reserve with knee injury (November 10-December 13, 2001). ... Released by Bengals (December 13, 2001).
PRO STATISTICS: 1999—Recovered one fumble for 21 yards.

			INTERCEPTIONS			
Year Team	G	GS	No.	Yds.	Avg.	TD
1993—Washington NFL	14	11	6	54	9.0	0
1994—Washington NFL	16	16	3	58	19.3	0
1995—Washington NFL	16	16	4	116	29.0	1
1996—Washington NFL	16	16	5	24	4.8	0
1997—Chicago NFL	16	16	3	12	4.0	0
1998—Chicago NFL	4	4	2	20	10.0	0
1999—Chicago NFL	12	6	1	36	36.0	0
—Cincinnati NFL	2	2	1	0	0.0	0
2000—Cincinnati NFL	16	11	2	40	20.0	0
2001—Cincinnati NFL	6	0	0	0	0.0	0
Pro totals (9 years)	118	98	27	360	13.3	1

CARTER, TONY — FB — BRONCOS

PERSONAL: Born August 23, 1972, in Columbus, Ohio. ... 6-0/235. ... Full name: Antonio Marcus Carter.
HIGH SCHOOL: South (Columbus, Ohio).
COLLEGE: Minnesota.

TRANSACTIONS/CAREER NOTES: Signed as non-drafted free agent by Chicago Bears (April 28, 1994). ... Granted unconditional free agency (February 13, 1998). ... Signed by New England Patriots (February 25, 1998). ... Granted unconditional free agency (March 2, 2001). ... Signed by Denver Broncos (May 4, 2001).
PRO STATISTICS: 1996—Recovered one fumble. 1997—Recovered one fumble. 1999—Recovered one fumble. 2001—Recovered one fumble.
SINGLE GAME HIGHS (regular season): Attempts—9 (December 17, 2000, vs. Buffalo); yards—37 (October 13, 1996, vs. New Orleans); and rushing touchdowns—1 (December 24, 2000, vs. Miami).

			RUSHING				RECEIVING				KICKOFF RETURNS				TOTALS			
Year Team	G	GS	Att.	Yds.	Avg.	TD	No.	Yds.	Avg.	TD	No.	Yds.	Avg.	TD	TD	2pt.	Pts.	Fum.
1994—Chicago NFL	14	0	0	0	0.0	0	1	24	24.0	0	6	99	16.5	0	0	0	0	0
1995—Chicago NFL	16	11	10	34	3.4	0	40	329	8.2	1	3	24	8.0	0	1	0	6	1
1996—Chicago NFL	16	11	11	43	3.9	0	41	233	5.7	0	0	0	0.0	0	0	0	0	1
1997—Chicago NFL	16	10	9	56	6.2	0	24	152	6.3	0	2	34	17.0	0	0	0	0	0
1998—New England NFL	11	7	2	3	1.5	0	18	166	9.2	0	0	0	0.0	0	0	0	0	0
1999—New England NFL	16	14	6	26	4.3	0	20	108	5.4	0	0	0	0.0	0	0	0	0	0
2000—New England NFL	16	6	37	90	2.4	2	9	73	8.1	0	1	16	16.0	0	2	0	12	0
2001—Denver NFL	16	6	1	4	4.0	0	11	83	7.5	0	2	44	22.0	0	0	0	0	1
Pro totals (8 years)	121	65	76	256	3.4	2	164	1168	7.1	1	14	217	15.5	0	3	0	18	3

CARTER, TYRONE   S   VIKINGS

PERSONAL: Born March 31, 1976, in Pompano Beach, Fla. ... 5-8/190.
HIGH SCHOOL: Ely (Pompano Beach, Fla.).
COLLEGE: Minnesota.
TRANSACTIONS/CAREER NOTES: Selected by Minnesota Vikings in fourth round (118th pick overall) of 2000 NFL draft. ... Signed by Vikings (July 5, 2000).
CHAMPIONSHIP GAME EXPERIENCE: Played in NFC championship game (2000 season).
HONORS: Jim Thorpe Award winner (1999). ... Named strong safety on THE SPORTING NEWS college All-America first team (1999).
PRO STATISTICS: 2001—Credited with one sack and recovered one fumble for 46 yards and a touchdown.

			INTERCEPTIONS				KICKOFF RETURNS				TOTALS			
Year Team	G	GS	No.	Yds.	Avg.	TD	No.	Yds.	Avg.	TD	TD	2pt.	Pts.	Fum.
2000—Minnesota NFL	15	7	0	0	0.0	0	17	389	22.9	0	0	0	0	0
2001—Minnesota NFL	15	7	0	0	0.0	0	0	0	0.0	0	1	0	6	0
Pro totals (2 years)	30	14	0	0	0.0	0	17	389	22.9	0	1	0	6	0

CARTY, JOHNDALE   S   FALCONS

PERSONAL: Born August 27, 1977, in Miami. ... 6-0/196.
HIGH SCHOOL: Hialeah (Fla.) Miami Lakes.
COLLEGE: Utah State.
TRANSACTIONS/CAREER NOTES: Selected by Atlanta Falcons in fourth round (126th pick overall) of 1999 NFL draft. ... Signed by Falcons (July 8, 1999).
PLAYING EXPERIENCE: Atlanta NFL, 1999-2001. ... Games/Games started: 1999 (14/0), 2000 (15/0), 2001 (16/2). Total: 45/2.
PRO STATISTICS: 2001—Intercepted one pass for no yards.

CASON, AVEION   RB   LIONS

PERSONAL: Born July 12, 1979, in St. Petersburg, Fla. ... 5-9/210. ... Full name: Aveion Marquel Cason.
HIGH SCHOOL: Lakewood (St. Petersburg, Fla.).
COLLEGE: Illinois State.
TRANSACTIONS/CAREER NOTES: Signed as non-drafted free agent by St. Louis Rams (April 23, 2001). ... Released by Rams (September 25, 2001). ... Re-signed by Rams to practice squad (September 26, 2001). ... Released by Rams (September 28, 2001). ... Signed by Detroit Lions (November 21, 2001).
SINGLE GAME HIGHS (regular season): Receptions—4 (January 6, 2002, vs. Dallas); yards—32 (January 6, 2002, vs. Dallas); and touchdown receptions—0.

			RUSHING				RECEIVING				KICKOFF RETURNS				TOTALS			
Year Team	G	GS	Att.	Yds.	Avg.	TD	No.	Yds.	Avg.	TD	No.	Yds.	Avg.	TD	TD	2pt.	Pts.	Fum.
2001—St. Louis NFL	1	0	0	0	0.0	0	0	0	0.0	0	4	73	18.3	0	0	0	0	1
—Detroit NFL	5	0	11	31	2.8	0	4	32	8.0	0	0	0	0.0	0	0	0	0	1
Pro totals (1 years)	6	0	11	31	2.8	0	4	32	8.0	0	4	73	18.3	0	0	0	0	2

CAVER, QUINTON   LB   EAGLES

PERSONAL: Born August 22, 1978, in Anniston, Ala. ... 6-4/230.
HIGH SCHOOL: Anniston (Ala.).
COLLEGE: Arkansas.
TRANSACTIONS/CAREER NOTES: Selected by Philadelphia Eagles in second round (55th pick overall) of 2001 NFL draft. ... Signed by Eagles (July 27, 2001).
PLAYING EXPERIENCE: Philadelphia NFL, 2001. ... Games/Games started: (11/0).
CHAMPIONSHIP GAME EXPERIENCE: Played in NFC championship game (2001 season).

CENTERS, LARRY — RB — BILLS

PERSONAL: Born June 1, 1968, in Tatum, Texas. ... 6-0/225. ... Full name: Larry E. Centers.
HIGH SCHOOL: Tatum (Texas).
COLLEGE: Stephen F. Austin State.
TRANSACTIONS/CAREER NOTES: Selected by Phoenix Cardinals in fifth round (115th pick overall) of 1990 NFL draft. ... Signed by Cardinals (July 23, 1990). ... On injured reserve with broken foot (September 11-October 30, 1991). ... Granted free agency (February 1, 1992). ... Re-signed by Cardinals (July 23, 1992). ... Granted unconditional free agency (February 17, 1994). ... Re-signed by Cardinals (March 15, 1994). ... Cardinals franchise renamed Arizona Cardinals for 1994 season. ... Granted unconditional free agency (February 14, 1997). ... Re-signed by Cardinals (March 14, 1997). ... Released by Cardinals (June 18, 1999). ... Signed by Washington Redskins (July 6, 1999). ... Released by Redskins (April 20, 2001). ... Signed by Buffalo Bills (May 8, 2001).
HONORS: Played in Pro Bowl (1995 and 1996 seasons).
PRO STATISTICS: 1991—Returned five punts for 30 yards and recovered two fumbles. 1993—Recovered two fumbles. 1994—Recovered two fumbles for 27 yards. 1995—Had only pass attempt intercepted and recovered one fumble. 1996—Recovered one fumble. 1999—Recovered one fumble. 2000—Recovered one fumble.
SINGLE GAME HIGHS (regular season): Attempts—15 (September 4, 1994, vs. Los Angeles Rams); yards—62 (November 26, 1995, vs. Atlanta); and rushing touchdowns—2 (December 4, 1994, vs. Houston).
STATISTICAL PLATEAUS: 100-yard receiving games: 1995 (2), 1996 (1). Total: 3.
MISCELLANEOUS: Holds Cardinals franchise all-time record for most receptions (535).

			RUSHING				RECEIVING				KICKOFF RETURNS				TOTALS			
Year Team	G	GS	Att.	Yds.	Avg.	TD	No.	Yds.	Avg.	TD	No.	Yds.	Avg.	TD	TD	2pt.	Pts.	Fum.
1990—Phoenix NFL	6	0	0	0	0.0	0	0	0	0.0	0	16	272	17.0	0	0	0	0	1
1991—Phoenix NFL	9	2	14	44	3.1	0	19	176	9.3	0	16	330	20.6	0	0	0	0	4
1992—Phoenix NFL	16	1	37	139	3.8	0	50	417	8.3	2	0	0	0.0	0	2	0	12	0
1993—Phoenix NFL	16	9	25	152	6.1	0	66	603	9.1	3	0	0	0.0	0	3	0	18	1
1994—Arizona NFL	16	5	115	336	2.9	5	77	647	8.4	2	0	0	0.0	0	7	0	42	2
1995—Arizona NFL	16	10	78	254	3.3	2	101	962	9.5	2	1	15	15.0	0	4	0	24	2
1996—Arizona NFL	16	14	116	425	3.7	2	99	766	7.7	7	0	0	0.0	0	9	0	54	1
1997—Arizona NFL	15	14	101	276	2.7	1	54	409	7.6	1	0	0	0.0	0	2	0	12	1
1998—Arizona NFL	16	12	31	110	3.5	0	69	559	8.1	2	0	0	0.0	0	2	0	12	1
1999—Washington NFL	16	12	13	51	3.9	0	69	544	7.9	3	0	0	0.0	0	3	0	18	1
2000—Washington NFL	15	5	19	103	5.4	0	81	600	7.4	3	0	0	0.0	0	3	0	18	1
2001—Buffalo NFL	16	13	34	160	4.7	2	80	620	7.8	2	0	0	0.0	0	4	0	24	2
Pro totals (12 years)	173	97	583	2050	3.5	12	765	6303	8.2	27	33	617	18.7	0	39	0	234	19

CERQUA, MARQ — LB — COWBOYS

PERSONAL: Born April 3, 1977, in Miami. ... 5-11/223. ... Full name: Marq Vincent Cerqua.
HIGH SCHOOL: Daniel (Central, S.C.).
COLLEGE: Furman, then Carson-Newman.
TRANSACTIONS/CAREER NOTES: Signed as non-drafted free agent by Tampa Bay Buccaneers (April 23, 2001). ... Claimed on waivers by Dallas Cowboys (December 24, 2001); did not play.
PLAYING EXPERIENCE: Tampa Bay NFL, 2001. ... Games/Games started: 2001 (3/0).

CESARIO, ANTHONY — G — DOLPHINS

PERSONAL: Born July 19, 1976, in Pueblo, Colo. ... 6-5/305. ... Full name: Anthony Angelo Cesario Jr. ... Name pronounced Sess-ARE-ee-oh.
HIGH SCHOOL: South (Pueblo, Colo.).
COLLEGE: Colorado State.
TRANSACTIONS/CAREER NOTES: Selected by Jacksonville Jaguars in third round (88th pick overall) of 1999 NFL draft. ... Signed by Jaguars (June 18, 1999). ... Inactive for all 16 games (1999). ... Released by Jaguars (August 27, 2000). ... Signed by Miami Dolphins (October 25, 2000). ... Released by Dolphins (September 2, 2001). ... Re-signed by Dolphins to practice squad (November 21, 2001). ... Activated (December 31, 2001).
CHAMPIONSHIP GAME EXPERIENCE: Member of Jaguars for AFC championship game (1999 season); inactive.
HONORS: Named offensive guard on THE SPORTING NEWS college All-America second team (1997 and 1998).

CHAMBERLAIN, BYRON — TE — VIKINGS

PERSONAL: Born October 17, 1971, in Honolulu. ... 6-1/264.
HIGH SCHOOL: Eastern Hills (Fort Worth, Texas).
COLLEGE: Missouri, then Wayne State (Neb.).
TRANSACTIONS/CAREER NOTES: Selected by Denver Broncos in seventh round (222nd pick overall) of 1995 NFL draft. ... Signed by Broncos (August 27, 1995). ... Released by Broncos (August 27, 1995). ... Re-signed by Broncos to practice squad (August 28, 1995). ... Activated (November 24, 1995). ... Assigned by Broncos to Rhein Fire in 1996 World League enhancement allocation program (February 19, 1996). ... Granted unconditional free agency (March 2, 2001). ... Signed by Minnesota Vikings (March 16, 2001). ... Granted unconditional free agency (March 1, 2002). ... Re-signed by Vikings (March 20, 2002).
CHAMPIONSHIP GAME EXPERIENCE: Played in AFC championship game (1997 and 1998 seasons). ... Member of Super Bowl championship team (1997 season); did not play. ... Member of Super Bowl championship team (1998 season).
PRO STATISTICS: W.L.: 1996—Rushed once for four yards and returned one kickoff for eight yards. NFL: 1996—Returned three kickoffs for 49 yards. 1997—Returned one kickoff for 13 yards. 2000—Returned two kickoffs for 25 yards. 2001—Recovered one fumble.
SINGLE GAME HIGHS (regular season): Receptions—7 (December 23, 2001, vs. Jacksonville); yards—123 (October 17, 1999, vs. Green Bay); and touchdown receptions—1 (December 30, 2001, vs. Green Bay).
STATISTICAL PLATEAUS: 100-yard receiving games: 1999 (1).

Year	Team	G	GS	No.	Receiving Yds.	Avg.	TD	TD	2pt	Pts.	Fum.
1995	Denver NFL	5	0	1	11	11.0	0	0	0	0	0
1996	Rhein W.L.	10	10	58	685	11.8	8	8	0	48	0
—	Denver NFL	11	0	12	129	10.8	0	0	0	0	1
1997	Denver NFL	10	0	2	18	9.0	0	0	0	0	1
1998	Denver NFL	16	0	3	35	11.7	0	0	0	0	0
1999	Denver NFL	16	0	32	488	15.3	2	2	0	12	0
2000	Denver NFL	15	0	22	283	12.9	1	1	0	6	0
2001	Minnesota NFL	16	15	57	666	11.7	3	3	0	18	1
W.L. totals (1 year)		10	10	58	685	11.8	8	8	0	48	0
NFL totals (7 years)		89	15	129	1630	12.6	6	6	0	36	3
Pro totals (8 years)		99	25	187	2315	12.4	14	14	0	84	3

CHAMBERLIN, FRANK   LB   TITANS

PERSONAL: Born January 2, 1978, in Paramus, N.J. ... 6-1/246. ... Full name: Frank Jacob Chamberlin.
HIGH SCHOOL: Mahwah (N.J.).
COLLEGE: Boston College.
TRANSACTIONS/CAREER NOTES: Selected by Tennessee Titans in fifth round (160th pick overall) of 2000 NFL draft. ... Signed by Titans (July 7, 2000).
PLAYING EXPERIENCE: Tennessee NFL, 2000 and 2001. ... Games/Games started: 2000 (12/0), 2001 (16/0). Total: 28/0.
PRO STATISTICS: 2001—Credited with one sack.

CHAMBERS, CHRIS   WR   DOLPHINS

PERSONAL: Born August 12, 1978, in Cleveland. ... 5-11/210.
HIGH SCHOOL: Bedford (Ohio).
COLLEGE: Wisconsin.
TRANSACTIONS/CAREER NOTES: Selected by Miami Dolphins in second round (52nd pick overall) of 2001 NFL draft. ... Signed by Dolphins (July 23, 2001).
PRO STATISTICS: 2001—Rushed once for minus 11 yards and fumbled twice.
SINGLE GAME HIGHS (regular season): Receptions—7 (December 22, 2001, vs. New England); yards—124 (December 22, 2001, vs. New England); and touchdown receptions—2 (December 10, 2001, vs. Indianapolis).
STATISTICAL PLATEAUS: 100-yard receiving games: 2001 (3).

Year	Team	G	GS	No.	Receiving Yds.	Avg.	TD
2001	Miami NFL	16	7	48	883	*18.4	7

CHANDLER, CHRIS   QB   BEARS

PERSONAL: Born October 12, 1965, in Everett, Wash. ... 6-4/228. ... Full name: Christopher Mark Chandler. ... Brother of Greg Chandler, catcher with San Francisco Giants organization (1978); and son-in-law of John Brodie, quarterback with San Francisco 49ers (1957-73).
HIGH SCHOOL: Everett (Wash.).
COLLEGE: Washington (degree in economics, 1988).
TRANSACTIONS/CAREER NOTES: Selected by Indianapolis Colts in third round (76th pick overall) of 1988 NFL draft. ... Signed by Colts (July 23, 1988). ... On injured reserve with knee injury (October 3, 1989-remainder of season). ... Traded by Colts to Tampa Bay Buccaneers for first round pick (LB Quentin Coryatt) in 1992 draft (August 7, 1990). ... Claimed on waivers by Phoenix Cardinals (November 6, 1991). ... Granted unconditional free agency (February 17, 1994). ... Signed by Los Angeles Rams (May 6, 1994). ... Granted unconditional free agency (February 17, 1995). ... Signed by Houston Oilers (March 10, 1995). ... Traded by Oilers to Atlanta Falcons for fourth- (WR Derrick Mason) and sixth- round (traded to New Orleans) picks in 1997 draft (February 24, 1997). ... Released by Falcons (February 25, 2002). ... Signed by Chicago Bears (April 12, 2002).
CHAMPIONSHIP GAME EXPERIENCE: Played in NFC championship game (1998 season). ... Played in Super Bowl XXXIII (1998 season).
HONORS: Played in Pro Bowl (1997 and 1998 seasons).
PRO STATISTICS: 1988—Fumbled eight times and recovered five fumbles for minus six yards. 1990—Fumbled five times and recovered one fumble for minus two yards. 1991—Fumbled six times and recovered two fumbles for minus seven yards. 1992—Fumbled nine times and recovered two fumbles for minus 11 yards. 1993—Fumbled twice. 1994—Fumbled three times. 1995—Tied for AFC lead with 12 fumbles and recovered five fumbles for minus nine yards. 1996—Fumbled eight times and recovered three fumbles for minus four yards. 1997—Fumbled nine times and recovered three fumbles for minus 18 yards. 1998—Caught one pass for 22 yards, fumbled six times and recovered one fumble for minus four yards. 1999—Fumbled seven times and recovered four fumbles for minus 14 yards. 2000—Caught one pass for minus four yards, fumbled seven times and recovered four fumbles for minus 13 yards. 2001—Fumbled eight times and recovered four fumbles for minus eight yards.
SINGLE GAME HIGHS (regular season): Attempts—50 (November 18, 2001, vs. Green Bay); completions—29 (November 18, 2001, vs. Green Bay); yards—431 (December 23, 2001, vs. Buffalo); and touchdown passes—4 (November 28, 1999, vs. Carolina).
STATISTICAL PLATEAUS: 300-yard passing games: 1992 (1), 1995 (1), 1998 (1), 1999 (2), 2001 (2). Total: 7.
MISCELLANEOUS: Regular-season record as starting NFL quarterback: 62-75 (.453). ... Postseason record as starting NFL quarterback: 2-1 (.667).

Year	Team	G	GS	Att.	Cmp.	Pct.	Passing Yds.	TD	Int.	Avg.	Rat.	Att.	Rushing Yds.	Avg.	TD	TD	2pt.	Totals Pts.
1988	Indianapolis NFL	15	13	233	129	55.4	1619	8	12	6.95	67.2	46	139	3.0	3	3	0	18
1989	Indianapolis NFL	3	3	80	39	48.8	537	2	3	6.71	63.4	7	57	8.1	1	1	0	6
1990	Tampa Bay NFL	7	3	83	42	50.6	464	1	6	5.59	41.4	13	71	5.5	1	1	0	6
1991	Tampa Bay NFL	6	3	104	53	51.0	557	4	8	5.36	47.6	18	79	4.4	0	0	0	0
—	Phoenix NFL	3	2	50	25	50.0	289	1	2	5.78	57.8	8	32	4.0	0	0	0	0
1992	Phoenix NFL	15	13	413	245	59.3	2832	15	15	6.86	77.1	36	149	4.1	1	1	0	6
1993	Phoenix NFL	4	2	103	52	50.5	471	3	2	4.57	64.8	3	2	0.7	0	0	0	0

– 69 –

				PASSING						RUSHING				TOTALS		
Year Team	G	GS	Att.	Cmp.	Pct.	Yds.	TD	Int.	Avg.	Rat.	Att.	Yds.	Avg.	TD	TD	2pt.	Pts.
1994—L.A. Rams NFL	12	6	176	108	61.4	1352	7	2	7.68	93.8	18	61	3.4	1	1	0	6
1995—Houston NFL	13	13	356	225	63.2	2460	17	10	6.91	87.8	28	58	2.1	2	2	1	14
1996—Houston NFL	12	12	320	184	57.5	2099	16	11	6.56	79.7	28	113	4.0	0	0	0	0
1997—Atlanta NFL	14	14	342	202	59.1	2692	20	7	7.87	95.1	43	158	3.7	0	0	0	0
1998—Atlanta NFL	14	14	327	190	58.1	3154	25	12	*9.65	100.9	36	121	3.4	2	2	0	12
1999—Atlanta NFL	12	12	307	174	56.7	2339	16	11	7.62	83.5	16	57	3.6	1	1	0	6
2000—Atlanta NFL	14	13	331	192	58.0	2236	10	12	6.76	73.5	21	60	2.9	0	0	0	0
2001—Atlanta NFL	14	14	365	223	61.1	2847	16	14	7.80	84.1	25	84	3.4	0	0	0	0
Pro totals (14 years)	158	137	3590	2083	58.0	25948	161	127	7.23	80.8	346	1241	3.6	12	12	1	74

CHANOINE, ROGER   OT   BROWNS

PERSONAL: Born August 11, 1976, in Linden, N.J. ... 6-4/295. ... Full name: Roger Chanoine Jr. ... Name pronounced SHAN-wah.
HIGH SCHOOL: Linden (N.J.).
COLLEGE: Temple.
TRANSACTIONS/CAREER NOTES: Signed as non-drafted free agent by St. Louis Rams (April 20, 1998). ... On injured reserve with ankle injury (August 25, 1998-entire season). ... Released by Rams (August 30, 1999). ... Signed by Cleveland Browns to practice squad (September 7, 1999). ... Activated (December 8, 1999). ... Granted free agency (March 1, 2002). ... Re-signed by Browns (April 20, 2002).
PLAYING EXPERIENCE: Cleveland NFL, 1999-2001. ... Games/Games started: 1999 (1/0), 2000 (7/0), 2001 (16/16). Total: 24/16.
PRO STATISTICS: 2000—Recovered one fumble.

CHAPMAN, DOUG   RB   VIKINGS

PERSONAL: Born August 22, 1977, in Chesterfield, Va. ... 5-10/213.
HIGH SCHOOL: Lloyd C. Bird (Chesterfield, Va.).
COLLEGE: Marshall.
TRANSACTIONS/CAREER NOTES: Selected by Minnesota Vikings in third round (88th pick overall) of 2000 NFL draft. ... Signed by Vikings (July 23, 2000). ... Inactive for all 16 games (2000).
CHAMPIONSHIP GAME EXPERIENCE: Member of Vikings for NFC championship game (2000 season); inactive.
PRO STATISTICS: 2001—Recovered two fumbles.
SINGLE GAME HIGHS (regular season): Attempts—22 (October 21, 2001, vs. Green Bay); yards—90 (October 21, 2001, vs. Green Bay); and rushing touchdowns—0.

			RUSHING				RECEIVING			TOTALS			
Year Team	G	GS	Att.	Yds.	Avg.	TD	No.	Yds.	Avg.	TD	TD	2pt.	Pts.	Fum.
2000—Minnesota NFL							Did not play.						
2001—Minnesota NFL	16	3	63	195	3.1	0	16	135	8.4	1	1	0	6	1
Pro totals (1 years)	16	3	63	195	3.1	0	16	135	8.4	1	1	0	6	1

CHAPMAN, LAMAR   DB   BROWNS

PERSONAL: Born November 6, 1976, in Liberal, Kan. ... 6-0/186.
HIGH SCHOOL: Liberal (Kan.).
COLLEGE: Kansas State.
TRANSACTIONS/CAREER NOTES: Selected by Cleveland Browns in fifth round (146th pick overall) of 2000 NFL draft. ... Signed by Browns (June 16, 2000). ... On injured reserve with knee injury (September 20, 2001-remainder of season).
HONORS: Named free safety on THE SPORTING NEWS college All-America second team (1999).
PRO STATISTICS: 2000—Returned one punt for five yards and fumbled once. 2001—Returned one punt for one yard.

			INTERCEPTIONS			
Year Team	G	GS	No.	Yds.	Avg.	TD
2000—Cleveland NFL	7	0	1	0	0.0	0
2001—Cleveland NFL	1	0	0	0	0.0	0
Pro totals (2 years)	8	0	1	0	0.0	0

CHARLTON, IKE   CB   SEAHAWKS

PERSONAL: Born October 6, 1977, in Orlando, Fla. ... 5-11/204. ... Full name: Isaac C. Charlton IV.
HIGH SCHOOL: Dr. Phillips (Orlando, Fla.).
COLLEGE: Virginia Tech.
TRANSACTIONS/CAREER NOTES: Selected after junior season by Seattle Seahawks in second round (52nd pick overall) of 2000 NFL draft. ... Signed by Seahawks (July 20, 2000).
PLAYING EXPERIENCE: Seattle NFL, 2000 and 2001. ... Games/Games started: 2000 (16/0), 2001 (15/1). Total: 31/1.
PRO STATISTICS: 2001—Intercepted two passes for 43 yards and a touchdown and credited with one sack.

CHASE, MARTIN   DT   SAINTS

PERSONAL: Born December 19, 1974, in Lawton, Okla. ... 6-2/310. ... Full name: Cecil Martin Chase.
HIGH SCHOOL: Eisenhower (Lawton, Okla.).
COLLEGE: Oklahoma.

TRANSACTIONS/CAREER NOTES: Selected by Baltimore Ravens in fifth round (124th pick overall) of 1998 NFL draft. ... Signed by Ravens (July 17, 1998). ... On injured reserve with ankle injury (August 25, 1998-entire season). ... Assigned by Ravens to Frankfurt Galaxy in 2000 NFL Europe enhancement allocation program (February 18, 2000). ... Claimed on waivers by New Orleans Saints (August 28, 2000). ... Granted free agency (March 2, 2001). ... Re-signed by Saints (April 16, 2001).
PLAYING EXPERIENCE: Baltimore NFL, 1999; New Orleans NFL, 2000 and 2001. ... Games/Games started: 1999 (3/0), 2000 (9/0), 2001 (16/3). Total: 28/3.
PRO STATISTICS: 2001—Credited with one sack.

CHATHAM, MATT   LB   PATRIOTS

PERSONAL: Born June 28, 1977, in Sioux City, Iowa. ... 6-4/250.
HIGH SCHOOL: Sioux City (Iowa).
COLLEGE: South Dakota.
TRANSACTIONS/CAREER NOTES: Signed as non-drafted free agent by St. Louis Rams (April 26, 1999). ... Released by Rams (June 26, 1999). ... Signed by Rams (February 11, 2000). ... Claimed on waivers by New England Patriots (August 28, 2000). ... Released by Patriots (September 2, 2001). ... Re-signed by Patriots to practice squad (September 4, 2001). ... Activated (September 22, 2001). ... Released by Patriots (September 25, 2001). ... Re-signed by Patriots to practice squad (September 26, 2001). ... Activated (October 3, 2001).
PLAYING EXPERIENCE: New England NFL, 2000 and 2001. ... Games/Games started: 2000 (6/0), 2001 (11/0). Total: 17/0.
CHAMPIONSHIP GAME EXPERIENCE: Played in AFC championship game (2001 season). ... Member of Super Bowl championship team (2001 season).

CHAVOUS, COREY   CB   VIKINGS

PERSONAL: Born January 15, 1976, in Petticoat Junction, S.C. ... 6-1/206. ... Cousin of Fred Vinson, cornerback, Carolina Panthers. ... Name pronounced CHAY-vus.
HIGH SCHOOL: Silver Bluff (Aiken, S.C.).
COLLEGE: Vanderbilt.
TRANSACTIONS/CAREER NOTES: Selected by Arizona Cardinals in second round (33rd pick overall) of 1998 NFL draft. ... Signed by Cardinals (July 23, 1998). ... Granted free agency (March 2, 2001). ... Re-signed by Cardinals (July 13, 2001). ... Granted unconditional free agency (March 1, 2002). ... Signed by Minnesota Vikings (March 22, 2002).

			INTERCEPTIONS			
Year Team	G	GS	No.	Yds.	Avg.	TD
1998—Arizona NFL	16	5	2	0	0.0	0
1999—Arizona NFL	15	4	1	1	1.0	0
2000—Arizona NFL	16	1	1	0	0.0	0
2001—Arizona NFL	14	14	1	0	0.0	0
Pro totals (4 years)	61	24	5	1	0.2	0

CHERRY, Je'ROD   S   PATRIOTS

PERSONAL: Born May 30, 1973, in Charlotte. ... 6-1/205. ... Full name: Je'Rod L. Cherry. ... Name pronounced juh-ROD.
HIGH SCHOOL: Berkeley (Calif.).
COLLEGE: California (degree in political science, 1995).
TRANSACTIONS/CAREER NOTES: Selected by New Orleans Saints in second round (40th pick overall) of 1996 NFL draft. ... Signed by Saints (July 3, 1996). ... Granted free agency (February 12, 1999). ... Re-signed by Saints (July 21, 1999). ... Granted unconditional free agency (February 11, 2000). ... Signed by Oakland Raiders (February 19, 2000). ... Released by Raiders (August 27, 2000). ... Signed by Philadelphia Eagles (September 20, 2000). ... Granted unconditional free agency (March 2, 2001). ... Signed by New England Patriots (July 25, 2001).
PLAYING EXPERIENCE: New Orleans NFL, 1996-1999; Philadelphia NFL, 2000; New England NFL, 2001. ... Games/Games started: 1996 (13/0), 1997 (16/0), 1998 (14/0), 1999 (16/0), 2000 (13/0), 2001 (16/0). Total: 88/0.
CHAMPIONSHIP GAME EXPERIENCE: Played in AFC championship game (2001 season). ... Member of Super Bowl championship team (2001 season).
PRO STATISTICS: 1996—Recovered one fumble. 1998—Credited with two sacks. 2000—Recovered one fumble.

CHESTER, LARRY   DT   DOLPHINS

PERSONAL: Born October 17, 1975, in Hammond, La. ... 6-2/310.
HIGH SCHOOL: Hammond (La.).
JUNIOR COLLEGE: Southwest Mississippi Junior College.
COLLEGE: Temple.
TRANSACTIONS/CAREER NOTES: Signed as non-drafted free agent by Indianapolis Colts (April 24, 1998). ... Released by Colts (August 31, 1998). ... Re-signed by Colts to practice squad (September 2, 1998). ... Activated (September 11, 1998). ... Granted free agency (March 2, 2001). ... Signed by Carolina Panthers (May 15, 2001). ... Granted unconditional free agency (March 1, 2002). ... Signed by Miami Dolphins (March 5, 2002).
PRO STATISTICS: 1999—Recovered one fumble. 2000—Recovered one fumble. 2001—Recovered one fumble.

Year Team	G	GS	SACKS
1998—Indianapolis NFL	14	2	3.0
1999—Indianapolis NFL	16	8	1.0
2000—Indianapolis NFL	16	0	2.5
2001—Carolina NFL	11	5	0.5
Pro totals (4 years)	57	15	7.0

CHEVRIER, RANDY   DT   BENGALS

PERSONAL: Born June 6, 1976, in St. Lenonard, Quebec. ... 6-2/291. ... Full name: Randy Robert Chevrier.
HIGH SCHOOL: MacDonald (Montreal).
JUNIOR COLLEGE: Vanier (Montreal).
COLLEGE: McGill (Quebec).
TRANSACTIONS/CAREER NOTES: Selected by Jacksonville Jaguars in seventh round (241st pick overall) of 2001 NFL draft. ... Signed by Jaguars (June 17, 2001). ... Claimed on waivers by Dallas Cowboys (September 3, 2001). ... Released by Cowboys (November 13, 2001). ... Signed by Cincinnati Bengals to practice squad (December 4, 2001). ... Activated (December 7, 2001).
PRO STATISTICS: 2001—Fumbled once for minus 26 yards.

Year Team	G	GS	SACKS
2001—Dallas NFL	8	0	0.0
—Cincinnati NFL	5	0	0.0
Pro totals (1 years)	13	0	0.0

CHIAVERINI, DARRIN   WR   COWBOYS

PERSONAL: Born October 12, 1977, in Orange County, Calif. ... 6-2/210. ... Name pronounced SHEVV-er-re-nee.
HIGH SCHOOL: Corona (Calif.).
COLLEGE: Colorado.
TRANSACTIONS/CAREER NOTES: Selected by Cleveland Browns in fifth round (148th pick overall) of 1999 NFL draft. ... Signed by Browns (July 22, 1999). ... Traded by Browns to Dallas Cowboys for conditional seventh-round pick (August 28, 2001). ... Granted free agency (March 1, 2002). ... Re-signed by Cowboys (April 26, 2002).
PRO STATISTICS: 1999—Returned two kickoffs for 35 yards and recovered one fumble. 2001—Rushed once for three yards.
SINGLE GAME HIGHS (regular season): Receptions—10 (December 19, 1999, vs. Jacksonville); yards—108 (December 19, 1999, vs. Jacksonville); and touchdown receptions—1 (December 30, 2001, vs. San Francisco).
STATISTICAL PLATEAUS: 100-yard receiving games: 1999 (1).

			RECEIVING				TOTALS			
Year Team	G	GS	No.	Yds.	Avg.	TD	TD	2pt.	Pts.	Fum.
1999—Cleveland NFL	16	8	44	487	11.1	4	4	0	24	0
2000—Cleveland NFL	10	2	8	68	8.5	1	1	0	6	1
2001—Dallas NFL	16	0	10	107	10.7	2	2	0	12	0
Pro totals (3 years)	42	10	62	662	10.7	7	7	0	42	1

CHREBET, WAYNE   WR   JETS

PERSONAL: Born August 14, 1973, in Garfield, N.J. ... 5-10/188. ... Name pronounced kra-BET.
HIGH SCHOOL: Garfield (N.J.).
COLLEGE: Hofstra.
TRANSACTIONS/CAREER NOTES: Signed as non-drafted free agent by New York Jets (April 25, 1995).
CHAMPIONSHIP GAME EXPERIENCE: Played in AFC championship game (1998 season).
PRO STATISTICS: 1995—Rushed once for one yard. 1996—Recovered two fumbles. 1997—Returned one kickoff for five yards. 2000—Rushed three times for minus three yards and recovered one fumble.
SINGLE GAME HIGHS (regular season): Receptions—12 (October 13, 1996, vs. Jacksonville); yards—162 (October 13, 1996, vs. Jacksonville); and touchdown receptions—2 (October 23, 2000, vs. Miami).
STATISTICAL PLATEAUS: 100-yard receiving games: 1996 (1), 1997 (1), 1998 (5), 1999 (1), 2000 (2). Total: 10.

			RECEIVING				PUNT RETURNS				TOTALS			
Year Team	G	GS	No.	Yds.	Avg.	TD	No.	Yds.	Avg.	TD	TD	2pt.	Pts.	Fum.
1995—New York Jets NFL	16	16	66	726	11.0	4	0	0	0.0	0	4	0	24	1
1996—New York Jets NFL	16	9	84	909	10.8	3	28	139	5.0	0	3	0	18	5
1997—New York Jets NFL	16	1	58	799	13.8	3	0	0	0.0	0	3	0	18	0
1998—New York Jets NFL	16	15	75	1083	14.4	8	0	0	0.0	0	8	0	48	0
1999—New York Jets NFL	11	11	48	631	13.1	3	0	0	0.0	0	3	0	18	0
2000—New York Jets NFL	16	16	69	937	13.6	8	0	0	0.0	0	8	0	48	0
2001—New York Jets NFL	15	15	56	750	13.4	1	0	0	0.0	0	1	0	6	0
Pro totals (7 years)	106	83	456	5835	12.8	30	28	139	5.0	0	30	0	180	6

CHRISTIAN, BOB   FB   FALCONS

PERSONAL: Born November 14, 1968, in St. Louis. ... 5-11/232. ... Full name: Robert Douglas Christian.
HIGH SCHOOL: McCluer North (Florissant, Mo.).
COLLEGE: Northwestern.
TRANSACTIONS/CAREER NOTES: Selected by Atlanta Falcons in 12th round (310th pick overall) of 1991 NFL draft. ... Signed by Falcons (July 18, 1991). ... Released by Falcons (August 20, 1991). ... Selected by London Monarchs in 16th round (175th pick overall) of 1992 World League draft. ... Signed by San Diego Chargers (July 10, 1992). ... Released by Chargers (August 25, 1992). ... Signed by Chicago Bears to practice squad (September 8, 1992). ... Activated (December 18, 1992). ... On injured reserve with knee injury (December 2, 1994-remainder of season). ... Selected by Carolina Panthers from Bears in NFL expansion draft (February 15, 1995). ... Granted free agency (February 16, 1996). ... Re-signed by Panthers (July 19, 1996). ... On injured reserve with shoulder injury (August 25, 1996-entire season). ... Granted unconditional free agency (February 14, 1997). ... Signed by Falcons (March 6, 1997). ... On injured reserve with knee injury (December 15, 1998-remainder of season).
PRO STATISTICS: 1995—Recovered one fumble. 1997—Recovered one fumble. 1998—Recovered two fumbles. 2000—Recovered one fumble for 10 yards.
SINGLE GAME HIGHS (regular season): Attempts—10 (December 30, 2001, vs. Miami); yards—78 (November 25, 2001, vs. Carolina); and rushing touchdowns—2 (December 26, 1999, vs. Arizona).

Year Team	G	GS	RUSHING Att.	Yds.	Avg.	TD	RECEIVING No.	Yds.	Avg.	TD	TOTALS TD	2pt.	Pts.	Fum.
1992—Chicago NFL	2	0	0	0	0.0	0	0	0	0.0	0	0	0	0	0
1993—Chicago NFL	14	1	8	19	2.4	0	16	160	10.0	0	0	0	0	0
1994—Chicago NFL	12	0	7	29	4.1	0	2	30	15.0	0	0	0	0	0
1995—Carolina NFL	14	12	41	158	3.9	0	29	255	8.8	1	1	1	8	1
1996—Carolina NFL								Did not play.						
1997—Atlanta NFL	16	12	7	8	1.1	0	22	154	7.0	1	1	0	6	3
1998—Atlanta NFL	14	11	8	21	2.6	2	19	214	11.3	1	3	0	18	1
1999—Atlanta NFL	16	14	38	174	4.6	5	40	354	8.9	2	7	0	42	1
2000—Atlanta NFL	16	14	9	19	2.1	0	44	315	7.2	0	0	0	0	0
2001—Atlanta NFL	16	8	44	284	6.5	2	45	392	8.7	2	4	0	24	0
Pro totals (9 years)	120	72	162	712	4.4	9	217	1874	8.6	7	16	1	98	6

CHRISTIE, STEVE   K   CHARGERS

PERSONAL: Born November 13, 1967, in Oakville, Ont. ... 6-0/195. ... Full name: Geoffrey Stephen Christie.
HIGH SCHOOL: Trafalgar (Oakville, Ont.).
COLLEGE: William & Mary.
TRANSACTIONS/CAREER NOTES: Signed as non-drafted free agent by Tampa Bay Buccaneers (May 8, 1990). ... Granted unconditional free agency (February 1, 1992). ... Signed by Buffalo Bills (February 5, 1992). ... Granted unconditional free agency (March 2, 2001). ... Re-signed by Bills (April 22, 2001). ... On injured reserve with groin injury (September 8-October 5, 2001). ... Released by Bills (October 3, 2001). ... Signed by San Diego Chargers (November 29, 2001). ... Granted unconditional free agency (March 1, 2002). ... Re-signed by Chargers (March 29, 2002).
CHAMPIONSHIP GAME EXPERIENCE: Played in AFC championship game (1992 and 1993 seasons). ... Played in Super Bowl XXVII (1992 season) and Super Bowl XXVIII (1993 season).
POST SEASON RECORDS: Holds Super Bowl single-game record for longest field goal—54 yards (January 30, 1994, vs. Dallas). ... Shares NFL postseason single-game record for most field goals made—5; and most field goals attempted—6 (January 17, 1993, at Miami).
PRO STATISTICS: 1994—Recovered one fumble. 1999—Recovered one fumble.

Year Team	G	XPM	XPA	KICKING FGM	FGA	Lg.	50+	Pts.
1990—Tampa Bay NFL	16	27	27	23	27	54	2-2	96
1991—Tampa Bay NFL	16	22	22	15	20	49	0-0	67
1992—Buffalo NFL	16	§43	§44	24	30	†54	3-5	115
1993—Buffalo NFL	16	36	37	23	32	*59	1-6	105
1994—Buffalo NFL	16	§38	§38	24	28	52	2-2	110
1995—Buffalo NFL	16	33	35	31	40	51	2-5	126
1996—Buffalo NFL	16	33	33	24	29	48	0-1	105
1997—Buffalo NFL	16	21	21	24	30	†55	1-2	93
1998—Buffalo NFL	16	41	41	33	*41	52	1-3	§140
1999—Buffalo NFL	16	33	33	25	34	52	3-3	108
2000—Buffalo NFL	16	31	31	26	35	48	0-1	109
2001—San Diego NFL	5	6	6	9	11	41	0-0	33
Pro totals (12 years)	181	364	368	281	357	59	15-30	1207

CHRISTY, JEFF   C   BUCCANEERS

PERSONAL: Born February 3, 1969, in Natrona Heights, Pa. ... 6-2/285. ... Full name: Jeffrey Allen Christy. ... Brother of Greg Christy, offensive tackle with Buffalo Bills (1985).
HIGH SCHOOL: Freeport (Pa.) Area.
COLLEGE: Pittsburgh.
TRANSACTIONS/CAREER NOTES: Selected by Phoenix Cardinals in fourth round (91st pick overall) of 1992 NFL draft. ... Signed by Cardinals (July 21, 1992). ... Released by Cardinals (August 31, 1992). ... Signed by Minnesota Vikings (March 16, 1993). ... On injured reserve with ankle injury (November 26, 1997-remainder of season). ... Granted unconditional free agency (February 11, 2000). ... Signed by Tampa Bay Buccaneers (February 15, 2000).
PLAYING EXPERIENCE: Minnesota NFL, 1993-1999; Tampa Bay NFL, 2000 and 2001. ... Games/Games started: 1993 (9/0), 1994 (16/16), 1995 (16/16), 1996 (16/16), 1997 (12/12), 1998 (16/16), 1999 (16/16), 2000 (16/16), 2001 (15/15). Total: 132/123.
CHAMPIONSHIP GAME EXPERIENCE: Played in NFC championship game (1998 season).
HONORS: Played in Pro Bowl (1998-2000 seasons).

CHUKWURAH, PATRICK   LB   VIKINGS

PERSONAL: Born March 1, 1979, in Nigeria. ... 6-1/238.
HIGH SCHOOL: MacArthur (Texas).
COLLEGE: Wyoming.
TRANSACTIONS/CAREER NOTES: Selected by Minnesota Vikings in fifth round (157th pick overall) of 2001 NFL draft. ... Signed by Vikings (July 24, 2001).

Year Team	G	GS	SACKS
2001—Minnesota NFL	16	3	2.5

CLAIBORNE, CHRIS   LB   LIONS

PERSONAL: Born July 26, 1978, in Riverdale, Calif. ... 6-3/255.
HIGH SCHOOL: John W. North (Riverside, Calif.).
COLLEGE: Southern California.

TRANSACTIONS/CAREER NOTES: Selected after junior season by Detroit Lions in first round (ninth pick overall) of 1999 NFL draft. ... Signed by Lions (July 24, 1999).
HONORS: Butkus Award winner (1998). ... Named inside linebacker on THE SPORTING NEWS college All-America first team (1998).
PRO STATISTICS: 1999—Recovered three fumbles for 27 yards. 2000—Intercepted one pass for one yard. 2001—Intercepted two passes for 11 yards and recovered one fumble.

Year Team	G	GS	SACKS
1999—Detroit NFL	15	13	1.5
2000—Detroit NFL	16	14	0.5
2001—Detroit NFL	16	16	4.0
Pro totals (3 years)	47	43	6.0

CLANCY, KENDRICK   NT   STEELERS

PERSONAL: Born September 17, 1978, in Tuscaloosa, Ala. ... 6-1/289.
HIGH SCHOOL: Holt (Tuscaloosa, Ala.).
JUNIOR COLLEGE: East Central Community College (Miss.).
COLLEGE: Mississippi.
TRANSACTIONS/CAREER NOTES: Selected by Pittsburgh Steelers in third round (72nd pick overall) of 2000 NFL draft. ... Signed by Steelers (July 16, 2000).
PLAYING EXPERIENCE: Pittsburgh NFL, 2000 and 2001. ... Games/Games started: 2000 (9/0), 2001 (16/6). Total: 25/6.
CHAMPIONSHIP GAME EXPERIENCE: Played in AFC championship game (2001 season).
HONORS: Named defensive tackle on THE SPORTING NEWS college All-America third team (1999).
PRO STATISTICS: 2001—Intercepted one pass for three yards.

CLARIDGE, TRAVIS   OT/G   FALCONS

PERSONAL: Born March 23, 1978, in Detroit. ... 6-5/300.
HIGH SCHOOL: Fort Vancouver (Vancouver, Wash.).
COLLEGE: Southern California.
TRANSACTIONS/CAREER NOTES: Selected by Atlanta Falcons in second round (37th pick overall) of 2000 NFL draft. ... Signed by Falcons (May 16, 2000).
PLAYING EXPERIENCE: Atlanta NFL, 2000 and 2001. ... Games/Games started: 2000 (16/16), 2001 (14/11). Total: 30/27.
HONORS: Named guard on THE SPORTING NEWS college All-America third team (1999).

CLARK, DANNY   LB   JAGUARS

PERSONAL: Born May 9, 1977, in Blue Island, Ill. ... 6-2/240. ... Full name: Daniel Clark IV.
HIGH SCHOOL: Hillcrest (Ill.).
COLLEGE: Illinois (degree in speech communications).
TRANSACTIONS/CAREER NOTES: Selected by Jacksonville Jaguars in seventh round (245th pick overall) of 2000 NFL draft. ... Signed by Jaguars (June 6, 2000).
PLAYING EXPERIENCE: Jacksonville NFL, 2000 and 2001. ... Games/Games started: 2000 (16/0), 2001 (13/3). Total: 29/3.
PRO STATISTICS: 2000—Recovered two fumbles for 44 yards.

CLARK, DARIUS   S   BRONCOS

PERSONAL: Born April 13, 1977, in Tampa, Fla. ... 5-10/210.
HIGH SCHOOL: Hillsborough (Fla.).
COLLEGE: Duke.
TRANSACTIONS/CAREER NOTES: Signed as non-drafted free agent by Denver Broncos (April 17, 2000). ... Rreleased by Broncos (August 27, 2000). ... Re-signed by Broncos to practice squad (August 28, 2000). ... Activated (December 21, 2000). ... Released by Broncos (September 2, 2001). ... Re-signed by Broncos to practice squad (September 4, 2001). ... Activated (October 23, 2001). ... On injured reserve with knee injury (December 10, 2001-remainder of season).
PLAYING EXPERIENCE: Denver NFL, 2001 ... Games/Games started: 2001 (7/0).

CLARK, DESMOND   TE   BRONCOS

PERSONAL: Born April 20, 1977, in Bartow, Fla. ... 6-3/255. ... Full name: Desmond Darice Clark.
HIGH SCHOOL: Kathleen (Lakeland, Fla.).
COLLEGE: Wake Forest.
TRANSACTIONS/CAREER NOTES: Selected by Denver Broncos in sixth round (179th pick overall) of 1999 NFL draft. ... Signed by Broncos (June 14, 1999). ... Granted free agency (March 1, 2002).
PRO STATISTICS: 2001—Returned one kickoff for 11 yards.
SINGLE GAME HIGHS (regular season): Receptions—7 (November 5, 2001, vs. Oakland); yards—94 (October 28, 2001, vs. New England); and touchdown receptions—1 (January 6, 2002, vs. Indianapolis).

			RECEIVING				TOTALS		
Year Team	G	GS	No.	Yds.	Avg.	TD	TD	2pt.	Pts.	Fum.
1999—Denver NFL	9	0	1	5	5.0	0	0	0	0	0
2000—Denver NFL	16	2	27	339	12.6	3	3	0	18	0
2001—Denver NFL	16	4	51	566	11.1	6	6	0	36	3
Pro totals (3 years)	41	6	79	910	11.5	9	9	0	54	3

CLARKE, PHIL   LB

PERSONAL: Born January 19, 1977, in Miami. ... 6-0/241.
HIGH SCHOOL: South Miami.
COLLEGE: Pittsburgh.
TRANSACTIONS/CAREER NOTES: Signed as non-drafted free agent by New Orleans Saints (May 17, 1999). ... Released by Saints (September 5, 1999). ... Re-signed by Saints to practice squad (September 6, 1999). ... Activated (November 10, 1999). ... Released by Saints (September 2, 2001). ... Re-signed by Saints (September 7, 2001). ... On injured reserve with knee injury (December 19, 2001-remainder of season). ... Granted free agency (March 1, 2002).
PLAYING EXPERIENCE: New Orleans NFL, 1999-2001. ... Games/Games started: 1999 (8/3), 2000 (14/4), 2001 (13/0). Total: 35/7.
PRO STATISTICS: 2000—Credited with one sack and recovered one fumble.

CLAYBROOKS, FELIPE   DL   BROWNS

PERSONAL: Born January 22, 1978, in Decatur, Ga. ... 6-4/260.
HIGH SCHOOL: Decatur (Ga.).
COLLEGE: Georgia Tech.
TRANSACTIONS/CAREER NOTES: Signed as non-drafted free agent by Arizona Cardinals (April 23, 2001). ... Released by Cardinals (August 27, 2001). ... Signed by Cleveland Browns to practice squad (November 7, 2001). ... Activated (December 11, 2001).
PLAYING EXPERIENCE: Cleveland NFL, 2001. ... Games/Games started: 2001 (4/0).

CLAYTON, CAREY   C   JAGUARS

PERSONAL: Born August 31, 1977, in Dyersburg, Tenn. ... 6-3/285.
HIGH SCHOOL: Carroll (Southlake, Texas).
COLLEGE: Texas-El Paso (degree in biology.).
TRANSACTIONS/CAREER NOTES: Signed as non-drafted free agent by San Diego Chargers (May 16, 2001). ... Released by Chargers (October 30, 2001). ... Re-signed by Chargers to practice squad (November 1, 2001). ... Released by Chargers (November 29, 2001). ... Signed by San Francisco 49ers to practice squad (December 5, 2001). ... Released by 49ers (December 31, 2001). ... Signed by Jacksonville Jaguars (January 17, 2002).
PLAYING EXPERIENCE: San Diego NFL, 2001. ... Games/Games started: 2001 (1/0).

CLEELAND, CAM   TE   PATRIOTS

PERSONAL: Born August 15, 1975, in Sedro Woolley, Wash. ... 6-4/272. ... Full name: Cameron Ross Cleeland. ... Nephew of Phil Misley, pitcher in Milwaukee Braves organization (1956-58).
HIGH SCHOOL: Sedro Woolley (Wash.).
COLLEGE: Washington.
TRANSACTIONS/CAREER NOTES: Selected by New Orleans Saints in second round (40th pick overall) of 1998 NFL draft. ... Signed by Saints (June 9, 1998). ... On injured reserve with Achilles' tendon injury (August 22, 2000-entire season). ... Granted free agency (March 2, 2001). ... Re-signed by Saints (March 19, 2001). ... On injured reserve with Achilles' tendon injury (December 26, 2001-remainder of season). ... Granted unconditional free agency (March 1, 2002). ... Signed by New England Patriots (March 28, 2002).
PRO STATISTICS: 1998—Recovered two fumbles for seven yards.
SINGLE GAME HIGHS (regular season): Receptions—10 (December 27, 1998, vs. Buffalo); yards—112 (December 27, 1998, vs. Buffalo); and touchdown receptions—2 (October 14, 2001, vs. Carolina).
STATISTICAL PLATEAUS: 100-yard receiving games: 1998 (1).

				RECEIVING			TOTALS			
Year Team	G	GS	No.	Yds.	Avg.	TD	TD	2pt.	Pts.	Fum.
1998—New Orleans NFL	16	16	54	684	12.7	6	6	0	36	1
1999—New Orleans NFL	11	8	26	325	12.5	1	1	†1	8	1
2000—New Orleans NFL						Did not play.				
2001—New Orleans NFL	9	7	13	138	10.6	4	4	0	24	1
Pro totals (3 years)	36	31	93	1147	12.3	11	11	1	68	3

CLEMENT, ANTHONY   OT   SEAHAWKS

PERSONAL: Born April 10, 1976, in Lafayette, La. ... 6-8/351.
HIGH SCHOOL: Cecilia (La.).
COLLEGE: Southwestern Louisiana.
TRANSACTIONS/CAREER NOTES: Selected by Arizona Cardinals in second round (36th pick overall) of 1998 NFL draft. ... Signed by Cardinals (June 16, 1998). ... On injured reserve with back injury (November 17, 1998-remainder of season). ... Granted free agency (March 2, 2001). ... Re-signed by Cardinals (May 7, 2001). ... Granted unconditional free agency (March 1, 2002). ... Signed by Seattle Seahawks (March 2, 2002).
PLAYING EXPERIENCE: Arizona NFL, 1998-2001. ... Games/Games started: 1998 (1/0), 1999 (16/14), 2000 (16/16), 2001 (16/16). Total: 49/46.
PRO STATISTICS: 2000—Recovered one fumble.

CLEMENTS, NATE   CB   BILLS

PERSONAL: Born December 12, 1979, in Shaker Heights, Ohio. ... 5-11/204.
HIGH SCHOOL: Shaker Heights (Ohio).
COLLEGE: Ohio State.
TRANSACTIONS/CAREER NOTES: Selected after junior season by Buffalo Bills in first round (21st pick overall) of 2001 NFL draft. ... Signed by Bills (July 28, 2001).
PRO STATISTICS: 2001—Returned four punts for 81 yards and one touchdown and credited with one sack.

			INTERCEPTIONS			KICKOFF RETURNS			TOTALS			
Year Team	G	GS	No.	Yds.	Avg.	TD	No.	Yds.	Avg.	TD	TD	2pt.	Pts.	Fum.
2001—Buffalo NFL	16	11	3	48	16.0	1	30	628	20.9	0	2	0	12	1

CLEMONS, CHARLIE — LB — SAINTS

PERSONAL: Born July 4, 1972, in Griffin, Ga. ... 6-2/250. ... Full name: Charlie Fitzgerald Clemons.
HIGH SCHOOL: Griffin (Ga.).
JUNIOR COLLEGE: Northeast Oklahoma Junior College.
COLLEGE: Georgia (degree in recreation and leisure studies, 1993).
TRANSACTIONS/CAREER NOTES: Signed by Winnipeg Blue Bombers of CFL (May 1994). ... Transferred to Ottawa Rough Riders of CFL (August 1995). ... Transferred back to Blue Bombers (January 1996). ... Signed as non-drafted free agent by St. Louis Rams (February 19, 1997). ... On injured reserve with hamstring injury (November 24, 1997-remainder of season). ... Granted free agency (February 11, 2000). ... Tendered offer sheet by New Orleans Saints (February 16, 2000). ... Rams declined to match offer (February 22, 2000). ... On injured reserve with Achilles' tendon injury (October 2, 2000-remainder of season).
CHAMPIONSHIP GAME EXPERIENCE: Played in NFC championship game (1999 season). ... Member of Super Bowl championship team (1999 season).
PRO STATISTICS: CFL: 1994—Recovered one fumble. 1995—Returned one kickoff for 10 yards. NFL: 1998—Returned one kickoff for no yards. 1999—Intercepted one pass for no yards and recovered one fumble. 2001—Intercepted one pass for three yards and recovered one fumble.

Year Team	G	GS	SACKS
1994—Winnipeg CFL	7	...	0.0
1995—Winnipeg CFL	6	...	3.0
—Ottawa CFL	7	...	3.0
1996—Winnipeg CFL	14	...	6.0
1997—St. Louis NFL	5	0	0.0
1998—St. Louis NFL	16	0	2.0
1999—St. Louis NFL	16	0	3.0
2000—New Orleans NFL	Did not play.		
2001—New Orleans NFL	16	15	13.5
CFL totals (3 years)	34	...	12.0
NFL totals (4 years)	53	15	18.5
Pro totals (7 years)	87	...	30.5

CLEMONS, DUANE — DE — CHIEFS

PERSONAL: Born May 23, 1974, in Riverside, Calif. ... 6-5/277.
HIGH SCHOOL: John W. North (Riverside, Calif.).
COLLEGE: California (degree in ethnic studies, 1993).
TRANSACTIONS/CAREER NOTES: Selected after junior season by Minnesota Vikings in first round (16th pick overall) of 1996 NFL draft. ... Signed by Vikings (July 25, 1996). ... Granted unconditional free agency (February 11, 2000). ... Signed by Kansas City Chiefs (March 24, 2000).
CHAMPIONSHIP GAME EXPERIENCE: Played in NFC championship game (1998 season).
PRO STATISTICS: 1996—Recovered one fumble for eight yards. 1997—Recovered one fumble. 1999—Recovered four fumbles. 2000—Recovered one fumble. 2001—Recovered one fumble.

Year Team	G	GS	SACKS
1996—Minnesota NFL	13	0	0.0
1997—Minnesota NFL	13	3	7.0
1998—Minnesota NFL	16	4	2.5
1999—Minnesota NFL	16	9	9.0
2000—Kansas City NFL	12	12	7.5
2001—Kansas City NFL	16	15	7.0
Pro totals (6 years)	86	43	33.0

CLIFTON, CHAD — OT — PACKERS

PERSONAL: Born June 26, 1976, in Martin, Tenn. ... 6-5/327. ... Full name: Jeffrey Chad Clifton.
HIGH SCHOOL: Westview (Martin, Tenn.).
COLLEGE: Tennessee.
TRANSACTIONS/CAREER NOTES: Selected by Green Bay Packers in second round (44th pick overall) of 2000 NFL draft. ... Signed by Packers (July 24, 2000).
PLAYING EXPERIENCE: Green Bay NFL, 2000 and 2001. ... Games/Games started: 2000 (13/10), 2001 (14/13). Total: 27/23.
HONORS: Named offensive tackle on THE SPORTING NEWS college All-America second team (1999).

CLOUD, MIKE — RB — CHIEFS

PERSONAL: Born July 1, 1975, in Charleston, S.C. ... 5-10/205. ... Full name: Michael Alexander Cloud.
HIGH SCHOOL: Portsmouth (R.I.).
COLLEGE: Boston College.
TRANSACTIONS/CAREER NOTES: Selected by Kansas City Chiefs in second round (54th pick overall) of 1999 NFL draft. ... Signed by Chiefs (July 30, 1999).
SINGLE GAME HIGHS (regular season): Attempts—11 (November 28, 1999, vs. Oakland); yards—58 (November 28, 1999, vs. Oakland); and rushing touchdowns—1 (November 25, 2001, vs. Seattle).

			RUSHING				RECEIVING				KICKOFF RETURNS				TOTALS		
Year Team	G	GS	Att.	Yds.	Avg.	TD	No.	Yds.	Avg.	TD	No.	Yds.	Avg.	TD	TD	2pt.	Pts.	Fum.
1999—Kansas City NFL	11	0	35	128	3.7	0	3	25	8.3	0	2	28	14.0	0	0	0	0	0
2000—Kansas City NFL	16	4	30	84	2.8	1	2	16	8.0	0	36	779	21.6	0	2	0	12	0
2001—Kansas City NFL	15	0	7	54	7.7	1	0	0	0.0	0	8	174	21.8	0	1	0	6	0
Pro totals (3 years)	42	4	72	266	3.7	2	5	41	8.2	0	46	981	21.3	0	3	0	18	0

COADY, RICH   S   RAMS

PERSONAL: Born January 26, 1976, in Dallas. ... 6-0/203. ... Full name: Richard Joseph Coady IV. ... Son of Rich Coady, tight end/center with Chicago Bears (1970-74).
HIGH SCHOOL: J.J. Pearce (Richardson, Texas).
COLLEGE: Texas A&M.
TRANSACTIONS/CAREER NOTES: Selected by St. Louis Rams in third round (68th pick overall) of 1999 NFL draft. ... Signed by Rams (July 16, 1999). ... On injured reserve with neck injury (December 13, 2000-remainder of season).
PLAYING EXPERIENCE: St. Louis NFL, 1999-2001. ... Games/Games started: 1999 (16/0), 2000 (12/2), 2001 (12/2). Total: 40/4.
CHAMPIONSHIP GAME EXPERIENCE: Played in NFC championship game (1999 season). ... Member of Super Bowl championship team (1999 season). ... Member of Rams for NFC championship game (2001 season); inactive. ... Member of Rams for Super Bowl XXXVI (2001 season); inactive.
PRO STATISTICS: 2001—Credited with one sack.

COAKLEY, DEXTER   LB   COWBOYS

PERSONAL: Born October 20, 1972, in Charleston, S.C. ... 5-10/230. ... Full name: William Dexter Coakley.
HIGH SCHOOL: Wando (Mt. Pleasant, S.C.), then Fork Union (Va.) Military Academy.
COLLEGE: Appalachian State (degree in communications and advertising.).
TRANSACTIONS/CAREER NOTES: Selected by Dallas Cowboys in third round (65th pick overall) of 1997 NFL draft. ... Signed by Cowboys (July 14, 1997). ... Granted free agency (February 11, 2000). ... Re-signed by Cowboys (April 28, 2000). ... Granted unconditional free agency (March 2, 2001). ... Re-signed by Cowboys (March 8, 2001).
HONORS: Played in Pro Bowl (1999 season).
PRO STATISTICS: 1997—Recovered one fumble for 16 yards and a touchdown. 1998—Recovered one fumble. 1999—Returned one kickoff for three yards. 2000—Rushed once for 26 yards and recovered one fumble for eight yards. 2001—Recovered one fumble.

			INTERCEPTIONS				SACKS
Year Team	G	GS	No.	Yds.	Avg.	TD	No.
1997—Dallas NFL	16	16	1	6	6.0	0	2.5
1998—Dallas NFL	16	16	1	18	18.0	0	2.0
1999—Dallas NFL	16	16	4	119	29.8	1	1.0
2000—Dallas NFL	16	16	0	0	0.0	0	0.0
2001—Dallas NFL	15	15	2	39	19.5	†2	0.0
Pro totals (5 years)	79	79	8	182	22.8	3	5.5

COCHRAN, ANTONIO   DT   SEAHAWKS

PERSONAL: Born June 21, 1976, in Montezuma, Ga. ... 6-4/290. ... Full name: Antonio Desez Cochran.
HIGH SCHOOL: Macon County (Montezuma, Ga.).
JUNIOR COLLEGE: Middle Georgia College.
COLLEGE: Georgia.
TRANSACTIONS/CAREER NOTES: Selected by Seattle Seahawks in fourth round (115th pick overall) of 1999 NFL draft. ... Signed by Seahawks (July 27, 1999). ... Granted free agency (March 1, 2002). ... Re-signed by Seahawks (May 2, 2002).
PLAYING EXPERIENCE: Seattle NFL, 1999-2001. ... Games/Games started: 1999 (4/0), 2000 (15/0), 2001 (16/2). Total: 35/2.
PRO STATISTICS: 2000—Credited with $1/2$ sack. 2001—Credited with $4 1/2$ sacks and recovered one fumble.

CODY, TAY   CB   CHARGERS

PERSONAL: Born October 6, 1977, in Blakely, Ga. ... 5-9/180.
HIGH SCHOOL: Earl County (Blakely, Ga.).
COLLEGE: Florida State.
TRANSACTIONS/CAREER NOTES: Selected by San Diego Chargers in third round (67th pick overall) of 2001 NFL draft. ... Signed by Chargers (July 24, 2001).
HONORS: Named cornerback on THE SPORTING NEWS college All-America first team (2000).

			INTERCEPTIONS			
Year Team	G	GS	No.	Yds.	Avg.	TD
2001—San Diego NFL	14	11	2	3	1.5	0

COGHILL, GEORGE   S   BRONCOS

PERSONAL: Born March 30, 1970, in Fredericksburg, Va. ... 6-0/210.
HIGH SCHOOL: James Madison (Vienna, Va.).
COLLEGE: Wake Forest.
TRANSACTIONS/CAREER NOTES: Signed as non-drafted free agent by New Orleans Saints (April 27, 1993). ... On injured reserve with knee injury (August 12, 1993-entire season). ... Released by Saints (August 22, 1994). ... Played for Scottish Claymores of World League (1995-97). ... Signed by Denver Broncos (July 16, 1997). ... Released by Broncos (August 24, 1997). ... Re-signed by Broncos to practice squad (August 25, 1997). ... Released by Broncos (January 26, 1998). ... Re-signed by Broncos (January 28, 1998).
PLAYING EXPERIENCE: Scottish W.L., 1995-1997; Denver NFL, 1998-2001. ... Games/Games started: 1995 (games played unavailable), 1996 (-), 1997 (-), 1998 (9/0), 1999 (13/5), 2000 (16/0), 2001 (16/0). Total NFL: 54/5.
CHAMPIONSHIP GAME EXPERIENCE: Played in AFC championship game (1998 season). ... Member of Super Bowl championship team (1998 season).
PRO STATISTICS: 1998—Intercepted one pass for 20 yards and returned three punts for 20 yards. 1999—Intercepted one pass for no yards and returned three punts for 25 yards. 2001—Intercepted one pass for no yards.

COHEN, DUSTIN — LB — RAMS

PERSONAL: Born December 22, 1976, in Cincinnati. ... 6-3/241. ... Full name: Dustin Will Cohen.
HIGH SCHOOL: Summit Country Day (Cincinnati).
COLLEGE: Miami of Ohio.
TRANSACTIONS/CAREER NOTES: Signed as non-drafted free agent by Buffalo Bills (April 28, 2000). ... Released by Bills (August 28, 2000). ... Signed by Chicago Bears to practice squad (September 13, 2000). ... Signed by St. Louis Rams off Bears practice squad (December 5, 2000). ... Released by Rams (September 2, 2001). ... Re-signed by Rams to practice sqaud (September 4, 2001). ... Activated (October 3, 2001). ... Granted free agency (March 1, 2002).
PLAYING EXPERIENCE: St. Louis NFL, 2001. ... Games/Games started: 2001(4/0).
CHAMPIONSHIP GAME EXPERIENCE: Played in NFC championship game (2001 season). ... Member of Rams for Super Bowl XXXVI (2001 season); inactive.

COLE, CHRIS — WR — BRONCOS

PERSONAL: Born November 12, 1977, in Orange, Texas. ... 6-0/195. ... Full name: Charles Christopher Cole.
HIGH SCHOOL: West Orange-Stark (Orange, Texas).
COLLEGE: Texas A&M.
TRANSACTIONS/CAREER NOTES: Selected by Denver Broncos in third round (70th pick overall) of 2000 NFL draft. ... Signed by Broncos (July 21, 2000).
SINGLE GAME HIGHS (regular season): Receptions—4 (December 2, 2001, vs. Miami); yards—43 (December 2, 2001, vs. Miami); and touchdown receptions—0.

			RECEIVING			KICKOFF RETURNS			TOTALS			
Year Team	G	GS	No.	Yds.	Avg.	TD	No.	Yds.	Avg.	TD	TD	2pt.	Pts.	Fum.
2000—Denver NFL	8	0	0	0	0.0	0	11	264	24.0	0	0	0	0	0
2001—Denver NFL	16	1	9	128	14.2	0	48	1127	23.5	0	0	0	0	2
Pro totals (2 years)	24	1	9	128	14.2	0	59	1391	23.6	0	0	0	0	2

COLEMAN, BEN — G/OT

PERSONAL: Born May 18, 1971, in South Hill, Va. ... 6-5/332. ... Full name: Benjamin Leon Coleman.
HIGH SCHOOL: Park View Senior (South Hill, Va.).
COLLEGE: Wake Forest.
TRANSACTIONS/CAREER NOTES: Selected by Phoenix Cardinals in second round (32nd pick overall) of 1993 NFL draft. ... Signed by Cardinals (July 6, 1993). ... Cardinals franchise renamed Arizona Cardinals for 1994 season. ... Claimed on waivers by Jacksonville Jaguars (September 27, 1995). ... Granted free agency (February 16, 1996). ... Re-signed by Jaguars (June 6, 1996). ... Granted unconditional free agency (February 14, 1997). ... Re-signed by Jaguars (March 3, 1997). ... Granted unconditional free agency (February 11, 2000). ... Signed by San Diego Chargers (June 15, 2000). ... Granted unconditional free agency (March 2, 2001). ... Signed by Washington Redskins (June 14, 2001). ... Granted unconditional free agency (March 1, 2002).
PLAYING EXPERIENCE: Phoenix NFL, 1993; Arizona NFL, 1994; Arizona (3)-Jacksonville (10) NFL, 1995; Jacksonville NFL, 1996-1999; San Diego NFL, 2000; Washington NFL, 2001. ... Games/Games started: 1993 (12/0), 1994 (15/13), 1995 (Ariz.-3/0; Jack.-10/5; Total: 13/5), 1996 (16/16), 1997 (16/16), 1998 (16/16), 1999 (16/12), 2000 (16/16), 2001 (15/10). Total: 135/104.
CHAMPIONSHIP GAME EXPERIENCE: Played in AFC championship game (1996 and 1999 seasons).
PRO STATISTICS: 1995—Recovered one fumble.

COLEMAN, CHRIS — WR — TITANS

PERSONAL: Born May 8, 1977, in Shelby, N.C. ... 6-0/202.
HIGH SCHOOL: Crest (Shelby, N.C.).
COLLEGE: North Carolina State.
TRANSACTIONS/CAREER NOTES: Signed as non-drafted free agent by Tennessee Titans (April 18, 2000). ... Claimed on waivers by Green Bay Packers (August 23, 2000). ... Released by Packers (August 25, 2000). ... Signed by Titans to practice squad (August 29, 2000). ... Released by Titans (September 5, 2000). ... Re-signed by Titans to practice squad (September 8, 2000). ... Activated (September 29, 2000). ... Assigned by Titans to Amsterdam Admirals in 2001 NFL Europe enhancement allocation program (February 17, 2001).
SINGLE GAME HIGHS (regular season): Receptions—1 (September 23, 2001, vs. Jacksonville); yards—19 (September 23, 2001, vs. Jacksonville); and touchdown receptions—0.

			RECEIVING			KICKOFF RETURNS			TOTALS			
Year Team	G	GS	No.	Yds.	Avg.	TD	No.	Yds.	Avg.	TD	TD	2pt.	Pts.	Fum.
2000—Tennessee NFL	13	0	0	0	0.0	0	2	54	27.0	0	0	0	0	0
2001—Amsterdam NFLE	...	...	51	710	13.9	8	0	0	0.0	0	8	0	48	0
—Tennessee NFL	16	0	1	19	19.0	0	11	251	22.8	0	0	0	0	0
NFL Europe totals (1 year)	...	...	51	710	13.9	8	0	0	0.0	0	8	0	48	0
NFL totals (2 years)	29	0	1	19	19.0	0	13	305	23.5	0	0	0	0	0
Pro totals (3 years)	...	...	52	729	14.0	8	13	305	23.5	0	8	0	48	0

COLEMAN, COSEY — G — BUCCANEERS

PERSONAL: Born October 27, 1978, in Clarkston, Ga. ... 6-4/322. ... Full name: Cosey Clinton Coleman.
HIGH SCHOOL: DeKalb (Clarkston, Ga.).
COLLEGE: Tennessee.
TRANSACTIONS/CAREER NOTES: Selected after junior season by Tampa Bay Buccaneers in second round (51st pick overall) of 2000 NFL draft. ... Signed by Buccaneers (July 23, 2000).
PLAYING EXPERIENCE: Tampa Bay NFL, 2000 and 2001. ... Games/Games started: 2000 (8/0), 2001 (16/16). Total: 24/16.

COLEMAN, FRED WR PATRIOTS

PERSONAL: Born January 31, 1975, in Tyler, Texas. ... 6-0/190. ... Full name: Fred Dewayne Coleman.
HIGH SCHOOL: Robert E. Lee (Tyler, Texas).
COLLEGE: Washington.
TRANSACTIONS/CAREER NOTES: Selected by Buffalo Bills in sixth round (160th pick overall) of 1998 NFL draft. ... Signed by Bills (June 19, 1998). ... Released by Bills (August 30, 1998). ... Re-signed by Bills to practice squad (August 31, 1998). ... Granted free agency after 1998 season. ... Signed by Philadelphia Eagles (January 11, 1999). ... Released by Eagles (August 31, 1999). ... Signed by New York Jets to practice squad (October 18, 1999). ... Released by Jets (August 20, 2000). ... Signed by Chicago Bears (April 24, 2001). ... Released by Bears (August 31, 2001). ... Signed by New England Patriots (November 8, 2001).
PLAYING EXPERIENCE: New England NFL, 2001. ... Games/Games started: (8/0).
CHAMPIONSHIP GAME EXPERIENCE: Played in AFC championship game (2001 season). ... Member of Super Bowl championship team (2001 season).
PRO STATISTICS: 2001—Caught two passes for 50 yards and recovered one fumble.
SINGLE GAME HIGHS (regular season): Receptions—1 (January 6, 2002, vs. Carolina); yards—46 (December 2, 2001, vs. New York Jets); and touchdown receptions—0.

COLEMAN, KARON RB BRONCOS

PERSONAL: Born May 22, 1978, in Missouri City, Texas. ... 5-7/198.
HIGH SCHOOL: Elkins (Missouri City, Texas).
COLLEGE: Stephen F. Austin State.
TRANSACTIONS/CAREER NOTES: Signed as non-drafted free agent by Denver Broncos (April 17, 2000). ... Released by Broncos (August 27, 2000). ... Re-signed by Broncos to practice squad (August 28, 2000). ... Activated (September 9, 2000). ... Released by Broncos (September 12, 2000). ... Re-signed by Broncos to practice squad (September 9, 2000). ... Activated (October 4, 2000). ... Released by Broncos (September 2, 2001). ... Re-signed by Broncos (November 26, 2001).
PRO STATISTICS: 2000—Recovered one fumble.
SINGLE GAME HIGHS (regular season): Attempts—14 (October 8, 2000, vs. San Diego); yards—52 (December 23, 2000, vs. San Francisco); and rushing touchdowns—1 (December 23, 2000, vs. San Francisco).

			RUSHING				RECEIVING				TOTALS		
Year Team	G	GS	Att.	Yds.	Avg.	TD	No.	Yds.	Avg.	TD	TD	2pt.	Pts.	Fum.
2000—Denver NFL	9	0	54	183	3.4	1	1	5	5.0	0	1	0	6	2
2001—Denver NFL	4	0	4	17	4.3	0	6	45	7.5	0	0	0	0	0
Pro totals (2 years)	13	0	58	200	3.4	1	7	50	7.1	0	1	0	6	2

COLEMAN, MARCO DE

PERSONAL: Born December 18, 1969, in Dayton, Ohio. ... 6-3/270. ... Full name: Marco Darnell Coleman.
HIGH SCHOOL: Patterson Co-op (Dayton, Ohio).
COLLEGE: Georgia Tech.
TRANSACTIONS/CAREER NOTES: Selected after junior season by Miami Dolphins in first round (12th pick overall) of 1992 NFL draft. ... Signed by Dolphins (August 1, 1992). ... Designated by Dolphins as transition player (February 25, 1993). ... Tendered offer sheet by San Diego Chargers (February 28, 1996). ... Dolphins declined to match offer (March 7, 1996). ... Granted unconditional free agency (February 12, 1999). ... Signed by Washington Redskins (June 3, 1999). ... Granted unconditional free agency (February 11, 2000). ... Re-signed by Redskins (February 29, 2000). ... Released by Redskins (June 3, 2002).
CHAMPIONSHIP GAME EXPERIENCE: Played in AFC championship game (1992 season).
HONORS: Named linebacker on THE SPORTING NEWS college All-America second team (1991). ... Played in Pro Bowl (2000 season).
PRO STATISTICS: 1997—Intercepted one pass for two yards. 1998—Recovered two fumbles. 1999—Recovered one fumble for 42 yards and a touchdown.

Year Team	G	GS	SACKS
1992—Miami NFL	16	15	6.0
1993—Miami NFL	15	15	5.5
1994—Miami NFL	16	16	6.0
1995—Miami NFL	16	16	6.5
1996—San Diego NFL	16	15	4.0
1997—San Diego NFL	16	16	2.0
1998—San Diego NFL	16	16	3.5
1999—Washington NFL	16	16	6.5
2000—Washington NFL	16	16	12.0
2001—Washington NFL	12	12	4.5
Pro totals (10 years)	155	153	56.5

COLEMAN, MARCUS CB TEXANS

PERSONAL: Born May 24, 1974, in Dallas. ... 6-2/210.
HIGH SCHOOL: Lake Highlands (Dallas).
COLLEGE: Texas Tech.
TRANSACTIONS/CAREER NOTES: Selected by New York Jets in fifth round (133rd pick overall) of 1996 NFL draft. ... Signed by Jets (July 11, 1996). ... Granted unconditional free agency (February 11, 2000). ... Re-signed by Jets (February 14, 2000). ... Selected by Houston Texans from Jets in NFL expansion draft (February 18, 2002).
CHAMPIONSHIP GAME EXPERIENCE: Played in AFC championship game (1998 season).
PRO STATISTICS: 1997—Recovered one fumble. 1999—Recovered one fumble. 2000—Caught one pass for 45 yards and a touchdown, converted two-point conversion and recovered one fumble. 2001—Recovered one fumble.

Year Team	G	GS	INTERCEPTIONS No.	Yds.	Avg.	TD
1996—New York Jets NFL	13	4	1	23	23.0	0
1997—New York Jets NFL	16	2	1	24	24.0	0
1998—New York Jets NFL	14	0	0	0	0.0	0
1999—New York Jets NFL	16	10	6	165	27.5	1
2000—New York Jets NFL	16	16	4	6	1.5	0
2001—New York Jets NFL	16	16	2	41	20.5	0
Pro totals (6 years)	91	48	14	259	18.5	1

COLEMAN, RODERICK DE RAIDERS

PERSONAL: Born August 16, 1976, in Philadelphia. ... 6-2/265.
HIGH SCHOOL: Simon Gratz (Philadelphia).
COLLEGE: East Carolina.
TRANSACTIONS/CAREER NOTES: Selected by Oakland Raiders in fifth round (153rd pick overall) of 1999 NFL draft. ... Signed by Raiders (July 24, 1999).
PLAYING EXPERIENCE: Oakland NFL, 1999-2001. ... Games/Games started: 1999 (3/0), 2000 (13/1), 2001 (14/6). Total: 30/7.
CHAMPIONSHIP GAME EXPERIENCE: Played in AFC championship game (2000 season).
PRO STATISTICS: 2000—Credited with six sacks and recovered one fumble. 2001—Credited with six sacks and recovered one fumble.

COLES, LAVERANUES WR/KR JETS

PERSONAL: Born December 29, 1977, in Jacksonville. ... 5-11/196.
HIGH SCHOOL: Jean Ribault (Jacksonville).
COLLEGE: Florida State.
TRANSACTIONS/CAREER NOTES: Selected by New York Jets in third round (78th pick overall) of 2000 NFL draft. ... Signed by Jets (May 1, 2000).
PRO STATISTICS: 2001—Recovered one fumble.
SINGLE GAME HIGHS (regular season): Receptions—7 (December 30, 2001, vs. Buffalo); yards—131 (October 29, 2000, vs. Buffalo); and touchdown receptions—2 (October 14, 2001, vs. Miami).
STATISTICAL PLATEAUS: 100-yard receiving games: 2000 (1), 2001 (1). Total: 2.

			RUSHING				RECEIVING				KICKOFF RETURNS				TOTALS			
Year Team	G	GS	Att.	Yds.	Avg.	TD	No.	Yds.	Avg.	TD	No.	Yds.	Avg.	TD	TD	2pt.	Pts.	Fum.
2000—New York Jets NFL	13	3	2	15	7.5	0	22	370	16.8	1	11	207	18.8	0	1	1	8	0
2001—New York Jets NFL	16	16	10	108	10.8	0	59	868	14.7	7	9	211	23.4	0	7	0	42	1
Pro totals (2 years)	29	19	12	123	10.3	0	81	1238	15.3	8	20	418	20.9	0	8	1	50	1

COLINET, STALIN DT JAGUARS

PERSONAL: Born July 17, 1974, in Bronx, N.Y. ... 6-6/288.
HIGH SCHOOL: Cardinal Hayes (Bronx, N.Y.).
COLLEGE: Boston College (degree in sociology, 1996).
TRANSACTIONS/CAREER NOTES: Selected by Minnesota Vikings in third round (78th pick overall) of 1997 NFL draft. ... Signed by Vikings (June 30, 1997). ... Traded by Vikings to Cleveland Browns for DT Jerry Ball (September 28, 1999). ... Granted free agency (February 11, 2000). ... Re-signed by Browns (April 18, 2000). ... Granted unconditional free agency (March 2, 2001). ... Re-signed by Browns (March 2, 2001). ... Traded by Browns to Vikings for future pick in draft (October 16, 2001). ... Released by Vikings (February 21, 2002). ... Signed by Jacksonville Jaguars (March 11, 2002).
PLAYING EXPERIENCE: Minnesota NFL, 1997 and 1998; Minnesota (3)-Cleveland (11) NFL, 1999; Cleveland NFL, 2000; Cleveland (5)-Minnesota (11) NFL, 2001. ... Games/games started: 1997 (10/2), 1998 (11/3), 1999 (Min.-3/1; Cle.-11/9; Total: 14/10), 2000 (16/16), 2001 (Cle.-5/0; Min.-11/11; Total: 16/11). Total: 67/42.
CHAMPIONSHIP GAME EXPERIENCE: Played in NFC championship game (1998 season).
PRO STATISTICS: 1998—Credited with one sack. 2000—Credited with $3^1/_2$ sacks and recovered one fumble. 2001—Credited with one sack and recovered one fumble.

COLLINS, BOBBY TE

PERSONAL: Born August 26, 1976, in York, Ala. ... 6-4/248. ... Full name: Bobby Eugene Collins.
HIGH SCHOOL: Sumter County (York, Ala.).
JUNIOR COLLEGE: East Mississippi Junior College.
COLLEGE: North Alabama.
TRANSACTIONS/CAREER NOTES: Selected by Buffalo Bills in fourth round (122nd pick overall) of 1999 NFL draft. ... Signed by Bills (July 12, 1999). ... Traded by Bills to Green Bay Packers for DE David Bowens (August 7, 2001). ... Released by Packers (October 14, 2001).
PRO STATISTICS: 1999—Returned one kickoff for six yards.
SINGLE GAME HIGHS (regular season): Receptions—3 (September 17, 2000, vs. New York Jets); yards—45 (November 28, 1999, vs. New England); and touchdown receptions—1 (January 2, 2000, vs. Indianapolis).

			RECEIVING			
Year Team	G	GS	No.	Yds.	Avg.	TD
1999—Buffalo NFL	14	4	9	124	13.8	2
2000—Buffalo NFL	12	2	6	72	12.0	0
2001—Green Bay NFL	4	0	1	3	3.0	0
Pro totals (3 years)	30	6	16	199	12.4	2

COLLINS, CALVIN — C — TEXANS

PERSONAL: Born January 5, 1974, in Beaumont, Texas. ... 6-2/310. ... Full name: Calvin Lewis Collins.
HIGH SCHOOL: West Brook (Beaumont, Texas).
COLLEGE: Texas A&M.
TRANSACTIONS/CAREER NOTES: Selected by Atlanta Falcons in sixth round (180th pick overall) of 1997 NFL draft. ... Signed by Falcons (June 22, 1997). ... Granted free agency (February 11, 2000). ... Re-signed by Falcons (June 24, 2000). ... Released by Falcons (August 20, 2001). ... Signed by Minnesota Vikings (October 15, 2001). ... Granted unconditional free agency (March 1, 2002). ... Signed by Houston Texans (June 5, 2002).
PLAYING EXPERIENCE: Atlanta NFL, 1997-2000; Minnesota NFL, 2001. ... Games/Games started: 1997 (15/13); 1998 (16/16), 1999 (14/8), 2000 (16/16), 2001 (7/3). Total: 68/56.
CHAMPIONSHIP GAME EXPERIENCE: Played in NFC championship game (1998 season). ... Played in Super Bowl XXXIII (1998 season).
PRO STATISTICS: 1998—Recovered one fumble.

COLLINS, KERRY — QB — GIANTS

PERSONAL: Born December 30, 1972, in Lebanon, Pa. ... 6-5/245. ... Full name: Kerry Michael Collins.
HIGH SCHOOL: Wilson (West Lawn, Pa.).
COLLEGE: Penn State.
TRANSACTIONS/CAREER NOTES: Selected by Carolina Panthers in first round (fifth pick overall) of 1995 NFL draft. ... Signed by Panthers (July 17, 1995). ... Granted free agency (February 13, 1998). ... Re-signed by Panthers (July 24, 1998). ... Claimed on waivers by New Orleans Saints (October 14, 1998). ... Granted unconditional free agency (February 12, 1999). ... Signed by New York Giants (February 19, 1999).
CHAMPIONSHIP GAME EXPERIENCE: Played in NFC championship game (1996 and 2000 season). ... Played in Super Bowl XXXV (2000 season).
HONORS: Maxwell Award winner (1994). ... Davey O'Brien Award winner (1994). ... Named quarterback on THE SPORTING NEWS college All-America first team (1994). ... Played in Pro Bowl (1996 season).
RECORDS: Holds NFL single-season record for most fumbles—22 (2001).
PRO STATISTICS: 1995—Fumbled 13 times and recovered four fumbles for minus 15 yards. 1996—Fumbled six times and recovered one fumble. 1997—Fumbled eight times and recovered two fumbles for minus 14 yards. 1998—Caught one pass for minus 11 yards, fumbled 13 times and recovered two fumbles for minus nine yards. 1999—Fumbled 11 times and recovered two fumbles for minus 27 yards. 2000—Fumbled seven times and recovered one fumble for minus 13 yards. 2001—Caught one pass for minus two yards, led league with 23 fumbles and recovered seven fumbles for minus 48 yards.
SINGLE GAME HIGHS (regular season): Attempts—59 (January 6, 2002, vs. Green Bay); completions—36 (January 6, 2002, vs. Green Bay); passing yards—386 (January 6, 2002, vs. Green Bay); and touchdown passes—3 (November 4, 2001, vs. Dallas).
STATISTICAL PLATEAUS: 300-yard passing games: 1995 (2), 1996 (1), 1997 (1), 1998 (2), 1999 (2), 2000 (3), 2001 (5). Total: 16.
MISCELLANEOUS: Selected by Detroit Tigers organization in 26th round of free-agent draft (June 4, 1990); did not sign. ... Selected by Toronto Blue Jays organization in 58th round of free-agent draft (June 4, 1994); did not sign. ... Regular-season record as starting NFL quarterback: 45-43 (.511). ... Postseason record as starting NFL quarterback: 3-2 (.600).

				PASSING							RUSHING				TOTALS		
Year Team	G	GS	Att.	Cmp.	Pct.	Yds.	TD	Int.	Avg.	Rat.	Att.	Yds.	Avg.	TD	TD	2pt.	Pts.
1995—Carolina NFL	15	13	433	214	49.4	2717	14	19	6.27	61.9	42	74	1.8	3	3	0	18
1996—Carolina NFL	13	12	364	204	56.0	2454	14	9	6.74	79.4	32	38	1.2	0	0	1	2
1997—Carolina NFL	13	13	381	200	52.5	2124	11	*21	5.57	55.7	26	65	2.5	0	1	0	6
1998—Carolina NFL	4	4	162	76	46.9	1011	8	5	6.24	70.8	7	40	5.7	0	0	1	2
—New Orleans NFL	7	7	191	94	49.2	1202	4	10	6.29	54.5	23	113	4.9	1	1	0	6
1999—N.Y. Giants NFL	10	7	331	190	57.4	2318	8	11	7.00	73.3	19	36	1.9	2	2	†1	14
2000—N.Y. Giants NFL	16	16	529	311	58.8	3610	22	13	6.82	83.1	41	65	1.6	1	1	0	6
2001—N.Y. Giants NFL	16	16	‡568	327	57.6	3764	19	16	6.63	77.1	39	73	1.9	0	0	0	0
Pro totals (7 years)	94	88	2959	1616	54.6	19200	100	104	6.49	71.3	229	504	2.2	8	8	3	54

COLLINS, MO — OT — RAIDERS

PERSONAL: Born September 22, 1976, in Charlotte. ... 6-4/335. ... Full name: Damon Jamal Collins.
HIGH SCHOOL: West Charlotte.
COLLEGE: Florida.
TRANSACTIONS/CAREER NOTES: Selected after junior season by Oakland Raiders in first round (23rd pick overall) of 1998 NFL draft. ... Signed by Raiders (July 15, 1998).
PLAYING EXPERIENCE: Oakland NFL, 1998-2001. ... Games/Games started: 1998 (16/11), 1999 (13/12), 2000 (16/16), 2001 (6/5). Total: 51/44.
CHAMPIONSHIP GAME EXPERIENCE: Played in AFC championship game (2000 season).

COLLINS, TODD — QB — CHIEFS

PERSONAL: Born November 5, 1971, in Walpole, Mass. ... 6-4/219.
HIGH SCHOOL: Walpole (Mass.).
COLLEGE: Michigan.
TRANSACTIONS/CAREER NOTES: Selected by Buffalo Bills in second round (45th pick overall) of 1995 NFL draft. ... Signed by Bills (July 10, 1995). ... Claimed on waivers by Kansas City Chiefs (August 25, 1998). ... Active for three games (1998); did not play. ... Active for all 16 games (1999); did not play. ... Active for all 16 games (2000); did not play.
PRO STATISTICS: 1996—Fumbled three times. 1997—Fumbled 10 times for minus 30 yards.
SINGLE GAME HIGHS (regular season): Attempts—44 (October 6, 1996, vs. Indianapolis); completions—25 (November 23, 1997, vs. Tennessee); yards—309 (October 6, 1996, vs. Indianapolis); and touchdown passes—3 (September 7, 1997, vs. New York Jets).
STATISTICAL PLATEAUS: 300-yard passing games: 1996 (1).
MISCELLANEOUS: Regular-season record as starting NFL quarterback: 7-10 (.412).

Year Team	G	GS	Att.	Cmp.	Pct.	PASSING Yds.	TD	Int.	Avg.	Rat.	Att.	RUSHING Yds.	Avg.	TD	TD	TOTALS 2pt.	Pts.
1995—Buffalo NFL	7	1	29	14	48.3	112	0	1	3.86	44.0	9	23	2.6	0	0	0	0
1996—Buffalo NFL	7	3	99	55	55.6	739	4	5	7.46	71.9	21	43	2.0	0	0	0	0
1997—Buffalo NFL	14	13	391	215	55.0	2367	12	13	6.05	69.5	30	77	2.6	0	0	0	0
1998—Kansas City NFL						Did not play.											
1999—Kansas City NFL						Did not play.											
2000—Kansas City NFL						Did not play.											
2001—Kansas City NFL	1	0	4	3	75.0	40	0	0	10.00	106.3	2	6	3.0	0	0	0	0
Pro totals (4 years)	29	17	523	287	54.9	3258	16	19	6.23	68.8	62	149	2.4	0	0	0	0

COLVIN, ROSEVELT LB BEARS

PERSONAL: Born September 5, 1977, in Indianapolis. ... 6-3/242.
HIGH SCHOOL: Broad Ripple (Indianapolis).
COLLEGE: Purdue.
TRANSACTIONS/CAREER NOTES: Selected by Chicago Bears in fourth round (111th pick overall) of 1999 NFL draft. ... Signed by Bears (July 21, 1999). ... Granted free agency (March 1, 2002).
PRO STATISTICS: 1999—Recovered one fumble. 2000—Recovered one fumble. 2001—Intercepted two passes for 22 yards and recovered one fumble.

Year Team	G	GS	SACKS
1999—Chicago NFL	11	0	2.0
2000—Chicago NFL	13	8	3.0
2001—Chicago NFL	16	13	10.5
Pro totals (3 years)	40	21	15.5

COMBS, CHRIS DE STEELERS

PERSONAL: Born December 15, 1976, in Roanoke, Va. ... 6-2/286. ... Full name: Christopher Brandon Combs. ... Son of Glen Combs, guard with five American Basketball Association teams (1968-69 through 1974-75).
HIGH SCHOOL: Patrick Henry (Roanoke, Va.).
COLLEGE: Duke (degree in sociology).
TRANSACTIONS/CAREER NOTES: Selected by Pittsburgh Steelers in sixth round (173rd pick overall) of 2000 NFL draft. ... Signed by Steelers (July 16, 2000).
PLAYING EXPERIENCE: Pittsburgh NFL, 2000 and 2001. ... Games/Games started: 2000 (6/0), 2001 (2/0). Total: 8/0.
CHAMPIONSHIP GAME EXPERIENCE: Member of Steelers for AFC championship game (2001 season); inactive.

COMELLA, GREG FB TITANS

PERSONAL: Born July 29, 1975, in Wellesley, Mass. ... 6-1/248. ... Name pronounced Ka-MELL-uh.
HIGH SCHOOL: Xaverian Brothers (Westwood, Mass.).
COLLEGE: Stanford.
TRANSACTIONS/CAREER NOTES: Signed as non-drafted free agent by New York Giants (April 24, 1998). ... Granted free agency (March 2, 2001). ... Re-signed by Giants (April 18, 2001). ... Granted unconditional free agency (March 1, 2002). ... Signed by Tennessee Titans (April 19, 2002).
CHAMPIONSHIP GAME EXPERIENCE: Played in NFC championship game (2000 season). ... Played in Super Bowl XXXV (2000 season).
PRO STATISTICS: 1998—Returned one kickoff for 12 yards and recovered one fumble. 1999—Returned two kickoffs for 31 yards. 2000—Returned two kickoffs for 20 yards, returned one punt for no yards and fumbled twice. 2001—Fumbled twice and recovered three fumbles.
SINGLE GAME HIGHS (regular season): Attempts—3 (November 5, 2000, vs. Cleveland); yards—19 (September 10, 2000, vs. Philadelphia); and rushing touchdowns—0.

Year Team	G	GS	RUSHING Att.	Yds.	Avg.	TD	RECEIVING No.	Yds.	Avg.	TD	TOTALS TD	2pt.	Pts.	Fum.
1998—New York Giants NFL	16	0	1	6	6.0	0	1	3	3.0	0	0	0	0	0
1999—New York Giants NFL	16	3	1	0	0.0	0	8	39	4.9	0	0	0	0	0
2000—New York Giants NFL	16	12	10	45	4.5	0	36	274	7.6	0	0	0	0	2
2001—New York Giants NFL	16	13	4	15	3.8	0	39	253	6.5	1	1	0	6	2
Pro totals (4 years)	64	28	16	66	4.1	0	84	569	6.8	1	1	0	6	4

COMPTON, MIKE OL PATRIOTS

PERSONAL: Born September 18, 1970, in Richlands, Va. ... 6-6/310. ... Full name: Michael Eugene Compton.
HIGH SCHOOL: Richlands (Va.).
COLLEGE: West Virginia.
TRANSACTIONS/CAREER NOTES: Selected by Detroit Lions in third round (68th pick overall) of 1993 NFL draft. ... Signed by Lions (June 4, 1993). ... Granted unconditional free agency (March 2, 2001). ... Signed by New England Patriots (April 2, 2001).
PLAYING EXPERIENCE: Detroit NFL, 1993-2000; New England NFL, 2001. ... Games/Games started: 1993 (8/0), 1994 (2/0), 1995 (16/8), 1996 (15/15), 1997 (16/16), 1998 (16/16), 1999 (15/15), 2000 (16/16), 2001 (16/16). Total: 120/102.
CHAMPIONSHIP GAME EXPERIENCE: Played in AFC championship game (2001 season). ... Member of Super Bowl championship team (2001 season).
HONORS: Named center on THE SPORTING NEWS college All-America first team (1992).
PRO STATISTICS: 1996—Fumbled once. 1999—Recovered two fumbles for eight yards. 2001—Fumbled once for minus 15 yards.

CONATY, BILLY   C   BILLS

PERSONAL: Born March 8, 1973, in Baltimore. ... 6-2/300. ... Full name: William B. Conaty. ... Name pronounced CON-uh-tee.
HIGH SCHOOL: Milford (Conn.) Academy, then Camden Catholic (Cherry Hill, N.J.).
COLLEGE: Virginia Tech.
TRANSACTIONS/CAREER NOTES: Signed as non-drafted free agent by Buffalo Bills (April 25, 1997). ... Released by Bills (August 24, 1997). ... Re-signed by Bills to practice squad (August 26, 1997). ... Activated (September 6, 1997). ... Released by Bills (September 22, 1997). ... Re-signed by Bills to practice squad (September 24, 1997). ... Granted free agency (March 2, 2001). ... Re-signed by Bills (June 12, 2001). ... Granted unconditional free agency (March 1, 2002). ... Re-signed by Bills (March 8, 2002).
PLAYING EXPERIENCE: Buffalo NFL, 1997-2001. ... Games/Games started: 1997 (1/0), 1998 (15/1), 1999 (7/1), 2000 (16/0), 2001 (16/16). Totals: 55/18.
HONORS: Named center on THE SPORTING NEWS college All-America first team (1996).
PRO STATISTICS: 2001—Recovered one fumble.

CONNELL, ALBERT   WR

PERSONAL: Born May 13, 1974, in Fort Lauderdale, Fla. ... 6-0/184. ... Full name: Albert Gene Anthony Connell.
HIGH SCHOOL: Piper (Fort Lauderdale, Fla.).
JUNIOR COLLEGE: Trinity Valley Community College (Texas).
COLLEGE: Texas A&M.
TRANSACTIONS/CAREER NOTES: Selected by Washington Redskins in fourth round (115th pick overall) of 1997 NFL draft. ... Signed by Redskins (May 28, 1997). ... Granted free agency (February 11, 2000). ... Re-signed by Redskins (April 21, 2000). ... Granted unconditional free agency (March 2, 2001). ... Signed by New Orleans Saints (March 30, 2001). ... On reserve/suspended list (December 17, 2001-remainder of season). ... Released by Saints (February 28, 2002).
PRO STATISTICS: 1997—Rushed once for three yards. 1999—Rushed once for eight yards and recovered one fumble. 2001—Rushed once for six yards and recovered one fumble.
SINGLE GAME HIGHS (regular season): Receptions—8 (October 17, 1999, vs. Arizona); yards—211 (October 22, 2000, vs. Jacksonville); and touchdown receptions—3 (October 22, 2000, vs. Jacksonville).
STATISTICAL PLATEAUS: 100-yard receiving games: 1998 (1), 1999 (4), 2000 (2). Total: 7.

			RECEIVING				TOTALS			
Year Team	G	GS	No.	Yds.	Avg.	TD	TD	2pt.	Pts.	Fum.
1997—Washington NFL	5	1	9	138	15.3	2	2	0	12	0
1998—Washington NFL	14	5	28	451	16.1	2	2	0	12	0
1999—Washington NFL	15	14	62	1132	18.3	7	7	0	42	1
2000—Washington NFL	16	13	39	762	19.5	3	3	0	18	0
2001—New Orleans NFL	11	1	12	191	15.9	2	2	0	12	0
Pro totals (5 years)	61	34	150	2674	17.8	16	16	0	96	1

CONWAY, BRETT   K   REDSKINS

PERSONAL: Born March 8, 1975, in Atlanta. ... 6-2/207. ... Full name: Brett Alan Conway.
HIGH SCHOOL: Parkview (Lilburn, Ga.).
COLLEGE: Penn State.
TRANSACTIONS/CAREER NOTES: Selected by Green Bay Packers in third round (90th pick overall) of 1997 NFL draft. ... Signed by Packers (July 8, 1997). ... On injured reserve with thigh injury (September 3, 1997-entire season). ... Traded by Packers to New York Jets for an undisclosed draft pick (August 21, 1998). ... Released by Jets (August 30, 1998). ... Re-signed by Jets to practice squad (September 1, 1998). ... Released by Jets (September 23, 1998). ... Signed by Washington Redskins (November 12, 1998). ... Granted free agency (February 11, 2000). ... Re-signed by Redskins (May 31, 2000). ... Released by Redskins (September 20, 2000). ... Signed by Oakland Raiders (November 11, 2000). ... Released by Raiders (November 21, 2000). ... Signed by Jets (December 18, 2000). ... Granted unconditional free agency (March 2, 2001). ... Signed by Redskins (March 15, 2001).
PRO STATISTICS: 1999—Attempted one pass without a completion and recovered one fumble. 2001—Punted once for 28 yards.

				KICKING				
Year Team	G	XPM	XPA	FGM	FGA	Lg.	50+	Pts.
1997—Green Bay NFL				Did not play.				
1998—Washington NFL	6	0	0	0	0	0	0-0	0
1999—Washington NFL	16	49	50	22	∞32	51	3-9	115
2000—Washington NFL	2	3	3	3	3	26	0-0	12
—Oakland NFL	1	3	3	1	1	19	0-0	6
—New York Jets NFL	1	2	2	2	2	40	0-0	8
2001—Washington NFL	16	22	22	26	33	†55	2-2	100
Pro totals (4 years)	42	79	80	54	71	55	5-11	241

CONWAY, CURTIS   WR   CHARGERS

PERSONAL: Born March 13, 1971, in Los Angeles. ... 6-1/196. ... Full name: Curtis LaMont Conway.
HIGH SCHOOL: Hawthorne (Calif.).
JUNIOR COLLEGE: El Camino College (Calif.).
COLLEGE: Southern California.
TRANSACTIONS/CAREER NOTES: Selected after junior season by Chicago Bears in first round (seventh pick overall) of 1993 NFL draft. ... Signed by Bears (May 24, 1993). ... Granted free agency (February 16, 1996). ... Re-signed by Bears (March 4, 1996). ... On injured reserve with (shoulder) injury (December 22, 1999-remainder of season). ... Granted unconditional free agency (February 11, 2000). ... Signed by San Diego Chargers (February 22, 2000).
HONORS: Named kick returner on THE SPORTING NEWS college All-America second team (1992).

PRO STATISTICS: 1994—Completed only pass attempt for 23 yards and a touchdown and recovered one fumble. 1994—Returned eight punts for 63 yards. 1995—Attempted one pass without a completion. 1996—Completed only pass attempt for 33 yards and a touchdown. 1997—Attempted one pass without a completion. 1998—Attempted one pass without a completion and recovered one fumble.
SINGLE GAME HIGHS (regular season): Receptions—11 (December 30, 2001, vs. Seattle); yards—156 (December 30, 2001, vs. Seattle); and touchdown receptions—3 (October 15, 1995, vs. Jacksonville).
STATISTICAL PLATEAUS: 100-yard receiving games: 1994 (1), 1995 (3), 1996 (4), 1997 (3), 1999 (1), 2000 (2), 2001 (4). Total: 18.

				RUSHING				RECEIVING				KICKOFF RETURNS				TOTALS		
Year Team	G	GS	Att.	Yds.	Avg.	TD	No.	Yds.	Avg.	TD	No.	Yds.	Avg.	TD	TD	2pt.	Pts.	Fum.
1993—Chicago NFL	16	7	5	44	8.8	0	19	231	12.2	2	21	450	21.4	0	2	0	12	1
1994—Chicago NFL	13	12	6	31	5.2	0	39	546	14.0	2	10	228	22.8	0	2	1	14	2
1995—Chicago NFL	16	16	5	77	15.4	0	62	1037	16.7	12	0	0	0.0	0	12	0	72	0
1996—Chicago NFL	16	16	8	50	6.3	0	81	1049	13.0	7	0	0	0.0	0	7	0	42	1
1997—Chicago NFL	7	7	3	17	5.7	0	30	476	15.9	1	0	0	0.0	0	1	0	6	0
1998—Chicago NFL	15	15	5	48	9.6	0	54	733	13.6	3	0	0	0.0	0	3	0	18	1
1999—Chicago NFL	9	8	1	-2	-2.0	0	44	426	9.7	4	0	0	0.0	0	4	0	24	2
2000—San Diego NFL	14	14	3	31	10.3	0	53	712	13.4	5	0	0	0.0	0	5	0	30	0
2001—San Diego NFL	16	16	7	116	16.6	1	71	1125	15.8	6	0	0	0.0	0	7	0	42	1
Pro totals (9 years)	122	111	43	412	9.6	1	453	6335	14.0	42	31	678	21.9	0	43	1	260	8

CONWELL, ERNIE — TE — RAMS

PERSONAL: Born August 17, 1972, in Renton, Wash. ... 6-2/265. ... Full name: Ernest Harold Conwell.
HIGH SCHOOL: Kentwood (Kent, Wash.).
COLLEGE: Washington (degree in sociology, 1995).
TRANSACTIONS/CAREER NOTES: Selected by St. Louis Rams in second round (59th pick overall) of 1996 NFL draft. ... Signed by Rams (June 25, 1996). ... On injured reserve with knee injury (October 28, 1998-remainder of season). ... On physically unable to perform list with knee injury (August 30-November 9, 1999). ... Granted unconditional free agency (February 11, 2000). ... Re-signed by Rams (February 11, 2000).
CHAMPIONSHIP GAME EXPERIENCE: Played in NFC championship game (1999 and 2001 seasons). ... Member of Super Bowl championship team (1999 season). ... Played in Super Bowl XXXVI (2001 season).
PRO STATISTICS: 1996—Recovered one fumble. 1997—Recovered one fumble. 2000—Rushed twice for 23 yards. 2001—Rushed seven times for 28 yards and one touchdown and recovered one fumble.
SINGLE GAME HIGHS (regular season): Receptions—6 (October 28, 2001, vs. New Orleans); yards—75 (January 6, 2002, vs. Atlanta); and touchdown receptions—1 (January 6, 2002, vs. Atlanta).

			RECEIVING				TOTALS			
Year Team	G	GS	No.	Yds.	Avg.	TD	TD	2pt.	Pts.	Fum.
1996—St. Louis NFL	10	8	15	164	10.9	0	0	0	0	0
1997—St. Louis NFL	16	16	38	404	10.6	4	4	0	24	0
1998—St. Louis NFL	7	7	15	105	7.0	0	0	0	0	0
1999—St. Louis NFL	3	0	1	11	11.0	0	0	0	0	0
2000—St. Louis NFL	16	1	5	40	8.0	0	0	0	0	0
2001—St. Louis NFL	16	13	38	431	11.3	4	5	0	30	2
Pro totals (6 years)	68	45	112	1155	10.3	8	9	0	54	2

COOK, JAMEEL — FB — BUCCANEERS

PERSONAL: Born February 8, 1979, in Miami. ... 5-10/237. ... Full name: Jameel A. Cook.
HIGH SCHOOL: Southridge (Miami).
COLLEGE: Illinois.
TRANSACTIONS/CAREER NOTES: Selected after junior season by Tampa Bay Buccaneers in sixth round (174th pick overall) of 2001 NFL draft. ... Signed by Buccaneers (July 16, 2001).
SINGLE GAME HIGHS (regular season): Attempts—2 (October 28, 2001, vs. Minnesota); yards—2 (October 28, 2001, vs. Minnesota); and rushing touchdowns—0.

			RUSHING				RECEIVING				TOTALS			
Year Team	G	GS	Att.	Yds.	Avg.	TD	No.	Yds.	Avg.	TD	TD	2pt.	Pts.	Fum.
2001—Tampa Bay NFL	16	3	2	2	1.0	0	17	89	5.2	0	0	0	0	0

COOK, RASHARD — S — EAGLES

PERSONAL: Born April 18, 1977, in San Diego. ... 5-11/197.
HIGH SCHOOL: Samuel F.B. Morse (San Diego).
COLLEGE: Southern California.
TRANSACTIONS/CAREER NOTES: Selected by Chicago Bears in sixth round (184th pick overall) of 1999 NFL draft. ... Signed by Bears (June 25, 1999). ... Claimed on waivers by Philadelphia Eagles (September 7, 1999). ... Granted free agency (March 1, 2002). ... Re-signed by Eagles (April 26, 2002).
CHAMPIONSHIP GAME EXPERIENCE: Played in NFC championship game (2001 season).
PRO STATISTICS: 1999—Credited with one sack. 2001—Ran 11 yards with lateral from punt return, credited with one sack and recovered one fumble.

			INTERCEPTIONS			
Year Team	G	GS	No.	Yds.	Avg.	TD
1999—Philadelphia NFL	13	0	1	29	29.0	0
2000—Philadelphia NFL	14	0	0	0	0.0	0
2001—Philadelphia NFL	16	3	1	11	11.0	0
Pro totals (3 years)	43	3	2	40	20.0	0

COOPER, CHRIS   DT   RAIDERS

PERSONAL: Born December 27, 1977, in Lincoln, Neb. ... 6-5/275.
HIGH SCHOOL: Lincoln Southeast (Neb.).
COLLEGE: Nebraska-Omaha.
TRANSACTIONS/CAREER NOTES: Selected by Oakland Raiders in sixth round (184th pick overall) of 2001 NFL draft. ... Signed by Raiders (July 21, 2001).
PLAYING EXPERIENCE: Oakland NFL, 2001. ... Games/Games started: (11/1).
PRO STATISTICS: 2001—Intercepted one pass for no yards.

COOPER, JARROD   S   PANTHERS

PERSONAL: Born March 31, 1978, in Pearland, Texas. ... 6-0/210.
HIGH SCHOOL: Pearland (Texas).
COLLEGE: Kansas State.
TRANSACTIONS/CAREER NOTES: Selected by Carolina Panthers in fifth round (143rd pick overall) of 2001 NFL draft. ... Signed by Panthers (July 19, 2001).
PLAYING EXPERIENCE: Carolina NFL, 2001. ... Games/Games started: (16/0).

CORTEZ, JOSE   K   49ERS

PERSONAL: Born May 27, 1975, in San Vicente, El Salvador. ... 5-11/205. ... Full name: Jose Antonio Cortez.
HIGH SCHOOL: Van Nuys (Calif.).
JUNIOR COLLEGE: Los Angeles Valley College.
COLLEGE: Oregon State.
TRANSACTIONS/CAREER NOTES: Signed as non-drafted free agent by Cleveland Browns (April 23, 1999). ... Released by Browns (June 3, 1999). ... Signed by San Diego Chargers (June 14, 1999). ... Released by Chargers (August 30, 1999). ... Signed by New York Giants to practice squad (December 14, 1999). ... Activated (December 17, 1999). ... Released by Giants (December 21, 1999). ... Signed by San Diego Chargers (January 18, 2000). ... Released by Chargers (August 27, 2000). ... Signed by San Francisco 49ers (May 9, 2001).

		KICKING						
Year Team	G	XPM	XPA	FGM	FGA	Lg.	50+	Pts.
1999—New York Giants NFL	1	0	0	0	0	0	0-0	0
2000—Amsterdam NFLE	...	0	0	9	13	0	0-0	27
2001—San Francisco NFL	16	47	47	18	25	52	1-1	101
NFL Europe totals (1 year)	...	0	0	9	13	0	0-0	27
NFL totals (2 years)	17	47	47	18	25	52	1-1	101
Pro totals (3 years)	...	47	47	27	38	52	1-0	128

COSTA, DAVE   OT   49ERS

PERSONAL: Born September 8, 1978, in Ellwood City, Pa. ... 6-5/307. ... Full name: David C. Costa.
HIGH SCHOOL: Ellwood City (Pa.).
COLLEGE: Wisconsin.
TRANSACTIONS/CAREER NOTES: Signed as non-drafted free agent by San Francisco 49ers (April 26, 2001). ... Released by 49ers (September 2, 2001). ... Signed by Tennessee Titans to practice squad (September 5, 2001). ... Signed by 49ers off Titans practice squad (September 26, 2001).
PLAYING EXPERIENCE: San Francisco NFL, 2001. ... Games/Games started: 2001 (14/0).

COTA, CHAD   DB

PERSONAL: Born August 8, 1971, in Ashland, Ore. ... 6-0/196. ... Full name: Chad Garrett Cota.
HIGH SCHOOL: Ashland (Ore.).
COLLEGE: Oregon (degree in sociology).
TRANSACTIONS/CAREER NOTES: Selected by Carolina Panthers in seventh round (209th pick overall) of 1995 NFL draft. ... Signed by Panthers (July 14, 1995). ... Granted free agency (February 13, 1998). ... Tendered offer sheet by New Orleans Saints (March 11, 1998). ... Panthers declined to match offer (March 19, 1998). ... Granted unconditional free agency (February 12, 1999). ... Signed by Indianapolis Colts (February 23, 1999). ... Released by Colts (February 21, 2002).
CHAMPIONSHIP GAME EXPERIENCE: Played in NFC championship game (1996 season).
PRO STATISTICS: 1995—Recovered one fumble. 1996—Credited with one sack, fumbled once and recovered one fumble. 1997—Credited with one sack and recovered one fumble. 1998—Credited with two sacks and recovered one fumble. 1999—Recovered one fumble for 25 yards and a touchdown. 2001—Returned one kickoff for no yards and recovered one fumble for nine yards.

			INTERCEPTIONS			
Year Team	G	GS	No.	Yds.	Avg.	TD
1995—Carolina NFL	16	0	0	0	0.0	0
1996—Carolina NFL	16	2	5	63	12.6	0
1997—Carolina NFL	16	16	2	28	14.0	0
1998—New Orleans NFL	16	16	4	16	4.0	0
1999—Indianapolis NFL	15	15	0	0	0.0	0
2000—Indianapolis NFL	16	16	2	3	1.5	0
2001—Indianapolis NFL	16	16	2	21	10.5	0
Pro totals (7 years)	111	81	15	131	8.7	0

COUCH, TIM — QB — BROWNS

PERSONAL: Born July 31, 1977, in Hyden, Ky. ... 6-4/227. ... Full name: Timothy Scott Couch.
HIGH SCHOOL: Leslie County (Hyden, Ky.).
COLLEGE: Kentucky.
TRANSACTIONS/CAREER NOTES: Selected after junior season by Cleveland Browns in first round (first pick overall) of 1999 NFL draft. ... Signed by Browns (April 17, 1999). ... On injured reserve with broken thumb (October 20, 2000-remainder of season).
HONORS: Named quarterback on THE SPORTING NEWS college All-America third team (1998).
PRO STATISTICS: 1999—Fumbled 14 times and recovered four fumbles for minus 11 yards. 2000—Fumbled twice for minus eight yards. 2001—Fumbled nine times and recovered six fumbles for minus 10 yards.
SINGLE GAME HIGHS (regular season): Attempts—46 (November 21, 1999, vs. Carolina); completions—29 (November 21, 1999, vs. Carolina); passing yards—336 (December 30, 2001, vs. Tennessee); and touchdown passes—3 (December 30, 2001, vs. Tennessee).
STATISTICAL PLATEAUS: 300-yard passing games: 2000 (1), 2001 (1). Total: 2.
MISCELLANEOUS: Regular-season record as starting NFL quarterback: 11-26 (.297).

			PASSING							RUSHING				TOTALS		
Year Team	G	GS	Att.	Cmp.	Pct.	Yds.	TD	Int.	Avg.	Rat.	Att.	Yds.	Avg.	TD	TD	2pt.	Pts.
1999—Cleveland NFL	15	14	399	223	55.9	2447	15	13	6.13	73.2	40	267	6.7	1	1	†1	8
2000—Cleveland NFL	7	7	215	137	63.7	1483	7	9	6.90	77.3	12	45	3.8	0	0	0	0
2001—Cleveland NFL	16	16	454	272	59.9	3040	17	21	6.70	73.1	38	128	3.4	0	0	0	0
Pro totals (3 years)	38	37	1068	632	59.2	6970	39	43	6.53	74.0	90	440	4.9	1	1	1	8

COUSIN, TERRY — CB — PANTHERS

PERSONAL: Born March 11, 1975, in Miami. ... 5-9/182.
HIGH SCHOOL: Miami Beach Senior.
COLLEGE: South Carolina.
TRANSACTIONS/CAREER NOTES: Signed as non-drafted free agent by Chicago Bears (April 25, 1997). ... Released by Bears (August 24, 1997). ... Re-signed by Bears to practice squad (August 26, 1997). ... Activated (October 25, 1997). ... Released by Bears (October 28, 1997). ... Re-signed by Bears to practice squad (October 30, 1997). ... Activated (November 15, 1997). ... Granted free agency (February 11, 2000). ... Re-signed by Bears (April 18, 2000). ... Claimed on waivers by Atlanta Falcons (August 28, 2000). ... Granted unconditional free agency (March 2, 2001). ... Signed by Miami Dolphins (March 15, 2001). ... Granted unconditional free agency (March 1, 2002). ... Signed by Carolina Panthers (March 19, 2002).
PRO STATISTICS: 1998—Recovered two fumbles. 1999—Recovered one fumble. 2001—Returned one punt for no yards, credited with two sacks and recovered one fumble.

			INTERCEPTIONS			
Year Team	G	GS	No.	Yds.	Avg.	TD
1997—Chicago NFL	6	0	0	0	0.0	0
1998—Chicago NFL	16	12	1	0	0.0	0
1999—Chicago NFL	16	9	2	1	0.5	0
2000—Atlanta NFL	15	0	0	0	0.0	0
2001—Miami NFL	16	3	0	0	0.0	0
Pro totals (5 years)	69	24	3	1	0.3	0

COWART, SAM — LB — JETS

PERSONAL: Born February 26, 1975, in Jacksonville. ... 6-2/245.
HIGH SCHOOL: Mandarin (Jacksonville).
COLLEGE: Florida State.
TRANSACTIONS/CAREER NOTES: Selected by Buffalo Bills in second round (39th pick overall) of 1998 NFL draft. ... Signed by Bills (July 20, 1998). ... On injured reserve with Achilles' tendon injury (September 26, 2001-remainder of season). ... Granted unconditional free agency (March 1, 2002). ... Signed by New York Jets (March 6, 2002).
PLAYING EXPERIENCE: Buffalo NFL, 1998 and 1999. ... Games/Games started: 1998 (16/11), 1999 (16/16). Total: 32/27.
HONORS: Named outside linebacker on THE SPORTING NEWS college All-America first team (1997). ... Played in Pro Bowl (2000 season).
PRO STATISTICS: 1998—Intercepted two passes for 23 yards. 1999—Recovered one fumble and credited with one sack. 2000—Intercepted two passes for four yards and recovered two fumbles for three yards.

Year Team	G	GS	SACKS
2000—Buffalo NFL	12	12	5.5
2001—Buffalo NFL	1	1	0.0
Pro totals (2 years)	13	13	5.5

COWSETTE, DELBERT — DT — REDSKINS

PERSONAL: Born September 3, 1977, in Cleveland. ... 6-1/288. ... Full name: Delbert Ray Cowsette.
HIGH SCHOOL: Central Catholic (Cleveland).
COLLEGE: Maryland.
TRANSACTIONS/CAREER NOTES: Selected by Washington Redskins in seventh round (216th pick overall) of 2000 NFL draft. ... Signed by Redskins (May 18, 2000). ... Released by Redskins (August 27, 2000). ... Re-signed by Redskins to practice squad (August 28, 2000). ... Released by Redskins (November 13, 2000). ... Signed by Indianapolis Colts to practice squad (December 7, 2000). ... Signed by Redskins off Colts practice squad (December 19, 2000).
PLAYING EXPERIENCE: Washington NFL, 2001. ... Games/Games started: (16/0).

– 86 –

COX, BRYAN — LB — SAINTS

PERSONAL: Born February 17, 1968, in St. Louis. ... 6-4/250. ... Full name: Bryan Keith Cox.
HIGH SCHOOL: East St. Louis (Ill.) Senior.
COLLEGE: Western Illinois (bachelor of science degree in mass communications).
TRANSACTIONS/CAREER NOTES: Selected by Miami Dolphins in fifth round (113th pick overall) of 1991 NFL draft. ... Signed by Dolphins (July 11, 1991). ... On injured reserve with sprained ankle (October 5-November 2, 1991). ... Granted unconditional free agency (February 16, 1996). ... Signed by Chicago Bears (February 20, 1996). ... On injured reserve with thumb injury (November 5, 1996-remainder of season). ... Released by Bears (June 2, 1998). ... Signed by New York Jets (August 1, 1998). ... On injured reserve with abdominal injury (December 10, 1999-remainder of season). ... On injured reserve with broken leg (December 18, 2000-remainder of season). ... Released by Jets (February 22, 2001). ... Signed by New England Patriots (July 31, 2001). ... Granted unconditional free agency (March 1, 2002). ... Signed by New Orleans Saints (March 28, 2002).
CHAMPIONSHIP GAME EXPERIENCE: Played in AFC championship game (1992, 1998 and 2001 seasons). ... Member of Super Bowl championship team (2001 season).
HONORS: Played in Pro Bowl (1992, 1994 and 1995 seasons).
PRO STATISTICS: 1992—Recovered one fumble. 1993—Recovered four fumbles for one yard. 1995—Recovered one fumble. 1996—Recovered three fumbles, including one in end zone for a touchdown. 1997—Recovered one fumble. 1998—Credited with a safety. 1999—Recovered one fumble. 2000—Recovered two fumbles. 2001—Caught one pass for seven yards and recovered one fumble for nine yards.

				INTERCEPTIONS				SACKS
Year Team	G	GS	No.	Yds.	Avg.	TD		No.
1991—Miami NFL	13	13	0	0	0.0	0		2.0
1992—Miami NFL	16	16	1	0	0.0	0		14.0
1993—Miami NFL	16	16	1	26	26.0	0		5.0
1994—Miami NFL	16	16	0	0	0.0	0		3.0
1995—Miami NFL	16	16	1	12	12.0	0		7.5
1996—Chicago NFL	9	9	0	0	0.0	0		3.0
1997—Chicago NFL	16	15	0	0	0.0	0		5.0
1998—New York Jets NFL	16	10	0	0	0.0	0		6.0
1999—New York Jets NFL	12	11	1	27	27.0	1		0.0
2000—New York Jets NFL	15	15	0	0	0.0	0		6.0
2001—New England NFL	11	7	0	0	0.0	0		0.0
Pro totals (11 years)	156	144	4	65	16.3	1		51.5

COX, RENARD — DB — JAGUARS

PERSONAL: Born March 3, 1978, in Richmond, Va. ... 6-0/191.
HIGH SCHOOL: Huguenot (Richmond, Va.).
JUNIOR COLLEGE: Lackawanna Community College (Scranton, Pa.).
COLLEGE: Maryland.
TRANSACTIONS/CAREER NOTES: Signed as non-drafted free agent by Arizona Cardinals (April 28, 2001). ... Released by Cardinals (August 21, 2000). ... Signed by New Orleans Saints (July 20, 2001). ... Released by Saints (September 2, 2001). ... Re-signed by Saints to practice squad (October 30, 2001). ... Signed by Jacksonville Jaguars off Saints practice squad (November 7, 2001). ... Released by Jaguars (December 11, 2001). ... Re-signed by Jaguars to practice squad (December 12, 2001). ... Activated (December 21, 2001).
PLAYING EXPERIENCE: Jacksonville NFL, 2001. ... Games/Games started: 2001 (6/0).

CRAFT, JASON — CB — JAGUARS

PERSONAL: Born February 13, 1976, in Denver. ... 5-10/178. ... Full name: Jason Donell Andre Craft.
HIGH SCHOOL: Denver East.
JUNIOR COLLEGE: Denver Community College.
COLLEGE: Colorado State.
TRANSACTIONS/CAREER NOTES: Selected by Jacksonville Jaguars in fifth round (160th pick overall) of 1999 NFL draft. ... Signed by Jaguars (May 18, 1999). ... Granted free agency (March 1, 2002). ... Tendered offer sheet by New Orleans Saints (March 5, 2002). ... Offer sheet matched by Jaguars (March 12, 2002).
PLAYING EXPERIENCE: Jacksonville NFL, 1999-2001. ... Games/Games started: 1999 (16/0), 2000 (16/3), 2001 (16/8). Total: 48/11.
CHAMPIONSHIP GAME EXPERIENCE: Played in AFC championship game (1999 season).
PRO STATISTICS: 1999—Recovered one fumble for 23 yards and a touchdown. 2000—Recovered one fumble for four yards. 2001—Intercepted two passes for four yards.

CRAIG, DAMEYUNE — QB — REDSKINS

PERSONAL: Born April 19, 1974, in Mobile, Ala. ... 6-1/200. ... Full name: Dameyune Vashon Craig. ... Name pronounced DAME-ee-un.
HIGH SCHOOL: Blount (Pritchard, Ala.).
COLLEGE: Auburn.
TRANSACTIONS/CAREER NOTES: Signed as non-drafted free agent by Carolina Panthers (April 18, 1998). ... Released by Panthers (August 30, 1998). ... Re-signed by Panthers to practice squad (September 1, 1998). ... Activated (December 5, 1998); did not play. ... Assigned by Panthers to Scottish Claymores in 1999 NFL Europe enhancement allocation program (February 22, 1999). ... Inactive for all 16 games (1999). ... On injured reserve with foot injury (November 6, 2001-remainder of season). ... Granted free agency (March 1, 2002). ... Signed by Washington Redskins (March 7, 2002).
PRO STATISTICS: 2000—Caught two passes for four yards. 2001—Fumbled once and recovered one fumble for minus 15 yards.
SINGLE GAME HIGHS (regular season): Attempts—8 (November 4, 2001, vs. Miami); completions—4 (November 4, 2001, vs. Miami); passing yards—34 (November 4, 2001, vs. Miami); and touchdown passes—0.

Year Team	G	GS	PASSING							RUSHING				TOTALS		
			Att.	Cmp.	Pct.	Yds.	TD	Int.	Avg.	Rat.	Att.	Yds.	Avg.	TD	TD	2pt.	Pts.
1999—Scottish NFLE	...	...	339	198	58.4	2932	21	12	8.65	92.7	53	276	5.2	3	3	0	18
2000—Carolina NFL	4	0	0	0	0.0	0	0	0	0.0	...	2	4	2.0	0	0	0	0
2001—Carolina NFL	2	0	8	4	50.0	34	0	0	4.25	61.5	3	20	6.7	0	0	0	0
NFL Europe totals (1 year)	...	...	339	198	58.4	2932	21	12	8.65	92.7	53	276	5.2	3	3	0	18
NFL totals (2 years)	6	0	8	4	50.0	34	0	0	4.25	61.5	5	24	4.8	0	0	0	0
Pro totals (3 years)	...	...	347	202	58.2	2966	21	12	8.55	92.0	58	300	5.2	3	3	0	18

CRAWFORD, CASEY — TE — PANTHERS

PERSONAL: Born August 1, 1977, in Washington, D.C. ... 6-6/255. ... Full name: Casey Stuart Crawford.
HIGH SCHOOL: Bishop O'Connell (Falls Church, Va.).
COLLEGE: Virginia.
TRANSACTIONS/CAREER NOTES: Signed as non-drafted free agent by Carolina Panthers (April 25, 2000).
PLAYING EXPERIENCE: Carolina NFL, 2000 and 2001. ... Games/Games started: 2000 (8/0), 2001 (3/1). Total: 11/1.
PRO STATISTICS: 2000—Caught four passes for 47 yards and one touchdown. 2001—Caught one pass for 10 yards, returned one kickoff for eight yards and recovered one fumble in end zone for touchdown.
SINGLE GAME HIGHS (regular season): Receptions—1 (December 23, 2001, vs. St. Louis); yards—16 (November 5, 2000, vs. St. Louis); and touchdown receptions—1 (November 5, 2000, vs. St. Louis).

CROCKETT, HENRI — LB — VIKINGS

PERSONAL: Born October 28, 1974, in Pompano Beach, Fla. ... 6-2/238. ... Full name: Henri W. Crockett. ... Brother of Zack Crockett, fullback, Oakland Raiders.
HIGH SCHOOL: Ely (Pompano Beach, Fla.).
COLLEGE: Florida State (degree in criminology, 1996).
TRANSACTIONS/CAREER NOTES: Selected by Atlanta Falcons in fourth round (100th pick overall) of 1997 NFL draft. ... Signed by Falcons (July 14, 1997). ... Granted free agency (February 11, 2000). ... Re-signed by Falcons (June 1, 2000). ... Granted unconditional free agency (March 2, 2001). ... Signed by Denver Broncos (May 4, 2001). ... Traded by Broncos to Falcons for conditional pick in 2002 draft (August 2, 2001). ... Granted unconditional free agency (March 1, 2002). ... Signed by Minnesota Vikings (March 13, 2002).
CHAMPIONSHIP GAME EXPERIENCE: Played in NFC championship game (1998 season). ... Played in Super Bowl XXXIII (1998 season).
PRO STATISTICS: 1997—Recovered one fumble. 2001—Intercepted one pass for seven yards.

Year Team	G	GS	SACKS
1997—Atlanta NFL	16	10	2.0
1998—Atlanta NFL	10	10	1.0
1999—Atlanta NFL	16	14	1.5
2000—Atlanta NFL	15	12	2.0
2001—Atlanta NFL	16	15	0.0
Pro totals (5 years)	73	61	6.5

CROCKETT, RAY — CB — CHIEFS

PERSONAL: Born January 5, 1967, in Dallas. ... 5-10/184. ... Full name: Donald Ray Crockett.
HIGH SCHOOL: Duncanville (Texas).
COLLEGE: Baylor.
TRANSACTIONS/CAREER NOTES: Selected by Detroit Lions in fourth round (86th pick overall) of 1989 NFL draft. ... Signed by Lions (July 18, 1989). ... Granted unconditional free agency (February 17, 1994). ... Signed by Denver Broncos (March 9, 1994). ... Granted unconditional free agency (March 2, 2001). ... Signed by Kansas City Chiefs (April 5, 2001).
CHAMPIONSHIP GAME EXPERIENCE: Played in NFC championship game (1991 season). ... Played in AFC championship game (1997 and 1998 seasons). ... Member of Super Bowl championship team (1997 and 1998 seasons).
PRO STATISTICS: 1989—Returned one kickoff for eight yards and recovered one fumble. 1990—Recovered two fumbles for 22 yards and a touchdown. 1992—Recovered one fumble for 15 yards. 1993—Recovered one fumble. 1994—Recovered two fumbles for 43 yards. 1995—Ran four yards with lateral from punt return and recovered one fumble for 50 yards and a touchdown. 1999—Recovered one fumble.

Year Team	G	GS	INTERCEPTIONS				SACKS
			No.	Yds.	Avg.	TD	No.
1989—Detroit NFL	16	0	1	5	5.0	0	0.0
1990—Detroit NFL	16	6	3	17	5.7	0	1.0
1991—Detroit NFL	16	16	∞6	141	23.5	∞1	1.0
1992—Detroit NFL	15	15	4	50	12.5	0	1.0
1993—Detroit NFL	16	16	2	31	15.5	0	1.0
1994—Denver NFL	14	14	2	6	3.0	0	0.0
1995—Denver NFL	16	16	0	0	0.0	0	3.0
1996—Denver NFL	15	15	2	34	17.0	0	4.0
1997—Denver NFL	16	16	4	18	4.5	0	0.0
1998—Denver NFL	16	16	3	105	35.0	1	0.5
1999—Denver NFL	16	16	2	14	7.0	0	2.0
2000—Denver NFL	13	11	4	31	7.8	0	1.0
2001—Kansas City NFL	14	12	1	8	8.0	0	0.0
Pro totals (13 years)	199	169	34	460	13.5	3	14.5

CROCKETT, ZACK — RB — RAIDERS

PERSONAL: Born December 2, 1972, in Pompano Beach, Fla. ... 6-2/245. ... Brother of Henri Crockett, linebacker, Minnesota Vikings.
HIGH SCHOOL: Ely (Pompano Beach, Fla.).
JUNIOR COLLEGE: Hinds Community College (Miss.).
COLLEGE: Florida State.

TRANSACTIONS/CAREER NOTES: Selected by Indianapolis Colts in third round (79th pick overall) of 1995 NFL draft. ... Signed by Colts (July 21, 1995). ... On injured reserve with knee injury (October 22, 1996-remainder of season). ... Granted free agency (February 13, 1998). ... Re-signed by Colts (July 23, 1998). ... Claimed on waivers by Jacksonville Jaguars (October 21, 1998). ... Granted unconditional free agency (February 12, 1999). ... Signed by Oakland Raiders (March 16, 1999).
CHAMPIONSHIP GAME EXPERIENCE: Played in AFC championship game (1995 and 2000 seasons).
PRO STATISTICS: 2000—Recovered one fumble.
SINGLE GAME HIGHS (regular season): Attempts—17 (October 28, 2001, vs. Philadelphia); yards—81 (November 2, 1997, vs. Tampa Bay); and rushing touchdowns—2 (November 5, 2001, vs. Denver).

				RUSHING				RECEIVING				TOTALS		
Year Team	G	GS	Att.	Yds.	Avg.	TD	No.	Yds.	Avg.	TD	TD	2pt.	Pts.	Fum.
1995—Indianapolis NFL	16	0	1	0	0.0	0	2	35	17.5	0	0	0	0	0
1996—Indianapolis NFL	5	5	31	164	5.3	0	11	96	8.7	1	1	0	6	2
1997—Indianapolis NFL	16	12	95	300	3.2	1	15	112	7.5	0	1	0	6	3
1998—Indianapolis NFL	2	1	2	5	2.5	0	1	1	1.0	0	0	0	0	1
—Jacksonville NFL	10	1	0	0	0.0	0	1	4	4.0	0	0	0	0	0
1999—Oakland NFL	13	1	45	91	2.0	4	8	56	7.0	1	5	0	30	0
2000—Oakland NFL	16	4	43	130	3.0	7	10	62	6.2	0	7	0	42	0
2001—Oakland NFL	16	0	57	145	2.5	6	2	10	5.0	0	6	0	36	1
Pro totals (7 years)	94	24	274	835	3.0	18	50	376	7.5	2	20	0	120	7

CROSBY, CLIFTON　　CB　　COLTS

PERSONAL: Born September 17, 1974, in Erie, Pa. ... 5-10/172.
HIGH SCHOOL: East (Erie, Pa.).
COLLEGE: Maryland.
TRANSACTIONS/CAREER NOTES: Signed as non-drafted free agent by St. Louis Rams (April 20, 1999). ... Released by Rams (September 5, 1999). ... Re-signed by Rams (September 6, 1999). ... Released by Rams (September 13, 1999). ... Re-signed by Rams to practice squad (September 30, 1999). ... Released by Rams (August 27, 2000). ... Re-signed by Rams to practice squad (August 29, 2000). ... Released by Rams (October 24, 2000). ... Signed by Indianapolis Colts (November 1, 2000).
PLAYING EXPERIENCE: St. Louis NFL, 1999; Indianapolis NFL, 2001. ... Games/Games started: 1999 (1/0), 2001 (14/0). Total: 15/0.
PRO STATISTICS: 2001—Recovered one fumble.

CROSBY, PHILLIP　　FB　　BILLS

PERSONAL: Born November 5, 1976, in Bessemer City, N.C. ... 6-0/242. ... Full name: Phillip Jermaine Crosby.
HIGH SCHOOL: Bessemer City (N.C.).
JUNIOR COLLEGE: Coffeyville Community College.
COLLEGE: Tennessee.
TRANSACTIONS/CAREER NOTES: Signed as non-drafted free agent by Buffalo Bills (April 22, 2000). ... Released by Bills (August 21, 2000). ... Re-signed by Bills (April 24, 2001).
PLAYING EXPERIENCE: Buffalo NFL, 2001. ... Games/Games started: 2001 (16/2).
PRO STATISTICS: 2001—Caught two passes for 16 yards and recovered one fumble.

CROSS, HOWARD　　TE

PERSONAL: Born August 8, 1967, in Huntsville, Ala. ... 6-5/270. ... Full name: Howard E. Cross.
HIGH SCHOOL: New Hope (Ala.).
COLLEGE: Alabama.
TRANSACTIONS/CAREER NOTES: Selected by New York Giants in sixth round (158th pick overall) of 1989 NFL draft. ... Signed by Giants (July 24, 1989). ... Granted free agency (February 1, 1991). ... Re-signed by Giants (July 24, 1991). ... Granted free agency (March 1, 1993). ... Re-signed by Giants (July 16, 1993). ... Designated by Giants as transition player (February 15, 1994). ... Announced retirement (February 28, 2002).
CHAMPIONSHIP GAME EXPERIENCE: Played in NFC championship game (1990 and 2000 season). ... Member of Super Bowl championship team (1990 season). ... Played in Super Bowl XXXV (2000 season).
PRO STATISTICS: 1992—Recovered one fumble. 1993—Recovered one fumble. 1994—Recovered one fumble. 1997—Recovered one fumble.
SINGLE GAME HIGHS (regular season): Receptions—6 (September 13, 1992, vs. Dallas); yards—77 (September 13, 1992, vs. Dallas); and touchdown receptions—2 (September 11, 1994, vs. Arizona).

			RECEIVING				KICKOFF RETURNS				TOTALS		
Year Team	G	GS	No.	Yds.	Avg.	TD	No.	Yds.	Avg.	TD	2pt.	Pts.	Fum.
1989—New York Giants NFL	16	4	6	107	17.8	1	0	0	0.0	0	1	0	6	1
1990—New York Giants NFL	16	8	8	106	13.3	0	1	10	10.0	0	0	0	0	0
1991—New York Giants NFL	16	16	20	283	14.2	2	1	11	11.0	0	2	0	12	1
1992—New York Giants NFL	16	16	27	357	13.2	2	0	0	0.0	0	2	0	12	2
1993—New York Giants NFL	16	16	21	272	13.0	5	2	15	7.5	0	5	0	30	0
1994—New York Giants NFL	16	16	31	364	11.7	4	0	0	0.0	0	4	0	24	0
1995—New York Giants NFL	15	15	18	197	10.9	0	0	0	0.0	0	0	0	0	0
1996—New York Giants NFL	16	16	22	178	8.1	1	0	0	0.0	0	1	0	6	0
1997—New York Giants NFL	16	16	21	150	7.1	2	0	0	0.0	0	2	0	12	1
1998—New York Giants NFL	16	16	13	90	6.9	0	0	0	0.0	0	0	0	0	2
1999—New York Giants NFL	16	15	9	55	6.1	0	0	0	0.0	0	0	0	0	0
2000—New York Giants NFL	16	11	4	30	7.5	0	0	0	0.0	0	0	0	0	0
2001—New York Giants NFL	16	6	1	5	5.0	0	0	0	0.0	0	0	0	0	0
Pro totals (13 years)	207	171	201	2194	10.9	17	4	36	9.0	0	17	0	102	8

CROWELL, GERMANE — WR — LIONS

PERSONAL: Born September 13, 1976, in Winston-Salem, N.C. ... 6-3/216. ... Full name: Germane L. Crowell.
HIGH SCHOOL: North Forsyth (Winston-Salem, N.C.).
COLLEGE: Virginia.
TRANSACTIONS/CAREER NOTES: Selected by Detroit Lions in second round (50th pick overall) of 1998 NFL draft. ... Signed by Lions (July 20, 1998). ... On injured reserve with knee injury (October 24, 2001-remainder of season). ... Granted unconditional free agency (March 1, 2002). ... Re-signed by Lions (March 26, 2002).
PRO STATISTICS: 1999—Recovered one fumble. 2001—Recovered one fumble.
SINGLE GAME HIGHS (regular season): Receptions—9 (October 14, 2001, vs. Minnesota); yards—163 (November 7, 1999, vs. St. Louis); and touchdown receptions—2 (September 12, 1999, vs. Seattle).
STATISTICAL PLATEAUS: 100-yard receiving games: 1999 (6), 2001 (1). Total: 7.

			RUSHING				RECEIVING				TOTALS			
Year Team	G	GS	Att.	Yds.	Avg.	TD	No.	Yds.	Avg.	TD	TD	2pt.	Pts.	Fum.
1998—Detroit NFL	14	2	1	35	35.0	0	25	464	18.6	3	3	0	18	1
1999—Detroit NFL	16	15	5	38	7.6	0	81	1338	16.5	7	7	†1	44	1
2000—Detroit NFL	9	7	1	12	12.0	0	34	430	12.6	3	3	0	18	0
2001—Detroit NFL	5	4	1	6	6.0	0	22	289	13.1	2	2	0	12	1
Pro totals (4 years)	44	28	8	91	11.4	0	162	2521	15.6	15	15	1	92	3

CRUMPLER, ALGE — TE — FALCONS

PERSONAL: Born December 23, 1977, in Wilmington, N.C. ... 6-2/262. ... Full name: Algernon Darius Crumpler.
HIGH SCHOOL: New Hanover (Wilmington, N.C.).
COLLEGE: North Carolina.
TRANSACTIONS/CAREER NOTES: Selected by Atlanta Falcons in second round (35th pick overall) of 2001 NFL draft. ... Signed by Falcons (May 29, 2001).
PRO STATISTICS: 2001—Returned three kickoffs for 32 yards, fumbled once and recovered two fumbles.
SINGLE GAME HIGHS (regular season): Receptions—5 (October 21, 2001, vs. New Orleans); yards—78 (October 21, 2001, vs. New Orleans); and touchdown receptions—1 (December 23, 2001, vs. Buffalo).

			RECEIVING			
Year Team	G	GS	No.	Yds.	Avg.	TD
2001—Atlanta NFL	16	12	25	330	13.2	3

CRUTCHFIELD, DARREL — CB — EAGLES

PERSONAL: Born February 26, 1979, in San Diego. ... 6-0/177.
HIGH SCHOOL: Raines (Jacksonville, Fla.).
COLLEGE: Clemson.
TRANSACTIONS/CAREER NOTES: Signed as non-drafted free agent by Philadelphia Eagles (April 23, 2001).
PLAYING EXPERIENCE: Philadelphia NFL, 2001. ... Games/Games started: 2001 (4/0).
CHAMPIONSHIP GAME EXPERIENCE: Member of Eagles for NFC championship game (2001 season); inactive.

CULPEPPER, DAUNTE — QB — VIKINGS

PERSONAL: Born January 28, 1977, in Ocala, Fla. ... 6-4/260.
HIGH SCHOOL: Vanguard (Ocala, Fla.).
COLLEGE: Central Florida.
TRANSACTIONS/CAREER NOTES: Selected by Minnesota Vikings in first round (11th pick overall) of 1999 NFL draft. ... Signed by Vikings (July 30, 1999).
CHAMPIONSHIP GAME EXPERIENCE: Played in NFC championship game (2000 season).
HONORS: Played in Pro Bowl (2000 season).
PRO STATISTICS: 1999—Fumbled once and recovered one fumble for minus two yards. 2000—Led NFC with 11 fumbles and recovered five fumbles for minus 23 yards. 2001—Fumbled 16 times and recovered seven fumbles for minus 17 yards.
SINGLE GAME HIGHS (regular season): Attempts—53 (October 29, 2000, vs. Tampa Bay); completions—30 (September 30, 2001, vs. Tampa Bay); yards—357 (November 19, 2000, vs. Carolina); and touchdown passes—4 (November 19, 2001, vs. New York Giants).
STATISTICAL PLATEAUS: 300-yard passing games: 2000 (5), 2001 (2). Total: 7.
MISCELLANEOUS: Selected by New York Yankees organization in 26th round of free-agent baseball draft (June 1, 1995); did not sign. ... Regular-season record as starting NFL quarterback: 15-12 (.556). ... Postseason record as starting NFL quarterback: 1-1 (.500).

			PASSING							RUSHING				TOTALS		
Year Team	G	GS	Att.	Cmp.	Pct.	Yds.	TD	Int.	Avg.	Rat.	Att.	Yds.	Avg.	TD	TD	2pt.	Pts.
1999—Minnesota NFL	1	0	0	0	0.00	0	0	0	0.0	...	3	6	2.0	0	0	0	0
2000—Minnesota NFL	16	16	474	297	62.7	3937	33	16	8.31	98.0	89	470	5.3	7	7	0	42
2001—Minnesota NFL	11	11	366	235	64.2	2612	14	13	7.14	83.3	71	416	5.9	5	5	†2	34
Pro totals (3 years)	28	27	840	532	63.3	6549	47	29	7.80	91.6	163	892	5.5	12	12	2	76

CUNNINGHAM, RANDALL — QB

PERSONAL: Born March 27, 1963, in Santa Barbara, Calif. ... 6-4/215. ... Brother of Sam Cunningham, running back with New England Patriots (1973-79 and 1981).
HIGH SCHOOL: Santa Barbara (Calif.).
COLLEGE: UNLV.

TRANSACTIONS/CAREER NOTES: Selected by Arizona Outlaws in 1985 USFL territorial draft. ... Selected by Philadelphia Eagles in second round (37th pick overall) of 1985 NFL draft. ... Signed by Eagles (July 22, 1985). ... On injured reserve with knee injury (September 3, 1991-remainder of season). ... Granted unconditional free agency (February 16, 1996). ... On retired list (August 30, 1996-April 15, 1997). ... Signed by Minnesota Vikings (April 15, 1997). ... Granted unconditional free agency (February 13, 1998). ... Re-signed by Vikings (March 24, 1998). ... Released by Vikings (June 2, 2000). ... Signed by Dallas Cowboys (June 8, 2000). ... Granted unconditional free agency (March 2, 2001). ... Signed by Baltimore Ravens (May 29, 2001). ... Granted unconditional free agency (March 1, 2002).
CHAMPIONSHIP GAME EXPERIENCE: Played in NFC championship game (1998 season).
HONORS: Named punter on THE SPORTING NEWS college All-America first team (1984). ... Played in Pro Bowl (1988-1990 and 1998 seasons). ... Named Outstanding Player of Pro Bowl (1988 season).
RECORDS: Holds NFL single-season record for most times sacked—72 (1986). ... Shares NFL single-game records for most own fumbles recovered—4 (November 30, 1986, OT, at Los Angeles Raiders); and most own and opponents' fumbles recovered—4 (November 30, 1986, OT, at Los Angeles Raiders).
PRO STATISTICS: 1985—Fumbled three times. 1986—Punted twice for 54 yards, fumbled seven times and recovered four fumbles. 1987—Caught one pass for minus three yards, led league with 12 fumbles and recovered six fumbles for minus seven yards. 1988—Punted three times for 167 yards, led league with 14 fumbles and recovered six fumbles. 1989—Punted six times for 319 yards, led the NFC with 17 fumbles and recovered four fumbles for minus six yards. 1990—Fumbled nine times and recovered three fumbles for minus four yards. 1992—Led league with 13 fumbles and recovered three fumbles. 1993—Fumbled three times. 1994—Punted once for 80 yards, fumbled 10 times and recovered five fumbles for minus 15 yards. 1995—Fumbled three times and recovered one fumble for minus five yards. 1997—Fumbled four times and recovered two fumbles. 1998—Caught one pass for minus three yards and fumbled twice. 1999—Fumbled twice for minus one yard. 2000—Fumbled four times and recovered three fumbles for minus two yards. 2001—Fumbled four times and recovered three fumbles for minus nine yards.
SINGLE GAME HIGHS (regular season): Attempts—62 (October 2, 1989, vs. Chicago); completions—34 (September 17, 1989, vs. Washington); passing yards—447 (September 17, 1989, vs. Washington); and touchdown passes—5 (September 17, 1989, vs. Washington).
STATISTICAL PLATEAUS: 300-yard passing games: 1987 (1), 1988 (2), 1989 (3), 1992 (1), 1993 (1), 1994 (4), 1998 (4), 1999 (2). Total: 18. ... 100-yard rushing games: 1986 (1), 1990 (1), 1992 (1). Total: 3.
MISCELLANEOUS: Regular-season record as starting NFL quarterback: 82-52-1 (.607). ... Postseason record as starting NFL quarterback: 3-6 (.333).

				PASSING							RUSHING			TOTALS		
Year Team	G	GS	Att.	Cmp.	Pct.	Yds.	TD	Int.	Avg.	Rat.	Att.	Yds.	Avg.	TD	TD	2pt.	Pts.
1985—Philadelphia NFL	6	4	81	34	42.0	548	1	8	6.77	29.8	29	205	7.1	0	0	0	0
1986—Philadelphia NFL	15	5	209	111	53.1	1391	8	7	6.66	72.9	66	540	8.2	5	5	0	30
1987—Philadelphia NFL	12	12	406	223	54.9	2786	23	12	6.86	83.0	76	505	6.6	3	3	0	18
1988—Philadelphia NFL	16	16	‡560	301	53.8	3808	24	16	6.80	77.6	93	624	6.7	6	6	0	36
1989—Philadelphia NFL	16	16	532	290	54.5	3400	21	15	6.39	75.5	104	621	*6.0	4	4	0	24
1990—Philadelphia NFL	16	16	465	271	58.3	3466	‡30	13	7.45	91.6	118	942	*8.0	5	5	0	30
1991—Philadelphia NFL	1	1	4	1	25.0	19	0	0	4.75	46.9	0	0	0.0	0	0	0	0
1992—Philadelphia NFL	15	15	384	233	60.7	2775	19	11	7.23	87.3	87	549	6.3	5	5	0	30
1993—Philadelphia NFL	4	4	110	76	69.1	850	5	5	7.73	88.1	18	110	6.1	1	1	0	6
1994—Philadelphia NFL	14	14	490	265	54.1	3229	16	13	6.59	74.4	65	288	4.4	3	3	0	18
1995—Philadelphia NFL	7	4	121	69	57.0	605	3	5	5.00	61.5	21	98	4.7	0	0	0	0
1996—								Did not play.									
1997—Minnesota NFL	6	3	88	44	50.0	501	6	4	5.69	71.3	19	127	6.7	0	0	0	0
1998—Minnesota NFL	15	14	425	259	60.9	3704	34	10	8.72	*106.0	32	132	4.1	1	1	1	8
1999—Minnesota NFL	6	6	200	124	62.0	1475	8	9	7.38	79.1	10	58	5.8	0	0	0	0
2000—Dallas NFL	6	3	125	74	59.2	849	6	4	6.79	82.4	23	89	3.9	1	1	0	6
2001—Baltimore NFL	6	2	89	54	60.7	573	3	2	6.44	81.3	14	40	2.9	1	1	0	6
Pro totals (16 years)	161	135	4289	2429	56.6	29979	207	134	6.99	81.5	775	4928	6.4	35	35	1	212

CURRY, DeMARCUS   OT

PERSONAL: Born April 30, 1975, in Columbus, Ga. ... 6-5/332.
HIGH SCHOOL: Kendrick (Columbus, Ga.).
COLLEGE: Auburn.
TRANSACTIONS/CAREER NOTES: Signed as non-drafted free agent by Tampa Bay Buccaneers (April 19, 1999). ... Released by Buccaneers (September 5, 1999). ... Re-signed by Buccaneers to practice squad (September 6, 1999). ... Released by Buccaneers (September 22, 1999). ... Re-signed by Buccaneers to practice squad (September 28, 1999). ... Activated (January 22, 2000). ... Released by Buccaneers (May 21, 2002).
PLAYING EXPERIENCE: Tampa Bay NFL, 2001. ... Games/Games started: 2001 (3/0).

CURRY, DONTE'   LB   REDSKINS

PERSONAL: Born July 22, 1978, in Savannah, Ga. ... 6-1/226.
HIGH SCHOOL: Savannah (Ga.).
JUNIOR COLLEGE: Middle Georgia Junior College.
COLLEGE: Morris Brown.
TRANSACTIONS/CAREER NOTES: Signed as non-drafted free agent by Green Bay Packers (April 24, 2001). ... Released by Packers (September 1, 2001). ... Re-signed by Packers to practice squad (September 3, 2001). ... Signed by Washington Redskins off Packers practice squad (October 3, 2001).
PLAYING EXPERIENCE: Washington NFL, 2001. ... Games/Games started: 2001 (8/0).

CURTIS, CANUTE   LB   BENGALS

PERSONAL: Born August 4, 1974, in Amityville, N.Y. ... 6-2/257. ... Name pronounced kuh-NOOT.
HIGH SCHOOL: Farmingdale (N.Y.).
COLLEGE: West Virginia.
TRANSACTIONS/CAREER NOTES: Selected by Cincinnati Bengals in sixth round (176th pick overall) of 1997 NFL draft. ... Signed by Bengals (July 11, 1997). ... Released by Bengals (August 24, 1997). ... Re-signed by Bengals to practice squad (August 26, 1997). ... Activated

(October 21, 1997). ... Released by Bengals (August 30, 1998). ... Re-signed by Bengals to practice squad (August 31, 1998). ... Activated (November 10, 1998). ... Granted free agency (February 11, 2000). ... Re-signed by Bengals (March 1, 2000).
PLAYING EXPERIENCE: Cincinnati NFL, 1997-2001. ... Games/games started: 1997 (3/0), 1998 (5/0), 1999 (15/0), 2000 (15/0), 2001 (16/4). Total: 54/4.
HONORS: Named outside linebacker on THE SPORTING NEWS college All-America first team (1996).
PRO STATISTICS: 1999—Credited with one sack. 2000—Credited with two sacks and recovered one fumble. 2001—Recovered one fumble for three yards.

CUSHING, MATT   TE   STEELERS

PERSONAL: Born July 2, 1975, in Chicago. ... 6-4/260. ... Full name: Matt Jay Cushing.
HIGH SCHOOL: Mount Carmel (Chicago).
COLLEGE: Illinois.
TRANSACTIONS/CAREER NOTES: Signed as non-drafted free agent by Pittsburgh Steelers (April 24, 1998). ... Released by Steelers (August 24, 1998). ... Re-signed by Steelers (February 22, 1999). ... Assigned to Amsterdam Admirals in 1999 NFL Europe enhancement allocation program (February 22, 1999). ... Released by Steelers (September 5, 1999). ... Re-signed by Steelers (October 28, 1999). ... Released by Steelers (August 27, 2000). ... Re-signed by Steelers (November 7, 2000). ... Granted free agency (March 1, 2002).
CHAMPIONSHIP GAME EXPERIENCE: Played in AFC championship game (2001 season).
SINGLE GAME HIGHS (regular season): Receptions—2 (December 23, 2001, vs. Detroit); yards—29 (January 2, 2000, vs. Tennessee); and touchdown receptions—1 (December 23, 2001, vs. Detroit).

			RECEIVING				TOTALS		
Year Team	G	GS	No.	Yds.	Avg.	TD	TD	2pt.	Pts.	Fum.
1999—Amsterdam NFLE	...	...	6	62	10.3	0	0	0	0	0
—Pittsburgh NFL	7	1	2	29	14.5	0	0	0	0	0
2000—Pittsburgh NFL	7	1	4	17	4.3	0	0	0	0	0
2001—Pittsburgh NFL	13	3	5	24	4.8	1	1	0	6	0
NFL Europe totals (1 year)	...	...	6	62	10.3	0	0	0	0	0
NFL totals (3 years)	27	5	11	70	6.4	1	1	0	6	0
Pro totals (4 years)	...	...	17	132	7.8	1	1	0	6	0

DALTON, LIONAL   DT   BRONCOS

PERSONAL: Born February 21, 1975, in Detroit. ... 6-1/309.
HIGH SCHOOL: Cooley (Detroit).
COLLEGE: Eastern Michigan.
TRANSACTIONS/CAREER NOTES: Signed as non-drafted free agent by Baltimore Ravens (April 23, 1998). ... Granted free agency (March 2, 2001). ... Re-signed by Ravens (March 29, 2001). ... Granted unconditional free agency (March 1, 2002). ... Signed by Denver Broncos (March 20, 2002).
PLAYING EXPERIENCE: Baltimore NFL, 1998-2001. ... Games/Games started: 1998 (2/1), 1999 (16/2), 2000 (16/1), 2001 (16/3). Total: 50/7.
CHAMPIONSHIP GAME EXPERIENCE: Played in AFC championship game (2000 season). ... Member of Super Bowl championship team (2000 season).
PRO STATISTICS: 1999—Credited with one sack.

DALUISO, BRAD   K

PERSONAL: Born December 31, 1967, in San Diego. ... 6-1/180. ... Full name: Bradley William Daluiso.
HIGH SCHOOL: Valhalla (El Cajon, Calif.).
JUNIOR COLLEGE: Grossmont College (Calif.).
COLLEGE: San Diego State, then UCLA.
TRANSACTIONS/CAREER NOTES: Signed as non-drafted free agent by Green Bay Packers (May 2, 1991). ... Traded by Packers to Atlanta Falcons for an undisclosed pick in 1992 draft (August 26, 1991). ... Claimed on waivers by Buffalo Bills (September 10, 1991). ... Granted unconditional free agency (February 1, 1992). ... Signed by Dallas Cowboys (February 18, 1992). ... Claimed on waivers by Denver Broncos (September 1, 1992). ... Released by Broncos (August 23, 1993). ... Signed by New York Giants (September 1, 1993). ... Granted free agency (February 17, 1994). ... Re-signed by Giants (June 21, 1994). ... Granted unconditional free agency (February 17, 1995). ... Re-signed by Giants (February 22, 1995). ... Granted unconditional free agency (February 13, 1998). ... Re-signed by Giants (February 13, 1998). ... On injured reserve with knee injury (October 20, 1999-remainder of season). ... Granted unconditional free agency (March 2, 2001). ... Signed by Oakland Raiders (January 4, 2002). ... Released by Raiders (January 8, 2002).
CHAMPIONSHIP GAME EXPERIENCE: Played in AFC championship game (1991 season). ... Played in Super Bowl XXVI (1991 season). ... Played in NFC championship game (2000 season). ... Played in Super Bowl XXXV (2000 season).
PRO STATISTICS: 1992—Punted 10 times for 467 yards.

				KICKING			
Year Team	G	XPM	XPA	FGM	FGA	Lg.	50+	Pts.
1991—Atlanta NFL	2	2	2	2	3	23	0-0	8
—Buffalo NFL	14	0	0	0	0	0	0-0	0
1992—Denver NFL	16	0	0	0	1	0	0-1	0
1993—New York Giants NFL	15	0	0	1	3	54	1-3	3
1994—New York Giants NFL	16	5	5	11	11	52	1-1	38
1995—New York Giants NFL	16	28	28	20	28	51	2-2	88
1996—New York Giants NFL	16	22	22	24	27	46	0-0	94
1997—New York Giants NFL	16	27	29	22	32	52	1-4	93
1998—New York Giants NFL	16	32	32	21	27	51	1-1	95
1999—New York Giants NFL	6	9	9	7	9	36	0-0	30
2000—New York Giants NFL	14	34	34	17	23	46	0-0	85
2001—Oakland NFL	1	1	2	3	4	44	0-0	10
Pro totals (11 years)	148	160	163	128	168	54	6-12	544

DANIELS, PHILLIP — DE — BEARS

PERSONAL: Born March 4, 1973, in Donaldsonville, Ga. ... 6-5/284. ... Full name: Phillip Bernard Daniels.
HIGH SCHOOL: Seminole County (Donaldsonville, Ga.).
COLLEGE: Georgia.
TRANSACTIONS/CAREER NOTES: Selected by Seattle Seahawks in fourth round (99th pick overall) of 1996 NFL draft. ... Signed by Seahawks (July 17, 1996). ... Granted free agency (February 12, 1999). ... Re-signed by Seahawks (April 6, 1999). ... Granted unconditional free agency (February 11, 2000). ... Signed by Chicago Bears (February 12, 2000). ... On injured reserve with ankle injury (December 13, 2000-remainder of season).
PRO STATISTICS: 1996—Recovered one fumble. 1997—Returned one kickoff for minus two yards and fumbled once. 1998—Recovered two fumbles. 2000—Recovered one fumble. 2001—Recovered two fumbles.

Year Team	G	GS	SACKS
1996—Seattle NFL	15	0	2.0
1997—Seattle NFL	13	10	4.0
1998—Seattle NFL	16	15	6.5
1999—Seattle NFL	16	16	9.0
2000—Chicago NFL	14	14	6.0
2001—Chicago NFL	16	16	9.0
Pro totals (6 years)	**90**	**71**	**36.5**

DARBY, CHARTRIC — DT — BUCCANEERS

PERSONAL: Born October 22, 1975, in North, S.C. ... 6-0/270. ... Full name: Chartric Terrell Darby.
HIGH SCHOOL: North (S.C.).
COLLEGE: South Carolina State.
TRANSACTIONS/CAREER NOTES: Signed as non-drafted free agent by Baltimore Ravens (April 23, 1998). ... Released by Ravens (August 30, 1998). ... Re-signed by Ravens to practice squad (September 1, 1998). ... Granted free agency after 1998 season. ... Signed by Indianapolis Colts (January 19, 1999). ... Claimed on waivers by Carolina Panthers (April 28, 1999). ... Released by Panthers (August 30, 1999). ... Selected by Rhein Fire in 2000 NFL Europe draft (February 22, 2000). ... Signed by Buccaneers (July 10, 2000). ... Released by Buccaneers (August 27, 2000). ... Re-signed by Buccaneers to practice squad (August 28, 2000).
PRO STATISTICS: 2001—Recovered one fumble.

Year Team	G	GS	SACKS
2000—Barcelona NFLE	...	...	8.5
2001—Tampa Bay NFL	13	0	2.0
NFL Europe totals (1 year)	...	...	8.5
NFL totals (1 year)	13	0	2.0
Pro totals (2 years)	...	...	**10.5**

DARCHE, JEAN-PHILIPE — TE — SEAHAWKS

PERSONAL: Born February 28, 1975, in Montreal. ... 6-0/239. ... Brother of Mathieu Darche, left winger, Columbus Blue Jackets.
HIGH SCHOOL: Andre Grassett Junior College (Montreal).
COLLEGE: McGill (Montreal).
TRANSACTIONS/CAREER NOTES: Signed as non-drafted free agent by Seattle Seahawks (May 11, 2000).
PLAYING EXPERIENCE: Seattle NFL, 2000 and 2001. ... Games/Games started: 2000 (16/0), 2001 (16/0). Total: 32/0.

DARIUS, DONOVIN — S — JAGUARS

PERSONAL: Born August 12, 1975, in Camden, N.J. ... 6-1/216. ... Full name: Donovin Lee Darius.
HIGH SCHOOL: Woodrow Wilson (Camden, N.J.).
COLLEGE: Syracuse (degree in exercise science, 1997).
TRANSACTIONS/CAREER NOTES: Selected by Jacksonville Jaguars in first round (25th pick overall) of 1998 NFL draft. ... Signed by Jaguars (July 23, 1998).
PLAYING EXPERIENCE: Jacksonville NFL, 1998-2001. ... Games/Games started: 1998 (14/14), 1999 (16/16), 2000 (16/16), 2001 (11/11). Total: 57/57.
CHAMPIONSHIP GAME EXPERIENCE: Played in AFC championship game (1999 season).
HONORS: Named free safety on The Sporting News college All-America first team (1997).
PRO STATISTICS: 1998—Recovered one fumble for 83 yards and a touchdown. 1999—Intercepted four passes for 37 yards. 2000—Intercepted two passes for 26 yards and credited with one sack. 2001—Intercepted one pass for 39 yards.

DARLING, JAMES — LB — JETS

PERSONAL: Born December 29, 1974, in Denver. ... 6-0/250. ... Full name: James Jackson Darling.
HIGH SCHOOL: Kettle Falls (Wash.).
COLLEGE: Washington State.
TRANSACTIONS/CAREER NOTES: Selected by Philadelphia Eagles in second round (57th pick overall) of 1997 NFL draft. ... Signed by Eagles (July 16, 1997). ... Granted free agency (February 11, 2000). ... Re-signed by Eagles (April 10, 2000). ... Granted unconditional free agency (March 2, 2001). ... Signed by New York Jets (March 21, 2001).
PLAYING EXPERIENCE: Philadelphia NFL, 1997-2000; New York Jets NFL, 2001. ... Games/Games started: 1997 (16/6), 1998 (12/8), 1999 (15/10), 2000 (16/0), 2001 (16/0). Total: 75/24.
HONORS: Named inside linebacker on The Sporting News college All-America second team (1996).
PRO STATISTICS: 1998—Credited with two sacks. 1999—Intercepted one pass for 33 yards. 2000—Credited with 1/2 sack.

DAVENPORT, JOE DEAN — TE — COLTS

PERSONAL: Born October 29, 1976, in Springdale, Ark. ... 6-6/273. ... Full name: Joe Dean Davenport.
HIGH SCHOOL: Springdale (Ark.).
COLLEGE: Arkansas.
TRANSACTIONS/CAREER NOTES: Signed as non-drafted free agent by Indianapolis Colts (May 9, 2001).
PLAYING EXPERIENCE: Indianapolis NFL, 2001. ... Games/Games started: 2001 (3/0).

DAVIS, DON — LB — RAMS

PERSONAL: Born December 17, 1972, in Olathe, Kan. ... 6-1/234.
HIGH SCHOOL: Olathe (Kan.) South.
COLLEGE: Kansas.
TRANSACTIONS/CAREER NOTES: Signed as non-drafted free agent by New York Jets (April 28, 1995). ... Released by Jets (August 27, 1995). ... Signed by Kansas City Chiefs (January 9, 1996). ... Released by Chiefs (August 20, 1996). ... Signed by New Orleans Saints to practice squad (August 27, 1996). ... Activated (October 4, 1996). ... On injured reserve with wrist injury (November 19, 1997-remainder of season). ... Claimed on waivers by Tampa Bay Buccaneers (November 25, 1998). ... Granted free agency (February 12, 1999). ... Re-signed by Buccaneers (May 21, 1999). ... Released by Buccaneers (October 9, 1999). ... Re-signed by Buccaneers (October 19, 1999). ... Granted unconditional free agency (February 11, 2000). ... Re-signed by Buccaneers (July 1, 2000). ... Granted unconditional free agency (March 2, 2001). ... Signed by St. Louis Rams (March 3, 2001).
PLAYING EXPERIENCE: New Orleans NFL, 1996 and 1997; New Orleans (4)-Tampa Bay (5) NFL, 1998; Tampa Bay NFL, 1999 and 2000; St. Louis NFL, 2001. ... Games/Games started: 1996 (11/0), 1997 (11/0), 1998 (N.O.-4/0; T.B.-5/0; Total: 9/0), 1999 (14/0), 2000 (16/0), 2001 (12/8). Total: 73/8.
CHAMPIONSHIP GAME EXPERIENCE: Played in NFC championship game (1999 and 2001 seasons). ... Played in Super Bowl XXXVI (2001 season).
PRO STATISTICS: 1996—Recovered one fumble. 2001—Recovered one fumble.

DAVIS, ERIC — CB

PERSONAL: Born January 26, 1968, in Anniston, Ala. ... 5-11/185. ... Full name: Eric Wayne Davis.
HIGH SCHOOL: Anniston (Ala.).
COLLEGE: Jacksonville (Ala.) State.
TRANSACTIONS/CAREER NOTES: Selected by San Francisco 49ers in second round (53rd pick overall) of 1990 NFL draft. ... Signed by 49ers (July 28, 1990). ... On injured reserve with shoulder injury (September 11, 1991-remainder of season). ... Granted free agency (March 1, 1993). ... Re-signed by 49ers (July 20, 1993). ... Granted unconditional free agency (February 16, 1996). ... Signed by Carolina Panthers (February 21, 1996). ... Released by Panthers (February 28, 2001). ... Signed by Denver Broncos (August 2, 2001). ... Granted unconditional free agency (March 1, 2002).
CHAMPIONSHIP GAME EXPERIENCE: Played in NFC championship game (1990, 1992-1994 and 1996 seasons). ... Member of Super Bowl championship team (1994 season).
HONORS: Played in Pro Bowl (1995 and 1996 seasons).
POST SEASON RECORDS: Shares NFL postseason career record for most consecutive games with one or more interception—3.
PRO STATISTICS: 1990—Returned five punts for 38 yards and recovered one fumble for 34 yards. 1992—Recovered two fumbles. 1993—Recovered one fumble for 47 yards and a touchdown. 1994—Recovered two fumbles. 1995—Credited with one sack. 1997—Recovered one fumble for two yards. 1998—Credited with one sack and recovered one fumble. 1999—Fumbled once and recovered one fumble. 2000—Returned two punts for 24 yards, fumbled once and recovered one fumble. 2001—Recovered one fumble.
MISCELLANEOUS: Holds Carolina Panthers all-time record for most interceptions (25).

			INTERCEPTIONS			
Year Team	G	GS	No.	Yds.	Avg.	TD
1990—San Francisco NFL	16	0	1	13	13.0	0
1991—San Francisco NFL	2	2	0	0	0.0	0
1992—San Francisco NFL	16	16	3	52	17.3	0
1993—San Francisco NFL	16	16	4	45	11.3	1
1994—San Francisco NFL	16	16	1	8	8.0	0
1995—San Francisco NFL	15	15	3	84	28.0	1
1996—Carolina NFL	16	16	5	57	11.4	0
1997—Carolina NFL	14	14	5	25	5.0	0
1998—Carolina NFL	16	16	5	81	16.2	2
1999—Carolina NFL	16	16	5	49	9.8	0
2000—Carolina NFL	16	16	5	14	2.8	0
2001—Denver NFL	16	0	0	0	0.0	0
Pro totals (12 years)	175	143	37	428	11.6	4

DAVIS, JOHN — TE — BEARS

PERSONAL: Born May 14, 1973, in Jasper, Texas. ... 6-4/264.
HIGH SCHOOL: Jasper (Texas).
JUNIOR COLLEGE: Cisco (Texas) Junior College.
COLLEGE: Emporia (Kan.) State.
TRANSACTIONS/CAREER NOTES: Selected by Dallas Cowboys in fifth round of 1994 supplemental draft. ... Signed by Cowboys for 1994 season. ... Released by Cowboys (August 28, 1994). ... Re-signed by Cowboys to practice squad (August 30, 1994). ... On injured reserve with ankle injury (prior to 1995 season-October 31, 1995). ... Released by Cowboys (October 31, 1995). ... Signed by New Orleans Saints (June 3, 1996). ... Released by Saints (August 12, 1996). ... Signed by Tampa Bay Buccaneers (January 20, 1997). ... Granted free agency (February 12, 1999). ... Re-signed by Buccaneers (April 18, 1999). ... Granted unconditional free agency (February 11, 2000). ... Signed by Minnesota Vikings (May 31, 2000). ... Released by Vikings (August 8, 2001). ... Signed by Chicago Bears (August 14, 2001).
CHAMPIONSHIP GAME EXPERIENCE: Played in NFC championship game (1999 and 2000 seasons).

SINGLE GAME HIGHS (regular season): Receptions—4 (October 1, 2000, vs. Detroit); yards—42 (September 10, 2000, vs. Miami); and touchdown receptions—1 (October 9, 2000, vs. Tampa Bay).

				RECEIVING				TOTALS		
Year Team	G	GS	No.	Yds.	Avg.	TD	TD	2pt.	Pts.	Fum.
1997—Tampa Bay NFL	8	2	3	35	11.7	0	0	0	0	0
1998—Tampa Bay NFL	16	0	2	12	6.0	1	1	0	6	0
1999—Tampa Bay NFL	16	0	2	7	3.5	1	1	0	6	0
2000—Minnesota NFL	15	9	17	202	11.9	0	1	0	6	0
2001—Chicago NFL	16	6	11	68	6.2	0	0	0	0	0
Pro totals (5 years)	71	17	35	324	9.3	3	3	0	18	0

DAVIS, LEONARD   OT   CARDINALS

PERSONAL: Born September 5, 1978, in Wortham, Texas. ... 6-6/370. ... Full name: Leonard Barnett Davis.
HIGH SCHOOL: Wortham (Texas).
COLLEGE: Texas.
TRANSACTIONS/CAREER NOTES: Selected by Arizona Cardinals in first round (second pick overall) of 2001 NFL draft. ... Signed by Cardinals (August 8, 2001).
PLAYING EXPERIENCE: Arizona NFL, 2001. ... Games/Games started: 2001 (16/16).
HONORS: Named offensive tackle on THE SPORTING NEWS college All-America first team (2000).

DAVIS, ROB   C   PACKERS

PERSONAL: Born December 10, 1968, in Washington, D.C. ... 6-3/286. ... Full name: Robert Emmett Davis.
HIGH SCHOOL: Eleanor Roosevelt (Greenbelt, Md.).
COLLEGE: Shippensburg, Pa. (degree in criminal justice/law enforcement).
TRANSACTIONS/CAREER NOTES: Signed as non-drafted free agent by New York Jets (April 27, 1993). ... Released by Jets (August 24, 1993). ... Re-signed by Jets (April 29, 1994). ... Released by Jets (August 22, 1994). ... Signed by Baltimore Stallions of CFL (April 1995). ... Signed by Kansas City Chiefs (April 22, 1996). ... Released by Chiefs (August 20, 1996). ... Signed by Chicago Bears (August 28, 1996). ... Released by Bears (August 27, 1997). ... Signed by Green Bay Packers (November 4, 1997). ... On physically unable to perform list with back injury (July 18-August 10, 1998). ... Granted unconditional free agency (March 2, 2001). ... Re-signed by Packers (March 20, 2001).
PLAYING EXPERIENCE: Baltimore CFL, 1995; Chicago NFL, 1996; Green Bay NFL, 1997-2001. ... Games/Games started: 1995 (18/games started unavailable), 1996 (16/0), 1997 (7/0), 1998 (16/0), 1999 (16/0), 2000 (16/0), 2001 (16/0). Total CFL: 18/-. Total NFL: 87/0. Total Pro: 105/-.
CHAMPIONSHIP GAME EXPERIENCE: Played in NFC championship game (1997 season). ... Played in Super Bowl XXXII (1997 season).
PRO STATISTICS: 2000—Recovered one fumble.

DAVIS, RUSSELL   DT   CARDINALS

PERSONAL: Born March 28, 1975, in Fayetteville, N.C. ... 6-4/306. ... Full name: Russell Morgan Davis.
HIGH SCHOOL: E.E. Smith (Fayetteville, N.C.).
COLLEGE: North Carolina.
TRANSACTIONS/CAREER NOTES: Selected by Chicago Bears in second round (48th pick overall) of 1999 NFL draft. ... Signed by Bears (July 22, 1999). ... Claimed on waivers by Arizona Cardinals (August 28, 2000).

Year Team	G	GS	SACKS
1999—Chicago NFL	11	8	2.0
2000—Arizona NFL	13	9	0.5
2001—Arizona NFL	16	16	2.0
Pro totals (3 years)	40	33	4.5

DAVIS, STEPHEN   RB   REDSKINS

PERSONAL: Born March 1, 1974, in Spartanburg, S.C. ... 6-0/234.
HIGH SCHOOL: Spartanburg (S.C.).
COLLEGE: Auburn (degree in vocational education, 1995).
TRANSACTIONS/CAREER NOTES: Selected by Washington Redskins in fourth round (102nd pick overall) of 1996 NFL draft. ... Signed by Redskins (July 16, 1996). ... Granted free agency (February 12, 1999). ... Re-signed by Redskins (May 12, 1999). ... Designated by Redskins as franchise player (February 11, 2000).
HONORS: Played in Pro Bowl (1999 and 2000 seasons).
PRO STATISTICS: 1997—Returned three kickoffs for 62 yards and recovered one fumble. 1999—Recovered two fumbles. 2000—Recovered one fumble. 2001—Recovered seven fumbles.
SINGLE GAME HIGHS (regular season): Attempts—38 (January 6, 2002, vs. Arizona); yards—189 (December 12, 1999, vs. Arizona); and rushing touchdowns—3 (September 26, 1999, vs. New York Jets).
STATISTICAL PLATEAUS: 100-yard rushing games: 1999 (6), 2000 (5), 2001 (6). Total: 17. ... 100-yard receiving games: 1998 (1).

			RUSHING				RECEIVING				TOTALS		
Year Team	G	GS	Att.	Yds.	Avg.	TD	No.	Yds.	Avg.	TD	TD	2pt.	Pts.	Fum.
1996—Washington NFL	12	0	23	139	6.0	2	0	0	0.0	0	2	0	12	0
1997—Washington NFL	14	6	141	567	4.0	3	18	134	7.4	0	3	0	18	1
1998—Washington NFL	16	12	34	109	3.2	0	21	263	12.5	2	2	0	12	0
1999—Washington NFL	14	14	290	‡1405	4.8	*17	23	111	4.8	0	†17	†1	104	4
2000—Washington NFL	15	15	332	1318	4.0	11	33	313	9.5	0	11	0	66	4
2001—Washington NFL	16	16	*356	‡1432	4.0	5	28	205	7.3	0	5	1	32	6
Pro totals (6 years)	87	63	1176	4970	4.2	38	123	1026	8.3	2	40	2	244	15

DAVIS, TERRELL — RB — BRONCOS

PERSONAL: Born October 28, 1972, in San Diego. ... 5-11/210.
HIGH SCHOOL: Abraham Lincoln Prep (San Diego).
COLLEGE: Long Beach State, then Georgia.
TRANSACTIONS/CAREER NOTES: Selected by Denver Broncos in sixth round (196th pick overall) of 1995 NFL draft. ... Signed by Broncos (June 30, 1995). ... On injured reserve with knee injury (October 6, 1999-remainder of season).
CHAMPIONSHIP GAME EXPERIENCE: Played in AFC championship game (1997 and 1998 seasons). ... Member of Super Bowl championship team (1997 and 1998 seasons).
HONORS: Named running back on The Sporting News NFL All-Pro team (1996-1998). ... Played in Pro Bowl (1996 and 1997 seasons). ... Named Most Valuable Player of Super Bowl XXXII (1997 season). ... Named to play in Pro Bowl (1998 season); replaced by Curtis Martin due to injury. ... Named NFL Player of the Year by The Sporting News (1998).
POST SEASON RECORDS: Holds Super Bowl single-game record for most rushing touchdowns—3 (January 25, 1998, vs. Green Bay). ... Shares Super Bowl single-game records for most points—18; and most touchdowns—3 (January 25, 1998, vs. Green Bay). ... Holds NFL postseason career record for highest average gain—5.41. ... Holds NFL postseason record for most consecutive games with 100 or more yards rushing—7 (1997-present). ... Shares NFL postseason career record for most games with 100 or more yards rushing—7.
PRO STATISTICS: 1995—Recovered one fumble. 1996—Recovered two fumbles. 1997—Recovered two fumbles for minus seven yards. 1998—Recovered one fumble. 1999—Recovered one fumble. 2001—Recovered one fumble.
SINGLE GAME HIGHS (regular season): Attempts—42 (October 26, 1997, vs. Buffalo); yards—215 (September 21, 1997, vs. Cincinnati); and rushing touchdowns—3 (December 6, 1998, vs. Kansas City).
STATISTICAL PLATEAUS: 100-yard rushing games: 1995 (3), 1996 (6), 1997 (10), 1998 (11), 2000 (1), 2001 (2). Total: 33.
MISCELLANEOUS: Holds Denver Broncos all-time records for most yards rushing (7,607), most touchdowns (65) and most rushing touchdowns (60).

			RUSHING				RECEIVING				TOTALS		
Year Team	G	GS	Att.	Yds.	Avg.	TD	No.	Yds.	Avg.	TD	TD	2pt.	Pts.	Fum.
1995—Denver NFL	14	14	237	1117	§4.7	7	49	367	7.5	1	8	0	48	5
1996—Denver NFL	16	16	§345	§1538	4.5	13	36	310	8.6	2	15	0	90	5
1997—Denver NFL	15	15	369	§1750	4.7	†15	42	287	6.8	0	15	3	†96	4
1998—Denver NFL	16	16	§392	*2008	*5.1	*21	25	217	8.7	2	*23	0	138	2
1999—Denver NFL	4	4	67	211	3.1	2	3	26	8.7	0	2	0	12	1
2000—Denver NFL	5	4	78	282	3.6	2	2	4	2.0	0	2	0	12	1
2001—Denver NFL	8	8	167	701	4.2	0	12	69	5.8	0	0	0	0	2
Pro totals (7 years)	78	77	1655	7607	4.6	60	169	1280	7.6	5	65	3	396	20

DAVIS, THABITI — WR — GIANTS

PERSONAL: Born March 24, 1975, in Charlotte, N.C. ... 6-2/205.
HIGH SCHOOL: West Charlotte (N.C), then Olympic (Charlotte, N.C.).
COLLEGE: Wake Forest.
TRANSACTIONS/CAREER NOTES: Signed as non-drafted free agent by New York Giants (June 29, 2000).
PLAYING EXPERIENCE: New York Giants NFL, 2000 and 2001. ... Games/Games started: 2000 (13/0), 2001 (16/0). Total: 29/0.
CHAMPIONSHIP GAME EXPERIENCE: Played in NFC championship game (2000 season). ... Played in Super Bowl XXXV (2000 season).
PRO STATISTICS: 2000—Caught two passes for 40 yards. 2001—Caught three passes for 34 yards.
SINGLE GAME HIGHS (regular season): Receptions—2 (January 6, 2002, vs. Green Bay); yards—27 (November 19, 2000, vs. Detroit); and touchdown receptions—0.

DAVIS, TYRONE — TE — PACKERS

PERSONAL: Born June 30, 1972, in Halifax, Va. ... 6-4/260.
HIGH SCHOOL: Halifax County (South Boston, Va.), then Fork Union (Va.) Military Academy.
COLLEGE: Virginia.
TRANSACTIONS/CAREER NOTES: Selected by New York Jets in fourth round (107th pick overall) of 1995 NFL draft. ... Signed by Jets (June 14, 1995). ... Released by Jets (September 13, 1995). ... Re-signed by Jets to practice squad (September 15, 1995). ... Activated (December 11, 1995). ... Granted free agency (February 14, 1997). ... Re-signed by Jets for 1997 season. ... Traded by Jets to Green Bay Packers for past considerations (August 25, 1997). ... Released by Packers (September 24, 1997). ... Re-signed by Packers (September 29, 1997). ... Granted unconditional free agency (March 2, 2001). ... Re-signed by Packers (March 21, 2001). ... On physically unable to perform list with hamstring injury (August 28-November 27, 2001). ... Granted unconditional free agency (March 1, 2002). ... Re-signed by Packers (April 23, 2002).
CHAMPIONSHIP GAME EXPERIENCE: Played in NFC championship game (1997 season). ... Played in Super Bowl XXXII (1997 season).
PRO STATISTICS: 1997—Recovered one fumble in end zone for a touchdown.
SINGLE GAME HIGHS (regular season): Receptions—5 (September 17, 2000, vs. Philadelphia); yards—83 (November 15, 1998, vs. New York Giants); and touchdown receptions—2 (November 22, 1998, vs. Minnesota).

			RECEIVING				TOTALS			
Year Team	G	GS	No.	Yds.	Avg.	TD	TD	2pt.	Pts.	Fum.
1995—New York Jets NFL	4	0	1	9	9.0	0	0	0	0	0
1996—New York Jets NFL	2	0	1	6	6.0	0	0	0	0	0
1997—Green Bay NFL	13	0	2	28	14.0	1	2	0	12	0
1998—Green Bay NFL	13	1	18	250	13.9	7	7	0	42	0
1999—Green Bay NFL	16	13	20	204	10.2	2	2	0	12	0
2000—Green Bay NFL	14	9	19	177	9.3	2	2	1	14	2
2001—Green Bay NFL	4	2	3	14	4.7	0	0	0	0	0
Pro totals (7 years)	66	25	64	688	10.8	12	13	1	80	3

DAWKINS, BRIAN — S — EAGLES

PERSONAL: Born October 13, 1973, in Jacksonville. ... 5-11/200.
HIGH SCHOOL: Raines (Jacksonville).
COLLEGE: Clemson (degree in education, 1995).

TRANSACTIONS/CAREER NOTES: Selected by Philadelphia Eagles in second round (61st pick overall) of 1996 NFL draft. ... Signed by Eagles (July 17, 1996).
CHAMPIONSHIP GAME EXPERIENCE: Played in NFC championship game (2001 season).
HONORS: Named defensive back on THE SPORTING NEWS college All-America second team (1995). ... Played in Pro Bowl (1999 season). ... Named safety on THE SPORTING NEWS NFL All-Pro team (2001).
PRO STATISTICS: 1996—Recovered two fumbles for 23 yards. 1998—Recovered one fumble. 1999—Recovered two fumbles. 2000—Recovered two fumbles. 2001—Recovered two fumbles for 49 yards and a touchdown.

				INTERCEPTIONS				SACKS
Year Team		G	GS	No.	Yds.	Avg.	TD	No.
1996—Philadelphia NFL		14	13	3	41	13.7	0	1.0
1997—Philadelphia NFL		15	15	3	76	25.3	1	0.0
1998—Philadelphia NFL		14	14	2	39	19.5	0	1.0
1999—Philadelphia NFL		16	16	4	127	31.8	1	1.5
2000—Philadelphia NFL		13	13	4	62	15.5	0	2.0
2001—Philadelphia NFL		15	15	2	15	7.5	0	1.5
Pro totals (6 years)		87	86	18	360	20.0	2	7.0

DAWKINS, SEAN — WR — VIKINGS

PERSONAL: Born February 3, 1971, in Red Bank, N.J. ... 6-4/218. ... Full name: Sean Russell Dawkins.
HIGH SCHOOL: Homestead (Cupertino, Calif.).
COLLEGE: California.
TRANSACTIONS/CAREER NOTES: Selected after junior season by Indianapolis Colts in first round (16th pick overall) of 1993 NFL draft. ... Signed by Colts (August 4, 1993). ... Granted unconditional free agency (February 13, 1998). ... Signed by New Orleans Saints (May 1, 1998). ... Granted unconditional free agency (February 12, 1999). ... Signed by Seattle Seahawks (April 15, 1999). ... Released by Seahawks (June 8, 2000). ... Re-signed by Seahawks (July 26, 2000). ... Released by Seahawks (March 1, 2001). ... Signed by Jacksonville Jaguars (May 30, 2001). ... Granted unconditional free agency (March 1, 2002). ... Signed by Minnesota Vikings (April 25, 2002).
CHAMPIONSHIP GAME EXPERIENCE: Played in AFC championship game (1995 season).
HONORS: Named wide receiver on THE SPORTING NEWS college All-America first team (1992).
SINGLE GAME HIGHS (regular season): Receptions—8 (November 22, 1998, vs. San Francisco); yards—148 (November 22, 1998, vs. San Francisco); and touchdown receptions—2 (December 10, 2000, vs. Denver).
STATISTICAL PLATEAUS: 100-yard receiving games: 1993 (1), 1994 (1), 1995 (2), 1997 (1), 1998 (3), 1999 (2), 2000 (1). Total: 11.

			RECEIVING				TOTALS			
Year Team	G	GS	No.	Yds.	Avg.	TD	TD	2pt.	Pts.	Fum.
1993—Indianapolis NFL	16	7	26	430	16.5	1	1	0	6	0
1994—Indianapolis NFL	16	16	51	742	14.5	5	5	0	30	1
1995—Indianapolis NFL	16	13	52	784	15.1	3	3	0	18	1
1996—Indianapolis NFL	15	14	54	751	13.9	1	1	0	6	1
1997—Indianapolis NFL	14	12	68	804	11.8	2	2	0	12	0
1998—New Orleans NFL	15	15	53	823	15.5	1	1	0	6	2
1999—Seattle NFL	16	13	58	992	17.1	7	7	0	42	1
2000—Seattle NFL	16	16	63	731	11.6	5	5	0	30	0
2001—Jacksonville NFL	16	3	20	234	11.7	0	0	0	0	1
Pro totals (9 years)	140	109	445	6291	14.1	25	25	0	150	7

DAWSON, JaJUAN — WR — BROWNS

PERSONAL: Born November 5, 1977, in Houston. ... 6-1/197. ... Full name: JaJuan LaTroy Dawson.
HIGH SCHOOL: H.L. Bourgeois (Gibson, La.).
COLLEGE: Tulane.
TRANSACTIONS/CAREER NOTES: Selected by Cleveland Browns in third round (79th pick overall) of 2000 NFL draft. ... Signed by Browns (June 3, 2000). ... On injured reserve with clavicle injury (September 20, 2000-remainder of season).
SINGLE GAME HIGHS (regular season): Receptions—6 (September 3, 2000, vs. Jacksonville); yards—83 (September 3, 2000, vs. Jacksonville); and touchdown receptions—1 (December 30, 2001, vs. Tennessee).

			RECEIVING			
Year Team	G	GS	No.	Yds.	Avg.	TD
2000—Cleveland NFL	2	2	9	97	10.8	1
2001—Cleveland NFL	14	0	22	281	12.8	1
Pro totals (2 years)	16	2	31	378	12.2	2

DAWSON, PHIL — K — BROWNS

PERSONAL: Born January 23, 1975, in West Palm Beach, Fla. ... 5-11/190.
HIGH SCHOOL: Lake Highlands (Dallas).
COLLEGE: Texas.
TRANSACTIONS/CAREER NOTES: Signed as non-drafted free agent by Oakland Raiders (April 24, 1998). ... Claimed on waivers by New England Patriots (August 21, 1998). ... Released by Patriots (August 30, 1998). ... Re-signed by Patriots to practice squad (August 31, 1998). ... Granted free agency after 1998 season. ... Signed by Cleveland Browns (March 25, 1999). ... Granted free agency (March 1, 2002). ... Re-signed by Browns (April 26, 2002).
PRO STATISTICS: 1999—Rushed once for four yards and a touchdown.

		KICKING						
Year Team	G	XPM	XPA	FGM	FGA	Lg.	50+	Pts.
1999—Cleveland NFL	15	23	24	8	12	49	0-0	53
2000—Cleveland NFL	16	17	17	14	17	45	0-0	59
2001—Cleveland NFL	16	29	30	22	25	48	0-0	95
Pro totals (3 years)	47	69	71	44	54	49	0-0	207

DAYNE, RON — RB — GIANTS

PERSONAL: Born March 14, 1978, in Berlin, N.J. ... 5-10/253.
HIGH SCHOOL: Overbrook (Berlin, N.J.).
COLLEGE: Wisconsin.
TRANSACTIONS/CAREER NOTES: Selected by New York Giants in first round (11th pick overall) of 2000 NFL draft. ... Signed by Giants (July 21, 2000).
CHAMPIONSHIP GAME EXPERIENCE: Played in NFC championship game (2000 season). ... Played in Super Bowl XXXV (2000 season).
HONORS: Heisman Trophy winner (1999). ... Doak Walker Award winner (1999). ... Maxwell Award winner (1999). ... Named running back on THE SPORTING NEWS college All-America first team (1999). ... Named College Football Player of the Year by THE SPORTING NEWS (1999).
PRO STATISTICS: 2001—Recovered two fumbles for minus 17 yards.
SINGLE GAME HIGHS (regular season): Attempts—25 (October 29, 2000, vs. Philadelphia); yards—111 (September 30, 2001, vs. New Orleans); and rushing touchdowns—1 (January 6, 2002, vs. Green Bay).
STATISTICAL PLATEAUS: 100-yard rushing games: 2000 (1), 2001 (1). Total: 2.

				RUSHING				RECEIVING				TOTALS		
Year Team	G	GS	Att.	Yds.	Avg.	TD	No.	Yds.	Avg.	TD	TD	2pt.	Pts.	Fum.
2000—New York Giants NFL	16	4	228	770	3.4	5	3	11	3.7	0	5	0	30	1
2001—New York Giants NFL	16	7	180	690	3.8	7	8	67	8.4	0	7	1	44	2
Pro totals (2 years)	32	11	408	1460	3.6	12	11	78	7.1	0	12	1	74	3

DEARTH, JAMES — TE — JETS

PERSONAL: Born January 22, 1976, in Scurry, Texas. ... 6-4/270.
HIGH SCHOOL: Scurry (Texas)-Rosser.
COLLEGE: Tulsa, then Tarleton State (Texas).
TRANSACTIONS/CAREER NOTES: Selected by Cleveland Browns in sixth round (191st pick overall) of 1999 NFL draft. ... Signed by Browns (July 22, 1999). ... Released by Browns (September 3, 1999). ... Re-signed by Browns to practice squad (November 23, 1999). ... Activated (December 14, 1999). ... Assigned by Browns to Scottish Claymores in 2000 NFL Europe enhancement allocation program (February 11, 2000). ... Released by Browns (April 18, 2000). ... Signed by Titans (July 14, 2000). ... Released by Titans (August 22, 2000). ... Re-signed by Titans to practice squad (November 8, 2000). ... Granted free agency following 2000 season. ... Signed by New York Jets (January 24, 2001).
PLAYING EXPERIENCE: Cleveland NFL, 1999; Scottish NFLE, 2000; New York Jets NFL, 2001. ... Games/Games started: 1999 (2/0), NFLE 2000 (games played unavailable), 2001 (16/1). Total: 18/1.
PRO STATISTICS: 2001—Caught three passes for 10 yards and one touchdown and returned one kickoff for seven yards.
SINGLE GAME HIGHS (regular season): Receptions—1 (December 16, 2001, vs. Cincinnati); yards—9 (November 11, 2001, vs. Kansas City); and touchdown receptions—1 (December 16, 2001, vs. Cincinnati).

DEESE, DERRICK — OT — 49ERS

PERSONAL: Born May 17, 1970, in Culver City, Calif. ... 6-3/289.
HIGH SCHOOL: Culver City (Calif.).
JUNIOR COLLEGE: El Camino Junior College (Calif.).
COLLEGE: Southern California.
TRANSACTIONS/CAREER NOTES: Signed as non-drafted free agent by San Francisco 49ers (May 8, 1992). ... On injured reserve with elbow injury (August 4, 1992-entire season). ... Inactive for six games (1993). ... On injured reserve with broken wrist (October 23, 1993-remainder of season). ... Granted free agency (February 17, 1995). ... Tendered offer sheet by St. Louis Rams (April 20, 1995). ... Offer matched by 49ers (April 21, 1995). ... Granted unconditional free agency (February 16, 1996). ... Re-signed by 49ers (June 4, 1996). ... Granted unconditional free agency (February 14, 1997). ... Re-signed by 49ers (April 22, 1997).
PLAYING EXPERIENCE: San Francisco NFL, 1994-2001. ... Games/Games started: 1994 (16/15), 1995 (2/2), 1996 (16/0), 1997 (16/13), 1998 (16/16), 1999 (16/16), 2000 (13/13), 2001 (16/16). Total: 111/91.
CHAMPIONSHIP GAME EXPERIENCE: Played in NFC championship game (1994 and 1997 seasons). ... Member of Super Bowl championship team (1994 season).
PRO STATISTICS: 1996—Returned two kickoffs for 20 yards. 1997—Recovered one fumble. 1998—Recovered one fumble. 1999—Recovered four fumbles. 2001—Recovered one fumble.

DeLOACH, JERRY — DT — TEXANS

PERSONAL: Born July 17, 1977, in Sacramento, Calif. ... 6-2/315.
HIGH SCHOOL: Valley (Calif.).
COLLEGE: California.
TRANSACTIONS/CAREER NOTES: Signed as non-drafted free agent by Washington Redskins (April 28, 2000). ... Traded by Redskins to Houston Texans for QB Danny Wuerffel (March 4, 2002).

Year Team	G	GS	SACKS
2001—Washington NFL	15	4	1.0

DeMULLING, RICK — G — COLTS

PERSONAL: Born July 21, 1977, in Cheney, Wash. ... 6-3/304. ... Full name: Rick Elwood DeMulling.
HIGH SCHOOL: Cheney (Wash.).
COLLEGE: Idaho.
TRANSACTIONS/CAREER NOTES: Selected by Indianapolis Colts in seventh round (220th pick overall) of 2001 NFL draft. ... Signed by Colts (June 19, 2001).
PLAYING EXPERIENCE: Indianapolis NFL, 2001. ... Games/Games started: 2001 (7/0).

DENMAN, ANTHONY — LB — BROWNS

PERSONAL: Born October 30, 1979, in Lufkin, Texas. ... 6-1/234. ... Full name: Anthony Ray Denman.
HIGH SCHOOL: Rusk (Texas).
COLLEGE: Notre Dame.
TRANSACTIONS/CAREER NOTES: Selected by Jacksonville Jaguars in seventh round (213th pick overall) of 2001 NFL draft. ... Signed by Jaguars (June 26, 2001). ... Claimed on waivers by Cleveland Browns (August 28, 2001). ... Released by Browns (September 1, 2001). ... Re-signed by Browns to practice squad (September 3, 2001). ... Activated (September 18, 2001).
PLAYING EXPERIENCE: Cleveland NFL, 2001. ... Games/Games started: (11/0).
HONORS: Named linebacker on THE SPORTING NEWS college All-America second team (2000).

DENNIS, PAT — CB — COWBOYS

PERSONAL: Born June 3, 1978, in Shreveport, La. ... 6-0/213. ... Full name: Patrick Dennis.
HIGH SCHOOL: Southwood (Shreveport, La.).
COLLEGE: Louisiana-Monroe.
TRANSACTIONS/CAREER NOTES: Selected after junior season by Kansas City Chiefs in fifth round (162nd pick overall) of 2000 NFL draft. ... Signed by Chiefs (July 20, 2000). ... On injured reserve with knee injury (September 1-October 3, 2001). ... Claimed on waivers by Dallas Cowboys (October 3, 2001).
PRO STATISTICS: 2000—Recovered two fumbles for minus five yards.

				INTERCEPTIONS			
Year Team	G	GS	No.	Yds.	Avg.	TD	
2000—Kansas City NFL	16	13	1	0	0.0	0	
2001—Dallas NFL	11	0	0	0	0.0	0	
Pro totals (2 years)	27	13	1	0	0.0	0	

DENSON, AUTRY — RB

PERSONAL: Born December 8, 1976, in Lauderhill, Fla. ... 5-10/203. ... Full name: Autry Lamont Denson.
HIGH SCHOOL: Nova (Fort Lauderdale, Fla.).
COLLEGE: Notre Dame.
TRANSACTIONS/CAREER NOTES: Selected by Tampa Bay Buccaneers in seventh round (233rd pick overall) of 1999 NFL draft. ... Signed by Buccaneers (July 29, 1999). ... Released by Buccaneers (September 5, 1999). ... Re-signed by Buccaneers to practice squad (September 6, 1999). ... Signed by Miami Dolphins off Buccaneers practice squad (October 20, 1999). ... Claimed on waivers by Chicago Bears (September 5, 2001). ... Granted free agency (March 1, 2002).
PRO STATISTICS: 2000—Returned 20 kickoffs for 495 yards. 2001—Returned one punt for five yards and returned 23 kickoffs for 534 yards.
SINGLE GAME HIGHS (regular season): Attempts—21 (January 2, 2000, vs. Washington); yards—80 (January 2, 2000, vs. Washington); and rushing touchdowns—0.

			RUSHING				RECEIVING			TOTALS			
Year Team	G	GS	Att.	Yds.	Avg.	TD	No.	Yds.	Avg.	TD	TD	2pt.	Pts.	Fum.
1999—Miami NFL	6	1	28	98	3.5	0	4	28	7.0	0	0	0	0	0
2000—Miami NFL	11	0	31	108	3.5	0	14	105	7.5	0	0	0	0	1
2001—Chicago NFL	16	0	1	4	4.0	0	0	0	0.0	0	0	0	0	1
Pro totals (3 years)	33	1	60	210	3.5	0	18	133	7.4	0	0	0	0	2

DETMER, KOY — QB — EAGLES

PERSONAL: Born July 5, 1973, in San Antonio. ... 6-1/195. ... Full name: Koy Dennis Detmer. ... Brother of Ty Detmer, quarterback, Detroit Lions.
HIGH SCHOOL: Mission (Texas).
COLLEGE: Colorado (degree in communications, 1996).
TRANSACTIONS/CAREER NOTES: Selected by Philadelphia Eagles in seventh round (207th pick overall) of 1997 NFL draft. ... Signed by Eagles (June 4, 1997). ... On injured reserve with knee injury (August 22, 1997-entire season). ... Granted free agency (February 11, 2000). ... Re-signed by Eagles (April 17, 2000).
CHAMPIONSHIP GAME EXPERIENCE: Played in NFC championship game (2001 season).
PRO STATISTICS: 1998—Fumbled once.
SINGLE GAME HIGHS (regular season): Attempts—43 (December 20, 1998, vs. Dallas); completions—24 (December 20, 1998, vs. Dallas); yards—231 (December 20, 1998, vs. Dallas); and touchdown passes—3 (December 19, 1999, vs. New England).
MISCELLANEOUS: Regular-season record as starting NFL quarterback: 2-4 (.333).

				PASSING						RUSHING			TOTALS		
Year Team	G	GS	Att.	Cmp.	Pct.	Yds.	TD	Int.	Avg.	Rat.	Att.	Yds.	Avg.	TD	2pt.	Pts.
1997—Philadelphia NFL						Did not play.									
1998—Philadelphia NFL	8	5	181	97	53.6	1011	5	5	5.59	67.7	7	20	2.9	0	0	0
1999—Philadelphia NFL	1	1	29	10	34.5	181	3	2	6.24	62.6	2	-2	-1.0	0	0	0
2000—Philadelphia NFL	16	0	1	0	0.0	0	0	1	0.0	0.0	1	8	8.0	0	0	0
2001—Philadelphia NFL	16	0	14	5	35.7	51	0	1	3.64	17.3	8	6	0.8	0	0	0
Pro totals (4 years)	41	6	225	112	49.8	1243	8	9	5.52	61.8	18	32	1.8	0	0	0

DETMER, TY — QB — LIONS

PERSONAL: Born October 30, 1967, in San Marcos, Texas. ... 6-0/194. ... Full name: Ty Hubert Detmer. ... Brother of Koy Detmer, quarterback, Philadelphia Eagles.
HIGH SCHOOL: Southwest (San Antonio).

COLLEGE: Brigham Young (degree in recreation administration, 1991).
TRANSACTIONS/CAREER NOTES: Selected by Green Bay Packers in ninth round (230th pick overall) of 1992 NFL draft. ... Signed by Packers (July 22, 1992). ... Active for two games (1992); did not play. ... Active for five games (1994); did not play. ... On injured reserve with thumb injury (November 8, 1995-remainder of season). ... Granted unconditional free agency (February 16, 1996). ... Signed by Philadelphia Eagles (March 1, 1996). ... Granted unconditional free agency (February 13, 1998). ... Signed by San Francisco 49ers (March 12, 1998). ... Traded by 49ers with fourth-round pick (LB Wali Rainer) in 1999 draft to Cleveland Browns for fourth- (traded to Indianapolis) and fifth-round (traded to Miami) picks in 1999 draft (February 23, 1999). ... On injured reserve with Achilles' tendon injury (August 16, 2000-entire season). ... Traded by Browns to Detroit Lions for undisclosed pick in 2002 draft (September 2, 2001).
HONORS: Heisman Trophy winner (1990). ... Maxwell Award winner (1990). ... Davey O'Brien Award winner (1990 and 1991). ... Named quarterback on THE SPORTING NEWS college All-America first team (1990 and 1991).
PRO STATISTICS: 1995—Fumbled once and recovered one fumble. 1996—Fumbled seven times and recovered one fumble. 1997—Fumbled six times and recovered one fumble for minus two yards. 1998—Fumbled once. 2001—Fumbled three times and recovered one fumble.
SINGLE GAME HIGHS (regular season): Attempts—51 (December 30, 2001, vs. Chicago); completions—31 (Decmeber 30, 2001, vs. Chicago); yards—342 (October 27, 1996, vs. Carolina); and touchdown passes—4 (October 20, 1996, vs. Miami).
STATISTICAL PLATEAUS: 300-yard passing games: 1996 (3), 2001 (1). Total: 4.
MISCELLANEOUS: Regular-season record as starting NFL quarterback: 11-14 (.440). ... Postseason record as starting NFL quarterback: 0-1.

				PASSING						RUSHING				TOTALS		
Year Team	G	GS	Att.	Cmp.	Pct.	Yds.	TD	Int.	Avg.	Rat.	Att.	Yds.	Avg.	TD	TD	2pt.	Pts.
1992—Green Bay NFL							Did not play.										
1993—Green Bay NFL	3	0	5	3	60.0	26	0	0	5.20	73.8	1	-2	-2.0	0	0	0	0
1994—Green Bay NFL							Did not play.										
1995—Green Bay NFL	4	0	16	8	50.0	81	1	1	5.06	59.6	3	3	1.0	0	0	0	0
1996—Philadelphia NFL	13	11	401	238	59.4	2911	15	13	7.26	80.8	31	59	1.9	1	1	0	6
1997—Philadelphia NFL	8	7	244	134	54.9	1567	7	6	6.42	73.9	14	46	3.3	1	1	0	6
1998—San Francisco NFL	16	1	38	24	63.2	312	4	3	8.21	91.1	8	7	0.9	0	0	0	0
1999—Cleveland NFL	5	2	91	47	51.6	548	4	2	6.02	75.7	6	38	6.3	1	1	0	6
2000—Cleveland NFL							Did not play.										
2001—Detroit NFL	4	4	151	92	60.9	906	3	10	6.00	56.9	9	26	2.9	0	0	0	0
Pro totals (7 years)	53	25	946	546	57.7	6351	34	35	6.71	74.7	72	177	2.5	3	3	0	18

DeVRIES, JARED   DE   LIONS

PERSONAL: Born June 11, 1976, in Aplington, Iowa. ... 6-4/280.
HIGH SCHOOL: Aplington-Parkersburg (Aplington, Iowa).
COLLEGE: Iowa.
TRANSACTIONS/CAREER NOTES: Selected by Detroit Lions in third round (70th pick overall) of 1999 NFL draft. ... Signed by Lions (July 28, 1999). ... On physically unable to perform list with blood clot (July 24-October 27, 2001). ... Granted free agency (March 1, 2002). ... Re-signed by Lions (April 16, 2002).
PLAYING EXPERIENCE: Detroit NFL, 1999-2001. ... Games/Games started: 1999 (2/0), 2000 (15/1), 2001 (11/0). Total: 28/1.
HONORS: Named defensive tackle on THE SPORTING NEWS college All-America third team (1997). ... Named defensive tackle on THE SPORTING NEWS college All-America first team (1998).
PRO STATISTICS: 2000—Recovered one fumble.

DIAZ-INFANTE, DAVID   G

PERSONAL: Born March 31, 1964, in San Jose, Calif. ... 6-3/296. ... Full name: Gustavo David Mienez Diaz-Infante. ... Name pronounced DEE-oz in-FON-tay.
HIGH SCHOOL: Bellarmine Prep (San Jose, Calif.).
COLLEGE: San Jose State.
TRANSACTIONS/CAREER NOTES: Signed as non-drafted free agent by San Diego Chargers prior to 1987 season. ... Released by Chargers prior to 1987 season. ... Re-signed by Chargers as replacement player for 1987 season. ... Released by Chargers (October 1987). ... Signed by Los Angeles Rams for 1988 season. ... Released by Rams prior to 1988 season. ... Re-signed by Rams for 1989 season. ... Released by Rams prior to 1989 season. ... Selected by Franfurt Galaxy in third round (fourth offensive lineman) of 1991 WLAF positional draft. ... Signed by Galaxy (January 11, 1991). ... Signed by San Francisco 49ers (May 25, 1993). ... Released by 49ers (August 22, 1993). ... Signed by Sacramento Gold Miners of CFL (September 1993). ... Signed by Denver Broncos (March 30, 1995). ... Released by Broncos (August 27, 1995). ... Re-signed by Broncos to practice squad (August 28, 1995). ... Released by Broncos (September 5, 1999). ... Signed by Philadelphia Eagles (September 14, 1999). ... Granted unconditional free agency (February 11, 2000). ... Signed by Broncos (May 25, 2000). ... Released by Broncos (August 27, 2000). ... Re-signed by Broncos (July 19, 2001). ... Granted unconditional free agency (March 1, 2002).
PLAYING EXPERIENCE: San Diego NFL, 1987; Frankfurt WL, 1991 and 1992; Sacramento CFL, 1993 and 1994; Denver NFL, 1996-1998 and 2001; Philadelphia NFL, 1999. ... Games/Games started: 1987 (3/0); replacement games), 1991, 1992 and 1994 games played unavailable, 1993 (8/-), 1996 (9/2), 1997 (16/7), 1998 (10/0), 1999 (15/0), 2000 (did not play), 2001 (16/0). Total NFL: 69/9; including 3/0 as replacement player.
CHAMPIONSHIP GAME EXPERIENCE: Played in AFC championship game (1997 and 1998 seasons). ... Member of Super Bowl championship team (1997 and 1998 seasons).

DIEM, RYAN   G   COLTS

PERSONAL: Born July 1, 1979, in Carol Stream, Ill. ... 6-6/332.
HIGH SCHOOL: Glenbard North (Carol Stream, Ill.).
COLLEGE: Northern Illinois.
TRANSACTIONS/CAREER NOTES: Selected by Indianapolis Colts in fourth round (118th pick overall) of 2001 NFL draft. ... Signed by Colts (July 19, 2001).
PLAYING EXPERIENCE: Indianapolis NFL, 2001. ... Games/Games started: 2001 (15/8).

DIGGS, NA'IL — LB — PACKERS

PERSONAL: Born July 8, 1978, in Phoenix. ... 6-4/238. ... Full name: Na'il Ronald Diggs.
HIGH SCHOOL: Dorsey (Los Angeles).
COLLEGE: Ohio State.
TRANSACTIONS/CAREER NOTES: Selected after junior season by Green Bay Packers in fourth round (98th pick overall) of 2000 NFL draft. ... Signed by Packers (June 19, 2000).
PLAYING EXPERIENCE: Green Bay NFL, 2000 and 2001. ... Games/Games started: 2000 (13/12); 2001 (16/16). Total: 29/28.
PRO STATISTICS: 2000—Recovered one fumble for 52 yards. 2001—Credited with two sacks.

DILFER, TRENT — QB — SEAHAWKS

PERSONAL: Born March 13, 1972, in Santa Cruz, Calif. ... 6-4/229. ... Full name: Trent Farris Dilfer.
HIGH SCHOOL: Aptos (Calif.).
COLLEGE: Fresno State.
TRANSACTIONS/CAREER NOTES: Selected after junior season by Tampa Bay Buccaneers in first round (sixth pick overall) of 1994 NFL draft. ... Signed by Buccaneers (August 3, 1994). ... Granted unconditional free agency (January 25, 2000). ... Signed by Baltimore Ravens (March 8, 2000). ... Granted unconditional free agency (March 2, 2001). ... Signed by Seattle Seahawks (August 3, 2001). ... Granted unconditional free agency (March 1, 2002). ... Re-signed by Seahawks (March 2, 2002).
CHAMPIONSHIP GAME EXPERIENCE: Member of Buccaneers for NFC championship game (1999 season); inactive. ... Played in AFC championship game (2000 season). ... Member of Super Bowl championship team (2000 season).
HONORS: Played in Pro Bowl (1997 season).
PRO STATISTICS: 1994—Fumbled twice. 1995—Fumbled 13 times and recovered one fumble for minus nine yards. 1996—Fumbled 10 times and recovered four fumbles for minus four yards. 1997—Fumbled nine times and recovered three fumbles for minus 22 yards. 1998—Fumbled nine times and recovered two fumbles for minus five yards. 1999—Fumbled six times for minus four yards. 2000—Fumbled eight times, recovered one fumble for minus seven yards and caught one pass for minus one yard. 2001—Caught one pass for minus five yards and fumbled three times for minus three yards.
SINGLE GAME HIGHS (regular season): Attempts—48 (November 26, 1995, vs. Green Bay); completions—30 (November 17, 1996, vs. San Diego); yards—327 (November 17, 1996, vs. San Diego); and touchdown passes—4 (September 21, 1997, vs. Miami).
STATISTICAL PLATEAUS: 300-yard passing games: 1995 (1), 1996 (1), 1999 (1). Total: 3.
MISCELLANEOUS: Regular-season record as starting NFL quarterback: 49-39 (.557). ... Postseason record as starting NFL quarterback: 5-1 (.833).

			PASSING							RUSHING				TOTALS		
Year Team	G	GS	Att.	Cmp.	Pct.	Yds.	TD	Int.	Avg.	Rat.	Att.	Yds.	Avg.	TD	TD	2pt.	Pts.
1994—Tampa Bay NFL	5	2	82	38	46.3	433	1	6	5.28	36.3	2	27	13.5	0	0	0	0
1995—Tampa Bay NFL	16	16	415	224	54.0	2774	4	18	6.68	60.1	23	115	5.0	2	2	0	12
1996—Tampa Bay NFL	16	16	482	267	55.4	2859	12	19	5.93	64.8	32	124	3.9	0	0	0	0
1997—Tampa Bay NFL	16	16	386	217	56.2	2555	21	11	6.62	82.8	33	99	3.0	1	1	0	6
1998—Tampa Bay NFL	16	16	429	225	52.4	2729	21	15	6.36	74.0	40	141	3.5	2	2	0	12
1999—Tampa Bay NFL	10	10	244	146	59.8	1619	11	11	6.64	75.8	35	144	4.1	0	0	0	0
2000—Baltimore NFL	11	8	226	134	59.3	1502	12	11	6.65	76.6	20	75	3.8	0	0	0	0
2001—Seattle NFL	7	4	122	73	59.8	1014	7	4	8.31	92.0	11	17	1.5	0	0	0	0
Pro totals (8 years)	97	88	2386	1324	55.5	15485	89	95	6.49	71.2	196	742	3.8	5	5	0	30

DILGER, KEN — TE — BUCCANEERS

PERSONAL: Born February 2, 1971, in Mariah Hill, Ind. ... 6-5/255. ... Full name: Kenneth Ray Dilger. ... Name pronounced DIL-gur.
HIGH SCHOOL: Heritage Hills (Lincoln City, Ind.).
COLLEGE: Illinois (degree in marketing).
TRANSACTIONS/CAREER NOTES: Selected by Indianapolis Colts in second round (48th pick overall) of 1995 NFL draft. ... Signed by Colts (July 15, 1995). ... Released by Colts (February 21, 2002). ... Signed by Tampa Bay Buccaneers (April 17, 2002).
CHAMPIONSHIP GAME EXPERIENCE: Played in AFC championship game (1995 season).
PRO STATISTICS: 1998—Returned one kickoff for 14 yards. 1999—Recovered one fumble. 2000—Returned one kickoff for no yards. 2001—Completed only pass attempt for 39 yards and a touchdown.
SINGLE GAME HIGHS (regular season): Receptions—8 (September 10, 2000, vs. Oakland); yards—156 (September 8, 1996, vs. New York Jets); and touchdown receptions—3 (December 14, 1997, vs. Miami).
STATISTICAL PLATEAUS: 100-yard receiving games: 1995 (1), 1996 (1), 1997 (1). Total: 3.

			RECEIVING				TOTALS			
Year Team	G	GS	No.	Yds.	Avg.	TD	TD	2pt.	Pts.	Fum.
1995—Indianapolis NFL	16	13	42	635	15.1	4	4	0	24	0
1996—Indianapolis NFL	16	16	42	503	12.0	4	4	0	24	1
1997—Indianapolis NFL	14	14	27	380	14.1	3	3	0	18	0
1998—Indianapolis NFL	16	16	31	303	9.8	1	1	1	8	0
1999—Indianapolis NFL	15	15	40	479	12.0	2	2	0	12	1
2000—Indianapolis NFL	16	16	47	538	11.4	3	3	0	18	1
2001—Indianapolis NFL	16	16	32	343	10.7	1	1	1	8	2
Pro totals (7 years)	109	106	261	3181	12.2	18	18	2	112	5

DILLON, COREY — RB — BENGALS

PERSONAL: Born October 24, 1974, in Seattle. ... 6-1/225.
HIGH SCHOOL: Franklin (Seattle).
JUNIOR COLLEGE: Garden City (Kan.) Community College, then Dixie College (Utah).
COLLEGE: Washington.

TRANSACTIONS/CAREER NOTES: Selected after junior season by Cincinnati Bengals in second round (43rd pick overall) of 1997 NFL draft. ... Signed by Bengals (July 21, 1997). ... Granted free agency (February 11, 2000). ... Re-signed by Bengals (August 9, 2000). ... Designated by Bengals as transition player (February 12, 2001). ... Re-signed by Bengals (May 11, 2001).
HONORS: Named running back on THE SPORTING NEWS college All-America second team (1996). ... Played in Pro Bowl (1999 and 2000 seasons).
PRO STATISTICS: 1997—Recovered one fumble for four yards. 1999—Recovered one fumble. 2001—Had only pass attempt intercepted and recovered one fumble.
SINGLE GAME HIGHS (regular season): Attempts—39 (December 4, 1997, vs. Tennessee); yards—278 (October 22, 2000, vs. Denver); and rushing touchdowns—4 (December 4, 1997, vs. Tennessee).
STATISTICAL PLATEAUS: 100-yard rushing games: 1997 (4), 1998 (4), 1999 (5), 2000 (5), 2001 (4). Total: 22.
MISCELLANEOUS: Selected by San Diego Padres organization in 34th round of free agent draft (June 3, 1993); did not sign.

				RUSHING				RECEIVING			KICKOFF RETURNS			TOTALS			
Year Team	G	GS	Att.	Yds.	Avg.	TD	No.	Yds.	Avg.	TD	No.	Yds.	Avg.	TD	TD	2pt.	Pts.	Fum.
1997—Cincinnati NFL	16	6	233	1129	4.8	10	27	259	9.6	0	6	182	30.3	0	10	0	60	1
1998—Cincinnati NFL	15	15	262	1130	4.3	4	28	178	6.4	0	0	0	0.0	0	5	0	30	2
1999—Cincinnati NFL	15	15	263	1200	4.6	5	31	290	9.4	1	1	4	4.0	0	6	0	36	3
2000—Cincinnati NFL	16	16	315	1435	4.6	7	18	158	8.8	0	0	0	0.0	0	7	0	42	4
2001—Cincinnati NFL	16	16	§340	1315	3.9	10	34	228	6.7	3	0	0	0.0	0	13	0	78	5
Pro totals (5 years)	78	68	1413	6209	4.4	36	138	1113	8.1	5	7	186	26.6	0	41	0	246	15

DiNAPOLI, GENNARO — C/G — TITANS

PERSONAL: Born May 25, 1975, in Manhassat, N.Y. ... 6-3/295. ... Full name: Gennaro L. DiNapoli. ... Name pronounced den-ah-POLE-e.
HIGH SCHOOL: Cazenovia (N.Y.), then Milford (Conn.) Academy.
COLLEGE: Virginia Tech.
TRANSACTIONS/CAREER NOTES: Selected by Oakland Raiders in fourth round (109th pick overall) of 1998 NFL draft. ... Signed by Raiders (July 24, 1998). ... Active for four games (1998); did not play. ... Traded by Raiders to Tennessee Titans for undisclosed pick (August 27, 2000). ... Granted unconditional free agency (March 1, 2002). ... Re-signed by Titans (April 19, 2002).
PLAYING EXPERIENCE: Oakland NFL, 1999; Tennessee NFL, 2001. ... Games/Games started: 1999 (11/9), 2000 (did not play), 2001 (5/2). Total: 16/11.

DINGLE, ADRIAN — DE — CHARGERS

PERSONAL: Born June 25, 1977, in Holly Hill, S.C. ... 6-3/272. ... Full name: Adrian Kennell Dingle.
HIGH SCHOOL: Holly Hill (S.C.)-Roberts.
COLLEGE: Clemson.
TRANSACTIONS/CAREER NOTES: Selected by San Diego Chargers in fifth round (139th pick overall) of 1999 NFL draft. ... Signed by Chargers (July 23, 1999). ... On physically unable to perform list with knee injury (August 31-November 17, 1999). ... Active for two games (1999); did not play. ... Granted free agency (March 1, 2002). ... Re-signed by Chargers (March 29, 2002).
PLAYING EXPERIENCE: San Diego NFL, 2000 and 2001. ... Games/Games started: 2000 (14/1), 2001 (14/0). Total: 28/1.
PRO STATISTICS: 2000—Credited with 2$1/2$ sacks. 2001—Credited with one sack.

DISHMAN, CHRIS — G — CARDINALS

PERSONAL: Born February 27, 1974, in Cozad, Neb. ... 6-3/332.
HIGH SCHOOL: Cozad (Neb.).
COLLEGE: Nebraska.
TRANSACTIONS/CAREER NOTES: Selected by Arizona Cardinals in fourth round (106th pick overall) of 1997 NFL draft. ... Signed by Cardinals (July 9, 1997). ... Granted free agency (February 11, 2000). ... Re-signed by Cardinals (April 28, 2000) ... Granted unconditional free agency (March 2, 2001). ... Re-signed by Cardinals (March 5, 2001).
PLAYING EXPERIENCE: Arizona NFL, 1997-2001. ... Games/Games started: 1997 (8/0), 1998 (12/11), 1999 (13/10), 2000 (14/12), 2001 (16/5). Total: 63/38.
PRO STATISTICS: 1998—Recovered one fumble. 1999—Returned one kickoff for nine yards. 2000—Fumbled once and recovered one fumble.

DIXON, DAVID — G — VIKINGS

PERSONAL: Born January 5, 1969, in Papakura, New Zealand. ... 6-5/359. ... Full name: David Tukatahi Dixon.
HIGH SCHOOL: Pukekohe (New Zealand).
JUNIOR COLLEGE: Ricks College (Idaho).
COLLEGE: Arizona State.
TRANSACTIONS/CAREER NOTES: Selected by New England Patriots in ninth-round (232nd pick overall) of 1992 draft. ... Signed by Patriots for 1992 season. ... Released by Patriots (August 1992). ... Signed by Minnesota Vikings to practice squad (October 20, 1992). ... Released by Vikings (August 23, 1993). ... Signed by Dallas Cowboys to practice squad (September 8, 1993). ... Granted free agency after 1993 season. ... Signed by Vikings (July 12, 1994). ... Granted free agency (February 14, 1997). ... Re-signed by Vikings (May 1, 1997). ... Granted unconditional free agency (February 13, 1998). ... Re-signed by Vikings (February 17, 1998). ... On physically unable to perform list with knee injury (August 1-10, 1998).
PLAYING EXPERIENCE: Minnesota NFL, 1994-2001. ... Games/Games started: 1994 (1/0), 1995 (15/6), 1996 (13/6), 1997 (13/13), 1998 (16/16), 1999 (16/16), 2000 (16/16), 2001 (15/14). Total: 105/87.
CHAMPIONSHIP GAME EXPERIENCE: Played in NFC championship game (1998 and 2000 seasons).
PRO STATISTICS: 1998—Recovered one fumble. 2000—Recovered one fumble. 2001—Recovered one fumble.

DIXON, GERALD   LB   RAIDERS

PERSONAL: Born June 20, 1969, in Charlotte. ... 6-3/250. ... Full name: Gerald Scott Dixon.
HIGH SCHOOL: Rock Hill (S.C.).
JUNIOR COLLEGE: Garden City (Kan.) Community College.
COLLEGE: South Carolina.
TRANSACTIONS/CAREER NOTES: Selected by Cleveland Browns in third round (78th pick overall) of 1992 NFL draft. ... Signed by Browns (July 15, 1992). ... On injured reserve with ankle injury (September 2, 1992-entire season). ... Granted free agency (February 17, 1995). ... Re-signed by Browns for 1995 season. ... Granted unconditional free agency (February 16, 1996). ... Signed by Cincinnati Bengals (March 14, 1996). ... Granted unconditional free agency (February 13, 1998). ... Signed by San Diego Chargers (March 24, 1998). ... Granted unconditional free agency (February 11, 2000). ... Re-signed by Chargers (March 15, 2000). ... Granted unconditional free agency (March 1, 2002). ... Signed by Oakland Raiders (April 10, 2002).
PRO STATISTICS: 1995—Intercepted two passes for 48 yards and one touchdown, returned one kickoff for 10 yards and recovered one fumble. 1996—Intercepted one pass for 10 yards. 1999—Recovered one fumble for 27 yards and a touchdown. 2000—Intercepted one pass for 36 yards and a touchdown and recovered one fumble. 2001—Intercepted one pass for six yards.

Year—Team	G	GS	SACKS
1992—Cleveland NFL	Did not play.		
1993—Cleveland NFL	11	0	0.0
1994—Cleveland NFL	16	0	1.0
1995—Cleveland NFL	16	9	0.0
1996—Cincinnati NFL	16	1	0.0
1997—Cincinnati NFL	15	12	8.5
1998—San Diego NFL	16	6	2.5
1999—San Diego NFL	14	1	4.0
2000—San Diego NFL	16	16	5.0
2001—San Diego NFL	16	15	2.0
Pro totals (9 years)	**136**	**60**	**23.0**

DIXON, MARK   G   DOLPHINS

PERSONAL: Born November 26, 1970, in Charlottesville, N.C. ... 6-4/300. ... Full name: Mark Keller Dixon.
HIGH SCHOOL: Ragsdale (Jamestown, N.C.).
COLLEGE: Virginia.
TRANSACTIONS/CAREER NOTES: Signed as non-drafted free agent by Philadelphia Eagles (April 1994). ... Released by Eagles (August 1994). ... Played with Frankfurt Galaxy of World League (1995). ... Signed by Atlanta Falcons (July 18, 1995). ... Released by Falcons (August 21, 1995). ... Signed by Baltimore Stallions of CFL (August 30, 1995). ... Signed by Miami Dolphins (January 22, 1998). ... On injured reserve with neck injury (November 24, 1998-remainder of season). ... On injured reserve with broken leg (December 4, 2001-remainder of season).
PLAYING EXPERIENCE: Frankfurt W.L., 1995; Baltimore Stallions CFL, 1995; Montreal Alouettes CFL, 1996 and 1997; Miami NFL, 1998-2001. ... Games/Games started: W.L. 1995 (games played unavailable); CFL 1995 (9/5), 1996 (18/18), 1997 (7/7), 1998 (11/10), 1999 (13/13), 2000 (15/15), 2001 (10/10). Total CFL: 33/30. Total NFL 49/48. Total Pro: 82/78.
CHAMPIONSHIP GAME EXPERIENCE: Member of CFL championship team (1995).
PRO STATISTICS: 1998—Recovered two fumbles.

DIXON, RON   WR/KR   GIANTS

PERSONAL: Born May 28, 1976, in Wildwood, Fla. ... 6-0/190. ... Full name: Ronald Dixon.
HIGH SCHOOL: Wildwood (Fla.).
JUNIOR COLLEGE: Itawamba Community College (Miss.).
COLLEGE: West Georgia, then Lambuth University.
TRANSACTIONS/CAREER NOTES: Selected by New York Giants in third round (73rd pick overall) of 2000 NFL draft.
CHAMPIONSHIP GAME EXPERIENCE: Played in NFC championship game (2000 season). ... Played in Super Bowl XXXV (2000 season).
PRO STATISTICS: 2000—Rushed twice for 13 yards. 2001—Rushed once for no yards and returned one punt for minus three yards.
SINGLE GAME HIGHS (regular season): Receptions—3 (January 6, 2002, vs. Green Bay); yards—62 (December 30, 2001, vs. Philadelphia); and touchdown receptions—1 (December 15, 2001, vs. Arizona).

			RECEIVING				KICKOFF RETURNS			TOTALS			
Year—Team	G	GS	No.	Yds.	Avg.	TD	No.	Yds.	Avg.	TD	TD	2pt.	Pts.	Fum.
2000—New York Giants NFL	12	0	6	92	15.3	1	31	658	21.2	0	1	0	6	0
2001—New York Giants NFL	15	0	8	227	28.4	1	34	645	19.0	0	1	0	6	2
Pro totals (2 years)	**27**	**0**	**14**	**319**	**22.8**	**2**	**65**	**1303**	**20.0**	**0**	**2**	**0**	**12**	**2**

DIXON, TONY   S   COWBOYS

PERSONAL: Born June 18, 1979, in Reform, Ala. ... 6-1/213.
HIGH SCHOOL: Pickens County (Reform, Ala.).
COLLEGE: Alabama (degree in management).
TRANSACTIONS/CAREER NOTES: Selected by Dallas Cowboys in second round (56th pick overall) of 2001 NFL draft. ... Signed by Cowboys (July 21, 2001).

Year—Team	G	GS	SACKS
2001—Dallas NFL	8	0	1.0

DOERING, JASON   DB   COLTS

PERSONAL: Born April 22, 1978, in Rhinelander, Wis. ... 6-0/200. ... Full name: Jason James Doering.
HIGH SCHOOL: Rhinelander (Wis.).
COLLEGE: Wisconsin.
TRANSACTIONS/CAREER NOTES: Selected by Indianapolis Colts in sixth round (193rd pick overall) of 2001 NFL draft. ... Signed by Colts (June 7, 2001).
PLAYING EXPERIENCE: Indianapolis NFL, 2001. ... Games/Games started: 2001 (16/1).

DOGINS, KEVIN — C — BEARS

PERSONAL: Born December 7, 1972, in Eagle Lake, Texas. ... 6-1/305. ... Full name: Kevin Ray Dogins.
HIGH SCHOOL: Rice (Texas).
COLLEGE: Texas A&M-Kingsville.
TRANSACTIONS/CAREER NOTES: Signed as non-drafted free agent by Dallas Cowboys (April 25, 1996). ... Released by Cowboys (August 19, 1996). ... Signed by Tampa Bay Buccaneers to practice squad (August 27, 1996). ... Activated (December 17, 1996). ... Inactive for all 16 games (1997). ... Granted free agency (February 11, 2000). ... Re-signed by Buccaneers (May 26, 2000). ... Granted unconditional free agency (March 2, 2001). ... Signed by Chicago Bears (June 22, 2001).
PLAYING EXPERIENCE: Tampa Bay NFL, 1996, 1998 and 1999; Chicago NFL, 2001. ... Games/Games started: 1996 (1/0), 1998 (6/4), 1999 (11/5), 2001 (15/0). Total: 33/9.
CHAMPIONSHIP GAME EXPERIENCE: Played in NFC championship game (1999 season).
PRO STATISTICS: 2001—Returned one kickoff for six yards.

DOMINGUEZ, MATT — TE — BRONCOS

PERSONAL: Born June 27, 1978, in Georgetown, Texas. ... 6-2/219.
HIGH SCHOOL: Georgetown (Texas).
COLLEGE: Sam Houston State.
TRANSACTIONS/CAREER NOTES: Signed as non-drafted free agent by Denver Broncos (April 27, 2001). ... Released by Broncos (September 2, 2001). ... Re-signed by Broncos to practice squad (September 4, 2001). ... Activated (October 5, 2001).
PLAYING EXPERIENCE: Denver NFL, 2001. ... Games/Games started: 2001 (12/0).
PRO STATISTICS: 2001—Caught three passes for 26 yards.
SINGLE GAME HIGHS (regular season): Receptions—1 (December 2, 2001, vs. Miami); yards—12 (December 2, 2001, vs. Miami); and touchdown receptions—0.

DONNALLEY, KEVIN — G — PANTHERS

PERSONAL: Born June 10, 1968, in St. Louis. ... 6-5/310. ... Full name: Kevin Thomas Donnalley. ... Brother of Rick Donnalley, center with Pittsburgh Steelers (1982 and 1983), Washington Redskins (1984 and 1985) and Kansas City Chiefs (1986 and 1987).
HIGH SCHOOL: Athens Drive Senior (Raleigh, N.C.).
COLLEGE: Davidson, then North Carolina (degree in economics).
TRANSACTIONS/CAREER NOTES: Selected by Houston Oilers in third round (79th pick overall) of 1991 NFL draft. ... Signed by Oilers (July 10, 1991). ... Granted free agency (February 17, 1994). ... Tendered offer sheet by Los Angeles Rams (March 17, 1994). ... Offer matched by Oilers (March 23, 1994). ... Oilers franchise moved to Tennessee for 1997 season. ... Granted unconditional free agency (February 13, 1998). ... Signed by Miami Dolphins (February 17, 1998). ... Released by Dolphins (June 2, 2000). ... Re-signed by Dolphins (June 13, 2000). ... Granted unconditional free agency (March 2, 2001). ... Signed by Carolina Panthers (March 16, 2001). ... On injured reserve with knee injury (October 23, 2001-remainder of season).
PLAYING EXPERIENCE: Houston NFL, 1991-1996; Tennessee NFL, 1997; Miami NFL, 1998-2000; Carolina NFL, 2001. ... Games/Games started: 1991 (16/0), 1992 (16/2), 1993 (16/6), 1994 (13/11), 1995 (16/16), 1996 (16/16), 1997 (16/16), 1998 (14/14), 1999 (16/9), 2000 (16/16), 2001 (6/6). Total: 161/112.
PRO STATISTICS: 1995—Recovered one fumble. 1998—Recovered one fumble.

DORSETT, ANTHONY — S — RAIDERS

PERSONAL: Born September 14, 1973, in Aliquippa, Pa. ... 5-11/200. ... Full name: Anthony Drew Dorsett Jr. ... Son of Tony Dorsett, Hall of Fame running back with Dallas Cowboys (1977-87) and Denver Broncos (1988).
HIGH SCHOOL: Richland (Dallas), then J.J. Pearce (Dallas).
COLLEGE: Pittsburgh.
TRANSACTIONS/CAREER NOTES: Selected by Houston Oilers in sixth round (177th pick overall) of 1996 NFL draft. ... Signed by Oilers (June 21, 1996). ... Assigned by Oilers to Barcelona Dragons in 1997 World League enhancement allocation program (February 19, 1997). ... Oilers franchise moved to Tennessee for 1997 season. ... Oilers franchise renamed Tennessee Titans for 1999 season (December 26, 1998). ... Granted free agency (February 12, 1999). ... Re-signed by Titans (June 15, 1999). ... Granted unconditional free agency (February 11, 2000). ... Signed by Oakland Raiders (March 21, 2000).
CHAMPIONSHIP GAME EXPERIENCE: Played in AFC championship game (1999 and 2000 seasons). ... Played in Super Bowl XXXIV (1999 season).
PRO STATISTICS: 2001—Recovered one fumble.

			INTERCEPTIONS				SACKS
Year Team	G	GS	No.	Yds.	Avg.	TD	No.
1996—Houston NFL	8	0	0	0	0.0	0	0.0
1997—Tennessee NFL	16	0	0	0	0.0	0	0.0
1998—Tennessee NFL	16	0	0	0	0.0	0	0.0
1999—Tennessee NFL	16	1	1	43	43.0	0	0.0
2000—Oakland NFL	16	16	0	0	0.0	0	1.0
2001—Oakland NFL	16	16	2	65	32.5	†2	1.0
Pro totals (6 years)	88	33	3	108	36.0	2	2.0

DORSEY, CHAR-RON — OT — COWBOYS

PERSONAL: Born November 5, 1977, in Jacksonville. ... 6-6/347.
HIGH SCHOOL: The Bolles School (Jacksonville).
COLLEGE: Florida State.
TRANSACTIONS/CAREER NOTES: Selected by Dallas Cowboys in seventh round (242nd pick overall) of 2001 NFL draft. ... Signed by Cowboys (July 17, 2001).
PLAYING EXPERIENCE: Dallas NFL, 2001. ... Games/Games started: 2001 (8/2).

DOTSON, EARL — OT — PACKERS

PERSONAL: Born December 17, 1970, in Beaumont, Texas. ... 6-4/317. ... Full name: Earl Christopher Dotson.
HIGH SCHOOL: Westbrook (Texas).
JUNIOR COLLEGE: Tyler (Texas) Junior College.
COLLEGE: Texas A&I.
TRANSACTIONS/CAREER NOTES: Selected by Green Bay Packers in third round (81st pick overall) of 1993 NFL draft. ... Signed by Packers (June 14, 1993). ... Released by Packers (February 27, 2001). ... Re-signed by Packers (March 8, 2001). ... Granted unconditional free agency (March 1, 2002). ... Re-signed by Packers (April 10, 2002).
PLAYING EXPERIENCE: Green Bay NFL, 1993-2001. ... Games/Games started: 1993 (13/0), 1994 (4/0), 1995 (16/16), 1996 (15/15), 1997 (13/13), 1998 (16/16), 1999 (15/15), 2000 (2/2), 2001 (12/0). Total: 106/77.
CHAMPIONSHIP GAME EXPERIENCE: Played in NFC championship game (1995-97 seasons). ... Member of Super Bowl championship team (1996 season). ... Played in Super Bowl XXXII (1997 season).
PRO STATISTICS: 1996—Recovered one fumble. 1997—Recovered one fumble. 2000—Recovered one fumble.

DOTSON, SANTANA — DT — REDSKINS

PERSONAL: Born December 19, 1969, in New Orleans. ... 6-5/285. ... Full name: Santana N. Dotson. ... Son of Alphonse Dotson, defensive tackle with Kansas City Chiefs (1965), Miami Dolphins (1966) and Oakland Raiders (1968-70).
HIGH SCHOOL: Jack Yates (Houston).
COLLEGE: Baylor.
TRANSACTIONS/CAREER NOTES: Selected by Tampa Bay Buccaneers in fifth round (132nd pick overall) of 1992 NFL draft. ... Signed by Buccaneers (July 7, 1992). ... Granted free agency (February 17, 1995). ... Re-signed by Buccaneers (June 14, 1995). ... Granted unconditional free agency (February 16, 1996). ... Signed by Green Bay Packers (March 7, 1996). ... Granted unconditional free agency (February 12, 1999). ... Re-signed by Packers (February 19, 1999). ... On injured reserve with knee injury (November 29, 2000-remainder of season). ... Released by Packers (February 27, 2002). ... Signed by Washington Redskins (June 4, 2002).
CHAMPIONSHIP GAME EXPERIENCE: Played in NFC championship game (1996 and 1997 seasons). ... Member of Super Bowl championship team (1996 season). ... Played in Super Bowl XXXII (1997 season).
HONORS: Named defensive lineman on THE SPORTING NEWS college All-America first team (1991). ... Named NFL Rookie of the Year by THE SPORTING NEWS (1992).
PRO STATISTICS: 1992—Recovered two fumbles for 42 yards and one touchdown. 1995—Recovered two fumbles. 1996—Recovered one fumble for eight yards. 1998—Recovered one fumble.

Year Team	G	GS	SACKS
1992—Tampa Bay NFL	16	16	10.0
1993—Tampa Bay NFL	16	13	5.0
1994—Tampa Bay NFL	16	9	3.0
1995—Tampa Bay NFL	16	8	5.0
1996—Green Bay NFL	16	15	5.5
1997—Green Bay NFL	16	16	5.5
1998—Green Bay NFL	16	16	3.0
1999—Green Bay NFL	12	12	2.5
2000—Green Bay NFL	12	11	6.0
2001—Green Bay NFL	16	13	3.5
Pro totals (10 years)	152	129	49.0

DOUGLAS, DAMEANE — WR — EAGLES

PERSONAL: Born March 15, 1976, in Hanford, Calif. ... 6-0/195.
HIGH SCHOOL: Hanford (Calif.).
COLLEGE: California.
TRANSACTIONS/CAREER NOTES: Selected by Oakland Raiders in fourth round (102nd pick overall) of 1999 NFL draft. ... Signed by Raiders for 1999 season. ... Claimed on waivers by Philadelphia Eagles (September 7, 1999).
CHAMPIONSHIP GAME EXPERIENCE: Played in NFC championship game (2001 season).
PRO STATISTICS: 2000—Returned two kickoffs for 50 yards. 2001—Returned two kickoffs for 32 yards.
SINGLE GAME HIGHS (regular season): Receptions—5 (January 6, 2002, vs. Tampa Bay); yards—77 (January 6, 2002, vs. Tampa Bay); and touchdown receptions—2 (January 6, 2002, vs. Tampa Bay).

			RECEIVING				TOTALS			
Year Team	G	GS	No.	Yds.	Avg.	TD	TD	2pt.	Pts.	Fum.
1999—Philadelphia NFL	14	0	8	79	9.9	1	1	0	6	0
2000—Philadelphia NFL	6	0	1	9	9.0	0	0	0	0	0
2001—Philadelphia NFL	16	0	5	77	15.4	2	2	0	12	0
Pro totals (3 years)	36	0	14	165	11.8	3	3	0	18	0

DOUGLAS, HUGH — LB/DE — EAGLES

PERSONAL: Born August 23, 1971, in Mansfield, Ohio. ... 6-2/280.
HIGH SCHOOL: Mansfield (Ohio).
COLLEGE: Central State (Ohio).
TRANSACTIONS/CAREER NOTES: Selected after junior season by New York Jets in first round (16th pick overall) of 1995 NFL draft. ... Signed by Jets (June 8, 1995). ... Traded by Jets to Philadelphia Eagles for second- (traded to Pittsburgh) and fifth-round (LB Casey Dailey) picks in 1998 draft (March 13, 1998). ... On injured reserve with bicep injury (October 20, 1999-remainder of season).
CHAMPIONSHIP GAME EXPERIENCE: Played in NFC championship game (2001 season).
HONORS: Named defensive end on THE SPORTING NEWS NFL All-Pro team (2000). ... Played in Pro Bowl (2000 season).
PRO STATISTICS: 1995—Recovered two fumbles. 1996—Recovered three fumbles for 64 yards and one touchdown. 2000—Intercepted one pass for nine yards.

Year Team	G	GS	SACKS
1995—New York Jets NFL	15	3	10.0
1996—New York Jets NFL	10	10	8.0
1997—New York Jets NFL	15	15	4.0
1998—Philadelphia NFL	15	13	12.5
1999—Philadelphia NFL	4	2	2.0
2000—Philadelphia NFL	16	15	15.0
2001—Philadelphia NFL	15	15	9.5
Pro totals (7 years)	90	73	61.0

DOUGLAS, MARQUES DE RAVENS

PERSONAL: Born March 5, 1977, in Greensboro, N.C. ... 6-2/270. ... Full name: Marques Lamont Douglas.
HIGH SCHOOL: Dudley (Greensboro, N.C.).
COLLEGE: Howard.
TRANSACTIONS/CAREER NOTES: Signed by Baltimore Ravens as non-drafted free agent (April 23, 1999). ... Released by Ravens (September 4, 1999). ... Re-signed by Ravens (December 22, 1999). ... Claimed on waivers by New Orleans Saints (August 28, 2000). ... Released by Saints (September 14, 2000). ... Re-signed by Saints (September 20, 2000). ... On injured reserve with knee injury (October 12, 2000-remainder of season). ... Released by Saints (September 2, 2001). ... Re-signed by Saints to practice squad (September 3, 2001). ... Signed by Baltimore Ravens off Saints practice squad (November 28, 2001).
PLAYING EXPERIENCE: New Orleans NFL, 2000; Baltimore NFL, 2001. ... Games/Games started: 2000 (1/0), 2001 (2/0). Total: 3/0.
PRO STATISTICS: 2001—Credited with one sack.

DOWNING, ERIC DT CHIEFS

PERSONAL: Born September 16, 1978, in Ahoskie, N.C. ... 6-3/314. ... Full name: Eric Lamont Downing.
HIGH SCHOOL: John F. Kennedy (Paterson, N.J.).
JUNIOR COLLEGE: Coffeyville (Kan.) Community College.
COLLEGE: Syracuse.
TRANSACTIONS/CAREER NOTES: Selected by Kansas City Chiefs in third round (75th pick overall) of 2001 NFL draft. ... Signed by Chiefs (May 23, 2001).

Year Team	G	GS	SACKS
2001—Kansas City NFL	15	9	1.5

DRAFT, CHRIS LB FALCONS

PERSONAL: Born February 26, 1976, in Anaheim. ... 5-11/232.
HIGH SCHOOL: Valencia (Placentia, Calif.).
COLLEGE: Stanford.
TRANSACTIONS/CAREER NOTES: Selected by Chicago Bears in sixth round (157th pick overall) of 1998 NFL draft. ... Signed by Bears (June 16, 1998). ... Released by Bears (August 30, 1998). ... Re-signed by Bears to practice squad (August 31, 1998). ... Activated (December 2, 1998). ... Released by Bears (August 30, 1999). ... Signed by San Francisco 49ers to practice squad (September 29, 1999). ... Activated (November 19, 1999). ... Released by 49ers (February 10, 2000). ... Signed by Atlanta Falcons (February 14, 2000). ... Granted free agency (March 1, 2002).
PLAYING EXPERIENCE: Chicago NFL, 1998; San Francisco NFL, 1999; Atlanta NFL, 2000 and 2001. ... Games/Games started: 1998 (1/0), 1999 (7/0), 2000 (13/8), 2001 (13/10). Total: 34/18.
PRO STATISTICS: 2000—Credited with one sack.

DRAGOS, SCOTT FB/TE PATRIOTS

PERSONAL: Born October 28, 1975, in Old Rochester, Mass. ... 6-2/245. ... Name pronounced DRAY-gos.
HIGH SCHOOL: Old Rochester (Mass.) Regional.
COLLEGE: Boston College.
TRANSACTIONS/CAREER NOTES: Signed as non-drafted free agent by New England Patriots (April 19, 1998). ... Released by Patriots (August 19, 1998). ... Signed by New York Giants (November 18, 1998). ... Assigned by Giants to Barcelona Dragons in 1999 NFL Europe enhancement allocation program (February 22, 1999). ... Released by Giants (September 5, 1999). ... Signed by Chicago Bears to practice squad (September 28, 1999). ... Released by Bears (August 27, 2000). ... Re-signed by Bears (October 10, 2000). ... Released by Bears (November 13, 2001). ... Re-signed by Bears (January 11, 2002). ... Granted free agency (March 1, 2002). ... Signed by New England Patriots (March 12, 2002).
SINGLE GAME HIGHS (regular season): Receptions—2 (December 10, 2000, vs. New England); yards—14 (December 10, 2000, vs. New England); and touchdown receptions—0

			RECEIVING			
Year Team	G	GS	No.	Yds.	Avg.	TD
1999—Barcelona NFLE	...	...	12	158	13.2	3
2000—Chicago NFL	9	2	4	28	7.0	0
2001—Chicago NFL	6	0	0	0	0.0	0
NFL Europe totals (1 year)	...	...	12	158	13.2	3
NFL totals (2 years)	15	2	4	28	7.0	0
Pro totals (3 years)	...	...	16	186	11.6	3

DRAKEFORD, TYRONNE CB

PERSONAL: Born June 21, 1971, in Camden, S.C. ... 5-11/185. ... Full name: Tyronne James Drakeford.
HIGH SCHOOL: North Central (Kershaw, S.C.).
COLLEGE: Virginia Tech (degree in finance).

TRANSACTIONS/CAREER NOTES: Selected by San Francisco 49ers in second round (62nd pick overall) of 1994 NFL draft. ... Signed by 49ers (July 20, 1994). ... Granted free agency (February 14, 1997). ... Re-signed by 49ers (April 8, 1997). ... Granted unconditional free agency (February 13, 1998). ... Signed by New Orleans Saints (February 19, 1998). ... Released by Saints (May 11, 2000). ... Signed by Washington Redskins (June 23, 2000). ... Granted unconditional free agency (March 2, 2001). ... Signed by 49ers (January 3, 2002). ... Granted unconditional free agency (March 1, 2002).
CHAMPIONSHIP GAME EXPERIENCE: Played in NFC championship game (1994 and 1997 seasons). ... Member of Super Bowl championship team (1994 season).
PRO STATISTICS: 1995—Credited with one sack, fumbled once and recovered one fumble for 12 yards. 1996—Credited with two sacks and recovered one fumble for eight yards. 1997—Returned one kickoff for 24 yards. 1999—Recovered one fumble for 20 yards.

				INTERCEPTIONS		
Year Team	G	GS	No.	Yds.	Avg.	TD
1994—San Francisco NFL	13	0	1	6	6.0	0
1995—San Francisco NFL	16	2	5	54	10.8	0
1996—San Francisco NFL	16	16	1	11	11.0	0
1997—San Francisco NFL	16	2	5	15	3.0	0
1998—New Orleans NFL	16	15	4	76	19.0	1
1999—New Orleans NFL	10	5	0	0	0.0	0
2000—Washington NFL	9	1	0	0	0.0	0
2001—San Francisco NFL	1	0	0	0	0.0	0
Pro totals (8 years)	**97**	**41**	**16**	**162**	**10.1**	**1**

DRIVER, DONALD — WR — PACKERS

PERSONAL: Born February 2, 1975, in Houston. ... 6-0/185. ... Full name: Donald Jerome Driver.
HIGH SCHOOL: Milby (Houston).
COLLEGE: Alcorn State (degree in accounting).
TRANSACTIONS/CAREER NOTES: Selected by Green Bay Packers in seventh round (213th pick overall) of 1999 NFL draft. ... Signed by Packers (June 2, 1999). ... Granted free agency (March 1, 2002). ... Re-signed by Packers (April 16, 2002).
PRO STATISTICS: 2000—Rushed once for four yards and recovered one fumble. 2001—Rushed three times for 38 yards and one touchdown.
SINGLE GAME HIGHS (regular season): Receptions—3 (October 14, 2001, vs. Baltimore); yards—69 (October 14, 2001, vs. Baltimore); and touchdown receptions—1 (December 16, 2001, vs. Tennessee).

			RECEIVING				TOTALS			
Year Team	G	GS	No.	Yds.	Avg.	TD	TD	2pt.	Pts.	Fum.
1999—Green Bay NFL	5	0	3	31	10.3	1	1	0	6	0
2000—Green Bay NFL	16	2	21	322	15.3	1	1	1	8	0
2001—Green Bay NFL	13	2	13	167	12.8	1	2	0	12	0
Pro totals (3 years)	**34**	**4**	**37**	**520**	**14.1**	**3**	**4**	**1**	**26**	**0**

DRIVER, TONY — S — BILLS

PERSONAL: Born August 4, 1977, in Louisville, Ky. ... 6-1/207.
HIGH SCHOOL: Male (Louisville, Ky.).
COLLEGE: Notre Dame.
TRANSACTIONS/CAREER NOTES: Selected by Buffalo Bills in sixth round (178th pick overall) of 2001 NFL draft. ... Signed by Bills (June 18, 2001). ... On injured reserve with shoulder and knee injuries (November 7, 2001-remainder of season).

			KICKOFF RETURNS				TOTALS			
Year Team	G	GS	No.	Yds.	Avg.	TD	TD	2pt.	Pts.	Fum.
2001—Buffalo NFL	5	0	7	130	18.6	0	0	0	0	0

DRONETT, SHANE — DT — FALCONS

PERSONAL: Born January 12, 1971, in Orange, Texas. ... 6-6/300.
HIGH SCHOOL: Bridge City (Texas).
COLLEGE: Texas.
TRANSACTIONS/CAREER NOTES: Selected after junior season by Denver Broncos in second round (54th pick overall) of 1992 NFL draft. ... Signed by Broncos (July 15, 1992). ... Granted free agency (February 17, 1995). ... Re-signed by Broncos (May 12, 1995). ... Granted unconditional free agency (February 16, 1996). ... Signed by Atlanta Falcons (April 9, 1996). ... Released by Falcons (October 7, 1996). ... Signed by Detroit Lions (October 9, 1996). ... Granted unconditional free agency (February 14, 1997). ... Signed by Lions for 1997 season. ... Released by Lions (August 24, 1997). ... Signed by Falcons (August 27, 1997). ... Granted unconditional free agency (February 13, 1998). ... Re-signed by Falcons (February 20, 1998). ... On injured reserve with knee injury (September 19, 2000-remainder of season).
CHAMPIONSHIP GAME EXPERIENCE: Played in NFC championship game (1998 season). ... Played in Super Bowl XXXIII (1998 season).
PRO STATISTICS: 1992—Recovered two fumbles for minus five yards. 1993—Intercepted two passes for 13 yards. 1998—Recovered one fumble. 1999—Recovered one fumble for 15 yards. 2001—Intercepted one pass for minus six yards, fumbled once and recovered one fumble.

Year Team	G	GS	SACKS
1992—Denver NFL	16	2	6.5
1993—Denver NFL	16	16	7.0
1994—Denver NFL	16	15	6.0
1995—Denver NFL	13	2	2.0
1996—Atlanta NFL	5	0	0.0
—Detroit NFL	7	0	0.0
1997—Atlanta NFL	16	1	3.0
1998—Atlanta NFL	16	16	6.5
1999—Atlanta NFL	16	16	6.5
2000—Atlanta NFL	3	3	1.0
2001—Atlanta NFL	15	15	5.5
Pro totals (10 years)	**139**	**86**	**44.0**

DROUGHNS, REUBEN — RB — BRONCOS

PERSONAL: Born August 21, 1978, in Chicago. ... 5-11/207.
HIGH SCHOOL: Anaheim (Calif.).
JUNIOR COLLEGE: Merced (Calif.) College.
COLLEGE: Oregon.
TRANSACTIONS/CAREER NOTES: Selected by Detroit Lions in third round (81st pick overall) of 2000 NFL draft. ... Signed by Lions (July 15, 2000). ... On injured reserve with shoulder injury (August 22, 2000-entire season). ... Released by Lions (September 12, 2001). ... Signed by Miami Dolphins to practice squad (September 18, 2001). ... Signed by Lions off Dolphins practice squad (October 9, 2001). ... Granted free agency (March 1, 2002). ... Signed by Denver Broncos (April 1, 2002).
SINGLE GAME HIGHS (regular season): Attempts—13 (November 11, 2001, vs. Tampa Bay); yards—36 (November 4, 2001, vs. San Francisco); and rushing touchdowns—0.

				RUSHING				RECEIVING				TOTALS		
Year Team	G	GS	Att.	Yds.	Avg.	TD	No.	Yds.	Avg.	TD	TD	2pt.	Pts.	Fum.
2000—Detroit NFL							Did not play.							
2001—Detroit NFL	9	3	30	72	2.4	0	4	21	5.3	1	1	0	6	0

DUDLEY, RICKEY — TE — BROWNS

PERSONAL: Born July 15, 1972, in Henderson, Texas. ... 6-6/255.
HIGH SCHOOL: Henderson (Texas).
COLLEGE: Ohio State.
TRANSACTIONS/CAREER NOTES: Selected by Oakland Raiders in first round (ninth pick overall) of 1996 NFL draft. ... Signed by Raiders (July 12, 1996). ... Granted unconditional free agency (March 2, 2001). ... Signed by Cleveland Browns (March 30, 2001). ... On injured reserve with foot injury (October 9, 2001-remainder of season).
CHAMPIONSHIP GAME EXPERIENCE: Played in AFC championship game (2000 season).
PRO STATISTICS: 1998—Rushed once for minus two yards. 2000—Rushed once for minus seven yards and recovered one fumble.
SINGLE GAME HIGHS (regular season): Receptions—6 (November 8, 1998, vs. Baltimore); yards—116 (November 9, 1997, vs. New Orleans); and touchdown receptions—2 (December 24, 2000, vs. Carolina).
STATISTICAL PLATEAUS: 100-yard receiving games: 1997 (2), 1998 (1). Total: 3.
MISCELLANEOUS: Member of Ohio State basketball team (1991-92 through 1993-94).

			RECEIVING				TOTALS			
Year Team	G	GS	No.	Yds.	Avg.	TD	TD	2pt.	Pts.	Fum.
1996—Oakland NFL	16	15	34	386	11.4	4	4	0	24	1
1997—Oakland NFL	16	16	48	787	16.4	7	7	0	42	0
1998—Oakland NFL	16	15	36	549	15.3	5	5	1	32	1
1999—Oakland NFL	16	16	39	555	14.2	9	9	0	54	0
2000—Oakland NFL	16	16	29	350	12.1	4	4	0	24	1
2001—Cleveland NFL	4	4	9	115	12.8	0	0	0	0	0
Pro totals (6 years)	84	82	195	2742	14.1	29	29	1	176	3

DUFFY, ROGER — G/C

PERSONAL: Born July 16, 1967, in Pittsburgh. ... 6-2/299. ... Full name: Roger Thomas Duffy.
HIGH SCHOOL: Canton (Ohio) Central Catholic.
COLLEGE: Penn State (degree in communications, 1990).
TRANSACTIONS/CAREER NOTES: Selected by New York Jets in eighth round (196th pick overall) of 1990 NFL draft. ... Signed by Jets (July 18, 1990). ... Granted free agency (February 1, 1992). ... Re-signed by Jets (May 15, 1992). ... Granted unconditional free agency (February 17, 1994). ... Re-signed by Jets (March 2, 1994). ... Granted unconditional free agency (February 16, 1996). ... Re-signed by Jets (April 1, 1996). ... Granted unconditional free agency (February 13, 1998). ... Signed by Pittsburgh Steelers (March 13, 1998). ... Released by Steelers (February 27, 2002).
PLAYING EXPERIENCE: New York Jets NFL, 1990-1997; Pittsburgh NFL, 1998-2001. ... Games/Games started: 1990 (16/2), 1991 (12/0), 1992 (16/6), 1993 (16/1), 1994 (16/14), 1995 (16/16), 1996 (16/16), 1997 (15/15), 1998 (15/4), 1999 (16/11), 2000 (13/7), 2001 (8/0). Total: 175/92.
CHAMPIONSHIP GAME EXPERIENCE: Member of Steelers for AFC championship game (2001 season); did not play.
PRO STATISTICS: 1991—Returned one kickoff for eight yards. 1992—Returned one kickoff for seven yards and recovered one fumble. 1993—Recovered one fumble. 1995—Recovered two fumbles. 1996—Recovered one fumble. 1997—Fumbled twice and recovered one fumble for minus 22 yards. 2000—Fumbled once for minus 10 yards.

DUGANS, RON — WR — BENGALS

PERSONAL: Born April 27, 1977, in Tallahassee, Fla. ... 6-2/205.
HIGH SCHOOL: Florida A&M University Develop Research (Tallahassee, Fla.).
COLLEGE: Florida State (degree in political science, 1999).
TRANSACTIONS/CAREER NOTES: Selected by Cincinnati Bengals in third round (66th pick overall) of 2000 NFL draft. ... Signed by Bengals (July 25, 2000).
PRO STATISTICS: 2001—Recovered one fumble.
SINGLE GAME HIGHS (regular season): Receptions—5 (November 18, 2001, vs. Tennessee); yards—51 (November 18, 2001, vs. Tennessee); and touchdown receptions—1 (December 30, 2001, vs. Pittsburgh).

			RECEIVING				TOTALS			
Year Team	G	GS	No.	Yds.	Avg.	TD	TD	2pt.	Pts.	Fum.
2000—Cincinnati NFL	14	5	14	125	8.9	1	1	0	6	0
2001—Cincinnati NFL	16	3	28	251	9.0	2	2	▲1	14	0
Pro totals (2 years)	30	8	42	376	9.0	3	3	1	20	0

DUNCAN, JAMIE   LB   RAMS

PERSONAL: Born July 20, 1975, in Wilmington, Del. ... 6-1/238. ... Full name: Jamie Robert Duncan.
HIGH SCHOOL: Christiana (Newark, Del.).
COLLEGE: Vanderbilt (degree in human and organizational development, 1998).
TRANSACTIONS/CAREER NOTES: Selected by Tampa Bay Buccaneers in third round (84th pick overall) of 1998 NFL draft. ... Signed by Buccaneers (July 10, 1998). ... Granted unconditional free agency (March 1, 2002). ... Signed by St. Louis Rams (March 3, 2002).
PLAYING EXPERIENCE: Tampa Bay NFL, 1998-2001. ... Games/Games started: 1998 (14/6), 1999 (16/0), 2000 (15/15), 2001 (15/15). Total: 60/36.
CHAMPIONSHIP GAME EXPERIENCE: Played in NFC championship game (1999 season).
HONORS: Named inside linebacker on THE SPORTING NEWS college All-America second team (1997).
PRO STATISTICS: 2000—Intercepted four passes for 55 yards and one touchdown and recovered one touchdown. 2001—Intercepted one pass for nine yards and credited with two sacks.

DUNN, DAVID   WR/KR

PERSONAL: Born June 10, 1972, in San Diego. ... 6-3/215.
HIGH SCHOOL: Samuel F.B. Morse (San Diego).
JUNIOR COLLEGE: Bakersfield (Calif.) College.
COLLEGE: Fresno State.
TRANSACTIONS/CAREER NOTES: Selected by Cincinnati Bengals in fifth round (139th pick overall) of 1995 NFL draft. ... Signed by Bengals (July 31, 1995). ... Granted free agency (February 13, 1998). ... Re-signed by Bengals (April 23, 1998). ... Released by Bengals (September 9, 1998). ... Signed by Pittsburgh Steelers (October 14, 1998). ... Released by Steelers (August 30, 1999). ... Signed by Cleveland Browns (September 28, 1999). ... Released by Browns (November 9, 1999). ... Signed by Oakland Raiders (February 29, 2000). ... Granted unconditional free agency (March 2, 2001). ... Re-signed by Raiders (March 22, 2001). ... Released by Raiders (December 5, 2001).
CHAMPIONSHIP GAME EXPERIENCE: Played in AFC championship game (2000 season).
HONORS: Named kick returner on THE SPORTING NEWS college All-America second team (1994).
PRO STATISTICS: 1995—Rushed once for minus 13 yards. 1997—Recovered one fumble. 1999—Recovered one fumble.
SINGLE GAME HIGHS (regular season): Receptions—7 (December 15, 1996, vs. Houston); yards—95 (December 15, 1996, vs. Houston); and touchdown receptions—1 (December 14, 1997, vs. Dallas).

			RECEIVING				PUNT RETURNS				KICKOFF RETURNS				TOTALS			
Year Team	G	GS	No.	Yds.	Avg.	TD	No.	Yds.	Avg.	TD	No.	Yds.	Avg.	TD	TD	2pt.	Pts.	Fum.
1995—Cincinnati NFL	16	0	17	209	12.3	1	0	0	0.0	0	50	1092	21.8	0	1	0	6	2
1996—Cincinnati NFL	16	0	32	509	15.9	1	7	54	7.7	0	35	782	22.3	▲1	3	0	18	1
1997—Cincinnati NFL	14	5	27	414	15.3	2	0	0	0.0	0	19	487	25.6	0	2	0	12	1
1998—Cincinnati NFL	1	0	0	0	0.0	0	0	0	0.0	0	0	0	0.0	0	0	0	0	0
—Pittsburgh NFL	10	0	9	87	9.7	0	0	0	0.0	0	21	525	25.0	0	0	0	0	1
1999—Cleveland NFL	6	0	1	4	4.0	0	4	25	6.3	0	9	180	20.0	0	0	0	0	3
2000—Oakland NFL	15	0	4	33	8.3	0	8	99	12.4	0	44	1073	24.4	▲1	1	0	6	0
2001—Oakland NFL	10	0	1	8	8.0	0	19	169	8.9	0	20	458	22.9	0	0	0	0	3
Pro totals (7 years)	88	5	91	1264	13.9	4	38	347	9.1	0	198	4597	23.2	2	7	0	42	11

DUNN, JASON   TE   CHIEFS

PERSONAL: Born November 15, 1973, in Harrodsburg, Ky. ... 6-6/273. ... Full name: Jason Adam Dunn.
HIGH SCHOOL: Harrodsburg (Ky.).
COLLEGE: Eastern Kentucky.
TRANSACTIONS/CAREER NOTES: Selected by Philadelphia Eagles in second round (54th pick overall) of 1996 NFL draft. ... Signed by Eagles (July 17, 1996). ... On injured reserve with knee injury (December 1, 1998-remainder of season). ... Granted free agency (February 12, 1999). ... Re-signed by Eagles for 1999 season. ... Released by Eagles (June 17, 1999). ... Signed by Kansas City Chiefs (July 11, 2000). ... Granted unconditional free agency (March 2, 2001). ... Re-signed by Chiefs (March 26, 2001). ... On injured reserve with elbow injury (January 4, 2001-remainder of season).
PRO STATISTICS: 1996—Recovered one fumble. 1997—Returned two kickoffs for 32 yards. 1998—Rushed once for minus five yards and recovered one fumble. 2001—Returned two kickoffs for 34 yards.
SINGLE GAME HIGHS (regular season): Receptions—4 (November 15, 1998, vs. Washington); yards—58 (September 22, 1996, vs. Atlanta); and touchdown receptions—1 (December 21, 1997, vs. Washington).

			RECEIVING				TOTALS			
Year Team	G	GS	No.	Yds.	Avg.	TD	TD	2pt.	Pts.	Fum.
1996—Philadelphia NFL	16	12	15	332	22.1	2	2	0	12	0
1997—Philadelphia NFL	15	4	7	93	13.3	2	2	0	12	0
1998—Philadelphia NFL	10	10	18	132	7.3	0	0	0	0	1
2000—Kansas City NFL	14	2	2	26	13.0	0	0	0	0	0
2001—Kansas City NFL	15	6	4	54	13.5	1	1	0	6	0
Pro totals (5 years)	70	34	46	637	13.8	5	5	0	30	1

DUNN, WARRICK   RB   FALCONS

PERSONAL: Born January 5, 1975, in Baton Rouge, La. ... 5-9/180. ... Full name: Warrick De'Mon Dunn.
HIGH SCHOOL: Catholic (Baton Rouge, La.).
COLLEGE: Florida State (degree in information studies, 1997).
TRANSACTIONS/CAREER NOTES: Selected by Tampa Bay Buccaneers in first round (12th pick overall) of 1997 NFL draft. ... Signed by Buccaneers (July 24, 1997). ... Granted unconditional free agency (March 1, 2002). ... Signed by Atlanta Falcons (March 15, 2002).
CHAMPIONSHIP GAME EXPERIENCE: Played in NFC championship game (1999 season).
HONORS: Named NFL Rookie of the Year by The Sporting News (1997). ... Played in Pro Bowl (1997 and 2000 seasons).
PRO STATISTICS: 1997—Returned five punts for 48 yards and recovered four fumbles. 1998—Recovered one fumble. 1999—Recovered one fumble.

SINGLE GAME HIGHS (regular season): Attempts—28 (December 10, 2000, vs. Miami); yards—210 (December 3, 2000, vs. Dallas); and rushing touchdowns—3 (December 18, 2000, vs. St. Louis).
STATISTICAL PLATEAUS: 100-yard rushing games: 1997 (5), 1998 (2), 2000 (3). Total: 10. ... 100-yard receiving games: 1997 (1), 1999 (1), 2001 (1). Total: 3.

				RUSHING				RECEIVING				KICKOFF RETURNS				TOTALS		
Year Team	G	GS	Att.	Yds.	Avg.	TD	No.	Yds.	Avg.	TD	No.	Yds.	Avg.	TD	TD	2pt.	Pts.	Fum.
1997—Tampa Bay NFL	16	10	224	978	4.4	4	39	462	11.8	3	6	129	21.5	0	7	0	42	4
1998—Tampa Bay NFL	16	14	245	1026	4.2	2	44	344	7.8	0	1	25	25.0	0	2	0	12	1
1999—Tampa Bay NFL	15	15	195	616	3.2	0	64	589	9.2	2	8	156	19.5	0	2	0	12	3
2000—Tampa Bay NFL	16	14	248	1133	4.6	8	44	422	9.6	1	0	0	0.0	0	9	0	54	1
2001—Tampa Bay NFL	13	12	158	447	2.8	3	68	557	8.2	3	0	0	0.0	0	6	0	36	2
Pro totals (5 years)	76	65	1070	4200	3.9	17	259	2374	9.2	9	15	310	20.7	0	26	0	156	11

DWIGHT, TIM   WR/PR   CHARGERS

PERSONAL: Born July 13, 1975, in Iowa City, Iowa. ... 5-9/180. ... Full name: Timothy John Dwight Jr.
HIGH SCHOOL: Iowa City (Iowa) High.
COLLEGE: Iowa.
TRANSACTIONS/CAREER NOTES: Selected by Atlanta Falcons in fourth round (114th pick overall) of 1998 NFL draft. ... Signed by Falcons (June 25, 1998). ... Granted free agency (March 2, 2001). ... Re-signed by Falcons (April 21, 2001). ... Traded by Falcons with first- (RB LaDainian Tomlinson) and third-round (DB Tay Cody) picks in 2001 draft and second-round pick in 2002 draft to San Diego Chargers for first-round pick (QB Michael Vick) in 2001 draft (April 20, 2001).
CHAMPIONSHIP GAME EXPERIENCE: Played in NFC championship game (1998 season). ... Played in Super Bowl XXXIII (1998 season).
HONORS: Named kick returner on THE SPORTING NEWS college All-America second team (1996). ... Named kick returner on THE SPORTING NEWS college All-America first team (1997).
POST SEASON RECORDS: Holds Super Bowl career record for highest kickoff return average (minimum four returns)—42.0. ... Shares Super Bowl single-game record for most touchdowns by kickoff return—1 (January 31, 1999, vs. Denver).
PRO STATISTICS: 1998—Attempted two passes with one completion for 22 yards and fumbled three times. 1999—Fumbled twice. 2000—Fumbled three times and recovered one fumble. 2001—Fumbled once and recovered one fumble.
SINGLE GAME HIGHS (regular season): Receptions—7 (January 3, 2000, vs. San Francisco); yards—162 (January 3, 2000, vs. San Francisco); and touchdown receptions—2 (January 3, 2000, vs. San Francisco).
STATISTICAL PLATEAUS: 100-yard receiving games: 1999 (2).

			RUSHING				RECEIVING				PUNT RETURNS				KICKOFF RETURNS				TOTALS		
Year Team	G	GS	Att.	Yds.	Avg.	TD	No.	Yds.	Avg.	TD	No.	Yds.	Avg.	TD	No.	Yds.	Avg.	TD	TD	2pt.	Pts.
1998—Atlanta NFL	12	0	8	19	2.4	0	4	94	23.5	1	31	263	8.5	0	36	973	27.0	1	2	0	12
1999—Atlanta NFL	12	8	5	28	5.6	1	32	669	*20.9	7	20	220	11.0	∞1	44	944	21.5	0	9	0	54
2000—Atlanta NFL	14	1	5	8	1.6	0	26	406	15.6	3	33	309	9.4	1	32	680	21.3	0	4	0	24
2001—San Diego NFL	10	2	2	24	12.0	1	25	406	16.2	0	24	271	11.3	1	0	0	0.0	0	2	0	12
Pro totals (4 years)	48	11	20	79	4.0	2	87	1575	18.1	11	108	1063	9.8	3	112	2597	23.2	1	17	0	102

DYER, DEON   FB   DOLPHINS

PERSONAL: Born October 2, 1977, in Chesapeake, Va. ... 5-11/255. ... Full name: Deon Joseph Dyer.
HIGH SCHOOL: Deep Creek (Chesapeake, Va.).
COLLEGE: North Carolina.
TRANSACTIONS/CAREER NOTES: Selected by Miami Dolphins in fourth round (117th pick overall) of 2000 NFL draft. ... Signed by Dolphins (June 2, 2000).
PRO STATISTICS: 2001—Returned two kickoffs for 24 yards and recovered one fumble.

			RUSHING				RECEIVING				TOTALS			
Year Team	G	GS	Att.	Yds.	Avg.	TD	No.	Yds.	Avg.	TD	TD	2pt.	Pts.	Fum.
2000—Miami NFL	16	1	0	0	0.0	0	2	14	7.0	0	0	0	0	0
2001—Miami NFL	16	0	0	0	0.0	0	0	0	0.0	0	0	0	0	0
Pro totals (2 years)	32	1	0	0	0.0	0	2	14	7.0	0	0	0	0	0

DYSON, ANDRE   CB   TITANS

PERSONAL: Born May 25, 1979, in Layton, Utah. ... 5-10/187. ... Brother of Kevin Dyson, wide receiver, Tennessee Titans.
HIGH SCHOOL: Clearfield (Utah).
COLLEGE: Utah.
TRANSACTIONS/CAREER NOTES: Selected by Tennessee Titans in second round (60th pick overall) of 2001 NFL draft. ... Signed by Titans (July 24, 2001).

			INTERCEPTIONS			
Year Team	G	GS	No.	Yds.	Avg.	TD
2001—Tennessee NFL	14	11	3	36	12.0	0

DYSON, KEVIN   WR   TITANS

PERSONAL: Born June 23, 1975, in Logan, Utah ... 6-1/201. ... Full name: Kevin Tyree Dyson. ... Brother of Andre Dyson, cornerback, Tennessee Titans.
HIGH SCHOOL: Clearfield (Utah).
COLLEGE: Utah.
TRANSACTIONS/CAREER NOTES: Selected by Tennessee Oilers in first round (16th pick overall) of 1998 NFL draft. ... Signed by Oilers (July 24, 1998). ... Oilers franchise renamed Tennessee Titans for 1999 season (December 26, 1998). ... On injured reserve with knee injury (September 29, 2000-remainder of season).
CHAMPIONSHIP GAME EXPERIENCE: Played in AFC championship game (1999 season). ... Played in Super Bowl XXXIV (1999 season).

PRO STATISTICS: 1998—Rushed once for four yards. 1999—Rushed once for three yards.
SINGLE GAME HIGHS (regular season): Receptions—9 (September 12, 1999, vs. Cincinnati); yards—162 (September 12, 1999, vs. Cincinnati); and touchdown receptions—2 (September 12, 1999, vs. Cincinnati).
STATISTICAL PLATEAUS: 100-yard receiving games: 1999 (1), 2000 (1), 2001 (2). Total: 4.

				RECEIVING				TOTALS		
Year Team	G	GS	No.	Yds.	Avg.	TD	TD	2pt.	Pts.	Fum.
1998—Tennessee NFL	13	9	21	263	12.5	2	2	0	12	0
1999—Tennessee NFL	16	16	54	658	12.2	4	4	0	24	0
2000—Tennessee NFL	2	2	6	104	17.3	1	1	0	6	0
2001—Tennessee NFL	16	16	54	825	15.3	7	7	1	44	0
Pro totals (4 years)	47	43	135	1850	13.7	14	14	1	86	0

EATON, CHAD   DT   SEAHAWKS

PERSONAL: Born April 6, 1972, in Exeter, N.H. ... 6-5/306. ... Full name: Chad Everett Eaton.
HIGH SCHOOL: Rogers (Puyallup, Wash.).
COLLEGE: Washington State.
TRANSACTIONS/CAREER NOTES: Selected by Arizona Cardinals in seventh round (241st pick overall) of 1995 NFL draft. ... Signed by Cardinals (July 24, 1995). ... Released by Cardinals (August 14, 1995). ... Signed by New York Jets (August 15, 1995). ... Released by Jets (August 27, 1995). ... Signed by Cleveland Browns to practice squad (September 28, 1995). ... Activated (December 15, 1995); did not play. ... Browns franchise moved to Baltimore and renamed Ravens for 1996 season (March 11, 1996). ... Released by Ravens (August 19, 1996). ... Signed by New England Patriots to practice squad (August 27, 1996). ... Activated (November 28, 1996). ... Granted unconditional free agency (March 2, 2001). ... Signed by Seattle Seahawks (March 9, 2001).
CHAMPIONSHIP GAME EXPERIENCE: Played in AFC championship game (1996 season). ... Played in Super Bowl XXXI (1996 season).
HONORS: Named defensive lineman on THE SPORTING NEWS college All-America second team (1994).
PRO STATISTICS: 1998—Returned one kickoff for 13 yards and recovered one fumble for two yards. 1999—Recovered three fumbles for 53 yards and one touchdown. 2001—Recovered one fumble.

Year Team	G	GS	SACKS
1995—Cleveland NFL		Did not play.	
1996—New England NFL	4	0	1.0
1997—New England NFL	16	1	1.0
1998—New England NFL	15	14	6.0
1999—New England NFL	16	16	3.0
2000—New England NFL	14	13	2.5
2001—Seattle NFL	16	16	1.0
Pro totals (6 years)	81	60	14.5

EDINGER, PAUL   K   BEARS

PERSONAL: Born January 17, 1978, in Frankfort, Mich. ... 5-8/163. ... Full name: Paul E. Edinger.
HIGH SCHOOL: Kathleen (Lakeland, Fla.).
COLLEGE: Michigan State.
TRANSACTIONS/CAREER NOTES: Selected by Chicago Bears in sixth round (174th pick overall) of 2000 NFL draft. ... Signed by Bears (June 8, 2000).
PRO STATISTICS: 2001—Punted once for 34 yards.

				KICKING				
Year Team	G	XPM	XPA	FGM	FGA	Lg.	50+	Pts.
2000—Chicago NFL	16	21	21	21	27	54	2-2	84
2001—Chicago NFL	16	34	34	26	31	48	0-0	112
Pro totals (2 years)	32	55	55	47	58	54	2-2	196

EDWARDS, ANTUAN   CB/SS   PACKERS

PERSONAL: Born May 26, 1977, in Starkville, Miss. ... 6-1/210. ... Full name: Antuan Minye' Edwards. ... Name pronounced AN-twan.
HIGH SCHOOL: Starkville (Miss.).
COLLEGE: Clemson.
TRANSACTIONS/CAREER NOTES: Selected by Green Bay Packers in first round (25th pick overall) of 1999 NFL draft. ... Signed by Packers (June 7, 1999). ... On injured reserve with knee injury (October 3, 2001-remainder of season).
PRO STATISTICS: 2001—Recovered one fumble for minus two yards.

			INTERCEPTIONS				PUNT RETURNS				TOTALS		
Year Team	G	GS	No.	Yds.	Avg.	TD	No.	Yds.	Avg.	TD	TD	2pt.	Pts.	Fum.
1999—Green Bay NFL	16	1	4	26	6.5	1	10	90	9.0	0	1	0	6	1
2000—Green Bay NFL	12	3	2	4	2.0	0	0	0	0.0	0	0	0	0	0
2001—Green Bay NFL	3	0	0	0	0.0	0	0	0	0.0	0	0	0	0	0
Pro totals (3 years)	31	4	6	30	5.0	1	10	90	9.0	0	1	0	6	1

EDWARDS, DONNIE   LB   CHARGERS

PERSONAL: Born April 6, 1973, in San Diego. ... 6-2/227. ... Full name: Donnie Lewis Edwards Jr.
HIGH SCHOOL: Chula Vista (San Diego).
COLLEGE: UCLA (degree in political science).
TRANSACTIONS/CAREER NOTES: Selected by Kansas City Chiefs in fourth round (98th pick overall) of 1996 NFL draft. ... Signed by Chiefs (July 24, 1996). ... Released by Chiefs (March 1, 2002). ... Signed by San Diego Chargers (April 20, 2002).
PRO STATISTICS: 1997—Recovered one fumble. 1998—Recovered one fumble. 1999—Recovered two fumbles for 79 yards and one touchdown. 2000—Recovered one fumble for 11 yards.

Year Team	G	GS	INTERCEPTIONS No.	Yds.	Avg.	TD	SACKS No.
1996—Kansas City NFL	15	1	1	22	22.0	0	0.0
1997—Kansas City NFL	16	16	2	15	7.5	0	2.5
1998—Kansas City NFL	15	15	0	0	0.0	0	6.0
1999—Kansas City NFL	16	16	5	50	10.0	1	3.0
2000—Kansas City NFL	16	16	2	45	22.5	1	1.0
2001—Kansas City NFL	16	16	0	0	0.0	0	2.0
Pro totals (6 years)	94	80	10	132	13.2	2	14.5

EDWARDS, MARC FB PATRIOTS

PERSONAL: Born November 17, 1974, in Cincinnati. ... 6-0/245. ... Full name: Marc Alexander Edwards.
HIGH SCHOOL: Norwood (Cincinnati).
COLLEGE: Notre Dame (degree in business management, 1996).
TRANSACTIONS/CAREER NOTES: Selected by San Francisco 49ers in second round (55th pick overall) of 1997 NFL draft. ... Signed by 49ers (July 23, 1997). ... On physically unable to perform list with back injury (July 17-August 10, 1998). ... Traded by 49ers to Cleveland Browns for fourth-round pick (DB Pierson Prioleau) in 1999 draft (April 18, 1999). ... Granted unconditional free agency (March 2, 2001). ... Signed by New England Patriots (March 19, 2001).
CHAMPIONSHIP GAME EXPERIENCE: Played in NFC championship game (1997 season). ... Played in AFC championship game (2001 season). ... Member of Super Bowl championship team (2001 season).
PRO STATISTICS: 1997—Returned one kickoff for 30 yards. 2000—Returned one kickoff for 24 yards and recovered one fumble. 2001—Returned one kickoff for 23 yards and recovered one fumble.
SINGLE GAME HIGHS (regular season): Attempts—6 (November 4, 2001, vs. Atlanta); yards—41 (September 27, 1998, vs. Atlanta); and rushing touchdowns—1 (December 2, 2001, vs. New York Jets).

			RUSHING				RECEIVING				TOTALS			
Year Team	G	GS	Att.	Yds.	Avg.	TD	No.	Yds.	Avg.	TD	TD	2pt.	Pts.	Fum.
1997—San Francisco NFL	15	1	5	17	3.4	0	6	48	8.0	0	0	0	0	0
1998—San Francisco NFL	16	11	22	94	4.3	1	22	218	9.9	2	3	0	18	0
1999—Cleveland NFL	16	14	6	35	5.8	0	27	212	7.9	2	2	0	12	1
2000—Cleveland NFL	16	8	2	9	4.5	0	16	128	8.0	2	2	0	12	2
2001—New England NFL	16	13	51	141	2.8	1	25	166	6.6	2	3	0	18	3
Pro totals (5 years)	79	47	86	296	3.4	2	96	772	8.0	8	10	0	60	6

EDWARDS, MARIO CB COWBOYS

PERSONAL: Born December 1, 1975, in Gautier, Miss. ... 6-0/191. ... Full name: Mario L. Edwards.
HIGH SCHOOL: Pascagoula (Miss.).
COLLEGE: Florida State.
TRANSACTIONS/CAREER NOTES: Selected by Dallas Cowboys in sixth round (180th pick overall) of 2000 NFL draft. ... Signed by Cowboys (July 14, 2000).
PLAYING EXPERIENCE: Dallas NFL, 2000 and 2001. ... Games/Games started: 2000 (11/1), 2001 (16/15). Total: 27/16.
PRO STATISTICS: 2001—Intercepted one pass for 71 yards and a touchdown and recovered one fumble for two yards.

EDWARDS, ROBERT RB DOLPHINS

PERSONAL: Born October 2, 1974, in Tennille, Ga. ... 5-11/220. ... Full name: Robert Lee Edwards III.
HIGH SCHOOL: Washington County (Sandersville, Ga.).
COLLEGE: Georgia.
TRANSACTIONS/CAREER NOTES: Selected by New England Patriots in first round (18th pick overall) of 1998 NFL draft. ... Signed by Patriots (July 17, 1998). ... On non-football injury list with knee injury (August 31, 1999-entire season). ... On non-football injury list with knee injury (August 22, 2000-entire season). ... On physically unable to perform list with knee injury (July 23-August 24, 2001). ... Released by Patriots (August 24, 2001). ... Signed by Miami Dolphins (March 6, 2002).
PRO STATISTICS: 1998—Recovered two fumbles.
SINGLE GAME HIGHS (regular season): Attempts—28 (December 6, 1998, vs. Pittsburgh); yards—196 (December 13, 1998, vs. St. Louis); and rushing touchdowns—1 (December 20, 1998, vs. San Francisco).
STATISTICAL PLATEAUS: 100-yard rushing games: 1998 (4).

			RUSHING				RECEIVING				TOTALS			
Year Team	G	GS	Att.	Yds.	Avg.	TD	No.	Yds.	Avg.	TD	TD	2pt.	Pts.	Fum.
1998—New England NFL	16	15	291	1115	3.8	9	35	331	9.5	3	12	0	72	5
1999—New England NFL							Did not play.							
2000—New England NFL							Did not play.							
2001—							Did not play.							
Pro totals (1 years)	16	15	291	1115	3.8	9	35	331	9.5	3	12	0	72	5

EDWARDS, RON DT BILLS

PERSONAL: Born July 12, 1979, in Houston. ... 6-3/305.
HIGH SCHOOL: Klein Forest (Houston).
COLLEGE: Texas A&M.
TRANSACTIONS/CAREER NOTES: Selected by Buffalo Bills in third round (76th pick overall) of 2001 NFL draft. ... Signed by Bills (June 1, 2001).
PLAYING EXPERIENCE: Buffalo NFL, 2001. ... Games/Games started: 2001 (7/3).

EDWARDS, TROY — WR — STEELERS

PERSONAL: Born April 7, 1977, in Shreveport, La. ... 5-9/192.
HIGH SCHOOL: Huntington (Shreveport, La.).
COLLEGE: Louisiana Tech.
TRANSACTIONS/CAREER NOTES: Selected by Pittsburgh Steelers in first round (13th pick overall) of 1999 NFL draft. ... Signed by Steelers (July 28, 1999).
CHAMPIONSHIP GAME EXPERIENCE: Played in AFC championship game (2001 season).
HONORS: Fred Biletnikoff Award winner (1998). ... Named wide receiver on THE SPORTING NEWS college All-America second team (1998).
PRO STATISTICS: 1999—Recovered three fumbles. 2001—Rushed five times for 28 yards and one touchdown and recovered one fumble for 32 yards and one touchdown.
SINGLE GAME HIGHS (regular season): Receptions—7 (November 28, 1999, vs. Cincinnati); yards—86 (November 28, 1999, vs. Cincinnati); and touchdown receptions—1 (December 18, 1999, vs. Kansas City).

			RECEIVING				PUNT RETURNS			KICKOFF RETURNS			TOTALS			
Year Team	G	GS	No.	Yds.	Avg.	TD	No.	Yds.	Avg.	TD	No.	Yds.	Avg.	TD	TD	2pt.	Pts.	Fum.
1999—Pittsburgh NFL	16	6	61	714	11.7	5	25	234	9.4	0	13	234	18.0	0	5	0	30	4
2000—Pittsburgh NFL	14	1	18	215	11.9	0	0	0	0.0	0	15	298	19.9	0	0	0	0	1
2001—Pittsburgh NFL	16	0	19	283	14.9	0	10	83	8.3	0	20	462	23.1	0	2	0	12	1
Pro totals (3 years)	46	7	98	1212	12.4	5	35	317	9.1	0	48	994	20.7	0	7	0	42	6

EKUBAN, EBENEZER — DE — COWBOYS

PERSONAL: Born May 29, 1976, in Ghana, Africa. ... 6-3/282. ... Full name: Ebenezer Ekuban Jr. ... Name pronounced ECK-you-bon.
HIGH SCHOOL: Bladensburg (Md.).
COLLEGE: North Carolina.
TRANSACTIONS/CAREER NOTES: Selected by Dallas Cowboys in first round (20th pick overall) of 1999 NFL draft. ... Signed by Cowboys (July 27, 1999). ... On injured reserve with back injury (December 21, 2001-remainder of season).
PRO STATISTICS: 2000—Recovered one fumble.

Year Team	G	GS	SACKS
1999—Dallas NFL	16	2	2.5
2000—Dallas NFL	12	2	6.5
2001—Dallas NFL	1	1	0.0
Pro totals (3 years)	29	5	9.0

ELAM, JASON — K — BRONCOS

PERSONAL: Born March 8, 1970, in Fort Walton Beach, Fla. ... 5-11/200. ... Name pronounced EE-lum.
HIGH SCHOOL: Brookwood (Snellville, Ga.).
COLLEGE: Hawaii.
TRANSACTIONS/CAREER NOTES: Selected by Denver Broncos in third round (70th pick overall) of 1993 NFL draft. ... Signed by Broncos (July 12, 1993). ... Granted free agency (March 1, 2002).
CHAMPIONSHIP GAME EXPERIENCE: Played in AFC championship game (1997 and 1998 seasons). ... Member of Super Bowl championship team (1997 and 1998 seasons).
HONORS: Named kicker on THE SPORTING NEWS college All-America second team (1989 and 1991). ... Played in Pro Bowl (1995 and 1998 seasons).
RECORDS: Holds NFL career record for most consecutive PATs made—313 (1993-current). ... Holds NFL career record for highest PAT percentage—99.65. ... Shares NFL career record for longest field goal—63 (October 25, 1998, vs. Jacksonville).
PRO STATISTICS: 1995—Punted once for 17 yards.

		KICKING						
Year Team	G	XPM	XPA	FGM	FGA	Lg.	50+	Pts.
1993—Denver NFL	16	§41	§42	26	35	54	4-6	119
1994—Denver NFL	16	29	29	30	37	†54	1-3	119
1995—Denver NFL	16	39	39	31	38	§56	5-7	132
1996—Denver NFL	16	§46	§46	21	28	51	1-3	109
1997—Denver NFL	15	§46	§46	26	36	53	3-5	124
1998—Denver NFL	16	§58	§58	23	27	*63	3-4	§127
1999—Denver NFL	16	29	29	29	36	*55	5-8	116
2000—Denver NFL	13	*49	*49	18	24	51	1-1	103
2001—Denver NFL	16	31	31	*31	36	50	2-4	124
Pro totals (9 years)	140	368	369	235	297	63	25-41	1073

ELAM, SHANE — LB

PERSONAL: Born November 6, 1977, in Covington, Tenn. ... 6-1/240. ... Full name: Shane Farrar Elam.
HIGH SCHOOL: Covington (Tenn.).
COLLEGE: Mississippi.
TRANSACTIONS/CAREER NOTES: Signed as non-drafted free agent by San Francisco 49ers (April 26, 2001). ... Released by 49ers (October 30, 2001). ... Signed by Houston Texans (January 22, 2002). ... Released by Texans (May 20, 2002).
PLAYING EXPERIENCE: San Francisco NFL, 2001. ... Games/Games started: 2001 (4/0).

ELLIOTT, JUMBO — OT — JETS

PERSONAL: Born April 1, 1965, in Lake Ronkonkoma, N.Y. ... 6-7/305. ... Full name: John Elliott.
HIGH SCHOOL: Sachem (Lake Ronkonkoma, N.Y.).
COLLEGE: Michigan.

TRANSACTIONS/CAREER NOTES: Selected by New York Giants in second round (36th pick overall) of 1988 NFL draft. ... Signed by Giants (July 18, 1988). ... Granted free agency (February 1, 1991). ... Re-signed by Giants (August 22, 1991). ... Designated by Giants as franchise player (February 25, 1993). ... On injured reserve with back injury (January 7, 1994-remainder of playoffs). ... Granted unconditional free agency (February 16, 1996). ... Signed by New York Jets (February 24, 1996). ... On injured reserve with ankle injury (December 1, 1997-remainder of season). ... Announced retirement (March 6, 2000). ... Re-signed by Jets (August 14, 2000). ... On suspended list (August 29-September 4, 2000). ... Released by Jets (July 19, 2001). ... Re-signed by Jets (April 5, 2002).
PLAYING EXPERIENCE: New York Giants NFL, 1988-1995; New York Jets NFL, 1996-2000. ... Games/Games started: 1988 (16/5), 1989 (13/11), 1990 (8/8), 1991 (16/16), 1992 (16/16), 1993 (11/11), 1994 (16/15), 1995 (16/16), 1996 (14/14), 1997 (13/13), 1998 (16/16), 1999 (16/15), 2000 (9/0), 2001 (did not play). Total: 180/156.
CHAMPIONSHIP GAME EXPERIENCE: Played in NFC championship game (1990 season). ... Member of Super Bowl championship team (1990 season). ... Played in AFC championship game (1998 season).
HONORS: Played in Pro Bowl (1993 season).
PRO STATISTICS: 1988—Recovered one fumble. 2000—Caught one pass for three yards and a touchdown.

ELLIS, ED　　　OT　　　CHARGERS

PERSONAL: Born October 13, 1975, in Hamden, Conn. ... 6-7/325. ... Full name: Edward Key Ellis.
HIGH SCHOOL: Hamden (Conn.).
COLLEGE: Buffalo.
TRANSACTIONS/CAREER NOTES: Selected by New England Patriots in fourth round (125th pick overall) of 1997 NFL draft. ... Signed by Patriots (June 19, 1997). ... Granted free agency (February 11, 2000). ... Assigned by Patriots to Barcelona Dragons in 2000 NFL Europe enhancement allocation program (February 18, 2000). ... Re-signed by Patriots (March 13, 2000). ... Released by Patriots (July 17, 2000). ... Signed by Washington Redskins (July 20, 2000). ... Granted unconditional free agency (March 2, 2001). ... Signed by San Diego Chargers (April 2, 2001).
PLAYING EXPERIENCE: New England NFL, 1997-1999; Barcelona NFLE, 2000; Washington NFL, 2000; San Diego NFL, 2001. ... Games/Games started: 1997 (1/0), 1998 (7/0), 1999 (1/1), NFLE 2000 (games played unavailable), NFL 2000 (12/0), 2001 (16/2). Total: 35/3.

ELLIS, GREG　　　DE　　　COWBOYS

PERSONAL: Born August 14, 1975, in Wendell. N.C. ... 6-6/275. ... Full name: Gregory Lemont Ellis.
HIGH SCHOOL: East Wake (Wendell, N.C.).
COLLEGE: North Carolina.
TRANSACTIONS/CAREER NOTES: Selected by Dallas Cowboys in first round (eighth pick overall) of 1998 NFL draft. ... Signed by Cowboys (July 13, 1998). ... On injured reserve with leg injury (December 16, 1999-remainder of season).
HONORS: Named defensive end on THE SPORTING NEWS college All-America second team (1996 and 1997).
PRO STATISTICS: 1998—Recovered one fumble for two yards. 1999—Intercepted one pass for 87 yards and a touchdown and recovered one fumble for 98 yards and a touchdown. 2000—Recovered two fumbles. 2001—Recovered two fumbles.

Year Team	G	GS	SACKS
1998—Dallas NFL	16	16	3.0
1999—Dallas NFL	13	13	7.5
2000—Dallas NFL	16	16	3.0
2001—Dallas NFL	16	16	6.0
Pro totals (4 years)	61	61	19.5

ELLIS, SHAUN　　　DT/DE　　　JETS

PERSONAL: Born June 24, 1977, in Anderson, S.C. ... 6-5/294. ... Full name: MeShaunda Pizarrur Ellis.
HIGH SCHOOL: Westside (Anderson, S.C.).
COLLEGE: Tennessee.
TRANSACTIONS/CAREER NOTES: Selected by New York Jets in first round (12th pick overall) of 2000 NFL draft. ... Signed by Jets (July 10, 2000).
PRO STATISTICS: 2000—Intercepted one pass for one yard and recovered two fumbles for two yards.

Year Team	G	GS	SACKS
2000—New York Jets NFL	16	3	8.5
2001—New York Jets NFL	16	15	5.0
Pro totals (2 years)	32	18	13.5

ELLISS, LUTHER　　　DT　　　LIONS

PERSONAL: Born March 22, 1973, in Mancos, Colo. ... 6-5/305.
HIGH SCHOOL: Mancos (Colo.).
COLLEGE: Utah.
TRANSACTIONS/CAREER NOTES: Selected by Detroit Lions in first round (20th pick overall) of 1995 NFL draft. ... Signed by Lions (July 19, 1995).
HONORS: Named defensive lineman on THE SPORTING NEWS college All-America first team (1994). ... Played in Pro Bowl (1999 and 2000 seasons).
PRO STATISTICS: 1997—Recovered two fumbles. 1998—Recovered one fumble. 1999—Recovered two fumbles for 11 yards and one touchdown. 2000—Recovered two fumbles for three yards.

Year Team	G	GS	SACKS
1995—Detroit NFL	16	16	0.0
1996—Detroit NFL	14	14	6.5
1997—Detroit NFL	16	16	8.5
1998—Detroit NFL	16	16	3.0
1999—Detroit NFL	15	14	3.5
2000—Detroit NFL	16	16	3.0
2001—Detroit NFL	14	13	0.0
Pro totals (7 years)	107	105	24.5

ELLSWORTH, PERCY — DB

PERSONAL: Born October 19, 1974, in Drewryville, Va. ... 6-2/225.
HIGH SCHOOL: Southhampton (Courtland, Va.).
COLLEGE: Virginia.
TRANSACTIONS/CAREER NOTES: Signed as non-drafted free agent by New York Giants (April 27, 1996). ... Granted free agency (February 12, 1999). ... Re-signed by Giants (July 19, 1999). ... Granted unconditional free agency (February 11, 2000). ... Signed by Cleveland Browns (February 18, 2000). ... On injured reserve with quadriceps injury (December 14-24, 2001). ... Released by Browns (December 24, 2001).
PRO STATISTICS: 1996—Recovered one fumble. 1997—Recovered two fumbles for 24 yards. 1999—Recovered one fumble for 15 yards. 2000—Recovered one fumble for 16 yards. 2001—Credited with one sack.

			INTERCEPTIONS			
Year Team	G	GS	No.	Yds.	Avg.	TD
1996—New York Giants NFL	14	4	3	62	20.7	0
1997—New York Giants NFL	16	1	4	40	10.0	0
1998—New York Giants NFL	16	9	5	92	18.4	2
1999—New York Giants NFL	14	14	6	80	13.3	0
2000—Cleveland NFL	16	16	1	33	33.0	1
2001—Cleveland NFL	11	9	1	19	19.0	0
Pro totals (6 years)	87	53	20	326	16.3	3

EMANUEL, BERT — WR

PERSONAL: Born October 26, 1970, in Kansas City, Mo. ... 5-10/185. ... Full name: Bert Tyrone Emanuel.
HIGH SCHOOL: Langham Creek (Houston).
COLLEGE: UCLA, then Rice (degree in business, 1993).
TRANSACTIONS/CAREER NOTES: Selected by Atlanta Falcons in second round (45th pick overall) of 1994 NFL draft. ... Signed by Falcons (July 11, 1994). ... Granted free agency (February 14, 1997). ... Re-signed by Falcons (July 16, 1997). ... Designated by Falcons as transition player (February 13, 1998). ... Tendered offer sheet by Tampa Bay Buccaneers (April 10, 1998). ... Falcons declined to match offer (April 14, 1998). ... Released by Buccaneers (April 12, 2000). ... Signed by Miami Dolphins (May 2, 2000). ... On injured reserve with broken rib (December 20, 2000-remainder of season). ... Granted unconditional free agency (March 2, 2001). ... Signed by New England Patriots (March 30, 2001). ... Released by Patriots (October 9, 2001). ... Signed by Detroit Lions (October 24, 2001). ... Granted unconditional free agency (March 1, 2002).
CHAMPIONSHIP GAME EXPERIENCE: Played in NFC championship game (1999 season).
PRO STATISTICS: 1994—Rushed twice for four yards and had only pass attempt intercepted. 1995—Rushed once for no yards. 1997—Recovered two fumbles. 1998—Rushed once for 11 yards. 2000—Rushed three times for minus two yards.
SINGLE GAME HIGHS (regular season): Receptions—9 (December 15, 1996, vs. St. Louis); yards—173 (December 15, 1996, vs. St. Louis); and touchdown receptions—2 (November 2, 1997, vs. St. Louis).
STATISTICAL PLATEAUS: 100-yard receiving games: 1994 (1), 1995 (4), 1996 (3), 1997 (1), 1998 (1). Total: 10.
MISCELLANEOUS: Selected by Toronto Blue Jays organization in 75th round of free-agent baseball draft (June 5, 1989); did not sign. ... Selected by Pittsburgh Pirates organization in 49th round of free-agent baseball draft (June 1, 1992); did not sign.

			RECEIVING				TOTALS			
Year Team	G	GS	No.	Yds.	Avg.	TD	TD	2pt.	Pts.	Fum.
1994—Atlanta NFL	16	16	46	649	14.1	4	4	0	24	0
1995—Atlanta NFL	16	16	74	1039	14.0	5	5	0	30	2
1996—Atlanta NFL	14	13	75	921	12.3	6	6	0	36	0
1997—Atlanta NFL	16	16	65	991	15.2	9	9	0	54	2
1998—Tampa Bay NFL	11	11	41	636	15.5	2	2	0	12	0
1999—Tampa Bay NFL	11	10	22	238	10.8	1	1	0	6	0
2000—Miami NFL	11	0	7	132	18.9	1	1	0	6	1
2001—New England NFL	2	1	4	25	6.3	0	0	0	0	0
—Detroit NFL	6	4	17	221	13.0	0	0	0	0	0
Pro totals (8 years)	103	87	351	4852	13.8	28	28	0	168	5

EMMONS, CARLOS — LB — EAGLES

PERSONAL: Born September 3, 1973, in Greenwood, Miss. ... 6-5/250. ... Name pronounced EM-mins.
HIGH SCHOOL: Greenwood (Miss.).
COLLEGE: Arkansas State (degree in business management, 1995).
TRANSACTIONS/CAREER NOTES: Selected by Pittsburgh Steelers in seventh round (242nd pick overall) of 1996 NFL draft. ... Signed by Steelers (July 16, 1996). ... Granted free agency (February 12, 1999). ... Re-signed by Steelers (April 23, 1999). ... Granted unconditional free agency (February 11, 2000). ... Signed by Philadelphia Eagles (March 23, 2000).
CHAMPIONSHIP GAME EXPERIENCE: Played in AFC championship game (1997 season). ... Played in NFC championship game (2001 season).
PRO STATISTICS: 1996—Recovered one fumble. 1998—Intercepted one pass for two yards and recovered one fumble. 1999—Intercepted one pass for 22 yards and recovered three fumbles for two yards. 2000—Intercepted two passes for eight yards and recovered one fumble for two yards.

Year Team	G	GS	SACKS
1996—Pittsburgh NFL	15	0	2.5
1997—Pittsburgh NFL	5	0	0.0
1998—Pittsburgh NFL	15	13	3.5
1999—Pittsburgh NFL	16	16	6.0
2000—Philadelphia NFL	16	13	0.5
2001—Philadelphia NFL	16	15	1.0
Pro totals (6 years)	83	57	13.5

ENGELBERGER, JOHN — DE — 49ERS

PERSONAL: Born October 18, 1976, in Heidelburg, Germany. ... 6-4/260. ... Full name: John Albert Engelberger.
HIGH SCHOOL: Robert E. Lee (Springfield, Va.).
COLLEGE: Virginia Tech.
TRANSACTIONS/CAREER NOTES: Selected by San Francisco 49ers in second round (35th pick overall) of 2000 NFL draft. ... Signed by 49ers (July 18, 2000).

Year Team	G	GS	SACKS
2000—San Francisco NFL	16	13	3.0
2001—San Francisco NFL	15	14	4.0
Pro totals (2 years)	31	27	7.0

ENGRAM, BOBBY — WR — SEAHAWKS

PERSONAL: Born January 7, 1973, in Camden, S.C. ... 5-10/185. ... Full name: Simon Engram III.
HIGH SCHOOL: Camden (S.C.).
COLLEGE: Penn State.
TRANSACTIONS/CAREER NOTES: Selected by Chicago Bears in second round (52nd pick overall) of 1996 NFL draft. ... Signed by Bears (July 17, 1996). ... Granted free agency (February 12, 1999). ... Re-signed by Bears (April 16, 1999). ... Granted unconditional free agency (February 11, 2000). ... Re-signed by Bears (April 26, 2000). ... On injured reserve with knee injury (September 19, 2000-remainder of season). ... Released by Bears (August 28, 2001). ... Signed by Seattle Seahawks (August 30, 2001).
HONORS: Named wide receiver on THE SPORTING NEWS college All-America second team (1994 and 1995).
PRO STATISTICS: 1997—Recovered one fumble. 1998—Rushed once for three yards. 1999—Rushed twice for 11 yards and recovered two fumbles. 2000—Rushed once for one yard and recovered one fumble.
SINGLE GAME HIGHS (regular season): Receptions—13 (December 26, 1999, vs. St. Louis); yards—143 (December 26, 1999, vs. St. Louis); and touchdown receptions—2 (December 26, 1999, vs. St. Louis).
STATISTICAL PLATEAUS: 100-yard receiving games: 1998 (3), 1999 (2). Total: 5.

			RECEIVING				PUNT RETURNS				KICKOFF RETURNS				TOTALS		
Year Team	G	GS	No.	Yds.	Avg.	TD	No.	Yds.	Avg.	TD	No.	Yds.	Avg.	TD	TD	2pt.	Pts.	Fum.
1996—Chicago NFL	16	2	33	389	11.8	6	31	282	9.1	0	25	580	23.2	0	6	0	36	2
1997—Chicago NFL	11	11	45	399	8.9	2	1	4	4.0	0	2	27	13.5	0	2	1	14	1
1998—Chicago NFL	16	16	64	987	15.4	5	0	0	0.0	0	0	0	0.0	0	5	0	30	1
1999—Chicago NFL	16	14	88	947	10.8	4	0	0	0.0	0	0	0	0.0	0	4	0	24	2
2000—Chicago NFL	3	3	16	109	6.8	0	0	0	0.0	0	0	0	0.0	0	0	0	0	1
2001—Seattle NFL	16	4	29	400	13.8	0	6	96	16.0	0	1	6	6.0	0	0	0	0	0
Pro totals (6 years)	78	50	275	3231	11.7	17	38	382	10.1	0	28	613	21.9	0	17	1	104	7

EVANS, DEMETRIC — DE — COWBOYS

PERSONAL: Born September 3, 1979, in Haynesville, La. ... 6-3/286. ... Full name: Demetric Untrell Evans.
HIGH SCHOOL: Haynesville (La.).
COLLEGE: Georgia.
TRANSACTIONS/CAREER NOTES: Signed as non-drafted free agent by Dallas Cowboys (April 27, 2001).
PLAYING EXPERIENCE: Dallas NFL, 2001. ... Games/Games started: 2001 (16/0).
PRO STATISTICS: 2001—Credited with one sack and returned one kickoff for seven yards.

EVANS, DOUG — CB — SEAHAWKS

PERSONAL: Born May 13, 1970, in Shreveport, La. ... 6-1/190. ... Full name: Douglas Edwards Evans. ... Brother of Bobby Evans, safety with Winnipeg Blue Bombers of the CFL (1990-94).
HIGH SCHOOL: Haynesville (La.).
COLLEGE: Louisiana Tech (degree in finance).
TRANSACTIONS/CAREER NOTES: Selected by Green Bay Packers in sixth round (141st pick overall) of 1993 NFL draft. ... Signed by Packers (July 9, 1993). ... Granted unconditional free agency (February 13, 1998). ... Signed by Carolina Panthers (February 18, 1998). ... On injured reserve with broken collarbone (November 10, 1998-remainder of season). ... Released by Panthers (February 22, 2002). ... Signed by Seattle Seahawks (April 5, 2002).
CHAMPIONSHIP GAME EXPERIENCE: Played in NFC championship game (1995-1997 seasons). ... Member of Super Bowl championship team (1996 season). ... Played in Super Bowl XXXII (1997 season).
PRO STATISTICS: 1993—Recovered two fumbles. 1994—Recovered one fumble for three yards. 1995—Returned one punt for no yards and fumbled once. 1996—Fumbled once and recovered one fumble for two yards. 2000—Recovered five fumbles for minus three yards and one touchdown.

			INTERCEPTIONS				SACKS
Year Team	G	GS	No.	Yds.	Avg.	TD	No.
1993—Green Bay NFL	16	0	1	0	0.0	0	0.0
1994—Green Bay NFL	16	15	1	0	0.0	0	1.0
1995—Green Bay NFL	16	16	2	24	12.0	0	1.0
1996—Green Bay NFL	16	16	5	102	20.4	1	3.0
1997—Green Bay NFL	15	15	3	33	11.0	0	1.0
1998—Carolina NFL	9	7	2	18	9.0	0	0.0
1999—Carolina NFL	16	16	2	1	0.5	0	0.0
2000—Carolina NFL	16	16	2	17	8.5	0	0.0
2001—Carolina NFL	16	16	8	126	15.8	1	0.0
Pro totals (9 years)	136	117	26	321	12.3	2	6.0

EVANS, HEATH   FB   SEAHAWKS

PERSONAL: Born December 30, 1978, in West Palm Beach, Fla. ... 6-0/249. ... Full name: Bryan Heath Evans.
HIGH SCHOOL: Kings Academy (Miami).
COLLEGE: Auburn.
TRANSACTIONS/CAREER NOTES: Selected by Seattle Seahawks in third round (82nd pick overall) of 2001 NFL draft. ... Signed by Seahawks (July 26, 2001).
PLAYING EXPERIENCE: New England NFL, 2001. ... Games/Games started: 2001 (16/0).
PRO STATISTICS: 2001—Rushed twice for 11 yards and returned three kickoffs for 40 yards.
SINGLE GAME HIGHS (regular season): Attempts—2 (December 16, 2001, vs. Dallas); yards—11 (December 16, 2001, vs. Dallas); and rushing touchdowns—0.

EVANS, JOSH   DT/DE

PERSONAL: Born September 6, 1972, in Langdale, Ala. ... 6-2/280. ... Full name: Mijoshki Antwon Evans.
HIGH SCHOOL: Lanett (Ala.).
COLLEGE: Alabama-Birmingham.
TRANSACTIONS/CAREER NOTES: Signed as non-drafted free agent by Dallas Cowboys (April 27, 1995). ... Released by Cowboys (August 22, 1995). ... Signed by Houston Oilers to practice squad (September 1, 1995). ... Activated (November 10, 1995). ... On injured reserve with knee injury (November 29, 1996-remainder of season). ... Oilers franchise moved to Tennessee for 1997 season. ... Granted free agency (February 13, 1998). ... Re-signed by Oilers (July 25, 1998). ... Oilers franchise renamed Tennessee Titans for 1999 season (December 26, 1998). ... On suspended list for violating league substance abuse policy (September 6-October 4, 1999). ... On suspended list for violating league substance abuse policy (March 1, 2000-April 13, 2001). ... Granted unconditional free agency (March 1, 2002).
CHAMPIONSHIP GAME EXPERIENCE: Played in AFC championship game (1999 season). ... Played in Super Bowl XXXIV (1999 season).
PRO STATISTICS: 1997—Recovered one fumble. 1999—Recovered two fumbles.

Year Team	G	GS	SACKS
1995—Houston NFL	7	0	0.0
1996—Houston NFL	8	0	0.0
1997—Tennessee NFL	15	0	2.0
1998—Tennessee NFL	14	11	3.5
1999—Tennessee NFL	11	10	3.5
2000—Tennessee NFL	Did not play.		
2001—Tennessee NFL	16	16	5.5
Pro totals (6 years)	71	37	14.5

FABINI, JASON   OT   JETS

PERSONAL: Born August 25, 1974, in Fort Wayne, Ind. ... 6-7/304.
HIGH SCHOOL: Bishop Dwenger (Fort Wayne, Ind.).
COLLEGE: Cincinnati.
TRANSACTIONS/CAREER NOTES: Selected by New York Jets in fourth round (111th pick overall) of 1998 NFL draft. ... Signed by Jets (July 13, 1998). ... On injured reserve with knee injury (November 16, 1999-remainder of season). ... Granted free agency (March 2, 2001). ... Re-signed by Jets (May 30, 2001).
PLAYING EXPERIENCE: New York Jets NFL, 1998-2001. ... Games/Games started: 1998 (16/16), 1999 (9/9), 2000 (16/16), 2001 (16/16). Total: 57/57.
CHAMPIONSHIP GAME EXPERIENCE: Played in AFC championship game (1998 season).
PRO STATISTICS: 2001—Recovered one fumble.

FAIR, CARL   RB   BROWNS

PERSONAL: Born June 8, 1979, in Starkville, Miss. ... 6-1/219.
HIGH SCHOOL: Starkville (Miss.).
JUNIOR COLLEGE: East Mississippi Community College.
COLLEGE: Alabama-Birmingham.
TRANSACTIONS/CAREER NOTES: Signed as non-drafted free agent by Cleveland Browns (April 26, 2001). ... Released by Browns (August 29, 2001). ... Re-signed by Browns to practice squad (September 3, 2001). ... Activated (December 20, 2001).
PLAYING EXPERIENCE: Cleveland NFL, 2001. ... Games/Games started: 2001 (3/0).

FAIR, TERRY   CB   LIONS

PERSONAL: Born July 20, 1976, in Phoenix. ... 5-9/184. ... Full name: Terrance Delon Fair.
HIGH SCHOOL: South Mountain (Phoenix).
COLLEGE: Tennessee.
TRANSACTIONS/CAREER NOTES: Selected by Detroit Lions in first round (20th pick overall) of 1998 NFL draft. ... Signed by Lions (July 20, 1998). ... On non-football injury list with hand injury (December 14, 1999-remainder of season).
HONORS: Named kick returner on THE SPORTING NEWS NFL All-Pro team (1998).
PRO STATISTICS: 1998—Credited with one sack and recovered one fumble. 1999—Recovered one fumble for 35 yards and a touchdown. 2000—Recovered one fumble for two yards.

			INTERCEPTIONS			PUNT RETURNS			KICKOFF RETURNS			TOTALS			
Year Team	G	GS	No.	Yds.	Avg.	TD	No.	Yds.	Avg.	TD	No.	Yds.	Avg.	TD	TD 2pt.	Pts. Fum.
1998—Detroit NFL	14	10	0	0	0.0	0	30	189	6.3	0	51	1428	*28.0	†2	2 0	12 5
1999—Detroit NFL	11	11	3	49	16.3	1	11	97	8.8	0	34	752	22.1	0	2 0	12 2
2000—Detroit NFL	15	15	2	0	0.0	0	2	15	7.5	0	6	149	24.8	0	0 0	0 1
2001—Detroit NFL	12	12	2	29	14.5	1	4	37	9.3	0	10	187	18.7	0	1 0	6 0
Pro totals (4 years)	52	48	7	78	11.1	2	47	338	7.2	0	101	2516	24.9	2	5 0	30 8

FANECA, ALAN G STEELERS

PERSONAL: Born December 7, 1976, in New Orleans. ... 6-5/305. ... Full name: Alan Joseph Faneca Jr.
HIGH SCHOOL: John Curtis Christian (New Orleans), then Lamar (Houston).
COLLEGE: Louisiana State.
TRANSACTIONS/CAREER NOTES: Selected after junior season by Pittsburgh Steelers in first round (26th pick overall) of 1998 NFL draft. ... Signed by Steelers (July 29, 1998).
PLAYING EXPERIENCE: Pittsburgh NFL, 1998-2001. ... Games/Games started: 1998 (16/12), 1999 (15/14), 2000 (16/16), 2001 (15/15). Total: 62/57.
CHAMPIONSHIP GAME EXPERIENCE: Played in AFC championship game (2001 season).
HONORS: Named guard on THE SPORTING NEWS college All-America first team (1997). ... Named guard on THE SPORTING NEWS NFL All-Pro team (2001).
PRO STATISTICS: 2000—Recovered one fumble.

FARMER, DANNY WR BENGALS

PERSONAL: Born May 21, 1977, in Los Angeles. ... 6-3/215. ... Full name: Daniel Steven Farmer. ... Son of George Farmer, wide receiver with Chicago Bears (1970-75) and Detroit Lions (1975); nephew of Dave Farmer, running back with Tampa Bay Buccaneers (1978).
HIGH SCHOOL: Loyola (Los Angeles).
COLLEGE: UCLA.
TRANSACTIONS/CAREER NOTES: Selected by Pittsburgh Steelers in fourth round (103rd pick overall) of 2000 NFL draft. ... Signed by Steelers (July 7, 2000). ... Claimed on waivers by Cincinnati Bengals (August 28, 2000).
PRO STATISTICS: 2000—Fumbled once. 2001—Returned one punt for 11 yards and fumbled once.
SINGLE GAME HIGHS (regular season): Receptions—5 (December 24, 2000, vs. Philadelphia); yards—102 (December 17, 2000, vs. Jacksonville); and touchdown receptions—1 (December 30, 2001, vs. Pittsburgh).
STATISTICAL PLATEAUS: 100-yard receiving games: 2000 (1).

			RECEIVING			
Year Team	G	GS	No.	Yds.	Avg.	TD
2000—Cincinnati NFL	13	2	19	268	14.1	0
2001—Cincinnati NFL	12	1	15	228	15.2	1
Pro totals (2 years)	25	3	34	496	14.6	1

FARRIOR, JAMES LB STEELERS

PERSONAL: Born January 6, 1975, in Ettrick, Va. ... 6-2/244. ... Full name: James Alfred Farrior.
HIGH SCHOOL: Matoaca (Ettrick, Va.).
COLLEGE: Virginia.
TRANSACTIONS/CAREER NOTES: Selected by New York Jets in first round (eighth pick overall) of 1997 NFL draft. ... Signed by Jets (July 20, 1997). ... Granted unconditional free agency (March 1, 2002). ... Signed by Pittsburgh Steelers (April 5, 2002).
CHAMPIONSHIP GAME EXPERIENCE: Played in AFC championship game (1998 season).
PRO STATISTICS: 1998—Recovered one fumble. 2000—Intercepted one pass for no yards and recovered one fumble. 2001—Intercepted two passes for 84 yards.

Year Team	G	GS	SACKS
1997—New York Jets NFL	16	15	1.5
1998—New York Jets NFL	12	2	0.0
1999—New York Jets NFL	16	4	2.0
2000—New York Jets NFL	16	6	1.0
2001—New York Jets NFL	16	16	1.0
Pro totals (5 years)	76	43	5.5

FARRIS, KRIS OT BILLS

PERSONAL: Born March 26, 1977, in St. Paul, Minn. ... 6-8/318. ... Full name: Kristofer Martin Farris.
HIGH SCHOOL: Santa Margarita (Rancho Santa Margarita, Calif.).
COLLEGE: UCLA.
TRANSACTIONS/CAREER NOTES: Selected after junior season by Pittsburgh Steelers in third round (74th pick overall) of 1999 NFL draft. ... Signed by Steelers (July 28, 1999). ... On injured reserve with broken foot (August 30, 1999-entire season). ... Claimed on waivers by Cincinnati Bengals (August 22, 2000). ... Released by Bengals (August 23, 2000). ... Signed by Buffalo Bills (April 23, 2001). ... On injured reserve with leg injury (October 3, 2001-remainder of season).
PLAYING EXPERIENCE: Buffalo NFL, 2001. ... Games/Games started: 2001 (3/1).
HONORS: Outland Trophy winner (1998). ... Named offensive tackle on THE SPORTING NEWS college All-America first team (1998).

FATAFEHI, MARIO DT CARDINALS

PERSONAL: Born January 27, 1979, in Chicago. ... 6-2/296.
HIGH SCHOOL: Ferrington (Honolulu, Hawaii).
JUNIOR COLLEGE: Snow College (Utah).
COLLEGE: Kansas State.
TRANSACTIONS/CAREER NOTES: Selected by Arizona Cardinals in fifth round (133rd pick overall) of 2001 NFL draft. ... Signed by Cardinals (June 5, 2001).

Year Team	G	GS	SACKS
2001—Arizona NFL	7	1	0.0

FAULK, KEVIN   RB   PATRIOTS

PERSONAL: Born June 5, 1976, in Lafayette, La. ... 5-8/202. ... Full name: Kevin Tony Faulk.
HIGH SCHOOL: Carencro (Lafayette, La.).
COLLEGE: Louisiana State (degree in kinesiology).
TRANSACTIONS/CAREER NOTES: Selected by New England Patriots in second round (46th pick overall) of 1999 NFL draft. ... Signed by Patriots (July 28, 1999). ... On injured reserve with broken ankle (December 15, 1999-remainder of season).
CHAMPIONSHIP GAME EXPERIENCE: Played in AFC championship game (2001 season). ... Member of Super Bowl championship team (2001 season).
HONORS: Named kick returner on THE SPORTING NEWS college All-America second team (1998).
PRO STATISTICS: 1999—Fumbled three times for minus nine yards. 2000—Fumbled six times and recovered one fumble. 2001—Completed only pass attempt for 23 yards, fumbled twice and recovered one fumble.
SINGLE GAME HIGHS (regular season): Attempts—22 (December 4, 2000, vs. Kansas City); yards—82 (September 11, 2000, vs. New York Jets); and rushing touchdowns—1 (September 30, 2001, vs. Indianapolis).

			RUSHING				RECEIVING				PUNT RETURNS				KICKOFF RETURNS				TOTALS		
Year Team	G	GS	Att.	Yds.	Avg.	TD	No.	Yds.	Avg.	TD	No.	Yds.	Avg.	TD	No.	Yds.	Avg.	TD	TD	2pt.	Pts.
1999—New England NFL	11	2	67	227	3.4	1	12	98	8.2	1	10	90	9.0	0	39	943	24.2	0	2	0	12
2000—New England NFL	16	9	164	570	3.5	4	51	465	9.1	1	6	58	9.7	0	38	816	21.5	0	5	1	32
2001—New England NFL	15	1	41	169	4.1	1	30	189	6.3	2	4	27	6.8	0	33	662	20.1	0	3	0	18
Pro totals (3 years)	42	12	272	966	3.6	6	93	752	8.1	4	20	175	8.8	0	110	2421	22.0	0	10	1	62

FAULK, MARSHALL   RB   RAMS

PERSONAL: Born February 26, 1973, in New Orleans. ... 5-10/211. ... Full name: Marshall William Faulk.
HIGH SCHOOL: G. W. Carver (New Orleans).
COLLEGE: San Diego State.
TRANSACTIONS/CAREER NOTES: Selected after junior season by Indianapolis Colts in first round (second pick overall) of 1994 NFL draft. ... Signed by Colts (July 24, 1994). ... Traded by Colts to St. Louis Rams for second- (LB Mike Peterson) and fifth-round (DE Brad Scioli) picks in 1999 draft (April 15, 1999).
CHAMPIONSHIP GAME EXPERIENCE: Member of Colts for AFC championship game (1995 season); inactive due to injury. ... Played in NFC championship game (1999 and 2001 seasons). ... Member of Super Bowl championship team (1999 season). ... Played in Super Bowl XXXVI (2001 season).
HONORS: Named running back on THE SPORTING NEWS college All-America first team (1991-1993). ... Named NFL Rookie of the Year by THE SPORTING NEWS (1994). ... Played in Pro Bowl (1994, 1995, 1998 and 1999 seasons). ... Named Outstanding Player of Pro Bowl (1994 season). ... Named running back on THE SPORTING NEWS NFL All-Pro team (1999-2001). ... Named NFL Player of the Year by THE SPORTING NEWS (2000 and 2001). ... Named to play in Pro Bowl (2000 season); replaced by Stephen Davis due to injury.
RECORDS: Holds NFL single-season record for most touchdowns—26 (2000).
PRO STATISTICS: 1994—Recovered one fumble. 1995—Recovered one fumble. 1997—Recovered one fumble. 1998—Recovered two fumbles for 13 yards. 1999—Attempted one pass without a completion. 2000—Returned one kickoff for 18 yards. 2000—Returned one kickoff for 18 yards and recovered two fumbles. 2001—Attempted one pass without a completion and recovered two fumbles.
SINGLE GAME HIGHS (regular season): Attempts—32 (December 24, 2000, vs. New Orleans); yards—220 (December 24, 2000, vs. New Orleans); and rushing touchdowns—4 (December 10, 2000, vs. Minnesota).
STATISTICAL PLATEAUS: 100-yard rushing games: 1994 (4), 1995 (1), 1996 (1), 1997 (4), 1998 (4), 1999 (7), 2000 (4), 2001 (5). Total: 30. ... 100-yard receiving games: 1994 (1), 1998 (3), 1999 (1), 2000 (2), 2001 (1). Total: 8.
MISCELLANEOUS: Holds St. Louis Rams all-time record for most touchdowns (59).

			RUSHING				RECEIVING				TOTALS			
Year Team	G	GS	Att.	Yds.	Avg.	TD	No.	Yds.	Avg.	TD	TD	2pt.	Pts.	Fum.
1994—Indianapolis NFL	16	16	314	1282	4.1	11	52	522	10.0	1	▲12	0	72	5
1995—Indianapolis NFL	16	16	289	1078	3.7	11	56	475	8.5	3	14	0	84	8
1996—Indianapolis NFL	13	13	198	587	3.0	7	56	428	7.6	0	7	0	42	2
1997—Indianapolis NFL	16	16	264	1054	4.0	7	47	471	10.0	1	8	0	48	5
1998—Indianapolis NFL	16	15	324	1319	4.1	6	86	908	10.6	4	10	0	60	3
1999—St. Louis NFL	16	16	253	1381	*5.5	7	87	1048	12.0	5	12	†1	74	2
2000—St. Louis NFL	14	14	253	1359	*5.4	*18	81	830	10.2	8	*26	2	*160	0
2001—St. Louis NFL	14	14	260	1382	*5.3	‡12	83	765	9.2	9	*21	1	*128	3
Pro totals (8 years)	121	120	2155	9442	4.4	79	548	5447	9.9	31	110	4	668	28

FAURIA, CHRISTIAN   TE   PATRIOTS

PERSONAL: Born September 22, 1971, in Harbor City, Calif. ... 6-4/245. ... Name pronounced FOUR-ee-ah.
HIGH SCHOOL: Crespi Carmelite (Encino, Calif.).
COLLEGE: Colorado (degree in communications, 1995).
TRANSACTIONS/CAREER NOTES: Selected by Seattle Seahawks in second round (39th pick overall) of 1995 NFL draft. ... Signed by Seahawks (July 17, 1995). ... Granted free agency (February 13, 1998). ... Re-signed by Seahawks (April 20, 1998). ... Granted unconditional free agency (February 12, 1999). ... Re-signed by Seahawks (March 5, 1999). ... Granted unconditional free agency (March 1, 2002). ... Signed by New England Patriots (March 22, 2002).
PRO STATISTICS: 1996—Returned one kickoff for eight yards. 1998—Returned one kickoff for no yards and recovered one fumble. 1999—Returned two kickoffs for 15 yards. 2000—Returned one kickoff for nine yards and recovered one fumble. 2001—Returned one kickoff for no yards.
SINGLE GAME HIGHS (regular season): Receptions—6 (December 26, 1999, vs. Kansas City); yards—84 (December 26, 1999, vs. Kansas City); and touchdown receptions—1 (September 30, 2001, vs. Oakland).

			RECEIVING				TOTALS		
Year Team	G	GS	No.	Yds.	Avg.	TD	TD	2pt.	Pts.	Fum.
1995—Seattle NFL	14	9	17	181	10.6	1	1	0	6	0
1996—Seattle NFL	10	9	18	214	11.9	1	1	0	6	0
1997—Seattle NFL	16	3	10	110	11.0	0	0	0	0	0
1998—Seattle NFL	16	15	37	377	10.2	2	2	0	12	1
1999—Seattle NFL	16	16	35	376	10.7	0	0	0	0	1
2000—Seattle NFL	15	10	28	237	8.5	2	2	0	12	1
2001—Seattle NFL	16	11	21	188	9.0	1	1	▲1	8	2
Pro totals (7 years)	103	73	166	1683	10.1	7	7	1	44	5

FAVORS, GREG — LB — COLTS

PERSONAL: Born September 30, 1974, in Atlanta. ... 6-1/244. ... Full name: Gregory Bernard Favors.
HIGH SCHOOL: Southside (Atlanta).
COLLEGE: Mississippi State (degree in correction, 1997).
TRANSACTIONS/CAREER NOTES: Selected by Kansas City Chiefs in fourth round (120th pick overall) of 1998 NFL draft. ... Signed by Chiefs (July 17, 1998). ... Claimed on waivers by Tennessee Titans (September 8, 1999). ... Granted free agency (March 2, 2001). ... Re-signed by Titans (May 9, 2001). ... Granted unconditional free agency (March 1, 2002). ... Signed by Indianapolis Colts (April 9, 2002).
CHAMPIONSHIP GAME EXPERIENCE: Played in AFC championship game (1999 season). ... Played in Super Bowl XXXIV (1999 season).
PRO STATISTICS: 1998—Recovered one fumble for 41 yards. 1999—Recovered one fumble. 2001—Intercepted one pass for no yards.

Year Team	G	GS	SACKS
1998—Kansas City NFL	16	4	2.0
1999—Tennessee NFL	15	0	0.0
2000—Tennessee NFL	16	15	5.5
2001—Tennessee NFL	16	13	1.5
Pro totals (4 years)	63	32	9.0

FAVRE, BRETT — QB — PACKERS

PERSONAL: Born October 10, 1969, in Gulfport, Miss. ... 6-2/225. ... Full name: Brett Lorenzo Favre. ... Name pronounced FARVE.
HIGH SCHOOL: Hancock North Central (Kiln, Miss.).
COLLEGE: Southern Mississippi.
TRANSACTIONS/CAREER NOTES: Selected by Atlanta Falcons in second round (33rd pick overall) of 1991 NFL draft. ... Signed by Falcons (July 18, 1991). ... Traded by Falcons to Green Bay Packers for first-round pick (OT Bob Whitfield) in 1992 draft (February 11, 1992). ... Granted free agency (February 17, 1994). ... Re-signed by Packers (July 14, 1994).
CHAMPIONSHIP GAME EXPERIENCE: Played in NFC championship game (1995-1997 seasons). ... Member of Super Bowl championship team (1996 season). ... Played in Super Bowl XXXII (1997 season).
HONORS: Played in Pro Bowl (1992, 1993, 1995 and 1996 seasons). ... Named NFL Player of the Year by THE SPORTING NEWS (1995 and 1996). ... Named quarterback on THE SPORTING NEWS NFL All-Pro team (1995-97). ... Named to play in Pro Bowl (1997 season); replaced by Chris Chandler due to injury.
RECORDS: Shares NFL record for longest pass completion (to Robert Brooks)—99 yards, touchdown (September 11, 1995, at Chicago).
POST SEASON RECORDS: Holds Super Bowl record for longest pass completion (to Antonio Freeman)—81 yards (January 26, 1997, vs. New England).
PRO STATISTICS: 1992—Caught one pass for minus seven yards, fumbled 12 times and recovered three fumbles for minus 12 yards. 1993—Fumbled 14 times and recovered two fumbles for minus one yard. 1994—Fumbled seven times and recovered one fumble for minus two yards. 1995—Fumbled eight times. 1996—Fumbled 11 times and recovered five fumbles for minus 10 yards. 1997—Fumbled seven times and recovered one fumble for minus 10 yards. 1998—Fumbled eight times and recovered three fumbles for minus one yard. 1999—Fumbled nine times and recovered one fumble for minus two yards. 2000—Fumbled nine times and recovered two fumbles for minus 12 yards. 2001—Fumbled 16 times and recovered six fumbles for minus 38 yards.
SINGLE GAME HIGHS (regular season): Attempts—61 (October 14, 1996, vs. San Francisco); completions—36 (December 5, 1993, vs. Chicago); yards—402 (December 5, 1993, vs. Chicago); and touchdown passes—5 (September 27, 1998, vs. Carolina).
STATISTICAL PLATEAUS: 300-yard passing games: 1993 (1), 1994 (4), 1995 (7), 1996 (2), 1997 (2), 1998 (4), 1999 (6), 2000 (2), 2001 (4). Total: 32.
MISCELLANEOUS: Regular-season record as starting NFL quarterback: 103-54 (.656). ... Postseason record as starting NFL quarterback: 10-6 (.625). ... Active NFL leader in touchdown passes (287). ... Holds Green Bay Packers all-time records for most yards passing (38,627) and most touchdown passes (287).

			PASSING							RUSHING				TOTALS		
Year Team	G	GS	Att.	Cmp.	Pct.	Yds.	TD	Int.	Avg.	Rat.	Att.	Yds.	Avg.	TD	TD	2pt.	Pts.
1991—Atlanta NFL	2	0	5	0	0.0	0	0	2	0.0	0.0	0	0	0.0	0	0	0	0
1992—Green Bay NFL	15	13	471	∞302	64.1	3227	18	13	6.85	85.3	47	198	4.2	1	1	0	6
1993—Green Bay NFL	16	16	‡522	‡318	60.9	3303	19	*24	6.33	72.2	58	216	3.7	1	1	0	6
1994—Green Bay NFL	16	16	582	363	62.4	3882	33	14	6.67	90.7	42	202	4.8	2	2	0	12
1995—Green Bay NFL	16	16	570	359	63.0	*4413	*38	13	‡7.74	‡99.5	39	181	4.6	3	3	0	18
1996—Green Bay NFL	16	16	‡543	‡325	59.9	‡3899	*39	13	7.18	95.8	49	136	2.8	2	2	0	12
1997—Green Bay NFL	16	16	513	‡304	59.3	‡3867	*35	16	7.54	92.6	58	187	3.2	1	1	0	6
1998—Green Bay NFL	16	16	‡551	*347	*63.0	*4212	31	‡23	7.64	87.8	40	133	3.3	1	1	0	6
1999—Green Bay NFL	16	16	*595	341	57.3	4091	22	23	6.88	74.7	28	142	5.1	0	0	0	0
2000—Green Bay NFL	16	16	*580	338	58.3	3812	20	16	6.57	78.0	27	108	4.0	0	0	0	0
2001—Green Bay NFL	16	16	510	314	61.6	3921	32	15	7.69	94.1	38	56	1.5	1	1	0	6
Pro totals (11 years)	161	157	5442	3311	60.8	38627	287	172	7.10	86.7	426	1559	3.7	12	12	0	72

FEAGLES, JEFF — P — SEAHAWKS

PERSONAL: Born March 7, 1966, in Anaheim. ... 6-1/207. ... Full name: Jeffrey Allan Feagles.
HIGH SCHOOL: Gerard Catholic (Phoenix).
JUNIOR COLLEGE: Scottsdale (Ariz.) Community College.
COLLEGE: Miami (Fla.) (degree in business administration, 1988).
TRANSACTIONS/CAREER NOTES: Signed as non-drafted free agent by New England Patriots (May 1, 1988). ... Claimed on waivers by Philadelphia Eagles (June 5, 1990). ... Granted unconditional free agency (February 1-April 1, 1992). ... Re-signed by Eagles for 1992 season. ... Granted unconditional free agency (February 17, 1994). ... Signed by Phoenix Cardinals (March 2, 1994). ... Cardinals franchise renamed Arizona Cardinals for 1994 season. ... Granted unconditional free agency (February 13, 1998). ... Signed by Seattle Seahawks (March 4, 1998).
HONORS: Played in Pro Bowl (1995 season).
PRO STATISTICS: 1988—Rushed once for no yards and recovered one fumble. 1989—Attempted two passes without a completion, fumbled once and recovered one fumble. 1990—Rushed twice for three yards and attempted one pass without a completion. 1991—Rushed three times for minus one yard, fumbled once and recovered one fumble. 1993—Rushed twice for six yards and recovered one fumble. 1994—Rushed twice for eight yards. 1995—Rushed twice for four yards and fumbled once for minus 22 yards. 1996—Rushed once for no yards

and fumbled once for minus seven yards. 1997—Fumbled once and recovered one fumble. 1999—Rushed twice for no yards. 2000—Attempted one pass without a completion. 2001—Attempted two passes without a completion, fumbled twice and recovered two fumbles.

			PUNTING					
Year Team		G	No.	Yds.	Avg.	Net avg.	In. 20	Blk.
1988—New England NFL		16	▲91	3482	38.3	34.1	24	0
1989—New England NFL		16	63	2392	38.0	31.3	13	1
1990—Philadelphia NFL		16	72	3026	42.0	35.5	20	2
1991—Philadelphia NFL		16	*87	3640	41.8	34.0	*29	1
1992—Philadelphia NFL		16	‡82	‡3459	42.2	36.9	‡26	0
1993—Philadelphia NFL		16	83	3323	40.0	35.3	*31	0
1994—Arizona NFL		16	*98	‡3997	40.8	36.0	‡33	0
1995—Arizona NFL		16	72	3150	43.8	‡38.2	20	0
1996—Arizona NFL		16	76	3328	43.8	36.4	23	1
1997—Arizona NFL		16	91	4028	44.3	36.8	24	1
1998—Seattle NFL		16	81	3568	44.0	36.5	27	0
1999—Seattle NFL		16	84	3425	40.8	35.2	34	0
2000—Seattle NFL		16	74	2960	40.0	36.9	24	▲1
2001—Seattle NFL		16	85	3730	43.9	36.4	26	1
Pro totals (14 years)		224	1139	47508	41.7	35.7	354	8

FEELEY, A.J.   QB   EAGLES

PERSONAL: Born May 16, 1977, in Caldwell, Idaho. ... 6-3/217. ... Full name: Adam Joshua Feeley.
HIGH SCHOOL: Ontario (Ore.).
COLLEGE: Oregon.
TRANSACTIONS/CAREER NOTES: Selected by Philadelphia Eagles in fifth round (155th pick overall) of 2001 NFL draft. ... Signed by Eagles (June 6, 2001).
CHAMPIONSHIP GAME EXPERIENCE: Member of Eagles for NFC championship game (2001 season); inactive.
SINGLE GAME HIGHS (regular season): Attempts—14 (January 6, 2002, vs. Tampa Bay); completions—10 (January 6, 2002, vs. Tampa Bay); passing yards—143 (January 6, 2002, vs. Tampa Bay); touchdown passes—2 (January 6, 2002, vs. Tampa Bay).

				PASSING						RUSHING			TOTALS		
Year Team	G	GS	Att.	Cmp.	Pct.	Yds.	TD	Int.	Avg.	Rat.	Att.	Yds.	Avg.	TD	TD	2pt.	Pts.
2001—Philadelphia NFL	1	0	14	10	71.4	143	2	1	10.21	114.0	0	0	0.0	0	0	0	0

FEELY, JAY   K   FALCONS

PERSONAL: Born May 23, 1976, in Odessa, Fla. ... 5-10/206.
HIGH SCHOOL: Tampa Jesuit (Fla.).
COLLEGE: Michigan.
TRANSACTIONS/CAREER NOTES: Signed as non-drafted free agent by Atlanta Falcons (April 12, 2001).

		KICKING					
Year Team	G	XPM	XPA	FGM	FGA	Lg.	50+	Pts.
2001—Atlanta NFL	16	28	28	‡29	‡37	†55	2-4	115

FENDERSON, JAMES   FB   SAINTS

PERSONAL: Born October 24, 1976, in Long Beach, Calif. ... 5-9/200. ... Full name: James E. Fenderson.
HIGH SCHOOL: Mililani (Oahu, Hawaii).
COLLEGE: Hawaii.
TRANSACTIONS/CAREER NOTES: Signed as non-drafted free agent by New Orleans Saints (April 26, 2001). ... Released by Saints (September 7, 2001). ... Re-signed by Saints (December 14, 2001).
PLAYING EXPERIENCE: New Orleans NFL, 2001. ... Games/Games started: 2001 (4/0).

FERGUSON, JASON   DT   JETS

PERSONAL: Born November 28, 1974, in Nettleton, Miss. ... 6-3/305. ... Full name: Jason O. Ferguson. ... Cousin of Terance Mathis, wide receiver with New York Jets (1990-93) and Atlanta Falcons (1994-2001).
HIGH SCHOOL: Nettleton (Miss.).
JUNIOR COLLEGE: Itawamba Community College (Miss.).
COLLEGE: Georgia.
TRANSACTIONS/CAREER NOTES: Selected by New York Jets in seventh round (229th pick overall) of 1997 NFL draft. ... Signed by Jets (April 30, 1997). ... On suspended list for violating league substance abuse policy (November 24-December 22, 1999). ... Granted free agency (February 11, 2000). ... Re-signed by Jets (May 24, 2000). ... Granted unconditional free agency (March 2, 2001). ... Re-signed by Jets (March 11, 2001). ... On injured reserve with shoulder injury (September 3, 2001-entire season).
CHAMPIONSHIP GAME EXPERIENCE: Played in AFC championship game (1998 season).
PRO STATISTICS: 1997—Returned one kickoff for one yard.

Year Team	G	GS	SACKS
1997—New York Jets NFL	13	1	3.5
1998—New York Jets NFL	16	16	4.0
1999—New York Jets NFL	9	9	1.0
2000—New York Jets NFL	15	11	1.0
2001—New York Jets NFL		Did not play.	
Pro totals (4 years)	53	37	9.5

FERGUSON, NICK — S — JETS

PERSONAL: Born November 27, 1973, in Miami. ... 5-11/201.
HIGH SCHOOL: Jackson (Miami).
COLLEGE: Morris Brown College, then Georgia Tech.
TRANSACTIONS/CAREER NOTES: Signed as non-drafted free agent by Cincinnati Bengals (April 23, 1996). ... Released by Bengals (August 5, 1996). ... Signed by Sasketchewan Roughriders of CFL (September 27, 1996). ... Traded by Roughriders to Winnipeg Blue Bombers (May 9, 1997). ... Signed by Chicago Bears (February 12, 1999). ... Assigned by Bears to Rhein Fire in 1999 NFL Europe enhancement allocation program (February 22, 1999). ... Released by Bears (August 30, 1999). ... Signed by Buffalo Bills (July 6, 2000). ... Released by Bills (August 27, 2000). ... Re-signed by Bills to practice squad (August 28, 2000). ... Signed by New York Jets off Bills practice squad (November 7, 2000).
PRO STATISTICS: 2001—Recovered one fumble.

				INTERCEPTIONS		
Year Team	G	GS	No.	Yds.	Avg.	TD
1996—Saskatchewan CFL	5	...	0	0	0.0	0
1997—Winnipeg CFL	15	...	2	35	17.5	0
1998—Winnipeg CFL	16	...	1	0	0.0	0
1999—Winnipeg CFL	3	...	0	0	0.0	0
—Rhein NFLE	...	...	0	0	0.0	0
2000—Rhein NFLE	...	...	2	0	0.0	0
—New York Jets NFL	7	0	1	20	20.0	0
2001—New York Jets NFL	16	1	0	0	0.0	0
NFL Europe totals (2 years)	...	...	2	0	0.0	0
CFL totals (4 years)	39	...	3	35	11.7	0
NFL totals (2 years)	23	1	1	20	20.0	0
Pro totals (8 years)	...	...	6	55	9.2	0

FERGUSON, ROBERT — WR — PACKERS

PERSONAL: Born December 17, 1979, in Houston. ... 6-1/209.
HIGH SCHOOL: Spring Woods (Houston).
JUNIOR COLLEGE: Tyler (Texas) Junior College.
COLLEGE: Texas A&M.
TRANSACTIONS/CAREER NOTES: Selected after junior season by Green Bay Packers in second round (41st pick overall) of 2001 NFL draft. ... Signed by Packers (July 23, 2001).
PLAYING EXPERIENCE: Green Bay NFL, 2001. ... Games/Games started: (1/0).
PRO STATISTICS: 2001—Returned one punt for four yards and returned two kickoffs for 32 yards.

FERRARA, FRANK — DE — GIANTS

PERSONAL: Born December 7, 1975, in Staten Island, N.Y. ... 6-3/270.
HIGH SCHOOL: New Dorp (N.Y.).
COLLEGE: Rhode Island.
TRANSACTIONS/CAREER NOTES: Signed as non-drafted free agent by New York Giants (April 19, 2000). ... Released by Giants (August 27, 2000). ... Re-signed by Giants to practice squad (August 29, 2000). ... Released by Giants (November 20, 2000). ... Re-signed by Giants to practice squad (December 13, 2000). ... Assigned by Giants to Amsterdam Admirals in 2000 NFL Europe enhancement allocation program (February 17, 2000).
PLAYING EXPERIENCE: Amsterdam NFLE, 2000; New York Giants NFL, 2001. ... Games/Games started: 2000 (games played unavailable), 2001 (9/0).
PRO STATISTICS: 2001—Credited with one sack.

FIALA, JOHN — LB — STEELERS

PERSONAL: Born November 25, 1973, in Fullerton, Calif. ... 6-3/237. ... Full name: John Charles Fiala. ... Name pronounced FEE-ah-lah.
HIGH SCHOOL: Lake Washington (Kirkland, Wash.).
COLLEGE: Washington.
TRANSACTIONS/CAREER NOTES: Selected by Miami Dolphins in sixth round (166th pick overall) of 1997 NFL draft. ... Signed by Dolphins (June 17, 1997). ... Released by Dolphins (July 31, 1997). ... Signed by Pittsburgh Steelers to practice squad (August 26, 1997). ... Granted free agency (March 2, 2001).
PLAYING EXPERIENCE: Pittsburgh NFL, 1998-2001. ... Games/Games started: 1998 (16/0), 1999 (16/0), 2000 (16/0), 2001 (16/0). Total: 64/0.
CHAMPIONSHIP GAME EXPERIENCE: Played in AFC championship game (2001 season).
PRO STATISTICS: 2001—Recovered one fumble.

FIEDLER, JAY — QB — DOLPHINS

PERSONAL: Born December 29, 1971, in Oceanside, N.Y. ... 6-2/225. ... Full name: Jay Brian Fiedler.
HIGH SCHOOL: Oceanside (N.Y.).
COLLEGE: Dartmouth (degree in engineering sciences).
TRANSACTIONS/CAREER NOTES: Signed as non-drafted free agent by Philadelphia Eagles (April 29, 1994). ... Inactive for all 16 games (1994). ... Claimed on waivers by Cincinnati Bengals (July 31, 1996). ... Released by Bengals (August 25, 1996). ... Played for Amsterdam Admirals of World League (1997). ... Signed by Minnesota Vikings (April 3, 1998). ... Released by Vikings (August 30, 1998). ... Re-signed by Vikings (September 15, 1998). ... Granted free agency (February 12, 1999). ... Signed by Jacksonville Jaguars (April 16, 1999). ... Granted unconditional free agency (February 11, 2000). ... Signed by Miami Dolphins (February 17, 2000).

CHAMPIONSHIP GAME EXPERIENCE: Member of Vikings for NFC championship game (1998 season); inactive. ... Member of Jaguars for AFC championship game (1999 season); did not play.
PRO STATISTICS: 1999—Fumbled once. 2000—Fumbled twice for minus eight yards. 2001—Fumbled six times.
SINGLE GAME HIGHS (regular season): Attempts—45 (December 24, 2000, vs. New England); completions—30 (December 24, 2000, vs. New England); yards—320 (December 22, 2001, vs. New England); and touchdown passes—3 (December 10, 2001, vs. Indianapolis).
STATISTICAL PLATEAUS: 300-yard passing games: 1999 (1), 2001 (1). Total: 2.
MISCELLANEOUS: Regular-season record as starting NFL quarterback: 22-10 (.688). ... Postseason record as starting NFL quarterback: 1-2 (.333).

				PASSING						RUSHING				TOTALS		
Year Team	G	GS	Att.	Cmp.	Pct.	Yds.	TD	Int.	Avg.	Rat.	Att.	Yds.	Avg.	TD	TD	2pt.	Pts.
1994—Philadelphia NFL									Did not play.								
1995—Philadelphia NFL									Did not play.								
1996—									Did not play.								
1997—Amsterdam W.L.			109	46	42.2	678	2	8	6.22	38.7	16	93	5.8	0	0	0	0
1998—Minnesota NFL	5	0	7	3	42.9	41	0	1	5.86	22.6	4	-6	-1.5	0	0	0	0
1999—Jacksonville NFL	7	1	94	61	64.9	656	2	2	6.98	83.5	13	26	2.0	0	0	0	0
2000—Miami NFL	15	15	357	204	57.1	2402	14	14	6.73	74.5	54	267	4.9	1	1	0	6
2001—Miami NFL	16	16	450	273	60.7	3290	20	19	7.31	80.3	73	321	4.4	4	4	0	24
W.L. totals (1 year)			109	46	42.2	678	2	8	6.22	38.7	16	93	5.8	0	0	0	0
NFL totals (4 years)	43	32	908	541	59.6	6389	36	36	7.04	77.7	144	608	4.2	5	5	0	30
Pro totals (5 years)			1017	587	57.7	7067	38	44	6.95	73.6	160	701	4.4	5	5	0	30

FIELDS, MARK — LB — PANTHERS

PERSONAL: Born November 9, 1972, in Los Angeles. ... 6-2/244. ... Full name: Mark Lee Fields.
HIGH SCHOOL: Washington (Cerritos, Calif.).
JUNIOR COLLEGE: Los Angeles Southwest Community College.
COLLEGE: Washington State.
TRANSACTIONS/CAREER NOTES: Selected by New Orleans Saints in first round (13th pick overall) of 1995 NFL draft. ... Signed by Saints (July 20, 1995). ... Released by Saints (March 30, 2001). ... Signed by St. Louis Rams (April 10, 2001). ... Released by Rams (March 9, 2002). ... Signed by Carolina Panthers (March 21, 2002).
CHAMPIONSHIP GAME EXPERIENCE: Played in NFC championship game (2001 season). ... Played in Super Bowl XXXVI (2001 season).
HONORS: Played in Pro Bowl (2000 season).
PRO STATISTICS: 1996—Recovered one fumble for 20 yards. 1997—Recovered two fumbles for 28 yards and one touchdown. 1998—Recovered one fumble for 36 yards and a touchdown. 1999—Intercepted two passes for no yards and recovered one fumble. 2001—Intercepted one pass for 30 yards.

Year Team	G	GS	SACKS
1995—New Orleans NFL	16	3	1.0
1996—New Orleans NFL	16	15	2.0
1997—New Orleans NFL	16	15	8.0
1998—New Orleans NFL	15	15	6.0
1999—New Orleans NFL	14	14	4.0
2000—New Orleans NFL	16	14	2.0
2001—St. Louis NFL	14	12	0.0
Pro totals (7 years)	107	88	23.0

FINA, JOHN — OT

PERSONAL: Born March 11, 1969, in Rochester, Minn. ... 6-5/300. ... Full name: John Joseph Fina. ... Name pronounced FEE-nuh.
HIGH SCHOOL: Salpointe Catholic (Tucson, Ariz.).
COLLEGE: Arizona.
TRANSACTIONS/CAREER NOTES: Selected by Buffalo Bills in first round (27th pick overall) of 1992 NFL draft. ... Signed by Bills (July 21, 1992). ... Designated by Bills as franchise player (February 16, 1996).... Released by Bills (June 3, 2002).
PLAYING EXPERIENCE: Buffalo NFL, 1992-2001. ... Games/Games started: 1992 (16/0), 1993 (16/16), 1994 (12/12), 1995 (16/16), 1996 (15/15), 1997 (16/16), 1998 (14/14), 1999 (16/16), 2000 (14/14), 2001 (13/12). Total: 148/131.
CHAMPIONSHIP GAME EXPERIENCE: Played in AFC championship game (1992 and 1993 seasons). ... Played in Super Bowl XXVII (1992 season) and Super Bowl XXVIII (1993 season).
PRO STATISTICS: 1992—Caught one pass for one yard and a touchdown. 1993—Rushed once for minus two yards. 1996—Recovered two fumbles for minus one yard. 1997—Recovered one fumble. 2000—Recovered one fumble.

FINN, JIM — RB — COLTS

PERSONAL: Born December 9, 1976, in Teaneck, N.J. ... 6-0/235.
HIGH SCHOOL: Bergen Catholic (Oradell, N.J.).
COLLEGE: Pennsylvania.
TRANSACTIONS/CAREER NOTES: Selected by Chicago Bears in seventh round (253rd pick overall) of 1999 NFL draft. ... Signed by Bears (June 3, 1999). ... Released by Bears (August 30, 1999). ... Re-signed by Bears to practice squad (September 21, 1999). ... Released by Bears (October 11, 1999). ... Signed by Indianapolis Colts (January 25, 2000).
PLAYING EXPERIENCE: Indianapolis NFL, 2000 and 2001. ... Games/Games started: 2000 (16/1), 2001 (15/0). Total: 31/1.
PRO STATISTICS: 2000—Rushed once for one yard, caught four passes for 13 yards and a touchdown and fumbled once. 2001—Returned three kickoffs for 29 yards.
SINGLE GAME HIGHS (regular season): Attempts—1 (November 12, 2000, vs. New York Jets); yards—1 (November 12, 2000, vs. New York Jets); and rushing touchdowns—0.

FINNERAN, BRIAN   WR   FALCONS

PERSONAL: Born January 31, 1976, in Mission Viejo, Calif. ... 6-5/210.
HIGH SCHOOL: Santa Margarita (Mission Viejo, Calif.).
COLLEGE: Villanova.
TRANSACTIONS/CAREER NOTES: Signed as non-drafted free agent by Seattle Seahawks (April 21, 1998). ... Released by Seahawks (August 24, 1998). ... Selected by Barcelona Dragons in 1999 NFL Europe draft (February 18, 1999). ... Signed by Philadelphia Eagles (July 6, 1999). ... Released by Eagles (October 12, 1999). ... Signed by Atlanta Falcons to practice squad (December 13, 1999).
HONORS: Won Walter Payton Award (1997).
PRO STATISTICS: NFLE: 1999—Returned one kickoff for no yards. 2000—Returned one kickoff for two yards.
SINGLE GAME HIGHS (regular season): Receptions—6 (December 9, 2001, vs. New Orleans); yards—93 (December 23, 2001, vs. Buffalo); and touchdown receptions—1 (December 16, 2001, vs. Indianapolis).

			RECEIVING				TOTALS		
Year Team	G	GS	No.	Yds.	Avg.	TD	TD	2pt.	Pts.	Fum.
1999—Barcelona NFLE	...	...	54	844	15.6	8	8	1	50	0
—Philadelphia NFL	3	0	2	21	10.5	0	0	0	0	0
2000—Atlanta NFL	12	0	7	60	8.6	0	0	0	0	0
2001—Atlanta NFL	16	1	23	491	21.3	3	3	0	18	0
NFL Europe totals (1 year)	...	...	54	844	15.6	8	8	1	50	0
NFL totals (3 years)	31	1	32	572	17.9	3	3	0	18	0
Pro totals (4 years)	...	...	86	1416	16.5	11	11	1	68	0

FIORE, DAVE   OT   49ERS

PERSONAL: Born August 10, 1974, in Hackensack, N.J. ... 6-4/290. ... Full name: David Allan Fiore. ... Name pronounced fee-OR-ee.
HIGH SCHOOL: Waldwick (N.J.).
COLLEGE: Hofstra.
TRANSACTIONS/CAREER NOTES: Signed as non-drafted free agent by San Francisco 49ers (April 23, 1996). ... Claimed on waivers by New York Jets (October 14, 1996). ... Active for nine games (1996); did not play. ... Released by Jets (July 31, 1997). ... Signed by 49ers (August 1, 1997). ... On injured reserve with knee injury (August 19, 1997-entire season).
PLAYING EXPERIENCE: San Francisco NFL, 1998-2001. ... Games/Games started: 1998 (9/3), 1999 (16/16), 2000 (15/15), 2001 (16/16). Total: 56/50.

FISHER, BRYCE   DT   BILLS

PERSONAL: Born May 12, 1977, in Renton, Wash. ... 6-3/268.
HIGH SCHOOL: Seattle Prep.
COLLEGE: Air Force.
TRANSACTIONS/CAREER NOTES: Selected by Buffalo Bills in seventh round (248th pick overall) of 1999 NFL draft. ... Signed by Bills (July 27, 1999). ... On military reserve list (August 30, 1999-entire season). ... On military reserve list (August 27, 2000-entire season).
PLAYING EXPERIENCE: Buffalo NFL, 2001. ... Games/Games started: 2001 (13/2).
PRO STATISTICS: 2001—Credited with three sacks.

FISK, JASON   DT   CHARGERS

PERSONAL: Born September 4, 1972, in Davis, Calif. ... 6-3/295.
HIGH SCHOOL: Davis (Calif.).
COLLEGE: Stanford.
TRANSACTIONS/CAREER NOTES: Selected by Minnesota Vikings in seventh round (243rd pick overall) of 1995 NFL draft. ... Signed by Vikings (July 24, 1995). ... Granted unconditional free agency (February 12, 1999). ... Signed by Tennessee Titans (March 3, 1999). ... Granted unconditional free agency (March 1, 2002). ... Signed by San Diego Chargers (March 7, 2002).
CHAMPIONSHIP GAME EXPERIENCE: Played in NFC championship game (1998 season). ... Played in AFC championship game (1999 season). ... Played in Super Bowl XXXIV (1999 season).
PRO STATISTICS: 1996—Intercepted one pass for no yards and recovered one fumble. 1997—Intercepted one pass for one yard and recovered one fumble. 1998—Recovered one fumble. 1999—Intercepted one pass for 17 yards. 2001—Recovered one fumble and credited with one safety.

Year Team	G	GS	SACKS
1995—Minnesota NFL	8	0	0.0
1996—Minnesota NFL	16	6	1.0
1997—Minnesota NFL	16	10	3.0
1998—Minnesota NFL	16	0	1.5
1999—Tennessee NFL	16	16	4.0
2000—Tennessee NFL	15	15	2.0
2001—Tennessee NFL	16	16	2.5
Pro totals (7 years)	103	63	14.0

FLANAGAN, MIKE   C   PACKERS

PERSONAL: Born November 10, 1973, in Washington, D.C. ... 6-5/297. ... Full name: Michael Christopher Flanagan.
HIGH SCHOOL: Rio Americano (Sacramento).
COLLEGE: UCLA.
TRANSACTIONS/CAREER NOTES: Selected by Green Bay Packers in third round (90th pick overall) of 1996 NFL draft. ... Signed by Packers (July 17, 1996). ... On injured reserve with leg injury (August 19, 1996-entire season). ... On physically unable to perform list with ankle injury (August 19, 1997-entire season). ... Traded by Packers to Carolina Panthers for an undisclosed draft pick (August 31, 1998); trade later voided because Flanagan failed physical (September 1, 1998). ... Granted free agency (February 12, 1999). ... Re-signed by Packers (March 25, 1999).
PLAYING EXPERIENCE: Green Bay NFL, 1998-2001. ... Games/Games started: 1998 (2/0), 1999 (15/0), 2000 (16/2), 2001 (16/16). Total: 49/18.
PRO STATISTICS: 2001—Fumbled twice for minus 18 yards.

FLANIGAN, JIM — DT

PERSONAL: Born August 27, 1971, in Green Bay. ... 6-2/290. ... Full name: James Michael Flanigan. ... Son of Jim Flanigan, linebacker with Green Bay Packers (1967-70) and New Orleans Saints (1971).
HIGH SCHOOL: Southern Door (Brussels, Wis.).
COLLEGE: Notre Dame.
TRANSACTIONS/CAREER NOTES: Selected by Chicago Bears in third round (74th pick overall) of 1994 NFL draft. ... Signed by Bears (July 14, 1994). ... Granted free agency (February 14, 1997). ... Re-signed by Bears (June 1, 1997). ... Granted unconditional free agency (February 13, 1998). ... Re-signed by Bears (February 13, 1998). ... Released by Bears (April 26, 2001). ... Signed by Green Bay Packers (May 29, 2001). ... Granted unconditional free agency (March 1, 2002).
PRO STATISTICS: 1994—Returned two kickoffs for 26 yards. 1995—Rushed once for no yards, caught two passes for six yards and two touchdowns and recovered one fumble. 1996—Caught one pass for one yard and a touchdown. 1997—Recovered three fumbles for three yards and credited with one two-point conversion. 1998—Recovered one fumble. 1999—Intercepted one pass for six yards and recovered one fumble. 2000—Recovered one fumble. 2001—Returned one kickoff for nine yards.

Year—Team	G	GS	SACKS
1994—Chicago NFL	14	0	0.0
1995—Chicago NFL	16	12	11.0
1996—Chicago NFL	14	14	5.0
1997—Chicago NFL	16	16	6.0
1998—Chicago NFL	16	16	8.5
1999—Chicago NFL	16	16	6.0
2000—Chicago NFL	16	14	4.0
2001—Green Bay NFL	16	8	4.5
Pro totals (8 years)	124	96	45.0

FLEMISTER, ZERON — TE — REDSKINS

PERSONAL: Born September 8, 1976, in Sioux City, Iowa. ... 6-4/249.
HIGH SCHOOL: West (Iowa).
COLLEGE: Iowa.
TRANSACTIONS/CAREER NOTES: Signed as non-drafted free agent by Washington Redskins (April 18, 2000).
SINGLE GAME HIGHS (regular season): Receptions—3 (December 30, 2001, vs. New Orleans); yards—44 (December 23, 2001, vs. Chicago); and touchdown receptions—1 (December 9, 2001, vs. Arizona).

			RECEIVING				TOTALS			
Year—Team	G	GS	No.	Yds.	Avg.	TD	TD	2pt.	Pts.	Fum.
2000—Washington NFL	5	0	1	8	8.0	0	0	0	0	0
2001—Washington NFL	16	1	18	196	10.9	2	2	0	12	0
Pro totals (2 years)	21	1	19	204	10.7	2	2	0	12	0

FLEMONS, RONALD — DE — FALCONS

PERSONAL: Born October 20, 1979, in San Antonio. ... 6-5/265.
HIGH SCHOOL: Marshall (San Antonio).
COLLEGE: Texas A&M.
TRANSACTIONS/CAREER NOTES: Selected by Atlanta Falcons in seventh round (226th pick overall) of 2001 NFL draft. ... Signed by Falcons (May 21, 2001).
PLAYING EXPERIENCE: Atlanta NFL, 2001. ... Games/Games started: 2001 (1/0).

FLETCHER, JAMAR — CB — DOLPHINS

PERSONAL: Born August 28, 1979, in St. Louis. ... 5-9/184. ... Full name: Jamar Mondell Fletcher.
HIGH SCHOOL: Hazelwood East (St. Louis).
COLLEGE: Wisconsin.
TRANSACTIONS/CAREER NOTES: Selected after junior season by Miami Dolphins in first round (26th pick overall) of 2001 NFL draft. ... Signed by Dolphins (July 25, 2001).
PLAYING EXPERIENCE: Miami NFL, 2001. ... Games/Games started: 2001 (14/2).
HONORS: Named cornerback on THE SPORTING NEWS college All-America first team (1999). ... Named cornerback on THE SPORTING NEWS college All-America second team (2000). ... Jim Thorpe Award winner (2000).

FLETCHER, LONDON — LB — BILLS

PERSONAL: Born May 19, 1975, in Cleveland. ... 5-10/241. ... Full name: London Levi Fletcher.
HIGH SCHOOL: Villa Angela-St. Joseph (Cleveland).
COLLEGE: John Carroll (degree in sociology).
TRANSACTIONS/CAREER NOTES: Signed as non-drafted free agent by St. Louis Rams (April 28, 1998). ... Granted free agency (March 2, 2001). ... Re-signed by Rams (May 9, 2001). ... Granted unconditional free agency (March 1, 2002). ... Signed by Buffalo Bills (March 7, 2002).
PLAYING EXPERIENCE: St. Louis NFL, 1998-2001. ... Games/Games started: 1998 (16/1), 1999 (16/16), 2000 (16/15), 2001 (16/16). Total: 64/48.
CHAMPIONSHIP GAME EXPERIENCE: Played in NFC championship game (1999 and 2001 seasons). ... Member of Super Bowl championship team (1999 season). ... Played in Super Bowl XXXVI (2001 season).
PRO STATISTICS: 1998—Returned five kickoffs for 72 yards and fumbled once. 1999—Returned two kickoffs for 13 yards, credited with three sacks and credited with a safety. 2000—Intercepted four passes for 33 yards, credited with $5^1/_2$ sacks, returned one kickoff for 17 yards and credited with a two-point conversion. 2001—Intercepted two passes for 18 yards and credited with $4^1/_2$ sacks.

FLETCHER, TERRELL — RB — CHARGERS

PERSONAL: Born September 14, 1973, in St. Louis. ... 5-8/196. ... Full name: Terrell Antoine Fletcher.
HIGH SCHOOL: Hazelwood East (St. Louis).
COLLEGE: Wisconsin (degree in English, 1994).
TRANSACTIONS/CAREER NOTES: Selected by San Diego Chargers in second round (51st pick overall) of 1995 NFL draft. ... Signed by Chargers (July 12, 1995). ... On injured reserve with knee injury (December 17, 1997-remainder of season). ... Granted free agency (February 13, 1998). ... Re-signed by Chargers (June 1998). ... Released by Chargers (April 20, 2001). ... Re-signed by Chargers (April 25, 2001).
PRO STATISTICS: 1995—Returned three punts for 12 yards and recovered two fumbles. 1996—Recovered one fumble. 1998—Completed only pass attempt for 23 yards and a touchdown and recovered two fumbles for 21 yards. 1999—Recovered one fumble.
SINGLE GAME HIGHS (regular season): Attempts—34 (December 6, 1998, vs. Washington); yards—127 (December 27, 1998, vs. Arizona); and rushing touchdowns—2 (November 22, 1998, vs. Kansas City).
STATISTICAL PLATEAUS: 100-yard rushing games: 1998 (2).

			RUSHING				RECEIVING			KICKOFF RETURNS				TOTALS			
Year Team	G	GS	Att.	Yds.	Avg.	TD	No.	Yds.	Avg.	TD	No.	Yds.	Avg.	TD	TD	2pt.	Pts.	Fum.
1995—San Diego NFL	16	0	26	140	5.4	1	3	26	8.7	0	4	65	16.3	0	1	0	6	2
1996—San Diego NFL	16	0	77	282	3.7	0	61	476	7.8	2	0	0	0.0	0	2	0	12	1
1997—San Diego NFL	13	1	51	161	3.2	0	39	292	7.5	0	0	0	0.0	0	0	0	0	4
1998—San Diego NFL	12	5	153	543	3.5	5	30	188	6.3	0	3	71	23.7	0	5	0	30	1
1999—San Diego NFL	15	2	48	126	2.6	0	45	360	8.0	0	7	112	16.0	0	0	0	0	1
2000—San Diego NFL	16	6	116	384	3.3	3	48	355	7.4	1	0	0	0.0	0	4	0	24	2
2001—San Diego NFL	13	0	29	107	3.7	0	23	184	8.0	0	1	11	11.0	0	0	0	0	1
Pro totals (7 years)	101	14	500	1743	3.5	9	249	1881	7.6	3	15	259	17.3	0	12	0	72	12

FLOWERS, ERIK — DE — BILLS

PERSONAL: Born March 1, 1978, in San Antonio, Texas. ... 6-4/273. ... Full name: Erik Mathews Flowers.
HIGH SCHOOL: Theodore Roosevelt (San Antonio, Texas).
JUNIOR COLLEGE: Trinity Valley Community College (Texas).
COLLEGE: Arizona State.
TRANSACTIONS/CAREER NOTES: Selected by Buffalo Bills in first round (26th pick overall) of 2000 NFL draft. ... Signed by Bills (July 23, 2000).
PRO STATISTICS: 2000—Intercepted one pass for no yards.

Year Team	G	GS	SACKS
2000—Buffalo NFL	16	0	2.0
2001—Buffalo NFL	15	6	2.0
Pro totals (2 years)	31	6	4.0

FLOWERS, LEE — S — STEELERS

PERSONAL: Born January 14, 1973, in Columbia, S.C. ... 6-0/214. ... Full name: Lethon Flowers III.
HIGH SCHOOL: Spring Valley (Columbia, S.C.).
COLLEGE: Georgia Tech.
TRANSACTIONS/CAREER NOTES: Selected by Pittsburgh Steelers in fifth round (151st pick overall) of 1995 NFL draft. ... Signed by Steelers (July 18, 1995). ... Granted free agency (February 13, 1998). ... Re-signed by Steelers (June 9, 1998). ... Granted unconditional free agency (February 12, 1999). ... Re-signed by Steelers (February 16, 1999).
PLAYING EXPERIENCE: Pittsburgh NFL, 1995-2001. ... Games/Games started: 1995 (10/0), 1996 (16/0), 1997 (10/0), 1998 (16/16), 1999 (15/15), 2000 (14/14), 2001 (15/15). Total: 96/60.
CHAMPIONSHIP GAME EXPERIENCE: Played in AFC championship game (1995, 1997 and 2001 seasons). ... Played in Super Bowl XXX (1995 season).
PRO STATISTICS: 1997—Recovered one fumble. 1998—Intercepted one pass for two yards, credited with one sack and recovered two fumbles. 1999—Credited with five sacks. 2000—Intercepted one pass for no yards, credited with one sack and recovered three fumbles. 2001—Credited with one sack.

FLUTIE, DOUG — QB — CHARGERS

PERSONAL: Born October 23, 1962, in Manchester, Md. ... 5-10/180. ... Full name: Douglas Richard Flutie. ... Brother of Darren Flutie, wide receiver with San Diego Chargers (1998), B.C. Lions of CFL (1991-95), Edmonton Eskimos of CFL (1996 and 1997) and Hamilton Tiger-Cats of CFL (1998).
HIGH SCHOOL: Natick (Mass.).
COLLEGE: Boston College (degrees in computer science and speech communications, 1984).
TRANSACTIONS/CAREER NOTES: Selected by New Jersey Generals in 1985 USFL territorial draft. ... Signed by Generals (February 4, 1985). ... Granted roster exemption (February 4-14, 1985). ... Activated (February 15, 1985). ... On developmental squad for three games with Generals (1985). ... Selected by Los Angeles Rams in 11th round (285th pick overall) of 1985 NFL draft. ... On developmental squad (June 10, 1995-remainder of season). ... Rights traded by Rams with fourth-round pick in 1987 draft to Chicago Bears for third- and sixth-round picks in 1987 draft (October 14, 1986). ... Signed by Bears (October 21, 1986). ... Granted roster exemption (October 21-November 3, 1986). ... Activated (November 4, 1986). ... Crossed picket line during players strike (October 13, 1987). ... Traded by Bears to New England Patriots for eighth-round pick in 1988 draft (October 13, 1987). ... Released by Patriots after 1989 season. ... Signed by B.C. Lions of CFL (June 1990). ... Granted free agency (February 1992). ... Signed by Calgary Stampeders of CFL (March 1992). ... Rights assigned to Toronto Argonauts of CFL (March 15, 1996). ... Signed by Buffalo Bills (January 16, 1998). ... Released by Bills (March 1, 2001). ... Signed by San Diego Chargers (March 9, 2001).
CHAMPIONSHIP GAME EXPERIENCE: Member of CFL championship team (1992, 1996 and 1997). ... Named Most Valuable Player of Grey Cup, CFL championship game (1992, 1996 and 1997). ... Played in Grey Cup (1993 and 1995).

HONORS: Heisman Trophy winner (1984). ... Named College Football Player of the Year by THE SPORTING NEWS (1984). ... Named quarterback on THE SPORTING NEWS college All-America first team (1984). ... Most Outstanding Player of CFL (1991-1994, 1996 and 1997). ... Played in Pro Bowl (1998 season).
PRO STATISTICS: USFL: 1985—Recovered two fumbles. NFL: 1986—Recovered two fumbles and fumbled three times for minus four yards. 1987—Recovered one fumble. 1988—Fumbled three times. 1989—Fumbled once. CFL: 1990—Fumbled six times. 1991—Fumbled seven times. 1992—Fumbled five times. 1993—Caught one pass for 11 yards and fumbled five times. 1994—Fumbled eight times. 1995—Fumbled twice. 1996—Fumbled once. 1997—Fumbled three times. NFL: 1998—Fumbled three times and recovered four fumbles for minus 13 yards. 1999—Fumbled six times and recovered one fumble for minus five yards. 2000—Fumbled five times and recovered two fumbles for nine yards. 2001—Fumbled seven times and recovered five fumbles for minus eight yards.
SINGLE GAME HIGHS (regular season): Attempts—53 (December 30, 2001, vs. Seattle); completions—34 (December 30, 2001, vs. Seattle); yards—377 (December 30, 2001, vs. Seattle); and touchdown passes—4 (October 30, 1988, vs. Chicago).
STATISTICAL PLATEAUS: 300-yard passing games: 1998 (2), 1999 (1), 2000 (1), 2001 (4). Total: 8.
MISCELLANEOUS: Regular-season record as starting NFL quarterback: 35-25 (.683). ... Postseason record as starting NFL quarterback: 0-2.

					PASSING						RUSHING				TOTALS	
Year Team	G	GS	Att.	Cmp.	Pct.	Yds.	TD	Int.	Avg.	Rat.	Att.	Yds.	Avg.	TD	TD 2pt.	Pts.
1985—New Jersey USFL......	15	...	281	134	47.7	2109	13	14	7.51	67.8	65	465	7.2	6	6 0	36
1986—Chicago NFL............	4	1	46	23	50.0	361	3	2	7.85	80.1	9	36	4.0	1	1 0	6
1987—Chicago NFL............						Did not play.										
—New England NFL......	1	1	25	15	60.0	199	1	0	7.96	98.6	6	43	7.2	0	0 0	0
1988—New England NFL......	11	9	179	92	51.4	1150	8	10	6.42	63.3	38	179	4.7	1	1 0	6
1989—New England NFL......	5	3	91	36	39.6	493	2	4	5.42	46.6	16	87	5.4	0	0 0	0
1990—British Columbia CFL..	16	...	392	207	52.8	2960	16	19	7.55	71.0	79	662	8.4	3	3 0	18
1991—British Columbia CFL..	18	...	730	466	63.8	6619	38	24	9.07	96.7	120	610	5.1	14	14 1	86
1992—Calgary CFL.............	18	...	688	396	57.6	5945	32	30	8.64	83.4	96	669	7.0	11	11 0	66
1993—Calgary CFL.............	18	...	703	416	59.2	6092	44	17	8.67	98.3	74	373	5.0	11	11 0	66
1994—Calgary CFL.............	18	...	659	403	61.2	5726	48	19	8.69	101.5	96	760	7.9	8	8 0	48
1995—Calgary CFL.............	12	...	332	223	67.2	2788	16	5	8.40	102.8	46	288	6.3	5	5 0	30
1996—Toronto CFL.............	18	...	677	434	64.1	5720	29	17	8.45	94.5	101	756	7.5	9	9 0	54
1997—Toronto CFL.............	18	18	673	430	63.9	5505	47	24	8.18	97.8	92	542	5.9	9	9 0	54
1998—Buffalo NFL..............	13	10	354	202	57.1	2711	20	11	7.66	87.4	48	248	5.2	1	1 0	6
1999—Buffalo NFL..............	15	15	478	264	55.2	3171	19	16	6.63	75.1	88	476	5.4	0	1 0	6
2000—Buffalo NFL..............	11	5	231	132	57.1	1700	8	3	7.36	86.5	36	161	4.5	1	1 0	6
2001—San Diego NFL.........	16	16	521	294	56.4	3464	15	18	6.65	72.0	53	192	3.6	1	1 0	6
USFL totals (1 year)............	15	...	281	134	47.7	2109	13	14	7.51	67.8	65	465	7.2	6	6 0	36
CFL totals (8 years)............	136	...	4854	2975	61.3	41355	270	155	8.52	93.9	704	4660	6.6	70	70 1	422
NFL totals (8 years)............	76	60	1925	1058	55.0	13249	76	64	6.88	75.9	294	1422	4.8	6	6 0	36
Pro totals (17 years)...........	227	...	7060	4167	59.0	56713	359	233	8.03	87.9	1063	6547	6.2	82	82 1	494

FLYNN, MIKE — OL — RAVENS

PERSONAL: Born June 15, 1974, in Doylestown, Pa. ... 6-3/300. ... Full name: Michael Patrick Flynn.
HIGH SCHOOL: Cathedral (Springfield, Mass.).
COLLEGE: Maine.
TRANSACTIONS/CAREER NOTES: Signed as non-drafted free agent by Baltimore Ravens (April 25, 1997). ... Released by Ravens (August 24, 1997). ... Signed by Tampa Bay Buccaneers to practice squad (August 27, 1997). ... Released by Buccaneers (September 2, 1997). ... Signed by Jacksonville Jaguars to practice squad (November 4, 1997). ... Signed by Ravens off Jaguars practice squad (December 3, 1997). ... Inactive for three games (1997). ... Granted free agency (March 2, 2001). ... Re-signed by Ravens (March 13, 2001).
PLAYING EXPERIENCE: Baltimore NFL, 1998-2001. ... Games/Games started: 1998 (2/0), 1999 (12/0), 2000 (16/16), 2001 (16/16). Total: 46/32.
CHAMPIONSHIP GAME EXPERIENCE: Played in AFC championship game (2000 season). ... Member of Super Bowl championship team (2000 season).
PRO STATISTICS: 2000—Fumbled once and recovered two fumbles for minus 18 yards. 2001—Fumbled once and recovered one fumble for minus three yards.

FOLAU, SPENCER — OT — SAINTS

PERSONAL: Born April 5, 1973, in Nuk 'Alofa, Tonga, Samoan Islands. ... 6-5/300. ... Full name: Spencer Sione Folau. ... Name pronounced fah-LOWE.
HIGH SCHOOL: Sequoia (Redwood City, Calif.).
COLLEGE: Idaho.
TRANSACTIONS/CAREER NOTES: Signed as non-drafted free agent by Baltimore Ravens (April 26, 1996). ... Released by Ravens (August 25, 1996). ... Re-signed by Ravens to practice squad (October 29, 1996). ... Assigned by Ravens to Rhein Fire in 1997 World League enhancement allocation program (February 1997). ... Released by Ravens (October 28, 1998). ... Re-signed by Ravens (November 3, 1998). ... Granted free agency (February 11, 2000). ... Tendered offer sheet by New England Patriots (April 10, 2000). ... Offer matched by Ravens (April 12, 2000). ... Released by Ravens (March 1, 2001). ... Signed by Miami Dolphins (July 28, 2001). ... Granted unconditional free agency (March 1, 2002). ... Signed by New Orleans Saints (April 1, 2002).
PLAYING EXPERIENCE: Rhein W.L., 1997; Baltimore NFL, 1997-2000; Miami NFL, 2001. ... Games/Games started: W.L. 1997 (games played unavailable), NFL 1997 (10/0), 1998 (3/3), 1999 (5/1), 2000 (11/4), 2001 (16/15). Total NFL: 45/23.
CHAMPIONSHIP GAME EXPERIENCE: Played in AFC championship game (2000 season). ... Member of Super Bowl championship team (2000 season).
PRO STATISTICS: 2001—Recovered one fumble.

FOLEY, STEVE — LB — BENGALS

PERSONAL: Born September 9, 1975, in Little Rock, Ark. ... 6-3/260.
HIGH SCHOOL: Hall (Little Rock, Ark.).
COLLEGE: Northeast Louisiana.

TRANSACTIONS/CAREER NOTES: Selected by Cincinnati Bengals in third round (75th pick overall) of 1998 NFL draft. ... Signed by Bengals (July 19, 1998).
PRO STATISTICS: 1999—Recovered two fumbles. 2000—Intercepted one pass for one yard and recovered one fumble.

Year Team	G	GS	SACKS
1998—Cincinnati NFL	10	1	2.0
1999—Cincinnati NFL	16	16	3.5
2000—Cincinnati NFL	16	16	4.0
2001—Cincinnati NFL	12	12	0.0
Pro totals (4 years)	**54**	**45**	**9.5**

FONTENOT, AL — DE — CHARGERS

PERSONAL: Born September 17, 1970, in Houston. ... 6-4/287. ... Full name: Albert Paul Fontenot.
HIGH SCHOOL: Jack Yates (Houston).
JUNIOR COLLEGE: Navarro College (Texas).
COLLEGE: Baylor (degree in communications).
TRANSACTIONS/CAREER NOTES: Selected by Chicago Bears in fourth round (112th pick overall) of 1993 NFL draft. ... Signed by Bears (July 16, 1993). ... Granted free agency (February 16, 1996). ... Re-signed by Bears (April 18, 1996). ... Granted unconditional free agency (February 14, 1997). ... Signed by Indianapolis Colts (April 3, 1997). ... On injured reserve with calf injury (November 25, 1998-remainder of season). ... Released by Colts (April 28, 1999). ... Signed by San Diego Chargers (May 12, 1999). ... Granted unconditional free agency (February 11, 2000). ... Re-signed by Chargers (March 10, 2000). ... Granted unconditional free agency (March 2, 2001). ... Re-signed by Chargers (April 10, 2001).
PRO STATISTICS: 1993—Returned one kickoff for eight yards. 1995—Credited with one safety and recovered one fumble. 1997—Recovered three fumbles for 35 yards and one touchdown. 1998—Recovered one fumble. 1999—Recovered one fumble. 2000—Credited with one safety. 2001—Intercepted one pass for no yards.

Year Team	G	GS	SACKS
1993—Chicago NFL	16	0	1.0
1994—Chicago NFL	16	8	4.0
1995—Chicago NFL	13	5	2.5
1996—Chicago NFL	16	15	4.5
1997—Indianapolis NFL	16	16	4.5
1998—Indianapolis NFL	7	5	1.0
1999—San Diego NFL	15	15	5.0
2000—San Diego NFL	15	15	4.0
2001—San Diego NFL	16	2	1.0
Pro totals (9 years)	**130**	**81**	**27.5**

FONTENOT, JERRY — C — SAINTS

PERSONAL: Born November 21, 1966, in Lafayette, La. ... 6-3/300. ... Full name: Jerry Paul Fontenot.
HIGH SCHOOL: Lafayette (La.).
COLLEGE: Texas A&M.
TRANSACTIONS/CAREER NOTES: Selected by Chicago Bears in third round (65th pick overall) of 1989 NFL draft. ... Signed by Bears (July 27, 1989). ... Granted free agency (March 1, 1993). ... Re-signed by Bears (June 16, 1993). ... Granted free agency (February 16, 1996). ... Re-signed by Bears (July 10, 1996). ... Granted unconditional free agency (February 14, 1997). ... Signed by New Orleans Saints (May 28, 1997). ... On injured reserve with knee injury (October 14, 1998-remainder of season). ... Granted unconditional free agency (February 12, 1999). ... Re-signed by Saints (February 15, 1999).
PLAYING EXPERIENCE: Chicago NFL, 1989-1996; New Orleans NFL, 1997-2001. ... Games/Games started: 1989 (16/0), 1990 (16/2), 1991 (16/7), 1992 (16/16), 1993 (16/16), 1994 (16/16), 1995 (16/16), 1996 (16/16), 1997 (16/16), 1998 (4/4), 1999 (16/16), 2000 (16/16), 2001 (16/16). Total: 196/157.
PRO STATISTICS: 1989—Recovered one fumble. 1990—Fumbled once. 1992—Fumbled once for minus two yards. 1993—Recovered one fumble. 1997—Fumbled three times. 1999—Recovered one fumble. 2000—Recovered one fumble.

FORD, HENRY — DT — TITANS

PERSONAL: Born October 30, 1971, in Fort Worth, Texas. ... 6-3/295.
HIGH SCHOOL: Trimble Technical (Fort Worth, Texas).
COLLEGE: Arkansas.
TRANSACTIONS/CAREER NOTES: Selected by Houston Oilers in first round (26th pick overall) of 1994 NFL draft. ... Signed by Oilers (June 16, 1994). ... Oilers franchise moved to Tennessee for 1997 season. ... Granted unconditional free agency (February 13, 1998). ... Re-signed by Oilers (March 2, 1998). ... Oilers franchise renamed Tennessee Titans for 1999 season (December 26, 1998).
CHAMPIONSHIP GAME EXPERIENCE: Played in AFC championship game (1999 season). ... Played in Super Bowl XXXIV (1999 season).
PRO STATISTICS: 1997—Recovered two fumbles for 13 yards. 1998—Recovered one fumble. 1999—Recovered two fumbles. 2000—Recovered one fumble for 30 yards for a touchdown.

Year Team	G	GS	SACKS
1994—Houston NFL	11	0	0.0
1995—Houston NFL	16	16	4.5
1996—Houston NFL	15	14	1.0
1997—Tennessee NFL	16	16	5.0
1998—Tennessee NFL	13	5	1.5
1999—Tennessee NFL	12	9	5.5
2000—Tennessee NFL	14	3	2.0
2001—Tennessee NFL	16	0	1.0
Pro totals (8 years)	**113**	**63**	**20.5**

FORDHAM, TODD — OT — JAGUARS

PERSONAL: Born October 9, 1973, in Atlanta. ... 6-5/315. ... Full name: Lindsey Todd Fordham.
HIGH SCHOOL: Tift County (Tifton, Ga.).
COLLEGE: Florida State (degree in business, 1996).
TRANSACTIONS/CAREER NOTES: Signed as non-drafted free agent by Jacksonville Jaguars (April 21, 1997). ... Released by Jaguars (August 24, 1997). ... Re-signed by Jaguars to practice squad (August 25, 1997). ... Activated (September 23, 1997). ... On injured reserve with knee injury (August 31, 1999-entire season). ... Granted free agency (February 11, 2000). ... Re-signed by Jaguars (February 24, 2000). ... Granted unconditional free agency (March 2, 2001). ... Signed by Denver Broncos (April 13, 2001). ... Released by Broncos (September 2, 2001). ... Signed by Jaguars (October 2, 2001). ... Granted unconditional free agency (March 1, 2002). ... Re-signed by Jaguars (April 16, 2002).
PLAYING EXPERIENCE: Jacksonville NFL, 1997, 1998, 2000 and 2001. ... Games/Games started: 1997 (1/0), 1998 (11/1), 2000 (16/8), 2001 (12/12). Total: 40/21.
PRO STATISTICS: 1998—Returned one kickoff for no yards and recovered one fumble. 2000—Returned one kickoff for no yards and fumbled once.

FOREMAN, JAY — LB — TEXANS

PERSONAL: Born February 18, 1976, in Eden Prairie, Minn. ... 6-1/240. ... Full name: Jamal A. Foreman. ... Son of Chuck Foreman, running back with Minnesota Vikings (1973-79) and New England Patriots (1980).
HIGH SCHOOL: Eden Prairie (Minn.).
COLLEGE: Nebraska (degree in business administration).
TRANSACTIONS/CAREER NOTES: Selected by Buffalo Bills in fifth round (156th pick overall) of 1999 NFL draft. ... Signed by Bills (July 27, 1999). ... Granted free agency (March 1, 2002). ... Re-signed by Bills (April 17, 2002). ... Traded by Bills to Houston Texans for KR/PR Charlie Rogers (April 17, 2002).
PLAYING EXPERIENCE: Buffalo NFL, 1999-2001. ... Games/Games started: 1999 (7/0), 2000 (15/4), 2001 (16/16). Total: 38/20.
PRO STATISTICS: 2000—Returned one kickoff for 19 yards. 2001—Credited with 2$\frac{1}{2}$ sacks and recovered two fumbles.

FORNEY, KYNAN — G — FALCONS

PERSONAL: Born September 8, 1978, in Nacogdoches, Texas. ... 6-2/305.
HIGH SCHOOL: Nacogdoches (Texas).
JUNIOR COLLEGE: Trinity Valley Community College (Texas).
COLLEGE: Hawaii.
TRANSACTIONS/CAREER NOTES: Selected by Atlanta Falcons in seventh round (219th pick overall) of 2001 NFL draft. ... Signed by Falcons (May 21, 2001).
PLAYING EXPERIENCE: Atlanta NFL, 2001. ... Games/Games started: 2001 (12/8).

FOSTER, LARRY — WR — LIONS

PERSONAL: Born November 7, 1976, in Shreveport, La. ... 5-10/196.
HIGH SCHOOL: West Jefferson (La.).
COLLEGE: Louisiana State.
TRANSACTIONS/CAREER NOTES: Signed as non-drafted free agent by Detroit Lions (April 28, 2000). ... Released by Lions (August 27, 2000). ... Re-signed by Lions to practice squad (August 29, 2000). ... Activated (October 16, 2000).
PRO STATISTICS: 2000—Fumbled twice and recovered one fumble. 2001—Fumbled once and recovered one fumble.
SINGLE GAME HIGHS (regular season): Receptions—8 (November 30, 2000, vs. Minnesota); yards—106 (November 30, 2000, vs. Minnesota); and touchdown receptions—1 (November 30, 2000, vs. Minnesota).
STATISTICAL PLATEAUS: 100-yard receiving games: 2000 (1).

			RUSHING				RECEIVING				PUNT RETURNS				KICKOFF RETURNS				TOTALS		
Year Team	G	GS	Att.	Yds.	Avg.	TD	No.	Yds.	Avg.	TD	No.	Yds.	Avg.	TD	No.	Yds.	Avg.	TD	TD	2pt.	Pts.
2000—Detroit NFL	10	0	2	31	15.5	0	17	175	10.3	1	0	0	0.0	0	0	0	0.0	0	1	0	6
2001—Detroit NFL	13	5	2	6	3.0	0	22	283	12.9	0	3	17	5.7	0	9	182	20.2	0	0	0	0
Pro totals (2 years)	23	5	4	37	9.3	0	39	458	11.7	1	3	17	5.7	0	9	182	20.2	0	1	0	6

FRALEY, HANK — C/G — EAGLES

PERSONAL: Born September 21, 1977, in Gaithersburg, Md. ... 6-2/300.
HIGH SCHOOL: Gaithersburg (Md.).
COLLEGE: Robert Morris.
TRANSACTIONS/CAREER NOTES: Signed as non-drafted free agent by Pittsburgh Steelers (April 21, 2000). ... Claimed on waivers by Philadelphia Eagles (August 28, 2000). ... Inactive for all 16 games (2000).
PLAYING EXPERIENCE: Philadelphia NFL, 2001. ... Games/Games started: 2001 (16/15).
CHAMPIONSHIP GAME EXPERIENCE: Played in NFC championship game (2001 season).
PRO STATISTICS: 2001—Fumbled once for minus 17 yards.

FRANKS, BUBBA — TE — PACKERS

PERSONAL: Born January 6, 1978, in Riverside, Calif. ... 6-6/260. ... Full name: Daniel Lamont Franks.
HIGH SCHOOL: Big Springs (Texas).
COLLEGE: Miami (Fla.).

TRANSACTIONS/CAREER NOTES: Selected after junior season by Green Bay Packers in first round (14th pick overall) of 2000 NFL draft. ... Signed by Packers (July 19, 2000).
HONORS: Named tight end on THE SPORTING NEWS college All-America first team (1999).
PRO STATISTICS: 2000—Fumbled once.
SINGLE GAME HIGHS (regular season): Receptions—5 (October 1, 2000, vs. Chicago); yards—54 (October 1, 2000, vs. Chicago); and touchdown receptions—2 (December 23, 2001, vs. Cleveland).

				RECEIVING		
Year Team	G	GS	No.	Yds.	Avg.	TD
2000—Green Bay NFL	16	13	34	363	10.7	1
2001—Green Bay NFL	16	14	36	322	8.9	9
Pro totals (2 years)	32	27	70	685	9.8	10

FREDRICKSON, ROB   LB   CARDINALS

PERSONAL: Born May 13, 1971, in Saint Joseph, Mich. ... 6-4/243. ... Full name: Robert J. Fredrickson.
HIGH SCHOOL: Saint Joseph (Mich.) Senior.
COLLEGE: Michigan State.
TRANSACTIONS/CAREER NOTES: Selected by Los Angeles Raiders in first round (22nd pick overall) of 1994 NFL draft. ... Signed by Raiders (July 19, 1994). ... Raiders franchise moved to Oakland (July 21, 1995). ... On injured reserve with shoulder injury (November 20, 1996-remainder of season). ... Traded by Raiders to Detroit Lions for fourth-round pick (traded to Washington) in 1998 draft (March 25, 1998). ... Granted unconditional free agency (February 12, 1999). ... Signed by Arizona Cardinals (March 26, 1999).
PRO STATISTICS: 1995—Recovered four fumbles for 35 yards and one touchdown. 1999—Recovered one fumble.

			INTERCEPTIONS				SACKS
Year Team	G	GS	No.	Yds.	Avg.	TD	No.
1994—Los Angeles Raiders NFL	16	12	0	0	0.0	0	3.0
1995—Oakland NFL	16	15	1	14	14.0	0	0.0
1996—Oakland NFL	10	10	0	0	0.0	0	0.0
1997—Oakland NFL	16	13	0	0	0.0	0	2.0
1998—Detroit NFL	16	16	1	0	0.0	0	2.5
1999—Arizona NFL	16	16	2	57	28.5	1	2.0
2000—Arizona NFL	13	12	1	8	8.0	0	1.0
2001—Arizona NFL	15	15	0	0	0.0	0	4.0
Pro totals (8 years)	118	109	5	79	15.8	1	14.5

FREEMAN, ANTONIO   WR

PERSONAL: Born May 27, 1972, in Baltimore. ... 6-1/198. ... Full name: Antonio Michael Freeman.
HIGH SCHOOL: Polytechnic (Baltimore).
COLLEGE: Virginia Tech.
TRANSACTIONS/CAREER NOTES: Selected by Green Bay Packers in third round (90th pick overall) of 1995 NFL draft. ... Signed by Packers (June 22, 1995). ... Granted free agency (February 13, 1998). ... Re-signed by Packers (June 16, 1998). ... Designated by Packers as franchise player (February 12, 1999). ... Released by Packers (June 3, 2002).
CHAMPIONSHIP GAME EXPERIENCE: Played in NFC championship game (1995-1997 seasons). ... Member of Super Bowl championship team (1996 season). ... Played in Super Bowl XXXII (1997 season).
HONORS: Named wide receiver on THE SPORTING NEWS NFL All-Pro team (1998). ... Played in Pro Bowl (1998 season).
POST SEASON RECORDS: Holds Super Bowl record for longest pass reception (from Brett Favre)—81 yards (January 26, 1997, vs. New England). ... Shares NFL postseason record for most touchdowns by punt return—1(December 31, 1995, vs. Atlanta).
PRO STATISTICS: 1995—Recovered four fumbles. 1996—Recovered one fumble for 14 yards. 1997—Rushed once for 14 yards. 1998—Rushed three times for five yards. 1999—Rushed once for minus two yards and recovered one fumble. 2000—Rushed twice for five yards. 2001—Rushed once for nine yards and recovered one fumble.
SINGLE GAME HIGHS (regular season): Receptions—10 (December 14, 1997, vs. Carolina); yards—193 (November 1, 1998, vs. San Francisco); and touchdown receptions—3 (December 20, 1998, vs. Tennessee).
STATISTICAL PLATEAUS: 100-yard receiving games: 1996 (4), 1997 (3), 1998 (6), 1999 (3), 2000 (2), 2001 (2). Total: 20.

			RECEIVING				PUNT RETURNS				KICKOFF RETURNS				TOTALS		
Year Team	G	GS	No.	Yds.	Avg.	TD	No.	Yds.	Avg.	TD	No.	Yds.	Avg.	TD	TD	2pt.	Pts. Fum.
1995—Green Bay NFL	11	0	8	106	13.3	1	37	292	7.9	0	24	556	23.2	0	1	0	6	7
1996—Green Bay NFL	12	12	56	933	16.7	9	0	0	0.0	0	1	16	16.0	0	9	0	54	3
1997—Green Bay NFL	16	16	81	1243	15.3	12	0	0	0.0	0	0	0	0.0	0	12	0	72	0
1998—Green Bay NFL	15	15	84	*1424	17.0	14	0	0	0.0	0	0	0	0.0	0	14	1	86	0
1999—Green Bay NFL	16	16	74	1074	14.5	6	0	0	0.0	0	0	0	0.0	0	6	0	36	1
2000—Green Bay NFL	15	15	62	912	14.7	9	0	0	0.0	0	0	0	0.0	0	9	0	54	1
2001—Green Bay NFL	16	16	52	818	15.7	6	17	114	6.7	0	2	28	14.0	0	6	1	38	1
Pro totals (7 years)	101	90	417	6510	15.6	57	54	406	7.5	0	27	600	22.2	0	57	2	346	14

FREEMAN, ARTURO   S   DOLPHINS

PERSONAL: Born October 27, 1976, in Orangeburg, S.C. ... 6-0/196. ... Full name: Arturo C. Freeman.
HIGH SCHOOL: Orangeburg-Wilkinson (Orangeburg, S.C.).
COLLEGE: South Carolina.
TRANSACTIONS/CAREER NOTES: Selected by Miami Dolphins in fifth round (152nd pick overall) of 2000 NFL draft. ... Signed by Dolphins (July 11, 2000).
PLAYING EXPERIENCE: Miami NFL, 2000 and 2001. ... Games/Games started: 2000 (8/0), 2001 (16/4). Total: 24/4.
PRO STATISTICS: 2001—Intercepted one pass for no yards, credited with one sack and recovered two fumbles for minus five yards.

FREROTTE, GUS — QB — BENGALS

PERSONAL: Born July 31, 1971, in Kittanning, Pa. ... 6-3/225. ... Full name: Gustave Joseph Frerotte. ... Cousin of Mitch Frerotte, guard with Buffalo Bills (1987 and 1990-92).
HIGH SCHOOL: Ford City (Pa.) Junior-Senior.
COLLEGE: Tulsa.
TRANSACTIONS/CAREER NOTES: Selected by Washington Redskins in seventh round (197th pick overall) of 1994 NFL draft. ... Signed by Redskins (July 19, 1994). ... Granted free agency (February 14, 1997). ... Re-signed by Redskins (July 18, 1997). ... On injured reserve with hip injury (December 2, 1997-remainder of season). ... Released by Redskins (February 11, 1999). ... Signed by Detroit Lions (March 3, 1999). ... Granted unconditional free agency (February 11, 2000). ... Signed by Denver Broncos (March 7, 2000). ... Granted unconditional free agency (March 2, 2001). ... Re-signed by Broncos (March 13, 2001). ... On injured reserve with shoulder injury (December 19, 2001-remainder of season). ... Granted unconditional free agency (March 1, 2002). ... Signed by Cincinnati Bengals (May 1, 2002).
HONORS: Played in Pro Bowl (1996 season).
PRO STATISTICS: 1994—Fumbled four times and recovered two fumbles for minus four yards. 1995—Fumbled seven times and recovered four fumbles for minus 16 yards. 1996—Fumbled 12 times and recovered one fumble for minus 12 yards. 1997—Fumbled eight times and recovered two fumbles for minus 16 yards. 1999—Fumbled three times and recovered one fumble. 2000—Fumbled five times. 2001—Fumbled twice and recovered one fumble.
SINGLE GAME HIGHS (regular season): Attempts—58 (November 19, 2000, vs. San Diego); completions—36 (November 19, 2000, vs. San Diego); yards—462 (November 19, 2000, vs. San Diego); and touchdown passes—5 (November 19, 2000, vs. San Diego).
STATISTICAL PLATEAUS: 300-yard passing games: 1995 (1), 1996 (1), 1999 (2), 2000 (1). Total: 5.
MISCELLANEOUS: Regular-season record as starting NFL quarterback: 25-33-1 (.424). ... Postseason record as starting NFL quarterback: 0-1.

			PASSING							RUSHING				TOTALS		
Year Team	G	GS	Att.	Cmp.	Pct.	Yds.	TD	Int.	Avg.	Rat.	Att.	Yds.	Avg.	TD	TD	2pt.	Pts.
1994—Washington NFL	4	4	100	46	46.0	600	5	5	6.00	61.3	4	1	0.3	0	0	0	0
1995—Washington NFL	16	11	396	199	50.3	2751	13	13	6.95	70.2	22	16	0.7	1	1	0	6
1996—Washington NFL	16	16	470	270	57.4	3453	12	11	7.35	79.3	28	16	0.6	0	0	0	0
1997—Washington NFL	13	13	402	204	50.7	2682	17	12	6.67	73.8	24	65	2.7	2	2	0	12
1998—Washington NFL	3	2	54	25	46.3	283	1	3	5.24	45.5	3	20	6.7	0	0	0	0
1999—Detroit NFL	9	6	288	175	60.8	2117	9	7	7.35	83.6	15	33	2.2	0	0	0	0
2000—Denver NFL	10	6	232	138	59.5	1776	9	8	7.66	82.1	22	64	2.9	1	1	0	6
2001—Denver NFL	4	1	48	30	62.5	308	3	0	6.42	101.7	10	9	0.9	1	1	0	6
Pro totals (8 years)	75	59	1990	1087	54.6	13970	69	59	7.02	76.1	128	224	1.8	5	5	0	30

FRICKE, BEN — G/C — COWBOYS

PERSONAL: Born November 3, 1975, in Austin, Texas. ... 6-0/280.
HIGH SCHOOL: L.C. Anderson (Austin, Texas).
COLLEGE: Houston.
TRANSACTIONS/CAREER NOTES: Selected by New York Giants in seventh round (213th pick overall) of 1998 NFL draft. ... Signed by Giants (July 20, 1998). ... Released by Giants (August 22, 1998). ... Selected by Amsterdam Admirals in 1999 NFL Europe draft (February 23, 1999). ... Signed by Dallas Cowboys (August 3, 1999). ... Released by Cowboys (September 22, 1999). ... Re-signed by Cowboys (October 5, 1999). ... Released by Cowboys (October 27, 1999). ... Re-signed by Cowboys to practice squad (October 28, 1999). ... Activated (November 19, 1999). ... Assigned by Cowboys to Admirals in 2000 NFL Europe enhancement allocation program (February 18, 2000). ... Granted free agency (March 1, 2002).
PLAYING EXPERIENCE: Amsterdam NFLE, 1999 and 2000; Dallas NFL, 1999-2001. ... Games/Games started: NFLE 1999 (games played unavailable), NFL 1999 (3/0), NFLE 2000 (-), NFL 2000 (8/5), 2001 (5/0). Total: NFL 16/5.
HONORS: Named center on THE SPORTING NEWS college All-America second team (1997).
PRO STATISTICS: 2000—Fumbled twice and recovered two fumbles.

FRIEDMAN, LENNIE — G — BRONCOS

PERSONAL: Born October 13, 1976, in Livingston, N.J. ... 6-3/285. ... Full name: Leonard Lebrecht Friedman.
HIGH SCHOOL: West Milford (N.J.).
COLLEGE: Duke.
TRANSACTIONS/CAREER NOTES: Selected by Denver Broncos in second round (61st pick overall) of 1999 NFL draft. ... Signed by Broncos (June 14, 1999). ... On injured reserve with knee injury (August 31, 1999-entire season). ... Assigned by Broncos to Barcelona Dragons in 2000 NFL Europe enhancement allocation program (February 18, 2000).
PLAYING EXPERIENCE: Barcelona NFLE, 2000; Denver NFL, 2000 and 2001. ... Games/Games started: NFLE 2000 (games played unavailable), NFL 2000 (16/8), 2001 (15/14). Total: 31/22.
PRO STATISTICS: 2000—Recovered two fumbles.

FRISCH, BYRON — DE — COWBOYS

PERSONAL: Born December 17, 1976, in Roseville, Calif. ... 6-5/267.
HIGH SCHOOL: Bonita Vista (Bonita, Calif.).
COLLEGE: Brigham Young.
TRANSACTIONS/CAREER NOTES: Selected by Tennessee Titans in third round (93rd pick overall) of 2000 NFL draft. ... Signed by Titans (July 19, 2000). ... Released by Titans (September 2, 2001). ... Signed by Dallas Cowboys (September 24, 2001).

Year Team	G	GS	SACKS
2001—Dallas NFL	13	0	3.0

FROST, SCOTT — S — PACKERS

PERSONAL: Born January 4, 1975, in Wood River, Neb. ... 6-3/219.
HIGH SCHOOL: Wood River (Neb.).
COLLEGE: Stanford, then Nebraska (degree in finance, 1997).
TRANSACTIONS/CAREER NOTES: Selected by New York Jets in third round (67th pick overall) of 1998 NFL draft. ... Signed by Jets (July 21, 1998). ... Granted free agency (March 2, 2001). ... Re-signed by Jets (April 12, 2001). ... On non-football injury list with ankle injury (July 28-August 18, 2001). ... Claimed on waivers by Cleveland Browns (August 29, 2001). ... Released by Browns (December 11, 2001). ... Signed by Green Bay Packers (December 19, 2001).
PLAYING EXPERIENCE: New York Jets NFL, 1998-2000; Cleveland NFL, 2001. ... Games/Games started: 1998 (13/0), 1999 (14/0), 2000 (16/1), 2001 (12/0). Total: 55/1.
CHAMPIONSHIP GAME EXPERIENCE: Played in AFC championship game (1998 season).
PRO STATISTICS: 1998—Returned one punt for no yards and fumbled once. 2000—Intercepted one pass for one yard and credited with one sack. 2001—Rushed once for one yard and recovered one fumble.

FUAMATU-MA'AFALA, CHRIS — RB — STEELERS

PERSONAL: Born March 4, 1977, in Honolulu. ... 6-0/255. ... Name pronounced fu-ah-MAH-tu ma-ah-FAH-la.
HIGH SCHOOL: St. Louis (Honolulu).
COLLEGE: Utah.
TRANSACTIONS/CAREER NOTES: Selected after junior season by Pittsburgh Steelers in sixth round (178th pick overall) of 1998 NFL draft. ... Signed by Steelers (July 10, 1998). ... On injured reserve with broken foot (Decemeber 20, 2000-remainder of season). ... Granted free agency (March 2, 2001). ... Tendered offer sheet by New England Patriots (April 14, 2001). ... Offer matched by Steelers (April 19, 2001).
CHAMPIONSHIP GAME EXPERIENCE: Played in AFC championship game (2001 season).
PRO STATISTICS: 1999—Returned one kickoff for nine yards.
SINGLE GAME HIGHS (regular season): Attempts—26 (December 23, 2001, vs. Detroit); yards—126 (December 23, 2001, vs. Detroit); and rushing touchdowns—1 (January 6, 2002, vs. Cleveland).
STATISTICAL PLATEAUS: 100-yard rushing games: 2001 (1).

			RUSHING				RECEIVING				TOTALS		
Year Team	G	GS	Att.	Yds.	Avg.	TD	No.	Yds.	Avg.	TD	TD	2pt.	Pts.	Fum.
1998—Pittsburgh NFL	12	0	7	30	4.3	2	9	84	9.3	1	3	0	18	0
1999—Pittsburgh NFL	10	0	1	4	4.0	0	0	0	0.0	0	0	0	0	0
2000—Pittsburgh NFL	7	1	21	149	7.1	0	11	107	9.7	0	1	0	6	0
2001—Pittsburgh NFL	16	5	120	453	3.8	3	16	127	7.9	1	4	0	24	0
Pro totals (4 years)	45	6	149	636	4.3	6	36	318	8.8	2	8	0	48	0

FULCHER, MONDRIEL — TE — RAIDERS

PERSONAL: Born October 15, 1976, in Coffeyville, Kan. ... 6-3/245. ... Full name: Mondriel DeCarlos A. Fulcher.
HIGH SCHOOL: Field Kindley (Coffeyville, Kan.).
COLLEGE: Miami (Fla.).
TRANSACTIONS/CAREER NOTES: Selected by Oakland Raiders in seventh round (227th pick overall) of 2000 NFL draft. ... Signed by Raiders (July 11, 2000).
PLAYING EXPERIENCE: Oakland NFL, 2000 amd 2001. ... Games/Games started: 2000 (10/0), 2001 (13/1). Total: 23/1.
CHAMPIONSHIP GAME EXPERIENCE: Member of Raiders for AFC Championship game (2000 season); inactive.

FULLER, COREY — DB — BROWNS

PERSONAL: Born May 1, 1971, in Tallahassee, Fla. ... 5-10/205.
HIGH SCHOOL: James S. Rickards (Tallahassee, Fla.).
COLLEGE: Florida State (degree in criminology and child development, 1994).
TRANSACTIONS/CAREER NOTES: Selected by Minnesota Vikings in second round (55th pick overall) of 1995 NFL draft. ... Signed by Vikings (July 24, 1995). ... Granted unconditional free agency (February 12, 1999). ... Signed by Cleveland Browns (February 18, 1999).
CHAMPIONSHIP GAME EXPERIENCE: Played in NFC championship game (1998 season).
PRO STATISTICS: 1995—Credited with $^{1}/_{2}$ sack and recovered one fumble for 12 yards and a touchdown. 1998—Credited with one sack. 1999—Recovered two fumbles. 2000—Recovered one fumble. 2001—Recovered one fumble.

			INTERCEPTIONS			
Year Team	G	GS	No.	Yds.	Avg.	TD
1995—Minnesota NFL	16	11	1	0	0.0	0
1996—Minnesota NFL	16	14	3	3	1.0	0
1997—Minnesota NFL	16	16	2	24	12.0	0
1998—Minnesota NFL	16	16	4	36	9.0	0
1999—Cleveland NFL	16	16	0	0	0.0	0
2000—Cleveland NFL	15	15	3	0	0.0	0
2001—Cleveland NFL	16	16	3	82	27.3	1
Pro totals (7 years)	111	104	16	145	9.1	1

FULLER, CURTIS — S — SEAHAWKS

PERSONAL: Born July 25, 1978, in North Richland Hill, Texas. ... 5-10/180.
HIGH SCHOOL: Christian (Fort Worth, Texas).
JUNIOR COLLEGE: Trinity Valley Community College (Texas).
COLLEGE: Texas Christian (degree in psychology).
TRANSACTIONS/CAREER NOTES: Selected by Seattle Seahawks in fourth round (127th pick overall) of 2001 NFL draft. ... Signed by Seahawks (June 8, 2001).
PLAYING EXPERIENCE: Seattle NFL, 2001. ... Games/Games started: 2001 (10/1).

GADSDEN, ORONDE — WR — DOLPHINS

PERSONAL: Born August 20, 1971, in Charleston, S.C. ... 6-2/215. ... Full name: Oronde Benjamin Gadsden. ... Name pronounced o-RON-day.
HIGH SCHOOL: Burke (Charleston, S.C.).
COLLEGE: Winston-Salem (degree in marketing).
TRANSACTIONS/CAREER NOTES: Signed by Dallas Cowboys as non-drafted free agent (August 1995). ... Released by Cowboys (August 22, 1995). ... Re-signed by Cowboys to practice squad (August 30, 1995). ... Activated (January 8, 1996). ... On injured reserve with left ankle sprain (January 11, 1996-remainder of playoffs). ... Released by Cowboys (August 27, 1996). ... Signed by Pittsburgh Steelers (February 4, 1997). ... Released by Steelers (August 19, 1997). ... Signed by Cowboys (August 21, 1997). ... Released by Cowboys (August 24, 1997). ... Played with Portland Forest Dragons of Arena League (1998). ... Signed by Miami Dolphins (August 3, 1998).
PRO STATISTICS: 2000—Recovered two fumbles. 2001—Recovered one fumble.
SINGLE GAME HIGHS (regular season): Receptions—9 (January 2, 2000, vs. Washington); yards—153 (December 27, 1998, vs. Atlanta); and touchdown receptions—2 (October 1, 2000, vs. Cincinnati).
STATISTICAL PLATEAUS: 100-yard receiving games: 1998 (1), 1999 (3), 2000 (1), 2001 (2). Total: 7.

				RECEIVING			TOTALS		
Year Team	G	GS	No.	Yds.	Avg.	TD	TD 2pt.	Pts.	Fum.
1995—Dallas NFL						Did not play.			
1996—						Did not play.			
1997—						Did not play.			
1998—Miami NFL	16	12	48	713	14.9	7	7 0	42	2
1999—Miami NFL	16	7	48	803	16.7	6	6 0	36	0
2000—Miami NFL	16	16	56	786	14.0	6	6 0	36	0
2001—Miami NFL	14	14	55	674	12.3	3	3 0	18	1
Pro totals (4 years)	62	49	207	2976	14.4	22	22 0	132	3

GALLOWAY, JOEY — WR — COWBOYS

PERSONAL: Born November 20, 1971, in Bellaire, Ohio. ... 5-11/197.
HIGH SCHOOL: Bellaire (Ohio).
COLLEGE: Ohio State (degree in business/marketing, 1994).
TRANSACTIONS/CAREER NOTES: Selected by Seattle Seahawks in first round (eighth pick overall) of 1995 NFL draft. ... Signed by Seahawks (July 20, 1995). ... On did not report list (September 4-November 9, 1999). ... Designated by Seahawks as franchise player (February 11, 2000). ... Traded by Seahawks to Dallas Cowboys for first-round pick (RB Shaun Alexander) in 2000 draft and first round pick (traded to San Francisco) in 2001 draft (February 12, 2000). ... On injured reserve with knee injury (September 8, 2000-remainder of season).
PRO STATISTICS: 1995—Returned two kickoffs for 30 yards. 1997—Recovered one fumble. 2001—Completed only pass attempt for minus one yard and recovered one fumble.
SINGLE GAME HIGHS (regular season): Receptions—8 (November 2, 1997, vs. Denver); yards—146 (December 30, 2001, vs. San Francisco); and touchdown receptions—3 (October 26, 1997, vs. Oakland).
STATISTICAL PLATEAUS: 100-yard receiving games: 1995 (3), 1996 (3), 1997 (3), 1998 (4), 2001 (1). Total: 13.

			RUSHING				RECEIVING				PUNT RETURNS				TOTALS		
Year Team	G	GS	Att.	Yds.	Avg.	TD	No.	Yds.	Avg.	TD	No.	Yds.	Avg.	TD	TD 2pt.	Pts.	Fum.
1995—Seattle NFL	16	16	11	154	14.0	1	67	1039	15.5	7	36	360	10.0	†1	9 0	54	1
1996—Seattle NFL	16	16	15	127	8.5	0	57	987	17.3	7	15	158	10.5	▲1	8 0	48	2
1997—Seattle NFL	15	15	9	72	8.0	0	72	1049	14.6 ▲	12	0	0	0.0	0	12 0	72	0
1998—Seattle NFL	16	16	9	26	2.9	0	65	1047	16.1 ▲	10	25	251	10.0	†2	12 0	72	1
1999—Seattle NFL	8	4	1	-1	-1.0	0	22	335	15.2	1	3	54	18.0	0	1 0	6	0
2000—Dallas NFL	1	1	0	0	0.0	0	4	62	15.5	1	1	2	2.0	0	1 0	6	0
2001—Dallas NFL	16	16	3	32	10.7	0	52	699	13.4	3	1	6	6.0	0	3 0	18	1
Pro totals (7 years)	88	84	48	410	8.5	1	339	5218	15.4	41	81	831	10.3	4	46 0	276	6

GALYON, SCOTT — LB — DOLPHINS

PERSONAL: Born March 23, 1974, in Seymour, Tenn. ... 6-2/238. ... Name pronounced GAL-yun.
HIGH SCHOOL: Seymour (Tenn.).
COLLEGE: Tennessee.
TRANSACTIONS/CAREER NOTES: Selected by New York Giants in sixth round (182nd pick overall) of 1996 NFL draft. ... Signed by Giants (July 17, 1996). ... On injured reserve with knee injury (December 8, 1998-remainder of season). ... Granted free agency (February 12, 1999). ... Re-signed by Giants (May 3, 1999). ... Granted unconditional free agency (February 11, 2000). ... Signed by Miami Dolphins (February 25, 2000). ... On injured reserve with knee injury (October 11, 2000-remainder of season). ... On physically unable to perform list with knee injury (July 24-31, 2001).
PLAYING EXPERIENCE: New York Giants NFL, 1996-1999; Miami NFL, 2000 and 2001. ... Games/Games started: 1996 (16/0), 1997 (16/0), 1998 (10/1), 1999 (16/0), 2000 (6/1), 2001 (16/2). Total: 80/4.
PRO STATISTICS: 1997—Credited with three sacks. 1998—Credited with one sack and recovered one fumble. 1999—Credited with one sack. 2001—Intercepted one pass for no yards, credited with one sack and recovered one fumble.

GAMBLE, TRENT — S — DOLPHINS

PERSONAL: Born July 24, 1977, in Denver. ... 5-9/195. ... Full name: Trent Ashford Gamble.
HIGH SCHOOL: Ponderosa (Parker, Colo.).
COLLEGE: Wyoming (degree in finance).
TRANSACTIONS/CAREER NOTES: Signed as non-drafted free agent by Miami Dolphins (April 25, 2000). ... On injured reserve with knee injury (October 23, 2001-remainder of season).
PLAYING EXPERIENCE: Miami NFL, 2000 and 2001. ... Games/Games started: 2000 (16/0), 2001 (1/0). Total: 17/0.
PRO STATISTICS: 2000—Recovered one fumble.

GAMMON, KENDALL TE CHIEFS

PERSONAL: Born October 23, 1968, in Wichita, Kan. ... 6-4/258. ... Full name: Kendall Robert Gammon.
HIGH SCHOOL: Rose Hill (Kan.).
COLLEGE: Pittsburg (Kan.) State (degree in physical education).
TRANSACTIONS/CAREER NOTES: Selected by Pittsburgh Steelers in 11th round (291st pick overall) of 1992 NFL draft. ... Signed by Steelers (July 14, 1992). ... Released by Steelers (August 30, 1993). ... Re-signed by Steelers (August 31, 1993). ... Granted unconditional free agency (February 17, 1995). ... Re-signed by Steelers (May 8, 1995). ... Released by Steelers (August 26, 1996). ... Signed by New Orleans Saints (August 28, 1996). ... Granted unconditional free agency (February 11, 2000). ... Signed by Kansas City Chiefs (February 23, 2000).
PLAYING EXPERIENCE: Pittsburgh NFL, 1992-1995; New Orleans NFL, 1996-1999; Kansas City NFL, 2000 and 2001. ... Games/Games started: 1992 (16/0), 1993 (16/0), 1994 (16/0), 1995 (16/0), 1996 (16/0), 1997 (16/0), 1998 (16/0), 1999 (16/0), 2000 (16/0), 2001 (16/0). Total: 160/0.
CHAMPIONSHIP GAME EXPERIENCE: Played in AFC championship game (1994 and 1995 seasons). ... Played in Super Bowl XXX (1995 season).
PRO STATISTICS: 1999—Returned one kickoff for nine yards.

GANDY, MIKE G BEARS

PERSONAL: Born January 3, 1979, in Rockford, Ill. ... 6-4/304. ... Full name: Michael Joseph Gandy.
HIGH SCHOOL: Garland (Texas).
COLLEGE: Notre Dame (degree in sociology and computer applications).
TRANSACTIONS/CAREER NOTES: Selected by Chicago Bears in third round (68th pick overall) of 2001 NFL draft. ... Signed by Bears (July 20, 2001). ... Inactive for 16 games (2001).
HONORS: Named guard on THE SPORTING NEWS college All-America first team (2000).

GANDY, WAYNE OT STEELERS

PERSONAL: Born February 10, 1971, in Haines City, Fla. ... 6-5/310. ... Full name: Wayne Lamar Gandy.
HIGH SCHOOL: Haines City (Fla.).
COLLEGE: Auburn.
TRANSACTIONS/CAREER NOTES: Selected by Los Angeles Rams in first round (15th pick overall) of 1994 NFL draft. ... Signed by Rams (July 23, 1994). ... Rams franchise moved to St. Louis (April 12, 1995). ... Granted unconditional free agency (February 12, 1999). ... Signed by Pittsburgh Steelers (April 6, 1999).
PLAYING EXPERIENCE: Los Angeles Rams NFL, 1994; St. Louis NFL, 1995-1998; Pittsburgh NFL, 1999-2001. ... Games/Games started: 1994 (16/9), 1995 (16/16), 1996 (16/16), 1997 (16/16), 1998 (16/16), 1999 (16/16), 2000 (16/16), 2001 (15/15). Total: 127/120.
CHAMPIONSHIP GAME EXPERIENCE: Played in AFC championship game (2001 season).
HONORS: Named offensive lineman on THE SPORTING NEWS college All-America first team (1993).
PRO STATISTICS: 2000—Recovered one fumble.

GANNON, RICH QB RAIDERS

PERSONAL: Born December 20, 1965, in Philadelphia. ... 6-3/210. ... Full name: Richard Joseph Gannon.
HIGH SCHOOL: St. Joseph's Prep (Philadelphia).
COLLEGE: Delaware (degree in criminal justice, 1987).
TRANSACTIONS/CAREER NOTES: Selected by New England Patriots in fourth round (98th pick overall) of 1987 NFL draft. ... Rights traded by Patriots to Minnesota Vikings for fourth- (WR Sammy Martin) and 11th-round (traded) picks in 1988 draft (May 6, 1987). ... Signed by Vikings (July 30, 1987). ... Active for 13 games (1989); did not play. ... Granted free agency (February 1, 1990). ... Re-signed by Vikings (July 30, 1990). ... Granted free agency (February 1, 1991). ... Re-signed by Vikings (July 25, 1991). ... Granted free agency (February 1, 1992). ... Re-signed by Vikings (August 8, 1992). ... Traded by Vikings to Washington Redskins for conditional draft pick (August 20, 1993). ... Granted unconditional free agency (February 17, 1994). ... Signed by Kansas City Chiefs (March 29, 1995). ... Released by Chiefs (February 15, 1996). ... Re-signed by Chiefs (April 3, 1996). ... Granted unconditional free agency (February 12, 1999). ... Signed by Oakland Raiders (February 16, 1999).
CHAMPIONSHIP GAME EXPERIENCE: Member of Vikings for NFC championship game (1987 season); did not play. ... Played in AFC championship game (2000 season).
HONORS: Played in Pro Bowl (1999 and 2000 seasons). ... Named quarterback on THE SPORTING NEWS NFL All-Pro team (2000). ... Named Outstanding Player of Pro Bowl (2000 and 2001).
PRO STATISTICS: 1990—Fumbled 10 times and recovered six fumbles for minus three yards. 1991—Fumbled twice and caught one pass for no yards. 1992—Fumbled five times. 1993—Fumbled three times and recovered one fumble. 1996—Fumbled once. 1997—Fumbled five times. 1998—Fumbled nine times and recovered four fumbles for minus 15 yards. 1999—Caught one pass for minus three yards, fumbled eight times and recovered one fumble for minus five yards. 2000—Fumbled nine times and recovered two fumbles for minus one yard. 2001—Tied for AFC lead with 13 fumbles and recovered three fumbles for minus eight yards.
SINGLE GAME HIGHS (regular season): Attempts—63 (October 20, 1991, vs. New England); completions—35 (October 20, 1991, vs. New England); yards—382 (November 13, 2000, vs. Denver); and touchdown passes—5 (December 24, 2000, vs. Carolina).
STATISTICAL PLATEAUS: 300-yard passing games: 1991 (1), 1992 (1), 1997 (1), 1998 (1), 1999 (2), 2000 (2), 2001 (4). Total: 12.
MISCELLANEOUS: Regular-season record as starting NFL quarterback: 61-45 (.575). ... Postseason record as starting NFL quarterback: 2-2 (.500).

				PASSING						RUSHING				TOTALS		
Year Team	G	GS	Att.	Cmp.	Pct.	Yds.	TD	Int.	Avg.	Rat.	Att.	Yds.	Avg.	TD	TD	2pt.	Pts.
1987—Minnesota NFL	4	0	6	2	33.3	18	0	1	3.00	2.8	0	0	0.0	0	0	0	0
1988—Minnesota NFL	3	0	15	7	46.7	90	0	0	6.00	66.0	4	29	7.3	0	0	0	0
1989—Minnesota NFL							Did not play.										
1990—Minnesota NFL	14	12	349	182	52.1	2278	16	16	6.53	68.9	52	268	5.2	1	1	0	6
1991—Minnesota NFL	15	11	354	211	59.6	2166	12	6	6.12	81.5	43	236	5.5	2	2	0	12
1992—Minnesota NFL	12	12	279	159	57.0	1905	12	13	6.83	72.9	45	187	4.2	0	0	0	0

Year	Team	G	GS	Att.	Cmp.	Pct.	Yds.	TD	Int.	Avg.	Rat.	Att.	Yds.	Avg.	TD	TD	2pt.	Pts.
						PASSING							RUSHING				TOTALS	
1993	Washington NFL	8	4	125	74	59.2	704	3	7	5.63	59.6	21	88	4.2	1	1	0	6
1994	—								Did not play.									
1995	Kansas City NFL	2	0	11	7	63.6	57	0	0	5.18	76.7	8	25	3.1	1	0	0	0
1996	Kansas City NFL	4	3	90	54	60.0	491	6	1	5.46	92.4	12	81	6.8	0	0	0	0
1997	Kansas City NFL	9	6	175	98	56.0	1144	7	4	6.54	79.8	33	109	3.3	2	2	0	12
1998	Kansas City NFL	12	10	354	206	58.2	2305	10	6	6.51	80.1	44	168	3.8	3	3	0	18
1999	Oakland NFL	16	16	515	304	59.0	3840	24	14	7.46	86.5	46	298	6.5	2	2	0	12
2000	Oakland NFL	16	16	473	284	60.0	3430	28	11	7.25	92.4	89	529	5.9	4	4	1	26
2001	Oakland NFL	16	16	549	§361	§65.8	3828	§27	9	6.97	§95.5	63	231	3.7	2	2	▲1	14
Pro totals (13 years)		131	106	3295	1949	59.2	22256	145	88	6.75	83.1	460	2249	4.9	18	17	2	106

GARCIA, FRANK   C   RAMS

PERSONAL: Born January 28, 1972, in Phoenix. ... 6-2/302. ... Full name: Frank Christopher Garcia.
HIGH SCHOOL: Maryvale (Phoenix).
COLLEGE: Washington.
TRANSACTIONS/CAREER NOTES: Selected by Carolina Panthers in fourth round (132nd pick overall) of 1995 NFL draft. ... Signed by Panthers (July 14, 1995). ... Granted free agency (February 13, 1998). ... Re-signed by Panthers (March 16, 1998). ... Granted unconditional free agency (March 2, 2001). ... Signed by St. Louis Rams (April 26, 2001).
PLAYING EXPERIENCE: Carolina NFL, 1995-2000; St. Louis NFL, 2001. ... Games/Games started: 1995 (15/14), 1996 (14/8), 1997 (16/16), 1998 (14/14), 1999 (16/16), 2000 (16/16), 2001 (13/3). Total: 104/87.
CHAMPIONSHIP GAME EXPERIENCE: Played in NFC championship game (1996 and 2001 seasons). ... Played in Super Bowl XXXVI (2001 season).
PRO STATISTICS: 1995—Fumbled once and recovered one fumble for 10 yards. 1996—Recovered two fumbles. 1997—Returned one kickoff for 11 yards. 1998—Recovered two fumbles for two yards. 1999—Recovered two fumbles. 2000—Recovered one fumble.

GARCIA, JEFF   QB   49ERS

PERSONAL: Born February 24, 1970, in Gilroy, Calif. ... 6-1/195.
HIGH SCHOOL: Gilroy (Calif.).
JUNIOR COLLEGE: Gavilan College (Calif.).
COLLEGE: San Jose State.
TRANSACTIONS/CAREER NOTES: Signed by Calgary Stampeders of CFL (1994). ... Granted free agency (February 16, 1997). ... Re-signed by Stampeders (April 30, 1997). ... Signed as non-drafted free agent by San Francisco 49ers (February 16, 1999).
CHAMPIONSHIP GAME EXPERIENCE: Played in Grey Cup (1995). ... Member of CFL Championship team (1998). ... Named Most Valuable Player of Grey Cup, CFL championship game (1998).
HONORS: Played in Pro Bowl (2000 season).
PRO STATISTICS: 1999—Fumbled five times and recovered one fumble for minus one yard. 2000—Fumbled seven times and recovered four fumbles for minus six yards. 2001—Fumbled nine times and recovered five fumbles for minus one yard.
SINGLE GAME HIGHS (regular season): Attempts—54 (November 18, 2001, vs. Carolina); completions—36 (December 17, 2000, vs. Chicago); passing yards—437 (December 5, 1999, vs. Cincinnati); and touchdown passes—4 (January 6, 2002, vs. New Orleans).
STATISTICAL PLATEAUS: 300-yard passing games: 1999 (3), 2000 (6), 2001 (3). Total: 12.
MISCELLANEOUS: Regular-season record as starting NFL quarterback: 20-22 (.476). ... Postseason record as starting NFL quarterback: 0-1.

Year	Team	G	GS	Att.	Cmp.	Pct.	Yds.	TD	Int.	Avg.	Rat.	Att.	Yds.	Avg.	TD	TD	2pt.	Pts.
						PASSING							RUSHING				TOTALS	
1994	Calgary CFL	7	...	3	2	66.7	10	0	0	3.33	71.5	2	3	1.5	0	0	0	0
1995	Calgary CFL	18	...	364	230	63.2	3358	25	7	9.23	108.1	61	396	6.5	5	5	0	30
1996	Calgary CFL	18	...	537	315	58.7	4225	25	16	7.87	86.9	92	657	7.1	6	6	0	36
1998	Calgary CFL	18	...	554	348	62.8	4276	28	15	7.72	92.2	94	575	6.1	6	6	0	36
1999	San Francisco NFL	13	10	375	225	60.0	2544	11	11	6.78	77.9	45	231	5.1	2	2	0	12
2000	San Francisco NFL	16	16	561	‡355	63.3	4278	‡31	10	7.63	97.6	72	414	5.8	4	4	0	24
2001	San Francisco NFL	16	16	504	316	62.7	3538	32	12	7.02	94.8	72	254	3.5	5	5	0	30
CFL totals (4 years)		61	...	1458	895	61.4	11869	78	38	8.14	94.1	249	1631	6.6	17	17	0	102
NFL totals (3 years)		45	42	1440	896	62.2	10360	74	33	7.19	91.5	189	899	4.8	11	11	0	66
Pro totals (7 years)		106	...	2898	1791	61.8	22229	152	71	7.67	92.8	438	2530	5.8	28	28	0	168

GARDENER, DARYL   DT   DOLPHINS

PERSONAL: Born February 25, 1973, in Baltimore. ... 6-6/310. ... Full name: Daryl Ronald Gardener.
HIGH SCHOOL: Lawton (Okla.).
COLLEGE: Baylor.
TRANSACTIONS/CAREER NOTES: Selected by Miami Dolphins in first round (20th pick overall) of 1996 NFL draft. ... Signed by Dolphins (June 6, 1996). ... On injured reserve with back injury (December 4, 2001-remainder of season).
PRO STATISTICS: 1996—Recovered one fumble. 1997—Recovered one fumble. 1998—Intercepted one pass for minus one yard. 1999—Recovered one fumble for 33 yards.

Year	Team	G	GS	SACKS
1996	Miami NFL	16	12	1.0
1997	Miami NFL	16	16	1.5
1998	Miami NFL	16	16	1.0
1999	Miami NFL	16	15	5.0
2000	Miami NFL	10	10	2.5
2001	Miami NFL	8	8	4.0
Pro totals (6 years)		82	77	15.0

GARDNER, BARRY   LB   EAGLES

PERSONAL: Born December 13, 1976, in Harvey, Ill. ... 6-0/248. ... Full name: Barry Allan Gardner.
HIGH SCHOOL: Thornton (Harvey, Ill.).
COLLEGE: Northwestern.
TRANSACTIONS/CAREER NOTES: Selected by Philadelphia Eagles in second round (35th pick overall) of 1999 NFL draft. ... Signed by Eagles (July 25, 1999).
PLAYING EXPERIENCE: Philadelphia NFL, 1999-2001. ... Games/Games started: 1999 (16/5), 2000 (16/13), 2001 (16/0). Total: 48/18.
CHAMPIONSHIP GAME EXPERIENCE: Played in NFC championship game (2001 season).
PRO STATISTICS: 1999—Recovered one fumble for 20 yards. 2000—Credited with one sack.

GARDNER, ROD   WR   REDSKINS

PERSONAL: Born October 26, 1977, in Jacksonville, Fla. ... 6-2/216. ... Full name: Roderick F. Gardner.
HIGH SCHOOL: Raines (Jacksonville, Fla.).
COLLEGE: Clemson.
TRANSACTIONS/CAREER NOTES: Selected by Washington Redskins in first round (15th pick overall) of 2001 NFL draft. ... Signed by Redskins (August 2, 2001).
PRO STATISTICS: 2001—Rushed once for 16 yards and fumbled once.
SINGLE GAME HIGHS (regular season): Receptions—6 (December 23, 2001, vs. Chicago); yards—208 (October 21, 2001, vs. Carolina); and touchdown receptions—1 (December 2, 2001, vs. Dallas).
STATISTICAL PLATEAUS: 100-yard receiving games: 2001 (1).

			RECEIVING			
Year Team	G	GS	No.	Yds.	Avg.	TD
2001—Washington NFL	16	16	46	741	16.1	4

GARDOCKI, CHRIS   P   BROWNS

PERSONAL: Born February 7, 1970, in Stone Mountain, Ga. ... 6-1/200. ... Full name: Christopher Allen Gardocki.
HIGH SCHOOL: Redan (Stone Mountain, Ga.).
COLLEGE: Clemson.
TRANSACTIONS/CAREER NOTES: Selected after junior season by Chicago Bears in third round (78th pick overall) of 1991 NFL draft. ... Signed by Bears (June 24, 1991). ... On injured reserve with groin injury (August 27-November 27, 1991). ... Granted unconditional free agency (February 17, 1995). ... Signed by Indianapolis Colts (February 24, 1995). ... Granted unconditional free agency (February 12, 1999). ... Signed by Cleveland Browns (February 16, 1999).
CHAMPIONSHIP GAME EXPERIENCE: Played in AFC championship game (1995 season).
HONORS: Named kicker on THE SPORTING NEWS college All-America second team (1990). ... Named punter on THE SPORTING NEWS NFL All-Pro team (1996). ... Played in Pro Bowl (1996 season).
RECORDS: Holds NFL career record for most consecutive punts without a block—825.
PRO STATISTICS: 1992—Attempted three passes with one completion for 43 yards and recovered one fumble. 1993—Attempted two passes without a completion, fumbled once and recovered one fumble. 1995—Attempted one pass without a completion.

				PUNTING			
Year Team	G	No.	Yds.	Avg.	Net avg.	In. 20	Blk.
1991—Chicago NFL	4	0	0	0.0	.0	0	0
1992—Chicago NFL	16	79	3393	42.9	36.2	19	0
1993—Chicago NFL	16	80	3080	38.5	36.6	28	0
1994—Chicago NFL	16	76	2871	37.8	37.3	23	0
1995—Indianapolis NFL	16	63	2681	42.6	33.3	16	0
1996—Indianapolis NFL	16	68	3105	45.7	§39.0	23	0
1997—Indianapolis NFL	16	67	3034	45.3	36.2	18	0
1998—Indianapolis NFL	16	79	3583	45.4	37.1	23	0
1999—Cleveland NFL	16	§106	*4645	43.8	34.6	20	0
2000—Cleveland NFL	16	*108	*4919	45.5	37.3	25	0
2001—Cleveland NFL	16	*99	§4249	42.9	34.6	25	0
Pro totals (11 years)	164	825	35560	43.1	35.7	220	0

GARMON, KELVIN   G   COWBOYS

PERSONAL: Born October 26, 1976, in Fort Worth, Texas ... 6-2/329.
HIGH SCHOOL: Haltom (Fort Worth, Texas).
COLLEGE: Baylor.
TRANSACTIONS/CAREER NOTES: Selected by Dallas Cowboys in seventh round (243rd pick overall) of 1999 NFL draft. ... Signed by Cowboys (August 8, 1999). ... On non-football injury list with leg injury (August 31, 1999-entire season). ... Active for one game (2000); did not play.
PLAYING EXPERIENCE: Dallas NFL, 2001. ... Games/Games started: 2001 (16/16).
PRO STATISTICS: 2001—Recovered one fumble.

GARNER, CHARLIE   RB   RAIDERS

PERSONAL: Born February 13, 1972, in Falls Church, Va. ... 5-10/195.
HIGH SCHOOL: Jeb Stuart (Falls Church, Va.).
JUNIOR COLLEGE: Scottsdale (Ariz.) Community College.
COLLEGE: Tennessee.

TRANSACTIONS/CAREER NOTES: Selected by Philadelphia Eagles in second round (42nd pick overall) of 1994 NFL draft. ... Signed by Eagles (July 18, 1994). ... Granted free agency (February 14, 1997). ... Re-signed by Eagles (June 16, 1997). ... Granted unconditional free agency (February 13, 1998). ... Re-signed by Eagles (February 23, 1998). ... On injured reserve with rib injury (December 10, 1998-remainder of season). ... Released by Eagles (April 20, 1999). ... Signed by San Francisco 49ers (July 19, 1999). ... Granted unconditional free agency (March 2, 2001). ... Signed by Oakland Raiders (April 13, 2001).
HONORS: Played in Pro Bowl (2000 season).
SINGLE GAME HIGHS (regular season): Attempts—36 (September 24, 2000, vs. Dallas); yards—201 (September 24, 2000, vs. Dallas); and rushing touchdowns—3 (October 8, 1995, vs. Washington).
STATISTICAL PLATEAUS: 100-yard rushing games: 1994 (2), 1995 (1), 1997 (1), 1998 (1), 1999 (3), 2000 (3). Total: 11. ... 100-yard receiving games: 2000 (1).

			RUSHING				RECEIVING				KICKOFF RETURNS				TOTALS			
Year Team	G	GS	Att.	Yds.	Avg.	TD	No.	Yds.	Avg.	TD	No.	Yds.	Avg.	TD	TD	2pt.	Pts.	Fum.
1994—Philadelphia NFL	10	8	109	399	3.7	3	8	74	9.3	0	0	0	0.0	0	3	0	18	3
1995—Philadelphia NFL	15	2	108	588	*5.4	6	10	61	6.1	0	29	590	20.3	0	6	0	36	2
1996—Philadelphia NFL	15	1	66	346	5.2	1	14	92	6.6	0	6	117	19.5	0	1	0	6	1
1997—Philadelphia NFL	16	2	116	547	4.7	3	24	225	9.4	0	0	0	0.0	0	3	0	18	1
1998—Philadelphia NFL	10	3	96	381	4.0	4	19	110	5.8	0	0	0	0.0	0	4	0	24	1
1999—San Francisco NFL	16	15	241	1229	5.1	4	56	535	9.6	2	0	0	0.0	0	6	0	36	4
2000—San Francisco NFL	16	14	258	1142	4.4	7	68	647	9.5	3	0	0	0.0	0	10	0	60	4
2001—Oakland NFL	16	15	211	839	4.0	1	72	578	8.0	2	0	0	0.0	0	3	0	18	2
Pro totals (8 years)	114	60	1205	5471	4.5	29	271	2322	8.6	7	35	707	20.2	0	36	0	216	18

GARNES, SAM   S   JETS

PERSONAL: Born July 12, 1974, in Bronx, N.Y. ... 6-3/225. ... Full name: Sam Aaron Garnes.
HIGH SCHOOL: DeWitt Clinton (Bronx, N.Y.).
COLLEGE: Cincinnati.
TRANSACTIONS/CAREER NOTES: Selected by New York Giants in fifth round (136th pick overall) of 1997 NFL draft. ... Signed by Giants for 1997 season. ... Granted free agency (February 11, 2000). ... Re-signed by Giants (February 12, 2000). ... Released by Giants (February 28, 2002). ... Signed by New York Jets (March 5, 2002).
PRO STATISTICS: 1999—Credited with one sack. 2000—Credited with one sack.

			INTERCEPTIONS			
Year Team	G	GS	No.	Yds.	Avg.	TD
1997—New York Giants NFL	16	15	1	95	95.0	1
1998—New York Giants NFL	11	11	1	13	13.0	0
1999—New York Giants NFL	16	16	2	7	3.5	0
2000—New York Giants NFL	15	14	1	4	4.0	0
2001—New York Giants NFL	16	16	1	5	5.0	0
Pro totals (5 years)	74	72	6	124	20.7	1

GARNETT, WINFIELD   DL   VIKINGS

PERSONAL: Born July 24, 1976, in Harvey, Ill. ... 6-6/320.
HIGH SCHOOL: Thornton (Harvey, Ill.).
COLLEGE: Ohio State.
TRANSACTIONS/CAREER NOTES: Signed as non-drafted free agent by Jacksonville Jaguars (April 23, 1998). ... Released by Jaguars (August 25, 1998). ... Signed by Seattle Seahawks (July 8, 1999). ... Assigned by Seahawks to Barcelona Dragons in 1999 NFL Europe enhancement allocation program (February 18, 1999). ... Released by Seahawks (September 5, 1999). ... Signed by New Orleans Saints (March 3, 2000). ... Released by Saints (August 22, 2000). ... Signed by Minnesota Vikings (February 19, 2001). ... Assigned by Vikings to Amsterdam Admirals in 2001 NFL Europe enhancement allocation program (February 20, 2001).

Year Team	G	GS	SACKS
1999—Barcelona NFLE	...	...	2.0
2000—	Did not play.		
2001—Amsterdam NFLE	...	...	8.0
—Minnesota NFL	12	2	2.0
NFL Europe totals (2 years)	...	...	10.0
NFL totals (1 year)	12	2	2.0
Pro totals (3 years)	...	...	12.0

GARRETT, JASON   QB

PERSONAL: Born March 28, 1966, in Abington, Pa. ... 6-2/200. ... Full name: Jason Calvin Garrett. ... Son of Jim Garrett, scout, Dallas Cowboys; brother of John Garrett, wide receiver with Cincinnati Bengals (1989) and San Antonio Riders of World League (1991); and brother of Judd Garrett, running back with London of World League (1991-92).
HIGH SCHOOL: University (Chargin Falls, Ohio).
COLLEGE: Princeton (degree in history).
TRANSACTIONS/CAREER NOTES: Signed as non-drafted free agent by New Orleans Saints (1989). ... Released by Saints (August 30, 1989). ... Re-signed by Saints to developmental squad (September 6, 1989). ... Released by Saints (December 29, 1989). ... Re-signed by Saints for 1990 season. ... Released by Saints (September 3, 1990). ... Signed by WLAF (January 3, 1991). ... Selected by San Antonio Riders in first round (seventh quarterback) of 1991 WLAF positional draft. ... Signed by Ottawa Rough Riders of CFL (1991). ... Released by San Antonio Riders (March 3, 1992). ... Signed by Dallas Cowboys (March 23, 1992). ... Released by Cowboys (August 31, 1992). ... Re-signed by Cowboys to practice squad (September 1, 1992). ... Granted unconditional free agency (February 16, 1996). ... Re-signed by Cowboys (April 3, 1996). ... Granted unconditional free agency (February 14, 1997). ... Re-signed by Cowboys (April 8, 1997). ... Granted unconditional free agency (February 11, 2000). ... Signed by New York Giants (February 22, 2000). ... Released by Giants (February 28, 2002).
CHAMPIONSHIP GAME EXPERIENCE: Member of Cowboys for NFC championship game (1993-1995 seasons); inactive. ... Member of Super Bowl championship team (1993 and 1995 seasons). ... Played in NFC championship game (2000 season). ... Member of Giants for Super Bowl XXXV (2000 season); did not play.

PRO STATISTICS: W.L.: 1991—Fumbled twice. CFL: 1991—Fumbled once. NFL: 1993—Fumbled once. 1994—Recovered one fumble. 1998—Fumbled four times for minus 17 yards.
SINGLE GAME HIGHS (regular season): Attempts—33 (September 27, 1998, vs. Oakland); completions—18 (September 27, 1998, vs. Oakland); yards—311 (November 24, 1994, vs. Green Bay); and touchdown passes—2 (November 14, 1999, vs. Green Bay).
STATISTICAL PLATEAUS: 300-yard passing games: 1994 (1).
MISCELLANEOUS: Regular-season record as starting NFL quarterback: 6-3 (.667).

				PASSING							RUSHING				TOTALS		
Year Team	G	GS	Att.	Cmp.	Pct.	Yds.	TD	Int.	Avg.	Rat.	Att.	Yds.	Avg.	TD	TD	2pt.	Pts.
1991—San Antonio W.L.	5	3	113	66	58.4	609	3	3	5.39	71.0	7	7	1.0	0	0	0	0
—Ottawa CFL	13	0	3	2	66.7	28	0	0	9.33	96.5	0	0	0.0	0	0	0	0
1992—Dallas NFL..................									Did not play.								
1993—Dallas NFL..................	5	1	19	9	47.4	61	0	0	3.21	54.9	8	-8	-1.0	0	0	0	0
1994—Dallas NFL..................	2	1	31	16	51.6	315	2	1	10.16	95.5	3	-2	-0.7	0	0	0	0
1995—Dallas NFL..................	1	0	5	4	80.0	46	1	0	9.20	144.5	1	-1	-1.0	0	0	0	0
1996—Dallas NFL..................	1	0	3	3	100.0	44	0	0	14.67	118.8	0	0	0.0	0	0	0	0
1997—Dallas NFL..................	1	0	14	10	71.4	56	0	0	4.00	78.3	0	0	0.0	0	0	0	0
1998—Dallas NFL..................	8	5	158	91	57.6	1206	5	3	7.63	84.5	11	14	1.3	0	0	0	0
1999—Dallas NFL..................	5	2	64	32	50.0	314	3	1	4.91	73.3	6	12	2.0	0	0	0	0
2000—N.Y. Giants NFL............	2	0	0	0	0.0	0	0	0	0.0	...	4	-4	-1.0	0	0	0	0
2001—N.Y. Giants NFL............	15	0	0	0	0.0	0	0	0	0.0	...	0	0	0.0	0	0	0	0
W.L. totals (1 year)	5	3	113	66	58.4	609	3	3	5.39	71.0	7	7	1.0	0	0	0	0
CFL totals (1 year)	13	0	3	2	66.7	28	0	0	9.33	96.5	0	0	0.0	0	0	0	0
NFL totals (9 years)	40	9	294	165	56.1	2042	11	5	6.95	83.2	33	11	0.3	0	0	0	0
Pro totals (11 years)	58	12	410	233	56.8	2679	14	8	6.53	79.9	40	18	0.5	0	0	0	0

GARY, OLANDIS — RB — BRONCOS

PERSONAL: Born May 18, 1975, in Washington, D.C. ... 5-11/218. ... Full name: Olandis C. Gary.
HIGH SCHOOL: Riverdale Baptist (Upper Marlboro, Md.).
COLLEGE: Marshall, then Georgia.
TRANSACTIONS/CAREER NOTES: Selected by Denver Broncos in fourth round (127th pick overall) of 1999 NFL draft. ... Signed by Broncos (July 20, 1999). ... On injured reserve with knee injury (September 8, 2000-remainder of season). ... On injured reserve with broken leg (November 26, 2001-remainder of season). ... Granted free agency (March 1, 2002).
PRO STATISTICS: 1999—Recovered one fumble. 2001—Returned one kickoff for 18 yards.
SINGLE GAME HIGHS (regular season): Attempts—37 (October 17, 1999, vs. Green Bay); yards—185 (December 25, 1999, vs. Detroit); and rushing touchdowns—2 (November 7, 1999, vs. San Diego).
STATISTICAL PLATEAUS: 100-yard rushing games: 1999 (4).

			RUSHING				RECEIVING				TOTALS			
Year Team	G	GS	Att.	Yds.	Avg.	TD	No.	Yds.	Avg.	TD	TD	2pt.	Pts.	Fum.
1999—Denver NFL...............................	12	12	276	1159	4.2	7	21	159	7.6	0	7	†1	44	2
2000—Denver NFL...............................	1	0	13	80	6.2	0	3	10	3.3	0	0	0	0	0
2001—Denver NFL...............................	9	1	57	228	4.0	1	4	29	7.3	0	1	0	6	0
Pro totals (3 years)	22	13	346	1467	4.2	8	28	198	7.1	0	8	1	50	2

GARY, WILLIE — S — RAMS

PERSONAL: Born November 1, 1978, in Valdosta, Ga. ... 5-10/195. ... Full name: Willie Frank Gary.
HIGH SCHOOL: Valdosta (Ga.).
COLLEGE: Kentucky.
TRANSACTIONS/CAREER NOTES: Signed as non-drafted free agent by St. Louis Rams (May 3, 2001). ... Released by Rams (September 1, 2001). ... Re-signed by Rams to practice squad (September 11, 2001). ... Released by Rams (October 23, 2001). ... Re-signed by Rams to practice squad (October 29, 2001). ... Activated (November 24, 2001).
PLAYING EXPERIENCE: St. Louis NFL, 2001. ... Games/Games started: 2001 (7/0).
CHAMPIONSHIP GAME EXPERIENCE: Played in NFC championship game (2001 season). ... Played in Super Bowl XXXVI (2001 season).

GARZA, ROBERT — C — FALCONS

PERSONAL: Born March 26, 1979, in Rio Hondo, Texas. ... 6-2/296.
HIGH SCHOOL: Rio Hondo (Texas).
COLLEGE: Texas A&M-Kingsville.
TRANSACTIONS/CAREER NOTES: Selected by Atlanta Falcons in fourth round (99th pick overall) of 2001 NFL draft. ... Signed by Falcons (May 21, 2001).
PLAYING EXPERIENCE: Atlanta NFL, 2001. ... Games/Games started: 2001 (16/4).
PRO STATISTICS: 2001—Returned one kickoff for one yard.

GASH, SAM — FB

PERSONAL: Born March 7, 1969, in Hendersonville, N.C. ... 6-0/240. ... Full name: Samuel Lee Gash Jr. ... Cousin of Thane Gash, safety with Cleveland Browns (1988-90) and San Francisco 49ers (1992).
HIGH SCHOOL: Hendersonville (N.C.).
COLLEGE: Penn State (degree in liberal arts).
TRANSACTIONS/CAREER NOTES: Selected by New England Patriots in eighth round (205th pick overall) of 1992 NFL draft. ... Signed by Patriots (June 10, 1992). ... Granted free agency (February 17, 1995). ... Re-signed by Patriots (May 5, 1995). ... On injured reserve with knee injury (December 10, 1996-remainder of season). ... Granted unconditional free agency (February 13, 1998). ... Signed by Buffalo Bills (March 5, 1998).

... Released by Bills (April 14, 2000). ... Signed by Baltimore Ravens (August 7, 2000). ... Granted unconditional free agency (March 2, 2001). ... Re-signed by Ravens (June 11, 2001). ... Released by Ravens (February 28, 2002).
CHAMPIONSHIP GAME EXPERIENCE: Played in AFC championship game (2000 season). ... Member of Super Bowl championship team (2000 season).
HONORS: Played in Pro Bowl (1998 and 1999 seasons).
PRO STATISTICS: 1992—Recovered two fumbles. 1994—Returned one kickoff for nine yards and recovered one fumble. 1998—Returned three kickoffs for 41 yards. 1999—Returned one kickoff for 13 yards and recovered one fumble.
SINGLE GAME HIGHS (regular season): Attempts—15 (December 18, 1994, vs. Buffalo); yards—56 (December 18, 1994, vs. Buffalo); and rushing touchdowns—1 (September 19, 1993, vs. Seattle).

				RUSHING				RECEIVING				TOTALS		
Year Team	G	GS	Att.	Yds.	Avg.	TD	No.	Yds.	Avg.	TD	TD	2pt.	Pts.	Fum.
1992—New England NFL	15	0	5	7	1.4	1	0	0	0.0	0	1	0	6	1
1993—New England NFL	15	4	48	149	3.1	1	14	93	6.6	0	1	0	6	1
1994—New England NFL	13	6	30	86	2.9	0	9	61	6.8	0	0	0	0	1
1995—New England NFL	15	12	8	24	3.0	0	26	242	9.3	1	1	0	6	0
1996—New England NFL	14	9	8	15	1.9	0	33	276	8.4	2	2	1	14	0
1997—New England NFL	16	5	6	10	1.7	0	22	154	7.0	3	3	0	18	0
1998—Buffalo NFL	16	13	11	32	2.9	0	19	165	8.7	3	3	0	18	0
1999—Buffalo NFL	15	11	0	0	0.0	0	20	163	8.2	2	2	0	12	0
2000—Baltimore NFL	15	4	2	2	1.0	0	6	30	5.0	1	1	0	6	0
2001—Baltimore NFL	16	4	2	-1	-0.5	0	9	80	8.9	1	1	0	6	0
Pro totals (10 years)	150	68	120	324	2.7	2	158	1264	8.0	13	15	1	92	3

GAY, BENJAMIN   RB   COLTS

PERSONAL: Born February 28, 1980, in Houston. ... 6-1/227.
HIGH SCHOOL: Spring (Houston).
JUNIOR COLLEGE: Garden City Community College.
COLLEGE: Baylor.
TRANSACTIONS/CAREER NOTES: Signed as non-drafted free agent by Cleveland Browns (July 20, 2001). ... Claimed on waivers by Indianapolis Colts (April 30, 2002).
PRO STATISTICS: 2001—Recovered one fumble.
SINGLE GAME HIGHS (regular season): Attempts—18 (November 18, 2001, vs. Baltimore); yards—56 (November 18, 2001, vs. Baltimore); and rushing touchdowns—1 (November 18, 2001, vs. Baltimore).

			RUSHING				RECEIVING				KICKOFF RETURNS				TOTALS			
Year Team	G	GS	Att.	Yds.	Avg.	TD	No.	Yds.	Avg.	TD	No.	Yds.	Avg.	TD	TD	2pt.	Pts.	Fum.
2001—Cleveland NFL	16	0	51	172	3.4	1	4	11	2.8	0	23	513	22.3	0	1	0	6	4

GAYLOR, TREVOR   WR   CHARGERS

PERSONAL: Born November 3, 1977, in St. Louis. ... 6-3/195. ... Full name: Trevor Alexander Gaylor.
HIGH SCHOOL: Hazelwood (Mo.) West.
COLLEGE: Miami of Ohio.
TRANSACTIONS/CAREER NOTES: Selected by San Diego Chargers in fourth round (111th pick overall) of 2000 NFL draft. ... Signed by Chargers (July 20, 2000).
PRO STATISTICS: 2000—Recovered one fumble for 13 yards.
SINGLE GAME HIGHS (regular season): Receptions—5 (December 30, 2001, vs. Seattle); yards—84 (December 30, 2001, vs. Seattle); and touchdown receptions—1 (October 1, 2000, vs. St. Louis).

			RECEIVING			
Year Team	G	GS	No.	Yds.	Avg.	TD
2000—San Diego NFL	14	2	13	182	14.0	1
2001—San Diego NFL	7	3	14	217	15.5	0
Pro totals (2 years)	21	5	27	399	14.8	1

GBAJA-BIAMILA, KABEER   DE   PACKERS

PERSONAL: Born September 24, 1977, in Los Angeles. ... 6-4/253. ... Full name: Muhammed-Kabeer Olarewaja Gbaja-Biamila.
HIGH SCHOOL: Crenshaw (Los Angeles).
COLLEGE: San Diego State.
TRANSACTIONS/CAREER NOTES: Selected by Green Bay Packers in fifth round (149th pick overall) of 2000 NFL draft. ... Signed by Packers (July 17, 2000). ... Released by Packers (August 27, 2000). ... Re-signed by Packers to practice squad (August 28, 2000). ... Activated (October 10, 2000).
PRO STATISTICS: 2001—Recovered one fumble.

Year Team	G	GS	SACKS
2000—Green Bay NFL	7	0	1.5
2001—Green Bay NFL	16	0	13.5
Pro totals (2 years)	23	0	15.0

GEASON, COREY   TE   STEELERS

PERSONAL: Born August 12, 1975, in St. James, La. ... 6-4/270.
HIGH SCHOOL: St. James (La.).
COLLEGE: Tulane.

TRANSACTIONS/CAREER NOTES: Signed as non-drafted free agent by Dallas Cowboys (April 21, 1998). ... Released by Cowboys (August 24, 1998). ... Signed by Tampa Bay Buccaneers (July 14, 1999). ... Released by Buccaneers (September 5, 1999). ... Signed by Pittsburgh Steelers to practice squad (December 21, 1999). ... On injured reserve with knee injury (November 7, 2000-remainder of season). ... Released by Steelers (September 2, 2001). ... Re-signed by Steelers (November 21, 2001).
PLAYING EXPERIENCE: Pittsburgh NFL, 2000 and 2001. ... Games/Games started: 2000 (9/3), 2001 (7/0). Total: 16/3.
CHAMPIONSHIP GAME EXPERIENCE: Member of Steelers for AFC championship game (2001 season); inactive.
PRO STATISTICS: 2000—Caught three passes for 66 yards.
SINGLE GAME HIGHS (regular season): Receptions—1 (November 5, 2000, vs. Tennessee); yards—36 (September 24, 2000, vs. Tennessee); and touchdown receptions—0.

GEORGE, EDDIE   RB   TITANS

PERSONAL: Born September 24, 1973, in Philadelphia. ... 6-3/240. ... Full name: Edward Nathan George.
HIGH SCHOOL: Abington (Philadelphia), then Fork Union (Va.) Military Academy.
COLLEGE: Ohio State.
TRANSACTIONS/CAREER NOTES: Selected by Houston Oilers in first round (14th pick overall) of 1996 NFL draft. ... Signed by Oilers (July 20, 1996). ... Oilers franchise moved to Tennessee for 1997 season. ... Oilers franchise renamed Tennessee Titans for 1999 season (December 26, 1998). ... On physically unable to perform list with toe injury (July 28-31, 2001).
CHAMPIONSHIP GAME EXPERIENCE: Played in AFC championship game (1999 season). ... Played in Super Bowl XXXIV (1999 season).
HONORS: Heisman Trophy winner (1995). ... Maxwell Award winner (1995). ... Doak Walker Award winner (1995). ... Named running back on THE SPORTING NEWS college All-America first team (1995). ... Named NFL Rookie of the Year by THE SPORTING NEWS (1996). ... Played in Pro Bowl (1997-2000 seasons).
PRO STATISTICS: 1996—Recovered one fumble. 1998—Recovered five fumbles. 1999—Recovered one fumble. 2000—Recovered two fumbles. 2001—Recovered three fumbles.
SINGLE GAME HIGHS (regular season): Attempts—36 (November 19, 2000, vs. Cleveland); yards—216 (August 31, 1997, vs. Oakland); and rushing touchdowns—3 (December 17, 2000, vs. Cleveland).
STATISTICAL PLATEAUS: 100-yard rushing games: 1996 (4), 1997 (8), 1998 (6), 1999 (5), 2000 (6), 2001 (1). Total: 30. ... 100-yard receiving games: 2000 (1).

				RUSHING				RECEIVING				TOTALS		
Year Team	G	GS	Att.	Yds.	Avg.	TD	No.	Yds.	Avg.	TD	TD	2pt.	Pts.	Fum.
1996—Houston NFL	16	16	335	1368	4.1	8	23	182	7.9	0	8	0	48	3
1997—Tennessee NFL	16	16	357	1399	3.9	6	7	44	6.3	1	7	1	44	4
1998—Tennessee NFL	16	16	348	1294	3.7	5	37	310	8.4	1	6	1	38	7
1999—Tennessee NFL	16	16	320	1304	4.1	9	47	458	9.7	4	13	0	78	5
2000—Tennessee NFL	16	16	*403	1509	3.7	14	50	453	9.1	2	16	0	96	5
2001—Tennessee NFL	16	16	315	939	3.0	5	37	279	7.5	0	5	0	30	8
Pro totals (6 years)	96	96	2078	7813	3.8	47	201	1726	8.6	8	55	2	334	32

GEORGE, JEFF   QB

PERSONAL: Born December 8, 1967, in Indianapolis. ... 6-4/215. ... Full name: Jeffrey Scott George.
HIGH SCHOOL: Warren Central (Indianapolis).
COLLEGE: Purdue, then Illinois (degree in speech communications, 1991).
TRANSACTIONS/CAREER NOTES: Signed after junior season by Indianapolis Colts (April 20, 1990). ... Selected officially by Colts in first round (first pick overall) of 1990 NFL draft. ... On reserve/did not report list (July 23-August 20, 1993). ... Traded by Colts to Atlanta Falcons for first- (LB Trev Alberts) and third-round (OT Jason Mathews) picks in 1994 draft and a first-round pick (WR Marvin Harrison) in 1996 draft (March 24, 1994). ... Designated by Falcons as transition player (February 16, 1996). ... Released by Falcons (October 22, 1996). ... Signed by Oakland Raiders (February 15, 1997). ... Granted unconditional free agency (February 12, 1999). ... Signed by Minnesota Vikings (April 6, 1999). ... Granted unconditional free agency (February 11, 2000). ... Signed by Washington Redskins (April 11, 2000). ... Released by Redskins (September 26, 2001).
PRO STATISTICS: 1990—Fumbled four times and recovered two fumbles. 1991—Fumbled eight times and recovered two fumbles for minus four yards. 1992—Fumbled six times and recovered one fumble for minus two yards. 1993—Fumbled four times. 1994—Led league with 12 fumbles and recovered six fumbles for minus 12 yards. 1995—Fumbled six times and recovered two fumbles for minus 15 yards. 1996—Fumbled three times and recovered two fumbles for minus 24 yards. 1997—Fumbled seven times and recovered three fumbles for minus 14 yards. 1998—Fumbled seven times and recovered one fumble for minus six yards. 1999—Fumbled eight times and recovered two fumbles. 2000—Fumbled three times and recovered one fumble for minus three yards. 2001—Fumbled twice and recovered one fumble.
SINGLE GAME HIGHS (regular season): Attempts—59 (November 7, 1993, vs. Washington); completions—37 (November 7, 1993, vs. Washington); yards—386 (September 17, 1995, vs. New Orleans); and touchdown passes—4 (November 28, 1999, vs. San Diego).
STATISTICAL PLATEAUS: 300-yard passing games: 1991 (2), 1992 (3), 1993 (2), 1994 (2), 1995 (3), 1997 (2), 1998 (1), 1999 (2). Total: 17.
MISCELLANEOUS: Regular-season record as starting NFL quarterback: 46-78 (.371). ... Postseason record as starting NFL quarterback: 1-2 (.333).

			PASSING							RUSHING				TOTALS		
Year Team	G	GS	Att.	Cmp.	Pct.	Yds.	TD	Int.	Avg.	Rat.	Att.	Yds.	Avg.	TD	TD	2pt.	Pts.
1990—Indianapolis NFL	13	12	334	181	54.2	2152	16	13	6.44	73.8	11	2	0.2	1	1	0	6
1991—Indianapolis NFL	16	16	485	292	60.2	2910	10	12	6.00	73.8	16	36	2.3	0	0	0	0
1992—Indianapolis NFL	10	10	306	167	54.6	1963	7	15	6.42	61.5	14	26	1.9	1	1	0	6
1993—Indianapolis NFL	13	11	407	234	57.5	2526	8	6	6.21	76.3	13	39	3.0	0	0	0	0
1994—Atlanta NFL	16	16	524	322	61.5	3734	23	18	7.13	83.3	30	66	2.2	0	0	0	0
1995—Atlanta NFL	16	16	557	336	60.3	4143	24	11	7.44	89.5	27	17	0.6	0	0	0	0
1996—Atlanta NFL	3	3	99	56	56.6	698	3	3	7.05	76.1	5	10	2.0	0	0	0	0
1997—Oakland NFL	16	16	521	290	55.7	*3917	§22	9	7.52	91.2	17	44	2.6	0	0	0	0
1998—Oakland NFL	8	7	169	93	55.0	1186	4	5	7.02	72.7	8	2	0.3	0	0	0	0
1999—Minnesota NFL	12	10	329	191	58.1	2816	23	12	8.56	94.2	16	41	2.6	0	0	0	0
2000—Washington NFL	8	5	194	113	58.2	1389	7	6	7.16	79.6	7	24	3.4	0	0	0	0
2001—Washington NFL	2	2	42	23	54.8	168	0	3	4.00	34.6	4	0	0.0	0	0	0	0
Pro totals (12 years)	133	124	3967	2298	57.9	27602	154	113	6.96	80.4	168	307	1.8	2	2	0	12

GERMAN, JAMMI   WR

PERSONAL: Born July 4, 1974, in Fort Myers, Fla. ... 6-1/191. ... Full name: Jammi Darnell German.
HIGH SCHOOL: Fort Myers (Fla.).
COLLEGE: Miami (Fla.).
TRANSACTIONS/CAREER NOTES: Selected by Atlanta Falcons in third round (74th pick overall) of 1998 NFL draft. ... Signed by Falcons (July 8, 1998). ... On injured reserve with knee injury (November 10, 1998-remainder of season). ... Released by Falcons (September 5, 1999). ... Re-signed by Falcons to practice squad (September 7, 1999). ... Activated (September 14, 1999). ... On injured reserve with ankle injury (December 13, 2000-remainder of season). ... Granted free agency (March 2, 2001). ... Re-signed by Falcons (April 5, 2001). ... Claimed on waivers by Cleveland Browns (August 4, 2001). ... On injured reserve with knee injury (December 6, 2001-remainder of season). ... Granted unconditional free agency (March 1, 2002).
PLAYING EXPERIENCE: Atlanta NFL, 1998-2000; Cleveland NFL, 2001. ... Games/Games started: 1998 (6/0), 1999 (14/0), 2000 (9/0), 2001 (6/0). Total: 35/0.
PRO STATISTICS: 1999—Caught 12 passes for 219 yards and three touchdowns and returned one kickoff for one yard. 2000—Caught one pass for 10 yards. 2001—Caught seven passes for 65 yards.
SINGLE GAME HIGHS (regular season): Receptions—3 (November 11, 2001, vs. Pittsburgh); yards—62 (October 10, 1999, vs. New Orleans); and touchdown receptions—2 (December 19, 1999, vs. Tennessee).

GERMANY, REGGIE   WR   BILLS

PERSONAL: Born March 19, 1978, in Hazelwood, Mo. ... 6-1/180.
HIGH SCHOOL: Hazelwood East (St. Louis).
COLLEGE: Ohio State.
TRANSACTIONS/CAREER NOTES: Selected by Buffalo Bills in seventh round (214th pick overall) of 2001 NFL draft. ... Signed by Bills (June 11, 2001).
PRO STATISTICS: 2001—Recovered one fumble.
SINGLE GAME HIGHS (regular season): Receptions—4 (November 11, 2001, vs. New England); yards—69 (November 11, 2001, vs. New England); and touchdown receptions—0.

			RECEIVING			
Year Team	G	GS	No.	Yds.	Avg.	TD
2001—Buffalo NFL	16	1	12	203	16.9	0

GIBSON, AARON   OT   COWBOYS

PERSONAL: Born September 27, 1977, in Indianapolis. ... 6-6/380.
HIGH SCHOOL: Decatur Central (Indianapolis).
COLLEGE: Wisconsin.
TRANSACTIONS/CAREER NOTES: Selected by Detroit Lions in first round (27th pick overall) of 1999 NFL draft. ... Signed by Lions (July 24, 1999). ... On injured reserve with shoulder injury (August 31, 1999-entire season). ... On injured reserve with shoulder injury (December 4, 2000-remainder of season). ... Claimed on waivers by Dallas Cowboys (October 31, 2001).
PLAYING EXPERIENCE: Detroit NFL, 2000; Detroit (6)-Dallas (1) NFL, 2001. ... Games/Games started: 2000 (10/10), 2001 (Det-6/5; Dal.-1/0; Total: 7/5). Total: 17/15.
HONORS: Named offensive tackle on THE SPORTING NEWS college All-America second team (1998).

GIBSON, DAMON   WR/KR   JAGUARS

PERSONAL: Born February 25, 1975, in Houston. ... 5-9/184.
HIGH SCHOOL: Forest Brook (Houston).
COLLEGE: Iowa.
TRANSACTIONS/CAREER NOTES: Signed as non-drafted free agent by Cincinnati Bengals (April 20, 1998). ... Selected by Cleveland Browns from Bengals in 1999 NFL expansion draft (February 9, 1999). ... Released by Browns (September 28, 1999). ... Selected by Scottish Claymores in 2000 NFL Europe draft (February 22, 2000). ... Signed by Jacksonville Jaguars (June 29, 2000). ... Released by Jaguars (August 22, 2000). ... Re-signed by Jaguars (June 29, 2001).
PRO STATISTICS: 1998—Rushed once for nine yards and recovered one fumble. 2001—Rushed twice for 19 yards and recovered one fumble.
SINGLE GAME HIGHS (regular season): Receptions—3 (November 1, 1998, vs. Denver); yards—76 (October 18, 1998, vs. Tennessee); and touchdown receptions—1 (November 8, 1998, vs. Jacksonville).

			RECEIVING				PUNT RETURNS				KICKOFF RETURNS				TOTALS			
Year Team	G	GS	No.	Yds.	Avg.	TD	No.	Yds.	Avg.	TD	No.	Yds.	Avg.	TD	TD	2pt.	Pts.	Fum.
1998—Cincinnati NFL	16	0	19	258	13.6	3	27	218	8.1	1	17	372	21.9	0	4	0	24	3
1999—Cleveland NFL	2	0	0	0	0.0	0	2	9	4.5	0	0	0	0.0	0	0	0	0	0
2000—Scottish NFLE	...	...	23	378	16.4	3	22	328	14.9	0	13	260	20.0	0	0	0	0	0
2001—Jacksonville NFL	16	0	2	13	6.5	0	38	333	8.8	0	26	511	19.7	0	0	0	0	3
NFL Europe totals (1 year)	...	...	23	378	16.4	3	22	328	14.9	0	13	260	20.0	0	0	0	0	0
NFL totals (3 years)	34	0	21	271	12.9	3	67	560	8.4	1	43	883	20.5	0	4	0	24	6
Pro totals (4 years)	...	...	44	649	14.8	6	89	888	10.0	1	56	1143	20.4	0	4	0	24	6

GIBSON, DAVID   S   BUCCANEERS

PERSONAL: Born November 5, 1977, in Santa Ana, Calif. ... 6-1/210.
HIGH SCHOOL: Mater Dei (Santa, Ana, Calif.).
COLLEGE: Southern California.
TRANSACTIONS/CAREER NOTES: Selected by Tampa Bay Buccaneers in sixth round (193rd pick overall) of 2000 NFL draft. ... Signed by Buccaneers (July 10, 2000).
PLAYING EXPERIENCE: Tampa Bay NFL, 2000 and 2001. ... Games/Games started: 2000 (9/0), 2001 (13/0). Total: 22/0.

GIBSON, DERRICK — S — RAIDERS

PERSONAL: Born March 22, 1979, in Miami. ... 6-2/215.
HIGH SCHOOL: Killian (Miami).
COLLEGE: Florida State.
TRANSACTIONS/CAREER NOTES: Selected by Oakland Raiders in first round (28th pick overall) of 2001 NFL draft. ... Signed by Raiders (July 21, 2001).

			INTERCEPTIONS		
Year Team	G	GS	No.	Yds.	Avg.	TD
2001—Oakland NFL	16	0	1	9	9.0	0

GIBSON, OLIVER — DT — BENGALS

PERSONAL: Born March 15, 1972, in Chicago. ... 6-2/315. ... Full name: Oliver Donnovan Gibson. ... Cousin of Godfrey Myles, linebacker with Dallas Cowboys (1991-96).
HIGH SCHOOL: Romeoville (Ill.).
COLLEGE: Notre Dame (degree in economics, 1994).
TRANSACTIONS/CAREER NOTES: Selected by Pittsburgh Steelers in fourth round (120th pick overall) of 1995 NFL draft. ... Signed by Steelers (July 18, 1995). ... Granted free agency (February 13, 1998). ... Re-signed by Steelers (June 9, 1998). ... Granted unconditional free agency (February 12, 1999). ... Signed by Cincinnati Bengals (March 9, 1999).
CHAMPIONSHIP GAME EXPERIENCE: Member of Steelers for AFC championship game (1995 season); inactive. ... Played in AFC championship game (1997 season).
HONORS: Earned first-team All-Independent honors from THE SPORTING NEWS (1994).
PRO STATISTICS: 1995—Returned one kickoff for 10 yards. 1997—Recovered one fumble. 1998—Returned one kickoff for nine yards. 1999—Recovered one fumble. 2001—Recovered one fumble.

Year Team	G	GS	SACKS
1995—Pittsburgh NFL	12	0	0.0
1996—Pittsburgh NFL	16	0	2.5
1997—Pittsburgh NFL	16	0	1.0
1998—Pittsburgh NFL	16	0	2.0
1999—Cincinnati NFL	16	16	4.5
2000—Cincinnati NFL	16	16	4.0
2001—Cincinnati NFL	16	16	3.0
Pro totals (7 years)	**108**	**48**	**17.0**

GILBERT, SEAN — DT — PANTHERS

PERSONAL: Born April 10, 1970, in Aliquippa, Pa. ... 6-5/318.
HIGH SCHOOL: Aliquippa (Pa.).
COLLEGE: Pittsburgh.
TRANSACTIONS/CAREER NOTES: Selected after junior season by Los Angeles Rams in first round (third pick overall) of 1992 NFL draft. ... Signed by Rams (July 28, 1992). ... Designated by Rams as transition player (February 25, 1993). ... Rams franchise moved to St. Louis (April 12, 1995). ... Traded by Rams to Washington Redskins for first-round pick (RB Lawrence Phillips) in 1996 draft (April 8, 1996). ... Designated by Redskins as franchise player (February 12, 1997). ... Sat out 1997 season due to contract dispute. ... Designated by Redskins as franchise player (February 11, 1998). ... Tendered offer sheet by Carolina Panthers (March 24, 1998). ... Redskins declined to match offer (April 21, 1998).
HONORS: Played in Pro Bowl (1993 season).
PRO STATISTICS: 1992—Recovered one fumble. 1994—Credited with one safety. 1995—Recovered one fumble. 1999—Intercepted one pass for four yards. 2000—Intercepted one pass for no yards and recovered one fumble.

Year Team	G	GS	SACKS
1992—Los Angeles Rams NFL	16	16	5.0
1993—Los Angeles Rams NFL	16	16	10.5
1994—Los Angeles Rams NFL	14	14	3.0
1995—St. Louis NFL	14	14	5.5
1996—Washington NFL	16	16	3.0
1997—Washington NFL		Did not play.	
1998—Carolina NFL	16	16	6.0
1999—Carolina NFL	16	16	2.5
2000—Carolina NFL	15	15	4.0
2001—Carolina NFL	9	9	2.0
Pro totals (9 years)	**132**	**132**	**41.5**

GILDON, JASON — LB — STEELERS

PERSONAL: Born July 31, 1972, in Altus, Okla. ... 6-4/250. ... Full name: Jason Larue Gildon. ... Related to Wendall Gaines, guard with Arizona Cardinals (1995).
HIGH SCHOOL: Altus (Okla.).
COLLEGE: Oklahoma State.
TRANSACTIONS/CAREER NOTES: Selected by Pittsburgh Steelers in third round (88th pick overall) of 1994 NFL draft. ... Signed by Steelers (July 15, 1994). ... Granted free agency (February 14, 1997). ... Re-signed by Steelers (July 21, 1997). ... Granted unconditional free agency (February 13, 1998). ... Re-signed by Steelers (April 7, 1998). ... Designated by Steelers as franchise player (February 21, 2002). ... Re-signed by Steelers (February 25, 2002).
CHAMPIONSHIP GAME EXPERIENCE: Played in AFC championship game (1994, 1995, 1997 and 2001 seasons). ... Played in Super Bowl XXX (1995 season).
HONORS: Played in Pro Bowl (2000 season).
PRO STATISTICS: 1995—Recovered one fumble. 1997—Recovered two fumbles for 32 yards and one touchdown. 1998—Recovered one fumble. 2000—Recovered four fumbles for 22 yards and one touchdown. 2001—Intercepted one pass for no yards and recovered two fumbles for 27 yards and one touchdown.

Year—Team	G	GS	SACKS
1994—Pittsburgh NFL	16	1	2.0
1995—Pittsburgh NFL	16	0	3.0
1996—Pittsburgh NFL	14	13	7.0
1997—Pittsburgh NFL	16	16	5.0
1998—Pittsburgh NFL	16	16	11.0
1999—Pittsburgh NFL	16	16	8.5
2000—Pittsburgh NFL	16	16	13.5
2001—Pittsburgh NFL	16	16	12.0
Pro totals (8 years)	126	94	62.0

GILMORE, BRYAN — WR — CARDINALS

PERSONAL: Born July 21, 1978, in Lufkin, Texas. ... 6-0/194.
HIGH SCHOOL: Lufkin (Texas).
COLLEGE: Midwestern State (Texas).
TRANSACTIONS/CAREER NOTES: Signed as non-drafted free agent by Arizona Cardinals (April 17, 2000). ... Released by Cardinals (August 27, 2000). ... Re-signed by Cardinals to practice squad (August 28, 2000). ... Activated (December 15, 2000). ... Assigned by Cardinals to Barcelona Dragons in 2001 NFL Europe enhancement allocation program (February 19, 2001). ... Released by Cardinals (September 2, 2001). ... Re-signed by Cardinals to practice squad (September 3, 2001). ... Activated (November 29, 2001).
PRO STATISTICS: NFLE: 2001—Rushed seven times for 30 yards and one touchdown.

			RECEIVING			
Year—Team	G	GS	No.	Yds.	Avg.	TD
2000—Arizona NFL	1	0	0	0	0.0	0
2001—Barcelona NFLE	...	...	30	403	13.4	5
—Arizona NFL	2	0	0	0	0.0	0
NFL Europe totals (1 year)	...	...	30	403	13.4	5
NFL totals (2 years)	3	0	0	0	0.0	0
Pro totals (3 years)	...	...	30	403	13.4	5

GIZZI, CHRIS — LB — PACKERS

PERSONAL: Born March 8, 1975, in Cleveland. ... 6-0/235.
HIGH SCHOOL: St. Ignatius (Cleveland).
COLLEGE: Air Force.
TRANSACTIONS/CAREER NOTES: Signed as non-drafted free agent by Denver Broncos (April 23, 1998). ... On military reserved list (June 10, 1998-entire season). ... On military reserved list (August 31, 1999-entire season). ... Claimed on waivers by Green Bay Packers (August 28, 2000). ... Released by Packers (October 3, 2000). ... Re-signed by Packers to practice squad (October 5, 2000). ... Activated (October 9, 2000). ... On injured reserve with back injury (December 19, 2001-remainder of season).
PLAYING EXPERIENCE: Green Bay NFL, 2000 and 2001. ... Games/Games started: 2000 (11/0), 2001 (12/1). Total: 23/1.

GLEASON, STEVE — DB — SAINTS

PERSONAL: Born March 19, 1977, in Spokane, Wash. ... 5-11/215. ... Full name: Stephen Gleason.
HIGH SCHOOL: Gonzaga (Wash.) Prep.
COLLEGE: Washington State.
TRANSACTIONS/CAREER NOTES: Signed as non-drafted free agent by Indianapolis Colts (April 16, 2000). ... Released by Colts (August 27, 2000). ... Signed by New Orleans Saints to practice squad (November 21, 2000). ... Activated (December 3, 2000). ... Released by Saints (September 2, 2001). ... Re-signed by Saints (November 23, 2001).
PLAYING EXPERIENCE: New Orleans NFL, 2000 and 2001. ... Games/Games started: 2000 (3/0), 2001 (7/0). Total: 10/0.
PRO STATISTICS: 2001—Recovered one fumble.

GLENN, AARON — CB/KR — TEXANS

PERSONAL: Born July 16, 1972, in Humble, Texas. ... 5-9/185. ... Full name: Aaron DeVon Glenn.
HIGH SCHOOL: Nimitz (Irving, Texas).
JUNIOR COLLEGE: Navarro College (Texas).
COLLEGE: Texas A&M.
TRANSACTIONS/CAREER NOTES: Selected by New York Jets in first round (12th pick overall) of 1994 NFL draft. ... Signed by Jets (July 21, 1994). ... Selected by Houston Texans from Jets in NFL expansion draft (February 18, 2002).
CHAMPIONSHIP GAME EXPERIENCE: Played in AFC championship game (1998 season).
HONORS: Named defensive back on THE SPORTING NEWS college All-America first team (1993). ... Played in Pro Bowl (1997 season). ... Named to play in Pro Bowl (1998 season); replaced by Charles Woodson due to injury.
PRO STATISTICS: 1994—Recovered one fumble. 1995—Recovered one fumble. 1998—Recovered one fumble and returned a missed field goal attempt 104 yards for a touchdown. 1999—Recovered one fumble. 2001—Returned two punts for six yards and recovered two fumbles for two yards.

			INTERCEPTIONS				KICKOFF RETURNS				TOTALS		
Year—Team	G	GS	No.	Yds.	Avg.	TD	No.	Yds.	Avg.	TD	2pt.	Pts.	Fum.
1994—New York Jets NFL	15	15	0	0	0.0	0	27	582	21.6	0	0	0	2
1995—New York Jets NFL	16	16	1	17	17.0	0	1	12	12.0	0	0	0	0
1996—New York Jets NFL	16	16	4	113	28.3	†2	1	6	6.0	0	2	0	12	0
1997—New York Jets NFL	16	16	1	5	5.0	0	28	741	§26.5	▲1	1	0	6	1
1998—New York Jets NFL	13	13	6	23	3.8	0	24	585	24.4	0	1	0	6	1
1999—New York Jets NFL	16	16	3	20	6.7	0	27	601	22.3	0	0	0	0	0
2000—New York Jets NFL	16	16	4	34	8.5	0	3	51	17.0	0	0	0	0	0
2001—New York Jets NFL	13	12	5	82	16.4	1	0	0	0.0	0	1	0	6	1
Pro totals (8 years)	121	120	24	294	12.3	3	111	2578	23.2	1	5	0	30	5

GLENN, JASON — LB — JETS

PERSONAL: Born August 20, 1979, in Aldine, Texas. ... 6-0/231.
HIGH SCHOOL: Nimitz (Aldine, Texas).
COLLEGE: Texas A&M.
TRANSACTIONS/CAREER NOTES: Selected by Detroit Lions in sixth round (173rd pick overall) of 2001 NFL draft. ... Signed by Lions (July 20, 2001). ... Claimed on waivers by New York Jets (September 3, 2001).
PLAYING EXPERIENCE: New York Jets NFL, 2001. ... Games/Games started: 2001 (15/0).
PRO STATISTICS: 2001—Ran four yards with blocked punt for a touchdown.

GLENN, TARIK — OT — COLTS

PERSONAL: Born May 25, 1976, in Cleveland. ... 6-5/332.
HIGH SCHOOL: Bishop O'Dowd (Oakland).
COLLEGE: California.
TRANSACTIONS/CAREER NOTES: Selected by Indianapolis Colts in first round (19th pick overall) of 1997 NFL draft. ... Signed by Colts (August 11, 1997). ... Granted free agency (March 1, 2002). ... Re-signed by Colts (March 15, 2002).
PLAYING EXPERIENCE: Indianapolis NFL, 1997-2001. ... Games/Games started: 1997 (16/16), 1998 (16/16), 1999 (16/16), 2000 (16/16), 2001 (16/16). Total: 80/80.
HONORS: Named offensive tackle on THE SPORTING NEWS college All-America second team (1996).
PRO STATISTICS: 1997—Caught one pass for three yards and recovered one fumble.

GLENN, TERRY — WR — PACKERS

PERSONAL: Born July 23, 1974, in Columbus, Ohio. ... 5-11/195.
HIGH SCHOOL: Brookhaven (Columbus, Ohio).
COLLEGE: Ohio State.
TRANSACTIONS/CAREER NOTES: Selected after junior season by New England Patriots in first round (seventh pick overall) of 1996 NFL draft. ... Signed by Patriots (July 12, 1996). ... On injured reserve with fractured ankle (December 18, 1998-remainder of season). ... On suspended list for violating league substance abuse policy (Sepetmber 9-October 7, 2001). ... On reserve/left squad list (August 15-September 13, 2001). ... Traded by Patriots to Green Bay Packers for fourth-round pick (DE Jarvis Green) in 2002 draft and conditional pick in 2003 draft (March 8, 2002).
CHAMPIONSHIP GAME EXPERIENCE: Played in AFC championship game (1996 season). ... Played in Super Bowl XXXI (1996 season).
HONORS: Fred Biletnikoff Award winner (1995). ... Named wide receiver on THE SPORTING NEWS college All-America first team (1995).
RECORDS: Holds NFL single-season record for most receptions by a rookie—90 (1996).
PRO STATISTICS: 1999—Recovered one fumble.
SINGLE GAME HIGHS (regular season): Receptions—13 (October 3, 1999, vs. Cleveland); yards—214 (October 3, 1999, vs. Cleveland); and touchdown receptions—1 (October 14, 2001, vs. San Diego).
STATISTICAL PLATEAUS: 100-yard receiving games: 1996 (2), 1997 (1), 1998 (4), 1999 (4), 2000 (1), 2001 (1). Total: 13.

			RUSHING				RECEIVING				TOTALS		
Year Team	G	GS	Att.	Yds.	Avg.	TD	No.	Yds.	Avg.	TD	TD	2pt.	Pts.	Fum.
1996—New England NFL	15	15	5	42	8.4	0	90	1132	12.6	6	6	0	36	1
1997—New England NFL	9	9	0	0	0.0	0	27	431	16.0	2	2	0	12	1
1998—New England NFL	10	9	2	-1	-0.5	0	50	792	15.8	3	3	0	18	0
1999—New England NFL	14	13	0	0	0.0	0	69	1147	16.6	4	4	0	24	2
2000—New England NFL	16	15	4	39	9.8	0	79	963	12.2	6	6	0	36	0
2001—New England NFL	4	1	0	0	0.0	0	14	204	14.6	1	1	0	6	0
Pro totals (6 years)	68	62	11	80	7.3	0	329	4669	14.2	22	22	0	132	4

GLOVER, La'ROI — DT — COWBOYS

PERSONAL: Born July 4, 1974, in San Diego. ... 6-2/285. ... Full name: La'Roi Damon Glover. ... Name pronounced la-ROY.
HIGH SCHOOL: Point Loma (San Diego).
COLLEGE: San Diego State.
TRANSACTIONS/CAREER NOTES: Selected by Oakland Raiders in fifth round (166th pick overall) of 1996 NFL draft. ... Signed by Raiders (July 12, 1996). ... Assigned by Raiders to Barcelona Dragons in 1997 World League enhancement allocation program (February 19, 1997). ... Claimed on waivers by New Orleans Saints (August 25, 1997). ... Granted unconditional free agency (March 1, 2002). ... Signed by Dallas Cowboys (March 12, 2002).
HONORS: Named defensive tackle on THE SPORTING NEWS NFL All-Pro team (2000). ... Played in Pro Bowl (2000 season).
PRO STATISTICS: 1997—Recovered one fumble. 1998—Intercepted one pass for no yards. 1999—Recovered one fumble for two yards. 2000—Recovered one fumble. 2001—Fumbled once and recovered two fumbles for 12 yards.

Year Team	G	GS	SACKS
1996—Oakland NFL	2	0	0.0
1997—Barcelona W.L.	10	10	6.5
—New Orleans NFL	15	2	6.5
1998—New Orleans NFL	16	15	10.0
1999—New Orleans NFL	16	16	8.5
2000—New Orleans NFL	16	16	*17.0
2001—New Orleans NFL	16	16	8.0
W.L. totals (1 year)	10	10	6.5
NFL totals (6 years)	81	65	50.0
Pro totals (7 years)	91	75	56.5

GODFREY, RANDALL — LB — TITANS

PERSONAL: Born April 6, 1973, in Valdosta, Ga. ... 6-2/245. ... Full name: Randall Euralentris Godfrey.
HIGH SCHOOL: Lowndes County (Valdosta, Ga.).
COLLEGE: Georgia.
TRANSACTIONS/CAREER NOTES: Selected by Dallas Cowboys in second round (49th pick overall) of 1996 NFL draft. ... Signed by Cowboys (July 17, 1996). ... Granted free agency (February 12, 1999). ... Re-signed by Cowboys (June 25, 1999). ... Granted unconditional free agency (February 11, 2000). ... Signed by Tennessee Titans (February 16, 2000).
PRO STATISTICS: 1997—Recovered one fumble. 1998—Recovered one fumble. 2000—Recovered one fumble.

				INTERCEPTIONS				SACKS
Year Team	G	GS	No.	Yds.	Avg.	TD	No.
1996—Dallas NFL	16	6	0	0	0.0	0	0.0
1997—Dallas NFL	16	16	0	0	0.0	0	1.0
1998—Dallas NFL	16	16	1	0	0.0	0	3.0
1999—Dallas NFL	16	16	1	10	10.0	0	1.0
2000—Tennessee NFL	16	16	2	25	12.5	1	3.0
2001—Tennessee NFL	14	14	1	5	5.0	0	1.0
Pro totals (6 years)	94	84	5	40	8.0	1	9.0

GOFF, MIKE — G — BENGALS

PERSONAL: Born January 6, 1976, in Spring Valley, Ill. ... 6-5/311. ... Full name: Michael J. Goff.
HIGH SCHOOL: Lasalle-Peru (Peru, Ill.).
COLLEGE: Iowa.
TRANSACTIONS/CAREER NOTES: Selected by Cincinnati Bengals in third round (78th pick overall) of 1998 NFL draft. ... Signed by Bengals (July 20, 1998).
PLAYING EXPERIENCE: Cincinnati NFL, 1998-2001. ... Games/Games started: 1998 (10/5), 1999 (12/1), 2000 (16/16), 2001 (16/16). Total: 54/38.
PRO STATISTICS: 1999—Recovered one fumble. 2000—Recovered two fumbles.

GOINGS, NICK — RB — PANTHERS

PERSONAL: Born January 26, 1978, in Dublin, Ohio. ... 6-0/225. ... Full name: Nick Aaron Goings.
HIGH SCHOOL: Dublin Scioto (Ohio).
COLLEGE: Ohio State, then Pittsburgh.
TRANSACTIONS/CAREER NOTES: Signed as non-drafted free agent by Carolina Panthers (April 23, 2001).
SINGLE GAME HIGHS (regular season): Attempts—25 (September 9, 2001, vs. Minnesota); yards—86 (September 9, 2001, vs. Minnesota); and rushing touchdowns—0.

			RUSHING				RECEIVING				TOTALS		
Year Team	G	GS	Att.	Yds.	Avg.	TD	No.	Yds.	Avg.	TD	TD	2pt.	Pts.	Fum.
2001—Carolina NFL	13	2	66	197	3.0	0	8	39	4.9	0	0	0	0	1

GOLD, IAN — LB — BRONCOS

PERSONAL: Born August 23, 1978, in Ann Arbor, Mich. ... 6-0/223. ... Full name: Ian Maurice Gold.
HIGH SCHOOL: Belleville (Mich.).
COLLEGE: Michigan.
TRANSACTIONS/CAREER NOTES: Selected by Denver Broncos in second round (40th pick overall) of 2000 NFL draft. ... Signed by Broncos (July 23, 2000).
PRO STATISTICS: 2000—Recovered two fumbles. 2001—Recovered two fumbles.

Year Team	G	GS	SACKS
2000—Denver NFL	16	0	2.0
2001—Denver NFL	16	0	3.0
Pro totals (2 years)	32	0	5.0

GOLDEN, JACK — LB — BUCCANEERS

PERSONAL: Born January 28, 1977, in Harvey, Ill. ... 6-1/240.
HIGH SCHOOL: Thornton (Harvey, Ill.).
COLLEGE: Oklahoma State.
TRANSACTIONS/CAREER NOTES: Signed as non-drafted free agent by New York Giants (April 20, 2000). ... Claimed on waivers by Tampa Bay Buccaneers (April 4, 2002).
PLAYING EXPERIENCE: New York Giants NFL, 2000 and 2001. ... Games/Games started: 2000 (16/0), 2001 (16/0). Total: 32/0.
CHAMPIONSHIP GAME EXPERIENCE: Played in NFC championship game (2000 season). ... Played in Super Bowl XXXV (2000 season).
PRO STATISTICS: 2000—Recovered one fumble.

GONZALEZ, TONY — TE — CHIEFS

PERSONAL: Born February 27, 1976, in Torrance, Calif. ... 6-4/249. ... Full name: Anthony Gonzalez.
HIGH SCHOOL: Huntington Beach (Calif.).
COLLEGE: California.
TRANSACTIONS/CAREER NOTES: Selected by Kansas City Chiefs in first round (13th pick overall) of 1997 NFL draft. ... Signed by Chiefs (July 29, 1997). ... Designated by Chiefs as franchise player (February 21, 2002).

HONORS: Named tight end on THE SPORTING NEWS college All-America first team (1996). ... Named tight end on THE SPORTING NEWS NFL All-Pro team (1999-2001). ... Played in Pro Bowl (1999 and 2000 seasons).
PRO STATISTICS: 1999—Recovered one fumble. 2000—Recovered one fumble. 2001—Rushed once for nine yards and completed only pass attempt for 40 yards.
SINGLE GAME HIGHS (regular season): Receptions—10 (December 4, 2000, vs. New England); yards—147 (December 4, 2000, vs. New England); and touchdown receptions—2 (December 30, 2001, vs. Jacksonville).
STATISTICAL PLATEAUS: 100-yard receiving games: 2000 (6), 2001 (1). Total: 7.

				RECEIVING				TOTALS		
Year Team	G	GS	No.	Yds.	Avg.	TD	TD	2pt.	Pts.	Fum.
1997—Kansas City NFL	16	0	33	368	11.2	2	2	1	14	0
1998—Kansas City NFL	16	16	59	621	10.5	2	2	0	12	3
1999—Kansas City NFL	15	15	76	849	11.2	11	11	0	66	2
2000—Kansas City NFL	16	16	93	1203	12.9	9	9	0	54	0
2001—Kansas City NFL	16	16	73	917	12.6	6	6	▲1	38	0
Pro totals (5 years)	79	63	334	3958	11.9	30	30	2	184	5

GOOCH, JEFF   LB   LIONS

PERSONAL: Born October 31, 1974, in Nashville. ... 5-11/225. ... Full name: Jeffery Lance Gooch.
HIGH SCHOOL: Overton (Nashville).
COLLEGE: Austin Peay State.
TRANSACTIONS/CAREER NOTES: Signed as non-drafted free agent by Tampa Bay Buccaneers (April 23, 1996). ... On injured reserve with knee injury (December 17, 1996-remainder of season). ... Granted free agency (February 12, 1999). ... Re-signed by Buccaneers (April 13, 1999). ... Traded by Buccaneers to St. Louis Rams for fifth-round pick in 2001 draft (March 19, 2001); trade voided because Gooch failed physical (March 23, 2001). ... Released by Buccaneers (February 26, 2002). ... Signed by Detroit Lions (April 16, 2002).
PLAYING EXPERIENCE: Tampa Bay NFL, 1996-2001. ... Games/Games started: 1996 (15/0), 1997 (14/5), 1998 (16/16), 1999 (15/0), 2000 (16/0), 2001 (13/0). Total: 89/21.
CHAMPIONSHIP GAME EXPERIENCE: Played in NFC championship game (1999 season).
PRO STATISTICS: 1996—Recovered one fumble. 1998—Credited with one sack and recovered one fumble. 2001—Credited with 1/2 sack.

GOODMAN, HERBERT   RB   PACKERS

PERSONAL: Born August 31, 1977, in Miami. ... 5-11/205.
HIGH SCHOOL: Homestead (Fla.).
COLLEGE: Graceland College (Iowa).
TRANSACTIONS/CAREER NOTES: Signed as non-drafted free agent by Green Bay Packers (April 20, 2000). ... Released by Packers (October 27, 2000). ... Re-signed by Packers to practice squad (November 1, 2000). ... Activated (November 29, 2000).
PLAYING EXPERIENCE: Green Bay NFL, 2000 and 2001. ... Games/Games started: 2000 (5/0), 2001 (7/0). Total: 12/0.
PRO STATISTICS: 2000—Rushed three times for minus two yards, caught one pass for no yards, returned four kickoffs for 129 yards and fumbled twice. 2001—Rushed once for minus one yard and returned one kickoff for 21 yards.
SINGLE GAME HIGHS (regular season): Attempts—2 (September 24, 2000, vs. Arizona); yards—4 (September 24, 2000, vs. Arizona); and rushing touchdowns—0.

GOODSPEED, DAN   OT/G   JETS

PERSONAL: Born May 20, 1977, in Cleveland. ... 6-6/300. ... Full name: Dan Edward Goodspeed.
HIGH SCHOOL: Lake (Uniontown, Ohio).
COLLEGE: Kent State.
TRANSACTIONS/CAREER NOTES: Signed as non-drafted free agent by San Francisco 49ers (April 26, 2001). ... Released by 49ers (September 25, 2001). ... Re-signed by 49ers to practice squad (September 26, 2001). ... Signed by New York Jets off 49ers practice squad (December 5, 2001).
PLAYING EXPERIENCE: New York Jets NFL, 2001. ... Games/Games started: 2001 (1/0).

GOODWIN, HUNTER   TE   VIKINGS

PERSONAL: Born October 10, 1972, in Bellville, Texas. ... 6-5/270. ... Full name: Robert Hunter Goodwin.
HIGH SCHOOL: Bellville (Texas).
COLLEGE: Texas A&M-Kingsville, then Texas A&M.
TRANSACTIONS/CAREER NOTES: Selected by Minnesota Vikings in fourth round (97th pick overall) of 1996 NFL draft. ... Signed by Vikings (July 20, 1996). ... Granted free agency (February 12, 1999). ... Tendered offer sheet by Miami Dolphins (April 8, 1999). ... Vikings declined to match offer (April 9, 1999). ... Released by Dolphins (March 14, 2001). ... Re-signed by Dolphins (March 16, 2001). ... Released by Dolphins (February 21, 2002). ... Signed by Vikings (April 19, 2002).
CHAMPIONSHIP GAME EXPERIENCE: Played in NFC championship game (1998 season).
PRO STATISTICS: 1998—Recovered one fumble. 2000—Returned two kickoffs for six yards.
SINGLE GAME HIGHS (regular season): Receptions—3 (December 27, 1999, vs. New York Jets); yards—24 (December 1, 1996, vs. Arizona); and touchdown receptions—1 (December 24, 2000, vs. New England).

				RECEIVING				TOTALS		
Year Team	G	GS	No.	Yds.	Avg.	TD	TD	2pt.	Pts.	Fum.
1996—Minnesota NFL	9	6	1	24	24.0	0	0	0	0	0
1997—Minnesota NFL	16	5	7	61	8.7	0	0	0	0	0
1998—Minnesota NFL	15	0	3	16	5.3	0	0	0	0	0
1999—Miami NFL	15	5	8	55	6.9	0	0	0	0	1
2000—Miami NFL	16	16	6	36	6.0	1	1	0	6	0
2001—Miami NFL	16	11	4	27	6.8	0	0	0	0	0
Pro totals (6 years)	87	43	29	219	7.6	1	1	0	6	1

GORDON, DARRIEN   CB/PR

PERSONAL: Born November 14, 1970, in Shawnee, Okla. ... 5-11/190. ... Full name: Darrien Jamal Gordon.
HIGH SCHOOL: Shawnee (Okla.).
COLLEGE: Stanford.
TRANSACTIONS/CAREER NOTES: Selected by San Diego Chargers in first round (22nd pick overall) of 1993 NFL draft. ... Signed by Chargers (July 16, 1993). ... Inactive for all 16 games due to shoulder injury (1995 season). ... Granted unconditional free agency (February 14, 1997). ... Signed by Denver Broncos (April 30, 1997). ... Granted unconditional free agency (February 12, 1999). ... Signed by Oakland Raiders (June 9, 1999). ... Released by Raiders (February 10, 2000). ... Re-signed by Raiders (February 28, 2000). ... Released by Raiders (March 1, 2001). ... Signed by Atlanta Falcons (August 15, 2001). ... Granted unconditional free agency (March 1, 2002).
CHAMPIONSHIP GAME EXPERIENCE: Played in AFC championship game (1994, 1997, 1998 and 2000 seasons). ... Played in Super Bowl XXIX (1994 season). ... Member of Super Bowl championship team (1997 and 1998 seasons).
HONORS: Named punt returner on THE SPORTING NEWS NFL All-Pro team (1997).
RECORDS: Shares NFL single-game records for most touchdowns by punt return—2; and most touchdowns by combined kick return—2 (November 9, 1997, vs. Carolina).
POST SEASON RECORDS: Holds Super Bowl career and single-game records for most interception return yards—108 (January 31, 1999, vs. Atlanta).
PRO STATISTICS: 1993—Recovered two fumbles for minus two yards. 1994—Recovered three fumbles for 15 yards. 1996—Credited with two sacks. 1997—Credited with two sacks and recovered four fumbles. 1998—Recovered one fumble. 1999—Credited with one sack and recovered two fumbles for 40 yards. 2000—Returned one kickoff for 17 yards and recovered one fumble for 74 yards and a touchdown. 2001—Recovered three fumbles.

			INTERCEPTIONS				PUNT RETURNS				TOTALS		
Year Team	G	GS	No.	Yds.	Avg.	TD	No.	Yds.	Avg.	TD	TD	2pt.	Pts.	Fum.
1993—San Diego NFL	16	7	1	3	3.0	0	31	395	12.7	0	0	0	0	4
1994—San Diego NFL	16	16	4	32	8.0	0	36	475	§13.2	†2	2	0	12	2
1995—San Diego NFL									Did not play.					
1996—San Diego NFL	16	6	2	55	27.5	0	36	537	§14.9	▲1	1	0	6	3
1997—Denver NFL	16	16	4	64	16.0	1	40	543	13.6	†3	4	0	24	3
1998—Denver NFL	16	16	4	125	31.3	0	34	379	11.1	0	1	0	6	1
1999—Oakland NFL	16	2	3	44	14.7	0	42	397	9.5	0	0	0	0	3
2000—Oakland NFL	13	0	0	0	0.0	0	29	258	8.9	0	1	0	6	2
2001—Atlanta NFL	16	2	1	7	7.0	0	31	437	‡14.1	0	0	0	0	4
Pro totals (8 years)	125	65	19	330	17.4	2	279	3421	12.3	6	9	0	54	22

GOWIN, TOBY   P   SAINTS

PERSONAL: Born March 30, 1975, in Jacksonville, Texas. ... 5-10/167. ... Name pronounced GO-in.
HIGH SCHOOL: Jacksonville (Texas).
COLLEGE: North Texas (degree in kinesiology).
TRANSACTIONS/CAREER NOTES: Signed as non-drafted free agent by Dallas Cowboys (April 24, 1997). ... Granted free agency (February 11, 2000). ... Tendered offer sheet by New Orleans Saints (April 6, 2000). ... Cowboys declined to match offer (April 6, 2000).
PRO STATISTICS: 1997—Missed only field-goal attempt. 2000—Rushed once for five yards.

				PUNTING			
Year Team	G	No.	Yds.	Avg.	Net avg.	In. 20	Blk.
1997—Dallas NFL	16	86	3592	41.8	35.4	26	0
1998—Dallas NFL	16	77	3342	43.4	36.6	31	∞1
1999—Dallas NFL	16	81	3500	43.2	35.1	24	0
2000—New Orleans NFL	16	74	3043	41.1	32.3	22	0
2001—New Orleans NFL	16	76	3180	41.8	35.8	24	0
Pro totals (5 years)	80	394	16657	42.3	35.1	127	1

GRAGG, SCOTT   OT   49ERS

PERSONAL: Born February 28, 1972, in Silverton, Ore. ... 6-8/325.
HIGH SCHOOL: Silverton (Ore.) Union.
COLLEGE: Montana.
TRANSACTIONS/CAREER NOTES: Selected by New York Giants in second round (54th pick overall) of 1995 NFL draft. ... Signed by Giants (July 23, 1995). ... Granted free agency (February 13, 1998). ... Re-signed by Giants (September 4, 1998). ... Released by Giants (March 28, 2000). ... Signed by San Francisco 49ers (July 19, 2000). ... Granted unconditional free agency (March 2, 2001). ... Re-signed by 49ers (April 5, 2001).
PLAYING EXPERIENCE: New York Giants NFL, 1995-1999; San Francisco NFL, 2000 and 2001. ... Games/Games started: 1995 (13/0), 1996 (16/16), 1997 (16/16), 1998 (16/16), 1999 (16/16), 2000 (16/16), 2001 (16/16). Total: 109/96.
PRO STATISTICS: 1997—Recovered one fumble. 1998—Recovered one fumble. 1999—Recovered one fumble. 2000—Recovered one fumble. 2001—Recovered one fumble.

GRAHAM, AARON   C/G

PERSONAL: Born May 22, 1973, in Las Vegas, N.M. ... 6-4/301.
HIGH SCHOOL: Denton (Texas).
COLLEGE: Nebraska.
TRANSACTIONS/CAREER NOTES: Selected by Arizona Cardinals in fourth round (112th pick overall) of 1996 NFL draft. ... Signed by Cardinals for 1996 season. ... Granted free agency (February 12, 1999). ... Re-signed by Cardinals (May 21, 1999). ... Granted unconditional free agency (February 11, 2000). ... Signed by Kansas City Chiefs (April 13, 2000) ... Released by Chiefs (August 22, 2000). ... Signed by Oakland Raiders (August 7, 2001). ... Released by Raiders (September 2, 2001). ... Re-signed by Raiders (September 26, 2001). ... Granted unconditional free agency (March 1, 2002).
PLAYING EXPERIENCE: Arizona NFL, 1996-1999; Oakland NFL, 2001. ... Games/Games started: 1996 (16/7), 1997 (16/4), 1998 (14/13), 1999 (16/16), 2001 (14/0). Total: 76/40.
PRO STATISTICS: 1997—Recovered one fumble. 1999—Fumbled once and recovered one fumble.

GRAHAM, DEMINGO — G — TEXANS

PERSONAL: Born September 10, 1973, in Newark, N.J. ... 6-3/310.
HIGH SCHOOL: Newark (N.J.) Central.
COLLEGE: Hofstra.
TRANSACTIONS/CAREER NOTES: Signed as non-drafted free agent by San Diego Chargers (April 20, 1998). ... Inactive for all 16 games (1998). ... Granted free agency (March 2, 2001). ... Re-signed by Chargers (April 19, 2001). ... Granted unconditional free agency (March 1, 2002). ... Signed by Houston Texans (April 9, 2002).
PLAYING EXPERIENCE: San Diego NFL, 1999-2001. ... Games/Games started: 1999 (16/10), 2000 (13/1), 2001 (16/16). Total: 45/27.
PRO STATISTICS: 2000—Returned one kickoff for no yards. 2001—Recovered one fumble.

GRAHAM, JAY — RB — SEAHAWKS

PERSONAL: Born July 14, 1975, in Concord, N.C. ... 6-0/224. ... Full name: Herman Jason Graham.
HIGH SCHOOL: Concord (N.C.).
COLLEGE: Tennessee.
TRANSACTIONS/CAREER NOTES: Selected by Baltimore Ravens in third round (64th pick overall) of 1997 NFL draft. ... Signed by Ravens (June 19, 1997). ... On injured reserve with knee injury (December 10, 1998-remainder of season). ... Granted free agency (February 11, 2000). ... Re-signed by Ravens (August 22, 2000). ... Released by Ravens (August 27, 2000). ... Signed by Seattle Seahawks (April 27, 2001). ... Released by Seahawks (September 2, 2001). ... Re-signed by Seahawks (October 2, 2001).
PRO STATISTICS: 1997—Returned six kickoffs for 115 yards and recovered one fumble. 1998—Returned three kickoffs for 52 yards. 2001—Returned three kickoffs for 56 yards.
SINGLE GAME HIGHS (regular season): Attempts—35 (November 16, 1997, vs. Philadelphia); yards—154 (November 16, 1997, vs. Philadelphia); and rushing touchdowns—1 (September 14, 1997, vs. New York Giants).
STATISTICAL PLATEAUS: 100-yard rushing games: 1997 (1).

			RUSHING				RECEIVING				TOTALS		
Year Team	G	GS	Att.	Yds.	Avg.	TD	No.	Yds.	Avg.	TD	TD	2pt.	Pts.	Fum.
1997—Baltimore NFL	13	3	81	299	3.7	2	12	51	4.3	0	2	0	12	2
1998—Baltimore NFL	5	2	35	109	3.1	0	5	41	8.2	0	0	0	0	0
1999—Baltimore NFL	4	0	0	0	0.0	0	0	0	0.0	0	0	0	0	0
2000—							Did not play.							
2001—Seattle NFL	11	0	12	43	3.6	0	1	6	6.0	0	0	0	0	0
Pro totals (4 years)	33	5	128	451	3.5	2	18	98	5.4	0	2	0	12	2

GRAHAM, JEFF — WR — FALCONS

PERSONAL: Born February 14, 1969, in Dayton, Ohio. ... 6-2/206. ... Full name: Jeff Todd Graham.
HIGH SCHOOL: Archbishop Hoban (Akron, Ohio).
COLLEGE: Ohio State.
TRANSACTIONS/CAREER NOTES: Selected by Pittsburgh Steelers in second round (46th pick overall) of 1991 NFL draft. ... Signed by Steelers (August 3, 1991). ... Traded by Steelers to Chicago Bears for fifth-round pick (DB Lethon Flowers) in 1995 draft (April 29, 1994). ... Granted unconditional free agency (February 16, 1996). ... Signed by New York Jets (March 14, 1996). ... Traded by Jets to Philadelphia Eagles for sixth-round pick (DE Eric Ogbogu) in 1998 draft (April 19, 1998). ... Released by Eagles (February 13, 1999). ... Signed by San Diego Chargers (March 19, 1999). ... Granted unconditional free agency (February 11, 2000). ... Re-signed by Chargers (February 21, 2000). ... Released by Chargers (February 27, 2002). ... Signed by Atlanta Falcons (April 26, 2002).
PRO STATISTICS: 1991—Returned three kickoffs for 48 yards. 1994—Recovered one fumble. 1995—Returned one kickoff for 12 yards. 1997—Recovered one fumble.
SINGLE GAME HIGHS (regular season): Receptions—9 (October 15, 2000, vs. Buffalo); yards—192 (December 19, 1993, vs. Houston); and touchdown receptions—3 (November 17, 1996, vs. Indianapolis).
STATISTICAL PLATEAUS: 100-yard receiving games: 1992 (2), 1993 (2), 1994 (2), 1995 (7), 1996 (3), 1997 (1), 1999 (4), 2000 (4), 2001 (2). Total: 27.

			RECEIVING				PUNT RETURNS				TOTALS		
Year Team	G	GS	No.	Yds.	Avg.	TD	No.	Yds.	Avg.	TD	TD	2pt.	Pts.	Fum.
1991—Pittsburgh NFL	13	1	2	21	10.5	0	8	46	5.8	0	0	0	0	0
1992—Pittsburgh NFL	14	10	49	711	14.5	1	0	0	0.0	0	1	0	6	0
1993—Pittsburgh NFL	15	12	38	579	15.2	0	0	0	0.0	0	0	0	0	0
1994—Chicago NFL	16	15	68	944	13.9	4	15	140	9.3	1	5	1	32	1
1995—Chicago NFL	16	16	82	1301	15.9	4	23	183	8.0	0	4	0	24	3
1996—New York Jets NFL	11	9	50	788	15.8	6	0	0	0.0	0	6	0	36	0
1997—New York Jets NFL	16	16	42	542	12.9	2	0	0	0.0	0	2	0	12	0
1998—Philadelphia NFL	15	15	47	600	12.8	2	0	0	0.0	0	2	0	12	0
1999—San Diego NFL	16	11	57	968	17.0	2	0	0	0.0	0	2	0	12	0
2000—San Diego NFL	14	13	55	907	16.5	4	3	7	2.3	0	4	0	24	1
2001—San Diego NFL	14	12	52	811	15.6	5	0	0	0.0	0	5	0	30	1
Pro totals (11 years)	160	130	542	8172	15.1	30	49	376	7.7	1	31	1	188	6

GRAHAM, KENT — QB — TEXANS

PERSONAL: Born November 1, 1968, in Wheaton, Ill. ... 6-6/248. ... Full name: Kent Douglas Graham.
HIGH SCHOOL: Wheaton (Ill.) North.
COLLEGE: Notre Dame, then Ohio State.
TRANSACTIONS/CAREER NOTES: Selected by New York Giants in eighth round (211th pick overall) of 1992 NFL draft. ... Signed by Giants (July 21, 1992). ... On injured reserve with elbow injury (September 18-October 14, 1992). ... Granted free agency (February 17, 1995). ... Re-signed by Giants (July 1995). ... Released by Giants (August 30, 1995). ... Signed by Detroit Lions (September 5, 1995). ... Granted unconditional free agency (February 16, 1996). ... Signed by Arizona Cardinals (March 7, 1996). ... Granted unconditional free agency (February 13, 1998). ... Signed by New York Giants (February 17, 1998). ... Released by Giants (February 10, 2000). ... Signed by Pittsburgh Steelers (February 28, 2000). ... Released by Steelers (September 2, 2001). ... Signed by Washington Redskins (September 26, 2001). ... Granted unconditional free agency (March 1, 2002). ... Signed by Houston Texans (April 8, 2002).

PRO STATISTICS: 1992—Fumbled once and recovered one fumble. 1994—Fumbled twice and recovered one fumble. 1996—Fumbled five times. 1997—Fumbled five times. 1998—Caught one pass for 16 yards and fumbled twice for minus three yards. 1999—Caught one pass for minus one yard, fumbled four times and recovered two fumbles. 2000—Fumbled once. 2001—Fumbled twice and recovered one fumble for minus three yards.
SINGLE GAME HIGHS (regular season): Attempts—58 (September 29, 1996, vs. St. Louis); completions—37 (September 29, 1996, vs. St. Louis); yards—366 (September 29, 1996, vs. St. Louis); and touchdown passes—4 (September 29, 1996, vs. St. Louis).
STATISTICAL PLATEAUS: 300-yard passing games: 1996 (1), 1997 (1). Total: 2.
MISCELLANEOUS: Regular-season record as starting NFL quarterback: 17-21 (.447).

				PASSING						RUSHING				TOTALS		
Year Team	G	GS	Att.	Cmp.	Pct.	Yds.	TD	Int.	Avg.	Rat.	Att.	Yds.	Avg.	TD	TD	2pt.	Pts.
1992—N.Y. Giants NFL..........	6	3	97	42	43.3	470	1	4	4.85	44.6	6	36	6.0	0	0	0	0
1993—N.Y. Giants NFL..........	9	0	22	8	36.4	79	0	0	3.59	47.3	2	-3	-1.5	0	0	0	0
1994—N.Y. Giants NFL..........	13	1	53	24	45.3	295	3	2	5.57	66.2	2	11	5.5	0	0	0	0
1995—Detroit NFL.................						Did not play.											
1996—Arizona NFL	10	8	274	146	53.3	1624	12	7	5.93	75.1	21	87	4.1	0	0	0	0
1997—Arizona NFL	8	6	250	130	52.0	1408	4	5	5.63	65.9	13	23	1.8	2	2	0	12
1998—N.Y. Giants NFL..........	11	6	205	105	51.2	1219	7	5	5.95	70.8	27	138	5.1	2	2	0	12
1999—N.Y. Giants NFL..........	9	9	271	160	59.0	1697	9	9	6.26	74.6	35	132	3.8	1	1	0	6
2000—Pittsburgh NFL............	14	5	148	66	44.6	878	1	1	5.93	63.4	8	7	0.9	0	0	0	0
2001—Washington NFL	3	0	19	13	68.4	131	2	0	6.89	122.9	7	-7	-1.0	0	0	0	0
Pro totals (9 years)	83	38	1339	694	51.8	7801	39	33	5.83	69.0	121	424	3.5	5	5	0	30

GRAHAM, SHAYNE   K

PERSONAL: Born December 9, 1977, in Radford, Va. ... 6-0/192. ... Full name: Michael Shayne Graham.
HIGH SCHOOL: Pulaski County (Va.).
COLLEGE: Virginia Tech.
TRANSACTIONS/CAREER NOTES: Signed as non-drafted free agent by New Orleans Saints (June 30, 2000). ... Released by Saints (August 22, 2000). ... Signed by Seattle Seahawks (April 27, 2001). ... Released by Seahawks (September 2, 2001). ... Signed by Buffalo Bills (November 27, 2001). ... Released by Bills (April 24, 2002).

			KICKING				
Year Team	G	XPM	XPA	FGM	FGA	Lg.	50+	Pts.
2001—Buffalo NFL	6	7	7	6	8	41	0-0	25

GRAMATICA, BILL   K   CARDINALS

PERSONAL: Born July 10, 1978, in Buenos Aires, Argentina. ... 5-10/194. ... Full name: Guillermo Gramatica. ... Brother of Martin Gramatica, kicker, Tampa Bay Buccaneers.
HIGH SCHOOL: LaBelle (Fla.).
COLLEGE: Florida State, then South Florida.
TRANSACTIONS/CAREER NOTES: Selected by Arizona Cardinals in fourth round (98th pick overall) of 2001 NFL draft. ... Signed by Cardinals (June 4, 2001). ... On injured reserve with knee injury (December 18, 2001-remainder of season).
PRO STATISTICS: 2001—Punted once for 41 yards.

			KICKING				
Year Team	G	XPM	XPA	FGM	FGA	Lg.	50+	Pts.
2001—Arizona NFL	13	25	25	16	20	50	1-1	73

GRAMATICA, MARTIN   K   BUCCANEERS

PERSONAL: Born November 27, 1975, in Buenos Aires, Argentina. ... 5-8/170. ... Name pronounced mar-TEEN gruh-MAT-ee-ka. ... Brother of Bill Gramatica, kicker, Arizona Cardinals.
HIGH SCHOOL: La Belle (Fla.).
COLLEGE: Kansas State.
TRANSACTIONS/CAREER NOTES: Selected by Tampa Bay Buccaneers in third round (80th pick overall) of 1999 NFL draft. ... Signed by Buccaneers (July 29, 1999).
CHAMPIONSHIP GAME EXPERIENCE: Played in NFC championship game (1999 season).
HONORS: Named kicker on THE SPORTING NEWS college All-America first team (1997). ... Named kicker on THE SPORTING NEWS college All-America second team (1998). ... Won Lou Groza Award (1997). ... Played in Pro Bowl (2000 season).
PRO STATISTICS: 1999—Recovered one fumble. 2001—Attempted one pass without a completion.

			KICKING				
Year Team	G	XPM	XPA	FGM	FGA	Lg.	50+	Pts.
1999—Tampa Bay NFL...............................	16	25	25	‡27	∞32	∞53	3-4	106
2000—Tampa Bay NFL...............................	16	42	42	28	34	*55	5-7	126
2001—Tampa Bay NFL...............................	14	28	28	23	29	49	0-3	97
Pro totals (3 years)	46	95	95	78	95	55	8-14	329

GRANT, DeLAWRENCE   DE   RAIDERS

PERSONAL: Born November 18, 1979, in Compton, Calif. ... 6-3/280. ... Full name: DeLawrence Grant Jr.
HIGH SCHOOL: Centennial (Compton, Calif.).
JUNIOR COLLEGE: El Camino College (Calif.).
COLLEGE: Oregon State.
TRANSACTIONS/CAREER NOTES: Selected by Oakland Raiders in third round (89th pick overall) of 2001 NFL draft. ... Signed by Raiders (July 22, 2001).
PLAYING EXPERIENCE: Oakland NFL, 2001. ... Games/Games started: 2001 (2/0).
HONORS: Named defensive end on THE SPORTING NEWS college All-America second team (2000).

GRANT, DEON   S   PANTHERS

PERSONAL: Born March 14, 1979, in Augusta, Ga. ... 6-2/207.
HIGH SCHOOL: Josey (Augusta, Ga.).
COLLEGE: Tennessee.
TRANSACTIONS/CAREER NOTES: Selected after junior season by Carolina Panthers in second round (57th pick overall) of 2000 NFL draft. ... Signed by Panthers (July 13, 2000). ... On injured reserve with hip injury (August 20, 2000-entire season).
HONORS: Named free safety on THE SPORTING NEWS college All-America first team (1999).
PRO STATISTICS: 2001—Credited with one sack.

				INTERCEPTIONS		
Year Team	G	GS	No.	Yds.	Avg.	TD
2000—Carolina NFL			Did not play.			
2001—Carolina NFL	16	16	5	96	19.2	0

GRANT, ERNEST   DT   DOLPHINS

PERSONAL: Born May 17, 1976, in Atlanta. ... 6-5/315. ... Full name: Ernest Jouoa Grant.
HIGH SCHOOL: Forest (Atlanta).
COLLEGE: Arkansas-Pine Bluff.
TRANSACTIONS/CAREER NOTES: Selected by Miami Dolphins in sixth round (167th pick overall) of 2000 NFL draft. ... Signed by Dolphins (July 17, 2000).
PLAYING EXPERIENCE: Miami NFL, 2000 and 2001. ... Games/Games started: 2000 (2/0), 2001 (11/3). Total: 13/3.
PRO STATISTICS: 2001—Credited with $1/2$ sack.

GRANT, ORANTES   LB   COWBOYS

PERSONAL: Born March 18, 1978, in Atlanta. ... 6-0/230. ... Full name: Orantes Laquay Grant.
HIGH SCHOOL: Dunwoody (Atlanta).
COLLEGE: Georgia.
TRANSACTIONS/CAREER NOTES: Selected by Dallas Cowboys in seventh round (219th pick overall) of 2000 NFL draft. ... Signed by Cowboys (July 17, 2000).
PLAYING EXPERIENCE: Dallas NFL, 2000 and 2001. ... Games/Games started: 2000 (13/0), 2001 (10/1). Total: 23/1.
PRO STATISTICS: 2000—Recovered two fumbles. 2001—Recovered one fumble.

GRANVILLE, BILLY   LB   TEXANS

PERSONAL: Born March 11, 1974, in Lawrenceville, N.J. ... 6-3/246.
HIGH SCHOOL: Lawrenceville (N.J.).
COLLEGE: Duke (degree in sociology, 1997).
TRANSACTIONS/CAREER NOTES: Signed as non-drafted free agent by Cincinnati Bengals (April 25, 1997). ... Granted free agency (February 11, 2000). ... Re-signed by Bengals (April 18, 2000). ... Granted unconditional free agency (March 2, 2001). ... Signed by Houston Texans (February 8, 2002).
PLAYING EXPERIENCE: Cincinnati NFL, 1997-2000. ... Games/Games started: 1997 (12/4), 1998 (16/0), 1999 (16/0), 2000 (14/0). Total: 58/4.
PRO STATISTICS: 1998—Recovered one fumble. 2000—Recovered one fumble.

GRASMANIS, PAUL   DT   EAGLES

PERSONAL: Born August 2, 1974, in Grand Rapids, Mich. ... 6-3/298. ... Full name: Paul Ryan Grasmanis.
HIGH SCHOOL: Jenison (Mich.).
COLLEGE: Notre Dame.
TRANSACTIONS/CAREER NOTES: Selected by Chicago Bears in fourth round (116th pick overall) of 1996 NFL draft. ... Signed by Bears (June 13, 1996). ... Granted free agency (February 12, 1999). ... Re-signed by Bears (April 13, 1999). ... Released by Bears (September 5, 1999). ... Signed by St. Louis Rams (September 7, 1999). ... Inactive for one game with Rams (1999). ... Released by Rams (September 13, 1999). ... Signed by Denver Broncos (November 1, 1999). ... Granted unconditional free agency (February 11, 2000). ... Signed by Philadelphia Eagles (March 3, 2000). ... Granted unconditional free agency (March 2, 2001). ... Re-signed by Eagles (April 24, 2001).
PLAYING EXPERIENCE: Chicago NFL, 1996-1998; Denver NFL, 1999; Philadelphia NFL, 2000 and 2001. ... Games/Games started: 1996 (14/3), 1997 (16/0), 1998 (15/0), 1999 (5/0), 2000 (16/0), 2001 (14/2). Total: 80/5.
CHAMPIONSHIP GAME EXPERIENCE: Played in NFC championship game (2001 season).
PRO STATISTICS: 1997—Credited with $1/2$ sack and recovered one fumble. 1998—Credited with one sack. 2000—Credited with $3 1/2$ sacks. 2001—Credited with two sacks.

GRAY, CHRIS   G/C   SEAHAWKS

PERSONAL: Born June 19, 1970, in Birmingham, Ala. ... 6-4/303. ... Full name: Christopher William Gray.
HIGH SCHOOL: Homewood (Ala.).
COLLEGE: Auburn (degree in marketing, 1992).
TRANSACTIONS/CAREER NOTES: Selected by Miami Dolphins in fifth round (132nd pick overall) of 1993 NFL draft. ... Signed by Dolphins (July 12, 1993). ... On injured reserve with ankle injury (November 15, 1995-remainder of season). ... On injured reserve with broken leg (November 19, 1996-remainder of season). ... Released by Dolphins (August 12, 1997). ... Signed by Chicago Bears (September 9, 1997). ... Granted unconditional free agency (February 13, 1998). ... Signed by Seattle Seahawks (February 20, 1998).
PLAYING EXPERIENCE: Miami NFL, 1993-1996; Chicago NFL, 1997; Seattle NFL, 1998-2001. ... Games/Games started: 1993 (5/0), 1994 (16/2), 1995 (10/10), 1996 (11/11), 1997 (8/2), 1998 (15/8), 1999 (16/10), 2000 (16/16), 2001 (16/16). Total: 113/75.
PRO STATISTICS: 1994—Recovered one fumble. 1999—Recovered one fumble. 2000—Recovered one fumble. 2001—Recovered two fumbles.

GRBAC, ELVIS — QB

PERSONAL: Born August 13, 1970, in Cleveland. ... 6-5/240. ... Name pronounced ger-BACK.
HIGH SCHOOL: St. Joseph (Cleveland).
COLLEGE: Michigan (degree in graphic design, 1993).
TRANSACTIONS/CAREER NOTES: Selected by San Francisco 49ers in eighth round (219th pick overall) of 1993 NFL draft. ... Signed by 49ers (July 13, 1993). ... Inactive for all 16 games (1993). ... Granted unconditional free agency (February 14, 1997). ... Signed by Kansas City Chiefs (March 17, 1997). ... Released by Chiefs (March 1, 2001). ... Signed by Baltimore Ravens (March 6, 2001). ... Released by Ravens (March 1, 2002).
CHAMPIONSHIP GAME EXPERIENCE: Member of 49ers for NFC championship game (1993 season); inactive. ... Member of 49ers for NFC championship game (1994 season); did not play. ... Member of Super Bowl championship team (1994 season).
HONORS: Played in Pro Bowl (2000 season).
PRO STATISTICS: 1994—Fumbled five times. 1995—Fumbled twice and recovered two fumbles for minus one yard. 1997—Fumbled once. 1998—Fumbled once and recovered one fumble. 1999—Fumbled seven times and recovered one fumble. 2000—Fumbled seven times and recovered two fumbles for minus six yards. 2001—Fumbled nine times and recovered two fumbles for minus two yards.
SINGLE GAME HIGHS (regular season): Attempts—63 (September 23, 2001, vs. Cincinnati); completions—39 (November 5, 2000, vs. Oakland); yards—504 (November 5, 2000, vs. Oakland); and touchdown passes—5 (September 19, 2000, vs. San Diego).
STATISTICAL PLATEAUS: 300-yard passing games: 1995 (3), 1997 (1), 1999 (1), 2000 (5), 2001 (1). Total: 11.
MISCELLANEOUS: Regular-season record as starting NFL quarterback: 40-30 (.571). ... Postseason record as starting NFL quarterback: 1-2 (.333).

			PASSING							RUSHING				TOTALS		
Year Team	G	GS	Att.	Cmp.	Pct.	Yds.	TD	Int.	Avg.	Rat.	Att.	Yds.	Avg.	TD	TD	2pt.	Pts.
1993—San Francisco NFL						Did not play.											
1994—San Francisco NFL	11	0	50	35	70.0	393	2	1	7.86	98.2	13	1	0.1	0	0	0	0
1995—San Francisco NFL	16	5	183	127	69.4	1469	8	5	8.03	96.6	20	33	1.7	2	2	0	12
1996—San Francisco NFL	15	4	197	122	61.9	1236	8	10	6.27	72.2	23	21	0.9	2	2	0	12
1997—Kansas City NFL	10	10	314	179	57.0	1943	11	6	6.19	79.1	30	168	5.6	1	1	0	6
1998—Kansas City NFL	8	6	188	98	52.1	1142	5	12	6.07	53.1	7	27	3.9	0	0	0	0
1999—Kansas City NFL	16	16	499	294	58.9	3389	22	15	6.79	81.7	19	10	0.5	0	0	0	0
2000—Kansas City NFL	15	15	547	326	59.6	4169	28	14	7.62	89.9	30	110	3.7	1	1	0	6
2001—Baltimore NFL	14	14	467	265	56.7	3033	15	18	6.49	71.1	21	18	0.9	1	1	0	6
Pro totals (8 years)	105	70	2445	1446	59.1	16774	99	81	6.86	79.6	163	388	2.4	7	7	0	42

GREEN, AHMAN — RB — PACKERS

PERSONAL: Born February 16, 1977, in Omaha, Neb. ... 6-0/217.
HIGH SCHOOL: North (Omaha, Neb.), then Central Christian (Omaha, Neb.).
COLLEGE: Nebraska.
TRANSACTIONS/CAREER NOTES: Selected after junior season by Seattle Seahawks in third round (76th pick overall) of 1998 NFL draft. ... Signed by Seahawks (July 18, 1998). ... Traded by Seahawks with fifth-round pick (WR/KR Joey Jamison) in 2000 draft to Green Bay Packers for CB Fred Vinson and sixth-round pick (DT Tim Watson) in 2000 draft (April 14, 2000). ... Granted free agency (March 2, 2001). ... Re-signed by Packers (July 24, 2001).
HONORS: Named running back on THE SPORTING NEWS college All-America second team (1997).
PRO STATISTICS: 1998—Recovered one fumble. 1999—Recovered one fumble. 2000—Attempted one pass without a completion and recovered one fumble. 2001—Recovered two fumbles.
SINGLE GAME HIGHS (regular season): Attempts—29 (December 9, 2001, vs. Chicago); yards—169 (November 4, 2001, vs. Tampa Bay); and rushing touchdowns—2 (January 2, 2002, vs. New York Giants).
STATISTICAL PLATEAUS: 100-yard rushing games: 1998 (1), 2000 (3), 2001 (7). Total: 11.

			RUSHING				RECEIVING				KICKOFF RETURNS				TOTALS			
Year Team	G	GS	Att.	Yds.	Avg.	TD	No.	Yds.	Avg.	TD	No.	Yds.	Avg.	TD	TD	2pt.	Pts.	Fum.
1998—Seattle NFL	16	0	35	209	6.0	1	3	2	0.7	0	27	620	23.0	0	1	0	6	1
1999—Seattle NFL	14	0	26	120	4.6	0	0	0	0.0	0	36	818	22.7	0	0	0	0	2
2000—Green Bay NFL	16	11	263	1175	4.5	10	73	559	7.7	3	0	0	0.0	0	13	0	78	6
2001—Green Bay NFL	16	16	304	1387	4.6	9	62	594	9.6	2	0	0	0.0	0	11	0	66	5
Pro totals (4 years)	62	27	628	2891	4.6	20	138	1155	8.4	5	63	1438	22.8	0	25	0	150	14

GREEN, BARRETT — LB — LIONS

PERSONAL: Born October 29, 1977, in West Palm Beach, Fla. ... 6-0/232. ... Son of Joe Green, defensive back with New York Giants (1970 and 1971).
HIGH SCHOOL: Suncoast (West Palm Beach, Fla.).
COLLEGE: West Virginia.
TRANSACTIONS/CAREER NOTES: Selected by Detroit Lions in second round (50th pick overall) of 2000 NFL draft. ... Signed by Lions (July 15, 2000).
PLAYING EXPERIENCE: Detroit NFL, 2000 and 2001. ... Games/Games started: 2000 (9/0), 2001 (14/10). Total: 23/10.
PRO STATISTICS: 2000—Recovered one fumble. 2001—Credited with one sack.

GREEN, DARRELL — CB — REDSKINS

PERSONAL: Born February 15, 1960, in Houston. ... 5-9/187.
HIGH SCHOOL: Jesse H. Jones Senior (Houston).
COLLEGE: Texas A&I.
TRANSACTIONS/CAREER NOTES: Selected by Denver Gold in 10th round (112th pick overall) of 1983 USFL draft. ... Selected by Washington Redskins in first round (28th pick overall) of 1983 NFL draft. ... Signed by Redskins (June 10, 1983). ... On injured reserve with broken hand (December 13, 1988-remainder of season). ... On injured reserve with broken bone in wrist (October 24, 1989-remainder of season). ...

G

Granted free agency (February 1, 1992). ... Re-signed by Redskins (August 25, 1992). ... On injured reserve with broken forearm (September 16-November 23, 1992). ... Granted unconditional free agency (February 17, 1995). ... Re-signed by Redskins (March 10, 1995). ... Granted unconditional free agency (February 14, 1997). ... Re-signed by Redskins (April 25, 1997).
CHAMPIONSHIP GAME EXPERIENCE: Played in NFC championship game (1983, 1986, 1987 and 1991 seasons). ... Played in Super Bowl XVIII (1983 season). ... Member of Super Bowl championship team (1987 and 1991 seasons).
HONORS: Played in Pro Bowl (1984, 1986, 1987, 1990, 1991, 1996 and 1997 seasons). ... Named cornerback on THE SPORTING NEWS NFL All-Pro team (1991).
POST SEASON RECORDS: Shares NFL postseason career record for most touchdowns by punt return—1 (January 10, 1988, at Chicago).
PRO STATISTICS: 1983—Recovered one fumble. 1985—Rushed once for six yards and recovered one fumble. 1986—Recovered one fumble. 1987—Recovered one fumble for 26 yards and a touchdown. 1988—Credited with one sack and recovered one fumble. 1989—Recovered one fumble. 1993—Recovered two fumbles for 78 yards and a touchdown. 1996—Recovered one fumble for 15 yards. 1997—Returned one kickoff for nine yards. 1999—Recovered one fumble for four yards.
MISCELLANEOUS: Holds Washington Redskins all-time record for most interceptions (54).

				INTERCEPTIONS				PUNT RETURNS				TOTALS		
Year Team	G	GS	No.	Yds.	Avg.	TD	No.	Yds.	Avg.	TD	TD	2pt.	Pts.	Fum.
1983—Washington NFL	16	16	2	7	3.5	0	4	29	7.3	0	0	0	0	1
1984—Washington NFL	16	16	5	91	18.2	1	2	13	6.5	0	1	0	6	0
1985—Washington NFL	16	16	2	0	0.0	0	16	214	13.4	0	0	0	0	2
1986—Washington NFL	16	15	5	9	1.8	0	12	120	10.0	0	0	0	0	1
1987—Washington NFL	12	12	3	65	21.7	0	5	53	10.6	0	1	0	6	0
1988—Washington NFL	15	15	1	12	12.0	0	9	103	11.4	0	0	0	0	1
1989—Washington NFL	7	7	2	0	0.0	0	1	11	11.0	0	0	0	0	1
1990—Washington NFL	16	16	4	20	5.0	1	1	6	6.0	0	1	0	6	0
1991—Washington NFL	16	16	5	47	9.4	0	0	0	0.0	0	0	0	0	0
1992—Washington NFL	8	7	1	15	15.0	0	0	0	0.0	0	0	0	0	0
1993—Washington NFL	16	16	4	10	2.5	0	1	27	27.0	0	1	0	6	0
1994—Washington NFL	16	16	3	32	10.7	1	0	0	0.0	0	1	0	6	0
1995—Washington NFL	16	16	3	42	14.0	1	0	0	0.0	0	1	0	6	0
1996—Washington NFL	16	16	3	84	28.0	1	0	0	0.0	0	1	0	6	0
1997—Washington NFL	16	16	1	83	83.0	1	0	0	0.0	0	1	0	6	0
1998—Washington NFL	16	16	3	36	12.0	0	0	0	0.0	0	0	0	0	0
1999—Washington NFL	16	16	3	33	11.0	0	0	0	0.0	0	0	0	0	0
2000—Washington NFL	13	2	3	35	11.7	0	0	0	0.0	0	0	0	0	0
2001—Washington NFL	16	4	1	0	0.0	0	0	0	0.0	0	0	0	0	0
Pro totals (19 years)	279	254	54	621	11.5	6	51	576	11.3	0	8	0	48	6

GREEN, DONNY — LB — CHARGERS

PERSONAL: Born September 18, 1977, in Hampton, Va. ... 6-2/238. ... Full name: Donny Jamal Green.
HIGH SCHOOL: Hampton (Va.).
COLLEGE: Virginia.
TRANSACTIONS/CAREER NOTES: Signed as non-drafted free agent by Buffalo Bills (April 24, 2001). ... Released by Bills (August 22, 2001). ... Signed by Washington Redskins (August 23, 2001). ... Released by Redskins (September 10, 2001). ... Signed by Dallas Cowboys to practice squad (November 29, 2001). ... Signed by Jacksonville Jaguars off Cowboys practice squad (December 12, 2001). ... Granted free agency following 2001 season. ... Signed by San Diego Chargers (June 5, 2002).
PLAYING EXPERIENCE: Washington (1)-Jacksonville (1) NFL, 2001. ... Games/Games started: 2001 (Was.-1/0; Jac.-1/0; Total: 2/0).

GREEN, JACQUEZ — WR — REDSKINS

PERSONAL: Born January 15, 1976, in Fort Valley, Ga. ... 5-10/175. ... Full name: D'Tanyian Jacquez Green.
HIGH SCHOOL: Peach County (Fort Valley, Ga.).
COLLEGE: Florida.
TRANSACTIONS/CAREER NOTES: Selected after junior season by Tampa Bay Buccaneers in second round (34th pick overall) of 1998 NFL draft. ... Signed by Buccaneers (July 19, 1998). ... Granted unconditional free agency (March 1, 2002). ... Signed by Washington Redskins (March 18, 2002).
CHAMPIONSHIP GAME EXPERIENCE: Played in NFC championship game (1999 season).
HONORS: Named wide receiver on THE SPORTING NEWS college All-America second team (1997).
PRO STATISTICS: 1998—Fumbled five times and recovered two fumbles. 1999—Fumbled once.
SINGLE GAME HIGHS (regular season): Receptions—11 (October 9, 2000, vs. Minnesota); yards—164 (November 14, 1999, vs. Kansas City); and touchdown receptions—1 (October 14, 2001, vs. Tennessee).
STATISTICAL PLATEAUS: 100-yard receiving games: 1999 (2), 2000 (2). Total: 4.

			RUSHING				RECEIVING				PUNT RETURNS				KICKOFF RETURNS				TOTALS		
Year Team	G	GS	Att.	Yds.	Avg.	TD	No.	Yds.	Avg.	TD	No.	Yds.	Avg.	TD	No.	Yds.	Avg.	TD	TD	2pt.	Pts.
1998—Tampa Bay NFL	12	1	3	12	4.0	0	14	251	17.9	2	30	453	15.1	1	10	229	22.9	0	3	0	18
1999—Tampa Bay NFL	16	10	3	8	2.7	0	56	791	14.1	3	23	204	8.9	0	10	185	18.5	0	3	0	18
2000—Tampa Bay NFL	16	16	5	13	2.6	0	51	773	15.2	1	2	1	0.5	0	1	11	11.0	0	1	0	6
2001—Tampa Bay NFL	12	10	0	0	0.0	0	36	402	11.2	1	0	0	0.0	0	0	0	0.0	0	1	0	6
Pro totals (4 years)	56	37	11	33	3.0	0	157	2217	14.1	7	55	658	12.0	1	21	425	20.2	0	8	0	48

GREEN, MIKE — RB — TITANS

PERSONAL: Born September 2, 1976, in Houston. ... 6-0/249. ... Full name: Mike Lewayne Green.
HIGH SCHOOL: Klein (Houston).
JUNIOR COLLEGE: Blinn College (Texas).
COLLEGE: Houston.
TRANSACTIONS/CAREER NOTES: Selected by Tennessee Titans in seventh round (213th pick overall) of 2000 NFL draft. ... Signed by Titans (July 10, 2000). ... Assigned by Titans to Barcelona Dragons in 2001 NFL Europe enhancement allocation program (February 19, 2001). ... Released by Titans (April 10, 2001). ... Re-signed by Titans (April 25, 2001).

PRO STATISTICS: NFLE: 2001—Completed only pass attempt for 44 yards and a touchdown. NFL: 2001—Attempted two passes with two interceptions, returned two kickoffs for 20 yards and recovered one fumble.
SINGLE GAME HIGHS (regular season): Attempts—5 (October 29, 2001, vs. Pittsburgh); yards—27 (October 29, 2001, vs. Pittsburgh); and rushing touchdowns—1 (December 30, 2001, vs. Cleveland).

				RUSHING				RECEIVING				TOTALS		
Year Team	G	GS	Att.	Yds.	Avg.	TD	No.	Yds.	Avg.	TD	TD	2pt.	Pts.	Fum.
2000—Tennessee NFL	2	0	0	0	0.0	0	0	0	0.0	0	0	0	0	0
2001—Barcelona NFLE	...	...	183	1057	5.8	8	12	67	5.6	0	8	0	48	0
—Tennessee NFL	16	1	15	71	4.7	1	12	64	5.3	1	2	0	12	1
NFL Europe totals (1 year)	...	...	183	1057	5.8	8	12	67	5.6	0	8	0	48	0
NFL totals (2 years)	18	1	15	71	4.7	1	12	64	5.3	1	2	0	12	1
Pro totals (3 years)	...	...	198	1128	5.7	9	24	131	5.5	1	10	0	60	1

GREEN, MIKE S BEARS

PERSONAL: Born December 6, 1976, in Ruston, La. ... 6-0/185.
HIGH SCHOOL: Ruston (La.).
COLLEGE: Louisiana-Lafayette.
TRANSACTIONS/CAREER NOTES: Selected by Chicago Bears in seventh round (254th pick overall) of 2000 NFL draft. ... Signed by Bears (May 30, 2000).
PLAYING EXPERIENCE: Chicago NFL, 2000 and 2001. ... Games/Games started: 2000 (7/0), 2001 (16/2). Total: 23/2.
PRO STATISTICS: 2001—Credited with three sacks and recovered one fumble.

GREEN, RAY CB DOLPHINS

PERSONAL: Born March 22, 1977, in Queens, New York. ... 6-3/187.
HIGH SCHOOL: Burke (Charleston, S.C.).
COLLEGE: South Carolina.
TRANSACTIONS/CAREER NOTES: Signed as non-drafted free agent by Carolina Panthers (April 17, 2000). ... Released by Panthers (September 1, 2001). ... Signed by Miami Dolphins (October 23, 2001).
PLAYING EXPERIENCE: Carolina NFL, 2000; Miami NFL, 2001. ... Games/Games started: 2000 (16/0), 2001 (4/0). Total: 20/0.
PRO STATISTICS: 2000—Returned one kickoff for one yards.

GREEN, TRENT QB CHIEFS

PERSONAL: Born July 9, 1970, in Cedar Rapids, Iowa. ... 6-3/210. ... Full name: Trent Jason Green.
HIGH SCHOOL: Vianney (St. Louis).
COLLEGE: Indiana.
TRANSACTIONS/CAREER NOTES: Selected by San Diego Chargers in eighth round (222nd pick overall) of 1993 NFL draft. ... Signed by Chargers (July 15, 1993). ... Inactive for all 16 games (1993). ... Released by Chargers (August 22, 1994). ... Signed by Washington Redskins (April 5, 1995). ... Inactive for all 16 games (1995). ... Inactive for all 16 games (1996). ... Granted free agency (February 14, 1997). ... Re-signed by Redskins (June 6, 1997). ... Granted unconditional free agency (February 12, 1999). ... Signed by St. Louis Rams (February 16, 1999). ... On injured reserve with knee injury (August 30, 1999-entire season). ... Traded by Rams with fifth-round pick (RB Derrick Blaylock) in 2001 draft to Kansas City Chiefs for first-round pick (DT Damione Lewis) in 2001 draft (April 20, 2001).
PRO STATISTICS: 1998—Caught two passes for minus eight yards, led NFL with 14 fumbles and recovered four fumbles. 2000—Fumbled three times. 2001—Caught one pass for one yard, fumbled 11 times and recovered five fumbles for minus five yards.
SINGLE GAME HIGHS (regular season): Attempts—54 (September 20, 1998, vs. Seattle); completions—30 (November 22, 1998, vs. Arizona); yards—431 (November 5, 2000, vs. Carolina); and touchdown passes—4 (November 11, 2000, vs. New York Giants).
STATISTICAL PLATEAUS: 300-yard passing games: 1998 (2), 2000 (3), 2001 (3). Total: 8.
MISCELLANEOUS: Regular-season record as starting NFL quarterback: 14-21 (.400).

			PASSING							RUSHING			TOTALS		
Year Team	G	GS	Att.	Cmp.	Pct.	Yds.	TD	Int.	Avg.	Rat.	Att.	Yds.	Avg.	TD	TD	2pt.	Pts.
1993—San Diego NFL									Did not play.							
1994—																
1995—Washington NFL									Did not play.							
1996—Washington NFL									Did not play.							
1997—Washington NFL	1	0	1	0	0.0	0	0	0	0.0	39.6	0	0	0.0	0	0	0	0
1998—Washington NFL	15	14	509	278	54.6	3441	23	11	6.76	81.8	42	117	2.8	2	2	0	12
1999—St. Louis NFL									Did not play.							
2000—St. Louis NFL	8	5	240	145	60.4	2063	16	5	8.60	‡101.8	20	69	3.5	0	1	0	6
2001—Kansas City NFL	16	16	523	296	56.6	3783	17	24	7.23	71.1	35	158	4.5	0	0	▲1	2
Pro totals (4 years)	40	35	1273	719	56.5	9287	56	40	7.30	81.1	97	344	3.5	3	3	1	20

GREEN, VICTOR S

PERSONAL: Born December 8, 1969, in Americus, Ga. ... 5-11/210. ... Full name: Victor Bernard Green. ... Cousin of Tommy Sims, defensive back with Indianapolis Colts (1986).
HIGH SCHOOL: Americus (Ga.).
JUNIOR COLLEGE: Copiah-Lincoln Junior College (Miss.).
COLLEGE: Akron (degree in criminal justice, 1993).
TRANSACTIONS/CAREER NOTES: Signed as non-drafted free agent by New York Jets (April 29, 1993). ... Released by Jets (August 30, 1993). ... Re-signed by Jets to practice squad (September 1, 1993). ... Activated (September 28, 1993). ... Released by Jets (February 28, 2002).
CHAMPIONSHIP GAME EXPERIENCE: Played in AFC championship game (1998 season).
PRO STATISTICS: 1994—Recovered one fumble. 1995—Recovered one fumble. 1996—Recovered three fumbles. 1998—Recovered one fumble. 1999—Recovered two fumbles for nine yards. 2000—Recovered four fumbles. 2001—Recovered one fumble.

Year Team	G	GS	INTERCEPTIONS No.	Yds.	Avg.	TD	SACKS No.
1993—New York Jets NFL	11	0	0	0	0.0	0	0.0
1994—New York Jets NFL	16	0	0	0	0.0	0	1.0
1995—New York Jets NFL	16	12	1	2	2.0	0	2.0
1996—New York Jets NFL	16	16	2	27	13.5	0	2.0
1997—New York Jets NFL	16	16	3	89	29.7	0	1.0
1998—New York Jets NFL	16	16	4	99	24.8	0	1.0
1999—New York Jets NFL	16	16	5	92	18.4	0	0.0
2000—New York Jets NFL	16	16	6	144	24.0	1	0.0
2001—New York Jets NFL	16	16	3	76	25.3	1	0.0
Pro totals (9 years)	139	108	24	529	22.0	2	7.0

GREENWOOD, MORLON LB DOLPHINS

PERSONAL: Born July 17, 1978, in Jamaica, West Indies. ... 6-0/242. ... Full name: Morlon O'Neil Greenwood.
HIGH SCHOOL: Freeport (N.Y.).
COLLEGE: Syracuse.
TRANSACTIONS/CAREER NOTES: Selected by Miami Dolphins in third round (88th pick overall) of 2001 NFL draft. ... Signed by Dolphins (July 23, 2001).

Year Team	G	GS	SACKS
2001—Miami NFL	14	12	1.5

GREER, DONOVAN DB REDSKINS

PERSONAL: Born September 11, 1974, in Houston. ... 5-9/178.
HIGH SCHOOL: Elsik (Alief, Texas).
COLLEGE: Texas A&M.
TRANSACTIONS/CAREER NOTES: Signed as non-drafted free agent by New Orleans Saints (April 25, 1997). ... Released by Saints (August 24, 1997). ... Signed by Atlanta Falcons (August 26, 1997). ... Released by Falcons (September 3, 1997). ... Signed by Saints to practice squad (September 4, 1997). ... Activated (November 15, 1997). ... Released by Saints (August 24, 1998). ... Signed by Buffalo Bills to practice squad (September 9, 1998). ... Activated (September 30, 1998). ... Granted free agency (February 11, 2000). ... Re-signed by Bills (April 14, 2000). ... Granted unconditional free agency (March 2, 2001). ... Signed by Washington Redskins (April 20, 2001). ... On injured reserve with knee injury (September 26, 2001-remainder of season).
PLAYING EXPERIENCE: Atlanta (1)-New Orleans (6) NFL, 1997; Buffalo NFL, 1998-2000; Washington NFL, 2001. ... Games/Games started: 1997 (Atl.-1/0; N.O.-6/1; Total: 7/1), 1998 (11/2), 1999 (16/0), 2000 (13/1), 2001 (2/0). Total: 49/4.
PRO STATISTICS: 1998—Recovered one fumble for 18 yards. 1999—Intercepted one pass for no yards. 2000—Recovered one fumble.

GREGG, KELLY DT RAVENS

PERSONAL: Born November 1, 1976, in Edmond, Okla. ... 6-0/285.
HIGH SCHOOL: Edmond (Okla.).
COLLEGE: Oklahoma.
TRANSACTIONS/CAREER NOTES: Selected by Cincinnati Bengals in sixth round (173rd pick overall) of 1999 NFL draft. ... Signed by Bengals (June 23, 1999). ... Released by Bengals (September 6, 1999). ... Re-signed by Bengals to practice squad (September 7, 1999). ... Signed by Philadelphia Eagles off Bengals practice squad (December 7, 1999). ... Released by Eagles (September 12, 2000). ... Signed by Baltimore Ravens to practice squad (September 13, 2000). ... Assigned by Ravens to Rhein Fire in 2001 NFL Europe enhancement allocation program (February 19, 2001).
PRO STATISTICS: NFLE: 2001—Returned one punt for 14 yards and one touchdown.

Year Team	G	GS	SACKS
1999—Philadelphia NFL	3	0	0.0
2000—Baltimore NFL	Did not play.		
2001—Rhein NFLE	...	...	6.0
—Baltimore NFL	8	1	1.0
NFL Europe totals (1 year)	...	...	6.0
NFL totals (2 years)	11	1	1.0
Pro totals (3 years)	...	...	7.0

GREGORY, DAMIAN DT BROWNS

PERSONAL: Born January 21, 1977, in Ann Arbor, Mich. ... 6-3/305. ... Full name: Damian K. Gregory.
HIGH SCHOOL: Sexton (Lansing, Mich.).
COLLEGE: Illinois State.
TRANSACTIONS/CAREER NOTES: Signed as non-drafted free agent by Miami Dolphins (April 27, 2000). ... On injured reserve with knee injury (August 22, 2000-remainder of season). ... On non-football injury list with spleen surgery (October 16, 2001-remainder of season). ... Claimed on waivers by Cleveland Browns (March 4, 2002).
PLAYING EXPERIENCE: Miami NFL, 2001. ... Games/Games started: 2001 (2/0).

GRICE, SHANE G BUCCANEERS

PERSONAL: Born December 20, 1976, in Tupelo, Miss. ... 6-1/307.
HIGH SCHOOL: Shannon (Miss.).
JUNIOR COLLEGE: Itawamba Community College.
COLLEGE: MIssissippi.

TRANSACTIONS/CAREER NOTES: Signed as non-drafted free agent by Tampa Bay Buccaneers (April 23, 2001). ... Released by Buccaneers (August 27, 2001). ... Re-signed by Buccaneers (September 26, 2001). ... Released by Buccaneers (November 10, 2001). ... Re-signed by Buccaneers to practice squad (November 13, 2001). ... Activated (December 22, 2001).
PLAYING EXPERIENCE: Tampa Bay NFL, 2001. ... Games/Games started: 2001 (1/0).

GRIESE, BRIAN   QB   BRONCOS

PERSONAL: Born March 18, 1975, in Miami. ... 6-3/215. ... Full name: Brian David Griese. ... Son of Bob Griese, Hall of Fame quarterback with Miami Dolphins (1967-80). ... Name pronounced GREE-see.
HIGH SCHOOL: Columbus (Miami).
COLLEGE: Michigan.
TRANSACTIONS/CAREER NOTES: Selected by Denver Broncos in third round (91st pick overall) of 1998 NFL draft. ... Signed by Broncos (July 22, 1998). ... Granted free agency (March 2, 2001). ... Re-signed by Broncos (April 11, 2001).
CHAMPIONSHIP GAME EXPERIENCE: Member of Broncos for AFC championship game (1998 season); inactive. ... Member of Super Bowl championship team (1998 season); inactive.
HONORS: Played in Pro Bowl (2000 season).
PRO STATISTICS: 1998—Fumbled once for minus one yard. 1999—Led league with 16 fumbles and recovered nine fumbles for minus 46 yards. 2000—Fumbled five times and recovered two fumbles for minus eight yards. 2001—Caught one pass for minus six yards, fumbled seven times and recovered two fumbles for minus one yard.
SINGLE GAME HIGHS (regular season): Attempts—50 (October 1, 2000, vs. New England); completions—31 (October 1, 2000, vs. New England); yards—365 (October 22, 2000, vs. Cincinnati); and touchdown passes—3 (September 23, 2001).
STATISTICAL PLATEAUS: 300-yard passing games: 1999 (2), 2000 (5), 2001 (1). Total: 8.
MISCELLANEOUS: Regular-season record as starting NFL quarterback: 19-19 (.500).

			PASSING							RUSHING				TOTALS		
Year Team	G	GS	Att.	Cmp.	Pct.	Yds.	TD	Int.	Avg.	Rat.	Att.	Yds.	Avg.	TD	TD	2pt.	Pts.
1998—Denver NFL	1	0	3	1	33.3	2	0	1	0.67	2.8	4	-4	-1.0	0	0	0	0
1999—Denver NFL	14	13	452	261	57.7	3032	14	14	6.71	75.6	46	138	3.0	2	2	0	12
2000—Denver NFL	10	10	336	216	§64.3	2688	19	4	§8.00	*102.9	29	102	3.5	1	1	0	6
2001—Denver NFL	15	15	451	275	61.0	2827	23	19	6.27	78.5	50	173	3.5	1	1	0	6
Pro totals (4 years)	40	38	1242	753	60.6	8549	56	38	6.88	83.6	129	409	3.2	4	4	0	24

GRIFFIN, CORNELIUS   DT   GIANTS

PERSONAL: Born December 3, 1976, in Brundidge, Ala. ... 6-3/300.
HIGH SCHOOL: Pike County (Brundidge, Ala.).
JUNIOR COLLEGE: Pearl River Community College (Miss.).
COLLEGE: Alabama.
TRANSACTIONS/CAREER NOTES: Selected by New York Giants in second round (42nd pick overall) of 2000 NFL draft. ... Signed by Giants (July 25, 2000).
CHAMPIONSHIP GAME EXPERIENCE: Played in NFC championship game (2000 season). ... Played in Super Bowl XXXV (2000 season).
PRO STATISTICS: 2001—Recovered one fumble.

Year Team	G	GS	SACKS
2000—New York Giants NFL	15	0	5.0
2001—New York Giants NFL	16	16	2.5
Pro totals (2 years)	31	16	7.5

GRIFFITH, ROBERT   S   BROWNS

PERSONAL: Born November 30, 1970, in Landham, Md. ... 5-11/198. ... Full name: Robert Otis Griffith.
HIGH SCHOOL: Mount Miguel (Spring Valley, Calif.).
COLLEGE: San Diego State.
TRANSACTIONS/CAREER NOTES: Signed by Sacramento Gold Miners of CFL to practice squad (August 8, 1993). ... Granted free agency after 1993 season. ... Signed as non-drafted free agent by Minnesota Vikings (April 21, 1994). ... Granted free agency (February 14, 1997). ... Re-signed by Vikings (May 7, 1997). ... Granted unconditional free agency (March 1, 2002). ... Signed by Cleveland Browns (March 6, 2002).
CHAMPIONSHIP GAME EXPERIENCE: Played in NFC championship game (1998 and 2000 seasons).
HONORS: Named safety on THE SPORTING NEWS NFL All-Pro team (1998). ... Played in Pro Bowl (2000 season).
PRO STATISTICS: 1996—Fumbled once. 2000—Recovered two fumbles.

			INTERCEPTIONS				SACKS
Year Team	G	GS	No.	Yds.	Avg.	TD	No.
1994—Minnesota NFL	15	0	0	0	0.0	0	0.0
1995—Minnesota NFL	16	0	0	0	0.0	0	0.5
1996—Minnesota NFL	14	14	4	67	16.8	0	2.0
1997—Minnesota NFL	16	16	2	26	13.0	0	0.0
1998—Minnesota NFL	16	16	5	25	5.0	0	0.0
1999—Minnesota NFL	16	16	3	0	0.0	0	4.0
2000—Minnesota NFL	16	16	1	25	25.0	0	1.0
2001—Minnesota NFL	10	9	2	25	12.5	0	0.0
Pro totals (8 years)	119	87	17	168	9.9	0	7.5

GROCE, CLIF   FB   TEXANS

PERSONAL: Born July 30, 1972, in College Station, Texas. ... 5-11/240. ... Full name: Clifton Allen Groce. ... Name pronounced gross.
HIGH SCHOOL: A&M Consolidated (College Station, Texas).
COLLEGE: Texas A&M.

TRANSACTIONS/CAREER NOTES: Signed as non-drafted free agent by Indianapolis Colts (April 27, 1995). ... Released by Colts (August 22, 1995). ... Re-signed by Colts to practice squad (August 28, 1995). ... Activated (December 7, 1995). ... Released by Colts (August 28, 1998). ... Signed by New England Patriots (December 16, 1998). ... Claimed on waivers by Cincinnati Bengals (December 24, 1998). ... Inactive for two games (1998). ... Released by Bengals (August 30, 1999). ... Re-signed by Bengals (September 2, 1999). ... Released by Bengals (September 2, 2001). ... Signed by Houston Texans (March 15, 2002).
CHAMPIONSHIP GAME EXPERIENCE: Played in AFC championship game (1995 season).
PRO STATISTICS: 1996—Returned one kickoff for 18 yards and recovered one fumble. 1997—Returned one kickoff for 15 yards.
SINGLE GAME HIGHS (regular season): Attempts—11 (October 13, 1996, vs. Baltimore); yards—55 (October 13, 196, vs. Baltimore); and rushing touchdowns—1 (December 12, 1999, vs. Cleveland).

				RUSHING				RECEIVING				TOTALS		
Year Team	G	GS	Att.	Yds.	Avg.	TD	No.	Yds.	Avg.	TD	TD	2pt.	Pts.	Fum.
1995—Indianapolis NFL	1	0	0	0	0.0	0	0	0	0.0	0	0	0	0	0
1996—Indianapolis NFL	15	8	46	184	4.0	0	13	106	8.2	0	0	0	0	2
1997—Indianapolis NFL	7	0	10	66	6.6	0	0	0	0.0	0	0	0	0	0
1998—Cincinnati NFL								Did not play.						
1999—Cincinnati NFL	16	15	8	22	2.8	1	25	154	6.2	0	1	0	6	0
2000—Cincinnati NFL	8	7	3	4	1.3	0	11	45	4.1	0	0	0	0	0
2001—								Did not play.						
Pro totals (5 years)	47	30	67	276	4.1	1	49	305	6.2	0	1	0	6	2

GRUTTADAURIA, MIKE   C   CARDINALS

PERSONAL: Born December 6, 1972, in Fort Lauderdale, Fla. ... 6-3/284. ... Full name: Michael Jason Gruttadauria. ... Name pronounced GRU-da-DOOR-ri-ah.
HIGH SCHOOL: Tarpon Springs (Fla.).
COLLEGE: Central Florida.
TRANSACTIONS/CAREER NOTES: Signed as non-drafted free agent by Dallas Cowboys (April 26, 1995). ... Released by Cowboys (August 22, 1995). ... Signed by St. Louis Rams (February 9, 1996). ... Granted free agency (February 12, 1999). ... Re-signed by Rams (June 8, 1999). ... Granted unconditional free agency (February 11, 2000). ... Signed by Arizona Cardinals (February 19, 2000). ... On injured reserve with neck injury (November 24, 2000-remainder of season).
PLAYING EXPERIENCE: St. Louis NFL, 1996-1999; Arizona NFL, 2000 and 2001. ... Games/Games started: 1996 (9/3), 1997 (14/14), 1998 (12/3), 1999 (16/16), 2000 (8/8), 2001 (15/15). Total: 74/59.
CHAMPIONSHIP GAME EXPERIENCE: Played in NFC championship game (1999 season). ... Member of Super Bowl championship team (1999 season).
PRO STATISTICS: 1997—Caught one pass for no yards. 2001—Fumbled once, rushed once for one yard and recovered one fumble.

GUTIERREZ, BROCK   C   BENGALS

PERSONAL: Born September 25, 1973, in Charlotte, Mich. ... 6-3/304.
HIGH SCHOOL: Charlotte (Mich.).
COLLEGE: Central Michigan.
TRANSACTIONS/CAREER NOTES: Signed as non-drafted free agent by Cincinnati Bengals (April 23, 1996). ... Active for two games (1996). ... Released by Bengals (August 30, 1998). ... Re-signed by Bengals (November 4, 1998). ... Released by Bengals (November 17, 1998). ... Signed by Jacksonville Jaguars to practice squad (November 30, 1998). ... Signed by Bengals off Jaguars practice squad (December 15, 1998). ... Granted free agency (February 11, 2000). ... Re-signed by Bengals (March 17, 2000).
PLAYING EXPERIENCE: Cincinnati NFL, 1997-2001. ... Games/Games started: 1997 (5/0), 1998 (1/0), 1999 (16/0), 2000 (16/7), 2001 (14/0). Total: 52/7.
PRO STATISTICS: 2001—Returned two kickoffs for 15 yards.

HAAYER, ADAM   OT   TITANS

PERSONAL: Born February 22, 1977, in Wyoming, Minn. ... 6-6/301.
HIGH SCHOOL: Forest Lake (Minn.).
COLLEGE: Minnesota.
TRANSACTIONS/CAREER NOTES: Selected by Tennessee Titans in sixth round (199th pick overall) of 2001 NFL draft. ... Signed by Titans (July 6, 2001). ... On injured reserve with knee injury (August 25, 2001-entire season).

HAGGANS, CLARK   DE   STEELERS

PERSONAL: Born January 10, 1977, in Torrance, Calif. ... 6-1/251. ... Full name: Clark Cromwell Haggans.
HIGH SCHOOL: Peninsula (Torrance, Calif.).
COLLEGE: Colorado State.
TRANSACTIONS/CAREER NOTES: Selected by Pittsburgh Steelers in fifth round (137th pick overall) of 2000 NFL draft. ... Signed by Steelers (July 7, 2000).
PLAYING EXPERIENCE: Pittsburgh NFL, 2000 and 2001. ... Games/Games started: 2000 (2/0), 2001 (16/1). Total: 18/1.
CHAMPIONSHIP GAME EXPERIENCE: Played in AFC championship game (2001 season).

HAKIM, Az-ZAHIR   WR   LIONS

PERSONAL: Born June 3, 1977, in Los Angeles. ... 5-10/178. ... Full name: Az-Zahir Ali Hakim. ... Name pronounced oz-za-HERE ha-KEEM.
HIGH SCHOOL: Fairfax (Los Angeles).
COLLEGE: San Diego State.

TRANSACTIONS/CAREER NOTES: Selected by St. Louis Rams in fourth round (96th pick overall) of 1998 NFL draft. ... Signed by Rams (July 13, 1998). ... Granted free agency (March 2, 2001). ... Re-signed by Rams (May 23, 2001). ... Granted unconditional free agency (March 1, 2002). ... Signed by Detroit Lions (March 7, 2002).
CHAMPIONSHIP GAME EXPERIENCE: Played in NFC championship game (1999 and 2001 seasons). ... Member of Super Bowl championship team (1999 season). ... Played in Super Bowl XXXVI (2001 season).
HONORS: Named punt returner on THE SPORTING NEWS NFL All-Pro team (2000).
PRO STATISTICS: 1998—Fumbled once. 1999—Fumbled six times and recovered three fumbles. 2000—Fumbled seven times and recovered one fumble. 2001—Completed only pass attempt for 51 yards and a touchdown, fumbled eight times and recovered one fumble for minus 12 yards.
SINGLE GAME HIGHS (regular season): Receptions—8 (November 5, 2000, vs. Carolina); yards—147 (November 5, 2000, vs. Carolina); and touchdown receptions—3 (October 3, 1999, vs. Cincinnati).
STATISTICAL PLATEAUS: 100-yard receiving games: 1999 (1), 2000 (3). Total: 4.

				RUSHING				RECEIVING				PUNT RETURNS				KICKOFF RETURNS				TOTALS		
Year Team	G	GS	Att.	Yds.	Avg.	TD	No.	Yds.	Avg.	TD	No.	Yds.	Avg.	TD	No.	Yds.	Avg.	TD	TD	2pt.	Pts.
1998—St. Louis NFL	9	4	2	30	15.0	1	20	247	12.4	1	0	0	0.0	0	0	0	0.0	0	2	0	12
1999—St. Louis NFL	15	0	4	44	11.0	0	36	677	18.8	8	∞44	461	10.5	∞1	2	35	17.5	0	9	0	54
2000—St. Louis NFL	16	4	5	19	3.8	0	53	734	13.8	4	32 ‡489‡	15.3		1	1	2	2.0	0	5	0	30
2001—St. Louis NFL	16	3	11	50	4.5	0	39	374	9.6	3	36	330	9.2	0	0	0	0.0	0	3	0	18
Pro totals (4 years)	56	11	22	143	6.5	1	148	2032	13.7	16	112	1280	11.4	2	3	37	12.3	0	19	0	114

HALEY, JERMAINE   DT   DOLPHINS

PERSONAL: Born February 13, 1973, in Fresno, Calif. ... 6-4/305.
HIGH SCHOOL: Hanford (Calif.).
JUNIOR COLLEGE: Butte Junior College (Calif.).
TRANSACTIONS/CAREER NOTES: Signed by Toronto Argonauts of CFL (May 1998). ... Selected by Miami Dolphins in seventh round (232nd pick overall) of 1999 NFL draft. ... Signed by Dolphins (March 2, 2000).
PRO STATISTICS: 2000—Credited with one safety.

			INTERCEPTIONS				SACKS
Year Team	G	GS	No.	Yds.	Avg.	TD	No.
1998—Toronto CFL	16	...	0	0	0.0	0	7.0
1999—Toronto CFL	15	...	1	0	0.0	0	3.0
2000—Miami NFL	15	4	0	0	0.0	0	1.5
2001—Miami NFL	12	5	0	0	0.0	0	0.5
CFL totals (2 years)	31	...	1	0	0.0	0	7.0
NFL totals (2 years)	27	9	0	0	0.0	0	2.0
Pro totals (4 years)	58	...	1	0	0.0	0	9.0

HALL, COREY   DB   FALCONS

PERSONAL: Born January 17, 1979, in Athens, Ga. ... 6-4/203.
HIGH SCHOOL: Clarke General (Ga.).
COLLEGE: Appalachian State.
TRANSACTIONS/CAREER NOTES: Selected by Atlanta Falcons in seventh round (215th pick overall) of 2001 NFL draft. ... Signed by Falcons (June 18, 2001). ... Released by Falcons (September 2, 2001). ... Re-signed by Falcons to practice squad (September 4, 2001). ... Activated (October 16, 2001).
PLAYING EXPERIENCE: Atlanta NFL, 2001. ... Games/Games started: 2001 (3/0).

HALL, CORY   S   BENGALS

PERSONAL: Born December 5, 1976, in Bakersfield, Calif. ... 6-0/213.
HIGH SCHOOL: South (Bakersfield, Calif.).
COLLEGE: Fresno State.
TRANSACTIONS/CAREER NOTES: Selected by Cincinnati Bengals in third round (65th pick overall) of 1999 NFL draft. ... Signed by Bengals (May 7, 1999). ... Granted free agency (March 1, 2002). ... Re-signed by Bengals (April 23, 2002).
PLAYING EXPERIENCE: Cincinnati NFL, 1999-2001. ... Games/Games started: 1999 (16/12), 2000 (16/6), 2001 (16/15). Total: 48/33.
PRO STATISTICS: 1999—Intercepted one pass for no yards and recovered one fumble. 2000—Intercepted one pass for 12 yards and credited with four sacks. 2001—Recovered one fumble for 73 yards.

HALL, DANTE   WR/KR   CHIEFS

PERSONAL: Born September 1, 1978, in Lufkin, Texas. ... 5-8/193. ... Full name: Damieon Dante Hall.
HIGH SCHOOL: Nimitz (Irving, Texas).
COLLEGE: Texas A&M.
TRANSACTIONS/CAREER NOTES: Selected by Kansas City Chiefs in fifth round (153rd pick overall) of 2000 NFL draft. ... Signed by Chiefs (July 6, 2000). ... Assigned by Chiefs to Scottish Claymores in 2001 NFL Europe enhancement allocation program (February 19, 2001).
PRO STATISTICS: NFL: 2001—Fumbled twice and recovered one fumble.

			RUSHING				RECEIVING				PUNT RETURNS				KICKOFF RETURNS				TOTALS		
Year Team	G	GS	Att.	Yds.	Avg.	TD	No.	Yds.	Avg.	TD	No.	Yds.	Avg.	TD	No.	Yds.	Avg.	TD	TD	2pt.	Pts.
2000—Kansas City NFL	5	0	0	0	0.0	0	0	0	0.0	0	6	37	6.2	0	17	358	21.1	0	0	0	0
2001—Scottish NFLE	...	...	4	12	3.0	0	34	462	13.6	5	15	177	11.8	0	26	635	24.4	0	5	0	30
—Kansas City NFL	13	0	2	10	5.0	0	0	0	0.0	0	32	235	7.3	0	43	969	22.5	0	0	0	0
NFLEurope totals (1 year)	...	...	4	12	3.0	0	34	462	13.6	5	15	177	11.8	0	26	635	24.4	0	5	0	30
NFL totals (2 years)	18	0	2	10	5.0	0	0	0	0.0	0	38	272	7.2	0	60	1327	22.1	0	0	0	0
Pro totals (3 years)	...	...	6	22	3.7	0	34	462	13.6	5	53	449	8.5	0	86	1962	22.8	0	5	0	30

HALL, JAMES   DE   LIONS

PERSONAL: Born February 4, 1977, in New Orleans. ... 6-2/271.
HIGH SCHOOL: St. Augustine (La.).
COLLEGE: Michigan.
TRANSACTIONS/CAREER NOTES: Signed as non-drafted free agent by Detroit Lions (April 28, 2000).
HONORS: Named linebacker on THE SPORTING NEWS college All-America third team (1999).
PRO STATISTICS: 2001—Recovered two fumbles for eight yards and one touchdown.

Year Team	G	GS	SACKS
2000—Detroit NFL	5	0	1.0
2001—Detroit NFL	15	0	4.0
Pro totals (2 years)	20	0	5.0

HALL, JOHN   K   JETS

PERSONAL: Born March 17, 1974, in Port Charlotte, Fla. ... 6-3/228.
HIGH SCHOOL: Port Charlotte (Fla.).
COLLEGE: Wisconsin.
TRANSACTIONS/CAREER NOTES: Signed as non-drafted free agent by New York Jets (April 25, 1997). ... Granted free agency (February 11, 2000). ... Re-signed by Jets (April 13, 2000).
CHAMPIONSHIP GAME EXPERIENCE: Played in AFC championship game (1998 season).
PRO STATISTICS: 1997—Punted three times for 144 yards. 1999—Punted once for 34 yards.

				KICKING				
Year Team	G	XPM	XPA	FGM	FGA	Lg.	50+	Pts.
1997—New York Jets NFL	16	36	36	28	†41	†55	4-6	120
1998—New York Jets NFL	16	45	46	25	35	54	1-3	120
1999—New York Jets NFL	16	27	29	27	33	48	0-0	108
2000—New York Jets NFL	15	30	30	21	32	51	1-3	93
2001—New York Jets NFL	16	32	32	24	31	53	3-6	104
Pro totals (5 years)	79	170	173	125	172	55	9-18	545

HALL, LAMONT   TE   SAINTS

PERSONAL: Born November 16, 1974, in Clover, S.C. ... 6-4/260. ... Full name: James Lamont Hall.
HIGH SCHOOL: Clover (S.C.).
COLLEGE: Clemson (degree in history).
TRANSACTIONS/CAREER NOTES: Signed as non-drafted free agent by Tampa Bay Buccaneers (April 24, 1998). ... Released by Buccaneers (August 25, 1998). ... Re-signed by Buccaneers to practice squad (October 21, 1998). ... Granted free agency following 1998 season. ... Selected by Rhein Fire in 1999 NFL Europe draft (February 18, 1999). ... Signed by Green Bay Packers (July 7, 1999). ... Traded by Packers with QB Aaron Brooks to New Orleans Saints for LB K.D. Williams and third-round pick (traded to San Francisco) in 2001 draft (July 31, 2000). ... Granted free agency (March 1, 2002).
PRO STATISTICS: 1999—Returned one kickoff for 15 yards.
SINGLE GAME HIGHS (regular season): Receptions—2 (October 22, 2000, vs. Atlanta); yards—20 (October 22, 2000, vs. Atlanta); touchdown receptions—1 (October 29, 2000, vs. Arizona).

			RECEIVING				TOTALS		
Year Team	G	GS	No.	Yds.	Avg.	TD	TD	2pt.	Pts.	Fum.
1998—Tampa Bay NFL					Did not play.					
1999—Rhein NFLE			5	60	12.0	0	0	0	0	0
—Green Bay NFL	14	0	3	33	11.0	0	0	0	0	0
2000—New Orleans NFL	16	5	5	33	6.6	1	1	0	6	0
2001—New Orleans NFL	16	6	2	15	7.5	0	0	0	0	1
NFL Europe totals (1 year)			5	60	12.0	0	0	0	0	0
NFL totals (2 years)	46	11	10	81	8.1	1	1	0	6	1
Pro totals (3 years)			15	141	9.4	1	1	0	6	1

HALL, LEMANSKI   LB   VIKINGS

PERSONAL: Born November 24, 1970, in Valley, Ala. ... 6-0/235. ... Full name: Lemanski S. Hall.
HIGH SCHOOL: Valley (Ala.).
COLLEGE: Alabama.
TRANSACTIONS/CAREER NOTES: Selected by Houston Oilers in seventh round (220th pick overall) of 1994 NFL draft. ... Signed by Oilers (June 20, 1994). ... Released by Oilers (August 28, 1994). ... Re-signed by Oilers to practice squad (August 30, 1994). ... Activated (December 23, 1994); did not play. ... Assigned by Oilers to Frankfurt Galaxy in 1995 World League enhancement allocation program (February 20, 1995). ... Assigned by Oilers to Amsterdam Admirals in 1996 World League enhancement allocation program (February 19, 1996). ... Oilers franchise moved to Tennessee for 1997 season. ... Granted free agency (February 13, 1998). ... Re-signed by Oilers (May 28, 1998). ... Traded by Oilers to Chicago Bears for seventh-round pick (RB Mike Green) in 2000 draft (September 1, 1998). ... Released by Bears (September 5, 1999). ... Signed by Dallas Cowboys (October 27, 1999). ... Granted unconditional free agency (February 11, 2000). ... Signed by Minnesota Vikings (February 24, 2000).
PLAYING EXPERIENCE: Frankfurt W.L., 1995; Houston NFL, 1995 and 1996; Amsterdam W.L., 1996; Tennessee NFL, 1997; Chicago NFL, 1998; Dallas NFL, 1999; Minnesota NFL, 2000 and 2001. ... Games/Games started: W.L.1995 (games played unavailable), NFL 1995 (12/0), W.L. 1996(-), NFL 1996 (3/0), 1997 (16/2), 1998 (15/0), 1999 (10/0), 2000 (15/1), 2001 (16/12). Total: 87/15.
CHAMPIONSHIP GAME EXPERIENCE: Played in NFC championship game (2000 season).
PRO STATISTICS: 1997—Credited with two sacks. 1998—Recovered one fumble for five yards. 2000—Recovered one fumble for one yards. 2001—Credited with two sacks and recovered two fumbles.

HALL, TRAVIS DT FALCONS

PERSONAL: Born August 3, 1972, in Kenai, Alaska. ... 6-5/295.
HIGH SCHOOL: West Jordan (Utah).
COLLEGE: Brigham Young.
TRANSACTIONS/CAREER NOTES: Selected by Atlanta Falcons in sixth round (181st pick overall) of 1995 NFL draft. ... Signed by Falcons (June 30, 1995).
CHAMPIONSHIP GAME EXPERIENCE: Played in NFC championship game (1998 season). ... Played in Super Bowl XXXIII (1998 season).
PRO STATISTICS: 1996—Recovered one fumble. 1997—Recovered one fumble. 1998—Recovered four fumbles. 1999—Recovered one fumble. 2000—Recovered one fumble. 2001—Recovered one fumble.

Year Team	G	GS	SACKS
1995—Atlanta NFL	1	0	0.0
1996—Atlanta NFL	14	13	6.0
1997—Atlanta NFL	16	16	10.5
1998—Atlanta NFL	14	13	4.5
1999—Atlanta NFL	16	15	4.5
2000—Atlanta NFL	16	15	4.5
2001—Atlanta NFL	16	16	2.5
Pro totals (7 years)	93	88	32.5

HALLEN, BOB G CHARGERS

PERSONAL: Born March 9, 1975, in Mentor, Ohio. ... 6-4/305. ... Full name: Robert Joseph Hallen.
HIGH SCHOOL: Mentor (Ohio).
COLLEGE: Kent.
TRANSACTIONS/CAREER NOTES: Selected by Atlanta Falcons in second round (53rd pick overall) of 1998 NFL draft. ... Signed by Falcons (June 3, 1998). ... Granted unconditional free agency (March 1, 2002). ... Signed by San Diego Chargers (May 1, 2002).
PLAYING EXPERIENCE: Atlanta NFL, 1998-2001. ... Games/Games started: 1998 (12/0), 1999 (16/14), 2000 (16/5), 2001 (15/12). Total: 59/31.
CHAMPIONSHIP GAME EXPERIENCE: Played in NFC championship game (1998 season). ... Played in Super Bowl XXXIII (1998 season).

HAM, DERRICK DE BROWNS

PERSONAL: Born March 23, 1975, in Merritt Island, Fla. ... 6-4/270. ... Full name: Derrick Jerome Ham.
HIGH SCHOOL: Merritt Island (Fla.).
COLLEGE: Miami (Fla.).
TRANSACTIONS/CAREER NOTES: Signed as non-drafted free agent by Washington Redskins (April 21, 1999). ... Released by Redskins (September 4, 1999). ... Re-signed by Redskins to practice squad (September 6, 1999). ... Released by Redskins (September 14, 1999). ... Re-signed by Redskins (February 10, 2000). ... Assigned by Redskins to Rhein Fire in 2000 NFL Europe enhancement allocation program (February 18, 2000). ... Released by Redskins (September 2, 2001). ... Signed by Cleveland Browns to practice squad (December 20, 2001). ... Activated (December 27, 2001).

Year Team	G	GS	SACKS
2000—Rhein NFLE	...	...	9.0
—Washington NFL	1	0	0.0
2001—Cleveland NFL	1	0	0.0
NFL Europe totals (1 year)	...	...	9.0
NFL totals (2 years)	2	0	0.0
Pro totals (3 years)	...	...	9.0

HAMBRICK, DARREN LB

PERSONAL: Born August 30, 1975, in Lacoochee, Fla. ... 6-2/227. ... Nephew of Mudcat Grant, pitcher for seven major league teams (1958-71).
HIGH SCHOOL: Pasco (Dade City, Fla.).
COLLEGE: Florida, then South Carolina.
TRANSACTIONS/CAREER NOTES: Selected by Dallas Cowboys in fifth round (130th pick overall) of 1998 NFL draft. ... Signed by Cowboys (July 14, 1998). ... Granted free agency (March 2, 2001). ... Re-signed by Cowboys (May 18, 2001). ... Claimed on waivers by Carolina Panthers (October 24, 2001). ... Granted unconditional free agency (March 1, 2002).
PLAYING EXPERIENCE: Dallas NFL, 1998-2000; Dallas (5)-Carolina (9) NFL, 2001. ... Games/Games started: 1998 (14/0), 1999 (16/12), 2000 (16/16), 2001 (Dal.-5/5; Car.-9/8; Total: 14/13). Total: 60/41.
PRO STATISTICS: 1999—Intercepted two passes for 44 yards, credited with 2$\frac{1}{2}$ sacks and credited with a safety. 2000—Credited with one sack. 2001—Recovered one fumble.

HAMBRICK, TROY RB COWBOYS

PERSONAL: Born November 6, 1976, in Pasco, Fla. ... 6-1/255.
HIGH SCHOOL: Pasco (Fla.).
COLLEGE: Savannah State.
TRANSACTIONS/CAREER NOTES: Signed as non-drafted free agent by Dallas Cowboys (June 1, 2000). ... Released by Cowboys (August 27, 2000). ... Re-signed by Cowboys to practice squad (August 29, 2000). ... Activated (December 8, 2000).
PRO STATISTICS: 2001—Fumbled once and recovered two fumbles.
SINGLE GAME HIGHS (regular season): Attempts—30 (November 4, 2001, vs. New York Giants); yards—127 (November 11, 2001, vs. Atlanta); and rushing touchdowns—2 (November 22, 2001, vs. Denver).
STATISTICAL PLATEAUS: 100-yard rushing games: 2001 (2).

Year	Team	G	GS	Att.	Rushing Yds.	Avg.	TD	No.	Receiving Yds.	Avg.	TD	TD	Totals 2pt.	Pts.	Fum.
2000	Dallas NFL	3	0	6	28	4.7	0	0	0	0.0	0	0	0	0	0
2001	Dallas NFL	16	11	113	579	5.1	2	4	62	15.5	0	2	0	12	1
Pro totals (2 years)		19	11	119	607	5.1	2	4	62	15.5	0	2	0	12	1

HAMILTON, BOBBY — DE — PATRIOTS

PERSONAL: Born July 1, 1971, in Columbia, Miss. ... 6-5/280.
HIGH SCHOOL: East Marion (Columbia, Miss.).
COLLEGE: Southern Mississippi.
TRANSACTIONS/CAREER NOTES: Signed as non-drafted free agent by Seattle Seahawks (April 19, 1994). ... On injured reserve with knee injury (August 17, 1994-entire season). ... Assigned by Seahawks to Amsterdam Admirals in 1995 World League enhancement allocation draft. ... Released by Seahawks (August 15, 1995). ... Signed by New York Jets (June, 1996). ... Released by Jets (August 24, 1996). ... Re-signed by Jets to practice squad (August 26, 1996). ... Activated (September 4, 1996). ... Granted unconditional free agency (February 11, 2000). ... Signed by New England Patriots (July 16, 2000).
CHAMPIONSHIP GAME EXPERIENCE: Played in AFC championship game (1998 and 2001 season). ... Member of Super Bowl championship team (2001 season).
PRO STATISTICS: 1996—Recovered one fumble for seven yards. 1997—Returned one kickoff for no yards. 2000—Returned one kickoff for no yards and recovered one fumble. 2001—Recovered one fumble.

Year	Team	G	GS	SACKS
1994	Seattle NFL	Did not play.		
1995	Amsterdam W.L.	10	9	5.0
1996	Amsterdam W.L.	11	9	5.0
	New York Jets NFL	15	11	4.5
1997	New York Jets NFL	16	0	1.0
1998	New York Jets NFL	16	1	0.0
1999	New York Jets NFL	7	0	0.0
2000	New England NFL	16	16	1.5
2001	New England NFL	16	15	7.0
W.L. totals (2 years)		21	18	10.0
NFL totals (5 years)		86	43	14.0
Pro totals (7 years)		107	61	24.0

HAMILTON, CONRAD — CB

PERSONAL: Born November 5, 1974, in Alamogordo, N.M. ... 5-10/185.
HIGH SCHOOL: Alamogordo (N.M.).
JUNIOR COLLEGE: New Mexico Military Institute.
COLLEGE: Eastern New Mexico.
TRANSACTIONS/CAREER NOTES: Selected by New York Giants in seventh round (214th pick overall) of 1996 NFL draft. ... Signed by Giants (July 18, 1996). ... Granted free agency (February 12, 1999). ... Re-signed by Giants (May 13, 1999). ... Granted unconditional free agency (February 11, 2000). ... Re-signed by Giants (February 22, 2000). ... Released by Giants (July 18, 2000). ... Signed by Atlanta Falcons (February 21, 2001). ... Released by Falcons (November 20, 2001).
PRO STATISTICS: 1998—Credited with one sack and recovered one fumble.

Year	Team	G	GS	Interceptions No.	Yds.	Avg.	TD	Kickoff Returns No.	Yds.	Avg.	TD	TD	Totals 2pt.	Pts.	Fum.
1996	New York Giants NFL	15	1	1	29	29.0	0	19	382	20.1	0	0	0	0	0
1997	New York Giants NFL	14	0	1	18	18.0	0	0	0	0.0	0	0	0	0	0
1998	New York Giants NFL	16	15	1	17	17.0	0	0	0	0.0	0	0	0	0	0
1999	New York Giants NFL	3	2	0	0	0.0	0	0	0	0.0	0	0	0	0	0
2000	—							Did not play.							
2001	Atlanta NFL	6	0	0	0	0.0	0	0	0	0.0	0	0	0	0	0
Pro totals (5 years)		54	18	3	64	21.3	0	19	382	20.1	0	0	0	0	0

HAMILTON, KEITH — DT — GIANTS

PERSONAL: Born May 25, 1971, in Paterson, N.J. ... 6-6/295. ... Full name: Keith Lamarr Hamilton.
HIGH SCHOOL: Heritage (Lynchburg, Va.).
COLLEGE: Pittsburgh.
TRANSACTIONS/CAREER NOTES: Selected after junior season by New York Giants in fourth round (99th pick overall) of 1992 NFL draft. ... Signed by Giants (July 21, 1992).
CHAMPIONSHIP GAME EXPERIENCE: Played in NFC championship game (2000 season). ... Played in Super Bowl XXXV (2000 season).
PRO STATISTICS: 1992—Recovered one fumble for four yards. 1993—Credited with a safety and recovered one fumble for 10 yards. 1994—Recovered three fumbles. 1995—Fumbled once and recovered three fumbles for 87 yards. 1997—Recovered three fumbles. 1998—Recovered one fumble. 1999—Recovered two fumbles.

Year	Team	G	GS	SACKS
1992	New York Giants NFL	16	0	3.5
1993	New York Giants NFL	16	16	11.5
1994	New York Giants NFL	15	15	6.5
1995	New York Giants NFL	14	14	2.0
1996	New York Giants NFL	14	14	3.0
1997	New York Giants NFL	16	16	8.0
1998	New York Giants NFL	16	16	7.0
1999	New York Giants NFL	16	16	4.0
2000	New York Giants NFL	16	16	10.0
2001	New York Giants NFL	13	13	6.0
Pro totals (10 years)		152	136	61.5

HAMITER, UHURU — DE — TEXANS

PERSONAL: Born March 14, 1973, in Kingstree, S.C. ... 6-4/280.
HIGH SCHOOL: Mastbaum Area Vo-Tech (Philadelphia).
COLLEGE: Delaware State.
TRANSACTIONS/CAREER NOTES: Selected by England Monarchs in 1998 NFL Europe draft (February 18, 1998). ... Signed as non-drafted free agent by Philadelphia Eagles (June 19, 1998). ... Claimed on waivers by New Orleans Saints (August 31, 1998). ... Active for one game (1998); did not play. ... Released by Saints (September 28, 1999). ... Re-signed by Saints to practice squad (September 30, 1999). ... Activated (November 19, 1999). ... Released by Saints (August 28, 2000). ... Signed by Eagles to practice squad (September 14, 2000). ... Activated (October 31, 2000). ... Claimed on waivers by Chicago Bears (August 27, 2001). ... Released by Bears (September 1, 2001). ... Signed by Eagles (December 31, 2001). ... Granted free agency (March 1, 2002). ... Signed by Houston Texans (May 30, 2002).
PLAYING EXPERIENCE: England NFLE, 1998; New Orleans NFL, 1999; Philadelphia NFL, 2000 and 2001. ... Games/Games started: 1998 (10/games started unavailable), 1999 (5/0), 2000 (7/0), 2001 (1/0). Total NFLE: (10/-). Total NFL: (13/0). Total Pro: (23/-).
CHAMPIONSHIP GAME EXPERIENCE: Member of Eagles for NFC championship game (2001 season); inactive.
PRO STATISTICS: 1998—Credited with seven sacks.

HAMPTON, CASEY — DT — STEELERS

PERSONAL: Born September 3, 1977, in Galveston, Texas. ... 6-1/321.
HIGH SCHOOL: Ball (Galveston, Texas).
COLLEGE: Texas.
TRANSACTIONS/CAREER NOTES: Selected by Pittsburgh Steelers in first round (19th pick overall) of 2001 NFL draft. ... Signed by Steelers (July 21, 2001).
CHAMPIONSHIP GAME EXPERIENCE: Played in AFC championship game (2001 season).
HONORS: Named defensive tackle on THE SPORTING NEWS college All-America second team (1999). ... Named defensive tackle on THE SPORTING NEWS college All-America first team (2000).
PRO STATISTICS: 2001—Recovered one fumble.

Year Team	G	GS	SACKS
2001—Pittsburgh NFL	16	9	1.0

HAMPTON, JERMAINE — DB — COLTS

PERSONAL: Born June 12, 1979, in Riverdale, Ill. ... 6-0/219.
HIGH SCHOOL: Harvey Thornton (Riverdale, Ill.).
COLLEGE: Northern Illinois.
TRANSACTIONS/CAREER NOTES: Signed as non-drafted free agent by Indianapolis Colts (April 26, 2001).
PLAYING EXPERIENCE: Indianapolis NFL, 2001. ... Games/Games started: 2001 (10/0).

HAMPTON, WILLIAM — CB — EAGLES

PERSONAL: Born March 7, 1975, in Little Rock, Ark. ... 5-10/190.
HIGH SCHOOL: McClellan (Little Rock, Ark.).
COLLEGE: Murray State.
TRANSACTIONS/CAREER NOTES: Signed as non-drafted free agent by Denver Broncos (January 25, 2000). ... Released by Broncos (August 21, 2000). ... Signed by Philadelphia Eagles to practice squad (August 31, 2000).
CHAMPIONSHIP GAME EXPERIENCE: Played in NFC championship game (2001 season).
PRO STATISTICS: 2001—Recovered one fumble.

			INTERCEPTIONS			
Year Team	G	GS	No.	Yds.	Avg.	TD
2000—Philadelphia NFL			Did not play.			
2001—Philadelphia NFL	13	0	1	33	33.0	1
Pro totals (1 years)	13	0	1	33	33.0	1

HAND, NORMAN — DT — SAINTS

PERSONAL: Born September 4, 1972, in Queens, N.Y. ... 6-3/310. ... Full name: Norman L. Hand.
HIGH SCHOOL: Walterboro (S.C.).
JUNIOR COLLEGE: Itawamba Community College (Miss.).
COLLEGE: Mississippi.
TRANSACTIONS/CAREER NOTES: Selected by Miami Dolphins in fifth round (158th pick overall) of 1995 NFL draft. ... Signed by Dolphins (May 17, 1995). ... Inactive for all 16 games (1995). ... Claimed on waivers by San Diego Chargers (August 25, 1997). ... Granted free agency (February 13, 1998). ... Re-signed by Chargers (July 14, 1998). ... Designated by Chargers as franchise player (February 11, 2000). ... Free agency status changed from franchise to unconditional (February 16, 2000). ... Signed by New Orleans Saints (February 23, 2000). ... On injured reserve with foot injury (January 4, 2002-remainder of season).
PRO STATISTICS: 1998—Intercepted two passes for 47 yards.

Year Team	G	GS	SACKS
1995—Miami NFL		Did not play.	
1996—Miami NFL	9	0	0.5
1997—San Diego NFL	15	1	1.0
1998—San Diego NFL	16	16	6.0
1999—San Diego NFL	14	14	4.0
2000—New Orleans NFL	15	15	3.0
2001—New Orleans NFL	13	13	3.5
Pro totals (6 years)	82	59	18.0

HANKTON, KARL — WR — PANTHERS

PERSONAL: Born July 24, 1970, in New Orleans. ... 6-2/202.
HIGH SCHOOL: De La Salle (New Orleans), then Valley Forge Military Academy (Wayne, Penn.).
COLLEGE: Louisiana State, then Trinity (Ill.).
TRANSACTIONS/CAREER NOTES: Signed as non-drafted free agent by Washington Redskins (April 1, 1997). ... Released by Redskins (February 25, 1998). ... Signed by Philadelphia Eagles (April 9, 1998). ... Released by Eagles (August 31, 1998). ... Re-signed by Eagles to practice squad (September 2, 1998). ... Released by Eagles (August 31, 1998). ... Re-signed by Eagles to practice squad (September 25, 1998). ... Activated (September 25, 1998). ... Released by Eagles (September 7, 1999). ... Signed by Carolina Panthers (February 29, 2000). ... Granted free agency (March 2, 2001).
PLAYING EXPERIENCE: Philadelphia NFL, 1998; Carolina NFL, 2000 and 2001. ... Games/Games started: 1998 (10/0), 2000 (16/0), 2001 (11/0). Total: 37/0.
PRO STATISTICS: 1998—Rushed once for minus four yards and returned one kickoff for 18 yards. 2000—Caught four passes for 38 yards and recovered one fumble.
SINGLE GAME HIGHS (regular season): Receptions—2 (November 27, 2000, vs. Green Bay); yards—14 (November 27, 2000, vs. Green Bay); and touchdown receptions—0.

HANSEN, PHIL — DE

PERSONAL: Born May 20, 1968, in Ellendale, N.D. ... 6-5/273. ... Full name: Phillip Allen Hansen.
HIGH SCHOOL: Oakes (N.D.).
COLLEGE: North Dakota State (degree in agricultural economics).
TRANSACTIONS/CAREER NOTES: Selected by Buffalo Bills in second round (54th pick overall) of 1991 NFL draft. ... Signed by Bills (July 10, 1991). ... Granted free agency (February 17, 1994). ... Re-signed by Bills (April 29, 1994). ... Announced retirement (January 7, 2002).
CHAMPIONSHIP GAME EXPERIENCE: Played in AFC championship game (1991-1993 seasons). ... Played in Super Bowl XXVI (1991 season), Super Bowl XXVII (1992 season) and Super Bowl XXVIII (1993 season).
PRO STATISTICS: 1991—Recovered one fumble. 1995—Recovered one fumble. 1996—Recovered two fumbles. 1997—Credited with a safety. 1998—Recovered three fumbles for 13 yards and one touchdown. 1999—Recovered two fumbles for 24 yards. 2000—Recovered one fumble for 29 yards. 2001—Intercepted one pass for 17 yards.

Year Team	G	GS	SACKS
1991—Buffalo NFL	14	10	2.0
1992—Buffalo NFL	16	16	8.0
1993—Buffalo NFL	11	9	3.5
1994—Buffalo NFL	16	16	5.5
1995—Buffalo NFL	16	16	10.0
1996—Buffalo NFL	16	16	8.0
1997—Buffalo NFL	16	16	6.0
1998—Buffalo NFL	15	15	7.5
1999—Buffalo NFL	14	14	6.0
2000—Buffalo NFL	10	9	2.0
2001—Buffalo NFL	12	12	3.0
Pro totals (11 years)	156	149	61.5

HANSON, CHRIS — P — JAGUARS

PERSONAL: Born October 25, 1976, in Riverdale, Ga. ... 6-1/214.
HIGH SCHOOL: East Coweta (Ga.).
COLLEGE: Marshall.
TRANSACTIONS/CAREER NOTES: Signed as non-drafted free agent by Cleveland Browns (April 23, 1999). ... Claimed on waivers by Green Bay Packers (September 1, 1999). ... Released by Packers (September 14, 1999). ... Re-signed by Packers to practice squad (September 16, 1999). ... Released by Packers (October 12, 1999). ... Signed by Miami Dolphins (February 8, 2000). ... Assigned by Dolphins to Barcelona Dragons in 2000 NFL Europe enhancement allocation program (February 18, 2000). ... On injured reserve with knee injury (July 21, 2000-entire season). ... Released by Dolphins (August 15, 2001). ... Signed by Jacksonville Jaguars (August 18, 2001).
PRO STATISTICS: 2001—Rushed twice for no yards, fumbled once and recovered one fumbled for minus 25 yards.

				PUNTING			
Year Team	G	No.	Yds.	Avg.	Net avg.	In. 20	Blk.
1999—Green Bay NFL	1	4	157	39.3	38.5	0	0
2000—Barcelona NFLE	...	50	2141	42.8	36.9	16	0
—Miami NFL				Did not play.			
2001—Jacksonville NFL	16	82	3577	43.6	37.1	24	0
NFL Europe totals (1 year)	...	50	2141	42.8	36.9	16	0
NFL totals (2 years)	17	86	3734	43.4	37.2	24	0
Pro totals (3 years)	...	136	5875	43.2	37.1	40	0

HANSON, JASON — K — LIONS

PERSONAL: Born June 17, 1970, in Spokane, Wash. ... 5-11/182. ... Full name: Jason Douglas Hanson.
HIGH SCHOOL: Mead (Spokane, Wash.).
COLLEGE: Washington State (degree in pre-med).
TRANSACTIONS/CAREER NOTES: Selected by Detroit Lions in second round (56th pick overall) of 1992 NFL draft. ... Signed by Lions (July 23, 1992). ... Designated by Lions as transition player (February 15, 1994).
HONORS: Named kicker on THE SPORTING NEWS college All-America first team (1989). ... Named kicker on THE SPORTING NEWS NFL All-Pro team (1993). ... Played in Pro Bowl (1997 and 1999 season).
PRO STATISTICS: 1995—Punted once for 34 yards. 1996—Punted once for 24 yards. 1998—Punted three times for 94 yards.

				KICKING				
Year Team	G	XPM	XPA	FGM	FGA	Lg.	50+	Pts.
1992—Detroit NFL	16	30	30	21	26	52	2-5	93
1993—Detroit NFL	16	28	28	‡34	‡43	53	3-7	‡130
1994—Detroit NFL	16	39	40	18	27	49	0-5	93
1995—Detroit NFL	16	*48	†48	28	34	56	1-1	132
1996—Detroit NFL	16	36	36	12	17	51	1-3	72
1997—Detroit NFL	16	39	40	26	29	†55	3-5	117
1998—Detroit NFL	16	27	29	29	33	51	1-3	114
1999—Detroit NFL	16	28	29	26	∞32	52	4-8	106
2000—Detroit NFL	16	29	29	24	30	54	2-2	101
2001—Detroit NFL	16	23	23	21	30	54	4-7	86
Pro totals (10 years)	160	327	332	239	301	56	21-46	1044

HAPE, PATRICK — FB/TE — BRONCOS

PERSONAL: Born June 6, 1974, in Killen, Ala. ... 6-4/262. ... Full name: Patrick Stephen Hape.
HIGH SCHOOL: Brooks (Killen, Ala.).
COLLEGE: Alabama.
TRANSACTIONS/CAREER NOTES: Selected by Tampa Bay Buccaneers in fifth round (137th pick overall) of 1997 NFL draft. ... Signed by Buccaneers (July 20, 1997). ... Granted free agency (February 11, 2000). ... Re-signed by Buccaneers (July 23, 2000). ... Granted unconditional free agency (March 2, 2001). ... Signed by Denver Broncos (March 14, 2001).
CHAMPIONSHIP GAME EXPERIENCE: Played in NFC championship game (1999 season).
PRO STATISTICS: 1997—Rushed once for one yard. 2001—Rushed twice for no yards.
SINGLE GAME HIGHS (regular season): Receptions—2 (October 1, 2000, vs. Washington); yards—13 (September 10, 2000, vs. Chicago); and touchdown receptions—1 (November 28, 1999, vs. Seattle). ... Attempts—2 (September 10, 2001, vs. New York Giants); yards—1 (August 31, 1997, vs. San Francisco); and rushing touchdowns—0.

			RECEIVING				TOTALS		
Year Team	G	GS	No.	Yds.	Avg.	TD	TD	2pt.	Pts.	Fum.
1997—Tampa Bay NFL	14	3	4	22	5.5	1	1	0	6	1
1998—Tampa Bay NFL	16	2	4	27	6.8	0	0	1	2	1
1999—Tampa Bay NFL	15	1	5	12	2.4	1	1	0	6	0
2000—Tampa Bay NFL	16	3	6	39	6.5	0	0	0	0	0
2001—Denver NFL	15	8	15	96	6.4	3	3	0	18	0
Pro totals (5 years)	76	17	34	196	5.8	5	5	1	32	2

HARDY, KEVIN — LB — COWBOYS

PERSONAL: Born July 24, 1973, in Evansville, Ind. ... 6-4/248. ... Full name: Kevin Lamont Hardy.
HIGH SCHOOL: Harrison (Evansville, Ind.).
COLLEGE: Illinois (degree in marketing, 1995).
TRANSACTIONS/CAREER NOTES: Selected by Jacksonville Jaguars in first round (second pick overall) of 1996 NFL draft. ... Signed by Jaguars (July 17, 1996). ... On injured reserve with knee injury (December 11, 2001-remainder of season). ... Granted unconditional free agency (March 1, 2002). ... Signed by Dallas Cowboys (April 14, 2002).
CHAMPIONSHIP GAME EXPERIENCE: Played in AFC championship game (1996 and 1999 seasons).
HONORS: Butkus Award winner (1995). ... Named linebacker on THE SPORTING NEWS college All-America first team (1995). ... Named linebacker on THE SPORTING NEWS NFL All-Pro team (1999). ... Played in Pro Bowl (1999 season).
PRO STATISTICS: 1996—Recovered one fumble for 13 yards. 1998—Recovered one fumble. 1999—Recovered one fumble. 2000—Recovered two fumbles for two yards. 2001—Recovered one fumble.

			INTERCEPTIONS				SACKS
Year Team	G	GS	No.	Yds.	Avg.	TD	No.
1996—Jacksonville NFL	16	15	2	19	9.5	0	5.5
1997—Jacksonville NFL	13	11	0	0	0.0	0	2.5
1998—Jacksonville NFL	16	16	2	40	20.0	0	1.5
1999—Jacksonville NFL	16	16	0	0	0.0	0	10.5
2000—Jacksonville NFL	16	16	1	0	0.0	0	3.0
2001—Jacksonville NFL	9	9	0	0	0.0	0	5.5
Pro totals (6 years)	86	83	5	59	11.8	0	28.5

HARDY, TERRY — TE

PERSONAL: Born May 31, 1976, in Montgomery, Ala. ... 6-4/270.
HIGH SCHOOL: Carver (Montgomery, Ala.).
COLLEGE: Southern Mississippi (degree in coaching and sports information, 1997).
TRANSACTIONS/CAREER NOTES: Selected by Arizona Cardinals in fifth round (125th pick overall) of 1998 NFL draft. ... Signed by Cardinals (June 15, 1998). ... Granted free agency (March 2, 2001). ... Re-signed by Cardinals (June 1, 2001). ... On injured reserve with knee injury (December 5, 2001-remainder of season). ... Granted unconditional free agency (March 1, 2002).
SINGLE GAME HIGHS (regular season): Receptions—7 (October 29, 2000, vs. New Orleans); yards—49 (September 12, 1999, vs. Philadelphia); and touchdown receptions—1 (September 30, 2001, vs. Atlanta).

			RECEIVING				TOTALS		
Year Team	G	GS	No.	Yds.	Avg.	TD	TD	2pt.	Pts.	Fum.
1998—Arizona NFL	9	0	0	0	0.0	0	0	0	0	0
1999—Arizona NFL	16	16	30	222	7.4	0	0	0	0	1
2000—Arizona NFL	16	15	27	160	5.9	1	1	0	6	2
2001—Arizona NFL	8	6	11	79	7.2	2	2	0	12	1
Pro totals (4 years)	49	37	68	461	6.8	3	3	0	18	4

HARPER, DEVERON — CB — PANTHERS

PERSONAL: Born November 15, 1977, in Orangeburg, S.C. ... 5-11/187. ... Full name: Deveron Alfredo Harper.
HIGH SCHOOL: Orangeburg-Wilkinson (Orangeburg, S.C.).
COLLEGE: Notre Dame.
TRANSACTIONS/CAREER NOTES: Signed as non-drafted free agent by Carolina Panthers (April 17, 2000).
PLAYING EXPERIENCE: Carolina NFL, 2000 and 2001. ... Games/Games started: 2000 (16/0), 2001 (8/1). Total: 24/1.

HARPER, NICK — DB — COLTS

PERSONAL: Born September 10, 1974, in Baldwin, Ga. ... 5-10/184. ... Full name: Nicholas Necosi Harper.
HIGH SCHOOL: Baldwin (Milledgeville, Ga.).
COLLEGE: Fort Valley State.
TRANSACTIONS/CAREER NOTES: Signed as non-drafted free agent by Indianapolis Colts (January 16, 2001).
PRO STATISTICS: 2001—Fumbled once, returned one punt for no yards and recovered one fumble.

Year Team	G	GS	No.	Yds.	Avg.	TD
2001—Indianapolis NFL	13	2	2	17	8.5	0

(INTERCEPTIONS)

HARRIS, AL — CB — EAGLES

PERSONAL: Born December 7, 1974, in Pompano Beach, Fla. ... 6-1/185. ... Full name: Alshinard Harris.
HIGH SCHOOL: Ely (Pompano Beach, Fla.).
JUNIOR COLLEGE: Trinity Valley Community College (Texas).
COLLEGE: Texas A&M-Kingsville.
TRANSACTIONS/CAREER NOTES: Selected by Tampa Bay Buccaneers in sixth round (169th pick overall) of 1997 NFL draft. ... Signed by Buccaneers (July 1, 1997). ... Released by Buccaneers (August 24, 1997). ... Re-signed by Buccaneers to practice squad (August 26, 1997). ... Claimed on waivers by Philadelphia Eagles (August 31, 1998).
PLAYING EXPERIENCE: Philadelphia NFL, 1998-2001. ... Games/Games started: 1998 (16/7), 1999 (16/6), 2000 (16/4), 2001 (16/2). Total: 64/19.
CHAMPIONSHIP GAME EXPERIENCE: Played in NFC championship game (2001 season).
PRO STATISTICS: 1998—Returned one punt for minus two yards and fumbled once. 1999—Intercepted four passes for 151 yards and one touchdown and fumbled once. 2000—Ran one yard with lateral from interception. 2001—Intercepted two passes for 22 yards.

HARRIS, ANTWAN — CB — PATRIOTS

PERSONAL: Born May 29, 1977, in Raleigh, N.C. ... 5-9/190. ... Full name: Melvin Antwan Harris.
HIGH SCHOOL: Ravenscroft (Raleigh, N.C.).
COLLEGE: Virginia.
TRANSACTIONS/CAREER NOTES: Selected by New England Patriots in sixth round (187th pick overall) of 2000 NFL draft. ... Signed by Patriots (July 14, 2000).
PRO STATISTICS: 2000—Recovered one fumble.

Year Team	G	GS	No.	Yds.	Avg.	TD	Sacks No.
2000—New England NFL	14	0	1	11	11.0	0	1.0
2001—New England NFL	11	1	0	0	0.0	0	0.0
Pro totals (2 years)	25	1	1	11	11.0	0	1.0

HARRIS, BERNARDO — LB

PERSONAL: Born October 15, 1971, in Chapel Hill, N.C. ... 6-2/250. ... Full name: Bernardo Jamaine Harris.
HIGH SCHOOL: Chapel Hill (N.C.).
COLLEGE: North Carolina.
TRANSACTIONS/CAREER NOTES: Signed as non-drafted free agent by Kansas City Chiefs (June 2, 1994). ... Released by Chiefs (August 2, 1994). ... Signed by Green Bay Packers (January 20, 1995). ... Released by Packers (February 27, 2002).
PLAYING EXPERIENCE: Green Bay NFL, 1995-2001. ... Games/Games started: 1995 (11/0), 1996 (16/0), 1997 (16/16), 1998 (16/16), 1999 (16/15), 2000 (16/16), 2001 (16/16). Total: 107/79.
CHAMPIONSHIP GAME EXPERIENCE: Played in NFC championship game (1995-1997 seasons). ... Member of Super Bowl championship team (1996 season). ... Played in Super Bowl XXXII (1997 season).
PRO STATISTICS: 1997—Intercepted one pass for no yards and credited with one sack. 1998—Credited with two sacks. 1999—Recovered one fumble. 2000—Credited with two sacks. 2001—Intercepted two passes for 12 yards, credited with 2$\frac{1}{2}$ sacks and recovered three fumbles.

HARRIS, COREY — CB — CHIEFS

PERSONAL: Born November 28, 1976, in Warner Robins, Ga. ... 5-10/191.
HIGH SCHOOL: Northside (Warner Robins, Ga.).
COLLEGE: The Citadel, then North Alabama.
TRANSACTIONS/CAREER NOTES: Signed as non-drafted free agent by New Orleans Saints (May 20, 1999). ... Released by Saints (September 5, 1999). ... Re-signed by Saints to practice squad (September 6, 1999). ... Released by Saints (September 28, 1999). ... Re-signed by Saints to practice squad (October 27, 1999). ... Activated (December 17, 1999). ... Released by Saints (September 20, 2000). ...

Assigned by Saints to Rhein Fire in 2001 NFL Europe enhancement allocation program (February 19, 2001). ... Released by Saints (May 8, 2001). ... Signed by Kansas City Chiefs (September 18, 2001).
PLAYING EXPERIENCE: New Orleans NFL, 1999 and 2000; Rhein NFLE, 2001; Kansas City NFL, 2001. ... Games/Games started: 1999 (3/0), 2000 (3/1), NFLE 2001 (games played unavailable), NFL 2001 (4/0). Total: 10/1.
PRO STATISTICS: NFLE: 2001—Intercepted two passes for 57 yards and one touchdown. NFL: 2001—Recovered one fumble for minus four yards.

HARRIS, COREY — S — LIONS

PERSONAL: Born October 25, 1969, in Indianapolis. ... 5-11/200. ... Full name: Corey Lamont Harris.
HIGH SCHOOL: Ben Davis (Indianapolis).
COLLEGE: Vanderbilt (degree in human resources).
TRANSACTIONS/CAREER NOTES: Selected by Houston Oilers in third round (77th pick overall) of 1992 NFL draft. ... Signed by Oilers (August 5, 1992). ... Claimed on waivers by Green Bay Packers (October 14, 1992). ... Granted free agency (February 17, 1995). ... Tendered offer sheet by Seattle Seahawks (March 3, 1995). ... Packers declined to match offer (March 10, 1995). ... Granted unconditional free agency (February 14, 1997). ... Signed by Miami Dolphins (March 17, 1997). ... Released by Dolphins (August 3, 1998). ... Signed by Baltimore Ravens (August 17, 1998). ... Granted unconditional free agency (February 12, 1999). ... Re-signed by Ravens (May 17, 1999). ... Granted unconditional free agency (February 11, 2000). ... Re-signed by Ravens (March 21, 2000). ... Granted unconditional free agency (March 1, 2002). ... Signed by Detroit Lions (April 2, 2002).
CHAMPIONSHIP GAME EXPERIENCE: Played in AFC championship game (2000 season). ... Member of Super Bowl championship team (2000 season).
PRO STATISTICS: 1992—Rushed twice for 10 yards and returned six punts for 17 yards. 1993—Caught two passes for 11 yards. 1994—Recovered one fumble. 1995—Recovered one fumble for 57 yards and a touchdown. 1996—Credited with one sack and recovered three fumbles for 28 yards. 1998—Credited with one sack and recovered one fumble. 1999—Credited with one sack. 2001—Recovered four fumbles for eight yards.
MISCELLANEOUS: Played wide receiver (1992 and 1993).

				INTERCEPTIONS				KICKOFF RETURNS				TOTALS			
Year Team	G	GS	No.	Yds.	Avg.	TD	No.	Yds.	Avg.	TD	TD	2pt.	Pts.	Fum.
1992—Houston NFL	5	0	0	0	0.0	0	0	0	0.0	0	0	0	0	0
—Green Bay NFL	10	0	0	0	0.0	0	33	691	20.9	0	0	0	0	0
1993—Green Bay NFL	11	0	0	0	0.0	0	16	482	30.1	0	0	0	0	0
1994—Green Bay NFL	16	2	0	0	0.0	0	29	618	21.3	0	0	0	0	1
1995—Seattle NFL	16	16	3	-5	-1.7	0	19	397	20.9	0	1	0	6	0
1996—Seattle NFL	16	16	1	25	25.0	0	7	166	23.7	0	0	0	0	0
1997—Miami NFL	16	7	0	0	0.0	0	11	224	20.4	0	0	0	0	0
1998—Baltimore NFL	16	6	0	0	0.0	0	35	965	§27.6	▲1	1	0	6	2
1999—Baltimore NFL	16	0	1	24	24.0	1	38	843	22.2	0	1	0	6	0
2000—Baltimore NFL	16	0	2	44	22.0	0	39	907	23.3	0	0	0	0	1
2001—Baltimore NFL	16	16	2	1	0.5	0	11	235	21.4	0	0	0	0	0
Pro totals (10 years)	154	63	9	89	9.9	1	238	5528	23.2	1	3	0	18	4

HARRIS, DERRICK — FB

PERSONAL: Born September 18, 1972, in Angleton, Texas. ... 6-0/252. ... Full name: Sidney Derrick Harris.
HIGH SCHOOL: Angleton (Texas), then Willowridge (Sugar Land, Texas).
COLLEGE: Miami, Fla. (degree in business management, 1995).
TRANSACTIONS/CAREER NOTES: Selected by St. Louis Rams in sixth round (175th pick overall) of 1996 NFL draft. ... Signed by Rams (July 9, 1996). ... Active for one game (1997); did not play. ... Granted free agency (February 12, 1999). ... Re-signed by Rams (June 14, 1999). ... Released by Rams (September 13, 1999). ... Signed by San Diego Chargers (January 18, 2000). ... Released by Chargers (September 7, 2000). ... Signed by New Orleans Saints (April 9, 2001). ... Released by Saints (August 28, 2001). ... Signed by San Diego Chargers (September 5, 2001). ... Granted unconditional free agency (March 1, 2002).
PRO STATISTICS: 1996—Recovered one fumble. 1998—Recovered two fumbles. 2001—Returned one kickoff for 19 yards and recovered one fumble for six yards and a touchdown.
SINGLE GAME HIGHS (regular season): Attempts—5 (October 11, 1998, vs. New York Jets); yards—15 (September 20, 1998, vs. Buffalo); and rushing touchdowns—0.

			RUSHING				RECEIVING				TOTALS			
Year Team	G	GS	Att.	Yds.	Avg.	TD	No.	Yds.	Avg.	TD	TD	2pt.	Pts.	Fum.
1996—St. Louis NFL	11	6	3	5	1.7	0	4	17	4.3	0	0	0	0	0
1997—St. Louis NFL							Did not play.							
1998—St. Louis NFL	16	14	14	38	2.7	0	12	57	4.8	2	2	0	12	1
1999—St. Louis NFL	1	0	0	0	0.0	0	0	0	0.0	0	0	0	0	0
2000—							Did not play.							
2001—San Diego NFL	16	0	0	0	0.0	0	1	7	7.0	0	1	0	6	0
Pro totals (4 years)	44	20	17	43	2.5	0	17	81	4.8	2	3	0	18	1

HARRIS, JACKIE — TE

PERSONAL: Born January 4, 1968, in Pine Bluff, Ark. ... 6-4/250. ... Full name: Jackie Bernard Harris. ... Second cousin of Chris Akins, safety, Cleveland Browns.
HIGH SCHOOL: Dollarway (Pine Bluff, Ark.).
COLLEGE: Northeast Louisiana.
TRANSACTIONS/CAREER NOTES: Selected by Green Bay Packers in fourth round (102nd pick overall) of 1990 NFL draft. ... Signed by Packers (July 22, 1990). ... Granted free agency (February 1, 1992). ... Re-signed by Packers (August 14, 1992). ... Designated by Packers as transition player (February 25, 1993). ... Tendered offer sheet by Tampa Bay Buccaneers (June 15, 1994). ... Packers declined to match offer (June 22, 1994). ... On injured reserve with shoulder injury (November 22, 1994-remainder of season). ... On injured reserve with hernia (January 2, 1998-remainder of 1997 playoffs). ... Granted unconditional free agency (February 13, 1998). ... Signed by Tennessee Oilers (March 11,

1998). ... Oilers franchise renamed Tennessee Titans for 1999 season (December 26, 1998). ... Granted unconditional free agency (February 11, 2000). ... Signed by Dallas Cowboys (March 17, 2000). ... Released by Cowboys (February 28, 2002).
CHAMPIONSHIP GAME EXPERIENCE: Played in AFC championship game (1999 season). ... Played in Super Bowl XXXIV (1999 season).
PRO STATISTICS: 1991—Rushed once for one yard and recovered one fumble. 1998—Returned one kickoff for three yards.
SINGLE GAME HIGHS (regular season): Receptions—10 (November 26, 1995, vs. Green Bay); yards—128 (October 10, 1993, vs. Denver); and touchdown receptions—2 (September 24, 2000, vs. San Francisco).
STATISTICAL PLATEAUS: 100-yard receiving games: 1993 (1), 1995 (2). Total: 3.

			RECEIVING				TOTALS		
Year Team	G	GS	No.	Yds.	Avg.	TD	TD	2pt.	Pts.	Fum.
1990—Green Bay NFL	16	3	12	157	13.1	0	0	0	0	0
1991—Green Bay NFL	16	6	24	264	11.0	3	3	0	18	1
1992—Green Bay NFL	16	11	55	595	10.8	2	2	0	12	1
1993—Green Bay NFL	12	12	42	604	14.4	4	4	0	24	0
1994—Tampa Bay NFL	9	9	26	337	13.0	3	3	1	20	0
1995—Tampa Bay NFL	16	16	62	751	12.1	1	1	0	6	2
1996—Tampa Bay NFL	13	12	30	349	11.6	1	1	1	8	1
1997—Tampa Bay NFL	12	11	19	197	10.4	1	1	0	6	0
1998—Tennessee NFL	16	16	43	412	9.6	2	2	0	12	0
1999—Tennessee NFL	12	1	26	297	11.4	1	1	†1	8	0
2000—Dallas NFL	16	7	39	306	7.8	5	5	1	32	0
2001—Dallas NFL	13	12	15	141	9.4	2	2	0	12	0
Pro totals (12 years)	167	116	393	4410	11.2	25	25	4	158	5

HARRIS, JOHNNIE — S — RAIDERS

PERSONAL: Born August 21, 1972, in Chicago. ... 6-2/210.
HIGH SCHOOL: Martin Luther King (Chicago).
JUNIOR COLLEGE: San Bernardino (Calif.) Valley.
COLLEGE: Mississippi State.
TRANSACTIONS/CAREER NOTES: Signed by San Antonio Texans of CFL (October 17, 1995). ... Selected by Edmonton Eskimos in 1996 U.S. Team Dispersal draft. ... Released by Eskimos (June 5, 1996). ... Played with Tampa Bay Storm of Arena League (1996-98). ... Signed by Toronto Argonauts of CFL (October 12, 1996). ... Released by Argonauts (May 15, 1997). ... Re-signed by Argonauts (June 2, 1997). ... Signed as non-drafted free agent by Oakland Raiders (February 28, 1999). ... Released by Raiders (September 5, 1999). ... Re-signed by Raiders to practice squad (September 7, 1999). ... Activated (December 1999).
PLAYING EXPERIENCE: Toronto Argonauts CFL, 1996 and 1997; Oakland NFL, 1999-2001. ... Games/Games started: 1996 (4/games started unavailable), 1997 (18/-), 1999 (4/0), 2000 (15/2), 2001 (16/5). Total CFL: 22/-. Total NFL: 35/7. Total Pro: 57/-.
CHAMPIONSHIP GAME EXPERIENCE: Member of CFL championship team (1996). ... Played in AFC championship game (2000 season).
PRO STATISTICS: CFL: 1996—Returned one kickoff for seven yards. 1997—Intercepted five passes for 72 yards. 2001—Credited with 1/2 sack.

HARRIS, NICK — P — BENGALS

PERSONAL: Born July 23, 1978, in Phoenix. ... 6-2/220.
HIGH SCHOOL: Westview (Phoenix).
COLLEGE: California (degree in business administration).
TRANSACTIONS/CAREER NOTES: Selected by Denver Broncos in fourth round (120th pick overall) of 2001 NFL draft. ... Signed by Broncos (May 22, 2001). ... Claimed on waivers by Cincinnati Bengals (August 29, 2001).

				PUNTING			
Year Team	G	No.	Yds.	Avg.	Net avg.	In. 20	Blk.
2001—Cincinnati NFL	16	84	3372	40.1	33.9	21	1

HARRIS, SEAN — LB

PERSONAL: Born February 25, 1972, in Tucson, Ariz. ... 6-3/252. ... Full name: Sean Eugene Harris.
HIGH SCHOOL: Magnet (Tucson, Ariz.).
COLLEGE: Arizona.
TRANSACTIONS/CAREER NOTES: Selected by Chicago Bears in third round (83rd pick overall) of 1995 NFL draft. ... Signed by Bears (July 18, 1995). ... Granted free agency (February 13, 1998). ... Re-signed by Bears (May 12, 1998). ... Granted unconditional free agency (February 12, 1999). ... Re-signed by Bears (March 11, 1999). ... Announced retirement (July 27, 2001). ... Released by Bears (July 31, 2001). ... Signed by Indianapolis Colts (August 13, 2001). ... Granted unconditional free agency (March 1, 2002).
PLAYING EXPERIENCE: Chicago NFL, 1995-2000; Indianapolis NFL, 2001. ... Games/Games started: 1995 (11/0), 1996 (15/0), 1997 (11/1), 1998 (16/14), 1999 (14/10), 2000 (15/13), 2001 (1/0). Total: 83/38.
PRO STATISTICS: 1998—Intercepted one pass for no yards and credited with one sack. 1999—Intercepted one pass for no yards and recovered two fumbles, including one in end zone for a touchdown. 2000—Credited with one sack.

HARRIS, WALT — CB — COLTS

PERSONAL: Born August 10, 1974, in La Grange, Ga. ... 5-11/195. ... Full name: Walter Lee Harris.
HIGH SCHOOL: La Grange (Ga.).
COLLEGE: Mississippi State.
TRANSACTIONS/CAREER NOTES: Selected by Chicago Bears in first round (13th pick overall) of 1996 NFL draft. ... Signed by Bears (July 11, 1996). ... On injured reserve with knee injury (December 22, 1998-remainder of season). ... On injured reserve with knee injury (December 22, 2000-remainder of season). ... Granted unconditional free agency (March 2, 2001). ... Re-signed by Bears (April 25, 2001). ... Granted unconditional free agency (March 1, 2002). ... Signed by Indianapolis Colts (March 15, 2002).

PRO STATISTICS: 1996—Recovered two fumbles for eight yards. 1997—Fumbled once and recovered one fumble. 1998—Recovered one fumble. 1999—Credited with one sack and recovered one fumble. 2000—Returned one punt for 14 yards. 2001—Recovered two fumbles.

				INTERCEPTIONS			
Year Team	G	GS	No.	Yds.	Avg.	TD	
1996—Chicago NFL	15	13	2	0	0.0	0	
1997—Chicago NFL	16	16	5	30	6.0	0	
1998—Chicago NFL	14	14	4	41	10.3	1	
1999—Chicago NFL	15	15	1	-1	-1.0	0	
2000—Chicago NFL	12	12	2	35	17.5	1	
2001—Chicago NFL	15	13	1	45	45.0	1	
Pro totals (6 years)	87	83	15	150	10.0	3	

HARRISON, LLOYD   CB   CHARGERS

PERSONAL: Born June 21, 1977, in Jamiaca. ... 5-10/190.
HIGH SCHOOL: Sewanhaka (Floral Park, N.Y.).
COLLEGE: North Carolina State.
TRANSACTIONS/CAREER NOTES: Selected by Washington Redskins in third round (64th pick overall) of 2000 NFL draft. ... Signed by Redskins (July 7, 2000). ... Claimed on waivers by San Diego Chargers (September 3, 2001).
PLAYING EXPERIENCE: Washington NFL, 2000; San Diego NFL, 2001. ... Games/Games started: 2000 (2/0), 2001 (12/1). Total: 14/1.
PRO STATISTICS: 2001—Credited with one sack.

HARRISON, MARVIN   WR   COLTS

PERSONAL: Born August 25, 1972, in Philadelphia. ... 6-0/178. ... Full name: Marvin Daniel Harrison.
HIGH SCHOOL: Roman Catholic (Philadelphia).
COLLEGE: Syracuse.
TRANSACTIONS/CAREER NOTES: Selected by Indianapolis Colts in first round (19th pick overall) of 1996 NFL draft. ... Signed by Colts (July 8, 1996). ... On injured reserve with shoulder injury (December 2, 1998-remainder of season).
HONORS: Named kick returner on THE SPORTING NEWS All-America first team (1995). ... Named wide receiver on THE SPORTING NEWS NFL All-Pro team (1999 and 2000). ... Played in Pro Bowl (1999 and 2000 seasons).
PRO STATISTICS: 1996—Rushed three times for 15 yards. 1997—Rushed twice for minus seven yards and recovered one fumble for five yards. 1999—Rushed once for four yards and recovered one fumble. 2001—Rushed once for three yards.
SINGLE GAME HIGHS (regular season): Receptions—14 (December 26, 1999, vs. Cleveland); yards—196 (September 26, 1999, vs. San Diego); and touchdown receptions—3 (November 11, 2001, vs. Miami).
STATISTICAL PLATEAUS: 100-yard receiving games: 1996 (2), 1998 (2), 1999 (9), 2000 (8), 2001 (6). Total: 27.

			RECEIVING				PUNT RETURNS				TOTALS		
Year Team	G	GS	No.	Yds.	Avg.	TD	No.	Yds.	Avg.	TD	TD	2pt.	Pts.	Fum.
1996—Indianapolis NFL	16	15	64	836	13.1	8	18	177	9.8	0	8	0	48	1
1997—Indianapolis NFL	16	15	73	866	11.9	6	0	0	0.0	0	6	2	40	2
1998—Indianapolis NFL	12	12	59	776	13.2	7	0	0	0.0	0	7	1	44	0
1999—Indianapolis NFL	16	16	115	*1663	14.5	§12	0	0	0.0	0	12	†1	74	2
2000—Indianapolis NFL	16	16	†102	1413	13.9	§14	0	0	0.0	0	14	0	84	2
2001—Indianapolis NFL	16	16	109	§1524	14.0	§15	0	0	0.0	0	15	0	90	0
Pro totals (6 years)	92	90	522	7078	13.6	62	18	177	9.8	0	62	4	380	7

HARRISON, RODNEY   S   CHARGERS

PERSONAL: Born December 15, 1972, in Markham, Ill. ... 6-1/218. ... Full name: Rodney Scott Harrison.
HIGH SCHOOL: Marian Catholic (Chicago Heights, Ill.).
COLLEGE: Western Illinois.
TRANSACTIONS/CAREER NOTES: Selected after junior season by San Diego Chargers in fifth round (145th pick overall) of 1994 NFL draft. ... Signed by Chargers (June 29, 1994).
CHAMPIONSHIP GAME EXPERIENCE: Played in AFC championship game (1994 season). ... Played in Super Bowl XXIX (1994 season).
HONORS: Named safety on THE SPORTING NEWS NFL All-Pro team (1998 and 2001). ... Played in Pro Bowl (1998 season).
PRO STATISTICS: 1994—Recovered one fumble. 1996—Returned one kickoff for 10 yards, fumbled once and recovered two fumbles for four yards. 1997—Returned one punt for no yards, returned one kickoff for 40 yards and a touchdown and recovered three fumbles, including one in the end zone for a touchdown. 2001—Recovered one fumble.

				INTERCEPTIONS			SACKS
Year Team	G	GS	No.	Yds.	Avg.	TD	No.
1994—San Diego NFL	15	0	0	0	0.0	0	0.0
1995—San Diego NFL	11	0	5	22	4.4	0	0.0
1996—San Diego NFL	16	16	5	56	11.2	0	1.0
1997—San Diego NFL	16	16	2	75	37.5	1	4.0
1998—San Diego NFL	16	16	3	42	14.0	0	4.0
1999—San Diego NFL	6	6	1	0	0.0	0	1.0
2000—San Diego NFL	16	16	6	97	16.2	1	6.0
2001—San Diego NFL	14	14	2	51	25.5	0	3.5
Pro totals (8 years)	110	84	24	343	14.3	2	19.5

HART, LAWRENCE   TE

PERSONAL: Born September 19, 1976, in New Orleans. ... 6-4/271. ... Full name: Lawrence Edward Hart Jr.
HIGH SCHOOL: Woodlawn (Shreveport, La.).
COLLEGE: Southern (La.).

TRANSACTIONS/CAREER NOTES: Selected by New York Jets in seventh round (195th pick overall) of 1998 NFL draft. ... Signed by Jets (June 15, 1998). ... Released by Jets (August 30, 1998). ... Re-signed by Jets to practice squad (August 31, 1998). ... Released by Jets (August 31, 1999). ... Signed by Green Bay Packers to practice squad (November 23, 1999). ... Assigned by Packers to Rhein Fire in 2000 NFL enhancement allocation program (February 18, 2000). ... Traded by Packers to New Orleans Saints for FB Marvin Powell (July 11, 2000). ... Traded by Saints to Dallas Cowboys for a conditional seventh-round draft choice (August 10, 2000). ... Released by Cowboys (August 21, 2000). ... Signed by Jacksonville Jaguars (May 3, 2001). ... Released by Jaguars (September 2, 2001). ... Signed by Arizona Cardinals (December 5, 2001). ... On injured reserve with ankle injury (January 4, 2002-remainder of season). ... Granted free agency (March 1, 2002).

				RECEIVING		
Year Team	G	GS	No.	Yds.	Avg.	TD
2000—Rhein NFLE	...	...	18	179	9.9	2
2001—Arizona NFL	1	0	0	0	0.0	0
NFL Europe totals (1 year)	...	...	18	179	9.9	2
NFL totals (1 year)	1	0	0	0	0.0	0
Pro totals (2 years)	...	...	18	179	9.9	2

HARTINGS, JEFF   G   STEELERS

PERSONAL: Born September 7, 1972, in St. Henry, Ohio. ... 6-3/295. ... Full name: Jeffrey Allen Hartings.
HIGH SCHOOL: St. Henry (Ohio).
COLLEGE: Penn State.
TRANSACTIONS/CAREER NOTES: Selected by Detroit Lions in first round (23rd pick overall) of 1996 NFL draft. ... Signed by Lions (September 27, 1996). ... Granted unconditional free agency (March 2, 2001). ... Signed by Pittsburgh Steelers (March 8, 2001).
PLAYING EXPERIENCE: Detroit NFL, 1996-2000; Pittsburgh NFL, 2001. ... Games/Games started: 1996 (11/10), 1997 (16/16), 1998 (13/13), 1999 (16/16), 2000 (16/16), 2001 (16/16). Total: 88/87.
CHAMPIONSHIP GAME EXPERIENCE: Played in AFC championship game (2001 season).
HONORS: Named offensive lineman on THE SPORTING NEWS college All-America second team (1994). ... Named offensive lineman on THE SPORTING NEWS college All-America first team (1995).
PRO STATISTICS: 1996—Recovered one fumble. 1999—Recovered two fumbles for one yard. 2000—Recovered one fumble in end zone for touchdown.

HARTS, SHAUNARD   DB   CHIEFS

PERSONAL: Born August 4, 1978, in Pittsburg, Calif. ... 5-11/207.
HIGH SCHOOL: Pittsburg (Calif.).
COLLEGE: Boise State.
TRANSACTIONS/CAREER NOTES: Selected by Kansas City Chiefs in seventh round (212th pick overall) of 2001 NFL draft. ... Signed by Chiefs (July 3, 2001). ... Released by Chiefs (September 2, 2001). ... Re-signed by Chiefs to practice squad (September 3, 2001). ... Activated (December 22, 2001).
PLAYING EXPERIENCE: Kansas City NFL, 2001. ... Games/Games started: 2001 (3/0).

HARTWELL, EDGERTON   LB   RAVENS

PERSONAL: Born May 27, 1978, in Las Vegas, Nev. ... 6-1/250.
HIGH SCHOOL: Cheyenne (Las Vegas, Nev.).
COLLEGE: Wisconsin, then Western Illinois.
TRANSACTIONS/CAREER NOTES: Selected by Baltimore Ravens in fourth round (126th pick overall) of 2001 NFL draft. ... Signed by Ravens (June 8, 2001).
PLAYING EXPERIENCE: Baltimore NFL, 2001. ... Games/Games started: 2001 (16/0).
PRO STATISTICS: 2001—Recovered one fumble.

HASSELBECK, MATT   QB   SEAHAWKS

PERSONAL: Born September 25, 1975, in Boulder, Colo. ... 6-4/233. ... Full name: Matthew Michael Hasselbeck. ... Son of Don Hasselbeck, tight end with New England Patriots (1977-85).
HIGH SCHOOL: Xaverian Brothers (Westwood, Mass.).
COLLEGE: Boston College (degree in marketing and finance, 1997).
TRANSACTIONS/CAREER NOTES: Selected by Green Bay Packers in sixth round (187th pick overall) of 1998 NFL draft. ... Signed by Packers (July 17, 1998). ... Released by Packers (September 3, 1998). ... Re-signed by Packers to practice squad (September 5, 1998). ... Traded by Packers with first-round pick (G Steve Hutchinson) in 2001 draft to Seattle Seahawks for first-round pick (DE Jamal Reynolds) in 2001 draft (March 2, 2001).
PRO STATISTICS: 1999—Fumbled once and recovered one fumble for minus 16 yards. 2001—Fumbled six times.
SINGLE GAME HIGHS (regular season): Attempts—37 (December 9, 2001, vs. Denver); completions—20 (September 9, 2001, vs. Cleveland); passing yards—243 (December 9, 2001, vs. Denver); and touchdown passes—2 (October 28, 2001, vs. Miami).
MISCELLANEOUS: Regular-season record as starting NFL quarterback: 5-7 (.417).

				PASSING						RUSHING			TOTALS		
Year Team	G	GS	Att.	Cmp.	Pct.	Yds.	TD	Int.	Avg.	Rat.	Att.	Yds.	Avg.	TD	TD	2pt.	Pts.
1999—Green Bay NFL	16	0	10	3	30.0	41	1	0	4.10	77.5	6	15	2.5	0	0	0	0
2000—Green Bay NFL	16	0	19	10	52.6	104	1	0	5.47	86.3	4	-5	-1.3	0	0	0	0
2001—Seattle NFL	13	12	321	176	54.8	2023	7	8	6.30	70.9	40	141	3.5	0	0	0	0
Pro totals (3 years)	45	12	350	189	54.0	2168	9	8	6.19	71.9	50	151	3.0	0	0	0	0

– 168 –

HASTY, JAMES — CB

PERSONAL: Born May 23, 1965, in Seattle. ... 6-0/213. ... Full name: James Edward Hasty.
HIGH SCHOOL: Franklin (Seattle).
COLLEGE: Central Washington, then Washington State (degree in communications, 1988).
TRANSACTIONS/CAREER NOTES: Selected by New York Jets in third round (74th pick overall) of 1988 NFL draft. ... Signed by Jets (July 12, 1988). ... Designated by Jets as transition player (February 25, 1993). ... Tendered offer sheet by Cincinnati Bengals (April 29, 1993). ... Offer matched by Jets (May 4, 1993). ... Granted unconditional free agency (February 17, 1995). ... Signed by Kansas City Chiefs (March 29, 1995). ... On reserve/did not report list (July 20-August 3, 1997). ... Granted unconditional free agency (February 13, 1998). ... Re-signed by Chiefs (February 17, 1998). ... Released by Chiefs (February 28, 2001). ... Signed by Oakland Raiders (November 8, 2001). ... On reserve/left squad list (November 21, 2001-remainder of season).
HONORS: Played in Pro Bowl (1997 and 1999 seasons).
PRO STATISTICS: 1988—Recovered three fumbles for 35 yards. 1989—Fumbled once and recovered two fumbles for two yards. 1990—Returned one punt for no yards, fumbled once and recovered three fumbles. 1991—Recovered four fumbles for seven yards. 1992—Recovered two fumbles. 1993—Recovered two fumbles for 28 yards. 1994—Recovered two fumbles. 1995—Recovered one fumble for 20 yards. 1996—Recovered one fumble for 80 yards and a touchdown. 1997—Recovered one fumble. 1998—Recovered one fumble. 2000—Recovered two fumbles.

			INTERCEPTIONS				SACKS
Year Team	G	GS	No.	Yds.	Avg.	TD	No.
1988—New York Jets NFL	15	15	5	20	4.0	0	1.0
1989—New York Jets NFL	16	16	5	62	12.4	1	0.0
1990—New York Jets NFL	16	16	2	0	0.0	0	0.0
1991—New York Jets NFL	16	16	3	39	13.0	0	0.0
1992—New York Jets NFL	16	16	2	18	9.0	0	0.0
1993—New York Jets NFL	16	16	2	22	11.0	0	0.0
1994—New York Jets NFL	16	16	5	90	18.0	0	3.0
1995—Kansas City NFL	16	16	3	89	29.7	▲1	0.0
1996—Kansas City NFL	15	14	0	0	0.0	0	1.0
1997—Kansas City NFL	16	15	3	22	7.3	0	2.0
1998—Kansas City NFL	16	14	4	42	10.5	0	1.0
1999—Kansas City NFL	15	15	†7	98	14.0	†2	1.0
2000—Kansas City NFL	16	15	4	53	13.3	0	1.0
2001—Oakland NFL	1	0	0	0	0.0	0	0.0
Pro totals (14 years)	206	200	45	555	12.3	4	10.0

HATCHETTE, MATTHEW — WR — RAIDERS

PERSONAL: Born May 1, 1974, in Cleveland. ... 6-3/193. ... Full name: Matthew Isaac Hatchette.
HIGH SCHOOL: Jefferson (Delphos, Ohio).
COLLEGE: Mercyhurst College (Pa.), then Langston University (Okla.).
TRANSACTIONS/CAREER NOTES: Selected by Minnesota Vikings in seventh round (235th pick overall) of 1997 NFL draft. ... Signed by Vikings (June 20, 1997). ... Granted free agency (February 11, 2000). ... Re-signed by Vikings (April 11, 2000). ... Granted unconditional free agency (March 2, 2001). ... Signed by New York Jets (March 20, 2001). ... Released by Jets (February 25, 2002). ... Signed by Oakland Raiders (March 22, 2002).
CHAMPIONSHIP GAME EXPERIENCE: Played in NFC championship game (1998 and 2000 seasons).
SINGLE GAME HIGHS (regular season): Receptions—6 (December 13, 1998, vs. Baltimore); yards—95 (December 13, 1998, vs. Baltimore); and touchdown receptions—1 (October 15, 2000, vs. Chicago).

			RECEIVING				TOTALS			
Year Team	G	GS	No.	Yds.	Avg.	TD	TD	2pt.	Pts.	Fum.
1997—Minnesota NFL	16	0	3	54	18.0	0	0	0	0	0
1998—Minnesota NFL	5	0	15	216	14.4	0	0	0	0	0
1999—Minnesota NFL	13	0	9	180	20.0	2	2	0	12	0
2000—Minnesota NFL	14	4	16	190	11.9	2	2	0	12	0
2001—New York Jets NFL	11	0	2	44	22.0	0	0	0	0	0
Pro totals (5 years)	59	4	45	684	15.2	4	4	0	24	0

HAUCK, TIM — S

PERSONAL: Born December 20, 1966, in Butte, Mont. ... 5-10/187. ... Full name: Timothy Christian Hauck. ... Name pronounced HOWK.
HIGH SCHOOL: Sweet Grass County (Big Timber, Mont.).
COLLEGE: Pacific (Ore.), then Montana.
TRANSACTIONS/CAREER NOTES: Signed as non-drafted free agent by New England Patriots (May 1, 1990). ... Released by Patriots (August 26, 1990). ... Re-signed by Patriots to practice squad (October 1, 1990). ... Activated (October 27, 1990). ... Granted unconditional free agency (February 1, 1991). ... Signed by Green Bay Packers (April 1, 1991). ... Granted unconditional free agency (February 1-April 1, 1992). ... Re-signed by Packers for 1992 season. ... Granted free agency (March 1, 1993). ... Re-signed by Packers (July 13, 1993). ... Granted unconditional free agency (February 17, 1994). ... Re-signed by Packers (July 20, 1994). ... Granted unconditional free agency (February 17, 1995). ... Signed by Denver Broncos (March 6, 1995). ... Granted unconditional free agency (February 14, 1997). ... Signed by Seattle Seahawks (June 2, 1997). ... Granted unconditional free agency (February 13, 1998). ... Signed by Indianapolis Colts (July 26, 1998). ... Granted unconditional free agency (February 12, 1999). ... Signed by Philadelphia Eagles (April 20, 1999). ... Granted unconditional free agency (February 11, 2000). ... Re-signed by Eagles (August 24, 2000). ... Granted unconditional free agency (March 2, 2001). ... Re-signed by Eagles (August 18, 2001). ... Granted unconditional free agency (March 1, 2002).
PLAYING EXPERIENCE: New England NFL, 1990; Green Bay NFL, 1991-1994; Denver NFL, 1995 and 1996; Seattle NFL, 1997; Indianapolis NFL, 1998; Philadelphia NFL, 1999-2001. ... Games/Games started: 1990 (10/0), 1991 (16/0), 1992 (16/0), 1993 (13/0), 1994 (13/3), 1995 (16/0), 1996 (16/0), 1997 (16/0), 1998 (16/7), 1999 (16/15), 2000 (16/3), 2001 (16/0). Total: 164/25.
CHAMPIONSHIP GAME EXPERIENCE: Played in NFC championship game (2001 season).
PRO STATISTICS: 1991—Recovered one fumble. 1992—Returned one punt for two yards. 1993—Recovered one fumble. 1997—Recovered one fumble for eight yards. 1999—Intercepted one pass for two yards and recovered one fumble. 2000—Recovered one fumble. 2001—Recovered one fumble.

HAWKES, MICHAEL — LB — RAMS

PERSONAL: Born April 11, 1977, in Richmond, Va. ... 6-0/242. ... Full name: Michael Tranzo Hawkes.
HIGH SCHOOL: Nottoway (Blackstone, Va.).
COLLEGE: Virginia Tech.
TRANSACTIONS/CAREER NOTES: Signed as non-drafted free agent by Carolina Panthers (April 25, 2000). ... Released by Panthers (August 27, 2000). ... Re-signed by Panthers to practice squad (August 29, 2000). ... Activated (December 19, 2000); did not play. ... Released by Panthers (September 2, 2001). ... Re-signed by Panthers to practice squad (September 4, 2001). ... Activated (October 12, 2001). ... Released by Panthers (October 24, 2001). ... Signed by St. Louis Rams (January 16, 2002).
PLAYING EXPERIENCE: Carolina NFL, 2000 and 2001. ... Games/Games started: 2000 (1/0), 2001 (2/0). Total: 3/0.
PRO STATISTICS: 2001—Recovered one fumble.

HAWKINS, ARTRELL — CB — BENGALS

PERSONAL: Born November 24, 1975, in Johnstown, Pa. ... 5-10/190. ... Cousin of Carlton Haselrig, guard with Pittsburgh Steelers (1990-93) and New York Jets (1995).
HIGH SCHOOL: Bishop McCort (Johnstown, Pa.).
COLLEGE: Cincinnati.
TRANSACTIONS/CAREER NOTES: Selected by Cincinnati Bengals in second round (43rd pick overall) of 1998 NFL draft. ... Signed by Bengals (May 14, 1998). ... Granted free agency (March 2, 2001). ... Re-signed by Bengals (April 4, 2001). ... Granted unconditional free agency (March 1, 2002). ... Re-signed by Bengals (March 18, 2002).
PRO STATISTICS: 1998—Credited with one sack and recovered one fumble for 25 yards. 1999—Recovered one fumble. 2000—Recovered one fumble for 12 yards. 2001—Recovered one fumble.

				INTERCEPTIONS		
Year Team	G	GS	No.	Yds.	Avg.	TD
1998—Cincinnati NFL	16	16	3	21	7.0	0
1999—Cincinnati NFL	14	13	0	0	0.0	0
2000—Cincinnati NFL	16	6	0	0	0.0	0
2001—Cincinnati NFL	14	13	3	26	8.7	0
Pro totals (4 years)	60	48	6	47	7.8	0

HAWTHORNE, DUANE — CB — COWBOYS

PERSONAL: Born August 26, 1976, in St. Louis. ... 5-10/175. ... Name pronounced DUH-wann.
HIGH SCHOOL: Ladue (Mo.).
COLLEGE: Northern Illinois.
TRANSACTIONS/CAREER NOTES: Signed as non-drafted free agent by Dallas Cowboys (April 23, 1999). ... Assigned by Cowboys to Scottish Claymores in 2000 NFL Europe enhancement allocation program (February 18, 2000). ... Granted free agency (March 1, 2002). ... Re-signed by Cowboys (April 25, 2002).

				INTERCEPTIONS		
Year Team	G	GS	No.	Yds.	Avg.	TD
1999—Dallas NFL	13	0	3	-2	-0.7	0
2000—Scottish NFLE	...	...	4	51	12.8	0
—Dallas NFL	14	0	0	0	0.0	0
2001—Dallas NFL	16	11	2	28	14.0	0
NFL Europe totals (1 year)	...	...	4	51	12.8	0
NFL totals (3 years)	43	11	5	26	5.2	0
Pro totals (4 years)	...	...	9	77	8.6	0

HAWTHORNE, MICHAEL — CB — SAINTS

PERSONAL: Born January 26, 1977, in Sarasota, Fla. ... 6-3/196. ... Full name: Michael Seneca Hawthorne.
HIGH SCHOOL: Booker (Sarasota, Fla.).
COLLEGE: Purdue.
TRANSACTIONS/CAREER NOTES: Selected by New Orleans Saints in sixth round (195th pick overall) of 2000 NFL draft. ... Signed by Saints (June 23, 2000).
PLAYING EXPERIENCE: New Orleans NFL, 2000 and 2001. ... Games/Games started: 2000 (11/0), 2001 (11/2). Total: 22/2.

HAYES, CHRIS — S — PATRIOTS

PERSONAL: Born May 7, 1972, in San Bernardino, Calif. ... 6-0/206.
HIGH SCHOOL: San Gorgonio (San Bernardino, Calif.).
COLLEGE: Washington State.
TRANSACTIONS/CAREER NOTES: Selected by New York Jets in seventh round (210th pick overall) of 1996 NFL draft. ... Signed by Jets (June 26, 1996). ... Released by Jets (August 19, 1996). ... Signed by Washington Redskins to practice squad (September 11, 1996). ... Released by Redskins (October 2, 1996). ... Signed by Green Bay Packers to practice squad (October 4, 1996). ... Activated (December 9, 1996). ... Traded by Packers to Jets for CB Carl Greenwood (June 5, 1997). ... Granted free agency (February 11, 2000). ... Re-signed by Jets (May 8, 2000). ... Granted unconditional free agency (March 2, 2001). ... Re-signed by Jets (March 13, 2001). ... Released by Jets (February 25, 2002). ... Signed by New England Patriots (March 12, 2002).
PLAYING EXPERIENCE: Green Bay NFL, 1996; New York Jets NFL, 1997-2001. ... Games/Games started: 1996 (2/0), 1997 (16/0), 1998 (15/0), 1999 (15/0), 2000 (16/8), 2001 (16/1). Total: 80/9.
CHAMPIONSHIP GAME EXPERIENCE: Played in NFC championship game (1996 season). ... Member of Super Bowl championship team (1996 season). ... Played in AFC championship game (1998 season).
PRO STATISTICS: 2000—Intercepted one pass for no yards and recovered one fumble.

HAYES, DONALD — WR — PATRIOTS

PERSONAL: Born July 13, 1975, in Madison, Wis. ... 6-4/208. ... Full name: Donald Ross Hayes Jr.
HIGH SCHOOL: Madison East (Wis.).
COLLEGE: Wisconsin.
TRANSACTIONS/CAREER NOTES: Selected by Carolina Panthers in fourth round (106th pick overall) of 1998 NFL draft. ... Signed by Panthers (July 8, 1998). ... Granted free agency (March 2, 2001). ... Re-signed by Panthers (March 2, 2001). ... Granted unconditional free agency (March 1, 2002). ... Signed by New England Patriots (March 12, 2002).
PRO STATISTICS: 2000—Fumbled once. 2001—Fumbled once and recovered one fumble.
SINGLE GAME HIGHS (regular season): Receptions—7 (October 14, 2001, vs. New Orleans); yards—133 (November 28, 1999, vs. Atlanta); and touchdown receptions—1 (December 30, 2001, vs. Arizona).
STATISTICAL PLATEAUS: 100-yard receiving games: 1999 (1), 2000 (1). Total: 2.

				RECEIVING		
Year Team	G	GS	No.	Yds.	Avg.	TD
1998—Carolina NFL	7	0	3	62	20.7	0
1999—Carolina NFL	13	1	11	270	24.5	2
2000—Carolina NFL	15	15	66	926	14.0	3
2001—Carolina NFL	16	15	52	597	11.5	2
Pro totals (4 years)	51	31	132	1855	14.1	7

HAYES, WINDRELL — WR — PACKERS

PERSONAL: Born December 14, 1976, in Stockton, Calif. ... 5-11/198.
HIGH SCHOOL: St. Mary's (Stockton, Calif.), then Franklin (Stockton, Calif.).
JUNIOR COLLEGE: San Joaquin Delta College, Calif. (did not play football).
COLLEGE: San Jose State, then Southern California.
TRANSACTIONS/CAREER NOTES: Selected by New York Jets in fifth round (143rd pick overall) of 2000 NFL draft. ... Signed by Jets (May 24, 2000). ... Released by Jets (October 29, 2001). ... Signed by Green Bay Packers (March 5, 2002).
PLAYING EXPERIENCE: New York Jets NFL, 2000 and 2001. ... Games/Games started: 2000 (8/1), 2001 (1/0). Total: 9/1.
PRO STATISTICS: 2000—Caught six passes for 126 yards and rushed once for two yards.
SINGLE GAME HIGHS (regular season): Receptions—4 (December 3, 2000, vs. Indianapolis); yards—84 (December 3, 2000, vs. Indianapolis); and touchdown receptions—0.

HAYWARD, REGGIE — DE — BRONCOS

PERSONAL: Born March 14, 1979, in Chicago. ... 6-5/255.
HIGH SCHOOL: Thornridge (Dolton, Ill.).
COLLEGE: Iowa State.
TRANSACTIONS/CAREER NOTES: Selected by Denver Broncos in third round (87th pick overall) of 2001 NFL draft. ... Signed by Broncos (July 26, 2001).

Year Team	G	GS	SACKS
2001—Denver NFL	6	2	3.0

HAZUGA, JEFF — DL — VIKINGS

PERSONAL: Born April 29, 1978, in Thorp, Wis. ... 6-5/277.
HIGH SCHOOL: Thorp (Wis.).
COLLEGE: St. Cloud State, then Wisconsin-Stout.
TRANSACTIONS/CAREER NOTES: Signed as non-drafted free agent by Minnesota Vikings (April 22, 2001). ... On injured reserve with shoulder injury (November 27, 2001-remainder of season).
PLAYING EXPERIENCE: Minnesota NFL, 2001. ... Games/Games started: 2001 (3/0).

HEAP, TODD — TE — RAVENS

PERSONAL: Born March 16, 1980, in Mesa, Ariz. ... 6-5/252. ... Full name: Todd Benjamin Heap.
HIGH SCHOOL: Mountain View (Mesa, Ariz.).
COLLEGE: Arizona State.
TRANSACTIONS/CAREER NOTES: Selected after junior season by Baltimore Ravens in first round (31st pick overall) of 2001 NFL draft. ... Signed by Ravens (July 28, 2001).
HONORS: Named tight end on THE SPORTING NEWS college All-America first team (2000).
PRO STATISTICS: 2001—Fumbled once.
SINGLE GAME HIGHS (regular season): Receptions—5 (September 9, 2001, vs. Chicago); yards—57 (September 9, 2001, vs. Chicago); and touchdown receptions—1 (November 18, 2001, vs. Cleveland).

				RECEIVING		
Year Team	G	GS	No.	Yds.	Avg.	TD
2001—Baltimore NFL	12	6	16	206	12.9	1

HEARD, RONNIE — S — 49ERS

PERSONAL: Born October 5, 1976, in Bay City, Texas. ... 6-3/215.
HIGH SCHOOL: Brazoswood (Clute, Texas).

COLLEGE: Mississippi.
TRANSACTIONS/CAREER NOTES: Signed as non-drafted free agent by San Francisco 49ers (April 20, 2000). ... Released by 49ers (August 27, 2000). ... Re-signed by 49ers to practice squad (August 29, 2000). ... Activated (October 16, 2000).
PLAYING EXPERIENCE: San Francisco NFL, 2000 and 2001. ... Games/Games started: 2000 (13/3), 2001 (16/0). Total: 29/3.
PRO STATISTICS: 2000—Credited with two sacks. 2001—Credited with one sack.

HEARST, GARRISON　　　RB　　　49ERS

PERSONAL: Born January 4, 1971, in Lincolnton, Ga. ... 5-11/215. ... Full name: Gerald Garrison Hearst.
HIGH SCHOOL: Lincoln County (Lincolnton, Ga.).
COLLEGE: Georgia.
TRANSACTIONS/CAREER NOTES: Selected after junior season by Phoenix Cardinals in first round (third pick overall) of 1993 NFL draft. ... Signed by Cardinals (August 28, 1993). ... On injured reserve with knee injury (November 4, 1993-remainder of season). ... Cardinals franchise renamed Arizona Cardinals for 1994 season. ... On physically unable to perform list with knee injury (August 23-October 13, 1994). ... Granted free agency (February 16, 1996). ... Re-signed by Cardinals (May 23, 1996). ... Claimed on waivers by Cincinnati Bengals (August 21, 1996). ... Granted unconditional free agency (February 14, 1997). ... Signed by San Francisco 49ers (March 7, 1997). ... On physically unable to perform list with leg injury (July 30, 1999-entire season). ... On physically unable to perform list with leg injury (August 22-November 21, 2000). ... Granted unconditional free agency (March 1, 2002). ... Re-signed by 49ers (March 13, 2002).
CHAMPIONSHIP GAME EXPERIENCE: Played in NFC championship game (1997 season).
HONORS: Doak Walker Award winner (1992). ... Named running back on THE SPORTING NEWS college All-America first team (1992). ... Named to play in Pro Bowl (1998 season); replaced by Emmitt Smith due to injury.
PRO STATISTICS: 1993—Had only pass attempt intercepted. 1994—Completed only pass attempt for 10 yards and a touchdown. 1995—Attempted two passes with one completion for 16 yards and recovered two fumbles. 1996—Recovered one fumble. 1997—Recovered two fumbles. 1998—Recovered one fumble. 2001—Recovered one fumble.
SINGLE GAME HIGHS (regular season): Attempts—28 (September 29, 1997, vs. Carolina); yards—198 (December 14, 1998, vs. Detroit); and rushing touchdowns—2 (November 25, 2001, vs. Indianapolis).
STATISTICAL PLATEAUS: 100-yard rushing games: 1995 (3), 1997 (3), 1998 (6), 2001 (4). Total: 16. ... 100-yard receiving games: 1998 (2), 2001 (1). Total: 3.

			RUSHING				RECEIVING				TOTALS			
Year Team	G	GS	Att.	Yds.	Avg.	TD	No.	Yds.	Avg.	TD	TD	2pt.	Pts.	Fum.
1993—Phoenix NFL	6	5	76	264	3.5	1	6	18	3.0	0	1	0	6	2
1994—Arizona NFL	8	0	37	169	4.6	1	6	49	8.2	0	1	0	6	0
1995—Arizona NFL	16	15	284	1070	3.8	1	29	243	8.4	1	2	0	12	12
1996—Cincinnati NFL	16	12	225	847	3.8	0	12	131	10.9	1	1	1	8	1
1997—San Francisco NFL	13	13	234	1019	4.4	4	21	194	9.2	2	6	0	36	2
1998—San Francisco NFL	16	16	310	1570	‡5.1	7	39	535	13.7	2	9	1	56	4
1999—San Francisco NFL								Did not play.						
2000—San Francisco NFL								Did not play.						
2001—San Francisco NFL	16	16	252	1206	4.8	4	41	347	8.5	1	5	0	30	1
Pro totals (7 years)	91	77	1418	6145	4.3	18	154	1517	9.9	7	25	2	154	22

HEATH, RODNEY　　　CB　　　BENGALS

PERSONAL: Born October 29, 1974, in Cincinnati. ... 5-10/177. ... Full name: Rodney Larece Heath.
HIGH SCHOOL: Western Hills (Cincinnati).
COLLEGE: Minnesota (degree in sports studies).
TRANSACTIONS/CAREER NOTES: Signed as non-drafted free agent by Cincinnati Bengals (January 27, 1999). ... On injured reserve with shoulder injury (December 4, 2000-remainder of season). ... On injured reserve with hamstring injury (October 16, 2001-remainder of season).
PRO STATISTICS: 1999—Recovered two fumbles for minus four yards. 2000—Returned one kickoff for 22 yards and recovered one fumble. 2001—Recovered one fumble.

			INTERCEPTIONS				TOTALS			
Year Team	G	GS	No.	Yds.	Avg.	TD	TD	2pt.	Pts.	Fum.
1999—Cincinnati NFL	16	9	3	72	24.0	1	1	0	6	0
2000—Cincinnati NFL	13	9	0	0	0.0	0	0	0	0	0
2001—Cincinnati NFL	5	5	0	0	0.0	0	0	0	0	0
Pro totals (3 years)	34	23	3	72	24.0	1	1	0	6	0

HEFFNER-LIDDIARD, BRODY　　　TE　　　VIKINGS

PERSONAL: Born June 12, 1977, in Salt Lake City. ... 6-4/250. ... Full name: Jon Brody Heffner-Liddiard.
HIGH SCHOOL: Torrey Pines (San Diego).
COLLEGE: Colorado.
TRANSACTIONS/CAREER NOTES: Signed as non-drafted free agent by Minnesota Vikings (April 25, 2000). ... Released by Vikings (August 14, 2000). ... Signed by New York Giants (August 20, 2000). ... Released by Giants (September 4, 2000). ... Re-signed by Giants to practice squad (September 5, 2000). ... Activated (September 9, 2000). ... Released by Giants (September 12, 2000). ... Signed by Miami Dolphins (November 23, 2000). ... Released by Dolphins (July 11, 2001). ... Signed by Minnesota Vikings (July 23, 2001).
PLAYING EXPERIENCE: Miami NFL, 2000; Minnesota NFL, 2001. ... Games/Games started: 2000 (5/0), 2001 (16/0). Total: 21/0.

HEIDEN, STEVE　　　TE　　　CHARGERS

PERSONAL: Born September 21, 1976, in Rushford, Minn. ... 6-5/270. ... Full name: Steve Allen Heiden. ... Name pronounced HIGH-den.
HIGH SCHOOL: Rushford-Peterson (Rushford, Minn.).
COLLEGE: South Dakota State.

TRANSACTIONS/CAREER NOTES: Selected by San Diego Chargers in third round (69th pick overall) of 1999 NFL draft. ... Signed by Chargers (July 22, 1999). ... Granted free agency (March 1, 2002). ... Re-signed by Chargers (April 3, 2002).
PLAYING EXPERIENCE: San Diego NFL, 1999-2001. ... Games/Games started: 1999 (11/0), 2000 (15/2), 2001 (16/9). Total: 42/11.
PRO STATISTICS: 2000—Caught six passes for 32 yards and one touchdown and recovered one fumble. 2001—Caught eight passes for 55 yards and one touchdown.
SINGLE GAME HIGHS (regular season): Receptions—2 (November 25, 2001, vs. Arizona); yards—24 (November 24, 2001, vs. Arizona); and touchdown receptions—1 (October 14, 2001, vs. New England).

HEIMBURGER, CRAIG   G

PERSONAL: Born February 3, 1977, in Belleville, Ill. ... 6-2/312. ... Full name: Craig Andre Heimburger. ... Name pronounced HIME-burger.
HIGH SCHOOL: Belleville (Ill.) East.
COLLEGE: Missouri.
TRANSACTIONS/CAREER NOTES: Selected by Green Bay Packers in fifth round (163rd pick overall) of 1999 NFL draft. ... Signed by Packers (July 13, 1999). ... Released by Packers (September 5, 1999). ... Re-signed by Packers to practice squad (September 7, 1999). ... Activated (November 23, 1999). ... Assigned by Packers to Rhein Fire in 2000 NFL Europe enhancement allocation program (February 18, 2000). ... Released by Packers (August 27, 2000). ... Re-signed by Packers to practice squad (August 28, 2000). ... Signed by Cincinnati Bengals off Packers practice squad (December 14, 2000). ... Claimed on waivers by Buffalo Bills (May 18, 2001). ... Granted free agency (March 1, 2002).
PLAYING EXPERIENCE: Green Bay NFL, 1999; Rhein NFLE, 2000; Buffalo NFL, 2001. ... Games/Games started: 1999 (2/0), 2000 (games played unavailable), 2001 (10/0). Total: 12/0.

HELLESTRAE, DALE   G/C   TEXANS

PERSONAL: Born July 11, 1962, in Phoenix. ... 6-5/291. ... Full name: Dale Robert Hellestrae. ... Name pronounced HELL-uh-stray.
HIGH SCHOOL: Saguaro (Scottsdale, Ariz.).
COLLEGE: Southern Methodist (degree in business administration).
TRANSACTIONS/CAREER NOTES: Selected by Houston Gamblers in 1985 USFL territorial draft. ... Selected by Buffalo Bills in fourth round (112th pick overall) of 1985 NFL draft. ... Signed by Bills (July 19, 1985). ... On injured reserve with broken thumb (October 4, 1985-remainder of season). ... On injured reserve with broken wrist (September 17-November 15, 1986). ... On injured reserve with hip injury (September 1, 1987-entire season). ... Granted unconditional free agency (February 1, 1989). ... Signed by Los Angeles Raiders (February 24, 1989). ... On injured reserve with broken leg (August 29, 1989-entire season). ... Traded by Raiders to Dallas Cowboys for seventh-round pick (traded to Chicago) in 1991 draft (August 20, 1990). ... Granted unconditional free agency (February 1-April 1, 1991). ... Re-signed by Cowboys for 1991 season. ... Granted unconditional free agency (February 1-April 1, 1992). ... Re-signed by Cowboys for 1992 season. ... Released by Cowboys (August 31, 1992). ... Re-signed by Cowboys (September 2, 1992). ... Granted unconditional free agency (March 1, 1993). ... Re-signed by Cowboys (June 2, 1993). ... Released by Cowboys (August 30, 1993). ... Re-signed by Cowboys (August 31, 1993). ... Granted unconditional free agency (February 17, 1994). ... Re-signed by Cowboys (July 14, 1994). ... Granted unconditional free agency (February 16, 1996). ... Re-signed by Cowboys (April 9, 1996). ... Granted unconditional free agency (February 13, 1998). ... Re-signed by Cowboys (April 7, 1998). ... Granted unconditional free agency (February 12, 1999). ... Re-signed by Cowboys (June 23, 1999). ... Granted unconditional free agency (February 11, 2000). ... Re-signed by Cowboys (June 19, 2000). ... Released by Cowboys (March 1, 2001). ... Signed by Baltimore Ravens (January 3, 2002). ... Granted unconditional free agency (March 1, 2002). ... Signed by Houston Texans (June 5, 2002).
PLAYING EXPERIENCE: Buffalo NFL, 1985, 1986 and 1988; Dallas NFL, 1990-2000; Baltimore NFL, 2001. ... Games/Games started: 1985 (4/0), 1986 (8/0), 1988 (16/2), 1990 (16/0), 1991 (16/0), 1992 (16/0), 1993 (16/0), 1994 (16/0), 1995 (16/0), 1996 (16/0), 1997 (16/0), 1998 (16/0), 1999 (16/0), 2000 (16/0), 2001 (1/0). Total: 205/2.
CHAMPIONSHIP GAME EXPERIENCE: Played in AFC championship game (1988 season). ... Played in NFC championship game (1992-1995 seasons). ... Member of Super Bowl championship team (1992, 1993 and 1995 seasons).
PRO STATISTICS: 1986—Fumbled once for minus 14 yards. 2001—Fumbled once for minus 11 yards.

HEMSLEY, NATE   LB   PANTHERS

PERSONAL: Born May 5, 1974, in Willingboro, N.J. ... 6-1/230. ... Full name: Nathaniel Richard Hemsley.
HIGH SCHOOL: Delran (N.J.).
COLLEGE: Syracuse.
TRANSACTIONS/CAREER NOTES: Signed as non-drafted free agent by Tennessee Oilers (April 23, 1997). ... Released by Oilers (August 13, 1997). ... Signed by Dallas Cowboys to practice squad (September 3, 1997). ... Activated (December 10, 1997). ... On injured reserve with ankle injury (October 5, 1998-remainder of season). ... Released by Cowboys (October 27, 1999). ... Signed by Miami Dolphins to practice squad (November 14, 2000). ... Released by Dolphins (August 28, 2001). ... Signed by Carolina Panthers (October 2, 2001).
PLAYING EXPERIENCE: Dallas NFL, 1997-1999; Carolina NFL, 2001. ... Games/Games started: 1997 (2/0), 1998 (3/0), 1999 (6/0), 2001 (9/3). Total: 20/3.

HENDERSON, JAMIE   CB   JETS

PERSONAL: Born January 1, 1979, in Carrolton, Ga. ... 6-2/202. ... Full name: Jamie Concepcion Henderson.
HIGH SCHOOL: Carrolton (Ga.).
JUNIOR COLLEGE: Mississippi Gulf Coast Junior College.
COLLEGE: Georgia.
TRANSACTIONS/CAREER NOTES: Selected by New York Jets in fourth round (101st pick overall) of 2001 NFL draft. ... Signed by Jets (June 28, 2001).
PRO STATISTICS: 2001—Returned one kickoff for no yards.

			INTERCEPTIONS			
Year Team	G	GS	No.	Yds.	Avg.	TD
2001—New York Jets NFL............................	16	0	1	5	5.0	0

HENDERSON, WILLIAM   FB   PACKERS

PERSONAL: Born February 19, 1971, in Richmond, Va. ... 6-1/253. ... Full name: William Terrelle Henderson.
HIGH SCHOOL: Thomas Dale (Chester, Va.).
COLLEGE: North Carolina.
TRANSACTIONS/CAREER NOTES: Selected by Green Bay Packers in third round (66th pick overall) of 1995 NFL draft. ... Signed by Packers (July 17, 1995). ... Granted free agency (February 13, 1998). ... Re-signed by Packers (June 15, 1998). ... Granted unconditional free agency (February 12, 1999). ... Re-signed by Packers (April 6, 1999). ... Granted unconditional free agency (March 1, 2002). ... Re-signed by Packers (March 1, 2002).
CHAMPIONSHIP GAME EXPERIENCE: Played in NFC championship game (1995-1997 seasons). ... Member of Super Bowl championship team (1996 season). ... Played in Super Bowl XXXII (1997 season).
PRO STATISTICS: 1996—Returned two kickoffs for 38 yards. 1997—Recovered two fumbles. 1999—Returned two kickoffs for 23 yards. 2000—Returned five kickoffs for 80 yards and recovered one fumble. 2001—Returned six kickoffs for 62 yards and recovered two fumbles.
SINGLE GAME HIGHS (regular season): Attempts—6 (September 7, 1997, vs. Philadelphia); yards—40 (September 9, 1996, vs. Philadelphia); and rushing touchdowns—1 (December 12, 1999, vs. Carolina).

			RUSHING				RECEIVING			TOTALS		
Year Team	G	GS	Att.	Yds.	Avg.	TD	No.	Yds.	Avg.	TD	TD	2pt.	Pts.	Fum.
1995—Green Bay NFL	15	2	7	35	5.0	0	3	21	7.0	0	0	0	0	0
1996—Green Bay NFL	16	11	39	130	3.3	0	27	203	7.5	1	1	0	6	1
1997—Green Bay NFL	16	14	31	113	3.6	0	41	367	9.0	1	1	0	6	1
1998—Green Bay NFL	16	10	23	70	3.0	2	37	241	6.5	1	3	0	18	1
1999—Green Bay NFL	16	13	7	29	4.1	2	30	203	6.8	1	3	0	18	1
2000—Green Bay NFL	16	7	2	16	8.0	0	35	234	6.7	1	1	0	6	1
2001—Green Bay NFL	16	8	6	11	1.8	0	21	193	9.2	0	0	0	0	0
Pro totals (7 years)	111	65	115	404	3.5	4	194	1462	7.5	5	9	0	54	5

HENDRICKS, TOMMY   LB   DOLPHINS

PERSONAL: Born October 23, 1978, in Houston. ... 6-2/233. ... Full name: Thomas Emmett Hendricks III.
HIGH SCHOOL: Scarborough (Texas), then Eiserhower (Houston).
COLLEGE: Michigan.
TRANSACTIONS/CAREER NOTES: Signed as non-drafted free agent by Miami Dolphins (April 25, 2000). ... Released by Dolphins (August 27, 2000). ... Re-signed by Dophins (September 26, 2000). ... Released by Dolphins (October 2, 2000). ... Re-signed by Dolphins to practice squad (October 4, 2000). ... Activated (November 10, 2000).
PLAYING EXPERIENCE: Miami NFL, 2000 and 2001. ... Games/Games started: 2000 (8/0), 2001 (16/1). Total: 24/1.

HENRY, ANTHONY   CB   BROWNS

PERSONAL: Born November 3, 1976, in Fort Myers, Fla. ... 6-0/198. ... Full name: Anthony Daniel Henry.
HIGH SCHOOL: Estero (Fla.).
COLLEGE: South Florida.
TRANSACTIONS/CAREER NOTES: Selected by Cleveland Browns in fourth round (97th pick overall) of 2001 NFL draft. ... Signed by Browns (June 15, 2001).

			INTERCEPTIONS		
Year Team	G	GS	No.	Yds.	Avg.	TD
2001—Cleveland NFL	16	2	†10	177	17.7	1

HENRY, TRAVIS   RB   BILLS

PERSONAL: Born October 29, 1978, in Frostproof, Fla. ... 5-9/220. ... Full name: Travis Deion Henry.
HIGH SCHOOL: Frostproof (Fla.).
COLLEGE: Tennessee.
TRANSACTIONS/CAREER NOTES: Selected by Buffalo Bills in second round (58th pick overall) of 2001 NFL draft. ... Signed by Bills (July 26, 2001).
PRO STATISTICS: 2001—Recovered two fumbles.
SINGLE GAME HIGHS (regular season): Attempts—27 (December 9, 2001, vs. Carolina); yards—113 (October 7, 2001, vs. New York Jets); and rushing touchdowns—1 (December 9, 2001, vs. Carolina).
STATISTICAL PLATEAUS: 100-yard rushing games: 2001 (2).

			RUSHING				RECEIVING			TOTALS		
Year Team	G	GS	Att.	Yds.	Avg.	TD	No.	Yds.	Avg.	TD	TD	2pt.	Pts.	Fum.
2001—Buffalo NFL	13	12	213	729	3.4	4	22	179	8.1	0	4	0	24	5

HENTRICH, CRAIG   P   TITANS

PERSONAL: Born May 18, 1971, in Alton, Ill. ... 6-3/198. ... Full name: Craig Anthony Hentrich. ... Name pronounced HEN-trick.
HIGH SCHOOL: Alton-Marquette (Ill.).
COLLEGE: Notre Dame.
TRANSACTIONS/CAREER NOTES: Selected by New York Jets in eighth round (200th pick overall) of 1993 NFL draft. ... Signed by Jets (July 14, 1993). ... Released by Jets (August 24, 1993). ... Signed by Green Bay Packers to practice squad (September 7, 1993). ... Activated (January 14, 1994); did not play. ... Granted unconditional free agency (February 13, 1998). ... Signed by Tennessee Oilers (February 19, 1998). ... Oilers franchise renamed Tennessee Titans for 1999 season (December 26, 1998).

CHAMPIONSHIP GAME EXPERIENCE: Played in NFC championship game (1995-1997 seasons). ... Member of Super Bowl championship team (1996 season). ... Played in Super Bowl XXXII (1997 season) and Super Bowl XXXIV (1999 season). ... Played in AFC championship game (1999 season).
HONORS: Named punter on THE SPORTING NEWS NFL All-Pro team (1998). ... Played in Pro Bowl (1998 season).
PRO STATISTICS: 1996—Attempted one pass without a completion and recovered one fumble. 1998—Rushed once for minus one yard and completed only pass attempt for 13 yards. 1999—Rushed twice for one yard and recovered two fumbles. 2001—Attempted two passes without a completion and one interception.

			PUNTING						KICKING				
Year Team	G	No.	Yds.	Avg.	Net avg.	In. 20	Blk.	XPM	XPA	FGM	FGA	Lg.	50+	Pts.
1993—Green Bay NFL								Did not play.						
1994—Green Bay NFL	16	81	3351	41.4	35.5	24	0	0	0	0	0	0	0-0	0
1995—Green Bay NFL	16	65	2740	42.2	34.6	26	2	5	5	3	5	49	0-0	14
1996—Green Bay NFL	16	68	2886	42.4	36.2	28	0	0	0	0	0	0	0-0	0
1997—Green Bay NFL	16	75	3378	45.0	36.0	26	0	0	0	0	0	0	0-0	0
1998—Tennessee NFL	16	69	3258	*47.2	*39.2	18	0	0	0	0	1	0	0-0	0
1999—Tennessee NFL	16	90	3824	42.5	38.1	35	0	0	0	0	0	0	0-0	0
2000—Tennessee NFL	16	76	3101	40.8	36.3	33	0	0	0	0	1	0	0-1	0
2001—Tennessee NFL	16	85	3567	42.0	37.0	28	0	0	0	0	0	0	0-0	0
Pro totals (8 years)	128	609	26105	42.9	36.7	218	2	5	5	3	7	49	0-1	14

HERNDON, JIMMY　　　OT　　　TEXANS

PERSONAL: Born August 30, 1973, in Baytown, Texas. ... 6-8/318.
HIGH SCHOOL: Lee (Baytown, Texas).
COLLEGE: Houston (degree in sociology, 1996).
TRANSACTIONS/CAREER NOTES: Selected by Jacksonville Jaguars in fifth round (146th pick overall) of 1996 NFL draft. ... Signed by Jaguars (May 24, 1996). ... Active for eight games (1996); did not play. ... Traded by Jaguars to Chicago Bears for seventh-round pick (WR Alvis Whitted) in 1998 draft (August 24, 1997). ... On injured reserve with knee injury (August 31, 1999-entire season). ... Granted unconditional free agency (March 1, 2002). ... Signed by Houston Texans (April 3, 2002).
PLAYING EXPERIENCE: Chicago NFL, 1997, 1998, 2000 and 2001. ... Games/Games started: 1997 (7/0), 1998 (9/2), 2000 (9/2), 2001 (16/0). Total: 41/4.
CHAMPIONSHIP GAME EXPERIENCE: Member of Jaguars for AFC championship game (1996 season); inactive.

HERNDON, STEVE　　　G　　　BRONCOS

PERSONAL: Born May 25, 1977, in LaGrange, Ga. ... 6-4/305. ... Full name: Steven Marshall Herndon.
HIGH SCHOOL: Troup County (LaGrange, Ga.).
COLLEGE: Georgia.
TRANSACTIONS/CAREER NOTES: Signed as non-drafted free agent by Miami Dolphins (April 25, 2000). ... Released by Dolphins (August 22, 2000). ... Signed by Denver Broncos to practice squad (August 29, 2000). ... Assigned by Broncos to Barcelona Dragons in 2001 NFL Europe enhancement allocation program (February 17, 2001).
PLAYING EXPERIENCE: Barcelona NFLE, 2000; Denver NFL, 2001. ... Games/Games started: 2000 (games played unavailable), 2001 (5/3).

HERRING, KIM　　　S　　　RAMS

PERSONAL: Born September 10, 1975, in Detroit. ... 6-0/200. ... Full name: Kimani Masai Herring.
HIGH SCHOOL: Solon (Ohio).
COLLEGE: Penn State.
TRANSACTIONS/CAREER NOTES: Selected by Baltimore Ravens in second round (58th pick overall) of 1997 NFL draft. ... Signed by Ravens (July 18, 1997). ... On injured reserve with shoulder injury (December 2, 1998-remainder of season). ... Granted free agency (February 11, 2000). ... Re-signed by Ravens (April 18, 2000) ... Granted unconditional free agency (March 2, 2001). ... Signed by St. Louis Rams (March 22, 2001).
PLAYING EXPERIENCE: Baltimore NFL, 1997-2000; St. Louis NFL, 2001. ... Games/Games started: 1997 (15/4), 1998 (7/7), 1999 (16/16), 2000 (16/16), 2001 (16/15). Total: 70/58.
CHAMPIONSHIP GAME EXPERIENCE: Member of Ravens for AFC Championship game (2000 season); inactive. ... Member of Super Bowl championship team (2000 season). ... Played in NFC championship game (2001 season). ... Played in Super Bowl XXXVI (2001 season).
HONORS: Named free safety on THE SPORTING NEWS college All-America first team (1996).
PRO STATISTICS: 1997—Credited with one sack and recovered one fumble. 1999—Recovered two fumbles. 2000—Intercepted three passes for 74 yards and credited with one sack. 2001—Intercepted one pass for 15 yards.

HERRON, ANTHONY　　　DE　　　LIONS

PERSONAL: Born September 24, 1979, in Bolingbrook, Ill. ... 6-3/280.
HIGH SCHOOL: Bolingbrook (Ill.).
COLLEGE: Iowa.
TRANSACTIONS/CAREER NOTES: Signed as non-drafted free agent by Detroit Lions (April 27, 2001). ... Released by Lions (September 2, 2001). ... Re-signed by Lions (November 27, 2001).
PLAYING EXPERIENCE: Detroit NFL, 2001. ... Games/Games started: 2001 (1/0).

HETHERINGTON, CHRIS　　　FB　　　RAMS

PERSONAL: Born November 27, 1972, in North Branford, Conn. ... 6-3/250. ... Full name: Christopher Raymond Hetherington.
HIGH SCHOOL: Avon (Conn.) Old Farms.
COLLEGE: Yale (degree in psychology).

TRANSACTIONS/CAREER NOTES: Signed as non-drafted free agent by Cincinnati Bengals (April 23, 1996). ... Released by Bengals (August 21, 1996). ... Re-signed by Bengals to practice squad (August 26, 1996). ... Signed by Indianapolis Colts off Bengals practice squad (October 22, 1996). ... Released by Colts (August 24, 1998). ... Re-signed by Colts (August 31, 1998). ... Released by Colts (February 12, 1999). ... Signed by Carolina Panthers (March 5, 1999). ... Granted unconditional free agency (February 11, 2000). ... Re-signed by Panthers (February 23, 2000). ... Granted unconditional free agency (March 1, 2002). ... Signed by St. Louis Rams (April 29, 2002).
PRO STATISTICS: 1999—Recovered one fumble. 2000—Recovered one fumble.
SINGLE GAME HIGHS (regular season): Attempts—5 (December 10, 2000, vs. Kansas City); yards—29 (December 24, 2000, vs. Oakland); and rushing touchdowns—1 (December 10, 2000, vs. Kansas City).

				RUSHING				RECEIVING				KICKOFF RETURNS			TOTALS			
Year Team	G	GS	Att.	Yds.	Avg.	TD	No.	Yds.	Avg.	TD	No.	Yds.	Avg.	TD	TD	2pt.	Pts.	Fum.
1996—Indianapolis NFL	6	0	0	0	0.0	0	0	0	0.0	0	1	16	16.0	0	0	0	0	0
1997—Indianapolis NFL	16	0	0	0	0.0	0	0	0	0.0	0	2	23	11.5	0	0	0	0	0
1998—Indianapolis NFL	14	1	0	0	0.0	0	0	0	0.0	0	5	71	14.2	0	0	0	0	1
1999—Carolina NFL	14	0	2	7	3.5	0	0	0	0.0	0	1	16	16.0	0	0	0	0	0
2000—Carolina NFL	16	5	23	65	2.8	2	14	116	8.3	1	2	21	10.5	0	3	0	18	0
2001—Carolina NFL	16	1	5	12	2.4	0	23	124	5.4	0	4	31	7.8	0	0	0	0	0
Pro totals (6 years)	82	7	30	84	2.8	2	37	240	6.5	1	15	178	11.9	0	3	0	18	1

HICKS, ERIC — DE — CHIEFS

PERSONAL: Born June 17, 1976, in Erie, Pa. ... 6-6/280. ... Full name: Eric David Hicks.
HIGH SCHOOL: Mercyhurst (Erie, Pa.).
COLLEGE: Maryland.
TRANSACTIONS/CAREER NOTES: Signed as non-drafted free agent by Kansas City Chiefs (April 25, 1998).
PRO STATISTICS: 1998—Recovered one fumble. 1999—Recovered two fumbles for 44 yards and one touchdown. 2000—Recovered one fumble. 2001—Recovered one fumble.

Year Team	G	GS	SACKS
1998—Kansas City NFL	3	0	0.0
1999—Kansas City NFL	16	16	4.0
2000—Kansas City NFL	13	11	14.0
2001—Kansas City NFL	16	16	3.5
Pro totals (4 years)	48	43	21.5

HICKS, SKIP — RB — TITANS

PERSONAL: Born October 13, 1974, in Corsicana, Texas. ... 6-0/203. ... Full name: Brian LaVell Hicks.
HIGH SCHOOL: Burkburnett (Texas).
COLLEGE: UCLA.
TRANSACTIONS/CAREER NOTES: Selected by Washington Redskins in third round (69th pick overall) of 1998 NFL draft. ... Signed by Redskins (July 7, 1998). ... Granted free agency (March 2, 2001). ... Signed by Chicago Bears (May 29, 2001). ... Claimed on waivers by Tennessee Titans (September 6, 2001). ... Granted unconditional free agency (March 1, 2002). ... Signed by Tennessee Titans (June 1, 2002).
HONORS: Named running back on THE SPORTING NEWS college All-America first team (1997).
PRO STATISTICS: 2000—Returned one kickoff for 17 yards.
SINGLE GAME HIGHS (regular season): Attempts—26 (November 15, 1998, vs. Philadelphia); yards—142 (December 16, 2001, vs. Green Bay); and rushing touchdowns—3 (November 15, 1998, vs. Philadelphia).
STATISTICAL PLATEAUS: 100-yard rushing games: 2001 (1).

			RUSHING				RECEIVING				TOTALS			
Year Team	G	GS	Att.	Yds.	Avg.	TD	No.	Yds.	Avg.	TD	TD	2pt.	Pts.	Fum.
1998—Washington NFL	9	5	122	433	3.5	8	4	23	5.8	0	8	0	48	0
1999—Washington NFL	10	2	78	257	3.3	3	8	72	9.0	0	3	0	18	1
2000—Washington NFL	10	1	29	78	2.7	1	5	43	8.6	0	1	0	6	1
2001—Tennessee NFL	9	0	56	341	6.1	1	5	22	4.4	0	1	0	6	0
Pro totals (4 years)	38	8	285	1109	3.9	13	22	160	7.3	0	13	0	78	2

HILBERT, JON — K — BEARS

PERSONAL: Born July 15, 1975, in West Palm Beach, Fla. ... 6-2/220. ... Full name: Jonathan Samuel Hilbert.
HIGH SCHOOL: Boonville (Ind.).
COLLEGE: Louisville.
TRANSACTIONS/CAREER NOTES: Signed as non-drafted free agent by Dallas Cowboys (April 15, 2000). ... Released by Cowboys (July 16, 2000). ... Signed by Buffalo Bills (July 20, 2000). ... Released by Bills (August 22, 2000). ... Signed by New Orleans Saints (March 26, 2001). ... Released by Saints (August 28, 2001). ... Signed by Cowboys (November 14, 2001). ... Granted free agency (March 1, 2002). ... Signed by Chicago Bears (March 15, 2002).

		KICKING						
Year Team	G	XPM	XPA	FGM	FGA	Lg.	50+	Pts.
2001—Dallas NFL	8	12	12	11	16	43	0-0	45

HILL, RAION — S

PERSONAL: Born September 2, 1976, in Marrero, La. ... 6-0/200.
HIGH SCHOOL: Brother Martin (New Orleans).
COLLEGE: Louisiana State.
TRANSACTIONS/CAREER NOTES: Signed as non-drafted free agent by Buffalo Bills (March 23, 1999). ... Released by Bills (August 30, 1999). ... Re-signed by Bills to practice squad (October 26, 1999). ... Released by Bills (April 24, 2002).
PLAYING EXPERIENCE: Buffalo NFL, 2000 and 2001. ... Games/Games started: 2000 (16/0), 2001 (15/13). Total: 31/13.
PRO STATISTICS: 2001—Recovered one fumble.

HILL, RENALDO — DB — CARDINALS

PERSONAL: Born November 12, 1978, in Detroit. ... 5-11/182.
HIGH SCHOOL: Chadsey (Mich.).
COLLEGE: Michigan State.
TRANSACTIONS/CAREER NOTES: Selected by Arizona Cardinals in seventh round (202nd pick overall) of 2001 NFL draft. ... Signed by Cardinals (May 29, 2001).

Year Team	G	GS	SACKS
2001—Arizona NFL	14	1	0.5

HILLIARD, IKE — WR — GIANTS

PERSONAL: Born April 5, 1976, in Patterson, La. ... 5-11/195. ... Full name: Isaac Jason Hilliard. ... Nephew of Dalton Hilliard, running back with New Orleans Saints (1986-93).
HIGH SCHOOL: Patterson (La.).
COLLEGE: Florida.
TRANSACTIONS/CAREER NOTES: Selected by New York Giants in first round (seventh pick overall) of 1997 NFL draft. ... Signed by Giants (July 19, 1997). ... On injured reserve with neck injury (September 30, 1997-remainder of season).
CHAMPIONSHIP GAME EXPERIENCE: Played in NFC championship game (2000 season).
PRO STATISTICS: 1998—Rushed once for four yards. 1999—Rushed three times for 16 yards. 2000—Rushed three times for 19 yards. 2001—Rushed once for 21 yards.
SINGLE GAME HIGHS (regular season): Receptions—8 (September 10, 2000, vs. Philadelphia); yards—141 (November 30, 1998, vs. San Francisco); and touchdown receptions—2 (November 12, 2000, vs. St. Louis).
STATISTICAL PLATEAUS: 100-yard receiving games: 1998 (1), 1999 (3), 2000 (1), 2001 (2). Total: 7.

			RECEIVING				TOTALS		
Year Team	G	GS	No.	Yds.	Avg.	TD	TD	2pt.	Pts.	Fum.
1997—New York Giants NFL	2	2	2	42	21.0	0	0	0	0	0
1998—New York Giants NFL	16	16	51	715	14.0	2	2	0	12	2
1999—New York Giants NFL	16	16	72	996	13.8	3	3	0	18	0
2000—New York Giants NFL	14	14	55	787	14.3	8	8	0	48	0
2001—New York Giants NFL	14	10	52	659	12.7	6	6	0	36	0
Pro totals (5 years)	62	58	232	3199	13.8	19	19	0	114	2

HILLIARD, JOHN — DE — SEAHAWKS

PERSONAL: Born April 16, 1976, in Coushatta, La. ... 6-2/294. ... Full name: John Edward Hilliard.
HIGH SCHOOL: Sterling (Houston).
COLLEGE: Mississippi State.
TRANSACTIONS/CAREER NOTES: Selected by Seattle Seahawks in sixth round (190th pick overall) of 2000 NFL draft. ... Signed by Seahawks (July 13, 2000).
PLAYING EXPERIENCE: Seattle NFL, 2000 and 2001. ... Games/Games started: 2000 (5/0), 2001 (16/7). Total: 21/7.

HITCHCOCK, JIMMY — CB

PERSONAL: Born November 9, 1970, in Concord, N.C. ... 5-10/187. ... Full name: Jimmy Davis Hitchcock Jr.
HIGH SCHOOL: Concord (N.C.).
COLLEGE: North Carolina.
TRANSACTIONS/CAREER NOTES: Selected by New England Patriots in third round (88th pick overall) of 1995 NFL draft. ... Signed by Patriots (July 19, 1995). ... Granted free agency (February 13, 1998). ... Re-signed by Patriots (April 18, 1998). ... Traded by Patriots to Minnesota Vikings for third-round pick (S Tony George) in 1999 draft (April 18, 1998). ... Granted unconditional free agency (February 11, 2000). ... Signed by Carolina Panthers (February 24, 2000). ... Released by Panthers (February 22, 2002).
CHAMPIONSHIP GAME EXPERIENCE: Member of Patriots for AFC championship game (1996 season); inactive. ... Member of Patriots for Super Bowl XXXI (1996 season); inactive. ... Played in NFC championship game (1998 season).
PRO STATISTICS: 1998—Recovered one fumble for one yard. 1999—Credited with two sacks. 2000—Returned one punt for no yards and fumbled once.

			INTERCEPTIONS			
Year Team	G	GS	No.	Yds.	Avg.	TD
1995—New England NFL	8	0	0	0	0.0	0
1996—New England NFL	13	5	2	14	7.0	0
1997—New England NFL	15	15	2	104	52.0	1
1998—Minnesota NFL	16	16	7	*242	‡34.6	*3
1999—Minnesota NFL	16	16	2	0	0.0	0
2000—Carolina NFL	16	2	3	116	38.7	1
2001—Carolina NFL	16	7	3	65	21.7	0
Pro totals (7 years)	100	61	19	541	28.5	5

HOBGOOD-CHITTICK, NATE — DT — CHIEFS

PERSONAL: Born November 30, 1974, in New Haven, Conn. ... 6-3/290. ... Full name: Nate Broe Hobgood-Chittick.
HIGH SCHOOL: William Allen (Allentown, Pa.).
COLLEGE: North Carolina.
TRANSACTIONS/CAREER NOTES: Signed as non drafted free agent by New York Giants (April 24, 1998). ... Inactive for four games with Giants (1998). ... Released by Giants (September 30, 1998). ... Re-signed by Giants to practice squad (October 2, 1998). ... Signed by Indianapolis

Colts off Giants practice squad (November 25, 1998). ... Inactive for five games with Colts (1998). ... Released by Colts (September 7, 1999). ... Signed by St. Louis Rams (September 13, 1999). ... Released by Rams (October 10, 2000). ... Signed by San Francisco 49ers (October 11, 2000). ... Granted free agency (March 2, 2001). ... Signed by Kansas City Chiefs (June 27, 2001). ... Released by Chiefs (September 18, 2001). ... Re-signed by Chiefs (October 3, 2001).
PLAYING EXPERIENCE: St. Louis NFL, 1999; St. Louis (5)-San Francisco (5) NFL, 2000; Kansas City NFL, 2001. ... Games/Games started: 1999 (10/1), 2000 (St.L-5/0; S.F.-5/0; Total: 10/0), 2001 (10/1). Total: 30/2.
CHAMPIONSHIP GAME EXPERIENCE: Played in NFC championship game (1999 season). ... Member of Super Bowl championship team (1999 season).
PRO STATISTICS: 1999—Credited with $1/2$ sack. 2000—Credited with one sack and recovered one fumble.

HOCHSTEIN, RUSS   G   BUCCANEERS

PERSONAL: Born October 7, 1977, in Hartington, Neb. ... 6-4/300.
HIGH SCHOOL: Cedar Catholic (Hartington, Neb.).
COLLEGE: Nebraska.
TRANSACTIONS/CAREER NOTES: Selected by Tampa Bay Buccaneers in fifth round (151st pick overall) of 2001 NFL draft. ... Signed by Buccaneers (July 16, 2001). ... Inactive for 16 games (2001).
HONORS: Named guard on THE SPORTING NEWS college All-America first team (2000).

HODGE, SEDRICK   LB   SAINTS

PERSONAL: Born September 13, 1978, in Fayettesville, Ga. ... 6-4/244. ... Full name: Sedrick Jamaine Hodge.
HIGH SCHOOL: Westminster (Atlanta).
COLLEGE: North Carolina.
TRANSACTIONS/CAREER NOTES: Selected by New Orleans Saints in third round (70th pick overall) of 2001 NFL draft. ... Signed by Saints (June 6, 2001).
PLAYING EXPERIENCE: New Orleans NFL, 2001. ... Games/Games started: 2001 (16/1).

HODGINS, JAMES   FB   RAMS

PERSONAL: Born April 30, 1977, in San Jose, Calif. ... 6-1/270.
HIGH SCHOOL: Oak Grove (San Jose, Calif.).
COLLEGE: San Jose State.
TRANSACTIONS/CAREER NOTES: Signed as non-drafted free agent by St. Louis Rams (April 20, 1999). ... Granted free agency (March 1, 2002). ... Tendered offer sheet by Denver Broncos (April 13, 2002). ... Offer matched by Rams (April 20, 2002).
CHAMPIONSHIP GAME EXPERIENCE: Played in NFC championship game (1999 and 2001 seasons). ... Member of Super Bowl championship team (1999 season). ... Played in Super Bowl XXXVI (2001 season).
PRO STATISTICS: 1999—Returned two kickoffs for four yards. 2000—Recovered one fumble.
SINGLE GAME HIGHS (regular season): Attempts—3 (November 28, 1999, vs. New Orleans); yards—5 (September 30, 2001, vs. Miami); and rushing touchdowns—1 (November 28, 1999, vs. New Orleans).

			RUSHING				RECEIVING			TOTALS			
Year Team	G	GS	Att.	Yds.	Avg.	TD	No.	Yds.	Avg.	TD	TD	2pt.	Pts.	Fum.
1999—St. Louis NFL	15	0	7	10	1.4	0	6	35	5.8	0	1	0	6	0
2000—St. Louis NFL	15	2	1	3	3.0	0	2	5	2.5	0	0	0	0	0
2001—St. Louis NFL	16	9	2	5	2.5	0	4	24	6.0	1	1	0	6	0
Pro totals (3 years)	46	11	10	18	1.8	0	12	64	5.3	1	2	0	12	0

HOLCOMB, KELLY   QB   BROWNS

PERSONAL: Born July 9, 1973, in Fayetteville, Tenn. ... 6-2/212. ... Full name: Bryan Kelly Holcomb.
HIGH SCHOOL: Lincoln County (Fayetteville, Tenn.).
COLLEGE: Middle Tennessee State.
TRANSACTIONS/CAREER NOTES: Signed as non-drafted free agent by Tampa Bay Buccaneers (May 1, 1995). ... Released by Buccaneers (August 22, 1995). ... Re-signed by Buccaneers to practice squad (August 29, 1995). ... Released by Buccaneers (September 19, 1995). ... Re-signed by Buccaneers to practice squad (October 4, 1995). ... Released by Buccaneers (October 17, 1995). ... Re-signed by Buccaneers to practice squad (December 19, 1995). ... Played for Barcelona Dragons of World League (1996). ... Released by Buccaneers (August 19, 1996). ... Re-signed by Indianapolis Colts to practice squad (November 27, 1996). ... Activated (December 12, 1996). ... Active for all 16 games (1998); did not play. ... Granted free agency (February 11, 2000). ... Re-signed by Colts (February 26, 2000). ... Released by Colts (February 28, 2001). ... Signed by Cleveland Browns (March 2, 2001).
PRO STATISTICS: W.L.: 1995—Caught one pass for minus eight yards. 1997—Fumbled four times and recovered one fumble for minus eight yards.
SINGLE GAME HIGHS (regular season): Attempts—32 (November 9, 1997, vs. Cincinnati); completions—19 (November 9, 1997, vs. Cincinnati); yards—236 (November 9, 1997, vs. Cincinnati); touchdown passes—1 (December 2, 2001, vs. Tennessee).
MISCELLANEOUS: Regular-season record as starting NFL quarterback: 0-1.

			PASSING							RUSHING				TOTALS		
Year Team	G	GS	Att.	Cmp.	Pct.	Yds.	TD	Int.	Avg.	Rat.	Att.	Yds.	Avg.	TD	TD	2pt.	Pts.
1995—Tampa Bay NFL								Did not play.									
1996—Barcelona W.L.	10	10	319	191	59.9	2382	14	16	7.47	76.8	38	111	2.9	2	2	0	12
—Indianapolis NFL								Did not play.									
1997—Indianapolis NFL	5	1	73	45	61.6	454	1	8	6.22	44.3	5	5	1.0	0	0	0	0
1998—Indianapolis NFL								Did not play.									
1999—Indianapolis NFL								Did not play.									
2000—Indianapolis NFL								Did not play.									
2001—Cleveland NFL	4	0	12	7	58.3	114	1	0	9.50	118.1	1	0	0.0	0	0	0	0
W.L. totals (1 year)	10	10	319	191	59.9	2382	14	16	7.47	76.8	38	111	2.9	2	2	0	12
NFL totals (3 years)	12	1	85	52	61.2	568	2	8	6.68	49.5	6	5	0.8	0	0	0	0
Pro totals (4 years)	22	11	404	243	60.1	2950	16	24	7.30	71.1	44	116	2.6	2	2	0	12

HOLCOMBE, ROBERT   RB   TITANS

PERSONAL: Born December 11, 1975, in Houston. ... 5-10/220. ... Full name: Robert Wayne Holcombe.
HIGH SCHOOL: Jeff Davis Senior (Houston), then Mesa (Ariz.).
COLLEGE: Illinois.
TRANSACTIONS/CAREER NOTES: Selected by St. Louis Rams in second round (37th pick overall) of 1998 NFL draft. ... Signed by Rams (July 2, 1998). ... Granted unconditional free agency (March 1, 2002). ... Signed by Tennessee Titans (May 23, 2002).
CHAMPIONSHIP GAME EXPERIENCE: Played in NFC championship game (1999 and 2001 seasons). ... Member of Super Bowl championship team (1999 season). ... Played in Super Bowl XXXVI (2001 season).
SINGLE GAME HIGHS (regular season): Attempts—21 (September 27, 1998, vs. Arizona); yards—86 (January 2, 2000); and rushing touchdowns—2 (September 27, 1998, vs. Arizona).

			RUSHING				RECEIVING				TOTALS		
Year Team	G	GS	Att.	Yds.	Avg.	TD	No.	Yds.	Avg.	TD	TD	2pt.	Pts.	Fum.
1998—St. Louis NFL	13	7	98	230	2.3	2	6	34	5.7	0	2	0	12	0
1999—St. Louis NFL	15	7	78	294	3.8	4	14	163	11.6	1	5	0	30	4
2000—St. Louis NFL	14	10	21	70	3.3	3	8	90	11.3	1	4	0	24	0
2001—St. Louis NFL	16	0	13	42	3.2	1	1	14	14.0	0	1	0	6	1
Pro totals (4 years)	58	24	210	636	3.0	10	29	301	10.4	2	12	0	72	5

HOLDEN, CURTIS   LB   SAINTS

PERSONAL: Born March 17, 1979, in San Francisco. ... 6-2/232.
HIGH SCHOOL: J. Eugene McAteer (San Francisco).
JUNIOR COLLEGE: San Francisco Community College.
COLLEGE: Washington State.
TRANSACTIONS/CAREER NOTES: Signed as non-drafted free agent by New Orleans Saints (July 26, 2001). ... Released by Saints (September 2, 2001). ... Re-signed by Saints to practice squad (September 3, 2001). ... Activated (October 17, 2001).
PLAYING EXPERIENCE: New Orleans NFL, 2001. ... Games/Games started: 2001 (12/0).

HOLDMAN, WARRICK   LB   BEARS

PERSONAL: Born November 22, 1975, in Alief, Texas. ... 6-1/230. ... Full name: Warrick Donte Holdman.
HIGH SCHOOL: Elsik (Alief, Texas).
COLLEGE: Texas A&M.
TRANSACTIONS/CAREER NOTES: Selected by Chicago Bears in fourth round (106th pick overall) of 1999 NFL draft. ... Signed by Bears (July 25, 1999). ... On injured reserve with knee injury (November 21, 2000-remainder of season). ... Granted free agency (March 1, 2002). ... Tendered offer sheet by Kansas City Chiefs (April 16, 2002). ... Offer matched by Bears (April 19, 2002).
PRO STATISTICS: 1999—Recovered one fumble for 33 yards. 2001—Intercepted one pass for no yards.

Year Team	G	GS	SACKS
1999—Chicago NFL	16	5	2.0
2000—Chicago NFL	10	10	0.0
2001—Chicago NFL	16	15	1.5
Pro totals (3 years)	42	30	3.5

HOLECEK, JOHN   LB   FALCONS

PERSONAL: Born May 7, 1972, in Steger, Ill. ... 6-2/242. ... Full name: John Francis Holecek. ... Name pronounced HOLL-uh-sek.
HIGH SCHOOL: Marian Catholic (Chicago Heights, Ill.).
COLLEGE: Illinois.
TRANSACTIONS/CAREER NOTES: Selected by Buffalo Bills in fifth round (144th pick overall) of 1995 NFL draft. ... Signed by Bills (June 12, 1995). ... On physically unable to perform list with hamstring injury (August 22-November 21, 1995). ... On injured reserve with knee injury (August 16, 1996-entire season). ... Granted free agency (February 13, 1998). ... Re-signed by Bills (April 27, 1998). ... Released by Bills (July 12, 2001). ... Signed by San Diego Chargers (July 31, 2001). ... On injured reserve with knee injury (November 28, 2001-remainder of season). ... Granted unconditional free agency (March 1, 2002). ... Signed by Atlanta Falcons (April 1, 2002).
PLAYING EXPERIENCE: Buffalo NFL, 1995 and 1997-2000; San Diego NFL, 2001. ... Games/Games started: 1995 (1/0), 1997 (14/8), 1998 (13/13), 1999 (14/14), 2000 (16/16), 2001 (11/0). Total: 69/51.
PRO STATISTICS: 1997—Credited with 1½ sacks. 1999—Intercepted one pass for 35 yards and credited with one sack. 2000—Intercepted one pass for no yards.

HOLLIDAY, VONNIE   DE   PACKERS

PERSONAL: Born December 11, 1975, in Camden, S.C. ... 6-5/290. ... Full name: Dimetry Giovonni Holliday. ... Cousin of Corey Holliday, wide receiver with Pittsburgh Steelers (1995-97).
HIGH SCHOOL: Camden (S.C.).
COLLEGE: North Carolina.
TRANSACTIONS/CAREER NOTES: Selected by Green Bay Packers in first round (19th pick overall) of 1998 NFL draft. ... Signed by Packers (June 15, 1998).
PRO STATISTICS: 1998—Recovered two fumbles. 1999—Recovered one fumble. 2000—Intercepted one pass for three yards. 2001—Recovered three fumbles for 11 yards.

Year Team	G	GS	SACKS
1998—Green Bay NFL	12	12	8.0
1999—Green Bay NFL	16	16	6.0
2000—Green Bay NFL	12	9	5.0
2001—Green Bay NFL	16	16	7.0
Pro totals (4 years)	56	53	26.0

HOLLIS, MIKE K BILLS

PERSONAL: Born May 22, 1972, in Kellogg, Idaho. ... 5-7/178. ... Full name: Michael Shane Hollis.
HIGH SCHOOL: Central Valley (Veradale, Wash.).
COLLEGE: Idaho (degree in sports science, 1996).
TRANSACTIONS/CAREER NOTES: Signed as non-drafted free agent by San Diego Chargers (May 6, 1994). ... Released by Chargers (August 22, 1994). ... Signed by Jacksonville Jaguars (June 5, 1995). ... Granted unconditional free agency (March 1, 2002). ... Signed by Buffalo Bills (April 9, 2002).
CHAMPIONSHIP GAME EXPERIENCE: Played in AFC championship game (1996 and 1999 seasons).
HONORS: Played in Pro Bowl (1997 season).

Year — Team	G	XPM	XPA	FGM	FGA	Lg.	50+	Pts.
1995—Jacksonville NFL	16	27	28	20	27	53	2-3	87
1996—Jacksonville NFL	16	27	27	30	36	53	2-3	117
1997—Jacksonville NFL	16	41	41	31	36	52	2-2	*134
1998—Jacksonville NFL	16	45	45	21	26	47	0-1	108
1999—Jacksonville NFL	16	37	37	31	38	50	1-1	130
2000—Jacksonville NFL	12	33	33	24	26	51	3-3	105
2001—Jacksonville NFL	16	29	31	18	28	48	0-1	83
Pro totals (7 years)	108	239	242	175	217	53	10-14	764

HOLMAN, RASHAD CB 49ERS

PERSONAL: Born January 17, 1978, in Louisville, Ky. ... 5-11/191.
HIGH SCHOOL: Male (Louisville, Ky.).
COLLEGE: Louisville.
TRANSACTIONS/CAREER NOTES: Selected by San Francisco 49ers in sixth round (179th pick overall) of 2001 NFL draft. ... Signed by 49ers (July 24, 2001).

Year — Team	G	GS	No.	Yds.	Avg.	TD
2001—San Francisco NFL	16	1	1	19	19.0	0

HOLMBERG, ROB LB PACKERS

PERSONAL: Born May 6, 1971, in McKeesport, Pa. ... 6-3/240. ... Full name: Robert Anthony Holmberg.
HIGH SCHOOL: Mt. Pleasant (Pa.).
COLLEGE: Navy, then Penn State.
TRANSACTIONS/CAREER NOTES: Selected by Los Angeles Raiders in seventh round (217th pick overall) of 1994 NFL draft. ... Signed by Raiders for 1994 season. ... Raiders franchise moved to Oakland (July 21, 1995). ... Released by Raiders (August 30, 1998). ... Signed by Indianapolis Colts (September 9, 1998). ... Released by Colts (September 29, 1998). ... Signed by New York Jets (October 27, 1998). ... Released by Jets (September 5, 1999). ... Signed by Minnesota Vikings (September 6, 1999). ... Released by Vikings (March 31, 2000). ... Signed by New England Patriots (July 23, 2000). ... Released by Patriots (September 2, 2001). ... Re-signed by Patriots (October 5, 2001). ... Released by Patriots (October 16, 2001). ... Signed by Carolina Panthers (October 23, 2001). ... Released by Panthers (October 31, 2001). ... Signed by Green Bay Packers (December 12, 2001). ... Granted unconditional free agency (March 1, 2002). ... Re-signed by Packers (April 10, 2002).
PLAYING EXPERIENCE: Los Angeles Raiders NFL, 1994; Oakland NFL, 1995-1997; Indianapolis (3)-New York Jets (9) NFL, 1998; Minnesota NFL, 1999; New England NFL, 2000; New England (2)-Carolina (1)-Green Bay (4) NFL, 2001. ... Games/Games started: 1994 (16/0), 1995 (16/0), 1996 (13/1), 1997 (16/0), 1998 (Ind.-3/0; NYJ-9/0; Total: 12/0), 1999 (16/0), 2000 (16/3), 2001 (N.E.-2/0; Car.-1/0; G.B.-4/2; Total: 7/2). Total: 112/6.
CHAMPIONSHIP GAME EXPERIENCE: Played in AFC championship game (1998 season).
PRO STATISTICS: 1995—Credited with one sack and recovered one fumble. 1996—Credited with one sack. 1997—Returned one kickoff for 15 yards and recovered one fumble.

HOLMES, EARL LB BROWNS

PERSONAL: Born April 28, 1973, in Tallahassee, Fla. ... 6-2/245. ... Full name: Earl L. Holmes.
HIGH SCHOOL: Florida A&M University (Tallahassee, Fla.).
COLLEGE: Florida A&M.
TRANSACTIONS/CAREER NOTES: Selected by Pittsburgh Steelers in fourth round (126th pick overall) of 1996 NFL draft. ... Signed by Steelers (July 16, 1996). ... Granted unconditional free agency (March 1, 2002). ... Signed by Cleveland Browns (April 5, 2002).
CHAMPIONSHIP GAME EXPERIENCE: Played in AFC championship game (1997 and 2001 seasons).
PRO STATISTICS: 1997—Recovered one fumble. 1998—Intercepted one pass for 36 yards. 1999—Recovered one fumble. 2000—Recovered one fumble for four yards. 2001—Recovered one fumble.

Year — Team	G	GS	SACKS
1996—Pittsburgh NFL	3	1	1.0
1997—Pittsburgh NFL	16	16	4.0
1998—Pittsburgh NFL	14	14	1.5
1999—Pittsburgh NFL	16	16	0.0
2000—Pittsburgh NFL	16	16	1.0
2001—Pittsburgh NFL	16	16	2.0
Pro totals (6 years)	81	79	9.5

HOLMES, JARET   K   JAGUARS

PERSONAL: Born March 3, 1976, in Clinton, Miss. ... 6-0/216. ... Full name: Jaret D. Holmes.
HIGH SCHOOL: Clinton (Miss.).
JUNIOR COLLEGE: Hinds Community College (Miss.).
COLLEGE: Auburn.
TRANSACTIONS/CAREER NOTES: Signed as non-drafted free agent by Philadelphia Eagles (April 21, 1998). ... Released by Eagles (August 17, 1998). ... Signed by Buffalo Bills (April 23, 1999). ... Released by Bills (August 30, 1999). ... Signed by Chicago Bears to practice squad (November 18, 1999). ... Released by Bears (November 23, 1999). ... Signed by New York Giants to practice squad (December 2, 1999). ... Signed by Bears off Giants practice squad (December 13, 1999). ... Released by Bears (August 27, 2000). ... Signed by Giants (September 30, 2000). ... Released by Giants (August 29, 2001). ... Signed by Cincinnati Bengals to practice squad (November 1, 2001). ... Released by Bengals (December 10, 2001). ... Signed by Jacksonville Jaguars (December 11, 2001).
CHAMPIONSHIP GAME EXPERIENCE: Member of Giants for NFC championship game (2000 season); inactive. ... Member of Giants for Super Bowl XXXV (2000 season); inactive.

				KICKING				
Year Team	G	XPM	XPA	FGM	FGA	Lg.	50+	Pts.
1999—Chicago NFL	3	0	0	2	2	39	0-0	6
2000—Berlin NFLE	...	0	0	9	12	0	0-0	27
—New York Giants NFL	4	3	3	2	2	34	0-0	9
2001—Jacksonville NFL	4	1	1	0	0	0	0-0	1
NFL Europe totals (1 year)	...	0	0	9	12	0	0-0	27
NFL totals (3 years)	11	4	4	4	4	39	0-0	16
Pro totals (4 years)	...	4	4	13	16	39	0-0	43

HOLMES, KENNY   DE   GIANTS

PERSONAL: Born October 24, 1973, in Vero Beach, Fla. ... 6-4/270. ... Full name: Kenneth Holmes.
HIGH SCHOOL: Vero Beach (Fla.).
COLLEGE: Miami, Fla. (degree in criminal justice).
TRANSACTIONS/CAREER NOTES: Selected by Houston Oilers in first round (18th pick overall) of 1997 NFL draft. ... Oilers franchise moved to Tennessee for 1997 season. ... Signed by Oilers (July 18, 1997). ... Oilers franchise renamed Tennessee Titans for 1999 season (December 26, 1998). ... Granted unconditional free agency (March 2, 2001). ... Signed by New York Giants (March 14, 2001).
CHAMPIONSHIP GAME EXPERIENCE: Played in AFC championship game (1999 season). ... Played in Super Bowl XXXIV (1999 season).
PRO STATISTICS: 1997—Recovered one fumble. 1999—Intercepted two passes for 17 yards. 2001—Recovered four fumbles for 12 yards.

Year Team	G	GS	SACKS
1997—Tennessee NFL	16	5	7.0
1998—Tennessee NFL	14	11	2.5
1999—Tennessee NFL	14	7	4.0
2000—Tennessee NFL	14	13	8.0
2001—New York Giants NFL	16	16	3.5
Pro totals (5 years)	74	52	25.0

HOLMES, PRIEST   RB   CHIEFS

PERSONAL: Born October 7, 1973, in Fort Smith, Ark. ... 5-9/213. ... Full name: Priest Anthony Holmes.
HIGH SCHOOL: Marshall (Texas).
COLLEGE: Texas.
TRANSACTIONS/CAREER NOTES: Signed as non-drafted free agent by Baltimore Ravens (April 25, 1997). ... Granted free agency (February 11, 2000). ... Re-signed by Ravens (June 9, 2000). ... Granted unconditional free agency (March 2, 2001). ... Signed by Kansas City Chiefs (April 1, 2001).
CHAMPIONSHIP GAME EXPERIENCE: Played in AFC championship game (2000 season). ... Member of Super Bowl championship team (2000 season).
PRO STATISTICS: 1997—Returned one kickoff for 14 yards. 1998—Had only pass attempt intercepted, returned two kickoffs for 30 yards and recovered one fumble for one yard. 1999—Recovered one fumble. 2000—Returned one kickoff for seven yards and recovered one fumble.
SINGLE GAME HIGHS (regular season): Attempts—36 (November 22, 1998, vs. Cincinnati); yards—227 (November 22, 1998, vs. Cincinnati); and rushing touchdowns—2 (October 14, 2001, vs. Pittsburgh).
STATISTICAL PLATEAUS: 100-yard rushing games: 1998 (4), 1999 (2), 2000 (1), 2001 (7). Total: 14. ... 100-yard receiving games: 2001 (2).
MISCELLANEOUS: Holds Baltimore Ravens all-time record for most yards rushing (2,102) and rushing touchdowns (10).

			RUSHING				RECEIVING				TOTALS		
Year Team	G	GS	Att.	Yds.	Avg.	TD	No.	Yds.	Avg.	TD	TD	2pt.	Pts.	Fum.
1997—Baltimore NFL	7	0	0	0	0.0	0	0	0	0.0	0	0	0	0	0
1998—Baltimore NFL	16	13	233	1008	4.3	7	43	260	6.0	0	7	0	42	3
1999—Baltimore NFL	9	4	89	506	5.7	1	13	104	8.0	1	2	0	12	0
2000—Baltimore NFL	16	2	137	588	4.3	2	32	221	6.9	0	2	0	12	2
2001—Kansas City NFL	16	16	327	*1555	4.8	8	62	614	9.9	2	10	0	60	4
Pro totals (5 years)	64	35	786	3657	4.7	18	150	1199	8.0	3	21	0	126	9

HOLT, TORRY   WR   RAMS

PERSONAL: Born June 5, 1976, in Greensboro, N.C. ... 6-0/190. ... Full name: Torry Jabar Holt.
HIGH SCHOOL: Eastern Guilford (Gibsonville, N.C.).
COLLEGE: North Carolina State.
TRANSACTIONS/CAREER NOTES: Selected by St. Louis Rams in first round (sixth pick overall) of 1999 NFL draft. ... Signed by Rams (June 5, 1999).

CHAMPIONSHIP GAME EXPERIENCE: Played in NFC championship game (1999 and 2001 seasons). ... Member of Super Bowl championship team (1999 season). ... Played in Super Bowl XXXVI (2001 season).
HONORS: Named wide receiver on THE SPORTING NEWS college All-America first team (1998). ... Played in Pro Bowl (2000 season).
PRO STATISTICS: 1999—Returned three punts for 15 yards and recovered one fumble. 2000—Recovered one fumble. 2001—Recovered one fumble for two yards.
SINGLE GAME HIGHS (regular season): Receptions—9 (December 18, 2000, vs. Tampa Bay); yards—203 (December 30, 2001, vs. Indianapolis); and touchdown receptions—2 (December 30, 2001, vs. Indianapolis).
STATISTICAL PLATEAUS: 100-yard receiving games: 1999 (2), 2000 (8), 2001 (3). Total: 13.

			RUSHING				RECEIVING				TOTALS			
Year Team	G	GS	Att.	Yds.	Avg.	TD	No.	Yds.	Avg.	TD	TD	2pt.	Pts.	Fum.
1999—St. Louis NFL	16	15	3	25	8.3	0	52	788	15.2	6	6	0	36	4
2000—St. Louis NFL	16	15	2	7	3.5	0	82	*1635	*19.9	6	6	0	36	2
2001—St. Louis NFL	16	15	2	0	0.0	0	81	1363	16.8	7	7	0	42	2
Pro totals (3 years)	48	45	7	32	4.6	0	215	3786	17.6	19	19	0	114	8

HOOVER, BRAD   FB   PANTHERS

PERSONAL: Born November 11, 1976, in High Point, N.C. ... 6-2/225. ... Full name: Bradley R. Hoover.
HIGH SCHOOL: Ledford (Thomasville, N.C.).
COLLEGE: Western Carolina.
TRANSACTIONS/CAREER NOTES: Signed as non-drafted free agent by Carolina Panthers (April 17, 2000).
PRO STATISTICS: 2000—Recovered one fumble. 2001—Returned one kickoff for eight yards.
SINGLE GAME HIGHS (regular season): Attempts—24 (November 27, 2000, vs. Green Bay); yards—117 (November 27, 2000, vs. Green Bay); and rushing touchdowns—1 (November 27, 2000, vs. Green Bay).
STATISTICAL PLATEAUS: 100-yard rushing games: 2000 (1).

			RUSHING				RECEIVING				TOTALS			
Year Team	G	GS	Att.	Yds.	Avg.	TD	No.	Yds.	Avg.	TD	TD	2pt.	Pts.	Fum.
2000—Carolina NFL	16	4	89	290	3.3	1	15	112	7.5	0	1	0	6	1
2001—Carolina NFL	16	7	17	71	4.2	0	26	185	7.1	0	0	0	0	1
Pro totals (2 years)	32	11	106	361	3.4	1	41	297	7.2	0	1	0	6	2

HOPKINS, BRAD   OT   TITANS

PERSONAL: Born September 5, 1970, in Columbia, S.C. ... 6-3/305. ... Full name: Bradley D. Hopkins.
HIGH SCHOOL: Moline (Ill.).
COLLEGE: Illinois (degree in speech communications, 1993).
TRANSACTIONS/CAREER NOTES: Selected by Houston Oilers in first round (13th pick overall) of 1993 NFL draft. ... Signed by Oilers (August 10, 1993). ... Granted unconditional free agency (February 14, 1997). ... Re-signed by Oilers (March 10, 1997). ... Oilers franchise moved to Tennessee for 1997 season. ... Oilers franchise renamed Tennessee Titans for 1999 season (December 26, 1998).
PLAYING EXPERIENCE: Houston NFL, 1993-1996; Tennessee NFL, 1997-2001. ... Games/Games started: 1993 (16/11), 1994 (16/15), 1995 (16/16), 1996 (16/16), 1997 (16/16), 1998 (13/13), 1999 (16/16), 2000 (15/15), 2001 (14/14). Total: 138/132.
CHAMPIONSHIP GAME EXPERIENCE: Played in AFC championship game (1999 season). ... Played in Super Bowl XXXIV (1999 season).
HONORS: Played in Pro Bowl (2000 season).
PRO STATISTICS: 1994—Recovered one fumble. 1995—Recovered three fumbles. 1996—Recovered one fumble. 1997—Recovered one fumble.

HORN, JOE   WR   SAINTS

PERSONAL: Born January 16, 1972, in New Haven, Conn. ... 6-1/206. ... Full name: Joseph Horn.
HIGH SCHOOL: Douglas Bird (Fayetteville, N.C.).
JUNIOR COLLEGE: Itawamba Community College (Miss.).
COLLEGE: None.
TRANSACTIONS/CAREER NOTES: Signed by Memphis Mad Dogs of CFL (March 25, 1995). ... Selected by Kansas City Chiefs in fifth round (135th pick overall) of 1996 NFL draft. ... Signed by Chiefs (June 25, 1996). ... Granted free agency (February 12, 1999). ... Re-signed by Chiefs (June 16, 1999). ... Granted unconditional free agency (February 11, 2000). ... Signed by New Orleans Saints (February 13, 2000).
HONORS: Played in Pro Bowl (2000 season).
PRO STATISTICS: 1996—Rushed once for eight yards. 1998—Rushed once for no yards, returned one punt for six yards and recovered three fumbles for minus eight yards. 1999—Rushed twice for 15 yards, returned one punt for 18 yards and recovered one fumble. 2000—Rushed six times for 10 yards and recovered one fumble. 2001—Rushed once for four yards and attempted one pass without a completion.
SINGLE GAME HIGHS (regular season): Receptions—13 (December 2, 2001, vs. Carolina); yards—180 (November 5, 2000, vs. San Francisco); and touchdown receptions—2 (December 23, 2001, vs. Tampa Bay).
STATISTICAL PLATEAUS: 100-yard receiving games: 2000 (5), 2001 (4). Total: 9.

			RECEIVING				KICKOFF RETURNS				TOTALS			
Year Team	G	GS	No.	Yds.	Avg.	TD	No.	Yds.	Avg.	TD	TD	2pt.	Pts.	Fum.
1995—Memphis CFL	17	17	71	1415	19.9	5	2	17	8.5	0	5	0	30	0
1996—Kansas City NFL	9	0	2	30	15.0	0	0	0	0.0	0	0	0	0	0
1997—Kansas City NFL	8	0	2	65	32.5	0	0	0	0.0	0	0	0	0	0
1998—Kansas City NFL	16	1	14	198	14.1	1	11	233	21.2	0	1	0	6	2
1999—Kansas City NFL	16	1	35	586	16.7	6	9	165	18.3	0	6	0	36	0
2000—New Orleans NFL	16	16	94	1340	14.3	8	0	0	0.0	0	8	0	48	1
2001—New Orleans NFL	16	16	83	1265	15.2	9	0	0	0.0	0	9	0	54	1
CFL totals (1 year)	17	17	71	1415	19.9	5	2	17	8.5	0	5	0	30	0
NFL totals (6 years)	81	34	230	3484	15.1	24	20	398	19.9	0	24	0	144	4
Pro totals (7 years)	98	51	301	4899	16.3	29	22	415	18.9	0	29	0	174	4

HOUSER, KEVIN   FB   SAINTS

PERSONAL: Born August 23, 1977, in Westlake, Ohio. ... 6-2/250. ... Full name: Kevin J. Houser.
HIGH SCHOOL: Westlake (Ohio).
COLLEGE: Ohio State.
TRANSACTIONS/CAREER NOTES: Selected by New Orleans Saints in seventh round (228th pick overall) of 2000 NFL draft. ... Signed by Saints (June 20, 2000).
PLAYING EXPERIENCE: New Orleans NFL, 2000 and 2001. ... Games/Games started: 2000 (16/0), 2001 (16/0). Total: 32/0.

HOUSHMANDZADEH, TJ   WR   BENGALS

PERSONAL: Born September 26, 1977, in Victor Valley, Calif. ... 6-1/197. ... Full name: Touraj Houshmandzadeh.
HIGH SCHOOL: Barstow (Calif.).
JUNIOR COLLEGE: Cerritos (Calif.).
COLLEGE: Oregon State.
TRANSACTIONS/CAREER NOTES: Selected by Cincinnati Bengals in seventh round (204th pick overall) of 2001 NFL draft. ... Signed by Bengals (July 18, 2001).
SINGLE GAME HIGHS (regular season): Receptions—9 (December 30, 2001, vs. Pittsburgh); yards—98 (December 30, 2001, vs. Pittsburgh); and touchdown receptions—0.

			RECEIVING			PUNT RETURNS			KICKOFF RETURNS			TOTALS			
Year Team	G	GS	No.	Yds.	Avg.	TD	No.	Yds.	Avg.	TD	No.	Yds.	Avg.	TD	TD 2pt. Pts. Fum.
2001—Cincinnati NFL	12	1	21	228	10.9	0	12	163	13.6	0	10	185	18.5	0	0 0 0 3

HOVAN, CHRIS   DT   VIKINGS

PERSONAL: Born May 12, 1978, in Rocky River, Ohio. ... 6-2/294. ... Full name: Christopher James Hovan.
HIGH SCHOOL: St. Ignatius (Cleveland).
COLLEGE: Boston College.
TRANSACTIONS/CAREER NOTES: Selected by Minnesota Vikings in first round (25th pick overall) of 2000 NFL draft. ... Signed by Vikings (July 24, 2000).
CHAMPIONSHIP GAME EXPERIENCE: Played in NFC championship game (2000 season).
HONORS: Named defensive end on THE SPORTING NEWS college All-America third team (1999).
PRO STATISTICS: 2001—Recovered one fumble.

Year Team	G	GS	SACKS
2000—Minnesota NFL	16	13	2.0
2001—Minnesota NFL	16	16	6.0
Pro totals (2 years)	32	29	8.0

HOWARD, BOBBIE   LB   BEARS

PERSONAL: Born June 14, 1977, in Charleston, W.Va. ... 5-10/230. ... Full name: Bobbie Allen Howard.
HIGH SCHOOL: DuPont (Belle, W.Va.).
COLLEGE: Notre Dame.
TRANSACTIONS/CAREER NOTES: Signed as non-drafted free agent by Tampa Bay Buccaneers (April 19, 1999). ... Released by Buccaneers (September 5,1999). ... Re-signed by Buccaneers (January 25, 2000). ... Assigned by Buccaneers to Frankfurt Galaxy in 2000 NFL Europe enhancement allocation program (February 18, 2000). ... Released by Buccaneers (August 27, 2000). ... Signed by Chicago Bears to practice squad (December 6, 2000). ... Activated (December 22, 2000); did not play.
PLAYING EXPERIENCE: Frankfurt NFLE, 2000; Chicago NFL, 2001. ... Games/Games started: 2000 (games played unavailable), 2001 (16/0).
PRO STATISTICS: 2001—Recovered one fumble.

HOWARD, DARREN   DE   SAINTS

PERSONAL: Born November 19, 1976, in St. Petersburg, Fla. ... 6-3/281.
HIGH SCHOOL: Boca Ciega (Fla.).
COLLEGE: Kansas State.
TRANSACTIONS/CAREER NOTES: Selected by New Orleans Saints in second round (33rd pick overall) of 2000 NFL draft. ... Signed by Saints (July 17, 2000).
PRO STATISTICS: 2000—Intercepted one pass for 46 yards, fumbled once and recovered two fumbles. 2001—Intercepted one pass for 37 yards.

Year Team	G	GS	SACKS
2000—New Orleans NFL	16	16	11.0
2001—New Orleans NFL	16	16	6.0
Pro totals (2 years)	32	32	17.0

HOWARD, DESMOND   WR   LIONS

PERSONAL: Born May 15, 1970, in Cleveland. ... 5-10/185. ... Full name: Desmond Kevin Howard.
HIGH SCHOOL: St. Joseph (Cleveland) Academy.
COLLEGE: Michigan (degree in communication studies).
TRANSACTIONS/CAREER NOTES: Selected by Washington Redskins in first round (fourth pick overall) of 1992 NFL draft. ... Signed by Redskins (August 25, 1992). ... On injured reserve with separated shoulder (December 29, 1992-remainder of 1992 playoffs). ... Selected by Jacksonville Jaguars from Redskins in NFL expansion draft (February 15, 1995). ... Granted unconditional free agency (February 16, 1996). ... Signed by Green Bay Packers (July 11, 1996). ... Granted unconditional free agency (February 14, 1997). ... Signed by Oakland Raiders (March 4, 1997). ...

Released by Raiders (June 9, 1999). ... Signed by Packers (June 29, 1999). ... Released by Packers (November 30, 1999). ... Signed by Detroit Lions (December 4, 1999). ... Granted unconditional free agency (February 11, 2000). ... Re-signed by Lions (July 19, 2000). ... Granted unconditional free agency (March 2, 2001). ... Re-signed by Lions (March 2, 2001).
CHAMPIONSHIP GAME EXPERIENCE: Played in NFC championship game (1996 season). ... Member of Super Bowl championship team (1996 season).
HONORS: Heisman Trophy winner (1991). ... Named College Football Player of the Year by THE SPORTING NEWS (1991). ... Maxwell Award winner (1991). ... Named wide receiver on THE SPORTING NEWS college All-America first team (1991). ... Named punt returner on THE SPORTING NEWS NFL All-Pro team (1996). ... Named Most Valuable Player of Super Bowl XXXI (1996 season). ... Played in Pro Bowl (2000 season).
RECORDS: Holds NFL single-season record for most yards by punt return—875 (1996).
POST SEASON RECORDS: Holds Super Bowl and NFL postseason record for longest kickoff return—99 yards (January 26, 1997, vs. New England). ... Holds Super Bowl single-game record for most yards by punt return—90 (January 26, 1997, vs. New England). ... Shares Super Bowl career and single-game records for most punt returns—6. ... Shares Super Bowl single-game record for most combined yards—244; most combined yards by kick returns—244; most touchdowns by kickoff return—1 (January 26, 1997, vs. New England). ... Shares NFL postseason single-game record for most combined yards —244; most combined kick return yards—244; and most touchdowns by kickoff return—1 (January 26, 1997, vs. New England).
PRO STATISTICS: 1992—Fumbled once. 1996—Fumbled twice and recovered one fumble. 1997—Fumbled twice and recovered two fumbles. 1998—Fumbled four times. 2000—Fumbled twice and recovered one fumble. 2001—Fumbled once.
SINGLE GAME HIGHS (regular season): Receptions—7 (November 20, 1994, vs. Dallas); yards—130 (December 4, 1994, vs. Tampa Bay); and touchdown receptions—1 (October 21, 2001, vs. Tennessee).
STATISTICAL PLATEAUS: 100-yard receiving games: 1994 (2).

				RUSHING				RECEIVING				PUNT RETURNS				KICKOFF RETURNS				TOTALS		
Year Team	G	GS	Att.	Yds.	Avg.	TD	No.	Yds.	Avg.	TD	No.	Yds.	Avg.	TD	No.	Yds.	Avg.	TD	TD	2pt.	Pts.
1992—Washington NFL .	16	1	3	14	4.7	0	3	20	6.7	0	6	84	14.0	1	22	462	21.0	0	1	0	6
1993—Washington NFL .	16	5	2	17	8.5	0	23	286	12.4	0	4	25	6.3	0	21	405	19.3	0	0	0	0
1994—Washington NFL .	16	15	1	4	4.0	0	40	727	18.2	5	0	0	0.0	0	0	0	0.0	0	5	1	32
1995—Jacksonville NFL .	13	7	1	8	8.0	0	26	276	10.6	1	24	246	10.3	0	10	178	17.8	0	1	0	6
1996—Green Bay NFL	16	0	0	0	0.0	0	13	95	7.3	0	*58	*875	*15.1	*3	22	460	20.9	0	3	0	18
1997—Oakland NFL........	15	0	0	0	0.0	0	4	30	7.5	0	27	210	7.8	0	*61	§1318	21.6	0	0	0	0
1998—Oakland NFL........	15	1	0	0	0.0	0	2	16	8.0	0	§45	541	12.0	†2	§49	1040	21.2	0	2	0	12
1999—Green Bay NFL.....	8	0	0	0	0.0	0	0	0	0.0	0	12	93	7.8	0	19	364	19.2	0	0	0	0
—Detroit NFL..........	5	0	0	0	0.0	0	0	0	0.0	0	6	115	19.2	∞1	15	298	19.9	0	1	0	6
2000—Detroit NFL..........	15	0	0	0	0.0	0	2	14	7.0	0	31	457	14.7	1	57	1401	24.6	0	1	0	6
2001—Detroit NFL..........	14	1	5	25	5.0	0	10	133	13.3	1	22	201	9.1	0	57	1446	25.4	0	1	0	6
Pro totals (10 years)	149	30	12	68	5.7	0	123	1597	13.0	7	235	2847	12.1	8	333	7372	22.1	0	15	1	92

HOWARD, REGGIE　　　CB　　　PANTHERS

PERSONAL: Born May 17, 1977, in Memphis, Tenn. ... 6-0/190. ... Full name: Reginald Clement Howard.
HIGH SCHOOL: Kirby (Memphis,Tenn.).
COLLEGE: Memphis.
TRANSACTIONS/CAREER NOTES: Signed as non-drafted free agent by Carolina Panthers (April 17, 2000). ... Released by Panthers (August 29, 2000). ... Signed by New Orleans Saints to practice squad (September 1, 2000). ... Activated (October 22, 2000). ... Claimed on waivers by Panthers (October 25, 2000).
PLAYING EXPERIENCE: New Orleans (1)-Carolina (1) NFL, 2000; Carolina NFL, 2001. ... Games/Games started: 2000 (N.O.-1/0; Caro.-1/0; Total: 2/0), 2001 (11/0). Total: 13/0.
PRO STATISTICS: 2001—Intercepted one pass for 16 yards and credited with one sack.

HOWARD, WILLIE　　　DE　　　VIKINGS

PERSONAL: Born December 26, 1977, in Mountain View, Calif. ... 6-3/298.
HIGH SCHOOL: Los Altos (Mountain View, Calif.).
COLLEGE: Stanford.
TRANSACTIONS/CAREER NOTES: Selected by Minnesota Vikings in second round (57th pick overall) of 2001 NFL draft. ... Signed by Vikings (July 28, 2001). ... On injured reserve with knee injury and broken leg (December 12, 2001-remainder of season).
PLAYING EXPERIENCE: Minnesota NFL, 2001. ... Games/Games started: 2001 (8/0).

HOWELL, JOHN　　　S　　　BUCCANEERS

PERSONAL: Born April 28, 1978, in North Platte, Neb. ... 5-11/204. ... Full name: John Thomas Howell.
HIGH SCHOOL: Mullen (Neb.).
COLLEGE: Colorado State.
TRANSACTIONS/CAREER NOTES: Selected by Tampa Bay Buccaneers in fourth round (117th pick overall) of 2001 NFL draft. ... Signed by Buccaneers (July 25, 2001).
PLAYING EXPERIENCE: Tampa Bay NFL, 2001. ... Games/Games started: 2001 (14/1).
PRO STATISTICS: 2001—Recovered one fumble.

HUARD, BROCK　　　QB　　　COLTS

PERSONAL: Born April 15, 1976, in Seattle. ... 6-4/232. ... Brother of Damon Huard, quarterback, New England Patriots.
HIGH SCHOOL: Puyallup (Wash.).
COLLEGE: Washington.
TRANSACTIONS/CAREER NOTES: Selected after junior season by Seattle Seahawks in third round (77th pick overall) of 1999 NFL draft. ... Signed by Seahawks (July 29, 1999). ... Inactive for all 16 games (1999). ... Granted free agency (March 1, 2002). ... Re-signed by Seahawks (April 19, 2002). ... Traded by Seahawks to Indianapolis Colts for fifth-round pick (DL Rocky Bernard) in 2002 draft (April 19, 2002).

PRO STATISTICS: 2000—Fumbled twice and recovered one fumble.
SINGLE GAME HIGHS (regular season): Attempts—34 (October 8, 2000, vs. Carolina); completions—19 (October 15, 2000, vs. Indianapolis); yards—226 (October 15, 2000, vs. Indianapolis); and touchdown passes—3 (October 15, 2000, vs. Indianapolis).
MISCELLANEOUS: Regular-season record as starting NFL quarterback: 0-5.

				PASSING						RUSHING				TOTALS	
Year Team	G	GS	Att.	Cmp.	Pct.	Yds.	TD	Int.	Avg.	Rat.	Att.	Yds.	Avg.	TD	TD	2pt.	Pts.
1999—Seattle NFL							Did not play.									
2000—Seattle NFL	5	4	87	49	56.3	540	3	2	6.21	76.8	5	29	5.8	0	0	0	0
2001—Seattle NFL	1	0	17	9	52.9	127	1	0	7.47	96.9	1	11	11.0	0	0	0	0
Pro totals (2 years)	6	4	104	58	55.8	667	4	2	6.41	80.1	6	40	6.7	0	0	0	0

HUDSON, CHRIS — S

PERSONAL: Born October 6, 1971, in Houston. ... 5-10/199. ... Full name: Christopher Reshard Hudson.
HIGH SCHOOL: E.E. Worthing (Houston).
COLLEGE: Colorado (degree in business, 1995).
TRANSACTIONS/CAREER NOTES: Selected by Jacksonville Jaguars in third round (71st pick overall) of 1995 NFL draft. ... Signed by Jaguars (June 1, 1995). ... On injured reserve with groin injury (September 28, 1995-remainder of season). ... Granted free agency (February 13, 1998). ... Re-signed by Jaguars (June 10, 1998). ... Granted unconditional free agency (February 12, 1999). ... Signed by Chicago Bears (April 22, 1999). ... Granted unconditional free agency (February 11, 2000). ... Signed by Atlanta Falcons (January 30, 2001). ... Granted unconditional free agency (March 1, 2002).
CHAMPIONSHIP GAME EXPERIENCE: Played in AFC championship game (1996 season).
HONORS: Jim Thorpe Award winner (1994).
PRO STATISTICS: 1996—Recovered two fumbles. 1997—Returned blocked field goal attempt 58 yards for a touchdown and recovered two fumbles for 32 yards and one touchdown. 1998—Recovered one fumble. 1999—Credited with one sack.

			INTERCEPTIONS				PUNT RETURNS				TOTALS			
Year Team	G	GS	No.	Yds.	Avg.	TD	No.	Yds.	Avg.	TD	TD	2pt.	Pts.	Fum.
1995—Jacksonville NFL	1	0	0	0	0.0	0	0	0	0.0	0	0	0	0	0
1996—Jacksonville NFL	16	16	2	25	12.5	0	32	348	10.9	0	0	0	0	3
1997—Jacksonville NFL	16	16	3	26	8.7	0	0	0	0.0	0	2	0	12	1
1998—Jacksonville NFL	13	13	3	10	3.3	0	0	0	0.0	0	0	0	0	0
1999—Chicago NFL	16	16	3	28	9.3	0	0	0	0.0	0	0	0	0	0
2000—							Did not play.							
2001—Atlanta NFL	15	2	0	0	0.0	0	2	26	13.0	0	0	0	0	0
Pro totals (6 years)	77	63	11	89	8.1	0	34	374	11.0	0	2	0	12	4

HUFF, ORLANDO — LB — SEAHAWKS

PERSONAL: Born August 14, 1978, in Mobile, Alabama. ... 6-2/246.
HIGH SCHOOL: Upland (Calif.).
JUNIOR COLLEGE: Eastern Arizona Junior College.
COLLEGE: Fresno State.
TRANSACTIONS/CAREER NOTES: Selected by Seattle Seahawks in fourth round (104th pick overall) of 2001 NFL draft. ... Signed by Seahawks (July 9, 2001).
PLAYING EXPERIENCE: Seattle NFL, 2001. ... Games/Games started: 2001 (12/0).

HUGGINS, JOHNNY — TE

PERSONAL: Born March 29, 1976, in Zachary, La. ... 6-3/245.
HIGH SCHOOL: Northwest (La.).
COLLEGE: Alabama State.
TRANSACTIONS/CAREER NOTES: Signed as non-drafted free agent by Dallas Cowboys (April 17, 2000). ... Released by Cowboys (September 1, 2000). ... Re-signed by Cowboys (February 7, 2001). ... Assigned by Cowboys to Rhein Fire in 2001 NFL Europe enhancement allocation program (February 12, 2001). ... Released by Cowboys (October 12, 2001). ... Re-signed by Cowboys to practice squad (October 15, 2001). ... Activated (October 22, 2001). ... Selected by Houston Texans from Cowboys in NFL expansion draft (February 18, 2002). ... Released by Texans (May 20, 2002).
SINGLE GAME HIGHS (regular season): Receptions—2 (December 16, 2001, vs. Seattle); yards—17 (November 11, 2001, vs. Atlanta); and touchdown receptions—0.

			RECEIVING			
Year Team	G	GS	No.	Yds.	Avg.	TD
2001—Rhein NFLE	...	...	16	167	10.4	0
—Dallas NFL	10	2	8	36	4.5	0
NFL Europe totals (1 year)	...	...	16	167	10.4	0
NFL totals (1 year)	10	2	8	36	4.5	0
Pro totals (2 years)	...	...	24	203	8.5	0

HULSEY, COREY — G — BILLS

PERSONAL: Born July 26, 1977, in Lula, Ga. ... 6-4/329. ... Full name: Corey Spear Hulsey.
HIGH SCHOOL: North Hall (Lula, Ga.).
COLLEGE: Clemson.
TRANSACTIONS/CAREER NOTES: Signed as non-drafted free agent by Buffalo Bills (April 19, 1999). ... Released by Bills (August 30, 1999). ... Re-signed by Bills (April 27, 2000). ... Released by Bills (August 27, 2000). ... Re-signed by Bills to practice squad (August 28, 2000).
PLAYING EXPERIENCE: Buffalo NFL, 2001. ... Games/Games started: 2001 (16/12).
PRO STATISTICS: 2001—Recovered one fumble.

HUMPHREY, DEON   LB   CHARGERS

PERSONAL: Born May 7, 1976, in Clewiston, Fla. ... 6-3/240. ... Full name: Deon Morie Humphrey.
HIGH SCHOOL: Lake Worth (Fla.).
COLLEGE: Florida State.
TRANSACTIONS/CAREER NOTES: Signed as non-drafted free agent by Green Bay Packers (April 19, 1999). ... Released by Packers (September 5, 1999). ... Re-signed by Packers to practice squad (December 1, 1999). ... Released by Packers (December 12, 1999). ... Selected by Amsterdam Admirals in NFL Europe draft (February 12, 2000). ... Signed by San Diego Chargers (June 28, 2000). ... Claimed on waivers by Carolina Panthers (August 28, 2000). ... Released by Panthers (September 30, 2000). ... Signed by Chargers to practice squad (October 4, 2000). ... Activated (October 24, 2000).
PLAYING EXPERIENCE: Amsterdam NFLE, 2000; Carolina (3)-San Diego (7) NFL, 2000; San Diego NFL, 2001. ... Games/Games started: NFLE 2000 (games played unavailable), NFL 2000 (Car.-3/0; S.D.-7/0; Total: 10/0), 2001 (11/0). Total: 21/0.
PRO STATISTICS: NFLE: 2000—Credited with $1/2$ sack. NFL: 2000—Recovered one fumble.

HUNT, CLETIDUS   DT/DE   PACKERS

PERSONAL: Born January 2, 1976, in Memphis, Tenn. ... 6-4/300. ... Full name: Cletidus Marquell Hunt.
HIGH SCHOOL: Whitehaven (Memphis, Tenn.).
JUNIOR COLLEGE: Northwest Mississippi Community College.
COLLEGE: Kentucky State.
TRANSACTIONS/CAREER NOTES: Selected by Green Bay Packers in third round (94th pick overall) of NFL draft. ... Signed by Packers (July 26, 1999). ... On suspended list for violating league substance abuse policy (July 20-October 14, 2001). ... Granted free agency (March 1, 2002). ... Re-signed by Packers (April 24, 2002).
PLAYING EXPERIENCE: Green Bay NFL, 1999-2001. ... Games/Games started: 1999 (11/1), 2000 (16/11), 2001 (12/4). Total: 39/16.
PRO STATISTICS: 1999—Credited with $1/2$ sack and recovered one fumble. 2000—Credited with five sacks. 2001—Recovered one fumble.

HUNTLEY, RICHARD   RB   BILLS

PERSONAL: Born September 18, 1972, in Monroe, N.C. ... 5-11/225. ... Full name: Richard Earl Huntley.
HIGH SCHOOL: Monroe (N.C.).
COLLEGE: Winston-Salem (N.C.) State.
TRANSACTIONS/CAREER NOTES: Selected by Atlanta Falcons in fourth round (117th pick overall) of 1996 NFL draft. ... Signed by Falcons for 1996 season. ... Released by Falcons (August 18, 1997). ... Signed by Pittsburgh Steelers (February 13, 1998). ... Granted free agency (February 11, 2000). ... Re-signed by Steelers (March 14, 2000). ... Released by Steelers (June 4, 2001). ... Signed by Carolina Panthers (June 6, 2001). ... Released by Panthers (March 22, 2002). ... Signed by Buffalo Bills (June 4, 2002).
PRO STATISTICS: 2001—Attempted one pass without a completion and recovered one fumble.
SINGLE GAME HIGHS (regular season): Attempts—21 (December 9, 2001, vs. Buffalo); yards—168 (January 6, 2002, vs. New England); and rushing touchdowns—2 (December 16, 2000, vs. Washington).
STATISTICAL PLATEAUS: 100-yard rushing games: 2001 (1).

			RUSHING				RECEIVING				KICKOFF RETURNS				TOTALS			
Year Team	G	GS	Att.	Yds.	Avg.	TD	No.	Yds.	Avg.	TD	No.	Yds.	Avg.	TD	TD	2pt.	Pts.	Fum.
1996—Atlanta NFL	1	0	2	8	4.0	0	1	14	14.0	0	0	0	0.0	0	0	0	0	0
1997—									Did not play.									
1998—Pittsburgh NFL	16	1	55	242	4.4	1	3	18	6.0	0	6	119	19.8	0	1	0	6	5
1999—Pittsburgh NFL	16	2	93	567	6.1	5	27	253	9.4	3	15	336	22.4	0	8	0	48	3
2000—Pittsburgh NFL	13	0	46	215	4.7	3	10	91	9.1	0	0	0	0.0	0	3	1	20	1
2001—Carolina NFL	14	9	165	665	4.0	2	21	101	4.8	1	1	20	20.0	0	3	0	18	3
Pro totals (5 years)	60	12	361	1697	4.7	11	62	477	7.7	4	22	475	21.6	0	15	1	92	12

HUTCHINSON, STEVE   G   SEAHAWKS

PERSONAL: Born November 1, 1977, in Coral Springs, Fla. ... 6-5/311.
HIGH SCHOOL: Coral Springs (Fla.).
COLLEGE: Michigan.
TRANSACTIONS/CAREER NOTES: Selected by Seattle Seahawks in first round (17th pick overall) of 2001 NFL draft. ... Signed by Seahawks (July 25, 2001).
PLAYING EXPERIENCE: Seattle NFL, 2001. ... Games/Games started: 2001 (16/16).
HONORS: Named guard on THE SPORTING NEWS college All-America first team (2000).
PRO STATISTICS: 2001—Recovered one fumble.

INSLEY, TREVOR   WR   TEXANS

PERSONAL: Born December 25, 1977, in San Clemente, Calif. ... 6-0/190.
HIGH SCHOOL: San Clemente (Calif.).
COLLEGE: Nevada-Reno.
TRANSACTIONS/CAREER NOTES: Signed as non-drafted free agent by Indianapolis Colts (April 17, 2000). ... Assigned by Colts to Barcelona Dragons in 2000 NFL Europe enhancement allocation program (February 17, 2000). ... On injured reserve with rib injury (August 29, 2000-remainder of season). ... Assigned by Colts to Barcelona Dragons in 2001 NFL Europe enhancement allocation program (February 19, 2001). ... Claimed on waivers by Houston Texans (March 1, 2002).
SINGLE GAME HIGHS (regular season): Receptions—5 (November 25, 2001, vs. San Francisco); yards—62 (November 25, 2001, vs. San Francisco); and touchdown receptions—1 (December 16, 2001, vs. Atlanta).

				RECEIVING			PUNT RETURNS				KICKOFF RETURNS				TOTALS		
Year Team	G	GS	No.	Yds.	Avg.	TD	No.	Yds.	Avg.	TD	No.	Yds.	Avg.	TD	TD	2pt.	Pts. Fum.
2000—Barcelona NFLE							Did not play.										
—Indianapolis NFL							Did not play.										
2001—Barcelona NFLE	...	...	61	658	10.8	2	19	267	14.1	1	0	0	0.0	0	3	0	18 0
—Indianapolis NFL	11	0	14	165	11.8	1	7	71	10.1	0	1	23	23.0	0	1	0	6 0
NFL Europe totals (1 year)	...	...	61	658	10.8	2	19	267	14.1	1	0	0	0.0	0	3	0	18 0
NFL totals (1 year)	11	0	14	165	11.8	1	7	71	10.1	0	1	23	23.0	0	1	0	6 0
Pro totals (2 years)	...	...	75	823	11.0	3	26	338	13.0	1	1	23	23.0	0	4	0	24 0

IOANE, JUNIOR   DT   RAIDERS

PERSONAL: Born July 21, 1977, in American Samoa. ... 6-4/320. ... Full name: Junior Burton Ioane.
HIGH SCHOOL: North Sanpete (Mount Pleasant, Utah).
JUNIOR COLLEGE: Snow College (Utah).
COLLEGE: Arizona State.
TRANSACTIONS/CAREER NOTES: Selected by Oakland Raiders in fourth round (107th pick overall) of 2000 NFL draft. ... Signed by Raiders (June 1, 2000). ... Inactive for all 16 games (2000).
PLAYING EXPERIENCE: Oakland NFL, 2001. ... Games/Games started: 2001 (3/0).

IRVIN, KEN   CB   SAINTS

PERSONAL: Born July 11, 1972, in Rome, Ga. ... 5-11/186. ... Full name: Kenneth Irvin.
HIGH SCHOOL: Pepperell (Lindale, Ga.).
COLLEGE: Memphis (degree in criminal justice, 1998).
TRANSACTIONS/CAREER NOTES: Selected by Buffalo Bills in fourth round (109th pick overall) of 1995 NFL draft. ... Signed by Bills (July 10, 1995). ... Granted free agency (February 13, 1998). ... Re-signed by Bills (April 17, 1998). ... Granted unconditional free agency (February 12, 1999). ... Re-signed by Bills (March 17, 1999). ... On injured reserve with foot injury (December 23, 1999-remainder of season). ... Released by Bills (February 28, 2002). ... Signed by New Orleans Saints (April 24, 2002).
PLAYING EXPERIENCE: Buffalo NFL, 1995-2001. ... Games/Games started: 1995 (16/3), 1996 (16/1), 1997 (16/0), 1998 (16/16), 1999 (14/14), 2000 (16/16), 2001 (14/4). Total: 108/54.
PRO STATISTICS: 1995—Returned one kickoff for 12 yards. 1996—Credited with two sacks and recovered one fumble. 1997—Intercepted two passes for 28 yards. 1998—Intercepted one pass for 43 yards. 1999—Intercepted one pass for one yard. 2000—Intercepted two passes for one yard. 2001—Intercepted one pass for no yards.

IRWIN, HEATH   G   RAMS

PERSONAL: Born June 27, 1973, in Boulder, Colo. ... 6-4/300. ... Nephew of Hale Irwin, professional golfer.
HIGH SCHOOL: Boulder (Colo.).
COLLEGE: Colorado.
TRANSACTIONS/CAREER NOTES: Selected by New England Patriots in fourth round (101st pick overall) of 1996 NFL draft. ... Signed by Patriots (July 17, 1996). ... Inactive for all 16 games (1996). ... Granted free agency (February 12, 1999). ... Re-signed by Patriots (June 24, 1999). ... Granted unconditional free agency (February 11, 2000). ... Signed by Miami Dolphins (February 25, 2000). ... Released by Dolphins (February 21, 2002). ... Signed by St. Louis Rams (June 4, 2002).
PLAYING EXPERIENCE: New England NFL, 1997-1999; Miami NFL, 2000 and 2001. ... Games/Games started: 1997 (16/1), 1998 (13/3), 1999 (15/13), 2000 (13/0), 2001 (16/7). Total: 73/24.
CHAMPIONSHIP GAME EXPERIENCE: Member of Patriots for AFC championship game (1996 season); inactive. ... Member of Patriots for Super Bowl XXXI (1996 season); inactive.

ISMAIL, QADRY   WR   COLTS

PERSONAL: Born November 8, 1970, in Newark, N.J. ... 6-0/200. ... Full name: Qadry Rahmadan Ismail. ... Brother of Rocket Ismail, wide receiver, Dallas Cowboys. ... Name pronounced KAH-dree ISS-my-el.
HIGH SCHOOL: Elmer L. Meyers (Wilkes-Barre, Pa.).
COLLEGE: Syracuse (degree in communications).
TRANSACTIONS/CAREER NOTES: Selected by Minnesota Vikings in second round (52nd pick overall) of 1993 NFL draft. ... Signed by Vikings (July 20, 1993). ... Granted unconditional free agency (February 14, 1997). ... Signed by Green Bay Packers (June 2, 1997). ... Traded by Packers to Miami Dolphins for first-round pick in (DT Vonnie Holliday) in 1998 draft (August 24, 1997). ... Granted unconditional free agency (February 13, 1998). ... Signed by New Orleans Saints (February 27, 1998). ... Released by Saints (February 10, 1999). ... Signed by Baltimore Ravens (April 27, 1999). ... Granted unconditional free agency (February 11, 2000). ... Re-signed by Ravens (April 28, 2000). ... Released by Ravens (March 1, 2002). ... Signed by Indianapolis Colts (March 18, 2002).
CHAMPIONSHIP GAME EXPERIENCE: Played in AFC championship game (2000 season). ... Member of Super Bowl championship team (2000 season).
HONORS: Named kick returner on THE SPORTING NEWS college All-America second team (1991).
PRO STATISTICS: 1993—Rushed three times for 14 yards. 1994—Recovered one fumble for one yard. 1995—Rushed once for seven yards. 1996—Recovered one fumble. 1999—Rushed once for four yards.
SINGLE GAME HIGHS (regular season): Receptions—9 (October 8, 2000, vs. Jacksonville); yards—258 (December 12, 1999, vs. Pittsburgh); and touchdown receptions—3 (December 12, 1999, vs. Pittsburgh).
STATISTICAL PLATEAUS: 100-yard receiving games: 1994 (2), 1995 (1), 1999 (3), 2000 (1), 2001 (1). Total: 8.
MISCELLANEOUS: Holds Baltimore Ravens all-time records for most receiving yards (2,819) and receptions (191). ... Shares Baltimore Ravens all-time record for most touchdown receptions (18).

Year Team	G	GS	RECEIVING No.	Yds.	Avg.	TD	KICKOFF RETURNS No.	Yds.	Avg.	TD	TOTALS TD	2pt.	Pts.	Fum.
1993—Minnesota NFL	15	3	19	212	11.2	1	‡42	902	21.5	0	1	0	6	1
1994—Minnesota NFL	16	3	45	696	15.5	5	35	807	23.1	0	5	0	30	2
1995—Minnesota NFL	16	2	32	597	18.7	3	42	1037	24.7	0	3	0	18	3
1996—Minnesota NFL	16	2	22	351	16.0	3	28	527	18.8	0	3	0	18	2
1997—Miami NFL	3	0	0	0	0.0	0	8	166	20.8	0	0	0	0	0
1998—New Orleans NFL	10	1	0	0	0.0	0	28	590	21.1	0	0	0	0	2
1999—Baltimore NFL	16	16	68	1105	16.3	6	4	55	13.8	0	6	0	36	2
2000—Baltimore NFL	15	13	49	655	13.4	5	2	51	25.5	0	5	0	30	0
2001—Baltimore NFL	16	15	74	1059	14.3	7	0	0	0.0	0	7	1	44	1
Pro totals (9 years)	123	55	309	4675	15.1	30	189	4135	21.9	0	30	1	182	13

ISMAIL, ROCKET   WR   COWBOYS

PERSONAL: Born November 18, 1969, in Elizabeth, N.J. ... 5-11/183. ... Full name: Raghib Ramadian Ismail. ... Brother of Qadry Ismail, wide receiver, Indianapolis Colts. ... Name pronounced rah-GIBB ISS-my-ell.
HIGH SCHOOL: Elmer L. Meyers (Wilkes-Barre, Pa.).
COLLEGE: Notre Dame (degree in sociology, 1994).
TRANSACTIONS/CAREER NOTES: Signed after junior season by Toronto Argonauts of CFL (April 21, 1991). ... Selected by Los Angeles Raiders in fourth round (100th pick overall) of 1991 NFL draft. ... Granted free agency from Argonauts (February 15, 1993). ... Signed by Raiders (August 30, 1993). ... Raiders franchise moved to Oakland (July 21, 1995). ... Granted free agency (February 16, 1996). ... Re-signed by Raiders (August 25, 1996). ... Traded by Raiders to Carolina Panthers for fifth-round pick (traded to Miami) in 1997 draft (August 25, 1996). ... Granted unconditional free agency (February 14, 1997). ... Re-signed by Panthers (February 26, 1997). ... Granted unconditional free agency (February 13, 1998). ... Re-signed by Panthers (June 2, 1998). ... Granted unconditional free agency (February 12, 1999). ... Signed by Dallas Cowboys (April 15, 1999). ... On injured reserve with knee injury (November 8, 2000-remainder of season).
CHAMPIONSHIP GAME EXPERIENCE: Played in Grey Cup, CFL championship game (1991). ... Played in NFC championship game (1996 season).
HONORS: Named kick returner on THE SPORTING NEWS college All-America first team (1989). ... Named College Football Player of the Year by THE SPORTING NEWS (1990). ... Named wide receiver on THE SPORTING NEWS college All-America first team (1990).
PRO STATISTICS: CFL: 1991—Returned two unsuccessful field-goals for 90 yards, attempted one pass without a completion, fumbled eight times and recovered two fumbles. 1992—Fumbled seven times and recovered two fumbles. NFL: 1993—Recovered one fumble. 1995—Fumbled four times and recovered one fumble. 1998—Fumbled twice and recovered one fumble. 1999—Fumbled once. 2000—Fumbled once.
SINGLE GAME HIGHS (regular season): Receptions—10 (December 9, 2001, vs. New York Giants); yards—149 (September 12, 1999, vs. Washington); and touchdown receptions—2 (October 11, 1998, vs. Dallas).
STATISTICAL PLATEAUS: 100-yard receiving games: 1995 (1), 1996 (1), 1997 (1), 1998 (3), 1999 (3), 2001 (2). Total: 11.

Year Team	G	GS	RUSHING Att.	Yds.	Avg.	TD	RECEIVING No.	Yds.	Avg.	TD	PUNT RETURNS No.	Yds.	Avg.	TD	KICKOFF RETURNS No.	Yds.	Avg.	TD	TOTALS TD	2pt.	Pts.
1991—Toronto CFL	17	17	36	271	7.5	3	64	1300	20.3	9	48	602	12.5	1	31	786	25.4	0	13	0	78
1992—Toronto CFL	16	16	34	154	4.5	3	36	651	18.1	4	59	614	10.4	1	43	*1139	26.5	0	8	0	48
1993—LA Raiders NFL	13	0	4	-5	-1.3	0	26	353	13.6	1	0	0	0.0	0	25	605	§24.2	0	1	0	6
1994—LA Raiders NFL	16	0	4	31	7.8	0	34	513	15.1	5	0	0	0.0	0	43	923	21.5	0	5	0	30
1995—Oakland NFL	16	16	6	29	4.8	0	28	491	17.5	3	0	0	0.0	0	36	706	19.6	0	3	0	18
1996—Carolina NFL	13	5	8	80	10.0	1	12	214	17.8	0	0	0	0.0	0	5	100	20.0	0	1	0	6
1997—Carolina NFL	13	2	4	32	8.0	0	36	419	11.6	2	0	0	0.0	0	0	0	0.0	0	2	0	12
1998—Carolina NFL	16	15	3	42	14.0	0	69	1024	14.8	8	0	0	0.0	0	0	0	0.0	0	8	0	48
1999—Dallas NFL	16	14	13	110	8.5	1	80	1097	13.7	6	0	0	0.0	0	0	0	0.0	0	7	0	42
2000—Dallas NFL	9	9	8	73	9.1	0	25	350	14.0	1	0	0	0.0	0	0	0	0.0	0	1	1	8
2001—Dallas NFL	14	13	8	31	3.9	0	53	834	15.7	2	1	20	20.0	0	0	0	0.0	0	2	0	12
CFL totals (2 years)	33	33	70	425	6.1	6	100	1951	19.5	13	107	1216	11.4	2	74	1925	26.0	0	21	0	126
NFL totals (9 years)	126	74	58	423	7.3	2	363	5295	14.6	28	1	20	20.0	0	109	2334	21.4	0	30	1	182
Pro totals (11 years)	159	107	128	848	6.6	8	463	7246	15.7	41	108	1236	11.4	2	183	4259	23.3	0	51	1	308

ISRAEL, STEVE   CB

PERSONAL: Born March 16, 1969, in Camden, N.J. ... 5-11/197. ... Full name: Steven Douglas Israel.
HIGH SCHOOL: Haddon Heights (N.J.).
COLLEGE: Pittsburgh (degree in economics).
TRANSACTIONS/CAREER NOTES: Selected by Los Angeles Rams in second round (30th pick overall) of 1992 NFL draft. ... Signed by Rams (August 23, 1992). ... Granted roster exemption (August 25-September 4, 1992). ... Claimed on waivers by Green Bay Packers (August 7, 1995). ... Released by Packers (August 25, 1995). ... Signed by San Francisco 49ers (October 3, 1995). ... Granted unconditional free agency (February 16, 1996). ... Re-signed by 49ers (March 1, 1996). ... Granted unconditional free agency (February 14, 1997). ... Signed by New England Patriots (March 24, 1997). ... Granted unconditional free agency (February 11, 2000). ... Signed by New Orleans Saints (April 21, 2000). ... On injured reserve with broken leg and ankle injury (August 7, 2000-entire season). ... Released by Saints (February 28, 2002).
PLAYING EXPERIENCE: Los Angeles Rams NFL, 1992-1994; San Francisco, NFL, 1995 and 1996; New England NFL, 1997-1999; New Orleans NFL, 2001. ... Games/Games started: 1992 (16/1), 1993 (16/12), 1994 (10/2), 1995 (8/0), 1996 (14/2), 1997 (5/0), 1998 (11/7), 1999 (13/13), 2000 (did not play), 2001 (9/1). Total: 102/38.
PRO STATISTICS: 1992—Returned one kickoff for minus three yards and recovered one fumble. 1993—Returned five kickoffs for 92 yards. 1996—Intercepted one pass for three yards and recovered one fumble. 1997—Credited with one sack. 1998—Intercepted three passes for 13 yards and credited with two sacks. 1999—Intercepted one pass for no yards, credited with one sack and recovered two fumbles.

ISSA, JABARI   DE   TEXANS

PERSONAL: Born April 18, 1978, in Foster City, Calif. ... 6-5/296.
HIGH SCHOOL: San Mateo (Calif.).
COLLEGE: Washington.
TRANSACTIONS/CAREER NOTES: Selected by Arizona Cardinals in sixth round (176th pick overall) of 2000 NFL draft. ... Signed by Cardinals (June 13, 2000). ... Selected by Houston Texans from Cardinals in NFL expansion draft (February 18, 2002).

Year Team	G	GS	SACKS
2000—Arizona NFL	10	0	1.0
2001—Arizona NFL	13	5	0.0
Pro totals (2 years)	23	5	1.0

IVY, COREY   CB   BUCCANEERS

PERSONAL: Born March 29, 1977, in St. Louis. ... 5-8/183. ... Full name: Corey Terrell Ivy.
HIGH SCHOOL: Moore (Oklahoma).
JUNIOR COLLEGE: Northeastern Oklahoma.
COLLEGE: Oklahoma.
TRANSACTIONS/CAREER NOTES: Signed as non-drafted free agent by New England Patriots (May 13, 1999). ... Released by Patriots (September 5, 1999). ... Re-signed by Patriots to practice squad (December 29, 1999). ... Signed by Cleveland Browns (July 12, 2000). ... Released by Browns (August 27, 2000). ... Signed by Tampa Bay Buccaneers (June 4, 2001). ... Released by Buccaneers (September 2, 2001). ... Re-signed by Buccaneers to practice squad (September 3, 2001). ... Activated (November 10, 2001). ... Released by Buccaneers (December 4, 2001). ... Re-signed by Buccaneers to practice squad (December 5, 2001).
PLAYING EXPERIENCE: Tampa Bay NFL, 2001. ... Games/Games started: 2001 (1/0).

IWUOMA, CHIDI   CB   LIONS

PERSONAL: Born February 19, 1978, in Pasadena, Calif. ... 5-8/180.
HIGH SCHOOL: Pasadena (Calif.).
COLLEGE: California.
TRANSACTIONS/CAREER NOTES: Signed as non-drafted free agent by Detroit Lions (April 27, 2000). ... Released by Lions (September 2, 2001). ... Re-signed by Lions to practice squad (September 4, 2001). ... Activated (September 8, 2001).
PLAYING EXPERIENCE: Detroit NFL, 2001. ... Games/Games started: 2001 (13/1).

IZZO, LARRY   LB   PATRIOTS

PERSONAL: Born September 26, 1974, in Fort Belvoir, Va. ... 5-10/228. ... Full name: Lawrence Alexander Izzo.
HIGH SCHOOL: McCullough (Houston).
COLLEGE: Rice.
TRANSACTIONS/CAREER NOTES: Signed as non-drafted free agent by Miami Dolphins (April 25, 1996). ... On injured reserve with foot injury (August 18, 1997-entire season). ... Granted free agency (February 12, 1999). ... Re-signed by Dolphins (March 31, 1999). ... Granted unconditional free agency (March 2, 2001). ... Signed by New England Patriots (March 6, 2001).
PLAYING EXPERIENCE: Miami NFL, 1996, 1998-2000; New England NFL, 2001. ... Games/Games started: 1996 (16/0), 1998 (13/0), 1999 (16/0), 2000 (16/0), 2001 (16/0). Total: 77/0.
CHAMPIONSHIP GAME EXPERIENCE: Played in AFC championship game (2001 season). ... Member of Super Bowl championship team (2001 season).
HONORS: Played in Pro Bowl (2000 season).
PRO STATISTICS: 1996—Rushed once for 26 yards. 1999—Recovered one fumble. 2000—Rushed once for 39 yards and fumbled once. 2001—Recovered one fumble.

JACKSON, ARNOLD   WR/PR   CARDINALS

PERSONAL: Born April 9, 1977, in Jacksonville. ... 5-8/163.
HIGH SCHOOL: Andrew Jackson (Fla.).
COLLEGE: Louisville.
TRANSACTIONS/CAREER NOTES: Signed as non-drafted free agent by Arizona Cardinals (April 23, 2001).
SINGLE GAME HIGHS (regular season): Receptions—4 (December 23, 2001, vs. Dallas); yards—17 (December 2, 2001, vs. Oakland); and touchdown receptions—0.

Year Team	G	GS	RECEIVING No.	Yds.	Avg.	TD	PUNT RETURNS No.	Yds.	Avg.	TD	KICKOFF RETURNS No.	Yds.	Avg.	TD	TOTALS TD	2pt.	Pts.	Fum.
2001—Arizona NFL	16	2	9	44	4.9	0	‡40	461	11.5	0	2	46	23.0	0	0	0	0	0

JACKSON, BRAD   LB   PANTHERS

PERSONAL: Born January 11, 1975, in Canton, Ohio. ... 6-0/230. ... Full name: Bradley Michael Jackson.
HIGH SCHOOL: Firestone (Akron, Ohio).
COLLEGE: Cincinnati.
TRANSACTIONS/CAREER NOTES: Selected by Miami Dolphins in third round (79th pick overall) of 1998 NFL draft. ... Signed by Dolphins (July 21, 1998). ... Released by Dolphins (August 25, 1998). ... Signed by Tennessee Oilers to practice squad (September 1, 1998). ... Released by Oilers (September 29, 1998). ... Signed by Baltimore Ravens to practice squad (September 30, 1998). ... Activated (December 17, 1998); did not play. ... Granted free agency (March 1, 2002). ... Signed by Carolina Panthers (March 13, 2002).
PLAYING EXPERIENCE: Baltimore NFL, 1999-2001. ... Games/Games started: 1999 (13/0), 2000 (10/0), 2001 (16/5). Total: 39/5.
CHAMPIONSHIP GAME EXPERIENCE: Played in AFC championship game (2000 season). ... Member of Super Bowl championship team (2000 season).
HONORS: Named outside linebacker on THE SPORTING NEWS college All-America third team (1997).
PRO STATISTICS: 1999—Recovered one fumble. 2000—Recovered two fumbles. 2001—Recovered one fumble.

JACKSON, CURTIS   WR   CHIEFS

PERSONAL: Born September 22, 1973, in Fort Worth, Texas. ... 5-10/194. ... Full name: Curtis Ray Jackson.
HIGH SCHOOL: Plano (Texas).
COLLEGE: Texas.

TRANSACTIONS/CAREER NOTES: Signed as non-drafted free agent by St. Louis Rams (April 18, 2000). ... Released by Rams (August 27, 2000). ... Re-signed by Rams to practice squad (August 29, 2000). ... Signed by New England Patriots off Rams practice squad (November 15, 2000). ... Released by Patriots (September 2, 2001). ... Re-signed by Patriots to practice squad (September 4, 2001). ... On injured reserve with ankle injury (November 7, 2001-remainder of season). ... Released by Patriots (February 25, 2002). ... Signed by Kansas City Chiefs (May 1, 2002).
PLAYING EXPERIENCE: New England NFL, 2000 and 2001. ... Games/Games started: 2000 (5/2), 2001 (2/0). Total: 7/2.
PRO STATISTICS: 2000—Caught five passes for 44 yards, returned 13 kickoffs for 323 yards and fumbled once. 2001—Caught two passes for 16 yards and returned two kickoffs for 30 yards.
SINGLE GAME HIGHS (regular season): Receptions—3 (December 10, 2000, vs. Chicago); yards—27 (December 10, 2000, vs. Chicago); and touchdown receptions—0.

JACKSON, DARRELL   WR   SEAHAWKS

PERSONAL: Born December 6, 1978, in Dayton, Ohio. ... 6-0/199. ... Full name: Darrell Lamont Jackson.
HIGH SCHOOL: Tampa Catholic.
COLLEGE: Florida.
TRANSACTIONS/CAREER NOTES: Selected after junior season by Seattle Seahawks in third round (80th pick overall) of 2000 NFL draft. ... Signed by Seahawks (July 19, 2000).
PRO STATISTICS: 2000—Rushed once for minus one yard, fumbled twice and recovered one fumble for 18 yards. 2001—Rushed once for nine yards.
SINGLE GAME HIGHS (regular season): Receptions—7 (November 11, 2001, vs. Oakland); yards—125 (September 30, 2001, vs. Oakland); and touchdown receptions—2 (January 6, 2002, vs. Kansas City).
STATISTICAL PLATEAUS: 100-yard receiving games: 2001 (5).

			RECEIVING		
Year Team	G	GS	No.	Yds.	Avg.	TD
2000—Seattle NFL	16	9	53	713	13.5	6
2001—Seattle NFL	16	16	70	1081	15.4	8
Pro totals (2 years)	32	25	123	1794	14.6	14

JACKSON, DEXTER   S   BUCCANEERS

PERSONAL: Born July 28, 1977, in Quincy, Fla. ... 6-1/203. ... Full name: Dexter Lamar Jackson.
HIGH SCHOOL: James A. Shanks (Quincy, Fla.).
COLLEGE: Florida State.
TRANSACTIONS/CAREER NOTES: Selected by Tampa Bay Buccaneers in fourth round (113th pick overall) of 1999 NFL draft. ... Signed by Buccaneers (July 29, 1999). ... Granted free agency (March 1, 2002). ... Re-signed by Buccaneers (April 26, 2002).
PLAYING EXPERIENCE: Tampa Bay NFL, 1999-2001. ... Games/Games started: 1999 (12/0), 2000 (13/0), 2001 (15/15). Total: 40/15.
CHAMPIONSHIP GAME EXPERIENCE: Played in NFC championship game (1999 season).
PRO STATISTICS: 2000—Recovered one fumble. 2001—Intercepted four passes for 42 yards, ran 18 yards with lateral from punt return and credited with 2½ sacks.

JACKSON, GRADY   DT   SAINTS

PERSONAL: Born January 21, 1973, in Greensboro, Ala. ... 6-2/330.
HIGH SCHOOL: Greensboro (Ala.) East.
JUNIOR COLLEGE: Hinds Community College (Miss.).
COLLEGE: Knoxville (Tenn.) College.
TRANSACTIONS/CAREER NOTES: Selected by Oakland Raiders in sixth round (193rd pick overall) of 1997 NFL draft. ... Signed by Raiders (July 18, 1997). ... Granted unconditional free agency (March 1, 2002). ... Signed by New Orleans Saints (April 11, 2002).
CHAMPIONSHIP GAME EXPERIENCE: Played in AFC championship game (2000 season).
PRO STATISTICS: 1998—Recovered one fumble for two yards. 1999—Recovered one fumble. 2000—Recovered one fumble. 2001—Recovered one fumble.

Year Team	G	GS	SACKS
1997—Oakland NFL	5	0	0.0
1998—Oakland NFL	15	1	3.0
1999—Oakland NFL	15	0	4.0
2000—Oakland NFL	16	15	8.0
2001—Oakland NFL	16	16	4.0
Pro totals (5 years)	67	32	19.0

JACKSON, JAMES   RB   BROWNS

PERSONAL: Born August 4, 1976, in Belle Glade, Fla. ... 5-10/209. ... Full name: James Shurrate Jackson.
HIGH SCHOOL: Glades Central (Belle Glade, Fla.).
COLLEGE: Miami.
TRANSACTIONS/CAREER NOTES: Selected by Cleveland Browns in third round (65th pick overall) of 2001 NFL draft. ... Signed by Browns (July 23, 2001). ... On injured reserve with ankle injury (December 20, 2001-remainder of season).
SINGLE GAME HIGHS (regular season): Attempts—31 (September 23, 2001, vs. Detroit); yards—124 (September 23, 2001, vs. Detroit); and rushing touchdowns—1 (October 21, 2001, vs. Baltimore).
STATISTICAL PLATEAUS: 100-yard rushing games: 2001 (1).

			RUSHING				RECEIVING				TOTALS		
Year Team	G	GS	Att.	Yds.	Avg.	TD	No.	Yds.	Avg.	TD	TD	2pt.	Pts.	Fum.
2001—Cleveland NFL	11	10	195	554	2.8	2	7	56	8.0	0	2	0	12	1

JACKSON, JARIOUS   QB   BRONCOS

PERSONAL: Born May 3, 1977, in Tupelo, Miss. ... 6-0/228. ... Full name: Jarious K. Jackson.
HIGH SCHOOL: Tupelo (Miss.).
COLLEGE: Notre Dame.
TRANSACTIONS/CAREER NOTES: Selected by Denver Broncos in seventh round (214th pick overall) of 2000 NFL draft. ... Signed by Broncos (July 20, 2000). ... Assigned by Broncos to Bracelona Dragons in 2001 NFL Europe enhancement allocation program (February 19, 2001).
PRO STATISTICS: NFL: 2001—Fumbled twice and recovered two fumbles for minus one yard.
SINGLE GAME HIGHS (regular season): Attempts—12 (December 16, 2001, vs. Kansas City); completions—7 (December 16, 2001, vs. Kansas City); yards—73 (December 16, 2001, vs. Kansas City); and touchdown passes—0.

				PASSING						RUSHING			TOTALS		
Year Team	G	GS	Att.	Cmp.	Pct.	Yds.	TD	Int.	Avg.	Rat.	Att.	Yds.	Avg.	TD	TD	2pt.	Pts.
2000—Denver NFL	2	0	1	0	0.0	0	0	0	0.0	39.6	1	-1	-1.0	0	0	0	0
2001—Barcelona NFLE	...	...	223	125	56.1	1544	13	6	6.92	85.9	43	287	6.7	2	2	0	12
—Denver NFL	1	0	12	7	58.3	73	0	0	6.08	76.0	5	7	1.4	0	0	0	0
NFL Europe totals (1 year)	...	...	223	125	56.1	1544	13	6	6.92	85.9	43	287	6.7	2	2	0	12
NFL totals (2 years)	3	0	13	7	53.8	73	0	0	5.62	70.4	6	6	1.0	0	0	0	0
Pro totals (3 years)	...	...	236	132	55.9	1617	13	6	6.85	85.0	49	293	6.0	2	2	0	12

JACKSON, JOHN   OT   BENGALS

PERSONAL: Born January 4, 1965, in Camp Kwe, Okinawa, Japan. ... 6-6/300.
HIGH SCHOOL: Woodward (Cincinnati).
COLLEGE: Eastern Kentucky (degree in police administration, 1991).
TRANSACTIONS/CAREER NOTES: Selected by Pittsburgh Steelers in 10th round (252nd pick overall) of 1988 NFL draft. ... Signed by Steelers (May 17, 1988). ... Granted unconditional free agency (February 13, 1998). ... Signed by San Diego Chargers (February 18, 1998). ... Released by Chargers (June 9, 2000). ... Signed by Cincinnati Bengals (July 23, 2000). ... Granted unconditional free agency (March 1, 2002). ... Re-signed by Bengals (March 6, 2002).
PLAYING EXPERIENCE: Pittsburgh NFL, 1988-1997; San Diego NFL, 1998 and 1999; Cincinnati NFL, 2000 and 2001. ... Games/Games started: 1988 (16/0), 1989 (14/12), 1990 (16/16), 1991 (16/16), 1992 (16/13), 1993 (16/16), 1994 (16/16), 1995 (11/9), 1996 (16/16), 1997 (16/16), 1998 (16/16), 1999 (15/15), 2000 (9/5), 2001 (11/0). Total: 204/166.
CHAMPIONSHIP GAME EXPERIENCE: Played in AFC championship game (1994, 1995 and 1997 seasons). ... Played in Super Bowl XXX (1995 season).
PRO STATISTICS: 1988—Returned one kickoff for 10 yards. 1991—Recovered one fumble. 1993—Recovered one fumble. 1994—Recovered two fumbles. 1996—Recovered one fumble.

JACKSON, JONATHAN   LB   SAINTS

PERSONAL: Born September 2, 1977, in Dayton, Ohio. ... 6-2/248. ... Full name: Jonathan Alexander Jackson.
HIGH SCHOOL: Bonanza (Las Vegas).
COLLEGE: Oregon State.
TRANSACTIONS/CAREER NOTES: Signed as non-drafted free agent by Kansas City Chiefs (April 24, 2000). ... Released by Chiefs (August 21, 2000). ... Signed by New Orleans Saints (April 26, 2001). ... Released by Saints (August 28, 2001). ... Re-signed by Saints (January 5, 2002).
PLAYING EXPERIENCE: New Orleans NFL, 2001. ... Games/Games started: 2001 (1/0).

JACKSON, LENZIE   WR   STEELERS

PERSONAL: Born June 17, 1977, in Santa Clara, Calif. ... 6-0/191. ... Full name: Lenzie Maurice Jackson.
HIGH SCHOOL: Milpitas (Calif.).
COLLEGE: Arizona State (degree in justice studies).
TRANSACTIONS/CAREER NOTES: Signed as non-drafted free agent by Jacksonville Jaguars (April 22, 1999). ... Released by Jaguars (September 5, 1999). ... Re-signed by Jaguars to practice squad (September 6, 1999). ... Activated (November 10, 1999). ... Released by Jaguars (August 22, 2000). ... Signed by Oakland Raiders to practice squad (August 30, 2000). ... Signed by Cleveland Browns off Raiders practice squad (September 13, 2000). ... On physically unable to perform list with toe injury (November 1, 2000-remainder of season). ... Released by Browns (September 3, 2001). ... Signed by Pittsburgh Steelers to practice squad (September 12, 2001). ... Activated (October 16, 2001).
PLAYING EXPERIENCE: Jacksonville NFL, 1999; Cleveland NFL, 2000; Pittsburgh NFL, 2001. ... Games/Games started: 1999 (4/0), 2000 (5/0), 2001 (11/0). Total: 20/0.
CHAMPIONSHIP GAME EXPERIENCE: Member of Jaguars for AFC championship game (1999 season); inactive. ... Played in AFC championship game (2001 season).
PRO STATISTICS: 1999—Returned three kickoffs for 58 yards. 2000—Caught one pass for five yards and returned nine kickoffs for 168 yards. 2001—Returned six kickoffs for 125 yards.
SINGLE GAME HIGHS (regular season): Receptions—1 (October 22, 2000, vs. Pittsburgh); yards—5 (October 22, 2000, vs. Pittsburgh); and touchdown receptions—0.

JACKSON, RAYMOND   DB

PERSONAL: Born February 17, 1973, in East Chicago, Ind. ... 5-10/189. ... Full name: Raymond DeWayne Jackson.
HIGH SCHOOL: Montbello (Denver).
COLLEGE: Colorado State.
TRANSACTIONS/CAREER NOTES: Selected by Buffalo Bills in fifth round (156th pick overall) of 1996 NFL draft. ... Signed by Bills (June 25, 1996). ... Selected by Cleveland Browns from Bills in NFL expansion draft (February 9, 1999). ... Granted free agency (February 12, 1999). ... Re-signed by Browns (April 14, 1999). ... Granted unconditional free agency (February 11, 2000). ... Re-signed by Browns (February 24, 2000). ... Released by Browns (August 31, 2001). ... Re-signed by Browns (September 20, 2001). ... Granted unconditional free agency (March 1, 2002).
PRO STATISTICS: 1997—Returned one punt for no yards and fumbled once. 2001—Returned one punt for 43 yards.

Year Team	G	GS	INTERCEPTIONS No.	Yds.	Avg.	TD
1996—Buffalo NFL	12	0	1	0	0.0	0
1997—Buffalo NFL	9	0	0	0	0.0	0
1998—Buffalo NFL	14	0	2	27	13.5	0
1999—Cleveland NFL	14	0	0	0	0.0	0
2000—Cleveland NFL	9	1	0	0	0.0	0
2001—Cleveland NFL	15	0	3	52	17.3	0
Pro totals (6 years)	73	1	6	79	13.2	0

JACKSON, SHELDON   TE   BILLS

PERSONAL: Born July 24, 1976, in Culver City, Calif. ... 6-3/242. ... Full name: Sheldon B. Jackson Jr.
HIGH SCHOOL: Damien (La Verne, Calif.).
COLLEGE: Nebraska (degree in psychology).
TRANSACTIONS/CAREER NOTES: Selected by Buffalo Bills in seventh round (230th pick overall) of 1999 NFL draft. ... Signed by Bills (June 22, 1999). ... Granted free agency (March 1, 2002).
PLAYING EXPERIENCE: Buffalo NFL, 1999-2001. ... Games/Games started: 1999 (13/4), 2000 (16/8), 2001 (16/1). Total: 45/13.
PRO STATISTICS: 1999—Caught four passes for 34 yards. 2000—Caught five passes for 36 yards and one touchdown and recovered one fumble. 2001—Caught one pass for one yard and one touchdown.
SINGLE GAME HIGHS (regular season): Receptions—2 (January 2, 2000, vs. Indianapolis); yards—22 (January 2, 2000, vs. Indianapolis); and touchdown receptions—1 (November 25, 2001, vs. Miami).

JACKSON, TERRY   RB   49ERS

PERSONAL: Born January 10, 1976, in Gainesville, Fla. ... 6-0/232. ... Full name: Terrance Bernard Jackson. ... Brother of Willie Jackson Jr., wide receiver with four NFL teams (1994-2001).
HIGH SCHOOL: P.K. Yonge (Gainesville, Fla.).
COLLEGE: Florida.
TRANSACTIONS/CAREER NOTES: Selected by San Francisco 49ers in fifth round (157th pick overall) of 1999 NFL draft. ... Signed by 49ers (July 26, 1999). ... Granted free agency (March 1, 2002).
PRO STATISTICS: 2000—Recovered one fumble.
SINGLE GAME HIGHS (regular season): Attempts—5 (December 2, 2001, vs. Buffalo); yards—37 (December 2, 2001, vs. Buffalo); and rushing touchdowns—1 (January 6, 2002, vs. New Orleans).

			RUSHING				RECEIVING				TOTALS		
Year Team	G	GS	Att.	Yds.	Avg.	TD	No.	Yds.	Avg.	TD	TD	2pt.	Pts.	Fum.
1999—San Francisco NFL	16	0	15	75	5.0	0	3	6	2.0	0	0	0	0	1
2000—San Francisco NFL	15	1	5	6	1.2	1	5	48	9.6	1	2	1	14	0
2001—San Francisco NFL	16	1	22	138	6.3	1	12	91	7.6	2	3	0	18	1
Pro totals (3 years)	47	2	42	219	5.2	2	20	145	7.3	3	5	1	32	2

JACKSON, TYOKA   DT   RAMS

PERSONAL: Born November 22, 1971, in Washington, D.C. ... 6-2/280. ... Name pronounced tie-OH-kah.
HIGH SCHOOL: Bishop McNamara (Forestville, Md.).
COLLEGE: Penn State.
TRANSACTIONS/CAREER NOTES: Signed as non-drafted free agent by Atlanta Falcons (May 2, 1994). ... Released by Falcons (August 29, 1994). ... Re-signed by Falcons to practice squad (August 30, 1994). ... Signed by Miami Dolphins off Falcons practice squad (November 16, 1994). ... Released by Dolphins (August 27, 1995). ... Signed by Tampa Bay Buccaneers (December 27, 1995). ... Granted free agency (February 13, 1998). ... Re-signed by Buccaneers (June 22, 1998). ... Granted unconditional free agency (March 2, 2001). ... Signed by St. Louis Rams (May 1, 2001).
CHAMPIONSHIP GAME EXPERIENCE: Member of Buccaneers for NFC championship game (1999 season); inactive. ... Played in NFC championship game (2001 season). ... Played in Super Bowl XXXVI (2001 season).
PRO STATISTICS: 1994—Recovered one fumble. 2001—Recovered one fumble.

Year Team	G	GS	SACKS
1994—Miami NFL	1	0	0.0
1995—	Did not play.		
1996—Tampa Bay NFL	13	2	0.0
1997—Tampa Bay NFL	12	0	2.5
1998—Tampa Bay NFL	16	12	3.0
1999—Tampa Bay NFL	6	0	1.0
2000—Tampa Bay NFL	16	1	2.0
2001—St. Louis NFL	16	0	3.0
Pro totals (7 years)	80	15	11.5

JACKSON, WAVERLY   G   COLTS

PERSONAL: Born December 19, 1972, in South Hill, Va. ... 6-2/343.
HIGH SCHOOL: Park View (Sterling, Va.).
COLLEGE: Virginia Tech.
TRANSACTIONS/CAREER NOTES: Signed as non-drafted free agent by Carolina Panthers (April 19, 1997). ... Released by Panthers (August 25, 1997). ... Re-signed by Panthers to practice squad (August 26, 1997). ... Granted free agency after 1997 season. ... Signed by Indianapolis Colts (January 12, 1998). ... Granted free agency (March 2, 2001). ... Re-signed by Colts (March 7, 2001).
PLAYING EXPERIENCE: Indianapolis NFL, 1998-2001. ... Games/Games started: 1998 (6/2), 1999 (16/16), 2000 (16/0), 2001 (16/0). Total: 54/18.

JACKSON, WILLIE — WR

PERSONAL: Born August 16, 1971, in Gainesville, Fla. ... 6-1/212. ... Full name: Willie Bernard Jackson Jr. ... Brother of Terry Jackson, running back, San Francisco 49ers.
HIGH SCHOOL: P.K. Yonge (Gainesville, Fla.).
COLLEGE: Florida (degree in telecommunications, 1993).
TRANSACTIONS/CAREER NOTES: Selected by Dallas Cowboys in fourth round (109th pick overall) of 1994 NFL draft. ... Signed by Cowboys (July 16, 1994). ... Inactive for 16 games (1994). ... Selected by Jacksonville Jaguars from Cowboys in NFL expansion draft (February 15, 1995). ... Granted free agency (February 14, 1997). ... Re-signed by Jaguars (March 26, 1997). ... Released by Jaguars (August 30, 1998). ... Signed by Cincinnati Bengals (September 10, 1998). ... Granted unconditional free agency (February 11, 2000). ... Signed by New Orleans Saints (April 28, 2000) ... Granted unconditional free agency (March 2, 2001). ... Re-signed by Saints (April 24, 2001). ... Granted unconditional free agency (March 1, 2002).
CHAMPIONSHIP GAME EXPERIENCE: Member of Cowboys for NFC championship game (1994 season); inactive. ... Played in AFC championship game (1996 season).
PRO STATISTICS: 1995—Returned one punt for minus two yards and recovered one fumble. 1996—Rushed once for two yards. 1997—Rushed three times for 14 yards. 1999—Returned two punts for six yards and recovered one fumble.
SINGLE GAME HIGHS (regular season): Receptions—11 (November 11, 2001, vs. San Francisco); yards—167 (November 11, 2001, vs. San Francisco); and touchdown receptions—2 (November 19, 2000, vs. Oakland).
STATISTICAL PLATEAUS: 100-yard receiving games: 1995 (1), 1996 (1), 2001 (3). Total: 5.

			RECEIVING				KICKOFF RETURNS				TOTALS			
Year Team	G	GS	No.	Yds.	Avg.	TD	No.	Yds.	Avg.	TD	TD	2pt.	Pts.	Fum.
1994—Dallas NFL								Did not play.						
1995—Jacksonville NFL	14	10	53	589	11.1	5	19	404	21.3	0	5	1	32	2
1996—Jacksonville NFL	16	2	33	486	14.7	3	7	149	21.3	0	3	1	20	0
1997—Jacksonville NFL	16	1	17	206	12.1	2	32	653	20.4	0	2	1	14	1
1998—Cincinnati NFL	8	0	7	165	23.6	0	0	0	0.0	0	0	0	0	0
1999—Cincinnati NFL	16	2	31	369	11.9	2	6	179	29.8	0	2	†1	14	1
2000—New Orleans NFL	15	6	37	523	14.1	6	0	0	0.0	0	6	0	36	2
2001—New Orleans NFL	16	16	81	1046	12.9	5	0	0	0.0	0	5	1	32	0
Pro totals (7 years)	101	37	259	3384	13.1	23	64	1385	21.6	0	23	5	148	6

JACOX, KENDYL — C — SAINTS

PERSONAL: Born June 10, 1975, in Dallas. ... 6-2/330. ... Full name: Kendyl LaMarc Jacox. ... Name pronounced JAY-cox.
HIGH SCHOOL: Carter (Dallas).
COLLEGE: Kansas State.
TRANSACTIONS/CAREER NOTES: Signed as non-drafted free agent by San Diego Chargers (April 20, 1998). ... On injured reserve with knee injury (December 4, 1999-remainder of season). ... Granted free agency (March 2, 2001). ... Re-signed by Chargers (April 10, 2001). ... Granted unconditional free agency (March 1, 2002). ... Signed by New Orleans Saints (May 28, 2002).
PLAYING EXPERIENCE: San Diego NFL, 1998-2001. ... Games/Games started: 1998 (16/6), 1999 (10/5), 2000 (15/3), 2001 (16/16). Total: 57/30.
PRO STATISTICS: 1998—Returned one kickoff for no yards. 2000—Returned one kickoff for eight yards. 2001—Fumbled once and recovered two fumbles for minus 18 yards.

JACQUET, NATE — WR

PERSONAL: Born September 2, 1975, in Duarte, Calif. ... 6-0/185. ... Full name: Nathaniel Martin Jacquet.
HIGH SCHOOL: Duarte (Calif.).
JUNIOR COLLEGE: Mount San Antonio College (Calif.).
COLLEGE: San Diego State.
TRANSACTIONS/CAREER NOTES: Selected by Indianapolis Colts in fifth round (150th pick overall) of 1997 NFL draft. ... Signed by Colts (June 26, 1997). ... Released by Colts (August 24, 1997). ... Re-signed by Colts to practice squad (August 25, 1997). ... Activated (November 4, 1997). ... Claimed on waivers by Miami Dolphins (August 26, 1998). ... Released by Dolphins (August 30, 1998). ... Re-signed by Dolphins to practice squad (August 31, 1998). ... Activated (September 9, 1998). ... Released by Dolphins (September 5, 1999). ... Re-signed by Dolphins (October 8, 1999). ... Granted free agency (February 11, 2000). ... Re-signed by Dolphins (April 28, 2000). ... Traded by Dolphins to San Diego Chargers for sixth-round pick (OT Brandon Winey) in 2001 (August 22, 2000). ... Released by Chargers (December 12, 2000). ... Signed by Minnesota Vikings (December 13, 2000). ... Granted unconditional free agency (March 2, 2001). ... Re-signed by Vikings (April 2, 2001). ... Released by Vikings (October 16, 2001). ... Re-signed by Vikings (October 25, 2001). ... Granted unconditional free agency (March 1, 2002).
PRO STATISTICS: 1997—Recovered one fumble. 1999—Rushed once for four yards. 2000—Recovered two fumbles. 2001—Recovered two fumbles.
SINGLE GAME HIGHS (regular season): Receptions—5 (December 13, 1998, vs. New York Jets); yards—68 (December 13, 1998, vs. New York Jets); and touchdown receptions—0.

			RECEIVING				PUNT RETURNS				KICKOFF RETURNS				TOTALS			
Year Team	G	GS	No.	Yds.	Avg.	TD	No.	Yds.	Avg.	TD	No.	Yds.	Avg.	TD	TD	2pt.	Pts.	Fum.
1997—Indianapolis NFL	5	0	0	0	0.0	0	13	96	7.4	0	8	156	19.5	0	0	0	0	1
1998—Miami NFL	15	0	8	122	15.3	0	0	0	0.0	0	4	103	25.8	0	0	0	0	0
1999—Miami NFL	13	0	1	18	18.0	0	28	351	12.5	0	1	26	26.0	0	0	0	0	1
2000—San Diego NFL	11	0	1	25	25.0	0	30	211	7.0	0	0	0	0.0	0	0	0	0	3
—Minnesota NFL	1	0	0	0	0.0	0	0	0	0.0	0	0	0	0.0	0	0	0	0	0
2001—Minnesota NFL	10	0	0	0	0.0	0	29	219	7.6	0	46	1012	22.0	0	0	0	0	4
Pro totals (5 years)	55	0	10	165	16.5	0	100	877	8.8	0	59	1297	22.0	0	0	0	0	9

JAMES, CEDRIC — WR — VIKINGS

PERSONAL: Born March 19, 1979, in Fort Worth, Texas. ... 6-1/199.
HIGH SCHOOL: Kennedale (Texas).
COLLEGE: Texas Christian.
TRANSACTIONS/CAREER NOTES: Selected by Minnesota Vikings in fourth round (131st pick overall) of 2001 NFL draft. ... Signed by Vikings (July 26, 2001). ... On injured reserve with leg injury (September 6, 2001-entire season).

			RECEIVING		
Year Team	G	GS	No.	Yds. Avg.	TD
2001—Minnesota NFL				Did not play.	

JAMES, EDGERRIN — RB — COLTS

PERSONAL: Born August 1, 1978, in Immokalee, Fla. ... 6-0/214. ... Full name: Edgerrin Tyree James. ... Name pronounced EDGE-rin.
HIGH SCHOOL: Immokalee (Fla.).
COLLEGE: Miami (Fla.).
TRANSACTIONS/CAREER NOTES: Selected after junior season by Indianapolis Colts in first round (fourth pick overall) of 1999 NFL draft. ... Signed by Colts (August 12, 1999). ... On injured reserve with knee injury (November 21, 2001-remainder of season).
HONORS: Named NFL Rookie of the Year by THE SPORTING NEWS (1999). ... Named running back on THE SPORTING NEWS NFL All-Pro team (1999 and 2000). ... Played in Pro Bowl (1999 and 2000 seasons).
PRO STATISTICS: 1999—Recovered two fumbles. 2001—Recovered one fumble.
SINGLE GAME HIGHS (regular season): Attempts—38 (October 15, 2000, vs. Seattle); yards—219 (October 15, 2000, vs. Seattle); and rushing touchdowns—3 (December 11, 2000, vs. Buffalo).
STATISTICAL PLATEAUS: 100-yard rushing games: 1999 (10), 2000 (9), 2001 (5). Total: 24.

			RUSHING				RECEIVING				TOTALS		
Year Team	G	GS	Att.	Yds.	Avg.	TD	No.	Yds.	Avg.	TD	TD	2pt.	Pts. Fum.
1999—Indianapolis NFL	16	16	*369	*1553	4.2	▲13	62	586	9.5	4	†17	0	102 8
2000—Indianapolis NFL	16	16	387	*1709	4.4	13	63	594	9.4	5	§18	1	110 5
2001—Indianapolis NFL	6	6	151	662	4.4	3	24	193	8.0	0	3	▲1	20 3
Pro totals (3 years)	38	38	907	3924	4.3	29	149	1373	9.2	9	38	2	232 16

JAMES, JENO — G — PANTHERS

PERSONAL: Born January 12, 1977, in Montgomery, Ala. ... 6-3/292. ... Full name: Jenorris James.
HIGH SCHOOL: Sidney Lanier (Montgomery, Ala.).
COLLEGE: Auburn.
TRANSACTIONS/CAREER NOTES: Selected by Carolina Panthers in sixth round (182nd pick overall) of 2000 NFL draft. ... Signed by Panthers (June 19, 2000).
PLAYING EXPERIENCE: Carolina NFL, 2000 and 2001. ... Games/Games started: 2000 (16/4), 2001 (14/6). Total: 30/10.

JAMES, TORY — CB — RAIDERS

PERSONAL: Born May 18, 1973, in New Orleans. ... 6-2/185. ... Full name: Tory Steven James.
HIGH SCHOOL: Archbishop Shaw (Marrero, La.).
COLLEGE: Louisiana State.
TRANSACTIONS/CAREER NOTES: Selected by Denver Broncos in second round (44th pick overall) of 1996 NFL draft. ... Signed by Broncos (July 22, 1996). ... On injured reserve with knee injury (August 18, 1997-entire season). ... Granted unconditional free agency (February 11, 2000). ... Signed by Oakland Raiders (February 28, 2000).
CHAMPIONSHIP GAME EXPERIENCE: Played in AFC championship game (1998 and 2000 seasons). ... Member of Super Bowl championship team (1998 season).
PRO STATISTICS: 1996—Recovered one fumble for 15 yards. 1998—Recovered one fumble.

			INTERCEPTIONS			
Year Team	G	GS	No.	Yds.	Avg.	TD
1996—Denver NFL	16	2	2	15	7.5	0
1997—Denver NFL				Did not play.		
1998—Denver NFL	16	0	0	0	0.0	0
1999—Denver NFL	16	4	5	59	11.8	0
2000—Oakland NFL	16	1	2	25	12.5	0
2001—Oakland NFL	16	1	5	72	14.4	0
Pro totals (5 years)	80	8	14	171	12.2	0

JANIKOWSKI, SEBASTIAN — K — RAIDERS

PERSONAL: Born March 2, 1978, in Poland. ... 6-1/255.
HIGH SCHOOL: Seabreeze (Daytona, Fla.).
COLLEGE: Florida State.
TRANSACTIONS/CAREER NOTES: Selected after junior season by Oakland Raiders in first round (17th pick overall) of 2000 NFL draft. ... Signed by Raiders (July 20, 2000).
CHAMPIONSHIP GAME EXPERIENCE: Played in AFC championship game (2000 season).
HONORS: Named kicker on THE SPORTING NEWS college All-America first team (1998 and 1999). ... Lou Groza Award winner (1998 and 1999).

		KICKING						
Year Team	G	XPM	XPA	FGM	FGA	Lg.	50+	Pts.
2000—Oakland NFL	14	46	46	22	32	▲54	1-4	112
2001—Oakland NFL	15	§42	▲42	23	28	52	1-2	111
Pro totals (2 years)	29	88	88	45	60	54	2-6	223

JANSEN, JON   OT   REDSKINS

PERSONAL: Born January 28, 1976, in Clawson, Mich. ... 6-6/311. ... Full name: Jonathan Ward Jansen.
HIGH SCHOOL: Clawson (Mich.).
COLLEGE: Michigan.
TRANSACTIONS/CAREER NOTES: Selected by Washington Redskins in second round (37th pick overall) of 1999 NFL draft. ... Signed by Redskins (July 9, 1999).
PLAYING EXPERIENCE: Washington NFL, 1999-2001. ... Games/Games started: 1999 (16/16), 2000 (16/16), 2001 (16/16). Total: 48/48.

JASPER, ED   DT   FALCONS

PERSONAL: Born January 18, 1973, in Tyler, Texas. ... 6-2/293. ... Full name: Edward Vidal Jasper.
HIGH SCHOOL: Troup (Texas).
COLLEGE: Texas A&M.
TRANSACTIONS/CAREER NOTES: Selected by Philadelphia Eagles in sixth round (198th pick overall) of 1997 NFL draft. ... Signed by Eagles (July 16, 1997). ... Released by Eagles (August 30, 1998). ... Re-signed by Eagles (September 17, 1998). ... Released by Eagles (October 23, 1998). ... Re-signed by Eagles (December 9, 1998). ... Released by Eagles (February 12, 1999). ... Signed by Atlanta Falcons (March 5, 1999).
PLAYING EXPERIENCE: Philadelphia NFL, 1997 and 1998; Atlanta NFL, 1999-2001. ... Games/Games started: 1997 (9/1), 1998 (7/0), 1999 (13/0), 2000 (15/15), 2001 (16/1). Total: 60/17.
PRO STATISTICS: 1997—Credited with one sack. 2000—Credited with 3½ sacks. 2001—Credited with 3½ sacks.

JEFFERS, PATRICK   WR   PANTHERS

PERSONAL: Born February 2, 1973, in Fort Campbell, Ky. ... 6-3/218. ... Full name: Patrick Christopher Jeffers.
HIGH SCHOOL: Fort Worth (Texas) Country Day.
COLLEGE: Virginia.
TRANSACTIONS/CAREER NOTES: Selected by Denver Broncos in fifth round (159th pick overall) of 1996 NFL draft. ... Signed by Broncos (July 17, 1996). ... Traded by Broncos to Dallas Cowboys for past considerations (August 30, 1998). ... Granted free agency (February 12, 1999). ... Tendered offer sheet by Carolina Panthers (April 12, 1999). ... Cowboys declined to match offer (April 15, 1999). ... On injured reserve with knee injury (August 13, 2000-entire season).
CHAMPIONSHIP GAME EXPERIENCE: Played in AFC championship game (1997 season). ... Member of Super Bowl championship team (1997 season).
PRO STATISTICS: 1996—Returned one kickoff for 18 yards. 1999—Rushed twice for 16 yards and recovered one fumble for three yards.
SINGLE GAME HIGHS (regular season): Receptions—8 (December 18, 1999, vs. San Francisco); yards—165 (January 2, 2000, vs. New Orleans); and touchdown receptions—2 (January 2, 2000, vs. New Orleans).
STATISTICAL PLATEAUS: 100-yard receiving games: 1999 (5).

				RECEIVING				TOTALS			
Year Team	G	GS	No.	Yds.	Avg.	TD	TD	2pt.	Pts.	Fum.
1996—Denver NFL	4	0	0	0	0.0	0	0	0	0	0
1997—Denver NFL	10	0	3	24	8.0	0	0	0	0	0
1998—Dallas NFL	8	1	18	330	18.3	2	2	0	12	0
1999—Carolina NFL	15	10	63	1082	17.2	12	12	0	72	0
2000—Carolina NFL					Did not play.					
2001—Carolina NFL	9	0	14	127	9.1	0	0	0	0	0
Pro totals (5 years)	46	11	98	1563	15.9	14	14	0	84	0

JEFFERSON, SHAWN   WR   FALCONS

PERSONAL: Born February 22, 1969, in Jacksonville. ... 5-11/185. ... Full name: Vanchi LaShawn Jefferson.
HIGH SCHOOL: Raines (Jacksonville).
COLLEGE: Central Florida.
TRANSACTIONS/CAREER NOTES: Selected by Houston Oilers in ninth round (240th pick overall) of 1991 NFL draft. ... Signed by Oilers (July 15, 1991). ... Traded by Oilers with first-round pick (DE Chris Mims) in 1992 draft to San Diego Chargers for DL Lee Williams (August 22, 1991). ... Granted free agency (March 1, 1993). ... Re-signed by Chargers (July 15, 1993). ... Granted free agency (February 17, 1994). ... Re-signed by Chargers (May 2, 1994). ... Released by Chargers (February 29, 1996). ... Signed by New England Patriots (March 14, 1996). ... Granted unconditional free agency (February 11, 2000). ... Signed by Atlanta Falcons (February 12, 2000).
CHAMPIONSHIP GAME EXPERIENCE: Played in AFC championship game (1994 and 1996 seasons). ... Played in Super Bowl XXIX (1994 season) and Super Bowl XXXI (1996 season).
PRO STATISTICS: 1998—Recovered one fumble. 1999—Recovered one fumble.
SINGLE GAME HIGHS (regular season): Receptions—7 (November 26, 2000, vs. Oakland); yards—148 (September 3, 2000, vs. San Francisco); and touchdown receptions—2 (October 31, 1999, vs. Arizona).
STATISTICAL PLATEAUS: 100-yard receiving games: 1995 (1), 1997 (1), 1998 (2), 1999 (1), 2000 (2). Total: 7.

			RUSHING				RECEIVING				TOTALS			
Year Team	G	GS	Att.	Yds.	Avg.	TD	No.	Yds.	Avg.	TD	TD	2pt.	Pts.	Fum.
1991—San Diego NFL	16	3	1	27	27.0	0	12	125	10.4	1	1	0	6	0
1992—San Diego NFL	16	1	0	0	0.0	0	29	377	13.0	2	2	0	12	0
1993—San Diego NFL	16	4	5	53	10.6	0	30	391	13.0	2	2	0	12	0
1994—San Diego NFL	16	16	3	40	13.3	0	43	627	14.6	3	3	0	18	0
1995—San Diego NFL	16	15	2	1	0.5	0	48	621	12.9	2	2	0	12	0
1996—New England NFL	15	15	1	6	6.0	0	50	771	15.4	4	4	0	24	2
1997—New England NFL	16	14	0	0	0.0	0	54	841	15.6	2	2	0	12	2
1998—New England NFL	16	16	1	15	15.0	0	34	771	*22.7	2	2	0	12	0
1999—New England NFL	16	16	0	0	0.0	0	40	698	§17.5	6	6	0	36	0
2000—Atlanta NFL	16	15	1	1	1.0	0	60	822	13.7	2	2	0	12	1
2001—Atlanta NFL	16	6	0	0	0.0	0	37	539	14.6	2	2	1	14	0
Pro totals (11 years)	175	121	14	143	10.2	0	437	6583	15.1	28	28	1	170	5

JENKINS, BILLY   S   BILLS

PERSONAL: Born July 8, 1974, in Los Angeles. ... 5-10/211.
HIGH SCHOOL: Albuquerque (N.M.).
COLLEGE: Howard.
TRANSACTIONS/CAREER NOTES: Signed as non-drafted free agent by St. Louis Rams (April 29, 1997). ... Granted free agency (February 11, 2000). ... Re-signed by Rams (March 3, 2000). ... Traded by Rams to Denver Broncos for fifth-round pick (DL Brian Young) in 2000 draft and fifth-round pick (traded to Washington) in 2001 draft (March 7, 2000). ... Released by Broncos (October 23, 2001). ... Signed by Green Bay Packers (November 19, 2001). ... Released by Packers (November 27, 2001). ... Re-signed by Packers (December 7, 2001). ... Granted unconditional free agency (March 1, 2002). ... Signed by Buffalo Bills (April 5, 2002).
CHAMPIONSHIP GAME EXPERIENCE: Played in NFC championship game (1999 season). ... Member of Super Bowl championship team (1999 season).
PRO STATISTICS: 2000—Fumbled once and recovered one fumble.

			INTERCEPTIONS			SACKS
Year Team	G	GS	No.	Yds.	Avg.	TD	No.
1997—St. Louis NFL	16	2	0	0	0.0	0	0.0
1998—St. Louis NFL	16	13	2	31	15.5	0	3.0
1999—St. Louis NFL	16	16	2	16	8.0	0	1.0
2000—Denver NFL	16	16	4	61	15.3	1	0.0
2001—Denver NFL	6	0	0	0	0.0	0	0.0
—Green Bay NFL	6	0	0	0	0.0	0	0.0
Pro totals (5 years)	76	47	8	108	13.5	1	4.0

JENKINS, DeRON   CB   PANTHERS

PERSONAL: Born November 14, 1973, in St. Louis. ... 5-11/192. ... Full name: DeRon Charles Jenkins.
HIGH SCHOOL: Ritenour (St. Louis).
COLLEGE: Tennessee.
TRANSACTIONS/CAREER NOTES: Selected by Baltimore Ravens in second round (55th pick overall) of 1996 NFL draft. ... Signed by Ravens (July 19, 1996). ... Granted free agency (February 12, 1999). ... Re-signed by Ravens (July 28, 1999). ... Granted unconditional free agency (February 11, 2000). ... Signed by San Diego Chargers (February 21, 2000). ... Released by Chargers (February 28, 2001). ... Signed by Tennessee Titans (June 29, 2001). ... Released by Titans (February 28, 2002). ... Signed by Carolina Panthers (March 15, 2002).
PLAYING EXPERIENCE: Baltimore NFL, 1996-1999; San Diego NFL, 2000; Tennessee NFL, 2001. ... Games/Games started: 1996 (15/2), 1997 (16/6), 1998 (16/7), 1999 (16/15), 2000 (15/14), 2001 (15/7). Total: 93/51.
PRO STATISTICS: 1996—Recovered one fumble. 1997—Intercepted one pass for 15 yards and recovered one fumble. 1998—Intercepted one pass for no yards and recovered one fumble. 1999—Credited with one sack. 2000—Intercepted one pass for 16 yards, returned one punt for no yards and fumbled once.

JENKINS, KERRY   G   BUCCANEERS

PERSONAL: Born September 6, 1973, in Tuscaloosa, Ala. ... 6-5/305.
HIGH SCHOOL: Holt (Ala.).
COLLEGE: Louisiana State, then Troy (Ala.) State.
TRANSACTIONS/CAREER NOTES: Signed as non-drafted free agent by Chicago Bears (April 25, 1997). ... Released by Bears (August 24, 1997). ... Re-signed by Bears to practice squad (August 27, 1997). ... Signed by New York Jets off Bears practice squad (December 3, 1997). ... Granted free agency (March 2, 2001). ... Re-signed by Jets (May 30, 2001). ... Granted unconditional free agency (March 1, 2002). ... Signed by Tampa Bay Buccaneers (March 6, 2002).
PLAYING EXPERIENCE: New York Jets NFL, 1997-2001. ... Games/Games started: 1997 (2/2), 1998 (16/0), 1999 (16/16), 2000 (16/16), 2001 (16/16). Total: 66/50.
CHAMPIONSHIP GAME EXPERIENCE: Played in AFC championship game (1998 season).
PRO STATISTICS: 1999—Recovered one fumble.

JENKINS, KRIS   DT   PANTHERS

PERSONAL: Born August 3, 1979, in Ypsilanti, Mich. ... 6-4/315. ... Full name: Kristopher Rudy-Charles Jenkins.
HIGH SCHOOL: Belleville (Ypsilanti, Mich.).
COLLEGE: Maryland.
TRANSACTIONS/CAREER NOTES: Selected by Carolina Panthers in second round (44th pick overall) of 2001 NFL draft. ... Signed by Panthers (July 13, 2001).
PRO STATISTICS: 2001—Recovered one fumble.

Year Team	G	GS	SACKS
2001—Carolina NFL	16	11	2.0

JENKINS, MARTAY   WR   CARDINALS

PERSONAL: Born February 28, 1975, in Waterloo, Iowa ... 6-0/201.
HIGH SCHOOL: Waterloo (Iowa) North.
JUNIOR COLLEGE: North Iowa Area Community College.
COLLEGE: Nebraska-Omaha (degree in sociology).
TRANSACTIONS/CAREER NOTES: Selected by Dallas Cowboys in sixth round (193rd pick overall) of 1999 NFL draft. ... Signed by Cowboys (July 27, 1999). ... Claimed on waivers by Arizona Cardinals (September 6, 1999).
PRO STATISTICS: 2000—Rushed once for minus four yards, returned one punt for one yard and fumbled three times. 2001—Rushed three times for four yards and recovered two fumbles.

SINGLE GAME HIGHS (regular season): Receptions—6 (December 2, 2001, vs. Oakland); yards—119 (October 7, 2001, vs. Philadelphia); and touchdown receptions—1 (December 9, 2001, vs. Washington).
STATISTICAL PLATEAUS: 100-yard receiving games: 2001 (1).

				RECEIVING				KICKOFF RETURNS				TOTALS		
Year Team	G	GS	No.	Yds.	Avg.	TD	No.	Yds.	Avg.	TD	TD	2pt.	Pts.	Fum.
1999—Arizona NFL	3	0	0	0	0.0	0	0	0	0.0	0	0	0	0	0
2000—Arizona NFL	16	2	17	219	12.9	0	*82	*2186	26.7	1	1	0	6	3
2001—Arizona NFL	13	3	32	518	16.2	3	49	1120	22.9	0	3	0	18	5
Pro totals (3 years)	32	5	49	737	15.0	3	131	3306	25.2	1	4	0	24	8

JENKINS, RONNEY　　　RB/KR　　　CHARGERS

PERSONAL: Born May 25, 1977, in Los Angeles. ... 5-11/188. ... Full name: Ronney Gene Jenkins.
HIGH SCHOOL: Point Hueneme (Oxnard, Calif.).
COLLEGE: Northern Arizona.
TRANSACTIONS/CAREER NOTES: Signed as non-drafted free agent by San Diego Chargers (April 17, 2000).
PRO STATISTICS: 2000—Rushed eight times for six yards, caught one pass for one yard and recovered two fumbles. 2001—Rushed once for minus one yard and recovered one fumble.
SINGLE GAME HIGHS (regular season): Attempts—3 (October 29, 2000, vs. Oakland); yards—6 (October 1, 2000, vs. St. Louis); and rushing touchdowns—0.

			KICKOFF RETURNS				TOTALS			
Year Team	G	GS	No.	Yds.	Avg.	TD	TD	2pt.	Pts.	Fum.
2000—San Diego NFL	16	0	§67	1531	22.9	▲1	1	0	6	3
2001—San Diego NFL	16	0	§58	*1541	*26.6	†2	2	0	12	1
Pro totals (2 years)	32	0	125	3072	24.6	3	3	0	18	4

JENNINGS, BRANDON　　　S　　　RAIDERS

PERSONAL: Born July 15, 1978, in Houston. ... 6-0/195.
HIGH SCHOOL: Channelview (Houston).
COLLEGE: Texas A&M.
TRANSACTIONS/CAREER NOTES: Signed as non-drafted free agent by Oakland Raiders (April 23, 2001). ... Released by Raiders (September 29, 2001). ... Re-signed by Raiders to practice squad (October 2, 2001). ... Activated (October 9, 2001). ... Claimed on waivers by Cleveland Browns (October 15, 2001). ... Released by Browns (October 24, 2001). ... Signed by Raiders to practice squad (November 7, 2001). ... Activated (November 23, 2001).
PLAYING EXPERIENCE: Oakland NFL, 2000 and 2001. ... Games/Games started: 2000 (2/0), 2001 (8/0). Total: 10/0.

JENNINGS, BRIAN　　　TE　　　49ERS

PERSONAL: Born October 14, 1976, in Mesa, Ariz. ... 6-5/245. ... Full name: Brian Lewis Jennings.
HIGH SCHOOL: Red Mountain (Mesa, Ariz.).
COLLEGE: Arizona State.
TRANSACTIONS/CAREER NOTES: Selected by San Francisco 49ers in seventh round (230th pick overall) of 2000 NFL draft. ... Signed by 49ers (July 10, 2000).
PLAYING EXPERIENCE: San Francisco NFL, 2000 and 2001. ... Games/Games started: 2000 (16/0), 2001 (16/0). Total: 32/0.
PRO STATISTICS: 2001—Fumbled once.

JENNINGS, JONAS　　　OT　　　BILLS

PERSONAL: Born November 21, 1977, in College Park, Ga. ... 6-3/320.
HIGH SCHOOL: Tri-Cities (East Point, Ga.).
COLLEGE: Georgia.
TRANSACTIONS/CAREER NOTES: Selected by Buffalo Bills in third round (95th pick overall) of 2001 NFL draft. ... Signed by Bills (June 22, 2001).
PLAYING EXPERIENCE: Buffalo NFL, 2001. ... Games/Games started: 2001 (12/12).

JENNINGS, LIGARIUS　　　CB　　　BENGALS

PERSONAL: Born November 3, 1977, in Birmingham, Ala. ... 5-8/202.
HIGH SCHOOL: Wenonah (Ala.).
COLLEGE: Tennessee State.
TRANSACTIONS/CAREER NOTES: Signed as non-drafted free agent by Detroit Lions (April 27, 2000). ... Released by Lions (September 2, 2001). ... Re-signed by Lions to practice squad (September 4, 2001). ... Signed by Cincinnati Bengals off Lions practice squad (October 16, 2001).
PLAYING EXPERIENCE: Cincinnati NFL, 2001. ... Games/Games started: 2001 (9/0).

JERVEY, TRAVIS　　　RB　　　FALCONS

PERSONAL: Born May 5, 1972, in Columbia, S.C. ... 6-0/222. ... Full name: Travis Richard Jervey.
HIGH SCHOOL: Wando (Mount Pleasant, S.C.).
COLLEGE: The Citadel.

TRANSACTIONS/CAREER NOTES: Selected by Green Bay Packers in fifth round (170th pick overall) of 1995 NFL draft. ... Signed by Packers (May 23, 1995). ... Granted free agency (February 13, 1998). ... Re-signed by Packers (June 16, 1998). ... On injured reserve with knee and ankle injuries (November 11, 1998-remainder of season). ... Granted unconditional free agency (February 12, 1999). ... Signed by San Francisco 49ers (March 22, 1999). ... On physically unable to perform list with ankle injury (July 27-August 26, 1999). ... On suspended list for violating league substance abuse policy (October 21-November 26, 1999). ... On injured reserve with broken collarbone (October 30, 2000-remainder of season). ... Released by 49ers (March 19, 2001). ... Signed by Atlanta Falcons (May 1, 2001). ... Granted unconditional free agency (March 1, 2002). ... Re-signed by Falcons (April 9, 2002).
CHAMPIONSHIP GAME EXPERIENCE: Played in NFC championship game (1995-97 seasons). ... Member of Super Bowl championship team (1996 season). ... Played in Super Bowl XXXII (1997 season).
HONORS: Played in Pro Bowl (1997 season).
PRO STATISTICS: 1995—Recovered one fumble. 1996—Recovered one fumble.
SINGLE GAME HIGHS (regular season): Attempts—29 (October 25, 1998, vs. Baltimore); yards—95 (November 1, 1998, vs. San Francisco); and rushing touchdowns—1 (January 3, 2000, vs. Atlanta).

				RUSHING			RECEIVING				KICKOFF RETURNS				TOTALS		
Year Team	G	GS	Att.	Yds.	Avg.	TD	No.	Yds.	Avg.	TD	No.	Yds.	Avg.	TD	TD	2pt.	Pts.	Fum.
1995—Green Bay NFL	16	0	0	0	0.0	0	0	0	0.0	0	8	165	20.6	0	0	0	0	0
1996—Green Bay NFL	16	0	26	106	4.1	0	0	0	0.0	0	1	17	17.0	0	0	0	0	4
1997—Green Bay NFL	16	0	0	0	0.0	0	0	0	0.0	0	0	0	0.0	0	0	0	0	0
1998—Green Bay NFL	8	5	83	325	3.9	1	9	33	3.7	0	0	0	0.0	0	1	0	6	0
1999—San Francisco NFL	8	0	6	49	8.2	1	1	2	2.0	0	8	191	23.9	0	1	0	6	0
2000—San Francisco NFL	8	0	1	0	0.0	0	0	0	0.0	0	8	209	26.1	0	0	0	0	0
2001—Atlanta NFL	16	0	3	6	2.0	0	0	0	0.0	0	0	0	0.0	0	0	0	0	0
Pro totals (7 years)	88	5	119	486	4.1	2	10	35	3.5	0	25	582	23.3	0	2	0	12	4

JETT, JAMES   WR   RAIDERS

PERSONAL: Born December 28, 1970, in Charlestown, W.Va. ... 5-10/170.
HIGH SCHOOL: Jefferson (Shenandoah Junction, W.Va.).
COLLEGE: West Virginia.
TRANSACTIONS/CAREER NOTES: Signed as non-drafted free agent by Los Angeles Raiders (May 1993). ... Raiders franchise moved to Oakland (July 21, 1995). ... Granted unconditional free agency (March 2, 2001). ... Re-signed by Raiders (March 2, 2001).
CHAMPIONSHIP GAME EXPERIENCE: Played in AFC championship game (2000 season).
PRO STATISTICS: 1993—Rushed once for no yards. 1994—Recovered two fumbles for 15 yards. 1997—Recovered one fumble. 1998—Rushed once for three yards and recovered one fumble for four yards.
SINGLE GAME HIGHS (regular season): Receptions—7 (October 13, 1996, vs. Detroit); yards—148 (September 21, 1997, vs. New York Jets); and touchdown receptions—2 (October 26, 1997, vs. Seattle).
STATISTICAL PLATEAUS: 100-yard receiving games: 1993 (2), 1996 (1), 1997 (1), 1998 (2). Total: 6.

			RECEIVING				TOTALS		
Year Team	G	GS	No.	Yds.	Avg.	TD	TD	2pt.	Pts.	Fum.
1993—Los Angeles Raiders NFL	16	1	33	771	*23.4	3	3	0	18	1
1994—Los Angeles Raiders NFL	16	1	15	253	16.9	0	0	0	0	0
1995—Oakland NFL	16	0	13	179	13.8	1	1	0	6	1
1996—Oakland NFL	16	16	43	601	14.0	4	4	0	24	0
1997—Oakland NFL	16	16	46	804	17.5	▲12	12	0	72	2
1998—Oakland NFL	16	16	45	882	19.6	6	6	0	36	0
1999—Oakland NFL	16	11	39	552	14.2	2	2	†1	14	0
2000—Oakland NFL	16	14	20	356	17.8	2	2	0	12	0
2001—Oakland NFL	10	0	2	19	9.5	0	0	0	0	0
Pro totals (9 years)	138	75	256	4417	17.3	30	30	1	182	4

JETT, JOHN   P   LIONS

PERSONAL: Born November 11, 1968, in Richmond, Va. ... 6-0/197.
HIGH SCHOOL: Northumberland (Heathsville, Va.).
COLLEGE: East Carolina.
TRANSACTIONS/CAREER NOTES: Signed as non-drafted free agent by Minnesota Vikings (June 22, 1992). ... Released by Vikings (August 25, 1992). ... Signed by Dallas Cowboys (March 10, 1993). ... Granted unconditional free agency (February 16, 1996). ... Re-signed by Cowboys (April 15, 1996). ... Granted unconditional free agency (February 14, 1997). ... Signed by Detroit Lions (March 7, 1997). ... Granted unconditional free agency (February 11, 2000). ... Re-signed by Lions (February 21, 2000).
CHAMPIONSHIP GAME EXPERIENCE: Played in NFC championship game (1993-1995 seasons). ... Member of Super Bowl championship team (1993 and 1995 seasons).
PRO STATISTICS: 1996—Rushed once for minus 23 yards. 1998—Attempted one pass without a completion. 1999—Rushed twice for minus eight yards and fumbled once. 2000—Rushed once for no yards, fumbled once and recovered one fumble for minus 10 yards. 2001—Rushed once for no yards.

		PUNTING					
Year Team	G	No.	Yds.	Avg.	Net avg.	In. 20	Blk.
1993—Dallas NFL	16	56	2342	41.8	37.7	22	0
1994—Dallas NFL	16	70	2935	41.9	35.3	26	0
1995—Dallas NFL	16	53	2166	40.9	34.5	17	0
1996—Dallas NFL	16	74	3150	42.6	36.7	22	0
1997—Detroit NFL	16	84	3576	42.6	35.6	24	†2
1998—Detroit NFL	14	66	2892	43.8	36.0	17	0
1999—Detroit NFL	16	86	3637	42.3	34.8	27	0
2000—Detroit NFL	16	‡93	‡4044	43.5	34.8	‡33	†2
2001—Detroit NFL	13	58	2512	43.3	35.5	16	0
Pro totals (9 years)	139	640	27254	42.6	35.6	204	4

JOHNSON, BRAD   QB   BUCCANEERS

PERSONAL: Born September 13, 1968, in Marietta, Ga. ... 6-5/226. ... Full name: James Bradley Johnson.
HIGH SCHOOL: Charles D. Owen (Black Mountain, N.C.).
COLLEGE: Florida State (degree in physical education, 1991).
TRANSACTIONS/CAREER NOTES: Selected by Minnesota Vikings in ninth round (227th pick overall) of 1992 NFL draft. ... Signed by Vikings (July 17, 1992). ... Active for one game (1992); did not play. ... Inactive for all 16 games (1993). ... Granted free agency (February 17, 1995). ... Assigned by Vikings to London Monarchs in 1995 World League enhancement allocation program (February 20, 1995). ... Re-signed by Vikings (March 27, 1995). ... On injured reserve with neck injury (December 5, 1997-remainder of season). ... Traded by Vikings to Washington Redskins for first- (QB Daunte Culpepper) and third-round (traded to Pittsburgh) picks in 1999 draft and second-round pick (DE Michael Boireau) in 2000 draft (February 15, 1999). ... Granted unconditional free agency (March 2, 2001). ... Signed by Tampa Bay Buccaneers (March 6, 2001).
CHAMPIONSHIP GAME EXPERIENCE: Member of Vikings for NFC championship game (1998 season); did not play.
HONORS: Played in Pro Bowl (1999 season).
PRO STATISTICS: 1995—Fumbled twice. 1996—Fumbled five times and recovered three fumbles for minus eight yards. 1997—Caught one pass for three yards and a touchdown, fumbled four times and recovered three fumbles. 1998—Fumbled once. 1999—Tied for NFC lead with 12 fumbles and recovered two fumbles for minus eight yards. 2000—Fumbled five times and recovered two fumbles for minus 14 yards. 2001—Fumbled four times and recovered two fumbles for minus one yard.
SINGLE GAME HIGHS (regular season): Attempts—56 (November 18, 2001, vs. Chicago); completions—40 (November 18, 2001, vs. Chicago); yards—471 (December 26, 1999, vs. San Francisco); and touchdown passes—4 (October 3, 1999, vs. Carolina).
STATISTICAL PLATEAUS: 300-yard passing games: 1997 (2), 1998 (1), 1999 (4), 2001 (2). Total: 9.
MISCELLANEOUS: Regular-season record as starting NFL quarterback: 41-25 (.621). ... Postseason record as starting NFL quarterback: 1-3 (.250).

				PASSING						RUSHING				TOTALS		
Year Team	G	GS	Att.	Cmp.	Pct.	Yds.	TD	Int.	Avg.	Rat.	Att.	Yds.	Avg.	TD	TD	2pt.	Pts.
1992—Minnesota NFL............						Did not play.											
1993—Minnesota NFL............						Did not play.											
1994—Minnesota NFL............	4	0	37	22	59.5	150	0	0	4.05	68.5	2	-2	-1.0	0	0	0	0
1995—London W.L.	...	...	328	194	59.1	2227	13	14	6.79	75.1	24	99	4.1	1	1	1	8
—Minnesota NFL	5	0	36	25	69.4	272	0	2	7.56	68.3	9	-9	-1.0	0	0	0	0
1996—Minnesota NFL............	12	8	311	195	62.7	2258	17	10	7.26	89.4	34	90	2.6	1	1	0	6
1997—Minnesota NFL............	13	13	452	275	60.8	3036	20	12	6.72	84.5	35	139	4.0	0	1	2	10
1998—Minnesota NFL............	4	2	101	65	64.4	747	7	5	7.40	89.0	12	15	1.3	0	0	0	0
1999—Washington NFL	16	16	519	316	60.9	4005	24	13	7.72	90.0	26	31	1.2	2	2	0	12
2000—Washington NFL	12	11	365	228	62.5	2505	11	15	6.86	75.7	22	58	2.6	1	1	0	6
2001—Tampa Bay NFL...........	16	16	559	340	60.8	3406	13	11	6.09	77.7	39	120	3.1	3	3	0	18
W.L. totals (1 year)	...	...	328	194	59.1	2227	13	14	6.79	75.1	24	99	4.1	1	1	1	8
NFL totals (8 years)................	82	66	2380	1466	61.6	16379	92	68	6.88	83.1	179	442	2.5	7	8	2	52
Pro totals (9 years)	...	...	2708	1660	61.3	18606	105	82	6.87	82.1	203	541	2.7	8	9	3	60

JOHNSON, BRYAN   FB   REDSKINS

PERSONAL: Born January 18, 1978, in Pocatello, Idaho. ... 6-1/234.
HIGH SCHOOL: Highland (Pocatello, Idaho).
COLLEGE: Boise State.
TRANSACTIONS/CAREER NOTES: Signed as non-drafted free agent by Washington Redskins (April 18, 2000). ... Released by Redskins (August 27, 2000). ... Re-signed by Redskins to practice squad (August 28, 2000). ... Activated (December 18, 2000).
PLAYING EXPERIENCE: Washington NFL, 2000 and 2001. ... Games/Games started: 2000 (1/0); 2001 (16/1). Total: 17/1.
PRO STATISTICS: 2001—Caught nine passes for 129 yards and returned four kickoffs for 51 yards.

JOHNSON, CHAD   WR   BENGALS

PERSONAL: Born January 9, 1978, in Los Angeles. ... 6-2/192.
HIGH SCHOOL: Miami Beach (Fla.).
JUNIOR COLLEGE: Santa Monica College (Calif.).
COLLEGE: Oregon State.
TRANSACTIONS/CAREER NOTES: Selected by Cincinnati Bengals in second round (36th pick overall) of 2001 NFL draft. ... Signed by Bengals (July 18, 2001).
SINGLE GAME HIGHS (regular season): Receptions—5 (October 14, 2001, vs. Cleveland); yards—68 (October 14, 2001, vs. Cleveland); and touchdown receptions—1 (September 30, 2001, vs. San Diego).

			RECEIVING			
Year Team	G	GS	No.	Yds.	Avg.	TD
2001—Cincinnati NFL..	12	3	28	329	11.8	1

JOHNSON, CHARLES   WR

PERSONAL: Born January 3, 1972, in San Bernardino, Calif. ... 6-0/205. ... Full name: Charles Everett Johnson.
HIGH SCHOOL: Cajon (San Bernardino, Calif.).
COLLEGE: Colorado (degree in marketing, 1993).
TRANSACTIONS/CAREER NOTES: Selected by Pittsburgh Steelers in first round (17th pick overall) of 1994 NFL draft. ... Signed by Steelers (July 21, 1994). ... On injured reserve with knee injury (December 23, 1995-remainder of season). ... Granted unconditional free agency (February 12, 1999). ... Signed by Philadelphia Eagles (February 16, 1999). ... On injured reserve with knee injury (December 3, 1999-remainder of season). ... Released by Eagles (April 24, 2001). ... Signed by New England Patriots (May 31, 2001). ... Released by Patriots (February 25, 2002).

CHAMPIONSHIP GAME EXPERIENCE: Played in AFC championship game (1994, 1997 and 2001 seasons). ... Member of Super Bowl championship team (2001 season).
HONORS: Named wide receiver on THE SPORTING NEWS college All-America second team (1993).
RECORDS: Shares NFL single-game record for most two-point conversions—2 (November 1, 1998).
PRO STATISTICS: 1994—Fumbled twice. 1995—Recovered one fumble. 1996—Fumbled once. 1999—Credited with a safety, fumbled twice and recovered one fumble.
SINGLE GAME HIGHS (regular season): Receptions—9 (November 1, 1998, vs. Tennessee); yards—165 (December 24, 1994, vs. San Diego); and touchdown receptions—3 (November 1, 1998, vs. Tennessee).
STATISTICAL PLATEAUS: 100-yard receiving games: 1994 (1), 1996 (4), 1997 (1), 1998 (1). Total: 7.

				RUSHING				RECEIVING				PUNT RETURNS				KICKOFF RETURNS				TOTALS		
Year Team	G	GS	Att.	Yds.	Avg.	TD	No.	Yds.	Avg.	TD	No.	Yds.	Avg.	TD	No.	Yds.	Avg.	TD	TD	2pt.	Pts.
1994—Pittsburgh NFL....	16	9	4	-1	-0.3	0	38	577	15.2	3	15	90	6.0	0	16	345	21.6	0	3	0	18
1995—Pittsburgh NFL....	15	12	1	-10	-10.0	0	38	432	11.4	0	0	0	0.0	0	2	47	23.5	0	0	0	0
1996—Pittsburgh NFL....	16	12	0	0	0.0	0	60	1008	16.8	3	0	0	0.0	0	6	111	18.5	0	3	1	20
1997—Pittsburgh NFL....	13	11	0	0	0.0	0	46	568	12.3	2	0	0	0.0	0	0	0	0.0	0	2	0	12
1998—Pittsburgh NFL....	16	16	1	4	4.0	0	65	815	12.5	7	0	0	0.0	0	0	0	0.0	0	7	†2	46
1999—Philadelphia NFL .	11	11	0	0	0.0	0	34	414	12.2	1	1	0	0.0	0	0	0	0.0	0	1	0	8
2000—Philadelphia NFL .	16	15	5	18	3.6	0	56	642	11.5	7	0	0	0.0	0	0	0	0.0	0	7	0	42
2001—New England NFL	14	3	0	0	0.0	0	14	111	7.9	1	0	0	0.0	0	0	0	0.0	0	1	0	6
Pro totals (8 years)........	117	89	11	11	1.0	0	351	4567	13.0	24	16	90	5.6	0	24	503	21.0	0	24	3	152

JOHNSON, DOUG   QB   FALCONS

PERSONAL: Born October 27, 1977, in Gainesville, Fla. ... 6-2/225.
HIGH SCHOOL: Buchholz (Gainesville, Fla.).
COLLEGE: Florida.
TRANSACTIONS/CAREER NOTES: Signed as non-drafted free agent by Atlanta Falcons (April 17, 2000).
PRO STATISTICS: 2000—Fumbled four times. 2001—Fumbled twice.
SINGLE GAME HIGHS (regular season): Attempts—33 (December 3, 2000, vs. Seattle); completions—17 (December 3, 2000, vs. Seattle); yards—233 (December 3, 2000, vs. Seattle); and touchdown passes—1 (November 11, 2001, vs. Dallas).
MISCELLANEOUS: Regular-season record as starting NFL quarterback: 0-2.

					PASSING						RUSHING			TOTALS		
Year Team	G	GS	Att.	Cmp.	Pct.	Yds.	TD	Int.	Avg.	Rat.	Att.	Yds.	Avg.	TD	TD	2pt.	Pts.
2000—Atlanta NFL	5	2	67	36	53.7	406	2	3	6.06	63.4	3	11	3.7	0	0	0	0
2001—Atlanta NFL	3	0	5	3	60.0	23	1	0	4.60	110.8	5	12	2.4	0	0	0	0
Pro totals (2 years)	8	2	72	39	54.2	429	3	3	5.96	68.6	8	23	2.9	0	0	0	0

JOHNSON, ELLIS   DT   COLTS

PERSONAL: Born October 30, 1973, in Wildwood, Fla. ... 6-2/288. ... Full name: Ellis Bernard Johnson.
HIGH SCHOOL: Wildwood (Fla.).
COLLEGE: Florida.
TRANSACTIONS/CAREER NOTES: Selected by Indianapolis Colts in first round (15th pick overall) of 1995 NFL draft. ... Signed by Colts (June 7, 1995). ... On physically unable to perform list with knee injury (July 27-August 20, 2001).
CHAMPIONSHIP GAME EXPERIENCE: Played in AFC championship game (1995 season).
PRO STATISTICS: 1997—Intercepted one pass for 18 yards and recovered two fumbles. 1999—Recovered one fumble. 2000—Intercepted one pass for minus one yard.

Year Team	G	GS	SACKS
1995—Indianapolis NFL...	16	2	4.5
1996—Indianapolis NFL...	12	6	0.0
1997—Indianapolis NFL...	15	15	4.5
1998—Indianapolis NFL...	16	16	8.0
1999—Indianapolis NFL...	16	16	7.5
2000—Indianapolis NFL...	13	13	5.0
2001—Indianapolis NFL...	16	16	3.5
Pro totals (7 years)...	104	84	33.0

JOHNSON, ERIC   TE   49ERS

PERSONAL: Born September 15, 1979, in Needham, Mass. ... 6-3/256.
HIGH SCHOOL: Needham (Mass.).
COLLEGE: Yale.
TRANSACTIONS/CAREER NOTES: Selected by San Francisco 49ers in seventh round (224th pick overall) of 2001 NFL draft. ... Signed by 49ers (July 24, 2001).
PRO STATISTICS: 2001—Fumbled once.
SINGLE GAME HIGHS (regular season): Receptions—4 (December 30, 2001, vs. Dallas); yards—38 (December 9, 2001, vs. St. Louis); and touchdown receptions—1 (December 16, 2001, vs. Miami).

			RECEIVING			
Year Team	G	GS	No.	Yds.	Avg.	TD
2001—San Francisco NFL..	16	14	40	362	9.1	3

JOHNSON, ERIC   S   RAIDERS

PERSONAL: Born April 30, 1976, in Phoenix, Ariz. ... 6-0/210.
HIGH SCHOOL: Alhambra (Arizona).
COLLEGE: Nebraska.

TRANSACTIONS/CAREER NOTES: Signed as non-drafted free agent by Oakland Raiders (March 23, 2000). ... On injured reserve with broken leg (November 7, 2001-remainder of season).
PLAYING EXPERIENCE: Oakland NFL, 2000 and 2001. ... Games/Games started: 2000 (16/0), 2001 (7/0). Total: 23/0.

JOHNSON, J.J. RB BROWNS

PERSONAL: Born April 20, 1974, in Mobile, Ala. ... 6-1/230. ... Full name: James E. Johnson.
HIGH SCHOOL: Dothan (Ala.), then Davidson (Mobile, Ala.).
JUNIOR COLLEGE: East Mississippi Junior College.
COLLEGE: Mississippi State.
TRANSACTIONS/CAREER NOTES: Selected by Miami Dolphins in second round (39th pick overall) of 1999 NFL draft. ... Signed by Dolphins (July 27, 1999). ... Traded by Dolphins to Cleveland Browns for conditional seventh-round pick in 2004 draft (March 8, 2002).
HONORS: Named running back on THE SPORTING NEWS college All-America second team (1998).
PRO STATISTICS: 1999—Returned two kickoffs for 26 yards and recovered one fumble. 2000—Returned two kickoffs for 26 yards. 2001—Returned one kickoff for 16 yards.
SINGLE GAME HIGHS (regular season): Attempts—31 (November 21, 1999, vs. New England); yards—106 (November 21, 1999, vs. New England); and rushing touchdowns—1 (November 26, 2000, vs. Indianapolis).
STATISTICAL PLATEAUS: 100-yard rushing games: 1999 (1).

				RUSHING				RECEIVING				TOTALS		
Year Team	G	GS	Att.	Yds.	Avg.	TD	No.	Yds.	Avg.	TD	TD	2pt.	Pts.	Fum.
1999—Miami NFL	13	4	164	558	3.4	4	15	100	6.7	0	4	0	24	2
2000—Miami NFL	13	1	50	168	3.4	1	10	61	6.1	0	1	0	6	0
2001—Miami NFL	10	0	5	22	4.4	0	4	21	5.3	0	0	0	0	0
Pro totals (3 years)	36	5	219	748	3.4	5	29	182	6.3	0	5	0	30	2

JOHNSON, JERRY DT BRONCOS

PERSONAL: Born July 11, 1977, in Fort Pierce, Fla. ... 6-0/290. ... Full name: Jerry M. Johnson Jr.
HIGH SCHOOL: Central (Fort Pierce, Fla.).
COLLEGE: Florida State.
TRANSACTIONS/CAREER NOTES: Selected by Denver Broncos in fourth round (101st pick overall) of 2000 NFL draft. ... Signed by Broncos (July 20, 2000). ... Inactive for all 16 games (2000).
PLAYING EXPERIENCE: Denver NFL, 2001. ... Games/Games started: 2001 (8/0).

JOHNSON, JOE DE PACKERS

PERSONAL: Born July 11, 1972, in St. Louis. ... 6-4/270. ... Full name: Joe T. Johnson.
HIGH SCHOOL: Jennings (Mo.).
COLLEGE: Louisville.
TRANSACTIONS/CAREER NOTES: Selected after junior season by New Orleans Saints in first round (13th pick overall) of 1994 NFL draft. ... Signed by Saints (June 7, 1994). ... Designated by Saints as franchise player (February 13, 1998). ... Re-signed by Saints (September 2, 1998). ... On injured reserve with knee injury (August 31, 1999-entire season). ... Granted unconditional free agency (March 1, 2002). ... Signed by Green Bay Packers (March 21, 2002).
HONORS: Played in Pro Bowl (1998 and 2000 seasons).
PRO STATISTICS: 1994—Recovered one fumble. 1997—Recovered one fumble. 1998—Recovered one fumble for five yards and a touchdown. 2000—Recovered two fumbles. 2001—Recovered two fumbles.

Year Team	G	GS	SACKS
1994—New Orleans NFL	15	14	1.0
1995—New Orleans NFL	14	14	5.5
1996—New Orleans NFL	13	13	7.5
1997—New Orleans NFL	16	16	8.5
1998—New Orleans NFL	16	16	7.0
1999—New Orleans NFL		Did not play.	
2000—New Orleans NFL	16	15	12.0
2001—New Orleans NFL	16	16	9.0
Pro totals (7 years)	106	104	50.5

JOHNSON, KEVIN WR BROWNS

PERSONAL: Born July 15, 1976, in Trenton, N.J. ... 5-11/195. ... Full name: Kevin L. Johnson.
HIGH SCHOOL: Hamilton West (Trenton, N.J.).
COLLEGE: Syracuse.
TRANSACTIONS/CAREER NOTES: Selected by Cleveland Browns in second round (32nd pick overall) of 1999 NFL draft. ... Signed by Browns (July 22, 1999).
PRO STATISTICS: 1999—Attempted one pass without a completion, returned one kickoff for 25 yards and recovered one fumble. 2000—Attempted three passes with one completion for 23 yards and one interception. 2001—Recovered two fumbles.
SINGLE GAME HIGHS (regular season): Receptions—8 (December 9, 2001, vs. New England); yards—153 (October 14, 2001, vs. Cincinnati); and touchdown receptions—2 (December 2, 2001, vs. Tennessee).
STATISTICAL PLATEAUS: 100-yard receiving games: 1999 (2), 2000 (1), 2001 (2). Total: 5.

			RUSHING				RECEIVING				PUNT RETURNS				TOTALS			
Year Team	G	GS	Att.	Yds.	Avg.	TD	No.	Yds.	Avg.	TD	No.	Yds.	Avg.	TD	TD	2pt.	Pts.	Fum.
1999—Cleveland NFL	16	16	1	-6	-6.0	0	66	986	14.9	8	19	128	6.7	0	8	0	48	1
2000—Cleveland NFL	16	16	0	0	0.0	0	57	669	11.7	0	0	0	0.0	0	0	0	0	0
2001—Cleveland NFL	16	16	0	0	0.0	0	84	1097	13.1	9	14	117	8.4	0	9	0	54	2
Pro totals (3 years)	48	48	1	-6	-6.0	0	207	2752	13.3	17	33	245	7.4	0	17	0	102	3

JOHNSON, KEYSHAWN — WR — BUCCANEERS

PERSONAL: Born July 22, 1972, in Los Angeles. ... 6-4/212. ... Cousin of Chris Miller, wide receiver with Green Bay Packers (1997), Detroit Lions (1997) and Chicago Bears (1998); and cousin of Ed Gray, guard with Atlanta Hawks (1997-98 and 1998-99).
HIGH SCHOOL: Dorsey (Los Angeles).
JUNIOR COLLEGE: West Los Angeles College.
COLLEGE: Southern California (degree in history).
TRANSACTIONS/CAREER NOTES: Selected by New York Jets in first round (first pick overall) of 1996 NFL draft. ... Signed by Jets (August 6, 1996). ... Traded by Jets to Tampa Bay Buccaneers for two first-round picks (LB John Abraham and TE Anthony Becht) in 2000 draft (April 12, 2000).
CHAMPIONSHIP GAME EXPERIENCE: Played in AFC championship game (1998 season).
HONORS: Named wide receiver on THE SPORTING NEWS college All-America first team (1995). ... Played in Pro Bowl (1998 and 1999 seasons). ... Named co-Oustanding Player of Pro Bowl (1998 season).
PRO STATISTICS: 1998—Rushed twice for 60 yards and one touchdown. 1999—Rushed five times for six yards and attempted one pass without a completion. 2000—Rushed twice for five yards.
SINGLE GAME HIGHS (regular season): Receptions—12 (November 18, 2001, vs. Chicago); yards—194 (September 12, 1999, vs. New England); and touchdown receptions—2 (December 18, 2000, vs. St. Louis).
STATISTICAL PLATEAUS: 100-yard receiving games: 1997 (1), 1998 (4), 1999 (2), 2000 (2), 2001 (4). Total: 13.

				RECEIVING				TOTALS		
Year Team	G	GS	No.	Yds.	Avg.	TD	TD	2pt.	Pts.	Fum.
1996—New York Jets NFL	14	11	63	844	13.4	8	8	1	50	0
1997—New York Jets NFL	16	16	70	963	13.8	5	5	0	30	0
1998—New York Jets NFL	16	16	83	1131	13.6	▲10	11	0	66	0
1999—New York Jets NFL	16	16	89	1170	13.1	8	8	0	48	0
2000—Tampa Bay NFL	16	16	71	874	12.3	8	8	0	48	2
2001—Tampa Bay NFL	15	15	‡106	1266	11.9	1	1	0	6	2
Pro totals (6 years)	93	90	482	6248	13.0	40	41	1	248	4

JOHNSON, LEE — P

PERSONAL: Born November 27, 1961, in Conroe, Texas. ... 6-2/200.
HIGH SCHOOL: McCullough (The Woodlands, Texas).
COLLEGE: Brigham Young.
TRANSACTIONS/CAREER NOTES: Selected by Houston Gamblers in ninth round (125th pick overall) of 1985 USFL draft. ... Selected by Houston Oilers in fifth round (138th pick overall) of 1985 NFL draft. ... Signed by Oilers (June 25, 1985). ... Crossed picket line during players strike (October 14, 1987). ... Claimed on waivers by Buffalo Bills (December 2, 1987). ... Claimed on waivers by Cleveland Browns (December 10, 1987). ... Claimed on waivers by Cincinnati Bengals (September 23, 1988). ... Granted free agency (February 1, 1991). ... Re-signed by Bengals (1991). ... Granted unconditional free agency (March 1, 1993). ... Re-signed by Bengals (May 10, 1993). ... Released by Bengals (December 7, 1998). ... Signed by New England Patriots (February 18, 1999). ... Released by Patriots (October 15, 2001). ... Signed by Minnesota Vikings (December 12, 2001). ... Granted unconditional free agency (March 1, 2002).
CHAMPIONSHIP GAME EXPERIENCE: Played in AFC championship game (1987 and 1988 seasons). ... Played in Super Bowl XXIII (1988 season).
RECORDS: Holds NFL career record for most punts—1,212.
POST SEASON RECORDS: Holds Super Bowl career record for longest punt—63 yards (January 22, 1989, vs. San Francisco).
PRO STATISTICS: 1985—Rushed once for no yards, fumbled twice and recovered one fumble for seven yards. 1987—Had 32.8-yard net punting average. 1988—Had 33.4-yard net punting average. 1989—Rushed once for minus seven yards. 1990—Attempted one pass with a completion for four yards and a touchdown. 1991—Attempted one pass with a completion for three yards, rushed once for minus two yards and fumbled once. 1993—Attempted one pass without a completion. 1994—Attempted one pass with a completion for seven yards and a touchdown. 1995—Attempted one pass with a completion for five yards, rushed once for minus 16 yards and fumbled once. 1997—Rushed once for no yards and recovered two fumbles. 1999—Rushed twice for 13 yards. 2000—Rushed twice for minus one yard, attempted one pass with a completion for 18 yards, fumbled twice and recovered one fumble for minus 12 yards. 2001—Rushed once for minus 19 yards and fumbled once.

		PUNTING						KICKING					
Year Team	G	No.	Yds.	Avg.	Net avg.	In. 20	Blk.	XPM	XPA	FGM	FGA	Lg.	50+	Pts.
1985—Houston NFL	16	83	3464	41.7	35.7	22	0	0	0	0	0	0	0-0	0
1986—Houston NFL	16	88	3623	41.2	35.7	26	0	0	0	0	0	0	0-0	0
1987—Houston NFL	9	41	1652	40.3	32.9	5	0	0	0	0	0	0	0-0	0
—Cleveland NFL	3	9	317	35.2	32.2	3	0	0	0	0	0	0	0-0	0
1988—Cleveland NFL	3	17	643	37.8	30.6	6	0	0	0	1	2	50	1-2	3
—Cincinnati NFL	12	14	594	42.4	36.7	4	0	0	0	0	0	0	0-0	0
1989—Cincinnati NFL	16	61	2446	40.1	30.1	14	2	0	1	0	0	0	0-0	0
1990—Cincinnati NFL	16	64	2705	42.3	34.2	12	0	0	0	1	0	0	0-0	0
1991—Cincinnati NFL	16	64	2795	43.7	34.7	15	0	0	0	1	3	53	1-3	3
1992—Cincinnati NFL	16	76	3196	42.1	35.8	15	0	0	0	0	1	0	0-1	0
1993—Cincinnati NFL	16	▲90	3954	43.9	36.6	24	0	0	0	0	0	0	0-0	0
1994—Cincinnati NFL	16	79	3461	43.8	35.2	19	1	0	0	0	0	0	0-0	0
1995—Cincinnati NFL	16	68	2861	42.1	38.6	26	0	0	0	0	0	0	0-0	0
1996—Cincinnati NFL	16	80	3630	45.4	34.3	16	1	0	0	0	0	0	0-0	0
1997—Cincinnati NFL	16	81	3471	42.9	35.9	27	0	0	0	0	0	0	0-0	0
1998—Cincinnati NFL	13	69	3083	44.7	35.6	14	1	0	0	0	0	0	0-0	0
1999—New England NFL	16	90	3735	41.5	34.6	23	0	0	0	0	0	0	0-0	0
2000—New England NFL	16	89	3798	42.7	36.8	31	▲1	0	0	0	0	0	0-0	0
2001—New England NFL	5	24	1045	43.5	38.3	9	0	0	0	0	0	0	0-0	0
—Minnesota NFL	4	25	983	39.3	34.4	9	0	0	0	0	0	0	0-0	0
Pro totals (17 years)	257	1212	51456	42.5	35.2	314	6	0	1	2	7	53	2-6	6

JOHNSON, LEON — RB/KR — BEARS

PERSONAL: Born July 13, 1974, in Morganton, N.C. ... 6-0/216. ... Full name: William Leon Johnson.
HIGH SCHOOL: Freedom (Morganton, N.C.).
COLLEGE: North Carolina.
TRANSACTIONS/CAREER NOTES: Selected by New York Jets in fourth round (104th pick overall) of 1997 NFL draft. ... Signed by Jets (July 17, 1997). ... On injured reserve with rib injury (December 16, 1998-remainder of season). ... On injured reserve with knee injury (September 13, 1999-remainder of season). ... Granted free agency (February 11, 2000). ... Re-signed by Jets (May 8, 2000). ... Released by Jets (June 27, 2000). ... Re-signed by Jets (November 28, 2000). ... Released by Jets (February 19, 2001). ... Signed by Chicago Bears (October 9, 2001).
PRO STATISTICS: 1997—Attempted two passes without a completion and one interception, fumbled five times and recovered five fumbles. 1998—Fumbled three times and recovered three fumbles. 1999—Fumbled once. 2001—Completed only pass attempt for 18 yards, fumbled twice and recovered two fumbles.
SINGLE GAME HIGHS (regular season): Attempts—13 (October 11, 1998, vs. St. Louis); yards—56 (October 11, 1998, vs. St. Louis); and rushing touchdowns—2 (September 20, 1998, vs Indianapolis).

			RUSHING				RECEIVING				PUNT RETURNS				KICKOFF RETURNS				TOTALS		
Year Team	G	GS	Att.	Yds.	Avg.	TD	No.	Yds.	Avg.	TD	No.	Yds.	Avg.	TD	No.	Yds.	Avg.	TD	TD	2pt.	Pts.
1997—N.Y. Jets NFL	16	1	48	158	3.3	2	16	142	8.9	0	§51	*619	12.1	1	12	319	26.6 ▲1		4	0	24
1998—N.Y. Jets NFL	12	2	41	185	4.5	2	13	222	17.1	2	29	203	7.0	0	16	366	22.9	0	4	0	24
1999—N.Y. Jets NFL	1	0	1	2	2.0	0	0	0	0.0	0	1	6	6.0	0	2	31	15.5	0	0	0	0
2000—N.Y. Jets NFL	3	0	0	0	0.0	0	0	0	0.0	0	10	62	6.2	0	6	117	19.5	0	0	0	0
2001—Chicago NFL	12	0	20	99	5.0	4	1	0	0.0	0	28	255	9.1	0	14	286	20.4	0	4	0	24
Pro totals (5 years)	44	3	110	444	4.0	8	30	364	12.1	2	119	1145	9.6	1	50	1119	22.4	1	12	0	72

JOHNSON, PATRICK — WR — JAGUARS

PERSONAL: Born August 10, 1976, in Gainesville, Ga. ... 5-10/191. ... Full name: Patrick Jevon Johnson.
HIGH SCHOOL: Redlands (Calif.).
COLLEGE: Oregon.
TRANSACTIONS/CAREER NOTES: Selected by Baltimore Ravens in second round (42nd pick overall) of 1998 NFL draft. ... Signed by Ravens (June 24, 1998). ... Granted free agency (March 2, 2001). ... Signed by Jacksonville Jaguars (March 18, 2002).
CHAMPIONSHIP GAME EXPERIENCE: Played in AFC championship game (2000 season). ... Member of Super Bowl championship team (2000 season).
HONORS: Named kick returner on THE SPORTING NEWS college All-America second team (1997).
PRO STATISTICS: 1998—Returned one punt for six yards. 1999—Rushed once for 12 yards and recovered one fumble for 12 yards. 2000—Rushed twice for 21 yards.
SINGLE GAME HIGHS (regular season): Receptions—9 (January 2, 2000, vs. New England); yards—114 (January 2, 2000, vs. New England); and touchdown receptions—1 (September 23, 2001, vs. Cincinnati).
STATISTICAL PLATEAUS: 100-yard receiving games: 1999 (1).

			RECEIVING				KICKOFF RETURNS				TOTALS			
Year Team	G	GS	No.	Yds.	Avg.	TD	No.	Yds.	Avg.	TD	TD	2pt.	Pts.	Fum.
1998—Baltimore NFL	13	0	12	159	13.3	1	16	399	24.9 ▲1		2	0	12	1
1999—Baltimore NFL	10	6	29	526	18.1	3	0	0	0.0	0	3	0	18	1
2000—Baltimore NFL	13	0	12	156	13.0	2	0	0	0.0	0	2	0	12	0
2001—Baltimore NFL	4	0	5	57	11.4	1	2	39	19.5	0	1	0	6	1
Pro totals (4 years)	40	15	58	898	15.5	7	18	438	24.3	1	8	0	48	3

JOHNSON, RAYLEE — DE — CHARGERS

PERSONAL: Born June 1, 1970, in Chicago. ... 6-3/272. ... Full name: Raylee Terrell Johnson.
HIGH SCHOOL: Fordyce (Ark.).
COLLEGE: Arkansas.
TRANSACTIONS/CAREER NOTES: Selected by San Diego Chargers in fourth round (95th pick overall) of 1993 NFL draft. ... Signed by Chargers (July 15, 1993). ... Granted unconditional free agency (February 14, 1997). ... Re-signed by Chargers (March 11, 1997). ... On injured reserve with knee injury (August 22, 2000-entire season).
CHAMPIONSHIP GAME EXPERIENCE: Played in AFC championship game (1994 season). ... Played in Super Bowl XXIX (1994 season).
PRO STATISTICS: 1999—Recovered one fumble. 2001—Recovered two fumbles for 46 yards and one touchdown.

Year Team	G	GS	SACKS
1993—San Diego NFL	9	0	0.0
1994—San Diego NFL	15	0	1.5
1995—San Diego NFL	16	1	3.0
1996—San Diego NFL	16	1	3.0
1997—San Diego NFL	16	0	2.5
1998—San Diego NFL	16	3	5.5
1999—San Diego NFL	16	16	10.5
2000—San Diego NFL		Did not play.	
2001—San Diego NFL	16	16	9.5
Pro totals (8 years)	120	37	35.5

JOHNSON, RIALL — LB — BENGALS

PERSONAL: Born April 20, 1978, in Lynnwood, Wash. ... 6-3/243.
HIGH SCHOOL: Mariner (Wash.).
COLLEGE: Stanford.
TRANSACTIONS/CAREER NOTES: Selected by Cincinnati Bengals in sixth round (168th pick overall) of 2001 NFL draft. ... Signed by Bengals (July 11, 2001). ... Released by Bengals (October 27, 2001). ... Re-signed by Bengals (October 30, 2001).
PLAYING EXPERIENCE: Cincinnati NFL, 2001. ... Games/Games started: 2001 (7/0).

JOHNSON, ROB   QB   BUCCANEERS

PERSONAL: Born March 18, 1973, in Newport Beach, Calif. ... 6-4/212. ... Full name: Rob Garland Johnson. ... Brother of Bret Johnson, quarterback with Toronto Argonauts of CFL (1993); and cousin of Bart Johnson, pitcher with Chicago White Sox (1969-74, 1976 and 1977).
HIGH SCHOOL: El Toro (Calif.).
COLLEGE: Southern California.
TRANSACTIONS/CAREER NOTES: Selected by Jacksonville Jaguars in fourth round (99th pick overall) of 1995 NFL draft. ... Signed by Jaguars (June 1, 1995). ... Traded by Jaguars to Buffalo Bills for first- (RB Fred Taylor) and fourth-round (RB Tavian Banks) picks in 1998 draft (February 13, 1998). ... Released by Bills (February 28, 2002). ... Signed by Tampa Bay Buccaneers (March 10, 2002).
CHAMPIONSHIP GAME EXPERIENCE: Member of Jaguars for AFC championship game (1996 season); did not play.
PRO STATISTICS: 1998—Fumbled twice and recovered one fumble for minus one yard. 2000—Fumbled four times, recovered two fumbles and caught one pass for minus six yards. 2001—Fumbled six times and recovered one fumble for minus four yards.
SINGLE GAME HIGHS (regular season): Attempts—47 (October 15, 2000, vs. San Diego); completions—29 (October 15, 2000, vs. San Diego); yards—321 (October 15, 2000, vs. San Diego); and touchdown passes—3 (September 10, 2000, vs. Green Bay).
STATISTICAL PLATEAUS: 300-yard passing games: 2000 (1), 2001 (1). Total: 2.
MISCELLANEOUS: Selected by Minnesota Twins organization in 16th round of free-agent draft (June 4, 1991); did not sign. ... Regular-season record as starting NFL quarterback: 10-17 (.370). ... Postseason record as starting NFL quarterback: 0-1.

			PASSING						RUSHING				TOTALS		
Year Team	G	GS	Att.	Cmp.	Pct.	Yds.	TD	Int.	Avg.	Rat.	Att.	Yds.	Avg.	TD	TD 2pt. Pts.
1995—Jacksonville NFL	1	0	7	3	42.9	24	0	1	3.43	12.5	3	17	5.7	0	0 0 0
1996—Jacksonville NFL	2	0	0	0	0.0	0	0	0	0.0	...	0	0	0.0	0	0 0 0
1997—Jacksonville NFL	5	1	28	22	78.6	344	2	2	12.29	111.9	10	34	3.4	1	1 0 6
1998—Buffalo NFL	8	6	107	67	62.6	910	8	3	8.50	102.9	24	123	5.1	1	1 0 6
1999—Buffalo NFL	2	1	34	25	73.5	298	2	0	8.76	119.5	8	61	7.6	0	0 0 0
2000—Buffalo NFL	12	11	306	175	57.2	2125	12	7	6.94	82.2	42	307	7.3	1	1 0 6
2001—Buffalo NFL	8	8	216	134	62.0	1465	5	7	6.78	76.3	36	241	6.7	1	1 0 6
Pro totals (7 years)	38	27	698	426	61.0	5166	29	20	7.40	85.7	123	783	6.4	4	4 0 24

JOHNSON, RUDI   RB   BENGALS

PERSONAL: Born October 1, 1979, in Ettrick, Va. ... 5-10/233. ... Full name: Rudi Ali Johnson.
HIGH SCHOOL: Thomas Dale (Ettrick, Va.).
JUNIOR COLLEGE: Butler County Community College (Kan.).
COLLEGE: Auburn.
TRANSACTIONS/CAREER NOTES: Selected by Cincinnati Bengals in fourth round (100th pick overall) of 2001 NFL draft. ... Signed by Bengals (July 17, 2001).
PLAYING EXPERIENCE: Cincinnati NFL, 2001. ... Games/Games started: 2001 (2/0).
HONORS: Named running back on THE SPORTING NEWS college All-America second team (2000).
PRO STATISTICS: 2001—Returned four kickoffs for 79 yards.

JOHNSON, TED   LB   PATRIOTS

PERSONAL: Born December 4, 1972, in Alameda, Calif. ... 6-4/255. ... Full name: Ted Curtis Johnson.
HIGH SCHOOL: Carlsbad (Calif.).
COLLEGE: Colorado.
TRANSACTIONS/CAREER NOTES: Selected by New England Patriots in second round (57th pick overall) of 1995 NFL draft. ... Signed by Patriots (July 18, 1995). ... On injured reserve with bicep injury (December 11, 1998-remainder of season).
CHAMPIONSHIP GAME EXPERIENCE: Played in AFC championship game (1996 and 2001 seasons). ... Played in Super Bowl XXXI (1996 season). ... Member of Super Bowl championship team (2001 season).
HONORS: Named linebacker on THE SPORTING NEWS college All-America second team (1994).
PRO STATISTICS: 1995—Recovered two fumbles. 1996—Intercepted one pass for no yards and recovered one fumble. 2000—Recovered three fumbles. 2001—Recovered one fumble.

Year Team	G	GS	SACKS
1995—New England NFL	12	11	0.5
1996—New England NFL	16	16	0.0
1997—New England NFL	16	16	4.0
1998—New England NFL	13	13	2.0
1999—New England NFL	5	5	2.0
2000—New England NFL	14	13	0.5
2001—New England NFL	12	5	0.0
Pro totals (7 years)	88	79	9.0

JOHNSON, TIM   LB   BEARS

PERSONAL: Born February 7, 1978, in Fairfield, Ala. ... 6-0/236.
HIGH SCHOOL: Fairfield (Ala.).
JUNIOR COLLEGE: East Mississippi Junior College.
COLLEGE: Youngstown State.
TRANSACTIONS/CAREER NOTES: Signed as non-drafted free agent by Baltimore Ravens (April 27, 2001). ... Released by Ravens (September 1, 2001). ... Re-signed by Ravens (September 5, 2001). ... Released by Ravens (September 10, 2001). ... Signed by Chicago Bears to practice squad (September 27, 2001). ... Released by Bears (October 30, 2001). ... Re-signed by Bears to practice squad (November 8, 2001).
PLAYING EXPERIENCE: Baltimore NFL, 2001. ... Games/Games started: 2001 (1/0).

JOHNSON, TRE' G BROWNS

PERSONAL: Born August 30, 1971, in Manhattan, N.Y. ... 6-2/326. ... Full name: Edward Stanton Johnson III.
HIGH SCHOOL: Peekskill (N.Y.).
COLLEGE: Temple (degree in social administration, 1993).
TRANSACTIONS/CAREER NOTES: Selected by Washington Redskins in second round (31st pick overall) of 1994 NFL draft. ... Signed by Redskins (July 22, 1994). ... On injured reserve with shoulder injury (December 16, 1997-remainder of season). ... Granted unconditional free agency (February 13, 1998). ... Re-signed by Redskins (February 13, 1998). ... On injured reserve with knee injury (November 24, 1998-remainder of season). ... On injured reserve with knee injury (October 9, 2000-remainder of season). ... Released by Redskins (February 21, 2001). ... Signed by Cleveland Browns (May 24, 2001). ... On physically unable to perform list with knee injury (July 23-28, 2001). ... On injured reserve with knee injury (October 2, 2001-remainder of season). ... Granted unconditional free agency (March 1, 2002). ... Re-signed by Browns (March 26, 2002).
PLAYING EXPERIENCE: Washington NFL, 1994-2000; Cleveland NFL, 2001. ... Games/Games started: 1994 (14/1), 1995 (10/9), 1996 (15/15), 1997 (11/10), 1998 (10/10), 1999 (16/16), 2000 (4/4), 2001 (3/3). Total: 83/68.
HONORS: Played in Pro Bowl (1999 season).
PRO STATISTICS: 1994—Ran four yards with lateral from kickoff return. 1996—Recovered one fumble. 1999—Recovered three fumbles.

JOHNSTONE, LANCE DE VIKINGS

PERSONAL: Born June 11, 1973, in Philadelphia. ... 6-4/253.
HIGH SCHOOL: Germantown (Philadelphia).
COLLEGE: Temple.
TRANSACTIONS/CAREER NOTES: Selected by Oakland Raiders in second round (57th pick overall) of 1996 NFL draft. ... Signed by Raiders for 1996 season. ... Granted unconditional free agency (March 2, 2001). ... Signed by Minnesota Vikings (March 30, 2001). ... Granted unconditional free agency (March 1, 2002). ... Re-signed by Vikings (March 28, 2002).
CHAMPIONSHIP GAME EXPERIENCE: Played in AFC championship game (2000 season).
PRO STATISTICS: 1996—Recovered one fumble for one yard and a touchdown. 1997—Recovered one fumble for two yards. 1998—Recovered one fumble for 40 yards and a touchdown. 1999—Intercepted one pass for no yards and recovered one fumble for 13 yards and a touchdown.

Year Team	G	GS	SACKS
1996—Oakland NFL	16	10	1.0
1997—Oakland NFL	14	6	3.5
1998—Oakland NFL	16	15	11.0
1999—Oakland NFL	16	16	10.0
2000—Oakland NFL	14	9	3.5
2001—Minnesota NFL	16	5	5.5
Pro totals (6 years)	92	61	34.5

JONES, DAMON TE

PERSONAL: Born September 18, 1974, in Evanston, Ill. ... 6-5/277.
HIGH SCHOOL: Evanston (Ill.).
COLLEGE: Michigan, then Southern Illinois (degree in consumer economics, 1997).
TRANSACTIONS/CAREER NOTES: Selected by Jacksonville Jaguars in fifth round (147th pick overall) of 1997 NFL draft. ... Signed by Jaguars (May 30, 1997). ... Granted free agency (February 11, 2000). ... Re-signed by Jaguars (April 10, 2000). ... On injured reserve with knee injury (September 5, 2000-remainder of season). ... Granted unconditional free agency (March 2, 2001). ... Re-signed by Jaguars (March 2, 2001). ... Released by Jaguars (November 22, 2001).
CHAMPIONSHIP GAME EXPERIENCE: Played in AFC championship game (1999 season).
PRO STATISTICS: 1998—Returned two kickoffs for minus one yard. 2001—Recovered one fumble.
SINGLE GAME HIGHS (regular season): Receptions—2 (October 18, 2001, vs. Buffalo); yards—58 (September 23, 2001, vs. Tennessee); and touchdown receptions—1 (September 9, 2001, vs. Pittsburgh).

			RECEIVING				TOTALS			
Year Team	G	GS	No.	Yds.	Avg.	TD	TD	2pt.	Pts.	Fum.
1997—Jacksonville NFL	11	3	5	87	17.4	2	2	0	12	0
1998—Jacksonville NFL	16	7	8	90	11.3	4	4	0	24	1
1999—Jacksonville NFL	15	8	19	221	11.6	4	4	0	24	0
2000—Jacksonville NFL	1	0	1	12	12.0	0	0	0	0	0
2001—Jacksonville NFL	7	4	8	140	17.5	1	1	0	6	1
Pro totals (5 years)	50	22	41	550	13.4	11	11	0	66	2

JONES, DHANI LB GIANTS

PERSONAL: Born February 22, 1978, in San Diego. ... 6-1/240. ... Full name: Dhani Makalani Jones.
HIGH SCHOOL: Winston Churchill (Potomac, Md.).
COLLEGE: Michigan.
TRANSACTIONS/CAREER NOTES: Selected by New York Giants in sixth round (177th pick overall) of 2000 NFL draft. ... Signed by Giants (July 18, 2000). ... On injured reserve with knee injury (August 20, 2000-entire season).

			INTERCEPTIONS		
Year Team	G	GS	No.	Yds.	Avg.	TD
2000—New York Giants NFL			Did not play.		
2001—New York Giants NFL	16	0	1	14	14.0	0

JONES, FRED — LB — BILLS

PERSONAL: Born October 18, 1977, in Subic Bay, The Phillipines. ... 6-2/246. ... Full name: Fred Allen Jones.
HIGH SCHOOL: St. Augustine (San Diego).
COLLEGE: Colorado.
TRANSACTIONS/CAREER NOTES: Signed as non-drafted free agent by Buffalo Bills (April 23, 2000).
PLAYING EXPERIENCE: Buffalo NFL, 2000 and 2001. ... Games/Games started: 2000 (15/0), 2001 (16/0). Total: 31/0.
PRO STATISTICS: 2000—Credited with one sack. 2001—Credited with 1/2 sack.

JONES, FREDDIE — TE — CARDINALS

PERSONAL: Born September 16, 1974, in Cheverly, Md. ... 6-5/270. ... Full name: Freddie Ray Jones Jr.
HIGH SCHOOL: McKinley (Landover, Md.).
COLLEGE: North Carolina.
TRANSACTIONS/CAREER NOTES: Selected by San Diego Chargers in second round (45th pick overall) of 1997 NFL draft. ... Signed by Chargers (May 21, 1997). ... On injured reserve with leg injury (December 12, 1997-remainder of season). ... Granted free agency (February 11, 2000). ... Re-signed by Chargers (April 29, 2000). ... Released by Chargers (February 27, 2002). ... Signed by Arizona Cardinals (March 18, 2002).
PRO STATISTICS: 2000—Recovered one fumble.
SINGLE GAME HIGHS (regular season): Receptions—10 (October 29, 2000, vs. Oakland); yards—111 (October 29, 2000, vs. Oakland); and touchdown receptions—2 (November 26, 2000, vs. Kansas City).
STATISTICAL PLATEAUS: 100-yard receiving games: 2000 (1).

				RECEIVING				TOTALS		
Year Team	G	GS	No.	Yds.	Avg.	TD	TD	2pt.	Pts.	Fum.
1997—San Diego NFL	13	8	41	505	12.3	2	2	0	12	0
1998—San Diego NFL	16	16	57	602	10.6	3	3	1	20	1
1999—San Diego NFL	16	16	56	670	12.0	2	2	0	12	0
2000—San Diego NFL	16	16	71	766	10.8	5	5	0	30	3
2001—San Diego NFL	14	9	35	388	11.1	4	4	0	24	0
Pro totals (5 years)	75	65	260	2931	11.3	16	16	1	98	4

JONES, GREG — LB — TEXANS

PERSONAL: Born May 22, 1974, in Denver. ... 6-4/248. ... Full name: Greg Phillip Jones.
HIGH SCHOOL: John F. Kennedy (Denver).
COLLEGE: Colorado (degree in small business management, 1996).
TRANSACTIONS/CAREER NOTES: Selected by Washington Redskins in second round (51st pick overall) of 1997 NFL draft. ... Signed by Redskins (July 11, 1997). ... Granted unconditional free agency (March 2, 2001). ... Signed by Chicago Bears (May 8, 2001). ... Granted unconditional free agency (March 1, 2002). ... Signed by Houston Texans (March 15, 2002).
PRO STATISTICS: 1997—Returned one kickoff for six yards. 1998—Intercepted one pass for nine yards. 2000—Recovered one fumble.

Year Team	G	GS	SACKS
1997—Washington NFL	16	3	3.5
1998—Washington NFL	16	5	1.0
1999—Washington NFL	15	15	0.5
2000—Washington NFL	16	4	1.0
2001—Chicago NFL	16	0	0.0
Pro totals (5 years)	79	27	6.0

JONES, HENRY — S

PERSONAL: Born December 29, 1967, in St. Louis. ... 6-0/200.
HIGH SCHOOL: St. Louis University High.
COLLEGE: Illinois (degree in psychology, 1990).
TRANSACTIONS/CAREER NOTES: Selected by Buffalo Bills in first round (26th pick overall) of 1991 NFL draft. ... Signed by Bills (August 30, 1991). ... Activated (September 7, 1991). ... Designated by Bills as transition player (February 15, 1994). ... On injured reserve with broken leg (October 1, 1996-remainder of season). ... Released by Bills (September 2, 2001). ... Signed by Minnesota Vikings (September 25, 2001). ... Released by Vikings (October 30, 2001).
CHAMPIONSHIP GAME EXPERIENCE: Played in AFC championship game (1991-1993 seasons). ... Played in Super Bowl XXVI (1991 season), Super Bowl XXVII (1992 season) and Super Bowl XXVIII (1993 season).
HONORS: Named strong safety on THE SPORTING NEWS NFL All-Pro team (1992). ... Played in Pro Bowl (1992 season).
RECORDS: Shares NFL single-game record for most touchdowns scored by interception—2 (September 20, 1992, vs. Indianapolis).
PRO STATISTICS: 1991—Recovered one fumble. 1992—Recovered two fumbles. 1993—Credited with a safety and recovered two fumbles. 1994—Recovered one fumble. 1995—Recovered one fumble. 1997—Returned one punt for no yards, fumbled once and recovered one fumble. 1999—Returned one kickoff for 37 yards and a touchdown. 2000—Returned one kickoff for four yards and recovered one fumble for 14 yards.

			INTERCEPTIONS				SACKS
Year Team	G	GS	No.	Yds.	Avg.	TD	No.
1991—Buffalo NFL	15	0	0	0	0.0	0	0.0
1992—Buffalo NFL	16	16	†8	*263	32.9	▲2	0.0
1993—Buffalo NFL	16	16	2	92	46.0	▲1	2.0
1994—Buffalo NFL	16	16	2	45	22.5	0	1.0
1995—Buffalo NFL	13	13	1	10	10.0	0	0.0
1996—Buffalo NFL	5	5	0	0	0.0	0	0.0
1997—Buffalo NFL	15	15	0	0	0.0	0	2.0
1998—Buffalo NFL	16	16	3	0	0.0	0	0.0
1999—Buffalo NFL	16	16	0	0	0.0	0	0.0
2000—Buffalo NFL	16	16	2	45	22.5	1	0.0
2001—Minnesota NFL	5	5	0	0	0.0	0	0.0
Pro totals (11 years)	149	134	18	455	25.3	4	5.0

JONES, JOHN — TE — RAVENS

PERSONAL: Born April 4, 1975, in Cleveland. ... 6-4/255.
HIGH SCHOOL: Glen Mills (Concordville, Pa.).
COLLEGE: Indiana (Pa.).
TRANSACTIONS/CAREER NOTES: Signed as non-drafted free agent by Baltimore Ravens (April 28, 2000). ... On injured reserve with ankle injury (January 3, 2000-remainder of season).
PLAYING EXPERIENCE: Baltimore NFL, 2000 and 2001. ... Games/Games started: 2000 (8/0), 2001 (15/2). Total: 23/2.
PRO STATISTICS: 2001—Caught two passes for 13 yards.
SINGLE GAME HIGHS (regular season): Receptions—2 (September 30, 2001, vs. Denver); yards—13 (September 30, 2001, vs. Denver); and touchdown receptions—0.

JONES, KENYATTA — OL — PATRIOTS

PERSONAL: Born January 18, 1979, in Gainesville, Fla. ... 6-3/305. ... Full name: Kenyatta Lapoleon Jones.
HIGH SCHOOL: Eastside (Gainesville, Fla.).
COLLEGE: South Florida.
TRANSACTIONS/CAREER NOTES: Selected by New England Patriots in fourth round (96th pick overall) of 2001 NFL draft. ... Signed by Patriots (July 19, 2001).
PLAYING EXPERIENCE: New England NFL, 2001. ... Games/Games started: 2001 (5/0).
CHAMPIONSHIP GAME EXPERIENCE: Member of Patriots for AFC championship game (2001 season); inactive. ... Member of Super Bowl championship team (2001 season); inactive.

JONES, LENOY — LB — BROWNS

PERSONAL: Born September 25, 1974, in Marlin, Texas. ... 6-1/236.
HIGH SCHOOL: Groesbeck (Texas).
COLLEGE: Texas Christian.
TRANSACTIONS/CAREER NOTES: Signed as non-drafted free agent by Houston Oilers (April 23, 1996). ... Released by Oilers (August 20, 1996). ... Re-signed by Oilers to practice squad (August 26, 1996). ... Activated (October 9, 1996). ... Oilers franchise moved to Tennessee for 1997 season. ... Oilers franchise renamed Tennessee Titans for 1999 season (December 26, 1998). ... Selected by Cleveland Browns from Titans in NFL expansion draft (February 9, 1999). ... Granted free agency (February 12, 1999). ... Re-signed by Browns (May 26, 1999). ... Granted unconditional free agency (February 11, 2000). ... Re-signed by Browns (March 6, 2000). ... On injured reserve with knee injury (November 28, 2000-remainder of season). ... On physically unable to perform list with knee injury (July 23-November 9, 2001). ... Granted unconditional free agency (March 1, 2002). ... Re-signed by Browns (April 1, 2002).
PLAYING EXPERIENCE: Houston NFL, 1996; Tennessee NFL, 1997 and 1998; Cleveland NFL, 1999-2001. ... Games/Games started: 1996 (11/0), 1997 (16/0), 1998 (9/0), 1999 (16/1), 2000 (8/0), 2001 (7/1). Total: 67/2.
PRO STATISTICS: 1996—Recovered one fumble. 1997—Credited with one sack. 1999—Intercepted one pass for three yards and fumbled once. 2000—Credited with $2^{1}/_{2}$ sacks and recovered one fumble.

JONES, MARCUS — DE — BUCCANEERS

PERSONAL: Born August 15, 1973, in Jacksonville, N.C. ... 6-6/278. ... Full name: Marcus Edward Jones.
HIGH SCHOOL: Southwest Onslow (Jacksonville, N.C.).
COLLEGE: North Carolina.
TRANSACTIONS/CAREER NOTES: Selected by Tampa Bay Buccaneers in first round (22nd pick overall) of 1996 NFL draft. ... Signed by Buccaneers (July 21, 1996). ... On injured reserve with ankle injury (December 23, 1997-remainder of season).
CHAMPIONSHIP GAME EXPERIENCE: Played in NFC championship game (1999 season).
HONORS: Named defensive lineman on THE SPORTING NEWS college All-America second team (1995).
PRO STATISTICS: 1997—Recovered one fumble. 1998—Recovered one fumble. 2000—Recovered one fumble. 2001—Recovered one fumble.

Year Team	G	GS	SACKS
1996—Tampa Bay NFL	16	3	1.0
1997—Tampa Bay NFL	7	1	0.0
1998—Tampa Bay NFL	15	0	0.0
1999—Tampa Bay NFL	16	4	7.0
2000—Tampa Bay NFL	16	16	13.0
2001—Tampa Bay NFL	15	15	3.0
Pro totals (6 years)	**85**	**39**	**24.0**

JONES, MARVIN — LB — JETS

PERSONAL: Born June 28, 1972, in Miami. ... 6-2/244. ... Full name: Marvin Maurice Jones.
HIGH SCHOOL: Miami Northwestern.
COLLEGE: Florida State.
TRANSACTIONS/CAREER NOTES: Selected after junior season by New York Jets in first round (fourth pick overall) of 1993 NFL draft. ... Signed by Jets (August 5, 1993). ... On injured reserve with hip injury (November 16, 1993-remainder of season). ... On injured reserve with knee injury (July 29, 1998-entire season). ... Released by Jets (February 26, 2002). ... Re-signed by Jets (March 6, 2002).
HONORS: Butkus Award winner (1992). ... Named College Football Player of the Year by THE SPORTING NEWS (1992). ... Named linebacker on THE SPORTING NEWS college All-America first team (1992).
PRO STATISTICS: 1993—Recovered one fumble. 1997—Recovered one fumble. 1999—Intercepted one pass for 15 yards and recovered one fumble. 2000—Recovered one fumble. 2001—Intercepted three passes for 27 yards, fumbled once and recovered one fumble.

Year	Team	G	GS	SACKS
1993	New York Jets NFL	9	0	0.0
1994	New York Jets NFL	15	11	0.5
1995	New York Jets NFL	10	10	1.5
1996	New York Jets NFL	12	12	1.0
1997	New York Jets NFL	16	16	3.0
1998	New York Jets NFL	Did not play.		
1999	New York Jets NFL	16	16	1.0
2000	New York Jets NFL	16	16	1.0
2001	New York Jets NFL	16	16	1.0
Pro totals (8 years)		110	97	9.0

JONES, MIKE — LB

PERSONAL: Born April 15, 1969, in Kansas City, Mo. ... 6-1/247. ... Full name: Michael Anthony Jones.
HIGH SCHOOL: Southwest (Kansas City, Mo.).
COLLEGE: Missouri.
TRANSACTIONS/CAREER NOTES: Signed as non-drafted free agent by Los Angeles Raiders (April 1991). ... Assigned by Raiders to Sacramento Surge in 1992 World League enhancement allocation program (February 20, 1992). ... Raiders franchise moved to Oakland (July 21, 1995). ... Granted unconditional free agency (February 14, 1997). ... Signed by St. Louis Rams (March 18, 1997). ... Granted unconditional free agency (March 2, 2001). ... Signed by Pittsburgh Steelers (April 20, 2001). ... Released by Steelers (June 3, 2002).
CHAMPIONSHIP GAME EXPERIENCE: Played in NFC championship game (1999 season). ... Member of Super Bowl championship team (1999 season). ... Played in AFC championship game (2001 season).
PRO STATISTICS: 1995—Recovered two fumbles for 52 yards and a touchdown. 1999—Fumbled once and recovered two fumbles for 42 yards and one touchdown.

				INTERCEPTIONS				SACKS
Year	Team	G	GS	No.	Yds.	Avg.	TD	No.
1991	Los Angeles Raiders NFL	16	0	0	0	0.0	0	0.0
1992	Sacramento W.L.	7	7	0	0	0.0	0	2.0
	—Los Angeles Raiders NFL	16	0	0	0	0.0	0	0.0
1993	Los Angeles Raiders NFL	16	2	0	0	0.0	0	0.0
1994	Los Angeles Raiders NFL	16	1	0	0	0.0	0	0.0
1995	Oakland NFL	16	16	1	23	23.0	0	0.0
1996	Oakland NFL	15	15	0	0	0.0	0	1.0
1997	St. Louis NFL	16	16	1	0	0.0	0	2.0
1998	St. Louis NFL	16	16	2	13	6.5	0	3.0
1999	St. Louis NFL	16	16	4	96	24.0	†2	1.0
2000	St. Louis NFL	16	16	0	0	0.0	0	2.0
2001	Pittsburgh NFL	15	0	0	0	0.0	0	0.0
W.L. totals (1 year)		7	7	0	0	0.0	0	2.0
NFL totals (11 years)		174	98	8	132	16.5	2	9.0
Pro totals (12 years)		181	105	8	132	16.5	2	11.0

JONES, REGGIE — WR — CHIEFS

PERSONAL: Born May 8, 1971, in Kansas City, Kan. ... 6-0/195. ... Full name: Reginald Lee Jones.
HIGH SCHOOL: Wyandotte (Kansas City, Kan.).
JUNIOR COLLEGE: Butler County (Kan.) Community College.
COLLEGE: Louisiana State (did not play football) (degree in business management).
TRANSACTIONS/CAREER NOTES: Signed as non-drafted free agent by Washington Redskins (April 27, 1995). ... Released by Redskins (August 22, 1995). ... Signed by Carolina Panthers to practice squad (September 4, 1995). ... Activated (October 21, 1995); did not play. ... Released by Panthers (August 22, 1996). ... Signed by Kansas City Chiefs (April 7, 1997). ... On injured reserve with thigh injury (August 15, 1997-entire season). ... Assigned by Chiefs to England Monarchs in 1998 NFL Europe enhancement allocation program (February 18, 1998). ... Released by Chiefs (August 30, 1998). ... Re-signed by Chiefs to practice squad (September 1, 1998). ... Released by Chiefs (August 30, 1999). ... Signed by Saskatchewan Roughriders of CFL (September 3, 1999). ... Signed by San Diego Chargers (February 28, 2000). ... Granted free agency (March 2, 2001). ... Re-signed by Chargers (April 30, 2001). ... Released by Chargers (November 13, 2001). ... Signed by Kansas City Chiefs (December 26, 2001).
PRO STATISTICS: NFLE: 1998—Rushed six time for 49 yards. 2000—Recovered one fumble. 2001—Recovered one fumble.
SINGLE GAME HIGHS (regular season): Receptions—7 (October 8, 2000, vs. Denver); yards—101 (October 8, 2000, vs. Denver); and touchdown receptions—0.
STATISTICAL PLATEAUS: 100-yard receiving games: 2000 (1).

				RECEIVING				PUNT RETURNS				KICKOFF RETURNS				TOTALS			
Year	Team	G	GS	No.	Yds.	Avg.	TD	No.	Yds.	Avg.	TD	No.	Yds.	Avg.	TD	TD	2pt.	Pts.	Fum.
1995	Carolina NFL	1	0	0	0	0.0	0	0	0	0.0	0	0	0	0.0	0	0	0	0	0
1996	—							Did not play.											
1997	Kansas City NFL							Did not play.											
1998	England NFLE	...	...	36	649	18.0	7	0	0	0.0	0	0	0	0.0	0	7	0	42	0
1999	Saskatchewan CFL	...	...	38	625	16.4	3	0	0	0.0	0	0	0	0.0	0	3	0	18	0
2000	San Diego NFL	11	3	22	253	11.5	0	9	53	5.9	0	1	11	11.0	0	0	0	0	1
2001	San Diego NFL	9	0	5	29	5.8	0	3	5	1.7	0	4	126	31.5	0	0	0	0	2
NFL Europe totals (1 year)		...	...	36	649	18.0	7	0	0	0.0	0	0	0	0.0	0	7	0	42	0
CFL totals (1 year)		...	...	38	625	16.4	3	0	0	0.0	0	0	0	0.0	0	3	0	18	0
NFL totals (3 years)		21	3	27	282	10.4	0	12	58	4.8	0	5	137	27.4	0	0	0	0	3
Pro totals (5 years)		...	...	101	1556	15.4	10	12	58	4.8	0	5	137	27.4	0	10	0	60	3

JONES, ROBERT   LB   PACKERS

PERSONAL: Born September 27, 1969, in Blackstone, Va. ... 6-3/245. ... Full name: Robert Lee Jones.
HIGH SCHOOL: Nottoway (Va.), then Fork Union (Va.) Military Academy.
COLLEGE: East Carolina.
TRANSACTIONS/CAREER NOTES: Selected by Dallas Cowboys in first round (24th pick overall) of 1992 NFL draft. ... Signed by Cowboys (April 26, 1992). ... Granted unconditional free agency (February 16, 1996). ... Signed by St. Louis Rams (March 5, 1996). ... Released by Rams (June 2, 1998). ... Signed by Miami Dolphins (June 10, 1998). ... Granted unconditional free agency (February 12, 1999). ... Re-signed by Dolphins (February 19, 1999). ... Released by Dolphins (March 1, 2001). ... Signed by Washington Redskins (June 14, 2001). ... Granted unconditional free agency (March 1, 2002). ... Signed by Houston Texans (April 25, 2002). ... Released by Texans (May 14, 2002). ... Signed by Green Bay Packers (May 23, 2002).
PLAYING EXPERIENCE: Dallas NFL, 1992-1995; St. Louis NFL, 1996 and 1997; Miami NFL, 1998-2000; Washington NFL, 2001. ... Games/Games started: 1992 (15/13), 1993 (13/3), 1994 (16/16), 1995 (12/12), 1996 (16/13), 1997 (16/15), 1998 (16/16), 1999 (16/15), 2000 (16/16), 2001 (15/9). Total: 151/128.
CHAMPIONSHIP GAME EXPERIENCE: Played in NFC championship game (1992-1995 seasons). ... Member of Super Bowl championship team (1992, 1993 and 1995 seasons).
HONORS: Named linebacker on THE SPORTING NEWS college All-America second team (1990). ... Named linebacker on THE SPORTING NEWS college All-America first team (1991).
PRO STATISTICS: 1992—Credited with one sack and recovered one fumble. 1993—Returned one kickoff for 12 yards. 1994—Returned one kickoff for eight yards and recovered one fumble. 1995—Credited with one sack. 1996—Intercepted one pass for no yards. 1997—Credited with one sack. 1998—Intercepted two passes for 14 yards and one touchdown and credited with five sacks. 2000—Recovered one fumble.

JONES, ROD   OT   REDSKINS

PERSONAL: Born January 11, 1974, in Detroit. ... 6-5/335. ... Full name: Rodrek Edward Jones.
HIGH SCHOOL: Henry Ford (Detroit).
COLLEGE: Kansas (degree in human development/family living).
TRANSACTIONS/CAREER NOTES: Selected by Cincinnati Bengals in seventh round (219th pick overall) of 1996 NFL draft. ... Signed by Bengals (July 15, 1996). ... Granted free agency (February 12, 1999). ... Re-signed by Bengals (April 15, 1999). ... Released by Bengals (May 31, 2001). ... Signed by St. Louis Rams (June 11, 2001). ... Granted unconditional free agency (March 1, 2002). ... Signed by Washington Redskins (April 2, 2002).
PLAYING EXPERIENCE: Cincinnati NFL, 1996-2000; St. Louis NFL, 2001. ... Games/Games started: 1996 (5/1), 1997 (13/8), 1998 (7/2), 1999 (16/15), 2000 (15/11), 2001 (6/1). Total: 62/38.
CHAMPIONSHIP GAME EXPERIENCE: Played in NFC championship game (2001 season). ... Played in Super Bowl XXXVI (2001 season).

JONES, TEBUCKY   S   PATRIOTS

PERSONAL: Born October 6, 1974, in New Britain, Conn. ... 6-2/220. ... Full name: Tebucky Shermaine Jones.
HIGH SCHOOL: New Britain (Conn.).
COLLEGE: Syracuse.
TRANSACTIONS/CAREER NOTES: Selected by New England Patriots in first round (22nd pick overall) of 1998 NFL draft. ... Signed by Patriots (July 18, 1998). ... On injured reserve with knee injury (December 31, 1999-remainder of season).
PLAYING EXPERIENCE: New England NFL, 1998-2001. ... Games/Games started: 1998 (16/0), 1999 (11/2), 2000 (15/9), 2001 (16/12). Total: 58/23.
CHAMPIONSHIP GAME EXPERIENCE: Played in AFC championship game (2001 season). ... Member of Super Bowl championship team (2001 season).
PRO STATISTICS: 1998—Recovered one fumble. 1999—Returned five kickoffs for 113 yards. 2000—Intercepted two passes for 20 yards. 2001—Intercepted one pass for minus four yards and credited with one sack.

JONES, THOMAS   RB   CARDINALS

PERSONAL: Born August 19, 1978, in Big Stone Gap, Va. ... 5-10/211. ... Full name: Thomas Quinn Jones.
HIGH SCHOOL: Powell Valley (Big Stone Gap, Va.).
COLLEGE: Virginia (degree in psychology, 1999).
TRANSACTIONS/CAREER NOTES: Selected by Arizona Cardinals in first round (seventh pick overall) of 2000 NFL draft. ... Signed by Cardinals (July 21, 2000).
HONORS: Named running back on THE SPORTING NEWS college All-America first team (1999).
PRO STATISTICS: 2000—Recovered one fumble. 2001—Recovered two fumbles.
SINGLE GAME HIGHS (regular season): Attempts—23 (September 10, 2000, vs. Dallas); yards—70 (September 10, 2000, vs. Dallas); and rushing touchdowns—1 (January 6, 2002, vs. Washington).

				RUSHING				RECEIVING				TOTALS		
Year Team	G	GS	Att.	Yds.	Avg.	TD	No.	Yds.	Avg.	TD	TD	2pt.	Pts.	Fum.
2000—Arizona NFL	14	4	112	373	3.3	2	32	208	6.5	0	2	0	12	4
2001—Arizona NFL	16	2	112	380	3.4	5	21	151	7.2	0	5	0	30	2
Pro totals (2 years)	30	6	224	753	3.4	7	53	359	6.8	0	7	0	42	6

JONES, WALTER   OT   SEAHAWKS

PERSONAL: Born January 19, 1974, in Aliceville, Ala. ... 6-5/307.
HIGH SCHOOL: Aliceville (Ala.).
JUNIOR COLLEGE: Holmes Junior College (Miss.).
COLLEGE: Florida State.
TRANSACTIONS/CAREER NOTES: Selected by Seattle Seahawks in first round (sixth pick overall) of 1997 NFL draft. ... Signed by Seahawks (August 6, 1997). ... Granted free agency (March 1, 2002).
PLAYING EXPERIENCE: Seattle NFL, 1997-2001. ... Games/Games started: 1997 (12/12), 1998 (16/16), 1999 (16/16), 2000 (16/16), 2001 (16/16). Total: 76/76.
HONORS: Played in Pro Bowl (1999 season).
PRO STATISTICS: 1999—Recovered one fumble.

JONES, WILLIE   OT   CHIEFS

PERSONAL: Born December 17, 1975, in Pahokee, Fla. ... 6-6/358.
HIGH SCHOOL: Glades (Belle Glade, Fla.).
COLLEGE: Grambling.
TRANSACTIONS/CAREER NOTES: Signed as non-drafted free agent by St. Louis Rams (April 30, 1999). ... On non-football injury list (November 24, 1999-remainder of season). ... Released by Rams (February 10, 2000). ... Signed by Miami Dolphins (March 23, 2000). ... Released by Dolphins (August 26, 2000). ... Signed by Kansas City Chiefs to practice squad (November 29, 2000). ... Granted free agency (March 1, 2002).
PLAYING EXPERIENCE: Kansas City NFL, 2001. ... Games/Games started: 2001 (12/0).
PRO STATISTICS: 2001—Recovered one fumble.

JORDAN, ANDREW   TE

PERSONAL: Born June 21, 1972, in Charlotte. ... 6-6/263. ... Full name: Andrew Jordan Jr.
HIGH SCHOOL: West Charlotte.
COLLEGE: North Greenville College (S.C.), then Western Carolina (degree in criminal justice, 1993).
TRANSACTIONS/CAREER NOTES: Selected by Minnesota Vikings in sixth round (179th pick overall) of 1994 NFL draft. ... Signed by Vikings (June 17, 1994). ... Released by Vikings (September 23, 1997). ... Signed by Tampa Bay Buccaneers (December 9, 1997). ... Released by Buccaneers (August 25, 1998). ... Signed by Philadelphia Eagles (December 1, 1998). ... Granted unconditional free agency (February 12, 1999). ... Re-signed by Eagles (February 18, 1999). ... Released by Eagles (September 7, 1999). ... Signed by Vikings (October 13, 1999). ... Granted unconditional free agency (March 2, 2001). ... Re-signed by Vikings (March 13, 2001). ... Granted unconditional free agency (March 1, 2002).
CHAMPIONSHIP GAME EXPERIENCE: Played in NFC championship game (2000 season).
PRO STATISTICS: 1994—Returned one kickoff for eight yards and recovered a fumble. 1999—Returned one kickoff for no yards.
SINGLE GAME HIGHS (regular season): Receptions—5 (November 13, 1994, vs. New England); yards—57 (November 13, 1994, vs. New England); and touchdown receptions—1 (September 23, 2001, vs. Chicago).

				RECEIVING				TOTALS		
Year Team	G	GS	No.	Yds.	Avg.	TD	TD	2pt.	Pts.	Fum.
1994—Minnesota NFL	16	12	35	336	9.6	0	0	1	2	1
1995—Minnesota NFL	13	7	27	185	6.9	2	2	0	12	1
1996—Minnesota NFL	13	9	19	128	6.7	0	0	1	2	0
1997—Minnesota NFL	2	0	0	0	0.0	0	0	0	0	0
—Tampa Bay NFL	2	0	1	0	0.0	0	0	0	0	0
1998—Philadelphia NFL	3	0	2	9	4.5	0	0	0	0	0
1999—Minnesota NFL	11	1	5	40	8.0	1	1	0	6	0
2000—Minnesota NFL	15	4	8	63	7.9	0	0	0	0	0
2001—Minnesota NFL	16	4	3	11	3.7	1	1	0	6	0
Pro totals (8 years)	91	37	100	772	7.7	4	4	2	28	2

JORDAN, LAMONT   RB   JETS

PERSONAL: Born November 11, 1978, in Forestville, Md. ... 5-10/230.
HIGH SCHOOL: Suitland (Forestville, Md.).
COLLEGE: Maryland.
TRANSACTIONS/CAREER NOTES: Selected by New York Jets in second round (49th pick overall) of 2001 NFL draft. ... Signed by Jets (July 25, 2001).
HONORS: Named running back on THE SPORTING NEWS college All-America third team (1999).
PRO STATISTICS: 2001—Attempted one pass without a completion and returned three kickoffs for 62 yards.
SINGLE GAME HIGHS (regular season): Attempts—10 (November 11, 2001, vs. Kansas City); yards—75 (November 4, 2001, vs. New Orleans); and rushing touchdowns—1 (January 6, 2002, vs. Oakland).

			RUSHING				RECEIVING				TOTALS		
Year Team	G	GS	Att.	Yds.	Avg.	TD	No.	Yds.	Avg.	TD	TD	2pt.	Pts.	Fum.
2001—New York Jets NFL	16	0	39	292	7.5	1	7	44	6.3	1	2	0	12	0

JORDAN, LEANDER   G   PANTHERS

PERSONAL: Born September 15, 1977, in Pittsburgh. ... 6-3/320. ... Full name: Leander James Jordan.
HIGH SCHOOL: Garfield (Pittsburgh), then Peabody (Pittsburgh), then Brashear (Pittsburgh).
COLLEGE: Indiana University (Pa.).
TRANSACTIONS/CAREER NOTES: Selected by Carolina Panthers in third round (82nd pick overall) of 2000 NFL draft. ... Signed by Panthers (June 8, 2000). ... Inactive for all 16 games (2000).
PLAYING EXPERIENCE: Carolina NFL, 2001. ... Games/Games started: 2001 (13/5).

JORDAN, RANDY   RB   RAIDERS

PERSONAL: Born June 6, 1970, in Manson, N.C. ... 5-11/215. ... Full name: Randy Loment Jordan.
HIGH SCHOOL: Warren County (Warrenton, N.C.).
COLLEGE: North Carolina.
TRANSACTIONS/CAREER NOTES: Signed as non-drafted free agent by Los Angeles Raiders (May 1993). ... Released by Raiders (August 25, 1993). ... Re-signed by Raiders to practice squad (August 31, 1993). ... Activated (October 30, 1993). ... Released by Raiders (August 28, 1994). ... Signed by Jacksonville Jaguars (December 15, 1994). ... Granted free agency (February 14, 1997). ... Re-signed by Jaguars (May 5, 1997). ...

Released by Jaguars (August 19, 1997). ... Re-signed by Jaguars (September 24, 1997). ... Granted unconditional free agency (February 13, 1998). ... Signed by Oakland Raiders (June 2, 1998).
CHAMPIONSHIP GAME EXPERIENCE: Played in AFC championship game (1996 and 2000 seasons).
PRO STATISTICS: 1996—Recovered one fumble.
SINGLE GAME HIGHS (regular season): Attempts—24 (December 20, 1998, vs. San Diego); yards—82 (December 20, 1998, vs. San Diego); and rushing touchdowns—2 (December 16, 2000, vs. Seattle).

			RUSHING				RECEIVING				KICKOFF RETURNS				TOTALS		
Year Team	G	GS	Att.	Yds.	Avg.	TD	No.	Yds.	Avg.	TD	No.	Yds.	Avg.	TD	TD	2pt.	Pts. Fum.
1993—LA Raiders NFL	10	2	12	33	2.8	0	4	42	10.5	0	0	0	0.0	0	0	0	0 2
1994—Jacksonville NFL									Did not play.								
1995—Jacksonville NFL	12	2	21	62	3.0	0	5	89	17.8	1	2	41	20.5	0	1	0	6 0
1996—Jacksonville NFL	15	0	0	0	0.0	0	0	0	0.0	0	26	553	21.3	0	0	0	0 1
1997—Jacksonville NFL	7	0	1	2	2.0	0	0	0	0.0	0	0	0	0.0	0	0	0	0 0
1998—Oakland NFL	16	0	47	159	3.4	1	3	2	0.7	0	0	0	0.0	0	1	0	6 1
1999—Oakland NFL	16	0	9	32	3.6	2	8	82	10.3	0	10	207	20.7	0	2	0	12 2
2000—Oakland NFL	16	0	46	213	4.6	3	27	299	11.1	1	0	0	0.0	0	5	0	30 1
2001—Oakland NFL	16	0	13	59	4.5	0	9	63	7.0	0	0	0	0.0	0	0	0	0 0
Pro totals (8 years)	108	4	149	560	3.8	6	56	577	10.3	2	38	801	21.1	0	9	0	54 7

JORDON, ANTONY — LB

PERSONAL: Born December 19, 1974, in Sewell, N.J. ... 6-3/235. ... Name pronounced ANT-knee.
HIGH SCHOOL: Washington Township (Sewell, N.J.).
COLLEGE: Vanderbilt.
TRANSACTIONS/CAREER NOTES: Selected by Indianapolis Colts in fifth round (135th pick overall) of 1998 NFL draft. ... Signed by Colts (July 24, 1998). ... Released by Colts (August 16, 1999). ... Signed by Chicago Bears (August 18, 1999). ... Released by Bears (September 5, 1999). ... Signed by Tampa Bay Buccaneers (January 22, 2000). ... Claimed on waivers by Philadelphia Eagles (August 23, 2000). ... Released by Eagles (August 27, 2000). ... Signed by Atlanta Falcons (October 25, 2000). ... On injured reserve with shoulder injury (November 27, 2001-remainder of season). ... Released by Falcons (February 21, 2002).
PLAYING EXPERIENCE: Indianapolis NFL, 1998; Atlanta NFL, 2000 and 2001. ... Games/Games started: 1998 (15/3), 2000 (8/0), 2001 (4/0). Total: 27/3.

JOSEPH, ELVIS — RB — JAGUARS

PERSONAL: Born August 30, 1978, in St. Michaels, Barbados. ... 6-1/213.
HIGH SCHOOL: John Ehret (Marrara, La.).
COLLEGE: Southern.
TRANSACTIONS/CAREER NOTES: Signed as non-drafted free agent by Jacksonville Jaguars (April 23, 2001).
PRO STATISTICS: 2001—Recovered one fumble.
SINGLE GAME HIGHS (regular season): Attempts—12 (October 7, 2001, vs. Seattle); yards—86 (December 23, 2001, vs. Minnesota); and rushing touchdowns—0.

			RUSHING				RECEIVING				KICKOFF RETURNS				TOTALS		
Year Team	G	GS	Att.	Yds.	Avg.	TD	No.	Yds.	Avg.	TD	No.	Yds.	Avg.	TD	TD	2pt.	Pts. Fum.
2001—Jacksonville NFL	14	3	68	294	4.3	0	18	183	10.2	2	17	428	25.2	1	3	0	18 2

JOSEPH, KERRY — S

PERSONAL: Born October 4, 1973, in New Iberia, La. ... 6-2/205.
HIGH SCHOOL: New Iberia (La.).
COLLEGE: McNeese State.
TRANSACTIONS/CAREER NOTES: Signed as non-drafted free agent by Cincinnati Bengals (April 22, 1996). ... Inactive for all 16 games (1996). ... Released by Bengals (May 6, 1997). ... Signed by Washington Redskins (May 16, 1997). ... Released by Redskins (August 25, 1997). ... Selected by Rhein Fire in 1998 NFL Europe draft (February 18, 1998). ... Signed by Seattle Seahawks (June 29, 1998). ... Granted free agency (February 11, 2000). ... Re-signed by Seahawks (April 19, 2000). ... Granted unconditional free agency (March 2, 2001). ... Re-signed by Seahawks (November 14, 2001). ... Granted free agency (March 2, 2002).
PRO STATISTICS: 1999—Recovered one fumble. 2001—Credited with one sack.

			INTERCEPTIONS				PUNT RETURNS				KICKOFF RETURNS				TOTALS		
Year Team	G	GS	No.	Yds.	Avg.	TD	No.	Yds.	Avg.	TD	No.	Yds.	Avg.	TD	TD	2pt.	Pts. Fum.
1996—Cincinnati NFL									Did not play.								
1997—									Did not play.								
1998—Rhein NFLE			4	25	6.3	0	4	43	10.8	0	0	0	0.0	0	0	0	0 0
—Seattle NFL	16	0	0	0	0.0	0	15	182	12.1	0	2	49	24.5	0	0	0	0 1
1999—Seattle NFL	16	4	3	82	27.3	0	0	0	0.0	0	6	132	22.0	0	0	0	0 0
2000—Seattle NFL	16	10	0	0	0.0	0	0	0	0.0	0	3	71	23.7	0	0	0	0 0
2001—Seattle NFL	8	0	0	0	0.0	0	2	12	6.0	0	4	83	20.8	0	0	0	0 1
NFL Europe totals (1 year)			4	25	6.3	0	4	43	10.8	0	0	0	0.0	0	0	0	0 0
NFL totals (3 years)	56	14	3	82	27.3	0	17	194	11.4	0	15	335	22.3	0	0	0	0 2
Pro totals (4 years)			7	107	15.3	0	21	237	11.3	0	15	335	22.3	0	0	0	0 2

JOYCE, MATT — G — LIONS

PERSONAL: Born March 30, 1972, in La Crosse, Wis. ... 6-7/305.
HIGH SCHOOL: New York Military Academy (Cornwall Hudson, N.Y.).
COLLEGE: Richmond (degree in health science, 1994).

JUE, BHAWOH CB/SS PACKERS

PERSONAL: Born May 24, 1979, in Bhawoh Papi Je in Monrovia, Liberia. ... 6-0/200. ... Full name: Bhawoh Papi Jue.
HIGH SCHOOL: Chantilly (Va.).
COLLEGE: Penn State (degree in telecommunications).
TRANSACTIONS/CAREER NOTES: Selected by Green Bay Packers in third round (71st pick overall) of 2001 NFL draft. ... Signed by Packers (July 11, 2001).

			INTERCEPTIONS			
Year Team	G	GS	No.	Yds.	Avg.	TD
2001—Green Bay NFL	15	7	2	35	17.5	0

JUNKIN, TREY TE

PERSONAL: Born January 23, 1961, in Conway, Ark. ... 6-2/247. ... Full name: Abner Kirk Junkin. ... Brother of Mike Junkin, linebacker with Cleveland Browns (1987 and 1988) and Kansas City Chiefs (1989).
HIGH SCHOOL: Northeast (North Little Rock, Ark.).
COLLEGE: Louisiana Tech.
TRANSACTIONS/CAREER NOTES: Selected by Buffalo Bills in fourth round (93rd pick overall) of 1983 NFL draft. ... Signed by Bills for 1983 season. ... Released by Bills (September 12, 1984). ... Signed by Washington Redskins (September 25, 1984). ... Rights relinquished by Redskins (February 1, 1985). ... Signed by Los Angeles Raiders (March 10, 1985). ... On injured reserve with knee injury (September 24, 1986-remainder of season). ... Released by Raiders (September 3, 1990). ... Signed by Seattle Seahawks (October 3, 1990). ... Granted unconditional free agency (February 1-April 1, 1991). ... Re-signed by Seahawks (July 9, 1991). ... Granted unconditional free agency (February 1-April 1, 1992). ... Re-signed by Seahawks for 1992 season. ... Granted unconditional free agency (March 1, 1993). ... Re-signed by Seahawks (March 11, 1993). ... Released by Seahawks (August 30, 1993). ... Re-signed by Seahawks (August 31, 1993). ... Granted unconditional free agency (February 17, 1994). ... Re-signed by Seahawks (May 31, 1994). ... Granted unconditional free agency (February 17, 1995). ... Re-signed by Seahawks (March 20, 1995). ... Granted unconditional free agency (February 16, 1996). ... Signed by Oakland Raiders (June 10, 1996). ... Claimed on waivers by Arizona Cardinals (October 14, 1996). ... Granted unconditional free agency (March 1, 2002).
PRO STATISTICS: 1983—Recovered one fumble. 1984—Recovered one fumble. 1989—Returned one kickoff for no yards.
SINGLE GAME HIGHS (regular season): Receptions—2 (November 22, 1992, vs. Kansas City); yards—38 (September 21, 1986, vs. New York Giants); and touchdown receptions—1 (September 25, 1994, vs. Pittsburgh).

			RECEIVING				TOTALS			
Year Team	G	GS	No.	Yds.	Avg.	TD	TD	2pt.	Pts.	Fum.
1983—Buffalo NFL	16	0	0	0	0.0	0	0	0	0	0
1984—Buffalo NFL	2	0	0	0	0.0	0	0	0	0	0
—Washington NFL	12	0	0	0	0.0	0	0	0	0	0
1985—Los Angeles Raiders NFL	16	0	2	8	4.0	1	1	0	6	0
1986—Los Angeles Raiders NFL	3	0	2	38	19.0	0	0	0	0	0
1987—Los Angeles Raiders NFL	12	1	2	15	7.5	0	0	0	0	0
1988—Los Angeles Raiders NFL	16	1	4	25	6.3	2	2	0	12	0
1989—Los Angeles Raiders NFL	16	0	3	32	10.7	2	2	0	12	0
1990—Seattle NFL	12	0	0	0	0.0	0	0	0	0	0
1991—Seattle NFL	16	0	0	0	0.0	0	0	0	0	0
1992—Seattle NFL	16	1	3	25	8.3	1	1	0	6	0
1993—Seattle NFL	16	1	0	0	0.0	0	0	0	0	0
1994—Seattle NFL	16	0	1	1	1.0	1	1	0	6	0
1995—Seattle NFL	16	0	0	0	0.0	0	0	0	0	0
1996—Oakland NFL	6	0	0	0	0.0	0	0	0	0	0
—Arizona NFL	10	0	0	0	0.0	0	0	0	0	0
1997—Arizona NFL	16	0	0	0	0.0	0	0	0	0	0
1998—Arizona NFL	16	0	0	0	0.0	0	0	0	0	0
1999—Arizona NFL	16	0	0	0	0.0	0	0	0	0	0
2000—Arizona NFL	16	0	0	0	0.0	0	0	0	0	0
2001—Arizona NFL	16	0	0	0	0.0	0	0	0	0	1
Pro totals (19 years)	281	4	17	144	8.5	7	7	0	42	1

JUREVICIUS, JOE WR BUCCANEERS

PERSONAL: Born December 23, 1974, in Cleveland. ... 6-5/230. ... Full name: Joe Michael Jurevicius. ... Name pronounced jur-uh-VISH-us.
HIGH SCHOOL: Lake Catholic (Mentor, Ohio).
COLLEGE: Penn State.
TRANSACTIONS/CAREER NOTES: Selected by New York Giants in second round (55th pick overall) of 1998 NFL draft. ... Signed by Giants (July 28, 1998). ... Granted free agency (March 2, 2001). ... Re-signed by Giants for 2001 season. ... Granted unconditional free agency (March 1, 2002). ... Signed by Tampa Bay Buccaneers (April 9, 2002).
CHAMPIONSHIP GAME EXPERIENCE: Played in NFC championship game (2000 season). ... Played in Super Bowl XXXV (2000 season).

PRO STATISTICS: 2000—Returned one kickoff for three yards.
SINGLE GAME HIGHS (regular season): Receptions—8 (January 6, 2002, vs. Green Bay); yards—93 (October 14, 2001, vs. St. Louis); and touchdown receptions—2 (November 4, 2001, vs. Dallas).

				RECEIVING			TOTALS			
Year Team	G	GS	No.	Yds.	Avg.	TD	TD	2pt.	Pts.	Fum.
1998—New York Giants NFL	14	1	9	146	16.2	0	0	0	0	0
1999—New York Giants NFL	16	1	18	318	17.7	1	1	0	6	1
2000—New York Giants NFL	14	3	24	272	11.3	1	1	0	6	1
2001—New York Giants NFL	14	9	51	706	13.8	3	3	0	18	0
Pro totals (4 years)	58	14	102	1442	14.1	5	5	0	30	2

KACYVENSKI, ISAIAH   LB   SEAHAWKS

PERSONAL: Born October 3, 1977, in Syracuse, N.Y. ... 6-1/250. ... Name pronounced kaz-uh-VEN-skee.
HIGH SCHOOL: Union Endicott (N.Y.).
COLLEGE: Harvard (degree in pre-med).
TRANSACTIONS/CAREER NOTES: Selected by Seattle Seahawks in fourth round (119th pick overall) of 2000 NFL draft. ... Signed by Seahawks (June 9, 2000).
PRO STATISTICS: 2000—Recovered one fumble.

			INTERCEPTIONS			
Year Team	G	GS	No.	Yds.	Avg.	TD
2000—Seattle NFL	16	0	1	0	0.0	0
2001—Seattle NFL	16	0	1	22	22.0	0
Pro totals (2 years)	32	0	2	22	11.0	0

KADELA, DAVE   OT   FALCONS

PERSONAL: Born May 6, 1978, in Dearborn, Mich. ... 6-6/294. ... Full name: David Richard Kadela.
HIGH SCHOOL: Coffman (Ohio).
COLLEGE: Virginia Tech.
TRANSACTIONS/CAREER NOTES: Signed as non-drafted free agent by Atlanta Falcons (April 24, 2001).
PLAYING EXPERIENCE: Atlanta NFL, 2001. ... Games/Games started: 2001 (1/0).

KAESVIHARN, KEVIN   CB   BENGALS

PERSONAL: Born August 29, 1976, in Paramount, Calif. ... 6-1/190. ... Full name: Kevin Robert Kaesviharn.
HIGH SCHOOL: Lakeville (Minn.).
COLLEGE: Augustana (S.D.).
TRANSACTIONS/CAREER NOTES: Signed as non-drafted free agent by Green Bay Packers (April 25, 2001). ... Released by Packers (August 27, 2001). ... Signed by Cincinnati Bengals to practice squad (October 23, 2001). ... Activated (October 27, 2001). ... Released by Bengals (October 30, 2001). ... Re-signed by Bengals to practice squad (October 31, 2001). ... Activated (November 10, 2001).

			INTERCEPTIONS			
Year Team	G	GS	No.	Yds.	Avg.	TD
2001—Cincinnati NFL	10	3	3	41	13.7	0

KALU, NDUKWE   DE   EAGLES

PERSONAL: Born August 3, 1975, in Baltimore. ... 6-3/265. ... Full name: Ndukwe Dike Kalu. ... Name pronounced EN-doo-kway ka-LOO.
HIGH SCHOOL: John Marshall (San Antonio).
COLLEGE: Rice.
TRANSACTIONS/CAREER NOTES: Selected by Philadelphia Eagles in fifth round (152nd pick overall) of 1997 NFL draft. ... Signed by Eagles (July 15, 1997). ... Released by Eagles (August 25, 1998). ... Signed by Washington Redskins (August 30, 1998). ... Granted free agency (February 11, 2000). ... Re-signed by Redskins (May 18, 2000). ... Granted unconditional free agency (March 2, 2001). ... Signed by Eagles (March 12, 2001).
CHAMPIONSHIP GAME EXPERIENCE: Played in NFC championship game (2001 season).
PRO STATISTICS: 2000—Recovered one fumble for four yards.

Year Team	G	GS	SACKS
1997—Philadelphia NFL	3	0	0.0
1998—Washington NFL	13	1	3.0
1999—Washington NFL	12	0	3.5
2000—Washington NFL	15	0	1.0
2001—Philadelphia NFL	14	1	3.0
Pro totals (5 years)	57	2	10.5

KASAY, JOHN   K   PANTHERS

PERSONAL: Born October 27, 1969, in Athens, Ga. ... 5-10/198. ... Full name: John David Kasay. ... Name pronounced CASEY.
HIGH SCHOOL: Clarke Central (Athens, Ga.).
COLLEGE: Georgia (degree in journalism, 1994).
TRANSACTIONS/CAREER NOTES: Selected by Seattle Seahawks in fourth round (98th pick overall) of 1991 NFL draft. ... Signed by Seahawks (July 19, 1991). ... Granted free agency (February 17, 1994). ... Re-signed by Seahawks (July 19, 1994). ... Granted unconditional free agency (February 17, 1995). ... Signed by Carolina Panthers (February 20, 1995). ... On injured reserve with knee injury (December 14, 1999-remainder of season). ... On injured reserve with knee injury (August 14, 2000-entire season).

CHAMPIONSHIP GAME EXPERIENCE: Played in NFC championship game (1996 season).
HONORS: Played in Pro Bowl (1996 season).
PRO STATISTICS: 1993—Recovered one fumble. 1995—Punted once for 32 yards. 1996—Punted once for 30 yards.

					KICKING				
Year Team	G	XPM	XPA	FGM	FGA	Lg.	50+	Pts.
1991—Seattle NFL	16	27	28	25	31	54	2-3	102
1992—Seattle NFL	16	14	14	14	22	43	0-0	56
1993—Seattle NFL	16	29	29	23	28	55	3-5	98
1994—Seattle NFL	16	25	26	20	24	50	1-2	85
1995—Carolina NFL	16	27	28	26	33	52	1-1	105
1996—Carolina NFL	16	34	35	*37	*45	53	3-7	*145
1997—Carolina NFL	16	25	25	22	26	54	3-6	91
1998—Carolina NFL	16	35	37	19	26	56	4-7	92
1999—Carolina NFL	13	33	33	22	25	52	2-4	99
2000—Carolina NFL				Did not play.				
2001—Carolina NFL	16	22	23	23	28	52	2-5	91
Pro totals (10 years)	157	271	278	231	288	56	21-40	964

KASPER, KEVIN   WR   BRONCOS

PERSONAL: Born December 23, 1977, in Hinsdale, Ill. ... 6-0/193.
HIGH SCHOOL: Hinsdale South (Burr Ridge, Ill.).
COLLEGE: Iowa.
TRANSACTIONS/CAREER NOTES: Selected by Denver Broncos in sixth round (190th pick overall) of 2001 NFL draft. ... Signed by Broncos (May 17, 2001).
PRO STATISTICS: 2001—Rushed three times for 19 yards.
SINGLE GAME HIGHS (regular season): Receptions—2 (December 30, 2001, vs. Oakland); yards—30 (December 16, 2001, vs. Kansas City); and touchdown receptions—0.

			RECEIVING				KICKOFF RETURNS				TOTALS		
Year Team	G	GS	No.	Yds.	Avg.	TD	No.	Yds.	Avg.	TD	TD	2pt.	Pts.	Fum.
2001—Denver NFL	10	5	8	84	10.5	0	14	372	26.6	0	0	0	0	0

KEARSE, JEVON   DE   TITANS

PERSONAL: Born September 3, 1976, in Fort Myers, Fla. ... 6-4/265. ... Name pronounced juh-VAUGHN CURSE.
HIGH SCHOOL: North Fort Myers (Fla.).
COLLEGE: Florida.
TRANSACTIONS/CAREER NOTES: Selected after junior season by Tennessee Titans in first round (16th pick overall) of 1999 NFL draft. ... Signed by Titans (July 27, 1999).
CHAMPIONSHIP GAME EXPERIENCE: Played in AFC championship game (1999 season). ... Played in Super Bowl XXXIV (1999 season).
HONORS: Named outside linebacker on THE SPORTING NEWS college All-America second team (1998). ... Named defensive end on THE SPORTING NEWS NFL All-Pro team (1999). ... Played in Pro Bowl (1999 and 2000 seasons).
RECORDS: Holds NFL rookie-season record for most sacks—14.5 (1999).
PRO STATISTICS: 1999—Recovered one fumble for 14 yards and a touchdown.

Year Team	G	GS	SACKS
1999—Tennessee NFL	16	16	§14.5
2000—Tennessee NFL	16	16	11.5
2001—Tennessee NFL	16	16	10.0
Pro totals (3 years)	48	48	36.0

KEATHLEY, MICHAEL   G   CHARGERS

PERSONAL: Born March 9, 1978, in Glen Rose, Texas. ... 6-4/296.
HIGH SCHOOL: Glen Rose (Texas).
COLLEGE: Texas Christian.
TRANSACTIONS/CAREER NOTES: Signed as non-drafted free agent by San Diego Chargers (April 27, 2001).
PLAYING EXPERIENCE: San Diego NFL, 2001. ... Games/Games started: 2001 (16/0).

KEATON, CURTIS   RB/KR   BENGALS

PERSONAL: Born October 18, 1976, in Columbus, Ohio. ... 5-10/219. ... Full name: Curtis Isaiah Keaton.
HIGH SCHOOL: Beechcroft (Columbus, Ohio).
COLLEGE: West Virginia, then James Madison.
TRANSACTIONS/CAREER NOTES: Selected by Cincinnati Bengals in fourth round (97th pick overall) of 2000 NFL draft. ... Signed by Bengals (June 23, 2000).
PLAYING EXPERIENCE: Cincinnati NFL, 2000 and 2001. ... Games/Games started: 2000 (6/0), 2001 (13/0). Total: 29/0.
PRO STATISTICS: 2000—Rushed six times for 24 yards. 2001—Rushed five times for 48 yards and caught one pass for nine yards.
SINGLE GAME HIGHS (regular season): Attempts—3 (September 30, 2001, vs. San Diego); yards—44 (September 30, 2001, vs. San Diego); and rushing touchdowns—0.

			KICKOFF RETURNS				TOTALS			
Year Team	G	GS	No.	Yds.	Avg.	TD	TD	2pt.	Pts.	Fum.
2000—Cincinnati NFL	6	0	6	100	16.7	0	0	0	0	0
2001—Cincinnati NFL	13	0	42	891	21.2	0	0	0	0	0
Pro totals (2 years)	19	0	48	991	20.6	0	0	0	0	0

KEITH, JOHN — S — 49ERS

PERSONAL: Born February 4, 1977, in Newman, Ga. ... 6-0/207. ... Full name: John Martin Keith.
HIGH SCHOOL: East Coweta (Ga.).
COLLEGE: Furman.
TRANSACTIONS/CAREER NOTES: Selected by San Francisco 49ers in fourth round (108th pick overall) of 2000 NFL draft. ... Signed by 49ers (July 16, 2000). ... On injured reserve with broken arm (October 10, 2000-remainder of season). ... On injured reserve with knee injury (September 12, 2001-remainder of season).

				INTERCEPTIONS			SACKS
Year Team	G	GS	No.	Yds.	Avg.	TD	No.
2000—San Francisco NFL	6	3	1	0	0.0	0	1.0
2001—San Francisco NFL	1	0	0	0	0.0	0	0.0
Pro totals (2 years)	7	3	1	0	0.0	0	1.0

KELLY, BEN — CB — PATRIOTS

PERSONAL: Born September 15, 1978, in Cleveland. ... 5-9/185. ... Full name: Ben O. Kelly.
HIGH SCHOOL: Mentor Lake (Cleveland).
COLLEGE: Colorado.
TRANSACTIONS/CAREER NOTES: Selected after junior season by Miami Dolphins in third round (84th pick overall) of 2000 NFL draft. ... Signed by Dolphins (July 24, 2000). ... On injured reserve with knee injury (September 26, 2000-remainder of season). ... Claimed on waivers by New England Patriots (November 2, 2001).
PLAYING EXPERIENCE: Miami NFL, 2000; Miami (2)-New England (2) NFL, 2001. ... Games/Games started: 2000 (2/0), 2001 (Mia.-2/0; N.E.-2/0; Total: 4/0). Total: 6/0.
PRO STATISTICS: 2000—Returned five punts for 31 yards. 2001—Returned seven kickoffs for 123 yards.

KELLY, BRIAN — CB — BUCCANEERS

PERSONAL: Born January 14, 1976, in Las Vegas, Nev. ... 5-11/193.
HIGH SCHOOL: Overland (Aurora, Colo.).
COLLEGE: Southern California.
TRANSACTIONS/CAREER NOTES: Selected by Tampa Bay Buccaneers in second round (45th pick overall) of 1998 NFL draft. ... Signed by Buccaneers (July 19, 1998). ... Granted free agency (March 2, 2001). ... Re-signed by Buccaneers (March 18, 2001). ... Granted unconditional free agency (March 1, 2002). ... Re-signed by Buccaneers (March 19, 2002).
PLAYING EXPERIENCE: Tampa Bay NFL, 1998-2001. ... Games/Games started: 1998 (16/3), 1999 (16/3), 2000 (16/3), 2001 (16/11). Total: 64/20.
CHAMPIONSHIP GAME EXPERIENCE: Played in NFC championship game (1999 season).
PRO STATISTICS: 1998—Intercepted one pass for four yards, fumbled once and recovered one fumble for 15 yards. 1999—Intercepted one pass for 26 yards. 2000—Intercepted one pass for nine yards and one touchdown and recovered two fumbles. 2001—Credited with $1\frac{1}{2}$ sacks.

KELLY, ERIC — CB — VIKINGS

PERSONAL: Born January 15, 1977, in Milwaukee. ... 5-10/197.
HIGH SCHOOL: Bay (Panama, Fla.).
COLLEGE: Kentucky.
TRANSACTIONS/CAREER NOTES: Selected by Minnesota Vikings in third round (64th pick overall) of 2001 NFL draft. ... Signed by Vikings (July 26, 2001).

				INTERCEPTIONS		
Year Team	G	GS	No.	Yds.	Avg.	TD
2001—Minnesota NFL	16	11	2	-7	-3.5	0

KELLY, LEWIS — G — VIKINGS

PERSONAL: Born April 21, 1977, in Lithonia, Ga. ... 6-4/306.
HIGH SCHOOL: Henderson (Lithonia, Ga.).
COLLEGE: South Carolina State.
TRANSACTIONS/CAREER NOTES: Selected by Minnesota Vikings in seventh round (248th pick overall) of 2000 NFL draft. ... Signed by Vikings (April 27, 2000). ... On injured reserve with knee injury (August 22, 2000-entire season).
PLAYING EXPERIENCE: Minnesota NFL, 2001. ... Games/Games started: 2001 (4/0).

KELLY, MAURICE — S — SEAHAWKS

PERSONAL: Born October 9, 1972, in Orangeburg, S.C. ... 6-2/209.
HIGH SCHOOL: Orangeburg-Wilkinson (Orangeburg, S.C.).
COLLEGE: East Tennessee State.
TRANSACTIONS/CAREER NOTES: Signed as non-drafted free agent by Seattle Seahawks (April 24, 2000). ... On injured reserve with toe injury (November 14, 2001-remainder of season).
PLAYING EXPERIENCE: Seattle NFL, 2000 and 2001. ... Games/Games started: 2000 (16/0), 2001 (8/3). Total: 24/3.

KELLY, REGGIE — TE — FALCONS

PERSONAL: Born February 22, 1977, in Aberdeen, Miss. ... 6-3/255. ... Full name: Reginald Kuta Kelly.
HIGH SCHOOL: Aberdeen (Miss.).
COLLEGE: Mississippi State.
TRANSACTIONS/CAREER NOTES: Selected by Atlanta Falcons in second round (42nd pick overall) of 1999 NFL draft. ... Signed by Falcons (June 25, 1999).
PRO STATISTICS: 2000—Fumbled once.
SINGLE GAME HIGHS (regular season): Receptions—4 (December 24, 2000, vs. Kansas City); yards—83 (September 24, 2000, vs. St. Louis); and touchdown receptions—1 (December 3, 2000, vs. Seattle).

				RECEIVING		
Year Team	G	GS	No.	Yds.	Avg.	TD
1999—Atlanta NFL	16	2	8	146	18.3	0
2000—Atlanta NFL	16	16	31	340	11.0	2
2001—Atlanta NFL	14	13	16	142	8.9	0
Pro totals (3 years)	46	31	55	628	11.4	2

KENDALL, PETE — G — CARDINALS

PERSONAL: Born July 9, 1973, in Quincy, Mass. ... 6-5/294. ... Full name: Peter Marcus Kendall.
HIGH SCHOOL: Archbishop Williams (Weymouth, Mass.).
COLLEGE: Boston College (degree in marketing, 1995).
TRANSACTIONS/CAREER NOTES: Selected by Seattle Seahawks in first round (21st pick overall) of 1996 NFL draft. ... Signed by Seahawks (July 21, 1996). ... Granted unconditional free agency (March 2, 2001). ... Signed by Arizona Cardinals (March 12, 2001). ... On injured reserve with foot injury (December 26, 2001-remainder of season).
PLAYING EXPERIENCE: Seattle NFL, 1996-2000; Seattle NFL, 2001. ... Games/Games started: 1996 (12/11), 1997 (16/16), 1998 (16/16), 1999 (16/16), 2000 (16/16), 2001 (11/11). Total: 87/86.
PRO STATISTICS: 2000—Recovered one fumble.

KENNEDY, KENOY — S — BRONCOS

PERSONAL: Born November 15, 1977, in Dallas. ... 6-1/215. ... Full name: Kenoy Wayne Kennedy.
HIGH SCHOOL: Terrell (Texas).
COLLEGE: Arkansas.
TRANSACTIONS/CAREER NOTES: Selected by Denver Broncos in second round (45th pick overall) of 2000 NFL draft. ... Signed by Broncos (June 1, 2000).
PRO STATISTICS: 2001—Credited with two sacks.

				INTERCEPTIONS		
Year Team	G	GS	No.	Yds.	Avg.	TD
2000—Denver NFL	13	0	1	0	0.0	0
2001—Denver NFL	16	16	1	6	6.0	0
Pro totals (2 years)	29	16	2	6	3.0	0

KENNEDY, LINCOLN — OT — RAIDERS

PERSONAL: Born February 12, 1971, in York, Pa. ... 6-6/340. ... Full name: Tamerlane Lincoln Kennedy.
HIGH SCHOOL: Samuel F.B. Morse (San Diego).
COLLEGE: Washington (degree in speech and drama, 1993).
TRANSACTIONS/CAREER NOTES: Selected by Atlanta Falcons in first round (ninth pick overall) of 1993 NFL draft. ... Signed by Falcons (August 2, 1993). ... Granted free agency (February 16, 1996). ... Re-signed by Falcons (May 13, 1996). ... Traded by Falcons to Oakland Raiders for fifth-round pick (traded to Washington) in 1997 draft (May 13, 1996).
PLAYING EXPERIENCE: Atlanta NFL, 1993-1995; Oakland NFL, 1996-2001. ... Games/Games started: 1993 (16/16), 1994 (16/2), 1995 (16/4), 1996 (16/16), 1997 (16/16), 1998 (16/16), 1999 (15/15), 2000 (16/16), 2001 (15/15). Total: 142/116.
CHAMPIONSHIP GAME EXPERIENCE: Played in AFC championship game (2000 season).
HONORS: Named offensive tackle on THE SPORTING NEWS college All-America first team (1992). ... Played in Pro Bowl (2000 season).
PRO STATISTICS: 1993—Recovered one fumble. 1994—Recovered one fumble. 1996—Recovered one fumble. 1998—Recovered one fumble for 27 yards. 2000—Recovered two fumbles. 2001—Recovered two fumbles for two yards.

KENNISON, EDDIE — WR — CHIEFS

PERSONAL: Born January 20, 1973, in Lake Charles, La. ... 6-1/190. ... Full name: Eddie Joseph Kennison III.
HIGH SCHOOL: Washington-Marion (Lake Charles, La.).
COLLEGE: Louisiana State.
TRANSACTIONS/CAREER NOTES: Selected after junior season by St. Louis Rams in first round (18th pick overall) of 1996 NFL draft. ... Signed by Rams (July 27, 1996). ... Traded by Rams to New Orleans Saints for second-round pick (DB Dre' Bly) in 1999 draft (February 18, 1999). ... Traded by Saints to Chicago Bears for fifth-round pick (traded to Indianapolis) in 2000 draft (February 21, 2000). ... Granted unconditional free agency (March 2, 2001). ... Signed by Denver Broncos (April 5, 2001). ... Released by Broncos (November 14, 2001). ... Signed by Kansas City Chiefs (December 3, 2001).
PRO STATISTICS: 1996—Fumbled five times. 1997—Fumbled twice. 1998—Fumbled four times and recovered one fumble. 1999—Fumbled six times and recovered four fumbles. 2000—Fumbled once and recovered one fumble. 2001—Fumbled once and recovered one fumble.
SINGLE GAME HIGHS (regular season): Receptions—8 (December 10, 2000, vs. New England); yards—226 (December 15, 1996, vs. Atlanta); and touchdown receptions—3 (December 15, 1996, vs. Atlanta).
STATISTICAL PLATEAUS: 100-yard receiving games: 1996 (2), 1999 (1), 2000 (1), 2001 (1). Total: 5.

Year	Team	G	GS	RUSHING Att.	Yds.	Avg.	TD	RECEIVING No.	Yds.	Avg.	TD	PUNT RETURNS No.	Yds.	Avg.	TD	KICKOFF RETURNS No.	Yds.	Avg.	TD	TOTALS TD	2pt.	Pts.
1996	St. Louis NFL	15	14	0	0	0.0	0	54	924	17.1	9	29	423	14.6	2	23	454	19.7	0	11	0	66
1997	St. Louis NFL	14	9	3	13	4.3	0	25	404	16.2	0	34	247	7.3	0	1	14	14.0	0	0	0	0
1998	St. Louis NFL	16	13	2	9	4.5	0	17	234	13.8	1	40	415	10.4	1	0	0	0.0	0	2	0	12
1999	New Orleans NFL	16	16	3	20	6.7	0	61	835	13.7	4	35	258	7.4	0	0	0	0.0	0	4	†1	26
2000	Chicago NFL	16	10	3	72	24.0	0	55	549	10.0	2	0	0	0.0	0	0	0	0.0	0	2	0	12
2001	Denver NFL	8	6	3	9	3.0	0	15	169	11.3	1	0	0	0.0	0	0	0	0.0	0	1	0	6
	Kansas City NFL	5	1	2	13	6.5	0	16	322	20.1	0	0	0	0.0	0	0	0	0.0	0	0	1	2
Pro totals (6 years)		90	69	16	136	8.5	0	243	3437	14.1	17	138	1343	9.7	3	24	468	19.5	0	20	2	124

KERNEY, PATRICK — DE — FALCONS

PERSONAL: Born December 30, 1976, in Trenton, N.J. ... 6-5/273. ... Full name: Patrick Manning Kerney.
HIGH SCHOOL: Taft Prep (Watertown, Conn.).
COLLEGE: Virginia.
TRANSACTIONS/CAREER NOTES: Selected by Atlanta Falcons in first round (30th pick overall) of 1999 NFL draft. ... Signed by Falcons (June 25, 1999).
HONORS: Named defensive end on THE SPORTING NEWS college All-America second team (1998).
PRO STATISTICS: 2000—Intercepted one pass for eight yards. 2001—Recovered one fumble.

Year	Team	G	GS	SACKS
1999	Atlanta NFL	16	2	2.5
2000	Atlanta NFL	16	16	2.5
2001	Atlanta NFL	16	16	12.0
Pro totals (3 years)		48	34	17.0

KIGHT, DANNY — K

PERSONAL: Born August 18, 1971, in Atlanta. ... 6-1/214.
HIGH SCHOOL: Druid Hills (Ga.).
COLLEGE: Augusta (Ga.) State.
TRANSACTIONS/CAREER NOTES: Signed as non-drafted free agent by San Diego Chargers (April 23, 1996). ... Released by Chargers (August 14, 1996). ... Signed by Dallas Cowboys (April 15, 1997). ... Released by Cowboys (August 12, 1997). ... Signed by Washington Redskins (February 11, 1998). ... On non-football injury list with leg injury (July 20-September 22, 1998). ... Released by Redskins (September 22, 1998). ... Signed by Tampa Bay Buccaneers (April 7, 1999). ... Claimed on waivers by Cleveland Browns (April 20, 1999). ... Released by Browns (August 25, 1999). ... Signed by Indianapolis Colts (October 13, 1999). ... Released by Colts (August 26, 2001). ... Signed by Baltimore Ravens (October 26, 2001). ... Granted free agency (March 1, 2002).
PLAYING EXPERIENCE: Indianapolis NFL, 1999 and 2000; Rhein NFLE, 2000; Baltimore NFL, 2001. ... Games/Games started: 1999 (12/0) NFLE 2000 (games played unavailable); NFL 2000 (16/0), 2001 (10/0). Total NFL: 38/0.
PRO STATISTICS: NFLE: 2000—Attempted five field goals with three completions for nine points.

KILLENS, TERRY — LB — BRONCOS

PERSONAL: Born March 24, 1974, in Cincinnati. ... 6-1/235. ... Full name: Terry Deleon Killens.
HIGH SCHOOL: Purcell (Cincinnati).
COLLEGE: Penn State.
TRANSACTIONS/CAREER NOTES: Selected by Houston Oilers in third round (74th pick overall) of 1996 NFL draft. ... Signed by Oilers (July 20, 1996). ... Oilers franchise moved to Tennessee for 1997 season. ... Oilers franchise renamed Tennessee Titans for 1999 season (December 26, 1998). ... Granted free agency (February 12, 1999). ... Re-signed by Titans (June 2, 1999). ... Granted unconditional free agency (February 11, 2000). ... Re-signed by Titans (May 26, 2000). ... Released by Titans (March 1, 2001). ... Signed by San Francisco 49ers (August 2, 2001). ... Granted unconditional free agency (March 1, 2002). ... Signed by Denver Broncos (March 22, 2002).
PLAYING EXPERIENCE: Houston NFL, 1996; Tennessee NFL, 1997-2000; San Francisco NFL, 2001. ... Games/Games started: 1996 (14/0), 1997 (16/0), 1998 (16/1), 1999 (16/1), 2000 (16/0), 2001 (16/2). Total: 94/4.
CHAMPIONSHIP GAME EXPERIENCE: Played in AFC championship game (1999 season). ... Played in Super Bowl XXXIV (1999 season).
PRO STATISTICS: 1999—Recovered one fumble. 2000—Credited with one sack.

KILLINGS, CEDRIC — DT

PERSONAL: Born December 14, 1977, in Miami. ... 6-2/290. ... Full name: Cedric Laquon Killings.
HIGH SCHOOL: Miami Central.
COLLEGE: Carson-Newman College (Tenn.).
TRANSACTIONS/CAREER NOTES: Signed as non-drafted free agent by San Francisco 49ers (April 27, 2000). ... Released by 49ers (August 29, 2001). ... Signed by Cleveland Browns (October 16, 2001). ... Released by Browns (November 7, 2001). ... Signed by Carolina Panthers (November 28, 2001). ... Granted free agency (March 1, 2002).
PLAYING EXPERIENCE: San Francisco NFL, 2000; Carolina NFL, 2001. ... Games/Games started: 2000 (14/1), 2001 (4/0). Total: 18/1.
PRO STATISTICS: 2000—Credited with three sacks.

KING, ANDRE — WR — BROWNS

PERSONAL: Born November 26, 1973, in Fort Lauderdale, Fla. ... 5-11/195.
HIGH SCHOOL: Stranahan (Fla.).
COLLEGE: Miami.
TRANSACTIONS/CAREER NOTES: Selected by Cleveland Browns in seventh round (245th pick overall) of 2001 NFL draft. ... Signed by Browns (July 18, 2001).
SINGLE GAME HIGHS (regular season): Receptions—4 (December 16, 2001, vs. Jacksonville); yards—61 (December 30, 2001, vs. Tennessee); and touchdown receptions—0.

Year	Team	G	GS	RECEIVING No.	Yds.	Avg.	TD	KICKOFF RETURNS No.	Yds.	Avg.	TD	TOTALS TD	2pt.	Pts.	Fum.
2001	Cleveland NFL	7	0	11	149	13.5	0	14	279	19.9	0	0	0	0	1

KING, LAMAR — DE — SEAHAWKS

PERSONAL: Born August 10, 1975, in Boston. ... 6-3/295.
HIGH SCHOOL: Chesapeake (Md.).
JUNIOR COLLEGE: Montgomery College (Md.).
COLLEGE: Saginaw Valley State (Mich.).
TRANSACTIONS/CAREER NOTES: Selected by Seattle Seahawks in first round (22nd pick overall) of 1999 NFL draft. ... Signed by Seahawks (August 12, 1999). ... On injured reserve with calf injury (January 4, 2001-remainder of season).
PRO STATISTICS: 2001—Recovered one fumble.

Year Team	G	GS	SACKS
1999—Seattle NFL	14	0	2.0
2000—Seattle NFL	14	14	6.0
2001—Seattle NFL	9	9	0.0
Pro totals (3 years)	37	23	8.0

KING, SHAUN — QB — BUCCANEERS

PERSONAL: Born May 29, 1977, in St. Petersburg, Fla. ... 6-0/225. ... Full name: Shaun Earl King.
HIGH SCHOOL: Gibbs (St. Petersburg, Fla.).
COLLEGE: Tulane.
TRANSACTIONS/CAREER NOTES: Selected by Tampa Bay Buccaneers in second round (50th pick overall) of 1999 NFL draft. ... Signed by Buccaneers (August 1, 1999).
CHAMPIONSHIP GAME EXPERIENCE: Played in NFC championship game (1999 season).
PRO STATISTICS: 1999—Fumbled four times and recovered one fumble. 2000—Fumbled four times and recovered three fumbles.
SINGLE GAME HIGHS (regular season): Attempts—42 (December 24, 2000, vs. Green Bay); completions—26 (October 9, 2000, vs. Minnesota); passing yards—297 (December 12, 1999, vs. Detroit); and touchdown passes—4 (October 29, 2000, vs. Minnesota).
MISCELLANEOUS: Regular-season record as starting NFL quarterback: 14-7 (.667). ... Postseason record as starting NFL quarterback: 1-2 (.333).

			PASSING							RUSHING				TOTALS		
Year Team	G	GS	Att.	Cmp.	Pct.	Yds.	TD	Int.	Avg.	Rat.	Att.	Yds.	Avg.	TD	TD	2pt.	Pts.
1999—Tampa Bay NFL	6	5	146	89	61.0	875	7	4	5.99	82.4	18	38	2.1	0	0	0	0
2000—Tampa Bay NFL	16	16	428	233	54.4	2769	18	13	6.47	75.8	73	353	4.8	5	5	1	32
2001—Tampa Bay NFL	3	0	31	21	67.7	210	0	1	6.77	73.3	5	-12	-2.4	0	0	1	2
Pro totals (3 years)	25	21	605	343	56.7	3854	25	18	6.37	77.2	96	379	3.9	5	5	2	34

KINNEY, ERRON — TE — TITANS

PERSONAL: Born July 28, 1977, in Richmond, Va. ... 6-5/280. ... Full name: Erron Quincy Kinney.
HIGH SCHOOL: Patrick Henry (Ashland, Va.).
COLLEGE: Florida.
TRANSACTIONS/CAREER NOTES: Selected by Tennessee Titans in third round (68th pick overall) of 2000 NFL draft. ... Signed by Titans (July 17, 2000).
PRO STATISTICS: 2000—Fumbled once and recovered one fumble. 2001—Returned one kickoff for 14 yards.
SINGLE GAME HIGHS (regular season): Receptions—7 (October 7, 2001, vs. Baltimore); yards—78 (October 7, 2001, vs. Baltimore); and touchdown receptions—1 (September 9, 2001, vs. Miami).

			RECEIVING			
Year Team	G	GS	No.	Yds.	Avg.	TD
2000—Tennessee NFL	16	10	19	197	10.4	1
2001—Tennessee NFL	13	12	25	263	10.5	1
Pro totals (2 years)	29	22	44	460	10.5	2

KIRBY, TERRY — RB — RAIDERS

PERSONAL: Born January 20, 1970, in Hampton, Va. ... 6-1/215. ... Full name: Terry Gayle Kirby. ... Brother of Wayne Kirby, outfielder with three major league teams (1991-98); and cousin of Chris Slade, linebacker with New England Patriots (1993-2000) and Carolina Panthers (2001).
HIGH SCHOOL: Tabb (Va.).
COLLEGE: Virginia (degree in psychology).
TRANSACTIONS/CAREER NOTES: Selected by Miami Dolphins in third round (78th pick overall) of 1993 NFL draft. ... Signed by Dolphins (July 19, 1993). ... On injured reserve with knee injury (September 26, 1994-remainder of season). ... Granted free agency (February 16, 1996). ... Traded by Dolphins to San Francisco 49ers for fourth-round pick in 1997 draft (August 19, 1996). ... Released by 49ers (March 3, 1998). ... Re-signed by 49ers (September 23, 1998). ... Granted unconditional free agency (February 12, 1999). ... Signed by Cleveland Browns (March 9, 1999). ... Released by Browns (August 29, 2000). ... Signed by Oakland Raiders (November 21, 2000).
CHAMPIONSHIP GAME EXPERIENCE: Played in NFC championship game (1997 season). ... Played in AFC championship game (2000 season).
PRO STATISTICS: 1993—Recovered four fumbles. 1995—Completed only pass attempt for 31 yards and a touchdown. 1996—Attempted two passes with one completion for 24 yards and a touchdown and returned one punt for three yards. 1997—Recovered two fumbles. 1998—Completed only pass attempt for 28 yards and a touchdown. 1999—Completed only pass attempt for two yards and recovered two fumbles.
SINGLE GAME HIGHS (regular season): Attempts—22 (October 17, 1999, vs. Jacksonville); yards—105 (December 2, 1996, vs. Atlanta); and rushing touchdowns—2 (December 26, 1999, vs. Indianapolis).
STATISTICAL PLATEAUS: 100-yard rushing games: 1994 (1), 1996 (1). Total: 2. ... 100-yard receiving games: 1993 (2).

				RUSHING				RECEIVING				KICKOFF RETURNS				TOTALS		
Year Team	G	GS	Att.	Yds.	Avg.	TD	No.	Yds.	Avg.	TD	No.	Yds.	Avg.	TD	TD	2pt.	Pts.	Fum.
1993—Miami NFL	16	8	119	390	3.3	3	75	874	11.7	3	4	85	21.3	0	6	0	36	5
1994—Miami NFL	4	4	60	233	3.9	2	14	154	11.0	0	0	0	0.0	0	2	1	14	2
1995—Miami NFL	16	4	108	414	3.8	4	66	618	9.4	3	0	0	0.0	0	7	0	42	2
1996—San Francisco NFL	14	10	134	559	4.2	3	52	439	8.4	1	1	22	22.0	0	4	0	24	1
1997—San Francisco NFL	16	3	125	418	3.3	6	23	279	12.1	1	3	124	41.3	1	8	2	52	3
1998—San Francisco NFL	9	0	48	258	5.4	3	16	134	8.4	0	17	340	20.0	0	3	0	18	0
1999—Cleveland NFL	16	10	130	452	3.5	6	58	528	9.1	3	11	230	20.9	0	9	0	54	4
2000—Oakland NFL	2	0	11	51	4.6	0	3	19	6.3	0	0	0	0.0	0	0	0	0	0
2001—Oakland NFL	11	0	10	49	4.9	0	9	62	6.9	0	46	1066	23.2	1	1	0	6	1
Pro totals (9 years)	104	39	745	2824	3.8	27	316	3107	9.8	11	82	1867	22.8	2	40	3	246	18

KIRKLAND, LEVON   LB   SEAHAWKS

PERSONAL: Born February 16, 1969, in Lamar, S.C. ... 6-1/275. ... Full name: Lorenzo Levon Kirkland. ... Name pronounced luh-VON.
HIGH SCHOOL: Lamar (S.C.).
COLLEGE: Clemson.
TRANSACTIONS/CAREER NOTES: Selected by Pittsburgh Steelers in second round (38th pick overall) of 1992 NFL draft. ... Signed by Steelers (July 25, 1992). ... Released by Steelers (March 8, 2001). ... Signed by Seattle Seahawks (April 9, 2001).
CHAMPIONSHIP GAME EXPERIENCE: Played in AFC championship game (1994, 1995 and 1997 seasons). ... Played in Super Bowl XXX (1995 season).
HONORS: Named linebacker on THE SPORTING NEWS college All-America first team (1991). ... Played in Pro Bowl (1996 and 1997 seasons). ... Named inside linebacker on THE SPORTING NEWS NFL All-Pro team (1997).
PRO STATISTICS: 1993—Recovered two fumbles for 24 yards and one touchdown. 1995—Recovered two fumbles. 1997—Recovered one fumble. 1999—Recovered two fumbles. 2000—Recovered one fumble.

			INTERCEPTIONS				SACKS
Year Team	G	GS	No.	Yds.	Avg.	TD	No.
1992—Pittsburgh NFL	16	0	0	0	0.0	0	0.0
1993—Pittsburgh NFL	16	13	0	0	0.0	0	1.0
1994—Pittsburgh NFL	16	15	2	0	0.0	0	3.0
1995—Pittsburgh NFL	16	16	0	0	0.0	0	1.0
1996—Pittsburgh NFL	16	16	4	12	3.0	0	4.0
1997—Pittsburgh NFL	16	16	2	14	7.0	0	5.0
1998—Pittsburgh NFL	16	16	1	1	1.0	0	2.5
1999—Pittsburgh NFL	16	16	1	23	23.0	0	2.0
2000—Pittsburgh NFL	16	16	1	1	1.0	0	1.0
2001—Seattle NFL	16	16	0	0	0.0	0	1.0
Pro totals (10 years)	160	140	11	51	4.6	0	19.5

KIRSCHKE, TRAVIS   DE   LIONS

PERSONAL: Born September 6, 1974, in Fullerton, Calif. ... 6-3/287.
HIGH SCHOOL: Esperanza (Anaheim, Calif.).
COLLEGE: UCLA.
TRANSACTIONS/CAREER NOTES: Signed as non-drafted free agent by Detroit Lions (April 24, 1997). ... Inactive for three games (1998). ... On injured reserve with abdominal injury (September 24, 1998-remainder of season). ... Granted free agency (February 11, 2000). ... Re-signed by Lions (April 25, 2000). ... Granted unconditional free agency (March 1, 2002). ... Re-signed by Lions (April 2, 2002).
PLAYING EXPERIENCE: Detroit NFL, 1997 and 1999-2001. ... Games/Games started: 1997 (3/0), 1999 (15/7), 2000 (13/0), 2001 (16/2). Total: 47/2.
PRO STATISTICS: 1999—Credited with two sacks and recovered one fumble. 2000—Credited with 1/2 sack and recovered one fumble.

KITNA, JON   QB   BENGALS

PERSONAL: Born September 21, 1972, in Tacoma, Wash. ... 6-2/217.
HIGH SCHOOL: Lincoln (Tacoma, Wash.).
COLLEGE: Central Washington (degree in math education, 1995).
TRANSACTIONS/CAREER NOTES: Signed as non-drafted free agent by Seattle Seahawks (April 25, 1996) ... Released by Seahawks (August 19, 1996) ... Re-signed by Seahawks to practice squad (August 20, 1996). ... Assigned by Seahawks to Barcelona Dragons in 1997 World League enhancement allocation program (April 7, 1997). ... Granted free agency (February 11, 2000). ... Re-signed by Seahawks (March 15, 2000). ... Granted unconditional free agency (March 2, 2001). ... Signed by Cincinnati Bengals (March 8, 2001).
PRO STATISTICS: 1997—Fumbled once and recovered one fumble for minus two yards. 1998—Fumbled six times and recovered four fumbles for minus 10 yards. 1999—Fumbled 14 times and recovered six fumbles for minus nine yards. 2000—Led league with 17 fumbles and recovered nine fumbles for minus 19 yards. 2001—Tied for AFC lead with 13 fumbles and recovered seven fumbles for minus 13 yards.
SINGLE GAME HIGHS (regular season): Attempts—68 (December 30, 2001, vs. Pittsburgh); completions—35 (December 30, 2001, vs. Pittsburgh); yards—411 (December 30, 2001, vs. Pittsburgh); and touchdown passes—3 (December 10, 2000, vs. Denver).
STATISTICAL PLATEAUS: 300-yard passing games: 2001 (3).
MISCELLANEOUS: Regular-season record as starting NFL quarterback: 24-24 (.500). ... Postseason record as starting NFL quarterback: 0-1.

					PASSING							RUSHING			TOTALS		
Year Team	G	GS	Att.	Cmp.	Pct.	Yds.	TD	Int.	Avg.	Rat.	Att.	Yds.	Avg.	TD	TD	2pt.	Pts.
1997—Barcelona W.L.	10	...	317	171	53.9	2448	22	15	7.72	82.6	50	334	6.7	3	3	0	18
—Seattle NFL	3	1	45	31	68.9	371	1	2	8.24	82.7	10	9	0.9	1	1	0	6
1998—Seattle NFL	6	5	172	98	57.0	1177	7	8	6.84	72.3	20	67	3.4	1	1	0	6
1999—Seattle NFL	15	15	495	270	54.5	3346	23	16	6.76	77.7	35	56	1.6	0	0	0	0
2000—Seattle NFL	15	12	418	259	62.0	2658	18	19	6.36	75.6	48	127	2.6	1	1	0	6
2001—Cincinnati NFL	16	15	*581	313	53.9	3216	12	22	5.54	61.1	27	73	2.7	1	1	0	6
W.L. totals (1 year)	10	...	317	171	53.9	2448	22	15	7.72	82.6	50	334	6.7	3	3	0	18
NFL totals (5 years)	55	48	1711	971	56.8	10768	61	67	6.29	71.2	140	332	2.4	4	4	0	24
Pro totals (6 years)	65	...	2028	1142	56.3	13216	83	82	6.52	73.0	190	666	3.5	7	7	0	42

KLEINSASSER, JIM   FB   VIKINGS

PERSONAL: Born January 31, 1977, in Carrington, N.D. ... 6-3/274.
HIGH SCHOOL: Carrington (N.D.).
COLLEGE: North Dakota.
TRANSACTIONS/CAREER NOTES: Selected by Minnesota Vikings in second round (44th pick overall) of 1999 NFL draft. ... Signed by Vikings (August 1, 1999).
CHAMPIONSHIP GAME EXPERIENCE: Played in NFC championship game (2000 season).
PRO STATISTICS: 1999—Returned one kickoff for no yards.
SINGLE GAME HIGHS (regular season): Attempts—5 (October 21, 2001, vs. Green Bay); yards—20 (October 21, 2001, vs. Green Bay); and rushing touchdowns—1 (October 21, 2001, vs. Green Bay).

				RUSHING				RECEIVING				TOTALS		
Year Team	G	GS	Att.	Yds.	Avg.	TD	No.	Yds.	Avg.	TD	TD	2pt.	Pts.	Fum.
1999—Minnesota NFL	13	7	0	0	0.0	0	6	13	2.2	0	0	0	0	2
2000—Minnesota NFL	14	8	12	43	3.6	0	10	98	9.8	0	0	0	0	0
2001—Minnesota NFL	11	11	23	72	3.1	1	24	184	7.7	0	1	0	6	2
Pro totals (3 years)	38	26	35	115	3.3	1	40	295	7.4	0	1	0	6	4

KNIGHT, MARCUS   WR   RAIDERS

PERSONAL: Born June 19, 1978, in Sylacauga, Ala. ... 6-1/180.
HIGH SCHOOL: Comer (Sylacauga, Ala.).
COLLEGE: Michigan.
TRANSACTIONS/CAREER NOTES: Signed as non-drafted free agent by Oakland Raiders (April 18, 2000) ... Released by Raiders (August 27, 2000). ... Re-signed by Raiders to practice squad (August 28, 2000).
PLAYING EXPERIENCE: Oakland NFL, 2001. ... Games/Games started: 2001 (5/1).

KNIGHT, ROGER   LB   SAINTS

PERSONAL: Born October 11, 1978, in St. Ann's, Jamaica. ... 6-0/245. ... Full name: Roger Oliver Knight.
HIGH SCHOOL: Brooklyn Tech (N.Y.).
COLLEGE: Wisconsin.
TRANSACTIONS/CAREER NOTES: Selected by Pittsburgh Steelers in sixth round (182nd pick overall) of 2001 NFL draft. ... Signed by Steelers (June 6, 2001). ... Released by Steelers (August 31, 2001). ... Signed by New Orleans Saints (December 4, 2001). ... On injured reserve with knee injury (December 12, 2001-remainder of season).
PLAYING EXPERIENCE: New Orleans NFL, 2001. ... Games/Games started: 2001 (1/0).

KNIGHT, SAMMY   S   SAINTS

PERSONAL: Born September 10, 1975, in Fontana, Calif. ... 6-0/205.
HIGH SCHOOL: Rubidoux (Riverside, Calif.).
COLLEGE: Southern California.
TRANSACTIONS/CAREER NOTES: Signed as non-drafted free agent by New Orleans Saints (April 25, 1997).
PRO STATISTICS: 1997—Recovered one fumble. 1998—Recovered two fumbles for three yards. 1999—Recovered one fumble. 2000—Credited with two sacks. 2001—Credited with one sack and recovered five fumbles.

			INTERCEPTIONS			
Year Team	G	GS	No.	Yds.	Avg.	TD
1997—New Orleans NFL	16	12	5	75	15.0	0
1998—New Orleans NFL	14	13	6	171	28.5	2
1999—New Orleans NFL	16	16	1	0	0.0	0
2000—New Orleans NFL	16	16	5	68	13.6	‡2
2001—New Orleans NFL	16	16	6	114	19.0	0
Pro totals (5 years)	78	73	23	428	18.6	4

KNIGHT, TOM   CB   PATRIOTS

PERSONAL: Born December 29, 1974, in Marlton, N.J. ... 6-0/196. ... Full name: Thomas Lorenzo Knight.
HIGH SCHOOL: Cherokee (Marlton, N.J.).
COLLEGE: Iowa.
TRANSACTIONS/CAREER NOTES: Selected by Arizona Cardinals in first round (ninth pick overall) of 1997 NFL draft. ... Signed by Cardinals (July 16, 1997). ... On injured reserve with hamstring injury (January 3, 2002-remainder of season). ... Granted unconditional free agency (March 1, 2002). ... Signed by New England Patriots (April 4, 2002).
PLAYING EXPERIENCE: Arizona NFL, 1997-2001. ... Games/Games Started: 1997 (15/14), 1998 (8/5), 1999 (16/11), 2000 (16/15), 2001 (8/8). Total: 63/53.
PRO STATISTICS: 1998—Credited with one sack. 1999—Intercepted two passes for 16 yards and returned three punts for 38 yards. 2000—Credited with one sack. 2001—Intercepted one pass for 43 yards.

KNORR, MICAH   P   COWBOYS

PERSONAL: Born January 9, 1975, in Orange, Calif. ... 6-2/199.
HIGH SCHOOL: Orange (Calif.).
COLLEGE: Utah State.

TRANSACTIONS/CAREER NOTES: Signed as non-drafted free agent by Dallas Cowboys (April 18, 2000).
PRO STATISTICS: 2001—Rushed once for no yards, attempted one pass without a completion and recovered one fumble.

				PUNTING			
Year Team	G	No.	Yds.	Avg.	Net avg.	In. 20	Blk.
2000—Dallas NFL	14	58	2485	42.8	35.7	12	0
2001—Dallas NFL	16	78	3135	40.2	31.1	25	*3
Pro totals (2 years)	30	136	5620	41.3	33.1	37	3

KOCH, AARON   G/T   JAGUARS

PERSONAL: Born February 21, 1978, in Portland, Ore. ... 6-3/300. ... Full name: Aaron Paul Koch. ... Name pronounced COOK.
HIGH SCHOOL: McNary (Kelzer, Ore.).
COLLEGE: Oregon State.
TRANSACTIONS/CAREER NOTES: Signed by Tennessee Titans as non-drafted free agent (April 18, 2000). ... Released by Titans (August 30, 2000). ... Re-signed by Titans to practice squad (September 5, 2000). ... Signed by Jacksonville Jaguars off Titans practice squad (September 27, 2000).
PLAYING EXPERIENCE: Jacksonville NFL, 2000 and 2001. ... Games/Games started: 2000 (8/0), 2001 (16/1). Total: 24/1.

KOCUREK, KRIS   DT   TITANS

PERSONAL: Born November 15, 1978, in Rockdale, Texas. ... 6-4/293.
HIGH SCHOOL: Caldwell (Texas).
COLLEGE: Texas Tech.
TRANSACTIONS/CAREER NOTES: Selected by Seattle Seahawks in seventh round (237th pick overall) of 2001 NFL draft. ... Signed by Seahawks (June 22, 2001). ... Released by Seahawks (September 2, 2001). ... Signed by Tennessee Titans to practice squad (October 25, 2001). ... Activated (December 20, 2001).
PLAYING EXPERIENCE: Tennessee NFL, 2001. ... Games/Games started: 2001 (1/0).

KOLODZIEJ, ROSS   DT   GIANTS

PERSONAL: Born May 11, 1978, in Stevens Point, Wis. ... 6-2/287.
HIGH SCHOOL: Stevens Point (Wis.).
COLLEGE: Wisconsin.
TRANSACTIONS/CAREER NOTES: Selected by New York Giants in seventh round (230th pick overall) of 2001 NFL draft. ... Signed by Giants (July 26, 2001).
PLAYING EXPERIENCE: New York Giants NFL, 2001. ... Games/Games started: 2001 (9/1).

KONRAD, ROB   FB   DOLPHINS

PERSONAL: Born November 12, 1976, in Rochester, N.Y. ... 6-3/255. ... Full name: Robert L. Konrad.
HIGH SCHOOL: St. John's (Andover, Mass.).
COLLEGE: Syracuse.
TRANSACTIONS/CAREER NOTES: Selected by Miami Dolphins in second round (43rd pick overall) of 1999 NFL draft. ... Signed by Dolphins (July 27, 1999). ... On injured reserve with rib injury (January 12, 2002-remainder of 2001 playoffs).
PRO STATISTICS: 1999—Recovered one fumble.
SINGLE GAME HIGHS (regular season): Attempts—7 (September 3, 2000, vs. Seattle); yards—19 (December 10, 2001, vs. Indianapolis); and rushing touchdowns—1 (December 10, 2001, vs. Indianapolis).

			RUSHING				RECEIVING				TOTALS		
Year Team	G	GS	Att.	Yds.	Avg.	TD	No.	Yds.	Avg.	TD	TD	2pt.	Pts.	Fum.
1999—Miami NFL	15	9	9	16	1.8	0	34	251	7.4	1	1	0	6	3
2000—Miami NFL	15	14	15	39	2.6	0	14	83	5.9	0	0	0	0	0
2001—Miami NFL	12	9	5	22	4.4	1	5	52	10.4	1	2	0	12	0
Pro totals (3 years)	42	32	29	77	2.7	1	53	386	7.3	2	3	0	18	3

KOWALKOWSKI, SCOTT   LB

PERSONAL: Born August 23, 1968, in Farmington Hills, Mich. ... 6-2/220. ... Full name: Scott Thomas Kowalkowski. ... Son of Bob Kowalkowski, guard with Detroit Lions (1966-76) and Green Bay Packers (1977). ... Name pronounced ko-wal-KOW-ski.
HIGH SCHOOL: St. Mary's Prep (Orchard Lake, Mich.).
COLLEGE: Notre Dame (degree in American studies).
TRANSACTIONS/CAREER NOTES: Selected by Philadelphia Eagles in eighth round (217th pick overall) of 1991 NFL draft. ... Signed by Eagles (July 10, 1991). ... On injured reserve with ankle injury (August 30-November 23, 1993). ... Released by Eagles (November 23, 1993). ... Signed by Detroit Lions (February 4, 1994). ... Granted unconditional free agency (February 17, 1995). ... Re-signed by Lions (March 24, 1995). ... Granted unconditional free agency (February 16, 1996). ... Re-signed by Lions (February 29,1996). ... Granted unconditional free agency (February 14, 1997). ... Re-signed by Lions (March 18, 1997). ... Granted unconditional free agency (February 11, 2000). ... Re-signed by Lions (April 26, 2000). ... Granted unconditional free agency (March 1, 2002).
PLAYING EXPERIENCE: Philadelphia NFL, 1991 and 1992; Detroit NFL, 1994-2001. ... Games/Games started: 1991 (16/0), 1992 (16/0), 1994 (16/0), 1995 (16/0), 1996 (16/1), 1997 (16/0), 1998 (15/0), 1999 (16/3), 2000 (16/2), 2001 (15/0). Total: 159/6.
PRO STATISTICS: 1991—Recovered one fumble. 1996—Recovered one fumble. 1998—Recovered one fumble. 1999—Intercepted one pass for 29 yards and credited with one sack. 2000—Recovered one fumble for two yards.

KOZLOWSKI, BRIAN   TE   FALCONS

PERSONAL: Born October 4, 1970, in Rochester, N.Y. ... 6-3/250. ... Full name: Brian Scott Kozlowski.
HIGH SCHOOL: Webster (N.Y.).
COLLEGE: Connecticut.
TRANSACTIONS/CAREER NOTES: Signed as non-drafted free agent by New York Giants (May 1, 1993). ... Released by Giants (August 16, 1993). ... Re-signed by Giants to practice squad (December 8, 1993). ... Granted unconditional free agency (February 14, 1997). ... Signed by Atlanta Falcons (March 21, 1997). ... Granted unconditional free agency (February 13, 1998). ... Re-signed by Falcons (March 4, 1998). ... Granted unconditional free agency (March 2, 2001). ... Re-signed by Falcons (April 5, 2001). ... Granted unconditional free agency (March 1, 2002). ... Re-signed by Falcons (April 4, 2002).
CHAMPIONSHIP GAME EXPERIENCE: Played in NFC championship game (1998 season). ... Played in Super Bowl XXXIII (1998 season).
PRO STATISTICS: 1995—Recovered one fumble. 2000—Recovered two fumbles. 2001—Returned one punt for no yards.
SINGLE GAME HIGHS (regular season): Receptions—4 (September 23, 2001, vs. Carolina); yards—86 (September 23, 2001, vs. Carolina); and touchdown receptions—1 (November 11, 2001, vs. Dallas).

			RECEIVING				KICKOFF RETURNS				TOTALS		
Year Team	G	GS	No.	Yds.	Avg.	TD	No.	Yds.	Avg.	TD	TD	2pt.	Pts.	Fum.
1993—New York Giants NFL								Did not play.						
1994—New York Giants NFL	16	3	1	5	5.0	0	2	21	10.5	0	0	0	0	0
1995—New York Giants NFL	16	0	2	17	8.5	0	5	75	15.0	0	0	0	0	1
1996—New York Giants NFL	5	0	1	4	4.0	1	1	16	16.0	0	1	0	6	0
1997—Atlanta NFL	16	5	7	99	14.1	1	2	49	24.5	0	1	0	6	0
1998—Atlanta NFL	16	4	10	103	10.3	1	1	12	12.0	0	1	0	6	0
1999—Atlanta NFL	16	3	11	122	11.1	2	2	19	9.5	0	2	0	12	1
2000—Atlanta NFL	16	2	15	151	10.1	2	7	77	11.0	0	2	0	12	0
2001—Atlanta NFL	16	0	15	270	18.0	1	3	35	11.7	0	1	0	6	0
Pro totals (8 years)	117	17	62	771	12.4	8	23	304	13.2	0	8	0	48	2

KREIDER, DAN   FB   STEELERS

PERSONAL: Born March 11, 1977, in Lancaster, Pa. ... 5-11/242.
HIGH SCHOOL: Manheim Central (Pa.).
COLLEGE: New Hampshire.
TRANSACTIONS/CAREER NOTES: Signed as non-drafted free agent by Pittsburgh Steelers (April 21, 2000). ... On physically unable to perform list with calf injury (July 20-September 2, 2001).
PLAYING EXPERIENCE: Pittsburgh NFL, 2000 and 2001. ... Games/Games started: 2000 (10/7), 2001 (13/1). Total: 23/8.
CHAMPIONSHIP GAME EXPERIENCE: Played in AFC championship game (2001 season).
PRO STATISTICS: 2000—Rushed two times for 24 yards, caught five passes for 42 yards and returned one kickoff for no yards. 2001—Rushed seven times for 29 yards and one touchdown and caught two passes for five yards.
SINGLE GAME HIGHS (regular season): Attempts—2 (December 23, 2001, vs. Detroit); yards—24 (December 3, 2000, vs. Oakland); and rushing touchdowns—1 (December 16, 2001, vs. Baltimore).

KREUTZ, OLIN   C   BEARS

PERSONAL: Born June 9, 1977, in Honolulu. ... 6-2/290.
HIGH SCHOOL: St. Louis (Honolulu).
COLLEGE: Washington.
TRANSACTIONS/CAREER NOTES: Selected after junior season by Chicago Bears in third round (64th pick overall) of 1998 NFL draft. ... Signed by Bears (July 20, 1998). ... On injured reserve with knee injury (November 21, 2000-remainder of season). ... Granted free agency (March 2, 2001). ... Re-signed by Bears (April 18, 2001). ... Granted unconditional free agency (March 1, 2002). ... Re-signed by Bears (March 8, 2002).
PLAYING EXPERIENCE: Chicago NFL, 1998-2001. ... Games/Games started: 1998 (9/0), 1999 (16/16), 2000 (7/7), 2001 (16/16). Total: 48/39.
HONORS: Named center on THE SPORTING NEWS college All-America first team (1997).
PRO STATISTICS: 1999—Fumbled once and recovered two fumbles for minus 17 yards. 2001—Fumbled once for minus nine yards.

KRIEWALDT, CLINT   LB   LIONS

PERSONAL: Born March 16, 1976, in Shiocton, Wis. ... 6-1/236.
HIGH SCHOOL: Shiocton (Wis.).
COLLEGE: Wisconsin-Stevens Point.
TRANSACTIONS/CAREER NOTES: Selected by Detroit Lions in sixth round (177th pick overall) of 1999 NFL draft. ... Signed by Lions (July 22, 1999). ... Granted free agency (March 1, 2002). ... Re-signed by Lions (April 16, 2002).
PLAYING EXPERIENCE: Detroit NFL, 1999-2001. ... Games/Games started: 1999 (12/0), 2000 (13/1), 2001 (14/1). Total: 39/2.
PRO STATISTICS: 1999—Intercepted one pass for two yards. 2000—Recovered one fumble.

KUEHL, RYAN   DT   BROWNS

PERSONAL: Born January 18, 1972, in Washington, D.C. ... 6-5/290. ... Full name: Ryan Philip Kuehl.
HIGH SCHOOL: Walt Whitman (Bethesda, Md.).
COLLEGE: Virginia (degree in marketing, 1994).
TRANSACTIONS/CAREER NOTES: Signed as non-drafted free agent by San Francisco 49ers (April 26, 1995). ... Released by 49ers (August 19, 1995). ... Re-signed by Redskins to practice squad (August 26, 1995). ... Signed by Washington Redskins (February 16, 1996). ... Released by Redskins (August 25, 1996). ... Re-signed by Redskins to practice squad (August 26, 1996). ... Activated (October 19, 1996). ... Released by Redskins (November 6, 1996). ... Re-signed by Redskins to practice squad (November 7, 1996). ... Activated (November 11, 1996). ... Released by Redskins (August 23, 1997). ... Re-signed by Redskins (September 9, 1997). ... Released by Redskins (August 30, 1998). ... Signed by Cleveland Browns (February 11, 1999).
PLAYING EXPERIENCE: Washington NFL, 1996 and 1997; Cleveland NFL, 1999-2001. ... Games/Games started: 1996 (2/0), 1997 (12/5), 1999 (16/0), 2000 (16/0), 2001 (16/0). Total: 62/5.

KURPEIKIS, JUSTIN — LB — STEELERS

PERSONAL: Born July 17, 1977, in Allison Park, Pa. ... 6-3/254. ... Full name: Justin William Kurpeikis.
HIGH SCHOOL: Central Catholic (Pittsburgh).
COLLEGE: Penn State.
TRANSACTIONS/CAREER NOTES: Signed as non-drafted free agent by Pittsburgh Steelers (April 23, 2001).
PLAYING EXPERIENCE: Pittsburgh NFL, 2001. ... Games/Games started: 2001 (3/0).
CHAMPIONSHIP GAME EXPERIENCE: Played in AFC championship game (2001 season).

KYLE, JASON — LB — PANTHERS

PERSONAL: Born May 12, 1972, in Tempe, Ariz. ... 6-3/242. ... Full name: Jason C. Kyle.
HIGH SCHOOL: McClintock (Tempe, Ariz.).
COLLEGE: Arizona State.
TRANSACTIONS/CAREER NOTES: Selected by Seattle Seahawks in fourth round (126th pick overall) of 1995 NFL draft. ... Signed by Seahawks (July 16, 1995). ... On injured reserve with shoulder injury (August 18, 1997-entire season). ... Granted free agency (February 13, 1998). ... Re-signed by Seahawks (April 16, 1998). ... Selected by Cleveland Browns from Seahawks in NFL expansion draft (February 9, 1999). ... On physically unable to perform list with knee injury (August 26, 1999-entire season). ... Released by Browns (August 27, 2000). ... Signed by St. Louis Rams (October 5, 2000). ... Released by Rams (October 16, 2000). ... Re-signed by Rams (October 24, 2000). ... Released by Rams (October 27, 2000). ... Signed by San Francisco 49ers (October 30, 2000). ... Granted unconditional free agency (March 2, 2001). ... Signed by Carolina Panthers (March 5, 2001).
PLAYING EXPERIENCE: Seattle NFL, 1995, 1996 and 1998; San Francisco NFL, 2000; Carolina NFL, 2001. ... Games/Games started: 1995 (16/0), 1996 (16/0), 1998 (16/0), 2000 (2/0), 2001 (16/0). Total: 66/0.
PRO STATISTICS: 2001—Fumbled once and recovered one fumble for minus 26 yards.

LaBOUNTY, MATT — DT

PERSONAL: Born January 3, 1969, in San Francisco. ... 6-4/275. ... Full name: Matthew James LaBounty.
HIGH SCHOOL: San Marin (Novato, Calif.).
COLLEGE: Oregon.
TRANSACTIONS/CAREER NOTES: Selected by San Francisco 49ers in 12th round (327th pick overall) of 1992 NFL draft. ... Signed by 49ers (July 13, 1992). ... Released by 49ers (August 31, 1992). ... Re-signed by 49ers to practice squad (September 1, 1992). ... Released by 49ers (October 17, 1993). ... Re-signed by 49ers to practice squad (October 20, 1993). ... Activated (December 2, 1993). ... Claimed on waivers by Green Bay Packers (December 8, 1993). ... On injured reserve with back injury (August 23, 1994-entire season). ... Traded by Packers to Seattle Seahawks for S Eugene Robinson (June 27, 1996). ... Granted unconditional free agency (February 13, 1998). ... Re-signed by Seahawks (February 11, 1998). ... Released by Seahawks (September 2, 2001). ... Re-signed by Seahawks (November 28, 2001). ... On injured reserve with shoulder injury (December 18, 2001-remainder of season). ... Released by Seahawks (April 22, 2002).
CHAMPIONSHIP GAME EXPERIENCE: Played in NFC championship game (1995 season).
PRO STATISTICS: 1998—Fumbled once and recovered one fumble for 13 yards.

Year Team	G	GS	SACKS
1992—San Francisco NFL	Did not play.		
1993—San Francisco NFL	6	0	0.0
1994—Green Bay NFL	Did not play.		
1995—Green Bay NFL	14	2	3.0
1996—Seattle NFL	3	0	0.0
1997—Seattle NFL	15	6	3.0
1998—Seattle NFL	16	1	6.0
1999—Seattle NFL	16	1	2.0
2000—Seattle NFL	12	2	0.5
2001—Seattle NFL	2	0	0.0
Pro totals (8 years)	84	12	14.5

LACINA, CORBIN — G — VIKINGS

PERSONAL: Born November 2, 1970, in Mankato, Minn. ... 6-4/314.
HIGH SCHOOL: Cretin-Derham Hall (St. Paul, Minn.).
COLLEGE: Augustana (S.D.).
TRANSACTIONS/CAREER NOTES: Selected by Buffalo Bills in sixth round (167th pick overall) of 1993 NFL draft. ... Signed by Bills (July 12, 1993). ... Released by Bills (August 30, 1993). ... Re-signed by Bills to practice squad (September 1, 1993). ... Activated (December 30, 1993); did not play. ... On injured reserve with foot injury (December 22, 1994-remainder of season). ... On injured reserve with groin injury (November 30, 1996-remainder of season). ... Granted free agency (February 14, 1997). ... Re-signed by Bills (June 12, 1997). ... Granted unconditional free agency (February 13, 1998). ... Signed by Carolina Panthers (February 26, 1998). ... Released by Panthers (June 16, 1999). ... Signed by Minnesota Vikings (June 18, 1999). ... Granted unconditional free agency (March 2, 2001). ... Re-signed by Vikings (June 19, 2001).
PLAYING EXPERIENCE: Buffalo NFL, 1994-1997; Carolina NFL, 1998; Minnesota NFL, 1999-2001. ... Games/Games started: 1994 (11/10), 1995 (16/3), 1996 (12/2), 1997 (16/3), 1998 (10/10), 1999 (14/0), 2000 (15/15), 2001 (11/10). Total: 105/63.
CHAMPIONSHIP GAME EXPERIENCE: Member of Bills for AFC championship game (1993 season); inactive. ... Member of Bills for Super Bowl XXVIII (1993 season); inactive. ... Played in NFC championship game (2000 season).
PRO STATISTICS: 1997—Recovered one fumble. 1998—Recovered one fumble.

LAKE, CARNELL — S

PERSONAL: Born July 15, 1967, in Salt Lake City. ... 6-1/213. ... Full name: Carnell Augustino Lake.
HIGH SCHOOL: Culver City (Calif.).
COLLEGE: UCLA (degree in political science, 1993).

TRANSACTIONS/CAREER NOTES: Selected by Pittsburgh Steelers in second round (34th pick overall) of 1989 NFL draft. ... Signed by Steelers (July 23, 1989). ... Granted free agency (February 1, 1992). ... Re-signed by Steelers (August 21, 1992). ... Granted roster exemption (August 21-28, 1992). ... Designated by Steelers as franchise player (February 15, 1995). ... Granted unconditional free agency (February 12, 1999). ... Signed by Jacksonville Jaguars (February 13, 1999). ... On injured reserve with foot injury (August 18, 2000-entire season). ... Released by Jaguars (September 2, 2001). ... Signed by Baltimore Ravens (September 11, 2001). ... Granted unconditional free agency (March 1, 2002).
CHAMPIONSHIP GAME EXPERIENCE: Played in AFC championship game (1994, 1995, 1997 and 1999 seasons). ... Played in Super Bowl XXX (1995 season).
HONORS: Named linebacker on THE SPORTING NEWS college All-America second team (1987). ... Played in Pro Bowl (1994-1997 and 1999 seasons). ... Named strong safety on THE SPORTING NEWS NFL All-Pro team (1997).
POST SEASON RECORDS: Shares NFL postseason single-game record for most safeties—1 (January 7, 1995, vs. Cleveland).
PRO STATISTICS: 1989—Recovered six fumbles for two yards. 1990—Recovered one fumble. 1992—Recovered one fumble for 12 yards. 1993—Recovered two fumbles. 1994—Recovered one fumble. 1995—Recovered one fumble. 1996—Recovered two fumbles for 85 yards and one touchdown. 1997—Recovered one fumble for 38 yards and a touchdown. 1998—Recovered one fumble for minus two yards. 2001—Returned one punt for no yards, fumbled once and recovered one fumble.

				INTERCEPTIONS			SACKS
Year Team	G	GS	No.	Yds.	Avg.	TD	No.
1989—Pittsburgh NFL	15	15	1	0	0.0	0	1.0
1990—Pittsburgh NFL	16	16	1	0	0.0	0	1.0
1991—Pittsburgh NFL	16	16	0	0	0.0	0	1.0
1992—Pittsburgh NFL	16	16	0	0	0.0	0	2.0
1993—Pittsburgh NFL	14	14	4	31	7.8	0	5.0
1994—Pittsburgh NFL	16	16	1	2	2.0	0	1.0
1995—Pittsburgh NFL	16	16	1	32	32.0	▲1	1.5
1996—Pittsburgh NFL	13	13	1	47	47.0	1	2.0
1997—Pittsburgh NFL	16	16	3	16	5.3	0	6.0
1998—Pittsburgh NFL	16	16	4	33	8.3	1	1.0
1999—Jacksonville NFL	16	16	0	0	0.0	0	3.5
2000—Jacksonville NFL			Did not play.				
2001—Baltimore NFL	15	1	0	0	0.0	0	0.0
Pro totals (12 years)	**185**	**171**	**16**	**161**	**10.1**	**3**	**25.0**

LANDETA, SEAN   P   EAGLES

PERSONAL: Born January 6, 1962, in Baltimore. ... 6-0/215. ... Full name: Sean Edward Landeta.
HIGH SCHOOL: Loch Raven (Baltimore).
COLLEGE: Towson State.
TRANSACTIONS/CAREER NOTES: Selected by Philadelphia Stars in 14th round (161st pick overall) of 1983 USFL draft. ... Signed by Stars (January 24, 1983). ... Stars franchise moved to Baltimore (November 1, 1984). ... Granted free agency (August 1, 1985). ... Signed by New York Giants (August 5, 1985). ... On injured reserve with back injury (September 7, 1988-remainder of season). ... Granted free agency (February 1, 1990). ... Re-signed by Giants (July 23, 1990). ... On injured reserve with knee injury (November 25, 1992-remainder of season). ... Granted unconditional free agency (March 1, 1993). ... Re-signed by Giants (March 18, 1993). ... Released by Giants (November 9, 1993). ... Signed by Los Angeles Rams (November 12, 1993). ... Granted unconditional free agency (February 17, 1994). ... Re-signed by Rams (May 10, 1994). ... Granted unconditional free agency (February 17, 1995). ... Rams franchise moved to St. Louis (April 12, 1995). ... Re-signed by Rams (May 8, 1995). ... Released by Rams (March 18, 1997). ... Signed by Tampa Bay Buccaneers (October 9, 1997). ... Granted unconditional free agency (February 13, 1998). ... Signed by Green Packers (February 26, 1998). ... Granted unconditional free agency (February 12, 1999). ... Signed by Philadelphia Eagles (February 26, 1999). ... Granted unconditional free agency (March 1, 2002). ... Re-signed by Eagles (March 21, 2002).
CHAMPIONSHIP GAME EXPERIENCE: Played in USFL championship game (1983-1985 seasons). ... Played in NFC championship game (1986, 1990 and 2001 seasons). ... Member of Super Bowl championship team (1986 and 1990 seasons).
HONORS: Named punter on THE SPORTING NEWS USFL All-Star team (1983 and 1984). ... Named punter on THE SPORTING NEWS NFL All-Pro team (1986, 1989 and 1990). ... Played in Pro Bowl (1986 and 1990 seasons).
PRO STATISTICS: USFL: 1983—Rushed once for minus five yards, fumbled once and recovered one fumble. 1984—Recovered one fumble. NFL: 1985—Attempted one pass without a completion. 1996—Rushed twice for no yards, fumbled once and recovered one fumble for minus 11 yards. 1999—Fumbled once and recovered one fumble.

			PUNTING			
Year Team	G	No.	Yds.	Avg.	Net avg.	In. 20	Blk.
1983—Philadelphia USFL	18	86	3601	41.9	36.5	31	0
1984—Philadelphia USFL	18	53	2171	41.0	*38.1	18	0
1985—Baltimore USFL	18	65	2718	41.8	33.2	18	0
—New York Giants NFL	16	81	3472	42.9	36.3	20	0
1986—New York Giants NFL	16	79	3539	‡44.8	‡37.1	24	0
1987—New York Giants NFL	12	65	2773	42.7	31.0	13	1
1988—New York Giants NFL	1	6	222	37.0	35.7	1	0
1989—New York Giants NFL	16	70	3019	43.1	*37.7	19	0
1990—New York Giants NFL	16	75	3306	‡44.1	37.2	†24	0
1991—New York Giants NFL	15	64	2768	43.3	35.2	16	0
1992—New York Giants NFL	11	53	2317	43.7	31.5	13	*2
1993—New York Giants NFL	8	33	1390	42.1	35.0	11	1
—Los Angeles Rams NFL	8	42	1825	43.5	32.8	7	0
1994—Los Angeles Rams NFL	16	78	3494	*44.8	34.2	23	0
1995—St. Louis NFL	16	83	3679	‡44.3	36.7	23	0
1996—St. Louis NFL	16	78	3491	44.8	36.1	23	0
1997—Tampa Bay NFL	10	54	2274	42.1	34.1	15	1
1998—Green Bay NFL	16	65	2788	42.9	37.1	30	0
1999—Philadelphia NFL	16	*107	‡4524	42.3	35.1	21	1
2000—Philadelphia NFL	16	86	3635	42.3	36.0	23	0
2001—Philadelphia NFL	16	‡97	4221	43.5	36.4	26	0
USFL totals (3 years)	**54**	**204**	**8490**	**41.6**	**35.9**	**67**	**0**
NFL totals (17 years)	**241**	**1216**	**52737**	**43.4**	**35.5**	**332**	**6**
Pro totals (20 years)	**295**	**1420**	**61227**	**43.1**	**35.5**	**399**	**6**

LANG, KENARD — DE — BROWNS

PERSONAL: Born January 31, 1975, in Orlando. ... 6-4/281. ... Full name: Kenard Dushun Lang.
HIGH SCHOOL: Maynard Evans (Orlando).
COLLEGE: Miami (Fla.).
TRANSACTIONS/CAREER NOTES: Selected by Washington Redskins in first round (17th pick overall) of 1997 NFL draft. ... Signed by Redskins (July 28, 1997). ... Granted unconditional free agency (March 1, 2002). ... Signed by Cleveland Browns (March 5, 2002).
PRO STATISTICS: 1997—Recovered two fumbles. 1999—Recovered one fumble. 2000—Recovered one fumble. 2001—Intercepted one pass for 14 yards and recovered two fumbles for minus three yards.

Year Team	G	GS	SACKS
1997—Washington NFL	11	11	1.5
1998—Washington NFL	16	16	7.0
1999—Washington NFL	16	9	6.0
2000—Washington NFL	16	0	3.0
2001—Washington NFL	16	16	4.0
Pro totals (5 years)	75	52	21.5

LANGFORD, JEVON — DE — BENGALS

PERSONAL: Born February 16, 1974, in Washington, D.C. ... 6-3/270.
HIGH SCHOOL: Bishop Carroll (Washington, D.C.).
COLLEGE: Oklahoma State.
TRANSACTIONS/CAREER NOTES: Selected after junior season by Cincinnati Bengals in fourth round (108th pick overall) of 1996 NFL draft. ... Signed by Bengals (August 5, 1996). ... Granted free agency (February 12, 1999). ... Re-signed by Bengals (May 25, 1999). ... Granted unconditional free agency (February 11, 2000). ... Re-signed by Bengals (May 5, 2000). ... Released by Bengals (September 2, 2001). ... Re-signed by Bengals (September 6, 2001).
PRO STATISTICS: 1996—Recovered one fumble.

Year Team	G	GS	SACKS
1996—Cincinnati NFL	12	3	2.0
1997—Cincinnati NFL	14	0	1.0
1998—Cincinnati NFL	14	1	0.5
1999—Cincinnati NFL	12	7	0.0
2000—Cincinnati NFL	11	3	0.0
2001—Cincinnati NFL	3	0	0.0
Pro totals (6 years)	66	14	3.5

LARRIMORE, KAREEM — CB

PERSONAL: Born April 21, 1976, in Los Angeles. ... 5-11/190. ... Full name: Kareem Maktrel Larrimore.
HIGH SCHOOL: Alain Locke Senior (Los Angeles).
JUNIOR COLLEGE: Cerritos College (Calif.).
COLLEGE: West Texas A&M.
TRANSACTIONS/CAREER NOTES: Selected by Dallas Cowboys in fourth round (109th pick overall) of 2000 NFL draft. ... Signed by Cowboys (July 14, 2000). ... Released by Cowboys (October 23, 2001).
PLAYING EXPERIENCE: Dallas NFL, 2000 and 2001. ... Games/Games started: 2000 (15/4), 2001 (4/2). Total: 19/6.
PRO STATISTICS: 2001—Returned one kickoff for 22 yards.

LARSEN, LEIF — DT — BILLS

PERSONAL: Born April 3, 1975, in Oslo, Norway. ... 6-4/300. ... Name pronounced LIFE.
HIGH SCHOOL: St. Halluard U.G.S. (Tofte, Norway).
COLLEGE: Texas-El Paso.
TRANSACTIONS/CAREER NOTES: Selected by Buffalo Bills in sixth round (194th pick overall) of 2000 NFL draft. ... Signed by Bills (June 20, 2000).

Year Team	G	GS	SACKS
2000—Buffalo NFL	6	0	1.0
2001—Buffalo NFL	9	5	1.0
Pro totals (2 years)	15	5	2.0

LASSITER, KWAMIE — S — CARDINALS

PERSONAL: Born December 3, 1969, in Hampton, Va. ... 6-0/203.
HIGH SCHOOL: Menchville (Newport News, Va.).
JUNIOR COLLEGE: Butler County Community College (Kan.).
COLLEGE: Kansas.
TRANSACTIONS/CAREER NOTES: Signed as non-drafted free agent by Arizona Cardinals (April 28, 1995). ... On injured reserve with ankle injury (October 5, 1995-remainder of season). ... Granted free agency (February 13, 1998). ... Re-signed by Cardinals (May 21, 1998). ... Granted unconditional free agency (February 12, 1999). ... Re-signed by Cardinals (March 9, 1999). ... Granted free agency (March 1, 2002). ... Re-signed by Cardinals (May 1, 2002).
PRO STATISTICS: 1995—Rushed once for one yard. 1997—Credited with three sacks. 1998—Recovered one fumble. 1999—Returned one kickoff for 13 yards and recovered two fumbles. 2000—Recovered one fumble. 2001—Returned three punts for 11 yards and credited with one sack.

Year Team	G	GS	INTERCEPTIONS No.	Yds.	Avg.	TD
1995—Arizona NFL	5	0	0	0	0.0	0
1996—Arizona NFL	14	0	1	20	20.0	0
1997—Arizona NFL	16	1	1	10	10.0	0
1998—Arizona NFL	16	6	‡8	80	10.0	0
1999—Arizona NFL	16	16	2	110	55.0	1
2000—Arizona NFL	16	16	1	11	11.0	0
2001—Arizona NFL	16	16	9	80	8.9	0
Pro totals (7 years)	99	55	22	311	14.1	1

LAW, TY — CB — PATRIOTS

PERSONAL: Born February 10, 1974, in Aliquippa, Pa. ... 5-11/200. ... Full name: Tajuan Law.
HIGH SCHOOL: Aliquippa (Pa.).
COLLEGE: Michigan.
TRANSACTIONS/CAREER NOTES: Selected after junior season by New England Patriots in first round (23rd pick overall) of 1995 NFL draft. ... Signed by Patriots (July 20, 1995). ... On injured reserve with hand injury (December 29, 1999-remainder of season).
CHAMPIONSHIP GAME EXPERIENCE: Played in AFC championship game (1996 and 2001 seasons). ... Played in Super Bowl XXXI (1996 season). ... Member of Super Bowl championship team (2001 season).
HONORS: Named cornerback on The Sporting News NFL All-Pro team (1998). ... Played in Pro Bowl (1998 season). ... Named co-Oustanding Player of Pro Bowl (1998 season).
POST SEASON RECORDS: Shares Super Bowl single-game record for most interceptions returned for touchdown—1 (February 3, 2002 vs. St. Louis Rams).
PRO STATISTICS: 1995—Credited with one sack. 1997—Credited with 1/2 sack, fumbled once and recovered one fumble. 1998—Recovered one fumble for 17 yards. 1999—Credited with 1/2 sack, fumbled once and recovered one fumble. 2001—Credited with one sack.

Year Team	G	GS	INTERCEPTIONS No.	Yds.	Avg.	TD
1995—New England NFL	14	7	3	47	15.7	0
1996—New England NFL	13	12	3	45	15.0	1
1997—New England NFL	16	16	3	70	23.3	0
1998—New England NFL	16	16	*9	133	14.8	1
1999—New England NFL	13	13	2	20	10.0	1
2000—New England NFL	15	15	2	32	16.0	0
2001—New England NFL	16	16	3	91	30.3	†2
Pro totals (7 years)	103	95	25	438	17.5	5

L

LAYNE, GEORGE — FB — FALCONS

PERSONAL: Born October 9, 1978, in Alvin, Texas. ... 5-11/250.
HIGH SCHOOL: Alvin (Texas).
COLLEGE: Texas Christian.
TRANSACTIONS/CAREER NOTES: Selected after junior season by Kansas City Chiefs in fourth round (108th pick overall) of 2001 NFL draft. ... Signed by Chiefs (July 23, 2001). ... Released by Chiefs (September 2, 2001). ... Re-signed by Chiefs to practice squad (September 4, 2001). ... Signed by Atlanta Falcons off Chiefs practice squad (October 2, 2001).
PLAYING EXPERIENCE: Atlanta NFL, 2001. ... Games/Games started: 2001 (2/0).

LEACH, MIKE — FB — BEARS

PERSONAL: Born October 18, 1976, in Lake Hopatcong, N.J. ... 6-2/240.
HIGH SCHOOL: Jefferson Township (N.J.).
COLLEGE: Boston University, then William and Mary.
TRANSACTIONS/CAREER NOTES: Signed as non-drafted free agent by Tennessee Titans (April 20, 2000). ... Released by Titans (October 16, 2001). ... Signed by Chicago Bears (January 10, 2001).
PLAYING EXPERIENCE: Tennessee NFL, 2000 and 2001. ... Games/Games started: 2000 (15/0), 2001 (4/0). Total: 19/0.
PRO STATISTICS: 2000—Returned one kickoff for 10 yards.

LEAF, RYAN — QB — SEAHAWKS

PERSONAL: Born May 15, 1976, in Great Falls, Mont. ... 6-5/248. ... Full name: Ryan David Leaf.
HIGH SCHOOL: Russell (Great Falls, Mont.).
COLLEGE: Washington State.
TRANSACTIONS/CAREER NOTES: Selected after junior season by San Diego Chargers in first round (second pick overall) of 1998 NFL draft. ... Signed by Chargers (July 28, 1998). ... Inactive for 15 games (1999). ... On injured reserve with shoulder injury (December 30, 1999-remainder of season). ... Claimed on waivers by Tampa Bay Buccaneers (March 2, 2001). ... Released by Buccaneers (September 3, 2001). ... Signed by Dallas Cowboys (October 12, 2001). ... Released by Cowboys (May 20, 2002).... Signed by Seattle Seahawks (May 21, 2002).
HONORS: Named quarterback on The Sporting News college All-America first team (1997).
PRO STATISTICS: 1998—Fumbled eight times and recovered two fumbles for minus 18 yards. 2000—Fumbled 12 times and recovered four fumbles for minus 18 yards. 2001—Fumbled four times for minus one yard.
SINGLE GAME HIGHS (regular season): Attempts—52 (October 25, 1998, vs. Seattle); completions—25 (October 25, 1998, vs. Seattle); yards—311 (November 19, 2000, vs. Denver); and touchdown passes—3 (November 19, 2000, vs. Denver).
STATISTICAL PLATEAUS: 300-yard passing games: 2000 (1).
MISCELLANEOUS: Regular-season record as starting NFL quarterback: 4-17 (.190).

					PASSING					RUSHING				TOTALS	
Year Team	G	GS	Att.	Cmp.	Pct.	Yds.	TD	Int.	Avg.	Rat.	Att.	Yds.	Avg.	TD	TD 2pt. Pts.
1998—San Diego NFL	10	9	245	111	45.3	1289	2	15	5.26	39.0	27	80	3.0	0	0 0 0
1999—San Diego NFL							Did not play.								
2000—San Diego NFL	11	9	322	161	50.0	1883	11	18	5.85	56.2	28	54	1.9	0	0 0 0
2001—Dallas NFL	4	3	88	45	51.1	494	1	3	5.61	57.7	4	-7	-1.8	0	0 0 0
Pro totals (3 years)	25	21	655	317	48.4	3666	14	36	5.60	50.0	59	127	2.2	0	0 0 0

LECHLER, SHANE   P   RAIDERS

PERSONAL: Born August 7, 1976, in Sealy, Texas. ... 6-2/225. ... Full name: Edward Shane Lechler.
HIGH SCHOOL: East Bernard (Texas).
COLLEGE: Texas A&M.
TRANSACTIONS/CAREER NOTES: Selected by Oakland Raiders in fifth round (142nd pick overall) of 2000 NFL draft. ... Signed by Raiders (July 22, 2000).
CHAMPIONSHIP GAME EXPERIENCE: Played in AFC championship game (2000 season).
HONORS: Named punter on THE SPORTING NEWS college All-America second team (1997). ... Named punter on THE SPORTING NEWS college All-America first team (1998). ... Named punter on THE SPORTING NEWS NFL All-Pro team (2000). ... Named punter on THE SPORTING NEWS college All-America third team (1999).
PRO STATISTICS: 2000—Missed only field-goal attempt and converted seven extra points. 2001—Rushed once for two yards, fumbled once and recovered one fumble.

			PUNTING				
Year Team	G	No.	Yds.	Avg.	Net avg.	In. 20	Blk.
2000—Oakland NFL	16	65	2984	45.9	*38.0	24	▲1
2001—Oakland NFL	16	73	3375	§46.2	35.6	23	1
Pro totals (2 years)	32	138	6359	46.1	36.7	47	2

LEE, CHARLES   WR   PACKERS

PERSONAL: Born November 19, 1977, in Miami. ... 6-2/205. ... Cousin of Harvey Clayton, defensive back with Pittsburgh Steelers (1983-86) and New York Giants (1987).
HIGH SCHOOL: Homestead (Fla.).
COLLEGE: Central Florida (degree in communications).
TRANSACTIONS/CAREER NOTES: Selected by Green Bay Packers in seventh round (242nd pick overall) of 2000 NFL draft. ... Signed by Packers (June 21, 2000).
PRO STATISTICS: 2000—Returned five punts for 52 yards. 2001—Returned three punts for six yards.
SINGLE GAME HIGHS (regular season): Receptions—3 (September 10, 2000, vs. Buffalo); yards—46 (October 8, 2000, vs. Detroit); and touchdown receptions—1 (October 21, 2001, vs. Minnesota).

			RECEIVING			
Year Team	G	GS	No.	Yds.	Avg.	TD
2000—Green Bay NFL	15	1	10	134	13.4	0
2001—Green Bay NFL	7	0	3	32	10.7	1
Pro totals (2 years)	22	1	13	166	12.8	1

LEGREE, LANCE   DT   GIANTS

PERSONAL: Born December 22, 1977, in Charleston, S.C. ... 6-1/285.
HIGH SCHOOL: St. Stephens (S.C.).
COLLEGE: Notre Dame.
TRANSACTIONS/CAREER NOTES: Signed as non-drafted free agent by New York Giants (April 27, 2001).
PLAYING EXPERIENCE: New York Giants NFL, 2001. ... Games/Games started: 2001 (13/2).
PRO STATISTICS: 2001—Recovered one fumble.

LEHR, MATT   G/C   COWBOYS

PERSONAL: Born April 25, 1979, in Jacksonville. ... 6-2/292. ... Full name: Matthew Steven Lehr.
HIGH SCHOOL: Woodbridge (Va.).
COLLEGE: Virginia Tech.
TRANSACTIONS/CAREER NOTES: Selected by Dallas Cowboys in fifth round (137th pick overall) of 2001 NFL draft. ... Signed by Cowboys (July 21, 2001).
PLAYING EXPERIENCE: Dallas NFL, 2001. ... Games/Games started: 2001 (8/0).

LEPSIS, MATT   OT   BRONCOS

PERSONAL: Born January 13, 1974, in Conroe, Texas. ... 6-4/290. ... Full name: Matthew Lepsis.
HIGH SCHOOL: Frisco (Texas).
COLLEGE: Colorado.
TRANSACTIONS/CAREER NOTES: Signed as non-drafted free agent by Denver Broncos (April 22, 1997). ... On non-football injury list with knee injury (July 16, 1997-entire season). ... Assigned by Broncos to Barcelona Dragons in 1998 NFL Europe enhancement allocation program (February 18, 1998). ... Granted free agency (March 2, 2001). ... Re-signed by Broncos (March 21, 2001).
PLAYING EXPERIENCE: Barcelona NFLE, 1998; Denver NFL, 1998-2001. ... Games/Games started: NFLE 1998 (games played unavailable), NFL 1998 (16/0), 1999 (16/16), 2000 (16/16), 2001 (16/16). Total NFL: 64/48.
CHAMPIONSHIP GAME EXPERIENCE: Played in AFC championship game (1998 season). ... Member of Super Bowl championship team (1998 season).
PRO STATISTICS: 2000—Recovered one fumble.

LETHRIDGE, ZEBBIE — CB — DOLPHINS

PERSONAL: Born January 31, 1975, in Lubbock, Texas. ... 6-0/190.
HIGH SCHOOL: Estacado (Lubbock,Texas).
COLLEGE: Texas Tech.
TRANSACTIONS/CAREER NOTES: Signed as non-drafted free agent by Dallas Cowboys (April 24, 1998). ... Released by Cowboys (August 30, 1998). ... Re-signed by Cowboys to practice squad (September 1, 1998). ... Released by Cowboys (September 4, 1999). ... Signed by Chicago Bears (November 9, 1999). ... Released by Bears (November 19, 1999). ... Re-signed by Bears to practice squad (November 22, 1999). ... Granted free agency following 1999 season. ... Signed by Jacksonville Jaguars (January 12, 2000). ... Assigned by Jaguars to Berlin Thunder in NFL Europe enhancement allocation program (February 18, 2000). ... Released by Jaguars (August 25, 2000). ... Signed by Miami Dolphins (April 26, 2001).
PLAYING EXPERIENCE: Berlin NFLE, 2000; Miami NFL, 2001. ... Games/Games started: 2000 (games played unavailable), 2001 (2/0).

LETT, LEON — DT

PERSONAL: Born October 12, 1968, in Mobile, Ala. ... 6-6/290. ... Full name: Leon Lett Jr.
HIGH SCHOOL: Fairhope (Ala.).
JUNIOR COLLEGE: Hinds Community College (Miss.).
COLLEGE: Emporia (Kan.) State.
TRANSACTIONS/CAREER NOTES: Selected by Dallas Cowboys in seventh round (173rd pick overall) of 1991 NFL draft. ... Signed by Cowboys (July 14, 1991). ... On injured reserve with back injury (August 27-November 21, 1991). ... On suspended list for violating league substance abuse policy (November 3-24, 1995). ... On suspended list for violating league substance abuse policy (December 3, 1996-December 1, 1997). ... On suspended list for violating league substance abuse policy (June 4-November 9, 1999). ... On injured reserve with knee injury (December 14, 2000-remainder of season). ... Granted unconditional free agency (March 2, 2001). ... Signed by Denver Broncos (March 22, 2001). ... Released by Broncos (February 21, 2002).
CHAMPIONSHIP GAME EXPERIENCE: Played in NFC championship game (1992-1995 seasons). ... Member of Super Bowl championship team (1992, 1993 and 1995 seasons).
HONORS: Played in Pro Bowl (1994 and 1998 seasons).
POST SEASON RECORDS: Holds Super Bowl career record for most yards by fumble recovery—64. ... Holds Super Bowl single-game record for most yards by fumble recovery—64 (January 31, 1993).
PRO STATISTICS: 1992—Recovered one fumble. 1993—Fumbled once. 1995—Recovered two fumbles. 1996—Recovered two fumbles. 1999—Recovered two fumbles.

Year — Team	G	GS	SACKS
1991—Dallas NFL	5	0	0.0
1992—Dallas NFL	16	0	3.5
1993—Dallas NFL	11	6	0.0
1994—Dallas NFL	16	16	4.0
1995—Dallas NFL	12	12	3.0
1996—Dallas NFL	13	13	3.5
1997—Dallas NFL	3	3	0.5
1998—Dallas NFL	16	15	4.0
1999—Dallas NFL	8	1	1.5
2000—Dallas NFL	9	7	2.5
2001—Denver NFL	12	0	0.0
Pro totals (11 years)	121	73	22.5

LEVENS, DORSEY — RB

PERSONAL: Born May 21, 1970, in Syracuse, N.Y. ... 6-1/230. ... Full name: Herbert Dorsey Levens.
HIGH SCHOOL: Nottingham (Syracuse, N.Y.).
COLLEGE: Notre Dame, then Georgia Tech (degree in business management).
TRANSACTIONS/CAREER NOTES: Selected by Green Bay Packers in fifth round (149th pick overall) of 1994 NFL draft. ... Signed by Packers (June 9, 1994). ... Granted free agency (February 14, 1997). ... Re-signed by Packers (June 20, 1997). ... Designated by Packers as franchise player (February 13, 1998). ... Re-signed by Packers (August 30, 1998). ... Released by Packers (February 28, 2002).
CHAMPIONSHIP GAME EXPERIENCE: Played in NFC championship game (1995-97 seasons). ... Member of Super Bowl championship team (1996 season). ... Played in Super Bowl XXXII (1997 season).
HONORS: Played in Pro Bowl (1997 season).
PRO STATISTICS: 1996—Recovered one fumble. 1997—Recovered one fumble for minus seven yards.
SINGLE GAME HIGHS (regular season): Attempts—33 (November 23, 1997, vs. Dallas); yards—190 (November 23, 1997, vs. Dallas); and rushing touchdowns—4 (January 2, 2000, vs. Arizona).
STATISTICAL PLATEAUS: 100-yard rushing games: 1997 (6), 1998 (1), 1999 (3). Total: 10.

			RUSHING				RECEIVING				KICKOFF RETURNS				TOTALS			
Year — Team	G	GS	Att.	Yds.	Avg.	TD	No.	Yds.	Avg.	TD	No.	Yds.	Avg.	TD	TD	2pt.	Pts.	Fum.
1994—Green Bay NFL	14	0	5	15	3.0	0	1	9	9.0	0	2	31	15.5	0	0	0	0	0
1995—Green Bay NFL	15	12	36	120	3.3	3	48	434	9.0	4	0	0	0.0	0	7	0	42	0
1996—Green Bay NFL	16	1	121	566	4.7	5	31	226	7.3	5	5	84	16.8	0	10	0	60	2
1997—Green Bay NFL	16	16	329	1435	4.4	7	53	370	7.0	5	0	0	0.0	0	12	1	74	5
1998—Green Bay NFL	7	4	115	378	3.3	1	27	162	6.0	0	0	0	0.0	0	1	0	6	0
1999—Green Bay NFL	14	14	279	1034	3.7	9	71	573	8.1	1	0	0	0.0	0	10	0	60	5
2000—Green Bay NFL	5	5	77	224	2.9	3	16	146	9.1	0	0	0	0.0	0	3	0	18	0
2001—Green Bay NFL	15	1	44	165	3.8	0	24	159	6.6	1	14	362	25.9	0	1	0	6	0
Pro totals (8 years)	102	53	1006	3937	3.9	28	271	2079	7.7	16	21	477	22.7	0	44	1	266	12

LEVERETTE, OTIS — DE — REDSKINS

PERSONAL: Born May 31, 1978, in Americus, Ga. ... 6-6/275. ... Full name: Otis Catrell Leverette.
HIGH SCHOOL: Americus (Ga.).
JUNIOR COLLEGE: Middle Georgia College.
COLLEGE: Alabama-Birmingham.
TRANSACTIONS/CAREER NOTES: Selected by Miami Dolphins in sixth round (187th pick overall) of 2001 NFL draft. ... Signed by Dolphins (July 12, 2001). ... Claimed on waivers by Washington Redskins (September 3, 2001).
PLAYING EXPERIENCE: Washington NFL, 2001. ... Games/Games started: 2001 (4/0).

LEWIS, CHAD — TE — EAGLES

PERSONAL: Born October 5, 1971, in Fort Dix, N.J. ... 6-6/252. ... Full name: Chad Wayne Lewis.
HIGH SCHOOL: Orem (Utah).
COLLEGE: Brigham Young (degrees in communications and Chinese).
TRANSACTIONS/CAREER NOTES: Signed as non-drafted free agent by Philadelphia Eagles (April 23, 1997). ... Released by Eagles (September 15, 1998). ... Signed by St. Louis Rams (December 9, 1998). ... Inactive for three games with Rams (1998). ... Claimed on waivers by Eagles (November 16, 1999). ... Granted free agency (February 11, 2000). ... Re-signed by Eagles (March 17, 2000).
CHAMPIONSHIP GAME EXPERIENCE: Played in NFC championship game (2001 season).
HONORS: Played in Pro Bowl (2000 season).
PRO STATISTICS: 1997—Returned one kickoff for 11 yards. 2001—Ran minus 10 yards with lateral from kickoff return and recovered one fumble.
SINGLE GAME HIGHS (regular season): Receptions—9 (December 24, 2000, vs. Cincinnati); yards—100 (December 10, 2000, vs. Cleveland); and touchdown receptions—2 (December 30, 2001, vs. New York Giants).
STATISTICAL PLATEAUS: 100-yard receiving games: 2000 (1).

			RECEIVING				TOTALS			
Year Team	G	GS	No.	Yds.	Avg.	TD	TD	2pt.	Pts.	Fum.
1997—Philadelphia NFL	16	3	12	94	7.8	4	4	0	24	0
1998—Philadelphia NFL	2	0	0	0	0.0	0	0	0	0	0
1999—St. Louis NFL	6	0	1	12	12.0	0	0	0	0	0
—Philadelphia NFL	6	4	7	76	10.9	3	3	0	18	0
2000—Philadelphia NFL	16	16	69	735	10.7	3	3	0	18	0
2001—Philadelphia NFL	15	15	41	422	10.3	6	6	0	36	2
Pro totals (5 years)	61	38	130	1339	10.3	16	16	0	96	2

LEWIS, DAMIONE — DT — RAMS

PERSONAL: Born March 1, 1978, in Sulphur Springs, Texas. ... 6-2/301. ... Full name: Damione Ramon Lewis.
HIGH SCHOOL: Sulphur Springs (Texas).
COLLEGE: Miami.
TRANSACTIONS/CAREER NOTES: Selected by St. Louis Rams in first round (12th pick overall) of 2001 NFL draft. ... Signed by Rams (July 27, 2001). ... On injured reserve with foot injury (November 20, 2001-remainder of season).
PLAYING EXPERIENCE: St. Louis NFL, 2001. ... Games/Games started: 2001 (9/3).
HONORS: Named defensive tackle on THE SPORTING NEWS college All-America third team (2000).
PRO STATISTICS: 2001—Recovered one fumble.

LEWIS, JAMAL — RB — RAVENS

PERSONAL: Born August 28, 1979, in Atlanta. ... 5-11/231. ... Full name: Jamal Lafitte Lewis.
HIGH SCHOOL: Douglass (Atlanta).
COLLEGE: Tennessee.
TRANSACTIONS/CAREER NOTES: Selected after junior season by Baltimore Ravens in first round (fifth pick overall) of 2000 NFL draft. ... Signed by Ravens (July 24, 2000). ... On injured reserve with knee injury (August 28, 2001-entire season). ... On suspended list for violating league substance abuse policy (November 17, 2001-present).
CHAMPIONSHIP GAME EXPERIENCE: Played in AFC championship game (2000 season). ... Member of Super Bowl championship team (2000 season).
HONORS: Named College Football Freshman of the Year by THE SPORTING NEWS (1997).
PRO STATISTICS: 2000—Recovered three fumbles.
SINGLE GAME HIGHS (regular season): Attempts—30 (November 26, 2000, vs. Cleveland); yards—187 (November 19, 2000, vs. Dallas); and rushing touchdowns—2 (November 26, 2000, vs. Cleveland).
STATISTICAL PLATEAUS: 100-yard rushing games: 2000 (5).

			RUSHING				RECEIVING			TOTALS			
Year Team	G	GS	Att.	Yds.	Avg.	TD	No.	Yds.	Avg.	TD	TD	2pt.	Pts.	Fum.
2000—Baltimore NFL	16	14	309	1364	4.4	6	27	296	11.0	0	6	1	38	6
2001—Baltimore NFL					Did not play.									
Pro totals (1 years)	16	14	309	1364	4.4	6	27	296	11.0	0	6	1	38	6

LEWIS, JERMAINE — WR/PR — TEXANS

PERSONAL: Born October 16, 1974, in Lanham, Md. ... 5-7/180. ... Full name: Jermaine Edward Lewis.
HIGH SCHOOL: Eleanor Roosevelt (Greenbelt, Md.).
COLLEGE: Maryland.

TRANSACTIONS/CAREER NOTES: Selected by Baltimore Ravens in fifth round (153rd pick overall) of 1996 NFL draft. ... Signed by Ravens (July 18, 1996). ... Selected by Houston Texans from Ravens in NFL expansion draft (February 18, 2002).
CHAMPIONSHIP GAME EXPERIENCE: Played in AFC championship game (2000 season). ... Member of Super Bowl championship team (2000 season).
HONORS: Named punt returner on THE SPORTING NEWS NFL All-Pro team (1998 and 2001). ... Played in Pro Bowl (1998 season).
RECORDS: Shares NFL single-game records for most touchdowns by punt returns—2; and most touchdowns by combined kick return—2 (December 7, 1997, vs. Seattle).
PRO STATISTICS: 1996—Fumbled four times and recovered one fumble. 1997—Fumbled three times and recovered two fumbles. 1998—Fumbled three times and recovered three fumbles. 1999—Fumbled once and recovered one fumble. 2000—Attempted one pass with a completion for three yards. 2001—Fumbled twice.
SINGLE GAME HIGHS (regular season): Receptions—8 (September 21, 1997, vs. Tennessee); yards—124 (September 21, 1997, vs. Tennessee); and touchdown receptions—2 (December 5, 1999, vs. Tennessee).
STATISTICAL PLATEAUS: 100-yard receiving games: 1997 (2), 1998 (2). Total: 4.

				RUSHING			RECEIVING				PUNT RETURNS				KICKOFF RETURNS				TOTALS		
Year Team	G	GS	Att.	Yds.	Avg.	TD	No.	Yds.	Avg.	TD	No.	Yds.	Avg.	TD	No.	Yds.	Avg.	TD	TD	2pt.	Pts.
1996—Baltimore NFL	16	1	1	-3	-3.0	0	5	78	15.6	1	36	339	9.4	0	41	883	21.5	0	1	0	6
1997—Baltimore NFL	14	7	3	35	11.7	0	42	648	15.4	6	28	437*15.6		2	41	905	22.1	0	8	0	48
1998—Baltimore NFL	13	13	5	20	4.0	0	41	784	19.1	6	32	405	12.7	†2	6	145	24.2	0	8	0	48
1999—Baltimore NFL	15	6	5	11	2.2	0	25	281	11.2	2	*57	452	7.9	0	8	158	19.8	0	2	0	12
2000—Baltimore NFL	15	1	3	38	12.7	0	19	161	8.5	1	36	578*16.1		†2	1	23	23.0	0	3	0	18
2001—Baltimore NFL	15	2	9	33	3.7	0	4	32	8.0	0	*42	*519	12.4	0	42	1039	24.7	0	0	0	0
Pro totals (6 years)	88	30	26	134	5.2	0	136	1984	14.6	16	231	2730	11.8	6	139	3153	22.7	0	22	0	132

LEWIS, JONAS — RB — 49ERS

PERSONAL: Born December 27, 1976, in Riverside, Calif. ... 5-9/210. ... Full name: Jonas W. Allen Lewis.
HIGH SCHOOL: Beaumont (Calif.).
COLLEGE: San Diego State.
TRANSACTIONS/CAREER NOTES: Signed by San Francisco 49ers as non-drafted free agent (April 24, 2000). ... On injured reserve with groin injury (January 3, 2002-remainder of season).
PLAYING EXPERIENCE: San Francisco NFL, 2000 and 2001. ... Games/Games started: 2000 (10/0), 2001 (1/0). Total: 11/0.
PRO STATISTICS: 2000—Rushed once for six yards, returned nine kickoffs for 168 yards and recovered one fumble. 2001—Returned two kickoffs for 32 yards.
SINGLE GAME HIGHS (regular season): Attempts—1 (September 24, 2000, vs. Dallas); yards—6 (September 24, 2000, vs. Dallas); and rushing touchdowns—0.

LEWIS, KEVIN — LB — GIANTS

PERSONAL: Born October 6, 1978, in Orlando, Fla. ... 6-1/230.
HIGH SCHOOL: Jones (Orlando, Fla.).
COLLEGE: Duke.
TRANSACTIONS/CAREER NOTES: Signed by New York Giants as non-drafted free agent (April 20, 2000). ... Released by Giants (September 2, 2001). ... Re-signed by Giants to practice squad (September 3, 2001). ... Activated (November 4, 2001).
PLAYING EXPERIENCE: New York Giants NFL, 2000 and 2001. ... Games/Games started: 2000 (7/0), 2001 (9/0). Total: 16/0.
CHAMPIONSHIP GAME EXPERIENCE: Member of Giants for Super Bowl XXXV (2000 season); inactive.

LEWIS, MICHAEL — WR — SAINTS

PERSONAL: Born November 14, 1971, in New Orleans. ... 5-8/165. ... Full name: Michael Lee Lewis.
HIGH SCHOOL: Grace King (Metairie, La.).
TRANSACTIONS/CAREER NOTES: Signed as non-drafted free agent by Philadelphia Eagles (July 14, 2000). ... Released by Eagles (August 21, 2000). ... Signed by New Orleans Saints (January 9, 2001). ... Assigned by Saints to Rhein Fire in 2001 NFL Europe enhancement allocation program (February 17, 2001). ... Released by Saints (October 30, 2001). ... Re-signed by Saints (December 21, 2001).
PRO STATISTICS: 2001—Recovered two fumbles.

			RECEIVING				PUNT RETURNS				KICKOFF RETURNS				TOTALS			
Year Team	G	GS	No.	Yds.	Avg.	TD	No.	Yds.	Avg.	TD	No.	Yds.	Avg.	TD	TD	2pt.	Pts.	Fum.
2001—Rhein NFLE	...	...	20	262	13.1	3	2	1	0.5	0	9	185	20.6	0	3	0	18	0
—New Orleans NFL	8	0	0	0	0.0	0	14	81	5.8	0	32	762	23.8	0	0	0	0	6
NFL Europe totals (1 year)	...	...	20	262	13.1	3	2	1	0.5	0	9	185	20.6	0	3	0	18	0
NFL totals (1 year)	8	0	0	0	0.0	0	14	81	5.8	0	32	762	23.8	0	0	0	0	6
Pro totals (2 years)	...	...	20	262	13.1	3	16	82	5.1	0	41	947	23.1	0	3	0	18	6

LEWIS, MO — LB — JETS

PERSONAL: Born October 21, 1969, in Atlanta. ... 6-3/258. ... Full name: Morris C. Lewis.
HIGH SCHOOL: J.C. Murphy (Atlanta).
COLLEGE: Georgia.
TRANSACTIONS/CAREER NOTES: Selected by New York Jets in third round (62nd pick overall) of 1991 NFL draft. ... Signed by Jets (July 18, 1991). ... Designated by Jets as franchise player (February 11, 2000).
CHAMPIONSHIP GAME EXPERIENCE: Played in AFC championship game (1998 season).
HONORS: Played in Pro Bowl (1998-2000 seasons).
PRO STATISTICS: 1991—Recovered one fumble. 1992—Recovered four fumbles for 22 yards. 1994—Recovered one fumble for 11 yards. 1997—Recovered one fumble for 26 yards. 1998—Fumbled once and recovered one fumble. 1999—Recovered one fumble. 2000—Rushed once for three yards and recovered two fumbles. 2001—Recovered two fumbles for 15 yards and a touchdown.

Year Team	G	GS	No.	Yds.	Avg.	TD	No.
1991—New York Jets NFL	16	16	0	0	0.0	0	2.0
1992—New York Jets NFL	16	16	1	1	1.0	0	1.0
1993—New York Jets NFL	16	16	2	4	2.0	0	4.0
1994—New York Jets NFL	16	16	4	106	26.5	2	6.0
1995—New York Jets NFL	16	16	2	22	11.0	▲1	5.0
1996—New York Jets NFL	9	9	0	0	0.0	0	0.5
1997—New York Jets NFL	16	16	1	43	43.0	1	8.0
1998—New York Jets NFL	16	16	1	11	11.0	0	7.0
1999—New York Jets NFL	16	16	0	0	0.0	0	5.5
2000—New York Jets NFL	16	16	1	23	23.0	0	10.0
2001—New York Jets NFL	16	16	1	17	17.0	0	3.0
Pro totals (11 years)	169	169	13	227	17.5	4	52.0

LEWIS, RAY LB RAVENS

PERSONAL: Born May 15, 1975, in Bartow, Fla. ... 6-1/245. ... Full name: Ray Anthony Lewis.
HIGH SCHOOL: Kathleen (Lakeland, Fla.).
COLLEGE: Miami (Fla.).
TRANSACTIONS/CAREER NOTES: Selected after junior season by Baltimore Ravens in first round (26th pick overall) of 1996 NFL draft. ... Signed by Ravens (July 15, 1996).
CHAMPIONSHIP GAME EXPERIENCE: Played in AFC championship game (2000 season). ... Member of Super Bowl championship team (2000 season).
HONORS: Named linebacker on THE SPORTING NEWS college All-America second team (1995). ... Played in Pro Bowl (1997, 1998 and 2000 seasons). ... Named linebacker on THE SPORTING NEWS NFL All-Pro team (1998-2001). ... Named to play in Pro Bowl (1999 season); replaced by Junior Seau due to personal reasons. ... Named Most Valuable Player of Super Bowl XXXV (2000 season).
PRO STATISTICS: 1997—Recovered one fumble. 1999—Credited with a safety and fumbled once. 2000—Recovered three fumbles. 2001—Recovered one fumble.

Year Team	G	GS	No.	Yds.	Avg.	TD	No.
1996—Baltimore NFL	14	13	1	0	0.0	0	2.5
1997—Baltimore NFL	16	16	1	18	18.0	0	4.0
1998—Baltimore NFL	14	14	2	25	12.5	0	3.0
1999—Baltimore NFL	16	16	3	97	32.3	0	3.5
2000—Baltimore NFL	16	16	2	1	0.5	0	3.0
2001—Baltimore NFL	16	16	3	115	38.3	0	3.5
Pro totals (6 years)	92	91	12	256	21.3	0	19.5

LIGHT, MATT OT PATRIOTS

PERSONAL: Born June 23, 1978, in Greenville, Ohio. ... 6-4/305. ... Full name: Matthew Charles Light.
HIGH SCHOOL: Greenville (Ohio).
COLLEGE: Purdue.
TRANSACTIONS/CAREER NOTES: Selected by New England Patriots in second round (48th pick overall) of 2001 NFL draft. ... Signed by Patriots (July 22, 2001).
PLAYING EXPERIENCE: New England NFL, 2001. ... Games/Games started: 2001 (14/12).
CHAMPIONSHIP GAME EXPERIENCE: Played in AFC championship game (2001 season). ... Member of Super Bowl championship team (2001 season).
HONORS: Named offensive tackle on THE SPORTING NEWS college All-America third team (2000).

LINDELL, RIAN K SEAHAWKS

PERSONAL: Born January 20, 1977, in Vancouver, Wash. ... 6-3/226. ... Full name: Rian David Lindell.
HIGH SCHOOL: Mountain View (Vancouver, Wash.).
COLLEGE: Washington State.
TRANSACTIONS/CAREER NOTES: Signed as non-drafted free agent by Seattle Seahawks (September 26, 2000).

Year Team	G	XPM	XPA	FGM	FGA	Lg.	50+	Pts.
2000—Seattle NFL	12	25	25	15	17	52	3-3	70
2001—Seattle NFL	16	33	33	20	32	54	3-5	93
Pro totals (2 years)	28	58	58	35	49	54	6-8	163

LINDSAY, EVERETT OL VIKINGS

PERSONAL: Born September 18, 1970, in Burlington, Iowa. ... 6-4/302. ... Full name: Everett Eric Lindsay.
HIGH SCHOOL: Millbrook (Raleigh, N.C.).
COLLEGE: Mississippi (degree in general business, 1992).
TRANSACTIONS/CAREER NOTES: Selected by Minnesota Vikings in fifth round (133rd pick overall) of 1993 NFL draft. ... Signed by Vikings (July 14, 1993). ... On injured reserve with shoulder injury (December 22, 1993-remainder of season). ... On injured reserve with shoulder injury (August 23, 1994-entire season). ... On physically unable to perform list with knee injury (July 22-August 20, 1996). ... On non-football injury list with knee injury (August 20, 1996-entire season). ... Assigned by Vikings to Barcelona Dragons in 1997 World League enhancement allocation program (February 19, 1997). ... Granted unconditional free agency (February 13, 1998). ... Re-signed by Vikings (February 17, 1998). ... Traded by Vikings to Baltimore Ravens for sixth-round pick (DE Talance Sawyer) in 1999 draft (April 17, 1999). ... Granted free agency (February 11, 2000). ... Signed by Cleveland Browns (February 15, 2000). ... Traded by Browns to Vikings for future draft pick (August 14, 2001).

PLAYING EXPERIENCE: Minnesota NFL, 1993, 1995, 1997 and 1998; Baltimore NFL, 1999; Cleveland NFL, 2000; Minnesota NFL, 2001. ... Games/Games started: 1993 (12/12), 1995 (16/0), 1997 (16/3), 1998 (16/3), 1999 (16/16), 2000 (16/16), 2001 (16/8). Total: 108/58.
CHAMPIONSHIP GAME EXPERIENCE: Played in NFC championship game (1998 season).
HONORS: Named offensive tackle on THE SPORTING NEWS college All-America second team (1992).
PRO STATISTICS: 2000—Recovered one fumble.

LITTLE, EARL DB BROWNS

PERSONAL: Born March 10, 1973, in Miami. ... 6-0/198. ... Full name: Earl Jerome Little.
HIGH SCHOOL: North Miami.
COLLEGE: Michigan, then Miami (Fla.).
TRANSACTIONS/CAREER NOTES: Signed as non-drafted free agent by Miami Dolphins (April 24, 1997). ... Released by Dolphins (August 24, 1997). ... Re-signed by Dolphins to practice squad (August 26, 1997). ... Released by Dolphins (August 29, 1997). ... Signed by New Orleans Saints to practice squad (October 1, 1997). ... Claimed on waivers by Cleveland Browns (October 25, 1999).
PLAYING EXPERIENCE: New Orleans NFL, 1998; New Orleans (1)-Cleveland (9) NFL, 1999; Cleveland NFL, 2000 and 2001. ... Games/Games started: 1998 (16/0), 1999 (N.O.- 1/0; Cle.-9/0; Total: 10/0), 2000 (16/0), 2001 (16/16). Total: 58/16.
PRO STATISTICS: 1998—Returned four kickoffs for 64 yards. 1999—Intercepted one pass for no yards, returned two kickoffs for 34 yards and fumbled once. 2000—Intercepted one pass for seven yards, returned two kickoffs for 20 yards, fumbled once and recovered one fumble. 2001—Intercepted five passes for 33 yards amd credited with one sack.

LITTLE, LEONARD DE RAMS

PERSONAL: Born October 19, 1974, in Asheville, N.C. ... 6-3/257. ... Full name: Leonard Antonio Little.
HIGH SCHOOL: Asheville (N.C.).
JUNIOR COLLEGE: Coffeyville (Kan.) Community College..
COLLEGE: Tennessee (degree in psychology, 1997).
TRANSACTIONS/CAREER NOTES: Selected by St. Louis Rams in third round (65th pick overall) of 1998 NFL draft. ... Signed by Rams (July 2, 1998). ... On non-football injury list for personal reasons (November 17, 1998-November 16, 1999). ... On suspended list for violating league substance abuse policy (July 16-November 9, 1999). ... Granted free agency (March 2, 2001). ... Re-signed by Rams (April 20, 2001). ... Granted unconditional free agency (March 1, 2002). ... Re-signed by Rams (March 3, 2002).
CHAMPIONSHIP GAME EXPERIENCE: Played in NFC championship game (1999 and 2001 seasons). ... Member of Super Bowl championship team (1999 season). ... Played in Super Bowl XXXVI (2001 season).
PRO STATISTICS: 2001—Recovered one fumble.

Year Team	G	GS	SACKS
1998—St. Louis NFL	6	0	0.5
1999—St. Louis NFL	6	0	0.0
2000—St. Louis NFL	14	0	5.0
2001—St. Louis NFL	13	0	14.5
Pro totals (4 years)	39	0	20.0

LIWIENSKI, CHRIS G VIKINGS

PERSONAL: Born August 2, 1975, in Sterling Heights, Mich. ... 6-5/321. ... Name pronounced Loo-win-ski.
HIGH SCHOOL: Stevenson (Sterling Heights, Mich.).
COLLEGE: Indiana.
TRANSACTIONS/CAREER NOTES: Selected by Detroit Lions in seventh round (207th pick overall) of 1998 NFL draft. ... Signed by Lions (July 15, 1998). ... Released by Lions (August 24, 1998). ... Signed by Minnesota Vikings to practice squad (August 31, 1998). ... Activated (November 18, 1998). ... Released by Vikings (September 9, 1999). ... Re-signed by Vikings to practice squad (September 10, 1999). ... Activated (December 10, 1999); did not play.
PLAYING EXPERIENCE: Minnesota NFL, 1998, 2000 and 2001. ... Games/Games started: 1998 (1/0), 1999 (did not play), 2000 (14/1), 2001 (16/16). Total: 31/17.
CHAMPIONSHIP GAME EXPERIENCE: Member of Vikings for NFC championship game (1998 season); inactive. ... Played in NFC championship game (2000 season).

LOCKETT, KEVIN WR REDSKINS

PERSONAL: Born September 4, 1974, in Tulsa, Okla. ... 6-0/187.
HIGH SCHOOL: Washington (Okla.).
COLLEGE: Kansas State (degree in accounting).
TRANSACTIONS/CAREER NOTES: Selected by Kansas City Chiefs in second round (47th pick overall) of 1997 NFL draft. ... Signed by Chiefs (July 25, 1997). ... Granted free agency (February 11, 2000). ... Re-signed by Chiefs (May 3, 2000) ... Granted unconditional free agency (March 2, 2001). ... Signed by Washington Redskins (April 9, 2001).
PRO STATISTICS: 1998—Recovered two fumbles. 2000—Returned one kickoff for 25 yards and recovered one fumble. 2001—Completed only pass attempt for 31 yards and a touchdown.
SINGLE GAME HIGHS (regular season): Receptions—7 (November 5, 2000, vs. Oakland); yards—77 (October 29, 2000, vs. Seattle); and touchdown receptions—1 (December 4, 2000, vs. New England).

			RECEIVING				PUNT RETURNS				TOTALS		
Year Team	G	GS	No.	Yds.	Avg.	TD	No.	Yds.	Avg.	TD	2pt.	Pts.	Fum.
1997—Kansas City NFL	9	0	1	35	35.0	0	0	0	0.0	0	0	0	0
1998—Kansas City NFL	13	3	19	281	14.8	0	7	36	5.1	0	0	0	2
1999—Kansas City NFL	16	1	34	426	12.5	2	1	10	10.0	0	2	12	0
2000—Kansas City NFL	16	2	33	422	12.8	2	26	208	8.0	0	2	12	3
2001—Washington NFL	16	0	22	293	13.3	0	5	14	2.8	0	0	0	1
Pro totals (5 years)	70	6	109	1457	13.4	4	39	268	6.9	0	4	24	6

LOGAN, MIKE — DB — STEELERS

PERSONAL: Born September 15, 1974, in Pittsburgh. ... 6-1/209. ... Full name: Michael V. Logan.
HIGH SCHOOL: McKeesport (Pa.).
COLLEGE: West Virginia.
TRANSACTIONS/CAREER NOTES: Selected by Jacksonville Jaguars in second round (50th pick overall) of 1997 NFL draft. ... Signed by Jaguars (May 23, 1997). ... On injured reserve with ankle injury (September 20, 1999-remainder of season). ... Granted free agency (February 11, 2000). ... Re-signed by Jaguars (March 10, 2000). ... Granted unconditional free agency (March 2, 2001). ... Signed by Pittsburgh Steelers (March 24, 2001).
CHAMPIONSHIP GAME EXPERIENCE: Played in AFC championship game (2001 season).
PRO STATISTICS: 1998—Recovered one fumble for two yards. 2000—Intercepted two passes for 14 yards and recovered one fumble for three yards. 2001—Intercepted two passes for two yards, credited with two sacks and recovered two fumbles for 14 yards.

			PUNT RETURNS				KICKOFF RETURNS				TOTALS		
Year Team	G	GS	No.	Yds.	Avg.	TD	No.	Yds.	Avg.	TD	TD	2pt.	Pts.	Fum.
1997—Jacksonville NFL	11	0	0	0	0.0	0	10	236	23.6	0	0	0	0	0
1998—Jacksonville NFL	15	0	2	26	13.0	0	18	414	23.0	0	0	0	0	1
1999—Jacksonville NFL	2	0	1	7	7.0	0	1	25	25.0	0	0	0	0	0
2000—Jacksonville NFL	15	11	0	0	0.0	0	0	0	0.0	0	0	0	0	0
2001—Pittsburgh NFL	16	1	0	0	0.0	0	1	9	9.0	0	0	0	0	0
Pro totals (5 years)	59	12	3	33	11.0	0	30	684	22.8	0	0	0	0	1

LONG, KEVIN — C

PERSONAL: Born May 2, 1975, in Summerville, S.C. ... 6-5/295. ... Full name: Kevin Dale Long.
HIGH SCHOOL: Summerville (S.C.).
COLLEGE: Florida State.
TRANSACTIONS/CAREER NOTES: Selected by Tennessee Oilers in seventh round (229th pick overall) of 1998 NFL draft. ... Signed by Oilers (July 2, 1998). ... Oilers franchise renamed Tennessee Titans for 1999 season (December 26, 1998). ... Granted unconditional free agency (March 1, 2002).
PLAYING EXPERIENCE: Tennessee NFL, 1998-2001. ... Games/Games started: 1998 (16/2), 1999 (16/12), 2000 (16/16), 2001 (15/5). Total: 63/35.
CHAMPIONSHIP GAME EXPERIENCE: Played in AFC championship game (1999 season). ... Played in Super Bowl XXXIV (1999 season).
PRO STATISTICS: 1999—Fumbled once for minus 10 yards. 2000—Recovered one fumble. 2001—Returned one kickoff for 10 yards and recovered one fumble.

LONGWELL, RYAN — K — PACKERS

PERSONAL: Born August 16, 1974, in Seattle. ... 6-0/200. ... Full name: Ryan Walker Longwell.
HIGH SCHOOL: Bend (Ore.).
COLLEGE: California (degree in English).
TRANSACTIONS/CAREER NOTES: Signed as non-drafted free agent by San Francisco 49ers (April 28, 1997). ... Claimed on waivers by Green Bay Packers (July 10, 1997).
CHAMPIONSHIP GAME EXPERIENCE: Played in NFC championship game (1997 season). ... Played in Super Bowl XXXII (1997 season).
PRO STATISTICS: 1999—Punted once for 19 yards. 2000—Punted once for 30 yards.

		KICKING						
Year Team	G	XPM	XPA	FGM	FGA	Lg.	50+	Pts.
1997—Green Bay NFL	16	*48	*48	24	30	50	1-1	120
1998—Green Bay NFL	16	41	43	29	33	45	0-1	128
1999—Green Bay NFL	16	38	38	25	30	50	1-2	113
2000—Green Bay NFL	16	32	32	‡33	‡38	52	3-5	131
2001—Green Bay NFL	16	44	45	20	31	54	1-3	104
Pro totals (5 years)	80	203	206	131	162	54	6-12	596

LOVERNE, DAVID — G — REDSKINS

PERSONAL: Born May 22, 1976, in San Ramon, Calif. ... 6-3/299. ... Name pronounced LAH-vern.
HIGH SCHOOL: De La Salle (Concord, Calif.).
COLLEGE: Idaho, then San Jose State.
TRANSACTIONS/CAREER NOTES: Selected by New York Jets in third round (90th pick overall) of 1999 NFL draft. ... Signed by Jets (July 1, 1999). ... Inactive for all 16 games (1999). ... Granted free agency (March 1, 2002). ... Re-signed by Jets (April 6, 2002). ... Traded by Jets with undisclosed draft pick to Washington Redskins for undisclosed draft pick (April 6, 2002).
PLAYING EXPERIENCE: New York Jets NFL, 2000 and 2001. ... Games/Games started: 2000 (16/0), 2001 (16/0). Total: 32/0.
PRO STATISTICS: 2000—Recovered one fumble.

LUCAS, ALBERT — DT

PERSONAL: Born September 1, 1978, in Macon, Ga. ... 6-1/294.
HIGH SCHOOL: Northeast (Macon, Ga.).
COLLEGE: Troy State.
TRANSACTIONS/CAREER NOTES: Signed as non-drafted free agent by Pittsburgh Steelers (April 21, 2000). ... Released by Steelers (August 27, 2000). ... Signed by Carolina Panthers to practice squad (September 20, 2000). ... Activated (September 30, 2000). ... On physically unable to perform list with back injury (September 1-November 10, 2001). ... Granted free agency (March 1, 2002).
PLAYING EXPERIENCE: Carolina NFL, 2000 and 2001. ... Games/Games started: 2000 (13/0), 2001 (7/0). Total: 20/0.
PRO STATISTICS: 2000—Recovered one fumble. 2001—Credited with one sack.

LUCAS, JUSTIN DB CARDINALS

PERSONAL: Born July 15, 1976, in Victoria, Texas. ... 5-10/197.
HIGH SCHOOL: Stroman (Victoria, Texas).
COLLEGE: Texas A&M, then Abilene Christian (degree in industrial technology).
TRANSACTIONS/CAREER NOTES: Signed as non-drafted free agent by Arizona Cardinals (April 23, 1999). ... Released by Cardinals (September 5, 1999). ... Re-signed by Cardinals to practice squad (September 7, 1999). ... Activated (October 17, 1999). ... Released by Cardinals (October 19, 1999). ... Re-signed by Cardinals to practice squad (October 20, 1999). ... Activated (December 31, 1999).
PLAYING EXPERIENCE: Arizona NFL, 1999-2001. ... Games/Games started: 1999 (2/0), 2000 (16/0), 2001 (13/4). Total: 31/4.

LUCAS, KEN CB SEAHAWKS

PERSONAL: Born January 23, 1979, in Cleveland, Miss. ... 6-0/203.
HIGH SCHOOL: East Side (Cleveland, Miss.).
COLLEGE: Mississippi.
TRANSACTIONS/CAREER NOTES: Selected by Seattle Seahawks in second round (40th pick overall) of 2001 NFL draft. ... Signed by Seahawks (July 26, 2001).
PRO STATISTICS: 2001—Recovered one fumble.

			INTERCEPTIONS		
Year Team	G	GS	No.	Yds.	Avg.	TD
2001—Seattle NFL	16	8	1	0	0.0	0

LUCAS, RAY QB DOLPHINS

PERSONAL: Born August 6, 1972, in Harrison, N.J. ... 6-3/225.
HIGH SCHOOL: Harrison (N.J.).
COLLEGE: Rutgers.
TRANSACTIONS/CAREER NOTES: Signed as non-drafted free agent by New England Patriots (May 1, 1996). ... Released by Patriots (August 25, 1996). ... Re-signed by Patriots to practice squad (August 27, 1996). ... Activated (December 12, 1996). ... Claimed on waivers by New York Jets (August 19, 1997). ... Released by Jets (August 24, 1997). ... Re-signed by Jets to practice squad (August 26, 1997). ... Activated (November 22, 1997). ... Granted free agency (March 2, 2001). ... Tendered offer sheet by Miami Dolphins (March 9, 2001). ... Jets declined to match offer (March 16, 2001).
CHAMPIONSHIP GAME EXPERIENCE: Played in AFC championship game (1996 season). ... Played in Super Bowl XXXI (1996 season). ... Member of Jets for AFC championship game (1998 season); did not play.
PRO STATISTICS: 1999—Fumbled eight times and recovered four fumbles for minus 28 yards. 2000—Fumbled twice and recovered one fumble.
SINGLE GAME HIGHS (regular season): Attempts—48 (December 5, 1999, vs. New York Giants); completions—31 (December 5, 1999, vs. New York Giants); yards—284 (December 5, 1999, vs. New York Giants); and touchdown passes—4 (December 5, 1999, vs. New York Giants).
MISCELLANEOUS: Regular-season record as starting NFL quarterback: 6-3 (.667).

			PASSING							RUSHING				TOTALS		
Year Team	G	GS	Att.	Cmp.	Pct.	Yds.	TD	Int.	Avg.	Rat.	Att.	Yds.	Avg.	TD	TD	2pt.	Pts.
1996—New England NFL	2	0	0	0	0.0	0	0	0	0.0	...	0	0	0.0	0	0	0	0
1997—New York Jets NFL	5	0	4	3	75.0	28	0	1	7.00	54.2	6	55	9.2	0	0	0	0
1998—New York Jets NFL	15	0	3	1	33.3	27	0	0	9.00	67.4	5	23	4.6	0	0	0	0
1999—New York Jets NFL	9	9	272	161	59.2	1678	14	6	6.17	85.1	41	144	3.5	1	1	0	6
2000—New York Jets NFL	6	0	41	21	51.2	206	0	4	5.02	26.1	6	42	7.0	0	0	0	0
2001—Miami NFL	10	0	3	2	66.7	45	0	0	15.00	109.7	8	6	0.8	1	1	0	6
Pro totals (6 years)	47	9	323	188	58.2	1984	14	11	6.14	76.4	66	270	4.1	2	2	0	12

LUCKY, MIKE TE COWBOYS

PERSONAL: Born November 23, 1975, in Antioch, Calif. ... 6-6/273. ... Full name: Michael Thomas Lucky.
HIGH SCHOOL: Antioch (Calif.).
COLLEGE: Arizona (degree in political science).
TRANSACTIONS/CAREER NOTES: Selected by Dallas Cowboys in seventh round (229th pick overall) of 1999 NFL draft. ... Signed by Cowboys (July 22, 1999). ... On injured reserve with knee injury (August 1, 2000-remainder of season). ... On physically unable to perform list with knee injury (July 22-August 14, 2001). ... Granted free agency (March 1, 2002). ... Re-signed by Cowboys (April 23, 2002).
PLAYING EXPERIENCE: Dallas NFL, 1999 and 2001. ... Games/Games started: 1999 (14/4), 2001 (16/5). Total: 30/11.
PRO STATISTICS: 1999—Caught five passes for 25 yards. 2001—Caught 13 passes for 96 yards and one touchdown.
SINGLE GAME HIGHS (regular season): Receptions—2 (December 23, 2001, vs. Arizona); yards—29 (December 23, 2001, vs. Arizona); and touchdown receptions—1 (September 23, 2001, vs. San Diego).

LYGHT, TODD CB LIONS

PERSONAL: Born February 9, 1969, in Kwajalein, Marshall Islands. ... 6-0/190. ... Full name: Todd William Lyght.
HIGH SCHOOL: Luke M. Powers Catholic (Flint, Mich.).
COLLEGE: Notre Dame.
TRANSACTIONS/CAREER NOTES: Selected by Los Angeles Rams in first round (fifth pick overall) of 1991 NFL draft. ... Signed by Rams (August 16, 1991). ... On injured reserve with shoulder injury (September 22-October 22, 1992). ... On injured reserve with knee injury (November 23, 1993-remainder of season). ... Designated by Rams as transition player (February 15, 1994). ... Rams franchise moved to St. Louis (April 12, 1995). ... Tendered offer sheet by Jacksonville Jaguars (April 12, 1996). ... Offer matched by Rams (April 15, 1996). ... Designated by Rams as transition player (February 11, 2000). ... Granted unconditional free agency (March 2, 2001). ... Signed by Detroit Lions (April 12, 2001).

CHAMPIONSHIP GAME EXPERIENCE: Played in NFC championship game (1999 season). ... Member of Super Bowl championship team (1999 season).
HONORS: Named defensive back on THE SPORTING NEWS college All-America first team (1989). ... Named defensive back on THE SPORTING NEWS college All-America second team (1990). ... Played in Pro Bowl (1999 season).
PRO STATISTICS: 1991—Fumbled once and recovered one fumble. 1993—Recovered one fumble for 13 yards. 1994—Returned one punt for 29 yards and recovered one fumble for 74 yards and a touchdown. 1995—Ran 16 yards with lateral from punt return. 1996—Fumbled once. 1997—Recovered two fumbles. 2000—Ran 16 yards with lateral from punt return. 2001—Recovered one fumble.

				INTERCEPTIONS				SACKS
Year	Team	G	GS	No.	Yds.	Avg.	TD	No.
1991—Los Angeles Rams NFL		12	8	1	0	0.0	0	0.0
1992—Los Angeles Rams NFL		12	12	3	80	26.7	0	0.0
1993—Los Angeles Rams NFL		9	9	2	0	0.0	0	0.0
1994—Los Angeles Rams NFL		16	16	1	14	14.0	0	0.0
1995—St. Louis NFL		16	16	4	34	8.5	1	0.0
1996—St. Louis NFL		16	16	5	43	8.6	1	0.0
1997—St. Louis NFL		16	16	4	25	6.3	0	1.0
1998—St. Louis NFL		16	16	3	30	10.0	0	1.5
1999—St. Louis NFL		16	16	6	112	18.7	1	2.5
2000—St. Louis NFL		14	12	2	21	10.5	0	1.0
2001—Detroit NFL		16	16	4	72	18.0	1	0.0
Pro totals (11 years)		159	153	35	431	12.3	4	6.0

LYLE, KEITH — S — FALCONS

PERSONAL: Born April 17, 1972, in Washington, D.C. ... 6-2/210. ... Full name: Keith Allen Lyle. ... Son of Garry Lyle, free safety/running back with Chicago Bears (1968-74).
HIGH SCHOOL: Mendon (N.Y.), then George C. Marshall (Falls Church, Va.).
COLLEGE: Virginia (degree in psychology, 1993).
TRANSACTIONS/CAREER NOTES: Selected by Los Angeles Rams in third round (71st pick overall) of 1994 NFL draft. ... Signed by Rams (July 8, 1994). ... Rams franchise moved to St. Louis (April 12, 1995). ... Granted free agency (February 14, 1997). ... Re-signed by Rams (April 15, 1997). ... Released by Rams (March 22, 2001). ... Signed by Washington Redskins (August 21, 2001). ... Granted unconditional free agency (March 1, 2002). ... Signed by Atlanta Falcons (April 8, 2002).
CHAMPIONSHIP GAME EXPERIENCE: Played in NFC championship game (1999 season). ... Member of Super Bowl championship team (1999 season).
PRO STATISTICS: 1995—Rushed once for four yards. 1996—Rushed three times for 39 yards and fumbled once. 2000—Rushed once for four yards and recovered one fumble for 94 yards and a touchdown.

				INTERCEPTIONS				SACKS
Year	Team	G	GS	No.	Yds.	Avg.	TD	No.
1994—Los Angeles Rams NFL		16	0	2	1	0.5	0	0.0
1995—St. Louis NFL		16	16	3	42	14.0	0	0.0
1996—St. Louis NFL		16	16	†9	‡152	16.9	0	0.0
1997—St. Louis NFL		16	16	8	102	12.8	0	2.0
1998—St. Louis NFL		16	16	3	20	6.7	0	1.0
1999—St. Louis NFL		9	9	2	10	5.0	0	1.0
2000—St. Louis NFL		16	16	1	9	9.0	0	0.0
2001—Washington NFL		16	0	1	0	0.0	0	1.0
Pro totals (8 years)		121	89	29	336	11.6	0	5.0

LYLE, RICK — DE/DT — PATRIOTS

PERSONAL: Born February 26, 1971, in Monroe, La. ... 6-5/290. ... Full name: Rick James Earl Lyle.
HIGH SCHOOL: Hickman Mills (Kansas City, Mo.).
COLLEGE: Missouri (degree in parks, recreation and tourism).
TRANSACTIONS/CAREER NOTES: Signed as non-drafted free agent by Cleveland Browns (May 2, 1994). ... On injured reserve with back injury (September 2, 1995-entire season). ... Browns franchise moved to Baltimore and renamed Ravens for 1996 season (March 11, 1996). ... Granted unconditional free agency (February 14, 1997). ... Signed by New York Jets (March 24, 1997). ... Granted unconditional free agency (March 2, 2001). ... Re-signed by Jets (May 14, 2001). ... Granted unconditional free agency (March 1, 2002). ... Signed by New England Patriots (March 12, 2002).
PLAYING EXPERIENCE: Cleveland NFL, 1994; Baltimore NFL, 1996; New York Jets NFL, 1997-2001. ... Games/Games started: 1994 (3/0), 1996 (11/3), 1997 (16/16), 1998 (16/16), 1999 (16/16), 2000 (14/14), 2001 (16/3). Total: 89/68.
CHAMPIONSHIP GAME EXPERIENCE: Played in AFC championship game (1998 season).
PRO STATISTICS: 1996—Credited with one sack. 1997—Credited with three sacks and recovered one fumble for two yards. 1998—Credited with 1$\frac{1}{2}$ sacks. 1999—Credited with one sack. 2000—Credited with one sack. 2001—Credited with 3$\frac{1}{2}$ sacks and recovered one fumble.

LYMAN, DUSTIN — TE — BEARS

PERSONAL: Born August 5, 1976, in Boulder, Colo. ... 6-4/249.
HIGH SCHOOL: Fairview (Boulder, Colo.).
COLLEGE: Wake Forest.
TRANSACTIONS/CAREER NOTES: Selected by Chicago Bears in third round (87th pick overall) of 2000 NFL draft. ... Signed by Bears (June 15, 2000).
PLAYING EXPERIENCE: Chicago NFL, 2000 and 2001. ... Games/Games started: 2000 (14/7). 2001 (4/0). Total: 18/7.
PRO STATISTICS: 2000—Caught one pass for four yards.
SINGLE GAME HIGHS (regular season): Receptions—1 (December 17, 2000, vs. San Francisco); yards—4 (December 17, 2000, vs. San Francisco); and touchdown receptions—0.

LYNCH, BEN — C

PERSONAL: Born November 18, 1972, in Santa Rosa, Calif. ... 6-4/295. ... Full name: Benjamin John Lynch.
HIGH SCHOOL: Analy (Sebastopol, Calif.).
COLLEGE: California.
TRANSACTIONS/CAREER NOTES: Selected by Kansas City Chiefs in seventh round (211th pick overall) of 1996 NFL draft. ... Signed by Chiefs (July 24, 1996). ... Released by Chiefs (August 20, 1996). ... Signed by Minnesota Vikings (February 10, 1997). ... Released by Vikings (August 18, 1997). ... Re-signed by Vikings to practice squad (December 11, 1997). ... Activated (December 30, 1997); did not play. ... Granted free agency (February 13, 1998). ... Selected by Frankfurt Galaxy in 1998 NFL Europe draft (February 18, 1998). ... Signed by Chicago Bears (July 1, 1998). ... On injured reserve with ankle injury (August 5-12, 1998). ... Released by Bears (August 12, 1998). ... Signed by San Francisco 49ers (May 4, 1999). ... Granted free agency (March 1, 2002).
PLAYING EXPERIENCE: Frankfurt NFL E, 1998; San Francisco NFL, 1999-2001. ... Games/Games started: 1998 (games played unavailable), 1999 (16/1), 2000 (11/0), 2001 (11/1). Total: 38/2.
PRO STATISTICS: 1999—Returned one kickoff for four yards.

LYNCH, JOHN — S — BUCCANEERS

PERSONAL: Born September 25, 1971, in Hinsdale, Ill. ... 6-2/220. ... Full name: John Terrence Lynch. ... Son of John Lynch, linebacker with Pittsburgh Steelers (1969); brother-in-law of John Allred, tight end, with Chicago Bears (1997-2000); and brother of Ryan Lynch, pitcher in Baltimore Orioles organization.
HIGH SCHOOL: Torrey Pines (Encinitas, Calif.).
COLLEGE: Stanford.
TRANSACTIONS/CAREER NOTES: Selected by Tampa Bay Buccaneers in third round (82nd pick overall) of 1993 NFL draft. ... Signed by Buccaneers (June 1, 1993). ... On injured reserve with knee injury (December 12, 1995-remainder of season). ... Granted free agency (February 16, 1996). ... Re-signed by Buccaneers (July 13, 1996).
CHAMPIONSHIP GAME EXPERIENCE: Played in NFC championship game (1999 season).
HONORS: Played in Pro Bowl (1997, 1999 and 2000 seasons). ... Named safety on The Sporting News NFL All-Pro team (1999 and 2000).
PRO STATISTICS: 1996—Rushed once for 40 yards, credited with one sack, fumbled once and recovered one fumble. 1997—Recovered two fumbles. 1998—Credited with two sacks and recovered one fumble. 1999—Credited with $1/2$ sack. 2000—Credited with one sack and recovered two fumbles for eight yards. 2001—Credited with one sack and recovered one fumble.

			INTERCEPTIONS			
Year Team	G	GS	No.	Yds.	Avg.	TD
1993—Tampa Bay NFL	15	4	0	0	0.0	0
1994—Tampa Bay NFL	16	0	0	0	0.0	0
1995—Tampa Bay NFL	9	6	3	3	1.0	0
1996—Tampa Bay NFL	16	14	3	26	8.7	0
1997—Tampa Bay NFL	16	16	2	28	14.0	0
1998—Tampa Bay NFL	15	15	2	29	14.5	0
1999—Tampa Bay NFL	16	16	2	32	16.0	0
2000—Tampa Bay NFL	16	16	3	43	14.3	0
2001—Tampa Bay NFL	16	16	3	21	7.0	0
Pro totals (9 years)	135	103	18	182	10.1	0

RECORD AS BASEBALL PLAYER

TRANSACTIONS/CAREER NOTES: Threw right, batted right. ... Selected by Florida Marlins organization in second round (66th pick overall) of free-agent draft (June 1, 1992).

					PITCHING TOTALS							
Year Team (League)	W	L	Pct.	ERA	G	GS	CG	ShO	Sv.	IP	H	R	ER	BB	SO
1992—Erie (N.Y.-Penn.)	0	3	.000	2.15	7	7	0	0	0	$29^{1}/_{3}$	24	15	7	17	16
1993—Kane County (Midwest)	1	0	1.000	3.00	2	2	0	0	0	9	4	4	3	12	3

LYON, BILLY — DE/DT — PACKERS

PERSONAL: Born December 10, 1973, in Ashland, Ky. ... 6-5/295. ... Full name: William Morton Lyon.
HIGH SCHOOL: Lloyd (Erlanger, Ky.).
COLLEGE: Marshall (degree in occupational safety).
TRANSACTIONS/CAREER NOTES: Signed as non-drafted free agent by Kansas City Chiefs (April 28, 1997). ... Released by Chiefs (August 15, 1997). ... Signed by Green Bay Packers to practice squad (November 20, 1997)
PLAYING EXPERIENCE: Green Bay NFL, 1998-2001. ... Games/Games started: 1998 (4/0), 1999 (16/4), 2000 (11/1), 2001 (12/0). Total: 43/5.
PRO STATISTICS: 1998—Credited with one sack. 1999—Intercepted one pass for no yards and credited with two sacks. 2000—Credited with one sack. 2001—Credited with two sacks.

LYTLE, MATT — QB

PERSONAL: Born September 4, 1975, in Wyomissing, Pa. ... 6-4/225.
HIGH SCHOOL: Wyomissing (Pa.).
COLLEGE: Pittsburgh.
TRANSACTIONS/CAREER NOTES: Signed as non-drafted free agent by Seattle Seahawks (August 28, 2000). ... Released by Seahawks (November 21, 2000). ... Re-signed by Seahawks to practice sqaud (November 23, 2000). ... Signed by Carolina Panthers off Seahawks practice squad (December 3, 2000). ... Granted free agency (March 2, 2002).
SINGLE GAME HIGHS (regular season): Attempts—25 (November 11, 2001, vs. St. Louis); completions—15 (November 11, 2001, vs. St. Louis); yards—126 (November 11, 2001, vs. St. Louis); and touchdown passes—1 (November 11, 2001, vs. St. Louis).
MISCELLANEOUS: Regular-season record as starting NFL quarterback: 0-1.

					PASSING						RUSHING			TOTALS		
Year Team	G	GS	Att.	Cmp.	Pct.	Yds.	TD	Int.	Avg.	Rat.	Att.	Yds.	Avg.	TD	TD	2pt.	Pts.
2000—Seattle NFL	1	0	0	0	0.0	0	0	0	0.0	...	0	0	0.0	0	0	0	0
2001—Carolina NFL	3	1	30	17	56.7	133	1	3	4.43	39.3	2	8	4.0	0	0	0	0
Pro totals (2 years)	4	1	30	17	56.7	133	1	3	4.43	39.3	2	8	4.0	0	0	0	0

MACHADO, J.P. C/G JETS

PERSONAL: Born January 6, 1976, in Monmouth, Ill. ... 6-4/300.
HIGH SCHOOL: Monmouth (Ill.).
COLLEGE: Illinois.
TRANSACTIONS/CAREER NOTES: Selected by New York Jets in sixth round (197th pick overall) of 1999 NFL draft. ... Signed by Jets (July 27, 1999).
PLAYING EXPERIENCE: New York Jets NFL, 1999-2001. ... Games/Games started: 1999 (5/0), 2000 (16/0), 2001 (16/3). Total: 37/3.
PRO STATISTICS: 1999—Recovered one fumble.

MACK, STACEY FB JAGUARS

PERSONAL: Born June 26, 1975, in Orlando, Fla. ... 6-1/237. ... Full name: Stacey Lamar Mack.
HIGH SCHOOL: Boone (Orlando, Fla.).
JUNIOR COLLEGE: Southwest Mississippi College.
COLLEGE: Temple.
TRANSACTIONS/CAREER NOTES: Signed as non-drafted free agent by Jacksonville Jaguars (April 22, 1999). ... On injured reserve with finger injury (October 12, 2000-remainder of season). ... Granted free agency (March 1, 2002).
CHAMPIONSHIP GAME EXPERIENCE: Member of Jaguars for AFC championship game (1999 season); inactive.
PRO STATISTICS: 1999—Returned six kickoffs for 112 yards. 2000—Returned six kickoffs for 104 yards and recovered one fumble. 2001—Returned two kickoffs for 49 yards and recovered two fumbles.
SINGLE GAME HIGHS (regular season): Attempts—28 (December 16, 2001, vs. Cleveland); yards—125 (December 30, 2001, vs. Kansas City); and rushing touchdowns—2 (December 23, 2001, vs. Minnesota).
STATISTICAL PLATEAUS: 100-yard rushing games: 2001 (3).

			RUSHING				RECEIVING				TOTALS		
Year Team	G	GS	Att.	Yds.	Avg.	TD	No.	Yds.	Avg.	TD	2pt.	Pts.	Fum.
1999—Jacksonville NFL	12	0	7	40	5.7	0	0	0	0.0	0	0	0	0
2000—Jacksonville NFL	6	2	54	145	2.7	1	0	0	0.0	0	1	0	6	3
2001—Jacksonville NFL	16	11	213	877	4.1	9	23	165	7.2	1	10	0	60	3
Pro totals (3 years)	34	13	274	1062	3.9	10	23	165	7.2	1	11	0	66	6

MACKEY, LOUIS LB COWBOYS

PERSONAL: Born December 29, 1977, in Richmond, Calif. ... 6-1/225.
HIGH SCHOOL: Richmond (Calif.), then Albany (Calif.).
JUNIOR COLLEGE: Gavilan Junior College (Calif.).
COLLEGE: Akron.
TRANSACTIONS/CAREER NOTES: Signed by Dallas Cowboys (August 10, 2001). ... Released by Cowboys (September 2, 2001). ... Re-signed by Cowboys to practice squad (September 3, 2001). ... Activated (November 17, 2001). ... On injured reserve with knee injury (November 21, 2001-remainder of season).
PLAYING EXPERIENCE: Dallas NFL, 2001. ... Games/Games started: 2001 (1/0).

MACKLIN, DAVID DB COLTS

PERSONAL: Born July 14, 1978, in Newport News, Va. ... 5-9/193. ... Full name: David Thurman Macklin.
HIGH SCHOOL: Menchville (Newport News, Va.).
COLLEGE: Penn State.
TRANSACTIONS/CAREER NOTES: Selected by Indianapolis Colts in third round (91st pick overall) of 2000 NFL draft. ... Signed by Colts (July 13, 2000).
PRO STATISTICS: 2000—Returned one kickoff for no yards. 2001—Credited with $1/2$ sack.

			INTERCEPTIONS			
Year Team	G	GS	No.	Yds.	Avg.	TD
2000—Indianapolis NFL	16	2	2	35	17.5	0
2001—Indianapolis NFL	16	16	3	15	5.0	0
Pro totals (2 years)	32	18	5	50	10.0	0

MADDOX, TOMMY QB STEELERS

PERSONAL: Born September 2, 1971, in Shreveport, La. ... 6-4/220. ... Full name: Thomas Alfred Maddox.
HIGH SCHOOL: L.D. Bell (Hurst, Texas).
COLLEGE: UCLA.
TRANSACTIONS/CAREER NOTES: Selected after sophomore season by Denver Broncos in first round (25th pick overall) of 1992 NFL draft. ... Signed by Broncos (July 22, 1992). ... Traded by Broncos to Los Angeles Rams for fourth-round pick (LB Ken Brown) in 1995 draft (August 27, 1994). ... Granted free agency (February 17, 1995). ... Rams franchise moved to St. Louis (April 12, 1995). ... Re-signed by Rams (July 7, 1995). ... Released by Rams (August 27, 1995). ... Signed by New York Giants (August 30, 1995). ... Released by Giants (August 19, 1996). ... Signed by Atlanta Falcons (April 19, 1997). ... Released by Falcons (August 18, 1997). ... Signed by New Jersey Red Dogs of Arena League (November 9, 1999). ... Signed by Pittsburgh Steelers (June 12, 2001).
CHAMPIONSHIP GAME EXPERIENCE: Member of Steelers for AFC championship game (2001 season); did not play.
PRO STATISTICS: 1992—Fumbled four times and recovered two fumbles. 1995—Fumbled once. 2001—Fumbled once.
SINGLE GAME HIGHS (regular season): Attempts—28 (December 2, 1992, vs. Buffalo); completions—18 (November 22, 1992, vs. Los Angeles Raiders); yards—207 (November 22, 1992 vs. Los Angeles Raiders); and touchdown passes—3 (December 6, 1992, vs. Dallas).
MISCELLANEOUS: Regular-season record as starting NFL quarterback: 0-4 (.000).

Year Team	G	GS	PASSING								RUSHING				TOTALS		
			Att.	Cmp.	Pct.	Yds.	TD	Int.	Avg.	Rat.	Att.	Yds.	Avg.	TD	TD	2pt.	Pts.
1992—Denver NFL	13	4	121	66	54.5	757	5	9	6.26	56.4	9	20	2.2	0	0	0	0
1993—Denver NFL	16	0	1	1	100.0	1	1	0	1.00	118.8	2	-2	-1.0	0	0	0	0
1994—L.A. Rams NFL	5	0	19	10	52.6	141	0	2	7.42	37.3	1	1	1.0	0	0	0	0
1995—N.Y. Giants NFL	16	0	23	6	26.1	49	0	3	2.13	0.0	1	4	4.0	0	0	0	0
1996—						Did not play.										
1997—						Did not play.										
1998—						Did not play.										
1999—						Did not play.										
2000—						Did not play.										
2001—Pittsburgh NFL	5	0	9	7	77.8	154	1	1	17.11	116.2	6	9	1.5	1	1	0	6
Pro totals (5 years)	55	4	173	90	52.0	1102	7	15	6.37	49.3	19	32	1.7	1	1	0	6

MADISON, SAM   CB   DOLPHINS

PERSONAL: Born April 23, 1974, in Thomasville, Ga. ... 5-11/185. ... Full name: Samuel A. Madison Jr.
HIGH SCHOOL: Florida A&M High (Monticello, Fla.).
COLLEGE: Louisville.
TRANSACTIONS/CAREER NOTES: Selected by Miami Dolphins in second round (44th pick overall) of 1997 NFL draft. ... Signed by Dolphins (June 16, 1997).
HONORS: Named cornerback on THE SPORTING NEWS NFL All-Pro team (1999 and 2000). ... Played in Pro Bowl (1999 and 2000 seasons).
PRO STATISTICS: 1998—Credited with one sack. 1999—Credited with a safety. 2000—Recovered two fumbles for 20 yards and a touchdown. 2001—Returned one punt for six yards.

Year Team	G	GS	INTERCEPTIONS				TOTALS			
			No.	Yds.	Avg.	TD	TD	2pt.	Pts.	Fum.
1997—Miami NFL	14	3	1	21	21.0	0	0	0	0	0
1998—Miami NFL	16	16	8	114	14.3	0	0	0	0	0
1999—Miami NFL	16	16	†7	164	23.4	1	1	0	8	0
2000—Miami NFL	16	16	5	80	16.0	0	1	0	6	1
2001—Miami NFL	13	13	2	0	0.0	0	0	0	0	0
Pro totals (5 years)	75	64	23	379	16.5	1	2	0	14	1

MAESE, JOE   C   RAVENS

PERSONAL: Born December 2, 1978, in Morenci, Ariz. ... 6-0/241.
HIGH SCHOOL: Cortez (Ariz.).
JUNIOR COLLEGE: Phoenix College.
COLLEGE: New Mexico.
TRANSACTIONS/CAREER NOTES: Selected by Baltimore Ravens in sixth round (194th pick overall) in 2001 NFL draft. ... Signed by Ravens (June 14, 2001). ... On injured reserve with knee injury (January 3, 2002-remainder of season).
PLAYING EXPERIENCE: Baltimore NFL, 2001. ... Games/Games started: 2001 (15/0).

MAKOVICKA, JOEL   FB   CARDINALS

PERSONAL: Born October 6, 1975, in Brainard, Neb. ... 5-11/196. ... Name pronounced mack-oh-VIK-uh.
HIGH SCHOOL: East Butler (Brainard, Neb.).
COLLEGE: Nebraska.
TRANSACTIONS/CAREER NOTES: Selected by Arizona Cardinals in fourth round (116th pick overall) of 1999 NFL draft. ... Signed by Cardinals (June 18, 1999). ... Granted free agency (March 1, 2002).
PRO STATISTICS: 1999—Returned one kickoff for 10 yards and recovered one fumble. 2001—Returned one kickoff for seven yards and recovered one fumble.
SINGLE GAME HIGHS (regular season): Attempts—2 (October 31, 1999, vs. New England); yards—7 (October 8, 2000, vs. Cleveland); and rushing touchdowns—0; receptions—3 (December 23, 2001, vs. Dallas); yards—25 (October 21, 2001, vs. Kansas City); and touchdown receptions—1 (October 7, 2001, vs. Philadelphia).

Year Team	G	GS	RUSHING				RECEIVING				TOTALS			
			Att.	Yds.	Avg.	TD	No.	Yds.	Avg.	TD	TD	2pt.	Pts.	Fum.
1999—Arizona NFL	16	10	8	7	0.9	0	10	70	7.0	1	1	0	6	1
2000—Arizona NFL	14	10	3	8	2.7	0	6	18	3.0	0	0	0	0	0
2001—Arizona NFL	16	14	1	19	19.0	0	16	95	5.9	1	1	0	6	1
Pro totals (3 years)	46	34	12	34	2.8	0	32	183	5.7	2	2	0	12	2

MANGUM, KRIS   TE   PANTHERS

PERSONAL: Born August 15, 1973, in Magee, Miss. ... 6-4/249. ... Full name: Kris Thomas Mangum. ... Son of John Mangum, defensive tackle with Boston Patriots (1966 and 1967) of AFL; and brother of John Mangum, cornerback with Chicago Bears (1990-98).
HIGH SCHOOL: Magee (Miss.).
COLLEGE: Mississippi.
TRANSACTIONS/CAREER NOTES: Selected by Carolina Panthers in seventh round (228th pick overall) of 1997 NFL draft. ... Signed by Panthers (May 20, 1997). ... Released by Panthers (September 2, 1997). ... Re-signed by Panthers to practice squad (September 4, 1997). ... Activated (December 5, 1997).
PRO STATISTICS: 1999—Returned two kickoffs for 20 yards.
SINGLE GAME HIGHS (regular season): Receptions—4 (December 30, 2001, vs. Arizona); yards—56 (December 20, 1997, vs. St. Louis); and touchdown receptions—1 (December 9, 2001, vs. Buffalo).

Year Team	G	GS	RECEIVING No.	Yds.	Avg.	TD	TOTALS TD	2pt.	Pts.	Fum.
1997—Carolina NFL	2	1	4	56	14.0	0	0	0	0	0
1998—Carolina NFL	6	0	1	5	5.0	0	0	0	0	0
1999—Carolina NFL	11	0	1	6	6.0	0	0	0	0	0
2000—Carolina NFL	15	7	19	215	11.3	1	1	0	6	0
2001—Carolina NFL	16	10	15	89	5.9	2	2	0	12	0
Pro totals (5 years)	50	18	40	371	9.3	3	3	0	18	0

MANNELLY, PATRICK   OT   BEARS

PERSONAL: Born April 18, 1975, in Atlanta. ... 6-5/269. ... Full name: James Patrick Mannelly.
HIGH SCHOOL: Marist (Atlanta).
COLLEGE: Duke.
TRANSACTIONS/CAREER NOTES: Selected by Chicago Bears in sixth round (189th pick overall) of 1998 NFL draft. ... Signed by Bears (June 11, 1998).
PLAYING EXPERIENCE: Chicago NFL, 1998-2001. ... Games/Games started: 1998 (16/0), 1999 (16/0), 2000 (16/0), 2001 (15/0). Total: 63/0.

MANNING, PEYTON   QB   COLTS

PERSONAL: Born March 24, 1976, in New Orleans. ... 6-5/230. ... Full name: Peyton Williams Manning. ... Son of Archie Manning, quarterback with New Orleans Saints (1971-82), Houston Oilers (1982-83) and Minnesota Vikings (1983-84).
HIGH SCHOOL: Isidore Newman (New Orleans).
COLLEGE: Tennessee (degree in speech communication).
TRANSACTIONS/CAREER NOTES: Selected by Indianapolis Colts in first round (first pick overall) of 1998 NFL draft. ... Signed by Colts (July 28, 1998).
HONORS: Davey O'Brien Award winner (1997). ... Named College Player of the Year by THE SPORTING NEWS (1997). ... Named quarterback on THE SPORTING NEWS college All-America second team (1997). ... Played in Pro Bowl (1999 and 2000 seasons).
RECORDS: Holds NFL rookie-season records for most passes attempted—575 (1998); most passes completed—326 (1998); and most yards passing—3,739.
PRO STATISTICS: 1998—Fumbled three times. 1999—Fumbled six times and recovered two fumbles for minus five yards. 2000—Fumbled five times and recovered one fumble for minus three yards. 2001—Fumbled seven times and recovered three fumbles for minus two yards.
SINGLE GAME HIGHS (regular season): Attempts—54 (October 8, 2000, vs. New England); completions—33 (September 10, 2000, vs. Oakland); yards—440 (September 25, 2000, vs. Jacksonville); and touchdown passes—4 (September 23, 2001, vs. Buffalo).
STATISTICAL PLATEAUS: 300-yard passing games: 1998 (4), 1999 (2), 2000 (5), 2001 (5). Total: 16.
MISCELLANEOUS: Regular-season record as starting NFL quarterback: 32-32 (.500). ... Postseason record as starting NFL quarterback: 0-2.

Year Team	G	GS	PASSING Att.	Cmp.	Pct.	Yds.	TD	Int.	Avg.	Rat.	RUSHING Att.	Yds.	Avg.	TD	TOTALS TD	2pt.	Pts.
1998—Indianapolis NFL	16	16	*575	§326	56.7	§3739	26	*28	6.50	71.2	15	62	4.1	0	0	0	0
1999—Indianapolis NFL	16	16	533	§331	§62.1	§4135	§26	15	§7.76	§90.7	35	73	2.1	2	2	0	12
2000—Indianapolis NFL	16	16	571	§357	62.5	4413	*33	15	7.73	94.7	37	116	3.1	1	1	0	6
2001—Indianapolis NFL	16	16	547	343	62.7	§4131	26	*23	7.55	84.1	35	157	4.5	4	4	0	24
Pro totals (4 years)	64	64	2226	1357	61.0	16418	111	81	7.38	85.1	122	408	3.3	7	7	0	42

MANUMALEUNA, BRANDON   TE   RAMS

PERSONAL: Born January 4, 1980, in Torrance, Calif. ... 6-2/288. ... Full name: Brandon Michael Manumaleuna.
HIGH SCHOOL: Narbonne (Calif.).
COLLEGE: Arizona.
TRANSACTIONS/CAREER NOTES: Selected by St. Louis Rams in fourth round (129th pick overall) of 2001 NFL draft. ... Signed by Rams (June 21, 2001).
PLAYING EXPERIENCE: St. Louis NFL, 2001. ... Games/Games started: (16/0).
CHAMPIONSHIP GAME EXPERIENCE: Played in NFC championship game (2001 season). ... Played in Super Bowl XXXVI (2001 season).
PRO STATISTICS: 2001—Caught one pass for one yard and a touchdown.
SINGLE GAME HIGHS (regular season): Receptions—1 (November 26, 2001, vs. Tampa Bay); yards—1 (November 26, 2001, vs. Tampa Bay); and touchdown receptions—1 (November 26, 2001, vs. Tampa Bay).

MARE, OLINDO   K   DOLPHINS

PERSONAL: Born June 6, 1973, in Hollywood, Fla. ... 5-10/195. ... Full name: Olindo Franco Mare. ... Name pronounced o-LEND-o MAR-ray.
HIGH SCHOOL: Cooper City (Fla.).
JUNIOR COLLEGE: Valencia Community College (Fla.).
COLLEGE: Syracuse.
TRANSACTIONS/CAREER NOTES: Signed as non-drafted free agent by New York Giants (May 2, 1996). ... Released by Giants (August 25, 1996). ... Re-signed by Giants to practice squad (August 27, 1996). ... Granted free agency after 1996 season. ... Signed by Miami Dolphins (February 27, 1997). ... Granted free agency (February 11, 2000). ... Re-signed by Dolphins (June 15, 2000). ... Granted unconditional free agency (March 2, 2001). ... Re-signed by Dolphins (March 2, 2001).
HONORS: Named kicker on THE SPORTING NEWS NFL All-Pro team (1999). ... Played in Pro Bowl (1999 season).
RECORDS: Holds NFL single-season record for most field goals made—39 (1999).
PRO STATISTICS: 2001—Rushed once for minus five yards.

Year Team	G	PUNTING No.	Yds.	Avg.	Net avg.	In. 20	Blk.	KICKING XPM	XPA	FGM	FGA	Lg.	50+	Pts.
1996—New York Giants NFL								Did not play.						
1997—Miami NFL	16	5	235	47.0	46.2	2	0	33	33	28	36	50	1-3	117
1998—Miami NFL	16	3	115	38.3	31.7	1	0	33	34	22	27	48	0-2	99
1999—Miami NFL	16	1	36	36.0	30.0	0	0	27	27	*39	*46	54	3-5	144
2000—Miami NFL	16	0	0	0.0	0	0	0	33	34	28	31	49	0-0	117
2001—Miami NFL	16	0	0	0.0	0	0	0	39	40	19	21	46	0-0	96
Pro totals (5 years)	80	9	386	42.9	39.6	3	0	165	168	136	161	54	4-10	573

MARION, BROCK — S — DOLPHINS

PERSONAL: Born June 11, 1970, in Bakersfield, Calif. ... 5-11/205. ... Full name: Brock Elliot Marion. ... Son of Jerry Marion, wide receiver with Pittsburgh Steelers (1967); and nephew of Brent McClanahan, running back with Minnesota Vikings (1973-79).
HIGH SCHOOL: West (Bakersfield, Calif.).
COLLEGE: Nevada.
TRANSACTIONS/CAREER NOTES: Selected by Dallas Cowboys in seventh round (196th overall) of 1993 NFL draft. ... Signed by Cowboys (July 14, 1993). ... Granted free agency (February 16, 1996). ... Re-signed by Cowboys (May 2, 1996). ... Granted unconditional free agency (February 14, 1997). ... Re-signed by Cowboys (April 7, 1997). ... Granted unconditional free agency (February 13, 1998). ... Signed by Miami Dolphins (March 3, 1998). ... Granted unconditional free agency (March 2, 2001). ... Re-signed by Dolphins (June 9, 2001). ... Released by Dolphins (February 28, 2002). ... Re-signed by Dolphins (March 10, 2002).
CHAMPIONSHIP GAME EXPERIENCE: Played in NFC championship game (1993-1995 seasons). ... Member of Super Bowl championship team (1993 and 1995 seasons).
HONORS: Played in Pro Bowl (2000 season).
PRO STATISTICS: 1993—Recovered one fumble. 1994—Credited with one sack and returned two kickoffs for 39 yards. 1996—Fumbled once and recovered one fumble for 45 yards. 1997—Recovered one fumble for 13 yards. 1998—Recovered one fumble for two yards. 1999—Credited with one sack and recovered one fumble. 2000—Recovered one fumble. 2001—Recovered one fumble for one yard.

				INTERCEPTIONS			KICKOFF RETURNS			TOTALS			
Year Team	G	GS	No.	Yds.	Avg.	TD	No.	Yds.	Avg.	TD	TD	2pt.	Pts.	Fum.
1993—Dallas NFL	15	0	1	2	2.0	0	0	0	0.0	0	0	0	0	0
1994—Dallas NFL	14	1	1	11	11.0	0	2	39	19.5	0	0	0	0	0
1995—Dallas NFL	16	16	6	40	6.7	1	1	16	16.0	0	1	0	6	0
1996—Dallas NFL	10	10	0	0	0.0	0	3	68	22.7	0	0	0	0	1
1997—Dallas NFL	16	16	0	0	0.0	0	10	311	31.1	0	0	0	0	0
1998—Miami NFL	16	16	0	0	0.0	0	6	109	18.2	0	0	0	0	0
1999—Miami NFL	16	16	2	30	15.0	0	*62	*1524	24.6	0	0	0	0	2
2000—Miami NFL	16	16	5	72	14.4	0	22	513	23.3	0	0	0	0	0
2001—Miami NFL	15	15	5	*227	45.4	†2	17	371	21.8	0	2	0	12	1
Pro totals (9 years)	134	106	20	382	19.1	3	123	2951	24.0	0	3	0	18	4

MARSHALL, TORRANCE — LB — PACKERS

PERSONAL: Born June 12, 1977, in Miami. ... 6-2/255.
HIGH SCHOOL: Sunset (Miami).
JUNIOR COLLEGE: Kemper Military Junior College (Mo.), then Miami-Dade Community College.
COLLEGE: Oklahoma.
TRANSACTIONS/CAREER NOTES: Selected by Green Bay Packers in third round (72nd pick overall) of 2001 NFL draft. ... Signed by Packers (July 24, 2001).
PLAYING EXPERIENCE: Green Bay NFL, 2001. ... Games/Games started: 2001 (14/1).
HONORS: Named linebacker on THE SPORTING NEWS college All-America third team (2000).
PRO STATISTICS: 2001—Recovered one fumble.

MARTIN, CECIL — FB — EAGLES

PERSONAL: Born July 8, 1975, in Chicago. ... 6-0/235.
HIGH SCHOOL: Evanston (Ill.).
COLLEGE: Wisconsin.
TRANSACTIONS/CAREER NOTES: Selected by Philadelphia Eagles in sixth round (172nd pick overall) of 1999 NFL draft. ... Signed by Eagles (July 25, 1999). ... Granted free agency (March 1, 2002). ... Re-signed by Eagles (April 26, 2002).
CHAMPIONSHIP GAME EXPERIENCE: Played in NFC championship game (2001 season).
SINGLE GAME HIGHS (regular season): Attempts—5 (September 30, 2001, vs. Dallas); yards—28 (December 24, 2000, vs. Cincinnati); and rushing touchdowns—0.

			RUSHING				RECEIVING				TOTALS			
Year Team	G	GS	Att.	Yds.	Avg.	TD	No.	Yds.	Avg.	TD	TD	2pt.	Pts.	Fum.
1999—Philadelphia NFL	12	5	3	3	1.0	0	11	22	2.0	0	0	0	0	0
2000—Philadelphia NFL	16	10	13	77	5.9	0	31	219	7.1	0	0	0	0	1
2001—Philadelphia NFL	16	15	9	27	3.0	0	24	124	5.2	2	2	0	12	0
Pro totals (3 years)	44	30	25	107	4.3	0	66	365	5.5	2	2	0	12	1

MARTIN, CURTIS — RB — JETS

PERSONAL: Born May 1, 1973, in Pittsburgh. ... 5-11/205.
HIGH SCHOOL: Taylor-Allderdice (Pittsburgh).
COLLEGE: Pittsburgh.
TRANSACTIONS/CAREER NOTES: Selected after junior season by New England Patriots in third round (74th pick overall) of 1995 NFL draft. ... Signed by Patriots (July 18, 1995). ... Granted free agency (February 13, 1998). ... Tendered offer sheet by New York Jets (March 20, 1998). ... Patriots declined to match offer (March 25, 1998).
CHAMPIONSHIP GAME EXPERIENCE: Played in AFC championship game (1996 and 1998 seasons). ... Played in Super Bowl XXXI (1996 season).
HONORS: Named NFL Rookie of the Year by THE SPORTING NEWS (1995). ... Played in Pro Bowl (1995, 1996 and 1998 seasons). ... Named running back on THE SPORTING NEWS NFL All-Pro team (2001).
PRO STATISTICS: 1995—Recovered three fumbles. 1996—Recovered one fumble. 1998—Recovered one fumble. 1999—Recovered two fumbles. 2000—Completed only pass attempt for 18 yards and a touchdown. 2001—Completed only pass attempt for 18 yards and a touchdown and recovered three fumbles.

SINGLE GAME HIGHS (regular season): Attempts—40 (September 14, 1997, vs. New York Jets); yards—203 (December 3, 2000, vs. Indianapolis); and rushing touchdowns—3 (November 11, 2001, vs. Kansas City).
STATISTICAL PLATEAUS: 100-yard rushing games: 1995 (9), 1996 (2), 1997 (3), 1998 (8), 1999 (6), 2000 (3), 2001 (7). Total: 38.

				RUSHING				RECEIVING				TOTALS		
Year Team	G	GS	Att.	Yds.	Avg.	TD	No.	Yds.	Avg.	TD	TD	2pt.	Pts.	Fum.
1995—New England NFL	16	15	§368	§1487	4.0	14	30	261	8.7	1	15	1	92	5
1996—New England NFL	16	15	316	1152	3.6	§14	46	333	7.2	3	§17	1	104	4
1997—New England NFL	13	13	274	1160	4.2	4	41	296	7.2	1	5	0	30	3
1998—New York Jets NFL	15	15	369	1287	3.5	8	43	365	8.5	1	9	0	54	5
1999—New York Jets NFL	16	16	367	1464	4.0	5	45	259	5.8	0	5	0	30	2
2000—New York Jets NFL	16	16	316	1204	3.8	9	70	508	7.3	2	11	0	66	2
2001—New York Jets NFL	16	16	333	1513	4.5	10	53	320	6.0	0	10	0	60	2
Pro totals (7 years)	108	106	2343	9267	4.0	64	328	2342	7.1	8	72	2	436	23

MARTIN, DAVID   TE   PACKERS

PERSONAL: Born March 13, 1979, in Fort Campbell, Va. ... 6-4/250. ... Full name: David Earl Martin.
HIGH SCHOOL: Norview (Norfolk, Va.).
COLLEGE: Tennessee.
TRANSACTIONS/CAREER NOTES: Selected by Green Bay Packers in sixth round (198th pick overall) of 2001 NFL draft. ... Signed by Packers (June 15, 2001).
SINGLE GAME HIGHS (regular season): Receptions—3 (November 11, 2001, vs. Chicago); yards—33 (October 7, 2001, vs. Tampa Bay); and touchdown receptions—1 (November 22, 2001, vs. Detroit).

			RECEIVING			
Year Team	G	GS	No.	Yds.	Avg.	TD
2001—Green Bay NFL	14	1	13	144	11.1	1

MARTIN, JAMIE   QB   RAMS

PERSONAL: Born February 8, 1970, in Orange, Calif. ... 6-2/205. ... Full name: Jamie Blane Martin.
HIGH SCHOOL: Arroyo Grande (Calif.).
COLLEGE: Weber State.
TRANSACTIONS/CAREER NOTES: Signed as non-drafted free agent by Los Angeles Rams (May 3, 1993). ... Released by Rams (August 24, 1993). ... Re-signed by Rams to practice squad (August 31, 1993). ... Activated (November 23, 1993). ... Inactive for five games (1993). ... Released by Rams (August 27, 1994). ... Re-signed by Rams (October 4, 1994). ... Released by Rams (October 12, 1994). ... Re-signed by Rams (November 15, 1994). ... Active for one game (1994); did not play. ... Assigned by Rams to Amsterdam Admirals of World Football League (1995). ... Rams franchise moved to St. Louis (April 12, 1995). ... On physically unable to perform list with broken collarbone (June 3, 1995-entire season). ... Released by Rams (August 17, 1997). ... Signed by Washington Redskins (December 2, 1997). ... Granted free agency (February 13, 1998). ... Signed by Jacksonville Jaguars (March 6, 1998). ... On injured reserve with knee injury (December 15, 1998-remainder of season). ... Granted unconditional free agency (February 12, 1999). ... Signed by Cleveland Browns (August 25, 1999). ... Granted unconditional free agency (February 11, 2000). ... Signed by Jaguars (February 22, 2000). ... Released by Jaguars (March 1, 2001). ... Re-signed by Jaguars (April 2, 2001). ... Released by Jaguars (September 2, 2001). ... Signed by Rams (September 3, 2001).
CHAMPIONSHIP GAME EXPERIENCE: Member of Rams for NFC championship game (2001 season); did not play. ... Member of Rams for Super Bowl XXXVI (2001 season); did not play.
HONORS: Walter Payton Award winner (1991).
PRO STATISTICS: 1996—Fumbled twice and recovered one fumble for minus two yards.
SINGLE GAME HIGHS (regular season): Attempts—23 (December 6, 1998, vs. Detroit); completions—15 (December 6, 1998, vs. Detroit); yards—228 (December 6, 1998, vs. Detroit); and touchdown passes—2 (December 6, 1998, vs. Detroit).
MISCELLANEOUS: Regular-season record as starting NFL quarterback: 0-1.

			PASSING							RUSHING			TOTALS		
Year Team	G	GS	Att.	Cmp.	Pct.	Yds.	TD	Int.	Avg.	Rat.	Att.	Yds.	Avg.	TD	TD	2pt.	Pts.
1993—L.A. Rams NFL						Did not play.									
1994—L.A. Rams NFL						Did not play.									
1995—Amsterdam W.L.	9	9	219	126	57.5	1433	11	6	6.54	82.6	0	0	0.0	0	0	0	0
—St. Louis NFL						Did not play.									
1996—St. Louis NFL	6	0	34	23	67.6	241	3	2	7.09	92.9	7	14	2.0	0	0	0	0
1997—Washington NFL						Did not play.									
1998—Jacksonville NFL	4	1	45	27	60.0	355	2	0	7.89	99.8	5	8	1.6	0	0	0	0
1999—Cleveland NFL						Did not play.									
2000—Jacksonville NFL	6	0	33	22	66.7	307	2	1	9.30	104.0	7	-6	-0.9	0	0	0	0
2001—St. Louis NFL	5	0	3	3	100.0	22	0	0	7.33	97.2	8	-9	-1.1	0	0	0	0
W.L. totals (1 year)	9	9	219	126	57.5	1433	11	6	6.54	82.6	0	0	0.0	0	0	0	0
NFL totals (4 years)	21	1	115	75	65.2	925	7	3	8.04	99.4	27	7	0.3	0	0	0	0
Pro totals (5 years)	30	10	334	201	60.2	2358	18	9	7.06	88.4	27	7	0.3	0	0	0	0

MARTIN, STEVE   DT   PATRIOTS

PERSONAL: Born May 31, 1974, in St. Paul, Minn. ... 6-4/312. ... Full name: Steven Albert Martin.
HIGH SCHOOL: Jefferson City (Mo.).
COLLEGE: Missouri.
TRANSACTIONS/CAREER NOTES: Selected by Indianapolis Colts in fifth round (151st pick overall) of 1996 NFL draft. ... Signed by Colts (July 5, 1996). ... Claimed on waivers by Philadelphia Eagles (October 23, 1998). ... Granted free agency (February 12, 1999). ... Re-signed by Eagles (April 9, 1999). ... Granted unconditional free agency (February 11, 2000). ... Signed by Kansas City Chiefs (February 24, 2000). ... Released by Chiefs (September 1, 2001). ... Signed by New York Jets (September 3, 2001). ... Granted unconditional free agency (March 1, 2002). ... Signed by New England Patriots (April 3, 2002).
PRO STATISTICS: 1996—Recovered one fumble. 1999—Recovered one fumble. 2001—Recovered two fumbles.

Year Team	G	GS	SACKS
1996—Indianapolis NFL	14	5	1.0
1997—Indianapolis NFL	12	0	0.0
1998—Indianapolis NFL	4	0	0.0
—Philadelphia NFL	9	3	1.0
1999—Philadelphia NFL	16	15	2.0
2000—Kansas City NFL	16	0	0.0
2001—New York Jets NFL	16	15	2.5
Pro totals (6 years)	87	38	6.5

MARTIN, TEE — QB — STEELERS

PERSONAL: Born July 25, 1978, in Mobile, Ala. ... 6-2/225. ... Full name: Tamaurice Nigel Martin.
HIGH SCHOOL: Williamson (Mobile, Ala.).
COLLEGE: Tennessee.
TRANSACTIONS/CAREER NOTES: Selected by Pittsburgh Steelers in fifth round (163rd pick overall) of 2000 NFL draft. ... Signed by Steelers (July 16, 2000). ... Inactive for 13 games (2000).
PLAYING EXPERIENCE: Pittsburgh NFL, 2001. ... Games/Games started: 2001 (1/0).
CHAMPIONSHIP GAME EXPERIENCE: Played in AFC championship game (2001 season).
PRO STATISTICS: 2001—Rushed once for eight yards.

MARTIN, TONY — WR

PERSONAL: Born September 5, 1965, in Miami. ... 6-1/175. ... Full name: Tony Derrick Martin.
HIGH SCHOOL: Miami Northwestern.
COLLEGE: Bishop (Texas), then Mesa State College (Colo.).
TRANSACTIONS/CAREER NOTES: Selected by New York Jets in fifth round (126th pick overall) of 1989 NFL draft. ... Signed by New York Jets for 1989 season. ... Released by Jets (September 4, 1989). ... Signed by Miami Dolphins to developmental squad (September 5, 1989). ... Activated (December 23, 1989); did not play. ... Granted free agency (February 1, 1992). ... Re-signed by Dolphins (March 10, 1992). ... Traded by Dolphins to San Diego Chargers for fourth-round pick (traded to Arizona) in 1994 draft (March 24, 1994). ... Designated by Chargers as franchise player (February 13, 1997). ... Re-signed by Chargers (May 1, 1997). ... Traded by Chargers to Atlanta Falcons for second-round pick (RB Jermaine Fazande) in 1999 draft (June 3, 1998). ... Released by Falcons (February 26, 1999). ... Signed by Dolphins (April 9, 1999). ... Released by Dolphins (February 22, 2001). ... Signed by Falcons (June 20, 2001). ... Released by Falcons (January 2, 2002).
CHAMPIONSHIP GAME EXPERIENCE: Played in AFC championship game (1992 and 1994 seasons). ... Played in Super Bowl XXIX (1994 season) and Super Bowl XXXIII (1998 season). ... Played in NFC championship game (1998 season).
HONORS: Played in Pro Bowl (1996 season).
RECORDS: Shares NFL record for longest pass reception (from Stan Humphries)—99 yards, touchdown (September 18, 1994, at Seattle).
PRO STATISTICS: 1990—Recovered two fumbles. 1992—Attempted one pass without a completion and recovered one fumble. 1994—Had only pass attempt intercepted and returned eight kickoffs for 167 yards. 1995—Attempted one pass without a completion. 1998—Attempted one pass without a completion.
SINGLE GAME HIGHS (regular season): Receptions—13 (September 10, 1995, vs. Seattle); yards—172 (December 11, 1994, vs. San Francisco); and touchdown receptions—3 (September 28, 1997, vs. Baltimore).
STATISTICAL PLATEAUS: 100-yard receiving games: 1991 (2), 1993 (1), 1994 (2), 1995 (4), 1996 (4), 1997 (2), 1998 (5), 1999 (5), 2000 (1). Total: 26.

			RUSHING				RECEIVING				PUNT RETURNS				TOTALS			
Year Team	G	GS	Att.	Yds.	Avg.	TD	No.	Yds.	Avg.	TD	No.	Yds.	Avg.	TD	TD	2pt.	Pts.	Fum.
1990—Miami NFL	16	5	1	8	8.0	0	29	388	13.4	2	26	140	5.4	0	2	0	12	4
1991—Miami NFL	16	0	0	0	0.0	0	27	434	16.1	2	1	10	10.0	0	2	0	12	2
1992—Miami NFL	16	3	1	-2	-2.0	0	33	553	16.8	2	0	0	0.0	0	2	0	12	2
1993—Miami NFL	12	0	1	6	6.0	0	20	347	17.4	3	0	0	0.0	0	3	0	18	1
1994—San Diego NFL	16	1	2	-9	-4.5	0	50	885	17.7	7	0	0	0.0	0	7	0	42	2
1995—San Diego NFL	16	16	0	0	0.0	0	90	1224	13.6	6	0	0	0.0	0	6	0	36	3
1996—San Diego NFL	16	16	0	0	0.0	0	85	1171	13.8	†14	0	0	0.0	0	14	0	84	0
1997—San Diego NFL	16	16	0	0	0.0	0	63	904	14.3	6	0	0	0.0	0	6	0	36	0
1998—Atlanta NFL	16	16	0	0	0.0	0	66	1181	17.9	6	0	0	0.0	0	6	0	36	0
1999—Miami NFL	16	13	1	-6	-6.0	0	67	1037	15.5	5	0	0	0.0	0	5	0	30	0
2000—Miami NFL	10	5	0	0	0.0	0	26	393	15.1	0	0	0	0.0	0	0	0	0	0
2001—Atlanta NFL	11	9	0	0	0.0	0	37	548	14.8	3	0	0	0.0	0	3	0	18	0
Pro totals (12 years)	177	100	6	-3	-0.5	0	593	9065	15.3	56	28	150	5.4	0	56	0	336	14

MASLOWSKI, MIKE — LB — CHIEFS

PERSONAL: Born July 11, 1974, in Thorp, Wis. ... 6-1/243. ... Full name: Michael John Maslowski.
HIGH SCHOOL: Thorp (Wis.).
COLLEGE: Wisconsin-La Crosse.
TRANSACTIONS/CAREER NOTES: Signed as non-drafted free agent by San Diego Chargers (April 21, 1997). ... Released by Chargers (August 1997). ... Played for San Jose Sabercats of Arena League (1998). ... Signed by Kansas City Chiefs (January 12, 1999). ... Assigned by Chiefs to Barcelona Dragons in 1999 NFL Europe enhancement allocation program (February 22, 1999). ... On injured reserve with knee injury (December 22, 2001-remainder of season). ... Granted free agency (March 1, 2002). ... Tendered offer sheet by New England Patriots (March 7, 2002). ... Offer matched by Chiefs (March 14, 2002).
PLAYING EXPERIENCE: Barcelona NFLE, 1999; Kansas City NFL, 1999-2001. ... Games/Games started: NFLE 1999 (games played unavailable); NFL 1999 (15/0), 2000 (16/5), 2001 (8/0). Total: 39/5.
PRO STATISTICS: NFLE: 1999—Intercepted four passes for 56 yards and one touchdown and credited with two sacks. NFL: 2000—Credited with two sacks and recovered one fumble. 2001—Credited with one sack.

MASON, DERRICK   WR   TITANS

PERSONAL: Born January 17, 1974, in Detroit. ... 5-10/188. ... Full name: Derrick James Mason.
HIGH SCHOOL: Mumford (Detroit).
COLLEGE: Michigan State.
TRANSACTIONS/CAREER NOTES: Selected by Houston Oilers in fourth round (98th pick overall) of 1997 NFL draft. ... Oilers franchise moved to Tennessee for 1997 season. ... Signed by Oilers (July 19, 1997). ... Oilers franchise renamed Tennessee Titans for 1999 season (December 26, 1998). ... Granted free agency (February 11, 2000). ... Re-signed by Titans (June 1, 2000). ... Granted unconditional free agency (March 2, 2001). ... Re-signed by Titans (March 2, 2001).
CHAMPIONSHIP GAME EXPERIENCE: Played in AFC championship game (1999 season). ... Played in Super Bowl XXXIV (1999 season).
HONORS: Named kick returner on THE SPORTING NEWS NFL All-Pro team (2000). ... Played in Pro Bowl (2000 season).
PRO STATISTICS: 1997—Rushed once for minus seven yards. 1998—Recovered one fumble. 2000—Rushed once for one yard and recovered one fumble. 2001—Recovered one fumble.
SINGLE GAME HIGHS (regular season): Receptions—12 (November 12, 2001, vs. Baltimore); yards—186 (January 6, 2002, vs. Cincinnati); and touchdown receptions—2 (January 6, 2002, vs. Cincinnati).
STATISTICAL PLATEAUS: 100-yard receiving games: 2000 (1), 2001 (4). Total: 5.

			RECEIVING			PUNT RETURNS				KICKOFF RETURNS				TOTALS			
Year Team	G	GS	No.	Yds.	Avg.	TD	No.	Yds.	Avg.	TD	No.	Yds.	Avg.	TD	TD	2pt.	Pts.	Fum.
1997—Tennessee NFL	16	2	14	186	13.3	0	13	95	7.3	0	26	551	21.2	0	0	0	0	5
1998—Tennessee NFL	16	0	25	333	13.3	3	31	228	7.4	0	8	154	19.3	0	3	0	18	1
1999—Tennessee NFL	13	0	8	89	11.1	0	26	225	8.7	0	41	805	19.6	0	1	0	6	0
2000—Tennessee NFL	16	10	63	895	14.2	5	*51	*662	13.0	1	42	1132	§27.0	0	6	0	36	1
2001—Tennessee NFL	15	15	73	1128	15.5	9	20	128	6.4	0	34	748	22.0	1	10	1	62	2
Pro totals (5 years)	76	27	183	2631	14.4	17	141	1338	9.5	2	151	3390	22.5	1	20	1	122	9

MASON, EDDIE   LB   REDSKINS

PERSONAL: Born January 9, 1972, in Siler City, N.C. ... 6-0/236. ... Full name: Eddie Lee Mason.
HIGH SCHOOL: Jordan-Matthews (Siler City, N.C.).
COLLEGE: North Carolina.
TRANSACTIONS/CAREER NOTES: Selected by New York Jets in sixth round (178th pick overall) of 1995 NFL draft. ... Signed by Jets (June 14, 1995). ... On injured reserve with knee injury (August 20, 1996-entire season). ... Granted unconditional free agency (February 14, 1997). ... Signed by Tampa Bay Buccaneers (April 21, 1997). ... Released by Buccaneers (August 17, 1997). ... Signed by Carolina Panthers (March 4, 1998). ... Released by Panthers (August 24, 1998). ... Signed by Jacksonville Jaguars (December 2, 1998). ... Released by Jaguars (September 5, 1999). ... Signed by Washington Redskins (September 21, 1999). ... Granted free agency (February 11, 2000). ... Re-signed by Redskins (April 10, 2000). ... Released by Redskins (September 2, 2001). ... Re-signed by Redskins (September 25, 2001). ... Granted unconditional free agency (March 1, 2002). ... Re-signed by Redskins (April 8, 2002).
PLAYING EXPERIENCE: New York Jets NFL, 1995; Jacksonville NFL, 1998; Washington NFL, 1999-2001. ... Games/Games started: 1995 (15/0), 1998 (4/0), 1999 (14/0), 2000 (16/2), 2001 (15/1). Total: 64/3.
PRO STATISTICS: 2000—Credited with two sacks. 2001—Credited with one sack.

MATHEWS, JASON   OT   TITANS

PERSONAL: Born February 9, 1971, in Orange, Texas. ... 6-5/304. ... Full name: Samuel Jason Mathews.
HIGH SCHOOL: Bridge City (Texas).
COLLEGE: Brigham Young, then Texas A&M.
TRANSACTIONS/CAREER NOTES: Selected by Indianapolis Colts in third round (67th pick overall) of 1994 NFL draft. ... Signed by Colts (July 23, 1994). ... Granted free agency (February 14, 1997). ... Re-signed by Colts (April 30, 1997). ... Granted unconditional free agency (February 13, 1998). ... Signed by Tampa Bay Buccaneers (May 7, 1998). ... Released by Buccaneers (August 30, 1998). ... Signed by Tennessee Oilers (September 1, 1998). ... Oilers franchise renamed Tennessee Titans for 1999 season (December 26, 1998).
PLAYING EXPERIENCE: Indianapolis NFL, 1994-1997; Tennessee NFL, 1998-2001. ... Games/Games started: 1994 (10/0), 1995 (16/16), 1996 (16/15), 1997 (16/0), 1998 (3/0), 1999 (5/0), 2000 (16/1), 2001 (16/2). Total: 98/34.
CHAMPIONSHIP GAME EXPERIENCE: Played in AFC championship game (1995 and 1999 seasons). ... Member of Titans for Super Bowl XXXIV (1999 season); did not play.
PRO STATISTICS: 1996—Recovered one fumble.

MATHIS, KEVIN   CB   SAINTS

PERSONAL: Born April 29, 1974, in Gainesville, Texas. ... 5-9/181.
HIGH SCHOOL: Gainesville (Texas).
COLLEGE: East Texas State.
TRANSACTIONS/CAREER NOTES: Signed as non-drafted free agent by Dallas Cowboys (April 24, 1997). ... Granted free agency (February 11, 2000). ... Re-signed by Cowboys (April 26, 2000). ... Traded by Cowboys to New Orleans Saints for LB Chris Bordano (April 26, 2000). ... Granted unconditional free agency (March 2, 2001). ... Re-signed by Saints (March 2, 2001).
PRO STATISTICS: 1997—Recovered two fumbles. 1998—Recovered four fumbles for six yards. 1999—Recovered one fumble. 2000—Intercepted one pass for no yards. 2001—Intercepted two passes and 34 yards and credited with one sack.

			PUNT RETURNS				KICKOFF RETURNS				TOTALS			
Year Team	G	GS	No.	Yds.	Avg.	TD	No.	Yds.	Avg.	TD	TD	2pt.	Pts.	Fum.
1997—Dallas NFL	16	3	11	91	8.3	0	0	0	0.0	0	0	0	0	2
1998—Dallas NFL	13	4	2	3	1.5	0	25	621	24.8	0	0	0	0	2
1999—Dallas NFL	8	4	0	0	0.0	0	18	408	22.7	0	0	0	0	1
2000—New Orleans NFL	16	16	1	5	5.0	0	8	187	23.4	0	0	0	0	1
2001—New Orleans NFL	14	13	0	0	0.0	0	0	0	0.0	0	0	0	0	0
Pro totals (5 years)	67	40	14	99	7.1	0	51	1216	23.8	0	0	0	0	6

– 243 –

MATHIS, TERANCE — WR

PERSONAL: Born June 7, 1967, in Detroit. ... 5-10/185. ... Cousin of Jason Ferguson, defensive tackle, New York Jets.
HIGH SCHOOL: Redan (Stone Mountain, Ga.).
COLLEGE: New Mexico.
TRANSACTIONS/CAREER NOTES: Selected by New York Jets in sixth round (140th pick overall) of 1990 NFL draft. ... Signed by Jets (July 12, 1990). ... Granted unconditional free agency (February 17, 1994). ... Signed by Atlanta Falcons (May 3, 1994). ... Granted unconditional free agency (February 16, 1996). ... Re-signed by Falcons (April 30, 1996). ... Released by Falcons (February 25, 2002).
CHAMPIONSHIP GAME EXPERIENCE: Played in NFC championship game (1998 season). ... Played in Super Bowl XXXIII (1998 season).
HONORS: Named wide receiver on THE SPORTING NEWS college All-America first team (1989). ... Played in Pro Bowl (1994 season).
RECORDS: Holds NFL career record for most two-point conversions—6.
PRO STATISTICS: 1990—Fumbled once. 1991—Fumbled four times and recovered one fumble. 1992—Fumbled twice and recovered one fumble. 1993—Fumbled five times and recovered one fumble. 1994—Recovered one fumble. 1995—Fumbled once. 1996—Recovered one fumble. 1998—Recovered two fumbles. 2000—Fumbled once.
SINGLE GAME HIGHS (regular season): Receptions—13 (September 18, 1994, vs. Kansas City); yards—198 (December 13, 1998, vs. New Orleans); and touchdown receptions—3 (November 19, 1995, vs. St. Louis).
STATISTICAL PLATEAUS: 100-yard receiving games: 1992 (1), 1994 (5), 1995 (2), 1996 (2), 1997 (1), 1998 (3), 1999 (1). Total: 15.
MISCELLANEOUS: Holds Atlanta Falcons all-time records for most receptions (573), most touchdown receptions (57), most touchdowns (57) and yards receiving (7,349).

				RUSHING			RECEIVING				PUNT RETURNS				KICKOFF RETURNS				TOTALS		
Year	Team	G	GS	Att.	Yds.	Avg.	TD	No.	Yds.	Avg.	TD	No.	Yds.	Avg.	TD	No.	Yds.	Avg.	TD	TD	2pt.	Pts.
1990—N.Y. Jets NFL	16	1	2	9	4.5	0	19	245	12.9	0	11	165	15.0	†1	43	787	18.3	0	1	0	6
1991—N.Y. Jets NFL	16	0	1	19	19.0	0	28	329	11.8	1	23	157	6.8	0	29	599	20.7	0	1	0	6
1992—N.Y. Jets NFL	16	1	3	25	8.3	1	22	316	14.4	3	2	24	12.0	0	28	492	17.6	0	4	0	24
1993—N.Y. Jets NFL	16	3	2	20	10.0	1	24	352	14.7	0	14	99	7.1	0	7	102	14.6	0	1	0	6
1994—Atlanta NFL	16	16	0	0	0.0	0	111	1342	12.1	11	0	0	0.0	0	0	0	0.0	0	11	∞2	70
1995—Atlanta NFL	14	12	0	0	0.0	0	78	1039	13.3	9	0	0	0.0	0	0	0	0.0	0	9	*3	60
1996—Atlanta NFL	16	16	0	0	0.0	0	69	771	11.2	7	3	19	6.3	0	0	0	0.0	0	7	1	44
1997—Atlanta NFL	16	16	3	35	11.7	0	62	802	12.9	6	0	0	0.0	0	0	0	0.0	0	6	0	36
1998—Atlanta NFL	16	16	1	-6	-6.0	0	64	1136	17.8	11	1	0	0.0	0	0	0	0.0	0	11	0	66
1999—Atlanta NFL	16	16	1	0	0.0	0	81	1016	12.5	6	0	0	0.0	0	0	0	0.0	0	6	0	36
2000—Atlanta NFL	16	16	1	-5	-5.0	0	57	679	11.9	5	0	0	0.0	0	0	0	0.0	0	5	0	30
2001—Atlanta NFL	16	16	0	0	0.0	0	51	564	11.1	2	0	0	0.0	0	0	0	0.0	0	2	0	12
Pro totals (12 years)	190	129	14	97	6.9	2	666	8591	12.9	61	54	464	8.6	1	107	1980	18.5	0	64	6	396

MATTHEWS, BRUCE — G/C — TITANS

PERSONAL: Born August 8, 1961, in Raleigh, N.C. ... 6-5/305. ... Full name: Bruce Rankin Matthews. ... Son of Clay Matthews Sr., defensive end/tackle with San Francisco 49ers (1950 and 1953-55); and brother of Clay Matthews Jr., linebacker with Cleveland Browns (1978-93) and Atlanta Falcons (1994-96).
HIGH SCHOOL: Arcadia (Calif.).
COLLEGE: Southern California (degree in industrial engineering, 1983).
TRANSACTIONS/CAREER NOTES: Selected by Los Angeles Express in 1983 USFL territorial draft. ... Selected by Houston Oilers in first round (ninth pick overall) of 1983 NFL draft. ... Signed by Oilers (July 24, 1983). ... Granted free agency (February 1, 1987). ... On reserve/unsigned list (August 31-November 3, 1987). ... Re-signed by Oilers (November 4, 1987). ... Granted roster exemption (November 4-7, 1987). ... Granted unconditional free agency (February 17, 1995). ... Re-signed by Oilers (August 8, 1995). ... Oilers franchise moved to Tennessee for 1997 season. ... Oilers franchise renamed Tennessee Titans for 1999 season (December 26, 1998). ... Granted unconditional free agency (February 12, 1999). ... Re-signed by Titans (May 13, 1999).
PLAYING EXPERIENCE: Houston NFL, 1983-1996; Tennessee NFL, 1997-2001. ... Games/Games started: 1983 (16/15), 1984 (16/16), 1985 (16/16), 1986 (16/16), 1987 (8/5), 1988 (16/16), 1989 (16/16), 1990 (16/16), 1991 (16/16), 1992 (16/16), 1993 (16/16), 1994 (16/16), 1995 (16/16), 1996 (16/16), 1997 (16/16), 1998 (16/16), 1999 (16/16), 2000 (16/16), 2001 (16/16). Total: 296/292.
CHAMPIONSHIP GAME EXPERIENCE: Played in AFC championship game (1999 season). ... Played in Super Bowl XXXIV (1999 season).
HONORS: Named guard on THE SPORTING NEWS college All-America first team (1982). ... Named guard on THE SPORTING NEWS NFL All-Pro team (1988-1990, 1992, 1998 and 2000). ... Played in Pro Bowl (1988-1994, 1996, 1997 and 1999 seasons). ... Named center on THE SPORTING NEWS NFL All-Pro team (1993). ... Named to play in Pro Bowl (1995 season); replaced by Will Shields due to injury. ... Named to play in Pro Bowl (1998 season); replaced by Mark Schlereth due to injury. ... Named to play in Pro Bowl (2000 season); replaced by Will Shields due to injury.
PRO STATISTICS: 1985—Recovered three fumbles. 1986—Recovered one fumble for seven yards. 1989—Fumbled twice and recovered one fumble for minus 29 yards. 1990—Recovered one fumble. 1991—Fumbled once and recovered one fumble for minus three yards. 1994—Fumbled twice. 1997—Recovered two fumbles. 1998—Recovered one fumble.

MATTHEWS, SHANE — QB — REDSKINS

PERSONAL: Born June 1, 1970, in Pascagoula, Miss. ... 6-3/196. ... Full name: Michael Shane Matthews.
HIGH SCHOOL: Pascagoula (Miss.).
COLLEGE: Florida.
TRANSACTIONS/CAREER NOTES: Signed as non-drafted free agent by Chicago Bears (April 29, 1993). ... Released by Bears (August 30, 1993). ... Re-signed by Bears to practice squad (September 1, 1993). ... Activated (October 8, 1993); did not play. ... Active for two games (1994); did not play. ... Released by Bears (September 15, 1995). ... Re-signed by Bears (February 12, 1996). ... Released by Bears (June 7, 1996). ... Re-signed by Bears (October 9, 1996). ... Granted unconditional free agency (February 14, 1997). ... Assigned by Bears to Rhein Fire in 1997 World League enhancement allocation program (February 19, 1997). ... Signed by Carolina Panthers (August 25, 1997). ... Released by Panthers (September 17, 1997). ... Re-signed by Panthers (October 16, 1997). ... Active for two games (1997); did not play. ... Granted unconditional free agency (February 13, 1998). ... Re-signed by Panthers (March 19, 1998). ... Active for 12 games (1998); did not play. ... Granted unconditional free agency (February 12, 1999). ... Signed by Bears (April 3, 1999). ... Granted unconditional free agency (February 11, 2000). ... Re-signed by Bears (July 18, 2000). ... Granted unconditional free agency (March 2, 2001). ... Re-signed by Bears (March 14, 2001). ... Released by Bears (October 13, 2001). ... Re-signed by Bears (October 13, 2001). ... Released by Bears (April 24, 2002). ... Signed by Washington Redskins (April 29, 2002).

PRO STATISTICS: 1999—Fumbled seven times and recovered two fumbles for minus 14 yards. 2000—Fumbled twice and recovered one fumble. 2001—Fumbled four times and recovered two fumbles for minus six yards.
SINGLE GAME HIGHS (regular season): Attempts—50 (November 4, 2001, vs. Cleveland); completions—30 (November 4, 2001, vs. Cleveland); yards—357 (November 4, 2001, vs. Cleveland); and touchdown passes—3 (October 28, 2001, vs. San Francisco).
STATISTICAL PLATEAUS: 300-yard passing games: 2001 (1).
MISCELLANEOUS: Regular-season record as starting NFL quarterback: 8-7 (.533).

			PASSING							RUSHING				TOTALS		
Year Team	G	GS	Att.	Cmp.	Pct.	Yds.	TD	Int.	Avg.	Rat.	Att.	Yds.	Avg.	TD	TD	2pt.	Pts.
1993—Chicago NFL...............								Did not play.									
1994—Chicago NFL...............								Did not play.									
1995—								Did not play.									
1996—Chicago NFL...............	2	0	17	13	76.5	158	1	0	9.29	124.1	1	2	2.0	1	1	0	6
1997—Carolina NFL								Did not play.									
1998—Carolina NFL								Did not play.									
1999—Chicago NFL...............	8	7	275	167	60.7	1645	10	6	5.98	80.6	14	31	2.2	0	0	0	0
2000—Chicago NFL...............	6	5	178	102	57.3	964	3	6	5.42	64.0	10	35	3.5	0	0	0	0
2001—Chicago NFL...............	5	3	129	84	65.1	694	5	6	5.38	72.3	4	5	1.3	0	0	0	0
Pro totals (4 years)	21	15	599	366	61.1	3461	19	18	5.78	75.1	29	73	2.5	1	1	0	6

MAWAE, KEVIN   C   JETS

PERSONAL: Born January 23, 1971, in Savannah, Ga. ... 6-4/289. ... Full name: Kevin James Mawae. ... Name pronounced ma-WHY.
HIGH SCHOOL: Leesville (La.).
COLLEGE: Louisiana State (degree in general studies).
TRANSACTIONS/CAREER NOTES: Selected by Seattle Seahawks in second round (36th pick overall) of 1994 NFL draft. ... Signed by Seahawks (July 21, 1994). ... Granted free agency (February 14, 1997). ... Re-signed by Seahawks (May 5, 1997). ... Granted unconditional free agency (February 13, 1998). ... Signed by New York Jets (February 19, 1998).
PLAYING EXPERIENCE: Seattle NFL, 1994-1997; New York Jets NFL, 1998-2001. ... Games/Games started: 1994 (14/11), 1995 (16/16), 1996 (16/16), 1997 (16/16), 1998 (16/16), 1999 (16/16), 2000 (16/16), 2001 (16/16). Total: 126/123.
CHAMPIONSHIP GAME EXPERIENCE: Played in AFC championship game (1998 season).
HONORS: Named center on THE SPORTING NEWS NFL All-Pro team (1999 and 2001). ... Played in Pro Bowl (1999 and 2000 seasons).
PRO STATISTICS: 1994—Recovered one fumble. 1996—Recovered two fumbles. 1997—Recovered two fumbles. 2001—Fumbled once for minus five yards.

MAYBERRY, JERMANE   G/OT   EAGLES

PERSONAL: Born August 29, 1973, in Floresville, Texas. ... 6-4/325. ... Full name: Jermane Timothy Mayberry.
HIGH SCHOOL: Floresville (Texas).
JUNIOR COLLEGE: Navarro College (Texas).
COLLEGE: Texas A&M-Kingsville.
TRANSACTIONS/CAREER NOTES: Selected by Philadelphia Eagles in first round (25th pick overall) of 1996 NFL draft. ... Signed by Eagles (June 13, 1996).
PLAYING EXPERIENCE: Philadelphia NFL, 1996-2001. ... Games/Games started: 1996 (3/1), 1997 (16/16), 1998 (15/10), 1999 (13/5), 2000 (16/16), 2001 (16/15). Total: 79/63.
CHAMPIONSHIP GAME EXPERIENCE: Played in NFC championship game (2001 season).
PRO STATISTICS: 1997—Recovered one fumble.

M

MAYNARD, BRAD   P   BEARS

PERSONAL: Born February 9, 1974, in Tipton, Ind. ... 6-1/182. ... Full name: Bradley Alan Maynard.
HIGH SCHOOL: Sheridan (Ind.).
COLLEGE: Ball State.
TRANSACTIONS/CAREER NOTES: Selected by New York Giants in third round (95th pick overall) of 1997 NFL draft. ... Signed by Giants (July 19, 1997). ... Granted free agency (February 11, 2000). ... Re-signed by Giants (June 8, 2000). ... Granted unconditional free agency (March 2, 2001). ... Signed by Chicago Bears (March 3, 2001).
CHAMPIONSHIP GAME EXPERIENCE: Played in NFC championship game (2000 season). ... Played in Super Bowl XXXV (2000 season).
HONORS: Named punter on THE SPORTING NEWS college All-America second team (1996).
PRO STATISTICS: 1998—Rushed once for minus five yards and attempted one pass without a completion. 2001—Rushed once for minus 10 yards and completed only pass attempt for 27 yards and a touchdown.

		PUNTING					
Year Team	G	No.	Yds.	Avg.	Net avg.	In. 20	Blk.
1997—New York Giants NFL...........................	16	*111	*4531	40.8	34.6	*33	1
1998—New York Giants NFL...........................	16	101	*4566	45.2	37.8	∞33	0
1999—New York Giants NFL...........................	16	89	3651	41.0	35.1	‡31	0
2000—New York Giants NFL...........................	16	79	3210	40.6	33.7	26	1
2001—Chicago NFL.................................	16	87	3709	42.6	37.0	*36	0
Pro totals (5 years)	80	467	19667	42.1	35.7	159	2

McAFEE, FRED   RB   SAINTS

PERSONAL: Born June 20, 1968, in Philadelphia, Miss. ... 5-10/193. ... Full name: Fred Lee McAfee.
HIGH SCHOOL: Philadelphia (Miss.).
COLLEGE: Mississippi College (degree in mass communications, 1990).

TRANSACTIONS/CAREER NOTES: Selected by New Orleans Saints in sixth round (154th pick overall) of 1991 NFL draft. ... Signed by Saints (July 14, 1991). ... Released by Saints (August 26, 1991). ... Re-signed by Saints to practice squad (August 28, 1991). ... Activated (October 18, 1991). ... On injured reserve with shoulder injury (December 15, 1992-remainder of season). ... Granted free agency (February 17, 1994). ... Signed by Arizona Cardinals (August 2, 1994). ... Released by Cardinals (October 31, 1994). ... Signed by Pittsburgh Steelers (November 9, 1994). ... Granted unconditional free agency (February 16, 1996). ... Re-signed by Steelers (April 12, 1996). ... Granted unconditional free agency (February 12, 1999). ... Signed by Kansas City Chiefs (July 30, 1999). ... Released by Chiefs (August 31, 1999). ... Signed by Tampa Bay Buccaneers (December 28, 1999). ... Granted unconditional free agency (February 11, 2000). ... Signed by Saints (October 2, 2000). ... Granted unconditional free agency (March 2, 2001). ... Re-signed by Saints (June 6, 2001).
CHAMPIONSHIP GAME EXPERIENCE: Played in AFC championship game (1994, 1995 and 1997 seasons). ... Played in Super Bowl XXX (1995 season). ... Played in NFC championship game (1999 season).
PRO STATISTICS: 1995—Recovered one fumble. 1998—Recovered a blocked punt in end zone for a touchdown. 2000—Recovered one fumble. 2001—Recovered three fumbles.
SINGLE GAME HIGHS (regular season): Attempts—28 (November 24, 1991, vs. Atlanta); yards—138 (November 24, 1991, vs. Atlanta); and rushing touchdowns—1 (September 10, 1995, vs. Houston).
STATISTICAL PLATEAUS: 100-yard rushing games: 1991 (1).

			RUSHING				RECEIVING			KICKOFF RETURNS			TOTALS		
Year Team	G	GS	Att.	Yds.	Avg.	TD	No.	Yds.	Avg.	TD	No.	Yds.	Avg.	TD	TD	2pt.	Pts.	Fum.
1991—New Orleans NFL	9	0	109	494	4.5	2	1	8	8.0	0	1	14	14.0	0	2	0	12	2
1992—New Orleans NFL	14	1	39	114	2.9	1	1	16	16.0	0	19	393	20.7	0	1	0	6	0
1993—New Orleans NFL	15	4	51	160	3.1	1	1	3	3.0	0	28	580	20.7	0	1	0	6	3
1994—Arizona NFL	7	0	2	-5	-2.5	1	1	4	4.0	0	7	113	16.1	0	1	0	6	1
—Pittsburgh NFL	6	0	16	56	3.5	1	0	0	0.0	0	0	0	0.0	0	1	0	6	0
1995—Pittsburgh NFL	16	1	39	156	4.0	1	15	88	5.9	0	5	56	11.2	0	1	0	6	0
1996—Pittsburgh NFL	14	0	7	17	2.4	0	5	21	4.2	0	0	0	0.0	0	0	0	0	0
1997—Pittsburgh NFL	14	0	13	41	3.2	0	2	44	22.0	0	0	0	0.0	0	0	0	0	1
1998—Pittsburgh NFL	14	0	18	111	6.2	0	9	27	3.0	0	1	10	10.0	0	1	0	6	0
1999—Tampa Bay NFL	1	0	0	0	0.0	0	0	0	0.0	0	0	0	0.0	0	0	0	0	0
2000—New Orleans NFL	12	0	2	37	18.5	0	0	0	0.0	0	10	251	25.1	0	0	0	0	0
2001—New Orleans NFL	16	0	1	2	2.0	0	0	0	0.0	0	6	144	24.0	0	0	0	0	0
Pro totals (11 years)	138	6	297	1183	4.0	7	35	211	6.0	0	77	1561	20.3	0	8	0	48	7

McALISTER, CHRIS   CB   RAVENS

PERSONAL: Born June 14, 1977, in Pasadena, Calif. ... 6-1/206. ... Full name: Christopher James McAlister. ... Son of James McAlister, running back with Philadelphia Eagles (1975 and 1976) and New England Patriots (1978).
HIGH SCHOOL: Pasadena (Calif.).
JUNIOR COLLEGE: Mt. San Antonio College (Calif.).
COLLEGE: Arizona.
TRANSACTIONS/CAREER NOTES: Selected by Baltimore Ravens in first round (10th pick overall) of 1999 NFL draft. ... Signed by Ravens (July 23, 1999).
CHAMPIONSHIP GAME EXPERIENCE: Played in AFC championship game (2000 season). ... Member of Super Bowl championship team (2000 season).
HONORS: Named cornerback on THE SPORTING NEWS college All-America third team (1997). ... Named cornerback on THE SPORTING NEWS college All-America first team (1998).
PRO STATISTICS: 1999—Returned one kickoff for 12 yards. 2000—Recovered one fumble. 2001—Returned five punts for 44 yards.

			INTERCEPTIONS			
Year Team	G	GS	No.	Yds.	Avg.	TD
1999—Baltimore NFL	16	12	5	28	5.6	0
2000—Baltimore NFL	16	16	4	*165	41.3	1
2001—Baltimore NFL	16	16	1	0	0.0	0
Pro totals (3 years)	48	44	10	193	19.3	1

McALLISTER, DEUCE   RB   SAINTS

PERSONAL: Born December 27, 1978, in Morton, Miss. ... 6-1/222. ... Full name: Dulymus James McAllister.
HIGH SCHOOL: Morton (Miss.).
COLLEGE: Mississippi.
TRANSACTIONS/CAREER NOTES: Selected by New Orleans Saints in first round (23rd pick overall) of 2001 NFL draft. ... Signed by Saints (August 4, 2001).
PRO STATISTICS: 2001—Fumbled once, attempted two passes with one completion for 12 yards and one touchdown and recovered one fumble.
SINGLE GAME HIGHS (regular season): Attempts—4 (November 18, 2001, vs. Indianapolis); yards—54 (December 9, 2001, vs. Atlanta); and rushing touchdowns—1 (December 9, 2001, vs. Atlanta).

			RUSHING				RECEIVING			PUNT RETURNS			KICKOFF RETURNS			TOTALS		
Year Team	G	GS	Att.	Yds.	Avg.	TD	No.	Yds.	Avg.	TD	No.	Yds.	Avg.	TD	No.	Yds.	Avg.	TD	TD	2pt.	Pts.
2001—New Orleans NFL	16	4	16	91	5.7	1	15	166	11.1	1	4	24	6.0	0	45	1091	24.2	0	2	0	12

McBRIDE, TOD   CB   PACKERS

PERSONAL: Born January 26, 1976, in Los Angeles. ... 6-1/205. ... Full name: Tod Anthony McBride.
HIGH SCHOOL: Walnut (Calif.).
COLLEGE: UCLA.
TRANSACTIONS/CAREER NOTES: Signed as non-drafted free agent by Seattle Seahawks (April 23, 1999). ... Claimed on waivers by Green Bay Packers (June 23, 1999). ... Granted free agency (March 1, 2002). ... Re-signed by Packers (April 24, 2002).
PLAYING EXPERIENCE: Green Bay NFL, 1999-2001. ... Games/Games started: 1999 (15/0), 2000 (15/6), 2001 (16/0). Total: 46/6.
PRO STATISTICS: 1999—Recovered two fumbles. 2000—Intercepted two passes for 43 yards. 2001—Credited with two sacks.

McBURROWS, GERALD   S   FALCONS

PERSONAL: Born October 7, 1973, in Detroit. ... 5-11/208. ... Full name: Gerald Lance McBurrows.
HIGH SCHOOL: Martin Luther King (Detroit).
COLLEGE: Kansas.
TRANSACTIONS/CAREER NOTES: Selected by St. Louis Rams in seventh round (214th pick overall) of 1995 NFL draft. ... Signed by Rams (June 16, 1995). ... On injured reserve with knee injury (October 29, 1997-remainder of season). ... Granted free agency (February 13, 1998). ... Re-signed by Rams (April 24, 1998). ... On injured reserve with knee injury (November 17, 1998-remainder of season). ... Granted unconditional free agency (February 12, 1999). ... Signed by Atlanta Falcons (March 2, 1999). ... Granted unconditional free agency (March 2, 2001). ... Re-signed by Falcons (March 21, 2001).
PLAYING EXPERIENCE: St. Louis NFL, 1995-1998; Atlanta NFL, 1999-2001. ... Games/Games started: 1995 (14/3), 1996 (16/7), 1997 (8/3), 1998 (10/0), 1999 (16/4), 2000 (16/4), 2001 (14/8). Total: 94/29.
PRO STATISTICS: 1995—Credited with one sack. 1996—Intercepted one pass for three yards. 1998—Recovered one fumble. 1999—Intercepted two passes for 64 yards, credited with one sack and recovered one fumble. 2000—Credited with two sacks and recovered two fumbles. 2001—Recovered one fumble for 15 yards.

McCAFFREY, ED   WR   BRONCOS

PERSONAL: Born August 17, 1968, in Waynesboro, Pa. ... 6-5/215. ... Full name: Edward McCaffrey.
HIGH SCHOOL: Allentown (Pa.) Central Catholic.
COLLEGE: Stanford.
TRANSACTIONS/CAREER NOTES: Selected by New York Giants in third round (83rd pick overall) of 1991 NFL draft. ... Signed by Giants (July 23, 1991). ... Granted free agency (February 17, 1994). ... Signed by San Francisco 49ers (July 24, 1994). ... Granted unconditional free agency (February 17, 1995). ... Signed by Denver Broncos (March 7, 1995). ... On injured reserve with leg injury (September 12, 2001-remainder of season).
CHAMPIONSHIP GAME EXPERIENCE: Played in NFC championship game (1994 season). ... Member of Super Bowl championship team (1994, 1997 and 1998 seasons). ... Played in AFC championship game (1997 and 1998 seasons).
HONORS: Named wide receiver on THE SPORTING NEWS college All-America second team (1990). ... Played in Pro Bowl (1998 season).
PRO STATISTICS: 1995—Rushed once for minus one yard. 1997—Recovered two fumbles.
SINGLE GAME HIGHS (regular season): Receptions—10 (November 19, 2000, vs. San Diego); yards—148 (November 19, 2000, vs. San Diego); and touchdown receptions—3 (September 13, 1999, vs. Miami).
STATISTICAL PLATEAUS: 100-yard receiving games: 1992 (1), 1997 (1), 1998 (4), 1999 (4), 2000 (5). Total: 15.

			RECEIVING				TOTALS		
Year Team	G	GS	No.	Yds.	Avg.	TD	TD	2pt.	Pts.	Fum.
1991—New York Giants NFL	16	0	16	146	9.1	0	0	0	0	0
1992—New York Giants NFL	16	3	49	610	12.4	5	5	0	30	2
1993—New York Giants NFL	16	1	27	335	12.4	2	2	0	12	0
1994—San Francisco NFL	16	0	11	131	11.9	2	2	0	12	0
1995—Denver NFL	16	5	39	477	12.2	2	2	1	14	1
1996—Denver NFL	15	15	48	553	11.5	7	7	0	42	0
1997—Denver NFL	15	15	45	590	13.1	8	8	0	48	0
1998—Denver NFL	15	15	64	1053	16.5	▲10	10	1	62	1
1999—Denver NFL	15	15	71	1018	14.3	7	7	0	42	0
2000—Denver NFL	16	16	101	1317	13.0	9	9	1	56	0
2001—Denver NFL	1	1	6	94	15.7	1	1	0	6	0
Pro totals (11 years)	157	86	477	6324	13.3	53	53	3	324	4

McCARDELL, KEENAN   WR

PERSONAL: Born January 6, 1970, in Houston. ... 6-1/190. ... Full name: Keenan Wayne McCardell. ... Name pronounced mc-CAR-dell.
HIGH SCHOOL: Waltrip (Houston).
COLLEGE: UNLV (degree in business management, 1991).
TRANSACTIONS/CAREER NOTES: Selected by Washington Redskins in 12th round (326th pick overall) of 1991 NFL draft. ... Signed by Redskins for 1991 season. ... On injured reserve with knee injury (August 20, 1991-entire season). ... Granted unconditional free agency (February 1, 1992). ... Signed by Cleveland Browns (March 24, 1992). ... Released by Browns (September 1, 1992). ... Re-signed by Browns to practice squad (September 3, 1992). ... Activated (October 6, 1992). ... Released by Browns (October 13, 1992). ... Re-signed by Browns to practice squad (October 14, 1992). ... Activated (November 14, 1992). ... Released by Browns (November 19, 1992). ... Re-signed by Browns to practice squad (November 20, 1992). ... Activated (December 26, 1992). ... Released by Browns (September 23, 1993). ... Signed by Chicago Bears to practice squad (November 2, 1993). ... Signed by Browns off Bears practice squad (November 24, 1993). ... Granted free agency (February 17, 1994). ... Re-signed by Browns (March 4, 1994). ... Granted unconditional free agency (February 16, 1996). ... Signed by Jacksonville Jaguars (March 2, 1996). ... Released by Jaguars (June 3, 2002).
CHAMPIONSHIP GAME EXPERIENCE: Played in AFC championship game (1996 and 1999 seasons).
HONORS: Played in Pro Bowl (1996 season).
PRO STATISTICS: 1995—Returned 13 punts for 93 yards and returned nine kickoffs for 161 yards. 1996—Returned one punt for two yards and recovered three fumbles. 1998—Returned one kickoff for 15 yards. 1999—Returned six punts for 41 yards, returned two kickoffs for 19 yards and recovered one fumble. 2000—Returned three punts for 25 yards and recovered one fumble for four yards.
SINGLE GAME HIGHS (regular season): Receptions—16 (October 20, 1996, vs. St. Louis); yards—232 (October 20, 1996, vs. St. Louis); and touchdown receptions—2 (November 29, 1998, vs. Cincinnati).
STATISTICAL PLATEAUS: 100-yard receiving games: 1995 (1), 1996 (3), 1997 (4), 1998 (2), 1999 (3), 2000 (5), 2001 (2). Total: 20.

			RECEIVING				TOTALS		
Year Team	G	GS	No.	Yds.	Avg.	TD	TD	2pt.	Pts.	Fum.
1991—Washington NFL					Did not play.					
1992—Cleveland NFL	2	0	1	8	8.0	0	0	0	0	0
1993—Cleveland NFL	6	3	13	234	18.0	4	4	0	24	0
1994—Cleveland NFL	13	3	10	182	18.2	0	0	0	0	0
1995—Cleveland NFL	16	5	56	709	12.7	4	4	0	24	0

– 247 –

Year Team	G	GS	No.	Yds.	Avg.	TD	TD	2pt.	Pts.	Fum.
1996—Jacksonville NFL	16	15	85	1129	13.3	3	3	2	22	1
1997—Jacksonville NFL	16	16	85	1164	13.7	5	5	0	30	0
1998—Jacksonville NFL	15	15	64	892	13.9	6	6	1	38	0
1999—Jacksonville NFL	16	15	78	891	11.4	5	5	†1	32	1
2000—Jacksonville NFL	16	16	94	1207	12.8	5	5	0	30	3
2001—Jacksonville NFL	16	16	93	1110	11.9	6	6	1	38	1
Pro totals (10 years)	132	104	579	7526	13.0	38	38	5	238	6

McCAREINS, JUSTIN — WR — TITANS

PERSONAL: Born December 11, 1978, in Naperville, Ill. ... 6-2/205.
HIGH SCHOOL: Naperville (Ill.) North.
COLLEGE: Northern Illinois.
TRANSACTIONS/CAREER NOTES: Selected by Tennessee Titans in fourth round (124th pick overall) of 2001 NFL draft. ... Signed by Titans (July 9, 2001).
SINGLE GAME HIGHS (regular season): Receptions—2 (October 14, 2001, vs. Tampa Bay); yards—70 (October 14, 2001, vs. Tampa Bay); and touchdown receptions—0.

			RECEIVING				PUNT RETURNS			KICKOFF RETURNS			TOTALS			
Year Team	G	GS	No.	Yds.	Avg.	TD	No.	Yds.	Avg.	TD	No.	Yds.	Avg.	TD	TD 2pt.	Pts. Fum.
2001—Tennessee NFL	4	1	3	88	29.3	0	2	29	14.5	0	4	70	17.5	0	0 0	0 0

McCLEARY, NORRIS — DT — CHIEFS

PERSONAL: Born May 10, 1977, in Shelby, N.C. ... 6-6/305. ... Full name: Norris Ellington McCleary.
HIGH SCHOOL: Bessemer (N.C.).
COLLEGE: East Carolina.
TRANSACTIONS/CAREER NOTES: Signed as non-drafted free agent by Kansas City Chiefs (June 6, 2000). ... Released by Chiefs (August 27, 2000). ... Re-signed by Chiefs to practice squad (August 30, 2000). ... Acitvated (November 24, 2000).
PLAYING EXPERIENCE: Kansas City NFL, 2000 and 2001. ... Games/Games started: 2000 (3/0), 2001 (10/0). Total: 13/0.

McCLELLION, CENTRAL — DB — CHIEFS

PERSONAL: Born September 15, 1975, in Delray Beach, Fla. ... 6-0/190.
HIGH SCHOOL: Olympic Heights (Boca Raton, Fla.).
COLLEGE: Ohio State.
TRANSACTIONS/CAREER NOTES: Signed as non-drafted free agent by Washington Redskins (July 9, 2001). ... Released by Redskins (September 2, 2001). ... Re-signed by Redskins to practice squad (September 3, 2001). ... Activated (September 26, 2001). ... Released by Redskins (December 10, 2001). ... Re-signed by Redskins to practice squad (December 12, 2001). ... Granted free agency after 2001 season. ... Signed by Kansas City Chiefs (January 30, 2002).
PLAYING EXPERIENCE: Scottish NFLE, 2001; Washington NFL, 2001 ... Games/Games started: NFLE 2001 (games played unavailable), NFL 2001 (6/0).
PRO STATISTICS: NFLE: 2001—Intercepted one pass for 12 yards and returned one punt for no yards. NFL: 2001—Returned one punt for no yards and fumbled once.

McCLEON, DEXTER — CB — RAMS

PERSONAL: Born October 9, 1973, in Meridian, Miss. ... 5-10/195. ... Full name: Dexter Keith McCleon.
HIGH SCHOOL: Meridian (Miss.).
COLLEGE: Clemson (degree in management, 1996).
TRANSACTIONS/CAREER NOTES: Selected by St. Louis Rams in second round (40th pick overall) of 1997 NFL draft. ... Signed by Rams (July 3, 1997). ... Granted free agency (February 11, 2000). ... Re-signed by Rams (June 13, 2000).
CHAMPIONSHIP GAME EXPERIENCE: Played in NFC championship game (1999 and 2001 seasons). ... Member of Super Bowl championship team (1999 season). ... Played in Super Bowl XXXVI (2001 season).
PRO STATISTICS: 1997—Credited with one sack. 1999—Credited with 1½ sacks. 2000—Credited with two sacks, returned one punt for no yards, fumbled once and recovered one fumble for 21 yards. 2001—Recovered one fumble for 29 yards and a touchdown.
MISCELLANEOUS: Selected by Minnesota Twins organization in 13th round of free-agent baseball draft (June 3, 1993); did not sign.

				INTERCEPTIONS		
Year Team	G	GS	No.	Yds.	Avg.	TD
1997—St. Louis NFL	16	1	1	0	0.0	0
1998—St. Louis NFL	15	6	2	29	14.5	0
1999—St. Louis NFL	15	15	4	17	4.3	0
2000—St. Louis NFL	16	16	8	28	3.5	0
2001—St. Louis NFL	16	16	4	66	16.5	0
Pro totals (5 years)	78	54	19	140	7.4	0

McCLURE, TODD — C — FALCONS

PERSONAL: Born February 16, 1977, in Baton Rouge, La. ... 6-1/286.
HIGH SCHOOL: Central (Baton Rouge, La.).
COLLEGE: Louisiana State.
TRANSACTIONS/CAREER NOTES: Selected by Atlanta Falcons in seventh round (237th pick overall) of 1999 NFL draft. ... Signed by Falcons (June 25, 1999). ... On injured reserve with knee injury (August 30, 1999-entire season). ... Granted free agency (March 1, 2002).
PLAYING EXPERIENCE: Atlanta NFL, 2000 and 2001. ... Games/Games started: 2000 (9/7), 2001 (15/15). Total: 24/22.
PRO STATISTICS: 2001—Recovered one fumble.

McCOLLUM, ANDY — C — RAMS

PERSONAL: Born June 2, 1970, in Akron, Ohio. ... 6-4/300. ... Full name: Andrew Jon McCollum. ... Name pronounced Mc-COL-umn.
HIGH SCHOOL: Revere (Richfield, Ohio).
COLLEGE: Toledo.
TRANSACTIONS/CAREER NOTES: Played with Milwaukee Mustangs of Arena League (1994). ... Signed as non-drafted free agent by Cleveland Browns (June 1994). ... Released by Browns (August 28, 1994). ... Re-signed by Browns to practice squad (August 30, 1994). ... Signed by New Orleans Saints off Browns practice squad (November 15, 1994). ... Inactive for five games (1994). ... Assigned by Saints to Barcelona Dragons in 1995 World League enhancement allocation program (February 20, 1995). ... Granted unconditional free agency (February 12, 1999). ... Signed by St. Louis Rams (April 13, 1999). ... Granted unconditional free agency (February 11, 2000). ... Re-signed by Rams (February 22, 2000).
PLAYING EXPERIENCE: Barcelona W.L., 1995; New Orleans NFL, 1995-1998; St. Louis NFL, 1999-2001. ... Games/Games started: W.L. 1995 (games played unavailable), NFL 1995 (11/9), 1996 (16/16), 1997 (16/16), 1998 (16/5), 1999 (16/2), 2000 (16/16), 2001 (16/16). Total NFL: 107/80.
CHAMPIONSHIP GAME EXPERIENCE: Played in NFC championship game (1999 and 2001 seasons). ... Member of Super Bowl championship team (1999 season). ... Played in Super Bowl XXXVI (2001 season).
PRO STATISTICS: 1996—Recovered one fumble. 1998—Recovered one fumble. 1999—Returned one kickoff for three yards. 2000—Fumbled once for minus four yards.

McCORD, QUENTIN — WR — FALCONS

PERSONAL: Born June 26, 1978, in Troup County, Ga. ... 5-10/188.
HIGH SCHOOL: La Grange (Ga.).
COLLEGE: Kentucky.
TRANSACTIONS/CAREER NOTES: Selected by Atlanta Falcons in seventh round (236th pick overall) of 2001 NFL draft. ... Signed by Falcons (June 20, 2001).
PRO STATISTICS: 2001—Returned two kickoffs for 39 yards.
SINGLE GAME HIGHS (regular season): Receptions—3 (October 7, 2001, vs. Chicago); yards—53 (October 7, 2001, vs. Chicago); and touchdown receptions—0.

				RUSHING				RECEIVING				TOTALS		
Year Team	G	GS	Att.	Yds.	Avg.	TD	No.	Yds.	Avg.	TD	TD	2pt.	Pts.	Fum.
2001—Atlanta NFL	7	0	2	11	5.5	0	3	53	17.7	0	0	0	0	0

McCRARY, FRED — FB — CHARGERS

PERSONAL: Born September 19, 1972, in Naples, Fla. ... 6-0/235. ... Full name: Freddy Demetrius McCrary.
HIGH SCHOOL: Naples (Fla.).
COLLEGE: Mississippi State.
TRANSACTIONS/CAREER NOTES: Selected by Philadelphia Eagles in sixth round (208th pick overall) of 1995 NFL draft. ... Signed by Eagles (June 27, 1995). ... Released by Eagles (August 25, 1996). ... Signed by New Orleans Saints (March 5, 1997). ... Released by Saints (August 24, 1998). ... Signed by San Diego Chargers (March 26, 1999). ... Granted free agency (February 11, 2000). ... Re-signed by Chargers (May 22, 2000).
PRO STATISTICS: 1995—Returned one kickoff for one yard. 1997—Returned two kickoffs for 26 yards. 1999—Returned one kickoff for four yards.
SINGLE GAME HIGHS (regular season): Attempts—5 (September 24, 2000, vs. Seattle); yards—13 (November 23, 1997, vs. Atlanta); and rushing touchdowns—1 (September 10, 1995, vs. Arizona).

				RUSHING				RECEIVING				TOTALS		
Year Team	G	GS	Att.	Yds.	Avg.	TD	No.	Yds.	Avg.	TD	TD	2pt.	Pts.	Fum.
1995—Philadelphia NFL	13	5	3	1	0.3	1	9	60	6.7	0	1	0	6	0
1996—							Did not play.							
1997—New Orleans NFL	7	0	8	15	1.9	0	4	17	4.3	0	0	0	0	0
1998—							Did not play.							
1999—San Diego NFL	16	14	0	0	0.0	0	37	201	5.4	1	1	0	6	0
2000—San Diego NFL	15	13	7	8	1.1	0	18	141	7.8	2	2	0	12	1
2001—San Diego NFL	16	12	2	3	1.5	0	13	71	5.5	0	0	0	0	0
Pro totals (5 years)	67	44	20	27	1.4	1	81	490	6.0	3	4	0	24	1

McCRARY, MICHAEL — DE — RAVENS

PERSONAL: Born July 7, 1970, in Vienna, Va. ... 6-4/260. ... Full name: Michael Curtis McCrary.
HIGH SCHOOL: George C. Marshall (Falls Church, Va.).
COLLEGE: Wake Forest.
TRANSACTIONS/CAREER NOTES: Selected by Seattle Seahawks in seventh round (170th pick overall) of 1993 NFL draft. ... Signed by Seahawks (July 13, 1993). ... Granted free agency (February 16, 1996). ... Re-signed by Seahawks (June 6, 1996). ... Granted unconditional free agency (February 14, 1997). ... Signed by Baltimore Ravens (April 7, 1997). ... On injured reserve with knee injury (November 28, 2001-remainder of season).
CHAMPIONSHIP GAME EXPERIENCE: Played in AFC championship game (2000 season). ... Member of Super Bowl championship team (2000 season).
HONORS: Named defensive end on THE SPORTING NEWS NFL All-Pro team (1998). ... Played in Pro Bowl (1998 and 1999 seasons).
PRO STATISTICS: 1996—Recovered one fumble. 1997—Recovered two fumbles. 1999—Recovered one fumble. 2000—Credited with a safety and recovered three fumbles.

Year Team	G	GS	SACKS
1993—Seattle NFL	15	0	4.0
1994—Seattle NFL	16	0	1.5
1995—Seattle NFL	11	0	1.0
1996—Seattle NFL	16	13	▲13.5
1997—Baltimore NFL	15	15	9.0
1998—Baltimore NFL	16	16	14.5
1999—Baltimore NFL	16	16	11.5
2000—Baltimore NFL	16	16	6.5
2001—Baltimore NFL	10	10	7.5
Pro totals (9 years)	131	86	69.0

McCREE, MARLON — S — JAGUARS

PERSONAL: Born March 17, 1977, in Orlando, Fla. ... 5-11/192. ... Full name: Marlon Tarron McCree.
HIGH SCHOOL: Atlantic (Daytona, Fla.).
COLLEGE: Kentucky (degree in finance).
TRANSACTIONS/CAREER NOTES: Selected by Jacksonville Jaguars in seventh round (233rd pick overall) of 2001 NFL draft. ... Signed by Jaguars (May 30, 2001).
PRO STATISTICS: 2001—Recovered two fumbles for two yards.

			INTERCEPTIONS				SACKS
Year Team	G	GS	No.	Yds.	Avg.	TD	No.
2001—Jacksonville NFL	13	11	1	10	10.0	0	1.0

McCULLOUGH, GEORGE — CB

PERSONAL: Born February 18, 1975, in Galveston, Texas. ... 5-10/187. ... Full name: George Wayne McCullough Jr.
HIGH SCHOOL: Ball (Galveston, Texas).
COLLEGE: Baylor.
TRANSACTIONS/CAREER NOTES: Selected by Houston Oilers in fifth round (143rd pick overall) of 1997 NFL draft. ... Oilers franchise moved to Tennessee for 1997 season. ... Signed by Oilers (July 19, 1997). ... Released by Oilers (August 25, 1997). ... Re-signed by Oilers to practice squad (August 26, 1997). ... Activated (December 5, 1997). ... Assigned by Oilers to Barcelona Dragons in 1998 NFL Europe enhancement allocation program (February 18, 1998). ... Oilers franchise renamed Tennessee Titans for 1999 season (December 26, 1998). ... Granted free agency (March 2, 2001). ... Signed by Kansas City Chiefs (May 10, 2001). ... Released by Chiefs (September 2, 2001). ... Signed by San Francisco 49ers (September 12, 2001). ... Granted unconditional free agency (March 1, 2002).
PLAYING EXPERIENCE: Tennessee NFL, 1997-2000; Barcelona NFLE, 1998; San Francisco NFL, 2001. ... Games/Games started: 1997 (2/0), NFLE 1998 (games played unavailable), NFL 1998 (7/0), 1999 (5/0), 2000 (11/0), 2001 (15/0). Total NFL: 40/0.
CHAMPIONSHIP GAME EXPERIENCE: Member of Titans for AFC championship game (1999 season); inactive. ... Played in Super Bowl XXXIV (1999 season).
PRO STATISTICS: NFLE: 1998—Intercepted three passes for 89 yards and one touchdown and credited with two sacks.

McCUTCHEON, DAYLON — CB — BROWNS

PERSONAL: Born December 9, 1976, in Walnut, Calif. ... 5-10/180. ... Son of Lawrence McCutcheon, Director of Scouting, St. Louis Rams, and former running back with four NFL teams (1972-81). ... Name pronounced mc-CUTCH-in.
HIGH SCHOOL: Bishop Amat (La Puente, Calif.).
COLLEGE: Southern California.
TRANSACTIONS/CAREER NOTES: Selected by Cleveland Browns in third round (62nd pick overall) of 1999 NFL draft. ... Signed by Browns (July 22, 1999). ... Granted free agency (March 1, 2002).
HONORS: Named cornerback on THE SPORTING NEWS college All-America second team (1998).

			INTERCEPTIONS				SACKS
Year Team	G	GS	No.	Yds.	Avg.	TD	No.
1999—Cleveland NFL	16	15	1	12	12.0	0	1.0
2000—Cleveland NFL	15	15	1	20	20.0	0	4.0
2001—Cleveland NFL	16	15	4	62	15.5	1	2.0
Pro totals (3 years)	47	45	6	94	15.7	1	7.0

McDANIEL, ED — LB

PERSONAL: Born February 23, 1969, in Battesburg, S.C. ... 5-11/234.
HIGH SCHOOL: Battesburg (S.C.)-Leesville.
COLLEGE: Clemson (degree in human resource and development, 1991).
TRANSACTIONS/CAREER NOTES: Selected by Minnesota Vikings in fifth round (125th pick overall) of 1992 NFL draft. ... Signed by Vikings (July 20, 1992). ... Released by Vikings (August 31, 1992). ... Re-signed by Vikings to practice squad (September 1, 1992). ... Activated (November 5, 1992). ... On injured reserve with knee injury (August 25, 1996-entire season). ... Granted unconditional free agency (February 12, 1999). ... Re-signed by Vikings (February 18, 1999). ... On physically unable to perform list with knee injury (August 1-10, 1999). ... Released by Vikings (February 21, 2002).
CHAMPIONSHIP GAME EXPERIENCE: Played in NFC championship game (1998 and 2000 seasons).
HONORS: Named to play in Pro Bowl (1998 season); replaced by Hardy Nickerson due to injury.
PRO STATISTICS: 1995—Recovered one fumble. 1998—Recovered two fumbles for five yards. 1999—Recovered two fumbles.

			INTERCEPTIONS				SACKS
Year Team	G	GS	No.	Yds.	Avg.	TD	No.
1992—Minnesota NFL	8	0	0	0	0.0	0	0.0
1993—Minnesota NFL	7	1	0	0	0.0	0	0.0
1994—Minnesota NFL	16	16	1	0	0.0	0	1.5
1995—Minnesota NFL	16	16	1	3	3.0	0	4.5
1996—Minnesota NFL			Did not play.				
1997—Minnesota NFL	16	16	1	18	18.0	0	1.5
1998—Minnesota NFL	16	16	0	0	0.0	0	7.0
1999—Minnesota NFL	16	16	0	0	0.0	0	2.0
2000—Minnesota NFL	16	15	0	0	0.0	0	2.0
2001—Minnesota NFL	14	13	1	0	0.0	0	1.0
Pro totals (9 years)	125	109	4	21	5.3	0	19.5

McDANIEL, EMMANUEL   CB

PERSONAL: Born July 27, 1972, in Griffin, Ga. ... 5-9/180.
HIGH SCHOOL: Jonesboro (Ga.).
COLLEGE: East Carolina.
TRANSACTIONS/CAREER NOTES: Selected by Carolina Panthers in fourth round (111th pick overall) of 1996 NFL draft. ... Signed by Panthers (July 20, 1996). ... Released by Panthers (August 26, 1997). ... Signed by Indianapolis Colts (November 27, 1997). ... Released by Colts (August 24, 1998). ... Re-signed by Colts (September 3, 1998). ... Inactive for one game with Colts (1998). ... Released by Colts (September 9, 1998). ... Signed by Miami Dolphins (October 8, 1998). ... Inactive for one game with Dolphins (1998). ... Released by Dolphins (October 14, 1998). ... Re-signed by Dolphins to practice squad (October 15, 1998). ... Activated (January 7, 1999). ... Claimed on waivers by New York Giants (September 1, 1999). ... Released by Giants (September 5, 1999). ... Re-signed by Giants to practice squad (September 6, 1999). ... Activated (November 15, 1999). ... Granted free agency (March 2, 2001). ... Re-signed by Giants (April 19, 2001). ... Granted unconditional free agency (March 1, 2002).
PLAYING EXPERIENCE: Carolina NFL, 1996; Indianapolis NFL, 1997; New York Giants NFL, 1999-2001. ... Games/Games started: 1996 (2/0), 1997 (3/0), 1999 (7/2), 2000 (16/3), 2001 (16/0). Total: 44/5.
CHAMPIONSHIP GAME EXPERIENCE: Member of Panthers for NFC championship game (1996 season); inactive. ... Played in NFC championship game (2000 season). ... Played in Super Bowl XXXV (2000 season).
PRO STATISTICS: 2000—Intercepted six passes for 30 yards, credited with one sack and recovered one fumble. 2001—Returned one kickoff for 17 yards and recovered one fumble.

McDANIEL, JEREMY   WR   BILLS

PERSONAL: Born May 2, 1976, in New Bern, N.C. ... 6-1/195. ... Full name: Jeremy Dwayne McDaniel.
HIGH SCHOOL: New Bern (N.C.).
JUNIOR COLLEGE: Fort Scott (Kan.) Community College.
COLLEGE: Arizona.
TRANSACTIONS/CAREER NOTES: Signed as non-drafted free agent by Buffalo Bills (April 23, 1999). ... Released by Bills (September 4, 1999). ... Re-signed by Bills to practice squad (September 7, 1999). ... Activated (December 23, 1999).
SINGLE GAME HIGHS (regular season): Receptions—5 (October 22, 2000, vs. Minnesota); yards—93 (September 17, 2000, vs. New York Jets); and touchdown receptions—1 (September 17, 2000, vs. New York Jets).

			RECEIVING			
Year Team	G	GS	No.	Yds.	Avg.	TD
1999—Buffalo NFL	1	0	0	0	0.0	0
2000—Buffalo NFL	16	5	43	697	16.2	2
2001—Buffalo NFL	7	0	11	129	11.7	0
Pro totals (3 years)	24	5	54	826	15.3	2

McDANIEL, RANDALL   G

PERSONAL: Born December 19, 1964, in Phoenix. ... 6-3/279. ... Full name: Randall Cornell McDaniel.
HIGH SCHOOL: Agua Fria Union (Avondale, Ariz.).
COLLEGE: Arizona State (degree in physical education, 1988).
TRANSACTIONS/CAREER NOTES: Selected by Minnesota Vikings in first round (19th pick overall) of 1988 NFL draft. ... Signed by Vikings (July 22, 1988). ... Granted free agency (February 1, 1991). ... Re-signed by Vikings (July 22, 1991). ... Designated by Vikings as transition player (February 25, 1993). ... Free agency status changed by Vikings from transitional to unconditional (February 17, 1994). ... Re-signed by Vikings (April 21, 1994). ... Designated by Vikings as franchise player (February 13, 1997). ... Re-signed by Vikings (February 21, 1997). ... Released by Vikings (February 10, 2000). ... Signed by Tampa Bay Buccaneers (March 1, 2000). ... Announced retirement (February 25, 2002).
PLAYING EXPERIENCE: Minnesota NFL, 1988-1999; Tampa Bay NFL, 2000 and 2001. ... Games/Games started: 1988 (16/15), 1989 (14/13), 1990 (16/16), 1991 (16/16), 1992 (16/16), 1993 (16/16), 1994 (16/16), 1995 (16/16), 1996 (16/16), 1997 (16/16), 1998 (16/16), 1999 (16/16), 2000 (16/16), 2001 (16/16). Total: 222/220.
CHAMPIONSHIP GAME EXPERIENCE: Played in NFC championship game (1998 season).
HONORS: Named guard on THE SPORTING NEWS college All-America second team (1987). ... Played in Pro Bowl (1989-2000 seasons). ... Named guard on THE SPORTING NEWS NFL All-Pro team (1991-1994 and 1996-1998).
PRO STATISTICS: 1991—Recovered one fumble. 1994—Recovered one fumble. 1996—Rushed twice for one yard. 2000—Caught one pass for two yards and a touchdown.

McDERMOTT, SEAN   C   TEXANS

PERSONAL: Born December 5, 1976, in Lufkin, Texas. ... 6-4/250.
HIGH SCHOOL: Fort Worth Arlington Heights (Texas).
COLLEGE: Kansas.
TRANSACTIONS/CAREER NOTES: Signed as non-drafted free agent by Tampa Bay Buccaneers (June 4, 2001). ... Selected by Houston Texans from Buccaneers in NFL expansion draft (February 18, 2002).
PLAYING EXPERIENCE: Tampa Bay NFL, 2001. ... Games/Games started: 2001 (16/0).

McDOUGAL, KEVIN   RB   COLTS

PERSONAL: Born May 18, 1977, in Denver. ... 5-11/203. ... Full name: Kevin John McDougal.
HIGH SCHOOL: Arvada West (Colorado).
COLLEGE: Colorado State.
TRANSACTIONS/CAREER NOTES: Signed by Indianapolis Colts as non-drafted free agent (April 20, 2000). ... On injured reserve with neck injury (November 28, 2000-remainder of season). ... Released by Colts (September 1, 2001). ... Re-signed by Colts to practice squad (September 3, 2001). ... Released by Colts (October 1, 2001). ... Re-signed by Colts (November 3, 2001).

PLAYING EXPERIENCE: Indianapolis NFL, 2000. ... Games/Games started: 2000 (6/0).
SINGLE GAME HIGHS (regular season): Attempts—10 (November 11, 2001, vs. Miami); yards—23 (November 25, 2001, vs. San Francisco); and rushing touchdowns—0.

			RUSHING				RECEIVING				KICKOFF RETURNS				TOTALS		
Year Team	G	GS	Att.	Yds.	Avg.	TD	No.	Yds.	Avg.	TD	No.	Yds.	Avg.	TD	TD	2pt.	Pts.	Fum.
2000—Indianapolis NFL	6	0	0	0	0.0	0	0	0	0.0	0	0	0	0.0	0	0	0	0	0
2001—Indianapolis NFL	9	0	17	48	2.8	0	1	10	10.0	0	16	362	22.6	0	0	1	2	0
Pro totals (2 years)	15	0	17	48	2.8	0	1	10	10.0	0	16	362	22.6	0	0	1	2	0

McDOUGLE, STOCKAR OT LIONS

PERSONAL: Born January 11, 1977, in Deerfield Beach, Fla. ... 6-6/350.
HIGH SCHOOL: Deerfield Beach (Fla.).
JUNIOR COLLEGE: Navarro College (Texas).
COLLEGE: Oklahoma.
TRANSACTIONS/CAREER NOTES: Selected by Detroit Lions in first round (20th pick overall) of 2000 NFL draft. ... Signed by Lions (July 15, 2000).
PLAYING EXPERIENCE: Detroit NFL, 2000 and 2001. ... Games/Games started: 2000 (8/8), 2001 (9/3). Total: 17/11.

McELROY, RAY CB

PERSONAL: Born July 31, 1972, in Bellwood, Ill. ... 5-11/196. ... Full name: Raymond Edward McElroy. ... Name pronounced Mc-ELL-roy.
HIGH SCHOOL: Proviso West (Hillside, Ill.).
COLLEGE: Eastern Illinois.
TRANSACTIONS/CAREER NOTES: Selected by Indianapolis Colts in fourth round (114th pick overall) of 1995 NFL draft. ... Signed by Colts (July 12, 1995). ... Granted free agency (February 13, 1998). ... Re-signed by Colts (February 24, 1998). ... Released by Colts (August 24, 1998). ... Re-signed by Colts (August 28, 1998). ... Granted unconditional free agency (February 12, 1999). ... Re-signed by Colts (May 3, 1999). ... Released by Colts (August 9, 1999). ... Signed by Carolina Panthers (August 11, 1999). ... Released by Panthers (September 3, 1999). ... Signed by Chicago Bears (April 17, 2000). ... Released by Bears (August 27, 2000). ... Re-signed by Bears (September 19, 2000). ... Released by Bears (August 3, 2001). ... Signed by Detroit Lions (August 11, 2001). ... Released by Lions (September 2, 2001). ... Re-signed by Lions (December 12, 2001). ... Granted unconditional free agency (March 1, 2002).
PLAYING EXPERIENCE: Indianapolis NFL, 1995-1998; Chicago NFL, 2000; Detroit NFL, 2001. ... Games/Games started: 1995 (16/0), 1996 (16/5), 1997 (16/4), 1998 (16/0), 2000 (13/0), 2001 (4/0). Total: 81/9.
CHAMPIONSHIP GAME EXPERIENCE: Played in AFC championship game (1995 season).
PRO STATISTICS: 1997—Returned blocked field goal attempt 42 yards for a touchdown. 2000—Recovered one fumble.

McFARLAND, ANTHONY DT BUCCANEERS

PERSONAL: Born December 18, 1977, in Winnsboro, La. ... 6-0/300. ... Full name: Anthony Darelle McFarland.
HIGH SCHOOL: Winnsboro (La.).
COLLEGE: Louisiana State.
TRANSACTIONS/CAREER NOTES: Selected by Tampa Bay Buccaneers in first round (15th pick overall) of 1999 NFL draft. ... Signed by Buccaneers (August 3, 1999).
PLAYING EXPERIENCE: Tampa Bay NFL, 1999-2001. ... Games/Games started: 1999 (14/0), 2000 (16/16), 2001 (14/14). Total: 44/30.
CHAMPIONSHIP GAME EXPERIENCE: Played in NFC championship game (1999 season).
HONORS: Named defensive tackle on THE SPORTING NEWS college All-America second team (1998).
PRO STATISTICS: 1999—Credited with one sack. 2000—Credited with $6^{1}/_{2}$ sacks and recovered one fumble. 2001—Credited with $3^{1}/_{2}$ sacks.

McGARITY, WANE WR

PERSONAL: Born September 30, 1976, in San Antonio. ... 5-8/197. ... Full name: Wane Keith McGarity.
HIGH SCHOOL: Clark (San Antonio).
COLLEGE: Texas.
TRANSACTIONS/CAREER NOTES: Selected by Dallas Cowboys in fourth round (118th pick overall) of 1999 NFL draft. ... Signed by Cowboys (July 26, 1999). ... On injured reserve with finger injury (December 10, 1999-remainder of season). ... Released by Cowboys (October 3, 2001). ... Signed by New Orleans Saints (October 24, 2001). ... Released by Saints (October 27, 2001). ... Re-signed by Saints (October 30, 2001). ... Granted free agency (March 1, 2002).
PRO STATISTICS: 2000—Rushed six times for 49 yards and one touchdown and recovered two fumbles.
SINGLE GAME HIGHS (regular season): Receptions—6 (November 19, 2000, vs. Baltimore); yards—59 (December 3, 2000, vs. Tampa Bay); and touchdown receptions—1 (September 23, 2001, vs. San Diego).

			RECEIVING				PUNT RETURNS				TOTALS			
Year Team	G	GS	No.	Yds.	Avg.	TD	No.	Yds.	Avg.	TD	TD	2pt.	Pts.	Fum.
1999—Dallas NFL	5	1	7	70	10.0	0	3	16	5.3	0	0	0	0	0
2000—Dallas NFL	14	0	25	250	10.0	0	30	353	11.8	†2	3	0	18	2
2001—Dallas NFL	3	1	6	45	7.5	1	6	38	6.3	0	1	0	6	1
—New Orleans NFL	9	0	1	-2	-2.0	0	19	183	9.6	0	0	0	0	1
Pro totals (3 years)	31	2	39	363	9.3	1	58	590	10.2	2	4	0	24	4

McGARRAHAN, SCOTT S DOLPHINS

PERSONAL: Born February 12, 1974, in Arlington, Texas. ... 6-1/200. ... Full name: John Scott McGarrahan. ... Name pronounced ma-GAIR-a-han.
HIGH SCHOOL: Lamar (Arlington, Texas).
COLLEGE: New Mexico.

TRANSACTIONS/CAREER NOTES: Selected by Green Bay Packers in sixth round (156th pick overall) of 1998 NFL draft. ... Signed by Packers (July 17, 1998). ... On injured reserve with hamstring injury (December 29, 1999-remainder of season). ... Granted free agency (March 2, 2001). ... Re-signed by Packers (May 8, 2001). ... Released by Packers (September 1, 2001). ... Signed by Miami Dolphins (September 5, 2001). ... Granted unconditional free agency (March 1, 2002). ... Re-signed by Dolphins (March 21, 2002).
PLAYING EXPERIENCE: Green Bay NFL, 1998-2000; Miami NFL, 2001. ... Games/Games started: 1998 (15/0), 1999 (13/0), 2000 (16/0), 2001 (16/0). Total: 60/0.
PRO STATISTICS: 1999—Recovered one fumble. 2000—Credited with $1/2$ sack. 2001—Recovered one fumble.

McGEE, TONY   TE   COWBOYS

PERSONAL: Born April 21, 1971, in Terre Haute, Ind. ... 6-4/248.
HIGH SCHOOL: Terre Haute (Ind.) South.
COLLEGE: Michigan (degree in communications).
TRANSACTIONS/CAREER NOTES: Selected by Cincinnati Bengals in second round (37th pick overall) of 1993 NFL draft. ... Signed by Bengals (July 20, 1993). ... Granted free agency (February 16, 1996). ... Re-signed by Bengals for 1996 season. ... On injured reserve with broken ankle (December 14, 2000-remainder of season). ... On injured reserve with ankle injury (December 3, 2001-remainder of season). ... Released by Bengals (April 25, 2002). ... Signed by Dallas Cowboys (April 28, 2002).
PRO STATISTICS: 1994—Returned one kickoff for four yards.
SINGLE GAME HIGHS (regular season): Receptions—8 (December 22, 1996, vs. Indianapolis); yards—118 (September 3, 1995, vs. Indianapolis); and touchdown receptions—2 (November 9, 1997, vs. Indianapolis).
STATISTICAL PLATEAUS: 100-yard receiving games: 1993 (1), 1995 (1). Total: 2.

			RECEIVING				TOTALS			
Year Team	G	GS	No.	Yds.	Avg.	TD	TD	2pt.	Pts.	Fum.
1993—Cincinnati NFL	15	15	44	525	11.9	0	0	0	0	1
1994—Cincinnati NFL	16	16	40	492	12.3	1	1	0	6	0
1995—Cincinnati NFL	16	16	55	754	13.7	4	4	0	24	2
1996—Cincinnati NFL	16	16	38	446	11.7	4	4	0	24	0
1997—Cincinnati NFL	16	16	34	414	12.2	6	6	1	38	0
1998—Cincinnati NFL	16	16	22	363	16.5	1	1	0	6	0
1999—Cincinnati NFL	16	16	26	344	13.2	2	2	0	12	0
2000—Cincinnati NFL	14	14	26	309	11.9	1	1	0	6	0
2001—Cincinnati NFL	11	9	14	148	10.6	1	1	0	6	0
Pro totals (9 years)	136	134	299	3795	12.7	20	20	1	122	3

McGEOGHAN, PHIL   WR   BRONCOS

PERSONAL: Born July 8, 1979, in Freding Hills, Maine. ... 6-2/224.
HIGH SCHOOL: Agawam (Freding Hills, Maine).
COLLEGE: Maine.
TRANSACTIONS/CAREER NOTES: Signed as non-drafted free agent by New York Jets (April 26, 2001). ... Released by Jets (August 27, 2001). ... Signed by Denver Broncos to practice squad (October 31, 2001). ... Activated (November 15, 2001).
PLAYING EXPERIENCE: Denver NFL, 2001. ... Games/Games started: 2001 (1/0).

McGINEST, WILLIE   DE   PATRIOTS

PERSONAL: Born December 11, 1971, in Long Beach, Calif. ... 6-5/270. ... Full name: William Lee McGinest Jr.
HIGH SCHOOL: Polytechnic (Pasadena, Calif.).
COLLEGE: Southern California.
TRANSACTIONS/CAREER NOTES: Selected by New England Patriots in first round (fourth pick overall) of 1994 NFL draft. ... Signed by Patriots (May 17, 1994). ... Granted unconditional free agency (February 13, 1998). ... Re-signed by Patriots (February 12, 1998).
CHAMPIONSHIP GAME EXPERIENCE: Played in AFC championship game (1996 and 2001 seasons). ... Played in Super Bowl XXXI (1996 season). ... Member of Super Bowl championship team (2001 season).
PRO STATISTICS: 1994—Recovered two fumbles. 1996—Intercepted one pass for 46 yards and a touchdown and recovered two fumbles, including one in end zone for a touchdown. 1997—Recovered three fumbles. 1999—Recovered two fumbles for two yards and one touchdown. 2000—Recovered two fumbles.

Year Team	G	GS	SACKS
1994—New England NFL	16	7	4.5
1995—New England NFL	16	16	11.0
1996—New England NFL	16	16	9.5
1997—New England NFL	11	11	2.0
1998—New England NFL	9	8	3.5
1999—New England NFL	16	16	9.0
2000—New England NFL	14	14	6.0
2001—New England NFL	11	5	6.0
Pro totals (8 years)	109	93	51.5

McGLOCKTON, CHESTER   DT   BRONCOS

PERSONAL: Born September 16, 1969, in Whiteville, N.C. ... 6-4/334.
HIGH SCHOOL: Whiteville (N.C.).
COLLEGE: Clemson.
TRANSACTIONS/CAREER NOTES: Selected after junior season by Los Angeles Raiders in first round (16th pick overall) of 1992 NFL draft. ... Signed by Raiders for 1992 season. ... On injured reserve (January 11, 1994-remainder of 1993 playoffs). ... Raiders franchise moved to Oakland (July 21, 1995). ... Designated by Raiders as franchise player (February 12, 1998). ... Tendered offer sheet by Kansas City Chiefs (April 10, 1998). ... Raiders declined to match offer (April 17, 1998). ... Released by Chiefs (February 28, 2001). ... Signed by Denver Broncos (April 10, 2001).

HONORS: Named defensive tackle on THE SPORTING NEWS NFL All-Pro team (1994). ... Played in Pro Bowl (1994-1997 seasons).
PRO STATISTICS: 1993—Intercepted one pass for 19 yards and recovered one fumble. 1994—Recovered one fumble. 1995—Recovered two fumbles. 1997—Recovered one fumble. 1998—Recovered one fumble. 1999—Intercepted one pass for 30 yards, fumbled once and recovered one fumble for minus two yards. 2000—Recovered one fumble. 2001—Intercepted two passes for 17 yards.

Year Team	G	GS	SACKS
1992—Los Angeles Raiders NFL	10	0	3.0
1993—Los Angeles Raiders NFL	16	16	7.0
1994—Los Angeles Raiders NFL	16	16	9.5
1995—Oakland NFL	16	16	7.5
1996—Oakland NFL	16	16	8.0
1997—Oakland NFL	16	16	4.5
1998—Kansas City NFL	10	9	1.0
1999—Kansas City NFL	16	16	1.5
2000—Kansas City NFL	15	15	4.5
2001—Denver NFL	16	16	1.0
Pro totals (10 years)	147	136	47.5

McGREW, REGGIE DT 49ERS

PERSONAL: Born December 16, 1976, in Mayo, Fla. ... 6-1/312. ... Full name: Reginald Gerard McGrew.
HIGH SCHOOL: Lafayette (Mayo, Fla.).
COLLEGE: Florida.
TRANSACTIONS/CAREER NOTES: Selected after junior season by San Francisco 49ers in first round (24th pick overall) of 1999 NFL draft. ... Signed by 49ers (July 26, 1999). ... Inactive for four games (1999). ... On injured reserve with triceps injury (October 4, 1999-remainder of season).

Year Team	G	GS	SACKS
1999—San Francisco NFL	Did not play.		
2000—San Francisco NFL	10	0	0.0
2001—San Francisco NFL	12	0	1.0
Pro totals (2 years)	22	0	1.0

McGRIFF, TRAVIS WR FALCONS

PERSONAL: Born June 24, 1976, in Gainesville, Fla. ... 5-8/185. ... Full name: William Travis McGriff.
HIGH SCHOOL: P.K. Yonge (Gainesville, Fla.).
COLLEGE: Florida.
TRANSACTIONS/CAREER NOTES: Selected by Denver Broncos in third round (93rd pick overall) of 1999 NFL draft. ... Signed by Broncos (July 22, 1999). ... Released by Broncos (October 23, 2001). ... Signed by Atlanta Falcons (January 15, 2002).
PRO STATISTICS: 1999—Recovered one fumble.
SINGLE GAME HIGHS (regular season): Receptions—1 (November 5, 2000, vs. New York Jets); yards—43 (October 1, 2000, vs. New England); and touchdown receptions—1 (October 1, 2000, vs. New England).

			RECEIVING				PUNT RETURNS				TOTALS		
Year Team	G	GS	No.	Yds.	Avg.	TD	No.	Yds.	Avg.	TD	TD	2pt.	Pts.	Fum.
1999—Denver NFL	14	0	3	37	12.3	0	7	50	7.1	0	0	0	0	1
2000—Denver NFL	14	0	2	51	25.5	1	0	0	0.0	0	1	0	6	0
2001—Denver NFL	5	0	0	0	0.0	0	0	0	0.0	0	0	0	0	0
Pro totals (3 years)	33	0	5	88	17.6	1	7	50	7.1	0	1	0	6	1

McINTOSH, CHRIS OT SEAHAWKS

PERSONAL: Born February 20, 1977, in Pewaukee, Wis. ... 6-6/314.
HIGH SCHOOL: Pewaukee (Wis.).
COLLEGE: Wisconsin.
TRANSACTIONS/CAREER NOTES: Selected by Seattle Seahawks in first round (22nd pick overall) of 2000 NFL draft. ... Sigend by Seahawks (August 26, 2000). ... On injured reserve with neck injury (January 4, 2001-remainder of season).
PLAYING EXPERIENCE: Seattle NFL, 2000 and 2001. ... Games/Games started: 2000 (14/10), 2001 (10/3). Total: 24/13.
HONORS: Named offensive tackle on THE SPORTING NEWS college All-America first team (1999).

McINTOSH, DAMION OT CHARGERS

PERSONAL: Born March 25, 1977, in Kingston, Jamaica. ... 6-4/325. ... Full name: Damion Alexis McIntosh.
HIGH SCHOOL: McArthur (Hollywood, Fla.).
COLLEGE: Kansas State.
TRANSACTIONS/CAREER NOTES: Selected by San Diego Chargers in third round (83rd pick overall) of 2000 NFL draft. ... Signed by Chargers (July 20, 2000).
PLAYING EXPERIENCE: San Diego NFL, 2000 and 2001. ... Games/Games started: 2000 (3/0), 2001 (15/14). Total: 18/14.

McKENZIE, KAREEM OT JETS

PERSONAL: Born May 24, 1979, in Willingboro, N.J. ... 6-6/327. ... Full name: Kareem Michael McKenzie.
HIGH SCHOOL: Willingboro (N.J.).
COLLEGE: Penn State.
TRANSACTIONS/CAREER NOTES: Selected by New York Jets in third round (79th pick overall) of 2001 NFL draft. ... Signed by Jets (July 25, 2001).
PLAYING EXPERIENCE: New York Jets NFL, 2001. ... Games/Games started: 2001 (8/0).

McKENZIE, KEITH — DL

PERSONAL: Born October 17, 1973, in Detroit. ... 6-3/273. ... Full name: Keith Derrick McKenzie.
HIGH SCHOOL: Highland Park (Mich.).
COLLEGE: Ball State (degree in history).
TRANSACTIONS/CAREER NOTES: Selected by Green Bay Packers in seventh round (252nd pick overall) of 1996 NFL draft. ... Signed by Packers (July 15, 1996). ... Granted free agency (February 12, 1999). ... Re-signed by Packers (June 1, 1999). ... Granted unconditional free agency (February 11, 2000). ... Signed by Cleveland Browns (February 24, 2000). ... On injured reserve with ankle injury (November 9, 2001-remainder of season). ... Granted unconditional free agency (March 1, 2002).
CHAMPIONSHIP GAME EXPERIENCE: Member of Super Bowl championship team (1996 season). ... Played in NFC championship game (1996 and 1997 seasons). ... Played in Super Bowl XXXII (1997 season).
PRO STATISTICS: 1998—Intercepted one pass for 33 yards and a touchdown, returned one kickoff for 17 yards and recovered three fumbles for 88 yards and one touchdown. 1999—Recovered four fumbles for 63 yards and two touchdowns. 2000—Recovered one fumble for 29 yards.

Year Team	G	GS	SACKS
1996—Green Bay NFL	10	0	1.0
1997—Green Bay NFL	16	0	1.5
1998—Green Bay NFL	16	0	8.0
1999—Green Bay NFL	16	2	8.0
2000—Cleveland NFL	16	16	8.0
2001—Cleveland NFL	7	6	3.0
Pro totals (6 years)	**81**	**24**	**29.5**

McKENZIE, MIKE — CB — PACKERS

PERSONAL: Born April 26, 1976, in Miami. ... 6-0/190. ... Full name: Michael Terrance McKenzie.
HIGH SCHOOL: Norland (Miami).
COLLEGE: Memphis.
TRANSACTIONS/CAREER NOTES: Selected after junior season by Green Bay Packers in third round (87th pick overall) of 1999 NFL draft. ... Signed by Packers (July 8, 1999).
PRO STATISTICS: 2000—Returned one punt for no yards and fumbled once.

			INTERCEPTIONS			
Year Team	G	GS	No.	Yds.	Avg.	TD
1999—Green Bay NFL	16	16	6	4	0.7	0
2000—Green Bay NFL	10	8	1	26	26.0	0
2001—Green Bay NFL	16	16	2	38	19.0	1
Pro totals (3 years)	**42**	**40**	**9**	**68**	**7.6**	**1**

McKINLEY, ALVIN — DT — BROWNS

PERSONAL: Born June 9, 1978, in Kosciusko, Miss. ... 6-3/292. ... Full name: Alvin Jerome McKinley.
HIGH SCHOOL: Weir (Miss.).
JUNIOR COLLEGE: Holmes Junior College (Miss.).
COLLEGE: Mississippi State.
TRANSACTIONS/CAREER NOTES: Selected by Carolina Panthers in fourth round (120th pick overall) of 2000 NFL draft. ... Signed by Panthers (June 21, 2000). ... Claimed on waivers by Cleveland Browns (August 29, 2001). ... Released by Browns (September 1, 2001). ... Re-signed by Browns to practice squad (September 3, 2001). ... Activated (October 9, 2001).
PLAYING EXPERIENCE: Carolina NFL, 2000; Cleveland NFL, 2001. ... Games/Games started: 2000 (7/0), 2001 (7/0). Total: 14/0.

McKINLEY, DENNIS — FB — CARDINALS

PERSONAL: Born November 3, 1976, in Kosciusko, Miss. ... 6-2/248. ... Full name: Dennis L. McKinley.
HIGH SCHOOL: Weir (Miss.) Attendance Center.
COLLEGE: Mississippi State (degree in educational psychology).
TRANSACTIONS/CAREER NOTES: Selected by Arizona Cardinals in sixth round (206th pick overall) of 1999 NFL draft. ... Signed by Cardinals for 1999 season. ... Granted free agency (March 1, 2002).
PLAYING EXPERIENCE: Arizona NFL, 1999-2001. ... Games/Games started: 1999 (16/0), 2000 (16/0), 2001 (14/0). Total: 46/0.
PRO STATISTICS: 1999—Caught one pass for four yards and recovered two fumbles. 2000—Caught two passes for 13 yards and returned one kickoff for 20 yards. 2001—Rushed once for one yard, caught one pass for 10 yards and returned one kickoff for 11 yards.
SINGLE GAME HIGHS (regular season): Attempts—1 (December 30, 2001, vs. Carolina); yards—1 (December 30, 2001, vs. Carolina); and rushing touchdowns—0.

McKINNEY, JEREMY — G — TEXANS

PERSONAL: Born January 6, 1976, in Huntington Park, Calif. ... 6-6/301. ... Full name: Jeremy Adam McKinney.
HIGH SCHOOL: Horizon (Brighton, Colo.).
COLLEGE: Iowa.
TRANSACTIONS/CAREER NOTES: Signed as non-drafted free agent by St. Louis Rams (April 20, 1998). ... Released by Rams (August 31, 1998). ... Re-signed by Rams to practice squad (September 1, 1998). ... Activated (December 19, 1998); did not play. ... Released by Rams (September 7, 1998). ... Signed by Detroit Lions to practice squad (October 12, 1999). ... Released by Lions (November 9, 1999). ... Signed by Rams to practice squad (November 24, 1999). ... Signed by Cleveland Browns off Rams practice squad (December 16, 1999). ... On injured reserve with knee injury (August 16, 2000-remainder of season). ... Selected by Houston Texans from Browns in NFL expansion draft (February 18, 2002).
PLAYING EXPERIENCE: Cleveland NFL, 2001. ... Games/Games started: 2001 (15/9).

McKINNEY, STEVE — G — TEXANS

PERSONAL: Born October 15, 1975, in Galveston, Texas. ... 6-4/295. ... Full name: Stephen Michael McKinney.
HIGH SCHOOL: Clear Lake (Houston).
COLLEGE: Texas A&M.
TRANSACTIONS/CAREER NOTES: Selected by Indianapolis Colts in fourth round (93rd pick overall) of 1998 NFL draft. ... Signed by Colts (July 23, 1998). ... Granted free agency (March 2, 2001). ... Re-signed by Colts (May 9, 2001). ... Granted unconditional free agency (March 1, 2002). ... Signed by Houston Texans (March 6, 2002).
PLAYING EXPERIENCE: Indianapolis NFL, 1998-2001. ... Games/Games started: 1998 (16/16), 1999 (15/14), 2000 (16/16), 2001 (14/14). Total: 61/60.
PRO STATISTICS: 2000—Recovered one fumble. 2001—Caught one pass for five yards.

McKINNON, RONALD — LB — CARDINALS

PERSONAL: Born September 20, 1973, in Fort Rucker Army Base, Ala. ... 6-0/248.
HIGH SCHOOL: Elba (Ala.).
COLLEGE: North Alabama.
TRANSACTIONS/CAREER NOTES: Signed as non-drafted free agent by Arizona Cardinals (April 23, 1996). ... Granted free agency (February 12, 1999). ... Re-signed by Cardinals (June 14, 1999). ... Granted unconditional free agency (February 11, 2000). ... Re-signed by Cardinals (February 24, 2000).
HONORS: Harlon Hill Trophy winner (1995).
PRO STATISTICS: 1996—Rushed once for minus four yards. 1997—Rushed once for three yards. 1998—Fumbled once and recovered two fumbles. 1999—Recovered one fumble. 2000—Recovered one fumble. 2001—Recovered two fumbles for 25 yards and a touchdown.

			INTERCEPTIONS				SACKS
Year Team	G	GS	No.	Yds.	Avg.	TD	No.
1996—Arizona NFL	16	0	0	0	0.0	0	0.0
1997—Arizona NFL	16	16	3	40	13.3	0	1.0
1998—Arizona NFL	13	13	5	25	5.0	0	2.0
1999—Arizona NFL	16	16	1	0	0.0	0	1.0
2000—Arizona NFL	16	16	0	0	0.0	0	4.0
2001—Arizona NFL	16	16	1	24	24.0	1	2.0
Pro totals (6 years)	93	77	10	89	8.9	1	10.0

McKNIGHT, JAMES — WR — DOLPHINS

PERSONAL: Born June 17, 1972, in Orlando, Fla. ... 6-1/198.
HIGH SCHOOL: Apopka (Fla.).
COLLEGE: Liberty (Va.).
TRANSACTIONS/CAREER NOTES: Signed as non-drafted free agent by Seattle Seahawks (April 29, 1994). ... Released by Seahawks (August 28, 1994). ... Re-signed by Seahawks to practice squad (August 29, 1994). ... Activated (November 19, 1994). ... Granted unconditional free agency (February 13, 1998). ... Re-signed by Seahawks (February 17, 1998). ... Traded by Seahawks to Dallas Cowboys for third-round pick (WR Darrell Jackson) in 2000 draft (June 24, 1999). ... On injured reserve with knee injury (August 27, 1999-entire season). ... Granted unconditional free agency (March 2, 2001). ... Signed by Miami Dolphins (March 16, 2001).
PRO STATISTICS: 1995—Returned one kickoff for four yards and recovered one fumble. 1996—Returned three kickoffs for 86 yards and recovered one fumble. 1997—Returned one kickoff for 14 yards. 2001—Rushed six times for 39 yards.
SINGLE GAME HIGHS (regular season): Receptions—9 (November 18, 2001, vs. New York Jets); yards—164 (November 12, 2000, vs. Cincinnati); and touchdown receptions—1 (January 6, 2002, vs. Buffalo).
STATISTICAL PLATEAUS: 100-yard receiving games: 1997 (1), 1998 (1), 2000 (3). Total: 5.

			RECEIVING					TOTALS		
Year Team	G	GS	No.	Yds.	Avg.	TD	TD	2pt.	Pts.	Fum.
1994—Seattle NFL	2	0	1	25	25.0	1	1	0	6	0
1995—Seattle NFL	16	0	6	91	15.2	0	0	0	0	1
1996—Seattle NFL	16	0	1	73	73.0	0	0	0	0	0
1997—Seattle NFL	12	5	34	637	*18.7	6	6	0	36	1
1998—Seattle NFL	14	3	21	346	16.5	2	2	0	12	0
1999—Dallas NFL					Did not play.					
2000—Dallas NFL	16	15	52	926	17.8	2	2	0	12	1
2001—Miami NFL	16	15	55	684	12.4	3	3	▲1	20	3
Pro totals (7 years)	92	38	170	2782	16.4	14	14	1	86	6

McMAHON, MIKE — QB — LIONS

PERSONAL: Born February 8, 1979, in Wexford, Pa. ... 6-2/213. ... Full name: Michael Edward McMahon.
HIGH SCHOOL: North Allegheny (Pa.).
COLLEGE: Rutgers.
TRANSACTIONS/CAREER NOTES: Selected by Detroit Lions in fifth round (149th pick overall) of 2001 NFL draft. ... Signed by Lions (June 7, 2001).
PRO STATISTICS: 2001—Fumbled five times.
SINGLE GAME HIGHS (regular season): Attempts—28 (December 23, 2001, vs. Pittsburgh); completions—15 (December 16, 2001, vs. Minnesota); yards—241 (December 16, 2001, vs. Minnesota); and touchdown passes—2 (December 23, 2001, vs. Pittsburgh).
MISCELLANEOUS: Regular-season record as starting NFL quarterback: 1-2 (.333).

				PASSING						RUSHING			TOTALS		
Year Team	G	GS	Att.	Cmp.	Pct.	Yds.	TD	Int.	Avg.	Rat.	Att.	Yds.	Avg.	TD	TD 2pt. Pts.
2001—Detroit NFL	8	3	115	53	46.1	671	3	1	5.83	69.9	27	145	5.4	1	1 1 8

McMILLON, TODD — CB — BEARS

PERSONAL: Born September 26, 1973, in Bellflower, Calif. ... 5-11/182.
HIGH SCHOOL: Cerritus (Bellflower, Calif.).
COLLEGE: Northern Arizona.
TRANSACTIONS/CAREER NOTES: Signed as non-drafted free agent by Chicago Bears (February 16, 2000). ... Released by Bears (August 22, 2000). ... Re-signed by Bears to practice squad (August 29, 2000). ... Activated (November 15, 2000). ... Assigned by Bears to Frankfurt Galaxy in 2001 NFL Europe enhancement allocation program (February 19, 2001). ... Released by Bears (September 3, 2001). ... Re-signed by Bears to practice squad (September 5, 2001). ... Activated (November 13, 2001).
PLAYING EXPERIENCE: Chicago NFL, 2000 and 2001; Frankfurt NFLE, 2001. ... Games/Games started: 2000 (3/0), NFLE 2001 (games played unavailable), NFL 2001 (8/0). Total: 11/0.
PRO STATISTICS: NFLE: 2001—Intercepted one pass for 12 yards and credited with one sack.

McMULLEN, KIRK — TE — BENGALS

PERSONAL: Born July 19, 1977, in Imperial, Pa. ... 6-4/255. ... Full name: Kirk Lawrence McMullen.
HIGH SCHOOL: West Allegheny (Pa.).
COLLEGE: Pittsburgh.
TRANSACTIONS/CAREER NOTES: Signed as non-drafted free agent by Kansas City Chiefs (April 19, 2000). ... Released by Chiefs (August 22, 2000). ... Re-signed by Chiefs to practice squad (August 30, 2000). ... Released by Chiefs (September 5, 2000). ... Signed by Cincinnati Bengals to practice squad (November 29, 2000). ... Assigned by Bengals to Amsterdam Admirals in 2001 NFL Europe enhancement allocation program (February 19, 2001). ... Released by Bengals (September 2, 2001). ... Re-signed by Bengals to practice squad (September 3, 2001). ... Activated (November 17, 2001). ... Released by Bengals (November 27, 2001). ... Re-signed by Bengals to practice squad (November 28, 2001). ... Activated (December 4, 2001).
PLAYING EXPERIENCE: Amsterdam NFLE, 2001; Cincinnati NFL, 2001. ... Games/Games started: NFLE 2001 (games played unavailable), NFL 2001 (7/2).
PRO STATISTICS: NFLE: 2001—Caught three passes for 34 yards. NFL: 2001—Caught two passes for 15 yards.
SINGLE GAME HIGHS (regular season): Receptions—1 (January 6, 2002, vs. Tennessee); yards—11 (January 6, 2002, vs. Tennessee); and touchdown receptions—0.

McNABB, DONOVAN — QB — EAGLES

PERSONAL: Born November 25, 1976, in Chicago. ... 6-2/226. ... Full name: Donovan Jamal McNabb.
HIGH SCHOOL: Mount Carmel (Ill.).
COLLEGE: Syracuse (degree in speech communications).
TRANSACTIONS/CAREER NOTES: Selected by Philadelphia Eagles in first round (second pick overall) of 1999 NFL draft. ... Signed by Eagles (July 30, 1999).
CHAMPIONSHIP GAME EXPERIENCE: Played in NFC championship game (2001 season).
HONORS: Played in Pro Bowl (2000 season).
PRO STATISTICS: 1999—Caught one pass for minus six yards and fumbled eight times for minus three yards. 2000—Fumbled seven times, recovered two fumbles for minus five yards and caught two passes for five yards. 2001—Fumbled eight times and recovered three fumbles for minus seven yards.
SINGLE GAME HIGHS (regular season): Attempts—55 (November 12, 2000, vs. Pittsburgh); completions—32 (September 9, 2001, vs. St. Louis); passing yards—390 (December 10, 2000, vs. Cleveland); and touchdown passes—4 (December 10, 2000, vs. Cleveland).
STATISTICAL PLATEAUS: 300-yard passing games: 2000 (2), 2001 (1). Total: 3. ... 100-yard rushing games: 2000 (1).
MISCELLANEOUS: Regular-season record as starting NFL quarterback: 24-14 (.631). ... Postseason record as starting NFL quarterback: 3-2 (.600).

					PASSING						RUSHING				TOTALS	
Year Team	G	GS	Att.	Cmp.	Pct.	Yds.	TD	Int.	Avg.	Rat.	Att.	Yds.	Avg.	TD	TD	2pt.	Pts.
1999—Philadelphia NFL	12	6	216	106	49.1	948	8	7	4.39	60.1	47	313	6.7	0	0	†1	2
2000—Philadelphia NFL	16	16	569	330	58.0	3365	21	13	5.91	77.8	86	629	7.3	6	6	0	36
2001—Philadelphia NFL	16	16	493	285	57.8	3233	25	12	6.56	84.3	82	482	5.9	2	2	0	12
Pro totals (3 years)	44	38	1278	721	56.4	7546	54	32	5.90	77.4	215	1424	6.6	8	8	1	50

McNAIR, STEVE — QB — TITANS

PERSONAL: Born February 14, 1973, in Mount Olive, Miss. ... 6-2/225. ... Full name: Steve LaTreal McNair. ... Brother of Fred McNair, quarterback with Carolina Cobras of Arena League.
HIGH SCHOOL: Mount Olive (Miss.).
COLLEGE: Alcorn State.
TRANSACTIONS/CAREER NOTES: Selected by Houston Oilers in first round (third pick overall) of 1995 NFL draft. ... Signed by Oilers (July 25, 1995). ... Oilers franchise moved to Tennessee for 1997 season. ... Oilers franchise renamed Tennessee Titans for 1999 season (December 26, 1998).
CHAMPIONSHIP GAME EXPERIENCE: Played in AFC championship game (1999 season). ... Played in Super Bowl XXXIV (1999 season).
HONORS: Walter Payton Award winner (1994). ... Named to play in Pro Bowl (2000 season); replaced by Elvis Grbac due to injury.
PRO STATISTICS: 1995—Fumbled three times and recovered two fumbles for minus two yards. 1996—Fumbled seven times and recovered four fumbles. 1997—Led NFL with 16 fumbles and recovered seven fumbles for minus two yards. 1998—Fumbled five times and recovered three fumbles for minus seven yards. 1999—Fumbled three times and recovered one fumble. 2000—Fumbled 12 times and recovered three fumbles for minus 31 yards. 2001—Fumbled five times and recovered one fumble for minus 15 yards.
SINGLE GAME HIGHS (regular season): Attempts—49 (December 20, 1998, vs. Green Bay); completions—29 (December 20, 1998, vs. Green Bay); yards—341 (September 12, 1999, vs. Cincinnati); and touchdown passes—5 (December 26, 1999, vs. Jacksonville).
STATISTICAL PLATEAUS: 300-yard passing games: 1996 (1), 1999 (1), 2001 (2). Total: 4.
MISCELLANEOUS: Regular-season record as starting NFL quarterback: 48-31 (.608). ... Postseason record as starting NFL quarterback: 3-2 (.600).

				PASSING						RUSHING			TOTALS		
Year Team	G	GS	Att.	Cmp.	Pct.	Yds.	TD	Int.	Avg.	Rat.	Att.	Yds.	Avg.	TD	TD	2pt.	Pts.
1995—Houston NFL	4	2	80	41	51.3	569	3	1	7.11	81.7	11	38	3.5	0	0	0	0
1996—Houston NFL	9	4	143	88	61.5	1197	6	4	8.37	90.6	31	169	5.5	2	2	0	12
1997—Tennessee NFL	16	16	415	216	52.0	2665	14	13	6.42	70.4	101	674	*6.7	8	8	0	48
1998—Tennessee NFL	16	16	492	289	58.7	3228	15	10	6.56	80.1	77	559	7.3	4	4	0	24
1999—Tennessee NFL	11	11	331	187	56.5	2179	12	8	6.58	78.6	72	337	4.7	8	8	0	48
2000—Tennessee NFL	16	15	396	248	62.6	2847	15	13	7.19	83.2	72	403	5.6	0	0	0	0
2001—Tennessee NFL	15	15	431	264	61.3	3350	21	12	§7.77	90.2	75	414	5.5	5	5	0	30
Pro totals (7 years)	87	79	2288	1333	58.3	16035	86	61	7.01	81.3	439	2594	5.9	27	27	0	162

McNEIL, RYAN   CB   CHARGERS

PERSONAL: Born October 4, 1970, in Fort Pierce, Fla. ... 6-2/192. ... Full name: Ryan Darrell McNeil.
HIGH SCHOOL: Westwood Christian (Miami).
COLLEGE: Miami, Fla. (degree in psychology, 1992).
TRANSACTIONS/CAREER NOTES: Selected by Detroit Lions in second round (33rd pick overall) of 1993 NFL draft. ... Signed by Lions (August 25, 1993). ... Granted unconditional free agency (February 14, 1997). ... Signed by St. Louis Rams (July 7, 1997). ... Designated by Rams as franchise player (February 13, 1998). ... Re-signed by Rams (August 31, 1998). ... Granted unconditional free agency (February 12, 1999). ... Signed by Cleveland Browns (August 1, 1999). ... Granted unconditional free agency (February 11, 2000). ... Signed by Dallas Cowboys (March 2, 2000). ... Released by Cowboys (February 28, 2001). ... Signed by San Diego Chargers (March 6, 2001).
HONORS: Named defensive back on THE SPORTING NEWS college All-America second team (1992).
PRO STATISTICS: 1995—Recovered two fumbles. 1996—Recovered two fumbles. 1997—Fumbled once and recovered one fumble. 1998—Recovered one fumble. 1999—Credited with one sack and recovered four fumbles.

			INTERCEPTIONS			
Year Team	G	GS	No.	Yds.	Avg.	TD
1993—Detroit NFL	16	2	2	19	9.5	0
1994—Detroit NFL	14	13	1	14	14.0	0
1995—Detroit NFL	16	16	2	26	13.0	0
1996—Detroit NFL	16	16	5	14	2.8	0
1997—St. Louis NFL	16	16	*9	127	14.1	1
1998—St. Louis NFL	16	12	1	37	37.0	1
1999—Cleveland NFL	16	14	0	0	0.0	0
2000—Dallas NFL	16	16	2	4	2.0	0
2001—San Diego NFL	16	16	8	55	6.9	0
Pro totals (9 years)	142	121	30	296	9.9	2

McNOWN, CADE   QB   DOLPHINS

PERSONAL: Born January 12, 1977, in Portland, Ore. ... 6-1/210. ... Full name: Cade B. McNown.
HIGH SCHOOL: San Benito (Hollister, Calif.), then West Linn (Ore.).
COLLEGE: UCLA.
TRANSACTIONS/CAREER NOTES: Selected by Chicago Bears in first round (12th pick overall) of 1999 NFL draft. ... Signed by Bears (August 2, 1999). ... Traded by Bears with seventh-round pick (RB Adrian Peterson) in 2002 draft to Miami Dolphins for sixth-round pick (RB Leonard Henry) in 2002 draft and conditional seventh-round pick in 2003 draft (August 22, 2001). ... Active for all 16 games (2001); did not play.
HONORS: Named quarterback on THE SPORTING NEWS college All-America third team (1997). ... Named quarterback on THE SPORTING NEWS college All-America second team (1998).
PRO STATISTICS: 1999—Fumbled six times and recovered two fumbles for minus two yards. 2000—Fumbled eight times and recovered four fumbles for minus 17 yards.
SINGLE GAME HIGHS (regular season): Attempts—42 (January 2, 2000, vs. Tampa Bay); completions—27 (September 3, 2000, vs. Minnesota); passing yards—301 (December 19, 1999, vs. Detroit); and touchdown passes—4 (December 19, 1999, vs. Detroit).
STATISTICAL PLATEAUS: 300-yard passing games: 1999 (1).
MISCELLANEOUS: Regular-season record as starting NFL quarterback: 3-12 (.200).

				PASSING						RUSHING			TOTALS		
Year Team	G	GS	Att.	Cmp.	Pct.	Yds.	TD	Int.	Avg.	Rat.	Att.	Yds.	Avg.	TD	TD	2pt.	Pts.
1999—Chicago NFL	15	6	235	127	54.0	1465	8	10	6.23	66.7	32	160	5.0	0	0	†1	2
2000—Chicago NFL	10	9	280	154	55.0	1646	8	9	5.88	68.5	50	326	6.5	3	3	0	18
2001—Miami NFL						Did not play.										
Pro totals (2 years)	25	15	515	281	54.6	3111	16	19	6.04	67.7	82	486	5.9	3	3	1	20

McQUARTERS, R.W.   CB   BEARS

PERSONAL: Born December 21, 1976, in Tulsa, Okla. ... 5-10/198. ... Full name: Robert William McQuarters II.
HIGH SCHOOL: Washington (Okla.).
COLLEGE: Oklahoma State.
TRANSACTIONS/CAREER NOTES: Selected after junior season by San Francisco 49ers in first round (28th pick overall) of 1998 NFL draft. ... Signed by 49ers (July 28, 1998). ... On injured reserve with shoulder injury (November 30, 1999-remainder of season). ... Traded by 49ers to Chicago Bears for sixth-round pick (WR Cedrick Wilson) in 2001 draft (June 5, 2000).
PRO STATISTICS: 1998—Recovered two fumbles. 2000—Credited with one sack. 2001—Credited with one sack and recovered one fumble for 69 yards and a touchdown.

			INTERCEPTIONS				PUNT RETURNS				KICKOFF RETURNS				TOTALS		
Year Team	G	GS	No.	Yds.	Avg.	TD	No.	Yds.	Avg.	TD	No.	Yds.	Avg.	TD	TD	2pt.	Pts.	Fum.
1998—San Francisco NFL	16	7	0	0	0.0	0	*47	406	8.6	1	17	339	19.9	0	1	0	6	4
1999—San Francisco NFL	11	4	1	25	25.0	0	18	90	5.0	0	26	568	21.8	0	0	0	0	1
2000—Chicago NFL	15	2	1	61	61.0	1	0	0	0.0	0	0	0	0.0	0	1	0	6	0
2001—Chicago NFL	16	16	3	47	15.7	0	12	96	8.0	0	0	0	0.0	0	1	0	6	0
Pro totals (4 years)	58	29	5	133	26.6	1	77	592	7.7	1	43	907	21.1	0	3	0	18	5

MEADOWS, ADAM — OT — COLTS

PERSONAL: Born January 25, 1974, in Powder Springs, Ga. ... 6-5/289. ... Full name: Adam Jonathon Meadows.
HIGH SCHOOL: McEachern (Powder Springs, Ga.).
COLLEGE: Georgia.
TRANSACTIONS/CAREER NOTES: Selected by Indianapolis Colts in second round (48th pick overall) of 1997 NFL draft. ... Signed by Colts (July 8, 1997). ... Granted free agency (February 11, 2000). ... Re-signed by Colts (March 1, 2000).
PLAYING EXPERIENCE: Indianapolis NFL, 1997-2001. ... Games/Games started: 1997 (16/16), 1998 (14/14), 1999 (16/16), 2000 (16/16), 2001 (15/15). Total: 77/77.

MEALEY, RONDELL — RB — PACKERS

PERSONAL: Born February 24, 1977, in New Orleans. ... 6-0/224. ... Full name: Rondell Christopher Mealey.
HIGH SCHOOL: Destrehan (La.).
COLLEGE: Louisiana State (degree in sports administration).
TRANSACTIONS/CAREER NOTES: Selected by Green Bay Packers in seventh round (252nd pick overall) of 2000 NFL draft. ... Signed by Packers (June 29, 2000). ... On injured reserve with knee injury (August 18, 2000-entire season). ... On injured reserve with broken leg (December 12, 2001-remainder of season).
PRO STATISTICS: 2001—Recovered one fumble for 27 yards.
SINGLE GAME HIGHS (regular season): Attempts—7 (September 30, 2001, vs. Carolina); yards—19 (September 19, 2001, vs. Washington); and rushing touchdowns—0.

			RUSHING				RECEIVING				KICKOFF RETURNS				TOTALS		
Year Team	G	GS	Att.	Yds.	Avg.	TD	No.	Yds.	Avg.	TD	No.	Yds.	Avg.	TD	TD	2pt.	Pts.	Fum.
2000—Green Bay NFL							Did not play.											
2001—Green Bay NFL	11	0	11	37	3.4	0	2	31	15.5	0	4	63	15.8	0	1	0	6	0

MEESTER, BRAD — G/C — JAGUARS

PERSONAL: Born March 23, 1977, in Iowa Falls, Iowa. ... 6-3/308. ... Full name: Brad Ley Meester.
HIGH SCHOOL: Aplington-Parkersburg (Aplington, Iowa).
COLLEGE: Northern Iowa (degree in business management, 1999).
TRANSACTIONS/CAREER NOTES: Selected by Jacksonville Jaguars in second round (60th pick overall) of 2000 NFL draft. ... Signed by Jaguars (May 16, 2000).
PLAYING EXPERIENCE: Jacksonville NFL, 2000 and 2001. ... Games/Games started: 2000 (16/16), 2001 (16/16). Total: 32/32.
PRO STATISTICS: 2000—Recovered one fumble. 2001—Recovered one fumble for 21 yards.

MEIER, ROB — DE — JAGUARS

PERSONAL: Born August 29, 1977, in Vancouver, B.C. ... 6-5/285. ... Full name: Robert Jack Daniel Meier.
HIGH SCHOOL: Sentinel (West Vancouver, B.C.).
COLLEGE: Washington State (degree in business).
TRANSACTIONS/CAREER NOTES: Selected by Jacksonville Jaguars in seventh round (241st pick overall) of 2000 NFL draft. ... Signed by Jaguars (May 17, 2000).
PLAYING EXPERIENCE: Jacksonville NFL, 2000 and 2001. ... Games/Games started: 2000 (16/0), 2001 (16/0). Total: 32/0.
PRO STATISTICS: 2000—Credited with 1/2 sack. 2001—Returned two kickoffs for 14 yards.

MEIER, SHAD — TE — TITANS

PERSONAL: Born June 7, 1978, in Pittsburgh, Kan. ... 6-4/253.
HIGH SCHOOL: Pittsburgh (Kan.).
COLLEGE: Kansas State.
TRANSACTIONS/CAREER NOTES: Selected by Tennessee Titans in third round (90th pick overall) of 2001 NFL draft. ... Signed by Titans (July 24, 2001).
PLAYING EXPERIENCE: Tennessee NFL, 2001. ... Games/Games started: (11/1).
PRO STATISTICS: 2001—Caught three passes for 31 yards.
SINGLE GAME HIGHS (regular season): Receptions—2 (November 4, 2001, vs. Jacksonville); yards—27 (November 4, 2001, vs. Jacksonville); and touchdown receptions—0.

MERRILL, THAN — S — BEARS

PERSONAL: Born December 12, 1977, in Fresno, Calif. ... 6-2/212. ... Full name: Nathaniel Merrill.
HIGH SCHOOL: Fresno (Calif.).
COLLEGE: Stanford, then Yale.
TRANSACTIONS/CAREER NOTES: Selected by Tampa Bay Buccaneers in seventh round (223rd pick overall) of 2001 NFL draft. ... Signed by Buccaneers (July 16, 2001). ... Claimed on waivers by Chicago Bears (September 3, 2001).
PLAYING EXPERIENCE: Chicago NFL, 2001. ... Games/Games started: 2001 (15/0).

MERRITT, AHMAD — WR — BEARS

PERSONAL: Born February 5, 1977, in Chicago. ... 5-10/193.
HIGH SCHOOL: St. Rita (Chicago).
COLLEGE: Wisconsin.

TRANSACTIONS/CAREER NOTES: Signed as non-drafted free agent by Chicago Bears (May 22, 2000). ... Released by Bears (August 22, 2000). ... Re-signed by Bears to practice squad (December 6, 2000). ... Assigned by Bears to Berlin Thunder in 2001 NFL Europe enhancement allocation program (February 19, 2001). ... Released by Bears (September 2, 2001). ... Re-signed by Bears to practice squad (September 3, 2001).
PRO STATISTICS: NFLE: 2001—Rushed four times for 26 yards, returned one punt for two yards and returned six kickoffs for 126 yards.
SINGLE GAME HIGHS (regular season): Receptions—2 (January 6, 2002, vs. Jacksonville); yards—20 (January 6, 2002, vs. Jacksonville); and touchdown receptions—0.

				RECEIVING				TOTALS			
Year Team	G	GS	No.	Yds.	Avg.	TD	TD	2pt.	Pts.	Fum.
2001—Berlin NFLE	...	...	39	582	14.9	6	6	0	36	0
—Chicago NFL	2	0	2	20	10.0	0	0	0	0	0
NFL Europe totals (1 year)	...	...	39	582	14.9	6	6	0	36	0
NFL totals (1 year)	2	0	2	20	10.0	0	0	0	0	0
Pro totals (2 years)	...	...	41	602	14.7	6	6	0	36	0

METCALF, ERIC — WR

PERSONAL: Born January 23, 1968, in Seattle. ... 5-10/190. ... Full name: Eric Quinn Metcalf. ... Son of Terry Metcalf, running back with St. Louis Cardinals (1973-77), Toronto Argonauts of CFL (1978-80) and Washington Redskins (1981); and cousin of Ray Hall, defensive tackle with Jacksonville Jaguars (1995).
HIGH SCHOOL: Bishop Denis J. O'Connell (Arlington, Va.).
COLLEGE: Texas (degree in liberal arts, 1990).
TRANSACTIONS/CAREER NOTES: Selected by Cleveland Browns in first round (13th pick overall) of 1989 NFL draft. ... Signed by Browns (August 20, 1989). ... Granted free agency (February 1, 1991). ... Re-signed by Browns for 1991 season. ... On injured reserve with shoulder injury (November 2, 1991-remainder of season). ... Granted free agency (February 1, 1992). ... Re-signed by Browns (August 30, 1992). ... Granted roster exemption (August 30-September 5, 1992). ... Traded by Browns with first-round pick (DB Devin Bush) in 1995 draft to Atlanta Falcons for first-round pick (traded to San Francisco) in 1995 draft (March 25, 1995). ... Granted unconditional free agency (February 14, 1997). ... Signed by San Diego Chargers (May 8, 1997). ... Traded by Chargers with first- (DE Andre Wadsworth) and second-round (CB Corey Chavous) picks in 1998 draft, first-round pick (WR David Boston) in 1999 draft and LB Patrick Sapp to Arizona Cardinals for first-round pick (QB Ryan Leaf) in 1998 draft (March 12, 1998). ... Granted unconditional free agency (February 12, 1999). ... Signed by Baltimore Ravens (July 2, 1999). ... Released by Ravens (September 5, 1999). ... Signed by Carolina Panthers (September 7, 1999). ... Granted unconditional free agency (February 11, 2000). ... Signed by Oakland Raiders (February 6, 2001). ... Released by Raiders (September 2, 2001). ... Signed by Washington Redskins (October 24, 2001). ... Granted unconditional free agency (March 1, 2002).
CHAMPIONSHIP GAME EXPERIENCE: Played in AFC championship game (1989 season).
HONORS: Named all-purpose player on THE SPORTING NEWS college All-America second team (1987). ... Named punt returner on THE SPORTING NEWS NFL All-Pro team (1993 and 1994). ... Played in Pro Bowl (1993, 1994 and 1997 seasons).
RECORDS: Holds NFL career record for most touchdowns by punt return—9. ... Shares NFL single-game records for most touchdowns by punt return—2; most touchdowns by combined kick return—2 (October 24, 1993, vs. Pittsburgh and November 2, 1997, vs. Cincinnati); and most touchdowns by combined kick return—12.
POST SEASON RECORDS: Shares NFL postseason career record for most touchdowns by kickoff return—1 (January 6, 1990, vs. Buffalo).
PRO STATISTICS: 1989—Attempted two passes with one completion for 32 yards and a touchdown and fumbled five times. 1990—Fumbled eight times and recovered one fumble. 1991—Fumbled once. 1992—Attempted one pass without a completion, fumbled six times and recovered two fumbles. 1993—Fumbled four times. 1994—Attempted one pass without a completion and fumbled six times. 1995—Attempted one pass without a completion, fumbled four times and recovered two fumbles. 1996—Fumbled three times. 1997—Fumbled four times and recovered two fumbles. 1998—Fumbled five times and recovered two fumbles. 1999—Fumbled twice. 2001—Fumbled four times and recovered one fumble.
SINGLE GAME HIGHS (regular season): Receptions—11 (September 17, 1995, vs. New Orleans); yards—177 (September 20, 1992, vs. Los Angeles Raiders); and touchdown receptions—3 (September 20, 1992, vs. Los Angeles Raiders).
STATISTICAL PLATEAUS: 100-yard receiving games: 1992 (1), 1993 (1), 1995 (2), 1996 (1), 1997 (1). Total: 6.

			RUSHING				RECEIVING				PUNT RETURNS				KICKOFF RETURNS				TOTALS		
Year Team	G	GS	Att.	Yds.	Avg.	TD	No.	Yds.	Avg.	TD	No.	Yds.	Avg.	TD	No.	Yds.	Avg.	TD	TD	2pt.	Pts.
1989—Cleveland NFL	16	11	187	633	3.4	6	54	397	7.4	4	0	0	0.0	0	31	718	23.2	0	10	0	60
1990—Cleveland NFL	16	9	80	248	3.1	1	57	452	7.9	1	0	0	0.0	0	*52	*1052	20.2	*2	4	0	24
1991—Cleveland NFL	8	3	30	107	3.6	0	29	294	10.1	0	12	100	8.3	0	23	351	15.3	0	0	0	0
1992—Cleveland NFL	16	5	73	301	4.1	1	47	614	13.1	5	*44	§429	9.8	1	9	157	17.4	0	7	0	42
1993—Cleveland NFL	16	9	129	611	4.7	1	63	539	8.6	2	36	464	§12.9	†2	15	318	21.2	0	5	0	30
1994—Cleveland NFL	16	8	93	329	3.5	2	47	436	9.3	3	35	348	9.9	†2	9	210	23.3	0	7	0	42
1995—Atlanta NFL	16	14	28	133	4.8	1	104	1189	11.4	8	39	383	9.8	†1	12	278	23.2	0	10	0	60
1996—Atlanta NFL	16	11	3	8	2.7	0	54	599	11.1	6	27	296	11.0	0	49	1034	21.1	0	6	0	36
1997—San Diego NFL	16	1	3	-5	-1.7	0	40	576	14.4	2	45	489	10.9	†3	16	355	22.2	0	5	0	30
1998—Arizona NFL	16	3	0	0	0.0	0	31	324	10.5	0	43	295	6.9	0	57	1218	21.4	0	0	0	0
1999—Carolina NFL	16	1	2	20	10.0	0	11	133	12.1	0	34	238	7.0	0	4	56	14.0	0	0	0	0
2000—									Did not play.													
2001—Washington NFL	10	0	0	0	0.0	0	4	19	4.8	0	33	412	12.5	∞1	1	25	25.0	0	1	0	6
Pro totals (12 years)	178	75	628	2385	3.8	12	541	5572	10.3	31	348	3454	9.9	10	278	5772	20.8	2	55	0	330

MICKELL, DARREN — DE

PERSONAL: Born August 3, 1970, in Miami. ... 6-4/280.
HIGH SCHOOL: Miami Senior.
COLLEGE: Florida.
TRANSACTIONS/CAREER NOTES: Selected by Kansas City Chiefs in second round of 1992 NFL supplemental draft (second of two supplemental drafts in 1992). ... Signed by Chiefs (September 16, 1992). ... Granted roster exemption (September 16-29, 1992). ... On injured reserve with knee injury (September 30-November 11, 1992). ... On practice squad (November 11-December 26, 1992). ... Granted unconditional free agency (February 16, 1996). ... Signed by New Orleans Saints (March 12, 1996). ... On reserve did not report list (July 14-August 12, 1996). ... On physically unable to perform list (August 12-19, 1996). ... On suspended list for violating league substance abuse policy (October 4-November 10, 1996). ... Announced retirement (February 23, 1998). ... Activated from roster exempt list (September 28, 1999). ... Released by Saints (November 10, 1999). ... Signed by San Diego Chargers (February 28, 2000). ... Granted unconditional free agency (March 2, 2001). ...

Signed by Oakland Raiders (June 5, 2001). ... Released by Raiders (August 28, 2001). ... Re-signed by Raiders (October 2, 2001). ... Released by Raiders (October 9, 2001).
CHAMPIONSHIP GAME EXPERIENCE: Played in AFC championship game (1993 season).
PRO STATISTICS: 1993—Recovered one fumble. 1994—Recovered one fumble. 1995—Recovered one fumble. 1997—Recovered one fumble for 11 yards.

Year — Team	G	GS	SACKS
1992—Kansas City NFL	1	0	0.0
1993—Kansas City NFL	16	1	1.0
1994—Kansas City NFL	16	13	7.0
1995—Kansas City NFL	12	6	5.5
1996—New Orleans NFL	12	12	3.0
1997—New Orleans NFL	14	13	3.5
1998—	Did not play.		
1999—New Orleans NFL	1	0	0.0
2000—San Diego NFL	16	16	6.0
2001—Oakland NFL	1	0	0.0
Pro totals (9 years)	89	61	26.0

MICKENS, RAY   CB   JETS

PERSONAL: Born January 4, 1973, in Frankfurt, West Germany. ... 5-8/180.
HIGH SCHOOL: Andress (El Paso, Texas).
COLLEGE: Texas A&M.
TRANSACTIONS/CAREER NOTES: Selected by New York Jets in third round (62nd pick overall) of 1996 NFL draft. ... Signed by Jets (July 13, 1996). ... Granted free agency (February 12, 1999). ... Re-signed by Jets (April 9, 1999).
CHAMPIONSHIP GAME EXPERIENCE: Played in AFC championship game (1998 season).
HONORS: Named defensive back on THE SPORTING NEWS college All-America second team (1995).
PRO STATISTICS: 1997—Credited with one sack and returned blocked field-goal attempt 72 yards for a touchdown. 1998—Recovered one fumble. 1999—Credited with two sacks. 2001—Credited with one sack and recovered one fumble.

			\multicolumn{4}{c}{INTERCEPTIONS}
Year — Team	G	GS	No.	Yds.	Avg.	TD
1996—New York Jets NFL	15	10	0	0	0.0	0
1997—New York Jets NFL	16	0	4	2	0.5	0
1998—New York Jets NFL	16	3	3	10	3.3	0
1999—New York Jets NFL	15	5	2	2	1.0	0
2000—New York Jets NFL	16	0	0	0	0.0	0
2001—New York Jets NFL	16	4	0	0	0.0	0
Pro totals (6 years)	94	22	9	14	1.6	0

MIDDLEBROOKS, WILLIE   CB   BRONCOS

PERSONAL: Born February 12, 1979, in Miami. ... 6-1/200.
HIGH SCHOOL: Homestead (Fla.).
COLLEGE: Minnesota.
TRANSACTIONS/CAREER NOTES: Selected after junior season by Denver Broncos in first round (24th pick overall) of 2001 NFL draft. ... Signed by Broncos (July 27, 2001).
PLAYING EXPERIENCE: Denver NFL, 2001. ... Games/Games started: 2001 (8/0).

MIDDLETON, FRANK   G   RAIDERS

PERSONAL: Born October 25, 1974, in Beaumont, Texas. ... 6-3/330. ... Full name: Frank Middleton Jr.
HIGH SCHOOL: West Brook (Beaumont, Texas).
JUNIOR COLLEGE: Fort Scott (Kan.) Community College.
COLLEGE: Arizona.
TRANSACTIONS/CAREER NOTES: Selected by Tampa Bay Buccaneers in third round (63rd pick overall) of 1997 NFL draft. ... Signed by Buccaneers (July 20, 1997). ... Granted free agency (February 11, 2000). ... Re-signed by Buccaneers (May 2, 2000). ... Granted unconditional free agency (March 2, 2001). ... Signed by Oakland Raiders (April 26, 2001).
PLAYING EXPERIENCE: Tampa Bay NFL, 1997-2000; Oakland NFL, 2001. ... Games/Games started: 1997 (15/2), 1998 (16/16), 1999 (16/16), 2000 (16/16), 2001 (13/11). Total: 74/61.
CHAMPIONSHIP GAME EXPERIENCE: Played in NFC championship game (1999 season).
PRO STATISTICS: 2001—Recovered one fumble.

MILBURN, GLYN   RB/KR

PERSONAL: Born February 19, 1971, in Santa Monica, Calif. ... 5-8/176. ... Full name: Glyn Curt Milburn. ... Cousin of Rod Milburn, gold medalist in 110-meter high hurdles in 1972 Summer Olympics.
HIGH SCHOOL: Santa Monica (Calif.).
COLLEGE: Oklahoma, then Stanford (degree in public policy).
TRANSACTIONS/CAREER NOTES: Selected by Denver Broncos in second round (43rd pick overall) of 1993 NFL draft. ... Signed by Broncos (July 15, 1993). ... Traded by Broncos to Detroit Lions for second- (traded to Baltimore) and seventh-round (P Brian Gragert) picks in 1996 NFL draft (April 12, 1996). ... Traded by Lions to Green Bay Packers for seventh-round pick (traded to Miami) in 1999 draft (April 21, 1998). ... Traded by Packers to Chicago Bears for seventh-round pick (WR Donald Driver) in 1999 draft (August 30, 1998). ... Released by Bears (July 9, 2001). ... Re-signed by Bears (July 19, 2001). ... Released by Bears (October 17, 2001). ... Signed by San Diego Chargers (November 16, 2001). ... Granted unconditional free agency (March 1, 2002).

HONORS: Named kick returner on THE SPORTING NEWS NFL All-Pro team (1995). ... Played in Pro Bowl (1995 and 1999 seasons). ... Named punt returner on THE SPORTING NEWS NFL All-Pro team (1999).
RECORDS: Holds NFL single-season record for most combined kick returns—102. ... Holds NFL single-game record for most combined net yards gained—404 (December 10, 1995).
PRO STATISTICS: 1993—Fumbled nine times and recovered one fumble. 1994—Fumbled four times and recovered one fumble. 1995—Fumbled twice. 1997—Fumbled three times and recovered two fumbles. 1998—Fumbled once. 1999—Fumbled four times and recovered two fumbles. 2000—Fumbled four times and recovered three fumbles. 2001—Fumbled twice and recovered one fumble.
SINGLE GAME HIGHS (regular season): Attempts—18 (December 10, 1995, vs. Seattle); yards—131 (December 10, 1995, vs. Seattle); and rushing touchdowns—1 (November 7, 1999, vs. Green Bay). Receptions—9 (September 18, 1994 vs. Los Angeles Raiders); yards—85 (September 18, 1994 vs. Los Angeles Raiders); and touchdown receptions—1 (November 6, 1994 vs. Los Angeles Rams).
STATISTICAL PLATEAUS: 100-yard rushing games: 1995 (1).

				RUSHING				RECEIVING				PUNT RETURNS				KICKOFF RETURNS				TOTALS		
Year Team	G	GS	Att.	Yds.	Avg.	TD	No.	Yds.	Avg.	TD	No.	Yds.	Avg.	TD	No.	Yds.	Avg.	TD	TD	2pt.	Pts.
1993—Denver NFL	16	2	52	231	4.4	0	38	300	7.9	3	40	425	10.6	0	12	188	15.7	0	3	0	18
1994—Denver NFL	16	3	58	201	3.5	1	77	549	7.1	3	41	379	9.2	0	37	793	21.4	0	4	0	24
1995—Denver NFL	16	1	49	266	5.4	0	22	191	8.7	0	31	354	11.4	0	47	1269	27.0	0	0	0	0
1996—Detroit NFL	16	0	0	0	0.0	0	0	0	0.0	0	34	284	8.4	0	64	1627	25.4	0	0	0	0
1997—Detroit NFL	16	1	0	0	0.0	0	5	77	15.4	0	47	433	9.2	0	55	1315	23.9	0	0	0	0
1998—Chicago NFL	16	0	4	8	2.0	0	4	37	9.3	0	25	291	11.6	1	*62	*1550	25.0	†2	3	0	18
1999—Chicago NFL	16	1	16	102	6.4	1	20	151	7.6	0	30	346	11.5	0	‡61	‡1426	23.4	0	1	0	6
2000—Chicago NFL	16	0	1	6	6.0	0	1	8	8.0	0	35	300	8.6	0	63	1468	23.3	0	0	0	0
2001—Chicago NFL	4	0	3	3	1.0	0	3	9	3.0	0	4	33	8.3	0	6	152	25.3	0	0	0	0
—San Diego NFL	6	0	0	0	0.0	0	0	0	0.0	0	17	139	8.2	0	0	0	0.0	0	0	0	0
Pro totals (9 years)	138	8	183	817	4.5	2	170	1322	7.8	6	304	2984	9.8	1	407	9788	24.0	2	11	0	66

MILEM, JOHN   DE   PANTHERS

PERSONAL: Born June 9, 1975, in Concord, N.C. ... 6-7/290. ... Full name: John Ray Milem.
HIGH SCHOOL: Rowan (Salisbury, N.C.).
COLLEGE: Lenoir-Rhyne College (N.C.).
TRANSACTIONS/CAREER NOTES: Selected by San Francisco 49ers in fifth round (150th pick overall) of 2000 NFL draft. ... Signed by 49ers (July 16, 2000). ... Claimed on waivers by Carolina Panthers (October 31, 2001). ... On injured reserve with knee injury (November 20, 2001-remainder of season).
PLAYING EXPERIENCE: San Francisco NFL, 2000; San Francisco (2)-Carolina (2) NFL, 2001. ... Games/Games started: 2000 (16/0), 2001 (S.F.-2/0; Car.-2/0; Total: 4/0). Total: 20/0.
PRO STATISTICS: 2000—Returned one kickoff for 13 yards.

MILI, ITULA   TE   SEAHAWKS

PERSONAL: Born April 20, 1973, in Kahuku, Hawaii. ... 6-4/258. ... Name pronounced EE-too-la MEE-lee.
HIGH SCHOOL: Kahuku (Hawaii).
COLLEGE: Brigham Young.
TRANSACTIONS/CAREER NOTES: Selected by Seattle Seahawks in sixth round (174th pick overall) of 1997 NFL draft. ... Signed by Seahawks (June 11, 1997). ... On physically unable to perform list with knee injury (August 18, 1997-entire season). ... On injured reserve with knee injury (December 25, 1998-remainder of season). ... Granted free agency (March 2, 2001). ... Re-signed by Seahawks (April 13, 2001). ... Granted unconditional free agency (March 1, 2002). ... Re-signed by Seahawks (March 14, 2002).
PRO STATISTICS: 2000—Returned one kickoff for 19 yards.
SINGLE GAME HIGHS (regular season): Receptions—5 (October 22, 2000, vs. Oakland); yards—52 (September 10, 2000, vs. St. Louis); and touchdown receptions—1 (October 28, 2001, vs. Miami).

			RECEIVING				TOTALS			
Year Team	G	GS	No.	Yds.	Avg.	TD	TD	2pt.	Pts.	Fum.
1997—Seattle NFL						Did not play.				
1998—Seattle NFL	7	0	1	20	20.0	0	0	0	0	0
1999—Seattle NFL	16	1	5	28	5.6	1	1	0	6	1
2000—Seattle NFL	16	6	28	288	10.3	3	3	0	18	1
2001—Seattle NFL	16	5	8	98	12.3	2	2	0	12	0
Pro totals (4 years)	55	12	42	434	10.3	6	6	0	36	2

MILLER, BILLY   TE   TEXANS

PERSONAL: Born April 24, 1977, in Los Angeles. ... 6-3/230. ... Full name: Billy RoShawn Miller.
HIGH SCHOOL: Westlake (Westlake Village, Calif.).
COLLEGE: Southern California.
TRANSACTIONS/CAREER NOTES: Selected by Denver Broncos in seventh round (218th pick overall) of 1999 NFL draft. ... Signed by Broncos (July 20, 1999). ... Released by Broncos (September 5, 1999). ... Re-signed by Broncos to practice squad (September 6, 1999). ... Activated (October 19, 1999). ... Released by Broncos (September 2, 2001). ... Signed by Houston Texans (February 8, 2001).
PLAYING EXPERIENCE: Denver NFL, 1999 and 2000. ... Games/Games started: 1999 (10/0), 2000 (12/0). Total: 22/0.
PRO STATISTICS: 1999—Caught five passes for 59 yards and returned four kickoffs for 79 yards. 2000—Caught one pass for seven yards and returned one kickoff for 13 yards.
SINGLE GAME HIGHS (regular season): Receptions—2 (November 7, 1999, vs. San Diego); yards—36 (November 7, 1999, vs. San Diego); and touchdown receptions—0.

MILLER, FRED   OT   TITANS

PERSONAL: Born February 6, 1973, in Houston. ... 6-7/315. ... Full name: Fred J. Miller Jr.
HIGH SCHOOL: Aldine Eisenhower (Houston).
COLLEGE: Baylor (degree in sociology, 1995).

TRANSACTIONS/CAREER NOTES: Selected by St. Louis Rams in fifth round (141st pick overall) of 1996 NFL draft. ... Signed by Rams (July 15, 1996). ... Granted free agency (February 12, 1999). ... Re-signed by Rams (May 24, 1999). ... Granted unconditional free agency (February 11, 2000). ... Signed by Tennessee Titans (February 16, 2000).
PLAYING EXPERIENCE: St. Louis NFL, 1996-1999; Tennessee NFL, 2000 and 2001. ... Games/Games started: 1996 (14/0), 1997 (15/7), 1998 (15/15), 1999 (16/16), 2000 (16/16), 2001 (16/16). Total: 92/70.
CHAMPIONSHIP GAME EXPERIENCE: Played in NFC championship game (1999 season). ... Member of Super Bowl championship team (1999 season).
PRO STATISTICS: 2000—Recovered two fumbles.

MILLER, JAMIR   LB   BROWNS

PERSONAL: Born November 19, 1973, in Philadelphia. ... 6-5/266. ... Full name: Jamir Malik Miller. ... Cousin of Mark Gunn, defensive lineman with New York Jets (1991-94 and 1996) and Philadelphia Eagles (1995 and 1996). ... Name pronounced JA-meer.
HIGH SCHOOL: El Cerrito (Calif.).
COLLEGE: UCLA.
TRANSACTIONS/CAREER NOTES: Selected after junior season by Arizona Cardinals in first round (10th pick overall) of 1994 NFL draft. ... Signed by Cardinals (August 12, 1994). ... On suspended list for violating league substance abuse policy (September 4-October 3, 1995). ... Granted unconditional free agency (February 12, 1999). ... Signed by Cleveland Browns (May 13, 1999).
HONORS: Named linebacker on THE SPORTING NEWS college All-America first team (1993). ... Named linebacker on THE SPORTING NEWS NFL All-Pro team (2001).
PRO STATISTICS: 1995—Fumbled once and recovered two fumbles for 26 yards. 1996—Recovered one fumble for 26 yards and a touchdown. 1998—Recovered two fumbles. 2000—Intercepted one pass for no yards. 2001—Intercepted one pass for no yards.

Year — Team	G	GS	SACKS
1994—Arizona NFL	16	0	3.0
1995—Arizona NFL	10	8	1.0
1996—Arizona NFL	16	16	1.0
1997—Arizona NFL	16	16	5.5
1998—Arizona NFL	16	16	3.0
1999—Cleveland NFL	15	15	4.5
2000—Cleveland NFL	16	16	5.0
2001—Cleveland NFL	16	16	13.0
Pro totals (8 years)	**121**	**103**	**36.0**

MILLER, JIM   QB   BEARS

PERSONAL: Born February 9, 1971, in Grosse Pointe, Mich. ... 6-2/221. ... Full name: James Donald Miller.
HIGH SCHOOL: Kettering (Detroit).
COLLEGE: Michigan State (degree in financial administration).
TRANSACTIONS/CAREER NOTES: Selected by Pittsburgh Steelers in sixth round (178th pick overall) of 1994 NFL draft. ... Signed by Steelers (May 12, 1994). ... Inactive for all 16 games (1994). ... Assigned by Steelers to Frankfurt Galaxy in 1995 World League enhancement allocation program (February 20, 1995). ... Released by Steelers (August 23, 1997). ... Signed by Jacksonville Jaguars (September 2, 1997). ... Released by Jaguars (September 23, 1997). ... Signed by Atlanta Falcons (October 27, 1997). ... Granted unconditional free agency (February 13, 1998). ... Signed by Detroit Lions (March 2, 1998). ... Released by Lions (August 24, 1998). ... Signed by Dallas Cowboys (September 8, 1998). ... Released by Cowboys (October 1998). ... Signed by Chicago Bears (December 1, 1998). ... Active for four games (1998); did not play. ... On suspended list for violating league substance abuse policy (December 1, 1999-remainder of season). ... Granted unconditional free agency (February 11, 2000). ... Re-signed by Bears (February 17, 2000). ... On injured reserve with torn Achilles' tendon (November 13, 2000-remainder of season). ... Granted unconditional free agency (March 1, 2002). ... Re-signed by Bears (March 1, 2002).
CHAMPIONSHIP GAME EXPERIENCE: Member of Pittsburgh Steelers for AFC championship game (1994 and 1995 seasons); inactive. ... Member of Steelers for Super Bowl XXX (1995 season); inactive.
PRO STATISTICS: 1995—Fumbled once. 1996—Fumbled once for minus four yards. 1999—Fumbled four times and recovered three fumbles for minus 19 yards. 2000—Fumbled once. 2001—Fumbled seven times and recovered three fumbles for minus 17 yards.
SINGLE GAME HIGHS (regular season): Attempts—48 (November 14, 1999, vs. Minnesota); completions—34 (November 14, 1999, vs. Minnesota); yards—422 (November 14, 1999, vs. Minnesota); and touchdown passes—3 (November 18, 2001, vs. Tampa Bay).
STATISTICAL PLATEAUS: 300-yard passing games: 1999 (2).
MISCELLANEOUS: Regular-season record as starting NFL quarterback: 13-6 (.684). ... Postseason record as starting NFL quarterback: 0-1.

			PASSING							RUSHING				TOTALS		
Year — Team	G	GS	Att.	Cmp.	Pct.	Yds.	TD	Int.	Avg.	Rat.	Att.	Yds.	Avg.	TD	TD	2pt.	Pts.
1994—Pittsburgh NFL	...	...					Did not play.										
1995—Frankfurt W.L.	...	...	43	23	53.5	236	1	1	5.49	67.6	3	-2	-0.7	0	0	0	0
—Pittsburgh NFL	4	0	56	32	57.1	397	2	5	7.09	53.9	1	2	2.0	0	0	0	0
1996—Pittsburgh NFL	2	1	25	13	52.0	123	0	0	4.92	65.9	2	-4	-2.0	0	0	0	0
1997—Atlanta NFL							Did not play.										
—Jacksonville NFL							Did not play.										
1998—Chicago NFL							Did not play.										
1999—Chicago NFL	5	3	174	110	63.2	1242	7	6	7.14	83.5	3	9	3.0	0	0	0	0
2000—Chicago NFL	4	2	82	47	57.3	382	1	1	4.66	68.2	7	5	0.7	0	0	0	0
2001—Chicago NFL	14	13	395	228	57.7	2299	13	10	5.82	74.9	29	-19	-0.7	0	0	0	0
W.L. totals (1 year)	...	...	43	23	53.5	236	1	1	5.49	67.6	3	-2	-0.7	0	0	0	0
NFL totals (4 years)	29	19	732	430	58.7	4443	23	22	6.07	74.3	42	-7	-0.2	0	0	0	0
Pro totals (5 years)	...	...	775	453	58.5	4679	24	23	6.04	73.9	45	-9	-0.2	0	0	0	0

MILLER, JOSH   P   STEELERS

PERSONAL: Born July 14, 1970, in Rockway, N.Y. ... 6-4/220.
HIGH SCHOOL: East Brunswick (N.J.).
JUNIOR COLLEGE: Scottsdale (Ariz.) Community College.
COLLEGE: Arizona (degree in communications, 1993).

TRANSACTIONS/CAREER NOTES: Signed as non-drafted free agent by Green Bay Packers (April 1993). ... Released by Packers before 1993 season. ... Signed by Baltimore Stallions of CFL (June 1994). ... Signed by Seattle Seahawks (May 29, 1996). ... Released by Seahawks (August 13, 1996). ... Signed by Pittsburgh Steelers (August 15, 1996).
CHAMPIONSHIP GAME EXPERIENCE: Played in Grey Cup, CFL championship game (1994). ... Played in AFC championship game (1997 and 2001 seasons).
HONORS: Named punter on the Sporting News college All-America first team (1992).
PRO STATISTICS: CFL: 1994—Fumbled once. NFL: 1997—Rushed once for minus seven yards. 1999—Rushed twice for minus nine yards and recovered one fumble for minus 11 yards. 2000—Rushed once for no yards, fumbled once and recovered one fumbled for minus 18 yards. 2001—Rushed once for no yards and fumbled once for minus nine yards.

				PUNTING			
Year Team	G	No.	Yds.	Avg.	Net avg.	In. 20	Blk.
1994—Baltimore CFL	18	117	5024	42.9	36.9	0	0
1995—Baltimore CFL	18	118	5629	47.7	42.2	0	0
1996—Pittsburgh NFL	12	55	2256	41.0	33.6	18	0
1997—Pittsburgh NFL	16	64	2729	42.6	35.0	17	0
1998—Pittsburgh NFL	16	81	3530	43.6	36.8	*34	0
1999—Pittsburgh NFL	16	84	3795	45.2	38.1	27	0
2000—Pittsburgh NFL	16	90	3944	43.8	37.5	*34	▲1
2001—Pittsburgh NFL	16	59	2505	42.5	34.9	23	1
CFL totals (2 years)	36	235	10653	45.3	39.6	0	0
NFL totals (6 years)	92	433	18759	43.3	36.3	153	2
Pro totals (8 years)	128	668	29412	44.0	37.4	153	2

MILLER, ROMARO QB VIKINGS

PERSONAL: Born September 12, 1978, in Shannon, Miss. ... 6-1/195.
HIGH SCHOOL: Shannon (Miss.).
COLLEGE: Mississippi.
TRANSACTIONS/CAREER NOTES: Signed as non-drafted free agent by Minnesota Vikings (May 9, 2001). ... Released by Vikings (September 2, 2001). ... Re-signed by Vikings (December 18, 2001).
PLAYING EXPERIENCE: Minnesota NFL, 2001. ... Games/Games started: 2001 (1/0).

MILLOY, LAWYER S PATRIOTS

PERSONAL: Born November 14, 1973, in St. Louis. ... 6-0/210.
HIGH SCHOOL: Lincoln (Tacoma, Wash.).
COLLEGE: Washington.
TRANSACTIONS/CAREER NOTES: Selected after junior season by New England Patriots in second round (36th pick overall) of 1996 NFL draft. ... Signed by Patriots (June 5, 1996).
CHAMPIONSHIP GAME EXPERIENCE: Played in AFC championship game (1996 and 2001 seasons). ... Played in Super Bowl XXXI (1996 season). ... Member of Super Bowl championship team (2001 season).
HONORS: Named defensive back on The Sporting News college All-America first team (1995). ... Played in Pro Bowl (1998 and 1999 seasons). ... Named safety on The Sporting News NFL All-Pro team (1999).
PRO STATISTICS: 1996—Recovered one fumble. 1997—Recovered two fumbles. 1998—Recovered one fumble. 1999—Recovered two fumbles. 2001—Recovered one fumble.

			INTERCEPTIONS				SACKS
Year Team	G	GS	No.	Yds.	Avg.	TD	No.
1996—New England NFL	16	10	2	14	7.0	0	1.0
1997—New England NFL	16	16	3	15	5.0	0	0.0
1998—New England NFL	16	16	6	54	9.0	1	1.0
1999—New England NFL	16	16	4	17	4.3	0	2.0
2000—New England NFL	16	16	2	2	1.0	0	0.0
2001—New England NFL	16	16	2	21	10.5	0	3.0
Pro totals (6 years)	96	90	19	123	6.5	1	7.0

MINNIS, MARVIN WR CHIEFS

PERSONAL: Born February 6, 1977, in Miami. ... 6-1/171.
HIGH SCHOOL: Nortwestern (Miami).
COLLEGE: Florida State.
TRANSACTIONS/CAREER NOTES: Selected by Kansas City Chiefs in third round (77th pick overall) of 2001 NFL draft. ... Signed by Chiefs (May 25, 2001).
HONORS: Named wide receiver on The Sporting News college All-America first team (2000).
SINGLE GAME HIGHS (regular season): Receptions—6 (December 23, 2001, vs. San Diego); yards—89 (December 16, 2001, vs. Denver); and touchdown receptions—1 (September 9, 2001, vs. Oakland).

			RECEIVING			
Year Team	G	GS	No.	Yds.	Avg.	TD
2001—Kansas City NFL	13	11	33	511	15.5	1

MINOR, KORY LB PANTHERS

PERSONAL: Born December 14, 1976, in Inglewood, Calif. ... 6-1/247. ... Full name: Kory DeShaun Minor.
HIGH SCHOOL: Bishop Amat (La Puente, Calif.).
COLLEGE: Notre Dame.
TRANSACTIONS/CAREER NOTES: Selected by San Francisco 49ers in seventh round (234th pick overall) of 1999 NFL draft. ... Signed by 49ers (July 26, 1999). ... Released by 49ers (September 5, 1999). ... Signed by Carolina Panthers to practice squad (September 14, 1999). ... Activated (December 28, 1999); did not play. ... On injured reserve with knee injury (December 19, 2000-remainder of season).
PLAYING EXPERIENCE: Carolina NFL, 2000 and 2001. ... Games/Games started: 2000 (15/0), 2001 (11/2). Total: 26/2.

MINOR, TRAVIS — RB — DOLPHINS

PERSONAL: Born June 30, 1979, in New Orleans. ... 5-10/201. ... Full name: Travis D. Minor.
HIGH SCHOOL: Catholic (Baton, La.).
COLLEGE: Florida State.
TRANSACTIONS/CAREER NOTES: Selected by Miami Dolphins in third round (85th pick overall) of 2001 NFL draft. ... Signed by Dolphins (July 23, 2001).
PRO STATISTICS: 2001—Recovered one fumble.
SINGLE GAME HIGHS (regular season): Attempts—9 (December 30, 2001, vs. Atlanta); yards—71 (November 11, 2001, vs. Indianapolis); and rushing touchdowns—1 (November 11, 2001, vs. Indianapolis).

				RUSHING				RECEIVING				TOTALS		
Year Team	G	GS	Att.	Yds.	Avg.	TD	No.	Yds.	Avg.	TD	TD	2pt.	Pts.	Fum.
2001—Miami NFL	16	0	59	281	4.8	2	29	263	9.1	1	4	0	24	0

MINTER, BARRY — LB

PERSONAL: Born January 28, 1970, in Mount Pleasant, Texas. ... 6-2/250. ... Full name: Barry Antoine Minter.
HIGH SCHOOL: Mount Pleasant (Texas).
COLLEGE: Tulsa.
TRANSACTIONS/CAREER NOTES: Selected by Dallas Cowboys in sixth round (168th pick overall) of 1993 NFL draft. ... Signed by Cowboys (July 14, 1993). ... Traded by Cowboys with LB Vinson Smith and sixth-round pick (DE Carl Reeves) in 1995 draft to Chicago Bears for TE Kelly Blackwell, S Markus Paul and LB John Roper (August 17, 1993). ... Granted free agency (February 16, 1996). ... Re-signed by Bears (February 26, 1996). ... Granted unconditional free agency (February 13, 1998). ... Re-signed by Bears (February 20, 1998). ... Released by Bears (June 5, 2001). ... Signed by Cleveland Browns (August 13, 2001). ... Released by Browns (September 19, 2001).
PRO STATISTICS: 1994—Recovered one fumble. 1997—Recovered three fumbles. 1998—Recovered one fumble for 11 yards. 1999—Recovered one fumble.

			INTERCEPTIONS				SACKS
Year Team	G	GS	No.	Yds.	Avg.	TD	No.
1993—Chicago NFL	2	0	0	0	0.0	0	0.0
1994—Chicago NFL	13	1	0	0	0.0	0	0.0
1995—Chicago NFL	16	3	1	2	2.0	1	0.0
1996—Chicago NFL	16	7	1	5	5.0	0	1.5
1997—Chicago NFL	16	16	0	0	0.0	0	6.0
1998—Chicago NFL	16	16	1	17	17.0	0	1.0
1999—Chicago NFL	16	16	2	66	33.0	1	3.0
2000—Chicago NFL	14	2	0	0	0.0	0	0.0
2001—Cleveland NFL	1	0	0	0	0.0	0	0.0
Pro totals (9 years)	110	61	5	90	18.0	2	11.5

MINTER, MIKE — S — PANTHERS

PERSONAL: Born January 15, 1974, in Cleveland. ... 5-10/188. ... Full name: Michael Christopher Minter.
HIGH SCHOOL: Lawton (Okla.).
COLLEGE: Nebraska (degree in engineering, 1996).
TRANSACTIONS/CAREER NOTES: Selected by Carolina Panthers in second round (56th pick overall) of 1997 NFL draft. ... Signed by Panthers (June 12, 1997). ... Granted unconditional free agency (March 2, 2001). ... Re-signed by Panthers (March 3, 2001).
PRO STATISTICS: 1997—Recovered two fumbles. 1999—Recovered two fumbles for 30 yards. 2000—Recovered one fumble. 2001—Recovered two fumbles.

			INTERCEPTIONS				SACKS
Year Team	G	GS	No.	Yds.	Avg.	TD	No.
1997—Carolina NFL	16	11	0	0	0.0	0	3.5
1998—Carolina NFL	6	4	1	7	7.0	0	0.0
1999—Carolina NFL	16	16	3	69	23.0	0	1.0
2000—Carolina NFL	16	16	2	38	19.0	1	2.0
2001—Carolina NFL	14	14	2	32	16.0	0	0.0
Pro totals (5 years)	68	61	8	146	18.3	1	6.5

MIRANDA, PAUL — CB — SEAHAWKS

PERSONAL: Born May 2, 1976, in Brooklyn, N.Y. ... 5-10/178. ... Full name: Paul Nathaniel Miranda.
HIGH SCHOOL: Thomas County Central (Thomasville, Ga.).
JUNIOR COLLEGE: Holmes Junior College (Miss.).
COLLEGE: Central Florida (degree in health services administration).
TRANSACTIONS/CAREER NOTES: Selected by Indianapolis Colts in fourth round (96th pick overall) of 1999 NFL draft. ... Signed by Colts (July 22, 1999). ... Released by Colts (August 31, 2000). ... Signed by Seattle Seahawks (September 1, 2000). ... Released by Seahawks (September 19, 2000). ... Signed by San Francisco 49ers to practice squad (September 21, 2000). ... Signed by Seahawks off 49ers practice squad (November 29, 2000). ... Granted free agency (March 1, 2002).
PLAYING EXPERIENCE: Indianapolis NFL, 1999; Seattle NFL, 2000 and 2001. ... Games/Games started: 1999 (5/0), 2000 (3/0), 2001 (8/2). Total: 16/2.
PRO STATISTICS: 2001—Recovered one fumble.

MISSOURI, DWAYNE   DE   COWBOYS

PERSONAL: Born December 23, 1978, in Frankfurt, Germany. ... 6-5/260. ... Full name: Dwayne Anthony Missouri.
HIGH SCHOOL: Roosevelt (San Antonio).
COLLEGE: Northwestern.
TRANSACTIONS/CAREER NOTES: Selected by Baltimore Ravens in seventh round (231st pick overall) of 2001 NFL draft. ... Signed by Ravens (July 17, 2001). ... Released by Ravens (September 9, 2001). ... Re-signed by Ravens to practice squad (September 18, 2001). ... Signed by Dallas Cowboys off Ravens practice sqaud (October 29, 2001).
PLAYING EXPERIENCE: Dallas NFL, 2001. ... Games/Games started: 2001 (3/0).

MITCHELL, ANTHONY   S   RAVENS

PERSONAL: Born December 13, 1974, in Youngstown, Ohio. ... 6-1/211. ... Full name: Anthony Maurice Mitchell.
HIGH SCHOOL: West Lake (Atlanta, Ga.).
COLLEGE: Tuskegee.
TRANSACTIONS/CAREER NOTES: Signed as non-drafted free agent by Jacksonville Jaguars (April 26, 1999). ... Released by Jaguars (September 1, 1999). ... Signed by Baltimore Ravens to practice squad (September 7, 1999). ... Activated (December 7, 1999).
PLAYING EXPERIENCE: Baltimore NFL, 2000 and 2001. ... Games/Games started: 2000 (16/0), 2001 (16/0). Total: 32/0.
CHAMPIONSHIP GAME EXPERIENCE: Member of Super Bowl championship team (2000 season).
PRO STATISTICS: 2000—Recovered one fumble. 2001—Caught one pass for minus 11 yards.

MITCHELL, BRANDON   DE   SEAHAWKS

PERSONAL: Born June 19, 1975, in Abbeville, La. ... 6-3/280. ... Full name: Brandon Pete Mitchell.
HIGH SCHOOL: Abbeville (La.).
COLLEGE: Texas A&M.
TRANSACTIONS/CAREER NOTES: Selected by New England Patriots in second round (59th pick overall) of 1997 NFL draft. ... Signed by Patriots (June 6, 1997). ... On injured reserve with ankle injury (October 30, 1998-remainder of season). ... Granted free agency (February 11, 2000). ... Re-signed by Patriots (July 16, 2000). ... On injured reserve with leg injury (December 6, 2000-remainder of season). ... Granted unconditional free agency (March 2, 2001). ... Re-signed by Patriots (April 16, 2001). ... Granted unconditional free agency (March 1, 2002). ... Signed by Seattle Seahawks (April 10, 2002).
PLAYING EXPERIENCE: New England NFL, 1997-2001. ... Games/Games started: 1997 (12/0), 1998 (7/1), 1999 (16/16), 2000 (11/9), 2001 (16/11). Total: 62/37.
CHAMPIONSHIP GAME EXPERIENCE: Played in AFC championship game (2001 season). ... Member of Super Bowl championship team (2001 season).
PRO STATISTICS: 1998—Credited with two sacks. 1999—Credited with three sacks and recovered one fumble. 2001—Credited with one sack.

MITCHELL, BRIAN   RB/KR   EAGLES

PERSONAL: Born August 18, 1968, in Fort Polk, La. ... 5-10/221. ... Full name: Brian Keith Mitchell.
HIGH SCHOOL: Plaquemine (La.).
COLLEGE: Southwestern Louisiana.
TRANSACTIONS/CAREER NOTES: Selected by Washington Redskins in fifth round (130th pick overall) of 1990 NFL draft. ... Signed by Redskins (July 22, 1990). ... Granted free agency (February 1, 1992). ... Re-signed by Redskins for 1992 season. ... Granted unconditional free agency (February 17, 1994). ... Re-signed by Redskins (May 24, 1994). ... Granted free agency (February 17, 1995). ... Re-signed by Redskins (March 27, 1995). ... Granted unconditional free agency (February 13, 1998). ... Re-signed by Redskins (February 12, 1998). ... Released by Redskins (June 1, 2000). ... Signed by Philadelphia Eagles (June 9, 2000). ... Granted unconditional free agency (March 1, 2002). ... Re-signed by Eagles (March 27, 2002).
CHAMPIONSHIP GAME EXPERIENCE: Played in NFC championship game (1991 and 2001 seasons). ... Member of Super Bowl championship team (1991 season).
HONORS: Named punt returner on THE SPORTING NEWS NFL All-Pro team (1995). ... Played in Pro Bowl (1995 season).
RECORDS: Holds NFL career record for most punt returns—388; most combined kick returns—897; most yards by combined kick returns—16,013; most yards gained by punt return—4,278; most kickoff returns—509; and most yards gained by kick returns—11,735. ... Holds NFL single-season record for most yards by combined kick return—1,930 (1994). ... Shares NFL career records for most touchdowns by combined kick returns—12.
PRO STATISTICS: 1990—Attempted six passes with three completions for 40 yards and fumbled twice. 1991—Fumbled eight times and recovered one fumble. 1992—Attempted one pass without a completion, fumbled four times and recovered two fumbles. 1993—Attempted two passes with one completion for 50 yards and an interception, fumbled three times and recovered one fumble. 1994—Had only one pass attempt intercepted and fumbled four times. 1995—Fumbled twice and recovered one fumble. 1996—Attempted one pass without a completion, fumbled once and recovered two fumbles. 1997—Fumbled three times. 1998—Attempted two passes with one completion for no yards and fumbled three times. 1999—Fumbled twice and recovered two fumbles for five yards. 2000—Attempted four passes with one completion for 21 yards, fumbled three times and recovered one fumble. 2001—Fumbled three times and recovered one fumble.
SINGLE GAME HIGHS (regular season): Attempts—21 (September 6, 1993, vs. Dallas); yards—116 (September 6, 1993, vs. Dallas); and rushing touchdowns—2 (September 6, 1993, vs. Dallas).
STATISTICAL PLATEAUS: 100-yard rushing games: 1993 (1), 2000 (1). Total: 2.

			RUSHING				RECEIVING				PUNT RETURNS				KICKOFF RETURNS				TOTALS		
Year Team	G	GS	Att.	Yds.	Avg.	TD	No.	Yds.	Avg.	TD	No.	Yds.	Avg.	TD	No.	Yds.	Avg.	TD	TD	2pt.	Pts.
1990—Washington NFL	15	0	15	81	5.4	1	2	5	2.5	0	12	107	8.9	0	18	365	20.3	0	1	0	6
1991—Washington NFL	16	0	3	14	4.7	0	0	0	0.0	0	45 *600	13.3	*2	29	583	20.1	0	2	0	12
1992—Washington NFL	16	0	6	70	11.7	0	3	30	10.0	0	29	271	9.3	1	23	492	21.4	0	1	0	6
1993—Washington NFL	16	4	63	246	3.9	3	20	157	7.9	0	29	193	6.7	0	33	678	20.5	0	3	0	18
1994—Washington NFL	16	7	78	311	4.0	0	26	236	9.1	1	32 ‡452 *14.1	†2	58	1478	25.5	0	3	1	20
1995—Washington NFL	16	1	46	301	6.5	1	38	324	8.5	1	25	315	12.6	†1	55	1408	‡25.6	0	3	0	18
1996—Washington NFL	16	2	39	193	4.9	0	32	286	8.9	0	23	258	11.2	0	56	1258	22.5	0	0	0	0
1997—Washington NFL	16	1	23	107	4.7	1	36	438	12.2	1	38	442	11.6	∞1	47	1094	23.3	1	4	0	24
1998—Washington NFL	16	0	39	208	5.3	2	44	306	7.0	0	44 ‡506	11.5	0	59	1337	22.7	1	3	0	18
1999—Washington NFL	16	0	40	220	5.5	1	31	305	9.8	0	40	332	8.3	0	43	893	20.8	0	1	0	6
2000—Philadelphia NFL	16	1	25	187	7.5	2	13	89	6.8	1	32	335	10.5	1	47	1124	23.9	1	5	0	30
2001—Philadelphia NFL	16	0	7	9	1.3	0	6	122	20.3	0	39 ‡467	12.0	0	41	1025	25.0	1	1	0	6
Pro totals (12 years)	191	16	384	1947	5.1	11	251	2298	9.2	4	388	4278	11.0	8	509	11735	23.1	4	27	1	164

MITCHELL, DONALD — CB — TITANS

PERSONAL: Born December 14, 1976, in Beaumont, Texas. ... 5-9/185. ... Full name: Donald Roosevelt Mitchell.
HIGH SCHOOL: Central (Beaumont, Texas).
COLLEGE: Southern Methodist.
TRANSACTIONS/CAREER NOTES: Selected by Tennessee Titans in fourth round (117th pick overall) of 1999 NFL draft. ... Signed by Titans (July 27, 1999). ... On injured reserve with knee injury (August 22, 2000-entire season).
PLAYING EXPERIENCE: Tennessee NFL, 1999 and 2001. ... Games/Games started: 1999 (16/0), 2000 (did not play), 2001 (13/4). Total: 29/4.
CHAMPIONSHIP GAME EXPERIENCE: Played in AFC championship game (1999 season). ... Played in Super Bowl XXXIV (1999 season).
PRO STATISTICS: 1999—Intercepted one pass for 42 yards and a touchdown and recovered one fumble. 2001—Returned blocked punt for 26 yards and a touchdown and returned blocked field goal for 69 yards and a touchdown.

MITCHELL, FREDDIE — WR — EAGLES

PERSONAL: Born November 28, 1978, in Lakeland, Fla. ... 5-11/184. ... Full name: Freddie Lee Mitchell II.
HIGH SCHOOL: Kathleen (Lakeland, Fla.).
COLLEGE: UCLA.
TRANSACTIONS/CAREER NOTES: Selected after junior season by Philadelphia Eagles in first round (25th pick overall) of 2001 NFL draft. ... Signed by Eagles (July 26, 2001).
CHAMPIONSHIP GAME EXPERIENCE: Played in NFC championship game (2001 season).
HONORS: Named wide receiver on THE SPORTING NEWS college All-America first team (2000).
PRO STATISTICS: 2001—Rushed twice for minus four yards and attempted one pass without a completion.
SINGLE GAME HIGHS (regular season): Receptions—4 (November 4, 2001, vs. Arizona); yards—62 (November 4, 2001, vs. Arizona); and touchdown receptions—1 (December 16, 2001, vs. Washington).

			RECEIVING		
Year Team	G	GS	No.	Yds.	Avg.	TD
2001—Philadelphia NFL	15	1	21	283	13.5	1

MITCHELL, JEFF — C — PANTHERS

PERSONAL: Born January 29, 1974, in Dallas. ... 6-4/300. ... Full name: Jeffrey Clay Mitchell.
HIGH SCHOOL: Countryside (Clearwater, Fla.).
COLLEGE: Florida.
TRANSACTIONS/CAREER NOTES: Selected by Baltimore Ravens in fifth round (134th pick overall) of 1997 NFL draft. ... Signed by Ravens (July 10, 1997). ... On injured reserve with knee injury (August 18, 1997-entire season). ... Granted free agency (February 11, 2000). ... Re-signed by Ravens (April 17, 2000) ... Granted unconditional free agency (March 2, 2001). ... Signed by Carolina Panthers (March 12, 2001).
PLAYING EXPERIENCE: Baltimore NFL, 1998-2000; Carolina NFL, 2001. ... Games/Games started: 1998 (11/10), 1999 (16/16), 2000 (14/14), 2001 (15/15). Total: 56/55.
CHAMPIONSHIP GAME EXPERIENCE: Played in AFC championship game (2000 season). ... Member of Super Bowl championship team (2000 season).
PRO STATISTICS: 1998—Fumbled once for minus 11 yards. 1999—Fumbled twice for minus 36 yards. 2001—Recovered two fumbles.

MITCHELL, KEITH — LB — SAINTS

PERSONAL: Born July 24, 1974, in Garland, Texas ... 6-2/245. ... Full name: Clarence Marquis Mitchell.
HIGH SCHOOL: Lakeview (Garland, Texas).
COLLEGE: Texas A&M.
TRANSACTIONS/CAREER NOTES: Signed as non-drafted free agent by New Orleans Saints (April 25, 1997).
HONORS: Named outside linebacker on THE SPORTING NEWS college All-America second team (1996). ... Played in Pro Bowl (2000 season).
PRO STATISTICS: 1998—Recovered three fumbles for 63 yards and a touchdown. 1999—Intercepted three passes for 22 yards and recovered one fumble. 2000—Intercepted one pass for 40 yards and one touchdown and recovered four fumbles for 90 yards and one touchdown.

Year Team	G	GS	SACKS
1997—New Orleans NFL	16	2	4.0
1998—New Orleans NFL	16	15	2.5
1999—New Orleans NFL	16	16	3.5
2000—New Orleans NFL	16	15	6.5
2001—New Orleans NFL	15	14	2.0
Pro totals (5 years)	79	62	18.5

MITCHELL, KEVIN — LB — REDSKINS

PERSONAL: Born January 1, 1971, in Harrisburg, Pa. ... 6-1/254. ... Full name: Kevin Danyelle Mitchell. ... Cousin of Troy Drayton, tight end, Kansas City Chiefs.
HIGH SCHOOL: Harrisburg (Pa.).
COLLEGE: Syracuse (degree in sociology).
TRANSACTIONS/CAREER NOTES: Selected by San Francisco 49ers in second round (53rd pick overall) of 1994 NFL draft. ... Signed by 49ers (July 20, 1994). ... Granted free agency (February 14, 1997). ... Re-signed by 49ers (April 24, 1997). ... Granted free agency (February 13, 1998). ... Signed by New Orleans Saints (February 19, 1998). ... Granted unconditional free agency (February 11, 2000). ... Signed by Washington Redskins (February 29, 2000). ... Granted unconditional free agency (March 2, 2001). ... Re-signed by Redskins (March 29, 2001). ... On injured reserve with ankle injury (December 26, 2001-remainder of season).
PLAYING EXPERIENCE: San Francisco NFL, 1994-1997; New Orleans NFL, 1998 and 1999; Washington NFL, 2000 and 2001. ... Games/Games started: 1994 (16/0), 1995 (15/0), 1996 (12/3), 1997 (16/0), 1998 (8/8), 1999 (16/1), 2000 (16/0), 2001 (13/13). Total: 112/25.
CHAMPIONSHIP GAME EXPERIENCE: Played in NFC championship game (1994 and 1997 seasons). ... Member of Super Bowl championship team (1994 season).
HONORS: Named defensive lineman on THE SPORTING NEWS college All-America second team (1992 and 1993).
PRO STATISTICS: 1996—Credited with one sack and recovered one fumble. 1998—Credited with 2$\frac{1}{2}$ sacks. 2000—Intercepted one pass for no yards and credited with one sack. 2001—Credited with two sacks.

MITCHELL, PETE — TE — JAGUARS

PERSONAL: Born October 9, 1971, in Royal Oak, Mich. ... 6-2/248. ... Full name: Peter Clark Mitchell.
HIGH SCHOOL: Brother Rice (Bloomfield Hills, Mich.).
COLLEGE: Boston College (degree in communications, 1994).
TRANSACTIONS/CAREER NOTES: Selected by Miami Dolphins in fourth round (122nd pick overall) of 1995 NFL draft. ... Signed by Dolphins (July 14, 1995). ... Traded by Dolphins to Jacksonville Jaguars for WR Mike Williams (August 27, 1995). ... Granted free agency (February 13, 1998). ... Re-signed by Jaguars (April 13, 1998). ... Designated by Jaguars as transition player (February 12, 1999). ... Free agency status changed from transition to unconditional (February 18, 1999). ... Signed by New York Giants (March 23, 1999). ... Granted unconditional free agency (March 2, 2001). ... Signed by Detroit Lions (April 26, 2000). ... Released by Lions (November 14, 2001). ... Signed by Jacksonville Jaguars (March 22, 2002).
CHAMPIONSHIP GAME EXPERIENCE: Played in AFC championship game (1996 season). ... Played in NFC championship game (2000 season). ... Played in Super Bowl XXXV (2000 season).
HONORS: Named tight end on THE SPORTING NEWS college All-America first team (1993 and 1994).
PRO STATISTICS: 1997—Returned two kickoffs for 17 yards and recovered one fumble. 1998—Returned two kickoffs for 27 yards and recovered one fumble. 2000—Fumbled once and recovered one fumble.
SINGLE GAME HIGHS (regular season): Receptions—10 (November 19, 1995, vs. Tampa Bay); yards—161 (November 19, 1995, vs. Tampa Bay); and touchdown receptions—1 (October 15, 2000, vs. Dallas).
STATISTICAL PLATEAUS: 100-yard receiving games: 1995 (1).

			RECEIVING				TOTALS			
Year Team	G	GS	No.	Yds.	Avg.	TD	TD	2pt.	Pts.	Fum.
1995—Jacksonville NFL	16	4	41	527	12.9	2	2	0	12	0
1996—Jacksonville NFL	16	7	52	575	11.1	1	1	0	6	1
1997—Jacksonville NFL	16	12	35	380	10.9	4	4	0	24	0
1998—Jacksonville NFL	16	16	38	363	9.6	2	2	0	12	0
1999—New York Giants NFL	15	6	58	520	9.0	3	3	0	18	1
2000—New York Giants NFL	14	5	25	245	9.8	1	1	0	6	1
2001—Detroit NFL	5	1	5	29	5.8	0	0	0	0	0
Pro totals (7 years)	98	51	254	2639	10.4	13	13	0	78	3

MITCHELL, SCOTT — QB

PERSONAL: Born January 2, 1968, in Salt Lake City. ... 6-6/240. ... Full name: William Scott Mitchell.
HIGH SCHOOL: Springville (Utah).
COLLEGE: Utah.
TRANSACTIONS/CAREER NOTES: Selected after junior season by Miami Dolphins in fourth round (93rd pick overall) of 1990 NFL draft. ... Signed by Dolphins (July 20, 1990). ... Inactive for 16 games (1990). ... Granted free agency (February 1, 1992). ... Assigned by Dolphins to Orlando Thunder in 1992 World League enhancement allocation program (February 20, 1992). ... Re-signed by Dolphins (February 21, 1992). ... Granted unconditional free agency (February 17, 1994). ... Signed by Detroit Lions (March 6, 1994). ... On injured reserve with wrist injury (November 8, 1994-remainder of season). ... Traded by Lions to Baltimore Ravens for third-round pick (traded to Miami) in 1999 draft and fifth-round pick (traded to St. Louis) in 2000 draft (March 16, 1999). ... Granted unconditional free agency (February 11, 2000). ... Signed by Cincinnati Bengals (March 9, 2000). ... Granted unconditional free agency (March 2, 2001). ... Re-signed by Bengals (April 22, 2001). ... Granted unconditional free agency (March 1, 2002).
CHAMPIONSHIP GAME EXPERIENCE: Played in AFC championship game (1992 season).
PRO STATISTICS: W.L.: 1992—Fumbled six times and recovered two fumbles for minus 19 yards. NFL: 1992—Fumbled once. NFL: 1993—Fumbled three times and recovered one fumble for minus four yards. 1994—Fumbled eight times and recovered two fumbles for minus five yards. 1995—Fumbled nine times and recovered one fumble. 1996—Fumbled nine times and recovered two fumbles for minus three yards. 1997—Tied for NFC lead with 15 fumbles and recovered four fumbles for minus 15 yards. 1998—Fumbled once for minus nine yards. 1999—Fumbled once. 2000—Fumbled four times for minus six yards.
SINGLE GAME HIGHS (regular season): Attempts—50 (September 7, 1997, vs. Tampa Bay); completions—31 (October 13, 1996, vs. Oakland); yards—410 (November 23, 1995, vs. Minnesota); and touchdown passes—4 (September 22, 1996, vs. Chicago).
STATISTICAL PLATEAUS: 300-yard passing games: 1993 (1), 1995 (5), 1996 (2), 1997 (1). Total: 9.
MISCELLANEOUS: Regular-season record as starting NFL quarterback: 32-39 (.451). ... Postseason record as starting NFL quarterback: 0-2.

					PASSING						RUSHING				TOTALS		
Year Team	G	GS	Att.	Cmp.	Pct.	Yds.	TD	Int.	Avg.	Rat.	Att.	Yds.	Avg.	TD	TD	2pt.	Pts.
1990—Miami NFL							Did not play.										
1991—Miami NFL	2	0	0	0	0.0	0	0	0	0.0	...	0	0	0.0	0	0	0	0
1992—Orlando W.L.	10	10	*361	*201	55.7	2213	12	7	6.13	77.0	21	45	2.1	1	1	0	6
—Miami NFL	16	0	8	2	25.0	32	0	1	4.00	4.2	8	10	1.3	0	0	0	0
1993—Miami NFL	13	7	233	133	57.1	1773	12	8	7.61	84.2	21	89	4.2	0	0	0	0
1994—Detroit NFL	9	9	246	119	48.4	1456	10	11	5.92	62.0	15	24	1.6	1	1	0	6
1995—Detroit NFL	16	16	583	346	59.3	4338	32	12	7.44	92.3	36	104	2.9	4	4	0	24
1996—Detroit NFL	14	14	437	253	57.9	2917	17	17	6.68	74.9	37	83	2.2	4	4	0	24
1997—Detroit NFL	16	16	509	293	57.6	3484	19	14	6.84	79.6	37	83	2.2	1	1	0	6
1998—Detroit NFL	2	2	75	38	50.7	452	1	3	6.03	57.2	7	30	4.3	0	0	0	0
1999—Baltimore NFL	2	2	56	24	42.9	236	1	4	4.21	31.5	1	1	1.0	0	0	0	0
2000—Cincinnati NFL	8	5	187	89	47.6	966	3	8	5.17	50.8	10	61	6.1	1	1	0	6
2001—Cincinnati NFL	1	0	12	4	33.3	38	0	3	3.17	3.5	0	0	0.0	0	0	0	0
W.L. totals (1 year)	10	10	361	201	55.7	2213	12	7	6.13	77.0	21	45	2.1	1	1	0	6
NFL totals (11 years)	99	71	2346	1301	55.5	15692	95	81	6.69	75.3	172	485	2.8	11	11	0	66
Pro totals (12 years)	109	81	2707	1502	55.5	17905	107	88	6.61	75.5	193	530	2.7	12	12	0	72

MITCHELL, TYWAN — WR — CARDINALS

PERSONAL: Born December 10, 1975, in Crete, Ill. ... 6-5/250.
HIGH SCHOOL: Crete-Monee (Ill.).
COLLEGE: Minnesota State-Mankato.

TRANSACTIONS/CAREER NOTES: Signed as non-drafted free agent by Baltimore Ravens for 1999 season. ... Released by Ravens (June 19, 1999). ... Signed by Arizona Cardinals for 1999 season. ... Released by Cardinals (September 5, 1999). ... Re-signed by Cardinals to practice squad (September 7, 1999). ... Assigned by Cardinals to Berlin Thunder in 2000 NFL Europe enhancement allocation program (February 22, 2000). ... Released by Cardinals (September 8, 2000). ... Re-signed by Cardinals (September 11, 2000).
SINGLE GAME HIGHS (regular season): Receptions—7 (December 15, 2001, vs. New York Giants); yards—62 (December 15, 2001, vs. New York Giants); and touchdown receptions—1 (December 15, 2001, vs. New York Giants).

				RECEIVING		
Year Team	G	GS	No.	Yds.	Avg.	TD
1999—Arizona NFL				Did not play.		
2000—Arizona NFL	10	1	5	80	16.0	0
2001—Arizona NFL	16	4	25	196	7.8	2
Pro totals (2 years)	26	5	30	276	9.2	2

MIXON, KENNY DE VIKINGS

PERSONAL: Born May 31, 1975, in Sun Valley, Calif. ... 6-4/275. ... Full name: Kenneth Jermaine Mixon.
HIGH SCHOOL: Pineville (La.).
COLLEGE: Louisiana State.
TRANSACTIONS/CAREER NOTES: Selected by Miami Dolphins in second round (49th pick overall) of 1998 NFL draft. ... Signed by Dolphins (July 21, 1998). ... Granted unconditional free agency (March 1, 2002). ... Signed by Minnesota Vikings (March 10, 2002).
PLAYING EXPERIENCE: Miami NFL, 1998-2001. ... Games/Games started: 1998 (16/16), 1999 (11/2), 2000 (16/16), 2001 (16/16). Total: 59/50.
PRO STATISTICS: 1998—Credited with two sacks. 2000—Credited with 2½ sacks and recovered one fumble. 2001—Intercepted one pass for 56 yards and a touchdown and credited with two sacks.

MOBLEY, JOHN LB BRONCOS

PERSONAL: Born October 10, 1973, in Chester, Pa. ... 6-1/236. ... Full name: John Ulysses Mobley.
HIGH SCHOOL: Chichester (Marcus Hook, Pa.).
COLLEGE: Kutztown (Pa.) University.
TRANSACTIONS/CAREER NOTES: Selected by Denver Broncos in first round (15th pick overall) of 1996 NFL draft. ... Signed by Broncos (July 23, 1996). ... On injured reserve with knee injury (September 22, 1999-remainder of season). ... Granted unconditional free agency (March 2, 2001). ... Re-signed by Broncos (March 2, 2001).
CHAMPIONSHIP GAME EXPERIENCE: Played in AFC championship game (1997 and 1998 seasons). ... Member of Super Bowl championship team (1997 and 1998 seasons).
HONORS: Named outside linebacker on THE SPORTING NEWS NFL All-Pro team (1997).
PRO STATISTICS: 1997—Recovered one fumble. 1998—Recovered one fumble. 2001—Recovered three fumbles for eight yards.

			INTERCEPTIONS				SACKS
Year Team	G	GS	No.	Yds.	Avg.	TD	No.
1996—Denver NFL	16	16	1	8	8.0	0	1.5
1997—Denver NFL	16	16	1	13	13.0	1	4.0
1998—Denver NFL	16	15	1	-2	-2.0	0	1.0
1999—Denver NFL	2	2	0	0	0.0	0	0.0
2000—Denver NFL	15	14	1	9	9.0	0	2.0
2001—Denver NFL	16	16	1	17	17.0	0	1.0
Pro totals (6 years)	81	79	5	45	9.0	1	9.5

MOHR, CHRIS P FALCONS

PERSONAL: Born May 11, 1966, in Atlanta. ... 6-5/215. ... Full name: Christopher Garrett Mohr.
HIGH SCHOOL: Briarwood Academy (Warrenton, Ga.).
COLLEGE: Alabama (degree in criminal justice).
TRANSACTIONS/CAREER NOTES: Selected by Tampa Bay Buccaneers in sixth round (146th pick overall) of 1989 NFL draft. ... Signed by Buccaneers (July 15, 1989). ... Released by Buccaneers (September 2, 1990). ... Signed by WLAF (January 31, 1991). ... Selected by Montreal Machine in first round (eighth punter) of 1991 WLAF positional draft. ... Signed by Buffalo Bills (June 6, 1991). ... Granted unconditional free agency (February 17, 1994). ... Re-signed by Bills (March 3, 1994). ... Granted unconditional free agency (February 14, 1997). ... Re-signed by Bills (March 4, 1997). ... Released by Bills (February 22, 2001). ... Signed by Atlanta Falcons (March 13, 2001).
CHAMPIONSHIP GAME EXPERIENCE: Played in AFC championship game (1991-1993 seasons). ... Played in Super Bowl XXVI (1991 season), Super Bowl XXVII (1992 season) and Super Bowl XXVIII (1993 season).
HONORS: Named punter on All-World League team (1991).
PRO STATISTICS: NFL: 1989—Converted one extra point. W.L.: 1991—Had only pass attempt intercepted and rushed three times for minus four yards. 1991—Completed only pass attempt for minus nine yards. 1992—Rushed once for 11 yards and recovered one fumble. 1993—Fumbled once and recovered one fumble. 1994—Rushed once for minus nine yards. 1997—Rushed once for no yards, completed only pass attempt for 29 yards, fumbled once and recovered one fumble for minus 10 yards. 1999—Rushed once for no yards. 2000—Attempted one pass with a completion for 44 yards. 2001—Attempted two passes with two completions for 40 yards.

				PUNTING			
Year Team	G	No.	Yds.	Avg.	Net avg.	In. 20	Blk.
1989—Tampa Bay NFL	16	∞84	3311	39.4	32.1	10	2
1990—			Did not play.				
1991—Montreal W.L.	10	57	2436	*42.7	34.0	13	2
—Buffalo NFL	16	54	2085	38.6	36.1	12	0
1992—Buffalo NFL	15	60	2531	42.2	36.7	12	0
1993—Buffalo NFL	16	74	2991	40.4	36.0	19	0
1994—Buffalo NFL	16	67	2799	41.8	36.0	13	0
1995—Buffalo NFL	16	86	3473	40.4	36.2	23	0
1996—Buffalo NFL	16	§101	§4194	41.5	36.5	§27	0

				PUNTING			
Year Team	G	No.	Yds.	Avg.	Net avg.	In. 20	Blk.
1997—Buffalo NFL	16	90	3764	41.8	36.0	24	1
1998—Buffalo NFL	16	69	2882	41.8	33.2	18	0
1999—Buffalo NFL	16	73	2840	38.9	33.9	20	0
2000—Buffalo NFL	16	95	3661	38.5	31.4	19	▲1
2001—Atlanta NFL	16	69	2680	38.8	36.1	25	0
W.L. totals (1 year)	10	57	2436	42.7	34.0	13	2
NFL totals (12 years)	191	922	37211	40.4	34.9	222	4
Pro totals (13 years)	201	979	39647	40.5	34.9	235	6

MOHRING, MICHAEL   DT/DE   RAIDERS

PERSONAL: Born March 22, 1974, in Glen Cove, N.Y. ... 6-5/295. ... Full name: Michael Joseph Mohring. ... Cousin of John Mohring, linebacker with Detroit Lions (1980) and Cleveland Browns (1980). ... Name pronounced MORE-ing.
HIGH SCHOOL: West Chester (Pa.) East.
COLLEGE: Pittsburgh.
TRANSACTIONS/CAREER NOTES: Signed as non-drafted free agent by Miami Dolphins (April 24, 1997). ... Released by Dolphins (August 18, 1997). ... Signed by San Diego Chargers to practice squad (August 25, 1997). ... Activated (December 12, 1997). ... On injured reserve with knee injury (October 24, 2000-remainder of season). ... On physically unable to perform list with knee injury (August 28-November 3, 2001). ... Granted unconditional free agency (March 1, 2002). ... Signed by Oakland Raiders (March 21, 2002).
PLAYING EXPERIENCE: San Diego NFL, 1997-2001. ... Games/Games started: 1997 (2/0), 1998 (10/0), 1999 (16/1), 2000 (7/0), 2001 (9/0). Total: 44/1.
PRO STATISTICS: 1998—Credited with one sack. 1999—Credited with two sacks.

MOLDEN, ALEX   CB   CHARGERS

PERSONAL: Born August 4, 1973, in Detroit. ... 5-10/190. ... Full name: Alex M. Molden.
HIGH SCHOOL: Sierra (Colorado Springs, Colo.).
COLLEGE: Oregon.
TRANSACTIONS/CAREER NOTES: Selected by New Orleans Saints in first round (11th pick overall) of 1996 NFL draft. ... Signed by Saints (July 21, 1996). ... Granted unconditional free agency (March 2, 2001). ... Signed by San Diego Chargers (March 7, 2001). ... On injured reserve with ankle injury (December 14, 2001-remainder of season).
HONORS: Named defensive back on THE SPORTING NEWS college All-America second team (1995).
PRO STATISTICS: 1997—Recovered two fumbles.

			INTERCEPTIONS				SACKS
Year Team	G	GS	No.	Yds.	Avg.	TD	No.
1996—New Orleans NFL	14	2	2	2	1.0	0	2.0
1997—New Orleans NFL	16	15	0	0	0.0	0	4.0
1998—New Orleans NFL	16	15	2	35	17.5	0	0.0
1999—New Orleans NFL	13	0	1	2	2.0	0	0.0
2000—New Orleans NFL	15	5	3	24	8.0	0	0.0
2001—San Diego NFL	6	3	1	0	0.0	0	0.0
Pro totals (6 years)	80	40	9	63	7.0	0	6.0

MONDS, MARIO   DT   BENGALS

PERSONAL: Born November 10, 1976, in Pierce, Fla. ... 6-3/325.
HIGH SCHOOL: Westwood (Fla.).
JUNIOR COLLEGE: Hutchinson (Kan.) Community College.
COLLEGE: Cincinnati.
TRANSACTIONS/CAREER NOTES: Selected by Washington Redskins in sixth round (186th pick overall) of 2001 NFL draft. ... Signed by Redskins (June 13, 2001). ... Claimed on waivers by Cincinnati Bengals (September 4, 2001).
PLAYING EXPERIENCE: Cincinnati NFL, 2001. ... Games/Games started: 2001 (2/0).

MONROE, ROD   TE   BROWNS

PERSONAL: Born July 30, 1975, in Hearne, Texas. ... 6-5/254. ... Full name: Rodrick Monroe.
HIGH SCHOOL: Hearne (Texas).
JUNIOR COLLEGE: McLennan Community College (Texas); did not play.
COLLEGE: Cincinnati.
TRANSACTIONS/CAREER NOTES: Selected by Dallas Cowboys in seventh round (237th pick overall) of 1998 NFL draft. ... Signed by Cowboys (July 13, 1998). ... Released by Cowboys (August 24, 1998). ... Signed by Atlanta Falcons to practice squad (September 1, 1998). ... Activated (December 15, 1998); did not play. ... Claimed on waivers by Jacksonville Jaguars (August 22, 2000). ... Released by Jaguars (August 27, 2000). ... Re-signed by Jaguars to practice squad (August 28, 2000). ... Released by Jaguars (September 6, 2000). ... Signed by Miami Dolphins to practice squad (September 26, 2000). ... Released by Dolphins (October 10, 2000). ... Signed by Cleveland Browns to practice squad (December 7, 2000). ... Assigned by Browns to Frankfurt Galaxy in 2001 NFL Europe enhancement allocation program (February 19, 2001). ... Released by Browns (September 2, 2001). ... Re-signed by Browns (October 10, 2001).
PLAYING EXPERIENCE: Atlanta NFL, 1999; Frankfurt NFLE, 2001; Cleveland NFL, 2001. ... Games/Games started: 1999 (2/0), NFLE 2001 (games played unavailable), NFL 2001 (7/3). Total: 9/3.
CHAMPIONSHIP GAME EXPERIENCE: Member of Falcons for NFC championship game (1998 season); inactive. ... Member of Falcons for Super Bowl XXXIII (1998 season); inactive.
PRO STATISTICS: 1999—Caught one pass for eight yards. NFLE: 2001—Caught 23 passes for 362 yards and two touchdowns.
SINGLE GAME HIGHS (regular season): Receptions—1 (December 12, 1999, vs. San Francisco); yards—8 (December 12, 1999, vs. San Francisco); and touchdown receptions—0.

MONTGOMERY, SCOTTIE — WR — BRONCOS

PERSONAL: Born May 26, 1978, in Shelby, N.C. ... 6-1/195. ... Full name: Scottie Austin Montgomery.
HIGH SCHOOL: Burns (Cherryville, N.C.).
COLLEGE: Duke.
TRANSACTIONS/CAREER NOTES: Signed as non-drafted free agent by Carolina Panthers (April 27, 2000). ... Released by Panthers (August 27, 2000). ... Signed by Denver Broncos to practice squad (September 13, 2000). ... Activated (October 21, 2000). ... Released by Broncos (September 2, 2001). ... Re-signed by Broncos to practice squad (September 4, 2001). ... Activated (October 23, 2001).
PLAYING EXPERIENCE: Denver NFL, 2000 and 2001. ... Games/Games started: 2000 (4/0), 2001 (8/0). Total: 12/0.
PRO STATISTICS: 2000—Caught one pass for 10 yards. 2001—Rushed once for five yards and caught 11 passes for 99 yards.
SINGLE GAME HIGHS (regular season): Receptions—4 (December 30, 2001, vs. Oakland); yards—34 (December 30, 2001, vs. Oakland); and touchdown receptions—0.

MONTY, PETE — LB

PERSONAL: Born July 3, 1974, in Fort Collins, Colo. ... 6-2/250. ... Full name: Peter Monty.
HIGH SCHOOL: Fort Collins (Colo.).
COLLEGE: Wisconsin.
TRANSACTIONS/CAREER NOTES: Selected by New York Giants in fourth round (103rd pick overall) of 1997 NFL draft. ... Signed by Giants (July 19, 1997). ... On injured reserve with knee injury (September 30, 1997-remainder of season). ... Granted free agency (February 11, 2000). ... Re-signed by Giants (April 13, 2000). ... Granted unconditional free agency (March 2, 2001). ... Signed by Minnesota Vikings (November 27, 2001). ... Granted unconditional free agency (March 1, 2002).
PLAYING EXPERIENCE: New York Giants NFL, 1997-2000; Minnesota NFL, 2001. ... Games/Games started: 1997 (3/0), 1998 (11/0), 1999 (16/3), 2000 (16/1), 2001 (6/0). Total: 52/4.
CHAMPIONSHIP GAME EXPERIENCE: Played in NFC championship game (2000 season). ... Played in Super Bowl XXXV (2000 season).
PRO STATISTICS: 2000—Credited with two sacks and recovered one fumble.

MOORE, COREY — LB — DOLPHINS

PERSONAL: Born March 20, 1977, in Brownsville, Tenn. ... 5-11/225. ... Full name: Corey Antonio Moore.
HIGH SCHOOL: Haywood (Brownsville, Tenn.).
JUNIOR COLLEGE: Holmes Junior College (Miss.).
COLLEGE: Virginia Tech.
TRANSACTIONS/CAREER NOTES: Selected by Buffalo Bills in third round (89th pick overall) of 2000 NFL draft. ... Signed by Bills (July 17, 2000). ... On physically unable to perform list due to leg injury (July 25-August 1, 2001). ... Claimed on waivers by Cincinnati Bengals (August 23, 2001). ... Released by Bengals (September 2, 2001). ... Signed by Miami Dolphins (December 27, 2001).
PLAYING EXPERIENCE: Buffalo NFL, 2000; Miami NFL, 2001. ... Games/Games started: 2000 (9/4), 2001 (1/0). Total: 10/4.
HONORS: Named defensive end on THE SPORTING NEWS college All-America second team (1998). ... Lombardi Award winner (1999). ... Bronko Nagurski Award winner (1999). ... Named defensive end on THE SPORTING NEWS college All-America first team (1999).
PRO STATISTICS: 2000—Credited with one sack and recovered one fumble.

MOORE, DAMON — S — BEARS

PERSONAL: Born September 15, 1976, in Fostoria, Ohio. ... 5-11/215.
HIGH SCHOOL: Fostoria (Ohio).
COLLEGE: Ohio State.
TRANSACTIONS/CAREER NOTES: Selected by Philadelphia Eagles in fourth round (128th pick overall) of 1999 NFL draft. ... Signed by Eagles (July 28, 1999). ... Granted free agency (March 1, 2002). ... Signed by Chicago Bears (June 4, 2002).
PLAYING EXPERIENCE: Philadelphia NFL, 1999-2001. ... Games/Games started: 1999 (16/1), 2000 (16/16), 2001 (16/16). Total: 48/33.
CHAMPIONSHIP GAME EXPERIENCE: Played in NFC championship game (2001 season).
HONORS: Named strong safety on THE SPORTING NEWS college All-America first team (1998).
PRO STATISTICS: 1999—Intercepted one pass for 28 yards and recovered one fumble. 2000—Intercepted two passes for 24 yards and fumbled once. 2001—Intercepted two passes for two yards, credited with one sack and recovered two fumbles for 10 yards and one touchdown.

MOORE, DAVE — TE — BILLS

PERSONAL: Born November 11, 1969, in Morristown, N.J. ... 6-2/250. ... Full name: David Edward Moore.
HIGH SCHOOL: Roxbury (Succasunna, N.J.).
COLLEGE: Pittsburgh (degree in justice administration, 1991).
TRANSACTIONS/CAREER NOTES: Selected by Miami Dolphins in seventh round (191st pick overall) of 1992 NFL draft. ... Signed by Dolphins (July 15, 1992). ... Released by Dolphins (August 31, 1992). ... Re-signed by Dolphins to practice squad (September 1, 1992). ... Released by Dolphins (September 16, 1992). ... Re-signed by Dolphins to practice squad (October 21, 1992). ... Activated (October 24, 1992). ... Released by Dolphins (October 28, 1992). ... Re-signed by Dolphins to practice squad (October 28, 1992). ... Released by Dolphins (November 18, 1992). ... Signed by Tampa Bay Buccaneers to practice squad (November 24, 1992). ... Activated (December 4, 1992). ... Granted free agency (February 16, 1996). ... Re-signed by Buccaneers (May 31, 1996). ... Granted unconditional free agency (February 14, 1997). ... Re-signed by Buccaneers (February 18, 1997). ... Granted unconditional free agency (February 11, 2000). ... Re-signed by Buccaneers (March 20, 2000). ... Released by Buccaneers (February 27, 2002). ... Signed by Buffalo Bills (March 11, 2002).
CHAMPIONSHIP GAME EXPERIENCE: Played in NFC championship game (1999 season).
PRO STATISTICS: 1993—Attempted one pass without a completion and recovered one fumble. 1995—Rushed once for four yards.
SINGLE GAME HIGHS (regular season): Receptions—6 (November 2, 1997, vs. Indianapolis); yards—62 (November 3, 1996, vs. Chicago); and touchdown receptions—1 (December 23, 2001, vs. New Orleans).

Year Team	G	GS	No.	Yds.	Avg.	TD	TD	2pt.	Pts.	Fum.
1992—Miami NFL	1	0	0	0	0.0	0	0	0	0	0
—Tampa Bay NFL	4	2	1	10	10.0	0	0	0	0	0
1993—Tampa Bay NFL	15	1	4	47	11.8	1	1	0	6	0
1994—Tampa Bay NFL	15	5	4	57	14.3	0	0	0	0	0
1995—Tampa Bay NFL	16	9	13	102	7.8	0	0	0	0	0
1996—Tampa Bay NFL	16	8	27	237	8.8	3	3	0	18	0
1997—Tampa Bay NFL	16	7	19	217	11.4	4	4	0	24	0
1998—Tampa Bay NFL	16	16	24	255	10.6	4	4	0	24	1
1999—Tampa Bay NFL	16	16	23	276	12.0	5	5	0	30	0
2000—Tampa Bay NFL	16	16	29	288	9.9	3	3	0	18	0
2001—Tampa Bay NFL	16	16	35	285	8.1	4	4	0	24	0
Pro totals (10 years)	147	96	179	1774	9.9	24	24	0	144	1

MOORE, HERMAN   WR

PERSONAL: Born October 20, 1969, in Danville, Va. ... 6-4/218. ... Full name: Herman Joseph Moore.
HIGH SCHOOL: George Washington (Danville, Va.).
COLLEGE: Virginia (degree in rhetoric and communication studies, 1991).
TRANSACTIONS/CAREER NOTES: Selected after junior season by Detroit Lions in first round (10th pick overall) of 1991 NFL draft. ... Signed by Lions (July 19, 1991). ... On injured reserve with quadricep injury (September 11-October 9, 1992). ... On practice squad (October 9-14, 1992). ... Designated by Lions as transition player (February 25, 1993). ... On injured reserve with hip injury (October 17, 2001-remainder of season). ... Released by Lions (June 3, 2002).
CHAMPIONSHIP GAME EXPERIENCE: Played in NFC championship game (1991 season).
HONORS: Named wide receiver on THE SPORTING NEWS college All-America first team (1990). ... Played in Pro Bowl (1994-1997 seasons). ... Named wide receiver on THE SPORTING NEWS NFL All-Pro team (1995-1997).
RECORDS: Holds NFL single-season record for most pass receptions—123 (1995).
POST SEASON RECORDS: Shares NFL postseason career and single-game records for most two-point conversions—1 (December 30, 1995, vs. Philadelphia).
SINGLE GAME HIGHS (regular season): Receptions—14 (December 4, 1995, vs. Chicago); yards—183 (December 4, 1995, vs. Chicago); and touchdown receptions—3 (October 29, 1995, vs. Green Bay).
STATISTICAL PLATEAUS: 100-yard receiving games: 1992 (3), 1993 (3), 1994 (3), 1995 (10), 1996 (5), 1997 (6), 1998 (4). Total: 34.
MISCELLANEOUS: Holds Detroit Lions all-time records for most yards receiving (9,174), most receptions (670), and most touchdown receptions (62).

Year Team	G	GS	No.	Yds.	Avg.	TD	TD	2pt.	Pts.	Fum.
1991—Detroit NFL	13	1	11	135	12.3	0	0	0	0	0
1992—Detroit NFL	12	11	51	966	‡18.9	4	4	0	24	0
1993—Detroit NFL	15	15	61	935	15.3	6	6	0	36	2
1994—Detroit NFL	16	16	72	1173	16.3	11	11	0	66	1
1995—Detroit NFL	16	16	*123	1686	13.7	14	14	0	84	2
1996—Detroit NFL	16	16	106	1296	12.2	9	9	1	56	0
1997—Detroit NFL	16	16	†104	1293	12.4	8	8	1	50	0
1998—Detroit NFL	15	15	82	983	12.0	5	5	0	30	0
1999—Detroit NFL	8	4	16	197	12.3	2	2	0	12	0
2000—Detroit NFL	15	12	40	434	10.9	3	3	0	18	0
2001—Detroit NFL	3	1	4	76	19.0	0	0	0	0	0
Pro totals (11 years)	145	123	670	9174	13.7	62	62	2	376	5

MOORE, LARRY   G   REDSKINS

PERSONAL: Born June 1, 1975, in San Diego. ... 6-2/296. ... Full name: Larry Maceo Moore.
HIGH SCHOOL: Monte Vista (Spring Valley, Calif.).
JUNIOR COLLEGE: Grossmont College (Calif.).
COLLEGE: Brigham Young.
TRANSACTIONS/CAREER NOTES: Signed as non-drafted free agent by Seattle Seahawks (April 25, 1997). ... Released by Seahawks (August 17, 1997). ... Signed by Washington Redskins to practice squad (August 26, 1997). ... Released by Redskins (September 3, 1997). ... Signed by Indianapolis Colts (January 29, 1998). ... Granted free agency (March 2, 2001). ... Re-signed by Colts (April 21, 2001). ... Granted unconditional free agency (March 1, 2002). ... Signed by Redskins (March 13, 2002).
PLAYING EXPERIENCE: Indianapolis NFL, 1998-2001. ... Games/Games started: 1998 (6/5), 1999 (16/16), 2000 (16/16), 2001 (16/11). Total: 54/48.
PRO STATISTICS: 1999—Fumbled twice for minus 25 yards. 2000—Recovered one fumble. 2001—Recovered two fumbles.

MOORE, MARTY   LB   PATRIOTS

PERSONAL: Born March 19, 1971, in Phoenix. ... 6-1/245. ... Full name: Martin Neff Moore.
HIGH SCHOOL: Highlands (Fort Thomas, Ky.).
COLLEGE: Kentucky.
TRANSACTIONS/CAREER NOTES: Selected by New England Patriots in seventh round (222nd pick overall) of 1994 NFL draft. ... Signed by Patriots (June 1, 1994). ... Granted free agency (February 14, 1997). ... Re-signed by Patriots (June 6, 1997). ... Granted unconditional free agency (February 13, 1998). ... Re-signed by Patriots (April 3, 1998). ... Granted unconditional free agency (February 11, 2000). ... Signed by Cleveland Browns (March 2, 2000). ... Released by Browns (August 27, 2001). ... Signed by Patriots (August 28, 2001). ... Released by Patriots (September 2, 2001). ... Re-signed by Patriots (September 4, 2001). ... On injured reserve with torn Achilles' tendon (October 3, 2001-remainder of season). ... Released by Patriots (March 5, 2002). ... Re-signed by Patriots (May 31, 2002).
PLAYING EXPERIENCE: New England NFL, 1994-1999 and 2001; Cleveland NFL, 2000. ... Games/Games started: 1994 (16/4), 1995 (16/3), 1996 (16/0), 1997 (16/0), 1998 (14/2), 1999 (15/2), 2000 (16/9), 2001 (3/0). Total: 112/20.
CHAMPIONSHIP GAME EXPERIENCE: Played in AFC championship game (1996 season). ... Played in Super Bowl XXXI (1996 season).
PRO STATISTICS: 1997—Intercepted two passes for seven yards. 1998—Recovered one fumble. 2000—Intercepted one pass for three yards and credited with one sack.

MOORE, ROB — WR — BRONCOS

PERSONAL: Born September 27, 1968, in New York. ... 6-3/204. ... Full name: Robert S. Moore.
HIGH SCHOOL: Hempstead (N.Y.).
COLLEGE: Syracuse (degree in sociology, 1990).
TRANSACTIONS/CAREER NOTES: Selected by New York Jets in first round of 1990 NFL supplemental draft. ... Signed by Jets (July 22, 1990). ... Designated by Jets as transition player (February 25, 1993). ... Free agency status changed by Jets from transitional to restricted (February 17, 1994). ... Re-signed by Jets (July 12, 1994). ... Designated by Jets as franchise player (February 15, 1995). ... Traded by Jets to Arizona Cardinals for RB Ronald Moore and first- (DE Hugh Douglas) and fourth-round (OT Melvin Hayes) picks in 1995 draft (April 21, 1995). ... Designated by Cardinals as franchise player (February 12, 1999). ... On injured reserve with knee injury (August 22, 2000-entire season). ... On injured reserve with hamstring injury (November 29, 2001-remainder of season). ... Released by Cardinals (February 27, 2002). ... Signed by Denver Broncos (March 19, 2002).
HONORS: Named wide receiver on THE SPORTING NEWS college All-America first team (1989). ... Played in Pro Bowl (1994 and 1997 seasons).
PRO STATISTICS: 1990—Rushed twice for minus four yards. 1992—Rushed once for 21 yards. 1993—Rushed once for minus six yards. 1994—Rushed once for minus three yards and recovered one fumble. 1995—Attempted two passes with one completion for 33 yards and an interception.
SINGLE GAME HIGHS (regular season): Receptions—9 (December 20, 1998, vs. New Orleans); yards—188 (November 30, 1997, vs. Pittsburgh); and touchdown receptions—3 (December 7, 1997, vs. Washington).
STATISTICAL PLATEAUS: 100-yard receiving games: 1990 (1), 1993 (2), 1994 (2), 1995 (3), 1996 (3), 1997 (8), 1998 (2), 1999 (2). Total: 23.

			RECEIVING				TOTALS			
Year Team	G	GS	No.	Yds.	Avg.	TD	TD	2pt.	Pts.	Fum.
1990—New York Jets NFL	15	14	44	692	15.7	6	6	0	36	1
1991—New York Jets NFL	16	16	70	987	14.1	5	5	0	30	2
1992—New York Jets NFL	16	15	50	726	14.5	4	4	0	24	0
1993—New York Jets NFL	13	13	64	843	13.2	1	1	0	6	2
1994—New York Jets NFL	16	16	78	1010	12.9	6	6	2	40	0
1995—Arizona NFL	15	15	63	907	14.4	5	5	1	32	0
1996—Arizona NFL	16	16	58	1016	17.5	4	4	1	26	0
1997—Arizona NFL	16	16	97	*1584	16.3	8	8	1	50	0
1998—Arizona NFL	16	16	67	982	14.7	5	5	0	30	0
1999—Arizona NFL	14	10	37	621	16.8	5	5	0	30	0
2000—Arizona NFL					Did not play.					
2001—Arizona NFL					Did not play.					
Pro totals (10 years)	153	147	628	9368	14.9	49	49	5	304	5

MOORE, RON — DT — FALCONS

PERSONAL: Born August 10, 1977, in Sanford, Fla. ... 6-2/312. ... Full name: Ronald Demon Moore.
HIGH SCHOOL: Seminole (Sanford, Fla.).
JUNIOR COLLEGE: Hinds Community College (Miss.).
COLLEGE: Northwestern Oklahoma State.
TRANSACTIONS/CAREER NOTES: Selected by Green Bay Packers in seventh round (229th pick overall) of 2000 NFL draft. ... Signed by Packers (May 17, 2000). ... Released by Packers (August 27, 2000). ... Signed by Dallas Cowboys to practice squad (September 13, 2000). ... Released by Cowboys (September 27, 2000). ... Signed by Atlanta Falcons to practice squad (November 8, 2000). ... Released by Falcons (September 2, 2001). ... Re-signed by Falcons to practice squad (September 11, 2001). ... Activated (November 27, 2001).
PLAYING EXPERIENCE: Atlanta NFL, 2001. ... Games/Games started: 2001 (1/0).

MOORMAN, BRIAN — P — BILLS

PERSONAL: Born February 8, 1976, in Segdwick, Kan. ... 6-0/180.
HIGH SCHOOL: Segdwick (Kan.).
COLLEGE: Pittsburgh State.
TRANSACTIONS/CAREER NOTES: Signed as non-drafted free agent by Seattle Seahawks (February 24, 1999). ... Released by Seahawks (August 30, 1999). ... Re-signed by Seahawks (February 17, 2000). ... Assigned by Seahawks to Berlin Thunder in 2000 NFL Europe enhancement allocation program (February 18, 2000). ... Released by Seahawks (August 27, 2000). ... Signed by Buffalo Bills (July 20, 2001).
PRO STATISTICS: NFLE: 2001—Rushed three times for 46 yards. NFL: 2001—Rushed once for no yards and attempted one pass without a completion.

		PUNTING					
Year Team	G	No.	Yds.	Avg.	Net avg.	In. 20	Blk.
2001—Berlin NFLE	...	38	1645	43.3	37.0	7	0
—Buffalo NFL	16	80	3262	40.8	33.8	16	0
NFL Europe totals (1 year)	...	38	1645	43.3	37.0	7	0
NFL totals (1 year)	16	80	3262	40.8	33.8	16	0
Pro totals (2 years)	...	118	4907	41.6	34.8	23	0

MORAN, SEAN — DE — 49ERS

PERSONAL: Born June 5, 1973, in Aurora, Colo. ... 6-4/275. ... Full name: Sean Farrell Moran.
HIGH SCHOOL: Overland (Aurora, Colo.).
COLLEGE: Colorado State.
TRANSACTIONS/CAREER NOTES: Selected by Buffalo Bills in fourth round (120th pick overall) of 1996 NFL draft. ... Signed by Bills (July 9, 1996). ... Granted free agency (February 12, 1999). ... Re-signed by Bills (April 1, 1999). ... Granted unconditional free agency (February 11, 2000). ... Signed by St. Louis Rams (March 15, 2000). ... Granted unconditional free agency (March 1, 2002). ... Signed by San Francisco 49ers (April 2, 2002).
PLAYING EXPERIENCE: Buffalo NFL, 1996-1999; St. Louis NFL, 2000 and 2001. ... Games/Games started: 1996 (16/0), 1997 (16/7), 1998 (9/2), 1999 (16/0), 2000 (15/3), 2001 (16/1). Total: 88/13.
CHAMPIONSHIP GAME EXPERIENCE: Played in NFC championship game (2001 season). ... Played in Super Bowl XXXVI (2001 season).
PRO STATISTICS: 1997—Intercepted two passes for 12 yards, credited with 4½ sacks and recovered one fumble. 1999—Credited with ½ sack. 2000—Credited with two sacks and returned one kickoff for 17 yards. 2001—Credited with two sacks.

MOREAU, FRANK   RB   TEXANS

PERSONAL: Born September 9, 1976, in Elizabethtown, Ky. ... 6-2/230. ... Full name: Franklin H. Moreau.
HIGH SCHOOL: Central Hardin (Elizabethtown, Ky.).
COLLEGE: Louisville (degree in justice administration).
TRANSACTIONS/CAREER NOTES: Selected by Kansas City Chiefs in fourth round (115th pick overall) of 2000 NFL draft. ... Signed by Chiefs (June 6, 2000). ... Claimed on waivers by Jacksonville Jaguars (September 3, 2001). ... Released by Jaguars (November 27, 2001). ... Signed by Houston Texans (January 8, 2002).
SINGLE GAME HIGHS (regular season): Attempts—18 (September 17, 2000, vs. San Diego); yards—59 (December 17, 2000, vs. Denver); and rushing touchdowns—1 (November 4, 2001, vs. Tennessee).

			RUSHING				TOTALS		
Year Team	G	GS	Att.	Yds.	Avg.	TD	TD	2pt.	Pts.	Fum.
2000—Kansas City NFL	11	1	67	179	2.7	4	4	0	24	2
2001—Jacksonville NFL	4	1	8	27	3.4	1	1	0	6	1
Pro totals (2 years)	15	2	75	206	2.7	5	5	0	30	3

MORELAND, EARTHWIND   CB   BROWNS

PERSONAL: Born June 13, 1977, in Atlanta. ... 5-11/185. ... Full name: Earthwind C. Moreland.
HIGH SCHOOL: Grady (Atlanta).
COLLEGE: Georgia Southern (degree in business management.).
TRANSACTIONS/CAREER NOTES: Signed as non-drafted free agent by Tampa Bay Buccaneers (April 16, 2000). ... Released by Buccaneers (August 27, 2000). ... Signed by New York Jets (August 29, 2000). ... Traded by Jets with sixth-round pick (TE John Gilmore) in 2002 draft to New Orleans Saints for RB Chad Morton (August 23, 2001). ... Claimed on waivers by Jacksonville Jaguars (September 3, 2001). ... Released by Jaguars (September 12, 2001). ... Re-signed by Jaguars to practice squad (September 18, 2001). ... Released by Jaguars (October 14, 2001). ... Signed by Cleveland Browns to practice squad (October 24, 2001). ... Activated (November 7, 2001).
PLAYING EXPERIENCE: New York Jets NFL, 2000; Cleveland NFL, 2001. ... Games/Games started: 2000 (1/0), 2001 (2/0). Total: 3/0.

MORELAND, JAKE   TE   TEXANS

PERSONAL: Born January 18, 1977, in Milwaukee. ... 6-3/255.
HIGH SCHOOL: Marquette (Milwaukee).
COLLEGE: Western Michigan.
TRANSACTIONS/CAREER NOTES: Signed as non-drafted free agent by New York Jets (April 20, 2000). ... Released by Jets (September 4, 2000). ... Re-signed by Jets to practice squad (September 6, 2000). ... Activated (October 22, 2000). ... Released by Jets (September 18, 2001). ... Re-signed by Jets to practice squad (September 19, 2001). ... Activated (October 10, 2001); did not play. ... Claimed on waivers by Cleveland Browns (December 6, 2001). ... Granted free agency (March 1, 2002). ... Signed by Houston Texans (March 12, 2002).
PLAYING EXPERIENCE: New York Jets NFL, 2000; Cleveland NFL, 2001. ... Games/Games started: 2000 (7/1), 2001 (4/0). Total: 11/1.
PRO STATISTICS: 2001—Caught three passes for 15 yards and returned one kickoff for 14 yards.
SINGLE GAME HIGHS (regular season): Receptions—2 (January 6, 2002, vs. Pittsburgh); yards—10 (January 6, 2002, vs. Pittsburgh); and touchdown receptions—0.

MORENO, ZEKE   LB   CHARGERS

PERSONAL: Born October 10, 1978, in Chula Vista, Calif. ... 6-2/246. ... Full name: Ezekiel Aaron Moreno.
HIGH SCHOOL: Castle Park (Chula Vista, Calif.).
COLLEGE: Southern California.
TRANSACTIONS/CAREER NOTES: Selected by San Diego Chargers in fifth round (139th pick overall) of 2001 NFL draft. ... Signed by Chargers (July 19, 2001).

Year Team	G	GS	SACKS
2001—San Diego NFL	16	0	1.0

MORGAN, DAN   LB   PANTHERS

PERSONAL: Born December 19, 1978, in Coral Springs, Fla. ... 6-2/233. ... Full name: Daniel Thomas Morgan Jr.
HIGH SCHOOL: Taravella (Coral Springs, Fla.).
COLLEGE: Miami.
TRANSACTIONS/CAREER NOTES: Selected by Carolina Panthers in first round (11th pick overall) of 2001 NFL draft. ... Signed by Panthers (July 21, 2001).
HONORS: Named linebacker on THE SPORTING NEWS college All-America first team (2000). ... Butkus Award winner (2000). ... Chuck Bednarik Award winner (2000).
PRO STATISTICS: 2001—Recovered one fumble.

			INTERCEPTIONS			SACKS
Year Team	G	GS	No.	Yds.	Avg.	TD	No.
2001—Carolina NFL	11	11	1	10	10.0	0	1.0

MORGAN, DON   S   VIKINGS

PERSONAL: Born September 18, 1975, in Stockton, Calif. ... 5-11/202.
HIGH SCHOOL: Manteca (Calif.).
COLLEGE: Nevada-Reno.
TRANSACTIONS/CAREER NOTES: Signed as non-drafted free agent by Minnesota Vikings (April 19, 1999). ... Released by Vikings (September 5, 1999). ... Re-signed by Vikings to practice squad (September 6, 1999). ... Activated (December 23, 1999). ... Released by Vikings (August 27, 2000). ... Re-signed by Vikings to practice squad (August 28, 2000). ... Activated (December 5, 2000). ... Released by Vikings (December 19, 2000). ... Re-signed by Vikings to practice squad (December 20, 2000). ... Activated (January 10, 2001).

PLAYING EXPERIENCE: Minnesota NFL, 1999-2001. ... Games/Games started: 1999 (2/0), 2000 (2/0), 2001 (16/2). Total: 20/2.
CHAMPIONSHIP GAME EXPERIENCE: Played in NFC championship game (2000 season).
PRO STATISTICS: 2001—Returned four punts for 17 yards, returned four kickoffs for 78 yards and fumbled once.

MORGAN, QUINCY — WR — BROWNS

PERSONAL: Born September 23, 1977, in Garland, Texas. ... 6-1/209.
HIGH SCHOOL: South Garland (Texas).
COLLEGE: Kansas State.
TRANSACTIONS/CAREER NOTES: Selected by Cleveland Browns in second round (33rd pick overall) of 2001 NFL draft. ... Signed by Browns (July 23, 2001).
HONORS: Named wide receiver on THE SPORTING NEWS college All-America third team (2000).
PRO STATISTICS: 2001—Rushed twice for 27 yards.
SINGLE GAME HIGHS (regular season): Receptions—5 (November 25, 2001, vs. Cincinnati); yards—78 (December 30, 2001, vs. Tennessee); and touchdown receptions—1 (October 21, 2001, vs. Baltimore).

			RECEIVING				KICKOFF RETURNS			TOTALS			
Year Team	G	GS	No.	Yds.	Avg.	TD	No.	Yds.	Avg.	TD	TD	2pt.	Pts.	Fum.
2001—Cleveland NFL	16	9	30	432	14.4	2	7	175	25.0	0	2	0	12	3

MORRIS, ARIC — S — TITANS

PERSONAL: Born July 22, 1977, in Winston-Salem, N.C. ... 5-10/212.
HIGH SCHOOL: Berkley (Mich.).
COLLEGE: Michigan State.
TRANSACTIONS/CAREER NOTES: Selected by Tennessee Titans in fifth round (135th pick overall) of 2000 NFL draft. ... Signed by Titans (July 5, 2000).
PLAYING EXPERIENCE: Tennessee NFL, 2000 and 2001. ... Games/Games started: 2000 (15/0), 2001 (16/10). Total: 31/10.
PRO STATISTICS: 2000—Recovered one fumble. 2001—Credited with 1½ sacks.

MORRIS, ROB — LB — COLTS

PERSONAL: Born January 18, 1975, in Nampa, Idaho. ... 6-2/243. ... Full name: Robert Samuel Morris.
HIGH SCHOOL: Nampa (Idaho).
COLLEGE: Brigham Young.
TRANSACTIONS/CAREER NOTES: Selected by Indianapolis Colts in first round (28th pick overall) of 2000 NFL draft. ... Signed by Colts (July 26, 2000). ... On injured reserve with knee injury (October 25, 2000-remainder of season).
PLAYING EXPERIENCE: Indianapolis NFL, 2000. ... Games/Games started: 2000 (7/0).
HONORS: Named linebacker on THE SPORTING NEWS college All-America second team (1999).

Year Team	G	GS	SACKS
2000—Indianapolis NFL	7	0	0.0
2001—Indianapolis NFL	14	14	1.0
Pro totals (2 years)	21	14	1.0

MORRIS, SAMMY — RB — BILLS

PERSONAL: Born March 23, 1977, in San Antonio. ... 6-0/225. ... Full name: Samuel Morris III.
HIGH SCHOOL: John Jay (San Antonio).
COLLEGE: Texas Tech.
TRANSACTIONS/CAREER NOTES: Selected by Buffalo Bills in fifth round (156th pick overall) of 2000 NFL draft. ... Signed by Bills (June 21, 2000).
PRO STATISTICS: 2000—Returned one kickoff for 17 yards and recovered one fumble. 2001—Recovered one fumble.
SINGLE GAME HIGHS (regular season): Attempts—19 (October 29, 2000, vs. New York Jets); yards—60 (October 15, 2000, vs. San Diego); and rushing touchdowns—1 (December 11, 2000, vs. Indianapolis).

			RUSHING				RECEIVING				TOTALS			
Year Team	G	GS	Att.	Yds.	Avg.	TD	No.	Yds.	Avg.	TD	TD	2pt.	Pts.	Fum.
2000—Buffalo NFL	12	9	93	341	3.7	5	37	268	7.2	1	6	0	36	2
2001—Buffalo NFL	16	1	20	72	3.6	0	7	36	5.1	0	0	0	0	1
Pro totals (2 years)	28	10	113	413	3.7	5	44	304	6.9	1	6	0	36	3

MORRIS, SYLVESTER — WR — CHIEFS

PERSONAL: Born October 6, 1977, in New Orleans. ... 6-3/216.
HIGH SCHOOL: McDonogh 35 (New Orleans).
COLLEGE: Jackson State.
TRANSACTIONS/CAREER NOTES: Selected by Kansas City Chiefs in first round (21st pick overall) of 2000 NFL draft. ... Signed by Chiefs (August 9, 2000). ... On physically unable to perform list with knee injury (August 28, 2001-entire season).
PRO STATISTICS: 2000—Attempted one pass with one completion for 31 yards and fumbled three times.
SINGLE GAME HIGHS (regular season): Receptions—6 (November 5, 2000, vs. Oakland); yards—112 (September 17, 2000, vs. San Diego); and touchdown receptions—3 (September 17, 2000, vs. San Diego).
STATISTICAL PLATEAUS: 100-yard receiving games: 2000 (2).

			RECEIVING			
Year Team	G	GS	No.	Yds.	Avg.	TD
2000—Kansas City NFL	15	14	48	678	14.1	3
2001—Kansas City NFL				Did not play.		
Pro totals (1 year)	15	14	48	678	14.1	3

MORROW, HAROLD   FB

PERSONAL: Born February 24, 1973, in Maplesville, Ala. ... 5-11/232. ... Full name: Harold Morrow Jr. ... Cousin of Tommie Agee, fullback with Seattle Seahawks (1988), Kansas City Chiefs (1989) and Dallas Cowboys (1990-94).
HIGH SCHOOL: Maplesville (Ala.).
COLLEGE: Auburn.
TRANSACTIONS/CAREER NOTES: Signed as non-drafted free agent by Dallas Cowboys (April 25, 1996). ... Claimed on waivers by Minnesota Vikings (August 26, 1996). ... Granted free agency (February 12, 1999). ... Re-signed by Vikings (April 23, 1999). ... Granted unconditional free agency (February 11, 2000). ... Re-signed by Vikings (March 7, 2000). ... Granted unconditional free agency (March 1, 2002).
PLAYING EXPERIENCE: Minnesota NFL, 1996-2001. ... Games/Games started: 1996 (8/0), 1997 (16/0), 1998 (11/0), 1999 (16/0), 2000 (16/0), 2001 (16/2). Total: 83/2.
CHAMPIONSHIP GAME EXPERIENCE: Played in NFC championship game (1998 and 2000 seasons).
PRO STATISTICS: 1996—Returned six kickoffs for 117 yards. 1997—Returned five kickoffs for 99 yards. 1998—Rushed three times for seven yards and recovered one fumble. 1999—Rushed twice for one yard, returned one kickoff for 20 yards and recovered one fumble. 2000—Rushed once for two yards, returned one kickoff for 17 yards and recovered one fumble. 2001—Rushed 12 times for 67 yards, caught 13 passes for 142 yards, returned six kickoffs for 109 yards, fumbled once and recovered three fumbles.
SINGLE GAME HIGHS (regular season): Attempts—5 (January 7, 2002, vs. Baltimore); yards—24 (December 30, 2001, vs. Green Bay); and rushing touchdowns—0.

MORTON, CHAD   RB/KR   JETS

PERSONAL: Born April 4, 1977, in Torrance, Calif. ... 5-8/186. ... Brother of Johnnie Morton, wide receiver, Kansas City Chiefs; and half brother of Michael Morton, running back with Tampa Bay Buccaneers (1982-84), Washington Redskins (1985) and Seattle Seahawks (1987).
HIGH SCHOOL: South Torrance (Calif.).
COLLEGE: Southern California.
TRANSACTIONS/CAREER NOTES: Selected by New Orleans Saints in fifth round (166th pick overall) of 2000 NFL draft. ... Signed by Saints (July 11, 2000). ... Traded by Saints to New York Jets for CB Earthwind Moreland and sixth-round pick (TE John Gilmore) in 2002 draft (August 23, 2001).
PRO STATISTICS: 2000—Fumbled twice and recovered one fumble.
SINGLE GAME HIGHS (regular season): Attempts—12 (November 26, 2000, vs. St. Louis); yards—45 (November 19, 2000, vs. Oakland); and rushing touchdowns—0.

			RUSHING				RECEIVING				PUNT RETURNS				KICKOFF RETURNS				TOTALS		
Year Team	G	GS	Att.	Yds.	Avg.	TD	No.	Yds.	Avg.	TD	No.	Yds.	Avg.	TD	No.	Yds.	Avg.	TD	TD	2pt.	Pts.
2000—New Orleans NFL	16	3	36	136	3.8	0	30	213	7.1	0	30	278	9.3	0	44	1029	23.4	0	0	0	0
2001—N.Y. Jets NFL	9	0	0	0	0.0	0	0	0	0.0	0	13	113	8.7	0	12	247	20.6	0	0	0	0
Pro totals (2 years)	25	3	36	136	3.8	0	30	213	7.1	0	43	391	9.1	0	56	1276	22.8	0	0	0	0

MORTON, JOHNNIE   WR   CHIEFS

PERSONAL: Born October 7, 1971, in Inglewood, Calif. ... 6-0/190. ... Full name: Johnnie James Morton. ... Brother of Chad Morton, running back, New York Jets; half brother of Michael Morton, running back with Tampa Bay Buccaneers (1982-84), Washington Redskins (1985) and Seattle Seahawks (1987).
HIGH SCHOOL: South Torrance (Calif.).
COLLEGE: Southern California (degree in communications).
TRANSACTIONS/CAREER NOTES: Selected by Detroit Lions in first round (21st pick overall) of 1994 NFL draft. ... Signed by Lions (July 18, 1994). ... Released by Lions (March 14, 2002). ... Signed by Kansas City Chiefs (March 29, 2002).
HONORS: Named wide receiver on THE SPORTING NEWS college All-America first team (1993).
PRO STATISTICS: 1994—Recovered one fumble. 1995—Returned seven punts for 48 yards.
SINGLE GAME HIGHS (regular season): Receptions—10 (January 2, 2000, vs. Minnesota); yards—174 (September 22, 1996, vs. Chicago); and touchdown receptions—2 (January 2, 2000, vs. Minnesota).
STATISTICAL PLATEAUS: 100-yard receiving games: 1995 (1), 1996 (2), 1997 (3), 1998 (3), 1999 (5), 2001 (4). Total: 18.

			RUSHING				RECEIVING				KICKOFF RETURNS				TOTALS			
Year Team	G	GS	Att.	Yds.	Avg.	TD	No.	Yds.	Avg.	TD	No.	Yds.	Avg.	TD	TD	2pt.	Pts.	Fum.
1994—Detroit NFL	14	0	0	0	0.0	0	3	39	13.0	1	4	143	35.8	1	2	0	12	1
1995—Detroit NFL	16	14	0	0	0.0	0	44	590	13.4	8	18	390	21.7	0	8	0	48	1
1996—Detroit NFL	16	15	9	35	3.9	0	55	714	13.0	6	0	0	0.0	0	6	0	36	1
1997—Detroit NFL	16	16	3	33	11.0	0	80	1057	13.2	6	0	0	0.0	0	6	0	36	2
1998—Detroit NFL	16	16	1	11	11.0	0	69	1028	14.9	2	0	0	0.0	0	2	0	12	0
1999—Detroit NFL	16	12	0	0	0.0	0	80	1129	14.1	5	1	22	22.0	0	5	0	30	0
2000—Detroit NFL	16	16	4	25	6.3	0	61	788	12.9	3	0	0	0.0	0	3	1	20	1
2001—Detroit NFL	16	16	1	6	6.0	0	77	1154	15.0	4	1	4	4.0	0	4	0	24	1
Pro totals (8 years)	126	105	21	143	6.8	0	469	6499	13.9	35	24	559	23.3	1	36	1	218	7

MORTON, MIKE   LB

PERSONAL: Born March 28, 1972, in Concord, N.C. ... 6-4/235. ... Full name: Michael Anthony Morton Jr.
HIGH SCHOOL: A.L. Brown (Kannapolis, N.C.).
COLLEGE: North Carolina.
TRANSACTIONS/CAREER NOTES: Selected by Los Angeles Raiders in fourth round (118th pick overall) of 1995 NFL draft. ... Signed by Raiders (July 21, 1995). ... Raiders franchise moved to Oakland (July 21, 1995). ... Granted unconditional free agency (February 12, 1999). ... Signed by Green Bay Packers (April 30, 1999). ... Traded by Packers to St. Louis Rams for seventh-round pick (traded to San Francisco) in 2001 draft (July 23, 1999). ... Granted unconditional free agency (February 11, 2000). ... Signed by Packers (May 5, 2000). ... Granted unconditional free agency (March 2, 2001). ... Signed by Indianapolis Colts (June 12, 2001). ... Granted unconditional free agency (March 1, 2002).
PLAYING EXPERIENCE: Oakland NFL, 1995-1998; St. Louis NFL, 1999; Green Bay NFL, 2000; Indianapolis NFL, 2001. ... Games/Games started: 1995 (12/0), 1996 (16/6), 1997 (11/11), 1998 (16/0), 1999 (16/0), 2000 (16/0), 2001 (16/0). Total: 103/17.
CHAMPIONSHIP GAME EXPERIENCE: Played in NFC championship game (1999 season). ... Member of Super Bowl championship team (1999 season).
PRO STATISTICS: 1995—Recovered one fumble. 1996—Intercepted two passes for 13 yards and credited with one sack. 1997—Returned one kickoff for 14 yards and recovered one fumble. 1998—Returned one kickoff for three yards and recovered two fumbles. 2000—Returned one kickoff for 13 yards.

MOSES, KELVIN — LB — JETS

PERSONAL: Born September 3, 1976, in Hartsville, S.C. ... 6-0/239.
HIGH SCHOOL: Hartsville (S.C.).
COLLEGE: Wake Forest.
TRANSACTIONS/CAREER NOTES: Signed as non-drafted free agent by New York Jets (April 27, 2000). ... Released by Jets (August 21, 2000). ... Re-signed by Jets (January 3, 2001). ... Assigned by Jets to Frankfurt Galaxy in 2001 NFL Europe enhancement allocation program (February 19, 2001).
PLAYING EXPERIENCE: Frankfurt NFLE, 2001; New York Jets NFL, 2001. ... Games/Games started: NFLE 2001 (games played unavailable), NFL 2001 (16/0).
PRO STATISTICS: NFLE: 2001—Credited with three sacks.

MOSS, RANDY — WR — VIKINGS

PERSONAL: Born February 13, 1977, in Rand, W.Va. ... 6-4/204. ... Half brother of Eric Moss, offensive lineman with Minnesota Vikings (1997-99).
HIGH SCHOOL: DuPont (Belle, W.Va.).
COLLEGE: Florida State (did not play football), then Marshall.
TRANSACTIONS/CAREER NOTES: Selected after sophomore season by Minnesota Vikings in first round (21st pick overall) of 1998 NFL draft. ... Signed by Minnesota Vikings (July 26, 1998).
CHAMPIONSHIP GAME EXPERIENCE: Played in NFC championship game (1998 and 2000 seasons).
HONORS: Fred Biletnikoff Award winner (1997). ... Named wide receiver on THE SPORTING NEWS college All-America first team (1997). ... Named NFL Rookie of the Year by THE SPORTING NEWS (1998). ... Named wide receiver on THE SPORTING NEWS NFL All-Pro team (1998 and 2000). ... Played in Pro Bowl (1998 and 1999 seasons). ... Named Outstanding Player of Pro Bowl (1999). ... Named to play in Pro Bowl (2000 season); replaced by Joe Horn due to injury.
RECORDS: Holds NFL rookie-season record for most touchdowns—17 (1998).
PRO STATISTICS: 1998—Rushed once for four yards. 1999—Rushed four times for 43 yards and completed only pass attempt for 27 yards and a touchdown. 2000—Rushed three times for five yards. 2001—Rushed three times for 38 yards and completed only pass attempt for 29 yards.
SINGLE GAME HIGHS (regular season): Receptions—12 (November 14, 1999, vs. Chicago); yards—204 (November 14, 1999, vs. Chicago); and touchdown receptions—3 (November 19, 2001, vs. New York Giants).
STATISTICAL PLATEAUS: 100-yard receiving games: 1998 (4), 1999 (7), 2000 (8), 2001 (4). Total: 23.

				RECEIVING				PUNT RETURNS				TOTALS		
Year Team	G	GS	No.	Yds.	Avg.	TD	No.	Yds.	Avg.	TD	TD	2pt.	Pts.	Fum.
1998—Minnesota NFL	16	11	69	1313	‡19.0	*17	1	0	0.0	0	‡17	†2	106	2
1999—Minnesota NFL	16	16	80	‡1413	17.7	11	17	162	9.5	∞1	12	0	72	3
2000—Minnesota NFL	16	16	77	1437	18.7	*15	0	0	0.0	0	15	1	92	2
2001—Minnesota NFL	16	16	82	1233	15.0	10	0	0	0.0	0	10	0	60	0
Pro totals (4 years)	64	59	308	5396	17.5	53	18	162	9.0	1	54	3	330	7

MOSS, SANTANA — WR/PR — JETS

PERSONAL: Born June 1, 1979, in Miami. ... 5-10/185. ... Full name: Santana Terrell Moss.
HIGH SCHOOL: Carol City (Miami).
COLLEGE: Miami (Fla.).
TRANSACTIONS/CAREER NOTES: Selected by New York Jets in first round (16th pick overall) of 2001 NFL draft. ... Signed by Jets (July 28, 2001).
HONORS: Named kick returner on THE SPORTING NEWS college All-America first team (2000).
PRO STATISTICS: 2001—Rushed one for minus six yards.
SINGLE GAME HIGHS (regular season): Receptions—2 (December 2, 2001, vs. New England); yards—40 (December 2, 2001, vs. New England); and touchdown receptions—0.

			RECEIVING				PUNT RETURNS				TOTALS		
Year Team	G	GS	No.	Yds.	Avg.	TD	No.	Yds.	Avg.	TD	TD	2pt.	Pts.	Fum.
2001—New York Jets NFL	5	0	2	40	20.0	0	6	82	13.7	0	0	0	0	0

MOULDS, ERIC — WR — BILLS

PERSONAL: Born July 17, 1973, in Lucedale, Miss. ... 6-2/204. ... Full name: Eric Shannon Moulds.
HIGH SCHOOL: George County (Lucedale, Miss.).
COLLEGE: Mississippi State.
TRANSACTIONS/CAREER NOTES: Selected by Buffalo Bills in first round (24th pick overall) of 1996 NFL draft. ... Signed by Bills (July 16, 1996).
HONORS: Played in Pro Bowl (1998 and 2000 seasons).
POST SEASON RECORDS: Holds NFL postseason single-game record for most yards receiving—240 (January 2, 1999, vs. Miami).
PRO STATISTICS: 1997—Returned two punts for 20 yards and recovered one fumble. 2000—Recovered one fumble. 2001—Recovered one fumble.
SINGLE GAME HIGHS (regular season): Receptions—12 (October 22, 2000, vs. Minnesota); yards—196 (November 25, 2001, vs. Miami); and touchdown receptions—2 (November 25, 2001, vs. Miami).
STATISTICAL PLATEAUS: 100-yard receiving games: 1998 (4), 1999 (3), 2000 (7), 2001 (2). Total: 16.

			RUSHING				RECEIVING				KICKOFF RETURNS				TOTALS		
Year Team	G	GS	Att.	Yds.	Avg.	TD	No.	Yds.	Avg.	TD	No.	Yds.	Avg.	TD	TD	2pt.	Pts.	Fum.
1996—Buffalo NFL	16	5	12	44	3.7	0	20	279	14.0	2	52	1205	23.2	▲1	3	0	18	1
1997—Buffalo NFL	16	8	4	59	14.8	0	29	294	10.1	0	43	921	21.4	0	0	1	2	3
1998—Buffalo NFL	16	15	0	0	0.0	0	67	§1368	20.4	9	0	0	0.0	0	9	0	54	0
1999—Buffalo NFL	14	14	1	1	1.0	0	65	994	15.3	7	0	0	0.0	0	7	0	42	1
2000—Buffalo NFL	16	16	2	24	12.0	0	94	1326	14.1	5	0	0	0.0	0	5	0	30	1
2001—Buffalo NFL	16	16	3	3	1.0	0	67	904	13.5	5	0	0	0.0	0	5	1	32	1
Pro totals (6 years)	94	74	22	131	6.0	0	342	5165	15.1	28	95	2126	22.4	1	29	2	178	7

MUHAMMAD, MUHSIN   WR   PANTHERS

PERSONAL: Born May 5, 1973, in Lansing, Mich. ... 6-2/217. ... Full name: Muhsin Muhammad II. ... Name pronounced moo-SIN moo-HAH-med.
HIGH SCHOOL: Waverly (Lansing, Mich.).
COLLEGE: Michigan State.
TRANSACTIONS/CAREER NOTES: Selected by Carolina Panthers in second round (43rd pick overall) of 1996 NFL draft. ... Signed by Panthers (July 23, 1996).
CHAMPIONSHIP GAME EXPERIENCE: Played in NFC championship game (1996 season).
HONORS: Played in Pro Bowl (1999 season).
PRO STATISTICS: 1996—Rushed once for minus one yard. 1998—Recovered one fumble. 2000—Rushed twice for 12 yards, fumbled once and recovered one fumble. 2001—Recovered two fumbles.
SINGLE GAME HIGHS (regular season): Receptions—11 (November 27, 2000, vs. Green Bay); yards—192 (September 13, 1998, vs. New Orleans); and touchdown receptions—3 (December 18, 1999, vs. San Francisco).
STATISTICAL PLATEAUS: 100-yard receiving games: 1998 (3), 1999 (5), 2000 (5), 2001 (2). Total: 15.
MISCELLANEOUS: Holds Carolina Panthers all-time records for most receiving yards (4,686) and most receptions (368).

				RECEIVING				TOTALS		
Year Team	G	GS	No.	Yds.	Avg.	TD	TD	2pt.	Pts.	Fum.
1996—Carolina NFL	9	5	25	407	16.3	1	1	0	6	0
1997—Carolina NFL	13	5	27	317	11.7	0	0	1	2	0
1998—Carolina NFL	16	16	68	941	13.8	6	6	1	38	2
1999—Carolina NFL	15	15	‡96	1253	13.1	8	8	0	48	1
2000—Carolina NFL	16	16	†102	1183	11.6	6	6	0	36	1
2001—Carolina NFL	11	11	50	585	11.7	1	1	0	6	2
Pro totals (6 years)	80	68	368	4686	12.7	22	22	2	136	6

MULITALO, EDWIN   G   RAVENS

PERSONAL: Born September 1, 1974, in Daly City, Calif. ... 6-3/340. ... Full name: Edwin Moliki Mulitalo. ... Name pronounced moo-lih-TAHL-oh.
HIGH SCHOOL: Jefferson (Daly City, Calif.).
JUNIOR COLLEGE: Ricks College (Idaho).
COLLEGE: Arizona.
TRANSACTIONS/CAREER NOTES: Selected by Baltimore Ravens in fourth round (129th pick overall) of 1999 NFL draft. ... Signed by Ravens (July 29, 1999). ... Granted free agency (March 1, 2002).
PLAYING EXPERIENCE: Baltimore NFL, 1999-2001. ... Games/Games started: 1999 (10/8), 2000 (16/16), 2001 (14/14). Total: 40/38.
CHAMPIONSHIP GAME EXPERIENCE: Played in AFC championship game (2000 season). ... Member of Super Bowl championship team (2000 season).
PRO STATISTICS: 2000—Recovered two fumbles.

MURPHY, FRANK   WR   BUCCANEERS

PERSONAL: Born February 11, 1977, in Jacksonville, Fla. ... 6-0/206.
HIGH SCHOOL: West Nassau (Callahan, Fla.).
JUNIOR COLLEGE: Itawamba Community College (Miss.), then Garden City (Kan.) Commmunity College.
COLLEGE: Kansas State.
TRANSACTIONS/CAREER NOTES: Selected by Chicago Bears in sixth round (170th pick overall) of 2000 NFL draft. ... Signed by Bears (May 31, 2000). ... Released by Bears (August 27, 2000). ... Signed by Tampa Bay Buccaneers to practice squad (August 28, 2000). ... Activated (November 22, 2000).
SINGLE GAME HIGHS (regular season): Receptions—3 (January 6, 2002, vs. Philadelphia); yards—25 (January 6, 2002, vs. Philadelphia); and touchdown receptions—1 (October 21, 2001, vs. Pittsburgh).

			RECEIVING				KICKOFF RETURNS				TOTALS		
Year Team	G	GS	No.	Yds.	Avg.	TD	No.	Yds.	Avg.	TD	TD	2pt.	Pts.	Fum.
2000—Tampa Bay NFL	1	0	0	0	0.0	0	2	24	12.0	0	0	0	0	0
2001—Tampa Bay NFL	11	0	8	71	8.9	1	20	445	22.3	0	1	0	6	2
Pro totals (2 years)	12	0	8	71	8.9	1	22	469	21.3	0	1	0	6	2

MURPHY, YO   WR   RAMS

PERSONAL: Born May 11, 1971, in Moscow, Idaho. ... 5-10/187. ... Full name: Llewellyn Murphy.
HIGH SCHOOL: Idaho Falls (Idaho).
COLLEGE: Idaho.
TRANSACTIONS/CAREER NOTES: Signed by B.C. Lions of CFL (April 1993). ... Granted free agency (February 16, 1996). ... Re-signed by Lions (August 20, 1996). ... Released by Lions (August 26, 1996). ... Signed as non-drafted free agent by Minnesota Vikings (February 7, 1998). ... Released by Vikings (August 24, 1998). ... Selected by Scottish Claymores in NFL Europe draft (February 22, 1999). ... Signed by Tampa Bay Buccaneers (July 12, 1999). ... Claimed on waivers by Vikings (December 2, 1999). ... Released by Vikings (January 11, 1999). ... Signed by Buccaneers (February 2, 2000). ... Released by Buccaneers (August 27, 2000). ... Re-signed by Buccaneers to practice squad (October 5, 2000). ... Granted free agency after 2000 season. ... Signed by St. Louis Rams (July 23, 2001).
CHAMPIONSHIP GAME EXPERIENCE: Member of Grey Cup championship team (1994). ... Played in NFC championship game (2001 season). ... Played in Super Bowl XXXVI (2001 season).
PRO STATISTICS: CFL: 1995—Rushed once for fifteen yards. NFLE: 1999—Rushed once for two yards.
SINGLE GAME HIGHS (regular season): Receptions—4 (October 31, 1999, vs. Detroit); yards—28 (October 31, 1999, vs. Detroit); and touchdown receptions—0.

			RECEIVING				PUNT RETURNS				KICKOFF RETURNS				TOTALS		
Year Team	G	GS	No.	Yds.	Avg.	TD	No.	Yds.	Avg.	TD	No.	Yds.	Avg.	TD	TD	2pt.	Pts.	Fum.
1993—British Columbia CFL..	1	...	0	0	0.0	0	0	0	0.0	0	0	0	0.0	0	0	0	0	0
1994—British Columbia CFL..	7	...	14	127	9.1	0	0	0	0.0	0	0	0	0.0	0	0	0	0	0
1995—British Columbia CFL..	10	...	31	510	16.5	2	0	0	0.0	0	0	0	0.0	0	2	0	12	0
1996—									Did not play.									
1997—									Did not play.									
1998—									Did not play.									
1999—Scottish NFLE	...	...	45	752	16.7	4	7	65	9.3	0	23	600	26.1	1	5	0	30	0
—Tampa Bay NFL	7	0	4	28	7.0	0	0	0	0.0	0	14	307	21.9	0	0	0	0	0
—Minnesota NFL	1	0	0	0	0.0	0	3	14	4.7	0	4	80	20.0	0	0	0	0	1
2000—Tampa Bay NFL									Did not play.									
2001—St. Louis NFL	16	0	0	0	0.0	0	0	0	0.0	0	8	174	21.8	0	0	0	0	0
NFL Europe totals (1 year)	...	...	45	752	16.7	4	7	65	9.3	0	23	600	26.1	1	5	0	30	0
CFL totals (3 years)	18	...	45	637	14.2	2	0	0	0.0	0	0	0	0.0	0	2	0	12	0
NFL totals (2 years)	24	0	4	28	7.0	0	3	14	4.7	0	26	561	21.6	0	0	0	0	1
Pro totals (6 years)	...	...	94	1417	15.1	6	10	79	7.9	0	49	1161	23.7	1	7	0	42	1

MYERS, BOBBY — S — TITANS

PERSONAL: Born November 10, 1976, in New Haven, Conn. ... 6-1/191. ... Full name: Bobby Jermaine Myers.
HIGH SCHOOL: Hamden (Conn.).
COLLEGE: Wisconsin.
TRANSACTIONS/CAREER NOTES: Selected by Tennessee Titans in fourth round (124th pick overall) of 2000 NFL draft. ... Signed by Titans (July 7, 2000). ... On injured reserve with knee injury (September 13, 2001-remainder of season).
PLAYING EXPERIENCE: Tennessee NFL, 2000 and 2001. ... Games/Games started: 2000 (16/1), 2001 (1/1). Total: 17/2.
PRO STATISTICS: 2001—Recovered one fumble for 14 yards and a touchdown.

MYERS, LEONARD — CB — PATRIOTS

PERSONAL: Born December 18, 1978, in Fort Lauderdale, Fla. ... 5-10/195. ... Full name: Leonard Bernard Myers.
HIGH SCHOOL: Dillard (Fort Lauderdale, Fla.).
COLLEGE: Miami.
TRANSACTIONS/CAREER NOTES: Selected by New England Patriots in sixth round (200th pick overall) of 2001 NFL draft. ... Signed by Patriots (July 2, 2001).
PLAYING EXPERIENCE: New England NFL, 2001. ... Games/Games started: 2001 (7/0).
CHAMPIONSHIP GAME EXPERIENCE: Member of Patriots for AFC championship game (2001 season); inactive. ... Member of Super Bowl championship team (2001 season); inactive.

MYERS, MICHAEL — DL — COWBOYS

PERSONAL: Born January 20, 1976, in Vicksburg, Miss. ... 6-2/292.
HIGH SCHOOL: Vicksburg (Miss.).
JUNIOR COLLEGE: Hinds Community College (Miss.).
COLLEGE: Alabama.
TRANSACTIONS/CAREER NOTES: Selected by Dallas Cowboys in fourth round (100th pick overall) of 1998 NFL draft. ... Signed by Cowboys (July 10, 1998). ... Granted free agency (March 2, 2001). ... Re-signed by Cowboys (May 3, 2001). ... Granted unconditional free agency (March 1, 2002). ... Re-signed by Cowboys (April 14, 2002).
HONORS: Named defensive tackle on THE SPORTING NEWS college All-America first team (1996).
PRO STATISTICS: 2000—Recovered one fumble. 2001—Recovered one fumble.

Year Team	G	GS	SACKS
1998—Dallas NFL	16	1	3.0
1999—Dallas NFL	6	0	0.0
2000—Dallas NFL	13	7	0.0
2001—Dallas NFL	16	16	3.5
Pro totals (4 years)	51	24	6.5

MYLES, DESHONE — LB

PERSONAL: Born October 31, 1974, in Las Vegas, Nev. ... 6-2/235. ... Name pronounced da-SHAWN.
HIGH SCHOOL: Cheyenne (North Las Vegas, Nev.).
COLLEGE: Nevada.
TRANSACTIONS/CAREER NOTES: Selected by Seattle Seahawks in fourth round (108th pick overall) of 1998 NFL draft. ... Signed by Seahawks (July 15, 1998). ... On injured reserve with knee injury (December 7, 1999-remainder of season). ... On injured reserve with knee injury (July 26, 2000-entire season). ... Granted free agency (March 2, 2001). ... Signed by New Orleans Saints (July 18, 2001). ... Released by Saints (October 15, 2001). ... Re-signed by Saints (December 19, 2001). ... Released by Saints (December 25, 2001).
PLAYING EXPERIENCE: Seattle NFL, 1998 and 1999; New Orleans NFL, 2001. ... Games/Games started: 1998 (12/7), 1999 (5/0), 2001 (1/0). Total: 18/7.
PRO STATISTICS: 1998—Recovered one fumble.

MYLES, TOBY — OT

PERSONAL: Born July 23, 1975, in Jackson, Miss. ... 6-5/325. ... Full name: Tobiath Myles.
HIGH SCHOOL: Callaway (Jackson, Miss.).
COLLEGE: Mississippi State, then Jackson State.

TRANSACTIONS/CAREER NOTES: Selected by New York Giants in fifth round (147th pick overall) of 1998 NFL draft. ... Signed by Giants (July 24, 1998). ... Active for four games (1998); did not play. ... Released by Giants (March 6, 2000). ... Signed by Oakland Raiders (March 14, 2000). ... Granted free agency (March 2, 2001). ... Re-signed by Raiders for 2001 season. ... Released by Raiders (September 2, 2001). ... Signed by Cleveland Browns (September 19, 2001). ... Released by Browns (November 21, 2001). ... Signed by Raiders (November 21, 2001). ... Granted unconditional free agency (March 1, 2002).
PLAYING EXPERIENCE: New York Giants NFL, 1999; Cleveland (2)-Oakland (1) NFL, 2001. ... Games/Games started: 1999 (8/0), 2001 (Cle-2/0; Oak.-1/0; Total: 3/0). Total: 11/0.
CHAMPIONSHIP GAME EXPERIENCE: Member of Raiders for AFC Championship game (2000 season); inactive.

NAEOLE, CHRIS   G   JAGUARS

PERSONAL: Born December 25, 1974, in Kailua, Hawaii. ... 6-3/313. ... Full name: Chris Kealoha Naeole. ... Name pronounced NAY-oh-lee.
HIGH SCHOOL: Kahuka (Kaaava, Hawaii).
COLLEGE: Colorado.
TRANSACTIONS/CAREER NOTES: Selected by New Orleans Saints in first round (10th pick overall) of 1997 NFL draft. ... Signed by Saints (July 17, 1997). ... On injured reserve with ankle injury (October 17, 1997-remainder of season). ... Granted unconditional free agency (March 1, 2002). ... Signed by Jacksonville Jaguars (April 6, 2002).
PLAYING EXPERIENCE: New Orleans NFL, 1997-2001. ... Games/Games started: 1997 (4/0), 1998 (16/16), 1999 (15/15), 2000 (16/16), 2001 (16/16). Total: 67/63.
HONORS: Named guard on The Sporting News college All-America second team (1996).
PRO STATISTICS: 1998—Recovered one fumble. 2001—Recovered one fumble.

NALEN, TOM   C   BRONCOS

PERSONAL: Born May 13, 1971, in Foxboro, Mass. ... 6-3/286. ... Full name: Thomas Andrew Nalen.
HIGH SCHOOL: Foxboro (Mass.).
COLLEGE: Boston College.
TRANSACTIONS/CAREER NOTES: Selected by Denver Broncos in seventh round (218th pick overall) of 1994 NFL draft. ... Signed by Broncos (July 15, 1994). ... Released by Broncos (September 2, 1994). ... Re-signed by Broncos to practice squad (September 6, 1994). ... Activated (October 7, 1994).
PLAYING EXPERIENCE: Denver NFL, 1994-2001. ... Games/Games started: 1994 (7/1), 1995 (15/15), 1996 (16/16), 1997 (16/16), 1998 (16/16), 1999 (16/16), 2000 (16/16), 2001 (16/16). Total: 118/108.
CHAMPIONSHIP GAME EXPERIENCE: Played in AFC championship game (1997 and 1998 seasons). ... Member of Super Bowl championship team (1997 and 1998 seasons).
HONORS: Played in Pro Bowl (1997-1999 seasons). ... Named center on The Sporting News NFL All-Pro team (1999 and 2000). ... Named to play in Pro Bowl (2000 season); replaced by Tim Ruddy due to injury.
PRO STATISTICS: 1997—Caught one pass for minus one yard. 2000—Fumbled once for minus two yards.

NATKIN, BRIAN   TE   TITANS

PERSONAL: Born January 3, 1978, in San Antonio, Texas. ... 6-2/250.
HIGH SCHOOL: Churchill (Texas).
COLLEGE: Texas-El Paso.
TRANSACTIONS/CAREER NOTES: Signed as non-drafted free agent by Detroit Lions (April 27, 2001). ... Released by Lions (June 12, 2001). ... Signed by Tennessee Titans (July 26, 2001). ... Released by Titans (August 31, 2001). ... Re-signed by Titans to practice squad (September 5, 2001). ... Activated (November 8, 2001). ... Released by Titans (November 28, 2001). ... Re-signed by Titans to practice squad (November 29, 2001).
PLAYING EXPERIENCE: Tennessee NFL, 2001. ... Games/Games started: 2001 (3/1).
PRO STATISTICS: 2001—Caught two passes for 42 yards.
SINGLE GAME HIGHS (regular season): Receptions—1 (November 18, 2001, vs. Cincinnati); yards—27 (November 12, 2001, vs. Baltimore); and touchdown receptions—0.

NAVIES, HANNIBAL   LB   PANTHERS

PERSONAL: Born July 19, 1977, in Chicago. ... 6-2/240. ... Full name: Hannibal Carter Navies. ... Name pronounced NAY-vees.
HIGH SCHOOL: St. Patrick (Chicago), then Berkeley (Oakland).
COLLEGE: Colorado.
TRANSACTIONS/CAREER NOTES: Selected by Carolina Panthers in fourth round (100th pick overall) of 1999 NFL draft. ... Signed by Panthers (July 21, 1999). ... On injured reserve with broken arm (October 23, 2001-remainder of season). ... Granted free agency (March 1, 2002).
PLAYING EXPERIENCE: Carolina NFL, 1999-2001. ... Games/Games started: 1999 (9/0), 2000 (13/1), 2001 (5/5). Total: 27/6.
PRO STATISTICS: 2000—Intercepted one pass for no yards and credited with two sacks.

NEAL, LORENZO   FB   BENGALS

PERSONAL: Born December 27, 1970, in Hanford, Calif. ... 5-11/240. ... Full name: Lorenzo LaVonne Neal.
HIGH SCHOOL: Lemoore (Calif.).
COLLEGE: Fresno State.
TRANSACTIONS/CAREER NOTES: Selected by New Orleans Saints in fourth round (89th pick overall) of 1993 NFL draft. ... Signed by Saints (July 15, 1993). ... On injured reserve with ankle injury (September 15, 1993-remainder of season). ... Granted free agency (February 16, 1996). ... Re-signed by Saints (July 1, 1996). ... Granted unconditional free agency (February 14, 1997). ... Signed by New York Jets (March 31, 1997). ... Traded by Jets to Tampa Bay Buccaneers for fifth-round pick (TE Blake Spence) in 1998 draft (March 12, 1998). ... Released by Buccaneers (February 11, 1999). ... Signed by Tennessee Titans (March 2, 1999). ... Released by Titans (March 1, 2001). ... Signed by Cincinnati Bengals (May 7, 2001).

CHAMPIONSHIP GAME EXPERIENCE: Played in AFC championship game (1999 season). ... Played in Super Bowl XXXIV (1999 season).
PRO STATISTICS: 1994—Returned one kickoff for 17 yards. 1995—Returned two kickoffs for 28 yards. 1996—Recovered two fumbles. 1997—Returned two kickoffs for 22 yards. 1999—Returned two kickoffs for 15 yards. 2000—Returned one kickoff for 15 yards.
SINGLE GAME HIGHS (regular season): Attempts—14 (October 9, 1994, vs. Chicago); yards—89 (September 5, 1993, vs. Houston); and rushing touchdowns—1 (October 10, 1999, vs. Baltimore).

				RUSHING				RECEIVING				TOTALS		
Year Team	G	GS	Att.	Yds.	Avg.	TD	No.	Yds.	Avg.	TD	TD	2pt.	Pts.	Fum.
1993—New Orleans NFL	2	2	21	175	8.3	1	0	0	0.0	0	1	0	6	1
1994—New Orleans NFL	16	7	30	90	3.0	1	2	9	4.5	0	1	0	6	1
1995—New Orleans NFL	16	7	5	3	0.6	0	12	123	10.3	1	1	0	6	2
1996—New Orleans NFL	16	11	21	58	2.8	1	31	194	6.3	1	2	0	12	1
1997—New York Jets NFL	16	3	10	28	2.8	0	8	40	5.0	1	1	0	6	0
1998—Tampa Bay NFL	16	1	5	25	5.0	0	5	14	2.8	1	1	0	6	0
1999—Tennessee NFL	16	14	2	1	0.5	1	7	27	3.9	2	3	0	18	0
2000—Tennessee NFL	16	5	1	-2	-2.0	0	9	31	3.4	2	2	0	12	0
2001—Cincinnati NFL	16	10	5	10	2.0	0	19	101	5.3	1	1	0	6	0
Pro totals (9 years)	130	60	100	388	3.9	4	93	539	5.8	9	13	0	78	5

NEDNEY, JOE   K   TITANS

PERSONAL: Born March 22, 1973, in San Jose, Calif. ... 6-5/220. ... Full name: Joseph Thomas Nedney. ... Name pronounced NED-nee.
HIGH SCHOOL: Santa Teresa (San Jose, Calif.).
COLLEGE: San Jose State (degree in recreation administration, 1998).
TRANSACTIONS/CAREER NOTES: Signed as non-drafted free agent by Green Bay Packers (April 1995). ... Released by Packers (August 27, 1995). ... Signed by Oakland Raiders to practice squad (August 29, 1995). ... Released by Raiders (September 6, 1995). ... Signed by Miami Dolphins to practice squad (September 21, 1995). ... Claimed on waivers by New York Jets (August 12, 1997). ... Released by Jets (August 25, 1997). ... Signed by Dolphins (October 3, 1997). ... Released by Dolphins (October 6, 1997). ... Signed by Arizona Cardinals (October 15, 1997). ... On injured reserve with knee injury (December 1, 1998-remainder of season). ... Released by Cardinals (February 12, 1999). ... Re-signed by Cardinals (March 31, 1999). ... Claimed on waivers by Baltimore Ravens (October 6, 1999). ... Inactive for four games with Ravens (1999). ... Released by Ravens (November 9, 1999). ... Signed by Raiders (December 14, 1999). ... Released by Raiders (August 27, 2000). ... Signed by Denver Broncos (September 12, 2000). ... Released by Broncos (October 2, 2000). ... Signed by Carolina Panthers (October 3, 2000). ... Granted unconditional free agency (March 2, 2001). ... Signed by Tennessee Titans (March 9, 2001).

				KICKING				
Year Team	G	XPM	XPA	FGM	FGA	Lg.	50+	Pts.
1995—Miami NFL				Did not play.				
1996—Miami NFL	16	35	36	18	29	44	0-2	89
1997—Arizona NFL	10	19	19	11	17	45	0-2	52
1998—Arizona NFL	12	30	30	13	19	53	1-4	69
1999—Arizona NFL	1	0	0	0	0	0	0-0	0
—Oakland NFL	3	13	13	5	7	52	1-2	28
2000—Denver NFL	3	4	4	8	10	43	0-1	28
—Carolina NFL	12	20	20	26	28	52	2-2	98
2001—Tennessee NFL	16	34	35	20	28	51	1-2	94
Pro totals (6 years)	73	155	157	101	138	53	5-15	458

NEIL, DAN   G   BRONCOS

PERSONAL: Born October 21, 1973, in Houston. ... 6-2/285. ... Full name: Daniel Neil.
HIGH SCHOOL: Cypress Creek (Houston).
COLLEGE: Texas.
TRANSACTIONS/CAREER NOTES: Selected by Denver Broncos in third round (67th pick overall) of 1997 NFL draft. ... Signed by Broncos (July 17, 1997). ... Granted free agency (February 11, 2000). ... Re-signed by Broncos (April 28, 2000) ... Granted unconditional free agency (March 2, 2001). ... Re-signed by Broncos (March 2, 2001).
PLAYING EXPERIENCE: Denver NFL, 1997-2001. ... Games/Games started: 1997 (3/0), 1998 (16/16), 1999 (15/15), 2000 (16/16), 2001 (15/15). Total: 65/62.
CHAMPIONSHIP GAME EXPERIENCE: Member of Broncos for AFC championship game (1997 season); inactive. ... Member of Super Bowl championship team (1997 season); inactive. ... Played in AFC championship game (1998 season). ... Member of Super Bowl championship team (1998 season).
HONORS: Named guard on THE SPORTING NEWS college All-America first team (1996).
PRO STATISTICS: 2001—Recovered one fumble.

NELSON, JIM   LB   VIKINGS

PERSONAL: Born April 16, 1975, in Riverside, Calif. ... 6-1/234. ... Full name: James Robert Nelson.
HIGH SCHOOL: McDonough (Waldorf, Md.).
COLLEGE: Penn State (degree in criminal justice).
TRANSACTIONS/CAREER NOTES: Signed as non-drafted free agent by San Francisco 49ers (April 24, 1998). ... Claimed on waivers by Green Bay Packers (July 20, 1998). ... Released by Packers (August 25, 1998). ... Re-signed by Packers to practice squad (September 14, 1998). ... Activated (December 29, 1998); did not play. ... Claimed on waivers by Minnesota Vikings (August 28, 2000). ... Granted free agency (March 1, 2002).
PLAYING EXPERIENCE: Green Bay NFL, 1999; Minnesota NFL, 2000 and 2001. ... Games/Games started: 1999 (16/0), 2000 (16/0), 2001 (16/2). Total: 48/2.
CHAMPIONSHIP GAME EXPERIENCE: Played in NFC championship game (2000 season).
PRO STATISTICS: 1999—Intercepted one pass for no yards and recovered one fumble. 2001—Recovered one fumble for minus one yard.

NESBIT, JAMAR — G — PANTHERS

PERSONAL: Born December 17, 1976, in Summerville, S.C. ... 6-4/330. ... Full name: Jamar Kendric Nesbit.
HIGH SCHOOL: Summerville (S.C.).
COLLEGE: South Carolina.
TRANSACTIONS/CAREER NOTES: Signed as non-drafted free agent by Carolina Panthers (April 18, 1999). ... Granted free agency (March 1, 2002).
PLAYING EXPERIENCE: Carolina NFL, 1999-2001. ... Games/Games started: 1999 (7/0), 2000 (16/16), 2001 (16/16). Total: 39/32.
PRO STATISTICS: 2001—Recovered one fumble.

NEWBERRY, JEREMY — G — 49ERS

PERSONAL: Born March 23, 1976, in Antioch, Calif. ... 6-5/304. ... Full name: Jeremy David Newberry.
HIGH SCHOOL: Antioch (Calif.).
COLLEGE: California.
TRANSACTIONS/CAREER NOTES: Selected by after junior season San Francisco 49ers in second round (58th pick overall) of 1998 NFL draft. ... Signed by San Francisco 49ers (July 18, 1998). ... On physically unable to perform list with knee injury (July 17-November 7, 1998). ... Active for one game (1998); did not play. ... Granted unconditional free agency (March 1, 2002). ... Re-signed by 49ers (March 2, 2002).
PLAYING EXPERIENCE: San Francisco NFL, 1999-2001. ... Games/Games started: 1999 (16/16), 2000 (16/16), 2001 (15/15). Total: 47/47.

NEWKIRK, ROBERT — DT

PERSONAL: Born March 6, 1977, in Belle Glade, Fla. ... 6-3/290.
HIGH SCHOOL: Glade Central (Belle Glade, Fla.).
COLLEGE: Michigan State.
TRANSACTIONS/CAREER NOTES: Signed as non-drafted free agent by Dallas Cowboys (April 23, 1999). ... Released by Cowboys (September 5, 1999). ... Re-signed by Cowboys to practice squad (September 6, 1999). ... Signed by New Orleans Saints off Cowboys practice squad (December 1, 1999). ... Released by Saints (August 28, 2000). ... Signed by Chicago Bears to practice squad (September 7, 2000). ... Activated (September 27, 2000). ... On injured reserve with wrist injury (November 13, 2000-remainder of season). ... On injured reserve with knee injury (December 29, 2001-remainder of season). ... Granted free agency (March 1, 2002).
PLAYING EXPERIENCE: New Orleans NFL, 1999; Chicago NFL, 2000 and 2001. ... Games/Games started: 1999 (5/0), 2000 (4/0), 2001 (10/1). Total: 19/1.
PRO STATISTICS: 2001—Credited with one sack and returned one kickoff for eight yards.

NEWMAN, KEITH — LB — BILLS

PERSONAL: Born January 19, 1977, in Tampa. ... 6-2/248. ... Full name: Keith Anthony Newman.
HIGH SCHOOL: Thomas Jefferson (Tampa).
COLLEGE: North Carolina.
TRANSACTIONS/CAREER NOTES: Selected by Buffalo Bills in fourth round (119th pick overall) of 1999 NFL draft. ... Signed by Bills (July 27, 1999). ... Granted free agency (March 1, 2002).
PLAYING EXPERIENCE: Buffalo NFL, 1999-2001. ... Games/Games started: 1999 (3/0), 2000 (16/16), 2001 (16/16). Total: 35/32.
PRO STATISTICS: 2000—Credited with eight sacks, fumbled once and recovered one fumble for 25 yards. 2001—Credited with $3^{1}/_{2}$ sacks.

NEWSOME, RICHARD — S — SAINTS

PERSONAL: Born December 6, 1977, in Lima, Ohio. ... 5-11/202. ... Full name: Richard Lawrence Newsome.
HIGH SCHOOL: Fostoria (Ohio).
COLLEGE: Michigan State.
TRANSACTIONS/CAREER NOTES: Signed as non-drafted free agent by New Orleans Saints (April 26, 2001).
PLAYING EXPERIENCE: New Orleans NFL, 2001. ... Games/Games started: 2001 (11/0).
PRO STATISTICS: 2001—Recovered one fumble.

NGUYEN, DAT — LB — COWBOYS

PERSONAL: Born September 25, 1975, in Fulton, Texas. ... 5-11/243. ... Name pronounced WIN.
HIGH SCHOOL: Rockport-Fulton (Rockport, Texas).
COLLEGE: Texas A&M (degree in agricultural development).
TRANSACTIONS/CAREER NOTES: Selected by Dallas Cowboys in third round (85th pick overall) of 1999 NFL draft. ... Signed by Cowboys (July 26, 1999). ... Granted free agency (March 1, 2002). ... Re-signed by Cowboys (April 16, 2002).
PLAYING EXPERIENCE: Dallas NFL, 1999-2001. ... Games/Games started: 1999 (16/0), 2000 (10/5), 2001 (16/16). Total: 42/21.
HONORS: Lombardi Award winner (1998). ... Chuck Bednarik Award winner (1998). ... Named inside linebacker on THE SPORTING NEWS college All-America first team (1998).
PRO STATISTICS: 1999—Intercepted one pass for six yards and credited with one sack. 2000—Intercepted two passes for 31 yards and recovered one fumble.

NICKERSON, HARDY — LB

PERSONAL: Born September 1, 1965, in Compton, Calif. ... 6-2/228. ... Full name: Hardy Otto Nickerson.
HIGH SCHOOL: Verbum Dei (Los Angeles).
COLLEGE: California (degree in sociology, 1986).

TRANSACTIONS/CAREER NOTES: Selected by Pittsburgh Steelers in fifth round (122nd pick overall) of 1987 NFL draft. ... Signed by Steelers (July 26, 1987). ... On injured reserve with ankle and knee injuries (November 3-December 16, 1989). ... Granted free agency (February 1, 1992). ... Re-signed by Steelers (June 15, 1992). ... Granted unconditional free agency (March 1, 1993). ... Signed by Tampa Bay Buccaneers (March 18, 1993). ... Granted unconditional free agency (February 16, 1996). ... Re-signed by Buccaneers (February 22, 1996). ... On injured reserve with heart problems (November 25, 1998-remainder of season). ... Granted unconditional free agency (February 11, 2000). ... Signed by Jacksonville Jaguars (February 22, 2000). ... On injured reserve with knee injury (December 5, 2000-remainder of season). ... Released by Jaguars (June 3, 2002).
CHAMPIONSHIP GAME EXPERIENCE: Played in NFC championship game (1999 season).
HONORS: Named linebacker on THE SPORTING NEWS college All-America second team (1985). ... Named inside linebacker on THE SPORTING NEWS NFL All-Pro team (1993). ... Played in Pro Bowl (1993 and 1996-1999 seasons).
PRO STATISTICS: 1987—Recovered one fumble. 1988—Intercepted one pass for no yards and recovered one fumble. 1992—Recovered two fumbles for 44 yards. 1993—Intercepted one pass for six yards and recovered one fumble. 1994—Intercepted two passes for nine yards. 1995—Recovered three fumbles. 1996—Intercepted two passes for 24 yards and recovered two fumbles. 1997—Recovered two fumbles. 1998—Recovered one fumble. 1999—Intercepted two passes for 18 yards. 2000—Intercepted one pass for 10 yards. 2001—Intercepted three passes for four yards and recovered one fumble.

Year Team	G	GS	SACKS
1987—Pittsburgh NFL	12	0	0.0
1988—Pittsburgh NFL	15	10	3.5
1989—Pittsburgh NFL	10	8	1.0
1990—Pittsburgh NFL	16	14	2.0
1991—Pittsburgh NFL	16	14	1.0
1992—Pittsburgh NFL	15	15	2.0
1993—Tampa Bay NFL	16	16	1.0
1994—Tampa Bay NFL	14	14	1.0
1995—Tampa Bay NFL	16	16	1.5
1996—Tampa Bay NFL	16	16	3.0
1997—Tampa Bay NFL	16	16	1.0
1998—Tampa Bay NFL	10	10	1.0
1999—Tampa Bay NFL	16	16	0.5
2000—Jacksonville NFL	6	6	1.0
2001—Jacksonville NFL	15	14	0.0
Pro totals (15 years)	**209**	**185**	**19.5**

NIX, JOHN   DT   COWBOYS

PERSONAL: Born November 24, 1976, in Lucendale, Miss. ... 6-1/326.
HIGH SCHOOL: George County (Miss.).
COLLEGE: Southern Mississippi.
TRANSACTIONS/CAREER NOTES: Selected by Dallas Cowboys in seventh round (240th pick overall) of 2001 NFL draft. ... Signed by Cowboys (July 20, 2001).
PLAYING EXPERIENCE: Dallas NFL, 2001. ... Games/Games started: 2001 (16/0).

NKWENTI, MATHIAS   OT   STEELERS

PERSONAL: Born May 11, 1978, in Younda, Cameroon, Africa. ... 6-3/300. ... Full name: Mathias Fru Nkwenti.
HIGH SCHOOL: Thomas S. Wootton (Rockville, Md.).
COLLEGE: Temple.
TRANSACTIONS/CAREER NOTES: Selected by Pittsburgh Steelers in fourth round (111th pick overall) of 2001 NFL draft. ... Signed by Steelers (May 21, 2001).
PLAYING EXPERIENCE: Pittsburgh NFL, 2001. ... Games/Games started: (1/0).
CHAMPIONSHIP GAME EXPERIENCE: Member of Steelers for AFC championship game (2001 season); inactive.

NOBLE, BRANDON   DT   COWBOYS

PERSONAL: Born April 10, 1974, in San Rafael, Calif. ... 6-2/304. ... Full name: Brandon Patrick Noble.
HIGH SCHOOL: First Colonial (Virginia Beach, Va.).
COLLEGE: Penn State.
TRANSACTIONS/CAREER NOTES: Signed as non-drafted free agent by San Francisco 49ers (April 29, 1997). ... Released by 49ers (August 19, 1997). ... Re-signed by 49ers to practice squad (November 12, 1997). ... Released by 49ers (November 19, 1997). ... Re-signed by 49ers (January 13, 1998). ... Assigned by 49ers to Barcelona Dragons in 1998 NFL Europe enhancement allocation program (February 18, 1998). ... Released by 49ers (August 25, 1998). ... Re-signed by 49ers to practice squad (December 3, 1998). ... Granted free agency after 1998 season. ... Signed by Dallas Cowboys (February 2, 1999). ... Assigned by Cowboys to Barcelona Dragons in 1999 NFL Europe enhancement allocation program (February 22, 1999). ... Granted free agency (March 1, 2002).
PRO STATISTICS: 1998—Intercepted one pass for no yards, returned one kickoff for 12 yards and recovered one fumble for a touchdown. NFLE: 1999—Returned one kickoff for 17 yards. NFL: 1999—Returned one kickoff for nine yards and recovered one fumble. 2000—Returned one kickoff for eight yards. 2001—Recovered two fumbles for six yards.

Year Team	G	GS	SACKS
1998—Barcelona NFLE	...	...	2.0
1999—Barcelona NFLE	...	...	5.0
—Dallas NFL	16	0	3.0
2000—Dallas NFL	16	9	1.0
2001—Dallas NFL	16	16	3.5
NFL Europe totals (2 years)	...	...	**7.0**
NFL totals (3 years)	**48**	**25**	**7.5**
Pro totals (5 years)	...	...	**14.5**

NORRIS, MORAN — RB — SAINTS

PERSONAL: Born June 16, 1978, in Houston. ... 6-1/250. ... Full name: Torrance Moran Norris.
HIGH SCHOOL: James Madison (Houston).
COLLEGE: Kansas.
TRANSACTIONS/CAREER NOTES: Selected by New Orleans Saints in fourth round (115th pick overall) of 2001 NFL draft. ... Signed by Saints (July 27, 2001).
PLAYING EXPERIENCE: New Orleans NFL, 2001. ... Games/Games started: (5/0).

NORTHCUTT, DENNIS — WR — BROWNS

PERSONAL: Born December 22, 1977, in Los Angeles. ... 5-10/175.
HIGH SCHOOL: Dorsey (Los Angeles).
COLLEGE: Arizona.
TRANSACTIONS/CAREER NOTES: Selected by Cleveland Browns in second round (32nd pick overall) of 2000 NFL draft. ... Signed by Browns (July 19, 2000). ... On non-football injury list with shoulder injury (July 23-September 30, 2001).
HONORS: Named wide receiver on THE SPORTING NEWS college All-America second team (1999).
PRO STATISTICS: 2000—Rushed nine times for 33 yards. 2001—Rushed three times for 26 yards, returned one kickoff for 26 yards and recovered one fumble.
SINGLE GAME HIGHS (regular season): Receptions—6 (December 2, 2001, vs. Tennessee); yards—80 (October 15, 2000, vs. Denver); and touchdown receptions—0.

			RECEIVING				PUNT RETURNS				TOTALS		
Year Team	G	GS	No.	Yds.	Avg.	TD	No.	Yds.	Avg.	TD	TD	2pt.	Pts.	Fum.
2000—Cleveland NFL	15	8	39	422	10.8	0	27	289	10.7	0	0	0	0	1
2001—Cleveland NFL	12	7	18	211	11.7	0	15	86	5.7	0	0	0	0	3
Pro totals (2 years)	27	15	57	633	11.1	0	42	375	8.9	0	0	0	0	4

NUGENT, DAVID — DE — PATRIOTS

PERSONAL: Born October 27, 1977, in Cincinnati. ... 6-4/295. ... Full name: David Michael Nugent.
HIGH SCHOOL: Houston (Germantown, Tenn.).
COLLEGE: Purdue.
TRANSACTIONS/CAREER NOTES: Selected by New England Patriots in sixth round (201st pick overall) of 2000 NFL draft. ... Signed by Patriots (July 12, 2000). ... Released by Patriots (September 2, 2001). ... Re-signed by Patriots to practice squad (September 4, 2001). ... Activated (October 15, 2001).
PLAYING EXPERIENCE: New England NFL, 2000 and 2001. ... Games/Games started: 2000 (6/0), 2001 (9/1). Total: 15/1.
CHAMPIONSHIP GAME EXPERIENCE: Member of Patriots for AFC championship game (2001 season); inactive. ... Member of Super Bowl championship team (2001 season); inactive.

NUTTEN, TOM — G — RAMS

PERSONAL: Born June 8, 1971, in Magog, Quebec. ... 6-5/304. ... Full name: Thomas Nutten. ... Name pronounced NEW-ton.
HIGH SCHOOL: Champlain Regional (Lennoxville, Quebec).
COLLEGE: Western Michigan (degree in marketing, 1994).
TRANSACTIONS/CAREER NOTES: Selected by Hamilton Tiger-Cats in first round (first pick overall) of 1995 CFL draft. ... Selected by Buffalo Bills in seventh round (221st pick overall) of 1995 NFL draft. ... Signed by Bills (June 12, 1995). ... Released by Bills (August 27, 1995). ... Re-signed by Bills to practice squad (August 29, 1995). ... Activated (October 10, 1995). ... Released by Bills (August 26, 1996). ... Signed by Denver Broncos (January 14, 1997). ... Released by Broncos (July 16, 1997). ... Signed by Tiger-Cats of CFL (July 28, 1997). ... Signed by St. Louis Rams (January 16, 1998). ... Assigned by Rams to Amsterdam Admirals in 1998 NFL Europe enhancement allocation program (February 18, 1998). ... On injured reserve with neck injury (November 17, 1998-remainder of season). ... Granted free agency (February 11, 2000). ... Re-signed by Rams (February 12, 2000).
PLAYING EXPERIENCE: Buffalo NFL, 1995; Hamilton CFL, 1997; Amsterdam NFLE, 1998; St. Louis NFL, 1998-2001. ... Games/Games started: 1995 (1/0), 1997 (13/games started unavailable), NFLE 1998 (games played unavailable), NFL 1998 (4/2), 1999 (14/14), 2000 (16/16), 2001 (15/13). Total NFL: 50/45. Total CFL: 13/-.
CHAMPIONSHIP GAME EXPERIENCE: Played in NFC championship game (1999 and 2001 seasons). ... Member of Super Bowl championship team (1999 season). ... Played in Super Bowl XXXVI (2001 season).
PRO STATISTICS: 1997—Recovered one fumble. 1999—Recovered one fumble. 2000—Recovered one fumble.

NWOKORIE, CHUKIE — DE — COLTS

PERSONAL: Born July 10, 1975, in Tuskegee, Ala. ... 6-3/280. ... Full name: Chijioke Obinna Nwokorie. ... Name pronounced CHEW-key wuh-CORE-e.
HIGH SCHOOL: Lafayette-Jefferson (Lafayette, Ind.).
COLLEGE: Purdue.
TRANSACTIONS/CAREER NOTES: Signed as non-drafted free agent by Indianapolis Colts (April 20, 1999). ... Released by Colts (October 25, 2000). ... Re-signed by Colts to practice squad (October 26, 2000). ... Activated (December 22, 2000). ... Granted free agency (March 1, 2002).
PLAYING EXPERIENCE: Indianapolis NFL, 1999-2001. ... Games/Games started: 1999 (1/0), 2000 (1/0), 2001 (16/6). Total: 18/6.
PRO STATISTICS: 2001—Credited with five sacks, returned two kickoffs for 15 yards and recovered three fumbles for 95 yards and a touchdown.

OBEN, ROMAN — OT — BUCCANEERS

PERSONAL: Born October 9, 1972, in Cameroon, West Africa. ... 6-4/305. ... Name pronounced OH-bin.
HIGH SCHOOL: Gonzaga (Washington, D.C.), then Fork Union (Va.) Military Academy.
COLLEGE: Louisville (degree in economics).
TRANSACTIONS/CAREER NOTES: Selected by New York Giants in third round (66th pick overall) of 1996 NFL draft. ... Signed by Giants (July 20, 1996). ... Granted free agency (February 12, 1999). ... Re-signed by Giants (July 28, 1999). ... Granted unconditional free agency (February 11, 2000). ... Signed by Cleveland Browns (March 9, 2000). ... Released by Browns (February 25, 2002). ... Signed by Tampa Bay Buccaneers (May 20, 2002).
PLAYING EXPERIENCE: New York Giants NFL, 1996-1999; Cleveland NFL, 2000 and 2001. ... Games/Games started: 1996 (2/0), 1997 (16/16), 1998 (16/8), 1999 (16/16), 2000 (16/16), 2001 (16/14). Total: 82/78.
PRO STATISTICS: 1999—Recovered two fumbles.

O'DONNELL, NEIL — QB — TITANS

PERSONAL: Born July 3, 1966, in Morristown, N.J. ... 6-3/228. ... Full name: Neil Kennedy O'Donnell.
HIGH SCHOOL: Madison-Boro (Madison, N.J.).
COLLEGE: Maryland (degree in economics, 1990).
TRANSACTIONS/CAREER NOTES: Selected by Pittsburgh Steelers in third round (70th pick overall) of 1990 NFL draft. ... Signed by Steelers (August 8, 1990). ... Active for three games (1990); did not play. ... Granted free agency (March 1, 1993). ... Tendered offer sheet by Tampa Bay Buccaneers (April 2, 1993). ... Offer matched by Steelers (April 12, 1993). ... Granted unconditional free agency (February 16, 1996). ... Signed by New York Jets (February 29, 1996). ... Released by Jets (June 24, 1998). ... Signed by Cincinnati Bengals (July 7, 1998). ... On injured reserve with hand injury (December 9, 1998-remainder of season). ... Released by Bengals (April 19, 1999). ... Signed by Tennessee Titans (July 23, 1999). ... Granted unconditional free agency (February 11, 2000). ... Re-signed by Titans (April 25, 2000).
CHAMPIONSHIP GAME EXPERIENCE: Played in AFC championship game (1994, 1995 and 1999 seasons). ... Played in Super Bowl XXX (1995 season). ... Member of Titans for Super Bowl XXXIV (1999 season); did not play.
HONORS: Played in Pro Bowl (1992 season).
RECORDS: Holds NFL career record for lowest interception percentage—2.12.
POST SEASON RECORDS: Holds NFL postseason single-game record for most passes attempted without an interception—54 (January 15, 1995, vs. San Diego).
PRO STATISTICS: 1991—Fumbled 11 times and recovered two fumbles for minus three yards. 1992—Fumbled six times and recovered four fumbles for minus 20 yards. 1993—Fumbled five times. 1994—Fumbled four times and recovered one fumble. 1995—Fumbled twice and recovered one fumble. 1996—Fumbled twice. 1997—Fumbled nine times and recovered two fumbles for minus one yard. 1998—Fumbled six times and recovered one fumble for minus two yards. 1999—Fumbled five times and recovered three fumbles for minus 14 yards. 2001—Fumbled once.
SINGLE GAME HIGHS (regular season): Attempts—55 (December 24, 1995, vs. Green Bay); completions—34 (November 5, 1995, vs. Chicago); yards—377 (November 19, 1995, vs. Cincinnati); and touchdown passes—5 (August 31, 1997, vs. Seattle).
STATISTICAL PLATEAUS: 300-yard passing games: 1991 (1), 1993 (1), 1995 (4), 1996 (2), 1997 (1), 1998 (1), 1999 (2). Total: 12.
MISCELLANEOUS: Regular-season record as starting NFL quarterback: 54-45 (.545). ... Postseason record as starting NFL quarterback: 3-4 (.429).

				PASSING							RUSHING				TOTALS		
Year Team	G	GS	Att.	Cmp.	Pct.	Yds.	TD	Int.	Avg.	Rat.	Att.	Yds.	Avg.	TD	TD	2pt.	Pts.
1990—Pittsburgh NFL						Did not play.											
1991—Pittsburgh NFL	12	8	286	156	54.5	1963	11	7	6.86	78.8	18	82	4.6	1	1	0	6
1992—Pittsburgh NFL	12	12	313	185	59.1	2283	13	9	7.29	83.6	27	5	0.2	1	1	0	6
1993—Pittsburgh NFL	16	15	486	270	55.6	3208	14	7	6.60	79.5	26	111	4.3	0	0	0	0
1994—Pittsburgh NFL	14	14	370	212	57.3	2443	13	9	6.60	78.9	31	80	2.6	1	1	0	6
1995—Pittsburgh NFL	12	12	416	246	59.1	2970	17	7	7.14	87.7	24	45	1.9	0	0	0	0
1996—New York Jets NFL	6	6	188	110	58.5	1147	4	7	6.10	67.8	6	30	5.0	0	0	0	0
1997—New York Jets NFL	15	14	460	259	56.3	2796	17	7	6.08	80.3	32	36	1.1	1	1	0	6
1998—Cincinnati NFL	13	11	343	212	§61.8	2216	15	4	6.46	90.2	13	34	2.6	0	0	0	0
1999—Tennessee NFL	8	5	199	116	59.5	1382	10	5	7.09	87.6	19	1	0.1	0	0	0	0
2000—Tennessee NFL	8	1	64	36	56.3	530	2	3	8.28	74.3	9	-2	-0.2	0	0	0	0
2001—Tennessee NFL	5	1	76	42	55.3	496	2	2	6.53	73.1	6	28	4.7	0	0	0	0
Pro totals (11 years)	121	99	3197	1844	57.7	21434	118	67	6.70	81.7	211	450	2.1	4	4	0	24

O'DWYER, MATT — G — BENGALS

PERSONAL: Born September 1, 1972, in Lincolnshire, Ill. ... 6-5/313. ... Full name: Matthew Phillip O'Dwyer.
HIGH SCHOOL: Adlai E. Stevenson (Prairie View, Ill.).
COLLEGE: Northwestern.
TRANSACTIONS/CAREER NOTES: Selected by New York Jets in second round (33rd pick overall) of 1995 NFL draft. ... Signed by Jets (July 20, 1995). ... Granted unconditional free agency (February 12, 1999). ... Signed by Cincinnati Bengals (June 19, 1999). ... Suspended two games by NFL for involvement in bar fight (March 14, 2000). ... On injured reserve with broken ankle (November 20, 2000-remainder of season). ... Granted unconditional free agency (March 2, 2001). ... Re-signed by Bengals (March 2, 2001).
PLAYING EXPERIENCE: New York Jets NFL, 1995-1998; Cincinnati NFL, 1999-2001. ... Games/Games started: 1995 (12/2), 1996 (16/16), 1997 (16/16), 1998 (16/16), 1999 (16/16), 2000 (10/10), 2001 (12/12). Total: 98/88.
CHAMPIONSHIP GAME EXPERIENCE: Played in AFC championship game (1998 season).
PRO STATISTICS: 2001—Recovered one fumble.

OFFICE, KENDRICK — DE — BILLS

PERSONAL: Born August 2, 1978, in Butler, Ala. ... 6-5/270. ... Full name: Kendrick LaShawn Office.
HIGH SCHOOL: Choctaw (Ala.).
COLLEGE: West Alabama.
TRANSACTIONS/CAREER NOTES: Signed as non-drafted free agent by Buffalo Bills (April 24, 2001). ... Claimed on waivers by Cleveland Browns (August 29, 2001). ... Released by Browns (September 2, 2001). ... Signed by Bills to practice squad (September 4, 2001). ... Activated (October 3, 2001).
PLAYING EXPERIENCE: Buffalo NFL, 2001. ... Games/Games started: (7/1).
PRO STATISTICS: 2001—Credited with three sacks.

OGBOGU, ERIC — DE — BENGALS

PERSONAL: Born July 18, 1975, in Irvington, N.Y. ... 6-4/280. ... Name pronounced a-BAH-goo.
HIGH SCHOOL: Archbishop Stepinac (White Plains, N.Y.).
COLLEGE: Maryland.
TRANSACTIONS/CAREER NOTES: Selected by New York Jets in sixth round (163rd pick overall) of 1998 NFL draft. ... Signed by Jets (July 2, 1998). ... On injured reserve with shoulder injury (August 7, 2000-entire season). ... Granted unconditional free agency (March 1, 2002). ... Signed by Cincinnati Bengals (April 29, 2002).
PLAYING EXPERIENCE: New York Jets NFL, 1998, 1999 and 2001. ... Games/Games started: 1998 (12/0), 1999 (14/0), 2001 (15/0). Total: 41/0.
CHAMPIONSHIP GAME EXPERIENCE: Played in AFC championship game (1998 season).
PRO STATISTICS: 1999—Credited with one sack and recovered two fumbles, including one in end zone for a touchdown. 2001—Recovered one fumble.

OGDEN, JEFF — WR — DOLPHINS

PERSONAL: Born February 22, 1975, in Snohomish, Wash. ... 6-0/187. ... Full name: Jeffery Ogden.
HIGH SCHOOL: Snohomish (Wash.).
COLLEGE: Eastern Washington.
TRANSACTIONS/CAREER NOTES: Signed as non-drafted free agent by Dallas Cowboys (April 21, 1998). ... Assigned by Cowboys to Rhein Fire in 2000 NFL Europe enhancement allocation program (February 18, 2000). ... Traded by Cowboys to Miami Dolphins for future seventh-round pick (August 22, 2000). ... Granted free agency (March 2, 2001). ... Re-signed by Dolphins (April 20, 2001). ... Granted unconditional free agency (March 1, 2002). ... Re-signed by Dolphins (April 3, 2002).
PRO STATISTICS: 1998—Rushed once for 12 yards and returned three kickoffs for 65 yards. 1999—Returned 12 kickoffs for 252 yards. NFLE: 2000—Attempted one pass without a completion and returned four kickoffs for 141 yards.
SINGLE GAME HIGHS (regular season): Receptions—4 (November 22, 1998, vs. Seattle); yards—28 (December 28, 2001, vs. New England); and touchdown receptions—1 (December 22, 2001, vs. New England).

				RECEIVING				PUNT RETURNS				TOTALS			
Year Team	G	GS	No.	Yds.	Avg.	TD	No.	Yds.	Avg.	TD	TD	2pt.	Pts.	Fum.
1998—Dallas NFL	16	0	8	63	7.9	0	0	0	0.0	0	0	0	0	1
1999—Dallas NFL	16	0	12	144	12.0	0	4	28	7.0	0	0	0	0	0
2000—Rhein NFLE	...	...	44	635	14.4	7	4	28	7.0	0	0	0	0	0
—Miami NFL	16	0	2	24	12.0	0	19	323	17.0	1	1	0	6	1
2001—Miami NFL	16	0	6	73	12.2	1	32	377	11.8	0	1	0	6	3
NFL Europe totals (1 year)	...	...	44	635	14.4	7	4	28	7.0	0	0	0	0	0
NFL totals (4 years)	64	0	28	304	10.9	1	55	728	13.2	1	2	0	12	5
Pro totals (5 years)	...	...	72	939	13.0	8	59	756	12.8	1	2	0	12	5

OGDEN, JONATHAN — OT — RAVENS

PERSONAL: Born July 31, 1974, in Washington, D.C. ... 6-8/340. ... Full name: Jonathan Phillip Ogden.
HIGH SCHOOL: St. Alban's (Washington, D.C.).
COLLEGE: UCLA.
TRANSACTIONS/CAREER NOTES: Selected by Baltimore Ravens in first round (fourth pick overall) of 1996 NFL draft. ... Signed by Ravens (July 15, 1996).
PLAYING EXPERIENCE: Baltimore NFL, 1996-2001. ... Games/Games started: 1996 (16/16), 1997 (16/16), 1998 (13/13), 1999 (16/16), 2000 (15/15), 2001 (16/16). Total: 92/92.
CHAMPIONSHIP GAME EXPERIENCE: Played in AFC championship game (2000 season). ... Member of Super Bowl championship team (2000 season).
HONORS: Outland Trophy winner (1995). ... Named offensive lineman on THE SPORTING NEWS college All-America first team (1995). ... Named offensive tackle on THE SPORTING NEWS NFL All-Pro team (1997, 2000 and 2001). ... Played in Pro Bowl (1997-2000 seasons).
PRO STATISTICS: 1996—Caught one pass for one yard and a touchdown. 1999—Recovered two fumbles for two yards. 2000—Recovered two fumbles.

OGLESBY, CEDRIC — K

PERSONAL: Born July 26, 1977, in Decatur, Ga. ... 5-11/175.
HIGH SCHOOL: Southwest DeKalb (Decatur, Ga.).
COLLEGE: South Carolina.
TRANSACTIONS/CAREER NOTES: Signed as non-drafted free agent by Dallas Cowboys (April 17, 2000). ... Released by Cowboys (April 30, 2000). ... Signed by San Diego Chargers (May 4, 2001). ... Released by Chargers (August 27, 2001). ... Signed by Arizona Cardinals (December 18, 2001). ... Granted free agency (March 1, 2002).

				KICKING				
Year Team	G	XPM	XPA	FGM	FGA	Lg.	50+	Pts.
2001—Arizona NFL	3	7	7	5	6	41	0-0	22

OGUNLEYE, ADEWALE — DE — DOLPHINS

PERSONAL: Born August 9, 1977, in Brooklyn, N.Y. ... 6-4/270.
HIGH SCHOOL: Tottenville (Staten Island, N.Y.).
COLLEGE: Indiana.
TRANSACTIONS/CAREER NOTES: Signed as non-drafted free agent by Miami Dolphins (April 25, 2000). ... On non-football injury list with knee injury (August 22, 2000-entire season).
PLAYING EXPERIENCE: Miami NFL, 2001. ... Games/Games started: (7/0).
PRO STATISTICS: 2001—Credited with $1/2$ sack.

– 286 –

OHALETE, IFEANYI   S   REDSKINS

PERSONAL: Born May 22, 1979, in Los Alamitos, Calif. ... 6-2/217.
HIGH SCHOOL: Los Alamitos (Calif.).
COLLEGE: Southern California.
TRANSACTIONS/CAREER NOTES: Signed as non-drafted free agent by Washington Redskins (April 25, 2001).
PLAYING EXPERIENCE: Washington NFL, 2001. ... Games/Games started: (16/0).
PRO STATISTICS: 2001—Intercepted one pass for 12 yards and recovered one fumble.

O'HARA, SHAUN   C   BROWNS

PERSONAL: Born June 23, 1977, in Hillsborough, N.J. ... 6-3/287.
HIGH SCHOOL: Hillsborough (N.J.).
COLLEGE: Rutgers.
TRANSACTIONS/CAREER NOTES: Signed as non-drafted free agent by Cleveland Browns (April 17, 2000).
PLAYING EXPERIENCE: Cleveland NFL, 2000 and 2001. ... Games/Games started: 2000 (9/4), 2001 (16/4). Total: 25/8.
PRO STATISTICS: 2000—Fumbled once for minus seven yards. 2001—Caught one pass for two yards and a touchdown.

OKEAFOR, CHIKE   DE   49ERS

PERSONAL: Born March 27, 1976, in Grand Rapids, Mich. ... 6-4/254. ... Full name: Chikeze Russell Okeafor. ... Name pronounced chee-KAY oh-KEY-fer.
HIGH SCHOOL: West Lafayette (Ind.).
COLLEGE: Purdue.
TRANSACTIONS/CAREER NOTES: Selected by San Francisco 49ers in third round (89th pick overall) of 1999 NFL draft. ... Signed by 49ers (July 27, 1999). ... On non-football injury list with back injury (July 27-September 5, 1999). ... Granted free agency (March 1, 2002).
PLAYING EXPERIENCE: San Francisco NFL, 1999-2001. ... Games/Games started: 1999 (12/0), 2000 (15/0), 2001 (14/3). Total: 41/3.
PRO STATISTICS: 1999—Credited with one sack. 2000—Credited with two sacks and returned one kickoff for 17 yards. 2001—Credited with 2 1/2 sacks.

OKOBI, CHUKKY   C   STEELERS

PERSONAL: Born November 18, 1978, in Pittsburgh. ... 6-1/310. ... Full name: Chukwunweze Sonume Okobi.
HIGH SCHOOL: Trinity Prawling (N.Y.).
COLLEGE: Purdue.
TRANSACTIONS/CAREER NOTES: Selected by Pittsburgh Steelers in fifth round (146th pick overall) of 2001 NFL draft. ... Signed by Steelers (May 17, 2001). ... On physically unable to perform list with leg injury (July 20-August 14, 2001).
PLAYING EXPERIENCE: Pittsburgh NFL, 2001. ... Games/Games started: (1/0).
CHAMPIONSHIP GAME EXPERIENCE: Member of Steelers for AFC championship game (2001 season); inactive.

OLDHAM, CHRIS   DB

PERSONAL: Born October 26, 1968, in Sacramento. ... 5-9/200. ... Full name: Christopher Martin Oldham. ... Name pronounced OLD-um.
HIGH SCHOOL: Highlands (Sacramento).
COLLEGE: Oregon (degree in communications).
TRANSACTIONS/CAREER NOTES: Selected by Detroit Lions in fourth round (105th pick overall) of 1990 NFL draft. ... Signed by Lions (July 19, 1990). ... Released by Lions (August 26, 1991). ... Signed by Buffalo Bills (September 25, 1991). ... Released by Bills (October 8, 1991). ... Signed by Phoenix Cardinals (October 15, 1991). ... Released by Cardinals (November 13, 1991). ... Signed by San Diego Chargers (February 15, 1992). ... Assigned by Chargers to San Antonio Riders in 1992 World League enhancement allocation program (February 20, 1992). ... Released by Chargers (August 25, 1992). ... Signed by Cardinals (December 22, 1992). ... Granted unconditional free agency (February 17, 1994). ... Cardinals franchise renamed Arizona Cardinals for 1994 season. ... Re-signed by Cardinals (June 7, 1994). ... Granted unconditional free agency (February 17, 1995). ... Signed by Pittsburgh Steelers (April 12, 1995). ... Granted unconditional free agency (February 11, 2000). ... Signed by New Orleans Saints (February 14, 2000). ... Granted unconditional free agency (March 1, 2002).
CHAMPIONSHIP GAME EXPERIENCE: Played in AFC championship game (1995 and 1997 seasons). ... Played in Super Bowl XXX (1995 season).
PRO STATISTICS: NFL: 1990—Returned 13 kickoffs for 234 yards and fumbled twice. W.L.: 1992—Returned one kickoff for 11 yards, credited with one sack and recovered one fumble. 1995—Recovered one fumble for 23 yards and a touchdown. 1998—Recovered five fumbles for 79 yards and one touchdown. 1999—Recovered one fumble. 2000—Recovered two fumbles for two yards. 2001—Recovered two fumbles for 81 yards and one touchdown.

			INTERCEPTIONS				SACKS
Year Team	G	GS	No.	Yds.	Avg.	TD	No.
1990—Detroit NFL	16	0	1	28	28.0	0	0.0
1991—Buffalo NFL	2	0	0	0	0.0	0	0.0
—Phoenix NFL	2	0	0	0	0.0	0	0.0
1992—San Antonio W.L.	9	9	3	52	17.3	*1	0.0
—Phoenix NFL	1	0	0	0	0.0	0	0.0
1993—Phoenix NFL	16	6	1	0	0.0	0	1.0
1994—Arizona NFL	11	1	0	0	0.0	0	0.0
1995—Pittsburgh NFL	15	0	1	12	12.0	0	0.0
1996—Pittsburgh NFL	16	0	0	0	0.0	0	2.0
1997—Pittsburgh NFL	16	0	2	16	8.0	0	4.0
1998—Pittsburgh NFL	16	1	1	14	14.0	0	0.5
1999—Pittsburgh NFL	15	0	1	9	9.0	0	3.0
2000—New Orleans NFL	13	1	2	0	0.0	0	2.0
2001—New Orleans NFL	16	1	1	0	0.0	0	2.5
W.L. totals (1 year)	9	9	3	52	17.3	1	0.0
NFL totals (12 years)	155	10	10	79	7.9	0	15.0
Pro totals (13 years)	164	19	13	131	10.1	1	15.0

O'LEARY, DAN — TE — BILLS

PERSONAL: Born September 1, 1977, in Cleveland. ... 6-3/248. ... Full name: Daniel Edward O'Leary.
HIGH SCHOOL: St. Ignatius (Ohio).
COLLEGE: Notre Dame.
TRANSACTIONS/CAREER NOTES: Selected by Buffalo Bills in sixth round (195th pick overall) of 2001 NFL draft. ... Signed by Bills (June 12, 2001). ... On injured reserve with wrist injury (November 21, 2001-remainder of season).
PLAYING EXPERIENCE: Buffalo NFL, 2001. ... Games/Games started: (8/0).

OLIVO, BROCK — FB — LIONS

PERSONAL: Born June 24, 1976, in St. Louis. ... 6-0/232. ... Name pronounced o-LEEV-o.
HIGH SCHOOL: St. Francis Borgia (Washington, Mo.).
COLLEGE: Missouri.
TRANSACTIONS/CAREER NOTES: Signed as non-drafted free agent by San Francisco 49ers (April 24, 1998). ... Released by 49ers (August 30, 1998). ... Re-signed by 49ers to practice squad (September 1, 1998). ... Signed by Detroit Lions off 49ers practice squad (September 23, 1998). ... Released by Lions (December 8, 1998). ... Re-signed by Lions to practice squad (December 9, 1998). ... On injured reserve with knee injury (December 22, 1999-remainder of season).
PRO STATISTICS: 1999—Recovered one fumble. 2001—Recovered one fumble.
SINGLE GAME HIGHS (regular season): Attempts—1 (December 30, 2001, vs. Chicago); yards—6 (December 30, 2001, vs. Chicago); and rushing touchdowns—0.

			RUSHING				RECEIVING				KICKOFF RETURNS				TOTALS		
Year Team	G	GS	Att.	Yds.	Avg.	TD	No.	Yds.	Avg.	TD	No.	Yds.	Avg.	TD	TD	2pt.	Pts. Fum.
1998—Detroit NFL	1	0	0	0	0.0	0	0	0	0.0	0	0	0	0.0	0	0	0	0 0
1999—Detroit NFL	14	0	1	1	1.0	0	4	24	6.0	0	11	198	18.0	0	0	0	0 0
2000—Detroit NFL	13	0	0	0	0.0	0	3	50	16.7	0	3	25	8.3	0	0	0	0 0
2001—Detroit NFL	16	0	1	6	6.0	0	0	0	0.0	0	1	40	40.0	0	0	0	0 0
Pro totals (4 years)	44	0	2	7	3.5	0	7	74	10.6	0	15	263	17.5	0	0	0	0 0

OLSEN, HANS — DT — COLTS

PERSONAL: Born July 31, 1977, in Caldwell, Idaho. ... 6-4/298.
HIGH SCHOOL: Weiser (Idaho).
COLLEGE: Brigham Young.
TRANSACTIONS/CAREER NOTES: Signed as non-drafted free agent by Indianapolis Colts (April 26, 2001). ... Released by Colts (September 2, 2001). ... Re-signed by Colts to practice squad (September 4, 2001). ... Activated (November 25, 2001).
PLAYING EXPERIENCE: Indianapolis NFL, 2001. ... Games/Games started: (2/0).

OLSON, BENJI — G — TITANS

PERSONAL: Born June 5, 1975, in Bremerton, Wash. ... 6-3/315. ... Full name: Benji Dempsey Olson.
HIGH SCHOOL: South Kitsap (Port Orchard, Wash.).
COLLEGE: Washington.
TRANSACTIONS/CAREER NOTES: Selected after junior season by Tennessee Oilers in fifth round (139th pick overall) of 1998 NFL draft. ... Signed by Oilers (June 29, 1998). ... Oilers franchise renamed Tennessee Titans for 1999 season (December 26, 1998). ... Granted free agency (March 2, 2001). ... Re-signed by Titans (July 25, 2001).
PLAYING EXPERIENCE: Tennessee NFL, 1998-2001. ... Games/Games started: 1998 (13/1), 1999 (16/16), 2000 (16/16), 2001 (16/16). Total: 61/49.
CHAMPIONSHIP GAME EXPERIENCE: Played in AFC championship game (1999 season). ... Played in Super Bowl XXXIV (1999 season).
HONORS: Named guard on THE SPORTING NEWS college All-America first team (1996).
PRO STATISTICS: 1999—Recovered one fumble.

O'NEAL, ANDRE — LB — VIKINGS

PERSONAL: Born December 12, 1975, in Decatur, Ga. ... 6-1/235. ... Full name: Andre T. O'Neal.
HIGH SCHOOL: Cedar Grove (Decatur, Ga.).
COLLEGE: Marshall (degree in adult fitness).
TRANSACTIONS/CAREER NOTES: Signed as non-drafted free agent by Kansas City Chiefs (April 27, 2000). ... Claimed on waivers by Green Bay Packers (October 3, 2001). ... Released by Packers (October 29, 2001). ... Signed by Minnesota Vikings (December 4, 2001).
PLAYING EXPERIENCE: Kansas City NFL, 2000; Kansas City (3)-Green Bay (2)-Minnesota (4) NFL, 2001. ... Games/Games started: 2000 (10/0), 2001 (K.C.-3/0; G.B.-2/0; Min.-4/2; Total: 9/2). Total: 19/2.
PRO STATISTICS: 2001—Recovered one fumble.

O'NEAL, DELTHA — CB/PR — BRONCOS

PERSONAL: Born January 30, 1977, in Palo Alto, Calif. ... 5-10/196. ... Full name: Deltha Lee O'Neal III.
HIGH SCHOOL: West (Milpitas, Calif.).
COLLEGE: California.
TRANSACTIONS/CAREER NOTES: Selected by Denver Broncos in first round (15th pick overall) of 2000 NFL draft. ... Signed by Broncos (July 21, 2000).
HONORS: Named kick returner on THE SPORTING NEWS college All-America first team (1999). ... Named cornerback on THE SPORTING NEWS college All-America second team (1999).
PRO STATISTICS: 2000—Recovered three fumbles for six yards.

			INTERCEPTIONS				PUNT RETURNS				KICKOFF RETURNS				TOTALS		
Year Team	G	GS	No.	Yds.	Avg.	TD	No.	Yds.	Avg.	TD	No.	Yds.	Avg.	TD	TD	2pt.	Pts. Fum.
2000—Denver NFL	16	0	0	0	0.0	0	34	354	10.4	0	46	1102	24.0	▲1	1	0	6 6
2001—Denver NFL	16	16	9	115	12.8	0	31	405	13.1	1	0	0	0.0	0	1	0	6 2
Pro totals (2 years)	32	16	9	115	12.8	0	65	759	11.7	1	46	1102	24.0	1	2	0	12 8

OSTROSKI, JERRY   G   BILLS

PERSONAL: Born July 12, 1970, in Collegeville, Pa. ... 6-3/323. ... Full name: Gerald Ostroski Jr.
HIGH SCHOOL: Owen J. Roberts (Pottstown, Pa.).
COLLEGE: Tulsa.
TRANSACTIONS/CAREER NOTES: Selected by Kansas City Chiefs in 10th round (271st pick overall) of 1992 NFL draft. ... Signed by Chiefs (July 21, 1992). ... Released by Chiefs (August 25, 1992). ... Signed by Atlanta Falcons (May 7, 1993). ... Released by Falcons (August 24, 1993). ... Signed by Buffalo Bills to practice squad (November 18, 1993). ... Released by Bills (August 28, 1994). ... Re-signed by Bills to practice squad (August 29, 1994). ... Activated (November 30, 1994). ... Granted free agency (February 13, 1998). ... Re-signed by Bills (April 8, 1998). ... Granted unconditional free agency (February 12, 1999). ... Re-signed by Bills (February 17, 1999). ... On injured reserve with knee injury (January 4, 2001-remainder of season).
PLAYING EXPERIENCE: Buffalo NFL, 1994-2001. ... Games/Games started: 1994 (4/3), 1995 (16/13), 1996 (16/16), 1997 (16/16), 1998 (16/16), 1999 (15/15), 2000 (16/16), 2001 (7/7). Total: 106/102.
PRO STATISTICS: 1996—Recovered one fumble. 1997—Recovered three fumbles. 1999—Fumbled once for minus two yards. 2000—Fumbled once for minus 12 yards and recovered one fumble in end zone for touchdown. 2001—Recovered one fumble.

OURS, WES   RB   COLTS

PERSONAL: Born December 30, 1977, in Rawlings, Md. ... 6-0/284.
HIGH SCHOOL: Westmar (Rawlings, Md.).
COLLEGE: West Virginia.
TRANSACTIONS/CAREER NOTES: Signed as non-drafted free agent by Indianapolis Colts (April 27, 2001). ... Claimed on waivers by Tennessee Titans (September 26, 2001). ... Released by Titans (November 20, 2001). ... Claimed on waivers by Colts (November 21, 2001).
PLAYING EXPERIENCE: Tennessee NFL, 2001. ... Games/Games started: (3/1).
PRO STATISTICS: 2001—Caught one pass for three yards.

OWENS, RICH   DE   CHIEFS

PERSONAL: Born May 22, 1972, in Philadelphia. ... 6-6/288.
HIGH SCHOOL: Lincoln (Philadelphia).
COLLEGE: Lehigh.
TRANSACTIONS/CAREER NOTES: Selected by Washington Redskins in fifth round (152nd pick overall) of 1995 NFL draft. ... Signed by Redskins (May 23, 1995). ... Granted free agency (February 13, 1998). ... Re-signed by Redskins (May 7, 1998). ... On injured reserve with knee injury (August 25, 1998-entire season). ... Granted unconditional free agency (February 12, 1999). ... Signed by Miami Dolphins (March 16, 1999). ... Granted unconditional free agency (March 2, 2001). ... Signed by Kansas City Chiefs (April 6, 2001). ... Granted unconditional free agency (March 1, 2002). ... Re-signed by Chiefs (April 30, 2002).
PRO STATISTICS: 1997—Recovered one fumble. 1999—Recovered one fumble.

Year Team	G	GS	SACKS
1995—Washington NFL	10	3	3.0
1996—Washington NFL	16	16	11.0
1997—Washington NFL	16	15	2.5
1998—Washington NFL	Did not play.		
1999—Miami NFL	16	14	8.5
2000—Miami NFL	12	3	0.5
2001—Kansas City NFL	16	1	3.0
Pro totals (6 years)	86	52	28.5

OWENS, TERRELL   WR   49ERS

PERSONAL: Born December 7, 1973, in Alexander City, Ala. ... 6-3/226. ... Full name: Terrell Eldorado Owens. ... Name pronounced TARE-el.
HIGH SCHOOL: Benjamin Russell (Alexander City, Ala.).
COLLEGE: Tennessee-Chattanooga.
TRANSACTIONS/CAREER NOTES: Selected by San Francisco 49ers in third round (89th pick overall) of 1996 NFL draft. ... Signed by 49ers (July 18, 1996). ... On physically unable to perform list with foot injury (July 17-August 11, 1997). ... Designated by 49ers as franchise player (February 12, 1999). ... Re-signed by 49ers (June 4, 1999).
CHAMPIONSHIP GAME EXPERIENCE: Played in NFC championship game (1997 season).
HONORS: Played in Pro Bowl (2000 season). ... Named wide receiver on THE SPORTING NEWS NFL All-Pro team (2001).
PRO STATISTICS: 1996—Returned three kickoffs for 47 yards. 1997—Returned two kickoffs for 31 yards and recovered one fumble. 1998—Rushed four times for 53 yards and one touchdown and recovered one fumble for 13 yards. 2000—Rushed three times for 11 yards. 2001—Rushed four times for 21 yards.
SINGLE GAME HIGHS (regular season): Receptions—20 (December 17, 2000, vs. Chicago); yards—283 (December 17, 2000, vs. Chicago); and touchdown receptions—2 (October 14, 2001, vs. Atlanta).
STATISTICAL PLATEAUS: 100-yard receiving games: 1996 (1), 1998 (2), 1999 (2), 2000 (5), 2001 (6). Total: 16.

			RECEIVING				TOTALS			
Year Team	G	GS	No.	Yds.	Avg.	TD	TD	2pt.	Pts.	Fum.
1996—San Francisco NFL	16	10	35	520	14.9	4	4	0	24	1
1997—San Francisco NFL	16	15	60	936	15.6	8	8	0	48	1
1998—San Francisco NFL	16	8	67	1097	16.4	14	15	1	92	1
1999—San Francisco NFL	14	14	60	754	12.6	4	4	0	24	1
2000—San Francisco NFL	14	13	97	1451	15.0	13	13	1	80	3
2001—San Francisco NFL	16	16	93	1412	15.2	*16	16	0	96	0
Pro totals (6 years)	92	76	412	6170	15.0	59	60	2	364	7

O

PACE, ORLANDO — OT — RAMS

PERSONAL: Born November 4, 1975, in Sandusky, Ohio. ... 6-7/325. ... Full name: Orlando Lamar Pace.
HIGH SCHOOL: Sandusky (Ohio).
COLLEGE: Ohio State.
TRANSACTIONS/CAREER NOTES: Selected after junior season by St. Louis Rams in first round (first pick overall) of 1997 NFL draft. ... Signed by Rams (August 16, 1997).
PLAYING EXPERIENCE: St. Louis NFL, 1997-2001. ... Games/Games started: 1997 (13/9), 1998 (16/16), 1999 (16/16), 2000 (16/16), 2001 (16/16). Total: 77/73.
CHAMPIONSHIP GAME EXPERIENCE: Played in NFC championship game (1999 and 2001 seasons). ... Member of Super Bowl championship team (1999 season). ... Played in Super Bowl XXXVI (2001 season).
HONORS: Lombardi Award winner (1995 and 1996). ... Named offensive tackle on THE SPORTING NEWS college All-America first team (1995 and 1996). ... Outland Trophy winner (1996). ... Named offensive tackle on THE SPORTING NEWS NFL All-Pro team (1999-2001). ... Played in Pro Bowl (1999 and 2000 seasons).
PRO STATISTICS: 1997—Recovered one fumble. 1998—Recovered one fumble. 2001—Recovered one fumble.

PAGE, SOLOMON — G — COWBOYS

PERSONAL: Born February 27, 1976, in Pittsburgh. ... 6-4/321.
HIGH SCHOOL: Brashear (Pittsburgh).
COLLEGE: West Virginia.
TRANSACTIONS/CAREER NOTES: Selected after junior season by Dallas Cowboys in second round (55th pick overall) of 1999 NFL draft. ... Signed by Cowboys (July 28, 1999). ... On injured reserve with knee injury (December 24, 2001-remainder of season).
PLAYING EXPERIENCE: Dallas NFL, 1999-2001. ... Games/Games started: 1999 (14/6), 2000 (16/16), 2001 (14/14). Total: 44/36.

PALMER, JESSE — QB — GIANTS

PERSONAL: Born October 5, 1978, in Toronto. ... 6-2/219. ... Full name: Jesse James Palmer.
HIGH SCHOOL: St. Pius X (Ottawa).
COLLEGE: Florida.
TRANSACTIONS/CAREER NOTES: Selected by New York Giants in fourth round (125th pick overall) of 2001 NFL draft. ... Signed by Giants (July 26, 2001). ... Inactive for all 16 games (2001).

				PASSING						RUSHING				TOTALS	
Year Team	G	GS	Att.	Cmp.	Pct.	Yds.	TD	Int.	Avg.	Rat.	Att.	Yds.	Avg.	TD	TD 2pt. Pts.
2001—N.Y. Giants NFL							Did not play.								

PARKER, ANTHONY — CB — 49ERS

PERSONAL: Born December 4, 1975, in Denver. ... 6-1/200. ... Full name: Anthony E. Parker.
HIGH SCHOOL: Thornton (Colo.).
JUNIOR COLLEGE: Mesa State College (Colo.).
COLLEGE: Weber State.
TRANSACTIONS/CAREER NOTES: Selected by San Francisco 49ers in fourth round (99th pick overall) of 1999 NFL draft. ... Signed by 49ers (July 26, 1999). ... On injured reserve with knee injury (August 31, 1999-entire season).
PLAYING EXPERIENCE: San Francisco NFL, 2000 and 2001. ... Games/Games started: 2000 (16/0), 2001 (5/0). Total: 21/0.

PARKER, GLENN — G

PERSONAL: Born April 22, 1966, in Westminster, Calif. ... 6-5/312. ... Full name: Glenn Andrew Parker.
HIGH SCHOOL: Edison (Huntington Beach, Calif.).
JUNIOR COLLEGE: Golden West Junior College (Calif.).
COLLEGE: Arizona.
TRANSACTIONS/CAREER NOTES: Selected by Buffalo Bills in third round (69th pick overall) of 1990 NFL draft. ... Signed by Bills (July 26, 1990). ... Granted free agency (March 1, 1993). ... Re-signed by Bills (March 11, 1993). ... Released by Bills (August 24, 1997). ... Signed by Kansas City Chiefs (August 28, 1997). ... Granted unconditional free agency (February 11, 2000). ... Signed by New York Giants (March 26, 2000). ... Released by Giants (June 4, 2002).
PLAYING EXPERIENCE: Buffalo NFL, 1990-1996; Kansas City NFL, 1997-2000; New York Giants NFL, 2001. ... Games/Games started: 1990 (16/3), 1991 (16/5), 1992 (13/13), 1993 (16/9), 1994 (16/13), 1995 (13/13), 1996 (14/13), 1997 (15/15), 1998 (15/15), 1999 (12/11), 2000 (13/13), 2001 (15/15). Total: 174/141.
CHAMPIONSHIP GAME EXPERIENCE: Played in AFC championship game (1990, 1992 and 1993 seasons). ... Member of Bills for AFC championship game (1991 season); inactive. ... Played in Super Bowl XXV (1990 season), Super Bowl XXVI (1991 season), Super Bowl XXVII (1992 season), Super Bowl XXVIII (1993 season) and Super Bowl XXXV (2000 season) ... Played in NFC championship game (2000 season).
PRO STATISTICS: 1992—Recovered one fumble. 1995—Recovered one fumble. 1996—Recovered two fumbles. 1998—Recovered one fumble. 2001—Recovered one fumble.

PARKER, LARRY — WR — CHIEFS

PERSONAL: Born July 14, 1976, in Bakersfield, Calif. ... 6-1/205.
HIGH SCHOOL: Bakersfield (Calif.).
COLLEGE: Southern California.
TRANSACTIONS/CAREER NOTES: Selected by Kansas City Chiefs in fourth round (108th pick overall) of 1999 NFL draft. ... Signed by Chiefs (July 29, 1999). ... Granted free agency (March 1, 2002). ... Re-signed by Chiefs (May 24, 2002).

PRO STATISTICS: 2000—Rushed once for minus seven yards and caught three passes for 41 yards. 2001—Rushed three times for six yards and caught 15 passes for 199 yards and two touchdowns.
SINGLE GAME HIGHS (regular season): Receptions—6 (October 25, 2001, vs. Indianapolis); yards—76 (October 25, 2001, vs. Indianapolis); and touchdown receptions—2 (October 25, 2001, vs. Indianapolis).

				PUNT RETURNS				KICKOFF RETURNS				TOTALS		
Year Team	G	GS	No.	Yds.	Avg.	TD	No.	Yds.	Avg.	TD	TD	2pt.	Pts.	Fum.
1999—Kansas City NFL	10	0	5	51	10.2	0	1	24	24.0	0	0	0	0	1
2000—Kansas City NFL	16	0	5	50	10.0	0	14	279	19.9	0	0	0	0	1
2001—Kansas City NFL	12	4	11	91	8.3	0	1	22	22.0	0	2	0	12	0
Pro totals (3 years)	38	4	21	192	9.1	0	16	325	20.3	0	2	0	12	2

PARKER, RIDDICK   DL   JETS

PERSONAL: Born November 20, 1972, in Emporia, Va. ... 6-3/295.
HIGH SCHOOL: Southampton (Courtland, Va.).
COLLEGE: North Carolina.
TRANSACTIONS/CAREER NOTES: Signed as non-drafted free agent by San Diego Chargers (April 28, 1995). ... Released by Chargers (August 22, 1995). ... Signed by Seattle Seahawks (July 8, 1996). ... Released by Seahawks (August 24, 1996). ... Re-signed by Seahawks to practice squad (August 26, 1996). ... Granted free agency (February 11, 2000). ... Re-signed by Seahawks (May 12, 2000). ... Granted unconditional free agency (March 2, 2001). ... Signed by New England Patriots (June 5, 2001). ... Granted unconditional free agency (March 1, 2002). ... Signed by New York Jets (April 22, 2002).
PLAYING EXPERIENCE: Seattle NFL, 1997-2000; New England NFL, 2001. ... Games/Games started: 1997 (12/0), 1998 (8/0), 1999 (16/3), 2000 (16/16), 2001 (13/0). Total: 65/19.
CHAMPIONSHIP GAME EXPERIENCE: Played in AFC championship game (2001 season). ... Member of Super Bowl championship team (2001 season); did not play.
PRO STATISTICS: 1998—Credited with one sack. 1999—Credited with two sacks. 2001—Credited with one sack and recovered one fumble.

PARKER, VAUGHN   OT   CHARGERS

PERSONAL: Born June 5, 1971, in Buffalo. ... 6-3/300. ... Full name: Vaughn Antoine Parker.
HIGH SCHOOL: Saint Joseph's Collegiate Institute (Buffalo).
COLLEGE: UCLA.
TRANSACTIONS/CAREER NOTES: Selected by San Diego Chargers in second round (63rd pick overall) of 1994 NFL draft. ... Signed by Chargers (July 12, 1994). ... Granted free agency (February 14, 1997). ... Re-signed by Chargers (June 6, 1997). ... On injured reserve with leg injury (December 12, 1998-remainder of season). ... Granted unconditional free agency (February 11, 2000). ... Re-signed by Chargers (February 11, 2000).
PLAYING EXPERIENCE: San Diego NFL, 1994-2001. ... Games/Games started: 1994 (6/0), 1995 (14/7), 1996 (16/16), 1997 (16/16), 1998 (6/6), 1999 (15/15), 2000 (16/16), 2001 (16/16). Total: 105/92.
CHAMPIONSHIP GAME EXPERIENCE: Played in AFC championship game (1994 season). ... Played in Super Bowl XXIX (1994 season).
PRO STATISTICS: 1994—Returned one kickoff for one yard. 1996—Recovered one fumble. 1997—Recovered two fumbles. 1999—Recovered one fumble.

PARKS, TOMMY   P

PERSONAL: Born October 14, 1968, in Houston, Miss. ... 6-2/225.
HIGH SCHOOL: Houston (Houston, Miss.).
COLLEGE: Mississippi State.
TRANSACTIONS/CAREER NOTES: Signed as non-drafted free agent by San Francisco 49ers (April 24, 2000). ... Released by 49ers (August 15, 2000). ... Signed by New York Jets (April 21, 2001). ... Released by Jets (September 17, 2001).

				PUNTING			
Year Team	G	No.	Yds.	Avg.	Net avg.	In. 20	Blk.
2001—New York Jets NFL	1	5	238	47.6	22.6	1	0

PARRELLA, JOHN   DT

PERSONAL: Born November 22, 1969, in Topeka, Kan. ... 6-3/300. ... Full name: John Lorin Parrella.
HIGH SCHOOL: Grand Island (Neb.) Central Catholic.
COLLEGE: Nebraska.
TRANSACTIONS/CAREER NOTES: Selected by Buffalo Bills in second round (55th pick overall) of 1993 NFL draft. ... Signed by Bills (July 12, 1993). ... Released by Bills (August 28, 1994). ... Signed by San Diego Chargers (September 12, 1994). ... Granted free agency (February 16, 1996). ... Re-signed by Chargers (June 14, 1996). ... Granted unconditional free agency (March 1, 2002).
CHAMPIONSHIP GAME EXPERIENCE: Member of Bills for AFC championship game (1993 season); inactive. ... Member of Bills for Super Bowl XXVIII (1993 season); inactive. ... Played in AFC championship game (1994 season). ... Played in Super Bowl XXIX (1994 season).
PRO STATISTICS: 1997—Recovered one fumble. 1998—Recovered one fumble. 2001—Recovered one fumble.

Year Team	G	GS	SACKS
1993—Buffalo NFL	10	0	1.0
1994—San Diego NFL	13	1	1.0
1995—San Diego NFL	16	1	2.0
1996—San Diego NFL	16	9	2.0
1997—San Diego NFL	16	16	3.5
1998—San Diego NFL	16	16	1.5
1999—San Diego NFL	16	16	5.5
2000—San Diego NFL	16	16	7.0
2001—San Diego NFL	16	16	2.0
Pro totals (9 years)	135	91	25.5

PARRISH, TONY   S   49ERS

PERSONAL: Born November 23, 1975, in Huntington Beach, Calif. ... 6-0/210.
HIGH SCHOOL: Marina (Huntington Beach, Calif.).
COLLEGE: Washington.
TRANSACTIONS/CAREER NOTES: Selected by Chicago Bears in second round (35th pick overall) of 1998 NFL draft. ... Signed by Bears (July 20, 1998). ... Granted unconditional free agency (March 1, 2002). ... Signed by San Francisco 49ers (April 2, 2002).
PRO STATISTICS: 1998—Credited with one sack, fumbled once and recovered two fumbles for minus two yards. 2000—Credited with two sacks. 2001—Credited with one sack and recovered two fumbles for 35 yards.

			INTERCEPTIONS			
Year Team	G	GS	No.	Yds.	Avg.	TD
1998—Chicago NFL	16	16	1	8	8.0	0
1999—Chicago NFL	16	16	1	41	41.0	0
2000—Chicago NFL	16	16	3	81	27.0	1
2001—Chicago NFL	16	16	3	36	12.0	0
Pro totals (4 years)	64	64	8	166	20.8	1

PASS, PATRICK   RB   PATRIOTS

PERSONAL: Born December 31, 1977, in Scottsdale, Ga. ... 5-10/215. ... Full name: Patrick D. Pass.
HIGH SCHOOL: Tucker (Ga.).
COLLEGE: Georgia.
TRANSACTIONS/CAREER NOTES: Selected by New England Patriots in seventh round (239th pick overall) of 2000 NFL draft. ... Signed by Patriots (June 29, 2000). ... Released by Patriots (August 27, 2000). ... Re-signed by Patriots to practice squad (August 29, 2000). ... Activated (September 16, 2000).
CHAMPIONSHIP GAME EXPERIENCE: Played in AFC championship game (2001 season). ... Member of Super Bowl championship team (2001 season).
PRO STATISTICS: 2000—Recovered one fumble. 2001—Returned 10 kickoffs for 222 yards and recovered one fumble.
SINGLE GAME HIGHS (regular season): Attempts—12 (November 19, 2000, vs. Cincinnati); yards—39 (November 19, 2000, vs. Cincinnati); and rushing touchdowns—0.
MISCELLANEOUS: Selected by Florida Marlins organization in 44th round of free-agent draft (June 4, 1996).

			RUSHING				RECEIVING				TOTALS		
Year Team	G	GS	Att.	Yds.	Avg.	TD	No.	Yds.	Avg.	TD	TD	2pt.	Pts.	Fum.
2000—New England NFL	5	1	18	58	3.2	0	4	17	4.3	0	0	0	0	0
2001—New England NFL	16	0	1	7	7.0	0	6	66	11.0	1	1	0	6	0
Pro totals (2 years)	21	1	19	65	3.4	0	10	83	8.3	1	1	0	6	0

RECORD AS BASEBALL PLAYER

TRANSACTIONS/CAREER NOTES: Selected by Florida Marlins organization in 44th round of free-agent draft (June 4, 1996).

					BATTING								FIELDING		
Year Team (League)	Pos.	G	AB	R	H	2B	3B	HR	RBI	Avg.	BB	SO	SB	PO	A	E	Avg.
1996—GC Marlins (GCL)	OF	29	90	14	22	4	0	0	8	.244	15	27	5	27	0	2	.931

PATHON, JEROME   WR   SAINTS

PERSONAL: Born December 16, 1975, in Capetown, South Africa. ... 6-0/182. ... Name pronounced PAY-thin.
HIGH SCHOOL: Carson Graham Secondary School (North Vancouver).
COLLEGE: Acadia (Nova Scotia), then Washington.
TRANSACTIONS/CAREER NOTES: Selected by Indianapolis Colts in second round (32nd pick overall) of 1998 NFL draft. ... Signed by Colts (July 26, 1998). ... On injured reserve with foot injury (November 19, 2001-remainder of season). ... Granted unconditional free agency (March 1, 2002). ... Signed by New Orleans Saints (April 10, 2002).
HONORS: Named wide receiver on THE SPORTING NEWS college All-America second team (1997).
PRO STATISTICS: 1998—Rushed three times for minus two yards. 1999—Returned six kickoffs for 123 yards. 2000—Rushed once for three yards and returned 26 kickoffs for 583 yards. 2001—Rushed once for minus eight yards and returned one kickoff for 13 yards.
SINGLE GAME HIGHS (regular season): Receptions—9 (September 23, 2001, vs. Buffalo); yards—168 (September 23, 2001, vs. Buffalo); and touchdown receptions—1 (September 23, 2001, vs. Buffalo).
STATISTICAL PLATEAUS: 100-yard receiving games: 2001 (1).

			RECEIVING				TOTALS		
Year Team	G	GS	No.	Yds.	Avg.	TD	TD	2pt.	Pts.	Fum.
1998—Indianapolis NFL	16	15	50	511	10.2	1	1	0	6	0
1999—Indianapolis NFL	10	2	14	163	11.6	0	0	0	0	0
2000—Indianapolis NFL	16	10	50	646	12.9	3	3	0	18	0
2001—Indianapolis NFL	4	3	24	330	13.8	2	2	0	12	0
Pro totals (4 years)	46	30	138	1650	12.0	6	6	0	36	0

PATMON, DEWAYNE   S   GIANTS

PERSONAL: Born April 25, 1979, in San Diego. ... 6-0/190.
HIGH SCHOOL: Patrick Henry (San Diego).
COLLEGE: Michigan.
TRANSACTIONS/CAREER NOTES: Signed as non-drafted free agent by New York Giants (April 27, 2001).
PLAYING EXPERIENCE: New York Giants NFL, 2001. ... Games/Games started: (7/0).

PATTEN, DAVID — WR — PATRIOTS

PERSONAL: Born August 19, 1974, in Columbia, S.C. ... 5-10/195.
HIGH SCHOOL: Lower Richland (Hopkins, S.C.).
COLLEGE: Western Carolina.
TRANSACTIONS/CAREER NOTES: Played for Albany Firebirds of Arena League (1996). ... Signed as non-drafted free agent by New York Giants (March 24, 1997). ... Released by Giants (August 24, 1997). ... Re-signed by Giants to practice squad (August 25, 1997). ... Activated (August 27, 1997). ... On injured reserve with knee injury (December 16, 1998-remainder of season). ... Granted free agency (February 11, 2000). ... Signed by Cleveland Browns (March 16, 2000). ... Granted unconditional free agency (March 2, 2001). ... Signed by New England Patriots (April 2, 2001).
CHAMPIONSHIP GAME EXPERIENCE: Played in AFC championship game (2001 season). ... Member of Super Bowl championship team (2001 season).
PRO STATISTICS: 1997—Rushed once for two yards and recovered one fumble. 1999—Rushed once for 27 yards. 2001—Rushed five times for 67 yards and one touchdown and attempted two passes with one completion for 60 yards and a touchdown and one interception.
SINGLE GAME HIGHS (regular season): Receptions—7 (October 14, 2001, vs. San Diego); yards—117 (October 21, 2001, vs. Indianapolis); and touchdown receptions—2 (October 21, 2001, vs. Indianapolis).
STATISTICAL PLATEAUS: 100-yard receiving games: 2000 (2), 2001 (1). Total: 3.

				RECEIVING				KICKOFF RETURNS				TOTALS		
Year Team	G	GS	No.	Yds.	Avg.	TD	No.	Yds.	Avg.	TD	TD	2pt.	Pts.	Fum.
1997—New York Giants NFL	16	3	13	226	17.4	2	8	123	15.4	0	2	0	12	2
1998—New York Giants NFL	12	0	11	119	10.8	1	43	928	21.6	1	2	0	12	0
1999—New York Giants NFL	16	0	9	115	12.8	0	33	673	20.4	0	0	0	0	0
2000—Cleveland NFL	14	11	38	546	14.4	1	22	469	21.3	0	1	0	6	2
2001—New England NFL	16	14	51	749	14.7	4	2	44	22.0	0	5	0	30	1
Pro totals (5 years)	74	28	122	1755	14.4	8	108	2237	20.7	1	10	0	60	5

PATTON, MARVCUS — LB — CHIEFS

PERSONAL: Born May 1, 1967, in Los Angeles. ... 6-2/237. ... Full name: Marvcus Raymond Patton.
HIGH SCHOOL: Leuzinger (Lawndale, Calif.).
COLLEGE: UCLA (degree in political science, 1990).
TRANSACTIONS/CAREER NOTES: Selected by Buffalo Bills in eighth round (208th pick overall) of 1990 NFL draft. ... Signed by Bills (July 27, 1990). ... On injured reserve with broken leg (January 26, 1991-remainder of 1990 playoffs). ... Granted free agency (February 1, 1992). ... Re-signed by Bills (July 23, 1992). ... Granted unconditional free agency (February 17, 1995). ... Signed by Washington Redskins (February 22, 1995). ... Granted unconditional free agency (February 12, 1999). ... Signed by Kansas City Chiefs (April 27, 1999).
CHAMPIONSHIP GAME EXPERIENCE: Played in AFC championship game (1991-1993 seasons). ... Played in Super Bowl XXVI (1991 season), Super Bowl XXVII (1992 season) and Super Bowl XXVIII (1993 season).
PRO STATISTICS: 1993—Recovered three fumbles for five yards. 1994—Recovered one fumble and fumbled once. 1995—Recovered one fumble. 1997—Returned one kickoff for 10 yards and recovered one fumble. 1999—Recovered three fumbles. 2000—Recovered one fumble.

			INTERCEPTIONS				SACKS
Year Team	G	GS	No.	Yds.	Avg.	TD	No.
1990—Buffalo NFL	16	0	0	0	0.0	0	0.5
1991—Buffalo NFL	16	2	0	0	0.0	0	0.0
1992—Buffalo NFL	16	4	0	0	0.0	0	2.0
1993—Buffalo NFL	16	16	2	0	0.0	0	1.0
1994—Buffalo NFL	16	16	2	8	4.0	0	0.0
1995—Washington NFL	16	16	2	7	3.5	0	2.0
1996—Washington NFL	16	16	2	26	13.0	0	2.0
1997—Washington NFL	16	16	2	5	2.5	0	4.5
1998—Washington NFL	16	16	0	0	0.0	0	3.0
1999—Kansas City NFL	16	16	1	0	0.0	0	6.5
2000—Kansas City NFL	16	15	2	39	19.5	1	1.0
2001—Kansas City NFL	16	15	2	5	2.5	0	3.0
Pro totals (12 years)	192	148	15	90	6.0	1	25.5

PAXTON, LONIE — TE — PATRIOTS

PERSONAL: Born March 13, 1978, in Anaheim, Calif. ... 6-2/260. ... Full name: Leonidas E. Paxton.
HIGH SCHOOL: Centennial (Carona, Calif.).
COLLEGE: Sacramento State.
TRANSACTIONS/CAREER NOTES: Signed as non-drafted free agent by New England Patriots (April 19, 2000).
PLAYING EXPERIENCE: New England NFL, 2000 and 2001. ... Games/Games started: 2000 (16/0), 2001 (16/0). Total: 32/0.
CHAMPIONSHIP GAME EXPERIENCE: Played in AFC championship game (2001 season). ... Member of Super Bowl championship team (2001 season).

PAYNE, SETH — DT — TEXANS

PERSONAL: Born February 12, 1975, in Clifton Springs, N.Y. ... 6-4/303. ... Full name: Seth Copeland Payne.
HIGH SCHOOL: Victor (N.Y.) Central.
COLLEGE: Cornell.
TRANSACTIONS/CAREER NOTES: Selected by Jacksonville Jaguars in fourth round (114th pick overall) of 1997 NFL draft. ... Signed by Jaguars (May 23, 1997). ... On injured reserve with shoulder injury (November 17, 1998-remainder of season). ... Selected by Houston Texans from Jaguars in NFL expansion draft (February 18, 2002).
PLAYING EXPERIENCE: Jacksonville NFL, 1997-2001. ... Games/Games started: 1997 (12/5), 1998 (6/1), 1999 (16/16), 2000 (16/14), 2001 (16/16). Total: 66/52.
CHAMPIONSHIP GAME EXPERIENCE: Played in AFC championship game (1999 season).
PRO STATISTICS: 1999—Credited with $1^{1}/_{2}$ sacks. 2000—Credited with two sacks. 2001—Credited with five sacks.

PEDERSON, DOUG QB PACKERS

PERSONAL: Born January 31, 1968, in Bellingham, Wash. ... 6-3/220. ... Full name: Douglas Irvin Pederson.
HIGH SCHOOL: Ferndale (Wash.).
COLLEGE: Northeast Louisiana (degree in business management).
TRANSACTIONS/CAREER NOTES: Signed as non-drafted free agent by Miami Dolphins (April 30, 1991). ... Released by Dolphins (August 16, 1991). ... Selected by New York/New Jersey Knights in fifth round (49th pick overall) of 1992 World League draft. ... Re-signed by Dolphins (June 1, 1992). ... Released by Dolphins (August 31, 1992). ... Re-signed by Dolphins to practice squad (September 1, 1992). ... Released by Dolphins (October 7, 1992). ... Re-signed by Dolphins (March 3, 1993). ... Released by Dolphins (August 30, 1993). ... Re-signed by Dolphins to practice squad (August 31, 1993). ... Activated (October 22, 1993). ... Released by Dolphins (December 15, 1993). ... Re-signed by Dolphins (April 15, 1994). ... Inactive for all 16 games (1994). ... Selected by Carolina Panthers from Dolphins in NFL expansion draft (February 15, 1995). ... Released by Panthers (May 22, 1995). ... Signed by Dolphins (July 11, 1995). ... Released by Dolphins (August 21, 1995). ... Re-signed by Dolphins (October 10, 1995). ... Inactive for two games with Dolphins (1995). ... Released by Dolphins (October 25, 1995). ... Signed by Green Bay Packers (November 22, 1995). ... Inactive for five games with Packers (1995). ... Granted unconditional free agency (February 14, 1997). ... Re-signed by Packers (February 20, 1997). ... Granted unconditional free agency (February 12, 1999). ... Signed by Philadelphia Eagles (February 17, 1999). ... Released by Eagles (August 27, 2000). ... Signed by Cleveland Browns (September 1, 2000). ... Released by Browns (February 22, 2001). ... Signed by Packers (March 13, 2001). ... Granted unconditional free agency (March 1, 2002). ... Re-signed by Packers (April 2, 2002).
CHAMPIONSHIP GAME EXPERIENCE: Member of Packers for NFC championship game (1995-97 seasons); inactive. ... Member of Super Bowl championship team (1996 season); inactive. ... Member of Packers for Super Bowl XXXII (1997 season); inactive.
PRO STATISTICS: 1993—Fumbled twice and recovered one fumble for minus one yard. 1998—Fumbled once for minus two yards. 1999—Fumbled seven times. 2000—Fumbled four times and recovered three fumbles.
SINGLE GAME HIGHS (regular season): Attempts—40 (December 10, 2000, vs. Philadelphia); completions—29 (December 10, 2000, vs. Philadelphia); yards—309 (December 10, 2000, vs. Philadelphia); and touchdown passes—2 (October 17, 1999, vs. Chicago).
STATISTICAL PLATEAUS: 300-yard passing games: 2000 (1).
MISCELLANEOUS: Regular-season record as starting NFL quarterback: 3-14 (.176).

				PASSING							RUSHING				TOTALS	
Year Team	G	GS	Att.	Cmp.	Pct.	Yds.	TD	Int.	Avg.	Rat.	Att.	Yds.	Avg.	TD	TD	2pt.	Pts.
1992—NY/New Jersey W.L. ...	7	1	128	70	54.7	1077	8	3	8.41	93.8	15	46	3.1	0	0	0	0
1993—Miami NFL	7	0	8	4	50.0	41	0	0	5.13	65.1	2	-1	-0.5	0	0	0	0
1994—Miami NFL						Did not play.											
1995—Miami NFL						Did not play.											
—Green Bay NFL............						Did not play.											
1996—Green Bay NFL...........	1	0	0	0	0.0	0	0	0	0.0	...	0	0	0.0	0	0	0	0
1997—Green Bay NFL...........	1	0	0	0	0.0	0	0	0	0.0	...	3	-4	-1.3	0	0	0	0
1998—Green Bay NFL...........	12	0	24	14	58.3	128	2	0	5.33	100.7	8	-4	-0.5	0	0	0	0
1999—Philadelphia NFL	16	9	227	119	52.4	1276	7	9	5.62	62.9	20	33	1.7	0	0	0	0
2000—Cleveland NFL	11	8	210	117	55.7	1047	2	8	4.99	56.6	18	68	3.8	0	0	0	0
2001—Green Bay NFL...........	16	0	0	0	0.0	0	0	0	0.0	...	1	-1	-1.0	0	0	0	0
W.L. totals (1 year)	7	1	128	70	54.7	1077	8	3	8.41	93.8	15	46	3.1	0	0	0	0
NFL totals (7 years)	64	17	469	254	54.2	2492	11	17	5.31	62.1	52	91	1.8	0	0	0	0
Pro totals (8 years)	71	18	597	324	54.3	3569	19	20	5.98	68.9	67	137	2.0	0	0	0	0

PEETE, RODNEY QB PANTHERS

PERSONAL: Born March 16, 1966, in Mesa, Ariz. ... 6-0/230. ... Son of Willie Peete, former running backs coach and scout with Chicago Bears; cousin of Calvin Peete, professional golfer.
HIGH SCHOOL: Sahuaro (Tucson, Ariz.), then Shawnee Mission South (Overland Park, Kan.).
COLLEGE: Southern California (degree in communications, 1989).
TRANSACTIONS/CAREER NOTES: Selected by Detroit Lions in sixth round (141st pick overall) of 1989 NFL draft. ... Signed by Lions (July 13, 1989). ... On injured reserve with Achilles' tendon injury (October 30, 1991-remainder of season). ... Granted free agency (February 1, 1992). ... Re-signed by Lions (July 30, 1992). ... Granted unconditional free agency (February 17, 1994). ... Signed by Dallas Cowboys (May 4, 1994). ... Granted unconditional free agency (February 17, 1995). ... Signed by Philadelphia Eagles (April 22, 1995). ... Granted unconditional free agency (February 16, 1996). ... Re-signed by Eagles (March 14, 1996). ... On injured reserve with knee injury (October 3, 1996-remainder of season). ... Granted unconditional free agency (February 14, 1997). ... Re-signed by Eagles (April 1, 1997). ... Traded by Eagles to Washington Redskins for sixth-round pick (C John Romero) in 2000 draft (April 28, 1999). ... Released by Redskins (April 18, 2000). ... Signed by Oakland Raiders (July 13, 2000). ... Released by Raiders (September 2, 2001). ... Re-signed by Raiders (September 29, 2001). ... Granted unconditional free agency (March 1, 2002). ... Signed by Carolina Panthers (March 28, 2002).
CHAMPIONSHIP GAME EXPERIENCE: Member of Cowboys for NFC championship game (1994 season); did not play. ... Member of Raiders for AFC Championship game (2000 season); inactive.
HONORS: Named quarterback on THE SPORTING NEWS college All-America second team (1988).
PRO STATISTICS: 1989—Fumbled nine times and recovered three fumbles. 1990—Fumbled nine times and recovered one fumble. 1991—Fumbled twice and recovered four fumbles for minus one yard. 1992—Fumbled six times and recovered four fumbles for minus seven yards. 1993—Fumbled 11 times and recovered four fumbles for minus eight yards. 1994—Fumbled three times and recovered two fumbles for minus one yard. 1995—Fumbled 13 times and recovered five fumbles. 1996—Fumbled twice and recovered one fumble. 1997—Fumbled five times and recovered two fumbles for minus six yards. 1998—Fumbled once.
SINGLE GAME HIGHS (regular season): Attempts—45 (October 8, 1995, vs. Washington); completions—30 (October 8, 1995, vs. Washington); yards—323 (September 27, 1992, vs. Tampa Bay); and touchdown passes—4 (December 16, 1990, vs. Chicago).
STATISTICAL PLATEAUS: 300-yard passing games: 1990 (1), 1992 (1). Total: 2.
MISCELLANEOUS: Selected by Toronto Blue Jays organization in 30th round of free-agent baseball draft (June 4, 1984); did not sign. ... Selected by Oakland Athletics organization in 14th round of free-agent baseball draft (June 1, 1988); did not sign. ... Selected by Athletics organization in 13th round of free-agent baseball draft (June 5, 1989); did not sign. ... Regular-season record as starting NFL quarterback: 37-35 (.514). ... Postseason record as starting NFL quarterback: 1-1 (.500).

				PASSING						RUSHING			TOTALS		
Year Team	G	GS	Att.	Cmp.	Pct.	Yds.	TD	Int.	Avg.	Rat.	Att.	Yds.	Avg.	TD	TD	2pt.	Pts.
1989—Detroit NFL..............	8	8	195	103	52.8	1479	5	9	7.58	67.0	33	148	4.5	4	4	0	24
1990—Detroit NFL..............	11	11	271	142	52.4	1974	13	8	7.28	79.8	47	363	7.7	6	6	0	36
1991—Detroit NFL..............	8	8	194	116	59.8	1339	5	9	6.90	69.9	25	125	5.0	2	2	0	12
1992—Detroit NFL..............	10	10	213	123	57.7	1702	9	9	7.99	80.0	21	83	4.0	0	0	0	0
1993—Detroit NFL..............	10	10	252	157	62.3	1670	6	14	6.63	66.4	45	165	3.7	1	1	0	6
1994—Dallas NFL................	7	1	56	33	58.9	470	4	1	8.39	102.5	9	-2	-0.2	0	0	0	0
1995—Philadelphia NFL........	15	12	375	215	57.3	2326	8	14	6.20	67.3	32	147	4.6	1	1	0	6
1996—Philadelphia NFL........	5	5	134	80	59.7	992	3	5	7.40	74.6	20	31	1.6	1	1	0	6
1997—Philadelphia NFL........	5	3	118	68	57.6	869	4	4	7.36	78.0	8	37	4.6	0	0	0	0
1998—Philadelphia NFL........	5	4	129	71	55.0	758	2	4	5.88	64.7	5	30	6.0	1	1	0	6
1999—Washington NFL........	3	0	17	8	47.1	107	2	1	6.29	82.2	2	-1	-0.5	0	0	0	0
2000—Oakland NFL.............									Did not play.								
2001—Oakland NFL.............	1	0	0	0	0.0	0	0	0	0.0	...	0	0	0.0	0	0	0	0
Pro totals (12 years)	88	72	1954	1116	57.1	13686	61	78	7.00	72.6	247	1126	4.6	16	16	0	96

PENNINGTON, CHAD   QB   JETS

PERSONAL: Born June 26, 1976, in Knoxville, Tenn. ... 6-3/225. ... Full name: James Chad Pennington.
HIGH SCHOOL: Webb (Knoxville, Tenn.).
COLLEGE: Marshall.
TRANSACTIONS/CAREER NOTES: Selected by New York Jets in first round (18th pick overall) of 2000 NFL draft. ... Signed by Jets (July 13, 2000).
HONORS: Named quarterback on THE SPORTING NEWS college All-America third team (1999).
SINGLE GAME HIGHS (regular season): Attempts—14 (October 21, 2001, vs. St. Louis); completions—9 (October 21, 2001, vs. St. Louis); yards—68 (October 21, 2001, vs. St. Louis); and touchdown passes—1 (October 21, 2001, vs. St. Louis).

				PASSING						RUSHING			TOTALS		
Year Team	G	GS	Att.	Cmp.	Pct.	Yds.	TD	Int.	Avg.	Rat.	Att.	Yds.	Avg.	TD	TD	2pt.	Pts.
2000—New York Jets NFL......	2	0	5	2	40.0	67	1	0	13.40	127.1	1	0	0.0	0	0	0	0
2001—New York Jets NFL......	2	0	20	10	50.0	92	1	0	4.60	79.6	1	11	11.0	0	0	0	0
Pro totals (2 years)	4	0	25	12	48.0	159	2	0	6.36	95.3	2	11	5.5	0	0	0	0

PERRY, ED   TE   DOLPHINS

PERSONAL: Born September 1, 1974, in Richmond, Va. ... 6-4/270. ... Full name: Edward Lewis Perry.
HIGH SCHOOL: Highlands Springs (Va.).
COLLEGE: James Madison.
TRANSACTIONS/CAREER NOTES: Selected by Miami Dolphins in sixth round (177th pick overall) of 1997 NFL draft. ... Signed by Dolphins (June 13, 1997). ... Granted free agency (February 11, 2000). ... Re-signed by Dolphins (April 28, 2000). ... On injured reserve with shoulder injury (November 23, 2000-remainder of season). ... Granted unconditional free agency (March 2, 2001). ... Re-signed by Dolphins (March 16, 2001).
PRO STATISTICS: 1997—Returned one kickoff for seven yards and recovered one fumble. 2001—Returned one kickoff for no yards.
SINGLE GAME HIGHS (regular season): Receptions—4 (September 13, 1998, vs. Buffalo); yards—59 (November 23, 1998, vs. New England); and touchdown receptions—1 (December 27, 1999, vs. New York Jets).

			RECEIVING				TOTALS			
Year Team	G	GS	No.	Yds.	Avg.	TD	TD	2pt.	Pts.	Fum.
1997—Miami NFL..	16	4	11	45	4.1	1	1	0	6	0
1998—Miami NFL..	14	5	25	255	10.2	0	0	0	0	0
1999—Miami NFL..	16	1	3	8	2.7	1	1	0	6	0
2000—Miami NFL..	10	0	0	0	0.0	0	0	0	0	0
2001—Miami NFL..	16	0	0	0	0.0	0	0	0	0	1
Pro totals (5 years)	72	10	39	308	7.9	2	2	0	12	1

PERRY, JASON   S   CHARGERS

PERSONAL: Born August 1, 1976, in Passaic, N.J. ... 6-0/200. ... Full name: Jason Robert Perry.
HIGH SCHOOL: Paterson (N.J.) Catholic.
COLLEGE: North Carolina State.
TRANSACTIONS/CAREER NOTES: Selected by San Diego Chargers in fourth round (104th pick overall) of 1999 NFL draft. ... Signed by Chargers (July 22, 1999). ... On injured reserve with knee injury (September 26, 2000-remainder of season). ... Granted free agency (March 1, 2002). ... Re-signed by Chargers (April 2, 2002).
PLAYING EXPERIENCE: San Diego NFL, 1999-2001. ... Games/Games started: 1999 (16/5), 2000 (1/0), 2001 (14/3). Total: 31/8.
PRO STATISTICS: 1999—Recovered one fumble. 2001—Intercepted two passes for 37 yards and one touchdown and recovered one fumble for seven yards.

PERRY, TODD   G   DOLPHINS

PERSONAL: Born November 28, 1970, in Elizabethtown, Ky. ... 6-5/305. ... Full name: Todd Joseph Perry.
HIGH SCHOOL: North Hardin (Radcliff, Ky.).
COLLEGE: Kentucky.
TRANSACTIONS/CAREER NOTES: Selected by Chicago Bears in fourth round (97th pick overall) of 1993 NFL draft. ... Signed by Bears (June 16, 1993). ... On injured reserve with back injury (December 19, 1997-remainder of season). ... Granted unconditional free agency (February 11, 2000). ... Re-signed by Bears (May 4, 2000). ... Granted unconditional free agency (March 2, 2001). ... Signed by Miami Dolphins (March 3, 2001).
PLAYING EXPERIENCE: Chicago NFL, 1993-2000; Miami NFL, 2001. ... Games/Games started: 1993 (13/3), 1994 (15/4), 1995 (15/15), 1996 (16/16), 1997 (11/11), 1998 (16/16), 1999 (16/16), 2000 (16/16), 2001 (16/16). Total: 134/113.
PRO STATISTICS: 1996—Recovered one fumble. 1999—Recovered one fumble.

P

PETER, CHRISTIAN — DT

PERSONAL: Born October 5, 1972, in Locust, N.J. ... 6-3/292. ... Brother of Jason Peter, defensive end with Carolina Panthers (1998-2001).
HIGH SCHOOL: Middletown South (Middleton, N.J.), then Milford (Conn.) Academy.
COLLEGE: Nebraska.
TRANSACTIONS/CAREER NOTES: Selected by New England Patriots in fifth round (149th pick overall) of 1996 NFL draft. ... Patriots released rights (April 24, 1996). ... Signed by New York Giants (January 22, 1997). ... Granted free agency (February 11, 2000). ... Re-signed by Giants (April 12, 2000). ... Granted unconditional free agency (March 2, 2001). ... Signed by Indianapolis Colts (April 21, 2001). ... On injured reserve with neck injury (January 4, 2002-remainder of season). ... Released by Colts (February 28, 2002).
CHAMPIONSHIP GAME EXPERIENCE: Played in NFC championship game (2000 season). ... Played in Super Bowl XXXV (2000 season).
PRO STATISTICS: 1999—Recovered one fumble for 38 yards and a touchdown.

Year Team	G	GS	SACKS
1997—New York Giants NFL	7	0	0.5
1998—New York Giants NFL	16	6	1.0
1999—New York Giants NFL	16	10	0.0
2000—New York Giants NFL	16	15	1.0
2001—Indianapolis NFL	14	0	1.0
Pro totals (5 years)	69	31	3.5

PETER, JASON — DE

PERSONAL: Born September 13, 1974, in Locust, N.J. ... 6-4/275. ... Full name: Jason Michael Peter. ... Brother of Christian Peter, defensive tackle, New York Giants (1997-2000) and Indianapolis Colts (2001).
HIGH SCHOOL: Middletown South (Middleton, N.J.), then Milford (Conn.) Academy.
COLLEGE: Nebraska (degree in communication studies, 1997).
TRANSACTIONS/CAREER NOTES: Selected by Carolina Panthers in first round (14th pick overall) of 1998 NFL draft. ... Signed by Panthers (August 31, 1998). ... On injured reserve with neck injury (December 5, 2000-remainder of season). ... On injured reserve with neck injury (November 6, 2001-remainder of season). ... Granted unconditional free agency (March 1, 2002).
HONORS: Named defensive tackle on THE SPORTING NEWS college All-America first team (1997).
PRO STATISTICS: 1998—Recovered one fumble.

Year Team	G	GS	SACKS
1998—Carolina NFL	14	11	1.0
1999—Carolina NFL	9	9	4.5
2000—Carolina NFL	9	0	2.0
2001—Carolina NFL	6	0	0.0
Pro totals (4 years)	38	20	7.5

PETERSON, JULIAN — LB — 49ERS

PERSONAL: Born July 28, 1978, in Hillcrest Heights, Md. ... 6-3/235. ... Full name: Julian Thomas Peterson.
HIGH SCHOOL: Crossland (Temple Hills, Md.).
JUNIOR COLLEGE: Valley Forge Junior College (Pa.).
COLLEGE: Michigan State.
TRANSACTIONS/CAREER NOTES: Selected by San Francisco 49ers in first round (16th pick overall) of 2000 NFL draft. ... Signed by 49ers (July 27, 2000).
PRO STATISTICS: 2000—Intercepted two passes for 33 yards. 2001—Recovered two fumbles for 26 yards and one touchdown.

Year Team	G	GS	SACKS
2000—San Francisco NFL	13	8	4.0
2001—San Francisco NFL	14	14	3.0
Pro totals (2 years)	27	22	7.0

PETERSON, MIKE — LB — COLTS

PERSONAL: Born June 17, 1976, in Gainesville, Fla. ... 6-1/232. ... Full name: Porter Michael Peterson. ... Couson of Freddie Solomon, wide receiver with Philadelphia Eagles (1995-98).
HIGH SCHOOL: Santa Fe (Alachua, Fla.).
COLLEGE: Florida.
TRANSACTIONS/CAREER NOTES: Selected by Indianapolis Colts in second round (36th pick overall) of 1999 NFL draft. ... Signed by Colts (July 28, 1999).
HONORS: Named outside linebacker on THE SPORTING NEWS college All-America first team (1998).
PRO STATISTICS: 1999—Recovered one fumble. 2000—Intercepted two passes for eight yards. 2001—Intercepted two passes for 18 yards and recovered one fumble.

Year Team	G	GS	SACKS
1999—Indianapolis NFL	16	13	3.0
2000—Indianapolis NFL	16	16	0.0
2001—Indianapolis NFL	9	9	1.5
Pro totals (3 years)	41	38	4.5

PETERSON, TODD — K — STEELERS

PERSONAL: Born February 4, 1970, in Washington, D.C. ... 5-10/177. ... Full name: Joseph Todd Peterson.
HIGH SCHOOL: Valdosta (Ga.) State.
COLLEGE: Navy, then Georgia (degree in finance, 1992).

TRANSACTIONS/CAREER NOTES: Selected by New York Giants in seventh round (177th pick overall) of 1993 NFL draft. ... Signed by Giants (July 19, 1993). ... Released by Giants (August 24, 1993). ... Signed by New England Patriots to practice squad (November 30, 1993). ... Released by Patriots (December 6, 1993). ... Signed by Atlanta Falcons (May 3, 1994). ... Released by Falcons (August 29, 1994). ... Signed by Arizona Cardinals (October 12, 1994). ... Released by Cardinals (October 24, 1994). ... Signed by Seattle Seahawks (January 17, 1995). ... Granted free agency (February 13, 1998). ... Re-signed by Seahawks for 1998 season. ... Granted unconditional free agency (February 12, 1999). ... Re-signed by Seahawks (March 2, 1999). ... Released by Seahawks (August 27, 2000). ... Signed by Kansas City Chiefs (October 11, 2000). ... Granted unconditional free agency (March 1, 2002). ... Signed by Pittsburgh Steelers (March 25, 2002).
PRO STATISTICS: 2001—Punted twice for 61 yards.

				KICKING				
Year Team	G	XPM	XPA	FGM	FGA	Lg.	50+	Pts.
1993—New England NFL				Did not play.				
1994—Arizona NFL	2	4	4	2	4	35	0-0	10
1995—Seattle NFL	16	§40	§40	23	28	49	0-2	109
1996—Seattle NFL	16	27	27	28	34	54	2-3	111
1997—Seattle NFL	16	37	37	22	28	52	1-2	103
1998—Seattle NFL	16	41	41	19	24	51	3-7	98
1999—Seattle NFL	16	32	32	34	40	51	1-2	134
2000—Kansas City NFL	11	25	25	15	20	42	0-0	70
2001—Kansas City NFL	16	27	28	27	35	51	1-2	108
Pro totals (8 years)	109	233	234	170	213	54	8-18	743

PETERSON, WILL   CB   GIANTS

PERSONAL: Born June 15, 1979, in Uniontown, Pa. ... 6-0/197. ... Full name: William James Peterson Jr.
HIGH SCHOOL: Laurel Highlands (Pa.).
COLLEGE: Michigan, then Western Illinois.
TRANSACTIONS/CAREER NOTES: Selected by New Yorks Giants in third round (78th pick overall) of 2001 NFL draft. ... Signed by Giants (July 26, 2001).

			INTERCEPTIONS				SACKS
Year Team	G	GS	No.	Yds.	Avg.	TD	No.
2001—New York Giants NFL	16	5	1	0	0.0	0	0.0

PETITGOUT, LUKE   OT   GIANTS

PERSONAL: Born June 16, 1976, in Milford, Del. ... 6-6/310. ... Full name: Lucas George Petitgout. ... Name pronounced pet-ee-GOO.
HIGH SCHOOL: Sussex Central (Georgetown, Del.).
COLLEGE: Notre Dame.
TRANSACTIONS/CAREER NOTES: Selected by New York Giants in first round (19th pick overall) of 1999 NFL draft. ... Signed by Giants (July 29, 1999).
PLAYING EXPERIENCE: New York Giants NFL, 1999-2001. ... Games/Games started: 1999 (15/8), 2000 (16/16), 2001 (16/16). Total: 47/40.
CHAMPIONSHIP GAME EXPERIENCE: Played in NFC championship game (2000 season). ... Played in Super Bowl XXXV (2000 season).
PRO STATISTICS: 2000—Recovered one fumble. 2001—Recovered one fumble.

PHENIX, PERRY   S

PERSONAL: Born November 14, 1974, in Monroe, La. ... 5-11/210. ... Full name: Perry Lee Phenix.
HIGH SCHOOL: Hillcrest (Dallas).
JUNIOR COLLEGE: Trinity Valley Community College (Texas).
COLLEGE: Southern Mississippi.
TRANSACTIONS/CAREER NOTES: Signed as non-drafted free agent by Tennessee Oilers (April 20, 1998). ... Granted free agency (March 2, 2001). ... Re-signed by Titans (October 17, 2001). ... Traded by Titans to Carolina Panthers for conditional draft pick (September 2, 2001). ... Claimed on waivers by Cleveland Browns (October 4, 2001). ... Released by Browns (October 15, 2001). ... Signed by Titans (October 17, 2001). ... Granted unconditional free agency (March 1, 2002).
PLAYING EXPERIENCE: Tennessee NFL, 1998-2000; Carolina (2)-Tennessee (12) NFL, 2001. ... Games/Games started: 1998 (15/3), 1999 (16/1), 2000 (16/0), 2001 (Car.-2/0; Ten.-12/11; Total: 14/11). Total: 61/15.
CHAMPIONSHIP GAME EXPERIENCE: Played in AFC championship game (1999 season). ... Played in Super Bowl XXXIV (1999 season).
PRO STATISTICS: 1998—Recovered one fumble for 18 yards. 2000—Intercepted one pass for 87 yards and a touchdown and recovered one fumble.

PHIFER, ROMAN   LB

PERSONAL: Born March 5, 1968, in Plattsburgh, N.Y. ... 6-2/248. ... Full name: Roman Zubinsky Phifer.
HIGH SCHOOL: South Mecklenburg (Charlotte).
COLLEGE: UCLA.
TRANSACTIONS/CAREER NOTES: Selected by Los Angeles Rams in second round (31st pick overall) of 1991 NFL draft. ... Signed by Rams (July 19, 1991). ... On injured reserve with broken leg (November 26, 1991-remainder of season). ... Granted unconditional free agency (February 17, 1995). ... Re-signed by Rams (March 22, 1995). ... Rams franchise moved to St. Louis (April 12, 1995). ... Granted unconditional free agency (February 12, 1999). ... Signed by New York Jets (March 9, 1999). ... Released by Jets (February 22, 2001). ... Signed by New England Patriots (August 3, 2001). ... Granted unconditional free agency (March 1, 2002).
CHAMPIONSHIP GAME EXPERIENCE: Played in AFC championship game (2001 season). ... Member of Super Bowl championship team (2001 season).
PRO STATISTICS: 1992—Recovered two fumbles. 1993—Recovered two fumbles for 10 yards. 1995—Fumbled once. 1998—Fumbled once. 2001—Recovered two fumbles.

Year Team	G	GS	INTERCEPTIONS No.	Yds.	Avg.	TD	SACKS No.
1991—Los Angeles Rams NFL	12	5	0	0	0.0	0	2.0
1992—Los Angeles Rams NFL	16	14	1	3	3.0	0	0.0
1993—Los Angeles Rams NFL	16	16	0	0	0.0	0	0.0
1994—Los Angeles Rams NFL	16	15	2	7	3.5	0	1.5
1995—St. Louis NFL	16	16	3	52	17.3	0	3.0
1996—St. Louis NFL	15	15	0	0	0.0	0	1.5
1997—St. Louis NFL	16	15	0	0	0.0	0	2.0
1998—St. Louis NFL	13	13	1	41	41.0	0	6.5
1999—New York Jets NFL	16	12	2	20	10.0	0	4.5
2000—New York Jets NFL	16	10	0	0	0.0	0	4.0
2001—New England NFL	16	16	1	14	14.0	0	2.0
Pro totals (11 years)	168	147	10	137	13.7	0	27.0

PHILLIPS, RYAN — LB — PATRIOTS

PERSONAL: Born February 7, 1974, in Renton, Wash. ... 6-4/252.
HIGH SCHOOL: Auburn (Wash.).
COLLEGE: Idaho.
TRANSACTIONS/CAREER NOTES: Selected by New York Giants in third round (68th pick overall) of 1997 NFL draft. ... Signed by Giants (July 19, 1997). ... Granted free agency (February 11, 2000). ... Re-signed by Giants (April 12, 2000). ... Granted unconditional free agency (March 2, 2001). ... Signed by Oakland Raiders (April 26, 2001). ... Released by Raiders (September 2, 2001). ... Signed by Indianapolis Colts (September 25, 2001). ... Granted unconditional free agency (March 1, 2002). ... Signed by New England Patriots (April 3, 2002).
PLAYING EXPERIENCE: New York Giants NFL, 1997-2000; Indianapolis NFL, 2001. ... Games/Games started: 1997 (10/0), 1998 (16/3), 1999 (16/16), 2000 (16/16), 2001 (13/6). Total: 71/41.
CHAMPIONSHIP GAME EXPERIENCE: Played in NFC championship game (2000 season). ... Played in Super Bowl XXXV (2000 season).
PRO STATISTICS: 1997—Credited with one sack. 1999—Intercepted one pass for no yards. 2000—Intercepted two passes for 22 yards and credited with 1 1/2 sacks. 2001—Intercepted one pass for 18 yards and credited with one sack.

PICKETT, RYAN — DT — RAMS

PERSONAL: Born October 8, 1979, in Zephyrhills, Fla. ... 6-2/310.
HIGH SCHOOL: Zephyrhills (Fla.).
COLLEGE: Ohio State.
TRANSACTIONS/CAREER NOTES: Selected after junior season by St. Louis Rams in first round (29th pick overall) of 2001 NFL draft. ... Signed by Rams (July 29, 2001).
CHAMPIONSHIP GAME EXPERIENCE: Played in NFC championship game (2001 season). ... Played in Super Bowl XXXVI (2001 season).

Year Team	G	GS	SACKS
2001—St. Louis NFL	11	0	0.5

PIERCE, ANTONIO — LB — REDSKINS

PERSONAL: Born October 26, 1978, in Ontario, Calif. ... 6-1/232.
HIGH SCHOOL: Paramount (Calif.).
JUNIOR COLLEGE: Mount San Antonio College (Calif.).
COLLEGE: Arizona.
TRANSACTIONS/CAREER NOTES: Signed as non-drafted free agent by Washington Redskins (April 25, 2001).
PLAYING EXPERIENCE: Washington NFL, 2001. ... Games/Games started: (16/8).
PRO STATISTICS: 2001—Intercepted one pass for no yards, credited with one sack and recovered one fumble.

PIERSON, PETE — OT

PERSONAL: Born February 4, 1971, in Portland, Ore. ... 6-5/315. ... Full name: Peter Samuel Pierson.
HIGH SCHOOL: David Douglas (Portland, Ore.).
COLLEGE: Washington (degree in political science, 1994).
TRANSACTIONS/CAREER NOTES: Selected by Tampa Bay Buccaneers in fifth round (136th pick overall) of 1994 NFL draft. ... Signed by Buccaneers (July 6, 1994). ... Released by Buccaneers (August 28, 1994). ... Re-signed by Buccaneers to practice squad (September 2, 1994). ... Activated (November 22, 1994). ... Released by Buccaneers (August 18, 1996). ... Re-signed by Buccaneers (September 10, 1996). ... Granted free agency (February 13, 1998). ... Re-signed by Buccaneers (June 11, 1998). ... Granted unconditional free agency (March 1, 2002).
PLAYING EXPERIENCE: Tampa Bay NFL, 1995-2001. ... Games/Games started: 1995 (12/4), 1996 (11/2), 1997 (15/0), 1998 (16/0), 1999 (15/0), 2000 (15/15), 2001 (16/0). Total: 100/21.
CHAMPIONSHIP GAME EXPERIENCE: Played in NFC championship game (1999 season).
PRO STATISTICS: 1995—Recovered one fumble.

PILLER, ZACH — G — TITANS

PERSONAL: Born May 2, 1976, in St. Petersburg, Fla. ... 6-5/315. ... Full name: Zachary Paul Piller.
HIGH SCHOOL: Lincoln (Tallahassee, Fla.).
COLLEGE: Georgia Tech, then Florida.
TRANSACTIONS/CAREER NOTES: Selected by Tennessee Titans in third round (81st pick overall) of 1999 NFL draft. ... Signed by Titans (July 22, 1999).
PLAYING EXPERIENCE: Tennessee NFL, 1999-2001. ... Games/Games started: 1999 (8/0), 2000 (16/0), 2001 (14/9). Total: 38/9.
CHAMPIONSHIP GAME EXPERIENCE: Member of Titans for AFC championship game (1999 season); inactive. ... Member of Titans for Super Bowl XXXIV (1999 season); inactive.

PINKSTON, TODD   WR   EAGLES

PERSONAL: Born April 23, 1977, in Forest, Miss. ... 6-2/170.
HIGH SCHOOL: Forest (Miss.).
COLLEGE: Southern Mississippi.
TRANSACTIONS/CAREER NOTES: Selected by Philadelphia Eagles in second round (36th pick overall) of 2000 NFL draft. ... Signed by Eagles (July 16, 2000).
CHAMPIONSHIP GAME EXPERIENCE: Played in NFC championship game (2001 season).
PRO STATISTICS: 2001—Rushed once for five yards.
SINGLE GAME HIGHS (regular season): Receptions—7 (September 9, 2001, vs. St. Louis); yards—99 (September 9, 2001, vs. St. Louis); and touchdown receptions—2 (October 7, 2001, vs. Arizona).

				RECEIVING		
Year Team	G	GS	No.	Yds.	Avg.	TD
2000—Philadelphia NFL	16	1	10	181	18.1	0
2001—Philadelphia NFL	15	15	42	586	14.0	4
Pro totals (2 years)	31	16	52	767	14.8	4

PITTMAN, KAVIKA   DE   BRONCOS

PERSONAL: Born October 9, 1974, in Frankfurt, West Germany. ... 6-6/273. ... Name pronounced kuh-VEE-kuh.
HIGH SCHOOL: Leesville (La.).
COLLEGE: McNeese State.
TRANSACTIONS/CAREER NOTES: Selected by Dallas Cowboys in second round (37th pick overall) of 1996 NFL draft. ... Signed by Cowboys (July 16, 1996). ... Granted unconditional free agency (February 11, 2000). ... Signed by Denver Broncos (February 22, 2000). ... On injured reserve with calf injury (December 19, 2001-remainder of season).
PRO STATISTICS: 1997—Returned one punt for no yards. 1998—Recovered two fumbles for seven yards. 1999—Recovered two fumbles. 2000—Recovered one fumble. 2001—Recovered one fumble for nine yards.

Year Team	G	GS	SACKS
1996—Dallas NFL	15	0	0.0
1997—Dallas NFL	15	0	1.0
1998—Dallas NFL	15	15	6.0
1999—Dallas NFL	16	16	3.0
2000—Denver NFL	15	15	7.0
2001—Denver NFL	14	14	1.0
Pro totals (6 years)	90	60	18.0

PITTMAN, MICHAEL   RB   BUCCANEERS

PERSONAL: Born August 14, 1975, in New Orleans. ... 6-0/216.
HIGH SCHOOL: Mira Mesa (San Diego).
COLLEGE: Fresno State.
TRANSACTIONS/CAREER NOTES: Selected by Arizona Cardinals in fourth round (95th pick overall) of 1998 NFL draft. ... Signed by Cardinals (May 20, 1998). ... Granted free agency (March 2, 2001). ... Re-signed by Cardinals (May 11, 2001). ... On suspended list (September 9-23, 2001). ... Granted unconditional free agency (March 1, 2002). ... Signed by Tampa Bay Buccaneers (March 25, 2002).
PRO STATISTICS: 1998—Fumbled once and recovered one fumble. 1999—Completed only pass attempt for 26 yards, fumbled three times and recovered one fumble. 2000—Fumbled five times. 2001—Fumbled five times.
SINGLE GAME HIGHS (regular season): Attempts—26 (October 21, 2001, vs. Kansas City); yards—133 (November 14, 1999, vs. Detroit); and rushing touchdowns—1 (December 23, 2001, vs. Dallas).
STATISTICAL PLATEAUS: 100-yard rushing games: 1999 (1), 2000 (1). Total: 2.

			RUSHING				RECEIVING				PUNT RETURNS				KICKOFF RETURNS				TOTALS		
Year Team	G	GS	Att.	Yds.	Avg.	TD	No.	Yds.	Avg.	TD	No.	Yds.	Avg.	TD	No.	Yds.	Avg.	TD	TD	2pt.	Pts.
1998—Arizona NFL	15	0	29	91	3.1	0	0	0	0.0	0	0	0	0.0	0	4	84	21.0	0	0	0	0
1999—Arizona NFL	10	2	64	289	4.5	2	16	196	12.3	0	4	16	4.0	0	2	31	15.5	0	2	0	12
2000—Arizona NFL	16	12	184	719	3.9	4	73	579	7.9	2	0	0	0.0	0	0	0	0.0	0	6	0	36
2001—Arizona NFL	15	14	241	846	3.5	5	42	264	6.3	0	0	0	0.0	0	6	161	26.8	0	5	0	30
Pro totals (4 years)	56	28	518	1945	3.8	11	131	1039	7.9	2	4	16	4.0	0	12	276	23.0	0	13	0	78

PLAYER, SCOTT   P   CARDINALS

PERSONAL: Born December 17, 1969, in St. Augustine, Fla. ... 6-1/220.
HIGH SCHOOL: St. Augustine (Fla.).
JUNIOR COLLEGE: Florida Community College.
COLLEGE: Flagler College (Fla.), then Florida State (degree in education).
TRANSACTIONS/CAREER NOTES: Played with Birmingham Barracudas of CFL (1995). ... Granted free agency (March 7, 1996). ... Signed as non-drafted free agent by Arizona Cardinals (April 23, 1996). ... Released by Cardinals (August 19, 1996). ... Signed by New York Giants (February 14, 1997). ... Assigned by Giants to Frankfurt Galaxy in 1997 World League enhancement allocation program (February 18, 1997). ... Released by Giants (August 24, 1997). ... Signed by New York Jets to practice squad (August 26, 1997). ... Released by Jets (August 28, 1997). ... Re-signed by Cardinals (March 3, 1998). ... Granted free agency (March 2, 2001). ... Re-signed by Cardinals (July 13, 2001).
HONORS: Played in Pro Bowl (2000 season).
PRO STATISTICS: CFL: 1995—Attempted two passes with one completion for 52 yards. NFL: 1999—Rushed once for minus 18 yards. 2000—Rushed once for minus 11 yards. 2001—Rushed once for no yards.

				PUNTING				
Year Team	G	No.	Yds.	Avg.	Net avg.	In. 20	Blk.
1995—Birmingham CFL	18	143	6247	43.7	36.5	0	0
1996—			Did not play.				
1997—Frankfurt W.L.	...	60	2617	43.6	34.3	17	1
1998—Arizona NFL	16	81	3378	41.7	35.9	12	∞1
1999—Arizona NFL	16	94	3948	42.0	36.7	18	0
2000—Arizona NFL	16	65	2871	44.2	37.3	17	0
2001—Arizona NFL	12	67	2779	41.5	33.8	17	0
W.L. totals (1 year)	...	60	2617	43.6	34.3	17	1
CFL totals (1 year)	18	143	6247	43.7	36.5	0	0
NFL totals (4 years)	60	307	12976	42.3	36.0	64	1
Pro totals (6 years)	...	510	21840	42.8	35.9	81	2

PLEASANT, ANTHONY   DE   PATRIOTS

PERSONAL: Born January 27, 1968, in Century, Fla. ... 6-5/280. ... Full name: Anthony Devon Pleasant.
HIGH SCHOOL: Century (Fla.).
COLLEGE: Tennessee State.
TRANSACTIONS/CAREER NOTES: Selected by Cleveland Browns in third round (73rd pick overall) of 1990 NFL draft. ... Signed by Browns (July 22, 1990). ... Browns franchise moved to Baltimore and renamed Ravens for 1996 season (March 11, 1996). ... Granted unconditional free agency (February 14, 1997). ... Signed by Atlanta Falcons (June 21, 1997). ... Released by Falcons (February 11, 1998). ... Signed by New York Jets (March 12, 1998). ... Granted unconditional free agency (February 11, 2000). ... Signed by San Francisco 49ers (July 19, 2000). ... Granted unconditional free agency (March 2, 2001). ... Signed by New England Patriots (March 22, 2001).
CHAMPIONSHIP GAME EXPERIENCE: Played in AFC championship game (1998 and 2001 seasons). ... Member of Super Bowl championship team (2001 season).
PRO STATISTICS: 1991—Recovered one fumble for four yards. 1993—Credited with a safety. 1996—Recovered one fumble for 36 yards. 2001—Intercepted two passes for no yards and fumbled once.

Year Team	G	GS	SACKS
1990—Cleveland NFL	16	7	3.5
1991—Cleveland NFL	16	7	2.5
1992—Cleveland NFL	16	14	4.0
1993—Cleveland NFL	16	13	11.0
1994—Cleveland NFL	14	14	4.5
1995—Cleveland NFL	16	16	8.0
1996—Baltimore NFL	12	12	4.0
1997—Atlanta NFL	11	0	0.5
1998—New York Jets NFL	16	15	6.0
1999—New York Jets NFL	16	16	2.0
2000—San Francisco NFL	16	16	2.0
2001—New England NFL	16	16	6.0
Pro totals (12 years)	181	146	54.0

PLUMMER, AHMED   CB   49ERS

PERSONAL: Born March 26, 1976, in Wyoming, Ohio. ... 6-0/191. ... Full name: Ahmed Kamil Plummer.
HIGH SCHOOL: Wyoming (Ohio).
COLLEGE: Ohio State.
TRANSACTIONS/CAREER NOTES: Selected by San Francisco 49ers in first round (24th pick overall) of 2000 NFL draft. ... Signed by 49ers (July 15, 2000).
PLAYING EXPERIENCE: San Francisco NFL, 2000 and 2001. ... Games/Games started: 2000 (16/15), 2001 (15/15). Total: 31/30.
PRO STATISTICS: 2000—Returned one kickoff for no yards. 2001—Intercepted seven passes for 45 yards and recovered one fumble.

PLUMMER, JAKE   QB   CARDINALS

PERSONAL: Born December 19, 1974, in Boise, Idaho. ... 6-2/202. ... Full name: Jason Steven Plummer.
HIGH SCHOOL: Capital (Boise, Idaho).
COLLEGE: Arizona State.
TRANSACTIONS/CAREER NOTES: Selected by Arizona Cardinals in second round (42nd pick overall) of 1997 NFL draft. ... Signed by Cardinals (July 14, 1997).
HONORS: Named quarterback on THE SPORTING NEWS college All-America second team (1996).
PRO STATISTICS: 1997—Caught one pass for two yards, fumbled six times and recovered one fumble for minus one yard. 1998—Fumbled 12 times and recovered three fumbles for minus two yards. 1999—Fumbled seven times and recovered five fumbles for minus four yards. 2000—Fumbled eight times and recovered four fumbles for minus one yard. 2001—Fumbled eight times and recovered five fumbles for minus three yards.
SINGLE GAME HIGHS (regular season): Attempts—57 (January 2, 2000, vs. Green Bay); completions—35 (January 2, 2000, vs. Green Bay); yards—465 (November 15, 1998, vs. Dallas); and touchdown passes—4 (November 18, 2001, vs. Detroit).
STATISTICAL PLATEAUS: 300-yard passing games: 1997 (2), 1998 (2), 1999 (1), 2000 (1), 2001 (1). Total: 7.
MISCELLANEOUS: Regular-season record as starting NFL quarterback: 25-41 (.379). ... Postseason record as starting NFL quarterback: 1-1 (.500).

					PASSING					RUSHING				TOTALS		
Year Team	G	GS	Att.	Cmp.	Pct.	Yds.	TD	Int.	Avg.	Rat.	Att.	Yds.	Avg.	TD	TD	2pt.	Pts.
1997—Arizona NFL	10	9	296	157	53.0	2203	15	15	7.44	73.1	39	216	5.5	2	2	1	14
1998—Arizona NFL	16	16	547	324	59.2	3737	17	20	6.83	75.0	51	217	4.3	4	4	0	24
1999—Arizona NFL	12	11	381	201	52.8	2111	9	*24	5.54	50.8	39	121	3.1	2	2	0	12
2000—Arizona NFL	14	14	475	270	56.8	2946	13	21	6.20	66.0	37	183	4.9	0	0	0	0
2001—Arizona NFL	16	16	525	304	57.9	3653	18	14	6.96	79.6	35	163	4.7	0	0	1	2
Pro totals (5 years)	68	66	2224	1256	56.5	14650	72	94	6.59	69.8	201	900	4.5	8	8	2	52

POCHMAN, OWEN — K/P — GIANTS

PERSONAL: Born August 2, 1977, in Renton, Wash. ... 6-0/180.
HIGH SCHOOL: Mercer Island (Wash.).
COLLEGE: Brigham Young.
TRANSACTIONS/CAREER NOTES: Selected by New England Patriots in seventh round (216th pick overall) of 2001 NFL draft. ... Signed by Patriots (July 13, 2001). ... Claimed on waivers by New York Giants (September 3, 2001).
PRO STATISTICS: 2001—Attempted two field goals.

			PUNTING				
Year Team	G	No.	Yds.	Avg.	Net avg.	In. 20	Blk.
2001—New York Giants NFL	10	5	146	29.2	24.8	3	0

POLK, CARLOS — LB — CHARGERS

PERSONAL: Born February 22, 1977, in Memphis, Tenn. ... 6-2/250. ... Full name: Carlos Devonn Polk.
HIGH SCHOOL: Guilford (Rockford, Ill.).
COLLEGE: Nebraska (degree in sociology).
TRANSACTIONS/CAREER NOTES: Selected by San Diego Chargers in fourth round (112th pick overall) of 2001 NFL draft. ... Signed by Chargers (June 20, 2001). ... On injured reserve with shoulder injury (November 14, 2001-remainder of season).
PLAYING EXPERIENCE: San Diego NFL, 2001. ... Games/Games started: 2001 (6/0).
HONORS: Named linebacker on THE SPORTING NEWS college All-America third team (2000).

POLK, DaSHON — LB — BILLS

PERSONAL: Born March 13, 1977, in Pacoima, Calif. ... 6-2/240. ... Full name: DaShon Lamor Polk.
HIGH SCHOOL: Taft (Calif.).
COLLEGE: Arizona.
TRANSACTIONS/CAREER NOTES: Selected by Buffalo Bills in seventh round (251st pick overall) of 2000 NFL draft. ... Signed by Bills (June 22, 2000).
PLAYING EXPERIENCE: Buffalo NFL, 2000 and 2001. ... Games/Games started: 2000 (5/0), 2001 (16/1). Total: 21/1.

POLLARD, MARCUS — TE — COLTS

PERSONAL: Born February 8, 1972, in Valley, Ala. ... 6-3/248. ... Full name: Marcus LaJuan Pollard.
HIGH SCHOOL: Valley (Ala.).
JUNIOR COLLEGE: Seward County Community College, Kan. (did not play football).
COLLEGE: Bradley (did not play football).
TRANSACTIONS/CAREER NOTES: Signed as non-drafted free agent by Indianapolis Colts (January 24, 1995). ... Released by Colts (August 22, 1995). ... Re-signed by Colts to practice squad (August 28, 1995). ... Activated (October 10, 1995). ... Granted free agency (February 13, 1998). ... Tendered offer sheet by Philadelphia Eagles (March 4, 1998). ... Offer matched by Colts (March 9, 1998). ... Designated by Colts as franchise player (February 22, 2001).
CHAMPIONSHIP GAME EXPERIENCE: Played in AFC championship game (1995 season).
PRO STATISTICS: 1996—Recovered one fumble. 1998—Returned one kickoff for four yards.
SINGLE GAME HIGHS (regular season): Receptions—6 (September 13, 1998, vs. New England); yards—126 (November 18, 2001, vs. New Orleans); and touchdown receptions—2 (October 10, 1999, vs. Miami).
STATISTICAL PLATEAUS: 100-yard receiving games: 2001 (2).

			RECEIVING				TOTALS			
Year Team	G	GS	No.	Yds.	Avg.	TD	TD	2pt.	Pts.	Fum.
1995—Indianapolis NFL	8	0	0	0	0.0	0	0	0	0	0
1996—Indianapolis NFL	16	4	6	86	14.3	1	1	0	6	0
1997—Indianapolis NFL	16	5	10	116	11.6	0	0	1	2	0
1998—Indianapolis NFL	16	11	24	309	12.9	4	4	†2	28	0
1999—Indianapolis NFL	16	12	34	374	11.0	4	4	0	24	2
2000—Indianapolis NFL	16	11	30	439	14.6	3	3	1	20	0
2001—Indianapolis NFL	16	16	47	739	15.7	8	8	0	48	0
Pro totals (7 years)	104	59	151	2063	13.7	20	20	4	128	2

POLLEY, TOMMY — LB — RAMS

PERSONAL: Born January 11, 1978, in Baltimore. ... 6-3/240.
HIGH SCHOOL: Dunbar (Baltimore).
COLLEGE: Florida State.
TRANSACTIONS/CAREER NOTES: Selected by St. Louis Rams in second round (42nd pick overall) of 2001 NFL draft. ... Signed by Rams (July 23, 2001).
PLAYING EXPERIENCE: St. Louis NFL, 2001. ... Games/Games started: 2001 (16/11).
CHAMPIONSHIP GAME EXPERIENCE: Played in NFC championship game (2001 season). ... Played in Super Bowl XXXVI (2001 season).
HONORS: Named linebacker on THE SPORTING NEWS college All-America third team (2000).

POOLE, KEITH — WR — BUCCANEERS

PERSONAL: Born June 18, 1974, in San Jose, Calif. ... 6-0/193. ... Full name: Keith Robert Strohmaier Poole.
HIGH SCHOOL: Clovis (Calif.).
COLLEGE: Arizona State.
TRANSACTIONS/CAREER NOTES: Selected by New Orleans Saints in fourth round (116th pick overall) of 1997 NFL draft. ... Signed by Saints (June 10, 1997). ... Released by Saints (June 4, 2001). ... Signed by Denver Broncos (June 11, 2001). ... Released by Broncos (September 2, 2001). ... Re-signed by Broncos (September 12, 2001). ... Released by Broncos (December 24, 2001). ... Signed by Tampa Bay Buccaneers (March 22, 2002).
PRO STATISTICS: 1999—Rushed once for 14 yards. 2000—Recovered one fumble.
SINGLE GAME HIGHS (regular season): Receptions—6 (January 2, 2000, vs. Carolina); yards—154 (October 18, 1998, vs. Atlanta); and touchdown receptions—2 (October 18, 1998, vs. Atlanta).
STATISTICAL PLATEAUS: 100-yard receiving games: 1998 (1), 1999 (1). Total: 2.

				RECEIVING				TOTALS		
Year Team	G	GS	No.	Yds.	Avg.	TD	TD	2pt.	Pts.	Fum.
1997—New Orleans NFL	3	0	4	98	24.5	2	2	0	12	0
1998—New Orleans NFL	15	4	24	509	21.2	2	2	0	12	0
1999—New Orleans NFL	15	15	42	796	19.0	6	6	0	36	0
2000—New Orleans NFL	15	4	21	293	14.0	1	1	0	6	1
2001—Denver NFL	6	3	5	38	7.6	0	0	0	0	0
Pro totals (5 years)	54	26	96	1734	18.1	11	11	0	66	1

POPE, DANIEL — P

PERSONAL: Born March 28, 1975, in Alpharetta, Ga. ... 5-10/203.
HIGH SCHOOL: Milton (Alpharetta, Ga.).
COLLEGE: Alabama.
TRANSACTIONS/CAREER NOTES: Signed as non-drafted free agent by Detroit Lions (April 23, 1999). ... Released by Lions (August 26, 1999). ... Signed by Kansas City Chiefs (August 27, 1999). ... Claimed on waivers by Cincinnati Bengals (July 20, 2000). ... Released by Bengals (September 2, 2001). ... Signed by New York Jets (September 26, 2001). ... Released by Jets (October 2, 2001). ... Re-signed by Jets (February 28, 2002). ... Released by Jets (April 26, 2002).
PRO STATISTICS: 1999—Rushed once for no yards, fumbled once and recovered one fumble for minus 11 yards. 2000—Rushed twice for 22 yards, fumbled once and recovered one fumble for minus 19 yards.

			PUNTING				
Year Team	G	No.	Yds.	Avg.	Net avg.	In. 20	Blk.
1999—Kansas City NFL	16	101	4218	41.8	35.1	20	†2
2000—Cincinnati NFL	16	94	3775	40.2	33.1	18	0
2001—New York Jets NFL	1	4	153	38.3	36.3	2	0
Pro totals (3 years)	33	199	8146	40.9	34.2	40	2

POPE, MARQUEZ — DB

PERSONAL: Born October 29, 1970, in Nashville. ... 5-11/205. ... Full name: Marquez Phillips Pope. ... Name pronounced MAR-kez.
HIGH SCHOOL: Long Beach (Calif.) Polytechnic.
COLLEGE: Fresno State (degree in speech and mass communication, 1998).
TRANSACTIONS/CAREER NOTES: Selected by San Diego Chargers in second round (33rd pick overall) of 1992 NFL draft. ... Signed by Chargers (July 16, 1992). ... On non-football illness list with virus (September 1-28, 1992). ... On practice squad (September 28-November 7, 1992). ... Traded by Chargers to Los Angeles Rams for sixth-round pick (G Troy Sienkiewicz) in 1995 draft (April 11, 1994). ... Granted free agency (February 17, 1995). ... Tendered offer sheet by San Francisco 49ers (April 9, 1995). ... Rams declined to match offer (April 12, 1995); received second-round pick (OL Jesse James) in 1995 draft as compensation. ... Granted unconditional free agency (February 12, 1999). ... Signed by Cleveland Browns (March 8, 1999). ... Released by Browns (February 18, 2000). ... Signed by Oakland Raiders (May 22, 2000). ... Released by Raiders (February 27, 2002).
CHAMPIONSHIP GAME EXPERIENCE: Played in NFC championship game (1997 season). ... Played in AFC championship game (2000 season).
PRO STATISTICS: 1993—Credited with 1/2 sack. 1996—Recovered one fumble for four yards. 2000—Credited with one sack and recovered five fumbles for minus two yards.

			INTERCEPTIONS			
Year Team	G	GS	No.	Yds.	Avg.	TD
1992—San Diego NFL	7	0	0	0	0.0	0
1993—San Diego NFL	16	1	2	14	7.0	0
1994—Los Angeles Rams NFL	16	16	3	66	22.0	0
1995—San Francisco NFL	16	16	1	-7	-7.0	0
1996—San Francisco NFL	16	16	6	98	16.3	1
1997—San Francisco NFL	5	5	1	7	7.0	0
1998—San Francisco NFL	6	3	1	0	0.0	0
1999—Cleveland NFL	16	15	2	15	7.5	0
2000—Oakland NFL	15	14	2	25	12.5	0
2001—Oakland NFL	16	12	1	22	22.0	0
Pro totals (10 years)	129	98	19	240	12.6	1

PORCHER, ROBERT — DE — LIONS

PERSONAL: Born July 30, 1969, in Wando, S.C. ... 6-3/282. ... Full name: Robert Porcher III. ... Name pronounced por-SHAY.
HIGH SCHOOL: Cainhoy (Huger, S.C.).
COLLEGE: Tennessee State, then South Carolina State (degree in criminal justice).
TRANSACTIONS/CAREER NOTES: Selected by Detroit Lions in first round (26th pick overall) of 1992 NFL draft. ... Signed by Lions (July 25, 1992). ... Granted unconditional free agency (February 16, 1996). ... Re-signed by Lions (March 29, 1996). ... Granted unconditional free agency (February 14, 1997). ... Re-signed by Lions (March 4, 1997). ... Designated by Lions as franchise player (February 10, 2000).

HONORS: Played in Pro Bowl (1999 season).
PRO STATISTICS: 1994—Recovered one fumble. 1996—Recovered two fumbles. 1997—Intercepted one pass for five yards. 2000—Recovered one fumble.
MISCELLANEOUS: Holds Detroit Lions all-time record most touchdown sacks (85.5).

Year—Team	G	GS	SACKS
1992—Detroit NFL	16	1	1.0
1993—Detroit NFL	16	4	8.5
1994—Detroit NFL	15	15	3.0
1995—Detroit NFL	16	16	5.0
1996—Detroit NFL	16	16	10.0
1997—Detroit NFL	16	15	12.5
1998—Detroit NFL	16	16	11.5
1999—Detroit NFL	15	14	15.0
2000—Detroit NFL	16	16	8.0
2001—Detroit NFL	16	16	11.0
Pro totals (10 years)	**158**	**129**	**85.5**

PORTER, ALVIN   DB   RAVENS

PERSONAL: Born May 10, 1977, in Shreveport, La. ... 5-11/175. ... Full name: Alvin Guy Porter.
HIGH SCHOOL: Adamson (Dallas).
COLLEGE: Oklahoma State.
TRANSACTIONS/CAREER NOTES: Signed as non-drafted free agent by Baltimore Ravens (April 27, 2001).
PLAYING EXPERIENCE: Baltimore NFL, 2001. ... Games/Games started: (16/0).
PRO STATISTICS: 2001—Intercepted one pass for minus three yards.

PORTER, DARYL   CB

PERSONAL: Born January 16, 1974, in Fort Lauderdale, Fla. ... 5-9/190. ... Full name: Daryl Maurice Porter. ... Cousin of Bennie Blades, safety with Detroit Lions (1988-96) and Seattle Seahawks (1997); and cousin of Brian Blades, wide receiver with Seattle Seahawks (1988-98).
HIGH SCHOOL: St. Thomas Aquinas (Fort Lauderdale, Fla.).
COLLEGE: Boston College.
TRANSACTIONS/CAREER NOTES: Selected by Pittsburgh Steelers in sixth round (186th pick overall) of 1997 NFL draft. ... Signed by Steelers (June 6, 1997). ... Released by Steelers (August 19, 1997). ... Re-signed by Steelers to practice squad (August 26, 1997). ... Released by Steelers (October 20, 1997). ... Signed by Detroit Lions (October 21, 1997). ... Released by Lions (August 24, 1998). ... Signed by Steelers to practice squad (September 1, 1998). ... Signed by Buffalo Bills off Steelers practice squad (December 16, 1998). ... Granted free agency (March 2, 2001). ... Signed by Miami Dolphins (March 15, 2001). ... Released by Dolphins (September 2, 2001). ... Signed by Tennessee Titans (September 13, 2001). ... Granted unconditional free agency (March 1, 2002). ... Signed by New England Patriots (May 8, 2002).
PLAYING EXPERIENCE: Detroit NFL, 1997; Buffalo NFL, 1998-2000; Tennessee NFL, 2001. ... Games/Games started: 1997 (7/0), 1998 (2/0), 1999 (16/0), 2000 (16/0), 2001 (14/3). Total: 55/3.
PRO STATISTICS: 1999—Returned two kickoffs for 41 yards. 2000—Caught one pass for 44 yards, intercepted one pass for no yards and recovered two fumbles for 54 yards and one touchdown. 2001—Recovered two fumbles.

PORTER, JERRY   WR   RAIDERS

PERSONAL: Born July 14, 1978, in Washington, D.C. ... 6-2/225.
HIGH SCHOOL: Coolidge (Washington, D.C.).
COLLEGE: West Virginia.
TRANSACTIONS/CAREER NOTES: Selected by Oakland Raiders in second round (47th pick overall) of 2000 NFL draft. ... Signed by Raiders (July 22, 2000).
PLAYING EXPERIENCE: Oakland NFL, 2000 and 2001. ... Games/Games started: 2000 (12/0), 2001 (15/1). Total: 27/1.
CHAMPIONSHIP GAME EXPERIENCE: Played in AFC championship game (2000 season).
PRO STATISTICS: 2000—Caught one pass for six yards. 2001—Rushed twice for 13 yards, caught 19 passes for 220 yards and ran 12 yards with lateral from punt return.
SINGLE GAME HIGHS (regular season): Receptions—4 (December 2, 2001, vs. Arizona); yards—53 (December 2, 2001, vs. Arizona); and touchdown receptions—0.

PORTER, JOEY   LB   STEELERS

PERSONAL: Born March 22, 1977, in Bakersfield, Calif. ... 6-3/249. ... Full name: Joey Eugene Porter.
HIGH SCHOOL: Foothills (Calif.).
COLLEGE: Colorado State.
TRANSACTIONS/CAREER NOTES: Selected by Pittsburgh Steelers in third round (73rd pick overall) of 1999 NFL draft. ... Signed by Steelers (July 30, 1999). ... Granted free agency (March 1, 2002). ... Re-signed by Steelers (May 7, 2002).
CHAMPIONSHIP GAME EXPERIENCE: Played in AFC championship game (2001 season).
PRO STATISTICS: 1999—Recovered two fumbles for 50 yards and one touchdown. 2000—Intercepted one pass, recovered one fumble for 32 yards and one touchdown and credited with a safety. 2001—Recovered one fumble.

Year—Team	G	GS	SACKS
1999—Pittsburgh NFL	16	0	2.0
2000—Pittsburgh NFL	16	16	10.5
2001—Pittsburgh NFL	15	15	9.0
Pro totals (3 years)	**47**	**31**	**21.5**

POSEY, JEFF — DE — TEXANS

PERSONAL: Born August 14, 1975, in Bassfield, Miss. ... 6-4/249.
HIGH SCHOOL: Greenville (Miss.).
JUNIOR COLLEGE: Pearl River Community College (Miss.).
COLLEGE: Southern Mississippi.
TRANSACTIONS/CAREER NOTES: Signed as non-drafted free agent by San Francisco 49ers (May 2, 1997) ... Released by 49ers (August 19, 1997). ... Re-signed by 49ers to practice squad (August 25, 1997). ... Granted free agency (March 2, 2001). ... Signed by Philadelphia Eagles (June 18, 2001). ... Released by Eagles (August 31, 2001). ... Signed by Carolina Panthers (October 23, 2001). ... Claimed on waivers by Jacksonville Jaguars (November 21, 2001). ... Granted unconditional free agency (March 1, 2002). ... Signed by Houston Texans (April 19, 2002).
PLAYING EXPERIENCE: San Francisco NFL, 1998-2000; Carolina (4)-Jacksonville (7) NFL, 2001. ... Games/Games started: 1998 (16/0), 1999 (16/6), 2000 (16/8), 2001 (Car.-4/0; Jac.-7/5; Total: 11/5). Total: 59/19.
PRO STATISTICS: 1998—Credited with $1/2$ sack. 1999—Credited with two sacks. 2000—Credited with $1/2$ sack and recovered one fumble.

POTEAT, HANK — CB — STEELERS

PERSONAL: Born August 30, 1977, in Philadelphia. ... 5-10/198. ... Full name: Henry Major Poteat II.
HIGH SCHOOL: Harrisburg (Pa.).
COLLEGE: Pittsburgh.
TRANSACTIONS/CAREER NOTES: Selected by Pittsburgh Steelers in third round (77th pick overall) of 2000 NFL draft. ... Signed by Steelers (July 21, 2000).
CHAMPIONSHIP GAME EXPERIENCE: Member of Steelers for AFC championship game (2001 season); inactive.
PRO STATISTICS: 2001—Recovered two fumbles.

				INTERCEPTIONS			PUNT RETURNS				KICKOFF RETURNS				TOTALS			
Year Team	G	GS	No.	Yds.	Avg.	TD	No.	Yds.	Avg.	TD	No.	Yds.	Avg.	TD	TD	2pt.	Pts.	Fum.
2000—Pittsburgh NFL	15	0	0	0	0.0	0	36	467	13.0	1	24	465	19.4	0	1	0	6	3
2001—Pittsburgh NFL	13	0	0	0	0.0	0	36	292	8.1	0	16	250	15.6	0	0	0	0	4
Pro totals (2 years)	28	0	0	0	0.0	0	72	759	10.5	1	40	715	17.9	0	1	0	6	7

POWELL, CARL — DT — REDSKINS

PERSONAL: Born January 4, 1974, in Detroit. ... 6-2/264. ... Full name: Carl Demetris Powell.
HIGH SCHOOL: Northern (Detroit).
JUNIOR COLLEGE: Grand Rapids (Mich.) Community College.
COLLEGE: Louisville.
TRANSACTIONS/CAREER NOTES: Selected by Indianapolis Colts in fifth round (156th pick overall) of 1997 NFL draft. ... Signed by Colts (July 3, 1997). ... Released by Colts (August 28, 1998). ... Selected by Rhein Fire in 1999 NFL Europe draft (February 23, 1999). ... Signed by Baltimore Ravens (July 21, 2000). ... Released by Ravens (November 13, 2000). ... Signed by Chicago Bears (March 5, 2001). ... Granted unconditional free agency (March 1, 2002). ... Signed by Washington Redskins (March 28, 2002).
PLAYING EXPERIENCE: Indianapolis NFL, 1997; Rhein NFLE, 1999; Barcelona NFLE, 2000; Baltimore NFL, 2000; Chicago NFL, 2001. ... Games/Games started: 1997 (11/0), NFLE 1999 (games played unavailable), NFLE 2000 (-), NFL 2000 (2/0), 2001 (16/0). Total NFL: 29/0.
PRO STATISTICS: NFLE: 2000—Credited with one sack. 2001—Returned one kickoff for one yard.

PRENTICE, TRAVIS — RB — TEXANS

PERSONAL: Born December 8, 1976, in Louisville, Ky. ... 5-11/221. ... Full name: Travis Jason Prentice.
HIGH SCHOOL: Manual (Louisville, Ky.).
COLLEGE: Miami of Ohio.
TRANSACTIONS/CAREER NOTES: Selected by Cleveland Browns in third round (63rd pick overall) of 2000 NFL draft. ... Signed by Browns (July 16, 2000). ... Traded by Browns with QB Spergon Wynn to Minnesota Vikings for pick in 2002 draft (LB Andra Davis) and pick in 2003 draft (September 2, 2001). ... Claimed on waivers by Houston Texans (May 2, 2002).
HONORS: Named running back on THE SPORTING NEWS college All-America second team (1998 and 1999).
PRO STATISTICS: 2001—Returned one kickoff for two yards and recovered one fumble.
SINGLE GAME HIGHS (regular season): Attempts—28 (Ocotober 8, 2000, vs. Arizona); yards—97 (October 8, 2000, vs. Arizona); and rushing touchdowns—3 (October 8, 2000, vs. Arizona).

			RUSHING				RECEIVING				TOTALS			
Year Team	G	GS	Att.	Yds.	Avg.	TD	No.	Yds.	Avg.	TD	TD	2pt.	Pts.	Fum.
2000—Cleveland NFL	16	11	173	512	3.0	7	37	191	5.2	1	8	0	48	2
2001—Minnesota NFL	14	0	14	13	0.9	2	1	10	10.0	0	2	0	12	1
Pro totals (2 years)	30	11	187	525	2.8	9	38	201	5.3	1	10	0	60	3

PRICE, MARCUS — OT — BILLS

PERSONAL: Born March 3, 1972, in Port Arthur, Texas. ... 6-4/314. ... Full name: Marcus Raymond Price.
HIGH SCHOOL: Lincoln (Port Arthur, Texas).
COLLEGE: Louisiana State.
TRANSACTIONS/CAREER NOTES: Selected by Jacksonville Jaguars in sixth round (172nd pick overall) of 1995 NFL draft. ... Signed by Jaguars (June 1, 1995). ... On injured reserve with ankle injury (August 19, 1995-entire season). ... Released by Jaguars (August 25, 1996). ... Signed by Denver Broncos to practice squad (December 3, 1996). ... Released by Broncos (December 30, 1996). ... Signed by Jaguars (January 31, 1997). ... Released by Jaguars (August 19, 1997). ... Re-signed by Jaguars to practice squad (October 28, 1997). ... Signed by San Diego Chargers off Jaguars practice squad (November 26, 1997). ... Released by Chargers (September 21, 1999). ... Signed by New Orleans Saints (March 23, 2000). ... Released by Saints (December 3, 2000). ... Re-signed by Saints (December 5, 2000). ... Granted unconditional free agency (March 1, 2002). ... Signed by Buffalo Bills (March 13, 2002).
PLAYING EXPERIENCE: San Diego NFL, 1997 and 1998; New Orleans NFL, 2000 and 2001. ... Games/Games started: 1997 (2/0), 1998 (10/0), 2000 (7/0), 2001 (12/0). Total: 31/0.

PRICE, PEERLESS — WR — BILLS

PERSONAL: Born October 27, 1976, in Dayton, Ohio. ... 5-11/190. ... Full name: Peerless LeCross Price.
HIGH SCHOOL: Meadowdale (Dayton, Ohio).
COLLEGE: Tennessee.
TRANSACTIONS/CAREER NOTES: Selected by Buffalo Bills in second round (53rd pick overall) of 1999 NFL draft. ... Signed by Bills (July 30, 1999).
PRO STATISTICS: 2000—Fumbled four times and recovered one fumble. 2001—Fumbled twice and recovered one fumble.
SINGLE GAME HIGHS (regular season): Receptions—10 (November 18, 2001, vs. Seattle); yards—151 (October 28, 2001, vs. San Diego); and touchdown receptions—1 (December 30, 2001, vs. New York Jets).
STATISTICAL PLATEAUS: 100-yard receiving games: 1999 (1), 2000 (1), 2001 (3). Total: 5.

				RUSHING				RECEIVING				PUNT RETURNS				KICKOFF RETURNS				TOTALS		
Year	Team	G	GS	Att.	Yds.	Avg.	TD	No.	Yds.	Avg.	TD	No.	Yds.	Avg.	TD	No.	Yds.	Avg.	TD	TD	2pt.	Pts.
1999—Buffalo NFL		16	4	1	-7	-7.0	0	31	393	12.7	3	1	16	16.0	0	1	27	27.0	0	3	0	18
2000—Buffalo NFL		16	16	2	32	16.0	0	52	762	14.7	3	5	27	5.4	0	0	0	0.0	0	3	0	18
2001—Buffalo NFL		16	16	6	97	16.2	0	55	895	16.3	7	19	110	5.8	0	0	0	0.0	0	7	0	42
Pro totals (3 years)		48	36	9	122	13.6	0	138	2050	14.9	13	25	153	6.1	0	1	27	27.0	0	13	0	78

PRICE, SHAWN — DE

PERSONAL: Born March 28, 1970, in Van Nuys, Calif. ... 6-4/290. ... Full name: Shawn Sterling Price.
HIGH SCHOOL: North Tahoe (Nev.).
JUNIOR COLLEGE: Sierra College (Calif.).
COLLEGE: Pacific.
TRANSACTIONS/CAREER NOTES: Signed as non-drafted free agent by Tampa Bay Buccaneers (April 29, 1993). ... Released by Buccaneers (August 30, 1993). ... Re-signed by Buccaneers to practice squad (August 31, 1993). ... Activated (November 5, 1993). ... Selected by Carolina Panthers from Buccaneers in NFL expansion draft (February 15, 1995). ... Granted unconditional free agency (February 16, 1996). ... Signed by Buffalo Bills (April 12, 1996). ... Granted unconditional free agency (February 13, 1998). ... Re-signed by Bills (March 9, 1998). ... Granted unconditional free agency (March 2, 2001). ... Re-signed by Bills (April 27, 2001). ... On injured reserve with knee injury (January 4, 2001-remainder of season). ... Granted unconditional free agency (March 1, 2002).

Year Team	G	GS	SACKS
1993—Tampa Bay NFL	9	6	3.0
1994—Tampa Bay NFL	6	0	0.0
1995—Carolina NFL	16	0	1.0
1996—Buffalo NFL	15	0	0.0
1997—Buffalo NFL	10	0	0.0
1998—Buffalo NFL	14	2	5.0
1999—Buffalo NFL	15	1	2.5
2000—Buffalo NFL	13	6	1.0
2001—Buffalo NFL	11	11	2.0
Pro totals (9 years)	109	26	14.5

PRINCE, RYAN — TE — JAGUARS

PERSONAL: Born May 16, 1977, in Provo, Utah. ... 6-4/265. ... Full name: Ryan Scott Prince.
HIGH SCHOOL: Davis (Farmington, Utah).
COLLEGE: Weber State.
TRANSACTIONS/CAREER NOTES: Signed as non-drafted free agent by Jacksonville Jaguars (April 23, 2001).
PLAYING EXPERIENCE: Jacksonville NFL, 2001. ... Games/Games started: (8/2).
PRO STATISTICS: 2001—Returned one kickoff for four yards.

PRINGLEY, MIKE — DE

PERSONAL: Born May 22, 1976, in Linden, N.J. ... 6-4/277. ... Full name: Michael Charles Pringley.
HIGH SCHOOL: Linden (N.J.).
COLLEGE: North Carolina.
TRANSACTIONS/CAREER NOTES: Selected by Detroit Lions in seventh round (215th pick overall) of 1999 NFL draft. ... Signed by Lions (July 22, 1999). ... Released by Lions (September 19, 2000). ... Signed by San Diego Chagers (December 13, 2000). ... Released by Chargers (November 16, 2001).
PLAYING EXPERIENCE: Detroit NFL, 1999; San Diego NFL, 2000 and 2001. ... Games/Games started: 1999 (9/0), 2000 (2/0), 2001 (1/0). Total: 12/0.
PRO STATISTICS: 1999—Credited with 1 1/2 sacks.

PRIOLEAU, PIERSON — CB — BILLS

PERSONAL: Born August 6, 1977, in Alvin, S.C. ... 5-11/190. ... Full name: Pierson Olin Prioleau. ... Name pronounced pray-LOW.
HIGH SCHOOL: Macedonia (Saint Stephens, S.C.).
COLLEGE: Virginia Tech.
TRANSACTIONS/CAREER NOTES: Selected by San Francisco 49ers in fourth round (110th pick overall) of 1999 NFL draft. ... Signed by 49ers (July 27, 1999). ... Released by 49ers (September 2, 2001). ... Signed by Buffalo Bills (November 7, 2001). ... Granted free agency (March 1, 2002).
PLAYING EXPERIENCE: San Francisco NFL, 1999 and 2000; Buffalo NFL, 2001. ... Games/Games started: 1999 (14/5), 2000 (13/5), 2001 (6/2). Total: 33/12.
HONORS: Named strong safety on THE SPORTING NEWS college All-America third team (1997).
PRO STATISTICS: 1999—Returned three kickoffs for 73 yards. 2000—Intercepted one pass for 13 yards. 2001—Credited with one sack.

PRITCHETT, KELVIN — DT — LIONS

PERSONAL: Born October 24, 1969, in Atlanta. ... 6-3/319. ... Full name: Kelvin Bratodd Pritchett.
HIGH SCHOOL: Therrell (Atlanta).
COLLEGE: Mississippi.
TRANSACTIONS/CAREER NOTES: Selected by Dallas Cowboys in first round (20th pick overall) of 1991 NFL draft. ... Rights traded by Cowboys to Detroit Lions for second- (LB Dixon Edwards), third- (G James Richards) and fourth-round (DE Tony Hill) picks in 1991 draft (April 21, 1991). ... Granted free agency (February 17, 1994). ... Re-signed by Lions (August 12, 1994). ... Granted unconditional free agency (February 17, 1995). ... Signed by Jacksonville Jaguars (March 11, 1995). ... On injured reserve with knee injury (November 4, 1997-remainder of season). ... Granted unconditional free agency (February 12, 1999). ... Signed by Lions (April 22, 1999). ... Granted unconditional free agency (February 11, 2000). ... Re-signed by Lions (May 12, 2000). ... Granted unconditional free agency (March 2, 2001). ... Re-signed by Lions (July 11, 2001). ... Granted unconditional free agency (March 1, 2002). ... Re-signed by Lions (March 26, 2002).
CHAMPIONSHIP GAME EXPERIENCE: Played in NFC championship game (1991 season). ... Played in AFC championship game (1996 season).
PRO STATISTICS: 1994—Recovered one fumble. 1996—Recovered two fumbles. 1997—Recovered one fumble. 2000—Intercepted one pass for 78 yards.

Year Team	G	GS	SACKS
1991—Detroit NFL	16	0	1.5
1992—Detroit NFL	16	15	6.5
1993—Detroit NFL	16	5	4.0
1994—Detroit NFL	16	15	5.5
1995—Jacksonville NFL	16	16	1.5
1996—Jacksonville NFL	13	4	2.0
1997—Jacksonville NFL	8	5	3.0
1998—Jacksonville NFL	15	9	3.0
1999—Detroit NFL	16	2	1.0
2000—Detroit NFL	15	0	2.5
2001—Detroit NFL	16	1	0.0
Pro totals (11 years)	**163**	**72**	**30.5**

PRITCHETT, STANLEY — FB — BEARS

PERSONAL: Born December 22, 1973, in Atlanta. ... 6-2/242. ... Full name: Stanley Jerome Pritchett.
HIGH SCHOOL: Frederick Douglass (College Park, Ga.).
COLLEGE: South Carolina.
TRANSACTIONS/CAREER NOTES: Selected by Miami Dolphins in fourth round (118th pick overall) of 1996 NFL draft. ... Signed by Dolphins (July 10, 1996). ... Granted free agency (February 12, 1999). ... Re-signed by Dolphins (April 13, 1999). ... Granted unconditional free agency (February 11, 2000). ... Signed by Philadelphia Eagles (March 9, 2000). ... Released by Eagles (September 2, 2001). ... Signed by Chicago Bears (October 17, 2001).
PRO STATISTICS: 1996—Recovered one fumble. 1998—Recovered one fumble. 2000—Returned one kickoff for 15 yards.
SINGLE GAME HIGHS (regular season): Attempts—17 (December 12, 1999, vs. New York Jets); yards—68 (December 12, 1999, vs. New York Jets); and rushing touchdowns—1 (October 15, 2000, vs. Arizona).

			RUSHING				RECEIVING				TOTALS			
Year Team	G	GS	Att.	Yds.	Avg.	TD	No.	Yds.	Avg.	TD	TD	2pt.	Pts.	Fum.
1996—Miami NFL	16	16	7	27	3.9	0	33	354	10.7	2	2	0	12	3
1997—Miami NFL	6	5	3	7	2.3	0	5	35	7.0	0	0	0	0	0
1998—Miami NFL	16	12	6	19	3.2	1	17	97	5.7	0	1	0	6	0
1999—Miami NFL	14	7	47	158	3.4	1	43	312	7.3	4	5	0	30	0
2000—Philadelphia NFL	16	2	58	225	3.9	1	25	193	7.7	0	1	0	6	1
2001—Chicago NFL	7	0	0	0	0.0	0	0	0	0.0	0	0	0	0	0
Pro totals (6 years)	**75**	**42**	**121**	**436**	**3.6**	**3**	**123**	**991**	**8.1**	**6**	**9**	**0**	**54**	**4**

PROEHL, RICKY — WR — RAMS

PERSONAL: Born March 7, 1968, in Bronx, N.Y. ... 6-0/190. ... Full name: Richard Scott Proehl.
HIGH SCHOOL: Hillsborough (Belle Mead, N.J.).
COLLEGE: Wake Forest.
TRANSACTIONS/CAREER NOTES: Selected by Phoenix Cardinals in third round (58th pick overall) of 1990 NFL draft. ... Signed by Cardinals (July 23, 1990). ... Granted free agency (March 1, 1993). ... Tendered offer sheet by New England Patriots (April 13, 1993). ... Offer matched by Cardinals (April 19, 1993). ... Cardinals franchise renamed Arizona Cardinals for 1994 season. ... Traded by Cardinals to Seattle Seahawks for fourth-round pick (traded to New York Jets) in 1995 draft (April 3, 1995). ... Released by Seahawks (March 7, 1997). ... Signed by Chicago Bears (April 10, 1997). ... Granted unconditional free agency (February 13, 1998). ... Signed by St. Louis Rams (February 25, 1998). ... Granted unconditional free agency (March 1, 2002). ... Re-signed by Rams (April 2, 2002).
CHAMPIONSHIP GAME EXPERIENCE: Played in NFC championship game (1999 and 2001 seasons). ... Member of Super Bowl championship team (1999 season). ... Played in Super Bowl XXXVI (2001 season).
PRO STATISTICS: 1990—Returned one punt for two yards and returned four kickoffs for 53 yards. 1991—Returned four punts for 26 yards and recovered one fumble. 1992—Had only pass attempt intercepted and fumbled five times. 1993—Fumbled once. 1994—Fumbled twice and recovered two fumbles. 1997—Returned eight punts for 59 yards. 2000—Returned one kickoff for two yards.
SINGLE GAME HIGHS (regular season): Receptions—11 (November 16, 1997, vs. New York Jets); yards—164 (November 27, 1997, vs. Detroit); and touchdown receptions—2 (January 6, 2002, vs. Atlanta).
STATISTICAL PLATEAUS: 100-yard receiving games: 1990 (2), 1991 (1), 1992 (3), 1993 (1), 1997 (3), 1998 (1), 2001 (1). Total: 12.

				RUSHING				RECEIVING			TOTALS			
Year Team	G	GS	Att.	Yds.	Avg.	TD	No.	Yds.	Avg.	TD	TD	2pt.	Pts.	Fum.
1990—Phoenix NFL	16	2	1	4	4.0	0	56	802	14.3	4	4	0	24	0
1991—Phoenix NFL	16	16	3	21	7.0	0	55	766	13.9	2	2	0	12	0
1992—Phoenix NFL	16	15	3	23	7.7	0	60	744	12.4	3	3	0	18	5
1993—Phoenix NFL	16	16	8	47	5.9	0	65	877	13.5	7	7	0	42	1
1994—Arizona NFL	16	16	0	0	0.0	0	51	651	12.8	5	5	0	30	2
1995—Seattle NFL	8	0	0	0	0.0	0	5	29	5.8	0	0	0	0	0
1996—Seattle NFL	16	7	0	0	0.0	0	23	309	13.4	2	2	0	12	0
1997—Chicago NFL	15	10	0	0	0.0	0	58	753	13.0	7	7	1	44	2
1998—St. Louis NFL	16	10	1	14	14.0	0	60	771	12.9	3	3	1	20	0
1999—St. Louis NFL	15	2	0	0	0.0	0	33	349	10.6	0	0	0	0	0
2000—St. Louis NFL	12	4	0	0	0.0	0	31	441	14.2	4	4	0	24	0
2001—St. Louis NFL	16	3	1	5	5.0	0	40	563	14.1	5	5	1	32	0
Pro totals (12 years)	178	101	17	114	6.7	0	537	7055	13.1	42	42	3	258	10

PRYCE, TREVOR — DT — BRONCOS

PERSONAL: Born August 3, 1975, in Brooklyn, N.Y. ... 6-5/295.
HIGH SCHOOL: Lake Howell (Casselberry, Fla.).
COLLEGE: Clemson.
TRANSACTIONS/CAREER NOTES: Selected by Denver Broncos in first round (28th pick overall) of 1997 NFL draft. ... Signed by Broncos (July 24, 1997).
CHAMPIONSHIP GAME EXPERIENCE: Played in AFC championship game (1997 and 1998 seasons). ... Member of Super Bowl championship team (1997 and 1998 seasons).
HONORS: Played in Pro Bowl (1999 and 2000 seasons).
PRO STATISTICS: 1998—Intercepted one pass for one yard. 1999—Intercepted one pass for no yards, credited with a safety and recovered one fumble. 2000—Recovered one fumble for 28 yards and a touchdown.

Year Team	G	GS	SACKS
1997—Denver NFL	8	3	2.0
1998—Denver NFL	16	15	8.5
1999—Denver NFL	15	15	13.0
2000—Denver NFL	16	16	12.0
2001—Denver NFL	16	16	7.0
Pro totals (5 years)	71	65	42.5

PYNE, JIM — OL — COLTS

PERSONAL: Born November 23, 1971, in Milford, Conn. ... 6-2/297. ... Full name: James M. Pyne. ... Son of George Pyne III, tackle with Boston Patriots of AFL (1965); and grandson of George Pyne Jr., tackle with Providence Steamrollers of NFL (1931).
HIGH SCHOOL: Choate Prep (Wallingford, Conn.), then Milford (Mass.).
COLLEGE: Virginia Tech.
TRANSACTIONS/CAREER NOTES: Selected by Tampa Bay Buccaneers in seventh round (200th pick overall) of 1994 NFL draft. ... Signed by Buccaneers (July 14, 1994). ... On injured reserve with broken leg (December 17, 1996-remainder of season). ... Granted free agency (February 14, 1997). ... Re-signed by Buccaneers (April 18, 1997). ... Granted unconditional free agency (February 13, 1998). ... Signed by Detroit Lions (February 21, 1998). ... Selected by Cleveland Browns from Lions in NFL expansion draft (February 9, 1999). ... On injured reserve with knee injury (September 11, 2000-remainder of season). ... Released by Browns (August 22, 2001). ... Signed by Philadelphia Eagles (August 31, 2001). ... Granted unconditional free agency (March 1, 2002). ... Signed by Indianapolis Colts (April 27, 2002).
PLAYING EXPERIENCE: Tampa Bay NFL, 1995-1997; Detroit NFL, 1998; Cleveland NFL, 1999 and 2000; Philadelphia NFL, 2001. ... Games/Games started: 1995 (15/13), 1996 (12/11), 1997 (15/14), 1998 (16/16), 1999 (16/16), 2000 (2/2), 2001 (5/1). Total: 81/73.
CHAMPIONSHIP GAME EXPERIENCE: Member of Eagles for NFC championship game (2001 season); did not play.
HONORS: Named offensive lineman on THE SPORTING NEWS college All-America first team (1993).
PRO STATISTICS: 1995—Recovered one fumble. 1997—Fumbled once for minus five yards.

QUARLES, SHELTON — LB — BUCCANEERS

PERSONAL: Born September 11, 1971, in Nashville. ... 6-1/225. ... Full name: Shelton Eugene Quarles.
HIGH SCHOOL: Whites Creek (Tenn.).
COLLEGE: Vanderbilt (degree in human and organized development).
TRANSACTIONS/CAREER NOTES: Signed as non-drafted free agent by Miami Dolphins (April 29, 1994). ... Released by Dolphins (August 15, 1994). ... Signed by B.C. Lions of CFL (December 1, 1994). ... Granted free agency (February 16, 1997). ... Signed by Tampa Bay Buccaneers (March 21, 1997).
PLAYING EXPERIENCE: B.C. CFL, 1995 and 1996; Tampa Bay NFL, 1997-2001. ... Games/Games started: 1995 (16/games started unavailable), 1996 (16/-), 1997 (16/0), 1998 (16/0), 1999 (16/14), 2000 (14/13), 2001 (16/16). Total CFL: 32/-. Total NFL: 78/43. Total Pro: 110/-.
CHAMPIONSHIP GAME EXPERIENCE: Played in NFC championship game (1999 season).
PRO STATISTICS: 1995—Intercepted one pass for no yards and recovered one fumble for 14 yards. 1996—Credited with 10 sacks and intercepted one pass for 22 yards. 1997—Recovered two fumbles. 1998—Credited with one sack. 1999—Recovered one fumble. 2000—Intercepted one pass for five yards, credited with two sacks and recovered two fumbles for five yards. 2001—Intercepted one pass for 98 yards and a touchdown and credited with two sacks.

QUINN, JONATHAN — QB — CHIEFS

PERSONAL: Born February 27, 1975, in Turlock, Calif. ... 6-6/239. ... Full name: Jonathan Ryan Quinn.
HIGH SCHOOL: McGavock (Nashville).
COLLEGE: Tulane, then Middle Tennessee State (degree in business administration, 1997).
TRANSACTIONS/CAREER NOTES: Selected by Jacksonville Jaguars in third round (86th pick overall) of 1998 NFL draft. ... Signed by Jaguars (May 19, 1998). ... Active for one game (1999); did not play. ... Assigned by Jaguars to Berlin Thunder in 2001 NFL Europe enhancement allocation program (February 19, 2001). ... Granted unconditional free agency (March 1, 2002). ... Signed by Kansas City Chiefs (May 1, 2002).
CHAMPIONSHIP GAME EXPERIENCE: Member of Jaguars for AFC championship game (1999 season); inactive.

PRO STATISTICS: 1998—Fumbled three times. 2001—Fumbled four times.
SINGLE GAME HIGHS (regular season): Attempts—31 (November 18, 2001, vs. Pittsburgh); completions—17 (November 18, 2001, vs. Pittsburgh); yards—225 (November 18, 2001, vs. Pittsburgh); and touchdown passes—1 (September 30, 2001, vs. Cleveland).
MISCELLANEOUS: Regular-season record as starting NFL quarterback: 1-2 (.333).

					PASSING						RUSHING				TOTALS	
Year Team	G	GS	Att.	Cmp.	Pct.	Yds.	TD	Int.	Avg.	Rat.	Att.	Yds.	Avg.	TD	TD	2pt.	Pts.
1998—Jacksonville NFL	4	2	64	34	53.1	387	2	3	6.05	62.4	11	77	7.0	1	1	0	6
1999—Jacksonville NFL								Did not play.									
2000—Jacksonville NFL	2	0	0	0	0.0	0	0	0	0.0	...	2	-2	-1.0	0	0	0	0
2001—Berlin NFLE	...	...	296	167	56.4	2257	24	9	7.63	95.2	33	112	3.4	0	0	0	0
—Jacksonville NFL	6	1	61	32	52.5	361	1	1	5.92	69.1	8	42	5.3	0	0	0	0
NFL Europe totals (1 year)	...	...	296	167	56.4	2257	24	9	7.63	95.2	33	112	3.4	0	0	0	0
NFL totals (3 years)	12	3	125	66	52.8	748	3	4	5.98	65.7	21	117	5.6	1	1	0	6
Pro totals (4 years)	...	...	421	233	55.3	3005	27	13	7.14	86.5	54	229	4.2	1	1	0	6

RABACH, CASEY — C — RAVENS

PERSONAL: Born September 24, 1977, in Sturgeon Bay, Wis. ... 6-4/301.
HIGH SCHOOL: Sturgeon Bay (Wis.).
COLLEGE: Wisconsin.
TRANSACTIONS/CAREER NOTES: Selected by Baltimore Ravens in third round (92nd pick overall) of 2001 NFL draft. ... Signed by Ravens (July 21, 2001). ... Active for two games (2001); did not play.

RACKERS, NEIL — K — BENGALS

PERSONAL: Born August 16, 1976, in Florissant, Mo. ... 6-0/205. ... Full name: Neil W. Rackers.
HIGH SCHOOL: Aquinas-Mercy (Florissant, Mo.).
COLLEGE: Illinois (degree in speech communication.).
TRANSACTIONS/CAREER NOTES: Selected by Cincinnati Bengals in sixth round (169th pick overall) of 2000 NFL draft. ... Signed by Bengals (July 21, 2000).
PRO STATISTICS: 2000—Rushed once for minus five yards. 2001—Punted once for 32 yards.

		KICKING					
Year Team	G	XPM	XPA	FGM	FGA	Lg.	50+	Pts.
2000—Cincinnati NFL	16	21	21	12	21	45	0-0	57
2001—Cincinnati NFL	16	23	24	17	28	52	1-2	74
Pro totals (2 years)	32	44	45	29	49	52	1-2	131

RACKLEY, DEREK — TE — FALCONS

PERSONAL: Born July 18, 1977, in Apple Valley, Minn. ... 6-4/250.
HIGH SCHOOL: Apple Valley (Minn.).
COLLEGE: Minnesota.
TRANSACTIONS/CAREER NOTES: Signed as non-drafted free agent by Atlanta Falcons (April 17, 2000).
PLAYING EXPERIENCE: Atlanta NFL, 2000 and 2001. ... Games/Games started: 2000 (16/0), 2001 (16/0). Total: 32/0.
PRO STATISTICS: 2001—Caught one pass for one yard and a touchdown.
SINGLE GAME HIGHS (regular season): Receptions—1 (December 30, 2001, vs. Miami); yards—1 (December 30, 2001, vs. Miami); and touchdown receptions—1 (December 30, 2001, vs. Miami).

RAINER, WALI — LB — JAGUARS

PERSONAL: Born April 19, 1977, in Rockingham, N.C. ... 6-2/245. ... Full name: Wali Rashid Rainer.
HIGH SCHOOL: West Charlotte (N.C.).
COLLEGE: Virginia.
TRANSACTIONS/CAREER NOTES: Selected by Cleveland Browns in fourth round (124th pick overall) of 1999 NFL draft. ... Signed by Browns (July 22, 1999). ... Granted free agency (March 1, 2002). ... Re-signed by Browns (April 20, 2002). ... Traded by Browns with third-round pick (traded to Washington) in 2002 draft to Jacksonville Jaguars for third-round pick (C Melvin Fowler) in 2002 draft (April 20, 2002).
PLAYING EXPERIENCE: Cleveland NFL, 1999-2001. ... Games/Games started: 1999 (16/15), 2000 (16/16), 2001 (14/13). Total: 46/44.
PRO STATISTICS: 1999—Credited with one sack. 2000—Credited with one sack, intercepted one pass for five yards and recovered one fumble. 2001—Credited with one sack and recovered one fumble.

RAIOLA, DOMINIC — C — LIONS

PERSONAL: Born December 30, 1978, in Honolulu, Hawaii. ... 6-1/303.
HIGH SCHOOL: St. Louis (Honolulu, Hawaii).
COLLEGE: Nebraska (degree in communication studies).
TRANSACTIONS/CAREER NOTES: Selected by Detroit Lions in second round (50th pick overall) of 2001 NFL draft. ... Signed by Lions (July 23, 2001).
PLAYING EXPERIENCE: Detroit NFL, 2001. ... Games/Games started: (16/0).
HONORS: Named center on THE SPORTING NEWS college All-America second team (2000).
PRO STATISTICS: 2001—Returned one kickoff for 11 yards.

RAMBO, KEN-YON   WR   COWBOYS

PERSONAL: Born October 4, 1978, in Cerritos, Calif. ... 6-1/195.
HIGH SCHOOL: Polytechnic (Long Beach, Calif.).
COLLEGE: Ohio State.
TRANSACTIONS/CAREER NOTES: Selected by Oakland Raiders in seventh round (229th pick overall) of 2001 NFL draft. ... Signed by Raiders (July 21, 2001). ... Released by Raiders (August 28, 2001). ... Signed by Dallas Cowboys (September 5, 2001).
SINGLE GAME HIGHS (regular season): Receptions—1 (December 30, 2001, vs. San Francisco); yards—14 (December 9, 2001, vs. New York Giants); and touchdown receptions—0.

			RECEIVING			PUNT RETURNS			KICKOFF RETURNS			TOTALS		
Year Team	G	GS	No.	Yds.	Avg.	TD	No.	Yds.	Avg.	TD	No.	Yds.	Avg.	TD	TD	2pt.	Pts.	Fum.
2001—Dallas NFL	13	0	3	28	9.3	0	2	15	7.5	0	2	30	15.0	0	0	0	0	0

RANDLE, JOHN   DT   SEAHAWKS

PERSONAL: Born December 12, 1967, in Hearne, Texas. ... 6-1/287. ... Brother of Ervin Randle, linebacker with Tampa Bay Buccaneers (1985-90) and Kansas City Chiefs (1991 and 1992).
HIGH SCHOOL: Hearne (Texas).
JUNIOR COLLEGE: Trinity Valley Community College (Texas).
COLLEGE: Texas A&I.
TRANSACTIONS/CAREER NOTES: Signed as non-drafted free agent by Minnesota Vikings (May 4, 1990). ... Designated by Vikings as transition player (January 15, 1994). ... Designated by Vikings as transition player (February 13, 1998). ... Tendered offer sheet by Miami Dolphins (February 16, 1998). ... Offer matched by Vikings (February 18, 1998). ... Released by Vikings (March 1, 2001). ... Signed by Seattle Seahawks (March 3, 2001).
CHAMPIONSHIP GAME EXPERIENCE: Played in NFC championship game (1998 and 2000 seasons).
HONORS: Played in Pro Bowl (1993-1998 seasons). ... Named defensive tackle on THE SPORTING NEWS NFL All-Pro team (1994-1998).
PRO STATISTICS: 1992—Recovered one fumble. 1994—Recovered two fumbles. 1997—Recovered two fumbles for five yards. 1998—Recovered one fumble. 1999—Intercepted one pass for one yard and recovered three fumbles. 2001—Recovered one fumble in end zone for a touchdown.

Year Team	G	GS	SACKS
1990—Minnesota NFL	16	0	1.0
1991—Minnesota NFL	16	8	9.5
1992—Minnesota NFL	16	14	11.5
1993—Minnesota NFL	16	16	12.5
1994—Minnesota NFL	16	16	∞13.5
1995—Minnesota NFL	16	16	10.5
1996—Minnesota NFL	16	16	11.5
1997—Minnesota NFL	16	16	*15.5
1998—Minnesota NFL	16	16	10.5
1999—Minnesota NFL	16	16	10.0
2000—Minnesota NFL	16	16	8.0
2001—Seattle NFL	15	14	11.0
Pro totals (12 years)	191	164	125.0

RANSOM, DERRICK   DT   CHIEFS

PERSONAL: Born September 13, 1976, in Indianapolis. ... 6-3/310. ... Full name: Derrick Wayne Ransom Jr.
HIGH SCHOOL: Lawrence Central (Indianapolis).
COLLEGE: Cincinnati (degree in finance).
TRANSACTIONS/CAREER NOTES: Selected by Kansas City Chiefs in sixth round (181st pick overall) of 1998 NFL draft. ... Signed by Chiefs (June 3, 1998). ... Granted free agency (March 2, 2001). ... Re-signed by Chiefs (April 3, 2001). ... Granted unconditional free agency (March 1, 2002). ... Re-signed by Chiefs (April 3, 2002).
PLAYING EXPERIENCE: Kansas City NFL, 1998-2001. ... Games/Games started: 1998 (7/0), 1999 (10/0), 2000 (10/0), 2001 (16/16). Total: 43/16.
PRO STATISTICS: 1998—Returned one kickoff for no yards. 1999—Credited with one sack. 2001—Credited with three sacks and recovered one fumble.

RASBY, WALTER   TE   REDSKINS

PERSONAL: Born September 7, 1972, in Washington, D.C. ... 6-3/256. ... Full name: Walter Herbert Rasby.
HIGH SCHOOL: Washington (N.C.).
COLLEGE: Wake Forest.
TRANSACTIONS/CAREER NOTES: Signed as non-drafted free agent by Pittsburgh Steelers (April 29, 1994). ... Released by Steelers (August 27, 1995). ... Signed by Carolina Panthers (October 17, 1995). ... Granted free agency (February 14, 1997). ... Re-signed by Panthers (June 3, 1997). ... On injured reserve with knee injury (December 10, 1997-remainder of season). ... Granted unconditional free agency (February 13, 1998). ... Signed by Detroit Lions (April 13, 1998). ... Granted unconditional free agency (March 2, 2001). ... Signed by Washington Redskins (April 10, 2001).
CHAMPIONSHIP GAME EXPERIENCE: Played in AFC championship game (1994 season). ... Played in NFC championship game (1996 season).
PRO STATISTICS: 1996—Recovered one fumble. 1997—Returned three kickoffs for 32 yards. 2000—Recovered one fumble.
SINGLE GAME HIGHS (regular season): Receptions—5 (October 4, 1998, vs. Chicago); yards—45 (January 6, 2002, vs. Arizona); and touchdown receptions—1 (January 6, 2002, vs. Arizona).

			RECEIVING				TOTALS			
Year Team	G	GS	No.	Yds.	Avg.	TD	TD	2pt.	Pts.	Fum.
1994—Pittsburgh NFL	2	0	0	0	0.0	0	0	0	0	0
1995—Carolina NFL	9	2	5	47	9.4	0	0	1	2	0
1996—Carolina NFL	16	1	0	0	0.0	0	0	0	0	0
1997—Carolina NFL	14	2	1	1	1.0	0	0	0	0	0
1998—Detroit NFL	16	16	15	119	7.9	1	1	0	6	0
1999—Detroit NFL	16	6	3	19	6.3	1	1	0	6	0
2000—Detroit NFL	16	8	10	78	7.8	1	1	0	6	0
2001—Washington NFL	16	11	10	128	12.8	2	2	0	12	0
Pro totals (8 years)	105	46	44	392	8.9	5	5	1	32	0

RATTAY, TIM — QB — 49ERS

PERSONAL: Born March 15, 1977, in Elyria, Ohio. ... 6-0/215.
HIGH SCHOOL: Phoenix (Ariz.) Christian.
JUNIOR COLLEGE: Scottsdale (Ariz.) Community College.
COLLEGE: Louisiana Tech.
TRANSACTIONS/CAREER NOTES: Selected by San Francisco 49ers in seventh round (212th pick overall) of 2000 NFL draft. ... Signed by 49ers (July 16, 2000).
PRO STATISTICS: 2001—Fumbled once and recovered one fumble.
SINGLE GAME HIGHS (regular season): Attempts—2 (January 6, 2002, vs. New Orleans); completions—2 (January 6, 2002, vs. New Orleans); yards—21 (January 6, 2002, vs. New Orleans); and touchdown passes—0.

			PASSING						RUSHING				TOTALS		
Year Team	G	GS	Att.	Cmp.	Pct.	Yds.	TD	Int.	Avg.	Rat.	Att.	Yds.	Avg.	TD	TD	2pt.	Pts.
2000—San Francisco NFL	1	0	1	1	100.0	-4	0	0	-4.00	79.2	2	-1	-0.5	0	0	0	0
2001—San Francisco NFL	3	0	2	2	100.0	21	0	0	10.50	110.4	5	-3	-0.6	0	0	0	0
Pro totals (2 years)	4	0	3	3	100.0	17	0	0	5.67	90.3	7	-4	-0.6	0	0	0	0

RAYMER, CORY — C — CHARGERS

PERSONAL: Born March 3, 1973, in Fond du Lac, Wis. ... 6-3/300.
HIGH SCHOOL: Goodrich (Fond du Lac, Wis.).
COLLEGE: Wisconsin.
TRANSACTIONS/CAREER NOTES: Selected by Washington Redskins in second round (37th pick overall) of 1995 NFL draft. ... Signed by Redskins (July 24, 1995). ... On injured reserve with back injury (November 25, 1996-remainder of season). ... Granted unconditional free agency (February 12, 1999). ... Re-signed by Redskins (March 16, 1999). ... Granted unconditional free agency (February 11, 2000). ... Re-signed by Redskins (February 26, 2000). ... On injured reserve with knee injury (September 28, 2000-remainder of season). ... Granted unconditional free agency (March 1, 2002). ... Signed by San Diego Chargers (March 7, 2002).
PLAYING EXPERIENCE: Washington NFL, 1995-1999 and 2001. ... Games/Games started: 1995 (3/2), 1996 (6/5), 1997 (6/3), 1998 (16/16), 1999 (16/16), 2001 (16/16). Total: 63/58.
HONORS: Named offensive lineman on THE SPORTING NEWS college All-America first team (1994).
PRO STATISTICS: 1996—Recovered one fumble. 1998—Recovered one fumble. 1999—Recovered one fumble.

READER, JAMIE — FB — EAGLES

PERSONAL: Born May 4, 1974, in Washington, D.C. ... 6-0/238.
HIGH SCHOOL: Monessen (Pa.).
COLLEGE: Akron.
TRANSACTIONS/CAREER NOTES: Signed as non-drafted free agent by Arizona Cardinals (May 3, 1998). ... Claimed on waivers by Miami Dolphins (July 24, 1998). ... Released by Dolphins (August 30, 1998). ... Re-signed by Dolphins to practice squad (August 31, 1998). ... Assigned by Dolphins to Scottish Claymores in 1999 NFL Europe enhancement allocation program (February 22, 1999). ... Released by Dolphins (September 4, 1999). ... Signed by Philadelphia Eagles to practice squad (September 30, 1999). ... Released by Eagles (August 27, 2000). ... Signed by New York Jets (April 28, 2001). ... Claimed on waivers by Eagles (May 10, 2001).
PLAYING EXPERIENCE: Scottish NFLE, 1999; Philadelphia NFL, 2001. ... Games/Games started: 1999 (10/10), 2001 (16/0).
CHAMPIONSHIP GAME EXPERIENCE: Played in NFC championship game (2001 season).
PRO STATISTICS: 1999—Rushed 27 times for 43 yards and caught 16 passes for 187 yards. 2001—Caught two passes for 14 yards and recovered one fumble.

REAGOR, MONTAE — DE — BRONCOS

PERSONAL: Born June 29, 1977, in Waxahachie, Texas. ... 6-3/285. ... Full name: Willie Montae Reagor. ... Name pronounced MON-tay RAY-ger.
HIGH SCHOOL: Waxahachie (Texas).
COLLEGE: Texas Tech (degree in exercise and sports sciences).
TRANSACTIONS/CAREER NOTES: Selected by Denver Broncos in second round (58th pick overall) of 1999 NFL draft. ... Signed by Broncos (July 13, 1999).
PLAYING EXPERIENCE: Denver NFL, 1999-2001. ... Games/Games started: 1999 (9/0), 2000 (13/0), 2001 (8/0). Total: 30/0.
HONORS: Named defensive end on THE SPORTING NEWS college All-America second team (1997). ... Named defensive end on THE SPORTING NEWS college All-America first team (1998).
PRO STATISTICS: 2000—Credited with two sacks. 2001—Credited with one sack.

REDMAN, CHRIS — QB — RAVENS

PERSONAL: Born July 7, 1977, in Louisville, Ky. ... 6-3/223.
HIGH SCHOOL: Male (Louisville, Ky.).
COLLEGE: Louisville.
TRANSACTIONS/CAREER NOTES: Selected by Baltimore Ravens in third round (75th pick overall) of 2000 NFL draft. ... Signed by Ravens (July 24, 2000). ... Inactive for 14 games (2001).
PLAYING EXPERIENCE: Baltimore NFL, 2000. ... Games/Games started: 2000 (3/0).
CHAMPIONSHIP GAME EXPERIENCE: Member of Ravens for AFC Championship game (2000 season); inactive. ... Member of Super Bowl championship team (2000 season); inactive.
PRO STATISTICS: 2000—Attempted three passes with two completions for 19 yards and rushed once for no yards.
SINGLE GAME HIGHS (regular season): Attempts—3 (September 24, 2000, vs. Cincinnati); completions—2 (September 24, 2000, vs. Cincinnati); yards—19 (September 24, 2000, vs. Cincinnati); and touchdown passes—0.

REDMOND, J.R. — RB — PATRIOTS

PERSONAL: Born September 28, 1977, in Los Angeles. ... 5-11/215. ... Full name: Joseph Robert Redmond.
HIGH SCHOOL: Carson (Calif.).
COLLEGE: Arizona State.
TRANSACTIONS/CAREER NOTES: Selected by New England Patriots in third round (76th pick overall) of 2000 NFL draft. ... Signed by Patriots (July 23, 2000).
CHAMPIONSHIP GAME EXPERIENCE: Played in AFC championship game (2001 season). ... Member of Super Bowl championship team (2001 season).
PRO STATISTICS: 2000—Returned one kickoff for 25 yards. 2001—Reurned two kickoffs for 57 yards.
SINGLE GAME HIGHS (regular season): Attempts—24 (November 5, 2000, vs. Buffalo); yards—97 (October 22, 2000, vs. Indianapolis); and rushing touchdowns—1 (November 5, 2000 vs. Buffalo).

			RUSHING				RECEIVING				TOTALS			
Year Team	G	GS	Att.	Yds.	Avg.	TD	No.	Yds.	Avg.	TD	TD	2pt.	Pts.	Fum.
2000—New England NFL	12	6	125	406	3.2	1	20	126	6.3	2	3	0	18	2
2001—New England NFL	12	0	35	119	3.4	0	13	132	10.2	0	0	0	0	0
Pro totals (2 years)	24	6	160	525	3.3	1	33	258	7.8	2	3	0	18	2

REED, JAKE — WR — SAINTS

PERSONAL: Born September 28, 1967, in Covington, Ga. ... 6-3/213. ... Full name: Willis Reed. ... Brother of Dale Carter, cornerback, New Orleans Saints.
HIGH SCHOOL: Newton County (Covington, Ga.).
COLLEGE: Grambling (degree in criminal justice, 1990).
TRANSACTIONS/CAREER NOTES: Selected by Minnesota Vikings in third round (68th pick overall) of 1991 NFL draft. ... Signed by Vikings (July 22, 1991). ... On injured reserve with ankle injury (November 2, 1991-remainder of season). ... Granted free agency (February 17, 1994). ... Re-signed by Vikings (May 6, 1994). ... Granted unconditional free agency (February 17, 1995). ... Re-signed by Vikings (February 28, 1995). ... Released by Vikings (February 10, 2000). ... Signed by New Orleans Saints (February 21, 2000). ... Released by Saints (March 1, 2001). ... Signed by Vikings (March 27, 2001). ... Granted unconditional free agency (March 1, 2002). ... Signed by Saints (March 12, 2002).
CHAMPIONSHIP GAME EXPERIENCE: Member of Vikings for NFC championship game (1998 season); inactive.
PRO STATISTICS: 1992—Returned one kickoff for one yard. 1995—Recovered one fumble.
SINGLE GAME HIGHS (regular season): Receptions—12 (September 7, 1997, vs. Chicago); yards—157 (November 6, 1994, vs. New Orleans); and touchdown receptions—2 (November 1, 1998, vs. Tampa Bay).
STATISTICAL PLATEAUS: 100-yard receiving games: 1994 (3), 1995 (3), 1996 (3), 1997 (5), 1998 (1), 1999 (2). Total: 17.

			RECEIVING				TOTALS			
Year Team	G	GS	No.	Yds.	Avg.	TD	TD	2pt.	Pts.	Fum.
1991—Minnesota NFL	1	0	0	0	0.0	0	0	0	0	0
1992—Minnesota NFL	16	0	6	142	23.7	0	0	0	0	0
1993—Minnesota NFL	10	1	5	65	13.0	0	0	0	0	0
1994—Minnesota NFL	16	16	85	1175	13.8	4	4	0	24	3
1995—Minnesota NFL	16	16	72	1167	16.2	9	9	0	54	1
1996—Minnesota NFL	16	15	72	1320	18.3	7	7	0	42	0
1997—Minnesota NFL	16	16	68	1138	16.7	6	6	0	36	0
1998—Minnesota NFL	11	11	34	474	13.9	4	4	0	24	0
1999—Minnesota NFL	16	8	44	643	14.6	2	2	0	12	0
2000—New Orleans NFL	7	6	16	206	12.9	0	0	0	0	0
2001—Minnesota NFL	16	0	27	309	11.4	1	1	1	8	0
Pro totals (11 years)	141	89	429	6639	15.5	33	33	1	200	4

REED, JAMES — DT — JETS

PERSONAL: Born February 3, 1977, in Saginaw, Mich. ... 6-0/286. ... Full name: James Reed Jr.
HIGH SCHOOL: Saginaw (Mich.).
COLLEGE: Iowa State.
TRANSACTIONS/CAREER NOTES: Selected by New York Jets in seventh round (206th pick overall) of 2001 NFL draft. ... Signed by Jets (June 28, 2001).
PRO STATISTICS: 2001—Recovered one fumble.

Year Team	G	GS	SACKS
2001—New York Jets NFL	16	2	1.0

REESE, IKE — LB — EAGLES

PERSONAL: Born October 16, 1973, in Jacksonville, N.C. ... 6-2/222. ... Full name: Isaiah Reese.
HIGH SCHOOL: Woodward (Cincinnati), then Aiken (Cincinnati).
COLLEGE: Michigan State.
TRANSACTIONS/CAREER NOTES: Selected by Philadelphia Eagles in fifth round (142nd pick overall) of 1998 NFL draft. ... Signed by Eagles (July 14, 1998). ... Granted free agency (March 2, 2001). ... Re-signed by Eagles (March 20, 2001).
PLAYING EXPERIENCE: Philadelphia NFL, 1998-2001. ... Games/Games started: 1998 (16/0), 1999 (16/0), 2000 (16/0), 2001 (16/0). Total: 64/0.
CHAMPIONSHIP GAME EXPERIENCE: Member of Eagles for NFC championship game (2001 season); inactive.
PRO STATISTICS: 1999—Credited with three sacks. 2001—Ran minus 11 yards with lateral from kick return.

REESE, IZELL — S — BRONCOS

PERSONAL: Born May 7, 1974, in Dothan, Ala. ... 6-2/190.
HIGH SCHOOL: Northview (Dothan, Ala.).
COLLEGE: Alabama-Birmingham.
TRANSACTIONS/CAREER NOTES: Selected by Dallas Cowboys in sixth round (188th pick overall) of 1998 NFL draft. ... Signed by Cowboys (July 15, 1998). ... On injured reserve with neck injury (November 19, 1999-remainder of season). ... Granted free agency (March 2, 2001). ... Re-signed by Cowboys (April 30, 2001). ... Granted unconditional free agency (March 1, 2002). ... Signed by Denver Broncos (April 1, 2002).
PRO STATISTICS: 2000—Credited with one safety. 2001—Credited with three sacks.

				INTERCEPTIONS		
Year Team	G	GS	No.	Yds.	Avg.	TD
1998—Dallas NFL	16	0	1	6	6.0	0
1999—Dallas NFL	8	4	3	28	9.3	0
2000—Dallas NFL	16	7	2	60	30.0	0
2001—Dallas NFL	16	4	1	42	42.0	0
Pro totals (4 years)	56	15	7	136	19.4	0

REHBERG, SCOTT — G — BENGALS

PERSONAL: Born November 17, 1973, in Kalamazoo, Mich. ... 6-8/315. ... Full name: Scott Joseph Rehberg. ... Name pronounced RAY-berg.
HIGH SCHOOL: Central (Kalamazoo, Mich.).
COLLEGE: Central Michigan.
TRANSACTIONS/CAREER NOTES: Selected by New England Patriots in seventh round (230th pick overall) of 1997 NFL draft. ... Signed by Patriots (June 19, 1997). ... Selected by Cleveland Browns from Patriots in NFL expansion draft (February 9, 1999). ... Granted free agency (February 11, 2000). ... Signed by Cincinnati Bengals (March 2, 2000).
PLAYING EXPERIENCE: New England NFL, 1997 and 1998; Cleveland NFL, 1999; Cincinnati NFL, 2000 and 2001. ... Games/Games started: 1997 (6/0), 1998 (2/0), 1999 (15/13), 2000 (10/6), 2001 (15/4). Total: 48/23.
PRO STATISTICS: 1999—Recovered one fumble.

REYES, TUTAN — OT — SAINTS

PERSONAL: Born October 28, 1977, in Queens, N.Y. ... 6-3/299.
HIGH SCHOOL: August Martin (Queens, N.Y.).
COLLEGE: Mississippi.
TRANSACTIONS/CAREER NOTES: Selected by New Orleans Saints in fifth round (131st pick overall) of 2000 NFL draft. ... Signed by Saints (July 14, 2000). ... Inactive for all 16 games (2000).
PLAYING EXPERIENCE: New Orleans NFL, 2001. ... Games/Games started: (1/0).

REYNOLDS, JAMAL — DE — PACKERS

PERSONAL: Born February 20, 1979, in Aiken, S.C. ... 6-3/266.
HIGH SCHOOL: Aiken (S.C.).
COLLEGE: Florida State.
TRANSACTIONS/CAREER NOTES: Selected by Green Bay Packers in first round (10th pick overall) of 2001 NFL draft. ... Signed by Packers (July 25, 2001).
HONORS: Named defensive end on THE SPORTING NEWS college All-America first team (2000). ... Lombardi Trophy winner (2000).

Year Team	G	GS	SACKS
2001—Green Bay NFL	6	0	2.0

RHINEHART, COBY — CB — CARDINALS

PERSONAL: Born February 7, 1977, in Dallas. ... 5-11/191. ... Full name: Jacoby M. Rhinehart.
HIGH SCHOOL: Tyler Street Christian Academy (Dallas).
COLLEGE: Southern Methodist.
TRANSACTIONS/CAREER NOTES: Selected by Arizona Cardinals in sixth round (190th pick overall) of 1999 NFL draft. ... Signed by Cardinals (June 18, 1999). ... On injured reserve with knee injury (August 22, 2000-entire season). ... Granted free agency (March 1, 2002).
PLAYING EXPERIENCE: Arizona NFL, 1999 and 2001. ... Games/Games started: 1999 (16/0), 2001 (13/0). Total: 29/0.

RHODES, DOMINIC — RB — COLTS

PERSONAL: Born January 17, 1979, in Waco, Texas. ... 5-9/208. ... Full name: Dominic Dondrell Rhodes.
HIGH SCHOOL: Cooper (Texas).
JUNIOR COLLEGE: Tyler Junior College.
COLLEGE: Midwestern State.
TRANSACTIONS/CAREER NOTES: Signed as non-drafted free agent by Indianapolis Colts (April 22, 2001).
SINGLE GAME HIGHS (regular season): Attempts—34 (November 4, 2001, vs. Buffalo); yards—177 (December 16, 2001, vs. Atlanta); and rushing touchdowns—2 (December 16, 2001, vs. Atlanta).
STATISTICAL PLATEAUS: 100-yard rushing games: 2001 (5).

				RUSHING				RECEIVING				KICKOFF RETURNS				TOTALS		
Year Team	G	GS	Att.	Yds.	Avg.	TD	No.	Yds.	Avg.	TD	No.	Yds.	Avg.	TD	TD	2pt.	Pts.	Fum.
2001—Indianapolis NFL	15	10	233	1104	4.7	9	34	224	6.6	0	14	356	25.4	1	10	0	60	6

RICARD, ALAN — FB — RAVENS

PERSONAL: Born January 17, 1977, in Independence, La. ... 5-11/237.
HIGH SCHOOL: Amite (La.).
COLLEGE: Northeast Louisiana.
TRANSACTIONS/CAREER NOTES: Signed as non-drafted free agent by Dallas Cowboys (April 30, 1999). ... Released by Cowboys (August 4, 1999). ... Signed by Baltimore Ravens (July 21, 2000). ... Released by Ravens (August 26, 2000). ... Re-signed by Ravens to practice squad (August 29, 2000).
PLAYING EXPERIENCE: Baltimore NFL, 2001. ... Games/Games started: (5/0).

RICE, JERRY — WR — RAIDERS

PERSONAL: Born October 13, 1962, in Starkville, Miss. ... 6-2/196. ... Full name: Jerry Lee Rice.
HIGH SCHOOL: Crawford MS Moor (Crawford, Miss.).
COLLEGE: Mississippi Valley State.
TRANSACTIONS/CAREER NOTES: Selected by Birmingham Stallions in first round (first pick overall) of 1985 USFL draft. ... Selected by San Francisco 49ers in first round (16th pick overall) of 1985 NFL draft. ... Signed by 49ers (July 23, 1985). ... Granted free agency (February 1, 1992). ... Re-signed by 49ers (August 25, 1992). ... On injured reserve with knee injury (December 23, 1997-remainder of season). ... Released by 49ers (June 4, 2001). ... Signed by Oakland Raiders (June 5, 2001).
CHAMPIONSHIP GAME EXPERIENCE: Played in NFC championship game (1988-1990 and 1992-1994 seasons). ... Member of Super Bowl championship team (1988, 1989 and 1994 seasons).
HONORS: Named wide receiver on THE SPORTING NEWS college All-America first team (1984). ... Named wide receiver on THE SPORTING NEWS NFL All-Pro team (1986-1996). ... Played in Pro Bowl (1986, 1987, 1989-1993, 1995 and 1998 seasons). ... Named NFL Player of the Year by THE SPORTING NEWS (1987 and 1990). ... Named Most Valuable Player of Super Bowl XXIII (1988 season). ... Named to play in Pro Bowl (1988 season); replaced by J.T. Smith due to injury. ... Named to play in Pro Bowl (1994 season); replaced by Herman Moore due to injury. ... Named Outstanding Player of Pro Bowl (1995 season). ... Named to play in Pro Bowl (1996 season); replaced by Irving Fryar due to injury.
RECORDS: Holds NFL career records for most touchdowns—196; most touchdown receptions—185; most receiving yards—20,386; most pass receptions—1,364; most seasons with 1,000 or more yards receiving—13; most games with 100 or more yards receiving—68; most consecutive games with one or more receptions—241 (December 9, 1985-present); most consecutive games with one or more touchdown reception—13 (December 19, 1986-December 27, 1987); and most seasons with 50 or more receptions—14. ... Holds NFL single-season record for most yards receiving—1,848 (1995); and most touchdown receptions—22 (1987). ... Shares NFL single-game record for most touchdown receptions—5 (October 14, 1990, at Atlanta).
POST SEASON RECORDS: Holds Super Bowl career records for most points—42; most touchdowns—7; most touchdown receptions—7; most receptions—28; most combined yards—527; and most yards receiving—512. ... Holds Super Bowl single-game records for most touchdowns receptions—3 (January 22, 1990, vs. Denver and January 29, 1995, vs. San Diego); and most yards receiving—215 (January 22, 1989, vs. Cincinnati). ... Shares Super Bowl single-game records for most points—18; most touchdowns—3 (January 28, 1990, vs. Denver and January 29, 1995, vs. San Diego); and most receptions—11 (January 22, 1989, vs. Cincinnati). ... Holds NFL postseason career records for most touchdown receptions—20; most touchdowns—137; most yards receiving—2,042; and most games with 100 or more yards receiving—8. ... Holds NFL postseason record for most consecutive games with one or more receptions—25 (1985-present). ... Shares NFL postseason career record for most consecutive games with 100 or more yards receiving—3 (1988-89). ... Shares NFL postseason single-game record for most touchdown receptions—3 (January 28, 1990, vs. Denver; January 1, 1989, vs. Minnesota; and January 29, 1995, vs. San Diego).
PRO STATISTICS: 1985—Returned one kickoff for six yards. 1986—Attempted two passes with one completion for 16 yards and recovered three fumbles. 1987—Recovered one fumble. 1988—Attempted three passes with one completion for 14 yards and one interception and recovered one fumble. 1993—Recovered one fumble. 1995—Completed only pass attempt for 41 yards and a touchdown and recovered one fumble in end zone for a touchdown. 1996—Attempted one pass without a completion. 1999—Attempted one pass without a completion. 2000—Attempted one pass without a completion and recovered one fumble. 2001—Recovered one fumble.
SINGLE GAME HIGHS (regular season): Receptions—16 (November 20, 1994, vs. Los Angeles Rams); yards—289 (December 18, 1995, vs. Minnesota); and touchdown receptions—5 (October 14, 1990, vs. Atlanta).
STATISTICAL PLATEAUS: 100-yard receiving games: 1985 (2), 1986 (6), 1987 (4), 1988 (5), 1989 (8), 1990 (7), 1991 (4), 1992 (3), 1993 (5), 1994 (5), 1995 (9), 1996 (3), 1998 (3), 1999 (2), 2001 (2). Total: 68.
MISCELLANEOUS: Active NFL leader for career receptions (1,364), receiving yards (20,386), touchdown receptions (185) and touchdowns (196). ... Holds San Francisco 49ers all-time records for most yards receiving (19,248), most touchdowns (187), most receptions (1,281) and most touchdown receptions (176).

				RUSHING				RECEIVING				TOTALS		
Year Team	G	GS	Att.	Yds.	Avg.	TD	No.	Yds.	Avg.	TD	TD	2pt.	Pts.	Fum.
1985—San Francisco NFL	16	4	6	26	4.3	1	49	927	18.9	3	4	0	24	1
1986—San Francisco NFL	16	15	10	72	7.2	1	‡86	*1570	18.3	*15	16	0	96	2
1987—San Francisco NFL	12	12	8	51	6.4	1	65	1078	16.6	*22	*23	0	*138	2
1988—San Francisco NFL	16	16	13	107	8.2	1	64	1306	20.4	9	10	0	60	2
1989—San Francisco NFL	16	16	5	33	6.6	0	82	*1483	18.1	*17	17	0	102	0
1990—San Francisco NFL	16	16	2	0	0.0	0	*100	*1502	15.0	*13	13	0	78	1

– 313 –

Year Team	G	GS	RUSHING Att.	Yds.	Avg.	TD	RECEIVING No.	Yds.	Avg.	TD	TOTALS TD	2pt.	Pts.	Fum
1991—San Francisco NFL	16	16	1	2	2.0	0	80	1206	15.1	*14	14	0	84	1
1992—San Francisco NFL	16	16	9	58	6.4	1	84	1201	14.3	10	11	0	66	2
1993—San Francisco NFL	16	16	3	69	23.0	1	98	*1503	15.3	†15	*16	0	96	3
1994—San Francisco NFL	16	16	7	93	13.3	2	112	*1499	13.4	13	15	1	92	1
1995—San Francisco NFL	16	16	5	36	7.2	1	122	*1848	15.1	15	17	1	104	3
1996—San Francisco NFL	16	16	11	77	7.0	1	*108	1254	11.6	8	9	0	54	0
1997—San Francisco NFL	2	1	1	-10	-10.0	0	7	78	11.1	1	1	0	6	0
1998—San Francisco NFL	16	16	0	0	0.0	0	82	1157	14.1	9	9	†2	58	2
1999—San Francisco NFL	16	16	2	13	6.5	0	67	830	12.4	5	5	0	30	0
2000—San Francisco NFL	16	16	1	-2	-2.0	0	75	805	10.7	7	7	0	42	3
2001—Oakland NFL	16	15	0	0	0.0	0	83	1139	13.7	9	9	0	54	1
Pro totals (17 years)	254	239	84	625	7.4	10	1364	20386	14.9	185	196	4	1184	24

RICE, RON   S

PERSONAL: Born November 9, 1972, in Detroit. ... 6-1/217. ... Full name: Ronald Wilson Rice.
HIGH SCHOOL: University of Detroit Jesuit.
COLLEGE: Eastern Michigan (degree in criminal justice).
TRANSACTIONS/CAREER NOTES: Signed as non-drafted free agent by Detroit Lions (April 24, 1995). ... Released by Lions (August 18, 1995). ... Re-signed by Lions to practice squad (August 29, 1995). ... Activated (November 1, 1995); did not play. ... Granted free agency (February 13, 1998). ... Re-signed by Lions (June 25, 1998). ... On injured reserve with neck injury (November 20, 2001-remainder of season). ... Released by Lions (March 6, 2002).
PRO STATISTICS: 1999—Recovered one fumble. 2000—Recovered one fumble for six yards.

Year Team	G	GS	INTERCEPTIONS No.	Yds.	Avg.	TD	SACKS No.
1995—Detroit NFL			Did not play.				
1996—Detroit NFL	13	2	0	0	0.0	0	0.0
1997—Detroit NFL	12	8	1	18	18.0	0	1.0
1998—Detroit NFL	16	16	3	25	8.3	0	3.5
1999—Detroit NFL	16	16	5	82	16.4	0	1.0
2000—Detroit NFL	14	14	1	7	7.0	0	0.0
2001—Detroit NFL	8	8	2	9	4.5	0	1.0
Pro totals (6 years)	79	64	12	141	11.8	0	6.5

RICE, SIMEON   DE   BUCCANEERS

PERSONAL: Born February 24, 1974, in Chicago. ... 6-5/268. ... Name pronounced simm-ee-ON.
HIGH SCHOOL: Mount Carmel (Chicago).
COLLEGE: Illinois (degree in speech communications, 1996).
TRANSACTIONS/CAREER NOTES: Selected by Arizona Cardinals in first round (third pick overall) of 1996 NFL draft. ... Signed by Cardinals (August 19, 1996). ... Designated by Cardinals as franchise player (February 11, 2000). ... Re-signed by Cardinals (September 7, 2000). ... Granted unconditional free agency (March 2, 2001). ... Signed by Tampa Bay Buccaneers (March 23, 2001).
HONORS: Played in Pro Bowl (1999 season). ... Named linebacker on THE SPORTING NEWS college All-America second team (1995).
PRO STATISTICS: 1996—Recovered one fumble. 1997—Intercepted one pass for no yards. 1998—Recovered four fumbles for 39 yards. 1999—Recovered one fumble. 2000—Recovered one fumble.

Year Team	G	GS	SACKS
1996—Arizona NFL	16	15	12.5
1997—Arizona NFL	16	15	5.0
1998—Arizona NFL	16	16	10.0
1999—Arizona NFL	16	16	16.5
2000—Arizona NFL	15	11	7.5
2001—Tampa Bay NFL	16	16	11.0
Pro totals (6 years)	95	89	62.5

RICHARDSON, DAMIEN   S   PANTHERS

PERSONAL: Born April 3, 1976, in Los Angeles. ... 6-1/210. ... Full name: Damien A. Richardson.
HIGH SCHOOL: Clovis West (Fresno, Calif.).
COLLEGE: Arizona State.
TRANSACTIONS/CAREER NOTES: Selected by Carolina Panthers in sixth round (165th pick overall) of 1998 NFL draft. ... Signed by Panthers (July 24, 1998). ... Granted free agency (March 2, 2001). ... Re-signed by Panthers (March 2, 2001). ... Granted unconditional free agency (March 1, 2002). ... Re-signed by Panthers (March 25, 2002).
PLAYING EXPERIENCE: Carolina NFL, 1998-2001. ... Games/Games started: 1998 (14/7), 1999 (15/0), 2000 (16/1), 2001 (16/2). Total: 61/10.
PRO STATISTICS: 1998—Recovered one fumble. 1999—Intercepted one pass for 27 yards and credited with one sack.

RICHARDSON, KYLE   P   VIKINGS

PERSONAL: Born March 2, 1973, in Farmington, Mo. ... 6-2/210. ... Full name: Kyle Davis Richardson.
HIGH SCHOOL: Farmington (Mo.).
COLLEGE: Arkansas State.
TRANSACTIONS/CAREER NOTES: Played for Rhein Fire of World League (1996). ... Signed as non-drafted free agent by Miami Dolphins (September 3, 1997). ... Released by Dolphins (September 8, 1997). ... Re-signed by Dolphins (September 18, 1997). ... Released by Dolphins (October 7, 1997). ... Signed by Seattle Seahawks (November 12, 1997). ... Released by Seahawks (November 25, 1997). ... Signed by Baltimore Ravens (March 25, 1998). ... Granted free agency (March 2, 2001). ... Re-signed by Ravens for 2001 season. ... Granted unconditional free agency (March 1, 2002). ... Signed by Minnesota Vikings (April 21, 2002).

CHAMPIONSHIP GAME EXPERIENCE: Played in AFC championship game (2000 season). ... Member of Super Bowl championship team (2000 season).
PRO STATISTICS: 1997—Rushed once for no yards and fumbled once for minus 13 yards. 1998—Rushed once for no yards and recovered one fumble. 2001—Rushed once for no yards, completed only pass attempt for minus 11 yards, fumbled once and recovered two fumbles.

					PUNTING		
Year Team	G	No.	Yds.	Avg.	Net avg.	In. 20	Blk.
1996—Rhein W.L.				Statistics unavailable.			
1997—Miami NFL	3	11	480	43.6	33.1	0	0
—Seattle NFL	2	8	324	40.5	23.8	2	†2
1998—Baltimore NFL	16	90	3948	43.9	38.3	25	*2
1999—Baltimore NFL	16	103	4355	42.3	35.5	*39	1
2000—Baltimore NFL	16	86	3457	40.2	33.9	35	0
2001—Baltimore NFL	16	85	3309	38.9	33.6	§29	§2
NFL totals (5 years)	69	383	15873	41.4	35.1	130	7
Pro totals (5 years)	69	383	15873	41.4	35.1	130	7

RICHARDSON, TONY   FB   CHIEFS

PERSONAL: Born December 17, 1971, in Frankfurt, West Germany. ... 6-1/233. ... Full name: Antonio Richardson.
HIGH SCHOOL: Daleville (Ala.).
COLLEGE: Auburn.
TRANSACTIONS/CAREER NOTES: Signed as non-drafted free agent by Dallas Cowboys (April 28, 1994). ... Released by Cowboys (August 28, 1994). ... Re-signed by Cowboys to practice squad (August 30, 1994). ... Granted free agency after 1994 season. ... Signed by Kansas City Chiefs (February 28, 1995). ... On injured reserve with wrist injury (December 11, 1996-remainder of season).
PRO STATISTICS: 1996—Recovered one fumble. 1998—Returned one punt for no yards and recovered one fumble. 2001—Recovered one fumble.
SINGLE GAME HIGHS (regular season): Attempts—23 (December 17, 2000, vs. Denver); yards—156 (December 17, 2000, vs. Denver); and rushing touchdowns—2 (November 4, 2001, vs. San Diego).
STATISTICAL PLATEAUS: 100-yard rushing games: 2000 (1).

			RUSHING				RECEIVING				TOTALS		
Year Team	G	GS	Att.	Yds.	Avg.	TD	No.	Yds.	Avg.	TD	TD	2pt.	Pts.	Fum.
1995—Kansas City NFL	14	1	8	18	2.3	0	0	0	0.0	0	0	0	0	0
1996—Kansas City NFL	13	0	4	10	2.5	0	2	18	9.0	1	1	0	6	0
1997—Kansas City NFL	14	0	2	11	5.5	0	3	6	2.0	3	3	0	18	0
1998—Kansas City NFL	14	1	20	45	2.3	2	2	13	6.5	0	2	0	12	0
1999—Kansas City NFL	16	15	84	387	4.6	1	24	141	5.9	0	1	0	6	1
2000—Kansas City NFL	16	16	147	697	4.7	3	58	468	8.1	3	6	0	36	3
2001—Kansas City NFL	14	8	66	191	2.9	7	30	265	8.8	0	7	0	42	0
Pro totals (7 years)	101	41	331	1359	4.1	13	119	911	7.7	7	20	0	120	4

RICHEY, WADE   K   CHARGERS

PERSONAL: Born May 19, 1976, in Lafayette, La. ... 6-3/205. ... Full name: Wade Edward Richey.
HIGH SCHOOL: Carencro (Lafayette, La.).
COLLEGE: Louisiana State.
TRANSACTIONS/CAREER NOTES: Signed as non-drafted free agent by Seattle Seahawks (April 21, 1998). ... Claimed on waivers by San Francisco 49ers (August 26, 1998). ... Granted free agency (March 2, 2001). ... Tendered offer sheet by San Diego Chargers (April 13, 2001). ... 49ers declined to match offer (April 18, 2001).
PRO STATISTICS: 1999—Punted four times for 146 yards.

				KICKING				
Year Team	G	XPM	XPA	FGM	FGA	Lg.	50+	Pts.
1998—San Francisco NFL	16	49	51	18	27	46	0-0	103
1999—San Francisco NFL	16	30	31	21	23	52	1-1	93
2000—San Francisco NFL	16	43	45	15	22	47	0-1	88
2001—San Diego NFL	16	26	26	21	32	51	1-3	89
Pro totals (4 years)	64	148	153	75	104	52	2-5	373

RICKS, MIKHAEL   TE   LIONS

PERSONAL: Born November 14, 1974, in Galveston, Texas. ... 6-5/237. ... Full name: Mikhael Roy Ricks. ... Name pronounced Michael.
HIGH SCHOOL: Anahuac (Texas).
COLLEGE: Stephen F. Austin State.
TRANSACTIONS/CAREER NOTES: Selected by San Diego Chargers in second round (59th pick overall) of 1998 NFL draft. ... Signed by Chargers (July 23, 1998). ... Released by Chargers (October 3, 2000). ... Signed by Kansas City Chiefs (October 11, 2000). ... Granted unconditional free agency (March 1, 2002). ... Signed by Detroit Lions (April 17, 2002).
PRO STATISTICS: 1999—Rushed twice for 11 yards and attempted one pass without a completion. 2001—Credited with one safety.
SINGLE GAME HIGHS (regular season): Receptions—6 (October 24, 1999, vs. Green Bay); yards—86 (September 19, 1999, vs. Cincinnati); and touchdown receptions—1 (January 6, 2002, vs. Seattle).

			RECEIVING				TOTALS		
Year Team	G	GS	No.	Yds.	Avg.	TD	TD	2pt.	Pts.	Fum.
1998—San Diego NFL	16	9	30	450	15.0	2	2	0	12	1
1999—San Diego NFL	16	15	40	429	10.7	0	0	†1	2	0
2000—San Diego NFL	3	1	3	35	11.7	0	0	0	0	0
—Kansas City NFL	1	0	0	0	0	0	0	0	0	0
2001—Kansas City NFL	16	0	18	252	14.0	1	1	0	8	0
Pro totals (4 years)	52	25	91	1166	12.8	3	3	1	22	1

– 315 –

RIEMERSMA, JAY — TE — BILLS

PERSONAL: Born May 17, 1973, in Evansville, Ind. ... 6-5/252. ... Full name: Allen Jay Riemersma. ... Name pronounced REEM-urz-muh.
HIGH SCHOOL: Zeeland (Mich.).
COLLEGE: Michigan.
TRANSACTIONS/CAREER NOTES: Selected by Buffalo Bills in seventh round (244th pick overall) of 1996 NFL draft. ... Signed by Bills (July 9, 1996). ... Released by Bills (August 25, 1996). ... Re-signed by Bills to practice squad (August 26, 1996). ... Activated (October 15, 1996); did not play. ... Granted free agency (February 12, 1999). ... Re-signed by Bills (April 26, 1999). ... Granted unconditional free agency (February 11, 2000). ... Re-signed by Bills (February 15, 2000).
PRO STATISTICS: 1998—Returned one kickoff for nine yards and recovered one fumble.
SINGLE GAME HIGHS (regular season): Receptions—6 (December 30, 2001, vs. New York Giants); yards—86 (November 7, 1999, vs. Washington); and touchdown receptions—2 (September 10, 2000, vs. Green Bay).

				RECEIVING				TOTALS		
Year Team	G	GS	No.	Yds.	Avg.	TD	TD	2pt.	Pts.	Fum.
1996—Buffalo NFL						Did not play.				
1997—Buffalo NFL	16	8	26	208	8.0	2	2	1	14	1
1998—Buffalo NFL	16	3	25	288	11.5	6	6	0	36	0
1999—Buffalo NFL	14	11	37	496	13.4	4	4	0	24	0
2000—Buffalo NFL	12	12	31	372	12.0	5	5	0	30	1
2001—Buffalo NFL	16	15	53	590	11.1	3	3	0	18	0
Pro totals (5 years)	74	49	172	1954	11.4	20	20	1	122	2

RILEY, KARON — DE — BEARS

PERSONAL: Born August 23, 1978, in Detroit. ... 6-2/264.
HIGH SCHOOL: Martin Luther King (Detroit).
COLLEGE: Southern Methodist, then Minnesota.
TRANSACTIONS/CAREER NOTES: Selected by Chicago Bears in fourth round (103rd pick overall) of 2001 NFL draft. ... Signed by Bears (June 18, 2001).
PLAYING EXPERIENCE: Chicago NFL, 2001. ... Games/Games started: 2001 (5/0).
HONORS: Named defensive end on THE SPORTING NEWS college All-America third team (2000).

RILEY, VICTOR — OT — SAINTS

PERSONAL: Born November 4, 1974, in Swansea, S.C. ... 6-5/328. ... Full name: Victor Allan Riley.
HIGH SCHOOL: Swansea (S.C.).
COLLEGE: Auburn.
TRANSACTIONS/CAREER NOTES: Selected by Kansas City Chiefs in first round (27th pick overall) of 1998 NFL draft. ... Signed by Chiefs (July 2, 1998). ... Granted unconditional free agency (March 1, 2002). ... Signed by New Orleans Saints (April 4, 2002).
PLAYING EXPERIENCE: Kansas City NFL, 1998-2001. ... Games/Games started: 1998 (16/15), 1999 (16/16), 2000 (16/16), 2001 (7/5). Total: 55/52.
PRO STATISTICS: 1998—Recovered one fumble.

RITCHIE, JON — RB — RAIDERS

PERSONAL: Born September 4, 1974, in Mechanicsburg, Pa. ... 6-1/250.
HIGH SCHOOL: Cumberland Valley (Mechanicsburg, Pa.).
COLLEGE: Michigan, then Stanford.
TRANSACTIONS/CAREER NOTES: Selected by Oakland Raiders in third round (63rd pick overall) of 1998 NFL draft. ... Signed by Raiders (July 18, 1998).
CHAMPIONSHIP GAME EXPERIENCE: Played in AFC championship game (2000 season).
SINGLE GAME HIGHS (regular season): Attempts—2 (September 12, 1999, vs. Green Bay); yards—14 (November 15, 1998, vs. Seattle); and rushing touchdowns—0.

			RUSHING				RECEIVING				TOTALS		
Year Team	G	GS	Att.	Yds.	Avg.	TD	No.	Yds.	Avg.	TD	TD	2pt.	Pts.	Fum.
1998—Oakland NFL	15	10	9	23	2.6	0	29	225	7.8	0	0	0	0	2
1999—Oakland NFL	16	14	5	12	2.4	0	45	408	9.1	1	1	0	6	0
2000—Oakland NFL	13	12	0	0	0.0	0	26	173	6.7	0	0	0	0	0
2001—Oakland NFL	15	10	0	0	0.0	0	19	154	8.1	2	2	0	12	0
Pro totals (4 years)	59	46	14	35	2.5	0	119	960	8.1	3	3	0	18	2

RIVERA, MARCO — G — PACKERS

PERSONAL: Born April 26, 1972, in Brooklyn, N.Y. ... 6-4/310. ... Full name: Marco Anthony Rivera.
HIGH SCHOOL: Elmont (N.Y.) Memorial.
COLLEGE: Penn State (degree in administration of justice).
TRANSACTIONS/CAREER NOTES: Selected by Green Bay Packers in sixth round (208th pick overall) of 1996 NFL draft. ... Signed by Packers (July 15, 1996). ... Inactive for all 16 games (1996). ... Assigned by Packers to Scottish Claymores in 1997 World League enhancement allocation program (February 19, 1997). ... Granted free agency (February 12, 1999). ... Re-signed by Packers (March 24, 1999).
PLAYING EXPERIENCE: Scottish W.L., 1997, Green Bay NFL, 1997-2001. ... Games/Games started: W.L. 1997 (10/10), NFL 1997 (14/0), 1998 (15/15), 1999 (16/16), 2000 (16/16), 2001 (16/16). Total W.L.:10/10. Total NFL: 77/63. Total Pro: 87/73.
CHAMPIONSHIP GAME EXPERIENCE: Member of Packers for NFC championship game (1996 season); inactive. ... Member of Super Bowl championship team (1996 season); inactive. ... Played in NFC championship game (1997 season). ... Played in Super Bowl XXXII (1997 season).
PRO STATISTICS: 1999—Recovered one fumble. 2001—Recovered one fumble.

RIVERS, MARCELLUS   TE   GIANTS

PERSONAL: Born October 26, 1978, in Oklahoma City, Okla. ... 6-4/231.
HIGH SCHOOL: Douglass (Oklahoma City, Okla.).
COLLEGE: Oklahoma State.
TRANSACTIONS/CAREER NOTES: Signed as non-drafted free agent by New York Giants (April 27, 2001).
PLAYING EXPERIENCE: New York Giants NFL, 2001. ... Games/Games started: 2001 (16/0).
PRO STATISTICS: 2001—Caught three passes for 11 yards and two touchdowns and returned one kickoff for 11 yards.
SINGLE GAME HIGHS (regular season): Receptions—1 (December 30, 2001, vs. Philadelphia); yards—8 (December 30, 2001, vs. Philadelphia); and touchdown receptions—1 (December 9, 2001, vs. Dallas).

ROAF, WILLIE   OT   CHIEFS

PERSONAL: Born April 18, 1970, in Pine Bluff, Ark. ... 6-5/312. ... Full name: William Layton Roaf.
HIGH SCHOOL: Pine Bluff (Ark.).
COLLEGE: Louisiana Tech.
TRANSACTIONS/CAREER NOTES: Selected by New Orleans Saints in first round (eighth pick overall) of 1993 NFL draft. ... Signed by Saints (July 15, 1993). ... Designated by Saints as transition player (February 15, 1994). ... On injured reserve with knee injury (November 28, 2001-remainder of season). ... Traded by Saints to Kansas City Chiefs for fourth-round pick in 2003 draft (March 26, 2002).
PLAYING EXPERIENCE: New Orleans NFL, 1993-2001. ... Games/Games started: 1993 (16/16), 1994 (16/16), 1995 (16/16), 1996 (13/13), 1997 (16/16), 1998 (15/15), 1999 (16/16), 2000 (16/16), 2001 (7/7). Total: 131/131.
HONORS: Named offensive tackle on The Sporting News college All-America second team (1992). ... Named offensive tackle on The Sporting News NFL All-Pro team (1994-1996). ... Played in Pro Bowl (1994-1997, 1999 and 2000 seasons). ... Named to play in Pro Bowl (1998 season); replaced by Bob Whitfield due to injury.
PRO STATISTICS: 1994—Recovered one fumble. 1996—Recovered one fumble. 1999—Recovered one fumble.

ROBBINS, BARRET   C   RAIDERS

PERSONAL: Born August 26, 1973, in Houston. ... 6-3/320.
HIGH SCHOOL: Sharpstown (Houston).
COLLEGE: Texas Christian.
TRANSACTIONS/CAREER NOTES: Selected by Los Angeles Raiders in second round (49th pick overall) of 1995 NFL draft. ... Signed by Raiders (June 20, 1995). ... Raiders franchise moved to Oakland (July 21, 1995). ... On injured reserve with knee injury (September 26, 2001-remainder of season).
PLAYING EXPERIENCE: Oakland NFL, 1995-2001. ... Games/Games started: 1995 (16/0), 1996 (14/14), 1997 (16/16), 1998 (16/16), 1999 (16/16), 2000 (16/16), 2001 (2/2). Total: 96/80.
CHAMPIONSHIP GAME EXPERIENCE: Played in AFC championship game (2000 season).
PRO STATISTICS: 1996—Recovered one fumble. 1999—Recovered one fumble.

ROBBINS, FRED   DT   VIKINGS

PERSONAL: Born March 25, 1977, in Pensacola, Fla. ... 6-4/313. ... Full name: Fredrick Robbins.
HIGH SCHOOL: Tate (Gonzalez, Fla.).
COLLEGE: Wake Forest.
TRANSACTIONS/CAREER NOTES: Selected by Minnesota Vikings in second round (55th pick overall) of 2000 NFL draft. ... Signed by Vikings (July 21, 2000).
CHAMPIONSHIP GAME EXPERIENCE: Member of Vikings for NFC championship game (2000 season); inactive.

Year Team	G	GS	SACKS
2000—Minnesota NFL	8	0	1.0
2001—Minnesota NFL	16	12	2.0
Pro totals (2 years)	24	12	3.0

ROBERG, MIKE   TE   BUCCANEERS

PERSONAL: Born September 18, 1977, in Kent, Wash. ... 6-4/263.
HIGH SCHOOL: University (Spokane, Wash.).
COLLEGE: Idaho.
TRANSACTIONS/CAREER NOTES: Selected by Carolina Panthers in seventh round (227th pick overall) of 2001 NFL draft. ... Signed by Panthers (June 21, 2001). ... Claimed on waivers by Tampa Bay Buccaneers (August 29, 2001). ... Released by Buccaneers (September 2, 2001). ... Re-signed by Buccaneers to practice squad (September 3, 2001). ... Activated (December 4, 2001).
PLAYING EXPERIENCE: Tampa Bay NFL, 2001. ... Games/Games started: (1/0).

ROBERTSON, BERNARD   OT   BEARS

PERSONAL: Born June 9, 1979, in New Orleans. ... 6-3/308. ... Full name: Bernard Robertson Jr.
HIGH SCHOOL: Karr (New Orleans).
COLLEGE: Tulane.
TRANSACTIONS/CAREER NOTES: Selected by Chicago Bears in fifth round (138th pick overall) of 2001 NFL draft. ... Signed by Bears (July 17, 2001). ... Active for one game (2001); did not play.

ROBERTSON, MARCUS — S — SEAHAWKS

PERSONAL: Born October 2, 1969, in Pasadena, Calif. ... 5-11/211. ... Full name: Marcus Aaron Robertson.
HIGH SCHOOL: John Muir (Pasadena, Calif.).
COLLEGE: Iowa State.
TRANSACTIONS/CAREER NOTES: Selected by Houston Oilers in fourth round (102nd pick overall) of 1991 NFL draft. ... Signed by Oilers (July 16, 1991). ... On injured reserve with knee injury (December 30, 1993-remainder of season). ... Granted free agency (February 17, 1994). ... Re-signed by Oilers (July 11, 1994). ... On injured reserve with knee injury (November 30, 1995-remainder of season). ... Oilers franchise moved to Tennessee for 1997 season. ... Oilers franchise renamed Tennessee Titans for 1999 season (December 26, 1998). ... Granted unconditional free agency (February 11, 2000). ... Re-signed by Titans (February 22, 2000). ... Released by Titans (March 1, 2001). ... Signed by Seattle Seahawks (April 12, 2001).
CHAMPIONSHIP GAME EXPERIENCE: Played in AFC championship game (1999 season). ... Member of Titans for Super Bowl XXXIV (1999 season); inactive.
HONORS: Named free safety on THE SPORTING NEWS NFL All-Pro team (1993).
PRO STATISTICS: 1991—Credited with one sack, returned one punt for no yards and fumbled once. 1993—Recovered three fumbles for 107 yards and one touchdown. 1994—Returned one punt for no yards, fumbled once and recovered one fumble. 1996—Recovered one fumble for five yards. 1997—Returned one punt for no yards and recovered three fumbles for 67 yards and two touchdowns. 1999—Credited with ¹/₂ sack. 2000—Recovered one fumble.

				INTERCEPTIONS		
Year Team	G	GS	No.	Yds.	Avg.	TD
1991—Houston NFL	16	0	0	0	0.0	0
1992—Houston NFL	16	14	1	27	27.0	0
1993—Houston NFL	13	13	7	137	19.6	0
1994—Houston NFL	16	16	3	90	30.0	0
1995—Houston NFL	2	2	0	0	0.0	0
1996—Houston NFL	16	16	4	44	11.0	0
1997—Tennessee NFL	14	14	5	127	25.4	0
1998—Tennessee NFL	12	12	1	0	0.0	0
1999—Tennessee NFL	15	15	1	3	3.0	0
2000—Tennessee NFL	15	15	0	0	0.0	0
2001—Seattle NFL	12	12	2	30	15.0	0
Pro totals (11 years)	147	129	24	458	19.1	0

ROBERTSON, TYRONE — DT — BILLS

PERSONAL: Born August 15, 1979, in Danville, Va. ... 6-4/295.
HIGH SCHOOL: George Washington (Va.).
JUNIOR COLLEGE: Hinds Community College (Miss.).
COLLEGE: Georgia.
TRANSACTIONS/CAREER NOTES: Selected by Buffalo Bills in seventh round (238th pick overall) of 2001 NFL draft. ... Signed by Bills (June 11, 2001).

Year Team	G	GS	SACKS
2001—Buffalo NFL	12	0	2.0

ROBINSON, BRYAN — DE — BEARS

PERSONAL: Born June 22, 1974, in Toledo, Ohio. ... 6-4/283. ... Full name: Bryan Keith Robinson.
HIGH SCHOOL: Woodward (Cincinnati).
JUNIOR COLLEGE: College of the Desert (Palm Desert, Calif.).
COLLEGE: Fresno State.
TRANSACTIONS/CAREER NOTES: Signed as non-drafted free agent by St. Louis Rams (April 29, 1997). ... Claimed on waivers by Chicago Bears (August 31, 1998). ... Granted free agency (February 11, 2000). ... Re-signed by Bears (April 19, 2000). ... Designated by Bears as transition player (February 22, 2001).
PRO STATISTICS: 2001—Recovered one fumble for one yard.

Year Team	G	GS	SACKS
1997—St. Louis NFL	11	0	1.0
1998—Chicago NFL	10	5	0.5
1999—Chicago NFL	16	16	5.0
2000—Chicago NFL	16	16	4.5
2001—Chicago NFL	16	16	4.5
Pro totals (5 years)	69	53	15.5

ROBINSON, DAMIEN — S — JETS

PERSONAL: Born December 23, 1973, in Dallas. ... 6-2/223. ... Full name: Damien Dion Robinson.
HIGH SCHOOL: Hillcrest (Dallas).
COLLEGE: Iowa.
TRANSACTIONS/CAREER NOTES: Selected by Philadelphia Eagles in fourth round (119th pick overall) of 1997 NFL draft. ... Signed by Eagles (June 4, 1997). ... Released by Eagles (August 25, 1997). ... Re-signed by Eagles to practice squad (August 27, 1997). ... Signed by Tampa Bay Buccaneers off Eagles practice squad (September 17, 1997). ... Inactive for 13 games (1997). ... On injured reserve with arm injury (October 27, 1998-remainder of season). ... Granted free agency (February 11, 2000). ... Re-signed by Buccaneers (May 15, 2000). ... Granted unconditional free agency (March 2, 2001). ... Signed by New York Jets (April 25, 2001).
PLAYING EXPERIENCE: Tampa Bay NFL, 1998-2000; New York Jets NFL, 2001. ... Games/Games started: 1998 (7/0), 1999 (16/16), 2000 (16/16), 2001 (14/14). Total: 53/46.
CHAMPIONSHIP GAME EXPERIENCE: Played in NFC championship game (1999 season).
PRO STATISTICS: 1999—Caught one pass for 17 yards, intercepted two passes for 36 yards, credited with ¹/₂ sack and recovered two fumbles. 2000—Caught one pass for 36 yards, intercepted six passes for one yard and recovered three fumbles for five yards. 2001—Intercepted two passes for 58 yards, fumbled once and recovered one fumble for four yards.

ROBINSON, EDDIE   LB   BILLS

PERSONAL: Born April 13, 1970, in New Orleans. ... 6-1/243. ... Full name: Eddie Joseph Robinson Jr.
HIGH SCHOOL: Brother Martin (New Orleans).
COLLEGE: Alabama State (degree in chemistry, 1993).
TRANSACTIONS/CAREER NOTES: Selected by Houston Oilers in second round (50th pick overall) of 1992 NFL draft. ... Signed by Oilers (July 16, 1992). ... Granted free agency (February 17, 1995). ... Re-signed by Oilers (July 1995). ... Granted unconditional free agency (February 16, 1996). ... Signed by Jacksonville Jaguars (March 1, 1996). ... Released by Jaguars (August 30, 1998). ... Signed by Tennessee Oilers (September 1, 1998). ... Oilers franchise renamed Tennessee Titans for 1999 season (December 26, 1998). ... Granted unconditional free agency (February 12, 1999). ... Re-signed by Titans (March 1, 1999). ... Released by Titans (February 28, 2002). ... Signed by Buffalo Bills (April 17, 2002).
CHAMPIONSHIP GAME EXPERIENCE: Played in AFC championship game (1996 and 1999 seasons). ... Played in Super Bowl XXXIV (1999 season).
PRO STATISTICS: 1995—Intercepted one pass for 49 yards and a touchdown and recovered one fumble. 1996—Recovered one fumble. 1997—Intercepted one pass for no yards and recovered two fumbles. 1998—Intercepted one pass for 11 yards. 1999—Recovered three fumbles for one yard. 2000—Recovered three fumbles. 2001—Intercepted two passes for 13 yards and recovered two fumbles for minus one yard.

Year—Team	G	GS	SACKS
1992—Houston NFL	16	11	1.0
1993—Houston NFL	16	15	1.0
1994—Houston NFL	15	15	0.0
1995—Houston NFL	16	16	3.5
1996—Jacksonville NFL	16	15	1.0
1997—Jacksonville NFL	16	14	2.0
1998—Tennessee NFL	16	16	3.5
1999—Tennessee NFL	16	16	6.0
2000—Tennessee NFL	16	16	4.0
2001—Tennessee NFL	16	16	1.0
Pro totals (10 years)	159	150	23.0

ROBINSON, JEFF   TE   COWBOYS

PERSONAL: Born February 20, 1970, in Kennewick, Wash. ... 6-4/275. ... Full name: Jeffrey William Robinson.
HIGH SCHOOL: Joel E. Ferris (Spokane, Wash.).
COLLEGE: Idaho (degree in finance, 1992).
TRANSACTIONS/CAREER NOTES: Selected by Denver Broncos in fourth round (98th pick overall) of 1993 NFL draft. ... Signed by Broncos (July 13, 1993). ... Granted free agency (February 16, 1996). ... Re-signed by Broncos (March 28, 1996). ... Granted unconditional free agency (February 14, 1997). ... Signed by St. Louis Rams (March 14, 1997). ... Granted unconditional free agency (March 1, 2002). ... Signed by Dallas Cowboys (March 5, 2002).
CHAMPIONSHIP GAME EXPERIENCE: Played in NFC championship game (1999 and 2001 seasons). ... Member of Super Bowl championship team (1999 season). ... Played in Super Bowl XXXVI (2001 season).
PRO STATISTICS: 1993—Recovered one fumble for minus 10 yards. 1995—Returned one kickoff for 14 yards and recovered one fumble. 1996—Recovered one fumble. 1998—Caught one pass for four yards and a touchdown. 1999—Caught six passes for 76 yards and two touchdowns. 2000—Caught five passes for 52 yards and recovered one fumble. 2001—Caught 11 passes for 108 yards and one touchdown.
SINGLE GAME HIGHS (regular season): Receptions—2 (November 18, 2001, vs. New England); yards—34 (December 10, 2000, vs. Minnesota); and touchdown receptions—1 (September 23, 2001, vs. San Francisco).
MISCELLANEOUS: Played defensive line (1993-98).

Year—Team	G	GS	SACKS
1993—Denver NFL	16	0	3.5
1994—Denver NFL	16	0	1.0
1995—Denver NFL	16	0	1.0
1996—Denver NFL	16	0	0.5
1997—St. Louis NFL	16	0	0.5
1998—St. Louis NFL	16	0	0.0
1999—St. Louis NFL	16	9	0.0
2000—St. Louis NFL	16	1	0.0
2001—St. Louis NFL	16	5	0.0
Pro totals (9 years)	144	15	6.5

ROBINSON, KOREN   WR   SEAHAWKS

PERSONAL: Born March 19, 1980, in Belmont, N.C. ... 6-1/213.
HIGH SCHOOL: South Point (N.C.).
COLLEGE: North Carolina State.
TRANSACTIONS/CAREER NOTES: Selected after sophomore season by Seattle Seahawks in first round (ninth pick overall) of 2001 NFL draft. ... Signed by Seahawks (July 27, 2001).
PRO STATISTICS: 2001—Recovered one fumble for minus three yards.
SINGLE GAME HIGHS (regular season): Receptions—5 (September 30, 2001, vs. Oakland); yards—78 (September 30, 2001, vs. Oakland); and touchdown receptions—1 (November 18, 2001, vs. Buffalo).

			RUSHING			RECEIVING			TOTALS			
Year—Team	G	GS	Att.	Yds.	Avg.	TD	No.	Yds.	Avg.	TD	TD	2pt.	Pts.	Fum.
2001—Seattle NFL	16	13	4	13	3.3	0	39	536	13.7	1	1	0	6	2

ROBINSON, MARCUS — WR — BEARS

PERSONAL: Born February 27, 1975, in Fort Valley, Ga. ... 6-3/213.
HIGH SCHOOL: Peach County (Fort Valley, Ga.).
COLLEGE: South Carolina.
TRANSACTIONS/CAREER NOTES: Selected by Chicago Bears in fourth round (108th pick overall) of 1997 NFL draft. ... Signed by Bears (July 11, 1997). ... Inactive for four games (1997). ... On injured reserve with thumb injury (September 24, 1997-remainder of season). ... Assigned by Bears to Rhein Fire in 1998 NFL Europe enhancement allocation program (February 18, 1998). ... On injured reserve with back injury (December 4, 2000-remainder of season). ... On injured reserve with knee injury (October 23, 2001-remainder of season).
PRO STATISTICS: 2000—Rushed once for nine yards.
SINGLE GAME HIGHS (regular season): Receptions—11 (December 19, 1999, vs. Detroit); yards—170 (December 19, 1999, vs. Detroit); and touchdown receptions—3 (December 19, 1999, vs. Detroit).
STATISTICAL PLATEAUS: 100-yard receiving games: 1999 (5), 2000 (1), 2001 (1). Total: 7.

			RECEIVING				TOTALS			
Year Team	G	GS	No.	Yds.	Avg.	TD	TD	2pt.	Pts.	Fum.
1997—Chicago NFL					Did not play.					
1998—Rhein NFLE	...	...	39	811	20.8	5	5	0	30	0
—Chicago NFL	3	0	4	44	11.0	1	1	0	6	0
1999—Chicago NFL	16	11	84	1400	16.7	9	9	0	54	0
2000—Chicago NFL	11	11	55	738	13.4	5	5	0	30	1
2001—Chicago NFL	5	4	23	269	11.7	2	2	0	12	0
NFL Europe totals (1 year)	...	...	39	811	20.8	5	5	0	30	0
NFL totals (3 years)	35	26	166	2451	14.8	17	17	0	102	1
Pro totals (4 years)	...	...	205	3262	15.9	22	22	0	132	1

ROBINSON-RANDALL, GREG — OT — PATRIOTS

PERSONAL: Born June 23, 1978, in Galveston, Texas. ... 6-5/322.
HIGH SCHOOL: La Marque (Texas).
JUNIOR COLLEGE: Coffeyville (Kan.) Community College.
COLLEGE: Michigan State.
TRANSACTIONS/CAREER NOTES: Selected by New England Patriots in fourth round (127th pick overall) of 2000 NFL draft. ... Signed by Patriots (July 12, 2000).
PLAYING EXPERIENCE: New England NFL, 2000 and 2001. ... Games/Games started: 2000 (12/4), 2001 (16/16). Total: 28/20.
CHAMPIONSHIP GAME EXPERIENCE: Played in AFC championship game (2001 season). ... Member of Super Bowl championship team (2001 season).

RODGERS, DERRICK — LB — DOLPHINS

PERSONAL: Born October 14, 1971, in Memphis, Tenn. ... 6-1/235. ... Full name: Derrick Andre Rodgers.
HIGH SCHOOL: St. Augustine (New Orleans).
JUNIOR COLLEGE: Riverside (Calif.) Community College.
COLLEGE: Arizona State.
TRANSACTIONS/CAREER NOTES: Selected by Miami Dolphins in third round (92nd pick overall) of 1997 NFL draft. ... Signed by Dolphins (July 8, 1997). ... Granted free agency (February 11, 2000). ... Re-signed by Dolphins (April 28, 2000). ... Granted unconditional free agency (March 2, 2001). ... Re-signed by Dolphins (March 3, 2001). ... On injured reserve with shoulder injury (December 27, 2001-remainder of season).
PRO STATISTICS: 1997—Recovered one fumble. 1999—Intercepted one pass for five yards and recovered two fumbles.

Year Team	G	GS	SACKS
1997—Miami NFL	15	14	5.0
1998—Miami NFL	16	16	2.5
1999—Miami NFL	16	15	0.0
2000—Miami NFL	16	15	0.5
2001—Miami NFL	14	14	1.0
Pro totals (5 years)	77	74	9.0

ROGERS, CHARLIE — KR/PR — BILLS

PERSONAL: Born June 19, 1976, in Cliffwood, N.J. ... 5-9/179. ... Full name: John Edward Rogers.
HIGH SCHOOL: Matawan Regional (Aberdeen, N.J.).
COLLEGE: Georgia Tech.
TRANSACTIONS/CAREER NOTES: Selected by Seattle Seahawks in fifth round (152nd pick overall) of 1999 NFL draft. ... Signed by Seahawks (July 29, 1999). ... Selected by Houston Texans from Seahawks in NFL expansion draft (February 18, 2002). ... Granted free agency (March 1, 2002). ... Re-signed by Texans (April 17, 2002). ... Traded by Texans to Buffalo Bills for LB Jay Foreman (April 17, 2002).
PRO STATISTICS: 2000—Recovered one fumble. 2001—Caught one pass for seven yards.

			PUNT RETURNS				KICKOFF RETURNS				TOTALS			
Year Team	G	GS	No.	Yds.	Avg.	TD	No.	Yds.	Avg.	TD	TD	2pt.	Pts.	Fum.
1999—Seattle NFL	12	0	22	318	*14.5	1	18	465	25.8	0	1	0	6	3
2000—Seattle NFL	15	0	26	363	14.0	0	66 §1629	24.7	▲1	1	0	6	5
2001—Seattle NFL	13	0	25	244	9.8	0	50	1120	22.4	0	0	0	0	2
Pro totals (3 years)	40	0	73	925	12.7	1	134	3214	24.0	1	2	0	12	10

– 320 –

ROGERS, SAM   LB   CHARGERS

PERSONAL: Born May 30, 1970, in Pontiac, Mich. ... 6-3/245. ... Full name: Sammy Lee Rogers.
HIGH SCHOOL: Saint Mary's Preparatory (Orchard Lake, Mich.).
JUNIOR COLLEGE: West Hills College (Calif.), then West Los Angeles College.
COLLEGE: Colorado.
TRANSACTIONS/CAREER NOTES: Selected by Buffalo Bills in second round (64th pick overall) of 1994 NFL draft. ... Signed by Bills (July 12, 1994). ... Granted free agency (February 14, 1997). ... Re-signed by Bills (June 12, 1997). ... Granted unconditional free agency (February 13, 1998). ... Re-signed by Bills (February 15, 1998). ... Released by Bills (March 1, 2001). ... Signed by San Diego Chargers (May 23, 2001).
PRO STATISTICS: 1995—Recovered one fumble. 1996—Recovered two fumbles. 1999—Intercepted one pass for 24 yards and recovered two fumbles for seven yards. 2000—Intercepted one pass for 10 yards and recovered one fumble.

Year Team	G	GS	SACKS
1994—Buffalo NFL	14	0	0.0
1995—Buffalo NFL	16	8	2.0
1996—Buffalo NFL	14	14	3.5
1997—Buffalo NFL	15	15	3.5
1998—Buffalo NFL	15	15	4.5
1999—Buffalo NFL	16	16	3.0
2000—Buffalo NFL	11	11	5.0
2001—San Diego NFL	15	0	1.0
Pro totals (8 years)	116	79	22.5

ROGERS, SHAUN   DT   LIONS

PERSONAL: Born March 12, 1979, in Houston. ... 6-4/331.
HIGH SCHOOL: LaPorte (Texas).
COLLEGE: Texas.
TRANSACTIONS/CAREER NOTES: Selected by Detroit Lions in second round (61st pick overall) of 2001 NFL draft. ... Signed by Lions (July 23, 2001). ... On physically unable to perfrom list with ankle injury (July 24-August 6, 2001).

Year Team	G	GS	SACKS
2001—Detroit NFL	16	16	3.0

ROGERS, TYRONE   DE   BROWNS

PERSONAL: Born October 11, 1976, in Montgomery, Ala. ... 6-5/236.
HIGH SCHOOL: Robert E. Lee (Montgomery, Ala.).
COLLEGE: Alabama State.
TRANSACTIONS/CAREER NOTES: Signed as non-drafted free agent by Cleveland Browns (April 23, 1999). ... Released by Browns (September 5, 1999). ... Re-signed by Browns to practice squad (September 6, 1999). ... Activated (November 23, 1999).
PLAYING EXPERIENCE: Cleveland NFL, 1999-2001. ... Games/Games started: 1999 (3/0), 2000 (16/0), 2001 (16/10). Total: 35/10.
PRO STATISTICS: 2000—Credited with two sacks and recovered three fumbles. 2001—Credited with six sacks.

ROLLE, SAMARI   CB   TITANS

PERSONAL: Born August 10, 1976, in Miami. ... 6-0/175. ... Full name: Samari Toure Rolle. ... Name pronounced suh-MARI ROLL.
HIGH SCHOOL: Miami Beach.
COLLEGE: Florida State.
TRANSACTIONS/CAREER NOTES: Selected by Tennessee Oilers in second round (46th pick overall) of 1998 NFL draft. ... Signed by Oilers (July 24, 1998). ... Oilers franchise renamed Tennessee Titans for 1999 season (December 26, 1998). ... Granted free agency (March 2, 2001). ... Re-signed by Titans (July 28, 2001). ... On physically unable to perform list with knee injury (July 28-August 14, 2001).
CHAMPIONSHIP GAME EXPERIENCE: Played in AFC championship game (1999 season). ... Played in Super Bowl XXXIV (1999 season).
HONORS: Named cornerback on THE SPORTING NEWS NFL All-Pro team (2000). ... Played in Pro Bowl (2000 season).
PRO STATISTICS: 1999—Returned one punt for 23 yards, fumbled once and recovered one fumble for three yards. 2000—Recovered one fumble. 2001—Returned one kickoff for three yards and recovered two fumbles for 34 yards.

			INTERCEPTIONS				SACKS
Year Team	G	GS	No.	Yds.	Avg.	TD	No.
1998—Tennessee NFL	15	1	0	0	0.0	0	2.0
1999—Tennessee NFL	16	16	4	65	16.3	0	3.0
2000—Tennessee NFL	15	15	▲7	140	20.0	0	1.5
2001—Tennessee NFL	14	13	3	3	1.0	0	2.0
Pro totals (4 years)	60	45	14	208	14.9	1	8.5

ROMAN, MARK   S   BENGALS

PERSONAL: Born March 26, 1977, in New Iberia, La. ... 5-11/184. ... Full name: Mark Emery Roman.
HIGH SCHOOL: New Iberia (La.).
COLLEGE: Louisiana State.
TRANSACTIONS/CAREER NOTES: Selected by Cincinnati Bengals in second round (34th pick overall) of 2000 NFL draft. ... Signed by Bengals (August 7, 2000). ... On injured reserve with finger injury (December 20, 2001-remainder of season).
PLAYING EXPERIENCE: Cincinnati NFL, 2000 and 2001. ... Games/Games started: 2000 (8/2), 2001 (13/8). Total: 21/10.
PRO STATISTICS: 2000—Recovered two fumbles. 2001—Intercepted one pass for no yards, credited with two sacks and recovered one fumble for minus one yard.

ROMANOWSKI, BILL — LB — RAIDERS

PERSONAL: Born April 2, 1966, in Vernon, Conn. ... 6-4/245. ... Full name: William Thomas Romanowski.
HIGH SCHOOL: Rockville (Vernon, Conn.).
COLLEGE: Boston College (degree in general management, 1988).
TRANSACTIONS/CAREER NOTES: Selected by San Francisco 49ers in third round (80th pick overall) of 1988 NFL draft. ... Signed by 49ers (July 15, 1988). ... Granted free agency (February 1, 1991). ... Re-signed by 49ers (July 17, 1991). ... Granted unconditional free agency (March 1, 1993). ... Re-signed by 49ers (March 23, 1993). ... Traded by 49ers to Philadelphia Eagles for third-(traded to Los Angeles Rams) and sixth-round (traded to Green Bay) picks in 1994 draft (April 24, 1994). ... Granted unconditional free agency (February 16, 1996). ... Signed by Denver Broncos (February 23, 1996). ... Released by Broncos (February 21, 2002). ... Signed by Oakland Raiders (February 27, 2002).
CHAMPIONSHIP GAME EXPERIENCE: Played in NFC championship game (1988-1990, 1992 and 1993 seasons). ... Member of Super Bowl championship team (1988, 1989, 1997 and 1998 seasons). ... Played in AFC championship game (1997 and 1998 seasons).
HONORS: Played in Pro Bowl (1996 and 1998 seasons).
PRO STATISTICS: 1988—Recovered one fumble. 1989—Returned one punt for no yards, fumbled once and recovered two fumbles. 1991—Recovered two fumbles. 1992—Recovered one fumble. 1993—Recovered one fumble. 1994—Recovered one fumble. 1995—Recovered one fumble. 1996—Recovered three fumbles. 1998—Recovered three fumbles. 1999—Fumbled once and recovered one fumble. 2000—Recovered two fumbles.

				INTERCEPTIONS				SACKS
Year Team	G	GS	No.	Yds.	Avg.	TD	No.
1988—San Francisco NFL	16	8	0	0	0.0	0	0.0
1989—San Francisco NFL	16	4	1	13	13.0	0	1.0
1990—San Francisco NFL	16	16	0	0	0.0	0	1.0
1991—San Francisco NFL	16	16	1	7	7.0	0	1.0
1992—San Francisco NFL	16	16	0	0	0.0	0	1.0
1993—San Francisco NFL	16	16	0	0	0.0	0	3.0
1994—Philadelphia NFL	16	15	2	8	4.0	0	2.5
1995—Philadelphia NFL	16	16	2	5	2.5	0	1.0
1996—Denver NFL	16	16	3	1	0.3	0	3.0
1997—Denver NFL	16	16	1	7	7.0	0	2.0
1998—Denver NFL	16	16	2	22	11.0	0	7.5
1999—Denver NFL	16	16	3	35	11.7	1	0.0
2000—Denver NFL	16	16	2	0	0.0	0	3.5
2001—Denver NFL	16	16	0	0	0.0	0	7.0
Pro totals (14 years)	224	203	17	98	5.8	1	33.5

ROSENTHAL, MIKE — G — GIANTS

PERSONAL: Born June 10, 1977, in Pittsburgh. ... 6-7/315. ... Full name: Michael Paul Rosenthal.
HIGH SCHOOL: Penn (Mishawaka, Ind.).
COLLEGE: Notre Dame.
TRANSACTIONS/CAREER NOTES: Selected by New York Giants in fifth round (149th pick overall) of 1999 NFL draft. ... Signed by Giants (July 26, 1999). ... Granted free agency (March 1, 2002).
PLAYING EXPERIENCE: New York Giants NFL, 1999-2001. ... Games/Games started: 1999 (9/7), 2000 (8/2), 2001 (7/0). Total: 24/9.
CHAMPIONSHIP GAME EXPERIENCE: Played in NFC championship game (2000 season). ... Played in Super Bowl XXXV (2000 season).

ROSS, ADRIAN — LB — BENGALS

PERSONAL: Born February 19, 1975, in Santa Clara, Calif. ... 6-2/256. ... Full name: Adrian Lamont Ross.
HIGH SCHOOL: Elk Grove (Calif.).
COLLEGE: Colorado State.
TRANSACTIONS/CAREER NOTES: Signed as non-drafted free agent by Cincinnati Bengals (April 21, 1998). ... Granted free agency (March 2, 2001). ... Re-signed by Bengals (May 1, 2001).
PLAYING EXPERIENCE: Cincinnati NFL, 1998-2001. ... Games/Games started: 1998 (14/1), 1999 (16/10), 2000 (13/4), 2001 (16/1). Total: 59/16.
PRO STATISTICS: 1998—Intercepted one pass for 11 yards. 1999—Credited with one sack. 2000—Credited with one sack. 2001—Credited with one sack and recovered one fumble.

ROSS, MICAH — WR — JAGUARS

PERSONAL: Born January 13, 1976, in Jacksonville. ... 6-3/220. ... Full name: Micah David Ross.
HIGH SCHOOL: Andrew Jackson (Fla.).
COLLEGE: Jacksonville.
TRANSACTIONS/CAREER NOTES: Signed as non-drafted free agent by Jacksonville Jaguars (August 17, 2001). ... Released by Jaguars (August 28, 2001). ... Re-signed by Jaguars to practice squad (October 31, 2001). ... Activated (December 8, 2001).
PLAYING EXPERIENCE: Jacksonville NFL, 2001. ... Games/Games started: 2001 (5/0).
PRO STATISTICS: 2001—Returned eight kickoffs for 150 yards and fumbled once.

ROSS, OLIVER — OT — STEELERS

PERSONAL: Born September 27, 1974, in Los Angeles. ... 6-5/309.
HIGH SCHOOL: Washington (Los Angeles).
JUNIOR COLLEGE: Southwestern College (Calif.).

COLLEGE: Iowa State.
TRANSACTIONS/CAREER NOTES: Selected by Dallas Cowboys in fifth round (138th pick overall) of 1998 NFL draft. ... Signed by Cowboys (July 16, 1998). ... Assigned by Cowboys to Rhein Fire in 1999 NFL Europe enhancement allocation program (February 22, 1999). ... Released by Cowboys (September 5, 1999). ... Signed by Philadelphia Eagles to practice squad (September 8, 1999). ... Activated (September 14, 1999); did not play. ... Assigned by Eagles to Amsterdam Admirals in 2000 NFL Europe enhancement allocation program (February 18, 2000). ... Released by Eagles (August 27, 2000). ... Signed by Chicago Bears to practice squad (September 4, 2000). ... Released by Bears (September 7, 2000). ... Signed by Steelers to practice squad (November 22, 2000). ... Activated (December 13, 2000). ... Granted free agency (March 1, 2002). ... Tendered offer sheet by Cleveland Browns (March 13, 2002). ... Offer matched by Steelers (March 15, 2002).
PLAYING EXPERIENCE: Dallas NFL, 1998; Rhein NFLE, 1999; Amsterdam NFLE, 2000; Pittsburgh NFL, 2001. ... Games/Games started: 1998 (2/0), NFLE 1999 (games played unavailable), NFLE 2000 (-), 2001 (16/8). Total: 18/8.
CHAMPIONSHIP GAME EXPERIENCE: Played in AFC championship game (2001 season).
PRO STATISTICS: 2001—Recovered two fumbles.

ROSSUM, ALLEN KR FALCONS

PERSONAL: Born October 22, 1975, in Dallas. ... 5-8/178.
HIGH SCHOOL: Skyline (Dallas).
COLLEGE: Notre Dame.
TRANSACTIONS/CAREER NOTES: Selected by Philadelphia Eagles in third round (85th pick overall) of 1998 NFL draft. ... Signed by Eagles (July 14, 1998). ... Traded by Eagles to Green Bay Packers for fifth-round pick (TE Tony Stewart) in 2001 draft (August 21, 2000). ... Granted free agency (March 2, 2001). ... Re-signed by Packers (April 23, 2001). ... Granted unconditional free agency (March 1, 2002). ... Signed by Atlanta Falcons (March 11, 2002).
PRO STATISTICS: 1998—Credited with one sack and recovered three fumbles. 1999—Recovered two fumbles. 2000—Rushed once for 16 yards, fumbled four times and recovered three fumbles.

				PUNT RETURNS				KICKOFF RETURNS				TOTALS		
Year	Team	G	GS	No.	Yds.	Avg.	TD	No.	Yds.	Avg.	TD	TD	2pt.	Pts.	Fum.
1998—Philadelphia NFL		15	2	22	187	8.5	0	44	1080	24.5	0	0	0	0	4
1999—Philadelphia NFL		16	0	28	250	8.9	0	54	1347	24.9	1	1	0	6	6
2000—Green Bay NFL		16	0	29	248	8.6	0	50	1288	25.8	1	1	0	6	4
2001—Green Bay NFL		6	0	11	109	9.9	∞1	23	431	18.7	0	1	0	6	0
Pro totals (4 years)		53	2	90	794	8.8	1	171	4146	24.2	2	3	0	18	14

ROUEN, TOM P BRONCOS

PERSONAL: Born June 9, 1968, in Hinsdale, Ill. ... 6-3/225. ... Full name: Thomas Francis Rouen Jr. ... Name pronounced RUIN.
HIGH SCHOOL: Heritage (Littleton, Colo.).
COLLEGE: Colorado State, then Colorado.
TRANSACTIONS/CAREER NOTES: Signed as non-drafted free agent by New York Giants (April 29, 1991). ... Released by Giants (August 19, 1991). ... Selected by Ohio Glory in fourth round (44th pick overall) of 1992 World League draft. ... Signed by Los Angeles Rams (July 1992). ... Released by Rams (August 24, 1992). ... Signed by Denver Broncos (April 29, 1993). ... Granted unconditional free agency (February 14, 1997). ... Re-signed by Broncos (March 6, 1997). ... Granted unconditional free agency (February 11, 2000). ... Re-signed by Broncos (February 24, 2000).
CHAMPIONSHIP GAME EXPERIENCE: Played in AFC championship game (1997 and 1998 seasons). ... Member of Super Bowl championship team (1997 and 1998 seasons).
HONORS: Named punter on THE SPORTING NEWS college All-America second team (1989).
PRO STATISTICS: 1993—Rushed once for no yards. 1998—Rushed once for no yards, missed one extra-point attempt and fumbled once for minus 15 yards. 1999—Rushed once for no yards and recovered one fumble. 2000—Rushed once for minus 11 yards.

			PUNTING			
Year Team	G	No.	Yds.	Avg.	Net avg.	In. 20	Blk.
1992—Ohio W.L.	10	48	1992	41.5	36.1	14	1
1993—Denver NFL	16	67	3017	45.0	37.1	17	1
1994—Denver NFL	16	76	3258	42.9	*37.1	23	0
1995—Denver NFL	16	52	2192	42.2	37.6	22	1
1996—Denver NFL	16	65	2714	41.8	36.2	16	0
1997—Denver NFL	16	60	2598	43.3	38.1	22	0
1998—Denver NFL	16	66	3097	46.9	37.6	14	1
1999—Denver NFL	16	84	3908	*46.5	35.6	19	0
2000—Denver NFL	16	61	2455	40.2	32.3	18	▲1
2001—Denver NFL	16	81	3668	45.3	36.5	25	1
W.L. totals (1 year)	10	48	1992	41.5	36.1	14	1
NFL totals (9 years)	144	612	26907	44.0	36.4	176	5
Pro totals (10 years)	154	660	28899	43.8	36.4	190	6

ROUNDTREE, RALEIGH G/OT

PERSONAL: Born August 31, 1975, in Augusta, Ga. ... 6-4/295. ... Full name: Raleigh Cito Roundtree.
HIGH SCHOOL: Josey (Augusta, Ga.).
COLLEGE: South Carolina State.
TRANSACTIONS/CAREER NOTES: Selected by San Diego Chargers in fourth round (109th pick overall) of 1997 NFL draft. ... Signed by Chargers (July 14, 1997). ... Inactive for all 16 games (1997). ... Granted free agency (February 11, 2000). ... Re-signed by Chargers (May 30, 2000). ... Granted unconditional free agency (March 2, 2001). ... Re-signed by Chargers (May 4, 2001). ... Granted unconditional free agency (March 1, 2002).
PLAYING EXPERIENCE: San Diego NFL, 1998-2001. ... Games/Games started: 1998 (15/5), 1999 (15/5), 2000 (16/15), 2001 (16/16). Total: 62/41.
PRO STATISTICS: 1998—Recovered one fumble. 2000—Recovered one fumble. 2001—Recovered one fumble for two yards.

ROYALS, MARK   P   DOLPHINS

PERSONAL: Born June 22, 1965, in Hampton, Va. ... 6-5/225. ... Full name: Mark Alan Royals.
HIGH SCHOOL: Mathews (Va.).
JUNIOR COLLEGE: Chowan College (N.C.).
COLLEGE: Appalachian State (degree in political science).
TRANSACTIONS/CAREER NOTES: Signed as non-drafted free agent by Dallas Cowboys (June 6, 1986). ... Released by Cowboys (August 8, 1986). ... Signed as replacement player by St. Louis Cardinals (September 30, 1987). ... Released by Cardinals (October 7, 1987). ... Signed as replacement player by Philadelphia Eagles (October 14, 1987). ... Released by Eagles (November 1987). ... Signed by Cardinals (December 12, 1987). ... Released by Cardinals (July 27, 1988). ... Signed by Miami Dolphins (May 2, 1989). ... Released by Dolphins (August 28, 1989). ... Signed by Tampa Bay Buccaneers (April 24, 1990). ... Granted unconditional free agency (February 1, 1992). ... Signed by Pittsburgh Steelers (March 15, 1992). ... Granted unconditional free agency (February 17, 1995). ... Signed by Detroit Lions (April 26, 1995). ... Granted free agency (February 16, 1996). ... Re-signed by Lions (June 19, 1996). ... Granted unconditional free agency (February 14, 1997). ... Signed by New Orleans Saints (April 25, 1997). ... Released by Saints (June 29, 1999). ... Signed by Buccaneers (August 4, 1999). ... Granted unconditional free agency (February 11, 2000). ... Re-signed by Buccaneers (March 24, 2000). ... Released by Buccaneers (February 26, 2002). ... Signed by Miami Dolphins (April 14, 2002).
CHAMPIONSHIP GAME EXPERIENCE: Played in AFC championship game (1994 season). ... Played in NFC championship game (1999 season).
PRO STATISTICS: 1987—Had 23.3-yard net punting average. 1992—Completed only pass attempt for 44 yards. 1994—Rushed once for minus 13 yards. 1995—Rushed once for minus seven yards. 1996—Completed only pass attempt for minus eight yards and recovered one fumble. 1999—Attempted two passes with one completion for 17 yards. 2000—Completed only pass attempt for 36 yards. 2001—Completed only pass attempt for five yards.

				PUNTING			
Year Team	G	No.	Yds.	Avg.	Net avg.	In. 20	Blk.
1987—St. Louis NFL	1	6	222	37.0	.0	2	0
—Philadelphia NFL	1	5	209	41.8	.0	1	0
1988—				Did not play.			
1989—				Did not play.			
1990—Tampa Bay NFL	16	72	2902	40.3	34.0	8	0
1991—Tampa Bay NFL	16	84	3389	40.3	32.2	22	0
1992—Pittsburgh NFL	16	73	3119	42.7	35.6	22	1
1993—Pittsburgh NFL	16	89	3781	42.5	34.2	§28	0
1994—Pittsburgh NFL	16	§97	3849	39.7	35.7	†35	0
1995—Detroit NFL	16	57	2393	42.0	31.0	15	2
1996—Detroit NFL	16	69	3020	43.8	33.3	11	1
1997—New Orleans NFL	16	88	4038	*45.9	34.9	21	0
1998—New Orleans NFL	16	88	4017	‡45.6	36.0	26	0
1999—Tampa Bay NFL	16	90	3882	43.1	37.4	23	0
2000—Tampa Bay NFL	16	85	3551	41.8	35.1	17	0
2001—Tampa Bay NFL	16	83	3382	40.7	34.2	26	0
Pro totals (13 years)	194	986	41754	42.3	34.2	257	4

ROYE, ORPHEUS   DL   BROWNS

PERSONAL: Born January 21, 1974, in Miami. ... 6-4/313. ... Full name: Orpheus Michael Roye. ... Name pronounced OR-fee-us ROY.
HIGH SCHOOL: Miami Springs.
JUNIOR COLLEGE: Jones County Junior College (Miss.).
COLLEGE: Florida State.
TRANSACTIONS/CAREER NOTES: Selected by Pittsburgh Steelers in sixth round (200th pick overall) of 1996 NFL draft. ... Signed by Steelers (July 16, 1996). ... Granted free agency (February 12, 1999). ... Re-signed by Steelers (April 23, 1999). ... Granted unconditional free agency (February 11, 2000). ... Signed by Cleveland Browns (February 12, 2000). ... On injured reserve with knee injury (December 11, 2001-remainder of season).
CHAMPIONSHIP GAME EXPERIENCE: Played in AFC championship game (1997 season).
PRO STATISTICS: 1996—Recovered one fumble. 1998—Returned one kickoff for no yards. 1999—Intercepted one pass for two yards and recovered one fumble. 2000—Recovered one fumble for eight yards. 2001—Intercepted one pass for no yards and credited with one safety.

Year Team	G	GS	SACKS
1996—Pittsburgh NFL	13	1	0.0
1997—Pittsburgh NFL	16	0	1.0
1998—Pittsburgh NFL	16	9	3.5
1999—Pittsburgh NFL	16	16	4.5
2000—Cleveland NFL	16	16	2.0
2001—Cleveland NFL	12	10	0.0
Pro totals (6 years)	89	52	11.0

RUCKER, MICHAEL   DE   PANTHERS

PERSONAL: Born February 28, 1975, in St. Joseph, Mo. ... 6-5/258. ... Full name: Michael Dean Rucker.
HIGH SCHOOL: Benton (St. Joseph, Mo.).
COLLEGE: Nebraska (degree in sociology).
TRANSACTIONS/CAREER NOTES: Selected by Carolina Panthers in second round (38th pick overall) of 1999 NFL draft. ... Signed by Panthers (July 13, 1999).
PRO STATISTICS: 2001—Recovered one fumble.

Year Team	G	GS	SACKS
1999—Carolina NFL	16	0	3.0
2000—Carolina NFL	16	1	2.5
2001—Carolina NFL	16	16	9.0
Pro totals (3 years)	48	17	14.5

RUDD, DWAYNE   LB   BROWNS

PERSONAL: Born February 3, 1976, in Batesville, Miss. ... 6-2/237. ... Full name: Dwayne Dupree Rudd.
HIGH SCHOOL: South Panola (Batesville, Miss.).
COLLEGE: Alabama.
TRANSACTIONS/CAREER NOTES: Selected by Minnesota Vikings in first round (20th pick overall) of 1997 NFL draft. ... Signed by Vikings (July 18, 1997). ... Granted unconditional free agency (March 2, 2001). ... Signed by Cleveland Browns (March 3, 2001).
CHAMPIONSHIP GAME EXPERIENCE: Played in NFC championship game (1998 and 2000 seasons).
RECORDS: Shares NFL single-season records for most touchdowns by fumble recovery—2 (1998); most touchdowns by recovery of opponents' fumbles—2 (1998).
PRO STATISTICS: 1998—Recovered three fumbles for 157 yards and two touchdowns. 1999—Recovered one fumble. 2001—Intercepted one pass for no yards.

Year Team	G	GS	SACKS
1997—Minnesota NFL	16	2	5.0
1998—Minnesota NFL	15	15	2.0
1999—Minnesota NFL	16	16	3.0
2000—Minnesota NFL	14	13	0.0
2001—Cleveland NFL	16	16	0.5
Pro totals (5 years)	77	62	10.5

RUDDY, TIM   C   DOLPHINS

PERSONAL: Born April 27, 1972, in Scranton, Pa. ... 6-3/300. ... Full name: Timothy Daniel Ruddy.
HIGH SCHOOL: Dunmore (Pa.).
COLLEGE: Notre Dame (degree in mechanical engineering).
TRANSACTIONS/CAREER NOTES: Selected by Miami Dolphins in second round (65th pick overall) of 1994 NFL draft. ... Signed by Dolphins (July 18, 1994). ... Granted unconditional free agency (February 11, 2000). ... Re-signed by Dolphins (February 24, 2000).
PLAYING EXPERIENCE: Miami NFL, 1994-2001. ... Games/Games started: 1994 (16/0), 1995 (16/16), 1996 (16/16), 1997 (15/15), 1998 (16/16), 1999 (16/16), 2000 (16/16), 2001 (15/15). Total: 126/110.
HONORS: Played in Pro Bowl (2000 season).
PRO STATISTICS: 1995—Fumbled once. 1996—Fumbled once for minus 14 yards. 1998—Fumbled once for minus three yards.

RUEGAMER, GREY   G   PATRIOTS

PERSONAL: Born June 1, 1976, in Las Vegas, Nev. ... 6-5/300. ... Full name: Christopher Grey Ruegamer.
HIGH SCHOOL: Bishop Gorman (Las Vegas, Nev.).
COLLEGE: Arizona State.
TRANSACTIONS/CAREER NOTES: Selected by Miami Dolphins in third round (72nd pick overall) of 1999 NFL draft. ... Signed by Dolphins (July 27, 1999). ... Active for one game (1999); did not play. ... Released by Dolphins (August 27, 2000). ... Signed by Pittsburgh Steelers to practice squad (August 29, 2000). ... Signed by New England Patriots off Steelers practice squad (November 16, 2000). ... Granted free agency (March 1, 2002).
PLAYING EXPERIENCE: New England NFL, 2000 and 2001. ... Games/Games started: 2000 (6/0), 2001 (14/1). Total: 20/1.
CHAMPIONSHIP GAME EXPERIENCE: Played in AFC championship game (2001 season). ... Member of Super Bowl championship team (2001 season).

RUFF, ORLANDO   LB   CHARGERS

PERSONAL: Born September 28, 1976, in Charleston, S.C. ... 6-3/250. ... Full name: Orlando Bernarda Ruff.
HIGH SCHOOL: Fairfield Central (Winnsboro, S.C.).
COLLEGE: Furman.
TRANSACTIONS/CAREER NOTES: Signed as non-drafted free agent by San Diego Chargers (April 20, 1999). ... Granted free agency (March 1, 2002). ... Re-signed by Chargers (April 2, 2002).
PLAYING EXPERIENCE: San Diego NFL, 1999-2001. ... Games/Games started: 1999 (14/0), 2000 (16/14), 2001 (16/14). Total: 46/28.
PRO STATISTICS: 2000—Intercepted one pass for 18 yards and recovered one fumble. 2001—Credited with one sack and recovered one fumble.

RUNYAN, JON   OT   EAGLES

PERSONAL: Born November 27, 1973, in Flint, Mich. ... 6-7/330. ... Full name: Jon Daniel Runyan.
HIGH SCHOOL: Carman-Ainsworth (Flint, Mich.).
COLLEGE: Michigan.
TRANSACTIONS/CAREER NOTES: Selected after junior season by Houston Oilers in fourth round (109th pick overall) of 1996 NFL draft. ... Signed by Oilers (July 20, 1996). ... Oilers franchise moved to Tennessee for 1997 season. ... Oilers franchise renamed Tennessee Titans for 1999 season (December 26, 1998). ... Granted free agency (February 12, 1999). ... Re-signed by Titans (June 23, 1999). ... Granted unconditional free agency (February 11, 2000). ... Signed by Philadelphia Eagles (February 14, 2000).
PLAYING EXPERIENCE: Houston NFL, 1996; Tennessee NFL, 1997-1999; Philadelphia NFL, 2000 and 2001. ... Games/Games started: 1996 (10/0), 1997 (16/16), 1998 (16/16), 1999 (16/16), 2000 (16/16), 2001 (16/16). Total: 90/80.
CHAMPIONSHIP GAME EXPERIENCE: Played in AFC championship game (1999 season). ... Played in Super Bowl XXXIV (1999 season). ... Played in NFC championship game (2001 season).
HONORS: Named offensive lineman on THE SPORTING NEWS college All-America second team (1995).
PRO STATISTICS: 2000—Recovered one fumble. 2001—Recovered one fumble.

RUSSELL, DARRELL   DT   RAIDERS

PERSONAL: Born May 27, 1976, in Pensacola, Fla. ... 6-5/325.
HIGH SCHOOL: St. Augustine (San Diego).
COLLEGE: Southern California.
TRANSACTIONS/CAREER NOTES: Selected by Oakland Raiders in first round (second pick overall) of 1997 NFL draft. ... Signed by Raiders (July 23, 1997). ... On suspended list for violating league substance abuse policy (September 9-October 14, 2001). ... On suspended list for violating league substance abuse policy (December 29, 2001-present).
HONORS: Played in Pro Bowl (1998 and 1999 seasons). ... Named defensive tackle on THE SPORTING NEWS NFL All-Pro team (1999).
PRO STATISTICS: 1998—Recovered one fumble. 1999—Recovered one fumble. 2000—Recovered one fumble and credited with one safety. 2001—Intercepted one pass for no yards.

Year Team	G	GS	SACKS
1997—Oakland NFL	16	10	3.5
1998—Oakland NFL	16	16	10.0
1999—Oakland NFL	16	16	9.5
2000—Oakland NFL	16	16	3.0
2001—Oakland NFL	11	7	2.5
Pro totals (5 years)	75	65	28.5

RUSSELL, TWAN   LB   DOLPHINS

PERSONAL: Born April 25, 1974, in Fort Lauderdale, Fla. ... 6-1/230. ... Full name: Twan Sanchez Russell.
HIGH SCHOOL: St. Thomas Aquinas (Fort Lauderdale, Fla.).
COLLEGE: Miami, Fla. (degree in broadcasting, 1996).
TRANSACTIONS/CAREER NOTES: Selected by Washington Redskins in fifth round (148th pick overall) of 1997 NFL draft. ... Signed by Redskins (May 9, 1997). ... On injured reserve with foot and knee injuries (September 23, 1998-remainder of season). ... On injured reserve with knee injury (November 16, 1999-remainder of season). ... Granted free agency (February 11, 2000). ... Signed by Miami Dolphins (March 23, 2000). ... Granted unconditional free agency (March 2, 2001). ... Re-signed by Dolphins (March 6, 2001).
PLAYING EXPERIENCE: Washington NFL, 1997-1999; Miami NFL, 2000 and 2001. ... Games/Games started: 1997 (15/0), 1998 (3/0), 1999 (9/0), 2000 (16/2), 2001 (16/2). Total: 59/4.
PRO STATISTICS: 2000—Recovered one fumble.

RUTLEDGE, JOHNNY   LB   CARDINALS

PERSONAL: Born January 4, 1977, in Belle Glade, Fla. ... 6-3/241. ... Full name: Johnny Boykins Rutledge III.
HIGH SCHOOL: Glades Central (Belle Glade, Fla.).
COLLEGE: Florida.
TRANSACTIONS/CAREER NOTES: Selected by Arizona Cardinals in second round (51st pick overall) of 1999 NFL draft. ... Signed by Cardinals (July 29, 1999).
PLAYING EXPERIENCE: Arizona NFL, 1999-2001. ... Games/Games started: 1999 (6/0), 2000 (11/3), 2001 (14/0). Total: 31/3.
PRO STATISTICS: 2000—Recovered one fumble.

RUTLEDGE, ROD   TE   TEXANS

PERSONAL: Born August 12, 1975, in Birmingham, Ala. ... 6-5/265. ... Full name: Rodrick Almar Rutledge.
HIGH SCHOOL: Erwin (Birmingham, Ala.).
COLLEGE: Alabama.
TRANSACTIONS/CAREER NOTES: Selected by New England Patriots in second round (54th pick overall) of 1998 NFL draft. ... Signed by Patriots (June 15, 1998). ... Granted unconditional free agency (March 1, 2002). ... Signed by Houston Texans (April 10, 2002).
PLAYING EXPERIENCE: New England NFL, 1998-2001. ... Games/Games started: 1998 (16/4), 1999 (16/2), 2000 (16/11), 2001 (15/14). Total: 63/31.
CHAMPIONSHIP GAME EXPERIENCE: Played in AFC championship game (2001 season). ... Member of Super Bowl championship team (2001 season).
PRO STATISTICS: 1999—Caught seven passes for 66 yards and fumbled once. 2000—Caught 15 passes for 103 yards and a touchdown and recovered one fumble. 2001—Caught five passes for 35 yards.
SINGLE GAME HIGHS (regular season): Receptions—4 (November 23, 2000, vs. Detroit); yards—27 (December 4, 2000, vs. Kansas City); and touchdown receptions—1 (November 12, 2000, vs. Cleveland).

RYPIEN, MARK   QB

PERSONAL: Born October 2, 1962, in Calgary, Alberta. ... 6-4/225. ... Full name: Mark Robert Rypien. ... Brother of Tim Rypien, catcher with Toronto Blue Jays organization (1984-1986); and cousin of Shane Churla, forward with six NHL teams (1986-96). ... Name pronounced RIP-in.
HIGH SCHOOL: Shadle Park (Spokane, Wash.).
COLLEGE: Washington State.
TRANSACTIONS/CAREER NOTES: Selected by Washington Redskins in sixth round (146th pick overall) of 1986 NFL draft. ... Signed by Redskins (July 18, 1986). ... On injured reserve with knee injury (September 5, 1986-entire season). ... On injured reserve with back injury (September 7-November 28, 1987). ... Active for one game with Redskins (1987); did not play. ... On injured reserve with knee injury (September 26-November 17, 1990). ... Granted free agency (February 1, 1991). ... Re-signed by Redskins (July 24, 1991). ... Granted free agency (February 1, 1992). ... Re-signed by Redskins (August 11, 1992). ... Released by Redskins (April 13, 1994). ... Signed by Cleveland Browns (May 10, 1994). ... Granted unconditional free agency (February 17, 1995). ... Signed by St. Louis Rams (May 8, 1995). ... Granted free agency (February 16, 1996). ... Signed by Philadelphia Eagles (October 3, 1996). ... Granted unconditional free agency (February 14, 1997). ... Signed by Rams (March 5, 1997). ... Granted unconditional free agency (February 13, 1998). ... Signed by Atlanta Falcons (April 3, 1998). ... Released by Falcons (July 20, 1998). ... Signed by Indianapolis Colts (July 31, 2001). ... Granted unconditional free agency (March 1, 2002).

CHAMPIONSHIP GAME EXPERIENCE: Played in NFC championship game (1991 season). ... Member of Super Bowl championship team (1987 and 1991 seasons).
HONORS: Played in Pro Bowl (1989 and 1991 seasons). ... Named Most Valuable Player of Super Bowl XXVI (1991 season).
PRO STATISTICS: 1988—Fumbled six times. 1989—Fumbled 14 times and recovered two fumbles. 1990—Fumbled twice. 1991—Fumbled nine times and recovered three fumbles for minus five yards. 1992—Fumbled four times and recovered two fumbles. 1993—Fumbled seven times. 1994—Fumbled twice. 1995—Fumbled once.
SINGLE GAME HIGHS (regular season): Attempts—55 (December 10, 1995, vs. Buffalo); completions—34 (December 17, 1995, vs. Washington); yards—442 (November 10, 1991, vs. Atlanta); and touchdown passes—6 (November 10, 1991, vs. Atlanta).
STATISTICAL PLATEAUS: 300-yard passing games: 1988 (2), 1989 (5), 1990 (1), 1991 (2), 1995 (3). Total: 13.
MISCELLANEOUS: Regular-season record as starting NFL quarterback: 47-31 (.603). Postseason record as starting NFL quarterback: 5-2 (.714).

					PASSING						RUSHING				TOTALS	
Year Team	G	GS	Att.	Cmp.	Pct.	Yds.	TD	Int.	Avg.	Rat.	Att.	Yds.	Avg.	TD	TD	2pt.	Pts.
1986—Washington NFL						Did not play.										
1987—Washington NFL						Did not play.										
1988—Washington NFL	9	6	208	114	54.8	1730	18	13	8.32	85.2	9	31	3.4	1	1	0	6
1989—Washington NFL	14	14	476	280	58.8	3768	22	13	7.92	88.1	26	56	2.2	1	1	0	6
1990—Washington NFL	10	10	304	166	54.6	2070	16	11	6.81	78.4	15	4	0.3	0	0	0	0
1991—Washington NFL	16	16	421	249	59.1	‡3564	‡28	11	8.47	97.9	15	6	0.4	1	1	0	6
1992—Washington NFL	16	16	‡479	269	56.2	3282	13	17	6.85	71.7	36	50	1.4	2	2	0	12
1993—Washington NFL	12	10	319	166	52.0	1514	4	10	4.75	56.3	9	4	0.4	3	3	0	18
1994—Cleveland NFL	6	3	128	59	46.1	694	4	3	5.42	63.7	7	4	0.6	0	0	0	0
1995—St. Louis NFL	11	3	217	129	59.4	1448	9	8	6.67	77.9	9	10	1.1	0	0	0	0
1996—Philadelphia NFL	1	0	13	10	76.9	76	1	0	5.85	116.2	0	0	0.0	0	0	0	0
1997—St. Louis NFL	5	0	39	19	48.7	270	0	2	6.92	50.2	1	1	1.0	0	0	0	0
1998—						Did not play.										
1999—						Did not play.										
2000—						Did not play.										
2001—Indianapolis NFL	4	0	9	5	55.6	57	0	0	6.33	74.8	0	0	0.0	0	0	0	0
Pro totals (11 years)	104	78	2613	1466	56.1	18473	115	88	7.07	78.9	127	166	1.3	8	8	0	48

SALAAM, EPHRAIM　　　　OT　　　　BRONCOS

PERSONAL: Born June 19, 1976, in Chicago. ... 6-7/300. ... Full name: Ephraim Mateen Salaam. ... Name pronounced EFF-rum sah-LAHM.
HIGH SCHOOL: Florin (Sacramento).
COLLEGE: San Diego State.
TRANSACTIONS/CAREER NOTES: Selected by Atlanta Falcons in seventh round (199th pick overall) of 1998 NFL draft. ... Signed by Falcons (June 3, 1998). ... Granted free agency (March 2, 2001). ... Re-signed by Falcons (April 6, 2001). ... Granted unconditional free agency (March 1, 2002). ... Signed by Denver Broncos (April 15, 2002).
PLAYING EXPERIENCE: Atlanta NFL, 1998-2001. ... Games/Games started: 1998 (16/16), 1999 (16/16), 2000 (14/10), 2001 (14/13). Total: 60/55.
CHAMPIONSHIP GAME EXPERIENCE: Played in NFC championship game (1998 season). ... Played in Super Bowl XXXIII (1998 season).

SALAVE'A, JOE　　　　DT　　　　TITANS

PERSONAL: Born March 23, 1975, in Leone, American Samoa. ... 6-3/295. ... Full name: Joe Fagaone Salave'a. ... Name pronounced sala-VAY-uh.
HIGH SCHOOL: Oceanside (Calif.).
COLLEGE: Arizona (degree in sociology, 1997).
TRANSACTIONS/CAREER NOTES: Selected by Tennessee Oilers in fourth round (107th pick overall) of 1998 NFL draft. ... Signed by Oilers (June 30, 1998). ... Oilers franchise renamed Tennessee Titans for 1999 season (December 26, 1998). ... Granted free agency (March 2, 2001). ... Re-signed by Titans (April 25, 2001). ... Granted unconditional free agency (March 1, 2002). ... Re-signed by Titans (May 9, 2002).
PLAYING EXPERIENCE: Tennessee NFL, 1998-2001. ... Games/Games started: 1998 (13/0), 1999 (10/0), 2000 (15/1), 2001 (11/0). Total: 49/1.
CHAMPIONSHIP GAME EXPERIENCE: Played in AFC championship game (1999 season). ... Played in Super Bowl XXXIV (1999 season).
HONORS: Named defensive tackle on THE SPORTING NEWS college All-America third team (1997).
PRO STATISTICS: 1998—Credited with one sack. 2000—Credited with four sacks.

SALEH, TAREK　　　　LB

PERSONAL: Born November 7, 1974, in Woodbridge, Conn. ... 6-0/240. ... Full name: Tarek Muhammad Saleh. ... Name pronounced TAR-ick sa-LAY.
HIGH SCHOOL: Notre Dame (West Haven, Conn.).
COLLEGE: Wisconsin.
TRANSACTIONS/CAREER NOTES: Selected by Carolina Panthers in fourth round (122nd pick overall) of 1997 NFL draft. ... Signed by Panthers for 1997 season. ... Selected by Cleveland Browns from Panthers in NFL expansion draft (February 9, 1999). ... Granted free agency (February 11, 2000). ... Re-signed by Browns (April 12, 2000) ... Granted unconditional free agency (March 2, 2001). ... Re-signed by Browns (March 5, 2001). ... Granted unconditional free agency (March 1, 2002).
PLAYING EXPERIENCE: Carolina NFL, 1997 and 1998; Cleveland NFL, 1999-2001. ... Games/Games started: 1997 (3/0), 1998 (11/1), 1999 (16/0), 2000 (16/0), 2001 (13/0). Total: 59/1.
PRO STATISTICS: 1997—Credited with one sack. 1998—Returned one kickoff for eight yards. 1999—Returned five kickoffs for 43 yards and recovered one fumble. 2000—Caught one pass for 22 yards, returned four kickoffs for 46 yards and recovered one fumble.

SAMUEL, KHARI — LB — TEXANS

PERSONAL: Born October 14, 1976, in New York. ... 6-3/240. ... Full name: Khari Iman Mitchell Samuel. ... Name pronounced CAR-ee.
HIGH SCHOOL: Framingham (Mass.).
COLLEGE: Massachusetts.
TRANSACTIONS/CAREER NOTES: Selected by Chicago Bears in fifth round (144th pick overall) of 1999 NFL draft. ... Signed by Bears (May 26, 1999). ... Released by Bears (September 28, 2001). ... Signed by Detroit Lions (October 17, 2001). ... Granted free agency (March 1, 2002). ... Signed by Houston Texans (March 20, 2002).
PLAYING EXPERIENCE: Chicago NFL, 1999 and 2000; Chicago (1)-Detroit (9) NFL, 2001. ... Games/Games started: 1999 (13/1), 2000 (16/0), 2001 (Chi.-1/0; Det.-9/0; Total: 10/0). Total: 39/1.
PRO STATISTICS: 1999—Recovered one fumble.

SAMUELS, CHRIS — OT — REDSKINS

PERSONAL: Born July 28, 1977, in Mobile, Ala. ... 6-5/303.
HIGH SCHOOL: Shaw (Mobile, Ala.).
COLLEGE: Alabama.
TRANSACTIONS/CAREER NOTES: Selected by Washington Redskins in first round (third pick overall) of 2000 NFL draft. ... Signed by Redskins (July 18, 2000).
PLAYING EXPERIENCE: Washington NFL, 2000 and 2001. ... Games/Games started: 2000 (16/16), 2001 (16/16). Total: 32/32.
HONORS: Outland Trophy winner (1999). ... Named offensive tackle on THE SPORTING NEWS college All-America first team (1999).
PRO STATISTICS: 2001—Recovered one fumble.

SANCHEZ, DAVIS — DB — CHARGERS

PERSONAL: Born August 7, 1974, in Vancouver. ... 5-10/190.
HIGH SCHOOL: North Delta (British Columbia).
JUNIOR COLLEGE: Butte Junior College.
COLLEGE: Oregon.
TRANSACTIONS/CAREER NOTES: Selected by Montreal Alouettes in first round (sixth pick overall) in 1999 CFL draft. ... Announced retirement (December 20, 1999). ... Signed as non-drafted free agent by San Diego Chargers (February 17, 2001).
PLAYING EXPERIENCE: Montreal CFL, 1999 and 2000; San Diego NFL, 2001. ... Games/Games started: 1999 (17/games started unavailable), 2000 (18/-), 2001 (12/2). Total CFL: 35/-. Total NFL: 12/2. Total Pro: 47/-.
PRO STATISTICS: 1999—Intercepted three passes for 42 yards. 2000—Intercepted nine passes for 163 yards and two touchdowns and returned one punt for no yards.

SANDERS, CHRIS — WR — BROWNS

PERSONAL: Born May 8, 1972, in Denver. ... 6-1/190. ... Full name: Christopher Dwayne Sanders.
HIGH SCHOOL: Montbello (Denver).
COLLEGE: Ohio State.
TRANSACTIONS/CAREER NOTES: Selected by Houston Oilers in third round (67th pick overall) of 1995 NFL draft. ... Signed by Oilers (July 20, 1995). ... Oilers franchise moved to Tennessee for 1997 season. ... Oilers franchise renamed Tennessee Titans for 1999 season (December 26, 1998). ... Released by Titans (February 28, 2002). ... Signed by Cleveland Browns (March 28, 2002).
CHAMPIONSHIP GAME EXPERIENCE: Played in AFC championship game (1999 season). ... Played in Super Bowl XXXIV (1999 season).
PRO STATISTICS: 1995—Rushed twice for minus 19 yards. 1997—Rushed once for minus eight yards. 1998—Rushed once for minus nine yards.
SINGLE GAME HIGHS (regular season): Receptions—7 (December 14, 1997, vs. Baltimore); yards—147 (November 26, 1995, vs. Denver); and touchdown receptions—2 (October 26, 1997, vs. Arizona).
STATISTICAL PLATEAUS: 100-yard receiving games: 1995 (1), 1996 (3), 1997 (1), 1998 (1), 1999 (1). Total: 7.

				RECEIVING			TOTALS			
Year Team	G	GS	No.	Yds.	Avg.	TD	TD	2pt.	Pts.	Fum.
1995—Houston NFL	16	10	35	823	*23.5	9	9	0	54	0
1996—Houston NFL	16	15	48	882	§18.4	4	4	0	24	0
1997—Tennessee NFL	15	14	31	498	16.1	3	3	0	18	1
1998—Tennessee NFL	14	1	5	136	27.2	0	0	0	0	0
1999—Tennessee NFL	16	0	20	336	16.8	1	1	0	6	0
2000—Tennessee NFL	16	14	33	536	16.2	0	0	0	0	1
2001—Tennessee NFL	4	0	5	74	14.8	0	0	0	0	0
Pro totals (7 years)	97	54	177	3285	18.6	17	17	0	102	3

SANDERS, FRANK — WR — CARDINALS

PERSONAL: Born February 17, 1973, in Fort Lauderdale, Fla. ... 6-2/200. ... Full name: Frank Vondel Sanders.
HIGH SCHOOL: Dillard (Fort Lauderdale, Fla.).
COLLEGE: Auburn.
TRANSACTIONS/CAREER NOTES: Selected by Arizona Cardinals in second round (47th pick overall) of 1995 NFL draft. ... Signed by Cardinals (July 17, 1995). ... Granted free agency (February 13, 1998). ... Re-signed by Cardinals (March 13, 1998).
HONORS: Named wide receiver on THE SPORTING NEWS college All-America second team (1994).
PRO STATISTICS: 1995—Rushed once for one yard. 1996—Rushed twice for minus four yards and recovered one fumble. 1997—Attempted one pass with a completion for 26 yards and rushed once for five yards. 1998—Rushed four times for no yards and recovered two fumbles. 1999—Attempted one pass without a completion and recovered one fumble. 2001—Attempted one pass without a completion.
SINGLE GAME HIGHS (regular season): Receptions—13 (January 2, 2000, vs. Green Bay); yards—190 (November 15, 1998, vs. Dallas); and touchdown receptions—2 (October 8, 2000, vs. Cleveland).
STATISTICAL PLATEAUS: 100-yard receiving games: 1995 (2), 1997 (2), 1998 (5), 1999 (2), 2001 (1). Total: 12.

Year Team	G	GS	No.	Yds.	Avg.	TD	TD	2pt.	Pts.	Fum.
1995—Arizona NFL	16	15	52	883	17.0	2	2	2	16	0
1996—Arizona NFL	16	16	69	813	11.8	4	4	0	24	1
1997—Arizona NFL	16	16	75	1017	13.6	4	4	1	26	3
1998—Arizona NFL	16	16	‡89	1145	12.9	3	3	0	18	3
1999—Arizona NFL	16	16	79	954	12.1	1	1	0	6	2
2000—Arizona NFL	16	16	54	749	13.9	6	6	0	36	0
2001—Arizona NFL	15	13	41	618	15.1	2	2	0	12	1
Pro totals (7 years)	111	108	459	6179	13.5	22	22	3	138	10

SANTIAGO, O.J. — TE

PERSONAL: Born April 4, 1974, in Whitby, Ont. ... 6-7/264. ... Full name: Otis Jason Santiago.
HIGH SCHOOL: St. Michael's (Toronto).
COLLEGE: Kent.
TRANSACTIONS/CAREER NOTES: Selected by Atlanta Falcons in third round (70th pick overall) of 1997 NFL draft. ... Signed by Falcons (July 11, 1997). ... On injured reserved with leg injury (November 20, 1997-remainder of season). ... Granted free agency (February 11, 2000). ... Re-signed by Falcons (June 5, 2000). ... Traded by Falcons to Dallas Cowboys for fourth round pick (LB Matt Stewart) in 2001 draft and seventh-round pick (WR Michael Coleman) in 2002 draft (August 27, 2000). ... Claimed on waivers by Cleveland Browns (November 22, 2000). ... Granted unconditional free agency (March 2, 2001). ... Re-signed by Browns (March 26, 2001). ... Granted unconditional free agency (March 1, 2002).
CHAMPIONSHIP GAME EXPERIENCE: Played in NFC championship game (1998 season). ... Played in Super Bowl XXXIII (1998 season).
PRO STATISTICS: 1998—Recovered one fumble. 2000—Returned one kickoff for 13 yards. 2001—Returned two kickoffs for one yard.
SINGLE GAME HIGHS (regular season): Reception—5 (September 14, 1997, vs. Oakland); yards—65 (December 27, 1998, vs. Miami); and touchdown receptions—2 (December 27, 1998, vs. Miami).

Year Team	G	GS	No.	Yds.	Avg.	TD	TD	2pt.	Pts.	Fum.
1997—Atlanta NFL	11	11	17	217	12.8	2	2	0	12	1
1998—Atlanta NFL	16	16	27	428	15.9	5	5	0	30	1
1999—Atlanta NFL	14	14	15	174	11.6	0	0	0	0	0
2000—Dallas NFL	11	0	0	0	0	0	0	0	0	0
2001—Cleveland NFL	14	12	17	153	9.0	2	2	0	12	0
Pro totals (5 years)	66	53	76	972	12.8	9	9	0	54	2

SANYIKA, SEKOU — LB — CARDINALS

PERSONAL: Born March 17, 1978, in New Orleans. ... 6-3/246.
HIGH SCHOOL: R.L. Stevenson (Hercules, Calif.).
COLLEGE: California.
TRANSACTIONS/CAREER NOTES: Selected by Arizona Cardinals in seventh round (215th pick overall) of 2000 NFL draft. ... Signed by Cardinals (June 19, 2000).
PLAYING EXPERIENCE: Arizona NFL, 2000 and 2001. ... Games/Games started: 2000 (16/0), 2001 (16/1). Total: 32/1.
PRO STATISTICS: 2001—Credited with one sack and recovered one fumble.

SAPP, WARREN — DT — BUCCANEERS

PERSONAL: Born December 19, 1972, in Orlando. ... 6-2/303. ... Full name: Warren Carlos Sapp.
HIGH SCHOOL: Apopka (Fla.).
COLLEGE: Miami (Fla.).
TRANSACTIONS/CAREER NOTES: Selected after junior season by Tampa Bay Buccaneers in first round (12th pick overall) of 1995 NFL draft. ... Signed by Buccaneers (April 27, 1995).
CHAMPIONSHIP GAME EXPERIENCE: Played in NFC championship game (1999 season).
HONORS: Lombardi Award winner (1994). ... Named defensive lineman on THE SPORTING NEWS college All-America first team (1994). ... Played in Pro Bowl (1997-2000 seasons). ... Named defensive tackle on THE SPORTING NEWS NFL All-Pro team (1999-2001).
PRO STATISTICS: 1995—Intercepted one pass for five yards and a touchdown. 1996—Recovered one fumble. 1997—Recovered one fumble for 23 yards. 1998—Recovered one fumble. 1999—Recovered two fumbles. 2000—Recovered one fumble. 2001—Recovered two fumbles.

Year Team	G	GS	SACKS
1995—Tampa Bay NFL	16	8	3.0
1996—Tampa Bay NFL	15	14	9.0
1997—Tampa Bay NFL	15	15	10.5
1998—Tampa Bay NFL	16	16	7.0
1999—Tampa Bay NFL	15	15	12.5
2000—Tampa Bay NFL	16	15	16.5
2001—Tampa Bay NFL	16	16	6.0
Pro totals (7 years)	109	99	64.5

SATURDAY, JEFF — C — COLTS

PERSONAL: Born June 8, 1975, in Atlanta. ... 6-2/293. ... Full name: Jeffrey Bryant Saturday.
HIGH SCHOOL: Shamrock (Tucker, Ga.).
COLLEGE: North Carolina.
TRANSACTIONS/CAREER NOTES: Signed as non-drafted free agent by Baltimore Ravens (April 27, 1998). ... Released by Ravens (June 12, 1998). ... Signed by Indianapolis Colts (January 7, 1999). ... Granted free agency (March 1, 2002).
PLAYING EXPERIENCE: Indianapolis NFL, 1999-2001. ... Games/Games started: 1999 (11/2), 2000 (16/16), 2001 (16/16). Total: 43/34.
PRO STATISTICS: 2000—Fumbled once and recovered one fumble.

SAUERBRUN, TODD — P — PANTHERS

PERSONAL: Born January 4, 1973, in Setauket, N.Y. ... 5-10/211. ... Name pronounced SOUR-brun.
HIGH SCHOOL: Ward Melville (Setauket, N.Y.).
COLLEGE: West Virginia.
TRANSACTIONS/CAREER NOTES: Selected by Chicago Bears in second round (56th pick overall) of 1995 NFL draft. ... Signed by Bears (July 20, 1995). ... Granted free agency (February 13, 1998). ... Re-signed by Bears (May 19, 1998). ... On injured reserve with knee injury (September 23, 1998-remainder of season). ... Granted unconditional free agency (February 11, 2000). ... Signed by Kansas City Chiefs (March 27, 2000). ... Released by Chiefs (March 13, 2001). ... Signed by Carolina Panthers (April 24, 2001).
HONORS: Named punter on THE SPORTING NEWS college All-America first team (1994). ... Named punter on THE SPORTING NEWS NFL All-Pro team (2001).
PRO STATISTICS: 1996—Rushed once for three yards, attempted two passes with two completions for 63 yards. 1997—Rushed twice for eight yards and fumbled once for minus nine yards. 1999—Rushed once for minus two yards and fumbled once. 2001—Rushed once for no yards.

			PUNTING				
Year Team	G	No.	Yds.	Avg.	Net avg.	In. 20	Blk.
1995—Chicago NFL	15	55	2080	37.8	31.1	16	0
1996—Chicago NFL	16	78	3491	44.8	34.9	15	0
1997—Chicago NFL	16	95	4059	42.7	32.8	26	0
1998—Chicago NFL	3	15	741	49.4	42.1	6	0
1999—Chicago NFL	16	85	3478	40.9	35.4	20	0
2000—Kansas City NFL	16	82	3656	44.6	35.8	28	0
2001—Carolina NFL	16	93	*4419	*47.5	*38.9	35	1
Pro totals (7 years)	98	503	21924	43.6	35.3	146	1

SAWYER, TALANCE — DE — VIKINGS

PERSONAL: Born June 14, 1976, in Bastrop, La. ... 6-2/270.
HIGH SCHOOL: Bastrop (La.).
COLLEGE: UNLV.
TRANSACTIONS/CAREER NOTES: Selected by Minnesota Vikings in sixth round (185th pick overall) of 1999 NFL draft. ... Signed by Vikings (June 4, 1999). ... Granted free agency (March 1, 2002).
PLAYING EXPERIENCE: Minnesota NFL, 1999-2001. ... Games/Games started: 1999 (2/0), 2000 (16/16), 2001 (16/16). Total: 34/32.
CHAMPIONSHIP GAME EXPERIENCE: Played in NFC championship game (2000 season).
PRO STATISTICS: 2000—Credited with six sacks and recovered two fumbles. 2001—Intercepted one pass for two yards, credited with five sacks and recovered two fumbles.

SAYLER, JACE — DL — PATRIOTS

PERSONAL: Born February 27, 1979, in Rockford, Ill. ... 6-5/295. ... Full name: Jace M. Sayler.
HIGH SCHOOL: McHenry (Ill.).
COLLEGE: Michigan State.
TRANSACTIONS/CAREER NOTES: Signed as non-drafted free agent by New England Patriots (April 27, 2001). ... On injured reserve with knee injury (October 5, 2001-remainder of season).
PLAYING EXPERIENCE: New England NFL, 2001. ... Games/Games started: 2001 (2/1).

SCHAU, RYAN — OT/G — TEXANS

PERSONAL: Born December 30, 1975, in Hammond, Ind. ... 6-6/300. ... Twin brother of Thomas Schau, center, Buffalo Bills.
HIGH SCHOOL: Bloomington (Ill.).
COLLEGE: Illinois.
TRANSACTIONS/CAREER NOTES: Signed as non-drafted free agent by Philadelphia Eagles (April 19, 1999). ... Selected by Houston Texans from Eagles in NFL expansion draft (February 18, 2002). ... Granted free agency (March 1, 2002).
PLAYING EXPERIENCE: Philadelphia NFL, 1999-2001. ... Games/Games started: 1999 (1/0), 2000 (10/0), 2001 (2/1). Total: 13/1.
CHAMPIONSHIP GAME EXPERIENCE: Member of Eagles for NFC championship game (2001 season); inactive.

SCHLECHT, JOHN — DT — 49ERS

PERSONAL: Born May 23, 1978, in St. Paul, Minn. ... 6-0/290. ... Full name: John James Schlecht.
HIGH SCHOOL: White Bear Lake (Minn.).
COLLEGE: Minnesota.
TRANSACTIONS/CAREER NOTES: Signed as non-drafted free agent by San Francisco 49ers (April 25, 2001).
PLAYING EXPERIENCE: San Francisco NFL, 2001. ... Games/Games started: 2001 (8/0).

SCHLESINGER, CORY — FB — LIONS

PERSONAL: Born June 23, 1972, in Columbus, Neb. ... 6-0/246.
HIGH SCHOOL: Columbus (Neb.).
COLLEGE: Nebraska (degree in indusrial technology education).
TRANSACTIONS/CAREER NOTES: Selected by Detroit Lions in sixth round (192nd pick overall) of 1995 NFL draft. ... Signed by Lions (July 19, 1995). ... Granted unconditional free agency (March 2, 2001). ... Re-signed by Lions (March 2, 2001).
PRO STATISTICS: 1995—Recovered one fumble for 11 yards. 1999—Returned two kickoffs for 33 yards and recovered one fumble. 2000—Returned two kickoffs for 25 yards. 2001—Returned one kickoff for 10 yards and recovered one fumble.
SINGLE GAME HIGHS (regular season): Attempts—10 (September 12, 1999, vs. Seattle); yards—50 (September 12, 1999, vs. Seattle); and rushing touchdowns—1 (December 16, 2001, vs. Minnesota).

				RUSHING				RECEIVING			TOTALS			
Year Team	G	GS	Att.	Yds.	Avg.	TD	No.	Yds.	Avg.	TD	TD	2pt.	Pts.	Fum.
1995—Detroit NFL	16	1	1	1	1.0	0	1	2	2.0	0	0	0	0	0
1996—Detroit NFL	16	1	0	0	0.0	0	0	0	0.0	0	0	0	0	0
1997—Detroit NFL	16	2	7	11	1.6	0	5	69	13.8	1	1	0	6	0
1998—Detroit NFL	15	2	5	17	3.4	0	3	16	5.3	1	1	0	6	0
1999—Detroit NFL	16	11	43	124	2.9	0	21	151	7.2	1	1	0	6	4
2000—Detroit NFL	16	6	1	3	3.0	0	12	73	6.1	0	0	0	0	0
2001—Detroit NFL	16	13	47	154	3.3	3	60	466	7.8	0	3	0	18	1
Pro totals (7 years)	111	36	104	310	3.0	3	102	777	7.6	3	6	0	36	5

SCHNECK, MIKE   C   STEELERS

PERSONAL: Born August 4, 1977, in Whitefish Bay, Wis. ... 6-1/246. ... Full name: Mike Louis Schneck.
HIGH SCHOOL: Whitefish Bay (Wis.).
COLLEGE: Wisconsin.
TRANSACTIONS/CAREER NOTES: Signed as non-drafted free agent by Pittsburgh Steelers (April 23, 1999); contract voided by NFL because he did not meet eligibility requirements. ... Re-signed by Steelers (July 12, 1999). ... Granted free agency (March 1, 2002). ... Re-signed by Steelers (April 24, 2002).
PLAYING EXPERIENCE: Pittsburgh NFL, 1999-2001. ... Games/Games started: 1999 (16/0), 2000 (16/0), 2001 (16/0). Total: 48/0.
CHAMPIONSHIP GAME EXPERIENCE: Played in AFC championship game (2001 season).

SCHOBEL, AARON   DE   BILLS

PERSONAL: Born April 1, 1977, in Columbus, Texas. ... 6-4/265.
HIGH SCHOOL: Columbus (Texas).
COLLEGE: Texas Christian.
TRANSACTIONS/CAREER NOTES: Selected by Buffalo Bills in second round (46th pick overall) of 2001 NFL draft. ... Signed by Bills (July 26, 2001).
HONORS: Named defensive end on THE SPORTING NEWS college All-America second team (2000).

Year Team	G	GS	SACKS
2001—Buffalo NFL	16	11	6.5

SCHROEDER, BILL   WR   LIONS

PERSONAL: Born January 9, 1971, in Eau Claire, Wis. ... 6-3/205. ... Full name: William Fredrich Schroeder. ... Name pronounced SHRAY-der.
HIGH SCHOOL: Sheboygan (Wis.) South.
COLLEGE: Wisconsin-La Crosse (degree in physical education/teaching).
TRANSACTIONS/CAREER NOTES: Selected by Green Bay Packers in sixth round (181st pick overall) of 1994 NFL draft. ... Signed by Packers (May 10, 1994). ... Released by Packers (August 28, 1994). ... Re-signed by Packers to practice squad (August 30, 1994). ... Activated (December 29, 1994). ... Traded by Packers with TE Jeff Wilner to New England Patriots for C Mike Arthur (August 11, 1995). ... On injured reserve with foot injury (August 27, 1995-entire season). ... Released by Patriots (August 14, 1996). ... Signed by Packers to practice squad (August 28, 1996). ... Assigned by Packers to Rhein Fire in 1997 World League enhancement allocation program (February 19, 1997). ... On injured reserve with broken collarbone (December 9, 1998-remainder of season). ... Granted unconditional free agency (March 1, 2002). ... Signed by Detroit Lions (March 14, 2002).
CHAMPIONSHIP GAME EXPERIENCE: Member of Packers for NFC championship game (1997 season); inactive. ... Member of Packers for Super Bowl XXXII (1997 season); inactive.
PRO STATISTICS: W.L.: 1997—Rushed twice of 18 yards. NFL: 1997—Recovered one fumble. 2000—Rushed twice for 11 yards. 2001—Rushed once for six yards.
SINGLE GAME HIGHS (regular season): Receptions—8 (December 17, 2000, vs. Minnesota); yards—158 (October 10, 1999, vs. Tampa Bay); and touchdown receptions—2 (October 1, 2000, vs. Chicago).
STATISTICAL PLATEAUS: 100-yard receiving games: 1998 (1), 1999 (1), 2000 (3), 2001 (5). Total: 10.

			RECEIVING				PUNT RETURNS				KICKOFF RETURNS				TOTALS			
Year Team	G	GS	No.	Yds.	Avg.	TD	No.	Yds.	Avg.	TD	No.	Yds.	Avg.	TD	TD	2pt.	Pts.	Fum.
1994—Green Bay NFL								Did not play.										
1995—New England NFL								Did not play.										
1996—Green Bay NFL								Did not play.										
1997—Rhein W.L.	...	...	43	702	16.3	6	0	0	0.0	0	1	20	20.0	0	6	0	36	0
—Green Bay NFL	15	1	2	15	7.5	0	33	342	10.4	0	24	562	23.4	0	1	0	6	4
1998—Green Bay NFL	13	3	31	452	14.6	1	2	5	2.5	0	0	0	0.0	0	1	0	6	1
1999—Green Bay NFL	16	16	74	1051	14.2	5	0	0	0.0	0	1	10	10.0	0	5	0	30	3
2000—Green Bay NFL	16	16	65	999	15.4	4	0	0	0.0	0	0	0	0.0	0	4	0	24	1
2001—Green Bay NFL	14	14	53	918	±17.3	9	0	0	0.0	0	0	0	0.0	0	9	0	54	1
W.L. totals (1 year)	...	...	43	702	16.3	6	0	0	0.0	0	1	20	20.0	0	6	0	36	0
NFL totals (4 years)	74	50	225	3435	15.3	20	35	347	9.9	0	25	572	22.9	0	20	0	120	10
Pro totals (5 years)	...	...	268	4137	15.4	26	35	347	9.9	0	26	592	22.8	0	26	0	156	10

SCHULTERS, LANCE   S   TITANS

PERSONAL: Born May 27, 1975, in Guyana. ... 6-2/207.
HIGH SCHOOL: Canarsie (Brooklyn, N.Y.).
JUNIOR COLLEGE: Nassau Community College (N.Y.).
COLLEGE: Hofstra.
TRANSACTIONS/CAREER NOTES: Selected by San Francisco 49ers in fourth round (119th pick overall) of 1998 NFL draft. ... Signed by 49ers (July 18, 1998). ... On injured reserve with knee injury (December 21, 2000-remainder of season). ... Granted free agency (March 2, 2001).

... Re-signed by 49ers (March 2, 2002). ... On physically unable to perform list with knee injury (July 29-August 6, 2001). ... Granted unconditional free agency (March 1, 2002). ... Signed by Tennessee Titans (April 11, 2002).
HONORS: Played in Pro Bowl (1999 season).
PRO STATISTICS: 2000—Credited with 1/2 sack and recovered one fumble for 16 yards. 2001—Credited with one sack and recovered two fumbles for 20 yards.

				INTERCEPTIONS		
Year Team	G	GS	No.	Yds.	Avg.	TD
1998—San Francisco NFL	15	0	0	0	0.0	0
1999—San Francisco NFL	13	13	6	127	21.2	1
2000—San Francisco NFL	12	12	0	0	0.0	0
2001—San Francisco NFL	16	16	3	0	0.0	0
Pro totals (4 years)	56	41	9	127	14.1	1

SCHULZ, KURT   S

PERSONAL: Born December 12, 1968, in Wenatchee, Wash. ... 6-1/208. ... Full name: Kurt Erich Schulz.
HIGH SCHOOL: Eisenhower (Yakima, Wash.).
COLLEGE: Eastern Washington.
TRANSACTIONS/CAREER NOTES: Selected by Buffalo Bills in seventh round (195th pick overall) of 1992 NFL draft. ... Signed by Bills (July 22, 1992). ... On injured reserve with knee injury (October 26-December 19, 1992). ... Granted unconditional free agency (February 11, 2000). ... Signed by Detroit Lions (February 18, 2000). ... Released by Lions (February 27, 2002).
CHAMPIONSHIP GAME EXPERIENCE: Played in AFC championship game (1993 season). ... Member of Bills for Super Bowl XXVII (1992 season); inactive. ... Played in Super Bowl XXVIII (1993 season).
PRO STATISTICS: 1992—Recovered two fumbles. 1998—Recovered one fumble for nine yards. 1999—Recovered one fumble.

				INTERCEPTIONS		
Year Team	G	GS	No.	Yds.	Avg.	TD
1992—Buffalo NFL	8	1	0	0	0.0	0
1993—Buffalo NFL	12	0	0	0	0.0	0
1994—Buffalo NFL	16	0	0	0	0.0	0
1995—Buffalo NFL	13	13	6	48	8.0	▲1
1996—Buffalo NFL	15	15	4	24	6.0	0
1997—Buffalo NFL	15	14	2	23	11.5	0
1998—Buffalo NFL	12	12	6	48	8.0	0
1999—Buffalo NFL	16	16	3	26	8.7	0
2000—Detroit NFL	11	11	7	53	7.6	0
2001—Detroit NFL	11	10	2	22	11.0	0
Pro totals (10 years)	129	92	30	244	8.1	1

SCIOLI, BRAD   DE   COLTS

PERSONAL: Born September 6, 1976, in Bridgeport, Pa. ... 6-3/280. ... Full name: Brad Elliott Scioli. ... Name pronounced SHE-o-lee.
HIGH SCHOOL: Upper Merion (King of Prussia, Pa.).
COLLEGE: Penn State.
TRANSACTIONS/CAREER NOTES: Selected by Indianapolis Colts in fifth round (138th pick overall) of 1999 NFL draft. ... Signed by Colts (July 22, 1999). ... Granted free agency (March 1, 2002).
PLAYING EXPERIENCE: Indianapolis NFL, 1999-2001. ... Games/Games started: 1999 (10/0), 2000 (16/2), 2001 (13/12). Total: 39/14.
PRO STATISTICS: 2000—Credited with two sacks. 2001—Credited with four sacks.

SCOTT, CAREY   CB   VIKINGS

PERSONAL: Born August 11, 1978, in Savannah, Ga. ... 5-11/207.
HIGH SCHOOL: Beach (Ga.).
COLLEGE: Kentucky State.
TRANSACTIONS/CAREER NOTES: Selected by Minnesota Vikings in sixth round (189th pick overall) of 2001 NFL draft. ... Signed by Vikings (July 30, 2001). ... On injured reserve with stomach injury (September 2, 2001-entire season).

				INTERCEPTIONS		
Year Team	G	GS	No.	Yds.	Avg.	TD
2001—Minnesota NFL				Did not play.		

SCOTT, CEDRIC   DE   GIANTS

PERSONAL: Born October 19, 1977, in Gulfport, Miss. ... 6-5/274.
HIGH SCHOOL: Gulfport (Miss.).
COLLEGE: Southern Mississippi (degree in exercise physiology).
TRANSACTIONS/CAREER NOTES: Selected by New York Giants in fourth round (114th pick overall) of 2001 NFL draft. ... Signed by Giants (July 26, 2001).
PLAYING EXPERIENCE: New York Giants NFL, 2001. ... Games/Games started: 2001 (9/0).

SCOTT, CHAD   DB   STEELERS

PERSONAL: Born September 6, 1974, in Capitol Heights, Md. ... 6-1/201. ... Full name: Chad Oliver Scott.
HIGH SCHOOL: Suitland (Forestville, Md.).
COLLEGE: Towson State, then Maryland.

TRANSACTIONS/CAREER NOTES: Selected by Pittsburgh Steelers in first round (24th pick overall) of 1997 NFL draft. ... Signed by Steelers (July 16, 1997). ... On injured reserve with knee injury (July 20, 1998-entire season).
CHAMPIONSHIP GAME EXPERIENCE: Played in AFC championship game (1997 and 2001 seasons).
PRO STATISTICS: 2000—Recovered two fumbles for six yards.

				INTERCEPTIONS			
Year Team	G	GS	No.	Yds.	Avg.	TD
1997—Pittsburgh NFL	13	9	2	-4	-2.0	0
1998—Pittsburgh NFL				Did not play.		
1999—Pittsburgh NFL	13	12	1	16	16.0	0
2000—Pittsburgh NFL	16	16	5	49	9.8	0
2001—Pittsburgh NFL	15	15	5	204	40.8	†2
Pro totals (4 years)	57	52	13	265	20.4	2

SCOTT, DARNAY   WR   BENGALS

PERSONAL: Born July 7, 1972, in St. Louis. ... 6-1/204.
HIGH SCHOOL: Kearny (San Diego).
COLLEGE: San Diego State.
TRANSACTIONS/CAREER NOTES: Selected after junior season by Cincinnati Bengals in second round (30th pick overall) of 1994 NFL draft. ... Signed by Bengals (July 18, 1994). ... Granted free agency (February 14, 1997). ... Re-signed by Bengals (June 16, 1997). ... On injured reserve with fractured leg (August 2, 2000-entire season).
PRO STATISTICS: 1994—Completed only pass attempt for 53 yards. 2001—Recovered one fumble.
SINGLE GAME HIGHS (regular season): Receptions—9 (January 6, 2002, vs. Tennessee); yards—157 (November 6, 1994, vs. Seattle); and touchdown receptions—2 (November 21, 1999, vs. Baltimore).
STATISTICAL PLATEAUS: 100-yard receiving games: 1994 (2), 1995 (1), 1996 (1), 1997 (2), 1998 (2), 1999 (2), 2001 (3). Total: 13.

			RUSHING				RECEIVING				KICKOFF RETURNS				TOTALS		
Year Team	G	GS	Att.	Yds.	Avg.	TD	No.	Yds.	Avg.	TD	No.	Yds.	Avg.	TD	TD	2pt.	Pts.	Fum.
1994—Cincinnati NFL	16	12	10	106	10.6	0	46	866	§18.8	5	15	342	22.8	0	5	0	30	0
1995—Cincinnati NFL	16	16	5	11	2.2	0	52	821	15.8	5	0	0	0.0	0	5	0	30	0
1996—Cincinnati NFL	16	16	3	4	1.3	0	58	833	14.4	5	0	0	0.0	0	5	0	30	0
1997—Cincinnati NFL	16	15	1	6	6.0	0	54	797	14.8	5	0	0	0.0	0	5	0	30	0
1998—Cincinnati NFL	13	13	2	10	5.0	0	51	817	16.0	7	0	0	0.0	0	7	0	42	0
1999—Cincinnati NFL	16	16	0	0	0.0	0	68	1022	15.0	7	0	0	0.0	0	7	0	42	0
2000—Cincinnati NFL									Did not play.									
2001—Cincinnati NFL	16	15	0	0	0.0	0	57	819	14.4	2	0	0	0.0	0	2	0	12	0
Pro totals (7 years)	109	103	21	137	6.5	0	386	5975	15.5	36	15	342	22.8	0	36	0	216	0

SCOTT, GARI   WR   EAGLES

PERSONAL: Born June 2, 1978, in West Palm Beach, Fla. ... 6-0/191. ... Full name: Gari J. Scott.
HIGH SCHOOL: Suncoast (Riviera Beach, Fla.).
COLLEGE: Michigan State.
TRANSACTIONS/CAREER NOTES: Selected by Philadelphia Eagles in fourth round (99th pick overall) of 2000 NFL draft. ... Signed by Eagles (June 16, 2000). ... Active for one game (2000); did not play.
CHAMPIONSHIP GAME EXPERIENCE: Member of Eagles for NFC championship game (2001 season); inactive.
SINGLE GAME HIGHS (regular season): Receptions—2 (January 6, 2002, vs. Tampa Bay); yards—26 (January 6, 2002, vs. Tampa Bay); and touchdown receptions—0.

			RECEIVING				TOTALS		
Year Team	G	GS	No.	Yds.	Avg.	TD	2pt.	Pts.	Fum.
2000—Philadelphia NFL				Did not play.					
2001—Philadelphia NFL	3	0	2	26	13.0	0	0	0	0
Pro totals (1 years)	3	0	2	26	13.0	0	0	0	0

SCOTT, LYNN   S   COWBOYS

PERSONAL: Born June 23, 1977, in Turpin, Okla. ... 6-0/210.
HIGH SCHOOL: Turpin (Okla.).
COLLEGE: Northwestern Oklahoma.
TRANSACTIONS/CAREER NOTES: Signed as non-drafted free agent by Dallas Cowboys (April 27, 2001).
PLAYING EXPERIENCE: Dallas NFL, 2001. ... Games/Games started: 2001 (14/0).
PRO STATISTICS: 2001—Recovered two fumbles.

SCOTT, TONY   CB   JETS

PERSONAL: Born October 3, 1976, in Lawndale, N.C. ... 5-10/193. ... Full name: Tony M. Scott.
HIGH SCHOOL: Lawndale (N.C.).
COLLEGE: North Carolina State.
TRANSACTIONS/CAREER NOTES: Selected by New York Jets in sixth round (179th pick overall) of 2000 NFL draft. ... Signed by Jets (May 9, 2000).
PRO STATISTICS: 2000—Returned one kickoff for no yards and recovered one fumble.

				INTERCEPTIONS			
Year Team	G	GS	No.	Yds.	Avg.	TD
2000—New York Jets NFL	16	0	1	0	0.0	0
2001—New York Jets NFL	7	0	0	0	0.0	0
Pro totals (2 years)	23	0	1	0	0.0	0

SCOTT, YUSUF — G

PERSONAL: Born November 30, 1976, in La Porte, Texas. ... 6-3/348. ... Full name: Yusuf Jamall Scott.
HIGH SCHOOL: La Porte (Texas).
COLLEGE: Arizona (degree in sociology).
TRANSACTIONS/CAREER NOTES: Selected after junior season by Arizona Cardinals in fifth round (168th pick overall) of 1999 NFL draft. ... Signed by Cardinals (June 18, 1999). ... Granted free agency (March 1, 2002).
PLAYING EXPERIENCE: Arizona NFL, 1999-2001. ... Games/Games started: 1999 (10/0), 2000 (9/0), 2001 (5/0). Total: 24/0.

SCROGGINS, TRACY — DE

PERSONAL: Born September 11, 1969, in Checotah, Okla. ... 6-3/273.
HIGH SCHOOL: Checotah (Okla.).
JUNIOR COLLEGE: Coffeyville (Kan.) Community College.
COLLEGE: Tulsa.
TRANSACTIONS/CAREER NOTES: Selected by Detroit Lions in second round (53rd pick overall) of 1992 NFL draft. ... Signed by Lions (July 23, 1992). ... Granted free agency (February 17, 1995). ... Re-signed by Lions (May 17, 1995). ... Granted unconditional free agency (March 2, 2001). ... Re-signed by Lions (May 3, 2001). ... Released by Lions (February 27, 2002).
PRO STATISTICS: 1993—Intercepted one pass for no yards and recovered one fumble. 1994—Recovered one fumble. 1995—Recovered one fumble for 81 yards and a touchdown. 1996—Recovered one fumble. 1997—Recovered one fumble for 17 yards and a touchdown and credited with a safety. 1999—Recovered two fumbles for four yards.

Year Team	G	GS	SACKS
1992—Detroit NFL	16	7	7.5
1993—Detroit NFL	16	0	8.0
1994—Detroit NFL	16	9	2.5
1995—Detroit NFL	16	16	9.5
1996—Detroit NFL	6	6	2.0
1997—Detroit NFL	15	6	7.5
1998—Detroit NFL	11	3	6.5
1999—Detroit NFL	14	11	8.5
2000—Detroit NFL	16	15	6.5
2001—Detroit NFL	16	16	2.0
Pro totals (10 years)	142	89	60.5

SEARCY, LEON — G — DOLPHINS

PERSONAL: Born December 21, 1969, in Washington, D.C. ... 6-4/320. ... Full name: Leon Searcy Jr.
HIGH SCHOOL: Maynard Evans (Orlando).
COLLEGE: Miami, Fla. (degree in sociology, 1992).
TRANSACTIONS/CAREER NOTES: Selected by Pittsburgh Steelers in first round (11th pick overall) of 1992 NFL draft. ... Signed by Steelers (August 3, 1992). ... Granted unconditional free agency (February 16, 1996). ... Signed by Jacksonville Jaguars (February 18, 1996). ... Inactive for 12 games (2000). ... On injured reserve with leg injury (November 29, 2000-remainder of season). ... Released by Jaguars (March 1, 2001). ... Signed by Baltimore Ravens (March 12, 2001). ... Suspended one game by NFL for violating league personal conduct policy (October 10, 2001). ... On injured reserve with arm injury (October 26, 2001-remainder of season). ... Released by Ravens (February 28, 2002). ... Signed by Miami Dolphins (March 8, 2002).
PLAYING EXPERIENCE: Pittsburgh NFL, 1992-1995; Jacksonville NFL, 1996-1999. ... Games/Games started: 1992 (15/0), 1993 (16/16), 1994 (16/16), 1995 (16/16), 1996 (16/16), 1997 (16/16), 1998 (15/15), 1999 (16/16). Total: 126/111.
CHAMPIONSHIP GAME EXPERIENCE: Played in AFC championship game (1994-1996 and 1999 seasons). ... Played in Super Bowl XXX (1995 season).
HONORS: Named offensive tackle on THE SPORTING NEWS college All-America second team (1991). ... Played in Pro Bowl (1999 season).
PRO STATISTICS: 1993—Recovered one fumble. 1995—Recovered one fumble. 1996—Recovered one fumble.

SEAU, JUNIOR — LB — CHARGERS

PERSONAL: Born January 19, 1969, in San Diego. ... 6-3/250. ... Full name: Tiaina Seau Jr. ... Name pronounced SAY-ow.
HIGH SCHOOL: Oceanside (Calif.).
COLLEGE: Southern California.
TRANSACTIONS/CAREER NOTES: Selected after junior season by San Diego Chargers in first round (fifth pick overall) of 1990 NFL draft. ... Signed by Chargers (August 27, 1990).
CHAMPIONSHIP GAME EXPERIENCE: Played in AFC championship game (1994 season). ... Played in Super Bowl XXIX (1994 season).
HONORS: Named linebacker on THE SPORTING NEWS college All-America first team (1989). ... Played in Pro Bowl (1991-2000 seasons). ... Named inside linebacker on THE SPORTING NEWS NFL All-Pro team (1992-1996, 1998 and 2000).
PRO STATISTICS: 1992—Recovered one fumble for 10 yards. 1993—Recovered one fumble for 21 yards. 1994—Recovered three fumbles. 1995—Recovered three fumbles for 30 yards and one touchdown. 1996—Recovered three fumbles. 1997—Fumbled once and recovered two fumbles for five yards. 1998—Recovered two fumbles. 1999—Caught two passes for eight yards and recovered one fumble.

			INTERCEPTIONS				SACKS
Year Team	G	GS	No.	Yds.	Avg.	TD	No.
1990—San Diego NFL	16	15	0	0	0.0	0	1.0
1991—San Diego NFL	16	16	0	0	0.0	0	7.0
1992—San Diego NFL	15	15	2	51	25.5	0	4.5
1993—San Diego NFL	16	16	2	58	29.0	0	0.0
1994—San Diego NFL	16	16	0	0	0.0	0	5.5
1995—San Diego NFL	16	16	2	5	2.5	0	2.0
1996—San Diego NFL	15	15	2	18	9.0	0	7.0
1997—San Diego NFL	15	15	2	33	16.5	0	7.0
1998—San Diego NFL	16	16	0	0	0.0	0	3.5
1999—San Diego NFL	14	14	1	16	16.0	0	3.5
2000—San Diego NFL	16	16	2	2	1.0	0	3.5
2001—San Diego NFL	16	16	1	2	2.0	0	1.0
Pro totals (12 years)	187	186	14	185	13.2	0	45.5

SEDER, TIM   K   COWBOYS

PERSONAL: Born September 17, 1974, in Ashland, Ohio. ... 5-9/197.
HIGH SCHOOL: Lucas (Ashland, Ohio).
COLLEGE: Ashland.
TRANSACTIONS/CAREER NOTES: Signed as non-drafted free agent by Dallas Cowboys (April 6, 2000). ... On injured reserve with ankle injury (November 14, 2001-remainder of season).
PRO STATISTICS: 2000—Rushed once for one yard and a touchdown. 2001—Rushed once for eight yards and a touchdown and recovered one fumble for minus six yards.

					KICKING			
Year Team	G	XPM	XPA	FGM	FGA	Lg.	50+	Pts.
2000—Dallas NFL	15	27	27	25	33	48	0-1	102
2001—Dallas NFL	8	12	12	11	17	46	0-1	51
Pro totals (2 years)	23	39	39	36	50	48	0-2	153

SEHORN, JASON   CB   GIANTS

PERSONAL: Born April 15, 1971, in Sacramento. ... 6-2/215.
HIGH SCHOOL: Mt. Shasta (Calif.).
JUNIOR COLLEGE: Shasta College (Calif.).
COLLEGE: Southern California.
TRANSACTIONS/CAREER NOTES: Selected by New York Giants in second round (59th pick overall) of 1994 NFL draft. ... Signed by Giants (July 17, 1994). ... Granted free agency (February 14, 1997). ... Re-signed by Giants (August 9, 1997). ... On injured reserve with knee injury (August 25, 1998-entire season). ... Granted unconditional free agency (March 2, 2001). ... Re-signed by Giants (March 2, 2001). ... On injured reserve with knee injury (January 2, 2002-remainder of season).
CHAMPIONSHIP GAME EXPERIENCE: Played in NFC championship game (2000 season). ... Played in Super Bowl XXXV (2000 season).
PRO STATISTICS: 1996—Credited with three sacks, returned one punt for no yards, fumbled once and recovered one fumble. 1997—Credited with 1½ sacks and recovered one fumble for two yards. 1999—Fumbled once for minus one yard. 2000—Returned two kickoffs for 31 yards and one touchdown and recovered one fumble for eight yards. 2001—Credited with one sack and recovered one fumble for 35 yards.

			INTERCEPTIONS			
Year Team	G	GS	No.	Yds.	Avg.	TD
1994—New York Giants NFL	8	0	0	0	0.0	0
1995—New York Giants NFL	14	0	0	0	0.0	0
1996—New York Giants NFL	16	15	5	61	12.2	1
1997—New York Giants NFL	16	16	6	74	12.3	1
1998—New York Giants NFL			Did not play.			
1999—New York Giants NFL	10	10	1	-4	-4.0	0
2000—New York Giants NFL	14	14	2	32	16.0	0
2001—New York Giants NFL	13	13	3	34	11.3	1
Pro totals (7 years)	91	68	17	197	11.6	3

RECORD AS BASEBALL PLAYER
TRANSACTIONS/CAREER NOTES: Threw right, batted right. ... Signed as non-drafted free agent by Chicago Cubs organization (July 24, 1989). ... Released by Cubs (April 4, 1991).

						BATTING							FIELDING		
Year Team (League)	Pos.	G	AB	R	H	2B	3B	HR	RBI	Avg.	BB	SO	SB	PO	A	E	Avg.
1990—Huntington (Appal.)	OF	49	125	21	23	3	1	1	10	.184	8	52	9	82	3	5	.944

SELLERS, MIKE   FB

PERSONAL: Born July 21, 1975, in Frankfurt, West Germany. ... 6-3/260.
HIGH SCHOOL: North Thurston (Lacey, Wash.).
JUNIOR COLLEGE: Walla Walla (Wash.) Community College.
COLLEGE: None.
TRANSACTIONS/CAREER NOTES: Signed by Edmonton Eskimos of CFL (March 21, 1995). ... Tranferred by Eskimos to reserve list (August 23, 1995). ... Transferred by Eskimos to injured list (October 12, 1995). ... Transferred by Eskimos to active roster (December 18, 1995). ... Signed as non-drafted free agent by Washington Redskins (February 11, 1998). ... Granted free agency (March 2, 2001). ... Signed by Cleveland Browns (March 15, 2001). ... Released by Browns (November 27, 2001). ... Signed by Winnipeg Blue Bombers of CFL (May 7, 2002).
PRO STATISTICS: CFL: 1997—Rushed 40 times for 133 yards, returned one kickoff for 14 yards and recovered one fumble for 43 yards. 1998—Returned two kickoffs for 33 yards and recovered one fumble. 1999—Returned three kickoffs for 32 yards. 2000—Rushed once for two yards and returned four kickoffs for 32 yards. 2001—Returned four kickoffs for 75 yards.
SINGLE GAME HIGHS (regular season): Attempts—1 (September 24, 2000, vs. New York Giants); yards—2 (September 24, 2000, vs. New York Giants); and rushing touchdowns—0; receptions—3 (December 27, 1998, vs. Dallas); yards—18 (December 27, 1998, vs. Dallas); and touchdown receptions—0.

			RECEIVING				TOTALS			
Year Team	G	GS	No.	Yds.	Avg.	TD	TD	2pt.	Pts.	Fum.
1996—Edmonton CFL	17	...	0	0	0.0	0	0	0	0	0
1997—Edmonton CFL	16	...	0	0	0.0	0	0	0	0	0
1998—Washington NFL	14	1	3	18	6.0	0	0	0	0	0
1999—Washington NFL	16	2	7	105	15.0	2	2	0	12	1
2000—Washington NFL	14	6	8	78	9.8	2	2	0	12	0
2001—Cleveland NFL	9	7	7	73	10.4	2	2	0	12	0
CFL totals (2 years)	33	...	0	0	0.0	0	0	0	0	0
NFL totals (4 years)	53	16	25	274	11.0	6	6	0	36	1
Pro totals (6 years)	86	...	25	274	11.0	6	6	0	36	1

SEMPLE, TONY   G   LIONS

PERSONAL: Born December 20, 1970, in Springfield, Ill. ... 6-5/303. ... Full name: Anthony Lee Semple.
HIGH SCHOOL: Lincoln (Ill.) Community.
COLLEGE: Memphis State (degree in sports administration).
TRANSACTIONS/CAREER NOTES: Selected by Detroit Lions in fifth round (154th pick overall) of 1994 NFL draft. ... Signed by Lions (July 21, 1994). ... On injured reserve with knee injury (August 19, 1994-entire season). ... Granted free agency (February 14, 1997). ... Re-signed by Lions (June 13, 1997). ... Granted unconditional free agency (February 13, 1998). ... Re-signed by Lions (February 21, 1998). ... Granted unconditional free agency (March 2, 2001). ... Re-signed by Lions (June 7, 2001). ... Granted unconditional free agency (March 1, 2002). ... Re-signed by Lions (April 1, 2002).
PLAYING EXPERIENCE: Detroit NFL, 1995-2001. ... Games/Games started: 1995 (16/0), 1996 (15/1), 1997 (16/1), 1998 (16/3), 1999 (12/12), 2000 (11/8), 2001 (15/12). Total: 101/37.

SERWANGA, KATO   CB   REDSKINS

PERSONAL: Born July 23, 1976, in Kampala, Uganda, Africa. ... 6-0/202. ... Twin brother of Wasswa Serwanga, cornerback with San Francisco 49ers (1999) and Minnesota Vikings (2000 and 2001). ... Name pronounced kah-TOE ser-WAN-guh.
HIGH SCHOOL: Sacramento (Calif.).
COLLEGE: Sacramento State, then Pacific, then California.
TRANSACTIONS/CAREER NOTES: Signed as non-drafted free agent by New England Patriots (April 24, 1998). ... Released by Patriots (August 30, 1998). ... Re-signed by Patriots to practice squad (August 31, 1998). ... Activated (December 12, 1998); did not play. ... Assigned by Patriots to Scottish Claymores in 2001 NFL Europe enhancement allocation program (February 19, 2001). ... Released by Patriots (September 2, 2001). ... Signed by Washington Redskins (October 16, 2001). ... Granted free agency (March 1, 2002). ... Re-signed by Redskins (April 11, 2002).
PRO STATISTICS: 1999—Credited with one sack and recovered one fumble. 2000—Credited with two sacks and recovered two fumbles.

			INTERCEPTIONS		
Year Team	G	GS	No.	Yds.	Avg.	TD
1998—New England NFL			Did not play.			
1999—New England NFL	16	3	3	2	0.7	0
2000—New England NFL	15	0	0	0	0.0	0
2001—Scottish NFLE			Statistics unavailable.			
—Washington NFL	11	0	0	0	0.0	0
Pro totals (3 years)	42	3	3	2	0.7	0

SERWANGA, WASSWA   CB

PERSONAL: Born July 23, 1976, in Kampala, Uganda, Africa. ... 5-11/203. ... Full name: Wasswa Kenneth Serwanga. ... Twin brother of Kato Serwanga, cornerback, Washington Redskins. ... Name pronounced ser-WAN-guh.
HIGH SCHOOL: Sacramento (Calif.).
COLLEGE: Sacramento State, then Pacific, then UCLA.
TRANSACTIONS/CAREER NOTES: Signed as non-drafted free agent by Chicago Bears (April 21, 1998). ... Released by Bears (August 21, 1998). ... Signed by San Francisco 49ers (April 23, 1999). ... Released by 49ers (September 5, 1999). ... Re-signed by 49ers to practice squad (September 7, 1999). ... Activated (October 12, 1999). ... Granted free agency (February 11, 2000). ... Selected by Amsterdam Admirals in 2000 NFL Europe draft (February 22, 2000). ... Signed by Kansas City Chiefs (April 24, 2000). ... Released by Chiefs (August 22, 2000). ... Signed by Minnesota Vikings (August 23, 2000). ... Released by Vikings (December 4, 2001).
PLAYING EXPERIENCE: San Francisco NFL, 1999; Minnesota NFL, 2000 and 2001. ... Games/Games started: 1999 (9/0), 2000 (7/2), 2001 (7/0). Total: 23/2.
CHAMPIONSHIP GAME EXPERIENCE: Played in NFC championship game (2000 season).

SETZER, BOBBY   DE   49ERS

PERSONAL: Born June 16, 1976, in Walnut Creek, Calif. ... 6-4/280. ... Full name: Robert Kelley Setzer Jr.
HIGH SCHOOL: South Salem (Kelso, Wash.).
JUNIOR COLLEGE: Walla Walla Community College.
COLLEGE: Boise State.
TRANSACTIONS/CAREER NOTES: Signed as non-drafted free agent by New York Giants (February 7, 2000). ... Released by Giants (February 9, 2000). ... Signed by New Orleans Saints (March 23, 2000). ... Released by Saints (August 27, 2000). ... Re-signed by Saints to practice squad (August 29, 2000). ... Released by Saints (September 2, 2001). ... Signed by San Francisco 49ers (September 5, 2001).
PLAYING EXPERIENCE: San Francisco NFL, 2001. ... Games/Games started: 2001 (14/0).
PRO STATISTICS: 2001—Credited with one sack.

SEUBERT, RICH   OT   GIANTS

PERSONAL: Born March 30, 1979, in Stratford, Wis. ... 6-5/295.
HIGH SCHOOL: Marsfield Columbus (Stratford, Wis.).
COLLEGE: Western Illinois.
TRANSACTIONS/CAREER NOTES: Signed as non-drafted free agent by New York Giants (April 27, 2001).
PLAYING EXPERIENCE: New York Giants NFL, 2001. ... Games/Games started: 2001 (2/0).

SEYMOUR, RICHARD   DT   PATRIOTS

PERSONAL: Born October 6, 1979, in Gadsden, S.C. ... 6-6/305.
HIGH SCHOOL: Lower Richland (S.C.).
COLLEGE: Georgia.

TRANSACTIONS/CAREER NOTES: Selected by New England Patriots in first round (sixth pick overall) of 2001 NFL draft. ... Signed by Patriots (July 24, 2001).
CHAMPIONSHIP GAME EXPERIENCE: Played in AFC championship game (2001 season). ... Member of Super Bowl championship team (2001 season).
HONORS: Named defensive tackle on THE SPORTING NEWS college All-America second team (2000).
PRO STATISTICS: 2001—Recovered one fumble.

Year Team	G	GS	SACKS
2001—New England NFL	13	10	3.0

SHADE, SAM — S — REDSKINS

PERSONAL: Born June 14, 1973, in Birmingham, Ala. ... 6-0/205.
HIGH SCHOOL: Wenonah (Birmingham, Ala.).
COLLEGE: Alabama.
TRANSACTIONS/CAREER NOTES: Selected by Cincinnati Bengals in fourth round (102nd pick overall) of 1995 NFL draft. ... Signed by Bengals (July 18, 1995). ... Granted free agency (February 13, 1998). ... Re-signed by Bengals (June 15, 1998). ... Granted unconditional free agency (February 12, 1999). ... Signed by Washington Redskins (February 18, 1999).
PRO STATISTICS: 1997—Fumbled once and recovered one fumble. 1998—Recovered two fumbles for 55 yards and one touchdown. 1999—Recovered one fumble. 2000—Recovered four fumbles for one yard. 2001—Recovered one fumble.

			INTERCEPTIONS				SACKS
Year Team	G	GS	No.	Yds.	Avg.	TD	No.
1995—Cincinnati NFL	16	2	0	0	0.0	0	0.0
1996—Cincinnati NFL	12	0	0	0	0.0	0	0.0
1997—Cincinnati NFL	16	12	1	21	21.0	0	4.0
1998—Cincinnati NFL	16	14	3	33	11.0	0	1.0
1999—Washington NFL	16	16	2	7	3.5	0	1.5
2000—Washington NFL	16	14	2	15	7.5	0	1.0
2001—Washington NFL	16	15	2	9	4.5	0	0.0
Pro totals (7 years)	108	73	10	85	8.5	0	7.5

SHARPE, SHANNON — TE — BRONCOS

PERSONAL: Born June 26, 1968, in Chicago. ... 6-2/230. ... Brother of Sterling Sharpe, wide receiver with Green Bay Packers (1988-94).
HIGH SCHOOL: Glennville (Ga.).
COLLEGE: Savannah (Ga.) State.
TRANSACTIONS/CAREER NOTES: Selected by Denver Broncos in seventh round (192nd pick overall) of 1990 NFL draft. ... Signed by Broncos (July 1990). ... Granted free agency (February 1, 1992). ... Re-signed by Broncos (July 31, 1992). ... Designated by Broncos as transition player (February 15, 1994). ... On injured reserve with broken collarbone (November 30, 1999-remainder of season). ... Granted unconditional free agency (February 12, 2000). ... Signed by Baltimore Ravens (February 16, 2000). ... Released by Ravens (March 1, 2002). ... Signed by Broncos (April 12, 2002).
CHAMPIONSHIP GAME EXPERIENCE: Played in AFC championship game (1991, 1997, 1998 and 2000 seasons). ... Member of Super Bowl championship team (1997, 1998 and 2000 seasons).
HONORS: Played in Pro Bowl (1992, 1993 and 1995-1997 seasons). ... Named tight end on THE SPORTING NEWS NFL All-Pro team (1993 and 1996-1998). ... Named to play in Pro Bowl (1994 season); replaced by Eric Green due to injury. ... Named to play in Pro Bowl (1998 season); replaced by Frank Wycheck due to injury.
POST SEASON RECORDS: Shares NFL postseason single-game record for most receptions—13 (January 9, 1994, vs. Los Angeles Raiders).
PRO STATISTICS: 1991—Rushed once for 15 yards and recovered one fumble. 1992—Rushed twice for minus six yards. 1993—Returned one kickoff for no yards. 1995—Recovered one fumble.
SINGLE GAME HIGHS (regular season): Receptions—13 (October 6, 1996, vs. San Diego); yards—180 (September 3, 1995, vs. Buffalo); and touchdown receptions—3 (October 6, 1996, vs. San Diego).
STATISTICAL PLATEAUS: 100-yard receiving games: 1992 (2), 1993 (2), 1994 (1), 1995 (2), 1996 (3), 1997 (4), 2000 (2). Total: 16.
MISCELLANEOUS: Holds Denver Broncos all-time records for most receiving yards (6,983) and most receptions (552). ... Shares Denver Broncos all-time record most touchdown receptions (44).

			RECEIVING				TOTALS			
Year Team	G	GS	No.	Yds.	Avg.	TD	TD	2pt.	Pts.	Fum.
1990—Denver NFL	16	2	7	99	14.1	1	1	0	6	1
1991—Denver NFL	16	9	22	322	14.6	1	1	0	6	0
1992—Denver NFL	16	11	53	640	12.1	2	2	0	12	1
1993—Denver NFL	16	12	81	995	12.3	§9	9	0	54	1
1994—Denver NFL	15	13	87	1010	11.6	4	4	2	28	1
1995—Denver NFL	13	12	63	756	12.0	4	4	0	24	1
1996—Denver NFL	15	15	80	1062	13.3	10	10	0	60	0
1997—Denver NFL	16	16	72	1107	15.4	3	3	1	20	1
1998—Denver NFL	16	16	64	768	12.0	▲10	10	0	60	0
1999—Denver NFL	5	5	23	224	9.7	0	0	0	0	0
2000—Baltimore NFL	16	15	67	810	12.1	5	5	0	30	0
2001—Baltimore NFL	16	15	73	811	11.1	2	2	0	12	1
Pro totals (12 years)	176	141	692	8604	12.4	51	51	3	312	8

SHARPER, DARREN — S — PACKERS

PERSONAL: Born November 3, 1975, in Richmond, Va. ... 6-2/205. ... Full name: Darren Mallory Sharper. ... Brother of Jamie Sharper, linebacker, Houston Texans.
HIGH SCHOOL: Hermitage (Richmond, Va.).
COLLEGE: William & Mary.

TRANSACTIONS/CAREER NOTES: Selected by Green Bay Packers in second round (60th pick overall) of 1997 NFL draft. ... Signed by Packers (July 11, 1997).
CHAMPIONSHIP GAME EXPERIENCE: Played in NFC championship game (1997 season). ... Played in Super Bowl XXXII (1997 season).
HONORS: Named safety on The Sporting News NFL All-Pro team (2000). ... Played in Pro Bowl (2000 season).
PRO STATISTICS: 1997—Returned one kickoff for three yards and recovered one fumble for 34 yards and a touchdown. 1999—Returned one kickoff for four yards, credited with one sack and recovered one fumble for nine yards. 2000—Credited with one sack. 2001—Credited with two sacks and recovered one fumble for 17 yards.

			INTERCEPTIONS				PUNT RETURNS				TOTALS		
Year Team	G	GS	No.	Yds.	Avg.	TD	No.	Yds.	Avg.	TD	TD	2pt.	Pts.	Fum.
1997—Green Bay NFL	14	0	2	70	35.0	∞2	7	32	4.6	0	3	0	18	1
1998—Green Bay NFL	16	16	0	0	0.0	0	0	0	0.0	0	0	0	0	0
1999—Green Bay NFL	16	16	3	12	4.0	0	0	0	0.0	0	0	0	0	0
2000—Green Bay NFL	16	16	*9	109	12.1	0	0	0	0.0	0	0	0	0	0
2001—Green Bay NFL	16	16	6	78	13.0	0	1	18	18.0	0	0	0	0	1
Pro totals (5 years)	78	64	20	269	13.5	2	8	50	6.3	0	3	0	18	2

SHARPER, JAMIE — LB — TEXANS

PERSONAL: Born November 23, 1974, in Richmond, Va. ... 6-3/240. ... Full name: Harry Jamie Sharper Jr. ... Brother of Darren Sharper, safety, Green Bay Packers.
HIGH SCHOOL: Hermitage (Richmond, Va.).
COLLEGE: Virginia (degree in psychology, 1996).
TRANSACTIONS/CAREER NOTES: Selected by Baltimore Ravens in second round (34th pick overall) of 1997 NFL draft. ... Signed by Ravens (July 23, 1997). ... Granted free agency (February 11, 2000). ... Re-signed by Ravens (June 16, 2000). ... Granted unconditional free agency (March 2, 2001). ... Re-signed by Ravens (April 3, 2001). ... Selected by Houston Texans from Ravens in NFL expansion draft (February 18, 2002).
CHAMPIONSHIP GAME EXPERIENCE: Played in AFC championship game (2000 season). ... Member of Super Bowl championship team (2000 season).
PRO STATISTICS: 1997—Intercepted one pass for four yards and fumbled once. 2000—Intercepted one pass for 45 yards and recovered two fumbles. 2001—Recovered one fumble for eight yards and one touchdown.

Year Team	G	GS	SACKS
1997—Baltimore NFL	16	15	3.0
1998—Baltimore NFL	16	16	1.0
1999—Baltimore NFL	16	16	4.0
2000—Baltimore NFL	16	16	0.0
2001—Baltimore NFL	16	16	6.0
Pro totals (5 years)	80	79	14.0

SHAW, BOBBY — WR — JAGUARS

PERSONAL: Born April 23, 1975, in San Francisco. ... 6-0/186.
HIGH SCHOOL: Galileo (San Francisco).
COLLEGE: California.
TRANSACTIONS/CAREER NOTES: Selected by Seattle Seahawks in sixth round (169th pick overall) of 1998 NFL draft. ... Signed by Seahawks (June 5, 1998). ... Released by Seahawks (August 30, 1998). ... Re-signed by Seahawks to practice squad (August 31, 1998). ... Activated (November 4, 1998); did not play. ... Released by Seahawks (November 18, 1998). ... Signed by Pittsburgh Steelers (November 20, 1998). ... Granted free agency (March 2, 2001). ... Re-signed by Steelers (March 2, 2001). ... Granted unconditional free agency (March 1, 2002). ... Signed by Jacksonville Jaguars (April 3, 2002).
CHAMPIONSHIP GAME EXPERIENCE: Played in AFC championship game (2001 season).
HONORS: Named wide receiver on The Sporting News college All-America first team (1997).
PRO STATISTICS: 2000—Ran minus eight yards with lateral. 2001—Returned one kickoff for two yards.
SINGLE GAME HIGHS (regular season): Receptions—7 (January 2, 2000, vs. Tennessee); yards—131 (January 2, 2000, vs. Tennessee); and touchdown receptions—1 (January 6, 2002, vs. Cleveland).
STATISTICAL PLATEAUS: 100-yard receiving games: 1999 (1), 2001 (1). Total: 2.

			RECEIVING				PUNT RETURNS				TOTALS		
Year Team	G	GS	No.	Yds.	Avg.	TD	No.	Yds.	Avg.	TD	TD	2pt.	Pts.	Fum.
1998—Seattle NFL							Did not play.							
1999—Pittsburgh NFL	15	1	28	387	13.8	3	4	53	13.3	0	3	0	18	0
2000—Pittsburgh NFL	16	0	40	672	16.8	4	2	17	8.5	0	4	0	24	2
2001—Pittsburgh NFL	16	0	24	409	17.0	2	4	45	11.3	0	2	0	12	1
Pro totals (3 years)	47	1	92	1468	16.0	9	10	115	11.5	0	9	0	54	3

SHAW, TERRANCE — CB — RAIDERS

PERSONAL: Born November 11, 1973, in Alameda, Calif. ... 5-11/200. ... Full name: Terrance Bernard Shaw.
HIGH SCHOOL: Marshall (Texas).
COLLEGE: Stephen F. Austin.
TRANSACTIONS/CAREER NOTES: Selected by San Diego Chargers in second round (34th pick overall) of 1995 NFL draft. ... Signed by Chargers (June 15, 1995). ... Released by Chargers (March 1, 2000). ... Signed by Miami Dolphins (June 13, 2000). ... Granted unconditional free agency (March 2, 2001). ... Signed by New England Patriots (March 22, 2001). ... Released by Patriots (February 25, 2002). ... Signed by Oakland Raiders (March 21, 2002).
CHAMPIONSHIP GAME EXPERIENCE: Played in AFC championship game (2001 season). ... Member of Super Bowl championship team (2001 season).
PRO STATISTICS: 1997—Recovered one fumble.

Year Team	G	GS	INTERCEPTIONS No.	Yds.	Avg.	TD
1995—San Diego NFL	16	14	1	31	31.0	0
1996—San Diego NFL	16	16	3	78	26.0	0
1997—San Diego NFL	16	16	1	11	11.0	0
1998—San Diego NFL	13	13	2	0	0.0	0
1999—San Diego NFL	8	8	0	0	0.0	0
2000—Miami NFL	11	3	1	0	0.0	0
2001—New England NFL	13	3	0	0	0.0	0
Pro totals (7 years)	93	73	8	120	15.0	0

SHEA, AARON   TE/FB   BROWNS

PERSONAL: Born December 5, 1976, in Ottawa, Ill. ... 6-3/244. ... Full name: Aaron T. Shea.
HIGH SCHOOL: Ottawa (Ill.).
COLLEGE: Michigan.
TRANSACTIONS/CAREER NOTES: Selected by Cleveland Browns in fourth round (110th pick overall) of 2000 NFL draft. ... Signed by Browns (July 13, 2000). ... On injured reserve with shoulder injury (December 27, 2001-remainder of season).
PRO STATISTICS: 2001—Recovered one fumble.
SINGLE GAME HIGHS (regular season): Receptions—6 (December 2, 2001, vs. Tennessee); yards—76 (October 15, 2000, vs. Denver); and touchdown receptions—1 (November 12, 2000, vs. New England).

Year Team	G	GS	RECEIVING No.	Yds.	Avg.	TD	TOTALS TD	2pt.	Pts.	Fum.
2000—Cleveland NFL	15	8	30	302	10.1	2	2	0	12	1
2001—Cleveland NFL	12	5	14	86	6.1	0	0	0	0	0
Pro totals (2 years)	27	13	44	388	8.8	2	2	0	12	1

SHELTON, DAIMON   FB   BEARS

PERSONAL: Born September 15, 1972, in Duarte, Calif. ... 6-0/258.
HIGH SCHOOL: Duarte (Calif.).
JUNIOR COLLEGE: Fresno (Calif.) City College.
COLLEGE: Cal State Sacramento.
TRANSACTIONS/CAREER NOTES: Selected by Jacksonville Jaguars in sixth round (184th pick overall) of 1997 NFL draft. ... Signed by Jaguars (May 23, 1997). ... Granted free agency (February 11, 2000). ... Re-signed by Jaguars (March 21, 2000). ... Granted unconditional free agency (March 2, 2001). ... Signed by Chicago Bears (May 23, 2001). ... On suspended list for violating league substance abuse policy (January 8, 2002-present). ... Granted unconditional free agency (March 1, 2002). ... Re-signed by Bears (April 2, 2002).
CHAMPIONSHIP GAME EXPERIENCE: Played in AFC championship game (1999 season).
PRO STATISTICS: 1999—Returned one kickoff for no yards and recovered one fumble. 2000—Recovered two fumbles.
SINGLE GAME HIGHS (regular season): Attempts—13 (October 18, 1998, vs. Buffalo); yards —44 (October 18, 1998, vs. Buffalo); and rushing touchdowns—1 (November 1, 1998, vs. Baltimore).

Year Team	G	GS	RUSHING Att.	Yds.	Avg.	TD	RECEIVING No.	Yds.	Avg.	TD	TOTALS TD	2pt.	Pts.	Fum.
1997—Jacksonville NFL	13	0	6	4	0.7	0	0	0	0.0	0	0	0	0	1
1998—Jacksonville NFL	14	8	30	95	3.2	1	10	79	7.9	0	1	0	6	0
1999—Jacksonville NFL	16	9	1	2	2.0	0	12	87	7.3	0	0	0	0	0
2000—Jacksonville NFL	16	9	2	3	1.5	0	4	48	12.0	0	0	0	0	0
2001—Chicago NFL	16	9	0	0	0.0	0	12	76	6.3	1	1	0	6	2
Pro totals (5 years)	75	35	39	104	2.7	1	38	290	7.6	1	2	0	12	3

SHELTON, L.J.   OT   CARDINALS

PERSONAL: Born March 21, 1976, in Rochester Hills, Mich. ... 6-6/335. ... Full name: Lonnie Jewel Shelton. ... Son of Lonnie Shelton, forward with New York Knicks (1976-77 and 1977-78), Seattle SuperSonics (1978-79 through 1982-83) and Cleveland Cavaliers (1983-84 through 1985-86).
HIGH SCHOOL: Rochester (Rochester Hills, Mich.).
COLLEGE: Eastern Michigan.
TRANSACTIONS/CAREER NOTES: Selected by Arizona Cardinals in first round (21st pick overall) of 1999 NFL draft. ... Signed by Cardinals (September 24, 1999).
PLAYING EXPERIENCE: Arizona NFL, 1999-2001. ... Games/Games started: 1999 (9/7), 2000 (14/14), 2001 (16/16). Total: 39/37.
PRO STATISTICS: 2000—Recovered one fumble.

SHEPHERD, GANNON   OT   FALCONS

PERSONAL: Born January 4, 1977, in Flint, Mich. ... 6-7/308.
HIGH SCHOOL: Marist (Ga.).
COLLEGE: Duke.
TRANSACTIONS/CAREER NOTES: Signed as non-drafted free agent by Chicago Bears (April 28, 2000). ... Released by Bears (August 23, 2000). ... Signed by Jacksonville Jaguars to practice squad (August 29, 2000). ... Released by Jaguars (September 26, 2000). ... Signed by Bears to practice squad (October 4, 2000). ... Released by Bears (October 10, 2000). ... Re-signed by Bears to practice squad (October 18, 2000). ... Signed off Bears practice squad by Jaguars (December 6, 2000). ... Released by Jaguars (October 3, 2001). ... Signed by Cleveland Browns to practice squad (November 21, 2001). ... Granted free agency after 2001 season. ... Signed by Atlanta Falcons (January 15, 2002).
PLAYING EXPERIENCE: Jacksonville NFL, 2001. ... Games/Games started: 2001 (1/0).

SHEPHERD, JACOBY — CB — TEXANS

PERSONAL: Born August 31, 1979, in Lufkin, Texas. ... 6-1/195. ... Full name: Jacoby Lamar Shepherd.
HIGH SCHOOL: Lufkin (Texas).
JUNIOR COLLEGE: Tyler (Texas) Junior College, then Cloud County Community College, Kan. (did not play football).
COLLEGE: Oklahoma State.
TRANSACTIONS/CAREER NOTES: Selected after junior season by St. Louis Rams in second round (62nd pick overall) of 2000 NFL draft. ... Signed by Rams (July 17, 2000). ... On injured reserve with quadriceps injury (November 27, 2001-remainder of season). ... Traded by Rams to Houston Texans for seventh round draft pick in 2003 draft (March 29, 2002).

				INTERCEPTIONS		
Year Team	G	GS	No.	Yds.	Avg.	TD
2000—St. Louis NFL	14	1	1	0	0.0	0
2001—St. Louis NFL	7	0	0	0	0.0	0
Pro totals (2 years)	21	1	1	0	0.0	0

SHIELDS, WILL — G — CHIEFS

PERSONAL: Born September 15, 1971, in Fort Riley, Kan. ... 6-3/311. ... Full name: Will Herthie Shields.
HIGH SCHOOL: Lawton (Okla.).
COLLEGE: Nebraska (degree in communications).
TRANSACTIONS/CAREER NOTES: Selected by Kansas City Chiefs in the third round (74th pick overall) of 1993 NFL draft. ... Signed by Chiefs (May 3, 1993). ... Designated by Chiefs as franchise player (February 11, 2000).
PLAYING EXPERIENCE: Kansas City NFL, 1993-2001. ... Games/Games started: 1993 (16/15), 1994 (16/16), 1995 (16/16), 1996 (16/16), 1997 (16/16), 1998 (16/16), 1999 (16/16), 2000 (16/16), 2001 (16/16). Total: 144/143.
CHAMPIONSHIP GAME EXPERIENCE: Played in AFC championship game (1993 season).
HONORS: Named guard on THE SPORTING NEWS college All-America second team (1991). ... Named guard on THE SPORTING NEWS college All-America first team (1992). ... Named guard on THE SPORTING NEWS NFL All-Pro team (1999). ... Played in Pro Bowl (1995-2000 seasons).
PRO STATISTICS: 1993—Recovered two fumbles. 1994—Recovered one fumble. 1995—Recovered one fumble. 1998—Caught one pass for four yards and recovered one fumble. 1999—Recovered one fumble. 2000—Recovered one fumble.

SHIPP, MARCEL — RB — CARDINALS

PERSONAL: Born August 8, 1978, in Paterson, N.J. ... 5-11/219.
HIGH SCHOOL: Milford (Conn.), then Passaic (N.J.).
COLLEGE: Massachusetts.
TRANSACTIONS/CAREER NOTES: Signed as non-drafted free agent by Arizona Cardinals (April 23, 2001).
PLAYING EXPERIENCE: Arizona NFL, 2001. ... Games/Games started: 2001 (11/0).
PRO STATISTICS: 2001—Returned six kickoffs for 118 yards.

SHORT, BRANDON — LB — GIANTS

PERSONAL: Born July 11, 1977, in McKeesport, Pa. ... 6-3/255. ... Full name: Brandon Darnell Short.
HIGH SCHOOL: McKeesport (Pa.).
COLLEGE: Penn State (degree in marketing, 1999).
TRANSACTIONS/CAREER NOTES: Selected by New York Giants in fourth round (105th pick overall) of 2000 NFL draft. ... Signed by Giants (July 25, 2000).
PLAYING EXPERIENCE: New York Giants NFL, 2000 and 2001. ... Games/Games started: 2000 (11/0), 2001 (16/16). Total: 27/16.
CHAMPIONSHIP GAME EXPERIENCE: Played in NFC championship game (2000 season). ... Played in Super Bowl XXXV (2000 season).
HONORS: Named linebacker on THE SPORTING NEWS college All-America second team (1999).
PRO STATISTICS: 2001—Intercepted one pass for 21 yards, credited with one sack and recovered one fumble.

SIDNEY, DAINON — CB — TITANS

PERSONAL: Born May 30, 1975, in Atlanta. ... 6-0/188. ... Full name: Dainon Tarquinius Sidney. ... Name pronounced DAY-nun.
HIGH SCHOOL: Riverdale (Ga.).
COLLEGE: East Tennessee State, then Alabama-Birmingham.
TRANSACTIONS/CAREER NOTES: Selected by Tennessee Oilers in third round (77th pick overall) of 1998 NFL draft. ... Signed by Oilers (July 21, 1998). ... Oilers franchise renamed Tennessee Titans for 1999 season (December 26, 1998). ... Granted free agency (March 2, 2001). ... On injured reserve with knee injury (September 26, 2001-remainder of season). ... Granted unconditional free agency (March 1, 2002). ... Re-signed by Titans (March 12, 2002).
PLAYING EXPERIENCE: Tennessee NFL, 1998-2001. ... Games/Games started: 1998 (16/1), 1999 (16/2), 2000 (11/2), 2001 (1/0). Total: 44/5.
CHAMPIONSHIP GAME EXPERIENCE: Played in AFC championship game (1999 season). ... Played in Super Bowl XXXIV (1999 season).
PRO STATISTICS: 1999—Intercepted three passes for 12 yards and returned one punt for four yards. 2000—Intercepted three passes for 19 yards and recovered two fumbles.

SIMMONS, ANTHONY — LB — SEAHAWKS

PERSONAL: Born June 20, 1976, in Spartanburg, S.C. ... 6-0/236.
HIGH SCHOOL: Spartanburg (S.C.).
COLLEGE: Clemson (degree in marketing, 1998).
TRANSACTIONS/CAREER NOTES: Selected after junior season by Seattle Seahawks in first round (15th pick overall) of 1998 NFL draft. ... Signed by Seahawks (July 18, 1998).
PLAYING EXPERIENCE: Seattle NFL, 1998-2001. ... Games/Games started: 1998 (11/4), 1999 (16/16), 2000 (16/16), 2001 (16/16). Total: 59/52.

HONORS: Named inside linebacker on THE SPORTING NEWS college All-America first team (1996 and 1997).
PRO STATISTICS: 1998—Intercepted one pass for 36 yards and a touchdown. 2000—Intercepted two passes for 15 yards and credited with four sacks. 2001—Credited with two sacks.

SIMMONS, BRIAN   LB   BENGALS

PERSONAL: Born June 21, 1975, in New Bern, N.C. ... 6-3/248. ... Full name: Brian Eugene Simmons.
HIGH SCHOOL: New Bern (N.C.).
COLLEGE: North Carolina.
TRANSACTIONS/CAREER NOTES: Selected by Cincinnati Bengals in first round (17th pick overall) of 1998 NFL draft. ... Signed by Bengals (July 27, 1998). ... On injured reserve with knee injury (November 9, 2000-remainder of season).
HONORS: Named outside linebacker on THE SPORTING NEWS college All-America second team (1996). ... Named outside linebacker on THE SPORTING NEWS college All-America third team (1997).
PRO STATISTICS: 1998—Intercepted one pass for 18 yards and recovered one fumble for 22 yards. 1999—Recovered one fumble. 2001—Intercepted one pass for five yards and ran 56 yards with lateral from fumble for one touchdown.

Year Team	G	GS	SACKS
1998—Cincinnati NFL	14	12	3.0
1999—Cincinnati NFL	16	16	3.0
2000—Cincinnati NFL	1	1	1.0
2001—Cincinnati NFL	16	16	6.5
Pro totals (4 years)	47	45	13.5

SIMMONS, JASON   CB   TEXANS

PERSONAL: Born March 30, 1976, in Inglewood, Calif. ... 5-9/198. ... Full name: Jason Lawrence Simmons.
HIGH SCHOOL: Leuzinger (Lawndale, Calif.).
COLLEGE: Arizona State.
TRANSACTIONS/CAREER NOTES: Selected by Pittsburgh Steelers in fifth round (137th pick overall) of 1998 NFL draft. ... Signed by Steelers (July 14, 1998). ... Granted free agency (March 2, 2001). ... Re-signed by Steelers (April 26, 2001). ... Granted unconditional free agency (March 1, 2002). ... Signed by Houston Texans (April 8, 2002).
PLAYING EXPERIENCE: Pittsburgh NFL, 1998-2001. ... Games/Games started: 1998 (6/0), 1999 (16/0), 2000 (15/0), 2001 (12/0). Total: 49/0.
CHAMPIONSHIP GAME EXPERIENCE: Played in AFC championship game (2001 season).
PRO STATISTICS: 1999—Recovered one fumble.

SIMMONS, TONY   WR   TEXANS

PERSONAL: Born December 8, 1974, in Chicago. ... 6-1/212. ... Full name: Tony Angelo Simmons.
HIGH SCHOOL: St. Rita (Chicago).
COLLEGE: Wisconsin (degree in construction administration).
TRANSACTIONS/CAREER NOTES: Selected by New England Patriots in second round (52nd pick overall) of 1998 NFL draft. ... Signed by Patriots (July 18, 1998). ... Assigned by Patriots to Barcelona Dragons in 2001 NFL Europe enhancement allocation program (February 19, 2001). ... Claimed on waivers by Cleveland Browns (September 3, 2001). ... Released by Browns (October 2, 2001). ... Signed by Indianapolis Colts (October 8, 2001). ... Released by Colts (November 7, 2001). ... Re-signed by Colts (November 21, 2001). ... Granted unconditional free agency (March 1, 2002). ... Signed by Houston Texans (March 26, 2002).
PRO STATISTICS: 1999—Returned six kickoffs for 132 yards. 2000—Returned four kickoffs for 82 yards. 2001—Returned two kickoffs for 27 yards.
SINGLE GAME HIGHS (regular season): Receptions—7 (October 10, 1999, vs. Kansas City); yards—109 (November 1, 1998, vs. Indianapolis); and touchdown receptions—1 (October 8, 2000, vs. Indianapolis).
STATISTICAL PLATEAUS: 100-yard receiving games: 1998 (1), 1999 (1). Total: 2.

			RECEIVING				TOTALS		
Year Team	G	GS	No.	Yds.	Avg.	TD	TD	2pt.	Pts.	Fum.
1998—New England NFL	11	6	23	474	20.6	3	3	0	18	0
1999—New England NFL	15	1	19	276	14.5	2	2	0	12	1
2000—New England NFL	12	2	14	231	16.5	1	1	0	6	0
2001—Barcelona NFLE	...	...	32	538	16.8	7	7	0	42	0
—Cleveland NFL	1	0	0	0	0.0	0	0	0	0	0
—Indianapolis NFL	6	0	2	17	8.5	0	0	0	0	0
NFL Europe totals (1 year)	...	...	32	538	16.8	7	7	0	42	0
NFL totals (4 years)	45	9	58	998	17.2	6	6	0	36	1
Pro totals (5 years)	...	...	90	1536	17.1	13	13	0	78	1

SIMON, COREY   DT   EAGLES

PERSONAL: Born March 2, 1977, in Boynton Beach, Fla. ... 6-2/293.
HIGH SCHOOL: Ely (Pompano Beach, Fla.).
COLLEGE: Florida State.
TRANSACTIONS/CAREER NOTES: Selected by Philadelphia Eagles in first round (sixth pick overall) of 2000 NFL draft. ... Signed by Eagles (July 28, 2000).
CHAMPIONSHIP GAME EXPERIENCE: Played in NFC championship game (2001 season).
HONORS: Named defensive tackle on THE SPORTING NEWS college All-America first team (1999).
PRO STATISTICS: 2000—Recovered one fumble for five yards.

Year Team	G	GS	SACKS
2000—Philadelphia NFL	16	16	9.5
2001—Philadelphia NFL	16	16	7.5
Pro totals (2 years)	32	32	17.0

SIMONEAU, MARK — LB — FALCONS

PERSONAL: Born January 16, 1977, in Phillipsburg, Kan. ... 6-0/234.
HIGH SCHOOL: Smith Center (Kan.).
COLLEGE: Kansas State.
TRANSACTIONS/CAREER NOTES: Selected by Atlanta Falcons in third round (67th pick overall) of 2000 NFL draft. ... Signed by Falcons (May 17, 2000).
HONORS: Named linebacker on THE SPORTING NEWS college All-America first team (1999).
PRO STATISTICS: 2001—Recovered one fumble.

Year Team	G	GS	SACKS
2000—Atlanta NFL	14	4	0.5
2001—Atlanta NFL	16	5	0.0
Pro totals (2 years)	30	9	0.5

SIMS, BARRY — G/OT — RAIDERS

PERSONAL: Born December 1, 1974, in Park City, Utah. ... 6-5/295.
HIGH SCHOOL: Park City (Utah).
JUNIOR COLLEGE: Dixie College (Utah).
COLLEGE: Utah.
TRANSACTIONS/CAREER NOTES: Selected by Scottish Claymores in 1999 NFL Europe draft (February 23, 1999). ... Signed as non-drafted free agent by Oakland Raiders (July, 1999).
PLAYING EXPERIENCE: Scottish NFLE, 1999; Oakland NFL, 1999-2001. ... Games/Games started: NFLE 1999 (games played unavailable), NFL 1999 (16/10), 2000 (16/9), 2001 (15/15). Total NFL: 47/34.
CHAMPIONSHIP GAME EXPERIENCE: Played in AFC championship game (2000 season).
PRO STATISTICS: 2000—Recovered one fumble. 2001—Recovered one fumble.

SINCLAIR, MICHAEL — DE

PERSONAL: Born January 31, 1968, in Galveston, Texas. ... 6-4/275. ... Full name: Michael Glenn Sinclair.
HIGH SCHOOL: Charlton-Pollard (Beaumont, Texas).
COLLEGE: Eastern New Mexico (degree in physical education).
TRANSACTIONS/CAREER NOTES: Selected by Seattle Seahawks in sixth round (155th pick overall) of 1991 NFL draft. ... Signed by Seahawks (July 18, 1991). ... Released by Seahawks (August 26, 1991). ... Re-signed by Seahawks to practice squad (August 28, 1991). ... Activated (November 30, 1991). ... On injured reserve with back injury (December 14, 1991-remainder of season). ... Active for two games (1991); did not play. ... Assigned by Seahawks to Sacramento Surge in 1992 World League enhancement allocation program (February 20, 1992). ... On injured reserve with ankle injury (September 1-October 3, 1992). ... On injured reserve with thumb injury (November 10, 1993-remainder of season). ... Granted free agency (February 17, 1995). ... Re-signed by Seahawks (May 24, 1995). ... Granted unconditional free agency (February 16, 1996). ... Re-signed by Seahawks (February 17, 1996). ... Released by Seahawks (February 22, 2002).
HONORS: Named defensive end on All-World League team (1992). ... Played in Pro Bowl (1996-1998 seasons).
PRO STATISTICS: W.L.: 1992—Recovered one fumble. NFL: 1995—Recovered two fumbles. 1997—Recovered one fumble in end zone for a touchdown. 1999—Recovered one fumble for 13 yards. 2000—Recovered four fumbles for 69 yards and a touchdown. 2001—Recovered one fumble for 12 yards.

Year Team	G	GS	SACKS
1991—Seattle NFL	Did not play.		
1992—Sacramento W.L.	10	10	10.0
—Seattle NFL	12	1	1.0
1993—Seattle NFL	9	1	8.0
1994—Seattle NFL	12	2	4.5
1995—Seattle NFL	16	15	5.5
1996—Seattle NFL	16	16	13.0
1997—Seattle NFL	16	16	12.0
1998—Seattle NFL	16	16	*16.5
1999—Seattle NFL	15	15	6.0
2000—Seattle NFL	16	16	3.5
2001—Seattle NFL	16	16	3.5
W.L. totals (1 year)	10	10	10.0
NFL totals (9 years)	144	114	73.5
Pro totals (10 years)	154	124	83.5

SINGLETON, ALSHERMOND — LB — BUCCANEERS

PERSONAL: Born August 7, 1975, in Newark, N.J. ... 6-2/228. ... Full name: Alshermond Glendale Singleton.
HIGH SCHOOL: Irvington (N.J.).
COLLEGE: Temple (degree in sports recreation management).
TRANSACTIONS/CAREER NOTES: Selected by Tampa Bay Buccaneers in fourth round (128th pick overall) of 1997 NFL draft. ... Signed by Buccaneers (July 17, 1997).
PLAYING EXPERIENCE: Tampa Bay NFL, 1997-2001. ... Games/Games started: 1997 (12/0), 1998 (15/0), 1999 (15/0), 2000 (13/1), 2001 (16/0). Total: 71/1.
CHAMPIONSHIP GAME EXPERIENCE: Member of Buccaneers for NFC championship game (1999 season); inactive.
PRO STATISTICS: 1997—Returned blocked punt 28 yards for a touchdown. 1999—Intercepted one pass for seven yards and credited with $^1/_2$ sack. 2001—Credited with one sack and recovered one fumble.

SIRAGUSA, TONY — DT

PERSONAL: Born May 14, 1967, in Kenilworth, N.J. ... 6-3/340. ... Full name: Anthony Siragusa.
HIGH SCHOOL: David Brearley Regional (Kenilworth, N.J.).
COLLEGE: Pittsburgh.
TRANSACTIONS/CAREER NOTES: Signed as non-drafted free agent by Indianapolis Colts (April 30, 1990). ... Granted unconditional free agency (February 14, 1997). ... Signed by Baltimore Ravens (April 24, 1997). ... Announced retirement effective at end of season (January 3, 2002).
CHAMPIONSHIP GAME EXPERIENCE: Played in AFC championship game (1995 and 2000 seasons). ... Member of Super Bowl championship team (2000 season).
PRO STATISTICS: 1990—Recovered one fumble. 1991—Recovered one fumble for five yards. 1992—Recovered one fumble. 1994—Recovered one fumble. 1996—Recovered one fumble. 1997—Recovered one fumble for seven yards. 1998—Recovered one fumble. 1999—Recovered one fumble. 2000—Recovered one fumble.

Year Team	G	GS	SACKS
1990—Indianapolis NFL	13	6	1.0
1991—Indianapolis NFL	13	6	2.0
1992—Indianapolis NFL	16	12	3.0
1993—Indianapolis NFL	14	14	1.5
1994—Indianapolis NFL	16	16	5.0
1995—Indianapolis NFL	14	14	2.0
1996—Indianapolis NFL	10	10	2.0
1997—Baltimore NFL	14	13	0.0
1998—Baltimore NFL	15	15	0.0
1999—Baltimore NFL	14	14	3.5
2000—Baltimore NFL	15	15	0.0
2001—Baltimore NFL	15	13	2.0
Pro totals (12 years)	169	148	22.0

SIRMON, PETER — LB — TITANS

PERSONAL: Born February 18, 1977, in Wenatchee, Wash. ... 6-2/246. ... Full name: Peter Anton Sirmon.
HIGH SCHOOL: Walla Walla (Wash.).
COLLEGE: Oregon.
TRANSACTIONS/CAREER NOTES: Selected by Tennessee Titans in fourth round (128th pick overall) of 2000 NFL draft. ... Signed by Titans (July 11, 2000).
PLAYING EXPERIENCE: Tennessee NFL, 2000 and 2001. ... Games/Games started: 2000 (5/0), 2001 (16/0). Total: 21/0.

SLADE, CHRIS — LB

PERSONAL: Born January 30, 1971, in Newport News, Va. ... 6-5/245. ... Full name: Christopher Carroll Slade. ... Cousin of Terry Kirby, running back, Oakland Raiders; and cousin of Wayne Kirby, outfielder, with four major league teams (1991-98).
HIGH SCHOOL: Tabb (Va.).
COLLEGE: Virginia.
TRANSACTIONS/CAREER NOTES: Selected by New England Patriots in second round (31st pick overall) of 1993 NFL draft. ... Signed by Patriots (July 24, 1993). ... Granted free agency (February 16, 1996). ... Re-signed by Patriots (May 28, 1996). ... Released by Patriots (February 27, 2001). ... Signed by Carolina Panthers (July 26, 2001). ... Granted unconditional free agency (March 1, 2002).
CHAMPIONSHIP GAME EXPERIENCE: Played in AFC championship game (1996 season). ... Played in Super Bowl XXXI (1996 season).
HONORS: Named defensive lineman on THE SPORTING NEWS college All-America first team (1992). ... Played in Pro Bowl (1997 season).
PRO STATISTICS: 1993—Recovered one fumble. 1995—Recovered two fumbles for 38 yards and one touchdown. 1996—Intercepted one pass for two yards and fumbled once. 1997—Intercepted one pass for one yard and a touchdown. 1999—Intercepted one pass for no yards.

Year Team	G	GS	SACKS
1993—New England NFL	16	5	9.0
1994—New England NFL	16	16	9.5
1995—New England NFL	16	16	4.0
1996—New England NFL	16	9	7.0
1997—New England NFL	16	16	9.0
1998—New England NFL	15	15	4.0
1999—New England NFL	16	16	4.5
2000—New England NFL	16	15	4.0
2001—Carolina NFL	15	0	2.5
Pro totals (9 years)	142	108	53.5

SLAUGHTER, T.J. — LB — JAGUARS

PERSONAL: Born February 20, 1977, in Birmingham, Ala. ... 6-0/239. ... Full name: Tavaris Jermell Slaughter.
HIGH SCHOOL: John Carroll (Birmingham, Ala.).
COLLEGE: Southern Mississippi.
TRANSACTIONS/CAREER NOTES: Selected by Jacksonville Jaguars in third round (92nd pick overall) of 2000 NFL draft. ... Signed by Jaguars (May 16, 2000). ... On injured reserve with knee injury (December 8, 2001-remainder of season).
PLAYING EXPERIENCE: Jacksonville NFL, 2000 and 2001. ... Games/Games started: 2000 (16/7), 2001 (9/8). Total: 25/15.
PRO STATISTICS: 2001—Credited with one sack.

SLOAN, DAVID — TE — SAINTS

PERSONAL: Born June 8, 1972, in Fresno, Calif. ... 6-6/260. ... Full name: David Lyle Sloan.
HIGH SCHOOL: Sierra Joint Union (Tollhouse, Calif.).
JUNIOR COLLEGE: Fresno (Calif.) City College.
COLLEGE: New Mexico.
TRANSACTIONS/CAREER NOTES: Selected by Detroit Lions in third round (70th pick overall) of 1995 NFL draft. ... Signed by Lions (July 20, 1995). ... Granted free agency (February 13, 1998). ... Re-signed by Lions (June 10, 1998). ... On physically unable to perform list with knee injury (August 25-October 23, 1998). ... Granted unconditional free agency (February 12, 1999). ... Re-signed by Lions (March 24, 1999). ... Granted unconditional free agency (March 1, 2002). ... Signed by New Orleans Saints (April 3, 2002).
HONORS: Played in Pro Bowl (1999 season).
PRO STATISTICS: 1995—Returned one kickoff for 14 yards. 1996—Recovered one fumble.
SINGLE GAME HIGHS (regular season): Receptions—7 (November 14, 1999, vs. Arizona); yards—88 (November 14, 1999, vs. Arizona); and touchdown receptions—1 (December 23, 2001, vs. Pittsburgh).

			RECEIVING					TOTALS		
Year Team	G	GS	No.	Yds.	Avg.	TD	TD	2pt.	Pts.	Fum.
1995—Detroit NFL	16	8	17	184	10.8	1	1	0	6	0
1996—Detroit NFL	4	4	7	51	7.3	0	0	0	0	0
1997—Detroit NFL	14	12	29	264	9.1	0	0	0	0	0
1998—Detroit NFL	10	2	11	146	13.3	1	1	0	6	0
1999—Detroit NFL	16	15	47	591	12.6	4	4	0	24	0
2000—Detroit NFL	15	10	32	379	11.8	2	2	0	12	0
2001—Detroit NFL	15	15	37	409	11.1	7	7	0	42	0
Pro totals (7 years)	90	66	180	2024	11.2	15	15	0	90	0

SMALL, TORRANCE — WR

PERSONAL: Born September 4, 1970, in Tampa. ... 6-3/220. ... Full name: Torrance Ramon Small.
HIGH SCHOOL: Thomas Jefferson (Tampa).
COLLEGE: Alcorn State.
TRANSACTIONS/CAREER NOTES: Selected by New Orleans Saints in fifth round (138th pick overall) of 1992 NFL draft. ... Signed by Saints (July 15, 1992). ... Released by Saints (September 3, 1992). ... Re-signed by Saints to practice squad (September 4, 1992). ... Activated (September 19, 1992). ... Granted free agency (February 17, 1995). ... Tendered offer sheet by Seattle Seahawks (March 8, 1995). ... Offer matched by Saints (March 15, 1995). ... Released by Saints (May 28, 1997). ... Signed by St. Louis Rams (June 7, 1997). ... Granted unconditional free agency (February 13, 1998). ... Signed by Indianapolis Colts (April 15, 1998). ... Granted unconditional free agency (February 12, 1999). ... Signed by Philadelphia Eagles (February 16, 1999). ... Released by Eagles (March 1, 2001). ... Signed by New England Patriots (May 31, 2001). ... Released by Patriots (September 22, 2001). ... Re-signed by Patriots (September 25, 2001). ... Released by Patriots (October 21, 2001).
PRO STATISTICS: 1994—Recovered one fumble. 1995—Rushed six times for 75 yards and one touchdown and recovered one fumble. 1996—Rushed four times for 51 yards and one touchdown. 1998—Rushed once for two yards and attempted one pass without a completion. 1999—Attempted two passes without a completion. 2000—Had only pass attempt intercepted and rushed once for one yard.
SINGLE GAME HIGHS (regular season): Receptions—9 (November 29, 1998, vs. Baltimore); yards—200 (December 24, 1994, vs. Denver); and touchdown receptions—2 (December 10, 2000, vs. Cleveland).
STATISTICAL PLATEAUS: 100-yard receiving games: 1994 (1), 1998 (2), 1999 (1), 2000 (1). Total: 5.

			RECEIVING					TOTALS		
Year Team	G	GS	No.	Yds.	Avg.	TD	TD	2pt.	Pts.	Fum.
1992—New Orleans NFL	13	2	23	278	12.1	3	3	0	18	0
1993—New Orleans NFL	11	0	16	164	10.3	1	1	0	6	0
1994—New Orleans NFL	16	0	49	719	14.7	5	5	1	32	0
1995—New Orleans NFL	16	1	38	461	12.1	5	6	0	36	0
1996—New Orleans NFL	16	13	50	558	11.2	2	3	0	18	1
1997—St. Louis NFL	13	7	32	488	15.3	1	1	0	6	0
1998—Indianapolis NFL	16	4	45	681	15.1	7	7	0	42	0
1999—Philadelphia NFL	15	15	49	655	13.4	4	4	0	24	0
2000—Philadelphia NFL	14	14	40	569	14.2	3	3	1	20	0
2001—New England NFL	3	0	4	29	7.3	0	0	0	0	0
Pro totals (10 years)	133	56	346	4602	13.3	31	33	2	202	1

SMART, ROD — RB — EAGLES

PERSONAL: Born January 9, 1977, in Lakeland, Fla. ... 5-11/191.
HIGH SCHOOL: Lakeland (Fla.).
COLLEGE: Western Kentucky.
TRANSACTIONS/CAREER NOTES: Signed as non-drafted free agent by San Diego Chargers (May 19, 2000). ... Released by Chargers (June 9, 2000). ... Signed by Philadelphia Eagles to practice squad (October 2, 2001). ... Activated (November 19, 2001). ... On injured reserve with foot injury (January 8, 2002-remainder of season).
PLAYING EXPERIENCE: Philadelphia NFL, 2001. ... Games/Games started: 2001 (6/0).
PRO STATISTICS: 2001—Rushed twice for six yards.
SINGLE GAME HIGHS (regular season): Attempts—2 (January 6, 2002, vs. Tampa Bay); yards—6 (January 6, 2002, vs. Tampa Bay); and rushing touchdowns—0.

SMITH, AARON — DE — STEELERS

PERSONAL: Born April 9, 1976, in Colorado Springs, Colo. ... 6-5/300. ... Full name: Aaron Douglas Smith.
HIGH SCHOOL: Sierra (Colorado Springs, Colo.).
COLLEGE: Northern Colorado.

TRANSACTIONS/CAREER NOTES: Selected by Pittsburgh Steelers in fourth round (109th pick overall) of 1999 NFL draft. ... Signed by Steelers (August 3, 1999). ... Granted free agency (March 1, 2002).
CHAMPIONSHIP GAME EXPERIENCE: Played in AFC championship game (2001 season).

Year—Team	G	GS	SACKS
1999—Pittsburgh NFL	6	0	0.0
2000—Pittsburgh NFL	16	15	4.0
2001—Pittsburgh NFL	16	16	8.0
Pro totals (3 years)	38	31	12.0

SMITH, AKILI   QB   BENGALS

PERSONAL: Born August 21, 1975, in San Diego. ... 6-3/220. ... Full name: Kabisa Akili Maradu Smith. ... Cousin of Marquis Smith, defensive back, Cleveland Browns. ... Name pronounced uh-KEE-lee.
HIGH SCHOOL: Lincoln (San Diego).
JUNIOR COLLEGE: Grossmont College (Calif.).
COLLEGE: Oregon.
TRANSACTIONS/CAREER NOTES: Selected by Cincinnati Bengals in first round (third pick overall) of 1999 NFL draft. ... Signed by Bengals (August 24, 1999). ... On injured reserve with hamstring injury (December 18, 2001-remainder of season).
PRO STATISTICS: 1999—Caught one pass for six yards, fumbled four times and recovered one fumble for minus three yards. 2000—Fumbled 14 times and recovered two fumbles for minus 14 yards. 2001—Recovered one fumble.
SINGLE GAME HIGHS (regular season): Attempts,—43 (September 10, 2000, vs. Cleveland); completions—25 (October 10, 1999, vs. Cleveland); passing yards—250 (September 10, 2000, vs. Cleveland); and touchdown passes—2 (October 10, 1999, vs. Cleveland).
MISCELLANEOUS: Regular-season record as starting NFL quarterback: 3-13 (.188).

					PASSING						RUSHING				TOTALS	
Year—Team	G	GS	Att.	Cmp.	Pct.	Yds.	TD	Int.	Avg.	Rat.	Att.	Yds.	Avg.	TD	TD	2pt.	Pts.
1999—Cincinnati NFL	7	4	153	80	52.3	805	2	6	5.26	55.6	19	114	6.0	1	1	0	6
2000—Cincinnati NFL	12	11	267	118	44.2	1253	3	6	4.69	52.8	41	232	5.7	0	0	0	0
2001—Cincinnati NFL	2	1	8	5	62.5	37	0	0	4.63	73.4	6	20	3.3	0	0	0	0
Pro totals (3 years)	21	16	428	203	47.4	2095	5	12	4.89	54.2	66	366	5.5	1	1	0	6

SMITH, ANTOWAIN   RB   PATRIOTS

PERSONAL: Born March 14, 1972, in Millbrook, Ala. ... 6-2/230. ... Full name: Antowain Drurell Smith. ... Name pronounced AN-twan.
HIGH SCHOOL: Elmore (Ala.).
JUNIOR COLLEGE: East Mississippi Junior College.
COLLEGE: Houston.
TRANSACTIONS/CAREER NOTES: Selected by Buffalo Bills in first round (23rd pick overall) of 1997 NFL draft. ... Signed by Bills (July 11, 1997). ... Released by Bills (May 18, 2001). ... Signed by New England Patriots (June 7, 2001). ... Granted unconditional free agency (March 1, 2002). ... Re-signed by Patriots (March 1, 2002).
CHAMPIONSHIP GAME EXPERIENCE: Played in AFC championship game (2001 season). ... Member of Super Bowl championship team (2001 season).
PRO STATISTICS: 1998—Recovered two fumbles. 2000—Returned one kickoff for no yards. 2001—Recovered one fumble.
SINGLE GAME HIGHS (regular season): Attempts—31 (October 11, 1998, vs. Indianapolis); yards—156 (December 22, 2001, vs. Miami); and rushing touchdowns—3 (December 23, 2000, vs. Seattle).
STATISTICAL PLATEAUS: 100-yard rushing games: 1997 (1), 1998 (3), 1999 (2), 2000 (1), 2001 (4). Total: 11.

			RUSHING				RECEIVING				TOTALS			
Year—Team	G	GS	Att.	Yds.	Avg.	TD	No.	Yds.	Avg.	TD	TD	2pt.	Pts.	Fum.
1997—Buffalo NFL	16	0	194	840	4.3	8	28	177	6.3	0	8	0	48	4
1998—Buffalo NFL	16	14	300	1124	3.7	8	5	11	2.2	0	8	0	48	5
1999—Buffalo NFL	14	11	165	614	3.7	6	2	32	16.0	0	6	0	36	4
2000—Buffalo NFL	11	3	101	354	3.5	4	3	20	6.7	0	4	0	24	1
2001—New England NFL	16	15	287	1157	4.0	12	19	192	10.1	1	13	0	78	4
Pro totals (5 years)	73	43	1047	4089	3.9	38	57	432	7.6	1	39	0	234	18

SMITH, BRADY   DE   FALCONS

PERSONAL: Born June 5, 1973, in Royal Oak, Mich. ... 6-5/274. ... Full name: Brady McKay Smith. ... Son of Steve Smith, offensive tackle with four NFL teams (1966-74).
HIGH SCHOOL: Barrington (Ill.).
COLLEGE: Colorado State (degree in liberal arts).
TRANSACTIONS/CAREER NOTES: Selected by New Orleans Saints in third round (70th pick overall) of 1996 NFL draft. ... Signed by Saints (July 12, 1996). ... Granted free agency (February 12, 1999). ... Re-signed by Saints (April 14, 1999). ... Granted unconditional free agency (February 11, 2000). ... Signed by Atlanta Falcons (February 19, 2000).
PRO STATISTICS: 1996—Returned two kickoffs for 14 yards. 1999—Recovered two fumbles.

Year—Team	G	GS	SACKS
1996—New Orleans NFL	16	4	2.0
1997—New Orleans NFL	16	2	5.0
1998—New Orleans NFL	14	5	0.0
1999—New Orleans NFL	16	16	6.0
2000—Atlanta NFL	15	15	4.5
2001—Atlanta NFL	15	15	8.0
Pro totals (6 years)	92	57	25.5

— 345 —

SMITH, BRUCE — DE — REDSKINS

PERSONAL: Born June 18, 1963, in Norfolk, Va. ... 6-4/261. ... Full name: Bruce Bernard Smith.
HIGH SCHOOL: Booker T. Washington (Norfolk, Va.).
COLLEGE: Virginia Tech.
TRANSACTIONS/CAREER NOTES: Selected by Baltimore Stars in 1985 USFL territorial draft. ... Signed by Buffalo Bills (February 28, 1985). ... Selected officially by Bills in first round (first pick overall) of 1985 NFL draft. ... On non-football injury list with substance abuse problem (September 2-28, 1988). ... Granted free agency (February 1, 1989). ... Tendered offer sheet by Denver Broncos (March 23, 1989). ... Offer matched by Bills (March 29, 1989). ... On injured reserve with knee injury (October 12-November 30, 1991). ... Released by Bills (February 10, 2000). ... Signed by Washington Redskins (February 14, 2000).
CHAMPIONSHIP GAME EXPERIENCE: Played in AFC championship game (1988 and 1990-1993 seasons). ... Played in Super Bowl XXV (1990 season), Super Bowl XXVI (1991 season), Super Bowl XXVII (1992 season) and Super Bowl XXVIII (1993 season).
HONORS: Named defensive lineman on THE SPORTING NEWS college All-America second team (1983 and 1984). ... Outland Trophy winner (1984). ... Named defensive end on THE SPORTING NEWS NFL All-Pro team (1987, 1988, 1990 and 1992-1997). ... Played in Pro Bowl (1987-1990, 1994, 1995, 1997 and 1998 seasons). ... Named Outstanding Player of Pro Bowl (1987 season). ... Named to play in Pro Bowl (1992 season); replaced by Howie Long due to injury. ... Named to play in Pro Bowl (1993 season); replaced by Sean Jones due to injury. ... Named to play in Pro Bowl (1996 season); replaced by Willie McGinest due to injury.
POST SEASON RECORDS: Shares Super Bowl single-game record for most safeties—1 (January 27, 1991, vs. New York Giants). ... Shares NFL postseason career record for most sacks—12. ... Shares NFL postseason single-game record for most safeties—1 (January 27, 1991, vs. New York Giants).
PRO STATISTICS: 1985—Rushed once for no yards and recovered four fumbles. 1987—Recovered two fumbles for 15 yards and one touchdown. 1988—Credited with one safety. 1993—Intercepted one pass for no yards and recovered one fumble. 1994—Intercepted one pass for no yards and recovered two fumbles. 1995—Recovered one fumble. 1996—Recovered one fumble. 1998—Recovered two fumbles for 18 yards. 1999—Recovered one fumble. 2000—Credited with one safety. 2001—Recovered one fumble.
MISCELLANEOUS: Active NFL leader for career sacks (171). ... Holds Buffalo Bills all-time record for most sacks (171).

Year—Team	G	GS	SACKS
1985—Buffalo NFL	16	13	6.5
1986—Buffalo NFL	16	15	15.0
1987—Buffalo NFL	12	12	12.0
1988—Buffalo NFL	12	12	11.0
1989—Buffalo NFL	16	16	13.0
1990—Buffalo NFL	16	16	19.0
1991—Buffalo NFL	5	5	1.5
1992—Buffalo NFL	15	15	14.0
1993—Buffalo NFL	16	16	14.0
1994—Buffalo NFL	15	15	10.0
1995—Buffalo NFL	15	15	10.5
1996—Buffalo NFL	16	16	▲13.5
1997—Buffalo NFL	16	16	§14.0
1998—Buffalo NFL	15	15	10.0
1999—Buffalo NFL	16	16	7.0
2000—Washington NFL	16	16	10.0
2001—Washington NFL	14	14	5.0
Pro totals (17 years)	247	243	186.0

SMITH, DARRIN — LB — SAINTS

PERSONAL: Born April 15, 1970, in Miami. ... 6-1/230. ... Full name: Darrin Andrew Smith.
HIGH SCHOOL: Miami Norland.
COLLEGE: Miami (Fla.) (degree in business management, 1991; master's degree in business administration, 1993).
TRANSACTIONS/CAREER NOTES: Selected by Dallas Cowboys in second round (54th pick overall) of 1993 NFL draft. ... Signed by Cowboys (July 21, 1993). ... On reserve/did not report list (July 20-October 14, 1995). ... Granted free agency (February 16, 1996). ... Re-signed by Cowboys (June 17, 1996). ... Granted unconditional free agency (February 14, 1997). ... Signed by Philadelphia Eagles (April 19, 1997). ... On injured reserve with ankle injury (November 19, 1997-remainder of season). ... Granted unconditional free agency (February 13, 1998). ... Signed by Seattle Seahawks (February 19, 1998). ... Released by Seahawks (February 10, 2000). ... Signed by New Orleans Saints (July 16, 2000). ... Granted unconditional free agency (March 2, 2001). ... Re-signed by Saints (April 10, 2001).
CHAMPIONSHIP GAME EXPERIENCE: Played in NFC championship game (1993 and 1995 seasons). ... Member of Super Bowl championship team (1993 and 1995 seasons).
PRO STATISTICS: 1993—Recovered one fumble. 1994—Recovered two fumbles for 11 yards. 1995—Recovered one fumble for 63 yards. 1997—Recovered one fumble. 1998—Recovered two fumbles.

			INTERCEPTIONS				SACKS
Year—Team	G	GS	No.	Yds.	Avg.	TD	No.
1993—Dallas NFL	16	13	0	0	0.0	0	1.0
1994—Dallas NFL	16	16	2	13	6.5	1	4.0
1995—Dallas NFL	9	9	0	0	0.0	0	3.0
1996—Dallas NFL	16	16	0	0	0.0	0	1.0
1997—Philadelphia NFL	7	7	0	0	0.0	0	1.0
1998—Seattle NFL	13	12	3	56	18.7	▲2	5.0
1999—Seattle NFL	15	15	1	0	0.0	0	1.0
2000—New Orleans NFL	16	11	2	56	28.0	1	2.0
2001—New Orleans NFL	16	16	0	0	0.0	0	1.5
Pro totals (9 years)	124	115	8	125	15.6	4	19.5

SMITH, DEREK — LB — 49ERS

PERSONAL: Born January 18, 1975, in American Fork, Utah. ... 6-2/245. ... Full name: Derek Mecham Smith.
HIGH SCHOOL: American Fork (Utah).
JUNIOR COLLEGE: Snow College (Utah).
COLLEGE: Arizona State.

TRANSACTIONS/CAREER NOTES: Selected by Washington Redskins in third round (80th pick overall) of 1997 NFL draft. ... Signed by Redskins (July 11, 1997). ... Granted free agency (February 11, 2000). ... Re-signed by Redskins (April 11, 2000). ... Granted unconditional free agency (March 2, 2001). ... Signed by San Francisco 49ers (March 23, 2001).
PRO STATISTICS: 1997—Recovered two fumbles for five yards. 1998—Recovered one fumble. 1999—Intercepted one pass for no yards and recovered one fumble. 2000—Recovered one fumble. 2001—Intercepted one pass for no yards and recovered two fumbles for three yards.

Year Team	G	GS	SACKS
1997—Washington NFL	16	16	2.0
1998—Washington NFL	16	15	0.5
1999—Washington NFL	16	16	1.0
2000—Washington NFL	16	14	1.0
2001—San Francisco NFL	14	14	3.0
Pro totals (5 years)	78	75	7.5

SMITH, DETRON   FB   JAGUARS

PERSONAL: Born February 25, 1974, in Dallas. ... 5-10/230. ... Full name: Detron Negil Smith. ... Name pronounced DEE-tron.
HIGH SCHOOL: Lake Highlands (Dallas).
COLLEGE: Texas A&M.
TRANSACTIONS/CAREER NOTES: Selected by Denver Broncos in third round (65th pick overall) of 1996 NFL draft. ... Signed by Broncos (July 20, 1996). ... Released by Broncos (February 28, 2002). ... Signed by Jacksonville Jaguars (April 8, 2002).
PLAYING EXPERIENCE: Denver NFL, 1996-2001. ... Games/Games started: 1996 (13/0), 1997 (16/0), 1998 (15/2), 1999 (16/0), 2000 (16/0), 2001 (15/0). Total: 91/2.
CHAMPIONSHIP GAME EXPERIENCE: Played in AFC championship game (1997 and 1998 seasons). ... Member of Super Bowl championship team (1997 and 1998 seasons).
HONORS: Played in Pro Bowl (1999 season).
PRO STATISTICS: 1997—Rushed four times for 10 yards, caught four passes for 41 yards and one touchdown and returned one kickoff for no yards. 1998—Caught three passes for 24 yards and returned three kickoffs for 51 yards. 1999—Rushed once for seven yards, caught four passes for 23 yards, returned one kickoff for 12 yards and recovered one fumble. 2000—Caught one pass for one yard and a touchdown and returned five kickoffs for 73 yards. 2001—Returned one kickoff for four yards and recovered one fumble.
SINGLE GAME HIGHS (regular season): Attempts—2 (December 21, 1997, vs. San Diego); yards—11 (December 21, 1997, vs. San Diego); and rushing touchdowns—0.

SMITH, DWIGHT   CB   BUCCANEERS

PERSONAL: Born August 13, 1978, in Detroit. ... 5-10/201.
HIGH SCHOOL: Central (Detroit).
COLLEGE: Akron.
TRANSACTIONS/CAREER NOTES: Selected by Tampa Bay Buccaneers in third round (84th pick overall) of 2001 NFL draft. ... Signed by Buccaneers (July 17, 2001).
HONORS: Named cornerback on The Sporting News college All-America third team (2000).
PRO STATISTICS: 2001—Recovered two fumbles.

			KICKOFF RETURNS				TOTALS			
Year Team	G	GS	No.	Yds.	Avg.	TD	TD	2pt.	Pts.	Fum.
2001—Tampa Bay NFL	15	0	16	355	22.2	0	0	0	0	2

SMITH, EMMITT   RB   COWBOYS

PERSONAL: Born May 15, 1969, in Pensacola, Fla. ... 5-9/216. ... Full name: Emmitt J. Smith III.
HIGH SCHOOL: Escambia (Pensacola, Fla.).
COLLEGE: Florida (degree in public recreation, 1996).
TRANSACTIONS/CAREER NOTES: Selected after junior season by Dallas Cowboys in first round (17th pick overall) of 1990 NFL draft. ... Signed by Cowboys (September 4, 1990). ... Granted roster exemption (September 4-8, 1990). ... Granted free agency (March 1, 1993). ... Re-signed by Cowboys (September 16, 1993).
CHAMPIONSHIP GAME EXPERIENCE: Played in NFC championship game (1992-1995 seasons). ... Member of Super Bowl championship team (1992, 1993 and 1995 seasons).
HONORS: Named running back on The Sporting News college All-America first team (1989). ... Played in Pro Bowl (1990-1992, 1995, 1998 and 1999 seasons). ... Named running back on The Sporting News NFL All-Pro team (1992-1995). ... Named NFL Player of the Year by The Sporting News (1993). ... Named Most Valuable Player of Super Bowl XXVIII (1993 season). ... Named to play in Pro Bowl (1993 season); replaced by Rodney Hampton due to injury. ... Named Sportsman of the Year by The Sporting News (1994). ... Named to play in Pro Bowl (1994 season); replaced by Ricky Watters due to injury.
RECORDS: Holds NFL career record for most rushing touchdowns—148; most consecutive seasons with 1,000 or more yards rushing—11 (1991-2001); and most seasons with 1,000 or more yards rushing—11 (1991-2001).
POST SEASON RECORDS: Holds Super Bowl career record for most rushing touchdowns—5. ... Holds NFL postseason career record for most rushing touchdowns—18. ... Holds NFL postseason career record for most yards rushing—1,586. ... Shares NFL postseason career record for most games with 100 or more yards rushing—7. ... Shares NFL postseason career records for most points scored—126; and most touchdowns—21.
PRO STATISTICS: 1991—Recovered one fumble. 1992—Recovered one fumble. 1993—Recovered three fumbles. 1996—Recovered one fumble. 1997—Recovered one fumble. 1998—Recovered one fumble. 1999—Recovered one fumble. 2000—Recovered one fumble. 2001—Recovered one fumble.
SINGLE GAME HIGHS (regular season): Attempts—35 (November 7, 1994, vs. New York Giants); yards—237 (October 31, 1993, vs. Philadelphia); and rushing touchdowns—4 (September 4, 1995, vs. New York Giants).
STATISTICAL PLATEAUS: 100-yard rushing games: 1990 (3), 1991 (8), 1992 (7), 1993 (7), 1994 (6), 1995 (11), 1996 (4), 1997 (2), 1998 (7), 1999 (9), 2000 (6), 2001 (4). Total: 74. ... 100-yard receiving games: 1990 (1), 1993 (1). Total: 2.
MISCELLANEOUS: Active NFL leader for career rushing yards (16,187) and rushing touchdowns (148). ... Holds Dallas Cowboys all-time records for most yards rushing (16,187), most touchdowns (159) and most rushing touchdowns (148).

Year Team	G	GS	RUSHING Att.	Yds.	Avg.	TD	RECEIVING No.	Yds.	Avg.	TD	TOTALS TD	2pt.	Pts.	Fum.
1990—Dallas NFL	16	15	241	937	3.9	11	24	228	9.5	0	11	0	66	7
1991—Dallas NFL	16	16	*365	*1563	4.3	12	49	258	5.3	1	13	0	78	8
1992—Dallas NFL	16	16	‡373	*1713	4.6	*18	59	335	5.7	1	*19	0	114	4
1993—Dallas NFL	14	13	283	*1486	*5.3	9	57	414	7.3	1	10	0	60	4
1994—Dallas NFL	15	15	*368	1484	4.0	*21	50	341	6.8	1	*22	0	132	1
1995—Dallas NFL	16	16	*377	*1773	4.7	*25	62	375	6.0	0	*25	0	*150	7
1996—Dallas NFL	15	15	327	1204	3.7	12	47	249	5.3	3	15	0	90	5
1997—Dallas NFL	16	16	261	1074	4.1	4	40	234	5.9	0	4	0	26	1
1998—Dallas NFL	16	16	319	1332	4.2	13	27	175	6.5	2	15	0	90	3
1999—Dallas NFL	15	15	‡329	1397	4.2	11	27	119	4.4	2	13	0	78	5
2000—Dallas NFL	16	16	294	1203	4.1	9	11	79	7.2	0	9	0	54	6
2001—Dallas NFL	14	14	261	1021	3.9	3	17	116	6.8	0	3	0	18	1
Pro totals (12 years)	185	183	3798	16187	4.3	148	470	2923	6.2	11	159	1	956	52

SMITH, HUNTER   P   COLTS

PERSONAL: Born August 9, 1977, in Sherman, Texas. ... 6-2/212. ... Full name: Hunter Dwight Smith.
HIGH SCHOOL: Sherman (Texas).
COLLEGE: Notre Dame.
TRANSACTIONS/CAREER NOTES: Selected by Indianapolis Colts in seventh round (210th pick overall) of 1999 NFL draft. ... Signed by Colts (July 22, 1999). ... Granted free agency (March 1, 2002).
PRO STATISTICS: 2000—Rushed once for 11 yards.

Year Team	G	PUNTING No.	Yds.	Avg.	Net avg.	In. 20	Blk.
1999—Indianapolis NFL	16	58	2467	42.5	30.6	16	†2
2000—Indianapolis NFL	16	65	2906	44.7	36.4	20	0
2001—Indianapolis NFL	16	68	3023	44.5	33.8	12	0
Pro totals (3 years)	48	191	8396	44.0	33.7	48	2

SMITH, JEFF   C/G   TITANS

PERSONAL: Born May 25, 1973, in Decatur, Tenn. ... 6-3/320. ... Full name: Jeffery Lee Smith.
HIGH SCHOOL: Meigs County (Decatur, Tenn.).
COLLEGE: Tennessee.
TRANSACTIONS/CAREER NOTES: Selected by Kansas City Chiefs in seventh round (241st pick overall) of 1996 NFL draft. ... Signed by Chiefs (July 24, 1996). ... Active for one game (1996); did not play. ... Assigned by Chiefs to Scottish Claymores in 1997 World League enhancement allocation program (February 19, 1997). ... Granted free agency (February 12, 1999). ... Re-signed by Chiefs (June 16, 1999). ... Granted unconditional free agency (February 11, 2000). ... Re-signed by Chiefs (March 21, 2000). ... Released by Chiefs (August 27, 2000). ... Signed by Jacksonville Jaguars (August 29, 2000). ... Granted unconditional free agency (March 2, 2001). ... Re-signed by Jaguars (April 16, 2001). ... Granted unconditional free agency (March 1, 2002). ... Signed by Tennessee Titans (May 17, 2002).
PLAYING EXPERIENCE: Scottish W.L., 1997; Kansas City NFL, 1997-1999; Jacksonville NFL, 2000 and 2001. ... Games/Games started: W.L. 1997 (10/games started unavailable), NFL 1997 (3/0), 1998 (11/3), 1999 (15/2), 2000 (14/12), 2001 (16/16). Total: NFL 59/33.
PRO STATISTICS: 2000—Fumbled once.

SMITH, JIMMY   WR   JAGUARS

PERSONAL: Born February 9, 1969, in Detroit. ... 6-1/213. ... Full name: Jimmy Lee Smith Jr.
HIGH SCHOOL: Callaway (Jackson, Miss.).
COLLEGE: Jackson State (degree in business management, 1992).
TRANSACTIONS/CAREER NOTES: Selected by Dallas Cowboys in second round (36th pick overall) of 1992 NFL draft. ... Signed by Cowboys (April 26, 1992). ... On injured reserve with fibula injury (September 2-October 7, 1992); on practice squad (September 28-October 7, 1992). ... On non-football injury list with appendicitis (September 2, 1993-entire season). ... Released by Cowboys (July 11, 1994). ... Signed by Philadelphia Eagles (July 19, 1994). ... Released by Eagles (August 29, 1994). ... Signed by Jacksonville Jaguars (February 28, 1995). ... Granted free agency (February 16, 1996). ... Re-signed by Jaguars (May 28, 1996).
CHAMPIONSHIP GAME EXPERIENCE: Played in NFC championship game (1992 season). ... Member of Super Bowl championship team (1992 season). ... Played in AFC championship game (1996 and 1999 seasons).
HONORS: Played in Pro Bowl (1997-2000 seasons).
PRO STATISTICS: 1995—Recovered blocked punt in end zone for a touchdown and recovered one fumble. 1997—Recovered one fumble. 1998—Recovered two fumbles. 2001—Rushed once for minus three yards and recovered one fumble.
SINGLE GAME HIGHS (regular season): Receptions—15 (September 10, 2000, vs. Baltimore); yards—291 (September 10, 2000, vs. Baltimore); and touchdown receptions—3 (September 10, 2000, vs. Baltimore).
STATISTICAL PLATEAUS: 100-yard receiving games: 1996 (4), 1997 (6), 1998 (5), 1999 (9), 2000 (5), 2001 (6). Total: 35.
MISCELLANEOUS: Holds Jacksonville Jaguars all-time record for most receptions (584), most yards receiving (8,260), most touchdowns (46) and most touchdown receptions (44).

Year Team	G	GS	RECEIVING No.	Yds.	Avg.	TD	KICKOFF RETURNS No.	Yds.	Avg.	TD	TOTALS TD	2pt.	Pts.	Fum.
1992—Dallas NFL	7	0	0	0	0.0	0	0	0	0.0	0	0	0	0	0
1993—Dallas NFL							Did not play.							
1994—							Did not play.							
1995—Jacksonville NFL	16	4	22	288	13.1	3	24	540	22.5	1	5	0	30	2
1996—Jacksonville NFL	16	9	83	§1244	15.0	7	2	49	24.5	0	7	0	42	1
1997—Jacksonville NFL	16	16	82	1324	16.1	4	0	0	0.0	0	4	0	24	1
1998—Jacksonville NFL	16	15	78	1182	15.2	8	0	0	0.0	0	8	0	48	2
1999—Jacksonville NFL	16	16	*116	1636	14.1	6	0	0	0.0	0	6	†1	38	0
2000—Jacksonville NFL	15	14	91	1213	13.3	8	0	0	0.0	0	8	0	48	1
2001—Jacksonville NFL	16	16	112	1373	12.3	8	0	0	0.0	0	8	0	48	1
Pro totals (8 years)	118	90	584	8260	14.1	44	26	589	22.7	1	46	1	278	9

SMITH, JUSTIN — DE — BENGALS

PERSONAL: Born September 30, 1979, in Jefferson City, Mo. ... 6-4/270.
HIGH SCHOOL: Jefferson City (Mo.).
COLLEGE: Missouri.
TRANSACTIONS/CAREER NOTES: Selected after junior season by Cincinnati Bengals in first round (fourth pick overall) of 2001 NFL draft. ... Signed by Bengals (September 8, 2001).
HONORS: Named defensive end on THE SPORTING NEWS college All-America third team (2000).
PRO STATISTICS: 2001—Intercepted two passes for 28 yards.

Year Team	G	GS	SACKS
2001—Cincinnati NFL	15	11	8.5

SMITH, KENNY — DT — SAINTS

PERSONAL: Born September 8, 1977, in Meridian, Miss. ... 6-3/289.
HIGH SCHOOL: Meridian (Miss.).
COLLEGE: Alabama.
TRANSACTIONS/CAREER NOTES: Selected by New Orleans Saints in third round (81st pick overall) of 2001 NFL draft. ... Signed by Saints (July 28, 2001).
PLAYING EXPERIENCE: New Orleans NFL, 2001. ... Games/Games started: 2001 (6/0).

SMITH, LAMAR — RB — PANTHERS

PERSONAL: Born November 29, 1970, in Fort Wayne, Ind. ... 5-11/224.
HIGH SCHOOL: South Side (Fort Wayne, Ind.).
COLLEGE: Houston.
TRANSACTIONS/CAREER NOTES: Selected by Seattle Seahawks in third round (73rd pick overall) of 1994 NFL draft. ... Signed by Seahawks (July 19, 1994). ... On non-football injury list with back injury (December 13, 1994-remainder of season). ... Granted free agency (February 14, 1997). ... Re-signed by Seahawks (February 1997). ... Granted unconditional free agency (February 13, 1998). ... Signed by New Orleans Saints (February 28, 1998). ... Released by Saints (February 24, 2000). ... Signed by Miami Dolphins (March 15, 2000). ... Granted unconditional free agency (March 1, 2002). ... Signed by Carolina Panthers (March 20, 2002).
PRO STATISTICS: 1995—Returned one kickoff for 20 yards. 1996—Recovered one fumble. 1997—Returned one kickoff for 14 yards. 1998—Attempted two passes with one completion for 20 yards and a touchdown. 1999—Attempted one pass without a completion. 2000—Attempted one pass without a completion.
SINGLE GAME HIGHS (regular season): Attempts—33 (November 17, 1996, vs. Detroit); yards—158 (January 6, 2002, vs. Buffalo); and rushing touchdowns—2 (December 24, 2000, vs. New England).
STATISTICAL PLATEAUS: 100-yard rushing games: 1996 (1), 1998 (1), 2000 (4), 2001 (3). Total: 9.

			RUSHING				RECEIVING				TOTALS		
Year Team	G	GS	Att.	Yds.	Avg.	TD	No.	Yds.	Avg.	TD	TD	2pt.	Pts.	Fum.
1994—Seattle NFL	2	0	2	-1	-0.5	0	0	0	0.0	0	0	0	0	0
1995—Seattle NFL	12	0	36	215	6.0	0	1	10	10.0	0	0	0	0	1
1996—Seattle NFL	16	2	153	680	4.4	8	9	58	6.4	0	8	*3	54	4
1997—Seattle NFL	12	2	91	392	4.3	2	23	183	8.0	0	2	1	14	0
1998—New Orleans NFL	14	9	138	457	3.3	1	24	249	10.4	2	3	0	18	4
1999—New Orleans NFL	13	2	60	205	3.4	0	20	151	7.6	1	1	0	6	1
2000—Miami NFL	15	15	309	1139	3.7	14	31	201	6.5	2	16	0	96	3
2001—Miami NFL	16	16	313	968	3.1	6	30	234	7.8	2	8	0	48	6
Pro totals (8 years)	100	46	1102	4055	3.7	31	138	1086	7.9	7	38	4	236	19

SMITH, LARRY — DT — JAGUARS

PERSONAL: Born December 4, 1974, in Kingsland, Ga. ... 6-5/300. ... Full name: Larry Smith Jr.
HIGH SCHOOL: Charlton County (Folkston, Ga.), then Valley Forge (Pa.).
COLLEGE: Florida State.
TRANSACTIONS/CAREER NOTES: Selected after junior season by Jacksonville Jaguars in second round (56th pick overall) of 1999 NFL draft. ... Signed by Jaguars (April 26, 1999).
CHAMPIONSHIP GAME EXPERIENCE: Played in AFC championship game (1999 season).
PRO STATISTICS: 2000—Recovered three fumbles for one yard. 2001—Recovered one fumble.

Year Team	G	GS	SACKS
1999—Jacksonville NFL	15	0	3.0
2000—Jacksonville NFL	14	4	0.0
2001—Jacksonville NFL	7	0	0.0
Pro totals (3 years)	36	4	3.0

SMITH, MARK — DT — BROWNS

PERSONAL: Born August 28, 1974, in Vicksburg, Miss. ... 6-4/294. ... Full name: Mark Anthony Smith.
HIGH SCHOOL: Vicksburg (Miss.).
JUNIOR COLLEGE: Navarro College (Texas), then Hinds Community College (Miss.).
COLLEGE: Auburn.
TRANSACTIONS/CAREER NOTES: Selected by Arizona Cardinals in seventh round (212th pick overall) of 1997 NFL draft. ... Signed by Cardinals (May 5, 1997). ... On injured reserve with knee injury (November 1, 1999-remainder of season). ... Granted free agency (February 11, 2000). ... Re-signed by Cardinals (June 27, 2000). ... Granted unconditional free agency (March 2, 2001). ... Signed by Cleveland Browns (March 13, 2001). ... Granted unconditional free agency (March 1, 2002). ... Re-signed by Browns (March 20, 2002).
PRO STATISTICS: 1998—Recovered one fumble. 2001—Recovered one fumble.

Year Team	G	GS	SACKS
1997—Arizona NFL	16	4	6.0
1998—Arizona NFL	14	13	9.0
1999—Arizona NFL	2	0	0.0
2000—Arizona NFL	14	7	3.0
2001—Cleveland NFL	16	11	2.0
Pro totals (5 years)	62	35	20.0

SMITH, MARQUIS DB BROWNS

PERSONAL: Born January 13, 1975, in San Diego. ... 6-2/213. ... Cousin of Akili Smith, quarterback, Cincinnati Bengals. ... Name pronounced mar-KEYS.
HIGH SCHOOL: Patrick Henry (San Diego).
COLLEGE: California.
TRANSACTIONS/CAREER NOTES: Selected by Cleveland Browns in third round (76th pick overall) of 1999 NFL draft. ... Signed by Browns (July 15, 1999). ... Granted free agency (March 1, 2002). ... Re-signed by Browns (April 20, 2002).
PLAYING EXPERIENCE: Cleveland NFL, 1999-2001. ... Games/Games started: 1999 (16/2), 2000 (16/16), 2001 (14/2). Total: 46/20.
PRO STATISTICS: 2000—Credited with one sack.

SMITH, MARVEL OT STEELERS

PERSONAL: Born August 6, 1978, in Oakland. ... 6-5/308. ... Full name: Marvel Amos Smith.
HIGH SCHOOL: Skyline (Oakland).
COLLEGE: Arizona State.
TRANSACTIONS/CAREER NOTES: Selected after junior season by Pittsburgh Steelers in second round (38th pick overall) of 2000 NFL draft. ... Signed by Steelers (July 16, 2000).
PLAYING EXPERIENCE: Pittsburgh NFL, 2000 and 2001. ... Games/Games started: 2000 (12/9), 2001 (16/16). Total: 28/25.
CHAMPIONSHIP GAME EXPERIENCE: Played in AFC championship game (2001 season).
HONORS: Named offensive tackle on THE SPORTING NEWS college All-America third team (1999).

SMITH, MAURICE RB FALCONS

PERSONAL: Born September 7, 1976, in Palmyra, North Carolina. ... 6-0/235.
HIGH SCHOOL: S.E. Halifax (N.C.).
COLLEGE: North Carolina A&T.
TRANSACTIONS/CAREER NOTES: Signed as non-drafted free agent by Atlanta Falcons (April 17, 2000).
PRO STATISTICS: 2001—Recovered two fumbles.
SINGLE GAME HIGHS (regular season): Attempts—27 (November 11, 2001, vs. Dallas); yards—148 (November 11, 2001, vs. Dallas); and rushing touchdowns—1 (December 30, 2001, vs. Miami).
STATISTICAL PLATEAUS: 100-yard rushing games: 2001 (1). ... 100-yard receiving games: 2001 (1).

			RUSHING				RECEIVING				TOTALS		
Year Team	G	GS	Att.	Yds.	Avg.	TD	No.	Yds.	Avg.	TD	TD	2pt.	Pts.	Fum.
2000—Atlanta NFL	11	0	19	69	3.6	0	1	5	5.0	0	0	0	0	0
2001—Atlanta NFL	16	12	237	760	3.2	5	19	230	12.1	1	6	0	36	1
Pro totals (2 years)	27	12	256	829	3.2	5	20	235	11.8	1	6	0	36	1

SMITH, OTIS CB PATRIOTS

PERSONAL: Born October 22, 1965, in New Orleans. ... 5-11/195. ... Full name: Otis Smith III.
HIGH SCHOOL: East Jefferson (Metairie, La.).
JUNIOR COLLEGE: Taft (Calif.) College.
COLLEGE: Missouri.
TRANSACTIONS/CAREER NOTES: Signed as non-drafted free agent by Philadelphia Eagles (April 25, 1990). ... On physically unable to perform list with appendectomy (August 2, 1990-entire season). ... Granted free agency (February 1, 1992). ... Re-signed by Eagles (August 11, 1992). ... Granted unconditional free agency (February 17, 1994). ... Re-signed by Eagles (April 25, 1994). ... Released by Eagles (March 22, 1995). ... Signed by New York Jets (April 13, 1995). ... Released by Jets (September 24, 1996). ... Signed by New England Patriots (October 9, 1996). ... Granted unconditional free agency (February 14, 1997). ... Re-signed by Jets (May 20, 1997). ... Granted unconditional free agency (February 13, 1998). ... Re-signed by Jets (April 9, 1998). ... On injured reserve with broken collarbone (October 5, 1999-remainder of season). ... Released by Jets (August 20, 2000). ... Signed by Patriots (August 23, 2000).
CHAMPIONSHIP GAME EXPERIENCE: Played in AFC championship game (1996, 1998 and 2001 seasons). ... Played in Super Bowl XXXI (1996 season). ... Member of Super Bowl championship team (2001 season).
PRO STATISTICS: 1991—Recovered one fumble. 1994—Credited with one sack and returned one kickoff for 14 yards. 1995—Returned one kickoff for six yards. 1996—Credited with one sack. 1997—Recovered two fumbles for 40 yards. 2000—Recovered one fumble for 12 yards. 2001—Credited with two sacks and recovered two fumbles.

			INTERCEPTIONS			
Year Team	G	GS	No.	Yds.	Avg.	TD
1990—Philadelphia NFL			Did not play.			
1991—Philadelphia NFL	15	1	2	74	37.0	∞1
1992—Philadelphia NFL	16	1	1	0	0.0	0
1993—Philadelphia NFL	15	0	1	0	0.0	0
1994—Philadelphia NFL	16	2	0	0	0.0	0
1995—New York Jets NFL	11	10	6	101	16.8	▲1
1996—New York Jets NFL	2	0	0	0	0.0	0
—New England NFL	11	6	2	20	10.0	0
1997—New York Jets NFL	16	16	6	158	26.3	†3
1998—New York Jets NFL	16	16	2	34	17.0	0
1999—New York Jets NFL	1	1	0	0	0.0	0
2000—New England NFL	16	14	1	56	56.0	0
2001—New England NFL	15	15	5	181	36.2	†2
Pro totals (11 years)	150	82	26	624	24.0	7

SMITH, PAUL   RB   49ERS

PERSONAL: Born January 31, 1978, in El Paso, Texas. ... 5-11/234.
HIGH SCHOOL: Andress (El Paso, Texas).
COLLEGE: Texas-El Paso.
TRANSACTIONS/CAREER NOTES: Selected by San Francisco 49ers in fifth round (132nd pick overall) of 2000 NFL draft. ... Signed by 49ers (July 21, 2000).
PRO STATISTICS: 2000—Returned nine kickoffs for 167 yards and recovered two fumbles. 2001—Returned three kickoffs for 37 yards and recovered one fumble.
SINGLE GAME HIGHS (regular season): Attempts—5 (December 3, 2000, vs. San Diego); yards—27 (December 2, 2001, vs. Buffalo); and rushing touchdowns—1 (December 2, 2001, vs. Buffalo).

				RUSHING				RECEIVING				TOTALS		
Year Team	G	GS	Att.	Yds.	Avg.	TD	No.	Yds.	Avg.	TD	TD	2pt.	Pts.	Fum.
2000—San Francisco NFL	10	0	18	72	4.0	0	2	55	27.5	0	0	0	0	2
2001—San Francisco NFL	15	0	4	27	6.8	1	0	0	0.0	0	1	0	6	1
Pro totals (2 years)	25	0	22	99	4.5	1	2	55	27.5	0	1	0	6	3

SMITH, ROBAIRE   DE/DT   TITANS

PERSONAL: Born November 15, 1977, in Flint, Mich. ... 6-4/280. ... Full name: Robaire Freddick Smith. ... Brother of Fernando Smith, defensive end, with four NFL teams (1994-2000).
HIGH SCHOOL: Flint (Mich.).
COLLEGE: Michigan State.
TRANSACTIONS/CAREER NOTES: Selected by Tennessee Titans in sixth round (197th pick overall) of 2000 NFL draft. ... Signed by Titans (July 5, 2000).
HONORS: Named defensive end on THE SPORTING NEWS college All-America second team (1999).

Year Team	G	GS	SACKS
2000—Tennessee NFL	7	0	2.5
2001—Tennessee NFL	10	0	2.0
Pro totals (2 years)	17	0	4.5

SMITH, ROD   WR   BRONCOS

PERSONAL: Born May 15, 1970, in Texarkana, Ark. ... 6-0/200.
HIGH SCHOOL: Texarkana (Ark.).
COLLEGE: Missouri Southern.
TRANSACTIONS/CAREER NOTES: Signed as non-drafted free agent by Denver Broncos (March 23, 1995).
CHAMPIONSHIP GAME EXPERIENCE: Played in AFC championship game (1997 and 1998 seasons). ... Member of Super Bowl championship team (1997 and 1998 seasons).
HONORS: Played in Pro Bowl (2000 season).
PRO STATISTICS: 1996—Rushed once for one yard. 1997—Rushed five times for 16 yards and recovered one fumble. 1998—Rushed six times for 63 yards, completed only pass attempt for 14 yards and recovered two fumbles for 11 yards and one touchdown. 1999—Attempted one pass without a completion. 2000—Rushed six times for 99 yards and a touchdown.
SINGLE GAME HIGHS (regular season): Receptions—13 (September 23, 2001, vs. Arizona); yards—187 (November 19, 2000, vs. San Diego); and touchdown receptions—3 (October 15, 2000, vs. Cleveland).
STATISTICAL PLATEAUS: 100-yard receiving games: 1997 (6), 1998 (4), 1999 (3), 2000 (8), 2001 (5). Total: 26.
MISCELLANEOUS: Shares Denver Broncos all-time record most touchdown receptions (44).

			RECEIVING				PUNT RETURNS				KICKOFF RETURNS				TOTALS		
Year Team	G	GS	No.	Yds.	Avg.	TD	No.	Yds.	Avg.	TD	No.	Yds.	Avg.	TD	TD	2pt.	Pts.	Fum.
1995—Denver NFL	16	1	6	152	25.3	1	0	0	0.0	0	4	54	13.5	0	1	0	6	0
1996—Denver NFL	10	1	16	237	14.8	2	23	283	12.3	0	1	29	29.0	0	2	0	12	1
1997—Denver NFL	16	16	70	1180	16.9▲	12	1	12	12.0	0	0	0	0.0	0	12	0	72	3
1998—Denver NFL	16	16	86	1222	14.2	6	0	0	0.0	0	0	0	0.0	0	7	0	42	0
1999—Denver NFL	15	15	79	1020	12.9	4	0	0	0.0	0	1	10	10.0	0	4	0	24	1
2000—Denver NFL	16	16	100	§1602	16.0	8	0	0	0.0	0	0	0	0.0	0	9	0	54	1
2001—Denver NFL	15	14	*113	1343	11.9	11	0	0	0.0	0	0	0	0.0	0	11▲	1	68	1
Pro totals (7 years)	104	79	470	6756	14.4	44	24	295	12.3	0	6	93	15.5	0	46	1	278	7

SMITH, STEVE   WR   PANTHERS

PERSONAL: Born May 12, 1979, in Lynwood, Calif. ... 5-9/179. ... Full name: Stevonne Smith.
HIGH SCHOOL: University (Los Angeles).
JUNIOR COLLEGE: Santa Monica Junior College.
COLLEGE: Utah.
TRANSACTIONS/CAREER NOTES: Selected by Carolina Panthers in third round (74th pick overall) of 2001 NFL draft. ... Signed by Panthers (June 19, 2001).
HONORS: Named kick returner on THE SPORTING NEWS NFL All-Pro team (2001).
PRO STATISTICS: 2001—Rushed four times for 43 yards and recovered four fumbles for two yards.
SINGLE GAME HIGHS (regular season): Receptions—3 (January 6, 2002, vs. New England); yards—36 (January 6, 2002, vs. New England); and touchdown receptions—0.

			RECEIVING				PUNT RETURNS				KICKOFF RETURNS				TOTALS		
Year Team	G	GS	No.	Yds.	Avg.	TD	No.	Yds.	Avg.	TD	No.	Yds.	Avg.	TD	TD	2pt.	Pts.	Fum.
2001—Carolina NFL	15	1	10	154	15.4	0	34	364	10.7	†1	56	1431	‡25.6	†2	3	0	18	8

SMITH, TERRELLE — FB — SAINTS

PERSONAL: Born March 12, 1978, in West Covina, Calif. ... 6-0/246. ... Full name: Terrelle Vernon Smith.
HIGH SCHOOL: Canyon Springs (Moreno Valley, Calif.).
COLLEGE: Arizona State.
TRANSACTIONS/CAREER NOTES: Selected by New Orleans Saints in fourth round (96th pick overall) of 2000 NFL draft. ... Signed by Saints (July 11, 2000).
PRO STATISTICS: 2001—Recovered one fumble.
SINGLE GAME HIGHS (regular season): Attempts—6 (December 10, 2000, vs. San Francisco); yards—42 (November 19, 2000, vs. Oakland); and rushing touchdowns—0.

			RUSHING				RECEIVING				TOTALS		
Year Team	G	GS	Att.	Yds.	Avg.	TD	No.	Yds.	Avg.	TD	TD	2pt.	Pts.	Fum.
2000—New Orleans NFL	14	9	29	131	4.5	0	12	65	5.4	0	0	0	0	1
2001—New Orleans NFL	14	9	5	8	1.6	0	4	30	7.5	2	2	0	12	1
Pro totals (2 years)	28	18	34	139	4.1	0	16	95	5.9	2	2	0	12	2

SMITH, THOMAS — CB

PERSONAL: Born December 5, 1970, in Gates, N.C. ... 5-11/190. ... Full name: Thomas Lee Smith Jr. ... Cousin of Sam Perkins, forward/center, with four NBA teams (1984-85 through 2000-01).
HIGH SCHOOL: Gates County (Gatesville, N.C.).
COLLEGE: North Carolina.
TRANSACTIONS/CAREER NOTES: Selected by Buffalo Bills in first round (28th pick overall) of 1993 NFL draft. ... Signed by Bills (July 16, 1993). ... Granted free agency (February 16, 1996). ... Re-signed by Bills (February 27, 1996). ... Granted unconditional free agency (February 11, 2000). ... Signed by Chicago Bears (February 12, 2000). ... Released by Bears (August 28, 2001). ... Signed by Indianapolis Colts (September 3, 2001). ... Released by Colts (December 5, 2001).
PRO STATISTICS: 1993—Recovered one fumble. 1997—Fumbled once and recovered one fumble for one yard. 1998—Recovered one fumble. 1999—Recovered one fumble. 2000—Recovered one fumble.

			INTERCEPTIONS			
Year Team	G	GS	No.	Yds.	Avg.	TD
1993—Buffalo NFL	16	1	0	0	0.0	0
1994—Buffalo NFL	16	16	1	4	4.0	0
1995—Buffalo NFL	16	16	2	23	11.5	0
1996—Buffalo NFL	16	16	1	0	0.0	0
1997—Buffalo NFL	16	16	0	0	0.0	0
1998—Buffalo NFL	14	14	1	0	0.0	0
1999—Buffalo NFL	16	16	1	29	29.0	0
2000—Chicago NFL	16	16	0	0	0.0	0
2001—Indianapolis NFL	11	0	0	0	0.0	0
Pro totals (9 years)	137	111	6	56	9.3	0

SMITH, TRAVIAN — LB — RAIDERS

PERSONAL: Born August 26, 1975, in Good Shepard, Texas. ... 6-4/240.
HIGH SCHOOL: Tatum (Texas).
COLLEGE: Oklahoma.
TRANSACTIONS/CAREER NOTES: Selected by Oakland Raiders in fifth round (152nd pick overall) of 1998 NFL draft. ... Signed by Raiders (July 6, 1998). ... Released by Raiders (August 26, 1998). ... Re-signed by Raiders to practice squad (August 31, 1998). ... Activated (December 15, 1998).
PLAYING EXPERIENCE: Oakland NFL, 1998-2001. ... Games/Games started: 1998 (2/0), 1999 (16/1), 2000 (16/0), 2001 (16/2). Total: 50/3.
CHAMPIONSHIP GAME EXPERIENCE: Played in AFC championship game (2000 season).
PRO STATISTICS: 1999—Recovered one fumble for one yard. 2001—Intercepted one pass for nine yards, credited with $2^{1}/_{2}$ sacks, fumbled once and recovered one fumble.

SMOOT, FRED — CB — REDSKINS

PERSONAL: Born April 17, 1979, in Jackson, Miss. ... 5-11/179. ... Full name: Fredrick D. Smoot.
HIGH SCHOOL: Provine (Jackson, Miss.).
JUNIOR COLLEGE: Hinds Community College (Miss.).
COLLEGE: Mississippi State.
TRANSACTIONS/CAREER NOTES: Selected by Washington Redskins in second round (45th pick overall) of 2001 NFL draft. ... Signed by Redskins (July 31, 2001).
HONORS: Named cornerback on THE SPORTING NEWS college All-America first team (2000).
PRO STATISTICS: 2001—Recovered one fumble.

			INTERCEPTIONS			
Year Team	G	GS	No.	Yds.	Avg.	TD
2001—Washington NFL	14	13	5	36	7.2	0

SNIDER, MATT — FB — TEXANS

PERSONAL: Born January 26, 1976, in Des Moines, Iowa. ... 6-3/242. ... Full name: Matthew Kale Snider.
HIGH SCHOOL: Lower Merion (Wynnewood, Pa.).
COLLEGE: Richmond.
TRANSACTIONS/CAREER NOTES: Signed as non-drafted free agent by Carolina Panthers (April 27, 1999). ... Claimed on waivers by Green Bay Packers (July 1, 1999). ... Released by Packers (September 1, 2001). ... Signed by Minnesota Vikings (September 6, 2001). ... Released by Vikings (October 9, 2001). ... Signed by Houston Texans (December 29, 2001).
PLAYING EXPERIENCE: Green Bay NFL, 1999 and 2000; Minnesota NFL, 2001. ... Games/Games started: 1999 (8/0), 2000 (16/0), 2001 (4/0). Total: 28/0.

SNOW, JUSTIN — TE — COLTS

PERSONAL: Born December 21, 1976, in Ft. Worth, Texas. ... 6-3/234.
HIGH SCHOOL: Cooper (Abilene, Texas.).
COLLEGE: Baylor.
TRANSACTIONS/CAREER NOTES: Signed as non-drafted free agent by Indianapolis Colts (April 20, 2000).
PLAYING EXPERIENCE: Indianapolis NFL, 2000 and 2001. ... Games/Games started: 2000 (16/0), 2001 (16/0). Total: 32/0.

SOLWOLD, MIKE — C — COWBOYS

PERSONAL: Born September 30, 1977, in Hartland, Wis. ... 6-6/244.
HIGH SCHOOL: Arrowhead (Wis.).
COLLEGE: Wisconsin.
TRANSACTIONS/CAREER NOTES: Signed as non-drafted free agent by Minnesota Vikings (April 22, 2001). ... Claimed on waivers by Dallas Cowboys (August 28, 2001). ... Released by Cowboys (September 3, 2001). ... Re-signed by Cowboys (November 14, 2001).
PLAYING EXPERIENCE: Dallas NFL, 2001. ... Games/Games started: 2001 (8/0).

SORENSEN, NICK — S — RAMS

PERSONAL: Born July 31, 1978, in Winter Haven, Fla. ... 6-2/205. ... Full name: Nicholas Carl Sorensen.
HIGH SCHOOL: George C. Marshall (Vienna, Va.).
COLLEGE: Virginia Tech.
TRANSACTIONS/CAREER NOTES: Signed as non-drafted free agent by Miami Dolphins (April 26, 2001). ... Released by Dolphins (August 26, 2001). ... Signed by St. Louis Rams to practice squad (October 16, 2001). ... Activated (November 16, 2001). ... Released by Rams (November 24, 2001). ... Re-signed by Rams (November 27, 2001).
PLAYING EXPERIENCE: St. Louis NFL, 2001. ... Games/Games started: 2001 (7/0).
CHAMPIONSHIP GAME EXPERIENCE: Played in NFC championship game (2001 season). ... Played in Super Bowl XXXVI (2001 season).

SOWELL, JERALD — FB — JETS

PERSONAL: Born January 21, 1974, in Baton Rouge, La. ... 6-0/237. ... Full name: Jerald Monye Sowell.
HIGH SCHOOL: Baker (La.).
COLLEGE: Tulane (degree in exercise science/kinesiology).
TRANSACTIONS/CAREER NOTES: Selected by Green Bay Packers in seventh round (231st pick overall) of 1997 NFL draft. ... Signed by Packers (July 10, 1997). ... Claimed on waivers by New York Jets (August 25, 1997). ... Granted free agency (February 11, 2000). ... Re-signed by Jets (April 25, 2000).
CHAMPIONSHIP GAME EXPERIENCE: Member of Jets for AFC championship game (1998 season); inactive.
PRO STATISTICS: 1999—Attempted one pass without a completion. 2000—Returned one kickoff for nine yards. 2001—Returned one kickoff for six yards.
SINGLE GAME HIGHS (regular season): Attempts—14 (November 8, 1998, vs. Buffalo); yards—82 (September 20, 1998, vs. Indianapolis); and rushing touchdowns—0.

			RUSHING				RECEIVING				TOTALS		
Year Team	G	GS	Att.	Yds.	Avg.	TD	No.	Yds.	Avg.	TD	TD	2pt.	Pts.	Fum.
1997—New York Jets NFL	9	0	7	35	5.0	0	1	8	8.0	0	0	0	0	0
1998—New York Jets NFL	16	2	40	164	4.1	0	10	59	5.9	0	0	0	0	2
1999—New York Jets NFL	16	0	3	5	1.7	0	0	0	0.0	0	0	0	0	0
2000—New York Jets NFL	16	0	2	0	0.0	0	6	84	14.0	0	0	0	0	0
2001—New York Jets NFL	16	0	4	9	2.3	0	1	19	19.0	0	0	0	0	0
Pro totals (5 years)	73	2	56	213	3.8	0	18	170	9.4	0	0	0	0	2

SPEARMAN, ARMEGIS — LB — BENGALS

PERSONAL: Born April 5, 1978, in Bruce, Miss. ... 6-1/258.
HIGH SCHOOL: Bruce (Miss.).
COLLEGE: Mississippi.
TRANSACTIONS/CAREER NOTES: Signed as non-drafted free agent by Cincinnati Bengals as non-drafted free agent (April 27, 2000). ... On injured reserve list with torn pectoral muscle (September 2, 2001-entire season).
PLAYING EXPERIENCE: Cincinnati NFL, 2000. ... Games/Games started: 2000 (15/11).
PRO STATISTICS: 2000—Credited with one sack.

SPEARS, MARCUS — G/OT — CHIEFS

PERSONAL: Born September 28, 1971, in Baton Rouge, La. ... 6-4/312. ... Full name: Marcus DeWayne Spears.
HIGH SCHOOL: Belaire (Baton Rouge, La.).
COLLEGE: Northwestern State (La.).
TRANSACTIONS/CAREER NOTES: Selected by Chicago Bears in second round (39th pick overall) of 1994 NFL draft. ... Signed by Bears (July 16, 1994). ... Inactive for all 16 games (1994). ... Active for five games (1995); did not play. ... Assigned by Bears to Amsterdam Admirals in 1996 World League enhancement allocation program (February 19, 1996). ... Granted unconditional free agency (February 14, 1997). ... Signed by Green Bay Packers (March 12, 1997). ... Released by Packers (August 19, 1997). ... Signed by Kansas City Chiefs (September 16, 1997). ... On injured reserve with hand injury (December 9, 1998-remainder of season). ... Granted unconditional free agency (February 12, 1999). ... Re-signed by Chiefs (February 16, 1999). ... On injured reserve with arm injury (December 15, 2000-remainder of season). ... Granted unconditional free agency (March 1, 2002). ... Re-signed by Chiefs (May 7, 2002).
PLAYING EXPERIENCE: Amsterdam W.L., 1996; Chicago NFL, 1996; Kansas City NFL, 1997-2001. ... Games/Games started: W.L. 1996 (games played unavailable), NFL 1996 (9/0), 1997 (3/0), 1998 (12/0), 1999 (10/2), 2000 (13/0), 2001 (16/16). Total NFL: 63/18.
HONORS: Named offensive lineman on THE SPORTING NEWS college All-America second team (1993).
PRO STATISTICS: 1996—Caught one pass for one yard and a touchdown. 1999—Recovered one fumble. 2000—Returned one kickoff for 11 yards. 2001—Recovered two fumbles for one yard.

SPELLMAN, ALONZO — DL

PERSONAL: Born September 27, 1971, in Mount Holly, N.J. ... 6-4/292. ... Full name: Alonzo Robert Spellman.
HIGH SCHOOL: Rancocas Valley Regional (Mount Holly, N.J.).
COLLEGE: Ohio State.
TRANSACTIONS/CAREER NOTES: Selected after junior season by Chicago Bears in first round (22nd pick overall) of 1992 NFL draft. ... Signed by Bears (July 13, 1992). ... Designated by Bears as transition player (February 16, 1996). ... Tendered offer sheet by Jacksonville Jaguars (February 17, 1996). ... Offer matched by Bears (February 23, 1996). ... Released by Bears (June 12, 1998). ... Signed by Dallas Cowboys (July 29, 1999). ... Granted unconditional free agency (February 11, 2000). ... Re-signed by Cowboys (March 21, 2000). ... Granted unconditional free agency (March 2, 2001). ... Signed by Detroit Lions (August 11, 2001). ... Released by Lions (October 24, 2001).
PRO STATISTICS: 1994—Intercepted one pass for 31 yards. 1995—Recovered one fumble. 1999—Recovered one fumble.

Year — Team	G	GS	SACKS
1992—Chicago NFL	15	0	4.0
1993—Chicago NFL	16	0	2.5
1994—Chicago NFL	16	16	7.0
1995—Chicago NFL	16	16	8.5
1996—Chicago NFL	16	15	8.0
1997—Chicago NFL	7	5	2.0
1998—	Did not play.		
1999—Dallas NFL	16	16	5.0
2000—Dallas NFL	16	15	5.0
2001—Detroit NFL	5	0	1.0
Pro totals (9 years)	**123**	**83**	**43.0**

SPENCER, JIMMY — CB — BRONCOS

PERSONAL: Born March 29, 1969, in Manning, S.C. ... 5-9/188. ... Full name: James Arthur Spencer Jr.
HIGH SCHOOL: Glades Central (Belle Glade, Fla.).
COLLEGE: Florida.
TRANSACTIONS/CAREER NOTES: Selected by Washington Redskins in eighth round (215th pick overall) of 1991 NFL draft. ... Signed by Redskins for 1991 season. ... Released by Redskins (August 26, 1991). ... Signed by New Orleans Saints (April 2, 1992). ... Granted unconditional free agency (February 16, 1996). ... Signed by Cincinnati Bengals (March 21, 1996). ... Released by Bengals (August 25, 1998). ... Signed by San Diego Chargers (September 1, 1998). ... Granted unconditional free agency (February 12, 1999). ... Re-signed by Chargers (April 7, 1999). ... On injured reserve with broken arm (December 20, 1999-remainder of season). ... Released by Chargers (February 10, 2000). ... Signed by Denver Broncos (March 6, 2000).
PRO STATISTICS: 1992—Recovered one fumble. 1993—Recovered three fumbles for 53 yards. 1994—Recovered one fumble. 1996—Recovered one fumble for 59 yards. 2000—Credited with one sack and recovered one fumble. 2001—Recovered one fumble.

			INTERCEPTIONS			
Year — Team	G	GS	No.	Yds.	Avg.	TD
1992—New Orleans NFL	16	4	0	0	0.0	0
1993—New Orleans NFL	16	3	0	0	0.0	0
1994—New Orleans NFL	16	16	5	24	4.8	0
1995—New Orleans NFL	16	15	4	11	2.8	0
1996—Cincinnati NFL	15	14	5	48	9.6	0
1997—Cincinnati NFL	16	9	1	-2	-2.0	0
1998—San Diego NFL	15	4	1	0	0.0	0
1999—San Diego NFL	14	7	4	1	0.3	0
2000—Denver NFL	16	5	3	102	34.0	2
2001—Denver NFL	16	1	3	25	8.3	0
Pro totals (10 years)	**156**	**78**	**26**	**209**	**8.0**	**2**

SPICER, PAUL — DE — JAGUARS

PERSONAL: Born August 18, 1975, in Indianapolis. ... 6-4/292.
HIGH SCHOOL: Northwestern (Indianapolis).
COLLEGE: College of DuPage (Ill.), then Saginaw Valley State (Mich.).
TRANSACTIONS/CAREER NOTES: Signed as non-drafted free agent by Seattle Seahawks (April 20, 1998). ... Released by Seahawks (August 24, 1998). ... Signed by Sasketchewan Roughriders of CFL (September 26, 1998). ... Signed by Detroit Lions (February 24, 1999). ... Released by Lions (September 5, 1999). ... Re-signed by Lions to practice squad (September 7, 1999). ... Activated (October 8, 1999). ... Released by Lions (November 6, 1999). ... Re-signed by Lions to practice squad (November 10, 1999). ... Released by Lions (August 22, 2000). ... Signed by Jacksonville Jaguars to practice squad (August 30, 2000). ... Activated (October 4, 2000). ... Assigned by Jaguars to Frankfurt Galaxy in 2001 NFL Europe enhancement allocation program (February 19, 2001).
PLAYING EXPERIENCE: Saskatchewan CFL, 1998; Detroit NFL, 1999; Jacksonville NFL, 2000 and 2001; Frankfurt NFLE, 2001. ... Games/Games started: 1998 (7/games started unavailable), 1999 (2/0), 2000 (3/0), NFLE 2001 (games played unavailable), NFL 2001 (16/4). Total CFL: 7/-. Total NFL: 21/4. Total Pro: 28/-.
PRO STATISTICS: 2000—Credited with one sack. NFLE: 2001—Credited with 3$^{1}/_{2}$ sacks. NFL: 2001—Returned one kickoff for eight yards, credited with two sacks and recovered one fumble for three yards.

SPIKES, CAMERON — G — RAMS

PERSONAL: Born November 6, 1976, in Madisonville, Texas. ... 6-2/323. ... Full name: Cameron Wade Spikes.
HIGH SCHOOL: Bryan (Texas).
COLLEGE: Texas A&M.
TRANSACTIONS/CAREER NOTES: Selected by St. Louis Rams in fifth round (145th pick overall) of 1999 NFL draft. ... Signed by Rams (July 19, 1999). ... Granted free agency (March 1, 2002).
PLAYING EXPERIENCE: St. Louis NFL, 1999-2001. ... Games/Games started: 1999 (5/0), 2000 (9/0), 2001 (5/0). Total: 19/0.
CHAMPIONSHIP GAME EXPERIENCE: Member of Rams for NFC championship game (1999 and 2001 seasons); inactive. ... Member of Super Bowl championship team (1999 season); inactive. ... Played in Super Bowl XXXVI (2001 season).

SPIKES, TAKEO — LB — BENGALS

PERSONAL: Born December 17, 1976, in Sandersville, Ga. ... 6-2/245. ... Full name: Takeo Gerard Spikes. ... Name pronounced tuh-KEE-oh.
HIGH SCHOOL: Washington County (Sandersville, Ga.).
COLLEGE: Auburn.
TRANSACTIONS/CAREER NOTES: Selected after junior season by Cincinnati Bengals in first round (13th pick overall) of 1998 NFL draft. ... Signed by Bengals (July 25, 1998).
HONORS: Named inside linebacker on THE SPORTING NEWS college All-America first team (1997).
PRO STATISTICS: 1999—Intercepted two passes for seven yards and recovered four fumbles. 2000—Intercepted two passes for 12 yards and recovered three fumbles. 2001—Intercepted one pass for 66 yards and one touchdown.

Year — Team	G	GS	SACKS
1998—Cincinnati NFL	16	16	2.0
1999—Cincinnati NFL	16	16	3.0
2000—Cincinnati NFL	16	16	2.0
2001—Cincinnati NFL	15	15	6.0
Pro totals (4 years)	63	63	13.0

SPIRES, GREG — DE — BUCCANEERS

PERSONAL: Born August 12, 1974, in Mariana, Fla. ... 6-1/265. ... Full name: Greg Tyrone Spires.
HIGH SCHOOL: Mariner (Cape Coral, Fla.).
COLLEGE: Florida State.
TRANSACTIONS/CAREER NOTES: Selected by New England Patriots in third round (83rd pick overall) of 1998 NFL draft. ... Signed by Patriots (July 16, 1998). ... On injured reserve with knee injury (December 15, 1999-remainder of season). ... Granted free agency (March 2, 2001). ... Re-signed by Patriots (April 30, 2001). ... Claimed on waivers by Cleveland Browns (September 4, 2001). ... Granted unconditional free agency (March 1, 2002). ... Signed by Tampa Bay Buccaneers (March 22, 2002).
PRO STATISTICS: 2000—Recovered one fumble. 2001—Returned one kickoff for 13 yards and recovered one fumble.

Year — Team	G	GS	SACKS
1998—New England NFL	15	1	3.0
1999—New England NFL	11	0	0.5
2000—New England NFL	16	2	6.0
2001—Cleveland NFL	16	4	4.0
Pro totals (4 years)	58	7	13.5

SPOON, BRANDON — LB — BILLS

PERSONAL: Born July 5, 1978, in Burlington, N.C. ... 6-2/242. ... Full name: Thomas Brandon Spoon.
HIGH SCHOOL: Williams (Burlington, N.C.).
COLLEGE: North Carolina.
TRANSACTIONS/CAREER NOTES: Selected by Buffalo Bills in fourth round (110th pick overall) of 2001 NFL draft. ... Signed by Bills (June 12, 2001).

			INTERCEPTIONS			
Year — Team	G	GS	No.	Yds.	Avg.	TD
2001—Buffalo NFL	14	14	2	51	25.5	†2

SPRIGGS, MARCUS — OT — DOLPHINS

PERSONAL: Born May 17, 1974, in Hattiesburg, Miss. ... 6-3/315. ... Full name: Thomas Marcus Spriggs.
HIGH SCHOOL: Byram (Jackson, Miss.).
JUNIOR COLLEGE: Hinds Community College (Miss.).
COLLEGE: Houston.
TRANSACTIONS/CAREER NOTES: Selected by Buffalo Bills in sixth round (185th pick overall) of 1997 NFL draft. ... Signed by Bills (June 13, 1997). ... Granted free agency (February 11, 2000). ... Re-signed by Bills (April 10, 2000). ... Granted unconditional free agency (March 2, 2001). ... Signed by Miami Dolphins (April 19, 2001). ... On injured reserve with knee injury (September 11, 2001-remainder of season)
PLAYING EXPERIENCE: Buffalo NFL, 1997-2000; Miami NFL, 2001. ... Games/Games started: 1997 (2/0), 1998 (1/0), 1999 (11/2), 2000 (16/11), 2001 (1/1). Total: 31/14.

SPRIGGS, MARCUS — DT — BROWNS

PERSONAL: Born July 26, 1976, in Washington, D.C. ... 6-4/314.
HIGH SCHOOL: Woodson (Washington, D.C.).
COLLEGE: Ohio State, then Troy (Ala.) State.
TRANSACTIONS/CAREER NOTES: Selected by Cleveland Browns in sixth round (174th pick overall) of 1999 NFL draft. ... Signed by Browns (July 22, 1999). ... On injured reserve with shoulder injury (November 23, 1999-remainder of season). ... On injured reserve with forearm injury (October 9, 2001-remainder of season). ... Granted free agency (March 1, 2002). ... Re-signed by Browns (May 1, 2002).
PLAYING EXPERIENCE: Cleveland NFL, 1999 and 2000. ... Games/Games started: 1999 (10/0), 2000 (8/0). Total: 18/0.
PRO STATISTICS: 2000—Credited with two sacks and recovered one fumble.

SPRINGS, SHAWN — CB — SEAHAWKS

PERSONAL: Born March 11, 1975, in Williamsburg, W.Va. ... 6-0/196. ... Son of Ron Springs, running back with Dallas Cowboys (1979-84) and Tampa Bay Buccaneers (1985 and 1986).
HIGH SCHOOL: Springbrook (Silver Spring, Md.).
COLLEGE: Ohio State.
TRANSACTIONS/CAREER NOTES: Selected by Seattle Seahawks in first round (third pick overall) of 1997 NFL draft. ... Signed by Seahawks (August 4, 1997). ... On suspended list for violating league substance abuse policy (November 27-January 4, 2001).
HONORS: Named cornerback on THE SPORTING NEWS college All-America second team (1996). ... Played in Pro Bowl (1998 season).
PRO STATISTICS: 1998—Recovered two fumbles for 14 yards and one touchdown. 1999—Returned one kickoff for 15 yards, returned blocked field goal 61 yards for a touchdown and recovered one fumble. 2001—Recovered one fumble.

				INTERCEPTIONS				TOTALS		
Year Team	G	GS	No.	Yds.	Avg.	TD	TD	2pt.	Pts.	Fum.
1997—Seattle NFL	10	10	1	0	0.0	0	0	0	0	0
1998—Seattle NFL	16	16	7	142	20.3	▲2	3	0	18	0
1999—Seattle NFL	16	16	5	77	15.4	0	1	0	6	0
2000—Seattle NFL	16	16	2	8	4.0	0	0	0	0	0
2001—Seattle NFL	8	7	1	0	0.0	0	0	0	0	0
Pro totals (5 years)	66	65	16	227	14.2	2	4	0	24	0

ST. LOUIS, BRAD — TE — BENGALS

PERSONAL: Born August 19, 1976, in Waverly, Mo. ... 6-3/247. ... Full name: Brad Allen St. Louis.
HIGH SCHOOL: Belton (Mo.).
COLLEGE: Southwest Missouri State.
TRANSACTIONS/CAREER NOTES: Selected by Cincinnati Bengals in seventh round (210th pick overall) of 2000 NFL draft. ... Signed by Bengals (July 20, 2000). ... On injured reserve with leg injury (December 5, 2001-remainder of season).
PLAYING EXPERIENCE: Cincinnati NFL, 2000 and 2001. ... Games/Games started: 2000 (16/0), 2001 (11/0). Total: 27/0.

STACHELSKI, DAVE — TE

PERSONAL: Born March 1, 1977, in Chicago. ... 6-3/245.
HIGH SCHOOL: Marysville-Pilchuck (Marysville, Wash.).
COLLEGE: Boise State.
TRANSACTIONS/CAREER NOTES: Selected by New England Patriots in fifth round (141st pick overall) of 2000 NFL draft. ... Signed by Patriots (July 14, 2000). ... Released by Patriots (August 14, 2000). ... Signed by New Orleans Saints (August 15, 2000). ... Released by Saints (August 27, 2000). ... Re-signed by Saints to practice squad (August 29, 2000). ... Activated (September 14, 2000). ... Released by Saints (October 23, 2001).
PLAYING EXPERIENCE: New Orleans NFL, 2000 and 2001. ... Games/Games started: 2000 (4/0), 2001 (5/0). Total: 9/0.
PRO STATISTICS: 2000—Recovered one fumble. 2001—Caught one pass for five yards.
SINGLE GAME HIGHS (regular season): Receptions—1 (September 9, 2001, vs. Buffalo); yards—5 (September 9, 2001, vs. Buffalo); and touchdown receptions—0.

STAI, BRENDEN — G — LIONS

PERSONAL: Born March 30, 1972, in Phoenix. ... 6-4/312. ... Full name: Brenden Michael Stai. ... Name pronounced STY.
HIGH SCHOOL: Anaheim High.
COLLEGE: Nebraska.
TRANSACTIONS/CAREER NOTES: Selected by Pittsburgh Steelers in third round (91st pick overall) of 1995 NFL draft. ... Signed by Steelers (July 18, 1995). ... Granted free agency (February 13, 1998). ... Re-signed by Steelers (June 9, 1998). ... Released by Steelers (March 14, 2000). ... Signed by Kansas City Chiefs (May 4, 2000). ... Traded by Chiefs to Jacksonville Jaguars for fourth-round pick (RB George Layne) in 2001 draft (August 16, 2000). ... Released by Jaguars (March 1, 2001). ... Signed by Detroit Lions (March 12, 2001).
PLAYING EXPERIENCE: Pittsburgh NFL, 1995-1999; Jacksonville NFL, 2000; Detroit NFL, 2001. ... Games/Games started: 1995 (16/9), 1996 (9/9), 1997 (11/9), 1998 (16/16), 1999 (16/16), 2000 (16/16), 2001 (16/16). Total: 100/91.
CHAMPIONSHIP GAME EXPERIENCE: Played in AFC championship game (1995 and 1997 seasons). ... Played in Super Bowl XXX (1995 season).
HONORS: Named offensive lineman on THE SPORTING NEWS college All-America second team (1994).

STALEY, DUCE — RB — EAGLES

PERSONAL: Born February 27, 1975, in Columbia, S.C. ... 5-11/220. ... Name pronounced DEUCE.
HIGH SCHOOL: Airport (Columbia, S.C.).
JUNIOR COLLEGE: Itawamba Community College (Miss.).
COLLEGE: South Carolina.
TRANSACTIONS/CAREER NOTES: Selected by Philadelphia Eagles in third round (71st pick overall) of 1997 NFL draft. ... Signed by Eagles (June 12, 1997). ... On injured reserve with foot injury (October 10, 2000-remainder of season).
CHAMPIONSHIP GAME EXPERIENCE: Played in NFC championship game (2001 season).
PRO STATISTICS: 1997—Recovered one fumble. 1998—Recovered two fumbles. 1999—Recovered two fumbles. 2000—Recovered one fumble. 2001—Recovered one fumble for minus five yards.
SINGLE GAME HIGHS (regular season): Attempts—30 (December 13, 1998, vs. Arizona); yards—201 (September 3, 2000, vs. Dallas); and rushing touchdowns—2 (September 27, 1998, vs. Kansas City).
STATISTICAL PLATEAUS: 100-yard rushing games: 1998 (1), 1999 (5), 2000 (1), 2001 (2). Total: 9. ... 100-yard receiving games: 2001 (1).

Year Team	G	GS	RUSHING Att.	Yds.	Avg.	TD	RECEIVING No.	Yds.	Avg.	TD	KICKOFF RETURNS No.	Yds.	Avg.	TD	TOTALS TD	2pt.	Pts.	Fum.
1997—Philadelphia NFL	16	0	7	29	4.1	0	2	22	11.0	0	47	1139	24.2	0	0	0	0	0
1998—Philadelphia NFL	16	13	258	1065	4.1	5	57	432	7.6	1	1	19	19.0	0	6	0	36	2
1999—Philadelphia NFL	16	16	325	1273	3.9	4	41	294	7.2	2	0	0	0.0	0	6	0	36	5
2000—Philadelphia NFL	5	5	79	344	4.4	1	25	201	8.0	0	0	0	0.0	0	1	0	6	3
2001—Philadelphia NFL	13	10	166	604	3.6	2	63	626	9.9	2	0	0	0.0	0	4	0	24	3
Pro totals (5 years)	66	44	835	3315	4.0	12	188	1575	8.4	5	48	1158	24.1	0	17	0	102	13

STANLEY, CHAD — P — TEXANS

PERSONAL: Born January 29, 1976, in Ore City, Texas. ... 6-3/205. ... Full name: Benjamin Chadwick Stanley.
HIGH SCHOOL: Ore City (Texas).
COLLEGE: Stephen F. Austin State.
TRANSACTIONS/CAREER NOTES: Signed as non-drafted free agent by San Francisco 49ers (April 23, 1999). ... Released by 49ers (September 1, 2001). ... Signed by Arizona Cardinals (November 6, 2001). ... Released by Cardinals (December 5, 2001). ... Signed by Houston Texans (February 6, 2002).
PRO STATISTICS: 1999—Rushed once for no yards and recovered one fumble.

Year Team	G	No.	Yds.	PUNTING Avg.	Net avg.	In. 20	Blk.
1999—San Francisco NFL	16	69	2737	39.7	30.7	20	†2
2000—San Francisco NFL	16	69	2727	39.5	32.2	15	1
2001—Arizona NFL	4	19	751	39.5	34.2	4	0
Pro totals (3 years)	36	157	6215	39.6	31.8	39	3

STARKEY, JASON — C — CARDINALS

PERSONAL: Born July 17, 1977, in Barboursville, W.Va. ... 6-4/282.
HIGH SCHOOL: Cabell-Midland (W.Va.).
COLLEGE: Marshall.
TRANSACTIONS/CAREER NOTES: Signed as non-drafted free agent by Arizona Cardinals (June 1, 2000). ... Released by Cardinals (August 27, 2000). ... Re-signed by Cardinals to practice squad (August 28, 2000). ... Activated (September 8, 2000). ... Released by Cardinals (September 11, 2000). ... Re-signed by Cardinals to practice squad (September 13, 2000).
PLAYING EXPERIENCE: Arizona NFL, 2000 and 2001. ... Games/Games started: 2000 (2/0), 2001 (12/1). Total: 14/1.

STARKS, DUANE — CB — CARDINALS

PERSONAL: Born May 23, 1974, in Miami. ... 5-10/170. ... Full name: Duane Lonell Starks.
HIGH SCHOOL: Miami Beach Senior.
JUNIOR COLLEGE: Holmes Junior College (Miss.).
COLLEGE: Miami (Fla.).
TRANSACTIONS/CAREER NOTES: Selected by Baltimore Ravens in first round (10th pick overall) of 1998 NFL draft. ... Signed by Ravens (August 5, 1998). ... Granted unconditional free agency (March 1, 2002). ... Signed by Arizona Cardinals (March 18, 2002).
CHAMPIONSHIP GAME EXPERIENCE: Played in AFC championship game (2000 season). ... Member of Super Bowl championship team (2000 season).
POST SEASON RECORDS: Shares Super Bowl single-game record for most interceptions returned for touchdown—1 (January 28, 2001 vs. New York Giants).
PRO STATISTICS: 2000—Returned nine punts for 135 yards, fumbled once and recovered two fumbles.
MISCELLANEOUS: Shares Baltimore Ravens all-time record for most interceptions (20).

Year Team	G	GS	INTERCEPTIONS No.	Yds.	Avg.	TD
1998—Baltimore NFL	16	8	5	3	0.6	0
1999—Baltimore NFL	16	6	5	59	11.8	1
2000—Baltimore NFL	15	15	6	125	20.8	0
2001—Baltimore NFL	15	15	4	9	2.3	0
Pro totals (4 years)	62	44	20	196	9.8	1

STECKER, AARON — RB — BUCCANEERS

PERSONAL: Born November 13, 1975, in Green Bay. ... 5-10/205.
HIGH SCHOOL: Ashwaubenon (Green Bay).
COLLEGE: Western Illinois.
TRANSACTIONS/CAREER NOTES: Signed as non-drafted free agent by Chicago Bears (April 18, 1999). ... Released by Bears (August 30, 1999). ... Signed by Tampa Bay Buccaneers to practice squad (October 20, 1999).
PRO STATISTICS: 2000—Fumbled once. 2001—Recovered one fumble.
SINGLE GAME HIGHS (regular season): Attempts—12 (January 6, 2002, vs. Philadelphia); yards—35 (January 6, 2002, vs. Philadelphia); and rushing touchdowns—1 (January 6, 2002, vs. Philadelphia).

Year Team	G	GS	RUSHING Att.	Yds.	Avg.	TD	RECEIVING No.	Yds.	Avg.	TD	KICKOFF RETURNS No.	Yds.	Avg.	TD	TOTALS TD	2pt.	Pts.	Fum.
2000—Tampa Bay NFL	10	0	12	31	2.6	0	1	15	15.0	0	29	663	22.9	0	0	0	0	1
2001—Tampa Bay NFL	13	0	24	72	3.0	1	10	101	10.1	1	9	259	28.8	0	2	0	12	0
Pro totals (2 years)	23	0	36	103	2.9	1	11	116	10.5	1	38	922	24.3	0	2	0	12	1

STEELE, GLEN — DE — BENGALS

PERSONAL: Born October 4, 1974, in Ligonier, Ind. ... 6-4/300. ... Full name: James Lendale Steele Jr.
HIGH SCHOOL: West Noble (Ligonier, Ind.).
COLLEGE: Michigan.
TRANSACTIONS/CAREER NOTES: Selected by Cincinnati Bengals in fourth round (105th pick overall) of 1998 NFL draft. ... Signed by Bengals (July 14, 1998). ... On injured reserve with ankle injury (December 15, 1998-remainder of season).
PLAYING EXPERIENCE: Cincinnati NFL, 1998-2001. ... Games/Games started: 1998 (10/0), 1999 (16/1), 2000 (16/1), 2001 (16/1). Total: 58/1.
PRO STATISTICS: 2000—Credited with two sacks. 2001—Credited with one sack and recovered one fumble.

STEELE, MARKUS — LB — COWBOYS

PERSONAL: Born July 24, 1979, in Cleveland. ... 6-3/240.
HIGH SCHOOL: Chanel (New Bedford, Ohio).
JUNIOR COLLEGE: Long Beach City College.
COLLEGE: Southern California.
TRANSACTIONS/CAREER NOTES: Selected by Dallas Cowboys in fourth round (122nd pick overall) of 2001 NFL draft. ... Signed by Cowboys (July 20, 2001).
PLAYING EXPERIENCE: Dallas NFL, 2001. ... Games/Games started: 2001 (15/10).

STEPHENS, JAMAIN — OT — BENGALS

PERSONAL: Born January 9, 1974, in Lumberton, N.C. ... 6-6/340.
HIGH SCHOOL: Lumberton (N.C.).
COLLEGE: North Carolina A&T.
TRANSACTIONS/CAREER NOTES: Selected by Pittsburgh Steelers in first round (29th pick overall) of 1996 NFL draft. ... Signed by Steelers (July 17, 1996). ... Inactive for all 16 games (1996). ... Claimed on waivers by Cincinnati Bengals (August 3, 1999). ... On reserve/suspended list (September 5-October 11, 1999).
PLAYING EXPERIENCE: Pittsburgh NFL, 1997 and 1998; Cincinnati NFL, 1999-2001. ... Games/Games started: 1997 (7/1), 1998 (11/10), 1999 (7/2), 2000 (5/0), 2001 (9/2). Total: 39/15.
CHAMPIONSHIP GAME EXPERIENCE: Member of Steelers for AFC championship game (1997 season); inactive.

STEPNOSKI, MARK — C

PERSONAL: Born January 20, 1967, in Erie, Pa. ... 6-2/265. ... Full name: Mark Matthew Stepnoski.
HIGH SCHOOL: Cathedral Prep (Erie, Pa.).
COLLEGE: Pittsburgh (degree in communications).
TRANSACTIONS/CAREER NOTES: Selected by Dallas Cowboys in third round (57th pick overall) of 1989 NFL draft. ... Signed by Cowboys (July 23, 1989). ... Granted free agency (February 1, 1992). ... Re-signed by Cowboys (September 5, 1992). ... Granted roster exemption (September 5-14, 1992). ... On injured reserve with knee injury (December 22, 1993-remainder of season). ... Granted unconditional free agency (February 17, 1994). ... Re-signed by Cowboys (June 29, 1994). ... Granted unconditional free agency (February 17, 1995). ... Signed by Houston Oilers (March 11, 1995). ... Oilers franchise moved to Tennessee for 1997 season. ... Granted unconditional free agency (February 12, 1999). ... Signed by Cowboys (April 13, 1999). ... On injured reserve with knee injury (December 12, 2000-remainder of season). ... Released by Cowboys (February 28, 2002).
PLAYING EXPERIENCE: Dallas NFL, 1989-1994 and 1999-2001; Houston NFL, 1995 and 1996; Tennessee NFL, 1997 and 1998. ... Games/Games started: 1989 (16/4), 1990 (16/16), 1991 (16/16), 1992 (14/14), 1993 (13/13), 1994 (16/16), 1995 (16/16), 1996 (16/16), 1997 (16/16), 1998 (13/13), 1999 (15/15), 2000 (11/11), 2001 (16/16). Total: 194/182.
CHAMPIONSHIP GAME EXPERIENCE: Played in NFC championship game (1992 and 1994 seasons). ... Member of Super Bowl championship team (1992 season).
HONORS: Named guard on THE SPORTING NEWS college All-America first team (1988). ... Played in Pro Bowl (1992 and 1994-1996 seasons).
PRO STATISTICS: 1989—Recovered three fumbles. 1990—Returned one kickoff for 15 yards. 1992—Recovered one fumble. 1993—Fumbled once. 1994—Fumbled four times for minus three yards. 1997—Fumbled twice and recovered one fumble for minus seven yards. 1998—Rushed once for no yards, fumbled twice and recovered one fumble for minus six yards. 1999—Fumbled once and recovered one fumble for minus 26 yards. 2000—Fumbled once. 2001—Fumbled once.

STEUSSIE, TODD — OT — PANTHERS

PERSONAL: Born December 1, 1970, in Canoga Park, Calif. ... 6-6/308. ... Full name: Todd Edward Steussie. ... Name pronounced STEW-see.
HIGH SCHOOL: Agoura (Calif.).
COLLEGE: California.
TRANSACTIONS/CAREER NOTES: Selected by Minnesota Vikings in first round (19th pick overall) of 1994 NFL draft. ... Signed by Vikings (July 13, 1994). ... Released by Vikings (March 14, 2001). ... Signed by Carolina Panthers (March 29, 2001).
PLAYING EXPERIENCE: Minnesota NFL, 1994-2000; Carolina NFL, 2001. ... Games/Games started: 1994 (16/16), 1995 (16/16), 1996 (16/16), 1997 (16/16), 1998 (15/15), 1999 (16/16), 2000 (16/16), 2001 (16/16). Total: 127/127.
CHAMPIONSHIP GAME EXPERIENCE: Played in NFC championship game (1998 and 2000 seasons).
HONORS: Named offensive lineman on THE SPORTING NEWS college All-America second team (1993). ... Played in Pro Bowl (1997 and 1998 seasons).
PRO STATISTICS: 1994—Recovered one fumble. 1996—Recovered one fumble. 1999—Recovered one fumble.

STEVENS, MATT   S   TEXANS

PERSONAL: Born June 15, 1973, in Chapel Hill, N.C. ... 6-0/205. ... Full name: Matthew Brian Stevens.
HIGH SCHOOL: Chapel Hill (N.C.).
COLLEGE: Appalachian State.
TRANSACTIONS/CAREER NOTES: Selected by Buffalo Bills in third round (87th pick overall) of 1996 NFL draft. ... Signed by Bills (July 15, 1996). ... Claimed on waivers by Philadelphia Eagles (August 25, 1997). ... On suspended list for anabolic steroid use (August 27-September 29, 1997). ... Claimed on waivers by Washington Redskins (December 8, 1998). ... Granted free agency (February 12, 1999). ... Re-signed by Redskins (April 23, 1999). ... Granted unconditional free agency (February 11, 2000). ... Re-signed by Redskins (May 12, 2000). ... Claimed on waivers by New England Patriots (December 20, 2000). ... Granted unconditional free agency (March 2, 2001). ... Re-signed by Patriots (March 16, 2001). ... Selected by Houston Texans from Patriots in NFL expansion draft (February 18, 2002).
CHAMPIONSHIP GAME EXPERIENCE: Played in AFC championship game (2001 season). ... Member of Super Bowl championship team (2001 season).
PRO STATISTICS: 1996—Recovered one fumble. 1997—Recovered one fumble. 1999—Credited with one sack and recovered one fumble. 2000—Recovered one fumble for one yard. 2001—Recovered one fumble.

				INTERCEPTIONS		
Year Team	G	GS	No.	Yds.	Avg.	TD
1996—Buffalo NFL	13	11	2	0	0.0	0
1997—Philadelphia NFL	11	0	1	0	0.0	0
1998—Philadelphia NFL	7	1	0	0	0.0	0
—Washington NFL	3	0	0	0	0.0	0
1999—Washington NFL	15	1	6	61	10.2	0
2000—Washington NFL	15	4	1	0	0.0	0
—New England NFL	1	0	0	0	0.0	0
2001—New England NFL	15	4	1	9	9.0	0
Pro totals (6 years)	80	21	11	70	6.4	0

STEWART, JAMES   RB   LIONS

PERSONAL: Born December 27, 1971, in Morristown, Tenn. ... 6-1/226. ... Full name: James Ottis Stewart III.
HIGH SCHOOL: Morristown-Hamblen West (Morristown, Tenn.).
COLLEGE: Tennessee.
TRANSACTIONS/CAREER NOTES: Selected by Jacksonville Jaguars in first round (19th pick overall) of 1995 NFL draft. ... Signed by Jaguars (June 1, 1995). ... On injured reserve with knee injury (September 22, 1998-remainder of season). ... Granted unconditional free agency (February 11, 2000). ... Signed by Detroit Lions (February 14, 2000).
CHAMPIONSHIP GAME EXPERIENCE: Played in AFC championship game (1996 and 1999 seasons).
PRO STATISTICS: 1996—Recovered one fumble. 1999—Recovered one fumble. 2000—Recovered one fumble.
SINGLE GAME HIGHS (regular season): Attempts—37 (December 17, 2000, vs. New York Jets); yards—164 (December 17, 2000, vs. New York Jets); and rushing touchdowns—5 (October 12, 1997, vs. Philadelphia).
STATISTICAL PLATEAUS: 100-yard rushing games: 1996 (1), 1997 (1), 1998 (2), 1999 (2), 2000 (3), 2001 (2). Total: 11.
MISCELLANEOUS: Holds Jacksonville Jaguars all-time record for most rushing touchdowns (33).

			RUSHING				RECEIVING				TOTALS		
Year Team	G	GS	Att.	Yds.	Avg.	TD	No.	Yds.	Avg.	TD	TD	2pt.	Pts.	Fum.
1995—Jacksonville NFL	14	7	137	525	3.8	2	21	190	9.0	1	3	0	18	1
1996—Jacksonville NFL	13	11	190	723	3.8	8	30	177	5.9	2	10	0	60	2
1997—Jacksonville NFL	16	5	136	555	4.1	8	41	336	8.2	1	9	0	54	0
1998—Jacksonville NFL	3	3	53	217	4.1	2	6	42	7.0	1	3	0	18	2
1999—Jacksonville NFL	14	7	249	931	3.7	▲13	21	108	5.1	0	13	0	78	4
2000—Detroit NFL	16	16	‡339	1184	3.5	10	32	287	9.0	1	11	3	72	4
2001—Detroit NFL	11	10	143	685	4.8	1	23	242	10.5	1	2	0	12	0
Pro totals (7 years)	87	59	1247	4820	3.9	44	174	1382	7.9	7	51	3	312	13

STEWART, KORDELL   QB   STEELERS

PERSONAL: Born October 16, 1972, in New Orleans. ... 6-1/217.
HIGH SCHOOL: John Ehret (Marrero, La.).
COLLEGE: Colorado.
TRANSACTIONS/CAREER NOTES: Selected by Pittsburgh Steelers in second round (60th pick overall) of 1995 NFL draft. ... Signed by Steelers (July 17, 1995).
CHAMPIONSHIP GAME EXPERIENCE: Played in AFC championship game (1995, 1997 and 2001 seasons). ... Played in Super Bowl XXX (1995 season).
PRO STATISTICS: 1995—Compiled a quarterback rating of 136.9. 1996—Compiled a quarterback rating of 18.8 and fumbled once. 1997—Compiled a quarterback rating of 75.2, fumbled six times and recovered one fumble for minus one yard. 1998—Compiled a quarterback rating of 62.9, punted once for 35 yards, fumbled three times and recovered two fumbles. 1999—Compiled a quarterback rating of 64.9, fumbled four times and recovered one fumble. 2000—Compiled a quarterback rating of 73.6, fumbled eight times and recovered three fumbles for minus one yard. 2001—Compiled a quarterback rating of 81.7, fumbled 11 times and recovered five fumbles for minus 10 yards.
SINGLE GAME HIGHS (regular season): Attempts—48 (December 13, 1997, vs. New England); completions—26 (December 13, 1997, vs. New England); yards—333 (December 16, 2001, vs. Baltimore); and touchdown passes—3 (December 30, 2001, vs. Cincinnati).
STATISTICAL PLATEAUS: 300-yard passing games: 1997 (2), 2001 (1). Total: 3. ... 100-yard rushing games: 1996 (1), 1998 (1). Total: 2.
MISCELLANEOUS: Regular-season record as starting NFL quarterback: 43-27 (.614). ... Postseason record as starting NFL quarterback: 2-2 (.500). ... Started two games at wide receiver (1995). ... Started two games at wide receiver (1996). ... Started one game at wide receiver (1999).

Year	Team	G	GS	Att.	Cmp.	Pct.	Yds.	TD	Int.	Avg.	Att.	Yds.	Avg.	TD	No.	Yds.	Avg.	TD	TD	2pt.	Pts.
1995	Pittsburgh NFL	10	2	7	5	71.4	60	1	0	8.57	15	86	5.7	1	14	235	16.8	1	2	0	12
1996	Pittsburgh NFL	16	2	30	11	36.7	100	0	2	3.33	39	171	4.4	5	17	293	17.2	3	8	0	48
1997	Pittsburgh NFL	16	16	440	236	53.6	3020	21	§17	6.86	88	476	5.4	11	0	0	0.0	0	11	0	66
1998	Pittsburgh NFL	16	16	458	252	55.0	2560	11	18	5.59	81	406	5.0	2	1	17	17.0	0	2	0	12
1999	Pittsburgh NFL	16	12	275	160	58.2	1464	6	10	5.32	56	258	4.6	2	9	113	12.6	1	3	0	18
2000	Pittsburgh NFL	16	11	289	151	52.2	1860	11	8	6.44	78	436	5.6	7	0	0	0.0	0	7	0	42
2001	Pittsburgh NFL	16	16	442	266	60.2	3109	14	11	7.03	96	537	5.6	5	0	0	0.0	0	5	0	30
Pro totals (7 years)		106	75	1941	1081	55.7	12173	64	66	6.27	453	2370	5.2	33	41	658	16.0	5	38	0	228

STEWART, MATT — LB — FALCONS

PERSONAL: Born August 31, 1979, in Columbus, Ohio. ... 6-3/232.
HIGH SCHOOL: DeSales (Columbus, Ohio).
COLLEGE: Vanderbilt.
TRANSACTIONS/CAREER NOTES: Selected by Atlanta Falcons in fourth round (102nd pick overall) of 2001 NFL draft. ... Signed by Falcons (May 30, 2001).
PLAYING EXPERIENCE: Atlanta NFL, 2001. ... Games/Games started: 2001 (15/0).
PRO STATISTICS: 2001—Recovered one fumble.

STEWART, QUINCY — LB — 49ERS

PERSONAL: Born March 27, 1978, in Tyler, Texas. ... 6-1/220. ... Full name: Quincy Jermaine Stewart.
HIGH SCHOOL: John Tyler (Texas).
COLLEGE: Louisiana Tech.
TRANSACTIONS/CAREER NOTES: Signed as non-drafted free agent by San Francisco 49ers (April 25, 2001).
PLAYING EXPERIENCE: San Francisco NFL, 2001. ... Games/Games started: 2001 (16/0).

STEWART, TONY — TE — EAGLES

PERSONAL: Born August 9, 1979, in Lohne, Germany. ... 6-5/255. ... Full name: Tony Alexander Stewart.
HIGH SCHOOL: Allentown Central (Pa.).
COLLEGE: Penn State.
TRANSACTIONS/CAREER NOTES: Selected by Philadelphia Eagles in fifth round (147th pick overall) of 2001 NFL draft. ... Signed by Eagles (May 22, 2001).
CHAMPIONSHIP GAME EXPERIENCE: Member of Eagles for NFC championship game (2001 season); inactive.
SINGLE GAME HIGHS (regular season): Receptions—3 (January 6, 2002, vs. Tampa Bay); yards—41 (January 6, 2002, vs. Tampa Bay); and touchdown receptions—1 (November 29, 2001, vs. Kansas City).

Year Team	G	GS	No.	Yds.	Avg.	TD
2001—Philadelphia NFL	3	1	5	52	10.4	1

STILLS, GARY — LB — CHIEFS

PERSONAL: Born July 11, 1974, in Trenton, N.J. ... 6-2/235.
HIGH SCHOOL: Valley Forge (Pa.) Military Academy.
COLLEGE: West Virginia.
TRANSACTIONS/CAREER NOTES: Selected by Kansas City Chiefs in third round (75th pick overall) of 1999 NFL draft. ... Signed by Chiefs (July 26, 1999). ... Assigned by Chiefs to Frankfurt Galaxy in 2001 NFL Europe enhancement allocation program (February 19, 2001). ... Granted free agency (March 1, 2002).
PLAYING EXPERIENCE: Kansas City NFL, 1999-2001; Frankfurt NFLE, 2001. ... Games/Games started: 1999 (2/0), 2000 (11/0), NFLE 2001 (games played unavailable), NFL 2001 (10/0). Total: 23/0.
PRO STATISTICS: 2000—Recovered one fumble. NFLE: 2001—Intercepted one pass for no yards and credited with $9 1/2$ sacks. NFL: 2001—Recovered one fumble.

STINCHCOMB, MATT — OT — RAIDERS

PERSONAL: Born June 3, 1977, in Lilburn, Ga. ... 6-6/310. ... Full name: Matthew Douglass Stinchcomb.
HIGH SCHOOL: Parkview (Lilburn, Ga.).
COLLEGE: Georgia.
TRANSACTIONS/CAREER NOTES: Selected by Oakland Raiders in first round (18th pick overall) of 1999 NFL draft. ... Signed by Raiders (July 22, 1999). ... Inactive for three games (1999). ... On injured reserve with shoulder injury (October 1, 1999-remainder of season).
PLAYING EXPERIENCE: Oakland NFL, 2000 and 2001. ... Games/Games started: 2000 (13/9), 2001 (14/1). Total: 27/10.
CHAMPIONSHIP GAME EXPERIENCE: Member of Raiders for AFC Championship game (2000 season); did not play.
HONORS: Named offensive tackle on THE SPORTING NEWS college All-America second team (1997 and 1998).

STOERNER, CLINT — QB — COWBOYS

PERSONAL: Born December 29, 1977, in Baytown, Texas. ... 6-2/210.
HIGH SCHOOL: Lee (Baytown, Texas).
COLLEGE: Arkansas.
TRANSACTIONS/CAREER NOTES: Signed as non-drafted free agent by Dallas Cowboys (May 5, 2000). ... Released by Cowboys (August 27, 2000). ... Re-signed by Cowboys to practice squad (August 29, 2000). ... Activated (September 8, 2000). ... Released by Cowboys (October 10, 2000). ...

Re-signed by Cowboys to practice squad (October 11, 2000). ... Activated (November 1, 2000). ... Released by Cowboys (November 21, 2000). ... Re-signed by Cowboys to practice squad (November 27, 2000). ... Activated (December 13, 2000). ... Assigned by Cowboys to Scottish Claymores in 2001 NFL Europe enhancement allocation program (February 12, 2001).
PRO STATISTICS: NFLE: 2001—Caught one pass for 18 yards. NFL: 2001—Fumbled once for minus one yard.
SINGLE GAME HIGHS (regular season): Attempts—23 (November 4, 2001, vs. New York Giants); completions—13 (November 4, 2001, vs. New York Giants); passing yards—177 (November 4, 2001, vs. New York Giants); and touchdown passes—2 (September 30, 2001, vs. Philadelphia).
MISCELLANEOUS: Regular-season record as starting NFL quarterback: 1-1 (.500).

				PASSING						RUSHING			TOTALS		
Year Team	G	GS	Att.	Cmp.	Pct.	Yds.	TD	Int.	Avg.	Rat.	Att.	Yds.	Avg.	TD	TD	2pt.	Pts.
2000—Dallas NFL	2	0	5	3	60.0	53	1	0	10.60	135.8	0	0	0.0	0	0	0	0
2001—Scottish NFLE	...	...	307	171	55.7	1866	10	8	6.08	73.8	31	101	3.3	0	0	0	0
—Dallas NFL	4	2	49	26	53.1	314	3	5	6.41	53.8	9	27	3.0	1	1	0	6
NFL Europe totals (1 year)	...	...	307	171	55.7	1866	10	8	6.08	73.8	31	101	3.3	0	0	0	0
NFL totals (2 years)	6	2	54	29	53.7	367	4	5	6.80	61.3	9	27	3.0	1	1	0	6
Pro totals (3 years)	...	...	361	200	55.4	2233	14	13	6.19	71.9	40	128	3.2	1	1	0	6

STOKES, BARRY   OT/G   BROWNS

PERSONAL: Born December 20, 1973, in Flint, Mich. ... 6-4/310. ... Full name: Barry Wade Stokes.
HIGH SCHOOL: Davison (Mich.).
COLLEGE: Eastern Michigan.
TRANSACTIONS/CAREER NOTES: Signed as non-drafted free agent by Detroit Lions (April 26, 1996). ... Released by Lions (August 14, 1996). ... Signed by Jacksonville Jaguars to practice squad (October 23, 1996). ... Granted free agency after 1996 season. ... Signed by Atlanta Falcons (January 30, 1997). ... Released by Falcons (August 1997). ... Signed by St. Louis Rams to practice squad (August 26, 1997). ... Released by Rams (October 6, 1997). ... Signed by Miami Dolphins to practice squad (November 26, 1997). ... Assigned by Dolphins to Scottish Claymores in 1998 NFL Europe enhancement allocation program (February 18, 1998). ... Released by Dolphins (August 25, 1998). ... Re-signed by Dolphins (November 4, 1998). ... Assigned by Dolphins to Scottish Claymores in 1999 NFL Europe enhancement allocation program (February 22, 1999). ... Released by Dolphins (September 4, 1999). ... Signed by Green Bay Packers (September 8, 1999). ... Released by Packers (September 21, 1999). ... Re-signed by Packers (October 20, 1999). ... Inactive for five games (1999). ... Released by Packers (November 9, 1999). ... Signed by Oakland Raiders (January 2, 2000). ... Released by Raiders (July 21, 2000). ... Signed by Packers (July 22, 2000). ... Released by Packers (September 27, 2000). ... Re-signed by Packers (October 23, 2000). ... Granted unconditional free agency (March 1, 2002). ... Signed by Cleveland Browns (April 1, 2002).
PLAYING EXPERIENCE: Scottish NFLE, 1998; Miami NFL, 1998; Green Bay NFL, 2000 and 2001. ... Games/Games started: NFLE 1998 (10/10), NFL 1998 (3/0), 2000 (8/0), 2001 (16/3). Total NFL: 27/3. Total Pro: 37/13.

STOKES, J.J.   WR   49ERS

PERSONAL: Born October 6, 1972, in San Diego. ... 6-4/217. ... Full name: Jerel Jamal Stokes.
HIGH SCHOOL: Point Loma (San Diego).
COLLEGE: UCLA (degree in sociology, 1994).
TRANSACTIONS/CAREER NOTES: Selected by San Francisco 49ers in first round (10th pick overall) of 1995 NFL draft. ... Signed by 49ers (July 27, 1995). ... On injured reserve with wrist injury (October 26, 1996-remainder of season). ... Granted unconditional free agency (February 12, 1999). ... Re-signed by 49ers (March 8, 1999).
CHAMPIONSHIP GAME EXPERIENCE: Played in NFC championship game (1997 season).
HONORS: Named wide receiver on THE SPORTING NEWS college All-America first team (1993).
PRO STATISTICS: 1997—Recovered two fumbles. 1999—Recovered one fumble. 2000—Rushed once for six yards.
SINGLE GAME HIGHS (regular season): Receptions—9 (October 18, 1998, vs. Indianapolis); yards—130 (January 3, 2000, vs. Atlanta); and touchdown receptions—2 (December 30, 2001, vs. Dallas).
STATISTICAL PLATEAUS: 100-yard receiving games: 1995 (1), 1998 (2), 1999 (1). Total: 4.

			RECEIVING				TOTALS			
Year Team	G	GS	No.	Yds.	Avg.	TD	TD	2pt.	Pts.	Fum.
1995—San Francisco NFL	12	2	38	517	13.6	4	4	0	24	0
1996—San Francisco NFL	6	6	18	249	13.8	0	0	0	0	0
1997—San Francisco NFL	16	16	58	733	12.6	4	4	0	24	1
1998—San Francisco NFL	16	13	63	770	12.2	8	8	0	48	0
1999—San Francisco NFL	16	4	34	429	12.6	3	3	†1	20	1
2000—San Francisco NFL	16	4	30	524	17.5	3	3	1	20	0
2001—San Francisco NFL	16	16	54	585	10.8	7	7	0	42	0
Pro totals (7 years)	98	61	295	3807	12.9	29	29	2	178	2

STOKLEY, BRANDON   WR   RAVENS

PERSONAL: Born June 23, 1976, in Blacksburg, Va. ... 5-11/197.
HIGH SCHOOL: Comeaux (Lafayette, La.).
COLLEGE: Southwestern Louisiana.
TRANSACTIONS/CAREER NOTES: Selected by Baltimore Ravens in fourth round (105th pick overall) of 1999 NFL draft. ... Signed by Ravens (July 28, 1999). ... On injured reserve with shoulder injury (October 25, 1999-remainder of season). ... Granted free agency (March 1, 2002).
CHAMPIONSHIP GAME EXPERIENCE: Played in AFC championship game (2000 season). ... Member of Super Bowl championship team (2000 season).
PRO STATISTICS: 2000—Rushed once for six yards. 2001—Rushed once for one yard, fumbled once and recovered one fumble.
SINGLE GAME HIGHS (regular season): Receptions—5 (October 21, 2001, vs. Cleveland); yards—68 (October 21, 2001, vs. Cleveland); and touchdown receptions—1 (December 16, 2001, vs. Pittsburgh).

			RECEIVING			
Year Team	G	GS	No.	Yds.	Avg.	TD
1999—Baltimore NFL	2	0	1	28	28.0	1
2000—Baltimore NFL	7	1	11	184	16.7	2
2001—Baltimore NFL	16	5	24	344	14.3	2
Pro totals (3 years)	25	6	36	556	15.4	5

STONE, MICHAEL — CB — CARDINALS

PERSONAL: Born February 13, 1978, in Southfield, Mich. ... 5-11/189. ... Full name: Michael Ahmed Stone.
HIGH SCHOOL: Southfield-Lathrup (Southfield, Mich.).
COLLEGE: Memphis.
TRANSACTIONS/CAREER NOTES: Selected by Arizona Cardinals in second round (54th pick overall) of 2001 NFL draft. ... Signed by Cardinals (July 16, 2001).
PLAYING EXPERIENCE: Arizona NFL, 2001. ... Games/Games started: 2001 (7/0).

STONE, RON — G — 49ERS

PERSONAL: Born July 20, 1971, in West Roxbury, Mass. ... 6-5/320.
HIGH SCHOOL: West Roxbury (Mass.).
COLLEGE: Boston College.
TRANSACTIONS/CAREER NOTES: Selected by Dallas Cowboys in fourth round (96th pick overall) of 1993 NFL draft. ... Signed by Cowboys (July 16, 1993). ... Active for four games with Cowboys (1993); did not play. ... Granted free agency (February 16, 1996). ... Tendered offer sheet by New York Giants (March 1, 1996). ... Cowboys declined to match offer (March 7, 1996). ... Granted unconditional free agency (March 1, 2002). ... Signed by San Francisco 49ers (April 12, 2002).
PLAYING EXPERIENCE: Dallas NFL, 1994 and 1995; New York Giants NFL, 1996-2001. ... Games/Games started: 1994 (16/0), 1995 (16/1), 1996 (16/16), 1997 (16/16), 1998 (14/14), 1999 (16/16), 2000 (15/15), 2001 (15/15). Total: 124/93.
CHAMPIONSHIP GAME EXPERIENCE: Member of Cowboys for NFC championship game (1993 season); inactive. ... Member of Super Bowl championship team (1993 and 1995 seasons). ... Played in NFC championship game (1994, 1995 and 2000 seasons). ... Played in Super Bowl XXXV (2000 season).
HONORS: Played in Pro Bowl (2000 season).
PRO STATISTICS: 1994—Recovered one fumble. 1997—Recovered one fumble. 2001—Recovered one fumble for one yard.

STOUTMIRE, OMAR — S — GIANTS

PERSONAL: Born July 9, 1974, in Pensacola, Fla. ... 5-11/198.
HIGH SCHOOL: Polytechnic (Pasadena, Calif.).
COLLEGE: Fresno State.
TRANSACTIONS/CAREER NOTES: Selected by Dallas Cowboys in seventh round (224th pick overall) of 1997 NFL draft. ... Signed by Cowboys (July 14, 1997). ... Claimed on waivers by Cleveland Browns (September 6, 1999). ... Inactive for two games with Browns (1999). ... Released by Browns (September 21, 1999). ... Signed by New York Jets (October 6, 1999). ... Granted free agency (February 11, 2000). ... Re-signed by Jets (April 18, 2000). ... Released by Jets (August 27, 2000). ... Signed by New York Giants (August 30, 2000). ... Granted unconditional free agency (March 2, 2001). ... Re-signed by Giants (May 14, 2001).
CHAMPIONSHIP GAME EXPERIENCE: Played in NFC championship game (2000 season). ... Played in Super Bowl XXXV (2000 season).
PRO STATISTICS: 1997—Recovered one fumble. 1998—Recovered one fumble. 1999—Recovered one fumble. 2000—Returned six kickoffs for 140 yards. 2001—Returned eight kickoffs for 127 yards.

			INTERCEPTIONS				SACKS
Year Team	G	GS	No.	Yds.	Avg.	TD	No.
1997—Dallas NFL	16	2	2	8	4.0	0	2.0
1998—Dallas NFL	16	12	0	0	0.0	0	1.0
1999—New York Jets NFL	12	5	2	97	48.5	1	1.0
2000—New York Giants NFL	16	0	0	0	0.0	0	0.0
2001—New York Giants NFL	16	0	0	0	0.0	0	0.0
Pro totals (5 years)	76	19	4	105	26.3	1	4.0

STOVER, MATT — K — RAVENS

PERSONAL: Born January 27, 1968, in Dallas. ... 5-11/178. ... Full name: John Matthew Stover.
HIGH SCHOOL: Lake Highlands (Dallas).
COLLEGE: Louisiana Tech (degree in marketing, 1991).
TRANSACTIONS/CAREER NOTES: Selected by New York Giants in 12th round (329th pick overall) of 1990 NFL draft. ... Signed by Giants (July 23, 1990). ... On injured reserve with leg injury (September 4, 1990-entire season). ... Granted unconditional free agency (February 1, 1991). ... Signed by Cleveland Browns (March 15, 1991). ... Granted free agency (March 1, 1993). ... Re-signed by Browns (July 24, 1993). ... Released by Browns (August 30, 1993). ... Re-signed by Browns (August 31, 1993). ... Granted unconditional free agency (February 17, 1994). ... Re-signed by Browns (March 4, 1994). ... Browns franchise moved to Baltimore and renamed Ravens for 1996 season (March 11, 1996).
CHAMPIONSHIP GAME EXPERIENCE: Played in AFC championship game (2000 season). ... Member of Super Bowl championship team (2000 season).
HONORS: Named kicker on The Sporting News NFL All-Pro team (2000). ... Played in Pro Bowl (2000 season).
PRO STATISTICS: 1992—Had only pass attempt intercepted.

				KICKING				
Year Team	G	XPM	XPA	FGM	FGA	Lg.	50+	Pts.
1990—New York Giants NFL				Did not play.				
1991—Cleveland NFL	16	33	34	16	22	§55	2-2	81
1992—Cleveland NFL	16	29	30	21	29	51	1-3	92
1993—Cleveland NFL	16	36	36	16	22	53	1-4	84
1994—Cleveland NFL	16	32	32	26	28	45	0-1	110
1995—Cleveland NFL	16	26	26	29	33	47	0-1	113
1996—Baltimore NFL	16	34	35	19	25	50	1-1	91
1997—Baltimore NFL	16	32	32	26	34	49	0-2	110
1998—Baltimore NFL	16	24	24	21	28	48	0-0	87
1999—Baltimore NFL	16	32	32	28	33	50	2-5	116
2000—Baltimore NFL	16	30	30	*35	*39	51	2-3	135
2001—Baltimore NFL	16	25	25	30	35	49	0-0	115
Pro totals (11 years)	176	333	336	267	328	55	9-22	1134

STRAHAN, MICHAEL — DE — GIANTS

PERSONAL: Born November 21, 1971, in Houston. ... 6-5/275. ... Full name: Michael Anthony Strahan. ... Nephew of Art Strahan, defensive tackle with Atlanta Falcons (1968). ... Name pronounced STRAY-han.
HIGH SCHOOL: Westbury (Houston), then Mannheim (West Germany) American.
COLLEGE: Texas Southern.
TRANSACTIONS/CAREER NOTES: Selected by New York Giants in second round (40th pick overall) of 1993 NFL draft. ... Signed by Giants (July 25, 1993). ... On injured reserve with foot injury (January 13, 1994-remainder of playoffs). ... Granted free agency (February 16, 1996). ... Re-signed by Giants (July 8, 1996).
CHAMPIONSHIP GAME EXPERIENCE: Played in NFC championship game (2000 season). ... Played in Super Bowl XXXV (2000 season).
HONORS: Named defensive end on THE SPORTING NEWS NFL All-Pro team (1997 and 2001). ... Played in Pro Bowl (1997-1999 seasons).
RECORDS: Holds NFL single-season record for most sacks—22$^{1}/_{2}$ (2001).
PRO STATISTICS: 1995—Intercepted two passes for 56 yards and credited with one safety. 1997—Recovered one fumble. 1998—Intercepted one pass for 24 yards and a touchdown. 1999—Intercepted one pass for 44 yards and a touchdown and recovered two fumbles. 2000—Recovered four fumbles. 2001—Recovered one fumble for 13 yards and a touchdown.

Year — Team	G	GS	SACKS
1993—New York Giants NFL	9	0	1.0
1994—New York Giants NFL	15	15	4.5
1995—New York Giants NFL	15	15	7.5
1996—New York Giants NFL	16	16	5.0
1997—New York Giants NFL	16	16	14.0
1998—New York Giants NFL	16	15	15.0
1999—New York Giants NFL	16	16	5.5
2000—New York Giants NFL	16	16	9.5
2001—New York Giants NFL	16	16	*22.5
Pro totals (9 years)	135	125	84.5

STREETS, TAI — WR — 49ERS

PERSONAL: Born April 20, 1977, in Matteson, Ill. ... 6-2/206.
HIGH SCHOOL: Thornton Township (Harvey, Ill.).
COLLEGE: Michigan.
TRANSACTIONS/CAREER NOTES: Selected by San Francisco 49ers in sixth round (171st pick overall) of 1999 NFL draft. ... Signed by 49ers (July 30, 1999). ... On non-football injury list with Achilles' tendon injury (July 30-November 30, 1999).
PRO STATISTICS: 2000—Rushed once for no yards, returned eight kickoffs for 180 yards and fumbled once.
SINGLE GAME HIGHS (regular season): Receptions—4 (November 18, 2001, vs. Carolina); yards—81 (September 9, 2001, vs. Atlanta); and touchdown receptions—1 (December 2, 2001, vs. Buffalo).

			RECEIVING			
Year — Team	G	GS	No.	Yds.	Avg.	TD
1999—San Francisco NFL	2	0	2	25	12.5	0
2000—San Francisco NFL	15	1	19	287	15.1	0
2001—San Francisco NFL	16	3	28	345	12.3	1
Pro totals (3 years)	33	4	49	657	13.4	1

STRONG, MACK — FB — SEAHAWKS

PERSONAL: Born September 11, 1971, in Fort Benning, Ga. ... 6-0/238.
HIGH SCHOOL: Brookstone (Columbus, Ga.).
COLLEGE: Georgia.
TRANSACTIONS/CAREER NOTES: Signed as non-drafted free agent by Seattle Seahawks (April 28, 1993). ... Released by Seahawks (September 4, 1993). ... Re-signed by Seahawks to practice squad (September 6, 1993). ... Released by Seahawks (February 10, 2000). ... Re-signed by Seahawks (February 14, 2000). ... Granted unconditional free agency (March 1, 2002). ... Re-signed by Seahawks (May 1, 2002).
PRO STATISTICS: 1995—Returned four kickoffs for 65 yards and recovered one fumble. 1996—Recovered one fumble. 1997—Returned one kickoff for 16 yards and recovered one fumble. 1998—Recovered one fumble. 2000—Returned one kickoff for 26 yards. 2001—Returned one kickoff for 16 yards.
SINGLE GAME HIGHS (regular season): Attempts—10 (December 11, 1994, vs. Houston); yards—44 (December 11, 1994, vs. Houston); rushing touchdowns—1 (November 12, 1995, vs. Jacksonville).

			RUSHING				RECEIVING				TOTALS			
Year — Team	G	GS	Att.	Yds.	Avg.	TD	No.	Yds.	Avg.	TD	TD	2pt.	Pts.	Fum.
1993—Seattle NFL							Did not play.							
1994—Seattle NFL	8	1	27	114	4.2	2	3	3	1.0	0	2	0	12	1
1995—Seattle NFL	16	1	8	23	2.9	1	12	117	9.8	3	4	0	24	2
1996—Seattle NFL	14	8	5	8	1.6	0	9	78	8.7	0	0	0	0	0
1997—Seattle NFL	16	10	4	8	2.0	0	13	91	7.0	2	2	0	12	0
1998—Seattle NFL	16	5	15	47	3.1	0	8	48	6.0	2	2	0	12	2
1999—Seattle NFL	14	1	1	0	0.0	0	1	5	5.0	0	0	0	0	0
2000—Seattle NFL	16	13	3	9	3.0	0	23	141	6.1	1	1	0	6	0
2001—Seattle NFL	16	13	17	55	3.2	0	17	141	8.3	0	0	0	0	0
Pro totals (8 years)	116	52	80	264	3.3	3	86	624	7.3	8	11	0	66	5

STROUD, MARCUS — DT — JAGUARS

PERSONAL: Born June 25, 1978, in Thomasville, Ga. ... 6-6/321.
HIGH SCHOOL: Brooks County (Barney, Ga.).
COLLEGE: Georgia.
TRANSACTIONS/CAREER NOTES: Selected by Jacksonville Jaguars in first round (13th pick overall) of 2001 draft. ... Signed by Jaguars (July 26, 2001).
PLAYING EXPERIENCE: Jacksonville NFL, 2001. ... Games/Games started: 2001 (16/0).

STRYZINSKI, DAN   P   CHIEFS

PERSONAL: Born May 15, 1965, in Vincennes, Ind. ... 6-2/200. ... Full name: Daniel Thomas Stryzinski. ... Name pronounced stra-ZIN-ski.
HIGH SCHOOL: Lincoln (Vincennes, Ind.).
COLLEGE: Indiana (bachelor of science degree in public finance and management, 1988).
TRANSACTIONS/CAREER NOTES: Signed as non-drafted free agent by Indianapolis Colts (July 1988). ... Released by Colts (August 23, 1988). ... Signed by Cleveland Browns (August 25, 1988). ... Released by Browns (August 30, 1988). ... Re-signed by Browns for 1989 season. ... Released by Browns (August 30, 1989). ... Signed by New Orleans Saints to developmental squad (October 11, 1989). ... Granted free agency following 1989 season. ... Signed by Pittsburgh Steelers (March 14, 1990). ... Granted unconditional free agency (February 1, 1992). ... Signed by Tampa Bay Buccaneers (February 21, 1992). ... Granted unconditional free agency (February 17, 1995). ... Signed by Atlanta Falcons (February 20, 1995). ... Granted unconditional free agency (March 2, 2001). ... Signed by Kansas City Chiefs (March 9, 2001).
CHAMPIONSHIP GAME EXPERIENCE: Played in NFC championship game (1998 season). ... Played in Super Bowl XXXIII (1998 season).
PRO STATISTICS: 1990—Rushed three times for 17 yards and recovered one fumble. 1991—Rushed four times for minus 11 yards, fumbled once and recovered two fumbles. 1992—Attempted two passes with two completions for 14 yards and rushed once for seven yards. 1994—Completed only pass attempt for 21 yards. 1995—Rushed once for no yards. 2001—Rushed once for minus 10 yards.

					PUNTING		
Year Team	G	No.	Yds.	Avg.	Net avg.	In. 20	Blk.
1990—Pittsburgh NFL	16	65	2454	37.8	34.1	18	1
1991—Pittsburgh NFL	16	74	2996	40.5	36.2	10	1
1992—Tampa Bay NFL	16	74	3015	40.7	36.2	15	0
1993—Tampa Bay NFL	16	*93	3772	40.6	35.2	24	1
1994—Tampa Bay NFL	16	72	2800	38.9	35.8	20	0
1995—Atlanta NFL	16	67	2759	41.2	36.2	21	0
1996—Atlanta NFL	16	75	3152	42.0	35.5	22	0
1997—Atlanta NFL	16	89	3498	39.3	36.7	20	0
1998—Atlanta NFL	16	74	2963	40.0	36.6	25	0
1999—Atlanta NFL	16	80	3163	39.5	37.1	27	0
2000—Atlanta NFL	16	84	3447	41.0	‡37.9	27	1
2001—Kansas City NFL	16	73	2976	40.8	35.6	27	0
Pro totals (12 years)	192	920	36995	40.2	36.1	256	4

STUBBLEFIELD, DANA   DT   49ERS

PERSONAL: Born November 14, 1970, in Cleves, Ohio. ... 6-2/290. ... Full name: Dana William Stubblefield.
HIGH SCHOOL: Taylor (North Bend, Ohio).
COLLEGE: Kansas.
TRANSACTIONS/CAREER NOTES: Selected by San Francisco 49ers in first round (26th pick overall) of 1993 NFL draft. ... Signed by 49ers (July 14, 1993). ... Granted unconditional free agency (February 13, 1998). ... Signed by Washington Redskins (February 23, 1998). ... Released by Redskins (March 1, 2001). ... Signed by 49ers (April 25, 2001).
CHAMPIONSHIP GAME EXPERIENCE: Played in NFC championship game (1993, 1994 and 1997 seasons). ... Member of Super Bowl championship team (1994 season).
HONORS: Played in Pro Bowl (1994, 1995 and 1997 seasons). ... Named defensive tackle on THE SPORTING NEWS NFL All-Pro team (1997).
PRO STATISTICS: 1995—Intercepted one pass for 12 yards. 1996—Intercepted one pass for 15 yards and recovered one fumble. 1999—Recovered one fumble. 2000—Recovered one fumble.

Year Team	G	GS	SACKS
1993—San Francisco NFL	16	14	10.5
1994—San Francisco NFL	14	14	8.5
1995—San Francisco NFL	16	16	4.5
1996—San Francisco NFL	15	15	1.0
1997—San Francisco NFL	16	16	15.0
1998—Washington NFL	7	7	1.5
1999—Washington NFL	16	16	3.0
2000—Washington NFL	15	14	2.5
2001—San Francisco NFL	16	16	4.0
Pro totals (9 years)	131	128	50.5

SULLIVAN, MARQUES   OT   BILLS

PERSONAL: Born February 2, 1978, in Oak Park, Ill. ... 6-5/320.
HIGH SCHOOL: Fenwick (Oak Park, Ill.).
COLLEGE: Illinois.
TRANSACTIONS/CAREER NOTES: Selected by Buffalo Bills in fifth round (144th pick overall) of 2001 NFL draft. ... Signed by Bills (June 11, 2001).
PLAYING EXPERIENCE: Buffalo NFL, 2001. ... Games/Games started: 2001 (10/2).

SURTAIN, PATRICK   CB   DOLPHINS

PERSONAL: Born June 19, 1976, in New Orleans. ... 5-11/192. ... Full name: Patrick Frank Surtain. ... Name pronounced sir-TANE.
HIGH SCHOOL: Edna Karr (New Orleans).
COLLEGE: Southern Mississippi.
TRANSACTIONS/CAREER NOTES: Selected by Miami Dolphins in second round (44th pick overall) of 1998 NFL draft. ... Signed by Dolphins (July 21, 1998).
HONORS: Named cornerback on THE SPORTING NEWS college All-America second team (1997).
PRO STATISTICS: 1999—Credited with two sacks. 2000—Credited with one sack and recovered one fumble. 2001—Credited with one sack, fumbled once and recovered two fumbles.

Year Team	G	GS	INTERCEPTIONS No.	Yds.	Avg.	TD
1998—Miami NFL	16	0	2	1	0.5	0
1999—Miami NFL	16	6	2	28	14.0	0
2000—Miami NFL	16	16	5	55	11.0	0
2001—Miami NFL	16	16	3	74	24.7	1
Pro totals (4 years)	64	38	12	158	13.2	1

SUTHERLAND, VINNY   WR/KR   49ERS

PERSONAL: Born April 22, 1978, in West Palm Beach, Fla. ... 5-8/188. ... Full name: Vincent Joseph Sutherland.
HIGH SCHOOL: Palm Beach Lakes (Fla.).
COLLEGE: Purdue.
TRANSACTIONS/CAREER NOTES: Selected by Atlanta Falcons in fifth round (136th pick overall) of 2001 NFL draft. ... Signed by Falcons (May 29, 2001). ... Released by Falcons (August 27, 2001). ... Signed by San Francisco 49ers (September 3, 2001).
PRO STATISTICS: 2001—Fumbled once.
SINGLE GAME HIGHS (regular season): Receptions—1 (December 30, 2001, vs. Dallas); yards—5 (December 30, 2001, vs. Dallas); and touchdown receptions—0.

			RUSHING			RECEIVING			PUNT RETURNS			KICKOFF RETURNS			TOTALS		
Year Team	G	GS	Att.	Yds.	Avg. TD	No.	Yds.	Avg. TD	No.	Yds.	Avg. TD	No.	Yds.	Avg. TD	TD	2pt.	Pts.
2001—San Fran. NFL	15	0	1	16	16.0 0	1	5	5.0 0	21	147	7.0 0	50	1140	22.8 0	0	0	0

SUTTLE, JASON   CB   TEXANS

PERSONAL: Born December 2, 1974, in Minneapolis. ... 5-10/181. ... Full name: Jason John Suttle.
HIGH SCHOOL: Burnsville (Minn.).
COLLEGE: Wisconsin (degree in sociology).
TRANSACTIONS/CAREER NOTES: Signed as non-drafted free agent by San Diego Chargers (April 24, 1998). ... Released by Chargers (July 23, 1998). ... Signed by New England Patriots (August 4, 1998). ... Released by Patriots (August 24, 1998). ... Signed by Denver Broncos (March 9, 1999). ... Released by Broncos (September 5, 1999). ... Re-signed by Broncos to practice squad (September 6, 1999). ... Activated (September 18, 1999). ... Released by Broncos (November 9, 1999). ... Re-signed by Broncos to practice squad (November 10, 1999). ... Activated (December 31, 1999). ... Claimed on waivers by Green Bay Packers (August 23, 2000). ... Released by Packers (August 27, 2000). ... Signed by Broncos to practice squad (August 29, 2000). ... Activated (November 25, 2000). ... Claimed on waivers by San Francisco 49ers (September 3, 2001). ... Released by 49ers (September 11, 2001). ... Signed by Houston Texans (December 29, 2001).
PLAYING EXPERIENCE: Denver NFL, 1999 and 2000; San Francisco NFL, 2001. ... Games/Games started: 1999 (5/0), 2000 (5/0), 2001 (1/0). Total: 11/0.
PRO STATISTICS: 2000—Recovered one fumble in end zone for a touchdown.

SWAYDA, SHAWN   DT

PERSONAL: Born September 4, 1974, in Phoenix. ... 6-5/294. ... Full name: Shawn Gerald Swayda.
HIGH SCHOOL: Brophy Prep (Phoenix).
COLLEGE: Arizona State.
TRANSACTIONS/CAREER NOTES: Selected by Chicago Bears in sixth round (196th pick overall) of 1997 NFL draft. ... Signed by Bears (July 10, 1997). ... Released by Bears (August 18, 1997). ... Signed by Dallas Cowboys to practice squad (October 9, 1997). ... Released by Cowboys (November 4, 1997). ... Signed by Detroit Lions to practice squad (November 24, 1997). ... Granted free agency after 1997 season. ... Signed by Atlanta Falcons (March 24, 1998). ... Released by Falcons (September 14, 1999). ... Re-signed by Falcons (September 28, 1999). ... Granted free agency (March 2, 2001). ... Re-signed by Falcons (May 29, 2001). ... Granted unconditional free agency (March 1, 2002).
PLAYING EXPERIENCE: Atlanta NFL, 1998-2001. ... Games/Games started: 1998 (5/0), 1999 (4/0), 2000 (16/0), 2001 (10/0). Total: 35/0.
CHAMPIONSHIP GAME EXPERIENCE: Member of Falcons for NFC championship game (1998 season); inactive. ... Member of Falcons for Super Bowl XXXIII (1998 season); inactive.
PRO STATISTICS: 2000—Credited with 1 1/2 sacks.

SWAYNE, HARRY   OT

PERSONAL: Born February 2, 1965, in Philadelphia. ... 6-5/300. ... Full name: Harry Vonray Swayne.
HIGH SCHOOL: Cardinal Dougherty (Philadelphia).
COLLEGE: Rutgers.
TRANSACTIONS/CAREER NOTES: Selected by Tampa Bay Buccaneers in seventh round (190th pick overall) of 1987 NFL draft. ... Signed by Buccaneers (July 18, 1987). ... On injured reserve with fractured hand (September 8-October 31, 1987). ... On injured reserve with neck injury (November 18, 1988-remainder of season). ... Granted free agency (February 1, 1990). ... Re-signed by Buccaneers (July 19, 1990). ... Granted unconditional free agency (February 1, 1991). ... Signed by San Diego Chargers (April 1, 1991). ... On injured reserve with fractured leg (November 26, 1991-remainder of season). ... Designated by Chargers as transition player (February 25, 1993). ... Tendered offer sheet by Phoenix Cardinals (April 9, 1993). ... Offer matched by Chargers (April 15, 1993). ... On physically unable to perform list (July 24-August 21, 1995). ... Free agency status changed by Chargers from transitional to unconditional (February 16, 1996). ... Re-signed by Chargers (July 24, 1996). ... Granted unconditional free agency (February 14, 1997). ... Signed by Denver Broncos (April 17, 1997). ... Granted unconditional free agency (February 12, 1999). ... Signed by Baltimore Ravens (February 26, 1999). ... On injured reserve with foot injury (November 10, 1999-remainder of season). ... Released by Ravens (August 28, 2001). ... Signed by Miami Dolphins (September 11, 2001). ... Announced retirement (January 15, 2002).
PLAYING EXPERIENCE: Tampa Bay NFL, 1987-1990; San Diego NFL, 1991-1996; Denver NFL, 1997 and 1998; Baltimore NFL, 1999 and 2000; Miami NFL, 2001. ... Games/Games started: 1987 (8/2), 1988 (10/1), 1989 (16/0), 1990 (10/0), 1991 (12/12), 1992 (16/16), 1993 (11/11), 1994 (16/16), 1995 (16/16), 1996 (16/3), 1997 (7/0), 1998 (16/16), 1999 (6/6), 2000 (13/13), 2001 (13/1). Total: 186/113.
CHAMPIONSHIP GAME EXPERIENCE: Played in AFC championship game (1994, 1997, 1998 and 2000 seasons). ... Played in Super Bowl XXIX (1994 season). ... Member of Super Bowl championship team (1997, 1998 and 2000 seasons).
PRO STATISTICS: 1998—Recovered one fumble. 2000—Recovered one fumble.

SWAYNE, KEVIN — WR — JETS

PERSONAL: Born January 17, 1975, in Banning, Calif. ... 6-1/191.
HIGH SCHOOL: Banning (Calif.).
COLLEGE: Wayne State.
TRANSACTIONS/CAREER NOTES: Signed as non-drafted free agent by Chicago Bears (April 25, 1997). ... Released by Bears prior to 1997 season. ... Played in Arena Football League (1998-2000). ... Signed by Philadelphia Eagles to practice squad (November 17, 1999). ... Granted free agency after 1999 season. ... Signed by San Diego Chargers (February 10, 2000). ... Released by Chargers (August 23, 2000). ... Signed by New York Jets (May 30, 2001).
SINGLE GAME HIGHS (regular season): Receptions—4 (December 16, 2001, vs. Cincinnati); yards—74 (December 16, 2001, vs. Cincinnati); and touchdown receptions—0.

				RECEIVING		
Year Team	G	GS	No.	Yds.	Avg.	TD
2001—New York Jets NFL	15	2	13	203	15.6	0

SWIFT, JUSTIN — TE — 49ERS

PERSONAL: Born August 14, 1975, in Kansas City, Kan. ... 6-3/265. ... Full name: Justin Charles Swift.
HIGH SCHOOL: Blue Valley (Overland Park, Kan.).
COLLEGE: Kansas State.
TRANSACTIONS/CAREER NOTES: Selected by Denver Broncos in seventh round (238th pick overall) of 1999 NFL draft. ... Signed by Broncos (July 20, 1999). ... Released by Broncos (August 27, 1999). ... Signed by Philadelphia Eagles (September 14, 1999). ... Released by Eagles (September 28, 1999). ... Signed by Broncos to practice squad (October 19, 1999). ... Released by Broncos (November 2, 1999). ... Signed by San Francisco 49ers to practice squad (November 15, 1999). ... Released by 49ers (February 10, 2000). ... Assigned by 49ers to Frankfurt Galaxy in 2000 NFL Europe enhancement allocation program (February 18, 2000). ... Re-signed by 49ers (February 22, 2000).
PLAYING EXPERIENCE: Philadelphia NFL, 1999; Frankfurt NFLE, 2000; San Francisco NFL, 2000 and 2001. ... Games/Games started: 1999 (1/0); 2000 NFLE (games played unavailable), 2000 NFL (16/1), 2001 (16/2). Total NFL: 33/3.
PRO STATISTICS: NFLE: 2000—Caught 27 passes for 260 yards and two touchdowns. NFL: 2000—Caught one pass for eight yards. 2001—Caught 11 passes for 66 yards and one touchdown.
SINGLE GAME HIGHS (regular season): Receptions—3 (September 23, 2001, vs. St. Louis); yards—13 (December 22, 2001, vs. Philadelphia); and touchdown receptions—1 (October 28, 2001, vs. Chicago).

SWINTON, REGGIE — WR — COWBOYS

PERSONAL: Born July 24, 1975, in Little Rock, Ark. ... 6-0/175.
HIGH SCHOOL: Central (Ark.).
COLLEGE: Murray State.
TRANSACTIONS/CAREER NOTES: Signed as non-drafted free agent by Jacksonville Jaguars (April 18, 1998). ... Released by Jaguars (August 25, 1998). ... Signed by Toronto Argonauts of CFL (February 19, 1999). ... Traded by Argonauts with QB Kerwin Bell to Winnipeg Blue Bombers for Eric Blount and RB Mitch Running (March 1, 1999). ... Released by Blue Bombers (August 16, 1999). ... Signed by Edmonton Eskimos of CFL (September 13, 1999). ... Released by Eskimos (October 12, 1999). ... Signed by Seattle Seahawks (February 24, 2000). ... Released by Seahawks (August 27, 2000). ... Signed by Dallas Cowboys (August 6, 2001).
PRO STATISTICS: 2001—Rushed once for minus four yards and recovered one fumble.
SINGLE GAME HIGHS (regular season): Receptions—3 (December 23, 2001, vs. Arizona); yards—72 (December 23, 2001, vs. Arizona); and touchdown receptions—1 (December 23, 2001, vs. Arizona).

			RECEIVING				KICKOFF RETURNS				PUNT RETURNS				TOTALS			
Year Team	G	GS	No.	Yds.	Avg.	TD	No.	Yds.	Avg.	TD	No.	Yds.	Avg.	TD	TD	2pt.	Pts.	Fum.
1999—Winnipeg CFL	4	...	11	162	14.7	1	7	235	33.6	1	5	18	3.6	0	2	0	12	0
—Toronto CFL	3	...	3	22	7.3	0	9	178	19.8	0	3	33	11.0	0	0	0	0	0
2000—								Did not play.										
2001—Dallas NFL	15	1	7	117	16.7	1	31	414	13.4	†1	56	1327	23.7	0	2	0	12	4
CFL total (1 year)	7	...	14	184	13.1	1	16	413	25.8	1	8	51	6.3	0	2	0	12	0
NFL total (1 year)	15	1	7	117	16.7	1	31	414	13.4	1	56	1327	23.7	0	2	0	12	4
Pro totals (2 years)	22	...	21	301	14.9	2	47	827	17.6	2	64	1378	21.5	0	4	0	24	4

SWORD, SAM — LB — COLTS

PERSONAL: Born December 4, 1974, in Saginaw, Mich. ... 6-1/245. ... Full name: Sam Lee-Arthur Sword.
HIGH SCHOOL: Arthur Hill (Saginaw, Mich.).
COLLEGE: Michigan.
TRANSACTIONS/CAREER NOTES: Signed as non-drafted free agent by Oakland Raiders (April 22, 1999). ... Released by Raiders (August 27, 2000). ... Signed by Indianapolis Colts (October 25, 2000). ... Released by Colts (November 24, 2000). ... Re-signed by Colts (November 30, 2000). ... Granted free agency (March 1, 2002).
PLAYING EXPERIENCE: Oakland NFL, 1999; Indianapolis NFL, 2000 and 2001. ... Games/Games started: 1999 (10/5), 2000 (4/0), 2001 (16/2). Total: 30/7.
PRO STATISTICS: 1999—Credited with one sack. 2001—Credited with one sack.

SZOTT, DAVE — G — JETS

PERSONAL: Born December 12, 1967, in Passaic, N.J. ... 6-4/289. ... Full name: David Andrew Szott. ... Name pronounced ZOT.
HIGH SCHOOL: Clifton (N.J.).
COLLEGE: Penn State (degree in political science).

TRANSACTIONS/CAREER NOTES: Selected by Kansas City Chiefs in seventh round (180th pick overall) of 1990 NFL draft. ... Signed by Chiefs (July 25, 1990). ... Granted free agency (March 1, 1993). ... Re-signed by Chiefs for 1993 season. ... On injured reserve with arm injury (December 2, 1998-remainder of season). ... On injured reserve with arm injury (October 11, 2000-remainder of season). ... Granted unconditional free agency (March 2, 2001). ... Signed by Washington Redskins (August 19, 2001). ... Granted unconditional free agency (March 1, 2002). ... Signed by New York Jets (March 21, 2002).
PLAYING EXPERIENCE: Kansas City NFL, 1990-2000; Washington NFL, 2001. ... Games/Games started: 1990 (16/11), 1991 (16/16), 1992 (16/16), 1993 (14/13), 1994 (16/16), 1995 (16/16), 1996 (16/16), 1997 (16/16), 1998 (1/1), 1999 (14/14), 2000 (1/1), 2001 (16/16). Total: 158/152.
CHAMPIONSHIP GAME EXPERIENCE: Played in AFC championship game (1993 season).
PRO STATISTICS: 1990—Recovered one fumble. 1991—Recovered one fumble. 1997—Recovered one fumble. 1999—Recovered one fumble.

TAFOYA, JOSEPH DE BEARS

PERSONAL: Born September 6, 1977, in Pittsburgh, Calif. ... 6-4/270. ... Full name: Joseph Peter Tafoya.
HIGH SCHOOL: Pittsburgh (Calif.).
COLLEGE: Arizona.
TRANSACTIONS/CAREER NOTES: Selected by Tampa Bay Buccaneers in seventh round (234th pick overall) of 2001 NFL draft. ... Signed by Buccaneers (July 18, 2001). ... Released by Buccaneers (September 2, 2001). ... Signed by Chicago Bears to practice squad (October 9, 2001). ... Activated (October 23, 2001).
PLAYING EXPERIENCE: Chicago NFL, 2001. ... Games/Games started: 2001 (5/0).

TAIT, JOHN OT CHIEFS

PERSONAL: Born January 26, 1975, in Phoenix. ... 6-6/316.
HIGH SCHOOL: McClintock (Tempe, Ariz.).
COLLEGE: Brigham Young (degree in communications).
TRANSACTIONS/CAREER NOTES: Selected after junior season by Kansas City Chiefs in first round (14th pick overall) of 1999 NFL draft. ... Signed by Chiefs (September 9, 1999).
PLAYING EXPERIENCE: Kansas City NFL, 1999-2001. ... Games/Games started: 1999 (12/3), 2000 (15/15), 2001 (16/16). Total: 43/34.
PRO STATISTICS: 2000—Recovered one fumble.

TANNER, BARRON DT CARDINALS

PERSONAL: Born September 14, 1973, in Athens, Texas. ... 6-3/347. ... Full name: Barron Keith Tanner.
HIGH SCHOOL: Athens (Texas).
COLLEGE: Oklahoma.
TRANSACTIONS/CAREER NOTES: Selected by Miami Dolphins in fifth round (149th pick overall) of 1997 NFL draft. ... Signed by Dolphins (July 8, 1997). ... Traded by Dolphins to Washington Redskins for seventh-round pick (traded to San Francisco) in 2001 draft (September 4, 1999). ... Inactive for all 16 games (1999). ... Granted free agency (February 11, 2000). ... Re-signed by Redskins (June 6, 2000). ... Released by Redskins (August 27, 2000). ... Signed by Arizona Cardinals (November 6, 2000).
PLAYING EXPERIENCE: Miami NFL, 1997 and 1998; Arizona NFL, 2000 and 2001. ... Games/Games started: 1997 (16/0), 1998 (13/0), 2000 (4/0), 2001 (16/16). Total: 49/16.

TANUVASA, MAA DT

PERSONAL: Born November 6, 1970, in America Samoa. ... 6-2/270. ... Full name: Maa Junior Tanuvasa. ... Name pronounced MAH-ah TAH-noo-VA-suh.
HIGH SCHOOL: Mililani (Wahiawa, Hawaii).
COLLEGE: Hawaii.
TRANSACTIONS/CAREER NOTES: Selected by Los Angeles Rams in eighth round (209th pick overall) of 1993 NFL draft. ... Signed by Rams for 1993 season. ... On injured reserve with knee injury (August 21, 1993-entire season). ... Released by Rams (August 23, 1994). ... Signed by Steelers to practice squad (December 1, 1994). ... Granted free agency after 1994 season. ... Signed by Denver Broncos (February 22, 1995). ... Released by Broncos (August 27, 1995). ... Re-signed by Broncos to practice squad (August 28, 1995). ... Activated (October 24, 1995). ... Granted free agency (February 14, 1997). ... Re-signed by Broncos (February 14, 1997). ... Released by Broncos (September 2, 2001). ... Signed by San Diego Chargers (October 3, 2001). ... On injured reserve with broken ankle (October 26, 2001-remainder of season). ... Granted unconditional free agency (March 1, 2002).
CHAMPIONSHIP GAME EXPERIENCE: Played in AFC championship game (1997 and 1998 seasons). ... Member of Super Bowl championship team (1997 and 1998 seasons).
PRO STATISTICS: 1996—Recovered one fumble. 1998—Returned one kickoff for 13 yards and recovered two fumbles for minus one yard. 2000—Recovered four fumbles for 38 yards.

Year Team	G	GS	SACKS
1993—Los Angeles Rams NFL	Did not play.		
1994—Pittsburgh NFL	Did not play.		
1995—Denver NFL	1	0	0.0
1996—Denver NFL	16	1	5.0
1997—Denver NFL	15	5	8.5
1998—Denver NFL	16	16	8.5
1999—Denver NFL	16	16	7.0
2000—Denver NFL	16	16	4.0
2001—San Diego NFL	2	0	1.0
Pro totals (7 years)	**82**	**54**	**34.0**

TARLE, JIM — K

PERSONAL: Born December 27, 1972, in Akron, Ohio. ... 6-0/221. ... Full name: James David Tarle.
HIGH SCHOOL: Bishop Kenny (Jacksonville).
COLLEGE: South Carolina, then Arkansas State.
TRANSACTIONS/CAREER NOTES: Signed as non-drafted free agent by Jacksonville Jaguars (November 15, 2000). ... Released by Jaguars (November 21, 2001).
PLAYING EXPERIENCE: Jacksonville NFL, 2000 and 2001. ... Games/Games started: 2000 (6/0), 2001 (9/0). Total: 15/0.

TATE, ROBERT — CB — VIKINGS

PERSONAL: Born October 19, 1973, in Harrisburg, Pa. ... 5-10/193.
HIGH SCHOOL: John Harris (Harrisburg, Pa.), then Milford (Conn.) Academy.
COLLEGE: Cincinnati.
TRANSACTIONS/CAREER NOTES: Selected by Minnesota Vikings in sixth round (183rd pick overall) of 1997 NFL draft. ... Signed by Vikings (June 17, 1997). ... On injured reserve with ankle injury (October 8, 1997-remainder of season).
CHAMPIONSHIP GAME EXPERIENCE: Member of Vikings for NFC championship game (1998 season); inactive. ... Played in NFC championship game (2000 season).
PRO STATISTICS: 1998—Caught one pass for 17 yards. 1999—Rushed once for four yards, caught one pass for three yards and intercepted one pass for 18 yards. 2000—Intercepted two passes for 12 yards and recovered one fumble.
SINGLE GAME HIGHS (regular season): Receptions—1 (November 22, 1998, vs. Green Bay); yards—17 (November 22, 1998, vs Green Bay); and touchdown receptions—0.

			KICKOFF RETURNS				TOTALS			
Year Team	G	GS	No.	Yds.	Avg.	TD	TD	2pt.	Pts.	Fum.
1997—Minnesota NFL	4	0	10	196	19.6	0	0	0	0	0
1998—Minnesota NFL	15	1	2	43	21.5	0	0	0	0	0
1999—Minnesota NFL	16	1	25	627	25.1	1	1	0	6	1
2000—Minnesota NFL	16	16	0	0	0.0	0	0	0	0	0
2001—Minnesota NFL	16	5	0	0	0.0	0	0	0	0	0
Pro totals (5 years)	67	23	37	866	23.4	1	1	0	6	1

TAUSCHER, MARK — OT/G — PACKERS

PERSONAL: Born June 17, 1977, in Marshfield, Wis. ... 6-3/320. ... Full name: Mark Gerald Tauscher.
HIGH SCHOOL: Auburndale (Wis.).
COLLEGE: Wisconsin.
TRANSACTIONS/CAREER NOTES: Selected by Green Bay Packers in seventh round (224th pick overall) of 2000 NFL draft. ... Signed by Packers (June 21, 2000).
PLAYING EXPERIENCE: Green Bay NFL, 2000 and 2001. ... Games/Games started: 2000 (16/14), 2001 (16/16). Total: 32/30.
PRO STATISTICS: 2001—Recovered one fumble.

TAVES, JOSH — DE — RAIDERS

PERSONAL: Born May 13, 1972, in Watsonville, Calif. ... 6-7/280. ... Name pronounced TAAVS. ... Full name: Josh Heinrich-Taves.
HIGH SCHOOL: Dennis-Yarmouth Regional (South Yarmouth, Mass.), then New Hampton Prep.
COLLEGE: Northeastern.
TRANSACTIONS/CAREER NOTES: Signed as non-drafted free agent by Detroit Lions (May 3, 1995). ... Released by Lions (August 28, 1995). ... Re-signed by Lions (August 30, 1995). ... Activated (December 21, 1995); did not play. ... Assigned by Lions to Barcelona Dragons in 1996 World League enhancement allocation program (February 1996). ... Released by Lions (August 21, 1996). ... Signed by Jacksonville Jaguars (November 13, 1996); did not play. ... Released by Jaguars (December 4, 1996). ... Signed by New England Patriots to practice squad (December 31, 1996). ... On injured reserve with ankle injury (August 21-September 22, 1997). ... Released by Patriots (September 22, 1997). ... Signed by Miami Dolphins (June 22, 1998). ... Claimed on waivers by New Orleans Saints (August 18, 1998). ... Released by Saints (September 5, 1998). ... Signed by Oakland Raiders (March 10, 1999). ... Released by Raiders (September 4, 1999). ... Re-signed by Raiders (February 17, 2000).
PLAYING EXPERIENCE: Barcelona W.L., 1996; Barcelona NFLE, 1998; Oakland NFL, 2000 and 2001. ... Games/Games started: 1996 (games played unavailable), 1998 (10/10), 2000 (16/0), 2001 (8/3). Total NFL: 24/3.
CHAMPIONSHIP GAME EXPERIENCE: Played in AFC championship game (2000 season).
PRO STATISTICS: W.L.: 1996—Credited with six sacks. NFLE: 1998—Tied for league lead with nine sacks. 2000—Intercepted one pass for 24 yards and credited with three sacks. 2001—Credited with one sack.

TAYLOR, BOBBY — CB — EAGLES

PERSONAL: Born December 28, 1973, in Houston. ... 6-3/216. ... Full name: Robert Taylor. ... Son of Robert Taylor, silver medalist in 100-meter dash and member of gold-medal winning 400-meter relay team at 1972 Summer Olympics.
HIGH SCHOOL: Longview (Texas).
COLLEGE: Notre Dame.
TRANSACTIONS/CAREER NOTES: Selected after junior season by Philadelphia Eagles in second round (49th pick overall) of 1995 NFL draft. ... Signed by Eagles (July 19, 1995). ... On injured reserve with knee injury (October 17, 1997-remainder of season). ... Granted free agency (February 13, 1998). ... Re-signed by Eagles (June 11, 1998). ... On injured reserve with fractured jaw (December 28, 1999-remainder of season).
CHAMPIONSHIP GAME EXPERIENCE: Played in NFC championship game (2001 season).
HONORS: Named defensive back on THE SPORTING NEWS college All-America first team (1993 and 1994).
PRO STATISTICS: 1996—Credited with one sack, fumbled once and recovered two fumbles for nine yards. 1997—Credited with two sacks. 1999—Recovered three fumbles. 2000—Recovered one fumble. 2001—Credited with one sack and recovered three fumbles.

Year Team	G	GS	INTERCEPTIONS No.	Yds.	Avg.	TD
1995—Philadelphia NFL	16	12	2	52	26.0	0
1996—Philadelphia NFL	16	16	3	-1	-0.3	0
1997—Philadelphia NFL	6	5	0	0	0.0	0
1998—Philadelphia NFL	11	10	0	0	0.0	0
1999—Philadelphia NFL	15	14	4	59	14.8	1
2000—Philadelphia NFL	16	15	3	64	21.3	0
2001—Philadelphia NFL	16	14	1	5	5.0	0
Pro totals (7 years)	96	86	13	179	13.8	1

TAYLOR, FRED   RB   JAGUARS

PERSONAL: Born January 27, 1976, in Pahokee, Fla. ... 6-1/231. ... Full name: Frederick Antwon Taylor.
HIGH SCHOOL: Glades Central (Belle Glade, Fla.).
COLLEGE: Florida.
TRANSACTIONS/CAREER NOTES: Selected by Jacksonville Jaguars in first round (ninth pick overall) of 1998 NFL draft. ... Signed by Jaguars (July 6, 1998).
CHAMPIONSHIP GAME EXPERIENCE: Played in AFC championship game (1999 season).
HONORS: Named running back on THE SPORTING NEWS college All-America third team (1997).
PRO STATISTICS: 1998—Recovered one fumble for nine yards. 2000—Recovered two fumbles for minus one yard.
SINGLE GAME HIGHS (regular season): Attempts—32 (December 17, 2000, vs. Cincinnati); yards—234 (November 19, 2000, vs. Pittsburgh); and rushing touchdowns—3 (December 3, 2000, vs. Cleveland).
STATISTICAL PLATEAUS: 100-yard rushing games: 1998 (6), 1999 (3), 2000 (9). Total: 18.
MISCELLANEOUS: Holds Jacksonville Jaguars all-time record for most yards rushing (3,470).

			RUSHING				RECEIVING				TOTALS			
Year Team	G	GS	Att.	Yds.	Avg.	TD	No.	Yds.	Avg.	TD	TD	2pt.	Pts.	Fum.
1998—Jacksonville NFL	15	12	264	1223	4.6	14	44	421	9.6	3	17	0	102	3
1999—Jacksonville NFL	10	9	159	732	4.6	6	10	83	8.3	0	6	0	36	0
2000—Jacksonville NFL	13	13	292	1399	4.8	12	36	240	6.7	2	14	0	84	4
2001—Jacksonville NFL	2	2	30	116	3.9	0	2	13	6.5	0	0	0	0	1
Pro totals (4 years)	40	36	745	3470	4.7	32	92	757	8.2	5	37	0	222	8

TAYLOR, HENRY   DT   DOLPHINS

PERSONAL: Born November 29, 1975, in Broward County, Fla. ... 6-2/295.
HIGH SCHOOL: Barnwell (S.C.).
COLLEGE: South Carolina.
TRANSACTIONS/CAREER NOTES: Signed as non-drafted free agent by San Diego Chargers (April 20, 1998). ... Released by Chargers (July 23, 1998). ... Re-signed by Chargers (July 31, 1998). ... Released by Chargers (August 25, 1998). ... Signed by Detroit Lions to practice squad (September 2, 1998). ... Activated (October 8, 1998); did not play. ... Released by Lions (October 19, 1998). ... Re-signed by Lions to practice squad (October 21, 1998). ... Activated (November 23, 1998). ... On injured reserve with groin injury (December 19, 1998-remainder of season). ... Assigned by Lions to Amsterdam Admirals in 1999 NFL Europe enhancement allocation program (February 17, 1999). ... Released by Lions (September 5, 1999). ... Re-signed by Lions to practice squad (September 7, 1999). ... Assigned by Lions to Frankfurt Galaxy in 2000 NFL Europe enhancement allocation program (February 18, 2000). ... Released by Lions (August 27, 2000). ... Signed by Atlanta Falcons (November 1, 2000). ... Signed by Chicago Bears (July 27, 2001). ... On suspended list for violating league substance abuse policy (October 5-29, 2001). ... Released by Bears (October 29, 2001). ... Signed by Miami Dolphins (December 4, 2001).
PLAYING EXPERIENCE: Detroit NFL, 1998; Amsterdam NFLE, 1999; Frankfurt NFLE, 2000; Atlanta NFL, 2000; Chicago (1)-Miami (1) NFL, 2001. ... Games/Games started: 1998 (1/0), 1999 (games played unavailable), NFLE 2000 (-), NFL 2000 (5/0), 2001 (Chi.-1/0; Mia.-2/0; Total: 3/0). Total NFL: 9/0.
PRO STATISTICS: NFLE: 2000—Credited with six sacks.

TAYLOR, JASON   DE   DOLPHINS

PERSONAL: Born September 1, 1974, in Pittsburgh. ... 6-6/260. ... Full name: Jason Paul Taylor.
HIGH SCHOOL: Woodland Hills (Pittsburgh).
COLLEGE: Akron.
TRANSACTIONS/CAREER NOTES: Selected by Miami Dolphins in third round (73rd pick overall) of 1997 NFL draft. ... Signed by Dolphins (July 9, 1997). ... On injured reserve with broken collarbone (December 29, 1998-remainder of playoffs). ... Granted free agency (February 11, 2000). ... Re-signed by Dolphins (April 13, 2000). ... Designated by Dolphins as franchise player (February 22, 2001).
HONORS: Named defensive end on THE SPORTING NEWS NFL All-Pro team (2000). ... Played in Pro Bowl (2000 season).
PRO STATISTICS: 1997—Recovered two fumbles. 1999—Intercepted one pass for no yards and recovered two fumbles for four yards and one touchdown. 2000—Intercepted one pass for two yards and recovered four fumbles for 29 yards and one touchdown. 2001—Intercepted one pass for four yards and recovered four fumbles for seven yards and one touchdown.

Year Team	G	GS	SACKS
1997—Miami NFL	13	11	5.0
1998—Miami NFL	16	15	9.0
1999—Miami NFL	15	15	2.5
2000—Miami NFL	16	16	14.5
2001—Miami NFL	16	16	8.5
Pro totals (5 years)	76	73	39.5

TAYLOR, SHANNON — LB — RAVENS

PERSONAL: Born February 16, 1975, in Roanoke, Va. ... 6-3/247. ... Full name: Shannon Andre Taylor.
HIGH SCHOOL: Patrick Henry (Roanoke, Va.).
COLLEGE: Virginia.
TRANSACTIONS/CAREER NOTES: Selected by San Diego Chargers in sixth round (184th pick overall) of 2000 NFL draft. ... Signed by Chargers (June 21, 2000). ... Released by Chargers (August 27, 2000). ... Re-signed by Chargers to practice squad (August 29, 2000). ... Activated (October 4, 2000). ... Released by Chargers (August 27, 2001). ... Signed by Baltimore Ravens (September 9, 2001). ... On injured reserve with shoulder injury (January 10, 2002-remainder of season).
PLAYING EXPERIENCE: San Diego NFL, 2000; Baltimore NFL, 2001. ... Games/Games started: 2000 (11/0), 2001 (11/0). Total: 22/0.
PRO STATISTICS: 2001—Credited with one sack and recovered one fumble.

TAYLOR, TONY — RB — COWBOYS

PERSONAL: Born March 9, 1978, in Pineville, La. ... 5-9/191.
HIGH SCHOOL: Pineville (La.).
COLLEGE: Northwestern State.
TRANSACTIONS/CAREER NOTES: Signed as non-drafted free agent by Dallas Cowboys (April 27, 2001). ... Released by Cowboys (September 2, 2001). ... Re-signed by Cowboys to practice squad (September 4, 2001). ... Activated (November 3, 2001). ... Released by Cowboys (November 17, 2001). ... Re-signed by Cowboys to practice squad (November 19, 2001).
PLAYING EXPERIENCE: Dallas NFL, 2001. ... Games/Games started: 2001 (1/0).
PRO STATISTICS: 2001—Rushed once for no yards.
SINGLE GAME HIGHS (regular season): Attempts—1 (November 11, 2001, vs. Atlanta); yards—0; and rushing touchdowns—0.

TAYLOR, TRAVIS — WR — RAVENS

PERSONAL: Born March 30, 1979, in Fernadina Beach, Fla. ... 6-1/200. ... Full name: Travis Lamont Taylor.
HIGH SCHOOL: Camden County (Ga.), then Jean Ribault (Jacksonville).
COLLEGE: Florida.
TRANSACTIONS/CAREER NOTES: Selected after junior season by Baltimore Ravens in first round (10th pick overall) of 2000 NFL draft. ... Signed by Ravens (August 1, 2000). ... On injured reserve with broken clavicle (November 8, 2000-remainder of season).
PRO STATISTICS: 2000—Rushed twice for 11 yards and fumbled once. 2001—Rushed five times for 46 yards.
SINGLE GAME HIGHS (regular season): Receptions—5 (November 18, 2001, vs. Cleveland); yards—90 (September 30, 2001, vs. Denver); and touchdown receptions—2 (September 10, 2000, vs. Jacksonville).

			RECEIVING		
Year Team	G	GS	No.	Yds.	Avg.	TD
2000—Baltimore NFL	9	8	28	276	9.9	3
2001—Baltimore NFL	16	13	42	560	13.3	3
Pro totals (2 years)	25	21	70	836	11.9	6

TEAGUE, GEORGE — S

PERSONAL: Born February 18, 1971, in Lansing, Mich. ... 6-1/196. ... Full name: George Theo Teague. ... Name pronounced TEEG.
HIGH SCHOOL: Jefferson Davis (Montgomery, Ala.).
COLLEGE: Alabama.
TRANSACTIONS/CAREER NOTES: Selected by Green Bay Packers in first round (29th pick overall) of 1993 NFL draft. ... Signed by Packers (July 9, 1993). ... Granted free agency (February 16, 1996). ... Re-signed by Packers (April 12, 1996). ... Traded by Packers to Atlanta Falcons for conditional draft pick (July 16, 1996). ... Released by Falcons (August 17, 1996). ... Signed by Dallas Cowboys (August 23, 1996). ... Granted unconditional free agency (February 14, 1997). ... Signed by Miami Dolphins (March 20, 1997). ... Traded by Dolphins to Cowboys (May 6, 1998), as compensation for Dolphins signing free agent S Brock Marion (March 3, 1998). ... Granted unconditional free agency (February 11, 2000). ... Re-signed by Cowboys (March 13, 2000). ... On injured reserve with broken foot (November 15, 2000-remainder of season). ... Released by Cowboys (February 28, 2002).
CHAMPIONSHIP GAME EXPERIENCE: Played in NFC championship game (1995 season).
POST SEASON RECORDS: Holds NFL postseason single-game record for longest interception return—101 yards, touchdown (January 8, 1994, at Detroit).
PRO STATISTICS: 1993—Returned one punt for minus one yard and recovered two fumbles. 1995—Recovered one fumble for four yards. 1998—Credited with two sacks. 1999—Recovered one fumble.

			INTERCEPTIONS		
Year Team	G	GS	No.	Yds.	Avg.	TD
1993—Green Bay NFL	16	12	1	22	22.0	0
1994—Green Bay NFL	16	16	3	33	11.0	0
1995—Green Bay NFL	15	15	2	100	50.0	0
1996—Dallas NFL	16	8	4	47	11.8	0
1997—Miami NFL	15	6	2	25	12.5	0
1998—Dallas NFL	16	5	0	0	0.0	0
1999—Dallas NFL	14	14	3	127	*42.3	†2
2000—Dallas NFL	9	9	0	0	0.0	0
2001—Dallas NFL	16	16	0	0	0.0	0
Pro totals (9 years)	133	101	15	354	23.6	2

TEAGUE, TREY   OT   BILLS

PERSONAL: Born December 27, 1974, in Jackson, Tenn. ... 6-5/292. ... Full name: Fred Everette Teague III. ... Name pronounced TEEG.
HIGH SCHOOL: University (Jackson, Tenn).
COLLEGE: Tennessee.
TRANSACTIONS/CAREER NOTES: Selected by Denver Broncos in seventh round (200th pick overall) of 1998 NFL draft. ... Signed by Broncos (July 23, 1998). ... Inactive for all 16 games (1998). ... On injured reserve with knee injury (September 12, 2000-remainder of season). ... Granted free agency (March 2, 2001). ... Re-signed by Broncos (May 3, 2001). ... Granted unconditional free agency (March 1, 2002). ... Signed by Buffalo Bills (March 27, 2002).
PLAYING EXPERIENCE: Denver NFL, 1999-2001. ... Games/Games started: 1999 (16/4), 2000 (2/0), 2001 (16/16). Total: 34/20.
CHAMPIONSHIP GAME EXPERIENCE: Member of Broncos for AFC championship game (1998 season); inactive. ... Member of Super Bowl championship team (1998 season); inactive.
PRO STATISTICS: 1999—Fumbled once for minus nine yards. 2001—Recovered one fumble.

TERRELL, DARYL   OT

PERSONAL: Born January 25, 1975, in Vossburg, Miss. ... 6-5/296.
HIGH SCHOOL: Heidelberg (Miss.).
JUNIOR COLLEGE: Jones County Community College (Miss.).
COLLEGE: Southern Mississippi.
TRANSACTIONS/CAREER NOTES: Signed as non-drafted free agent by Baltimore Ravens (June 3, 1997). ... Released by Ravens (July 8, 1997). ... Signed by New Orleans Saints (April 27, 1998). ... Released by Saints (August 24, 1998). ... Re-signed by Saints to practice squad (September 2, 1998). ... Assigned by Saints to Amsterdam Admirals in 1999 NFL Europe enhancement allocation program (February 22, 1999). ... Granted free agency (March 1, 2002).
PLAYING EXPERIENCE: Amsterdam NFLE, 1999; New Orleans NFL, 1999-2001. ... Games/Games started: NFLE 1999 (games played unavailable), NFL 1999 (12/1), 2000 (16/0), 2001 (16/10). Total NFL: 34/11.

TERRELL, DAVID   WR   BEARS

PERSONAL: Born March 13, 1979, in Richmond, Va. ... 6-3/215.
HIGH SCHOOL: Huguenot (Richmond, Va.).
COLLEGE: Michigan.
TRANSACTIONS/CAREER NOTES: Selected after junior season by Chicago Bears in first round (eighth pick overall) of 2001 NFL draft. ... Signed by Bears (July 31, 2001).
HONORS: Named wide receiver on THE SPORTING NEWS college All-America second team (2000).
PRO STATISTICS: 2001—Returned one kickoff for eight yards.
SINGLE GAME HIGHS (regular season): Receptions—7 (October 21, 2001, vs. Cincinnati); yards—94 (December 16, 2001, vs. Tampa Bay); and touchdown receptions—2 (October 28, 2001, vs. San Francisco).

			RECEIVING				TOTALS		
Year Team	G	GS	No.	Yds.	Avg.	TD	TD	2pt.	Pts.	Fum.
2001—Chicago NFL	16	6	34	415	12.2	4	4	0	24	0

TERRELL, DAVID   CB   REDSKINS

PERSONAL: Born July 8, 1975, in Floyada, Texas. ... 6-0/188.
HIGH SCHOOL: Sweetwater (Texas).
COLLEGE: Texas-El Paso.
TRANSACTIONS/CAREER NOTES: Selected by Washington Redskins in seventh round (191st pick overall) of 1998 NFL draft. ... Signed by Redskins (May 13, 1998). ... Released by Redskins (August 25, 1998). ... Selected by Rhein Fire in 1999 NFL Europe draft (February 23, 1999). ... Released by Redskins (September 4, 1999). ... Re-signed by Redskins to practice squad (September 14, 1999).
PLAYING EXPERIENCE: Rhein NFLE 1999; Washington NFL, 2000 and 2001. ... Games/Games started: 1999 (games played unavailable), 2000 (16/0), 2001 (16/16). Total: 32/16.
PRO STATISTICS: 2000—Recovered two fumbles. 2001—Intercepted two passes for no yards, credited with one sack and recovered one fumble.

TERRY, CHRIS   OT   PANTHERS

PERSONAL: Born August 8, 1975, in Jacksonville. ... 6-5/295. ... Full name: Christopher Alexander Terry.
HIGH SCHOOL: Jean Ribault (Jacksonville).
COLLEGE: Georgia.
TRANSACTIONS/CAREER NOTES: Selected by Carolina Panthers in second round (34th pick overall) of 1999 NFL draft. ... Signed by Panthers (May 24, 1999).
PLAYING EXPERIENCE: Carolina NFL, 1999-2001. ... Games/Games started: 1999 (16/16), 2000 (16/16), 2001 (15/15). Total: 47/47.
PRO STATISTICS: 1999—Recovered two fumbles.

TERRY, TIM   LB   SEAHAWKS

PERSONAL: Born July 26, 1974, in Hempstead, N.Y. ... 6-2/243.
HIGH SCHOOL: Hempstead (N.Y.).
COLLEGE: Temple.
TRANSACTIONS/CAREER NOTES: Signed as non-drafted free agent by Cincinnati Bengals (April 25, 1997). ... Released by Bengals (August 24, 1997). ... Re-signed by Bengals to practice squad (August 26, 1997). ... Activated (September 27, 1997). ... On injured reserve with knee

injury (December 8, 1997-remainder of season). ... Released by Bengals (August 19, 1998). ... Re-signed by Bengals to practice squad (December 16, 1998). ... Claimed on waivers by Kansas City Chiefs (August 10, 1999). ... Released by Chiefs (August 31, 1999). ... Re-signed by Chiefs (March 6, 2000). ... Released by Chiefs (August 27, 2000). ... Signed by Seattle Seahawks to practice squad (August 30, 2000). ... Activated (November 10, 2000). ... Granted free agency (March 1, 2002). ... Re-signed by Seahawks (May 2, 2002).
PLAYING EXPERIENCE: Cincinnati NFL, 1997; Seattle NFL, 2000 and 2001. ... Games/Games started: 1997 (5/0), 2000 (6/0), 2001 (16/0). Total: 27/0.
PRO STATISTICS: 2001—Credited with 2½ sacks.

TESTAVERDE, VINNY QB JETS

PERSONAL: Born November 13, 1963, in Brooklyn, N.Y. ... 6-5/235. ... Full name: Vincent Frank Testaverde. ... Name pronounced TESS-tuh-VER-dee.
HIGH SCHOOL: Sewanhaka (Floral Park, N.Y.), then Fork Union (Va.) Military Academy.
COLLEGE: Miami (Fla.).
TRANSACTIONS/CAREER NOTES: Signed by Tampa Bay Buccaneers (April 3, 1987). ... Selected officially by Buccaneers in first round (first pick overall) of 1987 NFL draft. ... On injured reserve with ankle injury (December 20, 1989-remainder of season). ... Granted unconditional free agency (March 1, 1993). ... Signed by Cleveland Browns (March 31, 1993). ... Browns franchise moved to Baltimore and renamed Ravens for 1996 season (March 11, 1996). ... Released by Ravens (June 2, 1998). ... Signed by New York Jets (June 24, 1998). ... Granted free agency (February 12, 1999). ... Re-signed by Jets (March 1, 1999). ... On injured reserve with torn Achilles' tendon (September 13, 1999-remainder of season).
CHAMPIONSHIP GAME EXPERIENCE: Played in AFC championship game (1998 season).
HONORS: Named quarterback on THE SPORTING NEWS college All-America second team (1985). ... Heisman Trophy winner (1986). ... Named College Football Player of the Year by THE SPORTING NEWS (1986). ... Maxwell Award winner (1986). ... Davey O'Brien Award winner (1986). ... Named quarterback on THE SPORTING NEWS college All-America first team (1986). ... Played in Pro Bowl (1996 and 1998 seasons).
PRO STATISTICS: 1987—Fumbled seven times and recovered four fumbles for minus three yards. 1988—Fumbled eight times and recovered two fumbles. 1989—Fumbled four times and recovered two fumbles. 1990—Caught one pass for three yards, fumbled 10 times and recovered three fumbles. 1991—Fumbled five times and recovered three fumbles. 1992—Fumbled four times and recovered four fumbles for minus eight yards. 1993—Fumbled four times. 1994—Fumbled three times and recovered two fumbles for two yards. 1995—Caught one pass for seven yards and fumbled four times for minus four yards. 1996—Fumbled nine times for minus 11 yards. 1997—Caught one pass for minus four yards, fumbled 11 times and recovered five fumbles for minus nine yards. 1998—Fumbled seven times and recovered three fumbles for minus six yards. 2000—Fumbled seven times for minus five yards. 2001—Fumbled 12 times and recovered five fumbles for minus 28 yards.
SINGLE GAME HIGHS (regular season): Attempts—69 (December 24, 2000, vs. Baltimore); completions—42 (December 6, 1998, vs. Seattle); yards—481 (December 24, 2000, vs. Baltimore); and touchdown passes—5 (October, 23, 2000, vs. Miami).
STATISTICAL PLATEAUS: 300-yard passing games: 1987 (1), 1988 (4), 1989 (4), 1991 (1), 1992 (1), 1993 (1), 1995 (2), 1996 (5), 1997 (3), 1998 (1), 2000 (2). Total: 25. ... 100-yard rushing games: 1990 (1).
MISCELLANEOUS: Regular-season record as starting NFL quarterback: 79-98-1 (.446). ... Postseason record as starting NFL quarterback: 2-3 (.400). ... Holds Tampa Bay Buccaneers all-time records for most yards passing (14,820) and most touchdown passes (77). ... Holds Baltimore Ravens all-time records for most yards passing (7,148) and most touchdown passes (51).

				PASSING							RUSHING				TOTALS		
Year Team	G	GS	Att.	Cmp.	Pct.	Yds.	TD	Int.	Avg.	Rat.	Att.	Yds.	Avg.	TD	TD	2pt.	Pts.
1987—Tampa Bay NFL	6	4	165	71	43.0	1081	5	6	6.55	60.2	13	50	3.8	1	1	0	6
1988—Tampa Bay NFL	15	15	466	222	47.6	3240	13	*35	6.95	48.8	28	138	4.9	1	1	0	6
1989—Tampa Bay NFL	14	14	480	258	53.8	3133	20	†22	6.53	68.9	25	139	5.6	0	0	0	0
1990—Tampa Bay NFL	14	13	365	203	55.6	2818	17	∞18	‡7.72	75.6	38	280	7.4	1	1	0	6
1991—Tampa Bay NFL	13	12	326	166	50.9	1994	8	15	6.12	59.0	32	101	3.2	0	0	0	0
1992—Tampa Bay NFL	14	14	358	206	57.5	2554	14	16	7.13	74.2	36	197	5.5	2	2	0	12
1993—Cleveland NFL	10	6	230	130	56.5	1797	14	9	‡7.81	85.7	18	74	4.1	0	0	0	0
1994—Cleveland NFL	14	13	376	207	55.1	2575	16	18	6.85	70.7	21	37	1.8	2	2	0	12
1995—Cleveland NFL	13	12	392	241	61.5	2883	17	10	7.35	87.8	18	62	3.4	2	2	0	12
1996—Baltimore NFL	16	16	549	325	59.2	4177	§33	19	7.61	88.7	34	188	5.5	2	2	1	14
1997—Baltimore NFL	13	13	470	271	57.7	2971	18	15	6.32	75.9	34	138	4.1	0	0	0	0
1998—New York Jets NFL	14	13	421	259	61.5	3256	§29	7	7.73	§101.6	24	104	4.3	1	1	0	6
1999—New York Jets NFL	1	1	15	10	66.7	96	1	1	6.40	78.8	0	0	0.0	0	0	0	0
2000—New York Jets NFL	16	16	*590	328	55.6	3732	21	25	6.33	69.0	25	32	1.3	0	0	0	0
2001—New York Jets NFL	16	16	441	260	59.0	2752	15	14	6.24	75.3	31	25	0.8	0	0	0	0
Pro totals (15 years)	189	178	5644	3157	55.9	39059	241	230	6.92	74.8	377	1565	4.2	12	12	1	74

THIBODEAUX, KEITH CB PACKERS

PERSONAL: Born May 16, 1974, in Opelousas, La. ... 5-11/189. ... Full name: Keith Trevis Thibodeaux. ... Name pronounced TEE-bo-do.
HIGH SCHOOL: Beau Chene (Opelousas, La.).
COLLEGE: Northwestern (La.) State.
TRANSACTIONS/CAREER NOTES: Selected by Washington Redskins in fifth round (140th pick overall) of 1997 NFL draft. ... Signed by Redskins (May 28, 1997). ... Released by Redskins (August 25, 1998). ... Signed by Atlanta Falcons (February 5, 1999). ... Released by Falcons (November 2, 1999). ... Signed by Minnesota Vikings (November 4, 1999). ... On injured reserve with shoulder injury (December 23, 1999-remainder of season). ... Released by Vikings (February 19, 2001). ... Re-signed by Vikings (July 27, 2001). ... Released by Vikings (October 15, 2001). ... Signed by Green Bay Packers (October 29, 2001). ... Released by Packers (November 13, 2001). ... Re-signed by Packers (November 19, 2001).
PLAYING EXPERIENCE: Washington NFL, 1997; Atlanta (8)-Minnesota (3) NFL, 1999, Minnesota NFL, 2000; Minnesota (5)-Green Bay (7) NFL, 2001. ... Games/Games started: 1997 (15/0), 1999 (Atl.-8/0; Min.-3/0; Total: 11/0), 2000 (16/0), 2001 (Min.-5/1; G.B.-7/0; Total: 12/1). Total: 54/1.
CHAMPIONSHIP GAME EXPERIENCE: Played in NFC championship game (2000 season).
PRO STATISTICS: 2000—Intercepted one pass for no yards. 2001—Intercepted one pass for nine yards.

THIERRY, JOHN　　　　　　DE　　　　　　　　　　FALCONS

PERSONAL: Born September 4, 1971, in Houston. ... 6-4/262. ... Full name: John Fitzgerald Thierry. ... Name pronounced Theory.
HIGH SCHOOL: Plaisance (Opelousas, La.).
COLLEGE: Alcorn State.
TRANSACTIONS/CAREER NOTES: Selected by Chicago Bears in first round (11th pick overall) of 1994 NFL draft. ... Signed by Bears (June 21, 1994). ... On injured reserve with knee injury (November 5, 1997-remainder of season). ... Granted unconditional free agency (February 12, 1999). ... Signed by Cleveland Browns (February 26, 1999). ... Granted unconditional free agency (February 11, 2000). ... Signed by Green Bay Packers (February 17, 2000). ... On injured reserve with knee injury (January 2, 2002-remainder of season). ... Released by Packers (February 27, 2002). ... Signed by Atlanta Falcons (March 27, 2002).
PRO STATISTICS: 1994—Returned one kickoff for no yards. 1995—Recovered four fumbles. 1998—Intercepted one pass for 14 yards and credited with a safety. 1999—Intercepted one pass for eight yards. 2001—Recovered two fumbles and credited with a safety.

Year Team	G	GS	SACKS
1994—Chicago NFL	16	1	0.0
1995—Chicago NFL	16	7	4.0
1996—Chicago NFL	16	2	2.0
1997—Chicago NFL	9	9	3.0
1998—Chicago NFL	16	9	3.5
1999—Cleveland NFL	16	10	7.0
2000—Green Bay NFL	16	16	6.5
2001—Green Bay NFL	12	12	3.5
Pro totals (8 years)	117	66	29.5

THOMAS, ADALIUS　　　　　DE　　　　　　　　　　RAVENS

PERSONAL: Born August 17, 1977, in Equality, Ala. ... 6-2/270. ... Full name: Adalius Donquail Thomas.
HIGH SCHOOL: Central Coosa (Equality, Ala.).
COLLEGE: Southern Mississippi.
TRANSACTIONS/CAREER NOTES: Selected by Baltimore Ravens in sixth round (186th pick overall) of 2000 NFL draft. ... Signed by Ravens (July 6, 2000).
PLAYING EXPERIENCE: Baltimore NFL, 2000 and 2001. ... Games/Games started: 2000 (3/0); 2001 (16/3). Total: 19/3.
CHAMPIONSHIP GAME EXPERIENCE: Played in AFC championship game (2000 season). ... Member of Super Bowl championship team (2000 season); inactive.
HONORS: Named defensive end on THE SPORTING NEWS college All-America second team (1999).
PRO STATISTICS: 2001—Credited with $3^1/_2$ sacks.

THOMAS, ANTHONY　　　　　RB　　　　　　　　　　BEARS

PERSONAL: Born November 11, 1977, in Winnfield, La. ... 6-2/227. ... Full name: Anthony Jermaine Thomas.
HIGH SCHOOL: Winnfield (La.).
COLLEGE: Michigan (degree in sports management and communications).
TRANSACTIONS/CAREER NOTES: Selected by Chicago Bears in second round (38th pick overall) of 2001 NFL draft. ... Signed by Bears (July 20, 2001).
HONORS: Named running back to THE SPORTING NEWS college All-America third team (2000).
PRO STATISTICS: 2001—Recovered one fumble.
SINGLE GAME HIGHS (regular season): Attempts—33 (January 6, 2002, vs. Jacksonville); yards—188 (October 21, 2001, vs. Cincinnati); and rushing touchdowns—1 (January 6, 2002, vs. Jacksonville).
STATISTICAL PLATEAUS: 100-yard rushing games: 2001 (4).

			RUSHING				RECEIVING				TOTALS		
Year Team	G	GS	Att.	Yds.	Avg.	TD	No.	Yds.	Avg.	TD	TD	2pt.	Pts.	Fum.
2001—Chicago NFL	14	10	278	1183	4.3	7	22	178	8.1	0	7	1	44	0

THOMAS, CHRIS　　　　　　WR

PERSONAL: Born July 16, 1971, in Burbank, Calif. ... 6-0/190. ... Full name: Chris Eric Thomas.
HIGH SCHOOL: Ventura (Calif.).
COLLEGE: Cal Poly-SLO (degree in English, 1994).
TRANSACTIONS/CAREER NOTES: Signed as non-drafted free agent by San Diego Chargers (May 6, 1993). ... Released by Chargers (August 30, 1993). ... Re-signed by Chargers to practice squad (September 1, 1993). ... Granted free agency after 1993 season. ... Signed by San Francisco 49ers (May 16, 1995). ... Released by 49ers (February 15, 1996). ... Re-signed by 49ers (May 15, 1996). ... Released by 49ers (August 20, 1996). ... Selected by Rhein Fire in 1997 World League draft (February 17, 1997). ... Signed by Washington Redskins (February 25, 1997). ... Released by Redskins (August 19, 1997). ... Re-signed by Redskins (August 21, 1997). ... Released by Redskins (August 23, 1997). ... Re-signed by Redskins (September 22, 1997). ... Granted free agency (February 12, 1999). ... Re-signed by Redskins (April 23, 1999). ... Released by Redskins (September 21, 1999). ... Signed by St. Louis Rams (October 20, 1999). ... Granted unconditional free agency (February 11, 2000). ... Signed by Minnesota Vikings (February 29, 2000). ... Released by Vikings (August 19, 2000). ... Signed by Rams (August 21, 2000). ... Granted unconditional free agency (March 2, 2001). ... Signed by Kansas City Chiefs (April 1, 2001). ... Released by Chiefs (December 3, 2001).
CHAMPIONSHIP GAME EXPERIENCE: Member of Rams for NFC championship game (1999 season); inactive. ... Member of Super Bowl championship team (1999 season); inactive.
PRO STATISTICS: 1995—Returned one punt for 25 yards and returned three kickoffs for 49 yards. 1998—Recovered one fumble. 2000—Recovered one fumble.
SINGLE GAME HIGHS (regular season): Receptions—4 (September 30, 2001, vs. Washington); yards—62 (September 23, 2001, vs. New York Giants); and touchdown receptions—1 (September 30, 2001, vs. Washington).

Year Team	G	GS	RECEIVING No.	Yds.	Avg.	TD	TOTALS TD	2pt.	Pts.	Fum.
1993—San Diego NFL							Did not play.			
1994—							Did not play.			
1995—San Francisco NFL	15	0	6	73	12.2	0	0	0	0	0
1996—							Did not play.			
1997—Washington NFL	13	0	11	93	8.5	0	0	0	0	0
1998—Washington NFL	14	0	14	173	12.4	0	0	0	0	0
1999—Washington NFL	2	0	0	0	0.0	0	0	0	0	0
—St. Louis NFL	6	0	1	6	6.0	0	0	0	0	0
2000—St. Louis NFL	16	0	0	0	0.0	0	0	0	0	0
2001—Kansas City NFL	10	5	19	247	13.0	1	1	0	6	0
Pro totals (6 years)	76	5	51	592	11.6	1	1	0	6	0

THOMAS, DAVE   CB

PERSONAL: Born August 25, 1968, in Miami. ... 6-3/218. ... Full name: Dave G. Thomas.
HIGH SCHOOL: Miami Beach.
JUNIOR COLLEGE: Butler Community College (Kan.).
COLLEGE: Tennessee.
TRANSACTIONS/CAREER NOTES: Selected by Dallas Cowboys in eighth round (203rd pick overall) of 1993 NFL draft. ... Signed by Cowboys (July 15, 1993). ... Selected by Jacksonville Jaguars from Cowboys in NFL expansion draft (February 15, 1995). ... Granted free agency (February 16, 1996). ... Re-signed by Jaguars (June 3, 1996). ... On injured reserve with broken leg (October 29, 1996-remainder of season). ... Granted unconditional free agency (February 14, 1997). ... Re-signed by Jaguars (March 3, 1997). ... Granted unconditional free agency (February 11, 2000). ... Signed by New York Giants (April 10, 2000). ... Released by Giants (February 28, 2002).
CHAMPIONSHIP GAME EXPERIENCE: Played in NFC championship game (1993, 1994 and 2000 seasons). ... Member of Super Bowl championship team (1993 season). ... Played in AFC championship game (1999 season). ... Played in Super Bowl XXXV (2000 season).
PRO STATISTICS: 1995—Recovered one fumble. 1996—Returned one punt for one yard and fumbled once. 1997—Recovered one fumble. 1998—Recovered one fumble.

Year Team	G	GS	INTERCEPTIONS No.	Yds.	Avg.	TD
1993—Dallas NFL	12	0	0	0	0.0	0
1994—Dallas NFL	16	0	0	0	0.0	0
1995—Jacksonville NFL	16	2	0	0	0.0	0
1996—Jacksonville NFL	9	5	2	7	3.5	0
1997—Jacksonville NFL	16	15	2	34	17.0	0
1998—Jacksonville NFL	14	13	1	0	0.0	0
1999—Jacksonville NFL	15	0	2	36	18.0	0
2000—New York Giants NFL	16	16	1	0	0.0	0
2001—New York Giants NFL	16	2	1	3	3.0	0
Pro totals (9 years)	130	53	9	80	8.9	0

THOMAS, EDWARD   LB   JAGUARS

PERSONAL: Born September 27, 1974, in Thomasville, Ga. ... 6-1/229. ... Full name: Edward Tervin Thomas.
HIGH SCHOOL: C.L. Harper (Atlanta).
COLLEGE: Georgia Southern.
TRANSACTIONS/CAREER NOTES: Signed by Montreal Alouettes of CFL (May 9, 1997). ... Released by Alouettes (June 20, 1997). ... Re-signed by Alouettes (July 14, 1997). ... Signed as non-drafted free agent by San Francisco 49ers (June 7, 2000). ... Released by 49ers (September 19, 2000). ... Re-signed by 49ers to practice squad (September 21, 2001). ... Activated (October 14, 2000). ... Released by 49ers (November 2, 2000). ... Re-signed by 49ers to practice squad (November 7, 2000). ... Released by 49ers (November 14, 2000). ... Signed by Jacksonville Jaguars to practice squad (November 21, 2000). ... Activated (November 29, 2000). ... Released by Jaguars (March 1, 2001). ... Re-signed by Jaguars (April 2, 2001).
PRO STATISTICS: CFL 1997: Recovered one fumble for three yards.

Year Team	G	GS	INTERCEPTIONS No.	Yds.	Avg.	TD	SACKS No.
1997—Montreal CFL	7	...	1	0	0.0	0	1.0
1998—Montreal CFL	3	...	0	0	0.0	0	0.0
1999—Montreal CFL	12	...	0	0	0.0	0	2.0
2000—San Francisco NFL	4	0	0	0	0.0	0	0.0
—Jacksonville NFL	4	0	0	0	0.0	0	0.0
2001—Jacksonville NFL	16	4	0	0	0.0	0	0.0
CFL totals (3 years)	22	...	1	0	0.0	0	3.0
NFL totals (2 years)	24	4	0	0	0.0	0	0.0
Pro totals (5 years)	46	...	1	0	0.0	0	3.0

THOMAS, FRED   CB   SAINTS

PERSONAL: Born September 11, 1973, in Bruce, Miss. ... 5-9/172.
HIGH SCHOOL: Bruce (Miss.).
JUNIOR COLLEGE: Northwest Mississippi Community College.
COLLEGE: Mississippi Valley State (did not play football), then Mississippi, then Tennessee-Martin.
TRANSACTIONS/CAREER NOTES: Selected by Seattle Seahawks in second round (47th pick overall) of 1996 NFL draft. ... Signed by Seahawks (July 19, 1996). ... Granted free agency (February 12, 1999). ... Re-signed by Seahawks (May 27, 1999). ... On injured reserve with broken leg (September 17, 1999-remainder of season). ... Granted unconditional free agency (February 11, 2000). ... Signed by New Orleans Saints (February 14, 2000).
PLAYING EXPERIENCE: Seattle NFL, 1996-1999; New Orleans NFL, 2000 and 2001. ... Games/Games started: 1996 (15/0), 1997 (16/3), 1998 (15/2), 1999 (1/0), 2000 (11/0), 2001 (16/16). Total: 74/21.
PRO STATISTICS: 1998—Recovered one fumble. 2001—Intercepted one pass for no yards.

THOMAS, HOLLIS DT EAGLES

PERSONAL: Born January 10, 1974, in Abilene, Texas. ... 6-0/306.
HIGH SCHOOL: Sumner (St. Louis).
COLLEGE: Northern Illinois.
TRANSACTIONS/CAREER NOTES: Signed as non-drafted free agent by Philadelphia Eagles (April 26, 1996). ... On injured reserve with arm/shoulder injury (December 2, 1998-remainder of season). ... On injured reserve with foot injury (December 31, 2001-remainder of season).
PRO STATISTICS: 1997—Recovered one fumble. 1998—Recovered one fumble. 1999—Recovered one fumble for two yards. 2000—Recovered one fumble. 2001—Recovered one fumble.

Year Team	G	GS	SACKS
1996—Philadelphia NFL	16	5	1.0
1997—Philadelphia NFL	16	16	2.5
1998—Philadelphia NFL	12	12	5.0
1999—Philadelphia NFL	16	16	1.0
2000—Philadelphia NFL	16	16	4.0
2001—Philadelphia NFL	14	14	0.0
Pro totals (6 years)	**90**	**79**	**13.5**

THOMAS, JASON G RAVENS

PERSONAL: Born June 10, 1977, in Savannah, Ga. ... 6-3/300.
HIGH SCHOOL: A.E. Beach (Savannah, Ga.).
COLLEGE: South Carolina, then Hampton.
TRANSACTIONS/CAREER NOTES: Selected by San Diego Chargers in seventh round (222nd pick overall) of 2000 NFL draft. ... Signed by Chargers (July 19, 2000). ... Released by Chargers (August 27, 2000). ... Re-signed by Chargers to practice squad (August 29, 2000). ... Activated (December 23, 2000); did not play. ... Released by Chargers (September 2, 2001). ... Re-signed by Chargers to practice squad (September 4, 2001). ... Signed by Baltimore Ravens off Chargers practice squad (November 21, 2001); did not play.

THOMAS, JUQUA DE TITANS

PERSONAL: Born May 15, 1978, in Houston. ... 6-2/252. ... Full name: Juqua Demail Thomas.
HIGH SCHOOL: Aldine (Texas).
JUNIOR COLLEGE: Northeastern Oklahoma.
COLLEGE: Oklahoma State.
TRANSACTIONS/CAREER NOTES: Signed as non-drafted free agent by Tennessee Titans (April 27, 2001).
PLAYING EXPERIENCE: Tennessee NFL, 2001. ... Games/Games started: 2001 (7/0).

THOMAS, KIWAUKEE CB JAGUARS

PERSONAL: Born June 19, 1977, in Warner Robins, Ga. ... 5-11/190. ... Full name: Kiwaukee Sanchez Thomas. ... Name pronounced kee-WA-kee.
HIGH SCHOOL: Perry (Ga.).
COLLEGE: Georgia Southern.
TRANSACTIONS/CAREER NOTES: Selected by Jacksonville Jaguars in fifth round (159th pick overall) of 2000 NFL draft. ... Signed by Jaguars (May 25, 2000).
PLAYING EXPERIENCE: Jacksonville NFL, 2000 and 2001. ... Games/Games started: 2000 (16/3), 2001 (16/5). Total: 32/8.
PRO STATISTICS: 2000—Recovered one fumble. 2001—Credited with three sacks and recovered one fumble.

THOMAS, MARK DE

PERSONAL: Born May 6, 1969, in Lilburn, Ga. ... 6-5/265. ... Full name: Mark Andrew Thomas.
HIGH SCHOOL: Lilburn (Ga.).
COLLEGE: North Carolina State.
TRANSACTIONS/CAREER NOTES: Selected by San Francisco 49ers in fourth round (89th pick overall) of 1992 NFL draft. ... Signed by 49ers (July 16, 1992). ... On injured reserve with ankle injury (September 1-October 7, 1992). ... On practice squad (October 7-November 11, 1992). ... On injured reserve (November 11, 1992-remainder of season). ... Selected by Carolina Panthers from 49ers in NFL expansion draft (February 15, 1995). ... Granted free agency (February 17, 1995). ... On injured reserve with thumb injury (November 27, 1995-remainder of season). ... Granted unconditional free agency (February 16, 1996). ... Re-signed by Panthers (February 20, 1996). ... Granted unconditional free agency (February 14, 1997). ... Signed by Chicago Bears (March 30, 1997). ... Claimed on waivers by Indianapolis Colts (December 2, 1998). ... Granted unconditional free agency (February 12, 1999). ... Re-signed by Colts (February 12, 1999). ... Granted unconditional free agency (March 1, 2002).
CHAMPIONSHIP GAME EXPERIENCE: Member of 49ers for NFC championship game (1993 and 1994 seasons); inactive. ... Member of Super Bowl championship team (1994 season). ... Played in NFC championship game (1996 season).
PRO STATISTICS: 1993—Recovered one fumble. 1996—Recovered one fumble for 18 yards. 1997—Recovered one fumble. 1999—Recovered one fumble.

Year Team	G	GS	SACKS
1992—San Francisco NFL	\multicolumn{3}{c}{Did not play.}		
1993—San Francisco NFL	11	1	0.5
1994—San Francisco NFL	9	0	1.0
1995—Carolina NFL	10	0	2.0
1996—Carolina NFL	12	0	4.0
1997—Chicago NFL	16	7	4.5
1998—Chicago NFL	10	4	4.5
—Indianapolis NFL	4	1	1.0
1999—Indianapolis NFL	15	2	3.0
2000—Indianapolis NFL	14	1	5.0
2001—Indianapolis NFL	12	0	1.5
Pro totals (9 years)	**113**	**16**	**27.0**

THOMAS, ORLANDO   S

PERSONAL: Born October 21, 1972, in Crowley, La. ... 6-1/225.
HIGH SCHOOL: Crowley (La.).
COLLEGE: Southwestern Louisiana.
TRANSACTIONS/CAREER NOTES: Selected by Minnesota Vikings in second round (42nd pick overall) of 1995 NFL draft. ... Signed by Vikings (July 25, 1995). ... Granted unconditional free agency (February 12, 1999). ... Re-signed by Vikings (February 24, 1999). ... On injured reserve with shoulder injury (December 22, 1999-remainder of season). ... On injured reserve with leg injury (January 10, 2001-remainder of playoffs). ... Released by Vikings (February 21, 2002).
CHAMPIONSHIP GAME EXPERIENCE: Played in NFC championship game (1998 season).
PRO STATISTICS: 1995—Fumbled once and recovered four fumbles for 19 yards and one touchdown. 1996—Recovered one fumble. 1997—Fumbled once and recovered two fumbles for 26 yards and one touchdown. 1998—Credited with $1/2$ sack. 1999—Recovered one fumble. 2000—Returned one kickoff for 15 yards, credited with one sack and recovered two fumbles.

				INTERCEPTIONS				TOTALS		
Year Team	G	GS	No.	Yds.	Avg.	TD	TD	2pt.	Pts.	Fum.
1995—Minnesota NFL	16	11	*9	108	12.0	1	2	0	12	1
1996—Minnesota NFL	16	16	5	57	11.4	0	0	0	0	0
1997—Minnesota NFL	15	13	2	1	0.5	0	1	0	6	1
1998—Minnesota NFL	16	16	2	27	13.5	0	0	0	0	0
1999—Minnesota NFL	13	12	2	32	16.0	1	1	0	6	0
2000—Minnesota NFL	9	9	1	0	0.0	0	0	0	0	0
2001—Minnesota NFL	13	10	1	0	0.0	0	0	0	0	0
Pro totals (7 years)	98	87	22	225	10.2	2	4	0	24	2

THOMAS, RANDY   G   JETS

PERSONAL: Born January 19, 1976, in East Point, Ga. ... 6-4/301.
HIGH SCHOOL: Tri-Cities (East Point, Ga.).
JUNIOR COLLEGE: Copiah-Lincoln Junior College (Miss.).
COLLEGE: Mississippi State.
TRANSACTIONS/CAREER NOTES: Selected by New York Jets in second round (57th pick overall) of 1999 NFL draft. ... Signed by Jets (July 20, 1999).
PLAYING EXPERIENCE: New York Jets NFL, 1999-2001. ... Games/Games started: 1999 (16/16), 2000 (16/16), 2001 (13/13). Total: 45/45.
HONORS: Named offensive guard on THE SPORTING NEWS college All-America second team (1998).
PRO STATISTICS: 2001—Recovered one fumble.

THOMAS, ROBERT   FB   COWBOYS

PERSONAL: Born December 1, 1974, in Jacksonville, Ark. ... 6-1/273.
HIGH SCHOOL: Jacksonville (Ark.).
COLLEGE: Henderson State (Ark.).
TRANSACTIONS/CAREER NOTES: Signed as non-drafted free agent by Dallas Cowboys (February 24, 1998). ... Assigned by Cowboys to Rhein Fire in 1999 NFL Europe enhancement allocation program (February 22, 1999). ... Granted free agency (March 2, 2001). ... Re-signed by Cowboys (March 21, 2001). ... On injured reserve with ankle injury (October 22, 2001-remainder of season).
PLAYING EXPERIENCE: Dallas NFL, 1998-2001; Rhein NFLE, 1999. ... Games/Games started: 1998 (16/0), NFLE 1999 (games played unavailable), NFL 1999 (16/7), 2000 (16/15), 2001 (5/5). Total NFL: 53/27.
PRO STATISTICS: NFLE: 1999—Intercepted one pass for 13 yards. NFL: 1999—Rushed eight times for 35 yards and caught 10 passes for 64 yards. 2000—Rushed 15 times for 51 yards, caught 23 passes for 117 yards and two touchdowns, fumbled twice and recovered one fumble. 2001—Rushed six times for 40 yards, caught five passes for 19 yards and one touchdown and recovered one fumble.
SINGLE GAME HIGHS (regular season): Attempts—4 (December 19, 1999, vs. New York Jets); yards—28 (September 9, 2001, vs. Tampa Bay); and rushing touchdowns—0.
MISCELLANEOUS: Played linebacker (1998 and 1999).

THOMAS, RODNEY   RB   FALCONS

PERSONAL: Born March 30, 1973, in Trinity, Texas. ... 5-10/210. ... Full name: Rodney Dejuane Thomas.
HIGH SCHOOL: Groveton (Texas).
COLLEGE: Texas A&M.
TRANSACTIONS/CAREER NOTES: Selected by Houston Oilers in third round (89th pick overall) of 1995 NFL draft. ... Signed by Oilers (August 1, 1995). ... Oilers franchise moved to Tennessee for 1997 season. ... Granted free agency (February 13, 1998). ... Re-signed by Oilers (June 2, 1998). ... Oilers franchise renamed Tennessee Titans for 1999 season (December 26, 1998). ... Released by Titans (March 1, 2001). ... Signed by Atlanta Falcons (May 1, 2001).
CHAMPIONSHIP GAME EXPERIENCE: Played in AFC championship game (1999 season). ... Played in Super Bowl XXXIV (1999 season).
PRO STATISTICS: 2000—Recovered one fumble.
SINGLE GAME HIGHS (regular season): Attempts—25 (November 19, 1995 vs. Kansas City); yards—108 (November 5, 1995, vs. Cleveland); and rushing touchdowns—2 (December 24, 1995, vs. Buffalo).
STATISTICAL PLATEAUS: 100-yard rushing games: 1995 (2).

			RUSHING				RECEIVING				KICKOFF RETURNS				TOTALS		
Year Team	G	GS	Att.	Yds.	Avg.	TD	No.	Yds.	Avg.	TD	No.	Yds.	Avg.	TD	TD 2pt.	Pts.	Fum.
1995—Houston NFL	16	10	251	947	3.8	5	39	204	5.2	2	3	48	16.0	0	7 1	44	8
1996—Houston NFL	16	0	49	151	3.1	1	13	128	9.8	0	5	80	16.0	0	1 0	6	0
1997—Tennessee NFL	16	1	67	310	4.6	3	14	111	7.9	0	17	346	20.4	0	3 0	18	1
1998—Tennessee NFL	11	0	24	100	4.2	2	6	55	9.2	0	3	64	21.3	0	2 0	12	0
1999—Tennessee NFL	16	0	43	164	3.8	1	9	72	8.0	0	0	0	0.0	0	1 0	6	0
2000—Tennessee NFL	16	0	61	175	2.9	0	8	35	4.4	1	0	0	0.0	0	1 0	6	1
2001—Atlanta NFL	12	0	37	126	3.4	0	2	26	13.0	0	0	0	0.0	0	0 0	0	0
Pro totals (7 years)	103	11	532	1973	3.7	12	91	631	6.9	3	28	538	19.2	0	15 1	92	10

THOMAS, TRA — OT — EAGLES

PERSONAL: Born November 20, 1974, in De Land, Fla. ... 6-7/349. ... Full name: William Thomas III. ... Name pronounced TRAY.
HIGH SCHOOL: De Land (Fla.).
COLLEGE: Florida State.
TRANSACTIONS/CAREER NOTES: Selected by Philadelphia Eagles in first round (11th pick overall) of 1998 NFL draft. ... Signed by Eagles (June 19, 1998).
PLAYING EXPERIENCE: Philadelphia NFL, 1998-2001. ... Games/Games started: 1998 (16/16), 1999 (16/15), 2000 (16/16), 2001 (15/15). Total: 63/62.
CHAMPIONSHIP GAME EXPERIENCE: Played in NFC championship game (2001 season).
PRO STATISTICS: 1998—Recovered one fumble. 1999—Recovered one fumble.

THOMAS, WILLIAM — LB — RAIDERS

PERSONAL: Born August 13, 1968, in Amarillo, Texas. ... 6-2/223. ... Full name: William Harrison Thomas Jr.
HIGH SCHOOL: Palo Duro (Amarillo, Texas).
COLLEGE: Texas A&M.
TRANSACTIONS/CAREER NOTES: Selected by Philadelphia Eagles in fourth round (105th pick overall) of 1991 NFL draft. ... Signed by Eagles (July 17, 1991). ... Granted free agency (February 17, 1994). ... Re-signed by Eagles (July 23, 1994). ... Released by Eagles (March 23, 2000). ... Signed by Raiders (July 21, 2000). ... Granted unconditional free agency (March 2, 2001). ... Re-signed by Raiders (May 9, 2001).
CHAMPIONSHIP GAME EXPERIENCE: Played in AFC championship game (2000 season).
HONORS: Played in Pro Bowl (1995 and 1996 seasons).
POST SEASON RECORDS: Shares NFL postseason record for most touchdowns by interception return—1 (December 30, 1995, vs. Detroit).
PRO STATISTICS: 1991—Recovered one fumble. 1992—Recovered two fumbles for two yards. 1993—Recovered three fumbles. 1995—Recovered one fumble. 1996—Recovered one fumble for 23 yards and a touchdown. 1997—Recovered one fumble for 37 yards and a touchdown. 1998—Blocked a punt out of end zone for a safety. 1999—Recovered one fumble for nine yards. 2001—Recovered two fumbles for 11 yards.

				INTERCEPTIONS				SACKS
Year Team		G	GS	No.	Yds.	Avg.	TD	No.
1991—Philadelphia NFL		16	7	0	0	0.0	0	2.0
1992—Philadelphia NFL		16	15	2	4	2.0	0	1.5
1993—Philadelphia NFL		16	16	2	39	19.5	0	6.5
1994—Philadelphia NFL		16	16	1	7	7.0	0	6.0
1995—Philadelphia NFL		16	16	7	104	14.9	1	2.0
1996—Philadelphia NFL		16	16	3	47	15.7	0	5.5
1997—Philadelphia NFL		14	14	2	11	5.5	0	5.0
1998—Philadelphia NFL		16	16	1	21	21.0	0	2.0
1999—Philadelphia NFL		14	13	0	0	0.0	0	2.5
2000—Oakland NFL		16	16	6	68	11.3	1	1.0
2001—Oakland NFL		16	15	3	46	15.3	0	3.0
Pro totals (11 years)		172	160	27	347	12.9	2	37.0

THOMAS, ZACH — LB — DOLPHINS

PERSONAL: Born September 1, 1973, in Pampa, Texas. ... 5-11/235. ... Full name: Zach Michael Thomas.
HIGH SCHOOL: White Deer (Texas), then Pampa (Texas).
COLLEGE: Texas Tech.
TRANSACTIONS/CAREER NOTES: Selected by Miami Dolphins in fifth round (154th pick overall) of 1996 NFL draft. ... Signed by Dolphins (July 10, 1996). ... Granted free agency (February 12, 1999). ... Re-signed by Dolphins (February 12, 1999).
HONORS: Named linebacker on THE SPORTING NEWS college All-America second team (1994). ... Named linebacker on THE SPORTING NEWS college All-America first team (1995). ... Played in Pro Bowl (1999 and 2000 seasons).
PRO STATISTICS: 1996—Returned one kickoff for 17 yards and recovered two fumbles for seven yards. 1999—Returned one kickoff for 15 yards. 2000—Recovered one fumble.

				INTERCEPTIONS				SACKS
Year Team		G	GS	No.	Yds.	Avg.	TD	No.
1996—Miami NFL		16	16	3	64	21.3	1	2.0
1997—Miami NFL		15	15	1	10	10.0	0	0.5
1998—Miami NFL		16	16	3	21	7.0	▲2	2.0
1999—Miami NFL		16	16	1	0	0.0	0	1.0
2000—Miami NFL		11	11	1	0	0.0	0	1.5
2001—Miami NFL		15	15	2	51	25.5	1	3.0
Pro totals (6 years)		89	89	11	146	13.3	4	10.0

THOMASON, JEFF — TE — EAGLES

PERSONAL: Born December 30, 1969, in San Diego. ... 6-5/255. ... Full name: Jeffrey David Thomason.
HIGH SCHOOL: Corona Del Mar (Newport Beach, Calif.).
COLLEGE: Oregon (degree in psychology).
TRANSACTIONS/CAREER NOTES: Signed as non-drafted free agent by Cincinnati Bengals (April 29, 1992). ... On injured reserve with sprained knee (September 1- December 5, 1992). ... Released by Bengals (August 30, 1993). ... Re-signed by Bengals (September 15, 1993). ... Claimed on waivers by Green Bay Packers (August 2, 1994). ... Released by Packers (August 21, 1994). ... Re-signed by Packers (January 20, 1995). ... Granted unconditional free agency (February 13, 1998). ... Re-signed by Packers (March 17, 1998). ... Traded by Packers to Philadelphia Eagles for TE Kaseem Sinceno (March 16, 2000). ... Granted unconditional free agency (March 2, 2001). ... Re-signed by Eagles (May 25, 2001).

CHAMPIONSHIP GAME EXPERIENCE: Played in NFC championship game (1995-1997 and 2001 seasons). ... Member of Super Bowl championship team (1996 season). ... Played in Super Bowl XXXII (1997 season).
PRO STATISTICS: 1995—Returned one kickoff for 16 yards and recovered one fumble. 1996—Returned one kickoff for 20 yards. 2000—Returned one kickoff for 10 yards. 2001—Recovered one fumble.
SINGLE GAME HIGHS (regular season): Receptions—5 (September 1, 1997, vs. Chicago); yards—58 (September 1, 1997, vs. Chicago); and touchdown receptions—1 (November 26, 2000, vs. Washington).

				RECEIVING			TOTALS			
Year Team	G	GS	No.	Yds.	Avg.	TD	TD	2pt.	Pts.	Fum.
1992—Cincinnati NFL	4	0	2	14	7.0	0	0	0	0	0
1993—Cincinnati NFL	3	0	2	8	4.0	0	0	0	0	0
1994—						Did not play.				
1995—Green Bay NFL	16	1	3	32	10.7	0	0	0	0	0
1996—Green Bay NFL	16	1	3	45	15.0	0	0	0	0	0
1997—Green Bay NFL	13	1	9	115	12.8	1	1	0	6	1
1998—Green Bay NFL	16	2	9	89	9.9	0	0	0	0	0
1999—Green Bay NFL	14	2	14	140	10.0	2	2	0	12	0
2000—Philadelphia NFL	16	5	10	46	4.6	5	5	0	30	0
2001—Philadelphia NFL	14	0	5	33	6.6	0	0	0	0	0
Pro totals (9 years)	**112**	**12**	**57**	**522**	**9.2**	**8**	**8**	**0**	**48**	**1**

THOMPSON, DERRIUS — WR — REDSKINS

PERSONAL: Born July 5, 1977, in Dallas. ... 6-2/215. ... Full name: Derrius Damon Thompson. ... Cousin of Reyna Thompson, cornerback with Miami Dolphins (1986-88), New York Giants (1989-92) and New England Patriots (1993-94).
HIGH SCHOOL: Cedar Hill (Texas).
COLLEGE: Baylor.
TRANSACTIONS/CAREER NOTES: Signed as non-drafted free agent by Washington Redskins (April 21, 1999). ... Released by Redskins (September 4, 1999). ... Re-signed by Redskins to practice squad (September 6, 1999). ... Activated (November 16, 1999). ... Released by Redskins (August 27, 2000). ... Re-signed by Redskins to practice squad (August 28, 2000). ... Activated (September 8, 2000). ... Released by Redskins (September 18, 2000). ... Re-signed by Redskins to practice squad (November 16, 2000). ... Activated (December 18, 2000). ... Granted free agency (March 1, 2002).
PLAYING EXPERIENCE: Washington NFL, 1999-2001. ... Games/Games started: 1999 (1/0), 2000 (4/0), 2001 (16/0). Total: 21/0.
PRO STATISTICS: 2001—Caught three passes for 52 yards and one touchdown, returned three kickoffs for 17 yards and recovered one fumble.
SINGLE GAME HIGHS (regular season): Receptions—1 (November 18, 2001, vs. Denver); yards—31 (October 28, 2001, vs. New York Giants); and touchdown receptions—1 (October 28, 2001, vs. New York Giants).

THOMPSON, DONNEL — LB — COLTS

PERSONAL: Born February 17, 1978, in Madison, Wis. ... 6-0/234.
HIGH SCHOOL: West (Madison, Wis.).
COLLEGE: Wisconsin.
TRANSACTIONS/CAREER NOTES: Signed as non-drafted free agent by Pittsburgh Steelers (April 21, 2000). ... Released by Steelers (September 2, 2001). ... Signed by Indianapolis Colts to practice squad (September 3, 2001). ... Activated (December 15, 2001).
PLAYING EXPERIENCE: Pittsburgh NFL, 2000; Indianapolis NFL, 2001. ... Games/Games started: 2000 (8/0), 2001 (4/0). Total: 12/0.

THOMPSON, MICHAEL — OT — FALCONS

PERSONAL: Born February 11, 1977, in Savannah, Ga. ... 6-4/295. ... Full name: Michael Anthony Thompson.
HIGH SCHOOL: Windsor Forest (Savannah, Ga.).
COLLEGE: Tennessee State.
TRANSACTIONS/CAREER NOTES: Selected by Atlanta Falcons in fourth round (100th pick overall) of 2000 NFL draft. ... Signed by Falcons (May 16, 2000). ... On injured reserve with torn Achilles' tendon (October 10, 2000-remainder of season).
PLAYING EXPERIENCE: Atlanta NFL, 2000 and 2001. ... Games/Games started: 2000 (3/2), 2001 (2/1). Total: 5/3.

THOMPSON, RAYNOCH — LB — CARDINALS

PERSONAL: Born November 21, 1977, in Los Angeles. ... 6-3/217. ... Full name: Raynoch Joseph Thompson.
HIGH SCHOOL: St. Augustine (New Orleans).
COLLEGE: Tennessee.
TRANSACTIONS/CAREER NOTES: Selected by Arizona Cardinals in second round (41st pick overall) of 2000 NFL draft. ... Signed by Cardinals (June 21, 2000). ... On injured reserve with knee injury (December 15, 2000-remainder of season).
PLAYING EXPERIENCE: Arizona NFL, 2000 and 2001. ... Games/Games started: 2000 (11/9), 2001 (14/14). Total: 25/23.
PRO STATISTICS: 2001—Credited with $1/2$ sack.

THORNTON, JOHN — DT — TITANS

PERSONAL: Born October 2, 1976, in Philadelphia. ... 6-2/300. ... Full name: John Jason Thornton.
HIGH SCHOOL: Scotland (Pa.) School for Veterans' Children.
COLLEGE: West Virginia.
TRANSACTIONS/CAREER NOTES: Selected by Tennessee Titans in second round (52nd pick overall) of 1999 NFL draft. ... Signed by Titans (July 26, 1999). ... On injured reserve with shoulder injury (November 8, 2001-remainder of season). ... Granted free agency (March 1, 2002).
CHAMPIONSHIP GAME EXPERIENCE: Played in AFC championship game (1999 season). ... Played in Super Bowl XXXIV (1999 season).

PRO STATISTICS: 1999—Credited with a safety. 2000—Returned one kickoff for 16 yards and recovered one fumble.

Year Team	G	GS	SACKS
1999—Tennessee NFL	16	3	4.5
2000—Tennessee NFL	16	16	4.0
2001—Tennessee NFL	3	0	0.0
Pro totals (3 years)	**35**	**19**	**8.5**

THRASH, JAMES   WR   EAGLES

PERSONAL: Born April 28, 1975, in Denver. ... 6-0/200.
HIGH SCHOOL: Wewoka (Okla.).
COLLEGE: Missouri Southern.
TRANSACTIONS/CAREER NOTES: Signed as non-drafted free agent by Philadelphia Eagles (April 22, 1997). ... Released by Eagles (July 8, 1997). ... Signed by Washington Redskins (July 11, 1997). ... On injured reserve with shoulder injury (December 8, 1998-remainder of season). ... Granted free agency (February 11, 2000). ... Re-signed with Redskins (April 21, 2000). ... Granted unconditional free agency (March 2, 2001). ... Signed by Eagles (March 9, 2001).
CHAMPIONSHIP GAME EXPERIENCE: Played in NFC championship game (2001 season).
PRO STATISTICS: 1999—Rushed once for 37 yards. 2000—Rushed 10 times for 82 yards, returned 10 punts for 106 yards and recovered one fumble. 2001—Rushed six times for 57 yards and recovered one fumble.
SINGLE GAME HIGHS (regular season): Receptions—10 (September 23, 2001, vs. Seattle); yards—165 (September 23, 2001, vs. Seattle); and touchdown receptions—2 (November 11, 2001, vs. Minnesota).
STATISTICAL PLATEAUS: 100-yard receiving games: 2000 (2), 2001 (2). Total: 4.

			RECEIVING				KICKOFF RETURNS			TOTALS			
Year Team	G	GS	No.	Yds.	Avg.	TD	No.	Yds.	Avg.	TD	TD	2pt.	Pts.	Fum.
1997—Washington NFL	4	0	2	24	12.0	0	0	0	0.0	0	0	0	0	0
1998—Washington NFL	10	1	10	163	16.3	1	6	129	21.5	0	1	0	6	0
1999—Washington NFL	16	0	3	44	14.7	0	14	355	25.4	1	1	0	6	0
2000—Washington NFL	16	8	50	653	13.1	2	45	1000	22.2	0	2	0	12	1
2001—Philadelphia NFL	15	15	63	833	13.2	8	5	101	20.2	0	8	0	48	1
Pro totals (5 years)	**61**	**24**	**128**	**1717**	**13.4**	**11**	**70**	**1585**	**22.6**	**1**	**12**	**0**	**72**	**2**

THWEATT, BYRON   LB   TITANS

PERSONAL: Born March 21, 1977, in Petersburg, Va. ... 6-2/233.
HIGH SCHOOL: Mataoca (Chesterfield, Va.).
COLLEGE: Virginia.
TRANSACTIONS/CAREER NOTES: Signed as non-drafted free agent by Tampa Bay Buccaneers (April 23, 2001). ... Released by Buccaneers (September 2, 2001). ... Re-signed by Buccaneers to practice squad (October 17, 2001). ... Released by Buccaneers (October 24, 2001). ... Re-signed by Buccaneers to practice squad (October 31, 2001). ... Released by Buccaneers (November 6, 2001). ... Signed by Tennessee Titans to practice squad (November 8, 2001). ... Activated (November 28, 2001).
PLAYING EXPERIENCE: Tennessee NFL, 2001. ... Games/Games started: 2001 (5/0).

TILLMAN, PAT   S

PERSONAL: Born November 6, 1976, in Fremont, Calif. ... 5-11/199. ... Full name: Patrick Daniel Tillman.
HIGH SCHOOL: Leland (San Jose, Calif.).
COLLEGE: Arizona State (degree in marketing, 1997).
TRANSACTIONS/CAREER NOTES: Selected by Arizona Cardinals in seventh round (226th pick overall) of 1998 NFL draft. ... Signed by Cardinals for 1998 season. ... Granted free agency (March 2, 2001). ... Re-signed by Cardinals (April 27, 2001). ... Granted unconditional free agency (March 1, 2002).
PLAYING EXPERIENCE: Arizona NFL, 1998-2001. ... Games/Games started: 1998 (16/10), 1999 (16/1), 2000 (16/16), 2001 (12/12). Total: 60/39.
HONORS: Named outside linebacker on THE SPORTING NEWS college All-America first team (1997).
PRO STATISTICS: 1998—Credited with one sack. 1999—Rushed once for four yards, intercepted two passes for seven yards, returned three kickoffs for 33 yards, fumbled once and recovered one fumble. 2000—Intercepted one pass for 30 yards, credited with 1 1/2 sacks and recovered two fumbles.

TILLMAN, TRAVARES   S   BILLS

PERSONAL: Born October 8, 1977, in Lyons, Ga. ... 6-1/194. ... Full name: Travares Arastius Tillman.
HIGH SCHOOL: Toombs County (Lyons, Ga.).
COLLEGE: Georgia Tech.
TRANSACTIONS/CAREER NOTES: Selected by Buffalo Bills in second round (58th pick overall) of 2000 NFL draft. ... Signed by Bills (July 20, 2000).
PRO STATISTICS: 2001—Recovered one fumble for 17 yards.

			INTERCEPTIONS			
Year Team	G	GS	No.	Yds.	Avg.	TD
2000—Buffalo NFL	15	4	0	0	0.0	0
2001—Buffalo NFL	13	6	1	0	0.0	0
Pro totals (2 years)	**28**	**10**	**1**	**0**	**0.0**	**0**

TIMMERMAN, ADAM   G   RAMS

PERSONAL: Born August 14, 1971, in Cherokee, Iowa. ... 6-4/310. ... Full name: Adam Larry Timmerman.
HIGH SCHOOL: Washington (Cherokee, Iowa).
COLLEGE: South Dakota State (degree in agriculture business).
TRANSACTIONS/CAREER NOTES: Selected by Green Bay Packers in seventh round (230th pick overall) of 1995 NFL draft. ... Signed by Packers (June 2, 1995). ... Granted free agency (February 13, 1998). ... Re-signed by Packers (April 15, 1998). ... Granted unconditional free agency (February 12, 1999). ... Signed by St. Louis Rams (February 15, 1999).
PLAYING EXPERIENCE: Green Bay NFL, 1995-1998; St. Louis NFL, 1999-2001. ... Games/Games started: 1995 (13/0), 1996 (16/16), 1997 (16/16), 1998 (16/16), 1999 (16/16), 2000 (16/15), 2001 (16/16). Total: 109/95.
CHAMPIONSHIP GAME EXPERIENCE: Played in NFC championship game (1995-97, 1999 and 2001 seasons). ... Member of Super Bowl championship team (1996 and 1999 seasons). ... Played in Super Bowl XXXII (1997 season). ... Played in Super Bowl XXXVI (2001 season).
HONORS: Played in Pro Bowl (1999 season).
PRO STATISTICS: 1999—Recovered one fumble. 2001—Recovered one fumble.

TOBECK, ROBBIE   C/G   SEAHAWKS

PERSONAL: Born March 6, 1970, in Tarpon Springs, Fla. ... 6-4/298. ... Full name: Robert L. Tobeck.
HIGH SCHOOL: New Port Richey (Fla.).
COLLEGE: Washington State.
TRANSACTIONS/CAREER NOTES: Signed as non-drafted free agent by Atlanta Falcons (May 7, 1993). ... Released by Falcons (August 30, 1993). ... Re-signed by Falcons to practice squad (August 31, 1993). ... Activated (January 1, 1994). ... Granted unconditional free agency (February 11, 2000). ... Signed by Seattle Seahawks (March 20, 2000). ... On physically unable to perform list with knee injury (August 20-October 14, 2000).
PLAYING EXPERIENCE: Atlanta NFL, 1994-1999; Seattle NFL, 2000 and 2001. ... Games/Games started: 1994 (5/0), 1995 (16/16), 1996 (16/16), 1997 (16/15), 1998 (16/16), 1999 (15/15), 2000 (4/0), 2001 (16/16). Total: 104/94.
CHAMPIONSHIP GAME EXPERIENCE: Played in NFC championship game (1998 season). ... Played in Super Bowl XXXIII (1998 season).
PRO STATISTICS: 1996—Caught two passes for 15 yards and a touchdown. 1997—Recovered one fumble. 1998—Recovered one fumble for one yard. 1999—Recovered one fumble.

TODD, JOE   LB

PERSONAL: Born April 17, 1979, in Mansfield, Maine ... 6-0/225.
HIGH SCHOOL: Mansfield (Maine).
COLLEGE: Hofstra.
TRANSACTIONS/CAREER NOTES: Signed as non-drafted free agent by New York Jets (April 30, 2001). ... Released by Jets (September 18, 2001).
PLAYING EXPERIENCE: New York Jets NFL, 2001. ... Games/Games started: 2001 (1/0).

TOMLINSON, LaDAINIAN   RB   CHARGERS

PERSONAL: Born June 23, 1979, in Rosebud, Texas. ... 5-10/221.
HIGH SCHOOL: Waco University (Texas).
COLLEGE: Texas Christian.
TRANSACTIONS/CAREER NOTES: Selected by San Diego Chargers in first round (fifth pick overall) of 2001 draft. ... Signed by Chargers (August 23, 2001).
HONORS: Named running back on THE SPORTING NEWS college All-America third team (1999). ... Named running back on THE SPORTING NEWS college All-America first team (2000). ... Doak Walker Award winner (2000).
SINGLE GAME HIGHS (regular season): Attempts—36 (September 9, 2001, vs. Washington); yards—145 (December 23, 2001, vs. Kansas City); and rushing touchdowns—3 (September 30, 2001, vs. Cincinnati).
STATISTICAL PLATEAUS: 100-yard rushing games: 2001 (4).

				RUSHING				RECEIVING				TOTALS		
Year Team	G	GS	Att.	Yds.	Avg.	TD	No.	Yds.	Avg.	TD	TD	2pt.	Pts.	Fum.
2001—San Diego NFL	16	16	339	1236	3.6	10	59	367	6.2	0	10	0	60	8

TONGUE, REGGIE   S   SEAHAWKS

PERSONAL: Born April 11, 1973, in Baltimore. ... 6-0/203. ... Full name: Reginald Clinton Tongue.
HIGH SCHOOL: Lathrop (Fairbanks, Alaska).
COLLEGE: Oregon State.
TRANSACTIONS/CAREER NOTES: Selected by Kansas City Chiefs in second round (58th pick overall) of 1996 NFL draft. ... Signed by Chiefs (July 26, 1996). ... Granted unconditional free agency (February 11, 2000). ... Signed by Seattle Seahawks (February 22, 2000).
PRO STATISTICS: 1998—Recovered one fumble. 1999—Advanced a lateral from an intercepted pass 46 yards for a touchdown and recovered three fumbles for nine yards. 2001—Recovered two fumbles for 23 yards.

			INTERCEPTIONS				SACKS
Year Team	G	GS	No.	Yds.	Avg.	TD	No.
1996—Kansas City NFL	16	0	0	0	0.0	0	0.0
1997—Kansas City NFL	16	16	1	0	0.0	0	2.5
1998—Kansas City NFL	15	15	0	0	0.0	0	2.0
1999—Kansas City NFL	16	16	1	80	80.0	1	2.0
2000—Seattle NFL	16	6	0	0	0.0	0	0.0
2001—Seattle NFL	16	16	3	67	22.3	1	1.0
Pro totals (6 years)	95	69	5	147	29.4	2	7.5

TOOMER, AMANI   WR   GIANTS

PERSONAL: Born September 8, 1974, in Berkely, Calif. ... 6-3/208. ... Name pronounced uh-MAHN-ee.
HIGH SCHOOL: De La Salle Catholic (Concord, Calif.).
COLLEGE: Michigan.
TRANSACTIONS/CAREER NOTES: Selected by New York Giants in second round (34th pick overall) of 1996 NFL draft. ... Signed by Giants (July 21, 1996). ... On injured reserve with knee injury (October 31, 1996-remainder of season). ... Granted free agency (February 12, 1999). ... Re-signed by Giants (July 31, 1999).
CHAMPIONSHIP GAME EXPERIENCE: Played in NFC championship game (2000 season). ... Played in Super Bowl XXXV (2000 season).
PRO STATISTICS: 1996—Recovered two fumbles. 1998—Attempted one pass without a completion. 1999—Rushed once for four yards. 2000—Rushed five times for 91 yards and a touchdown and recovered one fumble. 2001—Rushed three times for eight yards and recovered one fumble.
SINGLE GAME HIGHS (regular season): Receptions—9 (October 28, 2001, vs. Washington); yards—193 (December 10, 2000, vs. Pittsburgh); and touchdown receptions—3 (December 5, 1999, vs. New York Jets).
STATISTICAL PLATEAUS: 100-yard receiving games: 1999 (4), 2000 (5), 2001 (2). Total: 11.

				RECEIVING				PUNT RETURNS				KICKOFF RETURNS				TOTALS		
Year Team	G	GS	No.	Yds.	Avg.	TD	No.	Yds.	Avg.	TD	No.	Yds.	Avg.	TD	TD	2pt.	Pts.	Fum.
1996—New York Giants NFL..	7	1	1	12	12.0	0	18	298	16.6	2	11	191	17.4	0	2	0	12	1
1997—New York Giants NFL..	16	0	16	263	16.4	1	47	455	9.7	∞1	0	0	0.0	0	2	0	12	0
1998—New York Giants NFL..	16	0	27	360	13.3	5	35	252	7.2	0	4	66	16.5	0	5	0	30	0
1999—New York Giants NFL..	16	16	79	1183	15.0	6	1	14	14.0	0	0	0	0.0	0	6	0	36	0
2000—New York Giants NFL..	16	15	78	1094	14.0	7	0	0	0.0	0	0	0	0.0	0	8	0	48	1
2001—New York Giants NFL..	16	14	72	1054	14.6	5	8	41	5.1	0	0	0	0.0	0	5	0	30	2
Pro totals (6 years)	87	46	273	3966	14.5	24	109	1060	9.7	3	15	257	17.1	0	28	0	168	4

TOSI, MAO   DE/DT   CARDINALS

PERSONAL: Born December 12, 1976, in Manuía, American Samoa. ... 6-6/341. ... Full name: Falemao Tosi.
HIGH SCHOOL: East Anchorage (Alaska).
JUNIOR COLLEGE: Butler County Community College (Kan.).
COLLEGE: Idaho.
TRANSACTIONS/CAREER NOTES: Selected by Arizona Cardinals in fifth round (136th pick overall) of 2000 NFL draft. ... Signed by Cardinals (June 16, 2000).
PLAYING EXPERIENCE: Arizona NFL, 2000 and 2001. ... Games/Games started: 2000 (15/10), 2001 (11/1). Total: 26/11.
PRO STATISTICS: 2001—Credited with one sack.

TOWNS, LESTER   LB   PANTHERS

PERSONAL: Born August 28, 1977, in Pasadena, Calif. ... 6-1/252. ... Full name: Lester Towns III.
HIGH SCHOOL: Pasadena (Calif.).
COLLEGE: Washington.
TRANSACTIONS/CAREER NOTES: Selected by Carolina Panthers in seventh round (221st pick overall) of 2000 NFL draft. ... Signed by Panthers (July 14, 2000).
PLAYING EXPERIENCE: Carolina NFL, 2000 and 2001. ... Games/Games started: 2000 (16/14), 2001 (16/15). Total: 32/29.
PRO STATISTICS: 2000—Recovered two fumbles. 2001—Intercepted one pass for no yards.

TOWNSEND, DESHEA   CB   STEELERS

PERSONAL: Born September 8, 1975, in Batesville, Miss. ... 5-10/191. ... Full name: Trevor Deshea Townsend.
HIGH SCHOOL: South Panola (Batesville, Miss.).
COLLEGE: Alabama.
TRANSACTIONS/CAREER NOTES: Selected by Pittsburgh Steelers in fourth round (117th pick overall) of 1998 NFL draft. ... Signed by Steelers (July 6, 1998). ... Granted free agency (March 2, 2001). ... Re-signed by Steelers (March 2, 2001). ... Granted unconditional free agency (March 1, 2002). ... Re-signed by Steelers (March 24, 2002).
PLAYING EXPERIENCE: Pittsburgh NFL, 1998-2001. ... Games/Games started: 1998 (12/0), 1999 (16/4), 2000 (16/0), 2001 (16/1). Total: 60/5.
CHAMPIONSHIP GAME EXPERIENCE: Played in AFC championship game (2001 season).
PRO STATISTICS: 2000—Credited with 3$\frac{1}{2}$ sacks. 2001—Intercepted two passes for seven yards and credited with two sacks.

TRAPP, JAMES   CB   RAVENS

PERSONAL: Born December 28, 1969, in Greenville, S.C. ... 6-0/190. ... Full name: James Harold Trapp.
HIGH SCHOOL: Lawton (Okla.).
COLLEGE: Clemson.
TRANSACTIONS/CAREER NOTES: Selected by Los Angeles Raiders in third round (72nd pick overall) of 1993 NFL draft. ... Signed by Raiders (July 13, 1993). ... Raiders franchise moved to Oakland (July 21, 1995). ... Granted free agency (February 16, 1996). ... Re-signed by Raiders (March 30, 1996). ... Granted unconditional free agency (February 12, 1999). ... Signed by Baltimore Ravens (April 23, 1999). ... Granted unconditional free agency (February 11, 2000). ... Re-signed by Ravens (March 16, 2000). ... On injured reserve with groin injury (January 16, 2002-remainder of 2001 playoffs). ... Granted unconditional free agency (March 1, 2002). ... Re-signed by Ravens (May 20, 2002).
PLAYING EXPERIENCE: Los Angeles Raiders NFL, 1993 and 1994; Oakland NFL, 1995-1998; Baltimore NFL, 1999-2001. ... Games/Games started: 1993 (14/2), 1994 (16/2), 1995 (11/3), 1996 (12/4), 1997 (16/16), 1998 (16/0), 1999 (16/0), 2000 (16/1), 2001 (10/4). Total: 130/31.
CHAMPIONSHIP GAME EXPERIENCE: Played in AFC championship game (2000 season). ... Member of Super Bowl championship team (2000 season).
PRO STATISTICS: 1993—Intercepted one pass for seven yards. 1994—Credited with one sack. 1995—Recovered one fumble. 1996—Intercepted one pass for 23 yards. 1997—Intercepted two passes for 24 yards and recovered two fumbles. 1999—Credited with one sack. 2000—Credited with two sacks. 2001—Intercepted one pass for 15 yards and credited with one sack.

TRAYLOR, KEITH — DT — BEARS

PERSONAL: Born September 3, 1969, in Little Rock, Ark. ... 6-2/330. ... Full name: Byron Keith Traylor. ... Cousin of Isaac Davis, guard with San Diego Chargers (1994-97) and New Orleans Saints (1997).
HIGH SCHOOL: Malvern (Ark.).
JUNIOR COLLEGE: Coffeyville (Kan.) Community College.
COLLEGE: Oklahoma, then Central Oklahoma.
TRANSACTIONS/CAREER NOTES: Selected by Denver Broncos in third round (61st pick overall) of 1991 NFL draft. ... Signed by Broncos for 1991 season. ... Released by Broncos (June 7, 1993). ... Signed by Los Angeles Raiders (June 1993). ... Released by Raiders (August 30, 1993). ... Signed by Green Bay Packers (September 14, 1993). ... Released by Packers (November 9, 1993). ... Signed by Kansas City Chiefs (January 7, 1994). ... Released by Chiefs (January 14, 1994). ... Re-signed by Chiefs (May 18, 1994). ... Released by Chiefs (August 28, 1994). ... Re-signed by Chiefs (February 28, 1995). ... Granted unconditional free agency (February 14, 1997). ... Signed by Broncos (March 10, 1997). ... Released by Broncos (March 14, 2001). ... Signed by Chicago Bears (March 24, 2001).
CHAMPIONSHIP GAME EXPERIENCE: Played in AFC championship game (1991, 1997 and 1998 seasons). ... Member of Super Bowl championship team (1997 and 1998 seasons).
PRO STATISTICS: 1992—Returned one kickoff for 13 yards. 1995—Recovered one fumble. 1997—Intercepted one pass for 62 yards and a touchdown. 1998—Recovered one fumble. 2000—Recovered one fumble. 2001—Intercepted one pass for 67 yards.

Year Team	G	GS	SACKS
1991—Denver NFL	16	2	0.0
1992—Denver NFL	16	3	1.0
1993—Green Bay NFL	5	0	0.0
1994—	Did not play.		
1995—Barcelona W.L.	8	3	0.0
—Kansas City NFL	16	0	1.5
1996—Kansas City NFL	15	2	1.0
1997—Denver NFL	16	16	2.0
1998—Denver NFL	15	14	2.0
1999—Denver NFL	15	15	1.5
2000—Denver NFL	16	16	1.0
2001—Chicago NFL	16	15	2.0
W.L. totals (1 year)	8	3	0.0
NFL totals (10 years)	146	83	12.0
Pro totals (11 years)	154	86	12.0

TREJO, STEPHEN — TE — LIONS

PERSONAL: Born November 20, 1977, in Mesa, Ariz. ... 6-2/258. ... Full name: Stephen Nicholas Trejo.
HIGH SCHOOL: Casa Grande (Ariz.).
COLLEGE: Arizona State.
TRANSACTIONS/CAREER NOTES: Signed as non-drafted free agent by Detroit Lions (April 27, 2001).
PLAYING EXPERIENCE: Detroit NFL, 2001. ... Games/Games started: 2001 (14/0).
PRO STATISTICS: 2001—Caught five passes for 61 yards.

TREU, ADAM — C — RAIDERS

PERSONAL: Born June 24, 1974, in Lincoln, Neb. ... 6-5/300. ... Name pronounced TRUE.
HIGH SCHOOL: Pius X (Lincoln, Neb.).
COLLEGE: Nebraska.
TRANSACTIONS/CAREER NOTES: Selected by Oakland Raiders in third round (72nd pick overall) of 1997 NFL draft. ... Signed by Raiders for 1997 season.
PLAYING EXPERIENCE: Oakland NFL, 1997-2001. ... Games/Games started: 1997 (16/0), 1998 (16/0), 1999 (16/0), 2000 (16/0), 2001 (16/14). Total: 80/14.
CHAMPIONSHIP GAME EXPERIENCE: Played in AFC championship game (2000 season).
PRO STATISTICS: 1999—Returned one kickoff for six yards and fumbled once.

TROTTER, JEREMIAH — LB — REDSKINS

PERSONAL: Born January 20, 1977, in Hooks, Texas. ... 6-1/261.
HIGH SCHOOL: Hooks (Texas).
COLLEGE: Stephen F. Austin State.
TRANSACTIONS/CAREER NOTES: Selected after junior season by Philadelphia Eagles in third round (72nd pick overall) of 1998 NFL draft. ... Signed by Eagles (July 14, 1998). ... Granted free agency (March 2, 2001). ... Re-signed by Eagles (April 27, 2001). ... Designated by Eagles as franchise player (February 21, 2002). ... Granted unconditional free agency (April 5, 2002). ... Signed by Washington Redskins (April 19, 2002).
PLAYING EXPERIENCE: Philadelphia NFL, 1998-2001. ... Games/Games started: 1998 (8/0), 1999 (16/16), 2000 (16/16), 2001 (16/16). Total: 56/48.
CHAMPIONSHIP GAME EXPERIENCE: Played in NFC championship game (2001 season).
HONORS: Played in Pro Bowl (2000 season).
PRO STATISTICS: 1999—Intercepted two passes for 30 yards, credited with $2^1/_2$ sacks and recovered one fumble. 2000—Intercepted one pass for 27 yards and a touchdown and credited with three sacks. 2001—Intercepted two passes for 64 yards and one touchdown, credited with $3^1/_2$ sacks and recovered one fumble.

TUCKER, REX   G   BEARS

PERSONAL: Born December 20, 1976, in Midland, Texas. ... 6-5/315. ... Full name: Rex Truman Tucker. ... Brother of Ryan Tucker, offensive tackle, Cleveland Browns.
HIGH SCHOOL: Robert E. Lee (Midland, Texas).
COLLEGE: Texas A&M.
TRANSACTIONS/CAREER NOTES: Selected in third round by Chicago Bears (66th pick overall) of 1999 NFL draft. ... Signed by Bears (July 21, 1999). ... Granted free agency (March 1, 2002).
PLAYING EXPERIENCE: Chicago NFL, 1999-2001. ... Games/Games started: 1999 (2/1), 2000 (6/0), 2001 (16/16). Total: 24/17.
PRO STATISTICS: 2000—Returned one kickoff for no yards.

TUCKER, ROSS   G   REDSKINS

PERSONAL: Born March 2, 1979, in Wyomissing, Pa. ... 6-4/305.
HIGH SCHOOL: Wyomissing (Pa.).
COLLEGE: Princeton.
TRANSACTIONS/CAREER NOTES: Signed as non-drafted free agent by Washington Redskins (April 25, 2001).
PLAYING EXPERIENCE: Washington NFL, 2001. ... Games/Games started: 2001 (3/0).

TUCKER, RYAN   OT   BROWNS

PERSONAL: Born June 12, 1975, in Midland, Texas. ... 6-5/305. ... Full name: Ryan Huey Tucker. ... Brother of Rex Tucker, guard, Chicago Bears.
HIGH SCHOOL: Robert E. Lee (Midland, Texas).
COLLEGE: Texas Christian.
TRANSACTIONS/CAREER NOTES: Selected by St. Louis Rams in fourth round (112th pick overall) of 1997 NFL draft. ... Signed by Rams (July 3, 1997). ... On physically unable to perform list with knee injury (August 19-October 29, 1997). ... Granted free agency (February 11, 2000). ... Tendered offer sheet by Miami Dolphins (February 17, 2000). ... Offer matched by Rams (February 22, 2000). ... Released by Rams (March 1, 2002). ... Signed by Cleveland Browns (March 7, 2002).
PLAYING EXPERIENCE: St. Louis NFL, 1997-2001. ... Games/Games started: 1997 (7/0), 1998 (5/0), 1999 (16/0), 2000 (16/16), 2001 (15/15). Total: 59/31.
CHAMPIONSHIP GAME EXPERIENCE: Played in NFC championship game (1999 and 2001 seasons). ... Member of Super Bowl championship team (1999 season). ... Played in Super Bowl XXXVI (2001 season).
PRO STATISTICS: 1999—Caught one pass for two yards and a touchdown. 2001—Recovered one fumble.

TUIASOSOPO, MARQUES   QB   RAIDERS

PERSONAL: Born March 22, 1979, in Woodinville, Wash. ... 6-1/220.
HIGH SCHOOL: Woodinville (Wash.).
COLLEGE: Washington.
TRANSACTIONS/CAREER NOTES: Selected by Oakland Raiders in second round (59th pick overall) of 2001 NFL draft. ... Signed by Raiders (July 21, 2001).
SINGLE GAME HIGHS (regular season): Attempts—4 (September 30, 2001, vs. Seattle); completions—3 (September 30, 2001, vs. Seattle); yards—34 (September 30, 2001, vs. Seattle); and touchdown passes—0.

				PASSING						RUSHING			TOTALS		
Year Team	G	GS	Att.	Cmp.	Pct.	Yds.	TD	Int.	Avg.	Rat.	Att.	Yds.	Avg.	TD	TD	2pt.	Pts.
2001—Oakland NFL	1	0	4	3	75.0	34	0	0	8.50	100.0	1	1	1.0	0	0	0	0

TUIPALA, JOE   LB   JAGUARS

PERSONAL: Born September 13, 1976, in Honolulu, Hawaii. ... 6-1/244. ... Full name: Joseph Lafaele Tuipala.
HIGH SCHOOL: Burroughs (Ridgecrest, Calif.).
COLLEGE: San Diego State.
TRANSACTIONS/CAREER NOTES: Signed as non-drafted free agent by Detroit Lions (May 5, 1999). ... Released by Lions (August 31, 1999). ... Signed by New Orleans Saints to practice squad (December 15, 1999). ... Activated (December 23, 1999); did not play. ... Released by Saints (August 27, 2000). ... Signed by Jacksonville Jaguars (April 20, 2001).
PLAYING EXPERIENCE: Jacksonville NFL, 2001. ... Games/Games started: 2001 (12/0).

TUITELE, MAUGAULA   LB   PATRIOTS

PERSONAL: Born May 26, 1978, in Torrance, Calif. ... 6-2/255. ... Full name: Maugaula Norman Tuitele.
HIGH SCHOOL: Pacific (Calif.).
COLLEGE: Colorado State.
TRANSACTIONS/CAREER NOTES: Signed as non-drafted free agent by New England Patriots (April 19, 2000). ... Released by Patriots (August 28, 2001). ... Re-signed by Patriots to practice squad (September 25, 2001). ... Released by Patriots (September 26, 2001). ... Re-signed by Patriots to practice squad (November 20, 2001). ... Activated (December 2, 2001). ... Released by Patriots (December 5, 2001). ... Re-signed by Patriots to practice squad (December 6, 2001). ... Released by Patriots (December 27, 2001). ... Signed by Tampa Bay Buccaneers to practice squad (December 27, 2001). ... Granted free agency after 2001 season. ... Signed by Patriots (February 11, 2002). ... Assigned by Patriots to Rhein Fire in NFL Europe enhancement allocation program (February 12, 2002).
PLAYING EXPERIENCE: New England NFL, 2000 and 2001. ... Games/Games started: 2000 (1/0), 2001 (1/0). Total: 2/0.

TUMAN, JERAME — TE — STEELERS

PERSONAL: Born March 24, 1976, in Liberal, Kan. ... 6-4/270. ... Full name: Jerame Dean Tuman. ... Name pronounced Jeremy TOO-man.
HIGH SCHOOL: Liberal (Kan.).
COLLEGE: Michigan.
TRANSACTIONS/CAREER NOTES: Selected by Pittsburgh Steelers in fifth round (136th pick overall) of 1999 NFL draft. ... Signed by Steelers (July 19, 1999). ... On injured reserve with knee injury (October 27, 1999-remainder of season). ... Granted free agency (March 1, 2002).
PLAYING EXPERIENCE: Pittsburgh NFL, 1999-2001. ... Games/Games started: 1999 (7/0), 2000 (16/1), 2001 (16/7). Total: 39/8.
CHAMPIONSHIP GAME EXPERIENCE: Played in AFC championship game (2001 season).
HONORS: Named tight end on The Sporting News college All-America third team (1997).
PRO STATISTICS: 2000—Returned one kickoff for minus one yard. 2001—Caught seven passes for 96 yards and one touchdown.
SINGLE GAME HIGHS (regular season): Receptions—1 (December 16, 2001, vs. Baltimore); yards—32 (October 21, 2001, vs. Tampa Bay); and touchdown receptions—1 (October 21, 2001, vs. Tampa Bay).

TUPA, TOM — P/QB — BUCCANEERS

PERSONAL: Born February 6, 1966, in Cleveland. ... 6-4/225. ... Full name: Thomas Joseph Tupa Jr.
HIGH SCHOOL: Brecksville (Broadview Heights, Ohio).
COLLEGE: Ohio State.
TRANSACTIONS/CAREER NOTES: Selected by Phoenix Cardinals in third round (68th pick overall) of 1988 NFL draft. ... Signed by Cardinals (July 12, 1988). ... Granted free agency (February 1, 1991). ... Re-signed by Cardinals (July 17, 1991). ... Granted unconditional free agency (February 1, 1992). ... Signed by Indianapolis Colts (March 31, 1992). ... Released by Colts (August 30, 1993). ... Signed by Cleveland Browns (November 9, 1993). ... Released by Browns (November 24, 1993). ... Re-signed by Browns (March 30, 1994). ... Granted unconditional free agency (February 16, 1996). ... Signed by New England Patriots (March 15, 1996). ... Granted unconditional free agency (February 12, 1999). ... Signed by New York Jets (February 15, 1999). ... Released by Jets (February 25, 2002). ... Signed by Tampa Bay Buccaneers (May 10, 2002).
CHAMPIONSHIP GAME EXPERIENCE: Played in AFC championship game (1996 season). ... Played in Super Bowl XXXI (1996 season).
HONORS: Played in Pro Bowl (1999 season).
PRO STATISTICS: 1988—Attempted six passes with four completions for 49 yards. 1989—Rushed 15 times for 75 yards, attempted 134 passes with 65 completions for 973 yards (three touchdowns and nine interceptions), fumbled twice and recovered one fumble for minus six yards. 1990—Rushed once for no yards and fumbled once for minus seven yards. 1991—Rushed 28 times for 97 yards and a touchdown, attempted 315 passes with 165 completions for 2,053 yards (six touchdowns and 13 interceptions), fumbled eight times and recovered two fumbles. 1992—Rushed three times for nine yards, attempted 33 passes with 17 completions for 156 yards (one touchdown and two interceptions), fumbled once and recovered one fumble for minus one yard. 1995—Rushed once for nine yards, attempted one pass with a completion for 25 yards. 1996—Attempted two passes without a completion. 1998—Rushed twice for minus two yards. 1999—Rushed twice for eight yards, attempted 11 passes with six completions for 165 yards and two touchdowns and fumbled once. 2001—Completed only pass attempt for nine yards.
STATISTICAL PLATEAUS: 300-yard passing games: 1991 (1).
MISCELLANEOUS: Regular-season starting record as starting NFL quarterback: 4-9 (.308).

				PUNTING			
Year Team	G	No.	Yds.	Avg.	Net avg.	In. 20	Blk.
1988—Phoenix NFL	2	0	0	0.0	.0	0	0
1989—Phoenix NFL	14	6	280	46.7	39.7	2	0
1990—Phoenix NFL	15	0	0	0.0	.0	0	0
1991—Phoenix NFL	11	0	0	0.0	.0	0	0
1992—Indianapolis NFL	3	0	0	0.0	.0	0	0
1993—Cleveland NFL				Did not play.			
1994—Cleveland NFL	16	80	3211	40.1	35.3	27	0
1995—Cleveland NFL	16	65	2831	43.6	36.2	18	0
1996—New England NFL	16	63	2739	43.5	36.0	14	0
1997—New England NFL	16	78	3569	§45.8	36.1	24	1
1998—New England NFL	16	74	3294	44.5	35.4	13	0
1999—New York Jets NFL	16	81	3659	45.2	38.2	25	0
2000—New York Jets NFL	16	83	3714	44.7	33.2	18	0
2001—New York Jets NFL	15	67	2575	38.4	32.0	21	0
Pro totals (13 years)	172	597	25872	43.3	35.4	162	1

TURK, MATT — P — JETS

PERSONAL: Born June 6, 1968, in Greenfield, Wis. ... 6-5/250. ... Brother of Dan Turk, center with five NFL teams (1985-99).
HIGH SCHOOL: Greenfield (Wis.).
COLLEGE: Wisconsin-Whitewater.
TRANSACTIONS/CAREER NOTES: Signed as non-drafted free agent by Green Bay Packers (July 13, 1993). ... Released by Packers (August 4, 1993). ... Signed by Los Angeles Rams (April 1994). ... Released by Rams (August 22, 1994). ... Signed by Washington Redskins (April 5, 1995). ... Traded by Redskins to Miami Dolphins for sevnth-round pick (traded to San Francisco) in 2001 draft (March 9, 2000). ... Granted unconditional free agency (March 1, 2002). ... Signed by New York Jets (April 23, 2002).
HONORS: Played in Pro Bowl (1996-1998 seasons). ... Named punter on The Sporting News NFL All-Pro team (1997).
PRO STATISTICS: 1996—Rushed once for no yards and fumbled once. 1997—Rushed once for no yards and fumbled once for minus 16 yards. 1998—Rushed twice for minus 12 yards and fumbled once. 1999—Fumbled once.

				PUNTING			
Year Team	G	No.	Yds.	Avg.	Net avg.	In. 20	Blk.
1995—Washington NFL	16	74	3140	42.4	37.7	†29	0
1996—Washington NFL	16	75	3386	*45.1	*39.2	25	0
1997—Washington NFL	16	84	3788	45.1	*39.2	32	1
1998—Washington NFL	16	93	4103	44.1	‡39.0	∞33	∞1
1999—Washington NFL	14	62	2564	41.4	35.6	16	0
2000—Miami NFL	16	92	3870	42.1	36.2	25	0
2001—Miami NFL	16	81	3321	41.0	37.6	28	0
Pro totals (7 years)	110	561	24172	43.1	37.8	188	2

TURLEY, KYLE   OT   SAINTS

PERSONAL: Born September 24, 1975, in Provo, Utah. ... 6-5/300. ... Full name: Kyle John Turley.
HIGH SCHOOL: Valley View (Moreno Valley, Calif.).
COLLEGE: San Diego State.
TRANSACTIONS/CAREER NOTES: Selected by New Orleans Saints in first round (seventh pick overall) of 1998 NFL draft. ... Signed by Saints (July 23, 1998).
PLAYING EXPERIENCE: New Orleans NFL, 1998-2001. ... Games/Games started: 1998 (15/15), 1999 (16/16), 2000 (16/16), 2001 (16/16). Total: 63/63.
HONORS: Named offensive tackle on THE SPORTING NEWS college All-America first team (1997).
PRO STATISTICS: 2000—Recovered four fumbles for minus six yards and caught one pass for 16 yards. 2001—Recovered two fumbles.

TURNER, NATE   WR   CHARGERS

PERSONAL: Born May 26, 1978, in Gardena, Calif. ... 6-3/210.
HIGH SCHOOL: Jordan (Compton, Calif.).
JUNIOR COLLEGE: Compton Community College.
COLLEGE: UNLV.
TRANSACTIONS/CAREER NOTES: Signed as non-drafted free agent by San Diego Chargers (May 1, 2001). ... Released by Chargers (September 2, 2001). ... Re-signed by Chargers to practice squad (September 4, 2001). ... Released by Chargers (December 14, 2001). ... Re-signed by Chargers to practice squad (December 19, 2001). ... Activated (December 22, 2001).
PLAYING EXPERIENCE: San Diego NFL, 2001. ... Games/Games started: 2001 (1/0).

TURNER, SCOTT   CB

PERSONAL: Born February 26, 1972, in Richardson, Texas. ... 5-10/180.
HIGH SCHOOL: J.J. Pearce (Richardson, Texas).
COLLEGE: Illinois (degree in speech communications, 1994).
TRANSACTIONS/CAREER NOTES: Selected by Washington Redskins in seventh round (226th pick overall) of 1995 NFL draft. ... Signed by Redskins (July 18, 1995). ... On injured reserve with ankle injury (December 11, 1997-remainder of season). ... Granted free agency (February 13, 1998). ... Re-signed by Redskins (April 30, 1998). ... Claimed on waivers by San Diego Chargers (August 31, 1998). ... Granted unconditional free agency (February 11, 2000). ... Re-signed by Chargers (April 3, 2000). ... Granted unconditional free agency (March 2, 2001). ... Re-signed by Chargers (December 5, 2001). ... Granted unconditional free agency (March 1, 2002).
PRO STATISTICS: 1995—Returned one punt for no yards, credited with one sack, fumbled once and recovered one fumble. 1996—Recovered one fumble in end zone for a touchdown. 1998—Credited with one sack. 1999—Returned one punt for no yards and recovered one fumble.

			INTERCEPTIONS			
Year Team	G	GS	No.	Yds.	Avg.	TD
1995—Washington NFL	16	0	1	0	0.0	0
1996—Washington NFL	16	0	2	16	8.0	0
1997—Washington NFL	9	0	0	0	0.0	0
1998—San Diego NFL	16	1	1	0	0.0	0
1999—San Diego NFL	15	0	0	0	0.0	0
2000—San Diego NFL	16	2	1	75	75.0	1
2001—San Diego NFL	4	1	0	0	0.0	0
Pro totals (7 years)	92	4	5	91	18.2	1

TURNER, T.J.   LB

PERSONAL: Born October 1, 1978, in Dayton, Ohio. ... 6-3/255.
HIGH SCHOOL: Hillsboro (Ohio).
COLLEGE: Michigan State.
TRANSACTIONS/CAREER NOTES: Selected by New England Patriots in seventh round (239th pick overall) of 2001 NFL draft. ... Signed by Patriots (July 5, 2001). ... Released by Patriots (November 10, 2001).
PLAYING EXPERIENCE: New England NFL, 2001. ... Games/Games started: 2001 (2/0).

TUTEN, MELVIN   OT   PANTHERS

PERSONAL: Born November 11, 1971, in Washington, D.C. ... 6-7/320. ... Full name: Melvin Eugene Tuten Jr.
HIGH SCHOOL: Woodrow Wilson (Washington, D.C.).
COLLEGE: Syracuse.
TRANSACTIONS/CAREER NOTES: Selected by Cincinnati Bengals in third round (69th pick overall) of 1995 NFL draft. ... Signed by Bengals (July 18, 1995). ... Released by Bengals (August 18, 1997). ... Signed by Denver Broncos (February 5, 1998). ... Released by Broncos (August 25, 1998). ... Re-signed by Broncos (December 30, 1998). ... Assigned by Broncos to Barcelona Dragons in 1999 NFL Europe enhancement allocation program (February 22, 1999). ... Released by Broncos (September 5, 1999). ... Re-signed by Broncos (November 10, 1999). ... Released by Broncos (August 27, 2000). ... Re-signed by Broncos (September 12, 2000). ... Released by Broncos (October 14, 2000). ... Re-signed by Broncos (October 16, 2000). ... Claimed on waivers by Carolina Panthers (October 23, 2001).
PLAYING EXPERIENCE: Cincinnati NFL, 1995 and 1996; Barcelona NFLE, 1999; Denver NFL, 1999; Carolina NFL, 2000 and 2001. ... Games/Games started: 1995 (16/2), 1996 (13/7), NFLE 1999 (games played unavailable), NFL 1999 (2/0), 2000 (2/0), 2001 (15/1). Total NFL: 51/10.
PRO STATISTICS: 1995—Caught two passes for 12 yards and one touchdown.

TYLSKI, RICH   G   PATRIOTS

PERSONAL: Born February 27, 1971, in San Diego. ... 6-4/308. ... Full name: Richard Lee Tylski. ... Name pronounced TILL-skee.
HIGH SCHOOL: Madison (San Diego).
COLLEGE: Utah State (degree in sociology, 1994).
TRANSACTIONS/CAREER NOTES: Signed as non-drafted free agent by New England Patriots (April 25, 1994). ... Released by Patriots (August 20, 1994). ... Re-signed by Patriots to practice squad (August 30, 1994). ... Claimed on waivers by Jacksonville Jaguars (July 26, 1995). ... Released by Jaguars (August 27, 1995). ... Re-signed by Jaguars to practice squad (August 28, 1995). ... Granted free agency (February 12, 1999). ... Re-signed by Jaguars (May 5, 1999). ... Granted unconditional free agency (February 11, 2000). ... Signed by Pittsburgh Steelers (February 28, 2000). ... Released by Steelers (April 22, 2002). ... Signed by Patriots (May 31, 2002).
PLAYING EXPERIENCE: Jacksonville NFL, 1996-1999; Pittsburgh NFL, 2000 and 2001. ... Games/Games started: 1996 (16/7), 1997 (13/13), 1998 (12/8), 1999 (10/8), 2000 (16/16), 2001 (12/9). Total: 79/61.
CHAMPIONSHIP GAME EXPERIENCE: Played in AFC championship game (1999 and 2001 seasons).

ULBRICH, JEFF   LB   49ERS

PERSONAL: Born February 17, 1977, in San Jose, Calif. ... 6-0/249.
HIGH SCHOOL: Live Oak (Morgan Hill, Calif.).
JUNIOR COLLEGE: Gavilan College (Calif.).
COLLEGE: San Jose State, then Hawaii.
TRANSACTIONS/CAREER NOTES: Selected by San Francisco 49ers in third round (86th pick overall) of 2000 NFL draft. ... Signed by 49ers (July 13, 2000). ... On injured reserve with shoulder injury (November 20, 2000-remainder of season).
PLAYING EXPERIENCE: San Francisco NFL, 2000 and 2001. ... Games/Games started: 2000 (4/0), 2001 (14/14). Total: 18/4.
PRO STATISTICS: 2001—Credited with $1/2$ sack.

ULMER, ARTIE   LB   FALCONS

PERSONAL: Born July 30, 1973, in Rincon, Ga. ... 6-3/247. ... Full name: Charles Artie Ulmer.
HIGH SCHOOL: Effingham County (Springfield, Ga.).
COLLEGE: Georgia Southern, then Valdosta (Ga.) State.
TRANSACTIONS/CAREER NOTES: Selected by Minnesota Vikings in seventh round (220th pick overall) of 1997 NFL draft. ... On suspended list for violating league substance abuse policy (August 19-September 23, 1997). ... Signed by Vikings (June 17, 1997). ... Assigned by Vikings to Frankfurt Galaxy in 1998 NFL Europe enhancement allocation program (February 18, 1998). ... Released by Vikings (August 24, 1998). ... Signed by Denver Broncos (January 14, 1999). ... On injured reserve with knee injury (November 4, 1999-remainder of season). ... Granted free agency (February 11, 2000). ... Signed by San Francisco 49ers to practice squad (September 14, 2000). ... Activated (September 19, 2000). ... Released by 49ers (February 19, 2001). ... Signed by Atlanta Falcons (April 16, 2001). ... Granted unconditional free agency (March 1, 2002). ... Re-signed by Falcons (March 22, 2002).
PLAYING EXPERIENCE: Frankfurt NFLE, 1998; Denver NFL, 1999; San Francisco NFL, 2000; Atlanta NFL, 2001. ... Games/Games started: 1998 (games played unavailable), 1999 (7/0), 2000 (12/2), 2001 (15/0). Total NFL: 34/2.
PRO STATISTICS: NFLE: 1998—Credited with three sacks. 2000—Credited with one sack.

UNDERWOOD, DIMITRIUS   DL   COWBOYS

PERSONAL: Born March 29, 1977, in Philadelphia. ... 6-6/276. ... Full name: Dimitrius Paul Underwood.
HIGH SCHOOL: E.E. Smith (Fayetteville, N.C.).
COLLEGE: Michigan State.
TRANSACTIONS/CAREER NOTES: Selected after junior season by Minnesota Vikings in first round (29th pick overall) of 1999 NFL draft. ... Signed by Vikings (August 1, 1999). ... Left team and decided not to play football (August 11, 1999). ... Claimed on waivers by Miami Dolphins (August 16, 1999). ... On non-football injury list with neck injury (September 28-December 17, 1999). ... Released by Dolphins (December 17, 1999). ... Signed by Dallas Cowboys (March 10, 2000). ... On non-football illness list with illness (October 26, 2001-remainder of season).

Year Team	G	GS	SACKS
2000—Dallas NFL	15	0	4.0
2001—Dallas NFL	4	0	0.0
Pro totals (2 years)	19	0	4.0

UNUTOA, MORRIS   C

PERSONAL: Born March 10, 1971, in Torrance, Calif. ... 6-1/284. ... Full name: Morris Taua Unutoa. ... Name pronounced oo-nuh-TOE-uh.
HIGH SCHOOL: Carson (Calif.).
COLLEGE: Brigham Young.
TRANSACTIONS/CAREER NOTES: Signed as non-drafted free agent by Philadelphia Eagles (April 26, 1996). ... Granted free agency (February 12, 1999). ... Re-signed by Eagles (March 24, 1999). ... Released by Eagles (September 8, 1999). ... Signed by Tampa Bay Buccaneers (October 5, 1999). ... Granted unconditional free agency (March 2, 2001). ... Signed by Buffalo Bills (November 16, 2001). ... Granted unconditional free agency (March 1, 2002).
PLAYING EXPERIENCE: Philadelphia NFL, 1996-1998; Tampa Bay NFL, 1999 and 2000; Buffalo NFL, 2001. ... Games/Games started: 1996 (16/0), 1997 (16/0), 1998 (16/0), 1999 (12/0), 2000 (16/0), 2001 (8/0). Total: 84/0.
CHAMPIONSHIP GAME EXPERIENCE: Played in NFC championship game (1999 season).
PRO STATISTICS: 1996—Fumbled once. 2001—Fumbled once for minus 13 yards.

UPSHAW, REGAN — DE — RAIDERS

PERSONAL: Born August 12, 1975, in Barrien Springs, Mich. ... 6-4/260. ... Full name: Regan Charles Upshaw.
HIGH SCHOOL: Pittsburg (Calif.).
COLLEGE: California.
TRANSACTIONS/CAREER NOTES: Selected after junior season by Tampa Bay Buccaneers in first round (12th pick overall) of 1996 NFL draft. ... Signed by Buccaneers (July 21, 1996). ... Traded by Buccaneers to Jacksonville Jaguars for sixth-round pick (RB Jameel Cook) in 2001 draft (October 19, 1999). ... Granted unconditional free agency (February 11, 2000). ... Signed by Oakland Raiders (March 1, 2000).
CHAMPIONSHIP GAME EXPERIENCE: Played in AFC championship game (1999 and 2000 seasons).
PRO STATISTICS: 1996—Recovered one fumble. 1997—Recovered one fumble. 1998—Intercepted one pass for 26 yards. 2000—Recovered two fumbles for eight yards.

Year Team	G	GS	SACKS
1996—Tampa Bay NFL	16	16	4.0
1997—Tampa Bay NFL	15	15	7.5
1998—Tampa Bay NFL	16	16	7.0
1999—Tampa Bay NFL	1	0	0.0
—Jacksonville NFL	6	0	0.0
2000—Oakland NFL	16	7	6.0
2001—Oakland NFL	16	15	7.0
Pro totals (6 years)	86	69	31.5

URLACHER, BRIAN — LB — BEARS

PERSONAL: Born May 25, 1978, in Pasco, Wash. ... 6-4/251. ... Full name: Brian Keith Urlacher.
HIGH SCHOOL: Lovington (N.M.).
COLLEGE: New Mexico.
TRANSACTIONS/CAREER NOTES: Selected by Chicago Bears in first round (ninth pick overall) of 2000 NFL draft. ... Signed by Bears (June 16, 2000).
HONORS: Named strong safety on THE SPORTING NEWS college All-America second team (1999). ... Named NFL Rookie of the Year by THE SPORTING NEWS (2000). ... Played in Pro Bowl (2000 season). ... Named linebacker on THE SPORTING NEWS NFL All-Pro team (2001).
PRO STATISTICS: 2000—Recovered one fumble. 2001—Caught one pass for 27 yards and a touchdown and recovered two fumbles for 101 yards and one touchdown.

			INTERCEPTIONS				SACKS
Year Team	G	GS	No.	Yds.	Avg.	TD	No.
2000—Chicago NFL	16	14	2	19	9.5	0	8.0
2001—Chicago NFL	16	16	3	60	20.0	0	6.0
Pro totals (2 years)	32	30	5	79	15.8	0	14.0

VAN PELT, ALEX — QB — BILLS

PERSONAL: Born May 1, 1970, in Pittsburgh. ... 6-1/218. ... Full name: Gregory Alexander Van Pelt.
HIGH SCHOOL: Grafton (W.Va.), then Winston Churchill (San Antonio).
COLLEGE: Pittsburgh.
TRANSACTIONS/CAREER NOTES: Selected by Pittsburgh Steelers in eighth round (216th pick overall) of 1993 NFL draft. ... Signed by Steelers for 1993 season. ... Released by Steelers (August 30, 1993). ... Signed by Kansas City Chiefs to practice squad (November 3, 1993). ... Activated (November 8, 1993); did not play. ... Released by Chiefs (November 17, 1993). ... Re-signed by Chiefs (May 18, 1994). ... Released by Chiefs (August 23, 1994). ... Signed by Buffalo Bills to practice squad (December 14, 1994). ... Activated (December 17, 1994); did not play. ... Granted unconditional free agency (February 11, 2000). ... Re-signed by Bills (July 31, 2000). ... Granted unconditional free agency (March 2, 2001). ... Re-signed by Bills (March 19, 2001).
PRO STATISTICS: 1997—Fumbled three times and recovered three fumbles for minus seven yards. 2001—Fumbled five times and recovered one fumble.
SINGLE GAME HIGHS (regular season): Attempts—44 (December 16, 2001, vs. New England); completions—28 (November 18, 2001, vs. Seattle); yards—316 (November 18, 2001, vs. Seattle); and touchdown passes—3 (November 25, 2001, vs. Miami).
STATISTICAL PLATEAUS: 300-yard passing games: 2001 (2).
MISCELLANEOUS: Regular-season record as starting NFL quarterback: 3-8 (.273).

				PASSING							RUSHING				TOTALS		
Year Team	G	GS	Att.	Cmp.	Pct.	Yds.	TD	Int.	Avg.	Rat.	Att.	Yds.	Avg.	TD	TD	2pt.	Pts.
1993—Kansas City NFL								Did not play.									
1994—Buffalo NFL								Did not play.									
1995—Buffalo NFL	1	0	18	10	55.6	106	2	0	5.89	110.0	0	0	0.0	0	0	0	0
1996—Buffalo NFL	1	0	5	2	40.0	9	0	0	1.80	47.5	3	-5	-1.7	0	0	0	0
1997—Buffalo NFL	6	3	124	60	48.4	684	2	10	5.52	37.2	11	33	3.0	1	1	0	6
1998—Buffalo NFL	1	0	0	0	0.0	0	0	0	0.0	...	1	-1	-1.0	0	0	0	0
1999—Buffalo NFL	1	0	1	1	100.0	9	0	0	9.00	104.2	1	-1	-1.0	0	0	0	0
2000—Buffalo NFL	2	0	8	4	50.0	67	0	0	8.38	78.6	0	0	0.0	0	0	0	0
2001—Buffalo NFL	12	8	307	178	58.0	2056	12	11	6.70	76.4	12	33	2.8	0	0	0	0
Pro totals (7 years)	24	11	463	255	55.1	2931	16	21	6.33	67.0	28	59	2.1	1	1	0	6

VANCE, ERIC — S

PERSONAL: Born July 14, 1975, in Tampa. ... 6-2/218.
HIGH SCHOOL: L.D. Bell (Hurst, Texas).
COLLEGE: Vanderbilt.
TRANSACTIONS/CAREER NOTES: Signed as non-drafted free agent by Carolina Panthers (April 25, 1997). ... Released by Panthers (September 1, 1997). ... Signed by San Diego Chargers to practice squad (December 3, 1997). ... Granted free agency after 1997 season. ...

Signed by Tampa Bay Buccaneers (December 30, 1997). ... Released by Buccaneers (August 25, 1998). ... Signed by Indianapolis Colts to practice squad (August 31, 1998). ... Signed by Buccaneers off Colts practice squad (October 28, 1998). ... On injured reserve with foot injury (November 10-December 7, 1999). ... Released by Buccaneers (December 7, 1999). ... Signed by San Diego Chargers (February 22, 2000). ... Released by Chargers (August 27, 2000). ... Signed by Buccaneers (August 28, 2000). ... On injured reserve with knee injury (December 27, 2001-remainder of season). ... Released by Buccaneers (February 26, 2002).
PLAYING EXPERIENCE: Tampa Bay NFL, 1998-2001. ... Games/Games started: 1998 (3/1), 1999 (6/0), 2000 (14/0), 2001 (10/0). Total: 33/1.

VANDEN BOSCH, KYLE — DE — CARDINALS

PERSONAL: Born November 17, 1978, in Larchwood, Iowa. ... 6-4/270.
HIGH SCHOOL: West Lyon (Larchwood, Iowa).
COLLEGE: Nebraska (degree in finance).
TRANSACTIONS/CAREER NOTES: Selected by Arizona Cardinals in second round (34th pick overall) of 2001 NFL draft. ... Signed by Cardinals (July 12, 2001). ... On injured reserve with knee injury (October 25, 2001-remainder of season).
PRO STATISTICS: 2001—Recovered one fumble for nine yards and a touchdown.

Year Team	G	GS	SACKS
2001—Arizona NFL	3	3	0.5

VANDERJAGT, MIKE — K — COLTS

PERSONAL: Born March 24, 1970, in Oakville, Ont. ... 6-5/210. ... Name pronounced vander-JAT.
HIGH SCHOOL: White Oaks (Ont.).
JUNIOR COLLEGE: Allan Hancock College (Calif.).
COLLEGE: West Virginia.
TRANSACTIONS/CAREER NOTES: Signed by Saskatchewan Roughriders prior to 1993 season. ... Signed by Toronto Argonauts of CFL (February 15, 1994). ... Released by Argonauts (June 13, 1994). ... Signed by Hamilton Tiger-Cats of CFL (June 24, 1994). ... Released by Tiger-Cats (July 11, 1994). ... Signed by Argonauts of CFL (March 16, 1995). ... Released by Argonauts (June 25, 1995). ... Re-signed by Argonauts of CFL (May 10, 1996). ... Signed as non-drafted free agent by Indianapolis Colts (March 4, 1998).
CHAMPIONSHIP GAME EXPERIENCE: Member of CFL Championship team (1996 and 1997).
HONORS: Named Most Outstanding Canadian Player in Grey Cup (1996). ... Named to CFL All-Star team (1997).
RECORDS: Holds NFL career record for highest field-goal percentage—87.69.
PRO STATISTICS: CFL: 1996—Attempted two passes with one completion for 28 yards. 1997—Attempted one pass without a completion, rushed twice for 25 yards and fumbled once.

		PUNTING					KICKING						
Year Team	G	No.	Yds.	Avg.	Net avg.	In. 20	Blk.	XPM	XPA	FGM	FGA	Lg.	50+	Pts.
1993—Saskatchewan CFL	2	17	672	39.5	32.1	0	0	0	0	0	0	0	0-0	0
1994—								Did not play.						
1995—								Did not play.						
1996—Toronto CFL	18	103	4459	43.3	35.1	0	0	59	59	40	56	51	0-0	179
1997—Toronto CFL	18	118	5303	44.9	37.4	0	0	77	77	33	43	51	0-0	176
1998—Indianapolis NFL	14	0	0	0.0	.0	0	0	23	23	27	31	53	6-9	104
1999—Indianapolis NFL	16	0	0	0.0	0	0	0	43	43	34	38	53	1-2	*145
2000—Indianapolis NFL	16	0	0	0.0	0	0	0	46	46	25	27	48	0-1	121
2001—Indianapolis NFL	16	0	0	0.0	0	0	0	41	▲42	28	34	52	3-4	§125
CFL totals (3 years)	38	238	10434	43.8	36.0	0	0	136	136	73	99	51	0-0	355
NFL totals (4 years)	62	0	0	0.0	0.0	0	0	153	154	114	130	53	10-16	495
Pro totals (7 years)	100	238	10434	43.8	36.0	0	0	289	290	187	229	53	10-0	850

VAUGHN, DARRICK — CB/KR — FALCONS

PERSONAL: Born October 2, 1978, in Houston. ... 5-11/193.
HIGH SCHOOL: Aldine Nimitz (Houston).
COLLEGE: Southwest Texas State.
TRANSACTIONS/CAREER NOTES: Selected by Atlanta Falcons in seventh round (211th pick overall) of 2000 NFL draft. ... Signed by Falcons (May 17, 2000).
PRO STATISTICS: 2000—Recovered one fumble. 2001—Recovered two fumbles.

			INTERCEPTIONS			KICKOFF RETURNS				TOTALS			
Year Team	G	GS	No.	Yds.	Avg.	TD	No.	Yds.	Avg.	TD	TD	2pt.	Pts.	Fum.
2000—Atlanta NFL	16	0	0	0	0.0	0	39	1082	*27.7	*3	3	0	18	1
2001—Atlanta NFL	16	0	1	0	0.0	0	*61	‡1491	24.4	1	1	0	6	3
Pro totals (2 years)	32	0	1	0	0.0	0	100	2573	25.7	4	4	0	24	4

VERBA, ROSS — OL — BROWNS

PERSONAL: Born October 31, 1973, in Des Moines, Iowa. ... 6-4/308. ... Full name: Ross Robert Verba.
HIGH SCHOOL: Dowling (West Des Moines, Iowa).
COLLEGE: Iowa.
TRANSACTIONS/CAREER NOTES: Selected by Green Bay Packers in first round (30th pick overall) of 1997 NFL draft. ... Signed by Packers (July 31, 1997). ... Granted unconditional free agency (March 2, 2001). ... Signed by Cleveland Browns (March 23, 2001). ... On physically unable to perform list with back injury (July 23-August 13, 2001).
PLAYING EXPERIENCE: Green Bay NFL, 1997-2001. ... Games/Games started: 1997 (16/11), 1998 (16/16), 1999 (11/10), 2000 (16/16), 2001 (15/14). Total: 74/67.
CHAMPIONSHIP GAME EXPERIENCE: Played in NFC championship game (1997 season). ... Played in Super Bowl XXXII (1997 season).
PRO STATISTICS: 1999—Recovered one fumble for two yards.

VICK, MICHAEL QB FALCONS

PERSONAL: Born June 28, 1980, in Newport News, Va. ... 6-0/215. ... Full name: Michael Dwayne Vick.
HIGH SCHOOL: Warwick (Newport News, Va.).
COLLEGE: Virginia Tech.
TRANSACTIONS/CAREER NOTES: Selected after sophomore season by Atlanta Falcons in first round (first pick overall) of 2001 draft. ... Signed by Falcons (May 9, 2001).
HONORS: Named College Football Freshman of the Year by THE SPORTING NEWS (1999). ... Named quarterback on THE SPORTING NEWS college All-America first team (1999).
PRO STATISTICS: 2001—Fumbled six times.
SINGLE GAME HIGHS (regular season): Attempts—30 (January 6, 2002, vs. St. Louis); completions—12 (January 6, 2002, vs. St. Louis); yards—214 (December 30, 2001, vs. Miami); and touchdown passes—1 (December 30, 2001, vs. Miami).
MISCELLANEOUS: Regular-season record as starting NFL quarterback: 1-1 (.500).

				PASSING						RUSHING				TOTALS		
Year Team	G	GS	Att.	Cmp.	Pct.	Yds.	TD	Int.	Avg.	Rat.	Att.	Yds.	Avg.	TD	TD	2pt.	Pts.
2001—Atlanta NFL	8	2	113	50	44.2	785	2	3	6.95	62.7	31	289	9.3	1	1	0	6

VICKERS, KIPP OL REDSKINS

PERSONAL: Born August 27, 1969, in Tarpon Springs, Fla. ... 6-2/300. ... Full name: Kipp Emmanuel Vickers.
HIGH SCHOOL: Tarpon Springs (Holiday, Fla.).
COLLEGE: Miami (Fla.).
TRANSACTIONS/CAREER NOTES: Signed as non-drafted free agent by Indianapolis Colts (April 30, 1993). ... Released by Colts (August 30, 1993). ... Re-signed by Colts to practice squad (September 1, 1993). ... Activated (December 21, 1993); did not play. ... Released by Colts (August 28, 1994). ... Re-signed by Colts to practice squad (August 31, 1994). ... Released by Colts (November 1, 1994). ... Re-signed by Colts to practice squad (November 16, 1994). ... Activated (December 24, 1994); did not play. ... Assigned by Colts to Frankfurt Galaxy in 1995 World League enhancement allocation program (February 20, 1995). ... Released by Colts (February 4, 1997). ... Re-signed by Colts for 1997 season. ... Granted free agency (February 13, 1998). ... Re-signed by Colts (February 24, 1998). ... Released by Colts (August 24, 1998). ... Signed by Washington Redskins (November 24, 1998). ... Inactive for five games (1998). ... Granted free agency (February 12, 1999). ... Re-signed by Redskins (February 23, 1999). ... Granted unconditional free agency (February 11, 2000). ... Signed by Baltimore Ravens (February 17, 2000). ... Released by Ravens (March 1, 2002). ... Signed by Redskins (June 4, 2002).
PLAYING EXPERIENCE: Frankfurt W.L., 1995; Indianapolis NFL, 1995-1997; Washington NFL, 1999; Baltimore NFL, 2000 and 2001. ... Games/Games started: W.L. 1995 (games played unavailable), NFL 1995 (9/0), 1996 (10/6), 1997 (9/0), 1999 (11/0), 2000 (12/2), 2001 (16/14). Total NFL: 67/22.
CHAMPIONSHIP GAME EXPERIENCE: Played in AFC championship game (1995 and 2000 seasons). ... Member of Super Bowl championship team (2000 season).

VILLARRIAL, CHRIS G BEARS

PERSONAL: Born June 9, 1973, in Hummelstown, Pa. ... 6-3/309. ... Name pronounced vuh-LAR-ree-uhl.
HIGH SCHOOL: Hershey (Pa.).
COLLEGE: Indiana University (Pa.).
TRANSACTIONS/CAREER NOTES: Selected by Chicago Bears in fifth round (152nd pick overall) of 1996 NFL draft. ... Signed by Bears (July 11, 1996). ... Granted free agency (February 12, 1999). ... Re-signed by Bears (April 16, 1999).
PLAYING EXPERIENCE: Chicago NFL, 1996-2001. ... Games/Games started: 1996 (14/8), 1997 (11/11), 1998 (16/16), 1999 (15/15), 2000 (16/15), 2001 (16/16). Total: 88/81.
PRO STATISTICS: 1998—Recovered one fumble. 1999—Recovered two fumbles.

VINATIERI, ADAM K PATRIOTS

PERSONAL: Born December 28, 1972, in Yankton, S.D. ... 6-0/200. ... Full name: Adam Matthew Vinatieri. ... Name pronounced VIN-a-TERRY.
HIGH SCHOOL: Rapid City (S.D.) Central.
COLLEGE: South Dakota State (degree in fitness and wellness).
TRANSACTIONS/CAREER NOTES: Signed by Amsterdam Admirals of World League for 1996 season. ... Signed as non-drafted free agent by New England Patriots (June 28, 1996). ... Granted free agency (February 12, 1999). ... Re-signed by Patriots (March 12, 1999). ... Granted free agency (March 1, 2002). ... Re-signed by Patriots (March 15, 2002).
CHAMPIONSHIP GAME EXPERIENCE: Played in AFC championship game (1996 and 2001 seasons). ... Played in Super Bowl XXXI (1996 season). ... Member of Super Bowl championship team (2001 season).
PRO STATISTICS: 1996—Punted once for 27 yards. 1998—Credited with a two-point conversion. 2001—Punted once for 33 yards.

		KICKING						
Year Team	G	XPM	XPA	FGM	FGA	Lg.	50+	Pts.
1996—Amsterdam W.L.	10	4	4	9	10	43	0-0	31
—New England NFL	16	39	42	27	35	50	1-2	120
1997—New England NFL	16	40	40	25	29	52	1-1	115
1998—New England NFL	16	32	32	31	39	55	2-2	127
1999—New England NFL	16	29	30	26	33	51	1-2	107
2000—New England NFL	16	25	25	27	33	53	1-3	106
2001—New England NFL	16	41	▲42	24	30	54	1-1	113
W.L. totals (1 year)	10	4	4	9	10	43	0-0	31
NFL totals (6 years)	96	206	211	160	199	55	7-11	688
Pro totals (7 years)	106	210	215	169	209	55	7-0	719

VINCENT, KEYDRICK   G   STEELERS

PERSONAL: Born April 13, 1978, in Bartow, Fla. ... 6-5/330. ... Full name: Keydrick Trepell Vincent.
HIGH SCHOOL: Lake Gibson (Fla.).
COLLEGE: Mississippi.
TRANSACTIONS/CAREER NOTES: Signed as non-drafted free agent by Pittsburgh Steelers (April 23, 2001).
PLAYING EXPERIENCE: Pittsburgh NFL, 2001. ... Games/Games started: 2001 (5/1).
CHAMPIONSHIP GAME EXPERIENCE: Played in AFC championship game (2001 season).

VINCENT, TROY   CB   EAGLES

PERSONAL: Born June 8, 1971, in Trenton, N.J. ... 6-1/200. ... Full name: Troy D. Vincent. ... Nephew of Steve Luke, safety with Green Bay Packers (1975-80).
HIGH SCHOOL: Pennsbury (Fairless Hills, Pa.).
COLLEGE: Wisconsin.
TRANSACTIONS/CAREER NOTES: Selected by Miami Dolphins in first round (seventh pick overall) of 1992 NFL draft. ... Signed by Dolphins (August 8, 1992). ... Designated by Dolphins as transition player (February 25, 1993). ... On injured reserve with knee injury (December 15, 1993-remainder of season). ... Tendered offer sheet by Philadelphia Eagles (February 24, 1996). ... Dolphins declined to match offer (March 3, 1996).
CHAMPIONSHIP GAME EXPERIENCE: Played in AFC championship game (1992 season). ... Played in NFC championship game (2001 season).
HONORS: Named defensive back on THE SPORTING NEWS college All-America first team (1991). ... Played in Pro Bowl (1999 and 2000 seasons).
RECORDS: Holds NFL record for longest interception return for a touchdown—104 yards (November 3, 1996; with lateral from LB James Willis).
PRO STATISTICS: 1992—Returned five punts for 16 yards and recovered two fumbles. 1993—Recovered one fumble. 1994—Ran 58 yards with lateral from interception for a touchdown. 1996—Ran minus two yards with lateral from punt return. 1997—Returned one punt for minus eight yards, fumbled once and recovered two fumbles for five yards. 1998—Credited with one sack. 1999—Credited with one sack. 2000—Credited with one sack recovered two fumbles. 2001—Credited with $1\frac{1}{2}$ sacks and recovered one fumble.

			INTERCEPTIONS			
Year Team	G	GS	No.	Yds.	Avg.	TD
1992—Miami NFL	15	14	2	47	23.5	0
1993—Miami NFL	13	13	2	29	14.5	0
1994—Miami NFL	13	12	5	113	22.6	1
1995—Miami NFL	16	16	5	95	19.0	▲1
1996—Philadelphia NFL	16	16	3	144	*48.0	1
1997—Philadelphia NFL	16	16	3	14	4.7	0
1998—Philadelphia NFL	13	13	2	29	14.5	0
1999—Philadelphia NFL	14	14	†7	91	13.0	0
2000—Philadelphia NFL	16	16	5	34	6.8	0
2001—Philadelphia NFL	15	15	3	0	0.0	0
Pro totals (10 years)	147	145	37	596	16.1	3

VINSON, FRED   CB   PANTHERS

PERSONAL: Born April 2, 1977, in Aiken, S.C. ... 5-11/180. ... Full name: Fred Vinson Jr. ... Cousin of Corey Chavous, defensive back, Minnesota Vikings.
HIGH SCHOOL: North Augusta (S.C.).
COLLEGE: Vanderbilt (degree in engineering science and math).
TRANSACTIONS/CAREER NOTES: Selected by Green Bay Packers in second round (47th pick overall) of 1999 NFL draft. ... Signed by Packers (July 23, 1999). ... Traded by Packers with sixth-round pick (DT Tim Watson) in 2000 draft to Seattle Seahawks for RB Ahman Green and fifth-round pick (WR/KR Joey Jamison) in 2000 draft (April 14, 2000). ... On physically unable to perform list with knee injury (August 20, 2000-entire season). ... Released by Seahawks (June 7, 2001). ... Signed by Carolina Panthers (April 8, 2002).
PRO STATISTICS: 1999—Credited with one sack.

			INTERCEPTIONS			
Year Team	G	GS	No.	Yds.	Avg.	TD
1999—Green Bay NFL	16	1	2	21	10.5	0
2000—Seattle NFL			Did not play.			
2001—			Did not play.			
Pro totals (1 years)	16	1	2	21	10.5	0

VOLEK, BILLY   QB   TITANS

PERSONAL: Born April 28, 1976, in Hemit, Calif. ... 6-2/214. ... Full name: John William Volek.
HIGH SCHOOL: Clovis West (Fresno, Calif.).
COLLEGE: Fresno State.
TRANSACTIONS/CAREER NOTES: Signed as non-drafted free agent by Tennessee Titans (April 18, 2000). ... Active for one game (2000); did not play.
PLAYING EXPERIENCE: Tennessee NFL, 2001. ... Games/Games started: 2001 (1/0).
PRO STATISTICS: 2001—Attempted three passes without a completion.
SINGLE GAME HIGHS (regular season): Attempts—3 (December 9, 2001, vs. Minnesota); completions—0; yards—0; and touchdown passes—0.

VON OELHOFFEN, KIMO   DL   STEELERS

PERSONAL: Born January 30, 1971, in Kaunakaki, Hawaii. ... 6-4/300. ... Full name: Kimo K. von Oelhoffen. ... Name pronounced KEE-moe von OHL-hoffen.
HIGH SCHOOL: Molokai (Hoolehua, Hawaii).
JUNIOR COLLEGE: Walla Walla (Wash.) Community College.
COLLEGE: Hawaii, then Boise State.
TRANSACTIONS/CAREER NOTES: Selected by Cincinnati Bengals in sixth round (162nd pick overall) of 1994 NFL draft. ... Signed by Bengals (May 9, 1994). ... Granted unconditional free agency (February 11, 2000). ... Signed by Pittsburgh Steelers (February 14, 2000).
PLAYING EXPERIENCE: Cincinnati NFL, 1994-1999; Pittsburgh NFL, 2000 and 2001. ... Games/Games started: 1994 (7/0), 1995 (16/0), 1996 (11/1), 1997 (13/12), 1998 (16/16), 1999 (16/5), 2000 (16/16), 2001 (15/15). Total: 110/65.
CHAMPIONSHIP GAME EXPERIENCE: Played in AFC championship game (2001 season).
PRO STATISTICS: 1995—Returned one kickoff for 10 yards. 1996—Credited with one sack. 1999—Credited with four sacks and recovered one fumble. 2000—Credited with one sack. 2001—Credited with four sacks and recovered two fumbles.

VRABEL, MIKE   LB   PATRIOTS

PERSONAL: Born August 14, 1975, in Akron, Ohio. ... 6-4/250. ... Full name: Michael George Vrabel.
HIGH SCHOOL: Walsh Jesuit (Cuyahoga Falls, Ohio).
COLLEGE: Ohio State.
TRANSACTIONS/CAREER NOTES: Selected by Pittsburgh Steelers in third round (91st pick overall) of 1997 NFL draft. ... Signed by Steelers (July 15, 1997). ... Granted free agency (February 11, 2000). ... Re-signed by Steelers (April 20, 2000). ... Granted unconditional free agency (March 2, 2001). ... Signed by New England Patriots (March 16, 2001).
CHAMPIONSHIP GAME EXPERIENCE: Played in AFC championship game (1997 and 2001 seasons). ... Member of Super Bowl championship team (2001 season).
PRO STATISTICS: 1997—Returned one kickoff for no yards and recovered one fumble. 1999—Returned one kickoff for six yards and recovered one fumble. 2000—Recovered one fumble. 2001—Intercepted two passes for 27 yards.

Year Team	G	GS	SACKS
1997—Pittsburgh NFL	15	0	1.5
1998—Pittsburgh NFL	11	0	2.5
1999—Pittsburgh NFL	10	0	2.0
2000—Pittsburgh NFL	15	0	1.0
2001—New England NFL	16	12	3.0
Pro totals (5 years)	**67**	**12**	**10.0**

WADDELL, REGGIE   DB   RAVENS

PERSONAL: Born November 14, 1977, in Houston. ... 6-0/185. ... Full name: Reggie Duane Waddell.
HIGH SCHOOL: Willowridge (Houston).
JUNIOR COLLEGE: Dodge City Junior College (Kan.).
COLLEGE: Texas A&M, then Western Illinois.
TRANSACTIONS/CAREER NOTES: Signed as non-drafted free agent by Baltimore Ravens (April 27, 2001). ... Released by Ravens (September 9, 2001). ... Re-signed by Ravens to practice squad (September 18, 2001). ... Activated (January 22, 2002).
PLAYING EXPERIENCE: Baltimore NFL, 2001. ... Games/Games started: (1/0).

WADE, JOHN   C   JAGUARS

PERSONAL: Born January 25, 1975, in Harrisonburg, Va. ... 6-5/300. ... Full name: John Robert Wade.
HIGH SCHOOL: Harrisonburg (Va.).
COLLEGE: Marshall (degree in business management, 1997).
TRANSACTIONS/CAREER NOTES: Selected by Jacksonville Jaguars in fifth round (148th pick overall) of 1998 NFL draft. ... Signed by Jaguars (June 1, 1998). ... On injured reserve with broken foot (September 27, 2000-remainder of season). ... On physically unable to perform list with foot injury (July 27-September 2, 2001). ... Granted unconditional free agency (March 1, 2002). ... Re-signed by Jaguars (March 13, 2002).
PLAYING EXPERIENCE: Jacksonville NFL, 1998-2001. ... Games/Games started: 1998 (5/0), 1999 (16/16), 2000 (2/2), 2001 (15/0). Total: 38/18.
CHAMPIONSHIP GAME EXPERIENCE: Played in AFC championship game (1999 season).
PRO STATISTICS: 1999—Fumbled once for minus 14 yards.

WADE, TODD   OT   DOLPHINS

PERSONAL: Born October 30, 1976, in Greenwood, Miss. ... 6-8/325. ... Full name: Todd McLaurin Wade.
HIGH SCHOOL: Jackson (Miss.) Prep.
COLLEGE: Mississippi.
TRANSACTIONS/CAREER NOTES: Selected by Miami Dolphins in second round (53rd pick overall) of 2000 NFL draft. ... Signed by Dolphins (July 24, 2000).
PLAYING EXPERIENCE: Miami NFL, 2000 and 2001. ... Games/Games started: 2000 (16/16), 2001 (15/15). Total: 31/31.

WAERIG, JOHN   TE   LIONS

PERSONAL: Born April 8, 1976, in Philadelphia. ... 6-2/264.
HIGH SCHOOL: Cardinal Dougherty (Pa.).
COLLEGE: Wisconsin, then Maryland.

TRANSACTIONS/CAREER NOTES: Signed as non-drafted free agent by Jacksonville Jaguars (April 27, 2000). ... Released by Jaguars (July 6, 2000). ... Signed by Tampa Bay Buccaneers (July 25, 2000). ... Released by Buccaneers (August 21, 2000). ... Signed by Detroit Lions (February 19, 2001). ... Assigned by Lions to Barcelona Dragons in 2001 NFL Europe enhancement allocation program (February 19, 2001). ... Released by Lions (September 2, 2001). ... Re-signed by Lions to practice squad (September 4, 2001). ... Activated (November 15, 2001). ... Released by Lions (December 11, 2001). ... Re-signed by Lions to practice squad (December 18, 2001).
PLAYING EXPERIENCE: Barcelona NFLE, 2001; Detroit NFL, 2001. ... Games/Games started: NFLE 2001 (games played unavailable), NFL 2001 (1/0).
PRO STATISTICS: NFLE: 2001—Caught two passes for 43 yards and returned one kickoff for seven yards. NFL: 2001—Caught one pass for six yards.
SINGLE GAME HIGHS (regular season): Receptions—1 (December 2, 2001, vs. Chicago); yards—6 (December 2, 2001, vs. Chicago); and touchdown receptions—0.

WAHLE, MIKE   G   PACKERS

PERSONAL: Born March 29, 1977, in Portland, Ore. ... 6-6/310. ... Full name: Michael James Wahle. ... Name pronounced WALL.
HIGH SCHOOL: Rim of the World (Lake Arrowhead, Calif.).
COLLEGE: Navy.
TRANSACTIONS/CAREER NOTES: Selected by Green Bay Packers in second round of 1998 supplemental draft (July 9, 1998). ... Signed by Packers (August 6, 1998). ... Granted free agency (March 2, 2001). ... Re-signed by Packers (May 31, 2001). ... Granted unconditional free agency (March 1, 2002). ... Re-signed by Packers (March 8, 2002).
PLAYING EXPERIENCE: Green Bay NFL, 1998-2001. ... Games/Games started: 1998 (1/0), 1999 (16/13), 2000 (16/6), 2001 (16/16). Total: 33/29.
PRO STATISTICS: 1999—Recovered one fumble.

WAKEFIELD, FRED   DE   CARDINALS

PERSONAL: Born September 17, 1978, in Tuscola, Ill. ... 6-7/289.
HIGH SCHOOL: Tuscola (Ill.).
COLLEGE: Illinois.
TRANSACTIONS/CAREER NOTES: Signed as non-drafted free agent by Arizona Cardinals (April 23, 2001).
PLAYING EXPERIENCE: Arizona NFL, 2001. ... Games/Games started: (16/12).
PRO STATISTICS: 2001—Intercepted one pass for 20 yards and a touchdown and credited with $2^1/_2$ sacks.

WALKER, BRACEY   S   LIONS

PERSONAL: Born October 28, 1970, in Portsmouth, Va. ... 6-0/206. ... Full name: Bracey Wordell Walker.
HIGH SCHOOL: Pine Forest (Fayetteville, N.C.).
COLLEGE: North Carolina.
TRANSACTIONS/CAREER NOTES: Selected by Kansas City Chiefs in fourth round (127th pick overall) of 1994 NFL draft. ... Signed by Chiefs (July 20, 1994). ... Claimed on waivers by Cincinnati Bengals (October 12, 1994). ... Granted free agency (February 14, 1997). ... Re-signed by Bengals (April 18, 1997). ... Claimed on waivers by Miami Dolphins (August 20, 1997). ... On injured reserve with leg injury (December 2, 1997-remainder of season). ... Granted unconditional free agency (February 13, 1998). ... Re-signed by Dolphins (April 27, 1998). ... Released by Dolphins (August 19, 1998). ... Signed by Chiefs (November 3, 1998). ... Granted unconditional free agency (February 11, 2000). ... Re-signed by Chiefs (February 24, 2000). ... Granted unconditional free agency (March 2, 2002). ... Signed by Detroit Lions (April 15, 2002).
HONORS: Named defensive back on THE SPORTING NEWS college All-America second team (1993).
PRO STATISTICS: 1995—Recovered two fumbles. 1997—Recovered one fumble. 2001—Recovered one fumble.

				INTERCEPTIONS		
Year Team	G	GS	No.	Yds.	Avg.	TD
1994—Kansas City NFL	2	0	0	0	0.0	0
—Cincinnati NFL	7	0	0	0	0.0	0
1995—Cincinnati NFL	14	14	4	56	14.0	0
1996—Cincinnati NFL	16	16	2	35	17.5	0
1997—Miami NFL	12	0	0	0	0.0	0
1998—Kansas City NFL	8	0	0	0	0.0	0
1999—Kansas City NFL	16	1	0	0	0.0	0
2000—Kansas City NFL	15	0	0	0	0.0	0
2001—Kansas City NFL	15	0	0	0	0.0	0
Pro totals (8 years)	105	31	6	91	15.2	0

WALKER, BRIAN   S   LIONS

PERSONAL: Born May 31, 1972, in Colorado Springs, Colo. ... 6-1/205.
HIGH SCHOOL: Widefield (Colorado Springs, Colo.).
JUNIOR COLLEGE: Snow College (Utah).
COLLEGE: Washington State.
TRANSACTIONS/CAREER NOTES: Signed as non-drafted free agent by Washington Redskins (May 1, 1996). ... Released by Redskins (October 9, 1997). ... Signed by Miami Dolphins (December 9, 1997). ... Active for two games with Dolphins (1997); did not play. ... Claimed on waivers by Seattle Seahawks (September 6, 1999). ... Released by Seahawks (September 14, 1999). ... Re-signed by Seahawks (September 30, 1999). ... On injured reserve with hamstring injury (January 8, 2000-remainder of playoffs). ... Granted unconditional free agency (February 11, 2000). ... Signed by Dolphins (February 16, 2000). ... Granted unconditional free agency (March 2, 2001). ... Signed by Detroit Lions (March 5, 2002).
PLAYING EXPERIENCE: Washington NFL, 1996 and 1997; Miami NFL, 1998, 2000 and 2001; Seattle NFL, 1999. ... Games/Games started: 1996 (16/4), 1997 (5/0), 1998 (16/0), 1999 (5/0), 2000 (16/16), 2001 (13/13). Total: 71/33.
PRO STATISTICS: 1996—Credited with one sack. 1998—Intercepted four passes for 12 yards. 1999—Intercepted one pass for 21 yards and recovered one fumble. 2000—Intercepted seven passes for 80 yards and credited with two sacks. 2001—Intercepted one pass for no yards.

WALKER, DARWIN — DT — EAGLES

PERSONAL: Born June 15, 1977, in Walterboro, S.C. ... 6-3/294. ... Full name: Darwin Jamar Walker.
HIGH SCHOOL: Walterboro (S.C.).
COLLEGE: North Carolina State, then Tennessee.
TRANSACTIONS/CAREER NOTES: Selected by Arizona Cardinals in third round (71st pick overall) of 2000 NFL draft. ... Signed by Cardinals (June 19, 2000). ... Claimed on waivers by Philadelphia Eagles (September 12, 2000).
PLAYING EXPERIENCE: Arizona NFL, 2000; Philadelphia NFL, 2001. ... Games/Games started: 2000 (1/0), 2001 (10/0). Total: 11/0.
CHAMPIONSHIP GAME EXPERIENCE: Played in NFC championship game (2001 season).
HONORS: Named defensive tackle on THE SPORTING NEWS college All-America second team (1999).
PRO STATISTICS: 2001—Credited with one sack.

WALKER, DENARD — CB — BRONCOS

PERSONAL: Born August 9, 1973, in Dallas. ... 6-1/190. ... Full name: Denard Antuan Walker.
HIGH SCHOOL: South Garland (Texas), than Harlingen (Texas) Military Institute.
COLLEGE: Louisiana State.
TRANSACTIONS/CAREER NOTES: Selected by Houston Oilers in third round (75th pick overall) of 1997 NFL draft. ... Oilers franchise moved to Tennessee for 1997 season. ... Signed by Oilers (July 18, 1997). ... Oilers franchise renamed Tennessee Titans for 1999 season (December 26, 1998). ... Granted free agency (February 11, 2000). ... Re-signed by Titans (June 3, 2000). ... On suspended list (September 3-5, 2000). ... Granted unconditional free agency (March 2, 2001). ... Signed by Denver Broncos (March 19, 2001).
CHAMPIONSHIP GAME EXPERIENCE: Played in AFC championship game (1999 season). ... Played in Super Bowl XXXIV (1999 season).
PRO STATISTICS: 1999—Recovered one fumble for 83 yards and a touchdown. 2000—Returned one punt for no yards and fumbled once. 2001—Fumbled once and recovered one fumble.

			INTERCEPTIONS			
Year Team	G	GS	No.	Yds.	Avg.	TD
1997—Tennessee NFL	15	11	2	53	26.5	1
1998—Tennessee NFL	16	16	2	6	3.0	0
1999—Tennessee NFL	15	14	1	27	27.0	0
2000—Tennessee NFL	15	15	2	4	2.0	0
2001—Denver NFL	16	15	3	60	20.0	1
Pro totals (5 years)	77	71	10	150	15.0	2

WALKER, GARY — DT — TEXANS

PERSONAL: Born February 28, 1973, in Royston, Ga. ... 6-2/305. ... Full name: Gary Lamar Walker.
HIGH SCHOOL: Franklin County (Carnesville, Ga.).
JUNIOR COLLEGE: Hinds Community College (Miss.).
COLLEGE: Auburn.
TRANSACTIONS/CAREER NOTES: Selected by Houston Oilers in fifth round (159th pick overall) of 1995 NFL draft. ... Signed by Oilers (July 10, 1995). ... Oilers franchise moved to Tennessee for 1997 season. ... Granted free agency (February 13, 1998). ... Re-signed by Oilers (July 15, 1998). ... Granted unconditional free agency (February 12, 1999). ... Signed by Jacksonville Jaguars (February 15, 1999). ... Selected by Houston Texans from Jaguars in NFL expansion draft (February 18, 2002).
CHAMPIONSHIP GAME EXPERIENCE: Played in AFC championship game (1999 season).
PRO STATISTICS: 1996—Recovered one fumble. 2001—Recovered one fumble for three yards.

Year Team	G	GS	SACKS
1995—Houston NFL	15	9	2.5
1996—Houston NFL	16	16	5.5
1997—Tennessee NFL	15	15	7.0
1998—Tennessee NFL	16	16	1.0
1999—Jacksonville NFL	16	16	10.0
2000—Jacksonville NFL	15	14	5.0
2001—Jacksonville NFL	16	16	7.5
Pro totals (7 years)	109	102	38.5

WALKER, JOE — S — TITANS

PERSONAL: Born March 19, 1977, in Memphis. ... 5-10/204.
HIGH SCHOOL: Arlington-Lamar (Texas).
COLLEGE: Nebraska.
TRANSACTIONS/CAREER NOTES: Signed as non-drafted free agent by Tennessee Titans (April 27, 2001).
PLAYING EXPERIENCE: Tennessee NFL, 2001. ... Games/Games started: (16/3).
PRO STATISTICS: 2001—Returned 14 punts for 125 yards, returned three kickoffs for 33 yards, fumbled once and recovered one fumble.

WALKER, KENYATTA — OT — BUCCANEERS

PERSONAL: Born February 1, 1979, in Meridian, Miss. ... 6-5/302. ... Full name: Idrees Kenyatta Walker.
HIGH SCHOOL: Meridian (Miss.).
COLLEGE: Florida.
TRANSACTIONS/CAREER NOTES: Selected after junior season by Tampa Bay Buccaneers in first round (14th pick overall) of 2001 draft. ... Signed by Buccaneers (July 26, 2001).
PLAYING EXPERIENCE: Tampa Bay NFL, 2001. ... Games/Games started: (16/16).

WALKER, ROD — DT — PACKERS

PERSONAL: Born August 4, 1976, in Milton, Fla. ... 6-3/320. ... Full name: Roderick Dion Walker.
HIGH SCHOOL: Milton (Fla.).
COLLEGE: Troy State.
TRANSACTIONS/CAREER NOTES: Signed as non-drafted free agent by Washington Redskins (April 21, 1999). ... Released by Redskins (August 30, 1999). ... Re-signed by Redskins (September 2, 1999). ... Released by Redskins (September 4, 1999). ... Signed by Tennessee Titans to practice squad (October 26, 1999). ... Released by Titans (August 26, 2000). ... Re-signed by Titans to practice squad (August 30, 2000). ... Activated (December 1, 2000); did not play. ... Traded by Titans to Green Bay Packers for future draft pick (September 2, 2001).
PLAYING EXPERIENCE: Green Bay NFL, 2001. ... Games/Games started: (11/0).

WALLS, RAYMOND — CB — COLTS

PERSONAL: Born July 24, 1979, in Kentwood, La. ... 5-10/175. ... Full name: Raymond Omoncial Tyshone Walls.
HIGH SCHOOL: Kentwood (La.).
COLLEGE: Southern Mississippi.
TRANSACTIONS/CAREER NOTES: Selected by Indianapolis Colts in fifth round (152nd pick overall) of 2001 NFL draft. ... Signed by Colts (June 13, 2001). ... Released by Colts (September 1, 2001). ... Re-signed by Colts to practice squad (September 3, 2001). ... Activated (October 8, 2001).

			INTERCEPTIONS		
Year Team	G	GS	No.	Yds.	Avg.	TD
2001—Indianapolis NFL	4	0	1	0	0.0	0

WALLS, WESLEY — TE — PANTHERS

PERSONAL: Born February 26, 1966, in Pontotoc, Miss. ... 6-5/250. ... Full name: Charles Wesley Walls.
HIGH SCHOOL: Pontotoc (Miss.).
COLLEGE: Mississippi.
TRANSACTIONS/CAREER NOTES: Selected by San Francisco 49ers in second round (56th pick overall) of 1989 NFL draft. ... Signed by 49ers (July 26, 1989). ... Granted free agency (February 1, 1992). ... Re-signed by 49ers (July 18, 1992). ... On injured reserve with shoulder injury (September 1, 1992-January 16, 1993). ... On injured reserve with shoulder injury (October 27, 1993-remainder of season). ... Granted unconditional free agency (February 17, 1994). ... Signed by New Orleans Saints (April 27, 1994). ... Granted unconditional free agency (February 16, 1996). ... Signed by Carolina Panthers (February 21, 1996). ... On injured reserve with knee injury (October 31, 2000-remainder of season).
CHAMPIONSHIP GAME EXPERIENCE: Played in NFC championship game (1989, 1990 and 1996 seasons). ... Member of Super Bowl championship team (1989 season).
HONORS: Named tight end on The Sporting News college All-America second team (1988). ... Played in Pro Bowl (1996-1999 seasons).
PRO STATISTICS: 1989—Recovered one fumble. 1990—Returned one kickoff for 16 yards. 1993—Recovered one fumble. 1995—Returned one kickoff for six yards, fumbled once and recovered one fumble. 2001—Recovered one fumble.
SINGLE GAME HIGHS (regular season): Receptions—10 (October 7, 2001, vs. San Francisco); yards—147 (September 7, 1997, vs. Atlanta); and touchdown receptions—2 (January 2, 2000, vs. New Orleans).
STATISTICAL PLATEAUS: 100-yard receiving games: 1997 (2), 2000 (1). Total: 3.
MISCELLANEOUS: Holds Carolina Panthers all-time records for most touchdown receptions (40) and most touchdowns (40).

			RECEIVING				TOTALS			
Year Team	G	GS	No.	Yds.	Avg.	TD	TD	2pt.	Pts.	Fum.
1989—San Francisco NFL	16	0	4	16	4.0	1	1	0	6	1
1990—San Francisco NFL	16	0	5	27	5.4	0	0	0	0	0
1991—San Francisco NFL	15	0	2	24	12.0	0	0	0	0	0
1992—San Francisco NFL					Did not play.					
1993—San Francisco NFL	6	0	0	0	0.0	0	0	0	0	0
1994—New Orleans NFL	15	7	38	406	10.7	4	4	1	26	0
1995—New Orleans NFL	16	10	57	694	12.2	4	4	1	26	1
1996—Carolina NFL	16	15	61	713	11.7	10	10	0	60	0
1997—Carolina NFL	15	15	58	746	12.9	6	6	0	36	0
1998—Carolina NFL	14	14	49	506	10.3	5	5	0	30	0
1999—Carolina NFL	16	16	63	822	13.0	12	12	0	72	1
2000—Carolina NFL	8	8	31	422	13.6	2	2	0	12	0
2001—Carolina NFL	14	14	43	452	10.5	5	5	0	30	0
Pro totals (12 years)	167	99	411	4828	11.7	49	49	2	298	3

WALSH, CHRIS — WR — VIKINGS

PERSONAL: Born December 12, 1968, in Cleveland. ... 6-1/199. ... Full name: Christopher Lee Walsh.
HIGH SCHOOL: Ygnacio Valley (Concord, Calif.).
COLLEGE: Stanford (degree in quantitative economics, 1991).
TRANSACTIONS/CAREER NOTES: Selected by Buffalo Bills in ninth round (251st pick overall) of 1992 NFL draft. ... Signed by Bills (July 22, 1992). ... Released by Bills (August 31, 1992). ... Re-signed by Bills to practice squad (September 1, 1992). ... Activated (September 19, 1992). ... Released by Bills (October 2, 1992). ... Re-signed by Bills to practice squad (October 2, 1992). ... Released by Bills (March 10, 1994). ... Signed by Minnesota Vikings (May 6, 1994). ... Granted unconditional free agency (February 16, 1996). ... Re-signed by Vikings (March 4, 1996). ... Granted unconditional free agency (February 13, 1998). ... Re-signed by Vikings (March 4, 1998). ... Granted unconditional free agency (March 2, 2001). ... Re-signed by Vikings (June 11, 2001).
CHAMPIONSHIP GAME EXPERIENCE: Member of Bills for AFC championship game (1993 season); inactive. ... Member of Bills for Super Bowl XXVIII (1993 season); inactive. ... Played in NFC championship game (1998 and 2000 seasons).
PRO STATISTICS: 1994—Returned one kickoff for six yards. 1995—Returned three kickoffs for 42 yards. 1996—Attempted one pass without a completion and credited with one two-point conversion. 1997—Returned one kickoff for 10 yards. 2000—Returned one punt for 11 yards and returned two kickoffs for nine yards. 2001—Returned one punt for two yards, returned one kickoff for 10 yards and recovered one fumble.
SINGLE GAME HIGHS (regular season): Receptions—4 (December 24, 2000, vs. Indianapolis); yards—44 (December 17, 2000, vs. Green Bay); and touchdown receptions—1 (October 10, 1999, vs. Chicago).

Year Team	G	GS	RECEIVING No.	Yds.	Avg.	TD	TOTALS TD	2pt.	Pts.	Fum.
1992—Buffalo NFL	2	0	0	0	0.0	0	0	0	0	0
1993—Buffalo NFL	3	0	0	0	0.0	0	0	0	0	0
1994—Minnesota NFL	10	0	0	0	0.0	0	0	0	0	0
1995—Minnesota NFL	16	0	7	66	9.4	0	0	0	0	0
1996—Minnesota NFL	15	0	4	39	9.8	1	1	1	8	0
1997—Minnesota NFL	14	0	11	114	10.4	1	1	0	6	0
1998—Minnesota NFL	15	0	2	46	23.0	0	0	0	0	0
1999—Minnesota NFL	16	1	2	24	12.0	1	1	0	6	0
2000—Minnesota NFL	16	0	18	191	10.6	0	0	0	0	0
2001—Minnesota NFL	16	0	9	67	7.4	0	0	0	0	0
Pro totals (10 years)	123	1	53	547	10.3	3	3	1	20	0

WALTER, KEN — P — PATRIOTS

PERSONAL: Born August 15, 1972, in Cleveland. ... 6-1/195. ... Full name: Kenneth Matthew Walter Jr.
HIGH SCHOOL: Euclid (Ohio).
COLLEGE: Kent.
TRANSACTIONS/CAREER NOTES: Signed as non-drafted free agent by Carolina Panthers (April 14, 1997). ... Released by Panthers (April 24, 2001). ... Signed by New England Patriots (October 16, 2001).
CHAMPIONSHIP GAME EXPERIENCE: Played in AFC championship game (2001 season). ... Member of Super Bowl championship team (2001 season).
PRO STATISTICS: 1997—Rushed once for minus five yards. 1998—Rushed three times for no yards, attempted one pass without a completion, fumbled twice and recovered two fumbles for minus 20 yards. 2000—Rushed once for no yards, attempted one pass without a completion, fumbled twice and recovered two fumbles for minus 11 yards.

Year Team	G	No.	Yds.	PUNTING Avg.	Net avg.	In. 20	Blk.
1997—Carolina NFL	16	85	3604	42.4	36.4	29	0
1998—Carolina NFL	16	77	3131	40.7	38.1	20	0
1999—Carolina NFL	16	65	2562	39.4	36.7	18	0
2000—Carolina NFL	16	64	2459	38.4	33.8	19	†2
2001—New England NFL	11	49	1964	40.1	§38.1	24	0
Pro totals (5 years)	75	340	13720	40.4	36.6	110	2

WALTERS, TROY — WR/KR — COLTS

PERSONAL: Born December 15, 1976, in College Station, Texas. ... 5-7/173. ... Full name: Troy M. Walters.
HIGH SCHOOL: A&M Consolidated (College Station, Texas).
COLLEGE: Stanford.
TRANSACTIONS/CAREER NOTES: Selected by Minnesota Vikings in fifth round (165th pick overall) of 2000 NFL draft. ... Signed by Vikings (July 12, 2000). ... Claimed on waivers by Indianapolis Colts (February 24, 2002).
CHAMPIONSHIP GAME EXPERIENCE: Played in NFC championship game (2000 season).
HONORS: Named wide receiver on THE SPORTING NEWS college All-America first team (1999). ... Fred Biletnikoff Award winner (1999).
PRO STATISTICS: 2000—Rushed once for three yards, caught one pass for five yards and recovered one fumble.
SINGLE GAME HIGHS (regular season): Receptions—1 (October 1, 2000, vs. Tampa Bay); yards—5 (October 1, 2000, vs. Tampa Bay); and touchdown receptions—0.

Year Team	G	GS	PUNT RETURNS No.	Yds.	Avg.	TD	KICKOFF RETURNS No.	Yds.	Avg.	TD	TOTALS TD	2pt.	Pts.	Fum.
2000—Minnesota NFL	12	0	15	217	14.5	0	30	692	23.1	0	0	0	0	2
2001—Minnesota NFL	6	0	11	69	6.3	0	18	425	23.6	0	0	0	0	2
Pro totals (2 years)	18	0	26	286	11.0	0	48	1117	23.3	0	0	0	0	4

WALZ, ZACK — LB

PERSONAL: Born February 3, 1976, in Mountain View, Calif. ... 6-4/229. ... Full name: Zachary Christian Walz.
HIGH SCHOOL: Saint Francis (Mountain View, Calif.).
COLLEGE: Dartmouth (degree in government and economics, 1998).
TRANSACTIONS/CAREER NOTES: Selected by Arizona Cardinals in sixth round (158th pick overall) of 1998 NFL draft. ... Signed by Cardinals (June 4, 1998). ... On injured reserve with knee injury (November 17, 1999-remainder of season). ... On injured reserve with broken leg (November 24, 2000-remainder of season). ... Granted free agency (March 2, 2001). ... Re-signed by Cardinals (June 5, 2001). ... Granted unconditional free agency (March 1, 2002).
PLAYING EXPERIENCE: Arizona NFL, 1998-2001. ... Games/Games started: 1998 (16/0), 1999 (9/9), 2000 (6/5), 2001 (15/2). Total: 46/16.
PRO STATISTICS: 1998—Recovered one fumble. 1999—Credited with one sack. 2000—Intercepted one pass for no yards. 2001—Credited with one sack and recovered one fumble.

WARD, DEDRIC — WR/KR — DOLPHINS

PERSONAL: Born September 29, 1974, in Cedar Rapids, Iowa. ... 5-9/190. ... Full name: Dedric Lamar Ward. ... Name pronounced DEE-drick.
HIGH SCHOOL: Washington (Cedar Rapids, Iowa).
COLLEGE: Northern Iowa (degree in psychology).
TRANSACTIONS/CAREER NOTES: Selected by New York Jets in third round (88th pick overall) of 1997 NFL draft. ... Signed by Jets (July 17, 1997). ... Granted free agency (February 11, 2000). ... Re-signed by Jets (May 3, 2000). ... Granted unconditional free agency (March 2, 2001). ... Signed by Miami Dolphins (April 18, 2001).
CHAMPIONSHIP GAME EXPERIENCE: Played in AFC championship game (1998 season).

PRO STATISTICS: 1997—Rushed twice for 25 yards. 1998—Rushed twice for seven yards. 1999—Rushed once for minus one yard. 2000—Rushed four times for 23 yards. 2001—Rushed twice for 21 yards.
SINGLE GAME HIGHS (regular season): Receptions—8 (December 24, 2000, vs. Baltimore); yards—147 (December 24, 2000, vs. Baltimore); and touchdown receptions—1 (December 24, 2000, vs. Baltimore).
STATISTICAL PLATEAUS: 100-yard receiving games: 1997 (1), 2000 (3). Total: 4.

			RECEIVING				PUNT RETURNS				KICKOFF RETURNS				TOTALS		
Year Team	G	GS	No.	Yds.	Avg.	TD	No.	Yds.	Avg.	TD	No.	Yds.	Avg.	TD	TD	2pt.	Pts.	Fum.
1997—New York Jets NFL	11	1	18	212	11.8	1	8	55	6.9	0	2	10	5.0	0	1	0	6	1
1998—New York Jets NFL	16	2	25	477	19.1	4	8	72	9.0	0	3	60	20.0	0	4	0	24	0
1999—New York Jets NFL	16	10	22	325	14.8	3	38	288	7.6	0	0	0	0.0	0	3	0	18	2
2000—New York Jets NFL	16	16	54	801	14.8	3	27	214	7.9	0	0	0	0.0	0	3	0	18	1
2001—Miami NFL	13	1	21	209	10.0	0	9	88	9.8	0	0	0	0.0	0	0	0	0	1
Pro totals (5 years)	72	30	140	2024	14.5	11	90	717	8.0	0	5	70	14.0	0	11	0	66	5

WARD, HINES — WR — STEELERS

PERSONAL: Born March 8, 1976, in Forest Park, Ga. ... 6-0/200. ... Full name: Hines Ward Jr.
HIGH SCHOOL: Forest Park (Ga.).
COLLEGE: Georgia.
TRANSACTIONS/CAREER NOTES: Selected by Pittsburgh Steelers in third round (92nd pick overall) of 1998 NFL draft. ... Signed by Steelers (July 20, 1998). ... Granted free agency (March 2, 2001).
CHAMPIONSHIP GAME EXPERIENCE: Played in AFC championship game (2001 season).
PRO STATISTICS: 1998—Rushed once for 13 yards and attempted one pass with a completion for 17 yards. 1999—Rushed twice for minus two yards, returned one punt for two yards and returned one kickoff for 24 yards. 2000—Rushed four times for 53 yards, returned seven kickoffs for 186 yards and recovered one fumble. 2001—Rushed 10 times for 83 yards and attempted one pass without a completion.
SINGLE GAME HIGHS (regular season): Receptions—10 (December 9, 2001, vs. New York Jets); yards—124 (December 9, 2001, vs. New York Jets); and touchdown receptions—1 (December 23, 2001, vs. Detroit).
STATISTICAL PLATEAUS: 100-yard receiving games: 2001 (2).

			RECEIVING				TOTALS			
Year Team	G	GS	No.	Yds.	Avg.	TD	TD	2pt.	Pts.	Fum.
1998—Pittsburgh NFL	16	0	15	246	16.4	0	0	0	0	0
1999—Pittsburgh NFL	16	14	61	638	10.5	7	7	†1	44	1
2000—Pittsburgh NFL	16	15	48	672	14.0	4	4	0	24	2
2001—Pittsburgh NFL	16	16	94	1003	10.7	4	4	0	24	1
Pro totals (4 years)	64	45	218	2559	11.7	15	15	1	92	4

WARFIELD, ERIC — CB — CHIEFS

PERSONAL: Born March 3, 1976, in Vicksburg, Miss. ... 6-0/198. ... Full name: Eric Andrew Warfield.
HIGH SCHOOL: Arkansas (Texarkana, Ark.).
COLLEGE: Nebraska.
TRANSACTIONS/CAREER NOTES: Selected by Kansas City Chiefs in seventh round (216th pick overall) of 1998 NFL draft. ... Signed by Chiefs (May 27, 1998). ... Granted unconditional free agency (March 1, 2002). ... Re-signed by Chiefs (March 4, 2002).
PLAYING EXPERIENCE: Kansas City NFL, 1998-2001. ... Games/Games started: 1998 (12/0), 1999 (16/1), 2000 (13/4), 2001 (16/16). Total: 57/21.
PRO STATISTICS: 1999—Intercepted three passes for no yards. 2001—Intercepted four passes for 61 yards and one touchdown, returned one punt for no yards and fumbled once.

WARNER, KURT — QB — RAMS

PERSONAL: Born June 22, 1971, in Burlington, Iowa. ... 6-2/220. ... Full name: Kurtis Eugene Warner.
HIGH SCHOOL: Regis (Cedar Rapids, Iowa).
COLLEGE: Northern Iowa (degree in communications).
TRANSACTIONS/CAREER NOTES: Signed as non-drafted free agent by Green Bay Packers (April 28, 1994). ... Released by Packers prior to 1994 season. ... Played for Iowa Barnstormers of Arena Football League (1995-97). ... Signed by St. Louis Rams (December 26, 1997). ... Assigned by Rams to Amsterdam Admirals in 1998 NFL Europe enhancement allocation program (February 18, 1998).
CHAMPIONSHIP GAME EXPERIENCE: Played in NFC championship game (1999 and 2001 seasons). ... Member of Super Bowl championship team (1999 season). ... Played in Super Bowl XXXVI (2001 season).
HONORS: Named NFL Player of the Year by THE SPORTING NEWS (1999). ... Named quarterback on THE SPORTING NEWS NFL All-Pro team (1999 and 2001). ... Named Most Valuable Player of Super Bowl XXXIV (1999 season). ... Played in Pro Bowl (1999 season). ... Named to play in Pro Bowl (2000 season); replaced by Donovan McNabb due to injury.
RECORDS: Shares NFL single-season record for most games with 300 or more yards passing—9 (1999, 2001). ... Shares NFL record for most consecutive games with 300 or more yards passing—6 (September 4-October 15, 2000).
POST SEASON RECORDS: Holds Super Bowl single-game record for most yards passing—414 (January 30, 2000, vs. Tennessee).
PRO STATISTICS: 1999—Fumbled nine times for minus four yards. 2000—Fumbled four times for minus eight yards. 2001—Fumbled 10 times and recovered two fumbles for minus 14 yards.
SINGLE GAME HIGHS (regular season): Attempts—47 (October 29, 2001, vs. New Orleans); completions—35 (September 10, 2000, vs. Seattle); yards—441 (September 4, 2000, vs. Denver); and touchdown passes—5 (October 10, 1999, vs. San Francisco).
STATISTICAL PLATEAUS: 300-yard passing games: 1999 (9), 2000 (8), 2001 (9). Total: 26.
MISCELLANEOUS: Regular-season record as starting NFL quarterback: 35-8 (.814). ... Postseason record as starting NFL quarterback: 5-2 (.714).

Year	Team	G	GS	PASSING Att.	Cmp.	Pct.	Yds.	TD	Int.	Avg.	Rat.	RUSHING Att.	Yds.	Avg.	TD	TOTALS TD	2pt.	Pts.
1998	—Amsterdam NFLE	10	...	326	165	50.6	2101	15	6	6.44	78.8	19	17	0.9	1	1	0	6
	—St. Louis NFL	1	0	11	4	36.4	39	0	0	3.55	47.2	0	0	0.0	0	0	0	0
1999	—St. Louis NFL	16	16	499	325	*65.1	4353	*41	13	*8.72	*109.2	23	92	4.0	1	1	0	6
2000	—St. Louis NFL	11	11	347	235	*67.7	3429	21	18	*9.88	98.3	18	17	0.9	0	0	0	0
2001	—St. Louis NFL	16	16	546	*375	*68.7	*4830	*36	∞22	*8.85	*101.4	28	60	2.1	0	0	0	0
	NFL Europe totals (1 year)	10	...	326	165	50.6	2101	15	6	6.44	78.8	19	17	0.9	1	1	0	6
	NFL totals (4 years)	44	43	1403	939	66.9	12651	98	53	9.02	103.0	69	169	2.4	1	1	0	6
	Pro totals (5 years)	54	...	1729	1104	63.9	14752	113	59	8.53	98.4	88	186	2.1	2	2	0	12

WARREN, GERARD　　　DT　　　BROWNS

PERSONAL: Born July 25, 1978, in Lake City, Fla. ... 6-4/322. ... Full name: Gerard T. Warren.
HIGH SCHOOL: Union City (Raiford, Fla.).
COLLEGE: Florida.
TRANSACTIONS/CAREER NOTES: Selected by Cleveland Browns in first round (third pick overall) of 2001 draft. ... Signed by Browns (August 1, 2001).

Year Team	G	GS	SACKS
2001—Cleveland NFL	15	15	5.0

WARREN, LAMONT　　　RB　　　LIONS

PERSONAL: Born January 4, 1973, in Indianapolis. ... 5-11/202. ... Full name: Lamont Allen Warren.
HIGH SCHOOL: Dorsey (Los Angeles).
COLLEGE: Colorado.
TRANSACTIONS/CAREER NOTES: Selected after junior season by Indianapolis Colts in sixth round (164th pick overall) of 1994 NFL draft. ... Signed by Colts (July 13, 1994). ... Released by Colts (April 12, 1999). ... Signed by New England Patriots (April 17, 1999). ... Released by Patriots (February 22, 2000). ... Signed by Detroit Lions (February 14, 2001).
CHAMPIONSHIP GAME EXPERIENCE: Played in AFC championship game (1995 season).
PRO STATISTICS: 1994—Attempted one pass without a completion. 1996—Recovered one fumble. 1997—Attempted one pass without a completion and recovered one fumble. 2001—Attempted two passes without a completion and one interception and recovered one fumble.
SINGLE GAME HIGHS (regular season): Attempts—22 (December 23, 1995, vs. New England); yards—90 (December 23, 1995, vs. New England); and rushing touchdowns—1 (November 22, 2001, vs. Green Bay).

Year Team	G	GS	RUSHING Att.	Yds.	Avg.	TD	RECEIVING No.	Yds.	Avg.	TD	KICKOFF RETURNS No.	Yds.	Avg.	TD	TOTALS TD	2pt.	Pts.	Fum.
1994—Indianapolis NFL	11	0	18	80	4.4	0	3	47	15.7	0	2	56	28.0	0	0	0	0	0
1995—Indianapolis NFL	12	1	47	152	3.2	1	17	159	9.4	0	15	315	21.0	0	1	0	6	1
1996—Indianapolis NFL	13	3	67	230	3.4	1	22	174	7.9	0	3	54	18.0	0	1	0	6	3
1997—Indianapolis NFL	13	3	28	80	2.9	2	20	192	9.6	0	1	19	19.0	0	2	0	12	0
1998—Indianapolis NFL	12	2	25	61	2.4	1	11	44	4.0	1	8	152	19.0	0	2	0	12	0
1999—New England NFL	16	2	35	120	3.4	0	29	262	9.0	1	2	25	12.5	0	1	0	6	0
2000—											Did not play.							
2001—Detroit NFL	16	3	61	191	3.1	3	40	336	8.4	1	6	-4	0.0	0	4	1	26	1
Pro totals (7 years)	93	11	281	914	3.3	8	142	1214	8.5	3	31	617	19.9	0	11	1	68	5

WARRICK, PETER　　　WR/PR　　　BENGALS

PERSONAL: Born June 19, 1977, in Bradenton, Fla. ... 5-11/195.
HIGH SCHOOL: Southeast (Bradenton, Fla.).
COLLEGE: Florida State.
TRANSACTIONS/CAREER NOTES: Selected by Cincinnati Bengals in first round (fourth pick overall) of 2000 NFL draft. ... Signed by Bengals (June 4, 2000).
HONORS: Named wide receiver on THE SPORTING NEWS college All-America first team (1998 and 1999).
PRO STATISTICS: 2000—Recovered one fumble. 2001—Recovered one fumble.
SINGLE GAME HIGHS (regular season): Receptions—10 (December 30, 2001, vs. Pittsburgh); yards—109 (December 30, 2001, vs. Pittsburgh); and touchdown receptions—1 (September 30, 2001, vs. San Diego).
STATISTICAL PLATEAUS: 100-yard receiving games: 2001 (1).

Year Team	G	GS	RUSHING Att.	Yds.	Avg.	TD	RECEIVING No.	Yds.	Avg.	TD	PUNT RETURNS No.	Yds.	Avg.	TD	TOTALS TD	2pt.	Pts.	Fum.
2000—Cincinnati NFL	16	16	16	148	9.3	2	51	592	11.6	4	7	123	17.6	1	7	0	42	2
2001—Cincinnati NFL	16	14	8	14	1.8	0	70	667	9.5	1	18	116	6.4	0	1	0	6	3
Pro totals (2 years)	32	30	24	162	6.8	2	121	1259	10.4	5	25	239	9.6	1	8	0	48	5

WASHINGTON, DAMON　　　RB　　　GIANTS

PERSONAL: Born February 20, 1977, in Lockney, Texas. ... 5-11/193. ... Full name: Damon Keane Washington.
HIGH SCHOOL: Southwest (San Diego, Calif.).
COLLEGE: Colorado State.
TRANSACTIONS/CAREER NOTES: Signed as undrafted free agent by Chicago Bears (April 23, 1999). ... Released by Bears (September 6, 1999). ... Re-signed by Bears to practice squad (October 20, 1999). ... Released by Bears (November 8, 1999). ... Signed by St. Louis Rams (April 25, 2000). ... Released by Rams (August 28, 2000). ... Signed by New York Giants to practice squad (September 12, 2000). ... Activated (November 22, 2000).
PLAYING EXPERIENCE: New York Giants NFL, 2000 and 2001. ... Games/Games started: 2000 (3/0), 2001 (10/0). Total: 13/0.
PRO STATISTICS: 2001—Rushed 28 times for 89 yards, caught four passes for 25 yards, returned six kickoffs for 99 yards, fumbled twice and recovered one fumble.
SINGLE GAME HIGHS (regular season): Attempts—25 (October 7, 2001, vs. Washington); yards—90 (October 7, 2001, vs. Washington); and rushing touchdowns—0.

W

WASHINGTON, DEWAYNE   CB   STEELERS

PERSONAL: Born December 27, 1972, in Durham, N.C. ... 6-0/193. ... Full name: Dewayne Neron Washington.
HIGH SCHOOL: Northern (Durham, N.C.).
COLLEGE: North Carolina State.
TRANSACTIONS/CAREER NOTES: Selected by Minnesota Vikings in first round (18th pick overall) of 1994 NFL draft. ... Signed by Vikings (July 14, 1994). ... Granted unconditional free agency (February 13, 1998). ... Signed by Pittsburgh Steelers February 25, 1998).
CHAMPIONSHIP GAME EXPERIENCE: Played in AFC championship game (2001 season).
HONORS: Was a high school All-America selection by The Sporting News (1989).
PRO STATISTICS: 1994—Recovered two fumbles for 17 yards and one touchdown. 1998—Recovered two fumbles. 2001—Credited with one sack and recovered one fumble for 63 yards and a touchdown.

				INTERCEPTIONS		
Year Team	G	GS	No.	Yds.	Avg.	TD
1994—Minnesota NFL	16	16	3	135	45.0	2
1995—Minnesota NFL	15	15	1	25	25.0	0
1996—Minnesota NFL	16	16	2	27	13.5	1
1997—Minnesota NFL	16	16	4	71	17.8	0
1998—Pittsburgh NFL	16	16	5	§178	35.6	▲2
1999—Pittsburgh NFL	16	16	4	1	0.3	0
2000—Pittsburgh NFL	16	16	5	59	11.8	0
2001—Pittsburgh NFL	16	16	1	15	15.0	0
Pro totals (8 years)	127	127	25	511	20.4	5

WASHINGTON, KEITH   DE   BRONCOS

PERSONAL: Born December 18, 1972, in Dallas. ... 6-4/275. ... Full name: Keith L. Washington.
HIGH SCHOOL: Wilmer-Hutchins (Dallas).
COLLEGE: UNLV.
TRANSACTIONS/CAREER NOTES: Signed as non-drafted free agent by Minnesota Vikings (April 9, 1995). ... Released by Vikings (August 27, 1995). ... Re-signed by Vikings to practice squad (August 28, 1995). ... Activated (October 9, 1995); did not play. ... On injured reserve with ankle injury (November 15, 1995-remainder of season). ... Released by Vikings (August 25, 1996). ... Signed by Detroit Lions (August 26, 1996). ... Released by Lions (August 26, 1997). ... Signed by Baltimore Ravens (October 15, 1997). ... Granted free agency (February 13, 1998). ... Re-signed by Ravens (April 14, 1998). ... Granted unconditional free agency (February 11, 2000). ... Re-signed by Ravens (March 31, 2000). ... Released by Ravens (March 13, 2001). ... Signed by Denver Broncos (April 6, 2001).
PLAYING EXPERIENCE: Detroit NFL, 1996; Baltimore NFL, 1997-2000; Denver NFL, 2001. ... Games/Games started: 1996 (12/0), 1997 (10/1), 1998 (16/0), 1999 (16/0), 2000 (16/0), 2001 (16/16). Total: 86/17.
CHAMPIONSHIP GAME EXPERIENCE: Played in AFC championship game (2000 season). ... Member of Super Bowl championship team (2000 season).
PRO STATISTICS: 1996—Returned one kickoff for 14 yards. 1997—Credited with two sacks. 1998—Credited with one sack. 1999—Returned one kickoff for 12 yards, credited with one sack, fumbled once and recovered one fumble. 2000—Returned one kickoff for 17 yards and recovered one fumble. 2001—Credited with four sacks and recovered one fumble.

WASHINGTON, MARCUS   LB   COLTS

PERSONAL: Born October 17, 1977, in Auburn, Ala. ... 6-3/255. ... Full name: Marcus Cornelius Washington.
HIGH SCHOOL: Auburn (Ala.).
COLLEGE: Auburn.
TRANSACTIONS/CAREER NOTES: Selected by Indianapolis Colts in second round (59th pick overall) of 2000 NFL draft. ... Signed by Colts (July 13, 2000).
PRO STATISTICS: 2000—Intercepted one pass for one yard.

Year Team	G	GS	SACKS
2000—Indianapolis NFL	16	0	2.0
2001—Indianapolis NFL	16	16	8.0
Pro totals (2 years)	32	16	10.0

WASHINGTON, PATRICK   FB   JAGUARS

PERSONAL: Born March 4, 1978, in Washington, D.C. ... 6-2/244. ... Full name: Patrick Orlando Washington Jr.
HIGH SCHOOL: St. Albans (Washington, D.C.).
COLLEGE: Virginia.
TRANSACTIONS/CAREER NOTES: Signed as non-drafted free agent by Jacksonville Jaguars (April 23, 2001).
PLAYING EXPERIENCE: Jacksonville NFL, 2001. ... Games/Games started: (16/6).
PRO STATISTICS: 2001—Caught five passes for 36 yards.

WASHINGTON, TED   DT   BEARS

PERSONAL: Born April 13, 1968, in Tampa. ... 6-5/355. ... Full name: Theodore Washington. ... Son of Ted Washington, linebacker with New York Jets (1973) and Houston Oilers (1974-82).
HIGH SCHOOL: Tampa Bay Vocational Tech Senior.
COLLEGE: Louisville.
TRANSACTIONS/CAREER NOTES: Selected by San Francisco 49ers in first round (25th pick overall) of 1991 NFL draft. ... Signed by 49ers (July 10, 1991). ... Traded by 49ers to Denver Broncos for fifth-round pick (traded to Green Bay) in 1994 draft (April 19, 1994). ... Granted unconditional free agency (February 17, 1995). ... Signed by Buffalo Bills (February 25, 1995). ... Designated by Bills as franchise player

(February 13, 1998). ... Free agency status changed from franchise to transitional (February 27, 1998). ... Re-signed by Bills (March 2, 1998). ... Released by Bills (February 22, 2001). ... Signed by Chicago Bears (April 10, 2001).
CHAMPIONSHIP GAME EXPERIENCE: Played in NFC championship game (1992 and 1993 seasons).
HONORS: Played in Pro Bowl (1997, 1998 and 2000 seasons). ... Named defensive tackle on THE SPORTING NEWS NFL All-Pro team (2001).
PRO STATISTICS: 1993—Recovered one fumble. 1994—Intercepted one pass for five yards. 1997—Recovered one fumble. 1998—Intercepted one pass for no yards and credited with a safety. 2001—Recovered one fumble.

Year Team	G	GS	SACKS
1991—San Francisco NFL	16	0	1.0
1992—San Francisco NFL	16	6	2.0
1993—San Francisco NFL	12	12	3.0
1994—Denver NFL	15	15	2.5
1995—Buffalo NFL	16	15	2.5
1996—Buffalo NFL	16	16	3.5
1997—Buffalo NFL	16	16	4.0
1998—Buffalo NFL	16	16	4.5
1999—Buffalo NFL	16	16	2.5
2000—Buffalo NFL	16	16	2.5
2001—Chicago NFL	16	16	1.5
Pro totals (11 years)	**171**	**144**	**29.5**

WASHINGTON, TODD   C/G   BUCCANEERS

PERSONAL: Born July 19, 1976, in Nassawadox, Va. ... 6-3/324. ... Full name: Todd Page Washington.
HIGH SCHOOL: Nandua (Onley, Va.).
COLLEGE: Virginia Tech (degree in physical education and health, 1998).
TRANSACTIONS/CAREER NOTES: Selected by Tampa Bay Buccaneers in fourth round (104th pick overall) of 1998 NFL draft. ... Signed by Buccaneers (June 11, 1998). ... Granted free agency (March 2, 2001). ... Re-signed by Buccaneers (March 14, 2001). ... Granted unconditional free agency (March 1, 2002). ... Re-signed by Buccaneers (March 18, 2002).
PLAYING EXPERIENCE: Tampa Bay NFL, 1998-2001. ... Games/Games started: 1998 (4/0), 1999 (6/0), 2000 (9/0), 2001 (15/1). Total: 34/1.
CHAMPIONSHIP GAME EXPERIENCE: Played in NFC championship game (1999 season).
PRO STATISTICS: 2001—Returned one kickoff for 22 yards and fumbled once for minus nine yards.

WATERS, BRIAN   C   CHIEFS

PERSONAL: Born February 18, 1977, in Waxahachie, Texas. ... 6-3/315. ... Full name: Brian Demond Waters.
HIGH SCHOOL: Waxahachie (Texas).
COLLEGE: North Texas.
TRANSACTIONS/CAREER NOTES: Signed as non-drafted free agent by Dallas Cowboys (April 23, 1999). ... Released by Cowboys (September 5, 1999). ... Signed by Kansas City Chiefs (January 11, 2000).
PLAYING EXPERIENCE: Kansas City NFL, 2000 and 2001. ... Games/Games started: 2000 (6/0), 2001 (16/8). Total: 22/8.

WATSON, CHRIS   CB   BILLS

PERSONAL: Born June 30, 1977, in Chicago. ... 6-1/188.
HIGH SCHOOL: Leo (Chicago).
COLLEGE: Eastern Illinois.
TRANSACTIONS/CAREER NOTES: Selected by Denver Broncos in third round (67th pick overall) of 1999 NFL draft. ... Signed by Broncos (June 15, 1999). ... Traded by Broncos to Buffalo Bills for fourth-round pick (traded back to Buffalo) in 2001 draft (August 27, 2000). ... Granted free agency (March 1, 2002). ... Re-signed by Bills (March 27, 2002).
PRO STATISTICS: 1999—Recovered three fumbles. 2000—Recovered two fumbles. 2001—Intercepted one pass for 23 yards and recovered one fumble.

			PUNT RETURNS				KICKOFF RETURNS				TOTALS		
Year Team	G	GS	No.	Yds.	Avg.	TD	No.	Yds.	Avg.	TD	TD	2pt.	Pts.	Fum.
1999—Denver NFL	14	1	44	334	7.6	1	48	1138	23.7	0	1	0	6	5
2000—Buffalo NFL	16	4	33	163	4.9	0	44	894	20.3	0	0	0	0	4
2001—Buffalo NFL	14	0	0	0	0.0	0	5	96	19.2	0	0	0	0	1
Pro totals (3 years)	**44**	**5**	**77**	**497**	**6.5**	**1**	**97**	**2128**	**21.9**	**0**	**1**	**0**	**6**	**10**

WATSON, JUSTIN   RB

PERSONAL: Born January 7, 1975, in Bronx, N.Y. ... 6-0/230. ... Full name: Justin Sean Watson.
HIGH SCHOOL: Marshall (Pasadena, Calif.).
COLLEGE: San Diego State (degree in criminal justice).
TRANSACTIONS/CAREER NOTES: Signed as non-drafted free agent by San Diego Chargers (April 20, 1998). ... Released by Chargers (August 24, 1998). ... Re-signed by Chargers to practice squad (November 25, 1998). ... Assigned by Chargers to Berlin Thunder in 1999 NFL Europe enhancement allocation program (February 22, 1999). ... Released by Chargers (April 22, 1999). ... Signed by St. Louis Rams (July 1, 1999). ... Granted free agency (March 1, 2002).
CHAMPIONSHIP GAME EXPERIENCE: Member of Rams for NFC championship game (1999 and 2001 seasons); inactive. ... Member of Super Bowl championship team (1999 season); inactive. ... Member of Rams for Super Bowl XXXVI (2001 season); inactive.
SINGLE GAME HIGHS (regular season): Attempts—17 (November 12, 2000, vs. New York Giants); yards—102 (Ocotber 1, 2000, vs. San Diego); and rushing touchdowns—1 (December 10, 2000, vs. Minnesota).
STATISTICAL PLATEAUS: 100-yard rushing games: 2000 (1).

W

Year Team	G	GS	RUSHING Att.	Yds.	Avg.	TD	RECEIVING No.	Yds.	Avg.	TD	TOTALS TD	2pt.	Pts.	Fum.
1998—San Diego NFL							Did not play.							
1999—Berlin NFLE	...	...	81	333	4.1	2	18	188	10.4	1	3	0	18	0
—St. Louis NFL	8	0	47	179	3.8	0	0	0	0.0	0	0	0	0	2
2000—St. Louis NFL	14	2	54	249	4.6	4	10	56	5.6	0	4	0	24	0
2001—St. Louis NFL	11	0	1	0	0.0	0	0	0	0.0	0	0	0	0	0
NFL Europe totals (1 year)	...	...	81	333	4.1	2	18	188	10.4	1	3	0	18	0
NFL totals (2 years)	33	2	102	428	4.2	4	10	56	5.6	0	4	0	24	2
Pro totals (3 years)	...	...	183	761	4.2	6	28	244	8.7	1	7	0	42	2

WATTERS, RICKY — RB

PERSONAL: Born April 7, 1969, in Harrisburg, Pa. ... 6-1/211. ... Full name: Richard James Watters.
HIGH SCHOOL: Bishop McDevitt (Harrisburg, Pa.).
COLLEGE: Notre Dame (degree in design, 1990).
TRANSACTIONS/CAREER NOTES: Selected by San Francisco 49ers in second round (45th pick overall) of 1991 NFL draft. ... Signed by 49ers (July 11, 1991). ... On injured reserve with foot injury (August 27, 1991-entire season). ... Designated by 49ers as transition player (February 15, 1994). ... Tendered offer sheet by Philadelphia Eagles (March 18, 1995). ... 49ers declined to match offer (March 25, 1995). ... Granted unconditional free agency (February 13, 1998). ... Signed by Seattle Seahawks (March 4, 1998). ... On injured reserve with broken ankle (December 18, 2001-remainder of season). ... Granted unconditional free agency (March 1, 2002).
CHAMPIONSHIP GAME EXPERIENCE: Played in NFC championship game (1992-1994 seasons). ... Member of Super Bowl championship team (1994 season).
HONORS: Played in Pro Bowl (1992-1996 seasons).
POST SEASON RECORDS: Shares Super Bowl single-game records for most points—18; and most touchdowns—3 (January 29, 1995, vs. San Diego. ... Holds NFL postseason single-game records for most points—30; most touchdowns—5; and most rushing touchdowns—5 (January 15, 1994, vs. New York Giants).
PRO STATISTICS: 1992—Attempted one pass without a completion and recovered one fumble. 1993—Recovered one fumble. 1994—Recovered two fumbles. 1997—Recovered one fumble. 1998—Completed one pass for one yard and a touchdown and recovered one fumble. 2000—Recovered two fumbles. 2001—Recovered one fumble.
SINGLE GAME HIGHS (regular season): Attempts—33 (December 10, 1995, vs. Dallas); yards—178 (December 20, 1998, vs. Indianapolis); rushing touchdowns—3 (December 5, 1993, vs. Cincinnati).
STATISTICAL PLATEAUS: 100-yard rushing games: 1992 (4), 1993 (3), 1994 (2), 1995 (4), 1996 (6), 1997 (2), 1998 (4), 1999 (4), 2000 (2), 2001 (1). Total: 32. ... 100-yard receiving games: 1994 (1), 2000 (1). Total: 2.

Year Team	G	GS	RUSHING Att.	Yds.	Avg.	TD	RECEIVING No.	Yds.	Avg.	TD	TOTALS TD	2pt.	Pts.	Fum.
1991—San Francisco NFL							Did not play.							
1992—San Francisco NFL	14	13	206	1013	4.9	9	43	405	9.4	2	11	0	66	2
1993—San Francisco NFL	13	13	208	950	4.6	‡10	31	326	10.5	1	11	0	66	5
1994—San Francisco NFL	16	16	239	877	3.7	6	66	719	10.9	5	11	0	66	8
1995—Philadelphia NFL	16	16	337	1273	3.8	11	62	434	7.0	1	12	0	72	6
1996—Philadelphia NFL	16	16	*353	1411	4.0	13	51	444	8.7	0	13	0	78	5
1997—Philadelphia NFL	16	16	285	1110	3.9	7	48	440	9.2	0	7	0	42	3
1998—Seattle NFL	16	16	319	1239	3.9	9	52	373	7.2	0	9	1	56	4
1999—Seattle NFL	16	16	325	1210	3.7	5	40	387	9.7	2	5	0	42	4
2000—Seattle NFL	16	16	278	1242	4.5	7	63	613	9.7	2	9	0	54	5
2001—Seattle NFL	5	4	72	318	4.4	1	11	107	9.7	0	1	0	6	1
Pro totals (10 years)	144	142	2622	10643	4.1	78	467	4248	9.1	13	91	1	548	43

WAYNE, NATE — LB — PACKERS

PERSONAL: Born January 12, 1975, in Chicago. ... 6-0/237.
HIGH SCHOOL: Noxubee County (Macon, Miss.).
COLLEGE: Mississippi.
TRANSACTIONS/CAREER NOTES: Selected by Denver Broncos in seventh round (219th pick overall) of 1998 NFL draft. ... Signed by Broncos (June 9, 1998). ... Assigned by Broncos to Barcelona Dragons in 1999 NFL Europe enhancement allocation program (February 22, 1999). ... Released by Broncos (September 19, 1999). ... Re-signed by Broncos to practice squad (September 21, 1999). ... Activated (September 22, 1999). ... Traded by Broncos to Green Bay Packers for conditional future draft pick (August 15, 2000).
PLAYING EXPERIENCE: Denver NFL, 1998 and 1999; Barcelona NFLE, 1999; Green Bay NFL, 2000 and 2001. ... Games/Games started: 1998 (1/0), NFLE 1999 (games played unavailable); NFL 1999 (15/0), 2000 (16/13), 2001 (12/12). Total NFL: 44/25.
CHAMPIONSHIP GAME EXPERIENCE: Member of Broncos for AFC championship game (1998 season); inactive. ... Member of Super Bowl championship team (1998 season); inactive.
PRO STATISTICS: NFLE: 1999—Intercepted one pass for 31 yards and credited with one sack. NFL: 1999—Credited with two sacks. 2000—Credited with two sacks and recovered one fumble for nine yards. 2001—Intercepted three passes for 55 yards, credited with 5$^1/_2$ sacks and recovered two fumbles.

WAYNE, REGGIE — WR — COLTS

PERSONAL: Born November 17, 1978, in New Orleans. ... 6-0/203.
HIGH SCHOOL: Ehret (La.).
COLLEGE: Miami (Fla.).
TRANSACTIONS/CAREER NOTES: Selected by Indianapolis Colts in first round (30th pick overall) of 2001 NFL draft. ... Signed by Colts (July 26, 2001).
SINGLE GAME HIGHS (regular season): Receptions—5 (December 16, 2001, vs. Atlanta); yards—78 (December 16, 2001, vs. Atlanta); and touchdown receptions—0.

Year Team	G	GS	RECEIVING No.	Yds.	Avg.	TD
2001—Indianapolis NFL	13	9	27	345	12.8	0

WEARY, FRED   CB   FALCONS

PERSONAL: Born April 12, 1974, in Jacksonville. ... 5-10/181. ... Full name: Joseph Fredrick Weary.
HIGH SCHOOL: Mandarin (Jacksonville).
COLLEGE: Florida.
TRANSACTIONS/CAREER NOTES: Selected by New Orleans Saints in fourth round (97th pick overall) of 1998 NFL draft. ... Signed by Saints (July 10, 1998). ... On injured reserve with knee injury (November 29, 2000-remainder of season). ... Granted free agency (March 2, 2001). ... Re-signed by Saints (March 30, 2001). ... Granted unconditional free agency (March 1, 2002). ... Signed by Atlanta Falcons (April 9, 2002).
HONORS: Named cornerback on THE SPORTING NEWS college All-America first team (1997).
PRO STATISTICS: 1999—Recovered four fumbles for 60 yards. 2000—Credited with two sacks.

			INTERCEPTIONS			
Year Team	G	GS	No.	Yds.	Avg.	TD
1998—New Orleans NFL	14	1	2	64	32.0	1
1999—New Orleans NFL	16	11	2	49	24.5	0
2000—New Orleans NFL	12	12	2	27	13.5	0
2001—New Orleans NFL	14	1	0	0	0.0	0
Pro totals (4 years)	56	25	6	140	23.3	1

WEAVER, JED   TE   DOLPHINS

PERSONAL: Born August 11, 1976, in Bend, Ore. ... 6-4/262. ... Full name: Timothy Jed Weaver. ... Cousin of Jeff Weaver, pitcher, Detroit Tigers.
HIGH SCHOOL: Redmond (Ore.).
COLLEGE: Oregon.
TRANSACTIONS/CAREER NOTES: Selected by Philadelphia Eagles in seventh round (208th pick overall) of 1999 NFL draft. ... Signed by Eagles (July 16, 1999). ... Claimed on waivers by Miami Dolphins (August 23, 2000). ... Granted free agency (March 1, 2002). ... Re-signed by Dolphins (April 1, 2002).
PRO STATISTICS: 2000—Returned one kickoff for 15 yards.
SINGLE GAME HIGHS (regular season): Receptions—5 (December 24, 2000, vs. New England); yards—63 (December 24, 2000, vs. New England); and touchdown receptions—1 (November 25, 2001, vs. Buffalo).

			RECEIVING				TOTALS			
Year Team	G	GS	No.	Yds.	Avg.	TD	TD	2pt.	Pts.	Fum.
1999—Philadelphia NFL	16	10	11	91	8.3	0	0	†1	2	0
2000—Miami NFL	16	0	10	179	17.9	0	0	0	0	1
2001—Miami NFL	16	7	18	215	11.9	2	2	0	12	1
Pro totals (3 years)	48	17	39	485	12.4	2	2	1	14	2

WEBB, RICHMOND   OT   BENGALS

PERSONAL: Born January 11, 1967, in Dallas. ... 6-6/325. ... Full name: Richmond Jewel Webb Jr.
HIGH SCHOOL: Franklin D. Roosevelt (Dallas).
COLLEGE: Texas A&M (degree in industrial distribution).
TRANSACTIONS/CAREER NOTES: Selected by Miami Dolphins in first round (ninth pick overall) of 1990 NFL draft. ... Signed by Dolphins (July 27, 1990). ... Designated by Dolphins as franchise player (February 12, 1999). ... Designated by Dolphins as franchise player (February 11, 2000). ... Granted unconditional free agency (March 2, 2001). ... Signed by Cincinnati Bengals (April 30, 2001).
PLAYING EXPERIENCE: Miami NFL, 1990-2000; Cincinnati NFL, 2001. ... Games/Games started: 1990 (16/16), 1991 (14/14), 1992 (16/16), 1993 (16/16), 1994 (16/16), 1995 (16/16), 1996 (16/16), 1997 (16/16), 1998 (9/9), 1999 (15/14), 2000 (14/14), 2001 (16/16). Total: 180/179.
CHAMPIONSHIP GAME EXPERIENCE: Played in AFC championship game (1992 season).
HONORS: Named NFL Rookie of the Year by THE SPORTING NEWS (1990). ... Played in Pro Bowl (1990-1996 seasons). ... Named offensive tackle on THE SPORTING NEWS NFL All-Pro team (1992 and 1994).
PRO STATISTICS: 1995—Recovered one fumble. 2001—Recovered one fumble.

WEBSTER, JASON   CB   49ERS

PERSONAL: Born September 8, 1977, in Houston. ... 5-10/180. ... Full name: Jason Richmond Webster.
HIGH SCHOOL: Willowridge (Houston).
COLLEGE: Texas A&M.
TRANSACTIONS/CAREER NOTES: Selected by San Francisco 49ers in second round (48th pick overall) of 2000 NFL draft. ... Signed by 49ers (July 18, 2000).
PRO STATISTICS: 2000—Recovered one fumble for one yard. 2001—Credited with ½ sack.

			INTERCEPTIONS			
Year Team	G	GS	No.	Yds.	Avg.	TD
2000—San Francisco NFL	16	10	2	78	39.0	1
2001—San Francisco NFL	16	16	3	61	20.3	0
Pro totals (2 years)	32	26	5	139	27.8	1

WEBSTER, LARRY   DT   JETS

PERSONAL: Born January 18, 1969, in Elkton, Md. ... 6-5/315. ... Full name: Larry Melvin Webster Jr.
HIGH SCHOOL: Elkton (Md.).
COLLEGE: Maryland.
TRANSACTIONS/CAREER NOTES: Selected by Miami Dolphins in third round (70th pick overall) of 1992 NFL draft. ... Signed by Dolphins (July 10, 1992). ... Granted free agency (February 17, 1995). ... Signed by Cleveland Browns (May 4, 1995). ... On suspended list for violating league substance abuse policy (September 4-26, 1995). ... Browns franchise moved to Baltimore and renamed Ravens for 1996 season (March 11, 1996).

... On suspended list for violating league substance abuse policy (August 20, 1996-July 13, 1997). ... Granted unconditional free agency (February 13, 1998). ... Re-signed by Ravens (February 16, 1998). ... Granted unconditional free agency (February 11, 2000). ... Re-signed by Ravens (February 16, 2000). ... On suspended list for violating league substance abuse policy (July 6-November 13, 2000). ... Released by Ravens (March 1, 2002). ... Signed by New York Jets (April 28, 2002).
PLAYING EXPERIENCE: Miami NFL, 1992-1994; Cleveland NFL, 1995; Baltimore NFL, 1997-2001. ... Games/Games started: 1992 (16/0), 1993 (13/9), 1994 (16/7), 1995 (10/0), 1997 (16/3), 1998 (15/0), 1999 (16/16), 2000 (5/0), 2001 (15/0). Total: 122/35.
CHAMPIONSHIP GAME EXPERIENCE: Played in AFC championship game (1992 and 2000 seasons). ... Member of Super Bowl championship team (2000 season).
PRO STATISTICS: 1992—Credited with 1½ sacks. 1993—Recovered one fumble. 1999—Credited with two sacks. 2000—Recovered one fumble. 2001—Credited with ½ sack.

WEBSTER, NATE　　　LB　　　BUCCANEERS

PERSONAL: Born November 29, 1977, in Miami. ... 5-11/225. ... Full name: Nathaniel Webster Jr.
HIGH SCHOOL: Northwestern (Miami).
COLLEGE: Miami (Fla.).
TRANSACTIONS/CAREER NOTES: Selected after junior season by Tampa Bay Buccaneers in third round (90th pick overall) of 2000 NFL draft. ... Signed by Buccaneers (July 11, 2000).
PLAYING EXPERIENCE: Tampa Bay NFL, 2000 and 2001. ... Games/Games started: 2000 (16/0), 2001 (16/1). Total: 32/1.
HONORS: Named linebacker on THE SPORTING NEWS college All-America second team (1999).

WEDDERBURN, FLOYD　　　OT　　　SEAHAWKS

PERSONAL: Born May 5, 1976, in Kingston, Jamaica. ... 6-5/333. ... Full name: Floyd E. Wedderburn.
HIGH SCHOOL: Upper Darby (Drexel Hill, Pa.).
COLLEGE: Penn State.
TRANSACTIONS/CAREER NOTES: Selected by Seattle Seahawks in fifth round (140th pick overall) of 1999 NFL draft. ... Signed by Seahawks (July 29, 1999). ... Active for five games (1999); did not play. ... Granted free agency (March 1, 2002).
PLAYING EXPERIENCE: Seattle NFL, 2000 and 2001. ... Games/Games started: 2000 (16/16), 2001 (16/0). Total: 32/16.

WEINER, TODD　　　OT　　　FALCONS

PERSONAL: Born September 16, 1975, in Bristol, Pa. ... 6-4/297.
HIGH SCHOOL: Taravella (Coral Springs, Fla.).
COLLEGE: Kansas State.
TRANSACTIONS/CAREER NOTES: Selected by Seattle Seahawks in second round (47th pick overall) of 1998 NFL draft. ... Signed by Seahawks (July 15, 1998). ... Granted unconditional free agency (March 1, 2002). ... Signed by Atlanta Falcons (March 6, 2002).
PLAYING EXPERIENCE: Seattle NFL, 1998-2001. ... Games/Games started: 1998 (6/0), 1999 (11/1), 2000 (16/6), 2001 (16/13). Total: 49/20.
HONORS: Named offensive tackle on THE SPORTING NEWS college All-America second team (1997).
PRO STATISTICS: 2001—Recovered one fumble for minus three yards.

WEINKE, CHRIS　　　QB　　　PANTHERS

PERSONAL: Born July 31, 1972, in St. Paul, Minn. ... 6-4/232.
HIGH SCHOOL: Cretin-Derham (St. Paul, Minn.).
COLLEGE: Florida State (degree in sports management).
TRANSACTIONS/CAREER NOTES: Selected by Carolina Panthers in fourth round (106th pick overall) of 2001 NFL draft. ... Signed by Panthers (July 21, 2001).
HONORS: Named quarterback on THE SPORTING NEWS college All-America second team (2000). ... Heisman Trophy winner (2000). ... Davey O'Brien Award winner (2000).
PRO STATISTICS: 2001—Fumbled 11 times and recovered one fumble for minus two yards.
SINGLE GAME HIGHS (regular season): Attempts—63 (December 30, 2001, vs. Arizona); completions—36 (December 30, 2001, vs. Arizona); yards—312 (December 23, 2001, vs. St. Louis); and touchdown passes—2 (November 18, 2001, vs. San Francisco).
STATISTICAL PLATEAUS: 300-yard passing games: 2001 (1).
MISCELLANEOUS: Regular-season record as starting NFL quarterback: 1-14 (.067).

				PASSING							RUSHING				TOTALS	
Year Team	G	GS	Att.	Cmp.	Pct.	Yds.	TD	Int.	Avg.	Rat.	Att.	Yds.	Avg.	TD	TD	2pt.	Pts.
2001—Carolina NFL	15	15	540	293	54.3	2931	11	19	5.43	62.0	37	128	3.5	6	6	0	36

RECORD AS BASEBALL PLAYER

TRANSACTIONS/CAREER NOTES: Selected by Toronto Blue Jays organization in second round of free-agent draft (June 4, 1990).

					BATTING								FIELDING		
Year Team (League)	Pos.	G	AB	R	H	2B	3B	HR	RBI	Avg.	BB	SO	SB	PO	A	E	Avg.
1991—St. Cath. (NY-Penn)	1B	75	272	31	65	9	1	3	40	.239	41	61	12	56	132	21	.900
1992—Myrtle Beach (S.Atl.)	1B	135	458	61	110	16	2	13	63	.240	70	89	4	1141	85	26	.979
1993—Dunedin (FSL)	1B	128	476	68	135	16	2	17	98	.284	66	78	8	1142	101	20	.984
1994—Knoxville (Sou.)	1B	139	526	61	133	23	2	8	87	.253	45	121	12	1173	93	9	.993
1995—Syracuse (I.L.)	1B-3B	113	341	42	77	12	2	10	41	.226	44	74	4	1173	93	9	.993
1996—Syracuse (I.L.)	1B	51	161	21	30	8	1	3	18	.186	19	49	0	321	36	9	.975
—Knoxville (Sou.)	1B	75	265	48	70	18	2	15	55	.264	52	74	2	78	13	0	1.000

WELBOURN, JOHN   OT/G   EAGLES

PERSONAL: Born March 30, 1976, in Torrance, Calif. ... 6-5/318. ... Full name: John R. Welbourn.
HIGH SCHOOL: Palos Verdes Peninsula (Rolling Hills Estate, Calif.).
COLLEGE: California (degree in rhetoric).
TRANSACTIONS/CAREER NOTES: Selected by Philadelphia Eagles in fourth round (97th pick overall) of 1999 NFL draft. ... Signed by Eagles (July 25, 1999). ... On injured reserve with knee injury (September 13, 1999-remainder of season).
PLAYING EXPERIENCE: Philadelphia NFL, 1999-2001. ... Games/Games started: 1999 (1/1), 2000 (16/16), 2001 (15/15). Total: 32/32.
CHAMPIONSHIP GAME EXPERIENCE: Played in NFC championship game (2001 season).
PRO STATISTICS: 2000—Recovered one fumble.

WELLS, DEAN   LB

PERSONAL: Born July 20, 1970, in Louisville, Ky. ... 6-3/248. ... Full name: Donald Dean Wells.
HIGH SCHOOL: Holy Cross (Louisville, Ky.).
COLLEGE: Kentucky (degree in marketing, 1992).
TRANSACTIONS/CAREER NOTES: Selected by Seattle Seahawks in fourth round (85th pick overall) of 1993 NFL draft. ... Signed by Seahawks (July 13, 1993). ... Granted unconditional free agency (February 12, 1999). ... Signed by Carolina Panthers (April 7, 1999). ... Released by Panthers (February 22, 2002).
PLAYING EXPERIENCE: Seattle NFL, 1993-1998; Carolina NFL, 1999-2001. ... Games/Games started: 1993 (14/1), 1994 (15/0), 1995 (14/10), 1996 (16/15), 1997 (16/16), 1998 (9/8), 1999 (16/10), 2000 (16/14), 2001 (13/3). Total: 129/77.
PRO STATISTICS: 1995—Recovered one fumble. 1996—Credited with one sack and recovered two fumbles. 1997—Credited with one sack and recovered one fumble. 1998—Intercepted one pass for 25 yards. 1999—Intercepted one pass for one yard and credited with $^1\!/_2$ sack. 2000—Intercepted one pass for 14 yards.

WELLS, MIKE   DT

PERSONAL: Born January 6, 1971, in Arnold, Mo. ... 6-3/315. ... Full name: Mike Allan Wells.
HIGH SCHOOL: Fox (Arnold, Mo.).
COLLEGE: Iowa (degree in communication studies, 1994).
TRANSACTIONS/CAREER NOTES: Selected by Minnesota Vikings in fourth round (125th pick overall) of 1994 NFL draft. ... Signed by Vikings (June 24, 1994). ... Released by Vikings (August 28, 1994). ... Signed by Detroit Lions (August 29, 1994). ... Granted free agency (February 14, 1997). ... Re-signed by Lions (June 2, 1997). ... Granted unconditional free agency (February 13, 1998). ... Signed by Chicago Bears (February 17, 1998). ... Released by Bears (August 15, 2001). ... Signed by Indianapolis Colts (August 20, 2001). ... Released by Colts (February 21, 2002).
PLAYING EXPERIENCE: Detroit NFL, 1994-1997; Chicago NFL, 1998-2000; Indianapolis NFL, 2001. ... Games/Games started: 1994 (4/0), 1995 (15/0), 1996 (16/1), 1997 (16/16), 1998 (16/16), 1999 (16/16), 2000 (16/14), 2001 (6/0). Total: 115/63.
PRO STATISTICS: 1995—Credited with $^1\!/_2$ sack. 1996—Recovered one fumble in end zone for a touchdown. 1997—Credited with one sack and recovered one fumble. 1998—Credited with three sacks. 1999—Credited with one sack and recovered one fumble. 2000—Credited with one sack, intercepted one pass for 21 yards and caught one pass for 13 yards.

WESLEY, GREG   S   CHIEFS

PERSONAL: Born March 19, 1976, in Little Rock, Ark. ... 6-2/208. ... Full name: Gregory Lashon Wesley.
HIGH SCHOOL: England (Ark.).
COLLEGE: Arkansas-Pine Bluff.
TRANSACTIONS/CAREER NOTES: Selected by Kansas City Chiefs in third round (85th pick overall) of 2000 NFL draft. ... Signed by Chiefs (June 6, 2000).
PRO STATISTICS: 2000—Recovered one fumble. 2001—Recovered two fumbles.

			INTERCEPTIONS				SACKS
Year Team	G	GS	No.	Yds.	Avg.	TD	No.
2000—Kansas City NFL	16	16	2	28	14.0	0	1.0
2001—Kansas City NFL	16	16	2	44	22.0	0	2.0
Pro totals (2 years)	32	32	4	72	18.0	0	3.0

WESLEY, JOE   LB   JAGUARS

PERSONAL: Born November 10, 1976, in Jackson, Miss. ... 6-1/240.
HIGH SCHOOL: Brookhaven (Miss.).
COLLEGE: Louisiana State.
TRANSACTIONS/CAREER NOTES: Signed as non-drafted free agent by San Francisco 49ers (April 23, 1999). ... Released by 49ers (September 5, 1999). ... Re-signed by 49ers to practice squad (September 6, 1999). ... Activated (September 15, 1999). ... On injured reserve with groin injury (December 8, 1999-remainder of season). ... Released by 49ers (August 27, 2000). ... Selected by Berlin Thunder in 2001 NFL Europe draft (February 18, 2001). ... Signed by Jacksonville Jaguars (July 25, 2001). ... Released by Jaguars (September 2, 2001). ... Re-signed by Jaguars (September 11, 2001). ... Released by Jaguars (October 11, 2001). ... Re-signed by Jaguars to practice squad (October 22, 2001). ... Released by Jaguars (November 21, 2001). ... Re-signed by Jaguars to practice squad (November 28, 2001). ... Activated (December 4, 2001).
PLAYING EXPERIENCE: San Francisco NFL, 1999; Berlin NFLE, 2001; Jacksonville NFL, 2001. ... Games/Games started: 1999 (8/0), NFLE 2001 (games played unavailable), NFL 2001 (6/0). Total: 14/0.
PRO STATISTICS: NFLE: 2001—Intercepted one pass for 17 yards and credited with one sack.

WESTBROOK, BRYANT   CB   COWBOYS

PERSONAL: Born December 19, 1974, in Charlotte. ... 6-0/198. ... Full name: Bryant Antoine Westbrook.
HIGH SCHOOL: El Camino (Oceanside, Calif.).
COLLEGE: Texas.
TRANSACTIONS/CAREER NOTES: Selected by Detroit Lions in first round (fifth pick overall) of 1997 NFL draft. ... Signed by Lions (August 9, 1997). ... On injured reserve with Achilles' injury (December 4, 2000-remainder of season). ... Granted unconditional free agency (March 2, 2002). ... Signed by Dallas Cowboys (March 22, 2002).
PRO STATISTICS: 1999—Recovered one fumble.

				INTERCEPTIONS		
Year Team	G	GS	No.	Yds.	Avg.	TD
1997—Detroit NFL	15	14	2	64	32.0	1
1998—Detroit NFL	16	16	3	49	16.3	1
1999—Detroit NFL	10	8	0	0	0.0	0
2000—Detroit NFL	13	13	6	126	21.0	1
2001—Detroit NFL	10	3	1	0	0.0	0
Pro totals (5 years)	64	54	12	239	19.9	3

WESTBROOK, MICHAEL   WR

PERSONAL: Born July 7, 1972, in Detroit. ... 6-3/220.
HIGH SCHOOL: Chadsey (Detroit).
COLLEGE: Colorado.
TRANSACTIONS/CAREER NOTES: Selected by Washington Redskins in first round (fourth pick overall) of 1995 NFL draft. ... Signed by Redskins (August 14, 1995). ... On injured reserve with neck injury (December 8, 1998-remainder of season). ... On injured reserve with knee injury (September 12, 2000-remainder of season). ... Granted unconditional free agency (March 1, 2002).
HONORS: Named wide receiver on THE Sporting News college All-America first team (1994).
PRO STATISTICS: 1999—Recovered one fumble.
SINGLE GAME HIGHS (regular season): Receptions—10 (November 22, 1998, vs. Arizona); yards—159 (September 12, 1999, vs. Dallas); and touchdown receptions—3 (November 22, 1998, vs. Arizona).
STATISTICAL PLATEAUS: 100-yard receiving games: 1996 (1), 1997 (1), 1998 (4), 1999 (5), 2001 (1). Total: 12.

			RUSHING				RECEIVING				TOTALS			
Year Team	G	GS	Att.	Yds.	Avg.	TD	No.	Yds.	Avg.	TD	TD	2pt.	Pts.	Fum.
1995—Washington NFL	11	9	6	114	19.0	1	34	522	15.4	1	2	0	12	0
1996—Washington NFL	11	6	2	2	1.0	0	34	505	14.9	1	1	0	6	0
1997—Washington NFL	13	9	3	-11	-3.7	0	34	559	16.4	3	3	0	18	0
1998—Washington NFL	11	10	1	11	11.0	0	44	736	16.7	6	6	0	36	0
1999—Washington NFL	16	16	7	35	5.0	0	65	1191	18.3	9	9	†1	56	3
2000—Washington NFL	2	2	0	0	0.0	0	9	103	11.4	0	0	0	0	0
2001—Washington NFL	16	16	2	8	4.0	0	57	664	11.6	4	4	0	24	0
Pro totals (7 years)	80	68	21	159	7.6	1	277	4280	15.5	24	25	1	152	3

WESTMORELAND, ERIC   LB   JAGUARS

PERSONAL: Born March 11, 1977, in Jasper, Tenn. ... 6-0/234. ... Full name: Eric Lebron Westmoreland.
HIGH SCHOOL: Marion County (Tenn.).
COLLEGE: Tennessee.
TRANSACTIONS/CAREER NOTES: Selected by Jacksonville Jaguars in third round (73rd pick overall) of 2001 NFL draft. ... Signed by Jaguars (June 4, 2001).
PRO STATISTICS: 2001—Recovered one fumble.

Year Team	G	GS	SACKS
2001—Jacksonville NFL	11	2	1.0

WHEATLEY, TYRONE   RB   RAIDERS

PERSONAL: Born January 19, 1972, in Inkster, Mich. ... 6-0/235.
HIGH SCHOOL: Robichaud (Dearborn Heights, Mich.).
COLLEGE: Michigan.
TRANSACTIONS/CAREER NOTES: Selected by New York Giants in first round (17th pick overall) of 1995 NFL draft. ... Signed by Giants (August 9, 1995). ... Traded by Giants to Miami Dolphins for seventh-round pick (LB O.J. Childress) in 1999 draft (February 12, 1999). ... Released by Dolphins (August 3, 1999). ... Signed by Oakland Raiders (August 4, 1999).
CHAMPIONSHIP GAME EXPERIENCE: Played in AFC championship game (2000 season).
PRO STATISTICS: 1996—Completed only pass attempt for 24 yards and a touchdown and recovered one fumble for minus 18 yards. 1997—Recovered three fumbles. 1999—Recovered one fumble. 2000—Recovered one fumble.
SINGLE GAME HIGHS (regular season): Attempts—26 (December 16, 2000, vs. Seattle); yards—156 (October 22, 2000, vs. Seattle); and rushing touchdowns—2 (September 24, 2000, vs. Cleveland).
STATISTICAL PLATEAUS: 100-yard rushing games: 1997 (1), 1999 (2), 2000 (3). Total: 6.

			RUSHING				RECEIVING			KICKOFF RETURNS			TOTALS			
Year Team	G	GS	Att.	Yds.	Avg.	TD	No.	Yds.	Avg.	No.	Yds.	Avg.	TD	TD	2pt.	Pts.	Fum.
1995—New York Giants NFL	13	1	78	245	3.1	3	5	27	5.4	0	10	186	18.6	0	3	0	18	2
1996—New York Giants NFL	14	0	112	400	3.6	1	12	51	4.3	2	23	503	21.9	0	3	0	18	6
1997—New York Giants NFL	14	7	152	583	3.8	4	16	140	8.8	0	0	0	0.0	0	4	0	24	3
1998—New York Giants NFL	5	0	14	52	3.7	0	0	0	0.0	0	1	16	16.0	0	0	0	0	0
1999—Oakland NFL	16	9	242	936	3.9	8	21	196	9.3	3	0	0	0.0	0	11	0	66	3
2000—Oakland NFL	14	13	232	1046	4.5	9	20	156	7.8	1	0	0	0.0	0	10	0	60	4
2001—Oakland NFL	12	3	88	276	3.1	5	12	61	5.1	1	0	0	0.0	0	6	0	36	3
Pro totals (7 years)	88	33	918	3538	3.9	30	86	631	7.3	7	34	705	20.7	0	37	0	222	21

WHEELER, DAMEN — CB — JAGUARS

PERSONAL: Born September 3, 1977, in Sacramento. ... 5-9/180. ... Full name: Damen Keoki Wheeler.
HIGH SCHOOL: Valley (Sacramento).
COLLEGE: Colorado.
TRANSACTIONS/CAREER NOTES: Selected by San Diego Chargers in sixth round (203rd pick overall) of 2000 NFL draft. ... Signed by Chargers (July 18, 2000). ... Released by Chargers (July 24, 2000). ... Signed by Detroit Lions (August 31, 2000). ... Released by Lions (September 19, 2000). ... Signed by St. Louis Rams (May 5, 2001). ... Released by Rams (September 1, 2001). ... Signed by Jacksonville Jaguars to practice squad (October 14, 2001). ... Activated (December 7, 2001).
PLAYING EXPERIENCE: Jacksonville NFL, 2001. ... Games/Games started: 2001 (5/0).
HONORS: Named cornerback on THE SPORTING NEWS college All-America second team (1999).

WHIGHAM, LARRY — S — BEARS

PERSONAL: Born June 23, 1972, in Hattiesburg, Miss. ... 6-2/221. ... Full name: Larry Jerome Whigham.
HIGH SCHOOL: Hattiesburg (Miss.).
JUNIOR COLLEGE: Pearl River Community College (Poplarville, Miss.).
COLLEGE: Northeast Louisiana (degree in criminal justice).
TRANSACTIONS/CAREER NOTES: Selected by Seattle Seahawks in fourth round (110th pick overall) of 1994 NFL draft. ... Signed by Seahawks (June 9, 1994). ... Released by Seahawks (August 28, 1994). ... Re-signed by Seahawks to practice squad (August 29, 1994). ... Signed by New England Patriots off Seahawks practice squad (September 13, 1994). ... Granted free agency (February 14, 1997). ... Re-signed by Patriots (May 1, 1997). ... Granted unconditional free agency (February 12, 1999). ... Re-signed by Patriots (April 14, 1999). ... Released by Patriots (March 13, 2001). ... Signed by Chicago Bears (April 18, 2001).
CHAMPIONSHIP GAME EXPERIENCE: Played in AFC championship game (1996 season). ... Played in Super Bowl XXXI (1996 season).
HONORS: Played in Pro Bowl (1997 season).
PRO STATISTICS: 1994—Fumbled once. 1995—Recovered one fumble. 1996—Recovered one fumble. 1997—Credited with two sacks. 1998—Returned one kickoff for no yards. 1999—Credited with three sacks.

			INTERCEPTIONS			
Year Team	G	GS	No.	Yds.	Avg.	TD
1994—New England NFL	12	0	1	21	21.0	0
1995—New England NFL	16	0	0	0	0.0	0
1996—New England NFL	16	1	0	0	0.0	0
1997—New England NFL	16	0	2	60	30.0	1
1998—New England NFL	16	0	1	0	0.0	0
1999—New England NFL	16	0	0	0	0.0	0
2000—New England NFL	14	4	0	0	0.0	0
2001—Chicago NFL	14	0	0	0	0.0	0
Pro totals (8 years)	120	5	4	81	20.3	1

WHITE, CLAYTON — LB — GIANTS

PERSONAL: Born December 2, 1977, in Dunn, N.C. ... 5-11/225.
HIGH SCHOOL: Triton (Dunn, N.C.).
COLLEGE: North Carolina State.
TRANSACTIONS/CAREER NOTES: Signed as non-drafted free agent by New York Giants (April 27, 2001).
PLAYING EXPERIENCE: New York Giants NFL, 2001. ... Games/Games started: (16/0).

WHITE, DEZ — WR — BEARS

PERSONAL: Born August 23, 1979, in Orange Park, Fla. ... 6-1/215. ... Full name: Edward Dezmon White. ... Nephew of Adrian White, defensive back with New York Giants (1987-89 and 1991), Green Bay Packers (1992) and New England Patriots (1993).
HIGH SCHOOL: Bolles (Orange Park, Fla.).
COLLEGE: Georgia Tech.
TRANSACTIONS/CAREER NOTES: Selected after junior season by Chicago Bears in third round (69th pick overall) of 2000 NFL draft. ... Signed by Bears (July 19, 2000).
SINGLE GAME HIGHS (regular season): Receptions—7 (November 11, 2001, vs. Green Bay); yards—92 (November 4, 2001, vs. Cleveland); and touchdown receptions—1 (October 15, 2000, vs. Minnesota).

			RECEIVING				TOTALS			
Year Team	G	GS	No.	Yds.	Avg.	TD	TD	2pt.	Pts.	Fum.
2000—Chicago NFL	15	0	10	87	8.7	1	1	0	6	1
2001—Chicago NFL	14	6	45	428	9.5	0	0	0	0	0
Pro totals (2 years)	29	6	55	515	9.4	1	1	0	6	1

WHITE, JAMEL — RB — BROWNS

PERSONAL: Born February 11, 1977, in Los Angeles. ... 5-9/208.
HIGH SCHOOL: Palmdale (Calif.).
COLLEGE: South Dakota.
TRANSACTIONS/CAREER NOTES: Signed as non-drafted free agent by Indianapolis Colts (April 20, 2000). ... Released by Colts (August 27, 2000). ... Signed by Cleveland Browns (August 29, 2000).
SINGLE GAME HIGHS (regular season): Attempts—23 (September 30, 2001, vs. Jacksonville); yards—131 (December 23, 2001, vs. Green Bay); and rushing touchdowns—2 (December 30, 2001, vs. Tennessee).
STATISTICAL PLATEAUS: 100-yard rushing games: 2001 (1).

Year Team	G	GS	RUSHING Att.	Yds.	Avg.	TD	RECEIVING No.	Yds.	Avg.	TD	KICKOFF RETURNS No.	Yds.	Avg.	TD	TOTALS TD	2pt.	Pts.	Fum.
2000—Cleveland NFL	13	0	47	145	3.1	0	13	100	7.7	0	43	935	21.7	0	0	0	0	0
2001—Cleveland NFL	16	7	126	443	3.5	5	44	418	9.5	1	9	189	21.0	0	6	1	38	1
Pro totals (2 years)	29	7	173	588	3.4	5	57	518	9.1	1	52	1124	21.6	0	6	1	38	1

WHITE, REGGIE — RB — JAGUARS

PERSONAL: Born July 11, 1979, in Liberty, Texas. ... 6-0/228.
HIGH SCHOOL: Liberty (Texas).
COLLEGE: Oklahoma State.
TRANSACTIONS/CAREER NOTES: Signed as non-drafted free agent by New York Jets (April 26, 2001). ... Released by Jets (September 1, 2001). ... Signed by Tennessee Titans to practice squad (September 5, 2001). ... Released by Titans (October 16, 2001). ... Signed by Pittsburgh Steelers to practice squad (October 31, 2001). ... Released by Steelers (November 5, 2001). ... Signed by Jacksonville Jaguars (April 4, 2002).
PLAYING EXPERIENCE: Jacksonville NFL, 2001. ... Games/Games started: (5/0).

WHITE, STEVE — DE — JETS

PERSONAL: Born October 25, 1973, in Memphis, Tenn. ... 6-2/271. ... Full name: Stephen Gregory White.
HIGH SCHOOL: Westwood (Memphis, Tenn.).
COLLEGE: Tennessee (degree in psychology, 1996).
TRANSACTIONS/CAREER NOTES: Selected by Philadelphia Eagles in sixth round (194th pick overall) of 1996 NFL draft. ... Signed by Eagles (July 17, 1996). ... Released by Eagles (August 20, 1996). ... Signed by Tampa Bay Buccaneers to practice squad (August 27, 1996). ... Activated (October 15, 1996). ... Released by Buccaneers (November 9, 1996). ... Re-signed by Buccaneers (November 12, 1996). ... Granted unconditional free agency (March 1, 2002). ... Signed by New York Jets (March 7, 2002).
PLAYING EXPERIENCE: Tampa Bay NFL, 1996-2001. ... Games/Games started: 1996 (4/0), 1997 (15/1), 1998 (16/0), 1999 (13/13), 2000 (15/0), 2001 (16/1). Total: 79/15.
CHAMPIONSHIP GAME EXPERIENCE: Played in NFC championship game (1999 season).
PRO STATISTICS: 1997—Returned one kickoff for no yards. 1998—Credited with two sacks and recovered one fumble. 1999—Credited with two sacks and recovered one fumble. 2000—Credited with two sacks. 2001—Returned one kickoff for no yards, credited with five sacks and fumbled once.

WHITEHEAD, WILLIE — DE — SAINTS

PERSONAL: Born January 26, 1973, in Tuskegee, Ala. ... 6-3/285. ... Full name: William Whitehead.
HIGH SCHOOL: Tuskegee (Ala.) Institute.
COLLEGE: Auburn.
TRANSACTIONS/CAREER NOTES: Signed as non-drafted free agent by San Francisco 49ers (April 26, 1995). ... Released by 49ers (July 16, 1995). ... Signed by Baltimore Stallions of CFL (August 1995). ... Signed by Montreal Alouettes of CFL to practice squad (1996). ... Signed by Hamilton Tiger-Cats of CFL (May 14, 1997). ... Signed by Detroit Lions (February 11, 1998). ... Released by Lions (August 25, 1998). ... Signed by New Orleans Saints (January 27, 1999). ... Assigned by Saints to Frankfurt Galaxy in 1999 NFL Europe enhancement allocation program (February 22, 1999). ... Granted free agency (March 1, 2002).
PRO STATISTICS: 1997—Recovered one fumble. 2001—Returned two kickoffs for 19 yards.

Year Team	G	GS	SACKS
1995—Baltimore CFL	1	...	0.0
1996—Montreal CFL	Did not play.		
1997—Hamilton CFL	15	...	13.0
1998—	Did not play.		
1999—Frankfurt NFLE	...	...	2.0
—New Orleans NFL	16	3	7.0
2000—New Orleans NFL	16	2	5.5
2001—New Orleans NFL	14	0	2.0
NFL Europe totals (1 year)	...	...	2.0
CFL totals (2 years)	16	...	13.0
NFL totals (3 years)	46	5	14.5
Pro totals (6 years)	...	...	29.5

WHITFIELD, BOB — OT — FALCONS

PERSONAL: Born October 18, 1971, in Carson, Calif. ... 6-5/310. ... Full name: Bob Whitfield Jr.
HIGH SCHOOL: Banning (Los Angeles).
COLLEGE: Stanford.
TRANSACTIONS/CAREER NOTES: Selected after junior season by Atlanta Falcons in first round (eighth pick overall) of 1992 NFL draft. ... Signed by Falcons (September 4, 1992). ... Granted roster exemption for one game (September 1992).
PLAYING EXPERIENCE: Atlanta NFL, 1992-2001. ... Games/Games started: 1992 (11/0), 1993 (16/16), 1994 (16/16), 1995 (16/16), 1996 (16/16), 1997 (16/16), 1998 (16/16), 1999 (16/16), 2000 (15/15), 2001 (16/16). Total: 154/143.
CHAMPIONSHIP GAME EXPERIENCE: Played in NFC championship game (1998 season). ... Played in Super Bowl XXXIII (1998 season).
HONORS: Named offensive tackle on THE SPORTING NEWS college All-America first team (1991). ... Played in Pro Bowl (1998 season).
PRO STATISTICS: 1993—Recovered two fumbles. 1996—Recovered one fumble. 2001—Recovered two fumbles for five yards.

WHITING, BRANDON — DT/DE — EAGLES

PERSONAL: Born July 30, 1976, in Santa Rosa, Calif. ... 6-3/285. ... Name pronounced WHITE-ing.
HIGH SCHOOL: Polytechnic (Pasadena, Calif.).
COLLEGE: California.

TRANSACTIONS/CAREER NOTES: Selected by Philadelphia Eagles in fourth round (112th pick overall) of 1998 NFL draft. ... Signed by Eagles (July 14, 1998). ... Granted free agency (March 2, 2001). ... Re-signed by Eagles (March 20, 2001).
CHAMPIONSHIP GAME EXPERIENCE: Played in NFC championship game (2001 season).
PRO STATISTICS: 1998—Recovered one fumble for 24 yards. 1999—Intercepted one pass for 22 yards and a touchdown and returned three kickoffs for 49 yards. 2000—Returned one kickoff for 18 yards and recovered two fumbles. 2001—Recovered three fumbles.

Year Team	G	GS	SACKS
1998—Philadelphia NFL	16	5	1.5
1999—Philadelphia NFL	13	2	1.0
2000—Philadelphia NFL	16	10	3.5
2001—Philadelphia NFL	13	12	2.5
Pro totals (4 years)	58	29	8.5

WHITMAN, JOSH   TE   CHARGERS

PERSONAL: Born August 5, 1978, in Lafayette, Ind. ... 6-4/252. ... Full name: Joshua Harmon Whitman.
HIGH SCHOOL: Lafayette-Jefferson (Lafayette, Ind.).
COLLEGE: Illinois.
TRANSACTIONS/CAREER NOTES: Signed as non-drafted free agent by Buffalo Bills (April 24, 2001). ... Released by Bills (September 2, 2001). ... Signed by San Diego Chargers to practice squad (October 9, 2001). ... Activated (October 26, 2001).
PLAYING EXPERIENCE: San Diego NFL, 2001. ... Games/Games started: (4/1).
PRO STATISTICS: 2001—Returned one kickoff for nine yards.

WHITTED, ALVIS   WR   FALCONS

PERSONAL: Born September 4, 1974, in Durham, N.C. ... 6-0/186. ... Full name: Alvis James Whitted.
HIGH SCHOOL: Orange (Hillsborough, N.C.).
COLLEGE: North Carolina State.
TRANSACTIONS/CAREER NOTES: Selected by Jacksonville Jaguars in seventh round (192nd pick overall) of 1998 NFL draft. ... Signed by Jaguars (May 19, 1998). ... Released by Jaguars (December 4, 2001). ... Signed by Atlanta Falcons (January 10, 2002).
CHAMPIONSHIP GAME EXPERIENCE: Played in AFC championship game (1999 season).
PRO STATISTICS: 1998—Returned a blocked punt 24 yards for a touchdown. 1999—Returned eight kickoffs for 187 yards and one touchdown. 2000—Returned four kickoffs for 67 yards.
SINGLE GAME HIGHS (regular season): Receptions—4 (December 23, 2000, vs. New York Giants); yards—55 (October 29, 2000, vs. Dallas); and touchdown receptions—2 (October 29, 2000, vs. Dallas).

			RUSHING				RECEIVING			TOTALS		
Year Team	G	GS	Att.	Yds.	Avg.	TD	No.	Yds.	Avg.	TD	TD 2pt. Pts. Fum.
1998—Jacksonville NFL	16	0	3	13	4.3	0	2	61	30.5	0	1 0 6 0
1999—Jacksonville NFL	14	1	1	9	9.0	0	0	0	0.0	0	1 0 6 0
2000—Jacksonville NFL	16	3	0	0	0.0	0	13	137	10.5	3	3 0 18 1
2001—Jacksonville NFL	11	0	1	4	4.0	0	2	17	8.5	0	0 0 0 0
Pro totals (4 years)	57	4	5	26	5.2	0	17	215	12.6	3	5 0 30 1

WHITTINGTON, BERNARD   DT   BENGALS

PERSONAL: Born August 20, 1971, in St. Louis. ... 6-5/280. ... Full name: Bernard Maurice Whittington.
HIGH SCHOOL: Hazelwood East (St. Louis).
COLLEGE: Indiana (degree in sports management).
TRANSACTIONS/CAREER NOTES: Signed as non-drafted free agent by Indianapolis Colts (May 5, 1994). ... Granted free agency (February 14, 1997). ... Re-signed by Colts (June 13, 1997). ... Granted unconditional free agency (March 2, 2001). ... Signed by Cincinnati Bengals (July 12, 2001).
CHAMPIONSHIP GAME EXPERIENCE: Played in AFC championship game (1995 season).
PRO STATISTICS: 1995—Recovered one fumble. 1998—Recovered two fumbles.

Year Team	G	GS	SACKS
1994—Indianapolis NFL	13	8	0.0
1995—Indianapolis NFL	16	13	2.0
1996—Indianapolis NFL	16	14	3.0
1997—Indianapolis NFL	15	6	0.0
1998—Indianapolis NFL	15	11	4.0
1999—Indianapolis NFL	15	15	1.0
2000—Indianapolis NFL	15	12	1.0
2001—Cincinnati NFL	16	5	0.0
Pro totals (8 years)	121	84	11.0

WHITTLE, JASON   G   GIANTS

PERSONAL: Born March 7, 1975, in Springfield, Mo. ... 6-4/305.
HIGH SCHOOL: Camdenton (Mo.).
COLLEGE: Southwest Missouri State.
TRANSACTIONS/CAREER NOTES: Signed as non-drafted free agent by New York Giants (April 24, 1998). ... Released by Giants (August 30, 1998). ... Re-signed by Giants to practice squad (September 1, 1998). ... Activated (December 16, 1998). ... Granted free agency (March 1, 2002).
PLAYING EXPERIENCE: New York Giants NFL, 1998-2001. ... Games/Games started: 1998 (1/0), 1999 (16/1), 2000 (16/2), 2001 (16/2). Total: 49/5.
CHAMPIONSHIP GAME EXPERIENCE: Played in NFC championship game (2000 season). ... Played in Super Bowl XXXV (2000 season).

WIEGERT, ZACH   OT   JAGUARS

PERSONAL: Born August 16, 1972, in Fremont, Neb. ... 6-5/310. ... Full name: Zach Allen Wiegert. ... Name pronounced WEE-gert.
HIGH SCHOOL: Fremont (Neb.) Bergan.
COLLEGE: Nebraska.
TRANSACTIONS/CAREER NOTES: Selected by St. Louis Rams in second round (38th pick overall) of 1995 NFL draft. ... Signed by Rams (July 18, 1995). ... Granted free agency (February 13, 1998). ... Re-signed by Rams (June 17, 1998). ... Designated by Rams as transition player (February 12, 1999). ... Re-signed by Rams (March 24, 1999). ... Released by Rams (April 28, 1999). ... Signed by Jacksonville Jaguars (May 5, 1999). ... On injured reserve with knee injury (October 25, 2000-remainder of season).
PLAYING EXPERIENCE: St. Louis NFL, 1995-1998; Jacksonville NFL, 1999-2001. ... Games/Games started: 1995 (5/2), 1996 (16/16), 1997 (15/15), 1998 (13/13), 1999 (16/12), 2000 (8/8), 2001 (16/16). Total: 89/82.
CHAMPIONSHIP GAME EXPERIENCE: Played in AFC championship game (1999 season).
HONORS: Outland Trophy Award winner (1994). ... Named offensive lineman on THE SPORTING NEWS college All-America first team (1994).
PRO STATISTICS: 1996—Recovered two fumbles. 1997—Caught one pass for one yard and recovered four fumbles for no yards and one touchdown. 1998—Recovered one fumble. 1999—Caught one pass for minus three yards and recovered one fumble. 2000—Recovered one fumble.

WIEGMANN, CASEY   C   CHIEFS

PERSONAL: Born July 20, 1975, in Waterloo, Iowa. ... 6-2/285. ... Name pronounced WEG-man.
HIGH SCHOOL: Parkersburg (Iowa).
COLLEGE: Iowa.
TRANSACTIONS/CAREER NOTES: Signed as non-drafted free agent by Indianapolis Colts (April 26, 1996). ... Released by Colts (August 25, 1996). ... Re-signed by Colts to practice squad (August 27, 1996). ... Activated (September 10, 1996); did not play. ... Released by Colts (September 22, 1996). ... Re-signed by Colts to practice squad (September 23, 1996). ... Activated (October 15, 1996); did not play. ... Claimed on waivers by New York Jets (October 29, 1996). ... Released by Jets (September 21, 1997). ... Signed by Chicago Bears (September 24, 1997). ... Granted free agency (February 12, 1999). ... Tendered offer sheet by Miami Dolphins (April 5, 1999). ... Offer matched by Bears (April 8, 1999). ... Granted unconditional free agency (March 2, 2001). ... Signed by Kansas City Chiefs (March 15, 2001).
PLAYING EXPERIENCE: New York Jets (3)-Chicago (1) NFL, 1997; Chicago NFL, 1998-2000; Kansas City NFL, 2001. ... Games/Games started: 1997 (NYJ-3/0; Chi.-1/0; Total: 4/0), 1998 (16/16), 1999 (16/0), 2000 (16/10), 2001 (15/15). Total: 67/41.
PRO STATISTICS: 1998—Returned one kickoff for eight yards, fumbled once and recovered one fumble for minus three yards. 1999—Returned one kickoff for two yards. 2000—Recovered one fumble.

WIGGINS, JERMAINE   TE   COLTS

PERSONAL: Born January 18, 1975, in East Boston, Mass. ... 6-2/255.
HIGH SCHOOL: East Boston.
COLLEGE: Georgia.
TRANSACTIONS/CAREER NOTES: Signed by New York Jets as non-drafted free agent (April 19, 1999). ... Released by Jets (August 23, 1999). ... Re-signed by Jets to practice squad (August 28, 1999). ... Claimed on waivers by New England Patriots (November 28, 2000). ... Released by Patriots (May 2, 2002). ... Signed by Indianapolis Colts (May 14, 2002).
CHAMPIONSHIP GAME EXPERIENCE: Played in AFC championship game (2001 season). ... Member of Super Bowl championship team (2001 season).
PRO STATISTICS: 2000—Returned one kickoff for 12 yards and fumbled once. 2001—Recovered one fumble.
SINGLE GAME HIGHS (regular season): Receptions—5 (December 4, 2000, vs. Kansas City); yards—81 (December 24, 2000, vs. Miami); and touchdown receptions—1 (January 6, 2002, vs. Carolina).

			RECEIVING		
Year Team	G	GS	No.	Yds.	Avg.	TD
2000—New York Jets NFL	11	0	2	4	2.0	1
—New England NFL	4	2	16	203	12.7	1
2001—New England NFL	16	6	14	133	9.5	4
Pro totals (2 years)	31	8	32	340	10.6	6

WILCOX, DANIEL   TE   JETS

PERSONAL: Born March 23, 1977, in Atlanta. ... 6-1/229.
HIGH SCHOOL: Decatur (Ga.).
JUNIOR COLLEGE: Georgia Military College.
COLLEGE: Appalachian State.
TRANSACTIONS/CAREER NOTES: Signed as non-drafted free agent by New York Jets (April 26, 2001). ... Released by Jets (August 2, 2001). ... Re-signed by Jets (August 20, 2001). ... Released by Jets (September 2, 2001). ... Re-signed by Jets to practice squad (September 3, 2001). ... Activated (September 19, 2001); did not play. ... Released by Jets (October 10, 2001). ... Re-signed by Jets to practice squad (October 11, 2001). ... Activated (November 15, 2001).
PLAYING EXPERIENCE: New York Jets NFL, 2001. ... Games/Games started: (1/0).

WILEY, CHUCK   DE   VIKINGS

PERSONAL: Born March 6, 1975, in Baton Rouge, La. ... 6-5/277. ... Full name: Samuel Charles Wiley Jr. ... Cousin of Doug Williams, quarterback with Tampa Bay Buccaneers (1978-82), Oklahoma Outlaws of USFL (1984), Arizona Outlaws of USFL (1985) and Washington Redskins (1986-89).
HIGH SCHOOL: Southern University Lab (Baton Rouge, La.).
COLLEGE: Louisiana State (degree in pre-physical therapy).

TRANSACTIONS/CAREER NOTES: Selected by Carolina Panthers in third round (62nd pick overall) of 1998 NFL draft. ... Signed by Panthers (June 10, 1998). ... On injured reserve with heel injury (August 30, 1998-entire season). ... Claimed on waivers Atlanta Falcons (August 28, 2000). ... Granted unconditional free agency (March 1, 2002). ... Signed by Minnesota Vikings (May 2, 2002).
PLAYING EXPERIENCE: Carolina NFL, 1999; Atlanta NFL, 2000 and 2001. ... Games/Games started: 1999 (16/16), 2000 (16/0), 2001 (16/1). Total: 48/17.
PRO STATISTICS: 2000—Credited with four sacks. 2001—Intercepted one pass for one yard and credited with one sack.

WILEY, MARCELLUS — DE — CHARGERS

PERSONAL: Born November 30, 1974, in Compton, Calif. ... 6-4/275. ... Full name: Marcellus Vernon Wiley.
HIGH SCHOOL: Santa Monica (Calif.).
COLLEGE: Columbia (degree in sociology, 1997).
TRANSACTIONS/CAREER NOTES: Selected by Buffalo Bills in second round (52nd pick overall) of 1997 NFL draft. ... Signed by Bills (June 20, 1997). ... Granted unconditional free agency (March 2, 2001). ... Signed by San Diego Chargers (March 6, 2001).
PRO STATISTICS: 1997—Returned one kickoff for 12 yards, fumbled once and recovered two fumbles for 40 yards. 1998—Recovered one fumble for 15 yards. 1999—Intercepted one pass for 52 yards. 2000—Recovered one fumble.

Year — Team	G	GS	SACKS
1997—Buffalo NFL	16	0	0.0
1998—Buffalo NFL	16	3	3.5
1999—Buffalo NFL	16	1	5.0
2000—Buffalo NFL	16	15	10.5
2001—San Diego NFL	14	14	13.0
Pro totals (5 years)	78	33	32.0

WILEY, MICHAEL — RB — COWBOYS

PERSONAL: Born January 5, 1978, in Spring Valley, Calif. ... 5-11/203. ... Full name: Michael Deshawn Wiley.
HIGH SCHOOL: Monte Vista (Spring Valley, Calif.).
COLLEGE: Ohio State.
TRANSACTIONS/CAREER NOTES: Selected by Dallas Cowboys in fifth round (143rd pick overall) of 2000 NFL draft. ... Signed by Cowboys (July 14, 2000).
PRO STATISTICS: 2000—Recovered one fumble. 2001—Recovered one fumble.
SINGLE GAME HIGHS (regular season): Attempts—11 (December 10, 2000, vs. Washington); yards—85 (November 11, 2001, vs. Atlanta); and rushing touchdowns—0.

			RUSHING				RECEIVING				KICKOFF RETURNS				TOTALS		
Year — Team	G	GS	Att.	Yds.	Avg.	TD	No.	Yds.	Avg.	TD	No.	Yds.	Avg.	TD	TD	2pt.	Pts.	Fum.
2000—Dallas NFL	10	0	24	88	3.7	0	14	72	5.1	1	13	303	23.3	0	1	0	6	3
2001—Dallas NFL	16	0	34	247	7.3	0	16	99	6.2	1	4	90	22.5	0	1	0	6	1
Pro totals (2 years)	26	0	58	335	5.8	0	30	171	5.7	2	17	393	23.1	0	2	0	12	4

WILKINS, JEFF — K — RAMS

PERSONAL: Born April 19, 1972, in Youngstown, Ohio. ... 6-2/205. ... Full name: Jeff Allen Wilkins.
HIGH SCHOOL: Austintown Fitch (Youngstown, Ohio).
COLLEGE: Youngstown State (degree in communications, 1993).
TRANSACTIONS/CAREER NOTES: Signed as non-drafted free agent by Dallas Cowboys (April 28, 1994). ... Released by Cowboys (July 18, 1994). ... Signed by Philadelphia Eagles (November 14, 1994). ... Released by Eagles (August 14, 1995). ... Signed by San Francisco 49ers (November 8, 1995). ... Granted unconditional free agency (February 14, 1997). ... Signed by St. Louis Rams (March 6, 1997). ... Granted unconditional free agency (March 2, 2001). ... Re-signed by Rams (March 2, 2001).
CHAMPIONSHIP GAME EXPERIENCE: Played in NFC championship game (1999 and 2001 seasons). ... Member of Super Bowl championship team (1999 season). ... Played in Super Bowl XXXVI (2001 season).
PRO STATISTICS: 1999—Punted twice for 57 yards.

		KICKING						
Year — Team	G	XPM	XPA	FGM	FGA	Lg.	50+	Pts.
1994—Philadelphia NFL	6	0	0	0	0	0	0-0	0
1995—San Francisco NFL	7	27	29	12	13	40	0-0	63
1996—San Francisco NFL	16	40	40	30	34	49	0-0	130
1997—St. Louis NFL	16	32	32	25	∞37	52	2-2	107
1998—St. Louis NFL	16	25	26	20	26	‡57	3-6	§85
1999—St. Louis NFL	16	*64	*64	20	28	51	1-4	‡124
2000—St. Louis NFL	11	38	38	17	17	51	1-1	89
2001—St. Louis NFL	16	*58	*58	23	29	54	1-1	127
Pro totals (8 years)	104	284	287	147	184	57	8-14	725

WILKINS, TERRENCE — WR/KR — RAMS

PERSONAL: Born July 29, 1975, in Washington, D.C. ... 5-10/180. ... Full name: Terrence Olondo Wilkins.
HIGH SCHOOL: Bishop Denis J O'Connell (Arlington, Va.).
COLLEGE: Virginia.
TRANSACTIONS/CAREER NOTES: Signed as non-drafted free agent by Indianapolis Colts (April 22, 1999). ... Granted free agency (March 1, 2002). ... Re-signed by Colts (April 15, 2002). ... Traded by Colts to St. Louis Rams for undisclosed draft pick (April 15, 2002).
PRO STATISTICS: 1999—Rushed once for two yards and recovered one fumble in end zone for a touchdown. 2000—Rushed three times for eight yards and recovered one fumble.

SINGLE GAME HIGHS (regular season): Receptions—9 (September 25, 2000, vs. Jacksonville); yards—148 (September 25, 2000, vs. Jacksonville); and touchdown receptions—1 (December 3, 2000, vs. New York Jets).
STATISTICAL PLATEAUS: 100-yard receiving games: 1999 (1), 2000 (2). Total: 3.

			RECEIVING				PUNT RETURNS				KICKOFF RETURNS				TOTALS			
Year Team	G	GS	No.	Yds.	Avg.	TD	No.	Yds.	Avg.	TD	No.	Yds.	Avg.	TD	TD	2pt.	Pts.	Fum.
1999—Indianapolis NFL	16	11	42	565	13.5	4	41	388	9.5	1	51	1134	22.2	▲1	7	0	42	3
2000—Indianapolis NFL	14	7	43	569	13.2	3	29	240	8.3	0	15	279	18.6	0	3	0	18	4
2001—Indianapolis NFL	11	4	34	332	9.8	0	21	219	10.4	1	44	1007	22.9	0	1	0	6	1
Pro totals (3 years)	41	22	119	1466	12.3	7	91	847	9.3	2	110	2420	22.0	1	11	0	66	8

WILKINSON, DAN   DT   REDSKINS

PERSONAL: Born March 13, 1973, in Dayton, Ohio. ... 6-4/325. ... Nickname: Big Daddy.
HIGH SCHOOL: Paul L. Dunbar (Dayton, Ohio).
COLLEGE: Ohio State.
TRANSACTIONS/CAREER NOTES: Selected after sophomore season by Cincinnati Bengals in first round (first pick overall) of 1994 NFL draft. ... Signed by Bengals (May 5, 1994). ... Designated by Bengals as franchise player (February 11, 1998). ... Tendered offer sheet by Washington Redskins (February 25, 1998). ... Bengals declined to match offer (February 26, 1998); Bengals received first-(LB Brian Simmons) and third-round (G Mike Goff) picks as compensation.
HONORS: Named defensive lineman on THE SPORTING NEWS college All-America first team (1993).
PRO STATISTICS: 1996—Intercepted one pass for seven yards, fumbled once and recovered one fumble. 1998—Intercepted one pass for four yards and recovered one fumble. 1999—Intercepted one pass for 88 yards and a touchdown and recovered one fumble. 2001—Intercepted two passes for no yards.

Year Team	G	GS	SACKS
1994—Cincinnati NFL	16	14	5.5
1995—Cincinnati NFL	14	14	8.0
1996—Cincinnati NFL	16	16	6.5
1997—Cincinnati NFL	15	15	5.0
1998—Washington NFL	16	16	7.5
1999—Washington NFL	16	16	8.0
2000—Washington NFL	16	16	3.5
2001—Washington NFL	16	16	4.0
Pro totals (8 years)	125	123	48.0

WILLIAMS, AENEAS   CB   RAMS

PERSONAL: Born January 29, 1968, in New Orleans. ... 5-11/200. ... Full name: Aeneas Demetrius Williams. ... Name pronounced uh-NEE-us.
HIGH SCHOOL: Fortier (New Orleans).
COLLEGE: Southern (degree in accounting, 1990).
TRANSACTIONS/CAREER NOTES: Selected by Phoenix Cardinals in third round (59th pick overall) of 1991 NFL draft. ... Signed by Cardinals (July 26, 1991). ... Granted free agency (February 17, 1994). ... Cardinals franchise renamed Arizona Cardinals for 1994 season. ... Re-signed by Cardinals (June 1, 1994). ... Granted unconditional free agency (February 16, 1996). ... Re-signed by Cardinals (February 27, 1996). ... Designated by Cardinals as franchise player (February 22, 2001). ... Re-signed by Cardinals (April 21, 2001). ... Traded by Cardinals to St. Louis Rams for second- (DB Michael Stone) and fourth-round (DT Marcus Bell) picks in 2001 draft (April 21, 2001).
CHAMPIONSHIP GAME EXPERIENCE: Played in NFC championship game (2001 season). ... Played in Super Bowl XXXVI (2001 season).
HONORS: Named cornerback on THE SPORTING NEWS NFL All-Pro team (1995, 1997 and 2001). ... Played in Pro Bowl (1994-1999 seasons).
POST SEASON RECORDS: Holds NFL single-game postseason record for most interceptions returned for touchdown—2 (January 20, 2002, vs. Green Bay Packers).
PRO STATISTICS: 1991—Fumbled once and recovered two fumbles for 10 yards. 1992—Recovered one fumble for 39 yards. 1993—Recovered two fumbles for 20 yards and a touchdown. 1994—Recovered one fumble. 1995—Fumbled once and recovered three fumbles. 1996—Credited with one sack and recovered one fumble. 1998—Credited with one sack. 1999—Recovered two fumbles. 2000—Recovered two fumbles for 104 yards and one touchdown. 2001—Recovered four fumbles.

			INTERCEPTIONS			
Year Team	G	GS	No.	Yds.	Avg.	TD
1991—Phoenix NFL	16	15	∞6	60	10.0	0
1992—Phoenix NFL	16	16	3	25	8.3	0
1993—Phoenix NFL	16	16	2	87	43.5	1
1994—Arizona NFL	16	16	†9	89	9.9	0
1995—Arizona NFL	16	16	6	86	14.3	†2
1996—Arizona NFL	16	16	6	89	14.8	1
1997—Arizona NFL	16	16	6	95	15.8	∞2
1998—Arizona NFL	16	16	1	15	15.0	0
1999—Arizona NFL	16	16	2	5	2.5	0
2000—Arizona NFL	16	16	5	102	20.4	0
2001—St. Louis NFL	16	16	4	69	17.3	†2
Pro totals (11 years)	176	175	50	722	14.4	8

WILLIAMS, BOBBIE   G   EAGLES

PERSONAL: Born September 25, 1976, in Jefferson, Texas. ... 6-3/320.
HIGH SCHOOL: Jefferson (Texas).
COLLEGE: Arkansas.
TRANSACTIONS/CAREER NOTES: Selected by Philadelphia Eagles in second round (61st pick overall) of 2000 NFL draft. ... Signed by Eagles (July 17, 2000). ... Inactive for all 16 games (2000).
PLAYING EXPERIENCE: Philadelphia NFL, 2001. ... Games/Games started: (1/1).
CHAMPIONSHIP GAME EXPERIENCE: Member of Eagles for NFC championship game (2001 season); inactive.

– 410 –

WILLIAMS, BOO TE SAINTS

PERSONAL: Born June 22, 1979, in Tallahassee, Fla. ... 6-4/235. ... Full name: Eddie Lee Williams. ... Cousin of Tamarick Vanover, wide receiver, San Diego Chargers.
HIGH SCHOOL: Lincoln (Tallahassee, Fla.).
JUNIOR COLLEGE: Coffeyville (Kan.) Community College.
COLLEGE: Arkansas.
TRANSACTIONS/CAREER NOTES: Signed as non-drafted free agent by New Orleans Saints (April 26, 2000). ... Released by Saints (September 2, 2001). ... Re-signed by Saints to practice squad (September 3, 2001). ... Activated (October 27, 2001).

			RECEIVING		
Year Team	G	GS	No.	Yds.	Avg.	TD
2001—New Orleans NFL	11	4	20	202	10.1	3

WILLIAMS, BRIAN LB

PERSONAL: Born December 17, 1972, in Dallas. ... 6-1/257. ... Full name: Brian Marcee Williams.
HIGH SCHOOL: Bishop Dunne (Dallas).
COLLEGE: Southern California (degree in public administration).
TRANSACTIONS/CAREER NOTES: Selected by Green Bay Packers in third round (73rd pick overall) of 1995 NFL draft. ... Signed by Packers (May 9, 1995). ... Granted free agency (February 13, 1998). ... Re-signed by Packers (February 17, 1998). ... On injured reserve with knee injury (November 9, 1999-remainder of season). ... On injured reserve with knee injury (December 15, 2000-remainder of season). ... Released by Packers (February 22, 2001). ... Aigned by Jacksonville Jaguars (April 23, 2001). ... Released by Jaguars (July 18, 2001). ... Signed by New Orleans Saints (July 28, 2001). ... Claimed on waivers by Detroit Lions (December 5, 2001). ... Granted unconditional free agency (March 1, 2002).
CHAMPIONSHIP GAME EXPERIENCE: Played in NFC championship game (1995-97 seasons). ... Member of Super Bowl championship team (1996 season). ... Played in Super Bowl XXXII (1997 season).
PRO STATISTICS: 1996—Recovered three fumbles. 1997—Intercepted two passes for 30 yards and recovered one fumble. 1999—Intercepted two passes for 60 yards and recovered one fumble. 2000—Recovered one fumble. 2001—Recovered one fumble.

Year Team	G	GS	SACKS
1995—Green Bay NFL	13	0	0.0
1996—Green Bay NFL	16	16	0.5
1997—Green Bay NFL	16	16	1.0
1998—Green Bay NFL	16	15	2.0
1999—Green Bay NFL	7	7	2.0
2000—Green Bay NFL	4	3	0.5
2001—New Orleans NFL	4	0	0.0
—Detroit NFL	2	1	0.0
Pro totals (7 years)	78	58	6.0

WILLIAMS, DARRYL S

PERSONAL: Born January 8, 1970, in Miami. ... 6-0/205. ... Full name: Darryl Edwin Williams.
HIGH SCHOOL: American (Hialeah, Fla.).
COLLEGE: Miami (Fla.).
TRANSACTIONS/CAREER NOTES: Selected after junior season by Cincinnati Bengals in first round (28th pick overall) of 1992 NFL draft. ... Signed by Bengals (July 25, 1992). ... Designated by Bengals as transition player (February 15, 1994). ... Free agency status changed by Bengals from transitional to unconditional (February 16, 1996). ... Signed by Seattle Seahawks (February 21, 1996). ... Released by Seahawks (March 1, 2000). ... Signed by Bengals (March 6, 2000). ... Released by Bengals (May 1, 2002).
HONORS: Named defensive back on THE SPORTING NEWS college All-America second team (1991). ... Played in Pro Bowl (1997 season).
RECORDS: Shares NFL single-game record for most opponents' fumbles recovered—3 (October 4, 1998, vs. Kansas City).
PRO STATISTICS: 1992—Recovered one fumble. 1993—Recovered two fumbles. 1994—Returned one punt for four yards and recovered two fumbles. 1995—Credited with one safety and recovered three fumbles. 1996—Recovered one fumble for two yards. 1997—Recovered one fumble. 1998—Recovered three fumbles. 1999—Recovered one fumble. 2001—Recovered one fumble.

			INTERCEPTIONS				SACKS
Year Team	G	GS	No.	Yds.	Avg.	TD	No.
1992—Cincinnati NFL	16	12	4	65	16.3	0	2.0
1993—Cincinnati NFL	16	16	2	126	63.0	▲1	2.0
1994—Cincinnati NFL	16	16	2	45	22.5	0	1.0
1995—Cincinnati NFL	16	16	1	1	1.0	0	1.0
1996—Seattle NFL	16	16	5	148	29.6	1	0.0
1997—Seattle NFL	16	16	▲8	172	21.5	1	0.0
1998—Seattle NFL	16	16	3	41	13.7	0	0.0
1999—Seattle NFL	13	12	4	41	10.3	0	0.0
2000—Cincinnati NFL	16	16	1	36	36.0	1	0.0
2001—Cincinnati NFL	15	1	1	16	16.0	0	3.5
Pro totals (10 years)	156	137	31	691	22.3	4	9.5

WILLIAMS, ELIJAH CB

PERSONAL: Born August 20, 1975, in Milton, Fla. ... 5-10/180. ... Full name: Elijah Elgebra Williams.
HIGH SCHOOL: Milton (Fla.).
COLLEGE: Florida.
TRANSACTIONS/CAREER NOTES: Selected by Atlanta Falcons in sixth round (166th pick overall) of 1998 NFL draft. ... Signed by Falcons (June 11, 1998). ... Granted free agency (March 2, 2001). ... Re-signed by Falcons (April 16, 2001). ... Released by Falcons (September 2, 2001). ... Re-signed by Falcons (November 20, 2001). ... Granted unconditional free agency (March 1, 2002).
PLAYING EXPERIENCE: Atlanta NFL, 1998-2001. ... Games/Games started: 1998 (15/0), 1999 (15/2), 2000 (15/3), 2001 (5/1). Total: 50/6.
CHAMPIONSHIP GAME EXPERIENCE: Played in NFC championship game (1998 season). ... Played in Super Bowl XXXIII (1998 season).
PRO STATISTICS: 1998—Rushed twice for minus two yards and returned seven kickoffs for 132 yards. 1999—Returned three kickoffs for 37 yards. 2000—Intercepted one pass for one yard and returned two kickoffs for 34 yards.

WILLIAMS, ERIK   OT

PERSONAL: Born September 7, 1968, in Philadelphia. ... 6-6/311. ... Full name: Erik George Williams.
HIGH SCHOOL: John Bartram (Philadelphia).
COLLEGE: Central State (Ohio).
TRANSACTIONS/CAREER NOTES: Selected by Dallas Cowboys in third round (70th pick overall) of 1991 NFL draft. ... Signed by Cowboys (July 14, 1991). ... Designated by Cowboys as transition player (February 15, 1994). ... On non-football injury list with knee injury suffered in automobile accident (November 21, 1994-remainder of season). ... Released by Cowboys (March 7, 2001). ... Signed by Baltimore Ravens (August 28, 2001). ... Announced retirement (November 20, 2001).
PLAYING EXPERIENCE: Dallas NFL, 1991-2000; Baltimore NFL, 2001. ... Games/Games started: 1991 (11/3), 1992 (16/16), 1993 (16/16), 1994 (7/7), 1995 (15/15), 1996 (16/16), 1997 (15/15), 1998 (15/15), 1999 (14/14), 2000 (16/16), 2001 (5/0). Total: 146/133.
CHAMPIONSHIP GAME EXPERIENCE: Played in NFC championship game (1992, 1993 and 1995 seasons). ... Member of Super Bowl championship team (1992, 1993 and 1995 seasons).
HONORS: Named offensive tackle on THE SPORTING NEWS NFL All-Pro team (1993 and 1995). ... Played in Pro Bowl (1993, 1996, 1997 and 1999 seasons).
PRO STATISTICS: 1991—Recovered one fumble.

WILLIAMS, GRANT   OT   PATRIOTS

PERSONAL: Born May 10, 1974, in Hattiesburg, Miss. ... 6-7/320.
HIGH SCHOOL: Clinton (Miss.).
JUNIOR COLLEGE: Hinds Community College (Miss.).
COLLEGE: Louisiana Tech (degree in biology, 1995).
TRANSACTIONS/CAREER NOTES: Signed as non-drafted free agent by Seattle Seahawks (April 22, 1996). ... Granted unconditional free agency (February 11, 2000). ... Signed by New England Patriots (March 17, 2000). ... Granted unconditional free agency (March 1, 2002). ... Re-signed by Patriots (April 19, 2002).
PLAYING EXPERIENCE: Seattle NFL, 1996-1999; New England NFL, 2000 and 2001. ... Games/Games started: 1996 (8/0), 1997 (16/8), 1998 (16/0), 1999 (16/15), 2000 (16/9), 2001 (14/4). Total: 86/36.
CHAMPIONSHIP GAME EXPERIENCE: Played in AFC championship game (2001 season). ... Member of Super Bowl championship team (2001 season).
PRO STATISTICS: 1997—Recovered two fumbles.

WILLIAMS, JAMAL   DT   CHARGERS

PERSONAL: Born April 28, 1976, in Washington, D.C. ... 6-3/305.
HIGH SCHOOL: Archbishop Carroll (Washington, D.C.).
COLLEGE: Oklahoma State.
TRANSACTIONS/CAREER NOTES: Selected by San Diego Chargers in second round of 1998 supplemental draft (July 9, 1998). ... Signed by Chargers (August 7, 1998). ... Granted free agency (March 2, 2001). ... Re-signed by Chargers (May 11, 2001). ... On injured reserve with knee injury (October 3, 2001-remainder of season).
PLAYING EXPERIENCE: San Diego NFL, 1998-2001. ... Games/Games started: 1998 (9/0), 1999 (16/2), 2000 (16/16), 2001 (3/3). Total: 44/21.
PRO STATISTICS: 1998—Intercepted one pass for 14 yards and a touchdown. 1999—Credited with one sack. 2000—Credited with one sack. 2001—Recovered one fumble.

WILLIAMS, JAMES   WR   SEAHAWKS

PERSONAL: Born March 6, 1978, in Vicksburg, Miss. ... 5-10/188. ... Full name: James L. Williams.
HIGH SCHOOL: Warren Central (Vicksburg, Miss.).
JUNIOR COLLEGE: Hinds Community College (Miss.).
COLLEGE: Marshall.
TRANSACTIONS/CAREER NOTES: Selected by Seattle Seahawks in sixth round (175th pick overall) of 2000 NFL draft. ... Signed by Seahawks (June 22, 2000).
PRO STATISTICS: 2000—Rushed once for minus five yards and credited with one safety. 2001—Recovered one fumble for seven yards.
SINGLE GAME HIGHS (regular season): Receptions—4 (December 30, 2001, vs. San Diego); yards—101 (December 30, 2001, vs. San Diego); and touchdown receptions—1 (December 30, 2001, vs. San Diego).
STATISTICAL PLATEAUS: 100-yard receiving games: 2001 (1).

			RECEIVING				KICKOFF RETURNS			TOTALS			
Year Team	G	GS	No.	Yds.	Avg.	TD	No.	Yds.	Avg.	TD	TD	2pt.	Pts.	Fum.
2000—Seattle NFL	10	0	8	99	12.4	0	3	76	25.3	0	0	0	2	0
2001—Seattle NFL	6	2	12	212	17.7	1	9	175	19.4	0	1	0	6	1
Pro totals (2 years)	16	2	20	311	15.6	1	12	251	20.9	0	1	0	8	1

WILLIAMS, JAMES   OT   BEARS

PERSONAL: Born March 29, 1968, in Pittsburgh. ... 6-7/325. ... Full name: James Otis Williams.
HIGH SCHOOL: Allderdice (Pittsburgh).
COLLEGE: Cheyney (Pa.) State.
TRANSACTIONS/CAREER NOTES: Signed as non-drafted free agent by Chicago Bears (April 25, 1991). ... Granted free agency (February 16, 1996). ... Re-signed by Bears (March 15, 1996).
PLAYING EXPERIENCE: Chicago NFL, 1991-2001. ... Games/Games started: 1991 (14/0), 1992 (5/0), 1993 (3/0), 1994 (16/15), 1995 (16/10), 1996 (16/16), 1997 (16/16), 1998 (16/16), 1999 (16/16), 2000 (16/16), 2001 (16/16). Total: 150/127.
PRO STATISTICS: 1991—Credited with one sack. 1996—Recovered two fumbles. 2000—Recovered one fumble.
MISCELLANEOUS: Switched from defensive line to offensive line during the 1992 season.

WILLIAMS, JAY — DE — PANTHERS

PERSONAL: Born October 13, 1971, in Washington, D.C. ... 6-3/280. ... Full name: Jay Omar Williams.
HIGH SCHOOL: St. John's (Washington, D.C.).
COLLEGE: Wake Forest.
TRANSACTIONS/CAREER NOTES: Signed as non-drafted free agent by Miami Dolphins (April 28, 1994). ... Released by Dolphins (August 28, 1994). ... Signed by Los Angeles Rams to practice squad (September 27, 1994). ... Activated (December 7, 1994); did not play. ... Rams franchise moved from Los Angeles to St. Louis (April 12, 1995). ... On physically unable to perform list with forearm injury (July 31-November 18, 1996). ... Re-signed by Rams (November 20, 1996). ... Re-signed by Rams (December 11, 1996). ... Granted free agency (February 12, 1999). ... Re-signed by Rams (May 4, 1999). ... Granted unconditional free agency (February 11, 2000). ... Signed by Carolina Panthers (February 16, 2000).
CHAMPIONSHIP GAME EXPERIENCE: Played in NFC championship game (1999 season). ... Member of Super Bowl championship team (1999 season).
PRO STATISTICS: 1997—Returned one kickoff for 10 yards. 2001—Intercepted one pass for no yards.

Year Team	G	GS	SACKS
1994—Los Angeles Rams NFL	Did not play.		
1995—St. Louis NFL	7	0	0.0
1996—St. Louis NFL	2	0	0.0
1997—St. Louis NFL	16	2	1.0
1998—St. Louis NFL	16	1	1.0
1999—St. Louis NFL	16	0	4.0
2000—Carolina NFL	16	14	6.0
2001—Carolina NFL	16	13	1.0
Pro totals (7 years)	**89**	**30**	**13.0**

WILLIAMS, JERMAINE — RB

PERSONAL: Born August 14, 1973, in Greenville, N.C. ... 5-11/245.
HIGH SCHOOL: J.H. Rose (Greenville, N.C.).
JUNIOR COLLEGE: Butler County Community College (Kan.).
COLLEGE: Houston.
TRANSACTIONS/CAREER NOTES: Signed as non-drafted free agent by Tampa Bay Buccaneers (April 25, 1997). ... Released by Buccaneers (August 4, 1997). ... Signed by Oakland Raiders (April 25, 1998). ... Released by Raiders (September 1, 1998). ... Re-signed by Raiders to practice squad (September 2, 1998). ... Activated (October 24, 1998). ... Released by Raiders August 22, 2000). ... Signed by Jacksonville Jaguars (October 31, 2000). ... Released by Jaguars (February 27, 2001). ... Signed by Kansas City Chiefs (April 23, 2001). ... Released by Chiefs (December 3, 2001). ... Signed by Oakland Raiders (December 5, 2001). ... Granted unconditional free agency (March 1, 2002).
PLAYING EXPERIENCE: Oakland NFL, 1998 and 1999; Jacksonville NFL, 2000; Kansas City (11)-Oakland (1) NFL, 2001. ... Games/Games started: 1998 (10/0), 1999 (15/0), 2000 (7/0), 2001 (K.C.-11/2; Oak.-1/0; Total: 12/2). Total: 44/2.
PRO STATISTICS: 1999—Caught one pass for 20 yards. 2000—Rushed two times for eight yards and returned two kickoffs for 50 yards. 2001—Caught two passes for 11 yards.
SINGLE GAME HIGHS (regular season): Attempts—2 (December 10, 2000, vs. Arizona); yards—8 (December 10, 2000, vs. Arizona); and rushing touchdowns—0.

WILLIAMS, JIMMY — CB — 49ERS

PERSONAL: Born March 10, 1979, in Baton Rouge, La. ... 5-11/189.
HIGH SCHOOL: Episcopal (Baton Rouge, La.).
COLLEGE: Vanderbilt.
TRANSACTIONS/CAREER NOTES: Selected by Buffalo Bills in sixth round (196th pick overall) of 2001 NFL draft. ... Signed by Bills (June 13, 2001). ... Released by Bills (September 2, 2001). ... Signed by San Francisco 49ers to practice squad (September 5, 2001). ... Activated (October 16, 2001).
PLAYING EXPERIENCE: San Francisco NFL, 2001. ... Games/Games started: 2001 (10/0).

WILLIAMS, JOSH — DT — COLTS

PERSONAL: Born August 9, 1976, in Denver. ... 6-3/284. ... Full name: Josh Sinclair Williams.
HIGH SCHOOL: Cypress Creek (Houston).
COLLEGE: Michigan.
TRANSACTIONS/CAREER NOTES: Selected by Indianapolis Colts in fourth round (122nd pick overall) of 2000 NFL draft. ... Signed by Colts (June 27, 2000).
PRO STATISTICS: 2000—Credited with one safety and recovered one fumble. 2001—Recovered one fumble.

Year Team	G	GS	SACKS
2000—Indianapolis NFL	14	7	3.0
2001—Indianapolis NFL	16	16	3.0
Pro totals (2 years)	**30**	**23**	**6.0**

WILLIAMS, K.D. — LB

PERSONAL: Born April 22, 1973, in Tampa. ... 6-0/245. ... Full name: Kevin Williams. ... Cousin of Juran Bolden, cornerback with four NFL teams (1996-99).
HIGH SCHOOL: Jefferson (Tampa).
JUNIOR COLLEGE: Arizona West Junior College.
COLLEGE: Henderson State (Ark.).

TRANSACTIONS/CAREER NOTES: Signed by Winnipeg Blue Bombers of CFL (January 6, 1995). ... Traded by Blue Bombers of CFL with S Jason Mallett and DE Horace Morris to Sasketchewan Roughriders of CFL for LB Sheldon Benoit, CB Nick Ferguson and G John James (May 5, 1997). ... Traded by Roughriders of CFL with LB Lamar Griggs to Hamilton Tiger-Cats of CFL for second-round pick in 1998 CFL college draft and future considerations (September 4, 1997). ... Released by Tiger-Cats (October 9, 1997). ... Selected by Frankfurt Galaxy in 1998 NFL Europe draft (February 23, 1998). ... Signed as non-drafted free agent by Dallas Cowboys (July 21, 1998). ... Released by Cowboys (August 25, 1998). ... Signed by Kansas City Chiefs to practice squad (September 1, 1998). ... Released by Chiefs (November 3, 1998). ... Signed by Oakland Raiders (March 1999). ... Released by Raiders (December 14, 1999). ... Signed by New Orleans Saints (March 23, 2000). ... Traded by Saints with third-round pick (traded to San Francisco) in 2001 draft to Green Bay Packers for QB Aaron Brooks and TE Lamont Hall (July 31, 2000). ... Granted free agency (March 1, 2002).
PRO STATISTICS: CFL: 1995—Recovered three fumbles. 1996—Recovered two fumbles for seven yards. NFL: 1999—Recovered one fumble. 2000—Recovered one fumble. 2001—Recovered one fumble.

				INTERCEPTIONS			SACKS
Year Team	G	GS	No.	Yds.	Avg.	TD	No.
1995—Winnipeg CFL	15	...	1	0	0.0	0	5.0
1996—Winnipeg CFL	18	...	4	72	18.0	1	5.0
1997—Saskatchewan CFL	10	...	2	38	19.0	1	3.0
—Hamilton CFL	3	...	1	18	18.0	0	1.0
1998—Frankfurt NFLE	...	...	0	0	0.0	0	2.5
1999—Oakland NFL	9	8	1	14	14.0	0	1.0
2000—Green Bay NFL	16	3	0	0	0.0	0	0.5
2001—Green Bay NFL	12	0	0	0	0.0	0	0.0
NFL Europe totals (1 year)	...	...	0	0	0.0	0	2.5
CFL totals (3 years)	46	...	8	128	16.0	2	14.0
NFL totals (3 years)	37	11	1	14	14.0	0	1.5
Pro totals (7 years)	...	...	9	142	15.8	2	18.0

WILLIAMS, KARL　　WR　　BUCCANEERS

PERSONAL: Born April 10, 1971, in Albion, Mich. ... 5-10/177.
HIGH SCHOOL: Garland (Texas).
COLLEGE: Texas A&M-Kingsville.
TRANSACTIONS/CAREER NOTES: Signed as non-drafted free agent by Tampa Bay Buccaneers (April 23, 1996). ... Granted unconditional free agency (March 1, 2002). ... Re-signed by Buccaneers (April 17, 2002).
CHAMPIONSHIP GAME EXPERIENCE: Played in NFC championship game (1999 season).
PRO STATISTICS: 1996—Rushed once for minus three yards and recovered one fumble. 1997—Rushed once for five yards and recovered one fumble. 1999—Recovered one fumble. 2000—Recovered one fumble.
SINGLE GAME HIGHS (regular season): Receptions—6 (September 13, 1998, vs. Green Bay); yards—87 (December 7, 1997, vs. Green Bay); and touchdown receptions—2 (November 2, 1997, vs. Indianapolis).

			RECEIVING				PUNT RETURNS				KICKOFF RETURNS				TOTALS			
Year Team	G	GS	No.	Yds.	Avg.	TD	No.	Yds.	Avg.	TD	No.	Yds.	Avg.	TD	TD	2pt.	Pts.	Fum.
1996—Tampa Bay NFL	16	0	22	246	11.2	0	13	274	21.1	1	14	383	27.4	0	1	0	6	2
1997—Tampa Bay NFL	16	8	33	486	14.7	4	46	‡597	13.0	∞1	15	277	18.5	0	5	0	30	5
1998—Tampa Bay NFL	13	6	21	252	12.0	1	10	83	8.3	0	0	0	0.0	0	1	0	6	0
1999—Tampa Bay NFL	13	4	21	176	8.4	0	20	153	7.7	0	1	15	15.0	0	0	0	0	2
2000—Tampa Bay NFL	13	0	2	35	17.5	0	31	286	9.2	1	19	453	23.8	0	1	0	6	2
2001—Tampa Bay NFL	15	3	24	314	13.1	1	35	366	10.5	†1	2	35	17.5	0	2	0	12	3
Pro totals (6 years)	86	21	123	1509	12.3	6	155	1759	11.3	4	51	1163	22.8	0	10	0	60	14

WILLIAMS, MAURICE　　OT　　JAGUARS

PERSONAL: Born January 26, 1979, in Detroit. ... 6-5/307. ... Full name: Maurice Carlos Williams.
HIGH SCHOOL: Pershing (Detroit).
COLLEGE: Michigan.
TRANSACTIONS/CAREER NOTES: Selected by Jacksonville Jaguars in second round (43rd pick overall) of 2001 NFL draft. ... Signed by Jaguars (July 25, 2001).
PLAYING EXPERIENCE: Jacksonville NFL, 2001. ... Games/Games started: (16/16).
PRO STATISTICS: 2001—Recovered three fumbles.

WILLIAMS, MOE　　RB　　VIKINGS

PERSONAL: Born July 26, 1974, in Columbus, Ga. ... 6-1/210. ... Full name: Maurice Jabari Williams.
HIGH SCHOOL: Spencer (Columbus, Ga.).
COLLEGE: Kentucky.
TRANSACTIONS/CAREER NOTES: Selected after junior season by Minnesota Vikings in third round (75th pick overall) of 1996 NFL draft. ... Signed by Vikings (July 22, 1996). ... On injured reserve with foot injury (December 8, 1998-remainder of season). ... Granted free agency (February 12, 1999). ... Re-signed by Vikings (April 30, 1999). ... Granted unconditional free agency (February 11, 2000). ... Re-signed by Vikings (March 20, 2000). ... Released by Vikings (September 2, 2001). ... Signed by Baltimore Ravens (September 4, 2001). ... Granted unconditional free agency (March 1, 2002). ... Signed by Vikings (May 16, 2002).
CHAMPIONSHIP GAME EXPERIENCE: Played in NFC championship game (2000 season).
PRO STATISTICS: 1998—Recovered one fumble. 2000—Recovered one fumble.
SINGLE GAME HIGHS (regular season): Attempts—24 (December 2, 2001, vs. Indianapolis); yards—111 (December 2, 2001, vs. Indianapolis); and rushing touchdowns—1 (October 24, 1999, vs. San Francisco).
STATISTICAL PLATEAUS: 100-yard rushing games: 2001 (1).

Year Team	G	GS	RUSHING Att.	Yds.	Avg.	TD	RECEIVING No.	Yds.	Avg.	TD	KICKOFF RETURNS No.	Yds.	Avg.	TD	TOTALS TD	2pt.	Pts.	Fum.
1996—Minnesota NFL	9	0	0	0	0.0	0	0	0	0.0	0	0	0	0.0	0	0	0	0	0
1997—Minnesota NFL	14	0	22	59	2.7	1	4	14	3.5	0	16	388	24.3	0	1	0	6	0
1998—Minnesota NFL	12	1	0	0	0.0	0	1	64	64.0	0	2	19	9.5	0	0	0	0	1
1999—Minnesota NFL	14	0	24	69	2.9	0	1	12	12.0	0	10	240	24.0	1	2	0	12	0
2000—Minnesota NFL	16	0	23	67	2.9	0	4	31	7.8	0	10	214	21.4	0	0	1	2	0
2001—Baltimore NFL	15	2	65	291	4.5	0	23	210	9.1	0	0	0	0.0	0	0	0	0	1
Pro totals (6 years)	80	3	134	486	3.6	2	33	331	10.0	0	38	861	22.7	1	3	1	20	2

WILLIAMS, NICK — FB — BENGALS

PERSONAL: Born March 30, 1977, in Farmington Hills, Mich. ... 6-2/267. ... Full name: James Nicolas Williams.
HIGH SCHOOL: Harrison (Farmington Hills, Mich.).
COLLEGE: Miami (Fla.).
TRANSACTIONS/CAREER NOTES: Selected by Cincinnati Bengals in fifth round (135th pick overall) of 1999 NFL draft. ... Signed by Bengals (May 19, 1999). ... On physically unable to perform list with knee injury (July 22-November 27, 2001). ... Granted free agency (March 1, 2002). ... Re-signed by Bengals (April 23, 2002).
PRO STATISTICS: 2000—Recovered one fumble.
SINGLE GAME HIGHS (regular season): Attempts—5 (November 26, 2000, vs. Pittsburgh); yards—18 (October 24, 1999, vs. Indianapolis); and rushing touchdowns—0.

Year Team	G	GS	RUSHING Att.	Yds.	Avg.	TD	RECEIVING No.	Yds.	Avg.	TD	KICKOFF RETURNS No.	Yds.	Avg.	TD	TOTALS TD	2pt.	Pts.	Fum.
1999—Cincinnati NFL	11	0	10	30	3.0	0	10	96	9.6	0	8	109	13.6	0	0	0	0	1
2000—Cincinnati NFL	14	4	10	54	5.4	0	7	84	12.0	0	2	12	6.0	0	0	0	0	2
2001—Cincinnati NFL	4	2	0	0	0.0	0	0	0	0.0	0	0	0	0.0	0	0	0	0	0
Pro totals (3 years)	29	6	20	84	4.2	0	17	180	10.6	0	10	121	12.1	0	0	0	0	3

WILLIAMS, PAT — DT — BILLS

PERSONAL: Born October 24, 1972, in Monroe, La. ... 6-3/315. ... Full name: Patrick Williams.
HIGH SCHOOL: Wossman (Monroe, La.).
JUNIOR COLLEGE: Navarro College (Texas).
COLLEGE: Northeast Oklahoma, then Texas A&M.
TRANSACTIONS/CAREER NOTES: Signed as non-drafted free agent by Buffalo Bills (April 25, 1997). ... Granted free agency (February 11, 2000). ... Re-signed by Bills (March 23, 2000).
PRO STATISTICS: 2000—Recovered two fumbles.

Year Team	G	GS	SACKS
1997—Buffalo NFL	1	0	0.0
1998—Buffalo NFL	13	0	3.5
1999—Buffalo NFL	16	0	2.5
2000—Buffalo NFL	16	3	2.5
2001—Buffalo NFL	13	13	1.5
Pro totals (5 years)	59	16	10.0

WILLIAMS, RANDAL — WR — COWBOYS

PERSONAL: Born May 24, 1978, in Deerfield, Maine. ... 6-3/214. ... Full name: Randal Ellison Williams.
HIGH SCHOOL: Deerfield Academy (Maine).
COLLEGE: New Hampshire.
TRANSACTIONS/CAREER NOTES: Signed as non-drafted free agent by Jacksonville Jaguars (April 27, 2001). ... Claimed on waivers by Dallas Cowboys (October 29, 2001).
PLAYING EXPERIENCE: Dallas NFL, 2001. ... Games/Games started: (7/0).

WILLIAMS, RICKY — RB — DOLPHINS

PERSONAL: Born May 21, 1977, in San Diego. ... 5-10/230. ... Full name: Errick Lynne Williams.
HIGH SCHOOL: Patrick Henry (San Diego).
COLLEGE: Texas.
TRANSACTIONS/CAREER NOTES: Selected by New Orleans Saints in first round (fifth pick overall) of 1999 NFL draft. ... Signed by Saints (May 14, 1999). ... Traded by Saints with fourth-round pick (TE Randy McMichael) in 2002 draft to Miami Dolphins for first- (DE Charles Grant) and fourth-round (DB Keyon Craver) picks in 2002 draft and third-round pick in 2003 draft (March 8, 2002).
HONORS: Named running back on THE SPORTING NEWS college All-America first team (1997 and 1998). ... Doak Walker Award winner (1997 and 1998). ... Heisman Trophy winner (1998). ... Walter Camp Award winner (1998). ... Maxwell Award winner (1998). ... Named College Football Player of the Year by THE SPORTING NEWS (1998).
PRO STATISTICS: 1999—Attempted one pass without a completion and recovered one fumble. 2000—Attempted one pass with one completion for 34 yards and recovered two fumbles. 2001—Recovered two fumbles for four yards.
SINGLE GAME HIGHS (regular season): Attempts—40 (October 31, 1999, vs. Cleveland); yards—179 (October 31, 1999, vs. Cleveland); and rushing touchdowns—3 (October 22, 2000, vs. Atlanta).
STATISTICAL PLATEAUS: 100-yard rushing games: 1999 (2), 2000 (5), 2001 (5). Total: 12.

Year	Team	G	GS	Att.	Rushing Yds.	Avg.	TD	No.	Receiving Yds.	Avg.	TD	TD	Totals 2pt.	Pts.	Fum.
1999	New Orleans NFL	12	12	253	884	3.5	2	28	172	6.1	0	2	0	12	6
2000	New Orleans NFL	10	10	248	1000	4.0	8	44	409	9.3	1	9	0	54	6
2001	New Orleans NFL	16	16	313	1245	4.0	6	60	511	8.5	1	7	0	42	8
Pro totals (3 years)		38	38	814	3129	3.8	16	132	1092	8.3	2	18	0	108	20

RECORD AS BASEBALL PLAYER

TRANSACTIONS/CAREER NOTES: Batted right, threw right. ... Selected by Philadelphia Phillies organization in eighth round of free-agent draft (June 1, 1995). ... Selected by Montreal Expos from Phillies organization in Rule 5 major league draft (December 14, 1998). ... Traded by Expos to Texas Rangers for cash considerations (December 15, 1998).

Year	Team (League)	Pos.	G	AB	R	H	2B	3B	HR	RBI	Avg.	BB	SO	SB	PO	A	E	Avg.
1995	Martinsville (Appal.)	OF	36	113	19	27	1	0	0	11	.239	6	32	13	51	5	3	.949
1996	Piedmont (S. Atl.)	OF	84	266	30	50	4	3	3	20	.188	18	87	17	117	9	9	.933
1997	Piedmont (S. Atl.)	OF	37	136	12	28	5	0	1	6	.206	9	44	10	58	5	3	.955
1998	Batavia (NY-Penn)	OF	13	53	7	15	0	0	0	3	.283	2	16	6	17	1	0	1.000

WILLIAMS, RODNEY — P — GIANTS

PERSONAL: Born April 25, 1977, in Brooklyn, N.Y. ... 6-0/178. ... Full name: Rodney Colin Williams.
HIGH SCHOOL: DeKalb (Decatur, Ga.).
COLLEGE: Georgia Tech.
TRANSACTIONS/CAREER NOTES: Selected by St. Louis Rams in seventh round (252nd pick overall) of 1999 NFL draft. ... Signed by Rams (July 20, 1999). ... Released by Rams (August 30, 1999). ... Signed by Washington Redskins (January 24, 2000). ... Released by Redskins (August 27, 2000). ... Signed by New York Giants (February 28, 2001).
PRO STATISTICS: NFLE: 2001—Rushed once for eight yards. NFL: 2001—Rushed twice for 16 yards.

Year	Team	G	No.	Yds.	Avg.	Net avg.	In. 20	Blk.
2000	Rhein NFLE	...	42	1965	46.8	35.3	11	1
2001	Rhein NFLE	...	50	2014	40.3	33.6	12	0
	New York Giants NFL	15	91	3905	42.9	35.4	25	0
NFL Europe totals (2 years)		...	92	3979	43.3	34.4	23	1
NFL totals (1 year)		15	91	3905	42.9	35.4	25	0
Pro totals (3 years)		...	183	7884	43.1	34.9	48	1

WILLIAMS, ROLAND — TE — RAIDERS

PERSONAL: Born April 27, 1975, in Rochester, N.Y. ... 6-5/265. ... Full name: Roland Lamar Williams.
HIGH SCHOOL: East (Rochester, N.Y.).
COLLEGE: Syracuse (degree in speech communications, 1997).
TRANSACTIONS/CAREER NOTES: Selected by St. Louis Rams in fourth round (98th pick overall) of 1998 NFL draft. ... Signed by Rams (July 13, 1998). ... Granted free agency (March 2, 2001). ... Re-signed by Rams (April 20, 2001). ... Traded by Rams to Oakland Raiders for fourth-round pick (traded to Arizona) in 2001 draft (April 21, 2001).
CHAMPIONSHIP GAME EXPERIENCE: Played in NFC championship game (1999 season). ... Member of Super Bowl championship team (1999 season).
PRO STATISTICS: 1999—Recovered two fumbles.
SINGLE GAME HIGHS (regular season): Receptions—5 (December 22, 2001, vs. Tennessee); yards—50 (October 24, 1999, vs. Cleveland); and touchdown receptions—2 (October 24, 1999, vs. Cleveland).

Year	Team	G	GS	No.	Receiving Yds.	Avg.	TD	TD	Totals 2pt.	Pts.	Fum.
1998	St. Louis NFL	13	9	15	144	9.6	1	1	0	6	0
1999	St. Louis NFL	16	15	25	226	9.0	6	6	0	36	0
2000	St. Louis NFL	16	11	11	102	9.3	3	3	1	20	0
2001	Oakland NFL	16	15	33	298	9.0	3	3	0	18	0
Pro totals (4 years)		61	50	84	770	9.2	13	13	1	80	0

WILLIAMS, SAMMY — OL

PERSONAL: Born December 14, 1974, in Magnolia, Miss. ... 6-5/318.
HIGH SCHOOL: Thornton Township (Harvey, Ill.).
JUNIOR COLLEGE: Coffeyville (Kan.) Community College.
COLLEGE: Oklahoma.
TRANSACTIONS/CAREER NOTES: Selected by Baltimore Ravens in sixth round (164th pick overall) of 1998 NFL draft. ... Signed by Ravens (July 21, 1998). ... On injured reserve with knee and ankle injuries (August 30, 1998-entire season). ... Released by Ravens (September 4, 1999). ... Claimed on waivers by Kansas City Chiefs (September 6, 1999). ... Claimed on waivers by Ravens (November 10, 1999). ... Assigned by Ravens to Berlin Thunder in 2001 NFL Europe enhancement allocation program (February 19, 2001). ... Granted unconditional free agency (March 1, 2002).
PLAYING EXPERIENCE: Kansas City NFL, 1999 and 2000; Berlin NFLE, 2001; Baltimore NFL, 2001. ... Games/Games started: 1999 (1/0), 2000 (2/0), NFLE 2001 (games played unavailable), NFL 2001 (15/7). Total: 18/7.
CHAMPIONSHIP GAME EXPERIENCE: Member of Ravens for AFC Championship game (2000 season); inactive. ... Member of Super Bowl championship team (2000 season); inactive.

WILLIAMS, SHAUN — S — GIANTS

PERSONAL: Born October 10, 1976, in Los Angeles. ... 6-2/215. ... Full name: Shaun LeJon Williams.
HIGH SCHOOL: Crespi (Encino, Calif.).
COLLEGE: UCLA.
TRANSACTIONS/CAREER NOTES: Selected by New York Giants in first round (24th pick overall) of 1998 NFL draft. ... Signed by Giants (July 24, 1998). ... Granted unconditional free agency (March 1, 2002). ... Re-signed by Giants (March 29, 2002).
PLAYING EXPERIENCE: New York Giants NFL, 1998-2001. ... Games/Games started: 1998 (13/0), 1999 (11/0), 2000 (16/16), 2001 (16/16). Total: 56/32.
CHAMPIONSHIP GAME EXPERIENCE: Played in NFC championship game (2000 season). ... Played in Super Bowl XXXV (2000 season).
HONORS: Named free safety on THE SPORTING NEWS college All-America second team (1997).
PRO STATISTICS: 1998—Intercepted two passes for six yards. 2000—Intercepted three passes for 52 yards and recovered one fumble. 2001—Intercepted three passes for 25 yards and credited with one sack.

WILLIAMS, TONY — DT — BENGALS

PERSONAL: Born July 9, 1975, in Germantown, Tenn. ... 6-1/292. ... Full name: Anthony Demetric Williams.
HIGH SCHOOL: Oakhaven (Memphis, Tenn.), then Germantown (Tenn.).
COLLEGE: Memphis.
TRANSACTIONS/CAREER NOTES: Selected by Minnesota Vikings in fifth round (151st pick overall) of 1997 NFL draft. ... Signed by Vikings (June 17, 1997). ... Granted free agency (February 11, 2000). ... Re-signed by Vikings (May 18, 2000). ... Granted unconditional free agency (March 2, 2001). ... Signed by Cincinnati Bengals (March 6, 2001).
PLAYING EXPERIENCE: Minnesota NFL, 1997-2000; Cincinnati NFL, 2001. ... Games/Games started: 1997 (6/2), 1998 (14/9), 1999 (16/12), 2000 (14/12), 2001 (13/13). Total: 63/48.
CHAMPIONSHIP GAME EXPERIENCE: Played in NFC championship game (1998 and 2000 season).
PRO STATISTICS: 1998—Credited with one sack and recovered one fumble for six yards. 1999—Credited with five sacks and recovered one fumble. 2000—Credited with four sacks. 2001—Credited with five sacks and recovered two fumbles.

WILLIAMS, TYRONE — CB — PACKERS

PERSONAL: Born May 31, 1973, in Bradenton, Fla. ... 5-11/193. ... Full name: Upton Tyrone Williams.
HIGH SCHOOL: Manatee (Bradenton, Fla.).
COLLEGE: Nebraska.
TRANSACTIONS/CAREER NOTES: Selected by Green Bay Packers in third round (93rd pick overall) of 1996 NFL draft. ... Signed by Packers (May 15, 1996). ... Granted free agency (February 12, 1999). ... Re-signed by Packers (May 17, 1999).
CHAMPIONSHIP GAME EXPERIENCE: Played in NFC championship game (1996 and 1997 seasons). ... Member of Super Bowl championship team (1996 season). ... Played in Super Bowl XXXII (1997 season).
PRO STATISTICS: 1996—Recovered one fumble. 1999—Fumbled once and recovered two fumbles for 12 yards. 2001—Recovered one fumble.

Year Team	G	GS	No.	Yds.	Avg.	TD
1996—Green Bay NFL	16	0	0	0	0.0	0
1997—Green Bay NFL	16	15	1	0	0.0	0
1998—Green Bay NFL	16	16	5	40	8.0	0
1999—Green Bay NFL	16	16	4	12	3.0	0
2000—Green Bay NFL	16	16	4	105	26.3	1
2001—Green Bay NFL	16	16	4	117	29.3	1
Pro totals (6 years)	96	79	18	274	15.2	2

WILLIAMS, TYRONE — DE

PERSONAL: Born October 22, 1972, in Philadelphia. ... 6-4/292. ... Full name: Tyrone M. Williams Jr.
HIGH SCHOOL: LaVista (Papillion, Neb.).
COLLEGE: Wyoming.
TRANSACTIONS/CAREER NOTES: Signed as non-drafted free agent by St. Louis Rams (July 25, 1996). ... Released by Rams (August 25, 1996). ... Re-signed by Rams to practice squad (August 26, 1996). ... Allocated by Rams to Rhein Fire in 1997 World League enhancement allocation program (February 19, 1997). ... Released by Rams (August 19, 1997). ... Signed by Chicago Bears to practice squad (August 27, 1997). ... Released by Bears (September 9, 1997). ... Re-signed by Rams to practice squad (September 25, 1997). ... Released by Rams practice squad (October 29, 1997). ... Released by Bears (August 31, 1998). ... Signed by Philadelphia Eagles (July 6, 1999). ... Released by Eagles (September 4, 1999). ... Re-signed by Eagles (October 20, 1999). ... Released by Eagles (September 20, 2000). ... Signed by Kansas City Chiefs (September 27, 2000). ... Released by Chiefs (August 28, 2001). ... Signed by Washington Redskins (September 26, 2001). ... Claimed on waivers by Chiefs (October 25, 2001). ... Granted free agency (March 2, 2002).
PLAYING EXPERIENCE: Chicago NFL, 1997; Philadelphia NFL, 1999; Philadelphia (3)-Kansas City (10) NFL, 2000; Washington (4)-Kansas City (7) NFL, 2001. ... Games/Games started: 1997 (3/0), 1999 (4/0), 2000 (Phi.-3/0; K.C.-10/0; Total: 13/0), 2001 (Was.-4/0; K.C.-7/0; Total: 11/0). Total: 28/0.
PRO STATISTICS: 1999—Credited with three sacks and recovered one fumble. 2000—Credited with 1½ sacks.

WILLIAMS, WALLY — G/C — SAINTS

PERSONAL: Born February 20, 1971, in Tallahassee, Fla. ... 6-2/321. ... Full name: Wally James Williams Jr.
HIGH SCHOOL: James S. Rickards (Tallahassee, Fla.).
COLLEGE: Florida A&M.
TRANSACTIONS/CAREER NOTES: Signed as non-drafted free agent by Cleveland Browns (April 27, 1993). ... Browns franchise moved to Baltimore and renamed Ravens for 1996 season (March 11, 1996). ... Designated by Ravens as franchise player (February 13, 1998). ... Re-

signed by Ravens (August 18, 1998). ... Granted unconditional free agency (February 12, 1999). ... Signed by New Orleans Saints (February 15, 1999). ... On injured reserve with neck injury (November 19, 1999-remainder of season).
PLAYING EXPERIENCE: Cleveland NFL, 1993-1995; Baltimore NFL, 1996-1998; New Orleans NFL, 1999-2001. ... Games/Games started: 1993 (2/0), 1994 (11/7), 1995 (16/16), 1996 (15/13), 1997 (10/10), 1998 (13/13), 1999 (6/6), 2000 (16/16), 2001 (15/15). Total: 104/96.
PRO STATISTICS: 1994—Recovered one fumble. 1998—Recovered one fumble. 2000—Recovered one fumble.

WILLIAMS, WILLIE CB SEAHAWKS

PERSONAL: Born December 26, 1970, in Columbia, S.C. ... 5-9/181. ... Full name: Willie James Williams Jr.
HIGH SCHOOL: Spring Valley (Columbia, S.C.).
COLLEGE: Western Carolina.
TRANSACTIONS/CAREER NOTES: Selected by Pittsburgh Steelers in sixth round (162nd pick overall) of 1993 NFL draft. ... Signed by Steelers (July 9, 1993). ... Granted free agency (February 16, 1996). ... Re-signed by Steelers (June 12, 1996). ... Granted unconditional free agency (February 14, 1997). ... Signed by Seattle Seahawks (February 18, 1997). ... Granted unconditional free agency (March 2, 2001). ... Re-signed by Seahawks (May 3, 2001).
CHAMPIONSHIP GAME EXPERIENCE: Played in AFC championship game (1994 and 1995 seasons). ... Played in Super Bowl XXX (1995 season).
PRO STATISTICS: 1993—Returned one kickoff for 19 yards. 1996—Credited with one sack and recovered one fumble. 1998—Recovered one fumble. 2000—Credited with one sack and recovered one fumble. 2001—Recovered one fumble.

			INTERCEPTIONS		
Year Team	G	GS	No.	Yds.	Avg.	TD
1993—Pittsburgh NFL	16	0	0	0	0.0	0
1994—Pittsburgh NFL	16	1	0	0	0.0	0
1995—Pittsburgh NFL	16	15	§7	122	17.4	▲1
1996—Pittsburgh NFL	15	14	1	1	1.0	0
1997—Seattle NFL	16	16	1	0	0.0	0
1998—Seattle NFL	14	14	2	36	18.0	1
1999—Seattle NFL	15	14	5	43	8.6	1
2000—Seattle NFL	16	15	4	74	18.5	1
2001—Seattle NFL	14	14	4	24	6.0	0
Pro totals (9 years)	**138**	**103**	**24**	**300**	**12.5**	**4**

WILLIG, MATT OT 49ERS

PERSONAL: Born January 21, 1969, in Santa Fe Springs, Calif. ... 6-8/315. ... Full name: Matthew Joseph Willig.
HIGH SCHOOL: St. Paul (Santa Fe Springs, Calif.).
COLLEGE: Southern California.
TRANSACTIONS/CAREER NOTES: Signed as non-drafted free agent by New York Jets (May 5, 1992). ... Released by Jets (August 24, 1992). ... Re-signed by Jets to practice squad (September 2, 1992). ... Activated (December 24, 1992). ... Active for one game (1992); did not play. ... Signed by Jets (February 15, 1993). ... Released by Jets (April 23, 1996). ... Signed by Atlanta Falcons (May 2, 1996). ... Granted unconditional free agency (February 13, 1998). ... Signed by Green Bay Packers (May 5, 1998). ... Released by Packers (February 23, 1999). ... Signed by Cleveland Browns (August 17, 1999). ... Released by Browns (September 5, 1999). ... Signed by St. Louis Rams (November 30, 1999). ... Granted unconditional free agency (February 11, 2000). ... Signed by San Francisco 49ers (June 7, 2000). ... Granted unconditional free agency (March 1, 2002). ... Re-signed by 49ers (March 7, 2002).
PLAYING EXPERIENCE: New York Jets NFL, 1993-1995; Atlanta NFL, 1996 and 1997; Green Bay NFL, 1998; San Francisco NFL, 2000 and 2001. ... Games/Games started: 1993 (3/0), 1994 (16/3), 1995 (15/12), 1996 (12/0), 1997 (16/3), 1998 (16/0), 2000 (16/3), 2001 (15/0). Total: 109/31.
CHAMPIONSHIP GAME EXPERIENCE: Member of Rams for NFC championship game (1999 season); inactive. ... Member of Super Bowl championship team (1999 season); inactive.
PRO STATISTICS: 1998—Recovered one fumble.

WILLIS, DONALD G CHIEFS

PERSONAL: Born July 15, 1973, in Goleta, Calif. ... 6-3/330. ... Full name: Donald Kirk Willis.
HIGH SCHOOL: Cabrillo (Lompoc, Calif.).
COLLEGE: Washington, then North Carolina A&T.
TRANSACTIONS/CAREER NOTES: Signed as non-drafted free agent by Seattle Seahawks (April 27, 1995). ... Claimed on waivers by New Orleans Saints (December 1, 1995). ... Inactive for 16 games (1995). ... Released by Saints (September 8, 1997). ... Signed by Tampa Bay Buccaneers (December 30, 1997). ... Released by Buccaneers (August 30, 1998). ... Signed by Kansas City Chiefs (March 12, 1999). ... Released by Chiefs (September 6, 1999). ... Re-signed by Chiefs (March 6, 2000). ... Granted unconditional free agency (March 1, 2002). ... Re-signed by Chiefs (April 4, 2002).
PLAYING EXPERIENCE: New Orleans NFL, 1996; Kansas City NFL, 2000 and 2001. ... Games/Games started: 1996 (4/0), 2000 (16/2), 2001 (14/4). Total: 34/6.

WILSON, ADRIAN DB CARDINALS

PERSONAL: Born October 12, 1979, in High Point, N.C. ... 6-3/207.
HIGH SCHOOL: T.W. Andrews (High Point, N.C.).
COLLEGE: North Carolina State.
TRANSACTIONS/CAREER NOTES: Selected after junior season by Arizona Cardinals in third round (64th pick overall) of 2001 NFL draft. ... Signed by Cardinals (July 24, 2001).

			INTERCEPTIONS			SACKS
Year Team	G	GS	No.	Yds.	Avg.	TD	No.
2001—Arizona NFL	16	0	2	97	48.5	1	0.5

WILSON, AL   LB   BRONCOS

PERSONAL: Born June 21, 1977, in Jackson, Tenn. ... 6-0/240. ... Full name: Aldra Kauwa Wilson.
HIGH SCHOOL: Central Merry (Jackson, Tenn.).
COLLEGE: Tennessee.
TRANSACTIONS/CAREER NOTES: Selected by Denver Broncos in first round (31st pick overall) of NFL draft. ... Signed by Broncos (July 21, 1999).
PLAYING EXPERIENCE: Denver NFL, 1999-2001. ... Games/Games started: 1999 (16/12), 2000 (15/14), 2001 (16/16). Total: 47/42.
HONORS: Named inside linebacker on THE SPORTING NEWS college All-America second team (1998).
PRO STATISTICS: 1999—Credited with one sack and recovered two fumbles. 2000—Intercepted three passes for 21 yards and credited with five sacks. 2001—Credited with three sacks.

WILSON, ANTONIO   LB   VIKINGS

PERSONAL: Born December 29, 1977, in Seagoville, Texas. ... 6-2/247.
HIGH SCHOOL: Skyline (Dallas).
COLLEGE: Texas A&M-Commerce.
TRANSACTIONS/CAREER NOTES: Selected by Minnesota Vikings in fourth round (106th pick overall) of 2000 NFL draft. ... Signed by Vikings (July 21, 2000). ... Assigned by Vikings to Barcelona Dragons in 2001 NFL Europe enhancement allocation program (February 19, 2001). ... Released by Vikings (September 2, 2001). ... Re-signed by Vikings to practice squad (September 4, 2001). ... Activated (October 9, 2001). ... Released by Vikings (October 25, 2001). ... Re-signed by Vikings (October 30, 2001).
PLAYING EXPERIENCE: Minnesota NFL, 2000 and 2001; Barcelona NFLE, 2001. ... Games/Games started: 2000 (1/0), NFLE 2001 (games played unavailable), NFL 2001 (10/0). Total: 11/0.
CHAMPIONSHIP GAME EXPERIENCE: Member of Vikings for NFC championship game (2000 season); inactive.
PRO STATISTICS: NFLE: 2001—Intercepted one pass for six yards and credited with two sacks.

WILSON, CEDRICK   WR/KR   49ERS

PERSONAL: Born December 17, 1978, in Memphis, Tenn. ... 5-10/179.
HIGH SCHOOL: Melrose (Memphis, Tenn.).
COLLEGE: Tennessee.
TRANSACTIONS/CAREER NOTES: Selected by San Francisco 49ers in sixth round (169th pick overall) of 2001 NFL draft. ... Signed by 49ers (July 24, 2001).

			PUNT RETURNS				KICKOFF RETURNS				TOTALS		
Year Team	G	GS	No.	Yds.	Avg.	TD	No.	Yds.	Avg.	TD	TD	2pt.	Pts.	Fum.
2001—San Francisco NFL	6	0	2	4	2.0	0	6	127	21.2	0	0	0	0	0

WILSON, GILLIS   DE

PERSONAL: Born October 15, 1977, in Morgan City, La. ... 6-2/282. ... Full name: Gillis R. Wilson III.
HIGH SCHOOL: Patterson (La.).
COLLEGE: Southern.
TRANSACTIONS/CAREER NOTES: Selected by Carolina Panthers in fifth round (147th pick overall) of 2000 NFL draft. ... Signed by Panthers (June 8, 2000). ... Released by Panthers (August 26, 2000). ... Re-signed by Panthers to practice squad (August 29, 2000). ... Activated (December 20, 2000); did not play. ... Released by Panthers (August 28, 2001). ... Signed by New York Giants (September 18, 2001). ... Released by Giants (October 2, 2001). ... Re-signed by Giants to practice squad (October 3, 2001). ... Signed by Panthers off Giants practice squad (November 21, 2001). ... Granted free agency (March 1, 2002).

Year Team	G	GS	SACKS
2001—Carolina NFL	5	0	0.5

WILSON, JERRY   CB   SAINTS

PERSONAL: Born July 17, 1973, in Alexandria, La. ... 5-10/187. ... Full name: Jerry Lee Wilson Jr.
HIGH SCHOOL: La Grange (Lake Charles, La.).
COLLEGE: Southern (degree in rehabilitation counseling).
TRANSACTIONS/CAREER NOTES: Selected by Tampa Bay Buccaneers in fourth round (105th pick overall) of 1995 NFL draft. ... Signed by Buccaneers (May 9, 1995). ... On injured reserve with knee injury (August 31, 1995-entire season). ... Released by Buccaneers (August 20, 1996). ... Signed by Miami Dolphins to practice squad (October 29, 1996). ... Activated (November 5, 1996). ... Granted unconditional free agency (March 2, 2001). ... Signed by New Orleans Saints (January 2, 2001). ... Granted unconditional free agency (March 1, 2002). ... Re-signed by Saints (May 2, 2002).
PLAYING EXPERIENCE: Miami NFL, 1996-2000; New Orleans NFL, 2001. ... Games/Games started: 1996 (2/0), 1997 (16/0), 1998 (16/0), 1999 (16/1), 2000 (16/0), 2001 (1/0). Total: 67/1.
PRO STATISTICS: 1997—Credited with two sacks and recovered one fumble. 1998—Intercepted one pass for no yards. 1999—Intercepted one pass for 13 yards, returned three kickoffs for 50 yards and credited with three sacks. 2000—Intercepted one pass for 19 yards and credited with $1/2$ sack.

WILSON, REINARD   DE   BENGALS

PERSONAL: Born December 17, 1973, in Lake City, Fla. ... 6-2/272. ... Cousin of Brian Allen, linebacker, Houston Texans. ... Name pronounced ruh-NARD.
HIGH SCHOOL: Columbia (Lake City, Fla.).
COLLEGE: Florida State.

TRANSACTIONS/CAREER NOTES: Selected by Cincinnati Bengals in first round (14th pick overall) of 1997 NFL draft. ... Signed by Bengals (July 18, 1997). ... Granted unconditional free agency (March 1, 2002). ... Re-signed by Bengals (March 28, 2002).
HONORS: Named defensive end on THE SPORTING NEWS college All-America second team (1996).
PRO STATISTICS: 2000—Recovered one fumble for three yards. 2001—Recovered two fumbles.

Year Team	G	GS	SACKS
1997—Cincinnati NFL	16	4	3.0
1998—Cincinnati NFL	16	15	6.0
1999—Cincinnati NFL	15	0	3.0
2000—Cincinnati NFL	14	0	3.0
2001—Cincinnati NFL	16	5	9.0
Pro totals (5 years)	77	24	24.0

WILSON, ROBERT   WR

PERSONAL: Born June 23, 1974, in Tallahassee, Fla. ... 5-11/176.
HIGH SCHOOL: Jefferson County (Monticello, Fla.).
COLLEGE: Florida A&M.
TRANSACTIONS/CAREER NOTES: Signed as non-drafted free agent by Seattle Seahawks (April 25, 1997). ... Released by Seahawks (August 18, 1997). ... Re-signed by Seahawks to practice squad (August 19, 1997). ... Activated (December 17, 1997); did not play. ... Released by Seahawks (September 6, 1999). ... Re-signed by Seahawks (October 20, 1999). ... Released by Seahawks (November 13, 1999). ... Signed by New Orleans Saints (March 6, 2000). ... Granted free agency (March 1, 2002).
PLAYING EXPERIENCE: Seattle NFL, 1998 and 1999; New Orleans NFL, 2000 and 2001. ... Games/Games started: 1998 (16/0), 1999 (2/0), 2000 (16/0), 2001 (15/1). Total: 49/1.
PRO STATISTICS: 1998—Returned one kickoff for 16 yards. 2000—Caught 11 passes for 154 yards and ran 11 yards with lateral. 2001—Caught 21 passes for 277 yards.
SINGLE GAME HIGHS (regular season): Receptions—8 (December 3, 2000, vs. Denver); yards—122 (December 3, 2000, vs. Denver); and touchdown receptions—0.
STATISTICAL PLATEAUS: 100-yard receiving games: 2000 (1).

WINBORN, JAMIE   LB   49ERS

PERSONAL: Born May 14, 1979, in Wetumpka, Ala. ... 5-11/242.
HIGH SCHOOL: Wetumpka (Ala.).
COLLEGE: Vanderbilt.
TRANSACTIONS/CAREER NOTES: Selected after junior season by San Francisco 49ers in second round (47th pick overall) of 2001 NFL draft. ... Signed by 49ers (July 25, 2001).
PRO STATISTICS: 2001—Recovered one fumble for 17 yards.

			INTERCEPTIONS			SACKS
Year Team	G	GS	No.	Yds.	Avg.	TD	No.
2001—San Francisco NFL	14	4	2	40	20.0	0	0.5

WINFIELD, ANTOINE   CB   BILLS

PERSONAL: Born June 24, 1977, in Akron, Ohio. ... 5-9/180. ... Full name: Antoine D. Winfield.
HIGH SCHOOL: Garfield (Ohio).
COLLEGE: Ohio State.
TRANSACTIONS/CAREER NOTES: Selected by Buffalo Bills in first round (23rd pick overall) of 1999 NFL draft. ... Signed by Bills (July 30, 1999). ... On injured reserve list with shoulder injury (November 22, 2000-remainder of season).
HONORS: Named cornerback on THE SPORTING NEWS college All-America second team (1997). ... Jim Thorpe Award winner (1998). ... Named cornerback on THE SPORTING NEWS college All-America first team (1998).
PRO STATISTICS: 2001—Recovered one fumble for five yards.

			INTERCEPTIONS		
Year Team	G	GS	No.	Yds.	Avg.	TD
1999—Buffalo NFL	16	2	2	13	6.5	0
2000—Buffalo NFL	11	11	1	8	8.0	0
2001—Buffalo NFL	16	16	2	0	0.0	0
Pro totals (3 years)	43	29	5	21	4.2	0

WINTERS, FRANK   C   PACKERS

PERSONAL: Born January 23, 1964, in Hoboken, N.J. ... 6-3/305. ... Full name: Frank Mitchell Winters.
HIGH SCHOOL: Emerson (Union City, N.J.).
JUNIOR COLLEGE: College of Eastern Utah.
COLLEGE: Western Illinois (degree in political science administration, 1987).
TRANSACTIONS/CAREER NOTES: Selected by Cleveland Browns in 10th round (276th pick overall) of 1987 NFL draft. ... Signed by Browns (July 25, 1987). ... Granted unconditional free agency (February 1, 1989). ... Signed by New York Giants (March 17, 1989). ... Granted unconditional free agency (February 1, 1990). ... Signed by Kansas City Chiefs (March 26, 1990). ... Granted unconditional free agency (February 1, 1992). ... Signed by Green Bay Packers (March 17, 1992). ... Granted unconditional free agency (February 17, 1994). ... Re-signed by Packers (April 1, 1994). ... Granted unconditional free agency (February 14, 1997). ... Re-signed by Packers (March 26, 1997). ... On injured reserve with leg injury (December 16, 1998-remainder of season). ... Granted unconditional free agency (February 11, 2000). ... Re-signed by Packers (April 4, 2000).
PLAYING EXPERIENCE: Cleveland NFL, 1987 and 1988; New York Giants NFL, 1989; Kansas City NFL, 1990 and 1991; Green Bay NFL, 1992-2001. ... Games/Games started: 1987 (12/0), 1988 (16/0), 1989 (15/0), 1990 (16/6), 1991 (16/0), 1992 (16/11), 1993 (16/16), 1994 (16/16), 1995 (16/16), 1996 (16/16), 1997 (13/13), 1998 (13/13), 1999 (16/15), 2000 (14/14), 2001 (4/0). Total: 215/137.

– 420 –

CHAMPIONSHIP GAME EXPERIENCE: Played in AFC championship game (1987 season). ... Played in NFC championship game (1995-97 seasons). ... Member of Super Bowl championship team (1996 season). ... Played in Super Bowl XXXII (1997 season).
HONORS: Played in Pro Bowl (1996 season).
PRO STATISTICS: 1987—Fumbled once. 1990—Recovered two fumbles. 1992—Fumbled once. 1994—Fumbled once and recovered one fumble for minus two yards. 1996—Recovered one fumble. 1999—Recovered one fumble.

WISNIEWSKI, STEVE   G

PERSONAL: Born April 7, 1967, in Rutland, Vt. ... 6-4/305. ... Full name: Stephen Adam Wisniewski. ... Brother of Leo Wisniewski, nose tackle with Baltimore/Indianapolis Colts (1982-84). ... Name pronounced wiz-NEWS-key.
HIGH SCHOOL: Westfield (Houston).
COLLEGE: Penn State.
TRANSACTIONS/CAREER NOTES: Selected by Dallas Cowboys in second round (29th pick overall) of 1989 NFL draft. ... Draft rights traded by Cowboys with sixth-round pick (LB Jeff Francis) in 1989 draft to Los Angeles Raiders for second-(RB Darryl Johnston), third-(DE Rhondy Weston) and fifth-round (LB Willis Crockett) picks in 1989 draft (April 23, 1989). ... Signed by Raiders (July 22, 1989). ... Granted free agency (March 1, 1993). ... Re-signed by Raiders for 1993 season. ... Raiders franchise moved to Oakland (July 21, 1995). ... Announced retirement (January 21, 2002).
PLAYING EXPERIENCE: Los Angeles Raiders NFL, 1989-1994; Oakland NFL, 1995-2001. ... Games/Games started: 1989 (15/15), 1990 (16/16), 1991 (15/15), 1992 (16/16), 1993 (16/16), 1994 (16/16), 1995 (16/16), 1996 (16/16), 1997 (16/16), 1998 (16/16), 1999 (16/16), 2000 (16/16), 2001 (16/16). Total: 207/207.
CHAMPIONSHIP GAME EXPERIENCE: Played in AFC championship game (1990 and 2000 seasons).
HONORS: Named guard on THE SPORTING NEWS college All-America first team (1987 and 1988). ... Named guard on THE SPORTING NEWS NFL All-Pro team (1990-1994). ... Played in Pro Bowl (1990, 1991, 1993, 1995 and 2000 seasons). ... Named to play in Pro Bowl (1992 season); replaced by Jim Ritcher due to injury.
PRO STATISTICS: 1989—Recovered three fumbles. 1995—Recovered one fumble.

WISTROM, GRANT   DE   RAMS

PERSONAL: Born July 3, 1976, in Webb City, Mo. ... 6-4/272. ... Full name: Grant Alden Wistrom.
HIGH SCHOOL: Webb City (Mo.).
COLLEGE: Nebraska.
TRANSACTIONS/CAREER NOTES: Selected by St. Louis Rams in first round (sixth pick overall) of 1998 NFL draft. ... Signed by Rams (July 18, 1998).
CHAMPIONSHIP GAME EXPERIENCE: Played in NFC championship game (1999 and 2001 seasons). ... Member of Super Bowl championship team (1999 season). ... Played in Super Bowl XXXVI (2001 season).
HONORS: Named defensive end on THE SPORTING NEWS college All-America first team (1996 and 1997).
PRO STATISTICS: 1998—Recovered one fumble for four yards. 1999—Intercepted two passes for 131 yards and two touchdowns, fumbled once and recovered one fumble for 31 yards. 2001—Intercepted two passes for minus four yards and recovered one fumble for 17 yards.

Year Team	G	GS	SACKS
1998—St. Louis NFL	13	0	3.0
1999—St. Louis NFL	16	16	6.5
2000—St. Louis NFL	16	16	11.0
2001—St. Louis NFL	15	15	9.0
Pro totals (4 years)	60	47	29.5

WITHERSPOON, TERRY   FB   CHARGERS

PERSONAL: Born August 22, 1977, in Monroe, N.C. ... 5-11/250.
HIGH SCHOOL: Monroe (N.C.).
COLLEGE: Clemson.
TRANSACTIONS/CAREER NOTES: Signed as non-drafted free agent by San Diego Chargers (April 30, 2001). ... Released by Chargers (September 2, 2001). ... Re-signed by Chargers to practice squad (September 4, 2001). ... Released by Chargers (October 9, 2001). ... Signed by Dallas Cowboys to practice squad (October 18, 2001). ... Activated (December 21, 2001). ... Claimed on waivers by San Diego Chargers (April 23, 2002).
PLAYING EXPERIENCE: Dallas NFL, 2001. ... Games/Games started: (3/0).
PRO STATISTICS: 2001—Caught one pass for nine yards.

WITHROW, CORY   C   VIKINGS

PERSONAL: Born April 5, 1975, in Spokane, Wash. ... 6-2/281.
HIGH SCHOOL: Mead (Spokane, Wash.).
COLLEGE: Washington State.
TRANSACTIONS/CAREER NOTES: Signed as non-drafted free agent by Minnesota Vikings (April 23, 1998). ... Released by Vikings (August 30, 1998). ... Signed by Cincinnati Bengals to practice squad (December 18, 1998). ... Released by Bengals (April 15, 1999). ... Signed by Vikings (April 30, 1999). ... Released by Vikings (September 5, 1999). ... Re-signed by Vikings to practice squad (September 6, 1999). ... Activated (October 26, 1999); did not play. ... Released by Vikings (November 30, 1999). ... Re-signed by Vikings to practice squad (December 1, 1999).
PLAYING EXPERIENCE: Minnesota NFL, 2000 and 2001. ... Games/Games started: 2000 (12/0), 2001 (16/1). Total: 28/1.
CHAMPIONSHIP GAME EXPERIENCE: Played in NFC championship game (2000 season).

WITMAN, JON   FB

PERSONAL: Born June 1, 1972, in Wrightsville, Pa. ... 6-2/244. ... Full name: Jon Doyle Witman.
HIGH SCHOOL: Eastern York (Wrightsville, Pa.).
COLLEGE: Penn State.
TRANSACTIONS/CAREER NOTES: Selected by Pittsburgh Steelers in third round (92nd pick overall) of 1996 NFL draft. ... Signed by Steelers (July 16, 1996). ... Granted free agency (February 12, 1999). ... Re-signed by Steelers (March 10, 1999). ... On injured reserve with broken leg (October 17, 2000-remainder of season). ... Released by Steelers (March 1, 2001). ... Re-signed by Steelers (April 2, 2001). ... Granted unconditional free agency (March 1, 2002).
CHAMPIONSHIP GAME EXPERIENCE: Played in AFC championship game (1997 and 2001 seasons).
PRO STATISTICS: 1996—Returned one kickoff for 20 yards.
SINGLE GAME HIGHS (regular season): Attempts—7 (November 3, 1996, vs. St. Louis); yards—33 (November 3, 1996, vs. St. Louis); and rushing touchdowns—0.

			RUSHING				RECEIVING			TOTALS		
Year Team	G	GS	Att.	Yds.	Avg.	TD	No.	Yds.	Avg.	TD	2pt.	Pts. Fum.
1996—Pittsburgh NFL	16	4	17	69	4.1	0	2	15	7.5	0	0	0 0
1997—Pittsburgh NFL	16	2	5	11	2.2	0	1	3	3.0	0	0	0 0
1998—Pittsburgh NFL	16	8	1	2	2.0	0	13	74	5.7	0	0	0 0
1999—Pittsburgh NFL	16	11	6	18	3.0	0	12	106	8.8	0	0	0 0
2000—Pittsburgh NFL	6	5	3	5	1.7	0	5	33	6.6	0	0	0 0
2001—Pittsburgh NFL	15	12	5	24	4.8	0	6	32	5.3	0	0	0 0
Pro totals (6 years)	85	42	37	129	3.5	0	39	263	6.7	0	0	0 0

WOHLABAUGH, DAVE   C   BROWNS

PERSONAL: Born April 13, 1972, in Hamburg, N.Y. ... 6-3/292. ... Full name: David Vincent Wohlabaugh. ... Name pronounced WOOL-uh-buh.
HIGH SCHOOL: Frontier (Hamburg, N.Y.).
COLLEGE: Syracuse.
TRANSACTIONS/CAREER NOTES: Selected by New England Patriots in fourth round (112th pick overall) of 1995 NFL draft. ... Signed by Patriots (June 26, 1995). ... Granted free agency (February 13, 1998). ... Re-signed by Patriots (May 28, 1998). ... Granted unconditional free agency (February 12, 1999). ... Signed by Cleveland Browns (February 16, 1999).
PLAYING EXPERIENCE: New England NFL, 1995-1998; Cleveland NFL, 1999-2001. ... Games/Games started: 1995 (11/11), 1996 (16/16), 1997 (14/14), 1998 (16/16), 1999 (15/15), 2000 (12/12), 2001 (16/16). Total: 100/100.
CHAMPIONSHIP GAME EXPERIENCE: Played in AFC championship game (1996 season). ... Played in Super Bowl XXXI (1996 season).
PRO STATISTICS: 1995—Recovered one fumble. 1996—Recovered two fumbles for one yard.

WOMACK, FLOYD   OT   SEAHAWKS

PERSONAL: Born November 15, 1978, in Cleveland, Miss. ... 6-4/330. ... Full name: Floyd Seneca Womack.
HIGH SCHOOL: East Side (Cleveland, Miss.).
COLLEGE: Mississippi State.
TRANSACTIONS/CAREER NOTES: Selected by Seattle Seahawks in fourth round (128th pick overall) of 2001 NFL draft. ... Signed by Seahawks (June 22, 2001).
PLAYING EXPERIENCE: Seattle NFL, 2001. ... Games/Games started: (6/0).

WONG, KAILEE   LB   TEXANS

PERSONAL: Born May 23, 1976, in Eugene, Ore. ... 6-2/250.
HIGH SCHOOL: North Eugene (Ore.).
COLLEGE: Stanford.
TRANSACTIONS/CAREER NOTES: Selected by Minnesota Vikings in second round (51st pick overall) of 1998 NFL draft. ... Signed by Vikings (July 25, 1998). ... On injured reserve with leg injury (December 31, 1998-remainder of season). ... Granted free agency (March 2, 2001). ... Re-signed by Vikings (April 16, 2001). ... Granted unconditional free agency (March 1, 2002). ... Signed by Houston Texans (March 7, 2002).
PLAYING EXPERIENCE: Minnesota NFL, 1998-2001. ... Games/Games started: 1998 (15/0), 1999 (13/8), 2000 (16/16), 2001 (16/16). Total: 60/40.
CHAMPIONSHIP GAME EXPERIENCE: Played in NFC championship game (2000 season).
PRO STATISTICS: 1998—Credited with 1 1/2 sacks. 1999—Recovered one fumble for four yards. 2000—Intercepted two passes for 28 yards, credited with two sacks and fumbled once. 2001—Intercepted one pass for 27 yards and a touchdown and credited with three sacks.

WOODALL, LEE   LB

PERSONAL: Born October 31, 1969, in Carlisle, Pa. ... 6-1/230. ... Full name: Lee Artis Woodall.
HIGH SCHOOL: Carlisle (Pa.).
COLLEGE: West Chester (Pa.) University.
TRANSACTIONS/CAREER NOTES: Selected by San Francisco 49ers in sixth round (182nd pick overall) of 1994 NFL draft. ... Signed by 49ers (July 20, 1994). ... Released by 49ers (February 9, 2000). ... Signed by Carolina Panthers (March 22, 2000). ... Released by Panthers (February 28, 2001). ... Signed by Denver Broncos (May 4, 2001). ... Granted unconditional free agency (March 1, 2002).
CHAMPIONSHIP GAME EXPERIENCE: Played in NFC championship game (1994 and 1997 seasons). ... Member of Super Bowl championship team (1994 season).
HONORS: Played in Pro Bowl (1995 and 1997 seasons).
PRO STATISTICS: 1994—Recovered one fumble. 1995—Recovered two fumbles for 98 yards and one touchdown. 2000—Recovered one fumble.

Year Team	G	GS	INTERCEPTIONS No.	Yds.	Avg.	TD	SACKS No.
1994—San Francisco NFL	15	13	0	0	0.0	0	1.0
1995—San Francisco NFL	16	16	2	0	0.0	0	3.0
1996—San Francisco NFL	16	13	0	0	0.0	0	2.5
1997—San Francisco NFL	16	16	2	55	27.5	0	0.0
1998—San Francisco NFL	15	15	1	4	4.0	0	0.0
1999—San Francisco NFL	16	16	0	0	0.0	0	2.5
2000—Carolina NFL	16	16	1	0	0.0	0	0.0
2001—Denver NFL	14	0	0	0	0.0	0	1.0
Pro totals (8 years)	124	105	6	59	9.8	0	10.0

WOODARD, CEDRIC DT SEAHAWKS

PERSONAL: Born September 5, 1977, in Bay City, Texas. ... 6-2/311. ... Full name: Cedric Darnell Woodard. ... Cousin of Tracy Simien, linebacker with Pittsbrugh Steelers (1989), Kansas City Chiefs (1991-97) and San Diego Chargers (1999); and cousin of Elmo Wright, wide receiver with Kansas City Chiefs (1971-74), Houston Oilers (1975) and New England Patriots (1975).
HIGH SCHOOL: Sweeny (Texas).
COLLEGE: Texas.
TRANSACTIONS/CAREER NOTES: Selected by Baltimore Ravens in sixth round (191st pick overall) of 2000 NFL draft. ... Signed by Ravens (June 15, 2000). ... Claimed on waivers by Seattle Seahawks (September 6, 2000).
PLAYING EXPERIENCE: Seattle NFL, 2001. ... Games/Games started: 2001 (16/0).

WOODBURY, TORY QB JETS

PERSONAL: Born July 12, 1978, in Winston-Salem, N.C. ... 6-2/208.
HIGH SCHOOL: Glenn (Winston-Salem, N.C.).
COLLEGE: Winston-Salem State.
TRANSACTIONS/CAREER NOTES: Signed as non-drafted free agent by New York Jets (April 26, 2001).
PLAYING EXPERIENCE: New York Jets NFL, 2001. ... Games/Games started: (10/0).
PRO STATISTICS: 2001—Recovered one fumble.

WOODEN, SHAWN S DOLPHINS

PERSONAL: Born October 23, 1973, in Philadelphia. ... 5-11/205. ... Full name: Shawn Anthony Wooden.
HIGH SCHOOL: Abington (Pa.).
COLLEGE: Notre Dame (degree in computer science).
TRANSACTIONS/CAREER NOTES: Selected by Miami Dolphins in sixth round (189th pick overall) of 1996 NFL draft. ... Signed by Dolphins (July 10, 1996). ... On injured reserve with knee injury (September 15, 1998-remainder of season). ... Granted free agency (February 12, 1999). ... Re-signed by Dolphins (April 23, 1999). ... Granted unconditional free agency (February 11, 2000). ... Signed by Chicago Bears (March 6, 2000). ... Released by Bears (June 26, 2001). ... Signed by Dolphins (June 29, 2001).
PRO STATISTICS: 1996—Recovered two fumbles. 1997—Fumbled once and recovered two fumbles. 1999—Recovered two fumbles. 2000—Recovered one fumble for three yards.

Year Team	G	GS	INTERCEPTIONS No.	Yds.	Avg.	TD
1996—Miami NFL	16	11	2	15	7.5	0
1997—Miami NFL	16	15	2	10	5.0	0
1998—Miami NFL	2	1	0	0	0.0	0
1999—Miami NFL	15	6	0	0	0.0	0
2000—Chicago NFL	11	0	0	0	0.0	0
2001—Miami NFL	13	0	0	0	0.0	0
Pro totals (6 years)	73	33	4	25	6.3	0

WOODS, JEROME S CHIEFS

PERSONAL: Born March 17, 1973, in Memphis, Tenn. ... 6-2/207.
HIGH SCHOOL: Melrose (Memphis, Tenn.).
JUNIOR COLLEGE: Northeast Mississippi Community College.
COLLEGE: Memphis.
TRANSACTIONS/CAREER NOTES: Selected by Kansas City Chiefs in first round (28th pick overall) of 1996 NFL draft. ... Signed by Chiefs (August 12, 1996). ... Granted unconditional free agency (February 11, 2000). ... Re-signed by Chiefs (February 11, 2000).
PRO STATISTICS: 1996—Fumbled once and recovered one fumble. 1997—Credited with one sack and recovered two fumbles for 13 yards. 1999—Recovered one fumble for 19 yards. 2000—Credited with two sacks. 2001—Credited with one sack.

Year Team	G	GS	INTERCEPTIONS No.	Yds.	Avg.	TD
1996—Kansas City NFL	16	0	0	0	0.0	0
1997—Kansas City NFL	16	16	4	57	14.3	0
1998—Kansas City NFL	16	16	2	47	23.5	0
1999—Kansas City NFL	15	15	1	5	5.0	0
2000—Kansas City NFL	16	16	2	0	0.0	0
2001—Kansas City NFL	16	16	3	48	16.0	0
Pro totals (6 years)	95	79	12	157	13.1	0

WOODS, LEVAR — LB — CARDINALS

PERSONAL: Born March 15, 1978, in Larchwood, Iowa. ... 6-2/241.
HIGH SCHOOL: West Lyon (Inwood, Iowa).
COLLEGE: Iowa.
TRANSACTIONS/CAREER NOTES: Signed as non-drafted free agent by Arizona Cardinals (April 23, 2001).
PLAYING EXPERIENCE: Arizona NFL, 2001. ... Games/Games started: (15/0).
PRO STATISTICS: 2001—Recovered one fumble.

WOODSON, CHARLES — DB — RAIDERS

PERSONAL: Born October 7, 1976, in Fremont, Ohio. ... 6-1/205.
HIGH SCHOOL: Ross (Fremont, Ohio).
COLLEGE: Michigan.
TRANSACTIONS/CAREER NOTES: Selected after junior season by Oakland Raiders in first round (fourth pick overall) of 1998 NFL draft. ... Signed by Raiders (July 20, 1998).
CHAMPIONSHIP GAME EXPERIENCE: Played in AFC championship game (2000 season).
HONORS: Named cornerback on THE SPORTING NEWS college All-America second team (1996). ... Heisman Trophy winner (1997). ... Jim Thorpe Award winner (1997). ... Maxwell Award winner (1997). ... Chuck Bednarik Award winner (1997). ... Named College Football Player of the Year by The Sporting News (1997). ... Named cornerback on THE SPORTING NEWS college All-America first team (1997). ... Played in Pro Bowl (1998-2000 seasons). ... Named cornerback on THE SPORTING NEWS NFL All-Pro team (2001).
PRO STATISTICS: 1999—Caught one pass for 19 yards and recovered one fumble for 24 yards. 2000—Caught one pass for eight yards and recovered one fumble. 2001—Returned four punts for 47 yards and credited with two sacks.

				INTERCEPTIONS			
Year Team	G	GS	No.	Yds.	Avg.	TD
1998—Oakland NFL	16	16	5	118	23.6	1
1999—Oakland NFL	16	16	1	15	15.0	1
2000—Oakland NFL	16	16	4	36	9.0	0
2001—Oakland NFL	16	16	1	64	64.0	0
Pro totals (4 years)	64	64	11	233	21.2	2

WOODSON, DARREN — S — COWBOYS

PERSONAL: Born April 25, 1969, in Phoenix. ... 6-1/219. ... Full name: Darren Ray Woodson.
HIGH SCHOOL: Maryvale (Phoenix).
COLLEGE: Arizona State (degree in criminal justice).
TRANSACTIONS/CAREER NOTES: Selected by Dallas Cowboys in second round (37th pick overall) of 1992 NFL draft. ... Signed by Cowboys (April 26, 1992). ... On injured reserve with broken forearm (December 14, 2000-remainder of season). ... Granted unconditional free agency (March 1, 2002). ... Re-signed by Cowboys (March 1, 2002).
CHAMPIONSHIP GAME EXPERIENCE: Played in NFC championship game (1992-1995 seasons). ... Member of Super Bowl championship team (1992, 1993 and 1995 seasons).
HONORS: Named strong safety on THE SPORTING NEWS NFL All-Pro team (1994-1996 and 1998). ... Played in Pro Bowl (1994-1996 and 1998 seasons). ... Named to play in Pro Bowl (1997 season); replaced by John Lynch due to injury.
PRO STATISTICS: 1993—Recovered three fumbles for three yards. 1994—Recovered one fumble. 1996—Fumbled once and recovered one fumble. 1997—Fumbled once and recovered two fumbles. 2001—Recovered one fumble.

			INTERCEPTIONS				SACKS
Year Team	G	GS	No.	Yds.	Avg.	TD	No.
1992—Dallas NFL	16	2	0	0	0.0	0	1.0
1993—Dallas NFL	16	15	0	0	0.0	0	0.0
1994—Dallas NFL	16	16	5	140	28.0	1	0.0
1995—Dallas NFL	16	16	2	46	23.0	1	0.0
1996—Dallas NFL	16	16	5	43	8.6	0	3.0
1997—Dallas NFL	14	14	1	14	14.0	0	2.0
1998—Dallas NFL	16	15	1	1	1.0	0	3.0
1999—Dallas NFL	15	15	2	5	2.5	0	1.0
2000—Dallas NFL	11	11	2	12	6.0	0	0.0
2001—Dallas NFL	16	16	3	11	3.7	0	0.0
Pro totals (10 years)	152	136	21	272	13.0	2	10.0

WOODSON, ROD — S — RAIDERS

PERSONAL: Born March 10, 1965, in Fort Wayne, Ind. ... 6-0/205. ... Full name: Roderick Kevin Woodson.
HIGH SCHOOL: R. Nelson Snider (Fort Wayne, Ind.).
COLLEGE: Purdue.
TRANSACTIONS/CAREER NOTES: Selected by Pittsburgh Steelers in first round (10th pick overall) of 1987 NFL draft. ... On reserve/unsigned list (August 31-October 27, 1987). ... Signed by Steelers (October 28, 1987). ... Granted roster exemption (October 28-November 7, 1987). ... Granted free agency (February 1, 1991). ... Re-signed by Steelers (August 22, 1991). ... Granted unconditional free agency (February 14, 1997). ... Signed by San Francisco 49ers (July 17, 1997). ... Released by 49ers (February 9, 1998). ... Signed by Baltimore Ravens (February 20, 1998). ... Granted unconditional free agency (March 2, 2001). ... Re-signed by Ravens (May 7, 2001). ... Released by Ravens (March 1, 2002). ... Signed by Oakland Raiders (April 30, 2002).
CHAMPIONSHIP GAME EXPERIENCE: Played in AFC championship game (1994 and 2000 seasons). ... Member of Steelers for AFC championship game (1995 season); inactive. ... Played in Super Bowl XXX (1995 season). ... Played in NFC championship game (1997 season). ... Member of Super Bowl championship team (2000 season).

HONORS: Named defensive back on THE SPORTING NEWS college All-America second team (1985). ... Named kick returner on THE SPORTING NEWS college All-America first team (1986). ... Named kick returner on THE SPORTING NEWS NFL All-Pro team (1989). ... Played in Pro Bowl (1989-1994, 1996, 1999 and 2000 seasons). ... Named cornerback on THE SPORTING NEWS NFL All-Pro team (1990 and 1992-1994).
RECORDS: Holds NFL career record for most touchdowns by interception return—10.
PRO STATISTICS: 1987—Recovered two fumbles. 1988— Recovered three fumbles for two yards. 1989— Recovered four fumbles for one yard. 1990— Recovered three fumbles. 1991— Recovered three fumbles for 15 yards. 1992—Recovered one fumble for nine yards. 1993—Rushed once for no yards and recovered one fumble. 1994—Recovered one fumble. 1996—Recovered three fumbles for 42 yards and a touchdown. 1997—Recovered one fumble. 1999—Recovered two fumbles. 2000—Recovered three fumbles for four yards. 2001—Recovered one fumble.
MISCELLANEOUS: Active AFC leader for career interceptions (54). ... Shares Baltimore Ravens all-time record for most interceptions (20).

				INTERCEPTIONS			SACKS	PUNT RETURNS				KICKOFF RETURNS				TOTALS			
Year Team	G	GS	No.	Yds.	Avg.	TD	No.	No.	Yds.	Avg.	TD	No.	Yds.	Avg.	TD	TD	2pt.	Pts.	Fum.
1987—Pittsburgh NFL	8	0	1	45	45.0	1	0.0	16	135	8.4	0	13	290	22.3	0	1	0	6	3
1988—Pittsburgh NFL	16	16	4	98	24.5	0	0.5	33	281	8.5	0	37	850	23.0	†1	1	0	6	3
1989—Pittsburgh NFL	15	14	3	39	13.0	0	0.0	29	207	7.1	0	§36	§982	*27.3	†1	1	0	6	3
1990—Pittsburgh NFL	16	16	5	67	13.4	0	0.0	§38	§398	10.5	†1	35	764	21.8	0	1	0	6	3
1991—Pittsburgh NFL	15	15	3	72	24.0	0	1.0	28	320	§11.4	0	*44	§880	20.0	0	0	0	0	3
1992—Pittsburgh NFL	16	16	4	90	22.5	0	6.0	32	364	§11.4	1	25	469	18.8	0	1	0	6	2
1993—Pittsburgh NFL	16	16	8	§138	17.3	▲1	2.0	42	338	8.0	0	15	294	19.6	0	1	0	6	2
1994—Pittsburgh NFL	15	15	4	109	27.3	2	3.0	39	319	8.2	0	15	365	24.3	0	2	0	12	2
1995—Pittsburgh NFL	1	1	0	0	0.0	0	0.0	0	0	0.0	0	0	0	0.0	0	0	0	0	0
1996—Pittsburgh NFL	16	16	6	121	20.2	1	1.0	0	0	0.0	0	0	0	0.0	0	2	0	12	1
1997—San Francisco NFL	14	14	3	81	27.0	0	0.0	1	0	0.0	0	0	0	0.0	0	0	0	0	0
1998—Baltimore NFL	16	16	6	108	18.0	▲2	0.0	0	0	0.0	0	0	0	0.0	0	2	0	12	0
1999—Baltimore NFL	16	16	†7	195	27.9	†2	0.0	2	0	0.0	0	0	0	0.0	0	2	0	12	1
2000—Baltimore NFL	16	16	4	20	5.0	0	0.0	0	0	0.0	0	0	0	0.0	0	0	0	0	0
2001—Baltimore NFL	16	16	3	57	19.0	1	0.0	0	0	0.0	0	0	0	0.0	0	1	0	6	0
Pro totals (15 years)	212	203	61	1240	20.3	10	13.5	260	2362	9.1	2	220	4894	22.2	2	15	0	90	23

WOODY, DAMIEN   C   PATRIOTS

PERSONAL: Born November 3, 1977, in Beaverdam, Va. ... 6-3/320. ... Full name: Damien Michael Woody.
HIGH SCHOOL: Patrick Henry (Beaverdam, Va.).
COLLEGE: Boston College.
TRANSACTIONS/CAREER NOTES: Selected after junior season by New England Patriots in first round (17th pick overall) of 1999 NFL draft. ... Signed by Patriots (July 30, 1999).
PLAYING EXPERIENCE: New England NFL, 1999-2001. ... Games/Games started: 1999 (16/16), 2000 (16/16), 2001 (16/15). Total: 48/47.
CHAMPIONSHIP GAME EXPERIENCE: Played in AFC championship game (2001 season). ... Member of Super Bowl championship team (2001 season).
PRO STATISTICS: 1999—Fumbled once and recovered one fumble for minus 10 yards. 2001—Recovered one fumble.

WORTHEN, SHAWN   DT   VIKINGS

PERSONAL: Born September 12, 1978, in San Antonio. ... 6-0/316.
HIGH SCHOOL: Alamo Heights (San Antonio).
COLLEGE: Texas Christian.
TRANSACTIONS/CAREER NOTES: Selected by Minnesota Vikings in fourth round (130th pick overall) of 2001 NFL draft. ... Signed by Vikings (July 30, 2001).
PLAYING EXPERIENCE: Minnesota NFL, 2001. ... Games/Games started: 2001 (4/0).
PRO STATISTICS: 2001—Returned one kickoff for 11 yards.

WRIGHT, ANTHONY   QB   COWBOYS

PERSONAL: Born February 14, 1976, in Vanceboro, N.C. ... 6-1/207. ... Cousin of Jesse Campbell, safety with Philadelphia Eagles (1991 and 1992), New York Giants (1992-97) and Washington Redskins (1997 and 1998).
HIGH SCHOOL: West Craven (N.C.).
COLLEGE: South Carolina.
TRANSACTIONS/CAREER NOTES: Signed as non-drafted free agent by Pittsburgh Steelers (April 18, 1999). ... Active for one game (1999); did not play. ... Released by Steelers (August 27, 2000). ... Signed by Cowboys to practice squad (August 30, 2000). ... Activated (November 21, 2000). ... On injured reserve with knee injury (November 2, 2001-remainder of season).
PRO STATISTICS: 2000—Fumbled three times and recovered one fumble for minus three yards. 2001—Fumbled four times.
SINGLE GAME HIGHS (regular season): Attempts—28 (October 15, 2001, vs. Washington); completions—15 (October 15, 2001, vs. Washington); yards—193 (September 23, 2001, vs. San Diego); and touchdown passes—3 (September 23, 2001, vs. San Diego).
MISCELLANEOUS: Regular-season record as starting NFL quarterback: 1-4 (.200).

			PASSING						RUSHING				TOTALS		
Year Team	G	GS	Att.	Cmp.	Pct.	Yds.	TD	Int.	Avg.	Rat.	Att.	Yds.	Avg.	TD	TD	2pt.	Pts.
1999—Pittsburgh NFL							Did not play.									
2000—Dallas NFL	4	2	53	22	41.5	237	0	3	4.47	31.7	12	36	3.0	0	0	0	0
2001—Dallas NFL	4	3	98	48	49.0	529	5	5	5.40	61.1	17	57	3.4	0	0	0	0
Pro totals (2 years)	8	5	151	70	46.4	766	5	8	5.07	50.8	29	93	3.2	0	0	0	0

WRIGHT, FEARON — LB

PERSONAL: Born September 30, 1978, in Jamaica. ... 6-2/235.
HIGH SCHOOL: Inglewood (Calif.).
COLLEGE: Rhode Island.
TRANSACTIONS/CAREER NOTES: Signed as non-drafted free agent by Minnesota Vikings (May 31, 2001). ... On injured reserve with shoulder injury (November 8, 2001-remainder of season). ... Released by Vikings (February 21, 2002).
PLAYING EXPERIENCE: Minnesota NFL, 2001. ... Games/Games started: (7/0).

WRIGHT, KENNY — CB — VIKINGS

PERSONAL: Born September 14, 1977, in Ruston, La. ... 6-1/205. ... Full name: Kenneth D. Wright.
HIGH SCHOOL: Ruston (La.).
COLLEGE: Arkansas, then Northwestern (La.) State.
TRANSACTIONS/CAREER NOTES: Selected after junior season by Minnesota Vikings in fourth round (120th pick overall) of 1999 NFL draft. ... Signed by Vikings (July 21, 1999). ... Granted free agency (March 1, 2002). ... Re-signed by Vikings (April 16, 2002).
PLAYING EXPERIENCE: Minnesota NFL, 1999-2001. ... Games/Games started: 1999 (16/12), 2000 (16/7), 2001 (15/8). Total: 47/27.
CHAMPIONSHIP GAME EXPERIENCE: Member of Vikings for NFC championship game (2000 season); inactive.
PRO STATISTICS: 1999—Intercepted one pass for 11 yards. 2000—Recovered one fumble for 11 yards.

WRIGHT, KENYATTA — LB

PERSONAL: Born February 19, 1978, in Vian, Okla. ... 6-0/238.
HIGH SCHOOL: Vian (Okla.).
COLLEGE: Oklahoma State.
TRANSACTIONS/CAREER NOTES: Signed as non-drafted free agent by Buffalo Bills (April 23, 2000). ... Granted free agency (March 1, 2002).
PLAYING EXPERIENCE: Buffalo NFL, 2000 and 2001. ... Games/Games started: 2000 (16/0), 2001 (11/1). Total: 27/1.
PRO STATISTICS: 2001—Credited with $1^1/_2$ sacks and recovered one fumble.

WUERFFEL, DANNY — QB — REDSKINS

PERSONAL: Born May 27, 1974, in Pensacola, Fla. ... 6-1/212. ... Full name: Daniel Carl Wuerffel. ... Name pronounced WER-ful.
HIGH SCHOOL: Fort Walton Beach (Fla.).
COLLEGE: Florida.
TRANSACTIONS/CAREER NOTES: Selected by New Orleans Saints in fourth round (99th pick overall) of 1997 NFL draft. ... Signed by Saints (July 17, 1997). ... Released by Saints (February 11, 2000). ... Signed by Green Bay Packers (July 5, 2000). ... Granted unconditional free agency (March 2, 2001). ... Signed by Chicago Bears (July 10, 2001). ... Selected by Houston Texans from Bears in NFL expansion draft (February 18, 2002). ... Traded by Texans to Washington Redskins for DT Jerry DeLoach (March 4, 2002).
HONORS: Davey O'Brien Award winner (1995 and 1996). ... Heisman Trophy winner (1996). ... Named College Player of the Year by THE SPORTING NEWS (1996). ... Named quarterback on THE SPORTING NEWS college All-America first team (1996).
PRO STATISTICS: 1997—Fumbled twice and recovered two fumbles. 1998—Fumbled once and recovered one fumble.
SINGLE GAME HIGHS (regular season): Attempts—47 (October 4, 1998, vs. New England); completions—25 (October 4, 1998, vs. New England); yards—278 (October 4, 1998, vs. New England); and touchdown passes—2 (October 4, 1998, vs. New England).
MISCELLANEOUS: Regular-season record as starting NFL quarterback: 2-4 (.333).

				PASSING						RUSHING				TOTALS		
Year Team	G	GS	Att.	Cmp.	Pct.	Yds.	TD	Int.	Avg.	Rat.	Att.	Yds.	Avg.	TD	TD	2pt.	Pts.
1997—New Orleans NFL	7	2	91	42	46.2	518	4	8	5.69	42.3	6	26	4.3	0	0	0	0
1998—New Orleans NFL	5	4	119	62	52.1	695	5	5	5.84	66.3	11	60	5.5	0	0	0	0
1999—New Orleans NFL	4	0	48	22	45.8	191	0	3	3.98	30.8	2	29	14.5	1	1	0	6
2000—Rhein NFLE	...	...	260	161	61.9	2042	25	7	7.85	107.2	24	80	3.3	2	0	0	0
—Green Bay NFL	1	0	0	0	0.0	0	0	0	0.0	...	2	-2	-1.0	0	0	0	0
2001—Chicago NFL	1	0	0	0	0.0	0	0	0	0.0	...	0	0	0.0	0	0	0	0
NFL Europe totals (1 year)	...	...	260	161	61.9	2042	25	7	7.85	107.2	24	80	3.3	2	0	0	0
NFL totals (5 years)	18	6	258	126	48.8	1404	9	16	5.44	51.2	21	113	5.4	1	1	0	6
Pro totals (6 years)	...	...	518	287	55.4	3446	34	23	6.65	79.4	45	193	4.3	3	1	0	6

WUNSCH, JERRY — OT — BUCCANEERS

PERSONAL: Born January 21, 1974, in Eau Claire, Wis. ... 6-6/339. ... Full name: Gerald Wunsch. ... Name pronounced WUNCH.
HIGH SCHOOL: West (Wausau, Wis.).
COLLEGE: Wisconsin (degree in history).
TRANSACTIONS/CAREER NOTES: Selected by Tampa Bay Buccaneers in second round (37th pick overall) of 1997 NFL draft. ... Signed by Buccaneers (July 18, 1997). ... Granted unconditional free agency (March 2, 2001). ... Re-signed by Buccaneers (April 10, 2001).
PLAYING EXPERIENCE: Tampa Bay NFL, 1997-2001. ... Games/Games started: 1997 (16/0), 1998 (16/1), 1999 (16/13), 2000 (16/16), 2001 (16/16). Total: 80/46.
CHAMPIONSHIP GAME EXPERIENCE: Played in NFC championship game (1999 season).
PRO STATISTICS: 1997—Recovered one fumble.

WYCHECK, FRANK TE TITANS

PERSONAL: Born October 14, 1971, in Philadelphia. ... 6-3/250. ... Name pronounced WHY-check.
HIGH SCHOOL: Archbishop Ryan (Philadelphia).
COLLEGE: Maryland.
TRANSACTIONS/CAREER NOTES: Selected after junior season by Washington Redskins in sixth round (160th pick overall) of 1993 NFL draft. ... Signed by Redskins (July 15, 1993). ... On suspended list for anabolic steroid use (November 29, 1994-remainder of season). ... Released by Redskins (August 17, 1995). ... Signed by Houston Oilers (August 18, 1995). ... Granted free agency (February 16, 1996). ... Re-signed by Oilers (June 28, 1996). ... Oilers franchise moved to Tennessee for 1997 season. ... Oilers franchise renamed Tennessee Titans for 1999 season (December 26, 1998).
CHAMPIONSHIP GAME EXPERIENCE: Played in AFC championship game (1999 season). ... Played in Super Bowl XXXIV (1999 season).
HONORS: Played in Pro Bowl (1998-2000 seasons).
PRO STATISTICS: 1993—Recovered one fumble. 1995—Rushed once for one yard and a touchdown and recovered one fumble. 1996—Rushed twice for three yards. 1997—Recovered one fumble. 1998—Recovered two fumbles. 1999—Completed only pass attempt for 61 yards and a touchdown. 2000—Attempted two passes with two completions for 53 yards and a touchdown. 2001—Rushed once for one yard and completed only pass attempt for 21 yards.
SINGLE GAME HIGHS (regular season): Receptions—10 (December 5, 1999, vs. Baltimore); yards—100 (October 21, 2001, vs. Detroit); and touchdown receptions—2 (October 1, 2000, vs. New York Giants).
STATISTICAL PLATEAUS: 100-yard receiving games: 2001 (1).

				RECEIVING				KICKOFF RETURNS				TOTALS			
Year Team	G	GS	No.	Yds.	Avg.	TD	No.	Yds.	Avg.	TD	TD	2pt.	Pts.	Fum.
1993—Washington NFL	9	7	16	113	7.1	0	0	0	0.0	0	0	0	0	1
1994—Washington NFL	9	1	7	55	7.9	1	4	84	21.0	0	1	0	6	0
1995—Houston NFL	16	11	40	471	11.8	1	0	0	0.0	0	2	0	12	0
1996—Houston NFL	16	16	53	511	9.6	6	2	5	2.5	0	6	0	36	2
1997—Tennessee NFL	16	16	63	748	11.9	4	1	3	3.0	0	4	1	26	0
1998—Tennessee NFL	16	16	70	768	11.0	2	1	10	10.0	0	2	0	12	2
1999—Tennessee NFL	16	16	69	641	9.3	2	0	0	0.0	0	2	0	12	0
2000—Tennessee NFL	16	16	70	636	9.1	4	0	0	0.0	0	4	0	24	2
2001—Tennessee NFL	16	16	60	672	11.2	4	0	0	0.0	0	4	0	24	0
Pro totals (9 years)	130	115	448	4615	10.3	24	8	102	12.8	0	25	1	152	7

WYMS, ELLIS DE BUCCANEERS

PERSONAL: Born April 12, 1979, in Indianola, Miss. ... 6-3/279. ... Full name: Ellis Rashad Wyms.
HIGH SCHOOL: Gentry (Indianola, Miss.).
COLLEGE: Mississippi State.
TRANSACTIONS/CAREER NOTES: Selected by Tampa Bay Buccaneers in sixth round (183rd pick overall) of 2001 NFL draft. ... Signed by Buccaneers (July 16, 2001).
PLAYING EXPERIENCE: Tampa Bay NFL, 2001. ... Games/Games started: 2001 (4/0).

WYNN, MILTON WR BUCCANEERS

PERSONAL: Born September 21, 1978, in Mission Hills, Calif. ... 6-2/207. ... Full name: Milton Thomas Wynn.
HIGH SCHOOL: Antelope Valley (Calif.).
JUNIOR COLLEGE: Bakersfield (Calif.), then Los Angeles Valley.
COLLEGE: Washington State.
TRANSACTIONS/CAREER NOTES: Selected by St. Louis Rams in fourth round (116th pick overall) of 2001 NFL draft. ... Signed by Rams (July 19, 2001). ... Claimed on waivers by Tampa Bay Buccaneers (September 3, 2001).
SINGLE GAME HIGHS (regular season): Receptions—4 (January 6, 2002, vs. Philadelphia); yards—69 (January 6, 2002, vs. Philadelphia); and touchdown receptions—0.

			RECEIVING				TOTALS			
Year Team	G	GS	No.	Yds.	Avg.	TD	TD	2pt.	Pts.	Fum.
2001—Tampa Bay NFL	1	0	4	69	17.3	0	0	0	0	0

WYNN, RENALDO DE REDSKINS

PERSONAL: Born September 3, 1974, in Chicago. ... 6-3/280. ... Full name: Renaldo Levalle Wynn.
HIGH SCHOOL: De La Salle Institute (Chicago).
COLLEGE: Notre Dame (degree in sociology, 1996).
TRANSACTIONS/CAREER NOTES: Selected by Jacksonville Jaguars in first round (21st pick overall) of 1997 NFL draft. ... Signed by Jaguars (July 21, 1997). ... On injured reserve with groin injury (December 25, 1998-remainder of season). ... Granted unconditional free agency (March 1, 2002). ... Signed by Washington Redskins (March 28, 2002).
CHAMPIONSHIP GAME EXPERIENCE: Played in AFC championship game (1999 season).
PRO STATISTICS: 1997—Recovered one fumble. 1998—Recovered one fumble. 1999—Recovered one fumble.

Year Team	G	GS	SACKS
1997—Jacksonville NFL	16	8	2.5
1998—Jacksonville NFL	15	15	1.0
1999—Jacksonville NFL	12	10	1.5
2000—Jacksonville NFL	14	14	3.5
2001—Jacksonville NFL	16	16	5.0
Pro totals (5 years)	73	63	13.5

WYNN, SPERGON — QB — VIKINGS

PERSONAL: Born August 10, 1978, in Houston. ... 6-3/226. ... Full name: Spergon Wynn III.
HIGH SCHOOL: Episcopal (Bellaire, Texas).
COLLEGE: Minnesota, then Southwest Texas State.
TRANSACTIONS/CAREER NOTES: Selected by Cleveland Browns in sixth round (183rd pick overall) of 2000 NFL draft. ... Signed by Browns (July 11, 2000). ... On injured reserve with knee injury (December 8, 2000-remainder of season). ... Assigned by Browns to Amsterdam Admirals in 2001 NFL Europe enhancement allocation program (February 19, 2001). ... Traded by Browns with RB Travis Prentice to Minnesota Vikings for pick in 2002 draft and pick in 2003 draft (September 2, 2001).
PRO STATISTICS: 2000—Fumbled twice. 2001—Fumbled three times for minus two yards.
SINGLE GAME HIGHS (regular season): Attempts—39 (December 23, 2001, vs. Jacksonville); completions—24 (December 23, 2001, vs. Jacksonville); yards—218 (December 23, 2001, vs. Jacksonville); and touchdown passes—1 (December 30, 2001, vs. Green Bay).
MISCELLANEOUS: Regular-season record as starting NFL quarterback: 0-3.

				PASSING							RUSHING				TOTALS	
Year Team	G	GS	Att.	Cmp.	Pct.	Yds.	TD	Int.	Avg.	Rat.	Att.	Yds.	Avg.	TD	TD	2pt.	Pts.
2000—Cleveland NFL	7	1	54	22	40.7	167	0	1	3.09	41.2	3	15	5.0	0	0	0	0
2001—Amsterdam NFLE	...	...	337	193	57.3	2041	14	9	6.06	77.8	31	110	3.5	0	0	0	0
—Minnesota NFL	3	2	98	48	49.0	418	1	6	4.27	38.6	8	61	7.6	0	0	0	0
NFL Europe totals (1 year)	...	...	337	193	57.3	2041	14	9	6.06	77.8	31	110	3.5	0	0	0	0
NFL totals (2 years)	10	3	152	70	46.1	585	1	7	3.85	39.5	11	76	6.9	0	0	0	0
Pro totals (3 years)	...	...	489	263	53.8	2626	15	16	5.37	65.9	42	186	4.4	0	0	0	0

WYRICK, JIMMY — CB — LIONS

PERSONAL: Born December 31, 1976, in DeSoto, Texas. ... 5-9/179.
HIGH SCHOOL: DeSoto (Texas).
COLLEGE: Minnesota.
TRANSACTIONS/CAREER NOTES: Signed as non-drafted free agent by Detroit Lions (April 28, 2000). ... On injured reserve with ankle injury (October 16, 2000-remainder of season).
PLAYING EXPERIENCE: Detroit NFL, 2000 and 2001. ... Games/Games started: 2000 (6/0), 2001 (16/0). Total: 22/0.

YEAST, CRAIG — WR/KR

PERSONAL: Born November 20, 1976, in Danville, Ky. ... 5-8/170. ... Full name: Craig Nelson Yeast.
HIGH SCHOOL: Harrodsburg (Ky.).
COLLEGE: Kentucky.
TRANSACTIONS/CAREER NOTES: Selected by Cincinnati Bengals in fourth round (98th pick overall) of 1999 NFL draft. ... Signed by Bengals (July 28, 1999). ... Released by Bengals (August 27, 2001). ... Signed by New York Jets (October 10, 2001). ... Granted free agency (March 1, 2002).
PRO STATISTICS: 1999—Fumbled twice and recovered one fumble. 2000—Fumbled three times and recovered one fumble. 2001—Fumbled twice and recovered one fumble.
SINGLE GAME HIGHS (regular season): Receptions—4 (November 19, 2000, vs. New England); yards—57 (November 19, 2000, vs. New England); and touchdown receptions—0.

			RUSHING				RECEIVING				PUNT RETURNS				KICKOFF RETURNS				TOTALS		
Year Team	G	GS	Att.	Yds.	Avg.	TD	No.	Yds.	Avg.	TD	No.	Yds.	Avg.	TD	No.	Yds.	Avg.	TD	TD	2pt.	Pts.
1999—Cincinnati NFL	9	0	2	-16	-8.0	0	3	20	6.7	0	10	209	20.9	†2	3	50	16.7	0	2	0	12
2000—Cincinnati NFL	15	7	1	15	15.0	0	24	301	12.5	0	34	225	6.6	0	7	106	15.1	0	0	0	0
2001—N.Y. Jets NFL	11	0	0	0	0.0	0	0	0	0.0	0	13	122	9.4	0	29	663	22.9	0	0	0	0
Pro totals (3 years)	35	7	3	-1	-0.3	0	27	321	11.9	0	57	556	9.8	2	39	819	21.0	0	2	0	12

YODER, TODD — TE — BUCCANEERS

PERSONAL: Born March 18, 1978, in New Palestine, Ind. ... 6-4/250.
HIGH SCHOOL: New Palestine (Ind.).
COLLEGE: Vanderbilt.
TRANSACTIONS/CAREER NOTES: Signed as non-drafted free agent by Tampa Bay Buccaneers (April 17, 2000).
PLAYING EXPERIENCE: Tampa Bay NFL, 2000 and 2001. ... Games/Games started: 2000 (9/0), 2001 (16/1). Total: 25/1.
PRO STATISTICS: 2000—Caught one pass for one yard, returned one punt for no yards and fumbled once. 2001—Caught four passes for 48 yards.
SINGLE GAME HIGHS (regular season): Receptions—2 (January 6, 2002, vs. Philadelphia); yards—24 (December 9, 2001, vs. Detroit); and touchdown receptions—0.

YOUNG, BRIAN — DE — RAMS

PERSONAL: Born July 8, 1977, in Lawton, Okla. ... 6-2/290. ... Full name: James Brian Young.
HIGH SCHOOL: Andress (El Paso, Texas).
COLLEGE: Texas-El Paso.
TRANSACTIONS/CAREER NOTES: Selected by St. Louis Rams in fifth round (139th pick overall) of 2000 NFL draft. ... Signed by Rams (July 7, 2000).
PLAYING EXPERIENCE: St. Louis NFL, 2000 and 2001. ... Games/Games started: 2000 (11/0), 2001 (16/16). Total: 27/16.
CHAMPIONSHIP GAME EXPERIENCE: Played in NFC championship game (2001 season). ... Played in Super Bowl XXXVI (2001 season).
PRO STATISTICS: 2001—Intercepted one pass for 15 yards and credited with $6^{1}/_{2}$ sacks.

YOUNG, BRYANT — DT — 49ERS

PERSONAL: Born January 27, 1972, in Chicago Heights, Ill. ... 6-3/291. ... Full name: Bryant Colby Young.
HIGH SCHOOL: Bloom (Chicago Heights, Ill.).
COLLEGE: Notre Dame.
TRANSACTIONS/CAREER NOTES: Selected by San Francisco 49ers in first round (seventh pick overall) of 1994 NFL draft. ... Signed by 49ers (July 26, 1994). ... On injured reserve with broken leg (December 2, 1998-remainder of season). ... On physically unable to perform list with leg injury (July 30-August 10, 1999).
CHAMPIONSHIP GAME EXPERIENCE: Played in NFC championship game (1994 and 1997 seasons). ... Member of Super Bowl championship team (1994 season).
HONORS: Named defensive tackle on THE SPORTING NEWS NFL All-Pro team (1996 and 1998). ... Played in Pro Bowl (1996 and 1999 season).
PRO STATISTICS: 1994—Recovered one fumble. 1995—Recovered two fumbles. 1996—Credited with two safeties and recovered one fumble for 43 yards. 1998—Recovered one fumble. 1999—Credited with a safety. 2000—Recovered one fumble.

Year Team	G	GS	SACKS
1994—San Francisco NFL	16	16	6.0
1995—San Francisco NFL	12	12	6.0
1996—San Francisco NFL	16	16	11.5
1997—San Francisco NFL	12	12	4.0
1998—San Francisco NFL	12	12	9.5
1999—San Francisco NFL	16	16	11.0
2000—San Francisco NFL	15	15	9.5
2001—San Francisco NFL	16	16	3.5
Pro totals (8 years)	**115**	**115**	**61.0**

YOUNG, RYAN — OT — TEXANS

PERSONAL: Born June 28, 1976, in St. Louis. ... 6-5/320.
HIGH SCHOOL: Parkway Central (Chesterfield, Mo.).
COLLEGE: Kansas State.
TRANSACTIONS/CAREER NOTES: Selected by New York Jets in seventh round (223rd pick overall) of 1999 NFL draft. ... Signed by Jets (June 25, 1999). ... Selected by Houston Texans from Jets in NFL expansion draft (February 18, 2002). ... Granted free agency (March 1, 2002).
PLAYING EXPERIENCE: New York Jets NFL, 1999-2001. ... Games/Games started: 1999 (15/7), 2000 (16/16), 2001 (16/16). Total: 47/39.
PRO STATISTICS: 2001—Recovered one fumble.

ZAHURSKY, STEVE — G

PERSONAL: Born September 2, 1976, in Euclid, Ohio. ... 6-6/305. ... Name pronounced za-HER-ski.
HIGH SCHOOL: Euclid (Ohio).
COLLEGE: Kent.
TRANSACTIONS/CAREER NOTES: Signed as non-drafted free agent by Jacksonville Jaguars (April 23, 1998). ... Released by Jaguars (August 30, 1998). ... Signed by Philadelphia Eagles to practice squad (December 7, 1998). ... Granted free agency following 1998 season. ... Signed by Cleveland Browns (February 11, 1999). ... Claimed on waivers by Jaguars (August 29, 2001). ... Released by Jaguars (October 5, 2001).
PLAYING EXPERIENCE: Cleveland NFL, 1999 and 2000; Jacksonville NFL, 2001. ... Games/Games started: 1999 (9/7), 2000 (16/16), 2001 (1/0). Total: 26/23.
PRO STATISTICS: 2000—Recovered three fumbles.

ZEIGLER, DUSTY — C — GIANTS

PERSONAL: Born September 27, 1973, in Savannah, Ga. ... 6-5/303. ... Full name: Curtis Dustin Zeigler. ... Name pronounced ZIG-ler.
HIGH SCHOOL: Effingham County (Springfield, Ga.).
COLLEGE: Notre Dame.
TRANSACTIONS/CAREER NOTES: Selected by Buffalo Bills in sixth round (202nd pick overall) of 1996 NFL draft. ... Signed by Bills (June 25, 1996). ... Granted free agency (February 12, 1999). ... Re-signed by Bills (April 15, 1999). ... Granted unconditional free agency (February 11, 2000). ... Signed by New York Giants (March 6, 2000).
PLAYING EXPERIENCE: Buffalo NFL, 1996-1999; New York Giants NFL, 2000 and 2001. ... Games/Games started: 1996 (2/0), 1997 (13/13), 1998 (16/16), 1999 (15/15), 2000 (16/16), 2001 (16/16). Total: 78/76.
CHAMPIONSHIP GAME EXPERIENCE: Played in NFC championship game (2000 season). ... Played in Super Bowl XXXV (2000 season).
PRO STATISTICS: 1997—Fumbled once and recovered one fumble for minus 12 yards. 1998—Fumbled three times for minus 19 yards. 2001—Recovered one fumble.

ZELENKA, JOE — TE — JAGUARS

PERSONAL: Born March 9, 1976, in Cleveland. ... 6-3/280. ... Full name: Joseph John Zelenka.
HIGH SCHOOL: Benedictine (Cleveland).
COLLEGE: Wake Forest.
TRANSACTIONS/CAREER NOTES: Signed as non-drafted free agent by San Francisco 49ers (April 23, 1999). ... Traded by 49ers to Washington Redskins for seventh-round pick (TE Eric Johnson) in 2001 draft (April 17, 2000). ... Released by Redskins (March 9, 2001). ... Signed by Jacksonville Jaguars (August 13, 2001).
PLAYING EXPERIENCE: San Francisco NFL, 1999; Washington NFL, 2000; Jacksonville NFL, 2001. ... Games/Games started: 1999 (13/0), 2000 (16/0), 2001 (16/0). Total: 45/0.
PRO STATISTICS: 1999—Fumbled once and recovered one fumble for minus 15 yards. 2001—Fumbled once for minus 26 yards.

ZELLNER, PEPPI — DE — COWBOYS

PERSONAL: Born March 14, 1975, in Forsythe, Ga. ... 6-5/262. ... Full name: Hunndens Guiseppi Zellner.
HIGH SCHOOL: Mary Persons (Forsythe, Ga.).
JUNIOR COLLEGE: Georgia Military College.
COLLEGE: Fort Valley (Ga.) State.
TRANSACTIONS/CAREER NOTES: Selected by Dallas Cowboys in fourth round (132nd pick overall) of 1999 NFL draft. ... Signed by Cowboys (July 27, 1999). ... On injured reserve with knee injury (December 12, 2000-remainder of season). ... On physically unable to perform list with knee injury (July 22-August 14, 2001).
PLAYING EXPERIENCE: Dallas NFL, 1999-2001. ... Games/Games started: 1999 (13/0), 2000 (12/0), 2001 (16/15). Total: 41/15.
PRO STATISTICS: 1999—Credited with one sack. 2000—Credited with two sacks. 2001—Credited with three sacks and recovered one fumble.

ZEREOUE, AMOS — RB — STEELERS

PERSONAL: Born October 8, 1976, in Ivory Coast. ... 5-8/207. ... Name pronounced zer-O-way.
HIGH SCHOOL: W.C. Mepham (Hempstead, N.Y.).
COLLEGE: West Virginia.
TRANSACTIONS/CAREER NOTES: Selected after junior season by Pittsburgh Steelers in third round (95th pick overall) of 1999 NFL draft. ... Signed by Steelers (July 30, 1999). ... Granted free agency (March 1, 2002).
CHAMPIONSHIP GAME EXPERIENCE: Played in AFC championship game (2001 season).
HONORS: Named running back on THE SPORTING NEWS college All-America third team (1997).
PRO STATISTICS: 2001—Recovered one fumble.
SINGLE GAME HIGHS (regular season): Attempts—17 (September 12, 1999, vs. Cleveland); yards—73 (December 16, 2001, vs. Baltimore); and rushing touchdowns—1 (December 2, 2001, vs. Minnesota).

			RUSHING				RECEIVING			KICKOFF RETURNS			TOTALS			
Year Team	G	GS	Att.	Yds.	Avg.	TD	No.	Yds.	Avg.	TD	No.	Yds.	Avg.	TD	TD	2pt.	Pts.	Fum.
1999—Pittsburgh NFL	8	0	18	48	2.7	0	2	17	8.5	0	7	169	24.1	0	0	0	0	0
2000—Pittsburgh NFL	12	0	6	14	2.3	0	0	0	0.0	0	0	0	0.0	0	0	0	0	0
2001—Pittsburgh NFL	14	0	85	441	5.2	1	13	154	11.8	1	0	0	0.0	0	2	0	12	3
Pro totals (3 years)	34	0	109	503	4.6	1	15	171	11.4	1	7	169	24.1	0	2	0	12	3

ZGONINA, JEFF — DT — RAMS

PERSONAL: Born May 24, 1970, in Chicago. ... 6-2/305. ... Full name: Jeffrey Marc Zgonina. ... Name pronounced ska-KNEE-na.
HIGH SCHOOL: Mount Carmel (Chicago).
COLLEGE: Purdue (degree in community health promotion, 1992).
TRANSACTIONS/CAREER NOTES: Selected by Pittsburgh Steelers in seventh round (185th pick overall) of 1993 NFL draft. ... Signed by Steelers (July 16, 1993). ... Claimed on waivers by Carolina Panthers (August 28, 1995). ... Granted free agency (February 16, 1996). ... Re-signed by Panthers (April 11, 1996). ... Released by Panthers (August 19, 1996). ... Signed by Atlanta Falcons (October 8, 1996). ... Granted unconditional free agency (February 14, 1997). ... Signed by St. Louis Rams (March 17, 1997). ... Released by Rams (August 30, 1998). ... Signed by Oakland Raiders (October 13, 1998). ... Released by Raiders (October 18, 1998). ... Signed by Indianapolis Colts (November 25, 1998). ... Granted unconditional free agency (February 12, 1999). ... Signed by Rams (April 5, 1999).
PLAYING EXPERIENCE: Pittsburgh NFL, 1993 and 1994; Carolina NFL, 1995; Atlanta NFL, 1996; St. Louis NFL, 1997, 1999-2001; Indianapolis NFL, 1998. ... Games/Games started: 1993 (5/0), 1994 (16/0), 1995 (2/0), 1996 (8/0), 1997 (15/0), 1998 (2/0), 1999 (16/0), 2000 (16/11), 2001 (13/13). Total: 93/24.
CHAMPIONSHIP GAME EXPERIENCE: Played in AFC championship game (1994 season). ... Played in NFC championship game (1999 and 2001 seasons). ... Member of Super Bowl championship team (1999 season). ... Played in Super Bowl XXXVI (2001 season).
PRO STATISTICS: 1993—Recovered one fumble. 1994—Returned two kickoffs for eight yards, fumbled once and recovered one fumble. 1996—Credited with one sack and recovered one fumble. 1997—Returned one kickoff for five yards and credited with two sacks. 1999—Credited with 4$^1/_2$ sacks. 2000—Credited with two sacks and recovered three fumbles. 2001—Recovered two fumbles.

ZUKAUSKAS, PAUL — G — BROWNS

PERSONAL: Born July 12, 1979, in Weymouth, Mass. ... 6-5/306. ... Full name: Paul Malcolm Zukauskas.
HIGH SCHOOL: Boston College (Ma.).
COLLEGE: Boston College.
TRANSACTIONS/CAREER NOTES: Selected by Cleveland Browns in seventh round (203rd pick overall) of 2001 NFL draft. ... Signed by Browns (July 20, 2001). ... Released by Browns (September 1, 2001). ... Re-signed by Browns to practice squad (September 3, 2001). ... Activated (November 21, 2001).
PLAYING EXPERIENCE: Cleveland NFL, 2001. ... Games/Games started: (1/0).
HONORS: Named guard on THE SPORTING NEWS college All-America second team (2000).

2002 DRAFT PICKS

ALLEN, BRIAN — RB — COLTS

PERSONAL: Born April 20, 1980, in Ontario, Calif. ... 5-9/205.
HIGH SCHOOL: Damien (Calif.).
COLLEGE: Stanford.
TRANSACTIONS/CAREER NOTES: Selected by Indianapolis Colts in sixth round (204th pick overall) of 2002 NFL draft.

		RUSHING				RECEIVING				KICKOFF RETURNS				TOTALS	
Year Team	G	Att.	Yds.	Avg.	TD	No.	Yds.	Avg.	TD	No.	Yds.	Avg.	TD	TD	Pts.
1998—Stanford	11	76	154	2.0	0	5	19	3.8	0	8	136	17.0	0	0	0
1999—Stanford	11	115	604	5.3	4	4	39	9.8	0	1	15	15.0	0	4	24
2000—Stanford	11	174	460	2.6	0	10	105	10.5	0	2	25	12.5	0	0	0
2001—Stanford	11	174	899	5.2	9	4	63	15.8	0	15	399	26.6	0	9	54
College totals (4 years)	44	539	2117	3.9	13	23	226	9.8	0	26	575	22.1	0	13	78

ALLEN, JAMES — LB — SAINTS

PERSONAL: Born November 11, 1979, in Portland, Ore. ... 6-2/240.
HIGH SCHOOL: Thomas Jefferson (Portland, Ore.).
COLLEGE: Oregon State.
TRANSACTIONS/CAREER NOTES: Selected by New Orleans Saints in third round (82nd pick overall) of 2002 NFL draft.

		INTERCEPTIONS				SACKS
Year Team	G	No.	Yds.	Avg.	TD	No.
1997—Oregon State			Redshirted.			
1998—Oregon State	11	1	0	0.0	0	0.0
1999—Oregon State	12	1	0	0.0	0	4.0
2000—Oregon State	9	0	0	0.0	0	1.0
2001—Oregon State	11	0	0	0.0	0	2.0
College totals (4 years)	43	2	0	0.0	0	7.0

ANDERLE, MATT — OT — CHARGERS

PERSONAL: Born July 14, 1979, in St. Paul, Minn. ... 6-6/327.
HIGH SCHOOL: Mounds View (St. Paul, Minn.).
COLLEGE: Minnesota.
TRANSACTIONS/CAREER NOTES: Selected by San Diego Chargers in sixth round (178th pick overall) of 2002 NFL draft.
COLLEGE NOTES: Played defensive tackle, 1997-2000.

Year Team	G	SACKS
1997—Minnesota		Redshirted.
1998—Minnesota	11	1.0
1999—Minnesota	11	2.0
2000—Minnesota	10	1.0
2001—Minnesota	11	0.0
College totals (4 years)	43	4.0

ANDERON, MARQUES — S — PACKERS

PERSONAL: Born May 26, 1979, in Harbor City, Calif. ... 5-11/211. ... Full name: Marques Deon Anderson.
HIGH SCHOOL: Polytechnic (Pasadena, Calif.).
COLLEGE: UCLA.
TRANSACTIONS/CAREER NOTES: Selected by Green Bay Packers in third round (92nd pick overall) of 2002 NFL draft.

		INTERCEPTIONS				SACKS
Year Team	G	No.	Yds.	Avg.	TD	No.
1997—UCLA	11	3	32	10.7	0	0.0
1998—UCLA	12	0	0	0.0	0	0.0
1999—UCLA			Did not play.			
2000—UCLA	12	4	11	2.8	0	3.0
2001—UCLA	11	2	10	5.0	0	1.0
College totals (4 years)	46	9	53	5.9	0	4.0

ANELLI, MARK — TE — 49ERS

PERSONAL: Born June 5, 1979, in Addison, Ill. ... 6-3/265.
HIGH SCHOOL: Addison Trail (Addison, Ill.).
COLLEGE: Wisconsin.
TRANSACTIONS/CAREER NOTES: Selected by San Francisco 49ers in sixth round (201st pick overall) of 2002 NFL draft.

		RECEIVING			
Year Team	G	No.	Yds.	Avg.	TD
1997—Wisconsin			Redshirted.		
1998—Wisconsin	4	0	0	0.0	0
1999—Wisconsin	9	3	46	15.3	0
2000—Wisconsin	9	10	78	7.8	0
2001—Wisconsin	11	35	357	10.2	3
College totals (4 years)	33	48	481	10.0	3

– 431 –

AYODELE, AKIN — LB — JAGUARS

PERSONAL: Born September 17, 1979, in Grand Prairie, Texas. ... 6-2/257. ... Full name: Akinola James Ayodele.
HIGH SCHOOL: MacArthur (Irving, Texas).
COLLEGE: Purdue.
TRANSACTIONS/CAREER NOTES: Selected by Jacksonville Jaguars in third round (89th pick overall) of 2002 NFL draft.
COLLEGE NOTES: Returned two kickoffs for 23 yards (2001).

		INTERCEPTIONS				SACKS
Year Team	G	No.	Yds.	Avg.	TD	No.
1999—Purdue	11	0	0	0.0	0	11.0
2000—Purdue	12	2	3	1.5	0	9.0
2001—Purdue	12	0	0	0.0	0	9.0
College totals (3 years)	35	2	3	1.5	0	29.0

BAKER, CHRIS — TE — JETS

PERSONAL: Born November 18, 1979, in Saline, Mich. ... 6-3/258.
HIGH SCHOOL: Saline (Mich.).
COLLEGE: Michigan State.
TRANSACTIONS/CAREER NOTES: Selected by New York Jets in third round (88th pick overall) of 2002 NFL draft.
COLLEGE NOTES: Returned one kickoff for 10 yards (1998).

		RECEIVING			
Year Team	G	No.	Yds.	Avg.	TD
1998—Michigan State	12	22	305	13.9	3
1999—Michigan State	12	38	391	10.3	4
2000—Michigan State	11	33	461	14.0	2
2001—Michigan State	12	40	548	13.7	4
College totals (4 years)	47	133	1705	12.8	13

BALLARD, CLENTON — DT — JAGUARS

PERSONAL: Born April 17, 1979, in San Antonio. ... 6-3/315. ... Full name: Clenton Earl Ballard III.
HIGH SCHOOL: Taft (San Antonio).
COLLEGE: Southwest Texas State.
TRANSACTIONS/CAREER NOTES: Selected by Jacksonville Jaguars in sixth round (180th pick overall) of 2002 NFL draft.

		INTERCEPTIONS				SACKS
Year Team	G	No.	Yds.	Avg.	TD	No.
1998—Southwest Texas State	10	0	0	0.0	0	1.5
1999—Southwest Texas State	11	2	0	0.0	0	1.0
2000—Southwest Texas State	11	0	0	0.0	0	1.5
2001—Southwest Texas State	9	0	0	0.0	0	6.5
College totals (4 years)	41	2	0	0.0	0	10.5

BANKS, MIKE — TE — CARDINALS

PERSONAL: Born November 5, 1979, in Mason City, Iowa. ... 6-4/260.
HIGH SCHOOL: Ogden (Iowa).
COLLEGE: Iowa State.
TRANSACTIONS/CAREER NOTES: Selected by Arizona Cardinals in seventh round (223rd pick overall) of 2002 NFL draft. ... Signed by Cardinals (May 28, 2002).

		RECEIVING			
Year Team	G	No.	Yds.	Avg.	TD
1998—Iowa State	10	0	0	0.0	0
1999—Iowa State	...	9	99	11.0	0
2000—Iowa State	...	27	273	10.1	0
2001—Iowa State	...	23	212	9.2	0
College totals (4 years)	...	59	584	9.9	0

BANNAN, JUSTIN — DT — BILLS

PERSONAL: Born April 18, 1979, in Sacramento, Calif. ... 6-3/300.
HIGH SCHOOL: Bella Vista (Fair Oaks, Calif.).
COLLEGE: Colorado.
TRANSACTIONS/CAREER NOTES: Selected by Buffalo Bills in fifth round (139th pick overall) of 2002 NFL draft.

Year Team	G	SACKS
1998—Colorado	10	3.0
1999—Colorado	11	0.0
2000—Colorado	11	1.0
2001—Colorado	11	2.0
College totals (4 years)	43	6.0

BAUMAN, RASHAD — CB — REDSKINS

PERSONAL: Born May 7, 1979, in Tempe, Ariz. ... 5-8/186. ... Full name: Leddure Rashad Bauman.
HIGH SCHOOL: South Mountain (Phoenix).
COLLEGE: Oregon.
TRANSACTIONS/CAREER NOTES: Selected by Washington Redskins in third round (79th pick overall) of 2002 NFL draft.

				INTERCEPTIONS			SACKS
Year	Team	G	No.	Yds.	Avg.	TD	No.
1997—Oregon		12	2	61	30.5	1	0.0
1998—Oregon		12	3	115	38.3	1	0.0
1999—Oregon				Did not play.			
2000—Oregon		12	5	78	15.6	0	0.0
2001—Oregon		12	2	39	19.5	0	1.0
College totals (4 years)		48	12	293	24.4	2	1.0

BAXTER, JARROD — FB — TEXANS

PERSONAL: Born March 9, 1979, in Dayton, Ohio. ... 6-1/245. ... Full name: Jarrod Anthony Baxter.
HIGH SCHOOL: Highland (Albuquerque, N.M.).
COLLEGE: New Mexico.
TRANSACTIONS/CAREER NOTES: Selected by Houston Texans in fifth round (136th pick overall) of 2002 NFL draft.

			RUSHING				RECEIVING			TOTALS	
Year Team	G	Att.	Yds.	Avg.	TD	No.	Yds.	Avg.	TD	TD	Pts.
1998—New Mexico	12	38	190	5.0	0	0	0	0.0	0	0	0
1999—New Mexico	11	83	434	5.2	4	7	61	8.7	0	4	24
2000—New Mexico	12	138	559	4.1	4	1	4	4.0	0	4	24
2001—New Mexico	11	203	907	4.5	11	7	49	7.0	0	11	66
College totals (4 years)	46	462	2090	4.5	19	15	114	7.6	0	19	114

BEASLEY, CHAD — DT — VIKINGS

PERSONAL: Born November 13, 1978, in Upper St. Clair, Pa. ... 6-5/303. ... Full name: Thomas Chad Beasley.
HIGH SCHOOL: Gate City (Va.).
COLLEGE: Virginia Tech.
TRANSACTIONS/CAREER NOTES: Selected by Minnesota Vikings in seventh round (218th pick overall) of 2002 NFL draft.

			INTERCEPTIONS			SACKS
Year Team	G	No.	Yds.	Avg.	TD	No.
1998—Virginia Tech	11	1	0	0.0	0	1.0
1999—Virginia Tech	11	0	0	0.0	0	2.0
2000—Virginia Tech	11	1	15	15.0	0	1.0
2001—Virginia Tech	11	0	0	0.0	0	2.0
College totals (4 years)	44	2	15	7.5	0	6.0

BECKHAM, TONY — CB — TITANS

PERSONAL: Born October 1, 1978, in Ocala, Fla. ... 6-1/195.
HIGH SCHOOL: Forest (Ocala, Fla.).
COLLEGE: Wisconsin-Stout.
TRANSACTIONS/CAREER NOTES: Selected by Tennesse Titans in fourth round (115th pick overall) of 2002 NFL draft.
COLLEGE NOTES: Caught seven passes for 183 yards and three touchdowns (2001).

			INTERCEPTIONS			KICKOFF RETURNS			TOTALS	
Year Team	G	No.	Yds.	Avg.	TD	No.	Yds.	Avg.	TD	TD	Pts.
1997—Wisconsin-Stout					Redshirted.						
1998—Wisconsin-Stout	12	0	0	0.0	0	0	0	0.0	0	0	0
1999—Wisconsin-Stout	10	3	0	0.0	0	4	63	15.8	0	0	0
2000—Wisconsin-Stout	10	1	24	24.0	1	17	383	22.5	1	2	12
2001—Wisconsin-Stout	9	1	35	35.0	0	16	386	24.1	1	1	6
College totals (4 years)	41	5	59	11.8	1	37	832	22.5	2	3	18

BELLISARI, STEVE — S — RAMS

PERSONAL: Born April 21, 1980, in Boca Raton, Fla. ... 6-3/220.
HIGH SCHOOL: Boca Raton (Fla.).
COLLEGE: Ohio State.
TRANSACTIONS/CAREER NOTES: Selected by St. Louis Rams in sixth round (205th pick overall) of 2002 NFL draft.
COLLEGE NOTES: Intercepted one pass with 19 yard return (1998).

		PASSING								RUSHING			TOTALS	
Year Team	G	Att.	Cmp.	Pct.	Yds.	TD	Int.	Avg.	Rat.	Att.	Yds.	Avg.	TD	TD	Pts.
1998—Ohio State	...	...	...	...	0	0	0	0.0	...	0	0	0.0	0	0	0
1999—Ohio State	...	...	...	...	1616	12	...	...	...	...	332	...	0	0	0
2000—Ohio State	...	...	...	...	2319	...	...	...	...	...	179	...	0	0	0
2001—Ohio State	10	220	119	54.1	1919	10	7	8.72	136.0	83	280	3.4	3	3	18
College totals (4 years)	10	220	119	54.1	5854	22	7	26.61	304.2	83	791	9.5	3	3	18

BENTLEY, KEVIN — LB — BROWNS

PERSONAL: Born December 29, 1979, in Northridge, Calif. ... 6-0/243. ... Full name: Kevin Kinte Bentley.
HIGH SCHOOL: Montclair (Calif.).
COLLEGE: Northwestern.
TRANSACTIONS/CAREER NOTES: Selected by Cleveland Browns in fourth round (101st pick overall) of 2002 NFL draft.

Year Team	G	INTERCEPTIONS No.	Yds.	Avg.	TD	SACKS No.
1998—Northwestern	11	0	0	0.0	0	0.0
1999—Northwestern	11	2	40	20.0	1	2.0
2000—Northwestern	12	1	19	19.0	0	3.0
2001—Northwestern	11	0	0	0.0	0	1.0
College totals (4 years)	45	3	59	19.7	1	6.0

BENTLEY, LECHARLES — C — SAINTS

PERSONAL: Born November 7, 1979, in Cleveland. ... 6-3/299.
HIGH SCHOOL: St. Ignatius (Cleveland).
COLLEGE: Ohio State.
TRANSACTIONS/CAREER NOTES: Selected by New Orleans Saints in second round (44th pick overall) of 2002 NFL draft.
HONORS: Named center on THE SPORTING NEWS college All-America first team (2001).
COLLEGE PLAYING EXPERIENCE: Ohio State, 1998-2001. ... Games played: 1998 (12), 1999 (12), 2000 (12), 2001 (12). Total: 48.

BERNARD, ROCKY — DT — SEAHAWKS

PERSONAL: Born April 19, 1979, in Baytown, Texas. ... 6-3/294. ... Full name: Robert Bernard.
HIGH SCHOOL: Sterling (Baytown, Texas).
COLLEGE: Texas A&M.
TRANSACTIONS/CAREER NOTES: Selected by Seattle Seahawks in fifth round (146th pick overall) of 2002 NFL draft.

Year Team	G	SACKS
1997—Texas A&M	11	2.0
1998—Texas A&M	13	1.0
1999—Texas A&M	10	4.0
2000—Texas A&M	Redshirted.	
2001—Texas A&M	11	5.0
College totals (4 years)	45	12.0

BETTS, LADELL — RB — REDSKINS

PERSONAL: Born August 27, 1979, in Blue Springs, Mo. ... 5-10/220. ... Full name: Matthew Betts.
HIGH SCHOOL: Blue Springs (Mo.).
COLLEGE: Iowa.
TRANSACTIONS/CAREER NOTES: Selected by Washington Redskins in second round (56th pick overall) of 2002 NFL draft.
COLLEGE NOTES: Attemped one pass with one completion for 23 yards (1998). ... Returned one kickoff for nine yards (2001).

		RUSHING				RECEIVING				TOTALS	
Year Team	G	Att.	Yds.	Avg.	TD	No.	Yds.	Avg.	TD	TD	Pts.
1998—Iowa	11	188	679	3.6	5	20	259	12.9	0	5	30
1999—Iowa	11	189	857	4.5	5	20	195	9.8	1	6	36
2000—Iowa	12	232	1090	4.7	5	17	111	6.5	0	5	30
2001—Iowa	12	222	1060	4.8	10	15	137	9.1	1	11	66
College totals (4 years)	46	831	3686	4.4	25	72	702	9.8	2	27	162

BIBLA, MARTIN — G — FALCONS

PERSONAL: Born October 4, 1979, in Mountaintop, Pa. ... 6-3/306. ... Full name: Martin John Bibla.
HIGH SCHOOL: Crestwood (Mountaintop, Pa.).
COLLEGE: Miami (Fla.).
TRANSACTIONS/CAREER NOTES: Selected by Atlanta Falcons in fourth round (116th pick overall) of 2002 NFL draft.
COLLEGE PLAYING EXPERIENCE: Miami (Fla.), 1997-2001. ... Games played: 1997 (redshirted), 1998 (11), 1999 (12), 2000 (11), 2001 (11). Total: 45.

BIERRIA, TERREAL — S — SEAHAWKS

PERSONAL: Born October 10, 1980, in Slidell, La. ... 6-3/216.
HIGH SCHOOL: Salmen (Slidell, La.).
COLLEGE: Georgia.
TRANSACTIONS/CAREER NOTES: Selected after junior season by Seattle Seahawks in fourth round (120th pick overall) of 2002 NFL draft.

Year Team	G	INTERCEPTIONS No.	Yds.	Avg.	TD
1999—Georgia	11	1	4	4.0	0
2000—Georgia	11	3	96	32.0	1
2001—Georgia	11	0	0	0.0	0
College totals (3 years)	33	4	100	25.0	1

BOIMAN, ROCKY — LB — TITANS

PERSONAL: Born January 24, 1980, in Cincinnati. ... 6-4/242. ... Full name: Rocky Michael Boiman.
HIGH SCHOOL: St. Xavier (Cincinnati).
COLLEGE: Notre Dame.
TRANSACTIONS/CAREER NOTES: Selected by Tennessee Titans in fourth round (133rd pick overall) of 2002 NFL draft.

Year Team	G	SACKS
1998—Notre Dame	9	0.0
1999—Notre Dame	12	2.0
2000—Notre Dame	11	3.5
2001—Notre Dame	11	3.0
College totals (4 years)	43	8.5

BRANCH, ANTHONY — WR — PATRIOTS

PERSONAL: Born July 18, 1979, in Albany, Ga. ... 5-9/191.
HIGH SCHOOL: Monroe (Ga.).
JUNIOR COLLEGE: Jones County Junior College (Miss.).
COLLEGE: Louisville.
TRANSACTIONS/CAREER NOTES: Selected by New England Patriots in second round (65th pick overall) of 2002 NFL draft.
HONORS: Named wide receiver on The Sporting News college All-America third team (2001).

		RECEIVING				PUNT RETURNS				KICKOFF RETURNS				TOTALS	
Year Team	G	No.	Yds.	Avg.	TD	No.	Yds.	Avg.	TD	No.	Yds.	Avg.	TD	TD	Pts.
1997—Jones County Junior College	...	37	639	17.3	5	0	0	0.0	0	14	331	23.6	0	5	30
1998—Jones County Junior College	...	69	1012	14.7	9	15	192	12.8	0	17	333	19.6	0	9	54
1999—Louisville								Redshirted.							
2000—Louisville	10	71	1016	14.3	9	0	0	0.0	0	0	0	0.0	0	9	54
2001—Louisville	10	72	1188	16.5	9	0	0	0.0	0	0	0	0.0	0	9	54
Junior college totals (2 years)	...	106	1651	15.6	14	15	192	12.8	0	31	664	21.4	0	14	84
College totals (2 years)	20	143	2204	15.4	18	0	0	0.0	0	0	0	0.0	0	18	108

BRANDON, SAM — S — BRONCOS

PERSONAL: Born July 5, 1979, in Toledo, Ohio. ... 6-2/200.
HIGH SCHOOL: Riverside (Calif.).
COLLEGE: UNLV.
TRANSACTIONS/CAREER NOTES: Selected by Denver Broncos in fourth round (131st pick overall) of 2002 NFL draft.
COLLEGE NOTES: Played wide receiver (1998). ... Caught 12 passes for 122 yards and one touchdown (1998).

		INTERCEPTIONS			
Year Team	G	No.	Yds.	Avg.	TD
1998—Arizona State	9	0	0	0.0	0
1999—Arizona State			Did not play.		
2000—Arizona State	12	1	22	22.0	0
2001—Arizona State	11	2	90	45.0	1
College totals (3 years)	32	3	112	37.3	1

BRIGHTFUL, LAMONT — DB — RAVENS

PERSONAL: Born January 29, 1979, in Oak Harbor, Wash. ... 5-10/170. ... Full name: Lamont Eugene Brightful.
HIGH SCHOOL: Mariner (Everett, Wash.).
COLLEGE: Eastern Washington.
TRANSACTIONS/CAREER NOTES: Selected by Baltimore Ravens in sixth round (195th pick overall) of 2002 NFL draft.

		RUSHING				RECEIVING				PUNT RETURNS				KICKOFF RETURNS				TOTALS	
Year Team	G	Att.	Yds.	Avg.	TD	No.	Yds.	Avg.	TD	No.	Yds.	Avg.	TD	No.	Yds.	Avg.	TD	TD	Pts.
1997—Eastern Washington							Did not play.												
1998—Eastern Washington	11	1	12	12.0	0	24	384	16.0	4	0	0	0.0	0	0	0	0.0	0	0	0
1999—Eastern Washington	11	0	0	0.0	0	24	460	19.2	3	0	0	0.0	0	26	882	33.9	2	5	30
2000—Eastern Washington	11	7	128	18.3	2	32	413	12.9	2	15	166	11.1	0	15	483	32.2	2	6	30
2001—Eastern Washington	11	3	59	19.7	1	42	804	19.1	11	0	0	0.0	0	24	584	24.3	1	13	78
College totals (4 years)	44	11	199	18.1	3	122	2061	16.9	20	15	166	11.1	0	65	1949	30.0	5	24	138

BROCK, RAHEEM — DE — EAGLES

PERSONAL: Born June 10, 1978, in Philadelphia. ... 6-4/257.
HIGH SCHOOL: Dobbins (Germantown, Md.).
COLLEGE: Temple.
TRANSACTIONS/CAREER NOTES: Selected by Philadelphia Eagles in seventh round (238th pick overall) of 2002 NFL draft.

		INTERCEPTIONS				SACKS
Year Team	G	No.	Yds.	Avg.	TD	No.
1998—Temple	5	0	0	0.0	0	2.0
1999—Temple	10	0	0	0.0	0	1.0
2000—Temple	11	0	0	0.0	0	4.0
2001—Temple	11	1	59	59.0	1	4.0
College totals (4 years)	37	1	59	59.0	1	11.0

BROWN, ALEX — DE — BEARS

PERSONAL: Born June 4, 1979, in Jasper, Fla. ... 6-3/260. ... Full name: Alex James Brown.
HIGH SCHOOL: Hamilton County (White Springs, Fla.).
COLLEGE: Florida.
TRANSACTIONS/CAREER NOTES: Selected by Chicago Bears in fourth round (104th pick overall) of 2002 NFL draft.
HONORS: Named defensive end on The Sporting News college All-America first team (1999). ... Named defensive end on The Sporting News college All-America second team (2001).

Year Team	G	INTERCEPTIONS No. Yds. Avg. TD	SACKS No.
1998—Florida	11	0 0 0.0 0	2.0
1999—Florida	12	2 2 1.0 0	13.0
2000—Florida	12	1 22 22.0 0	7.5
2001—Florida	11	0 0 0.0 0	10.5
College totals (4 years)	46	3 24 8.0 0	33.0

BROWN, SHELDON CB EAGLES

PERSONAL: Born March 19, 1979, in Fort Lawn, S.C. ... 5-10/196.
HIGH SCHOOL: Lewisville (Richburg, S.C.).
COLLEGE: South Carolina.
TRANSACTIONS/CAREER NOTES: Selected by Philadelphia Eagles in second round (59th pick overall) of 2002 NFL draft.

Year Team	G	INTERCEPTIONS No. Yds. Avg. TD	SACKS No.
1998—South Carolina	11	1 30 30.0 0	0.0
1999—South Carolina	11	2 59 29.5 0	0.0
2000—South Carolina	11	4 71 17.8 0	0.0
2001—South Carolina	12	3 46 15.3 0	1.5
College totals (4 years)	45	10 206 20.6 0	1.5

BRYANT, ANTONIO WR COWBOYS

PERSONAL: Born March 9, 1981, in Miami. ... 6-1/188.
HIGH SCHOOL: Miami Northwestern.
COLLEGE: Pittsburgh.
TRANSACTIONS/CAREER NOTES: Selected after junior season by Dallas Cowboys in second round (63rd pick overall) of 2002 NFL draft.
HONORS: Named wide receiver on THE SPORTING NEWS college All-America second team (2000).

Year Team	G	RECEIVING No. Yds. Avg. TD	PUNT RETURNS No. Yds. Avg. TD	TOTALS TD Pts.
1999—Pittsburgh	11	51 844 16.5 6	0 0 0.0 0	6 36
2000—Pittsburgh	10	68 1302 19.1 11	16 181 11.3 0	11 66
2001—Pittsburgh	10	42 659 15.7 9	28 207 7.4 0	9 54
College totals (3 years)	31	161 2805 17.4 26	44 388 8.8 0	26 156

BRYANT, WENDELL DT CARDINALS

PERSONAL: Born September 12, 1980, in St. Louis. ... 6-4/308.
HIGH SCHOOL: Ritenour (St. Louis).
COLLEGE: Wisconsin.
TRANSACTIONS/CAREER NOTES: Selected by Arizona Cardinals in first round (12th pick overall) of 2002 NFL draft.
HONORS: Named defensive tackle on THE SPORTING NEWS college All-America second team (2001).

Year Team	G	SACKS
1998—Wisconsin	12	3.0
1999—Wisconsin	12	7.0
2000—Wisconsin	12	6.0
2001—Wisconsin	12	8.0
College totals (4 years)	48	24.0

BUCHANON, PHILLIP CB RAIDERS

PERSONAL: Born September 19, 1980, in Lehigh, Fla. ... 5-10/186. ... Full name: Phillip Darren Buchanon.
HIGH SCHOOL: Lehigh (Fla.).
COLLEGE: Miami (Fla.).
TRANSACTIONS/CAREER NOTES: Selected after junior season by Oakland Raiders in first round (17th pick overall) of 2002 NFL draft.

Year Team	G	INTERCEPTIONS No. Yds. Avg. TD	SACKS No.	PUNT RETURNS No. Yds. Avg. TD	KICKOFF RETURNS No. Yds. Avg. TD	TOTALS TD Pts.
1999—Miami (Fla.)	10	0 0 0.0 0	0.0	0 0 0.0 0	0 0 0.0 0	0 0
2000—Miami (Fla.)	11	2 78 39.0 1	0.0	1 13 13.0 0	0 0 0.0 0	2 12
2001—Miami (Fla.)	11	5 157 31.4 1	0.0	31 464 15.0 2	4 150 37.5 0	3 18
College totals (3 years)	32	7 235 33.6 2	0.0	32 477 14.9 2	4 150 37.5 0	5 30

BULLARD, COURTLAND LB RAMS

PERSONAL: Born August 2, 1978, in Miami. ... 6-3/234.
HIGH SCHOOL: Southridge (Miami).
COLLEGE: Ohio State.
TRANSACTIONS/CAREER NOTES: Selected by St. Louis Rams in fifth round (167th pick overall) of 2002 NFL draft.

Year Team	G	INTERCEPTIONS No. Yds. Avg. TD	SACKS No.
1997—Ohio State	13	0 0 0.0 0	0.0
1998—Ohio State	2	0 0 0.0 0	0.0
1999—Ohio State	11	0 0 0.0 0	3.0
2000—Ohio State	12	1 0 0.0 0	6.0
2001—Ohio State	12	0 0 0.0 0	2.0
College totals (5 years)	50	1 0 0.0 0	11.0

BURFORD, SETH — QB — CHARGERS

PERSONAL: Born March 11, 1979, in Oakdale, Calif. ... 6-3/241.
HIGH SCHOOL: Oakdale (Calif.).
COLLEGE: Idaho State, then Cal Poly-San Luis Obispo.
TRANSACTIONS/CAREER NOTES: Selected by San Diego Chargers in seventh round (216th pick overall) of 2002 NFL draft.

		PASSING								RUSHING			TOTALS	
Year Team	G	Att.	Cmp.	Pct.	Yds.	TD	Int.	Avg.	Rat.	Att.	Yds.	Avg.	TD	TD Pts.
1997—Idaho State	6	120	56	46.7	690	2	0	5.75	100.5	0	0	0.0	0	2 12
1998—Idaho State	11	139	75	54.0	951	7	3	6.84	123.7	62	124	2.0	2	2 12
1999—Cal Poly-San Luis Obispo						Did not play.								
2000—Cal Poly-San Luis Obispo	11	306	175	57.2	2672	23	7	8.73	150.8	109	252	2.3	6	6 42
2001—Cal Poly-San Luis Obispo	9	211	112	53.1	1610	13	5	7.63	132.8	125	328	2.6	8	8 48
College totals (4 years)	37	776	418	53.9	5923	45	15	7.63	133.3	296	704	2.4	16	18 114

CALDWELL, RECHE — WR — CHARGERS

PERSONAL: Born March 28, 1979, in Tampa, Fla. ... 5-11/194. ... Full name: Donald Reche Caldwell Jr.
HIGH SCHOOL: Jefferson (Tampa, Fla.).
COLLEGE: Florida.
TRANSACTIONS/CAREER NOTES: Selected after junior season by San Diego Chargers in second round (48th pick overall) of 2002 NFL draft.

		RUSHING				RECEIVING				PUNT RETURNS				KICKOFF RETURNS				TOTALS
Year Team	G	Att.	Yds.	Avg.	TD	No.	Yds.	Avg.	TD	No.	Yds.	Avg.	TD	No.	Yds.	Avg.	TD	TD Pts.
1999—Florida	12	4	19	4.8	0	27	269	10.0	2	5	49	9.8	0	3	52	17.3	0	2 12
2000—Florida	12	4	25	6.3	0	49	760	15.5	6	0	0	0.0	0	0	0	0.0	0	6 36
2001—Florida	11	5	47	9.4	0	65	1059	16.3	10	0	0	0.0	0	1	12	12.0	0	10 60
College totals (3 years)	35	13	91	7.0	0	141	2088	14.8	18	5	49	9.8	0	4	64	16.0	0	18 108

CALMUS, ROCKY — LB — TITANS

PERSONAL: Born August 1, 1979, in Tulsa, Okla. ... 6-3/243.
HIGH SCHOOL: Jenks (Okla.).
COLLEGE: Oklahoma.
TRANSACTIONS/CAREER NOTES: Selected by Tennessee Titans in third round (77th pick overall) of 2002 NFL draft.
HONORS: Named linebacker on THE SPORTING NEWS college All-America first team (2001). ... Butkus Award winner (2001).

		INTERCEPTIONS				SACKS
Year Team	G	No.	Yds.	Avg.	TD	No.
1998—Oklahoma	11	0	0	0.0	0	1.0
1999—Oklahoma	11	1	0	0.0	0	4.0
2000—Oklahoma	12	1	41	41.0	1	4.0
2001—Oklahoma	12	1	33	33.0	0	4.0
College totals (4 years)	46	3	74	24.7	1	13.0

CAMPION, PETE — G — PANTHERS

PERSONAL: Born December 3, 1979, in Fergus Falls, Minn. ... 6-4/307.
HIGH SCHOOL: Fergus Falls (Minn.).
COLLEGE: North Dakota State.
TRANSACTIONS/CAREER NOTES: Selected by Carolina Panthers in seventh round (213th pick overall) of 2002 NFL draft.
COLLEGE PLAYING EXPERIENCE: North Dakota State, 1998-2001. ... Games played: 1998 (11), 1999 (11), 2000 (11), 2001 (11). Total: 44.

CARR, DAVID — QB — TEXANS

PERSONAL: Born July 21, 1979, in Bakersfield, Calif. ... 6-3/223.
HIGH SCHOOL: Stockdale (Bakersfield, Calf.).
COLLEGE: Fresno State.
TRANSACTIONS/CAREER NOTES: Selected by Houston Texans in first round (first pick overall) of 2002 NFL draft.

		PASSING								RUSHING			TOTALS	
Year Team	G	Att.	Cmp.	Pct.	Yds.	TD	Int.	Avg.	Rat.	Att.	Yds.	Avg.	TD	TD Pts.
1997—Fresno State	4	11	5	45.5	53	0	1	4.82	67.7	5	-21	-4.2	0	0 0
1998—Fresno State	7	41	22	53.7	228	1	5	5.56	103.7	24	-31	-1.3	0	0 0
1999—Fresno State						Redshirted.								
2000—Fresno State	12	349	216	61.9	2729	23	12	7.82	142.4	74	83	1.1	4	4 24
2001—Fresno State	14	533	344	64.5	4839	46	9	9.08	165.9	94	67	0.7	5	5 30
College totals (4 years)	37	934	587	62.8	7849	70	23	8.40	153.2	197	98	0.5	9	9 54

CARTER, TIM — WR — GIANTS

PERSONAL: Born September 21, 1979, in Atlanta. ... 5-11/190. ... Full name: Timothy M. Carter.
HIGH SCHOOL: Lakewood (St. Petersburg, Fla.).
COLLEGE: Auburn.
TRANSACTIONS/CAREER NOTES: Selected by New York Giants in second round (46th pick overall) of 2002 NFL draft.

Year Team	G	RUSHING Att.	Yds.	Avg.	TD	RECEIVING No.	Yds.	Avg.	TD	PUNT RETURNS No.	Yds.	Avg.	TD	KICKOFF RETURNS No.	Yds.	Avg.	TD	TOTALS TD	Pts.
1998—Auburn	5	0	0	0.0	0	0	0	0.0	0	0	0	0.0	0	0	0	0.0	0	0	0
1999—Auburn	7	2	29	14.5	0	1	1	1.0	0	0	0	0.0	0	8	184	23.0	0	0	0
2000—Auburn	11	15	116	7.7	0	21	271	12.9	1	0	0	0.0	0	19	461	24.3	1	2	12
2001—Auburn	11	7	28	4.0	0	35	570	16.3	3	1	18	18.0	0	13	311	23.9	0	3	18
College totals (4 years)	34	24	173	7.2	0	57	842	14.8	4	1	18	18.0	0	40	956	23.9	1	5	30

CARTWRIGHT, ROCK — FB — REDSKINS

PERSONAL: Born December 3, 1979, in Conroe, Texas. ... 5-7/237.
HIGH SCHOOL: Conroe (Texas).
JUNIOR COLLEGE: Trinity Valley Community College (Texas).
COLLEGE: Kansas State.
TRANSACTIONS/CAREER NOTES: Selected by Washington Redskins in seventh round (257th pick overall) of 2002 NFL draft..

Year Team	G	RUSHING Att.	Yds.	Avg.	TD	RECEIVING No.	Yds.	Avg.	TD	TOTALS TD	Pts.
1998—Trinity Valley						Statistics unavailable.					
1999—Trinity Valley						Statistics unavailable.					
2000—Kansas State	12	46	278	6.0	5	5	78	15.6	0	5	30
2001—Kansas State	11	66	292	4.4	2	15	108	7.2	0	2	12
College totals (2 years)	23	112	570	5.1	7	20	186	9.3	0	7	42

CASH, CHRIS — CB — LIONS

PERSONAL: Born July 13, 1980, in Stockton, Calif. ... 5-11/170.
HIGH SCHOOL: Franklin (Stockton, Calif.).
JUNIOR COLLEGE: Palomar College (Calif.).
COLLEGE: Southern California.
TRANSACTIONS/CAREER NOTES: Selected by Detroit Lions in sixth round (175th pick overall) of 2002 NFL draft.

Year Team	G	INTERCEPTIONS No.	Yds.	Avg.	TD
1998—Palomar College		Statistics unavailable.			
1999—Palomar College		Statistics unavailable.			
2000—Southern California	11	2	0	0.0	1
2001—Southern California	9	2	0	0.0	0
College totals (2 years)	20	4	0	0.0	1

CHANDLER, JEFF — K — 49ERS

PERSONAL: Born June 18, 1979, in Jacksonville, Fla. ... 6-2/218. ... Full name: Jeffrey Robin Chandler.
HIGH SCHOOL: Mandarin (Jacksonville, Fla.).
COLLEGE: Florida.
TRANSACTIONS/CAREER NOTES: Selected by San Francisco 49ers in fourth round (102nd pick overall) of 2002 NFL draft.

Year Team	G	KICKING XPM	XPA	FGM	FGA	Lg.	50+	Pts.
1997—Florida	1	1	1	0	0	0	0-0	1
1998—Florida	11	33	37	11	15	46	0-0	66
1999—Florida	12	38	41	21	24	50	0-0	101
2000—Florida	12	49	53	16	19	54	0-0	97
2001—Florida	12	46	48	19	22	52	0-0	103
College totals (5 years)	48	167	180	67	80	54	0-0	368

CHARLES, TERRY — WR — CHARGERS

PERSONAL: Born July 8, 1979, in Long Beach, Calif. ... 6-3/207.
HIGH SCHOOL: Wilson (Long Beach, Calif.).
COLLEGE: Portland State.
TRANSACTIONS/CAREER NOTES: Selected by San Diego Chargers in fifth round (142nd pick overall) of 2002 NFL draft.

Year Team	G	RECEIVING No.	Yds.	Avg.	TD
1997—Portland State		Redshirted.			
1998—Portland State	6	5	96	19.2	0
1999—Portland State	11	62	1171	18.9	10
2000—Portland State	11	42	792	18.9	5
2001—Portland State	11	71	1096	15.4	12
College totals (4 years)	39	180	3155	17.5	27

COLEMAN, KENYON — DE — RAIDERS

PERSONAL: Born April 10, 1979, in Fontana, Calif. ... 6-4/284. ... Full name: Kenyon Octavia Coleman.
HIGH SCHOOL: Alta Loma (Calif.).
COLLEGE: UCLA.
TRANSACTIONS/CAREER NOTES: Selected by Oakland Raiders in fifth round (147th pick overall) of 2002 NFL draft.
HONORS: Named defensive end on THE SPORTING NEWS college All-America third team (2001).

Year Team	G	SACKS
1997—UCLA	12	0.0
1998—UCLA	10	4.5
1999—UCLA	11	3.5
2000—UCLA	3	0.0
2001—UCLA	11	8.5
College totals (5 years)	47	16.5

COLEMAN, MICHAEL — WR — FALCONS

PERSONAL: Born July 9, 1980, in Wilmington, Del. ... 5-11/190.
HIGH SCHOOL: Delcastle (Wilmington, Del.).
COLLEGE: Widener.
TRANSACTIONS/CAREER NOTES: Selected by Atlanta Falcons in seventh round (217th pick overall) of 2002 NFL draft.
COLLEGE NOTES: Intercepted two passes (2001).

			RUSHING				RECEIVING				KICKOFF RETURNS				TOTALS	
Year Team	G	Att.	Yds.	Avg.	TD	No.	Yds.	Avg.	TD	No.	Yds.	Avg.	TD	TD	Pts.
1998—Widener	3	0	0	0.0	0	7	145	20.7	0	0	0	0.0	0	0	0
1999—Widener	...	0	0	0.0	0	31	634	20.5	11	0	0	0.0	0	11	66
2000—Widener	...	0	0	0.0	0	66	1834	27.8	26	24	438	18.3	0	26	156
2001—Widener	...	4	32	8.0	0	74	1681	22.7	19	11	227	20.6	0	0	0
College totals (4 years)	...	4	32	8.0	0	178	4294	24.1	56	35	665	19.0	0	37	222

COLEMAN, REGGIE — OT — REDSKINS

PERSONAL: Born October 4, 1978, in Jonesboro, Ark. ... 6-5/315. ... Full name: Reginald Fernando Coleman.
HIGH SCHOOL: Jonesboro (Ark.).
COLLEGE: Tennessee.
TRANSACTIONS/CAREER NOTES: Selected by Washington Redskins in sixth round (192nd pick overall) of 2002 NFL draft.
COLLEGE PLAYING EXPERIENCE: Tennessee, 1999-2001. ... Games played: 1999 (10), 2000 (11), 2001 (10). Total: 31.

COLOMBO, MARC — OT — BEARS

PERSONAL: Born October 8, 1978, in Bridgewater, Mass. ... 6-7/313. ... Full name: Marc Edward Colombo.
HIGH SCHOOL: Bridgewater-Raynham (Bridgewater, Mass.).
COLLEGE: Boston College.
TRANSACTIONS/CAREER NOTES: Selected by Chicago Bears in first round (29th pick overall) of 2002 NFL draft.
COLLEGE PLAYING EXPERIENCE: Boston College, 1998-2001. ... Games played: 1998 (6); 1999 (7); 2000 (11); 2001 (8). Total: 32.

CRAVER, KEYUO — CB — SAINTS

PERSONAL: Born August 22, 1980, in Harleton, Texas. ... 5-10/195.
HIGH SCHOOL: Harleton (Texas).
COLLEGE: Nebraska.
TRANSACTIONS/CAREER NOTES: Selected by New Orleans Saints in fourth round (125th pick overall) of 2002 NFL draft.
HONORS: Named cornerback on THE SPORTING NEWS college All-America first team (2001).

			INTERCEPTIONS			SACKS		PUNT RETURNS			TOTALS	
Year Team	G	No.	Yds.	Avg.	TD	No.	No.	Yds.	Avg.	TD	TD	Pts.
1998—Nebraska	12	1	0	0.0	0	0.0	0	0	0.0	0	0	0
1999—Nebraska	12	3	18	6.0	0	0.0	10	106	10.6	0	0	0
2000—Nebraska	11	0	0	0.0	0	2.5	2	31	15.5	2	2	12
2001—Nebraska	12	3	97	32.3	1	0.0	21	246	11.7	0	0	0
College totals (4 years)	47	7	115	16.4	1	2.5	33	383	11.6	2	2	12

CROUCH, ERIC — WR — RAMS

PERSONAL: Born November 16, 1978, in Omaha, Neb. ... 6-0/205.
HIGH SCHOOL: Millard North (Omaha, Neb.).
COLLEGE: Nebraska.
TRANSACTIONS/CAREER NOTES: Selected by St. Louis Rams in third round (95th pick overall) of 2002 NFL draft.
HONORS: Heisman Trophy winner (2001). ... Davey O'Brien Award winner (2001). ... Named quarterback on THE SPORTING NEWS college All-America first team (2001).

					PASSING						RUSHING			TOTALS	
Year Team	G	Att.	Cmp.	Pct.	Yds.	TD	Int.	Avg.	Rat.	Att.	Yds.	Avg.	TD	TD	Pts.
1998—Nebraska	8	101	49	48.5	601	4	4	5.95	103.6	96	459	4.8	5	5	30
1999—Nebraska	12	160	83	51.9	1269	7	4	7.93	127.9	180	889	4.9	16	16	96
2000—Nebraska	11	156	75	48.1	1101	11	7	7.06	121.7	169	971	5.7	20	20	120
2001—Nebraska	12	189	105	55.6	1510	7	10	7.99	124.3	203	1115	5.5	18	18	108
College totals (4 years)	43	606	312	51.5	4481	29	25	7.39	121.7	648	3434	5.3	59	59	354

CURRY, RONALD — QB — RAIDERS

PERSONAL: Born May 28, 1979, in Hampton, Va. ... 6-1/220. ... Full name: Ronald Antonio Curry.
HIGH SCHOOL: Hampton (Va.).
COLLEGE: North Carolina.
TRANSACTIONS/CAREER NOTES: Selected by Oakland Raiders in seventh round (235th pick overall) of 2002 NFL draft.

			PASSING							RUSHING			TOTALS	
Year Team	G	Att.	Cmp.	Pct.	Yds.	TD	Int.	Avg.	Rat.	Att.	Yds.	Avg.	TD	TD	Pts.
1998—North Carolina	11	147	66	44.9	975	6	7	6.63	104.6	80	419	5.2	2	2	12
1999—North Carolina	5	110	54	49.1	682	3	10	6.20	92.0	60	226	3.8	2	2	12
2000—North Carolina	11	304	163	53.6	2325	11	12	7.65	121.9	119	351	2.9	6	6	36
2001—North Carolina	10	134	62	46.3	1005	8	6	7.50	120.0	89	253	2.8	3	3	18
College totals (4 years)	37	695	345	49.6	4987	28	35	7.18	113.1	348	1249	3.6	13	13	78

CURTIS, KEVIN — S — 49ERS

PERSONAL: Born July 28, 1980, in Frankfurt, West Germany. ... 6-2/212.
HIGH SCHOOL: Coronado (Lubbock, Texas).
COLLEGE: Texas Tech.
TRANSACTIONS/CAREER NOTES: Selected by San Francisco 49ers in fourth round (127th pick overall) of 2002 NFL draft.

		INTERCEPTIONS			SACKS
Year Team	G	No.	Yds.	Avg.	TD	No.
1997—Texas Tech			Redshirted.			
1998—Texas Tech	11	1	20	20.0	0	0.0
1999—Texas Tech	11	3	47	15.7	0	0.0
2000—Texas Tech	12	2	58	29.0	1	2.0
2001—Texas Tech	11	4	19	4.8	0	4.0
College totals (4 years)	45	10	144	14.4	1	6.0

DAVENPORT, NAJEH — FB — PACKERS

PERSONAL: Born February 8, 1979, in Miami. ... 6-1/246. ... Full name: Najeh Trenadious Monte Davenport.
HIGH SCHOOL: Miami Central (Fla.).
COLLEGE: Miami (Fla.).
TRANSACTIONS/CAREER NOTES: Selected by Green Bay Packers in fourth round (135th pick overall) of 2002 NFL draft.

		RUSHING				RECEIVING				KICKOFF RETURNS				TOTALS	
Year Team	G	Att.	Yds.	Avg.	TD	No.	Yds.	Avg.	TD	No.	Yds.	Avg.	TD	TD	Pts.
1998—Miami (Fla.)	10	55	387	7.0	6	5	41	8.2	0	12	319	26.6	0	6	36
1999—Miami (Fla.)	1	13	81	6.2	0	1	1	1.0	0	2	27	13.5	0	0	0
2000—Miami (Fla.)	10	65	308	4.7	4	15	149	9.9	1	0	0	0.0	0	5	30
2001—Miami (Fla.)	11	23	54	2.3	3	14	190	13.6	2	0	0	0.0	0	5	30
College totals (4 years)	32	156	830	5.3	13	35	381	10.9	3	14	346	24.7	0	16	96

DAVEY, ROHAN — QB — PATRIOTS

PERSONAL: Born April 14, 1978, in Claredon, Jamaica. ... 6-2/245. ... Full name: Rohan St. Patrick Davey.
HIGH SCHOOL: Miami Lakes (Fla.).
COLLEGE: Louisiana State.
TRANSACTIONS/CAREER NOTES: Selected by New England Patriots in fourth round (117th pick overall) of 2002 NFL draft.

			PASSING							RUSHING			TOTALS	
Year Team	G	Att.	Cmp.	Pct.	Yds.	TD	Int.	Avg.	Rat.	Att.	Yds.	Avg.	TD	TD	Pts.
1998—Louisiana State	2	0	0	0.0	0	0	0	0.0	...	1	-3	-3.0	0	0	0
1999—Louisiana State	7	52	31	59.6	491	4	4	9.44	148.9	19	27	1.4	0	0	0
2000—Louisiana State	4	59	38	64.4	577	7	1	9.78	182.3	8	49	6.1	0	0	0
2001—Louisiana State	12	367	217	59.1	3347	18	10	9.12	146.5	38	4	0.1	0	0	0
College totals (4 years)	25	478	286	59.8	4415	29	15	9.24	151.2	66	77	1.2	0	0	0

DAVIS, ANDRA — LB — BROWNS

PERSONAL: Born December 23, 1978, in Live Oak, Fla. ... 6-1/244. ... Full name: Andra Raynard Davis.
HIGH SCHOOL: Suwanee (Live Oak, Fla.).
COLLEGE: Florida.
TRANSACTIONS/CAREER NOTES: Selected by Cleveland Browns in fifth round (141st pick overall) of 2002 NFL draft.
HONORS: Named linebacker on THE SPORTING NEWS college All-America second team (2001).

		INTERCEPTIONS			SACKS
Year Team	G	No.	Yds.	Avg.	TD	No.
1997—Florida			Redshirted.			
1998—Florida	11	0	0	0.0	0	0.0
1999—Florida	12	0	0	0.0	0	3.0
2000—Florida	1	0	0	0.0	0	0.0
2001—Florida	11	1	25	25.0	1	2.0
College totals (4 years)	35	1	25	25.0	1	5.0

DAVIS, ANDRE' WR BROWNS

PERSONAL: Born June 12, 1979, in Niskayuna, N.Y. ... 6-1/194. ... Full name: Andre' N. Davis.
HIGH SCHOOL: Niskayuna (N.Y.).
COLLEGE: Virginia Tech.
TRANSACTIONS/CAREER NOTES: Selected by Cleveland Browns in second round (47th pick overall) of 2002 NFL draft.

			RUSHING				RECEIVING				PUNT RETURNS				KICKOFF RETURNS			TOTALS	
Year Team	G	Att.	Yds.	Avg.	TD	No.	Yds.	Avg.	TD	No.	Yds.	Avg.	TD	No.	Yds.	Avg.	TD	TD	Pts.
1998—Virginia Tech	8	0	0	0.0	0	5	83	16.6	0	1	36	36.0	0	0	0	0.0	0	0	0
1999—Virginia Tech	11	3	72	24.0	3	35	962	27.5	9	1	3	3.0	0	0	0	0.0	0	12	72
2000—Virginia Tech	9	3	51	17.0	1	24	318	13.3	2	18	396	22.0	3	0	0	0.0	0	6	36
2001—Virginia Tech	11	5	-2	-0.4	0	39	623	16.0	7	35	437	12.5	1	10	218	21.8	0	8	48
College totals (4 years)	39	11	121	11.0	4	103	1986	19.3	18	55	872	15.9	4	10	218	21.8	0	26	156

DAVIS, DORSETT DT BRONCOS

PERSONAL: Born January 24, 1979, in Shelby, Miss. ... 6-5/304. ... Full name: Dorsett Terrell Davis.
HIGH SCHOOL: East Side (Cleveland, Miss.).
JUNIOR COLLEGE: Mississippi Delta Community College.
COLLEGE: Mississippi State.
TRANSACTIONS/CAREER NOTES: Selected by Denver Broncos in third round (96th pick overall) of 2002 NFL draft.

Year Team	G	SACKS
1997—Mississippi Delta	Did not play.	
1998—Mississippi Delta	Statistics unavailable.	
1999—Mississippi State	11	2.0
2000—Mississippi State	10	1.0
2001—Mississippi State	11	1.0
College totals (3 years)	32	4.0

DENNEY, RYAN DE BILLS

PERSONAL: Born June 15, 1977, in Denver. ... 6-7/276.
HIGH SCHOOL: Horizon (Thornton, Colo.).
COLLEGE: Brigham Young.
TRANSACTIONS/CAREER NOTES: Selected by Buffalo Bills in second round (61st pick overall) of 2002 NFL draft.

		INTERCEPTIONS				SACKS
Year Team	G	No.	Yds.	Avg.	TD	No.
1998—Brigham Young	14	0	0	0.0	0	0.0
1999—Brigham Young	11	0	0	0.0	0	5.0
2000—Brigham Young	11	0	0	0.0	0	4.0
2001—Brigham Young	13	1	-1	-1.0	0	7.0
College totals (4 years)	49	1	-1	-1.0	0	16.0

DOMAN, BRANDON QB 49ERS

PERSONAL: Born December 29, 1976, in Salt Lake City, Utah. ... 6-1/210.
HIGH SCHOOL: Brighton (Salt Lake City, Utah).
COLLEGE: Brigham Young.
TRANSACTIONS/CAREER NOTES: Selected by San Francisco 49ers in fifth round (163rd pick overall) of 2002 NFL draft.

				PASSING					RUSHING			RECEIVING			TOTALS	
Year Team	G	Att.	Cmp.	Pct.	Yds.	TD	Int.	Avg.	Att.	Yds.	Avg.	TD	No.	Yds.	Avg.	TD	TD	Pts.
1998—Brigham Young	4	2	1	50.0	30	0	1	15.00	5	9	1.8	0	1	7	7.0	0	0	0
1999—Brigham Young	10	2	0	0.0	0	0	1	0.0	5	32	6.4	0	9	83	9.2	0	0	0
2000—Brigham Young	5	92	51	55.4	782	2	4	8.50	33	129	3.9	3	0	0	0.0	0	3	18
2001—Brigham Young	13	408	261	64.0	3542	33	8	8.68	141	503	3.6	8	1	17	17.0	0	0	0
College totals (4 years)	32	504	313	62.1	4354	35	14	8.64	184	673	3.7	11	11	107	9.7	0	3	18

DORSCH, TRAVIS P/K BENGALS

PERSONAL: Born September 4, 1979, in Bozeman, Mont. ... 6-6/221. ... Full name: Travis Edward Dorsch.
HIGH SCHOOL: Bozeman (Mont.).
COLLEGE: Purdue.
TRANSACTIONS/CAREER NOTES: Selected by Cincinnati Bengals in fourth round (109th pick overall) of 2002 NFL draft.
HONORS: Named kicker on THE SPORTING NEWS college All-America first team (2001). ... Named punter on THE SPORTING NEWS college All-America second team (2001).
COLLEGE NOTES: Attempted one pass with one completion for four yards and one touchdown (1999). ... Attempted one pass without a completion (2000).

				PUNTING						KICKING			
Year Team	G	No.	Yds.	Avg.	Net avg.	In. 20	Blk.	XPM	XPA	FGM	FGA	Lg.	50+	Pts.
1998—Purdue	...	0	0	0.0	.0	0	0	48	50	16	22	47	0-0	96
1999—Purdue	...	0	0	0.0	.0	0	0	38	39	18	31	47	0-0	92
2000—Purdue	...	13	652	50.2	.0	0	0	45	47	12	17	45	0-0	81
2001—Purdue	...	53	2547	48.1	.0	0	0	20	25	22	27	50	0-0	86
College totals (4 years)	...	66	3199	48.5	0.0	0	0	151	161	68	97	50	0-0	355

2002 DRAFT PICKS

DUCKETT, T.J.   RB   FALCONS

PERSONAL: Born February 17, 1981, in Kalamazoo, Mich. ... 6-0/254.
HIGH SCHOOL: Loy Norrix (Kalamazoo, Mich.).
COLLEGE: Michigan State.
TRANSACTIONS/CAREER NOTES: Selected after junior season by Atlanta Falcons in first round (18th pick overall) of 2002 NFL draft.

		RUSHING				RECEIVING			TOTALS	
Year Team	G	Att.	Yds.	Avg.	TD	No.	Yds.	Avg.	TD	TD	Pts.
1999—Michigan State	12	118	606	5.1	10	2	32	16.0	0	10	60
2000—Michigan State	11	240	1353	5.6	7	8	39	4.9	0	7	42
2001—Michigan State	12	263	1420	5.4	12	12	80	6.7	1	13	78
College totals (3 years)	35	621	3379	5.4	29	22	151	6.9	1	30	180

DWYER, NATE   DT   CARDINALS

PERSONAL: Born September 30, 1978, in Stillwater, Minn. ... 6-3/313.
HIGH SCHOOL: Stillwater (Minn.).
COLLEGE: Kansas.
TRANSACTIONS/CAREER NOTES: Selected by Arizona Cardinals in fourth round (113th pick overall) of 2002 NFL draft.

		INTERCEPTIONS				SACKS
Year Team	G	No.	Yds.	Avg.	TD	No.
1998—Kansas	11	2	43	21.5	1	3.0
1999—Kansas	12	0	0	0.0	0	3.0
2000—Kansas	11	0	0	0.0	0	7.0
2001—Kansas	11	0	0	0.0	0	3.0
College totals (4 years)	45	2	43	21.5	1	16.0

EASY, OMAR   RB   CHIEFS

PERSONAL: Born October 29, 1977, in Jamaica. ... 6-1/244. ... Full name: Omar Xavier Easy.
HIGH SCHOOL: Everett (Mass.).
COLLEGE: Penn State.
TRANSACTIONS/CAREER NOTES: Selected by Kansas City Chiefs in fourth round (107th pick overall) of 2002 NFL draft.

		RUSHING				RECEIVING			TOTALS	
Year Team	G	Att.	Yds.	Avg.	TD	No.	Yds.	Avg.	TD	TD	Pts.
1997—Penn State					Redshirted.						
1998—Penn State	9	39	141	3.6	2	2	10	5.0	0	2	12
1999—Penn State	11	27	146	5.4	2	1	17	17.0	0	2	12
2000—Penn State	11	44	176	4.0	0	14	153	10.9	1	1	6
2001—Penn State	11	45	196	4.4	1	9	70	7.8	0	1	6
College totals (4 years)	42	155	659	4.3	5	26	250	9.6	1	6	36

ECHOLS, MIKE   CB   TITANS

PERSONAL: Born October 13, 1978, in Youngstown, Ohio. ... 5-10/190.
HIGH SCHOOL: Ursuline (Youngstown, Ohio).
COLLEGE: Wisconsin.
TRANSACTIONS/CAREER NOTES: Selected by Tennessee Titans in fourth round (110th pick overall) of 2002 NFL draft.

		INTERCEPTIONS				SACKS
Year Team	G	No.	Yds.	Avg.	TD	No.
1998—Wisconsin	12	3	0	0.0	0	1.0
1999—Wisconsin	12	1	0	0.0	0	0.0
2000—Wisconsin	12	5	110	22.0	1	1.0
2001—Wisconsin	12	3	1	0.3	0	2.0
College totals (4 years)	48	12	111	9.3	1	4.0

EDWARDS, KALIMBA   DE   LIONS

PERSONAL: Born December 26, 1979, in East Point, Ga. ... 6-5/264.
HIGH SCHOOL: Tri-Cities (Atlanta).
COLLEGE: South Carolina.
TRANSACTIONS/CAREER NOTES: Selected by Detroit Lions in second round (35th pick overall) of 2002 NFL draft.
HONORS: Named linebacker on The Sporting News college All-America first team (2001).

		INTERCEPTIONS				SACKS
Year Team	G	No.	Yds.	Avg.	TD	No.
1998—South Carolina	11	0	0	0.0	0	1.0
1999—South Carolina	11	0	0	0.0	0	5.0
2000—South Carolina	12	1	81	81.0	0	7.0
2001—South Carolina	10	0	0	0.0	0	3.5
College totals (4 years)	44	1	81	81.0	1	16.5

ELLIOTT, JAMIN   WR   BEARS

PERSONAL: Born October 5, 1979, in Portsmouth, Va. ... 6-0/181.
HIGH SCHOOL: Churchland (Portsmouth, Va.).
COLLEGE: Delaware.
TRANSACTIONS/CAREER NOTES: Selected by Chicago Bears in sixth round (203rd pick overall) of 2002 NFL draft.

		RECEIVING			
	G	No.	Yds.	Avg.	TD
1998—Delaware State Hornets	11	23	367	16.0	4
1999—Delaware State Hornets	11	47	850	18.1	4
2000—Delaware State Hornets	14	58	1337	23.1	8
2001—Delaware State Hornets	11	30	514	17.1	3
College totals (4 years)	47	158	3068	19.4	19

EPSTEIN, HAYDEN   K/P   JAGUARS

PERSONAL: Born November 16, 1980, in San Diego. ... 6-2/214.
HIGH SCHOOL: Torrey Pines (Cardiff, Calif.).
COLLEGE: Michigan.
TRANSACTIONS/CAREER NOTES: Selected by Jacksonville Jaguars in seventh round (247th pick overall) of 2002 NFL draft.

		PUNTING						KICKING					
Year Team	G	No.	Yds.	Avg.	Net avg.	In. 20	Blk.	XPM	XPA	FGM	FGA	Lg.	50+	Pts.
1998—Michigan	...	9	361	40.1	.0	0	0	1	1	0	0	0	0-0	1
1999—Michigan	...	32	1282	40.1	.0	0	0	5	8	21	22	0	0-0	68
2000—Michigan	...	55	2224	40.4	.0	0	0	26	28	8	14	0	0-0	50
2001—Michigan	...	71	2790	39.3	.0	0	0	37	37	13	20	0	0-0	76
College totals (4 years)	...	167	6657	39.9	0.0	0	0	69	74	42	56	0	0-0	195

EVANS, JOEY   DE   BENGALS

PERSONAL: Born August 22, 1979, in Fayetteville, N.C. ... 6-4/264. ... Full name: Joseph Earl Evans Jr.
HIGH SCHOOL: E.E. Smith (Fayetteville, N.C.).
COLLEGE: North Carolina.
TRANSACTIONS/CAREER NOTES: Selected by Cincinnati Bengals in seventh round (219th pick overall) of 2002 NFL draft.

Year Team	G	SACKS
1997—North Carolina		Redshirted.
1998—North Carolina	11	0.0
1999—North Carolina	11	3.0
2000—North Carolina	11	8.0
2001—North Carolina	11	2.5
College totals (4 years)	44	13.5

FAGGINS, DEMARCUS   CB   TEXANS

PERSONAL: Born June 13, 1979, in Irving, Texas. ... 5-10/178.
HIGH SCHOOL: Irving (Texas).
JUNIOR COLLEGE: Navarro College (Texas).
COLLEGE: Kansas State.
TRANSACTIONS/CAREER NOTES: Selected by Houston Texans in sixth round (173rd pick overall) of 2002 NFL draft.

		INTERCEPTIONS				SACKS
Year Team	G	No.	Yds.	Avg.	TD	No.
1998—Navarro College		Statistics unavailable.				
1999—Navarro College		Statistics unavailable.				
2000—Kansas State	13	0	0	0.0	0	1.0
2001—Kansas State	11	5	89	17.8	0	0.0
College totals (2 years)	24	5	89	17.8	0	1.0

FASANI, RANDY   QB   PANTHERS

PERSONAL: Born September 18, 1978, in Granite City, Calif. ... 6-3/234.
HIGH SCHOOL: Del Oro (Loomis, Calif.).
COLLEGE: Stanford.
TRANSACTIONS/CAREER NOTES: Selected by Carolina Panthers in fifth round (137th pick overall) of 2002 NFL draft.
COLLEGE NOTES: Caught two passes for 48 yards (1998).

		PASSING								RUSHING				TOTALS	
Year Team	G	Att.	Cmp.	Pct.	Yds.	TD	Int.	Avg.	Rat.	Att.	Yds.	Avg.	TD	TD	Pts.
1998—Stanford	10	16	8	50.0	81	1	1	5.06	100.7	9	9	1.0	3	3	18
1999—Stanford	3	6	1	16.7	13	0	0	2.17	34.9	4	11	2.8	0	0	0
2000—Stanford	8	180	93	51.7	1400	11	6	7.78	130.5	55	123	2.2	2	2	12
2001—Stanford	8	167	86	51.5	1479	13	4	8.86	146.8	59	174	2.9	1	0	0
College totals (4 years)	29	369	188	50.9	2973	25	11	8.06	135.0	127	317	2.5	6	5	30

FERGUSON, JARRETT — FB — BILLS

PERSONAL: Born January 23, 1979, in Portsmouth, Va. ... 5-8/222. ... Full name: Jarrett Thomas Ferguson.
HIGH SCHOOL: Staunton River (Va.).
COLLEGE: Virginia Tech.
TRANSACTIONS/CAREER NOTES: Selected by Buffalo Bills in seventh round (251st pick overall) of 2002 NFL draft.

			RUSHING				RECEIVING			TOTALS	
Year Team	G	Att.	Yds.	Avg.	TD	No.	Yds.	Avg.	TD	TD	Pts.
1997—Virginia Tech					Redshirted.						
1998—Virginia Tech	11	34	199	5.9	3	7	99	14.1	1	4	24
1999—Virginia Tech	11	34	173	5.1	1	5	48	9.6	0	1	6
2000—Virginia Tech	11	40	210	5.3	6	3	40	13.3	0	6	36
2001—Virginia Tech	11	35	156	4.5	5	25	256	10.2	3	8	48
College totals (4 years)	44	143	738	5.2	15	40	443	11.1	4	19	114

FISHER, LEVAR — LB — CARDINALS

PERSONAL: Born November 29, 1979, in Beaufort, N.C. ... 6-1/228.
HIGH SCHOOL: East Carteret (Beaufort, N.C.).
COLLEGE: North Carolina State.
TRANSACTIONS/CAREER NOTES: Selected by Arizona Cardinals in second round (49th pick overall) of 2002 NFL draft.
HONORS: Named linebacker on THE SPORTING NEWS college All-America third team (2001). ... Named linebacker on THE SPORTING NEWS college All-America second team (2000).

		INTERCEPTIONS				SACKS
Year Team	G	No.	Yds.	Avg.	TD	No.
1998—North Carolina State	11	0	0	0.0	0	2.0
1999—North Carolina State	12	0	0	0.0	0	3.5
2000—North Carolina State	11	1	3	3.0	0	5.0
2001—North Carolina State	11	0	0	0.0	0	1.5
College totals (4 years)	45	1	3	3.0	0	12.0

FISHER, TRAVIS — CB — RAMS

PERSONAL: Born September 12, 1979, in Tallahassee, Fla. ... 5-10/189.
HIGH SCHOOL: Godby (Tallahassee, Fla.).
JUNIOR COLLEGE: Coffeyville (Kan.) Community College.
COLLEGE: Central Florida.
TRANSACTIONS/CAREER NOTES: Selected by St. Louis Rams in second round (64th pick overall) of 2002 NFL draft.

		INTERCEPTIONS			
Year Team	G	No.	Yds.	Avg.	TD
1997—Coffeyville		Statistics unavailable.			
1998—Coffeyville		Statistics unavailable.			
1999—Central Florida	11	0	0	0.0	0
2000—Central Florida	11	2	0	0.0	0
College totals (2 years)	22	2	0	0.0	0

FLETCHER, BRYAN — TE — BEARS

PERSONAL: Born March 23, 1979, in St. Louis. ... 6-5/235. ... Full name: Bryan Jamaile Fletcher.
HIGH SCHOOL: Hazelwood East (St. Louis).
COLLEGE: UCLA.
TRANSACTIONS/CAREER NOTES: Selected by Chicago Bears in sixth round (210th pick overall) of 2002 NFL draft.

		RECEIVING			
Year Team	G	No.	Yds.	Avg.	TD
1998—UCLA	11	0	0	0	0
1999—UCLA	8	9	90	10.0	0
2000—UCLA	12	10	144	14.4	2
2001—UCLA	11	11	189	17.2	1
College totals (4 years)	42	20	423	21.2	3

FONOTI, TONIU — G — CHARGERS

PERSONAL: Born November 26, 1981, in American Samoa. ... 6-4/349. ... Full name: Toniuolevaiavea Satele Fonoti.
HIGH SCHOOL: Kahuku (Hauula, Hawaii).
COLLEGE: Nebraska.
TRANSACTIONS/CAREER NOTES: Selected after junior season by San Diego Chargers in second round (39th pick overall) of 2002 NFL draft.
COLLEGE PLAYING EXPERIENCE: Nebraska, 1999-2001. ... Games played: 1999 (12), 2000 (11), 2001 (12). Total: 35.

FOOTE, LARRY — LB — STEELERS

PERSONAL: Born June 12, 1980, in Detroit. ... 6-1/234. ... Full name: Lawrence Edward Foote Jr.
HIGH SCHOOL: Pershing (Detroit).
COLLEGE: Michigan.
TRANSACTIONS/CAREER NOTES: Selected by Pittsburgh Steelers in fourth round (128th pick overall) of 2002 NFL draft.
HONORS: Named linebacker on THE SPORTING NEWS college All-America second team (2001).

Year	Team	G	INTERCEPTIONS No.	Yds.	Avg.	TD	SACKS No.
1998	Michigan	12	0	0	0.0	0	1.0
1999	Michigan	12	1	0	0.0	0	3.0
2000	Michigan	12	2	41	20.5	0	1.0
2001	Michigan	12	0	0	0.0	0	6.0
College totals (4 years)		48	3	41	13.7	0	11.0

FOSTER, DeSHAUN — RB — PANTHERS

PERSONAL: Born January 10, 1980, in Charlotte, N.C. ... 6-0/222. ... Full name: DeShaun Xavier Foster.
HIGH SCHOOL: Tustin (Calif.).
COLLEGE: UCLA.
TRANSACTIONS/CAREER NOTES: Selected by Carolina Panthers in second round (34th pick overall) of 2002 NFL draft.
HONORS: Named running back on THE SPORTING NEWS college All-America second team (2001).

Year Team	G	RUSHING Att.	Yds.	Avg.	TD	RECEIVING No.	Yds.	Avg.	TD	KICKOFF RETURNS No.	Yds.	Avg.	TD	TOTALS TD	Pts.
1998—UCLA	11	126	673	5.3	10	16	163	10.2	2	8	213	26.6	0	12	72
1999—UCLA	9	111	375	3.4	0	17	114	6.7	0	1	16	16.0	0	6	36
2000—UCLA	11	269	1037	3.9	12	16	142	8.9	1	0	0	0.0	0	13	78
2001—UCLA	8	216	1109	5.1	12	9	129	14.3	1	0	0	0.0	0	13	78
College totals (4 years)	39	722	3194	4.4	34	58	548	9.4	4	9	229	25.4	0	44	264

FOWLER, MELVIN — C — BROWNS

PERSONAL: Born March 31, 1979, in Wheatley Heights, N.Y. ... 6-3/300. ... Full name: Melvin Thaddeus Fowler Jr.
HIGH SCHOOL: Half Hollow Hills (Long Island, N.Y.).
COLLEGE: Maryland.
TRANSACTIONS/CAREER NOTES: Selected by Cleveland Browns in third round (76th pick overall) of 2002 NFL draft.
COLLEGE PLAYING EXPERIENCE: Maryland, 1997-2001. ... Games played: 1997 (redshirted), 1998 (11), 1999 (11), 2000 (11), 2001 (11). Total: 44.

FRANKLIN, BRAD — CB — PANTHERS

PERSONAL: Born December 22, 1979, in Baton Rouge, La. ... 6-1/190.
HIGH SCHOOL: Broadmoor (La.).
COLLEGE: Louisiana-Lafayette.
TRANSACTIONS/CAREER NOTES: Selected by Carolina Panthers in seventh round (258th pick overall) of 2002 NFL draft..

Year Team	G	INTERCEPTIONS No.	Yds.	Avg.	TD	KICKOFF RETURNS No.	Yds.	Avg.	TD	TOTALS TD	Pts.
1998—Louisiana-Lafayette	11	1	0	0.0	0	0	0	0.0	0	0	0
1999—Louisiana-Lafayette	9	1	0	0.0	0	4	59	14.8	0	0	0
2000—Louisiana-Lafayette	11	1	40	40.0	1	2	21	10.5	0	1	6
2001—Louisiana-Lafayette	11	0	0	0.0	0	0	0	0.0	0	1	6
College totals (4 years)	42	3	40	13.3	1	6	80	13.3	0	2	12

FREEMAN, EDDIE — DT — CHIEFS

PERSONAL: Born January 4, 1978, in Mobile, Ala. ... 6-5/310.
HIGH SCHOOL: B.C. Rain (Mobile, Ala.).
COLLEGE: Alabama-Birmingham.
TRANSACTIONS/CAREER NOTES: Selected by Kansas City Chiefs in second round (43rd pick overall) of 2002 NFL draft.

Year Team	G	SACKS
1997—Alabama-Birmingham		Redshirted.
1998—Alabama-Birmingham	11	4.0
1999—Alabama-Birmingham	11	2.0
2000—Alabama-Birmingham	11	5.5
2001—Alabama-Birmingham	11	3.0
College totals (4 years)	44	14.5

FREENEY, DWIGHT — DE — COLTS

PERSONAL: Born February 19, 1980, in Hartford, Conn. ... 6-1/266. ... Full name: Dwight Jason Freeney.
HIGH SCHOOL: Bloomfield (Conn.).
COLLEGE: Syracuse.
TRANSACTIONS/CAREER NOTES: Selected by Indianapolis Colts in first round (11th pick overall) of 2002 NFL draft.
HONORS: Named defensive end on THE SPORTING NEWS college All-America first team (2001).

Year Team	G	SACKS
1998—Syracuse	10	0.0
1999—Syracuse	10	3.5
2000—Syracuse	7	13.0
2001—Syracuse	12	17.5
College totals (4 years)	39	34.0

FUJITA, SCOTT — LB — CHIEFS

PERSONAL: Born April 28, 1979, in Ventura, Calif. ... 6-5/248.
HIGH SCHOOL: Rio Mesa (Calif.).
COLLEGE: California.
TRANSACTIONS/CAREER NOTES: Selected by Kansas City Chiefs in fifth round (143rd pick overall) of 2002 NFL draft.

Year Team	G	SACKS
1997—California	Redshirted.	
1998—California	7	0.0
1999—California	10	0.5
2000—California	11	4.0
2001—California	11	2.5
College totals (4 years)	39	7.0

GAFFNEY, JABAR　　　WR　　　TEXANS

PERSONAL: Born December 1, 1980, in San Antonio. ... 6-1/193. ... Full name: Derrick Jabar Gaffney.
HIGH SCHOOL: Raines (Jacksonville, Fla.).
COLLEGE: Florida.
TRANSACTIONS/CAREER NOTES: Selected after sophomore season by Houston Texans in second round (33rd pick overall) of 2002 NFL draft.
HONORS: Named wide receiver on THE SPORTING NEWS college All-America first team (2001).

		RECEIVING			
Year Team	G	No.	Yds.	Avg.	TD
2000—Florida	12	71	1184	16.7	14
2001—Florida	11	67	1191	17.8	13
College totals (2 years)	23	138	2375	17.2	27

GAINES, TEDDY　　　CB　　　49ERS

PERSONAL: Born September 12, 1979, in Kingsport, Tenn. ... 5-11/165. ... Full name: Wilford Teddy Gaines.
HIGH SCHOOL: Dobyns-Bennett (Kingsport, Tenn.).
COLLEGE: Tennessee.
TRANSACTIONS/CAREER NOTES: Selected by San Francisco 49ers in seventh round (256th pick overall) of 2002 NFL draft..

		INTERCEPTIONS			
Year Team	G	No.	Yds.	Avg.	TD
1998—Tennessee	0	0	0	0.0	0
1999—Tennessee	11	0	0	0.0	0
2000—Tennessee	11	1	0	0.0	0
2001—Tennessee	11	0	0	0.0	0
College totals (4 years)	33	1	0	0.0	0

GARRARD, DAVID　　　QB　　　JAGUARS

PERSONAL: Born February 14, 1978, in East Orange, N.J. ... 6-1/237. ... Full name: David Douglas Garrard.
HIGH SCHOOL: Southern Durham (N.C.).
COLLEGE: East Carolina.
TRANSACTIONS/CAREER NOTES: Selected by Jacksonville Jaguars in fourth round (108th pick overall) of 2002 NFL draft.

		PASSING							RUSHING				TOTALS	
Year Team	G	Att.	Cmp.	Pct.	Yds.	TD	Int.	Avg.	Rat.	Att.	Yds.	Avg.	TD	TD	Pts.
1998—East Carolina	11	255	157	61.6	2091	14	7	8.20	143.1	127	164	1.3	2	2	12
1999—East Carolina	11	312	181	58.0	2359	14	12	7.56	128.6	138	493	3.6	8	8	48
2000—East Carolina	11	312	164	52.6	2332	19	11	7.47	128.4	135	358	2.7	5	5	30
2001—East Carolina	11	290	164	56.6	2247	13	9	7.75	130.2	116	194	1.7	6	6	36
College totals (4 years)	44	1169	666	57.0	9029	60	39	7.72	132.1	516	1209	2.3	21	21	126

GILMORE, JOHN　　　TE　　　SAINTS

PERSONAL: Born September 21, 1979, in Marquette, Mich. ... 6-3/265. ... Full name: John Henry Gilmore.
HIGH SCHOOL: Wilson (West Lawn, Pa.).
COLLEGE: Penn State.
TRANSACTIONS/CAREER NOTES: Selected by New Orleans Saints in sixth round (196th pick overall) of 2002 NFL draft.

		RECEIVING			
Year Team	G	No.	Yds.	Avg.	TD
1997—Penn State	Redshirted.				
1998—Penn State	6	1	9	9.0	0
1999—Penn State	11	22	259	11.8	1
2000—Penn State	8	10	82	8.2	2
2001—Penn State	10	25	284	11.4	0
College totals (4 years)	35	58	634	10.9	3

GIVENS, DAVID　　　WR　　　PATRIOTS

PERSONAL: Born August 16, 1980, in Youngstown, Ohio. ... 6-0/217. ... Full name: David Lamar Givens.
HIGH SCHOOL: Humble (Texas).
COLLEGE: Notre Dame.
TRANSACTIONS/CAREER NOTES: Selected by New England Patriots in seventh round (253rd pick overall) of 2002 NFL draft.
COLLEGE NOTES: Attempted one pass with one completion for 21 yards and one touchdown (1999). ... Attempted two passes with one completion for 52 yards (2000). ... Attempted two passes with one completion for 29 yards (2001).

			RUSHING				RECEIVING				KICKOFF RETURNS				TOTALS	
Year	Team	G	Att.	Yds.	Avg.	TD	No.	Yds.	Avg.	TD	No.	Yds.	Avg.	TD	TD	Pts.
1998—Notre Dame		11	4	26	6.5	1	0	0	0.0	0	2	21	10.5	0	1	6
1999—Notre Dame		12	6	13	2.2	1	14	187	13.4	1	2	48	24.0	0	2	12
2000—Notre Dame		11	24	101	4.2	2	25	310	12.4	2	11	227	20.6	0	4	24
2001—Notre Dame		10	7	6	0.9	0	33	317	9.6	0	6	143	23.8	0	0	0
College totals (4 years)		44	41	146	3.6	4	72	814	11.3	3	21	439	20.9	0	7	42

GLOVER, LaVAR — CB — STEELERS

PERSONAL: Born December 17, 1978, in Dayton, Ohio. ... 5-9/175.
HIGH SCHOOL: Jefferson (Dayton, Ohio).
COLLEGE: Cincinnati.
TRANSACTIONS/CAREER NOTES: Selected by Pittsburgh Steelers in seventh round (212th pick overall) of 2002 NFL draft.

			INTERCEPTIONS			
Year	Team	G	No.	Yds.	Avg.	TD
1997—Cincinnati			Redshirted.			
1998—Cincinnati		11	0	0	0.0	0
1999—Cincinnati		11	0	0	0.0	0
2000—Cincinnati		11	1	30	30.0	1
2001—Cincinnati		11	1	38	38.0	1
College totals (4 years)		44	2	68	34.0	2

GONZALEZ, JOAQUIN — OT — BROWNS

PERSONAL: Born September 7, 1979, in Miami. ... 6-3/293. ... Full name: Joaquin Antonio Gonzalez.
HIGH SCHOOL: Columbus (Miami).
COLLEGE: Miami (Fla.).
TRANSACTIONS/CAREER NOTES: Selected by Cleveland Browns in seventh round (227th pick overall) of 2002 NFL draft.
HONORS: Named offensive tackle on THE SPORTING NEWS college All-America second team (2001).
COLLEGE PLAYING EXPERIENCE: Miami (Fla.), 1997-2001. ... Games played: 1997 (0), 1998 (11), 1999 (12), 2000 (11), 2001 (11). Total: 45.

GOODMAN, ANDRE' — CB — LIONS

PERSONAL: Born August 8, 1978, in Greenville, S.C. ... 5-10/182.
HIGH SCHOOL: Eastwood (Greenville, S.C.).
COLLEGE: South Carolina.
TRANSACTIONS/CAREER NOTES: Selected by Detroit Lions in third round (68th pick overall) of 2002 NFL draft.

			INTERCEPTIONS				SACKS
Year	Team	G	No.	Yds.	Avg.	TD	No.
1998—South Carolina		2	0	0	0.0	0	0.0
1999—South Carolina		6	0	0	0.0	0	0.0
2000—South Carolina		11	1	71	71.0	0	1.0
2001—South Carolina		11	3	13	4.3	0	0.0
College totals (4 years)		30	4	84	21.0	0	1.0

GOODWIN, JONATHAN — OL — JETS

PERSONAL: Born December 2, 1978, in Columbia, S.C. ... 6-3/318. ... Full name: Jonathan Scott Goodwin.
HIGH SCHOOL: Lower Richland (S.C.).
COLLEGE: Ohio, then Michigan.
TRANSACTIONS/CAREER NOTES: Selected by New York Jets in fifth round (154th pick overall) of 2002 NFL draft.
HONORS: Named guard on THE SPORTING NEWS college All-America third team (2001).
COLLEGE PLAYING EXPERIENCE: Ohio, 1997. ... Michigan, 1999-2001. ... Games played: 1997 (11), 1998 (did not play), 1999 (5), 2000 (12), 2001 (12). Total: 40.

GORDON, LAMAR — RB — RAMS

PERSONAL: Born January 7, 1980, in Milwaukee. ... 6-1/204.
HIGH SCHOOL: Cudahy (Milwaukee).
COLLEGE: North Dakota State.
TRANSACTIONS/CAREER NOTES: Selected by St. Louis Rams in third round (84th pick overall) of 2002 NFL draft.

			RUSHING				RECEIVING				KICKOFF RETURNS				TOTALS	
Year	Team	G	Att.	Yds.	Avg.	TD	No.	Yds.	Avg.	TD	No.	Yds.	Avg.	TD	TD	Pts.
1998—North Dakota	...	139	698	5.0	8	10	119	11.9	0	0	0	0.0	0	8	48
1999—North Dakota	...	259	1495	5.8	22	15	114	7.6	0	0	0	0.0	0	22	132
2000—North Dakota	...	256	1727	6.7	22	14	163	11.6	1	0	0	0.0	0	23	138
2001—North Dakota	...	129	780	6.0	10	5	66	13.2	1	4	101	25.3	0	11	66
College totals (4 years)	...	783	4700	6.0	62	44	462	10.5	2	4	101	25.3	0	64	384

GRAHAM, DANIEL — TE — PATRIOTS

PERSONAL: Born November 16, 1978, in Torrance, Calif. ... 6-3/248.
HIGH SCHOOL: Thomas Jefferson (Denver).
COLLEGE: Colorado.
TRANSACTIONS/CAREER NOTES: Selected by New England Patriots in first round (21st pick overall) of 2002 NFL draft.
HONORS: Named tight end on THE SPORTING NEWS college All-America first team (2001).

		RECEIVING			
Year Team	G	No.	Yds.	Avg.	TD
1998—Colorado	11	3	83	27.7	0
1999—Colorado	9	19	264	13.9	4
2000—Colorado	10	33	443	13.4	1
2001—Colorado	12	51	753	14.8	6
College totals (4 years)	42	106	1543	14.6	11

GRANT, CHARLES — DE — SAINTS

PERSONAL: Born September 3, 1978, in Colquitt, Ga. ... 6-3/282.
HIGH SCHOOL: Miller County (Colquitt, Ga.).
COLLEGE: Georgia.
TRANSACTIONS/CAREER NOTES: Selected by New Orleans Saints in first round (25th pick overall) of 2002 NFL draft.
COLLEGE NOTES: Rushed 17 times for 79 yards and three touchdowns (1999).

Year Team	G	SACKS
1999—Georgia	11	7.0
2000—Georgia	10	2.0
2001—Georgia	10	6.0
College totals (4 years)	31	15.0

GRAU, JEFF — TE — REDSKINS

PERSONAL: Born December 16, 1979, in Inglewood, Calif. ... 6-3/245. ... Full name: Jeffrey Alan Grau.
HIGH SCHOOL: Loyola (Torrance, Calif.).
COLLEGE: UCLA.
TRANSACTIONS/CAREER NOTES: Selected by Washington Redskins in seventh round (230th pick overall) of 2002 NFL draft.
COLLEGE PLAYING EXPERIENCE: UCLA, 1998-2001. ... Games played: (statistics unavailable).

GRAY, BOBBY — S — BEARS

PERSONAL: Born April 30, 1978, in Houston. ... 6-0/209. ... Full name: Bobby Wayne Gray.
HIGH SCHOOL: Aldine (Texas).
COLLEGE: Louisiana Tech.
TRANSACTIONS/CAREER NOTES: Selected by Chicago Bears in fifth round (140th pick overall) of 2002 NFL draft.

		INTERCEPTIONS			SACKS
Year Team	G	No.	Yds.	Avg.	TD	No.
1998—LouisianaTech	12	1	17	17.0	0	1.0
1999—LouisianaTech	11	1	0	0.0	0	0.0
2000—LouisianaTech	11	1	7	7.0	0	0.0
2001—LouisianaTech	11	2	38	19.0	0	0.0
College totals (4 years)	45	5	62	12.4	0	1.0

GREEN, HOWARD — DT — TEXANS

PERSONAL: Born January 12, 1979, in Donaldsonville, La. ... 6-2/331. ... Full name: Howard Green Jr.
HIGH SCHOOL: Donaldsonville (La.).
JUNIOR COLLEGE: Southwest Mississippi College.
COLLEGE: Louisiana State.
TRANSACTIONS/CAREER NOTES: Selected by Houston Texans in sixth round (190th pick overall) of 2002 NFL draft.

Year Team	G	SACKS
1998—Southwest Mississippi	Statistics unavailable.	
1999—Southwest Mississippi	Statistics unavailable.	
2000—Louisiana State	10	1.0
2001—Louisiana State	13	2.0
College totals (2 years)	23	3.0

GREEN, JARVIS — DE — PATRIOTS

PERSONAL: Born January 12, 1979, in Thibodaux, La. ... 6-3/272. ... Full name: Jarvis Pernell Green.
HIGH SCHOOL: Donaldsville (La.).
COLLEGE: Louisiana State.
TRANSACTIONS/CAREER NOTES: Selected by New England Patriots in fourth round (126th pick overall) of 2002 NFL draft.

Year Team	G	SACKS
1997—Louisiana State		Redshirted.
1998—Louisiana State	10	8.0
1999—Louisiana State	11	7.0
2000—Louisiana State	9	1.0
2001—Louisiana State	11	4.0
College totals (4 years)	41	20.0

GREEN, WILLIAM — RB — BROWNS

PERSONAL: Born December 17, 1979, in Atlantic City, N.J. ... 6-0/221.
HIGH SCHOOL: Holy Spirit (Atlantic City, N.J.).
COLLEGE: Boston College.
TRANSACTIONS/CAREER NOTES: Selected after junior season by Cleveland Browns in first round (16th pick overall) of 2002 NFL draft.
HONORS: Named running back on THE SPORTING NEWS college All-America first team (2001).

		RUSHING				RECEIVING				PUNT RETURNS				KICKOFF RETURNS				TOTALS	
Year Team	G	Att.	Yds.	Avg.	TD	No.	Yds.	Avg.	TD	No.	Yds.	Avg.	TD	No.	Yds.	Avg.	TD	TD	Pts.
1999—Boston College	10	49	251	5.1	4	2	5	2.5	0	1	11	11.0	0	13	342	26.3	0	4	24
2000—Boston College	11	187	1164	6.2	14	6	78	13.0	1	0	0	0.0	0	9	199	22.1	0	15	90
2001—Boston College	10	265	1559	5.9	15	23	260	11.3	2	0	0	0.0	0	9	199	22.1	0	17	102
College totals (3 years)	31	501	2974	5.9	33	31	343	11.1	3	1	11	11.0	0	31	740	23.9	0	36	216

GREISEN, NICK — LB — GIANTS

PERSONAL: Born August 10, 1979, in Sturgeon Bay, Wis. ... 6-1/242.
HIGH SCHOOL: Sturgeon Bay (Wis.).
COLLEGE: Wisconsin.
TRANSACTIONS/CAREER NOTES: Selected by New York Giants in fifth round (152nd pick overall) of 2002 NFL draft.

		INTERCEPTIONS				SACKS
Year Team	G	No.	Yds.	Avg.	TD	No.
1998—Wisconsin	5	0	0	0.0	0	0.0
1999—Wisconsin	12	0	0	0.0	0	1.0
2000—Wisconsin	13	3	0	0.0	0	6.0
2001—Wisconsin	12	2	0	0.0	0	4.0
College totals (4 years)	42	5	0	0.0	0	11.0

GURODE, ANDRE — G/C — COWBOYS

PERSONAL: Born March 6, 1978, in Houston. ... 6-4/316.
HIGH SCHOOL: North Shore (Houston).
COLLEGE: Colorado.
TRANSACTIONS/CAREER NOTES: Selected by Dallas Cowboys in second round (37th pick overall) of 2002 NFL draft.
HONORS: Named guard on THE SPORTING NEWS college All-America first team (2001).
COLLEGE PLAYING EXPERIENCE: Colorado, 1997-2001. ... Games played: 1997 (redshirted), 1998 (5), 1999 (11), 2000 (11), 2001 (12). Total: 39.

HALL, CARLOS — DE — TITANS

PERSONAL: Born January 16, 1979, in Moro, Ark. ... 6-4/259.
HIGH SCHOOL: Lee (Mariana, Ark.).
COLLEGE: Arkansas.
TRANSACTIONS/CAREER NOTES: Selected by Tennessee Titans in seventh round (240th pick overall) of 2002 NFL draft.

Year Team	G	SACKS
1997—Arkansas		Redshirted.
1998—Arkansas	11	5.0
1999—Arkansas	9	4.0
2000—Arkansas	11	2.0
2001—Arkansas	10	1.0
College totals (4 years)	41	12.0

HANNAM, RYAN — TE — SEAHAWKS

PERSONAL: Born February 24, 1980, in St. Ansgar, Iowa. ... 6-2/251.
HIGH SCHOOL: St. Ansgar (Iowa).
COLLEGE: Northern Iowa.
TRANSACTIONS/CAREER NOTES: Selected by Seattle Seahawks in fifth round (169th pick overall) of 2002 NFL draft.

		RECEIVING			
Year Team	G	No.	Yds.	Avg.	TD
1998—Northern Iowa	11	2	39	19.5	1
1999—Northern Iowa	11	23	253	11.0	5
2000—Northern Iowa	11	18	261	14.5	1
2001—Northern Iowa	14	43	404	9.4	0
College totals (4 years)	47	86	957	11.1	7

HARPER, ALAN — DT — JETS

PERSONAL: Born September 6, 1979, in Fontana, Calif. ... 6-1/285.
HIGH SCHOOL: Fontana (Calif.).
COLLEGE: Fresno State.
TRANSACTIONS/CAREER NOTES: Selected by New York Jets in fourth round (121st pick overall) of 2002 NFL draft.
HONORS: Named defensive tackle on THE SPORTING NEWS college All-America second team (2001).

		INTERCEPTIONS				SACKS
Year Team	G	No.	Yds.	Avg.	TD	No.
1998—Fresno State	11	0	0	0.0	0	1.0
1999—Fresno State	13	0	0	0.0	0	5.0
2000—Fresno State	12	0	0	0.0	0	3.0
2001—Fresno State	14	1	5	5.0	0	12.0
College totals (4 years)	50	1	5	5.0	0	21.0

HARRINGTON, JOEY — QB — LIONS

PERSONAL: Born October 21, 1978, in Portland, Ore. ... 6-4/215. ... Full name: John Joseph Harrington.
HIGH SCHOOL: Central Catholic (Portland, Ore.).
COLLEGE: Oregon.
TRANSACTIONS/CAREER NOTES: Selected by Detroit Lions in first round (third pick overall) of 2002 NFL draft.
HONORS: Named quarterback on THE SPORTING NEWS college All-America second team (2001).
COLLEGE NOTES: Caught one pass for 18 yards and touchdown (2000); caught one pass for one yard and intercepted one pass for 21 yards (2001).

		PASSING							RUSHING				TOTALS	
Year Team	G	Att.	Cmp.	Pct.	Yds.	TD	Int.	Avg.	Rat.	Att.	Yds.	Avg.	TD	TD	Pts.
1998—Oregon	1	1	0	0.0	0	0	0	0.0	0.0	0	0	0.0	0	0	0
1999—Oregon	8	158	84	53.2	1180	10	3	7.47	133.0	24	30	1.3	4	4	24
2000—Oregon	12	405	214	52.8	2967	22	14	7.33	125.4	66	124	1.9	7	8	48
2001—Oregon	12	364	214	58.8	2764	27	6	7.59	143.8	55	56	1.0	0	7	42
College totals (4 years)	33	928	512	55.2	6911	59	23	7.45	133.8	145	210	1.4	11	19	114

HARRIS, NAPOLEON — LB — RAIDERS

PERSONAL: Born February 25, 1979, in Dixmoor, Ill. ... 6-3/253. ... Full name: Napoleon Bill Harris.
HIGH SCHOOL: Thornton (Chicago).
COLLEGE: Northwestern.
TRANSACTIONS/CAREER NOTES: Selected by Oakland Raiders in first round (23rd pick overall) of 2002 NFL draft.

		INTERCEPTIONS				SACKS
Year Team	G	No.	Yds.	Avg.	TD	No.
1998—Northwestern	12	1	8	8.0	0	0.0
1999—Northwestern	10	0	0	0.0	0	3.0
2000—Northwestern	12	2	50	25.0	0	3.0
2001—Northwestern	11	1	0	0.0	0	3.0
College totals (4 years)	45	4	58	14.5	0	9.0

HARRISON, TYREO — LB — EAGLES

PERSONAL: Born May 15, 1980, in Sulphur Springs, Texas. ... 6-2/238. ... Full name: Tyreo Tremayne Harrison.
HIGH SCHOOL: Sulphur Springs (Texas).
COLLEGE: Notre Dame.
TRANSACTIONS/CAREER NOTES: Selected by Philadelphia Eagles in sixth round (198th pick overall) of 2002 NFL draft. ... Signed by Eagles (May 13, 2002).

Year Team	G	SACKS
1998—Notre Dame	6	1.0
1999—Notre Dame	12	0.0
2000—Notre Dame	11	1.0
2001—Notre Dame	11	2.0
College totals (4 years)	40	4.0

HARTWIG, JUSTIN — G — TITANS

PERSONAL: Born November 21, 1978, in Mankato, Minn. ... 6-4/300.
HIGH SCHOOL: Valley (West Des Moines, Iowa).
COLLEGE: Kansas.
TRANSACTIONS/CAREER NOTES: Selected by Tennessee Titans in sixth round (187th pick overall) of 2002 NFL draft.
COLLEGE PLAYING EXPERIENCE: Kansas, 1997-2001. ... Games played: 1997 (redshirted), 1998 (4), 1999 (12), 2000 (11), 2001 (11). Total: 38.

HATCH, JEFF — OT — GIANTS

PERSONAL: Born September 28, 1979, in Millersville, Md. ... 6-6/302.
HIGH SCHOOL: Severn (Millersville, Md.).
COLLEGE: Pennsylvania.
TRANSACTIONS/CAREER NOTES: Selected by New York Giants in third round (78th pick overall) of 2002 NFL draft.
COLLEGE NOTES: Played defensive tackle (1999). ... Credited with one sack for eight-yard loss (1999).
COLLEGE PLAYING EXPERIENCE: Pennsylvania, 1999-2001. ... Games played: 1999 (statistics unavailable), 2000 (10), 2001 (9). Total: 19.

HAYGOOD, HERB — WR — BRONCOS

PERSONAL: Born December 29, 1977, in Sarasota, Fla. ... 5-11/193.
HIGH SCHOOL: Sarasota (Fla.).
COLLEGE: Michigan State.
TRANSACTIONS/CAREER NOTES: Selected by Denver Broncos in fifth round (144th pick overall) of 2002 NFL draft.
HONORS: Named kick returner on THE SPORTING NEWS college All-America second team (2001).

		RUSHING				RECEIVING				KICKOFF RETURNS				TOTALS	
Year Team	G	Att.	Yds.	Avg.	TD	No.	Yds.	Avg.	TD	No.	Yds.	Avg.	TD	TD	Pts.
1998—Michigan State	11	2	16	8.0	0	12	148	12.3	0	11	258	23.5	0	0	0
1999—Michigan State	12	2	24	12.0	0	11	145	13.2	1	26	534	20.5	0	1	6
2000—Michigan State	11	3	-4	-1.3	0	35	539	15.4	2	15	346	23.1	0	2	12
2001—Michigan State	12	1	6	6.0	0	57	808	14.2	4	24	632	26.3	2	6	36
College totals (4 years)	46	8	42	5.3	0	115	1640	14.3	7	76	1770	23.3	2	9	54

HAYNES, VERRON — FB — STEELERS

PERSONAL: Born February 17, 1979, in Bronx, N.Y. ... 5-9/224.
HIGH SCHOOL: North Springs (Atlanta).
COLLEGE: Western Kentucky, then Georgia.
TRANSACTIONS/CAREER NOTES: Selected by Pittsburgh Steelers in fifth round (166th pick overall) of 2002 NFL draft.

		RUSHING				RECEIVING				TOTALS	
Year Team	G	Att.	Yds.	Avg.	TD	No.	Yds.	Avg.	TD	TD	Pts.
1997—Western Kentucky	9	59	305	5.2	2	0	0	0.0	0	2	12
1998—Georgia						Did not play.					
1999—Georgia	1	1	1	1.0	0	0	0	0.0	0	0	0
2000—Georgia	11	10	46	4.6	1	0	0	0.0	0	1	6
2001—Georgia	10	126	691	5.5	7	19	242	12.7	2	9	54
College totals (4 years)	31	196	1043	5.3	10	19	242	12.7	2	12	72

HAYNESWORTH, ALBERT — DT — TITANS

PERSONAL: Born June 17, 1981, in Hartsville, S.C. ... 6-6/320. ... Full name: Albert Haynesworth III.
HIGH SCHOOL: Hartsville (S.C.).
COLLEGE: Tennessee.
TRANSACTIONS/CAREER NOTES: Selected after junior season by Tennessee Titans in first round (15th pick overall) of 2002 NFL draft.

Year Team	G	SACKS
1999—Tennessee	10	0.0
2000—Tennessee	11	3.5
2001—Tennessee	12	1.5
College totals (3 years)	33	5.0

HEINRICH, KEITH — TE — PANTHERS

PERSONAL: Born March 19, 1979, in Tomball, Texas. ... 6-5/255.
HIGH SCHOOL: Tomball (Texas).
COLLEGE: Sam Houston State.
TRANSACTIONS/CAREER NOTES: Selected by Carolina Panthers in sixth round (174th pick overall) of 2002 NFL draft.

		RECEIVING			
Year Team	G	No.	Yds.	Avg.	TD
1998—Sam Houston State	5	7	56	8.0	0
1999—Sam Houston State	11	12	175	14.6	1
2000—Sam Houston State	11	25	224	9.0	1
2001—Sam Houston State	13	45	595	13.2	7
College totals (4 years)	40	89	1050	11.8	9

HEITMANN, ERIC — G — 49ERS

PERSONAL: Born February 24, 1980, in Brookshire, Texas. ... 6-3/305.
HIGH SCHOOL: Katy (Texas).
COLLEGE: Stanford.
TRANSACTIONS/CAREER NOTES: Selected by San Francisco 49ers in seventh round (239th pick overall) of 2002 NFL draft.
HONORS: Named guard on THE SPORTING NEWS college All-America second team (2001).
COLLEGE PLAYING EXPERIENCE: Stanford, 1998-2001. ... Games played: 1998 (11), 1999 (11), 2000 (11), 2001 (11). Total: 44.

HENDERSON, JOHN — DT — JAGUARS

PERSONAL: Born January 9, 1979, in Nashville, Tenn. ... 6-7/318. ... Full name: John Nathan Henderson.
HIGH SCHOOL: Pearl-Cohn (Nashville, Tenn.).
COLLEGE: Tennessee.
TRANSACTIONS/CAREER NOTES: Selected by Jacksonville Jaguars in first round (ninth pick overall) of 2002 NFL draft.
HONORS: Named defensive tackle on THE SPORTING NEWS college All-America first team (2000 and 2001).

Year Team	G	SACKS
1999—Tennessee	11	4.0
2000—Tennessee	11	12.0
2001—Tennessee	10	4.5
College totals (3 years)	32	20.5

HENRY, LEONARD — RB — DOLPHINS

PERSONAL: Born January 5, 1978, in Clinton, N.C. ... 6-1/206.
HIGH SCHOOL: Clinton (N.C.).
COLLEGE: East Carolina.
TRANSACTIONS/CAREER NOTES: Selected by Miami Dolphins in seventh round (241st pick overall) of 2002 NFL draft.
HONORS: Named running back on THE SPORTING NEWS college All-America third team (2001).

		RUSHING				RECEIVING			TOTALS	
Year Team	G	Att.	Yds.	Avg.	TD	No.	Yds.	Avg.	TD	TD	Pts.
1997—East Carolina						Redshirted.					
1998—East Carolina	10	125	634	5.1	4	2	18	9.0	0	4	24
1999—East Carolina	11	77	312	4.1	1	8	64	8.0	0	1	6
2000—East Carolina	11	133	711	5.3	8	18	137	7.6	1	9	54
2001—East Carolina	11	184	1432	7.8	16	26	210	8.1	2	18	108
College totals (4 years)	43	519	3089	6.0	29	54	429	7.9	3	32	192

HILL, CHARLES — DT — TEXANS

PERSONAL: Born November 1, 1980, in Palmer Park, Md. ... 6-2/293. ... Full name: Charles LeDawnta Hill.
HIGH SCHOOL: Eleanor Roosevelt (Palmer Park, Md.).
COLLEGE: Maryland.
TRANSACTIONS/CAREER NOTES: Selected by Houston Texans in third round (83rd pick overall) of 2002 NFL draft.

Year Team	G	SACKS
1998—Maryland	9	1.0
1999—Maryland	10	0.0
2000—Maryland	9	3.0
2001—Maryland	11	2.0
College totals (4 years)	39	6.0

HILL, DARRELL — WR — TITANS

PERSONAL: Born June 19, 1979, in Chicago. ... 6-3/197.
HIGH SCHOOL: Mount Carmel (Chicago).
COLLEGE: Northern Illinois.
TRANSACTIONS/CAREER NOTES: Selected by Tennessee Titans in seventh round (225th pick overall) of 2002 NFL draft.

		RECEIVING			
Year Team	G	No.	Yds.	Avg.	TD
1997—Northern Illinois		Did not play.			
1998—Northern Illinois	11	23	367	16.0	4
1999—Northern Illinois	11	47	850	18.1	4
2000—Northern Illinois	14	58	1337	23.1	8
2001—Northern Illinois	11	30	514	17.1	3
College totals (4 years)	47	158	3068	19.4	19

HILL, KAHLIL — WR — FALCONS

PERSONAL: Born March 18, 1979, in Iowa City, Iowa. ... 6-2/200.
HIGH SCHOOL: Iowa City (Iowa).
COLLEGE: Iowa.
TRANSACTIONS/CAREER NOTES: Selected by Atlanta Falcons in sixth round (184th pick overall) of 2002 NFL draft.

		RUSHING				RECEIVING				PUNT RETURNS				KICKOFF RETURNS				TOTALS	
Year Team	G	Att.	Yds.	Avg.	TD	No.	Yds.	Avg.	TD	No.	Yds.	Avg.	TD	No.	Yds.	Avg.	TD	TD	Pts.
1998—Iowa	11	1	6	6.0	0	35	432	12.3	2	10	177	17.7	2	18	465	25.8	1	5	30
1999—Iowa							Did not play.												
2000—Iowa	12	1	3	3.0	0	58	619	10.7	5	16	153	9.6	0	25	680	27.2	1	6	36
2001—Iowa	12	3	0	0.0	0	59	841	14.3	8	19	226	11.9	0	15	364	24.3	0	8	48
College totals (3 years)	35	5	9	1.8	0	152	1892	12.4	15	45	556	12.4	2	58	1509	26.0	2	19	114

HILL, MATT — OT — SEAHAWKS

PERSONAL: Born November 10, 1978, in Grangeville, Idaho. ... 6-6/300.
HIGH SCHOOL: Grangeville (Idaho).
COLLEGE: Boise State.
TRANSACTIONS/CAREER NOTES: Selected by Seattle Seahawks in fifth round (171st pick overall) of 2002 NFL draft.
COLLEGE NOTES: Played defensive tackle (1998 and 1999). ... Recorded $1^{1}/_{2}$ sacks (1999).
COLLEGE PLAYING EXPERIENCE: Boise State, 1998-2001. ... Games played: 1998 (5), 1999 (12), 2000 (12), 2001 (12). Total: 41.

HOPE, CHRIS — S — STEELERS

PERSONAL: Born September 29, 1980, in Rock Hill, S.C. ... 6-0/204.
HIGH SCHOOL: Rock Hill (S.C.).
COLLEGE: Florida State.
TRANSACTIONS/CAREER NOTES: Selected by Pittsburgh Steelers in third round (94th pick overall) of 2002 NFL draft.
HONORS: Named free safety on THE SPORTING NEWS college All-America second team (2000).
COLLEGE NOTES: Returned one punt for 10 yards (2001).

				INTERCEPTIONS		
Year	Team	G	No.	Yds.	Avg.	TD
1998—Florida State		12	0	0	0.0	0
1999—Florida State		11	4	17	4.3	0
2000—Florida State		12	2	11	5.5	0
2001—Florida State		11	3	0	0.0	0
College totals (4 years)		46	9	28	3.1	0

HOUGHTON, MIKE — G/OT — PACKERS

PERSONAL: Born December 1, 1979, in Northridge, Calif. ... 6-5/313. ... Full name: Michael Christopher Houghton.
HIGH SCHOOL: Mission Bay (San Diego).
COLLEGE: San Diego State.
TRANSACTIONS/CAREER NOTES: Selected by Green Bay Packers in sixth round (200th pick overall) of 2002 NFL draft.
COLLEGE PLAYING EXPERIENCE: San Diego State, 1997-2001. ... Games played: 1997 (redshirted), 1998 (did not play), 1999 (12), 2000 (12), 2001 (11). Total: 35.

HUNTER, JAVIN — WR — RAVENS

PERSONAL: Born May 9, 1980, in Detroit. ... 5-11/190. ... Full name: Javin Edward Hunter.
HIGH SCHOOL: Detroit Country Day (Beverly Hills, Mich.).
COLLEGE: Notre Dame.
TRANSACTIONS/CAREER NOTES: Selected by Baltimore Ravens in sixth round (206th pick overall) of 2002 NFL draft.

			RUSHING				RECEIVING				TOTALS	
Year	Team	G	Att.	Yds.	Avg.	TD	No.	Yds.	Avg.	TD	TD	Pts.
1998—Notre Dame		7	1	15	15.0	0	0	0	0.0	0	0	0
1999—Notre Dame		12	1	13	13.0	0	13	224	17.2	0	0	0
2000—Notre Dame		9	1	23	23.0	0	13	256	19.7	3	3	18
2001—Notre Dame		11	0	0	0.0	0	37	387	10.5	1	1	6
College totals (4 years)		39	3	51	17.0	0	63	867	13.8	4	4	24

HUNTER, PETE — CB — COWBOYS

PERSONAL: Born May 25, 1980, in Atlantic City, N.J. ... 6-2/202. ... Full name: Ralph Hunter.
HIGH SCHOOL: Atlantic City (N.J.).
COLLEGE: Virginia Union.
TRANSACTIONS/CAREER NOTES: Selected by Dallas Cowboys in fifth round (168th pick overall) of 2002 NFL draft.

			INTERCEPTIONS				SACKS
Year	Team	G	No.	Yds.	Avg.	TD	No.
1998—Virginia Union		10	0	0	0.0	0	0.0
1999—Virginia Union		10	6	133	22.2	0	2.0
2000—Virginia Union		11	3	56	18.7	0	1.0
2001—Virginia Union		11	11	93	8.5	0	0.0
College totals (4 years)		42	20	282	14.1	0	3.0

JAMMER, QUENTIN — CB — CHARGERS

PERSONAL: Born June 19, 1979, in Angleton, Texas. ... 5-11/204. ... Full name: Quentin T. Jammer.
HIGH SCHOOL: Angleton (Texas).
COLLEGE: Texas.
TRANSACTIONS/CAREER NOTES: Selected by San Diego Chargers in first round (fifth pick overall) of 2002 NFL draft.
HONORS: Named cornerback on THE SPORTING NEWS college All-America first team (2001).

			INTERCEPTIONS				SACKS
Year	Team	G	No.	Yds.	Avg.	TD	No.
1997—Texas		11	0	0	0.0	0	0.0
1998—Texas		11	2	18	9.0	0	1.0
1999—Texas		1	0	0	0.0	0	0.0
2000—Texas		11	3	11	3.7	0	1.0
2001—Texas		12	2	0	0.0	0	0.0
College totals (5 years)		46	7	29	4.1	0	2.0

JARRETT, CRAIG — P — SEAHAWKS

PERSONAL: Born July 17, 1979, in Martinsville, Ind. ... 6-2/215.
HIGH SCHOOL: Martinsville (Ind.).
COLLEGE: Michigan State.
TRANSACTIONS/CAREER NOTES: Selected by Seattle Seahawks in sixth round (194th pick overall) of 2002 NFL draft.

			PUNTING					
Year	Team	G	No.	Yds.	Avg.	Net avg.	In. 20	Blk.
1998—Michigan State	...	64	2803	43.8	...	17	2
1999—Michigan State	...	62	2699	43.5	...	14	1
2000—Michigan State	...	62	2528	40.8	...	17	1
2001—Michigan State	...	51	2225	43.6	...	15	7
College totals (4 years)	...	239	10255	42.9	...	63	11

JEFFERSON, JOSEPH — CB — COLTS

PERSONAL: Born February 15, 1980, in Russelville, Ky. ... 5-11/205. ... Full name: Joseph Jefferson Jr.
HIGH SCHOOL: Logan County (Adairville, Ky.).
COLLEGE: Western Kentucky.
TRANSACTIONS/CAREER NOTES: Selected by Indianapolis Colts in third round (74th pick overall) of 2002 NFL draft.

		INTERCEPTIONS			SACKS	PUNT RETURNS				KICKOFF RETURNS				TOTALS	
Year Team	G	No.	Yds.	Avg.	TD	No.	No.	Yds.	Avg.	TD	No.	Yds.	Avg.	TD	TD	Pts.
1998—Western Kentucky	11	1	0	0.0	0	1.0	3	113	37.7	0	0	0	0.0	0	0	0
1999—Western Kentucky	9	0	0	0.0	0	1.5	5	41	8.2	0	10	207	20.7	0	0	0
2000—Western Kentucky	13	6	137	22.8	0	0.0	19	215	11.3	1	4	124	31.0	0	1	6
2001—Western Kentucky	12	1	30	30.0	0	1.0	26	440	16.9	1	11	248	22.5	0	1	6
College totals (4 years)	45	8	167	20.9	0	3.5	53	809	15.3	2	25	579	23.2	0	2	12

JOHNSON, DENNIS — DE — CARDINALS

PERSONAL: Born December 4, 1979, in Danville, Ky. ... 6-5/258. ... Full name: Dennis Alan Johnson.
HIGH SCHOOL: Harrodburg (Ky.).
COLLEGE: Kentucky.
TRANSACTIONS/CAREER NOTES: Selected after junior season by Arizona Cardinals in third round (98th pick overall) of 2002 NFL draft.

Year Team	G	SACKS
1998—Kentucky	11	2.0
1999—Kentucky	11	5.0
2000—Kentucky	1	0.0
2001—Kentucky	11	12.0
College totals (4 years)	34	19.0

JOHNSON, DEVEREN — WR — COWBOYS

PERSONAL: Born January 1, 1980, in San Diego. ... 6-4/211.
JUNIOR COLLEGE: Champlain Junior College (Vt.).
COLLEGE: Sacred Heart.
TRANSACTIONS/CAREER NOTES: Selected by Dallas Cowboys in sixth round (208th pick overall) of 2002 NFL draft.

		RECEIVING			
Year Team	G	No.	Yds.	Avg.	TD
1998—Champlain Junior College		Statistics unavailable.			
1999—Champlain Junior College		Statistics unavailable.			
2000—Sacred Heart	11	38	593	15.6	6
2001—Sacred Heart	11	50	1157	23.1	13
College totals (2 years)	22	88	1750	19.9	19

JOHNSON, KYLE — FB — PANTHERS

PERSONAL: Born December 15, 1978, in Woodbridge, N.J. ... 6-0/242. ... Full name: Albert Kyle Johnson.
HIGH SCHOOL: Woodbridge (N.J.).
COLLEGE: Syracuse.
TRANSACTIONS/CAREER NOTES: Selected by Carolina Panthers in fifth round (145th pick overall) of 2002 NFL draft.

		RUSHING				RECEIVING				TOTALS	
Year Team	G	Att.	Yds.	Avg.	TD	No.	Yds.	Avg.	TD	TD	Pts.
1997—Syracuse	3	6	26	4.3	0	0	0	0.0	0	0	0
1998—Syracuse	6	6	33	5.5	1	0	0	0.0	0	1	6
1999—Syracuse	11	32	157	4.9	3	6	40	6.7	1	4	24
2000—Syracuse	1	5	27	5.4	1	1	1	1.0	0	1	6
2001—Syracuse	12	52	223	4.3	3	6	75	12.5	1	4	24
College totals (5 years)	33	101	466	4.6	8	13	116	8.9	2	10	60

JOHNSON, RON — WR — RAVENS

PERSONAL: Born May 23, 1980, in Detroit. ... 6-2/225.
HIGH SCHOOL: Martin Luther King (Detroit).
COLLEGE: Minnesota.
TRANSACTIONS/CAREER NOTES: Selected by Baltimore Ravens in fourth round (123rd pick overall) of 2002 NFL draft.
COLLEGE NOTES: Attempted one pass without a completion (1999). ... Attempted two passes with one completion for two yards and one touchdown (2001).

		RUSHING				RECEIVING				PUNT RETURNS				KICKOFF RETURNS				TOTALS	
Year Team	G	Att.	Yds.	Avg.	TD	No.	Yds.	Avg.	TD	No.	Yds.	Avg.	TD	No.	Yds.	Avg.	TD	TD	Pts.
1998—Minnesota	11	0	0	0.0	0	38	395	10.4	4	0	0	0.0	0	0	0	0.0	0	4	24
1999—Minnesota	12	0	0	0.0	0	43	574	13.3	7	0	0	0.0	0	0	0	0.0	0	7	42
2000—Minnesota	12	1	-27	-27.0	0	61	1125	18.4	11	8	69	8.6	0	3	53	17.7	0	11	66
2001—Minnesota	11	0	0	0.0	0	56	895	16.0	9	0	0	0.0	0	0	0	0.0	0	9	54
College totals (4 years)	46	1	-27	-27.0	0	198	2989	15.1	31	8	69	8.6	0	3	53	17.7	0	31	186

JOLLEY, DOUG — TE — RAIDERS

PERSONAL: Born January 2, 1979, in St. George, Utah. ... 6-4/251.
HIGH SCHOOL: Dixie (St. George, Utah).
COLLEGE: Brigham Young.
TRANSACTIONS/CAREER NOTES: Selected by Oakland Raiders in second round (55th pick overall) of 2002 NFL draft.
COLLEGE NOTES: Punted one time for 19 yards (1999). ... Rushed one time for nine yard loss (2000).

			RECEIVING		
Year Team	G	No.	Yds.	Avg.	TD
1999—Brigham Young	8	6	63	10.5	3
2000—Brigham Young	9	14	213	15.2	1
2001—Brigham Young	13	32	492	15.4	7
College totals (3 years)	30	52	768	14.8	11

JONES, DARYL — WR — GIANTS

PERSONAL: Born February 2, 1979, in Dallas. ... 5-9/175. ... Full name: Daryl Lawrence Jones.
HIGH SCHOOL: Carter (Dallas).
COLLEGE: Miami (Fla.).
TRANSACTIONS/CAREER NOTES: Selected by New York Giants in seventh round (226th pick overall) of 2002 NFL draft.

		RECEIVING				PUNT RETURNS				KICKOFF RETURNS				TOTALS	
Year Team	G	No.	Yds.	Avg.	TD	No.	Yds.	Avg.	TD	No.	Yds.	Avg.	TD	TD	Pts.
1997—Miami (Fla.)	11	16	252	15.8	2	0	0	0.0	0	0	0	0.0	0	2	12
1998—Miami (Fla.)	11	12	146	12.2	2	0	0	0.0	0	3	44	14.7	0	3	18
1999—Miami (Fla.)							Redshirted.								
2000—Miami (Fla.)	11	12	181	15.1	1	7	169	24.1	1	13	351	27.0	0	0	0
2001—Miami (Fla.)	6	19	240	12.6	0	4	20	5.0	0	0	0	0.0	0	0	0
College totals (4 years)	39	59	819	13.9	5	11	189	17.2	1	16	395	24.7	0	5	30

JONES, LEVI — OT — BENGALS

PERSONAL: Born August 24, 1979, in Eloy, Ariz. ... 6-5/304. ... Full name: Levi J. Jones.
HIGH SCHOOL: Santa Cruz (Eloy, Ariz.).
COLLEGE: Arizona State.
TRANSACTIONS/CAREER NOTES: Selected by Cincinnati Bengals in first round (10th pick overall) of 2002 NFL draft.
COLLEGE NOTES: Played defensive and offensive tackle (1998 and 2000). ... Credited with one sack (1998).
COLLEGE PLAYING EXPERIENCE: Arizona State, 1997-2001. ... Games: 1997 (redshirted), 1998 (10), 1999 (12), 2000 (12), 2001 (11). Total: 46.

JONES, TERRY — TE — RAVENS

PERSONAL: Born December 3, 1979, in Tuscaloosa, Ala. ... 6-3/265. ... Full name: Terry Jones Jr.
HIGH SCHOOL: Central (Tuscaloosa, Ala.).
COLLEGE: Alabama.
TRANSACTIONS/CAREER NOTES: Selected by Baltimore Ravens in fifth round (155th pick overall) of 2002 NFL draft.

			RECEIVING		
Year Team	G	No.	Yds.	Avg.	TD
1998—Alabama	11	0	0	0.0	0
1999—Alabama	11	13	201	15.5	1
2000—Alabama	5	6	123	20.5	0
2001—Alabama	11	12	156	13.0	2
College totals (4 years)	38	31	480	15.5	3

KAMPMAN, AARON — DT/DE — PACKERS

PERSONAL: Born November 30, 1979, in Kelsey, Iowa. ... 6-4/286.
HIGH SCHOOL: Aplington-Parkersburg (Parkersburg, Iowa).
COLLEGE: Iowa.
TRANSACTIONS/CAREER NOTES: Selected by Green Bay Packers in fifth round (156th pick overall) of 2002 NFL draft.

			INTERCEPTIONS			SACKS
Year Team	G	No.	Yds.	Avg.	TD	No.
1998—Iowa	9	0	0	0.0	0	6.0
1999—Iowa	11	0	0	0.0	0	0.0
2000—Iowa	12	1	0	0.0	0	3.0
2001—Iowa	12	2	14	7.0	0	9.0
College totals (4 years)	44	3	14	4.7	0	18.0

KEISEL, BRETT — DE — STEELERS

PERSONAL: Born September 19, 1978, in Provo, Utah. ... 6-5/269.
HIGH SCHOOL: Greybull (Wyo.).
JUNIOR COLLEGE: Snow Junior College (Utah).

COLLEGE: Brigham Young.
TRANSACTIONS/CAREER NOTES: Selected by Pittsburgh Steelers in seventh round (242nd pick overall) of 2002 NFL draft.

Year Team	G	SACKS
1998—Brigham Young	5	0.0
1999—Snow College	Statistics unavailable.	
2000—Brigham Young	12	5.0
2001—Brigham Young	13	4.0
College totals (3 years)	30	9.0

KELLY, JEFF — QB — SEAHAWKS

PERSONAL: Born September 7, 1979, in Deerpark, Ala. ... 6-1/210.
HIGH SCHOOL: Citronelle (Deerpark, Ark.).
COLLEGE: Southern Mississippi.
TRANSACTIONS/CAREER NOTES: Selected by Seattle Seahawks in seventh round (232nd pick overall) of 2002 NFL draft.

		PASSING							RUSHING				TOTALS	
Year Team	G	Att.	Cmp.	Pct.	Yds.	TD	Int.	Avg.	Rat.	Att.	Yds.	Avg.	TD	TD	Pts.
1998—Southern Mississippi	7	12	6	50.0	39	0	0	3.25	77.3	3	-10	-3.3	0	0	0
1999—Southern Mississippi	11	260	153	58.8	2062	21	11	7.93	143.7	50	-58	-1.2	1	1	6
2000—Southern Mississippi	11	341	198	58.1	2381	15	11	6.98	124.8	148	54	0.4	4	4	24
2001—Southern Mississippi	11	362	214	59.1	2613	15	11	7.22	127.3	95	32	0.3	3	3	18
College totals (4 years)	40	975	571	58.6	7095	51	33	7.28	130.2	296	18	0.1	8	8	48

KITTNER, KURT — QB — FALCONS

PERSONAL: Born January 23, 1980, in Schaumburg, Ill. ... 6-2/221.
HIGH SCHOOL: Schaumburg (Ill.).
COLLEGE: Illinois.
TRANSACTIONS/CAREER NOTES: Selected by Atlanta Falcons in fifth round (158th pick overall) of 2002 NFL draft.
COLLEGE NOTES: Caught one pass for 30 yards and a touchdown (1999).

		PASSING							RUSHING				TOTALS	
Year Team	G	Att.	Cmp.	Pct.	Yds.	TD	Int.	Avg.	Rat.	Att.	Yds.	Avg.	TD	TD	Pts.
1998—Illinois	9	162	72	44.4	782	1	7	4.83	78.4	43	28	0.7	2	2	12
1999—Illinois	12	396	216	54.5	2702	24	5	6.82	129.3	67	83	1.2	1	0	0
2000—Illinois	10	297	173	58.2	1982	18	8	6.67	124.8	44	61	1.4	2	2	12
2001—Illinois	12	409	221	54.0	3256	27	14	7.96	135.8	42	-14	-0.3	2	2	12
College totals (4 years)	43	1264	682	54.0	8722	70	34	6.90	124.8	196	158	0.8	7	6	36

KNIGHT, BRYAN — LB — BEARS

PERSONAL: Born January 22, 1979, in Buffalo. ... 6-2/240. ... Full name: Bryan Jerome Knight.
HIGH SCHOOL: St. Joseph (Buffalo).
COLLEGE: Pittsburgh.
TRANSACTIONS/CAREER NOTES: Selected by Chicago Bears in fifth round (165th pick overall) of 2002 NFL draft.

		INTERCEPTIONS				SACKS
Year Team	G	No.	Yds.	Avg.	TD	No.
1998—Pittsburgh	11	0	0	0.0	0	0.5
1999—Pittsburgh	11	1	-3	-3.0	0	3.0
2000—Pittsburgh	11	0	0	0.0	0	11.5
2001—Pittsburgh	11	0	0	0.0	0	8.5
College totals (4 years)	44	1	-3	-3.0	0	23.5

KOSIER, KYLE — OT — 49ERS

PERSONAL: Born January 27, 1978, in Peoria, Ariz. ... 6-5/293. ... Full name: Kyle Blaine Kosier.
HIGH SCHOOL: Cactus (Peoria, Ariz.).
COLLEGE: Arizona State.
TRANSACTIONS/CAREER NOTES: Selected by San Francisco 49ers in seventh round (248th pick overall) of 2002 NFL draft.
COLLEGE PLAYING EXPERIENCE: Arizona State, 1997-2001. ... Games played: 1997 (redshirted), 1998 (1), 1999 (10), 2000 (12), 2001 (11). Total: 34.

LEBER, BEN — LB — CHARGERS

PERSONAL: Born December 7, 1978, in Vermillion, S.D. ... 6-3/244.
HIGH SCHOOL: Vermillion (S.D.).
COLLEGE: Kansas State.
TRANSACTIONS/CAREER NOTES: Selected by San Diego Chargers in third round (71st pick overall) of 2002 NFL draft.

		INTERCEPTIONS				SACKS
Year Team	G	No.	Yds.	Avg.	TD	No.
1998—Kansas State	10	0	0	0.0	0	2.0
1999—Kansas State	11	0	0	0.0	0	2.0
2000—Kansas State	13	1	4	4.0	0	3.5
2001—Kansas State	11	0	0	0.0	0	6.0
College totals (4 years)	45	1	4	4.0	0	13.5

LELIE, ASHLEY — WR — BRONCOS

PERSONAL: Born February 16, 1980, in Bellflower, Calif. ... 6-3/200.
HIGH SCHOOL: Radford (Honolulu, Hawaii).
COLLEGE: Hawaii.
TRANSACTIONS/CAREER NOTES: Selected after junior season by Denver Broncos in first round (19th pick overall) of 2002 NFL draft.
HONORS: Named wide receiver on THE SPORTING NEWS college All-America third team (2001).

			RECEIVING			
Year Team	G	No.	Yds.	Avg.	TD	
1999—Hawaii	12	36	518	14.4	2	
2000—Hawaii	12	74	1110	15.0	11	
2001—Hawaii	12	84	1713	20.4	19	
College totals (3 years)	36	194	3341	17.2	32	

LEWIS, JAMES — S — COLTS

PERSONAL: Born December 19, 1978, in Piscataway, N.J. ... 5-10/192. ... Full name: James Christopher Lewis Jr.
HIGH SCHOOL: Piscataway (N.J.).
COLLEGE: Miami (Fla.).
TRANSACTIONS/CAREER NOTES: Selected by Indianapolis Colts in sixth round (183rd pick overall) of 2002 NFL draft.

		INTERCEPTIONS				SACKS
Year Team	G	No.	Yds.	Avg.	TD	No.
1998—Miami (Fla.)	11	0	0	0.0	0	1.0
1999—Miami (Fla.)	12	0	0	0.0	0	1.5
2000—Miami (Fla.)	11	0	0	0.0	0	0.0
2001—Miami (Fla.)	11	3	112	37.3	1	0.0
College totals (4 years)	45	3	112	37.3	1	2.5

LEWIS, MICHAEL — S — EAGLES

PERSONAL: Born April 29, 1980, in Houston. ... 6-1/211.
HIGH SCHOOL: Lamar Consolidated (Richmond, Texas).
COLLEGE: Colorado.
TRANSACTIONS/CAREER NOTES: Selected by Philadelphia Eagles in second round (58th pick overall) of 2002 NFL draft.
HONORS: Named safety on THE SPORTING NEWS college All-America third team (2001).
COLLEGE NOTES: Returned one punt for 39 yards (1998).

		INTERCEPTIONS				SACKS
Year Team	G	No.	Yds.	Avg.	TD	No.
1998—Colorado	8	1	0	0.0	0	2.5
1999—Colorado	9	0	0	0.0	0	2.0
2000—Colorado	11	3	34	11.3	0	1.0
2001—Colorado	12	5	78	15.6	1	1.0
College totals (4 years)	40	9	112	12.4	1	6.5

LOCKETT, AARON — WR — BUCCANEERS

PERSONAL: Born September 6, 1978, in Tulsa, Okla. ... 5-7/155.
HIGH SCHOOL: Booker T. Washington (Tulsa, Okla.).
COLLEGE: Kansas State.
TRANSACTIONS/CAREER NOTES: Selected by Tampa Bay Buccaneers in seventh round (254th pick overall) of 2002 NFL draft.

		RUSHING				RECEIVING				PUNT RETURNS				KICKOFF RETURNS				TOTALS	
Year Team	G	Att.	Yds.	Avg.	TD	No.	Yds.	Avg.	TD	No.	Yds.	Avg.	TD	No.	Yds.	Avg.	TD	TD	Pts.
1997—Kansas State							Redshirted.													
1998—Kansas State	12	1	12	12.0	0	44	928	21.1	6	0	0	0.0	0	0	0	0.0	0	6	36
1999—Kansas State	11	3	-9	-3.0	0	33	531	16.1	3	0	0	0.0	0	0	0	0.0	0	3	18
2000—Kansas State	13	7	62	8.9	0	36	584	16.2	2	22	501	22.8	3	14	312	22.3	0	5	30
2001—Kansas State	11	4	4	1.0	0	24	357	14.9	3	32	344	10.8	0	14	397	28.4	1	4	24
College totals (4 years)	47	15	69	4.6	0	137	2400	17.5	14	54	845	15.6	3	28	709	25.3	1	18	108

LOTT, ANDRE — CB — REDSKINS

PERSONAL: Born May 31, 1979, in Memphis, Tenn. ... 5-10/194. ... Full name: Andre Marquette Lott.
HIGH SCHOOL: Melrose (Memphis, Tenn.).
COLLEGE: Tennessee.
TRANSACTIONS/CAREER NOTES: Selected by Washington Redskins in fifth round (159th pick overall) of 2002 NFL draft.

		INTERCEPTIONS				SACKS
Year Team	G	No.	Yds.	Avg.	TD	No.
1998—Tennessee	12	0	0	0.0	0	0.0
1999—Tennessee	11	1	0	0.0	0	0.0
2000—Tennessee	10	2	18	9.0	0	1.0
2001—Tennessee	10	0	0	0.0	0	1.0
College totals (4 years)	43	3	18	6.0	0	2.0

LOWE, OMARE — CB — DOLPHINS

PERSONAL: Born April 20, 1978, in Maple Valley, Wash. ... 6-0/196.
HIGH SCHOOL: Tacoma (Wash.).
COLLEGE: Washington.
TRANSACTIONS/CAREER NOTES: Selected by Miami Dolphins in fifth round (161st pick overall) of 2002 NFL draft.
COLLEGE NOTES: Caught one pass for 24 yards (2001).

		INTERCEPTIONS			SACKS
Year Team	G	No.	Yds.	Avg. TD	No.
1997—Washington			Redshirted.		
1998—Washington	9	1	0	0.0 0	0.0
1999—Washington	10	1	24	24.0 0	0.0
2000—Washington	11	2	7	3.5 0	0.0
2001—Washington	10	1	21	21.0 1	1.0
College totals (4 years)	40	5	52	10.4 1	1.0

LUZAR, CHRIS — TE — JAGUARS

PERSONAL: Born February 12, 1979, in Newport News, Va. ... 6-7/260. ... Full name: Christopher Myers Luzar.
HIGH SCHOOL: Lafayette (Williamsburg, Va.).
COLLEGE: Virginia.
TRANSACTIONS/CAREER NOTES: Selected by Jacksonville in fourth round (118th pick overall) of 2002 NFL draft.

		RECEIVING			
Year Team	G	No.	Yds.	Avg.	TD
1998—Virginia	11	3	9	3.0	0
1999—Virginia	11	8	60	7.5	0
2000—Virginia	9	9	149	16.6	0
2001—Virginia	12	33	380	11.5	0
College totals (4 years)	43	53	598	11.3	0

MALLARD, JOSH — DE — COLTS

PERSONAL: Born March 21, 1979, in Savannah, Ga. ... 6-1/261. ... Full name: Joshua B. Mallard.
HIGH SCHOOL: Benedictine Military Academy (Ga.).
COLLEGE: Georgia.
TRANSACTIONS/CAREER NOTES: Selected by Indianapolis Colts in seventh round (220th pick overall) of 2002 NFL draft.

Year Team	G	SACKS
1997—Georgia		Redshirted.
1998—Georgia	10	6.0
1999—Georgia	11	4.0
2000—Georgia	11	3.0
2001—Georgia	11	5.0
College totals (4 years)	43	18.0

MALLARD, WESLY — LB — GIANTS

PERSONAL: Born November 21, 1978, in Hinesville, Ga. ... 6-1/221.
HIGH SCHOOL: Hardaway (Columbus, Ga.).
COLLEGE: Oregon.
TRANSACTIONS/CAREER NOTES: Selected by New York Giants in sixth round (188th pick overall) of 2002 NFL draft.

		INTERCEPTIONS			SACKS
Year Team	G	No.	Yds.	Avg. TD	No.
1998—Oregon	12	0	0	0.0 0	0.0
1999—Oregon	4	0	0	0.0 0	0.0
2000—Oregon	11	0	0	0.0 0	2.0
2001—Oregon	12	2	14	7.0 0	3.0
College totals (4 years)	39	2	14	7.0 0	5.0

MANUEL, MARQUAND — S — BENGALS

PERSONAL: Born July 11, 1979, in Miami. ... 6-0/209. ... Full name: Marquand Alexander Manuel.
HIGH SCHOOL: Miami Senior (Fla.).
COLLEGE: Florida.
TRANSACTIONS/CAREER NOTES: Selected by Cincinnati Bengals in sixth round (181st pick overall) of 2002 NFL draft. ... Signed by Bengals (May 13, 2002).

		INTERCEPTIONS			SACKS
Year Team	G	No.	Yds.	Avg. TD	No.
1997—Florida			Redshirted.		
1998—Florida	11	1	29	29.0 0	3.0
1999—Florida	12	3	21	7.0 0	2.0
2000—Florida	12	1	16	16.0 0	0.0
2001—Florida	11	1	18	18.0 0	3.0
College totals (4 years)	46	6	84	14.0 0	8.0

MARTIN, JAMAR   FB   COWBOYS

PERSONAL: Born April 12, 1980, in Canton, Ohio. ... 5-11/244.
HIGH SCHOOL: McKinley (Canton, Ohio).
COLLEGE: Ohio State.
TRANSACTIONS/CAREER NOTES: Selected by Dallas Cowboys in fourth round (129th pick overall) of 2002 NFL draft.

			RUSHING				RECEIVING			TOTALS	
Year Team	G	Att.	Yds.	Avg.	TD	No.	Yds.	Avg.	TD	TD	Pts.
1998—Ohio State	11	12	34	2.8	1	5	68	13.6	0	1	6
1999—Ohio State	12	19	100	5.3	1	3	10	3.3	1	2	12
2000—Ohio State	12	8	6	0.8	2	1	13	13.0	0	2	12
2001—Ohio State	12	22	86	3.9	0	13	120	9.2	1	1	6
College totals (4 years)	47	61	226	3.7	4	22	211	9.6	2	6	36

MASSEY, CHRIS   C   RAMS

PERSONAL: Born August 21, 1979, in Charleston, W.Va. ... 6-0/245. ... Full name: Christopher Todd Massey.
HIGH SCHOOL: East Bank (W.Va.).
COLLEGE: Marshall.
TRANSACTIONS/CAREER NOTES: Selected by St. Louis Rams in seventh round (243rd pick overall) of 2002 NFL draft.
COLLEGE PLAYING EXPERIENCE: Marshall, 1998-2001. ... Games played: 1998 (11), 1999 (11), 2000 (11), 2001 (11). Total: 44.

MAYS, LEE   WR   STEELERS

PERSONAL: Born September 18, 1978, in Houston. ... 6-2/192.
HIGH SCHOOL: Westfield (Houston).
COLLEGE: Texas-El Paso.
TRANSACTIONS/CAREER NOTES: Selected by Pittsburgh Steelers in sixth round (202nd pick overall) of 2002 NFL draft.

			RUSHING				RECEIVING			KICKOFF RETURNS			TOTALS	
Year Team	G	Att.	Yds.	Avg.	TD	No.	Yds.	Avg.	TD	No.	Yds.	Avg.	TD	TD Pts.
1997—Texas-El Paso							Redshirted.							
1998—Texas-El Paso	11	0	0	0.0	0	17	196	11.5	3	11	234	21.3	0	0 0
1999—Texas-El Paso	12	5	36	7.2	0	60	881	14.7	9	13	226	17.4	0	9 54
2000—Texas-El Paso	11	4	17	4.3	0	71	1098	15.5	15	3	32	10.7	0	15 90
2001—Texas-El Paso	11	0	0	0.0	0	53	732	13.8	1	4	84	21.0	0	1 6
College totals (4 years)	45	9	53	5.9	0	201	2907	14.5	28	31	576	18.6	0	25 150

McADDLEY, JASON   WR   CARDINALS

PERSONAL: Born July 28, 1979, in Oak Ridge, Tenn. ... 6-1/203.
HIGH SCHOOL: Oak Ridge (Tenn.).
COLLEGE: Alabama.
TRANSACTIONS/CAREER NOTES: Selected by Arizona Cardinals in fifth round (149th pick overall) of 2002 NFL draft. ... Signed by Cardinals (June 5, 2002).
COLLEGE NOTES: Returned one punt for six yards (2000).

			RUSHING				RECEIVING			KICKOFF RETURNS			TOTALS	
Year Team	G	Att.	Yds.	Avg.	TD	No.	Yds.	Avg.	TD	No.	Yds.	Avg.	TD	TD Pts.
1997—Alabama							Redshirted.							
1998—Alabama	11	1	-1	-1.0	0	2	14	7.0	0	0	0	0.0	0	0 0
1999—Alabama	12	1	25	25.0	0	24	334	13.9	3	0	0	0.0	0	3 18
2000—Alabama	11	3	53	17.7	0	27	413	15.3	3	5	93	18.6	0	3 18
2001—Alabama	11	0	0	0.0	0	18	259	14.4	2	8	148	18.5	0	2 12
College totals (4 years)	45	5	77	15.4	0	71	1020	14.4	8	13	241	18.5	0	8 48

McCADAM, KEVIN   S   FALCONS

PERSONAL: Born March 6, 1979, in La Mesa, Calif. ... 6-1/219. ... Full name: Kevin Edward McCadam.
HIGH SCHOOL: El Capitan (Calif.).
JUNIOR COLLEGE: Grossmont College.
COLLEGE: Colorado State, then Virginia Tech.
TRANSACTIONS/CAREER NOTES: Selected by Atlanta Falcons in fifth round (148th pick overall) of 2002 NFL draft.

		INTERCEPTIONS			SACKS	PUNT RETURNS				KICKOFF RETURNS				TOTALS	
Year Team	G	No.	Yds.	Avg.	TD	No.	No.	Yds.	Avg.	TD	No.	Yds.	Avg.	TD	TD Pts.
1997—Colorado State								Redshirted.								
1998—Grossmont College								Did not play.								
1999—Grossmont College	...	0	0	0.0	0	0.0	21	379	18.0	0	25	640	25.6	1	1 6
2000—Virginia Tech	9	0	0	0.0	0	0.0	0	0	0.0	0	0	0	0.0	0	0 0
2001—Virginia Tech	11	3	0	0.0	1	2.0	0	0	0.0	0	0	0	0.0	0	2 12
Junior college totals (1 year)	...	0	0	0.0	0	0.0	21	379	18.0	0	25	640	25.6	1	1 6
College totals (2 years)	20	3	0	0.0	1	2.0	0	0	0.0	0	0	0	0.0	0	2 12

McCOWN, JOSH   QB   CARDINALS

PERSONAL: Born July 4, 1979, in Jacksonville, Texas. ... 6-4/223. ... Full name: Joshua McCown.
HIGH SCHOOL: Jacksonville (Texas).
COLLEGE: Southern Methodist, then Sam Houston State.
TRANSACTIONS/CAREER NOTES: Selected by Arizona Cardinals in third round (81st pick overall) of 2002 NFL draft.

– 459 –

Year Team	G	PASSING Att.	Cmp.	Pct.	Yds.	TD	Int.	Avg.	Rat.	RUSHING Att.	Yds.	Avg.	TD	TOTALS TD	Pts.
1998—SMU	9	99	46	46.5	619	7	8	6.25	106.2	51	35	0.7	0	0	0
1999—SMU	10	234	125	53.4	1434	11	10	6.13	111.9	69	-9	-0.1	1	1	6
2000—SMU	11	331	169	51.1	1969	9	16	5.95	100.3	78	175	2.2	3	3	18
2001—Sam Houston State	13	429	259	60.4	3481	32	12	8.11	147.6	198	201	1.0	6	6	36
College totals (4 years)	43	1093	599	54.8	7503	59	46	6.86	121.9	396	402	1.0	10	10	60

McGRAW, JON   S   JETS

PERSONAL: Born April 2, 1979, in Manhattan, Kan. ... 6-3/206.
HIGH SCHOOL: Riley County (Manhattan, Kan.).
COLLEGE: Kansas State.
TRANSACTIONS/CAREER NOTES: Selected by New York Jets in second round (57th pick overall) of 2002 NFL draft.

Year Team	G	INTERCEPTIONS No.	Yds.	Avg.	TD	SACKS No.
1998—Kansas State	12	1	3	3.0	0	0.0
1999—Kansas State	10	1	0	0.0	0	0.0
2000—Kansas State	12	3	71	23.7	1	2.0
2001—Kansas State	9	4	54	13.5	0	1.0
College totals (4 years)	43	9	128	14.2	1	3.0

McKINNEY, SETH   C   DOLPHINS

PERSONAL: Born June 12, 1979, in Austin, Texas. ... 6-3/300.
HIGH SCHOOL: Westlake (Austin, Texas).
JUNIOR COLLEGE: Lackawanna Junior College (Pa.).
COLLEGE: Texas A&M.
TRANSACTIONS/CAREER NOTES: Selected by Miami Dolphins in third round (90th pick overall) of 2002 NFL draft.
HONORS: Named center on THE SPORTING NEWS college All-America second team (2001).
COLLEGE PLAYING EXPERIENCE: Texas A&M, 1998-2001. ... Games played: 1998 (14), 1999 (12), 2000 (12), 2001 (12). Total: 50.

McKINNIE, BRYANT   OT   VIKINGS

PERSONAL: Born September 23, 1979, in Woodbury, N.J. ... 6-8/343. ... Full name: Bryant Douglas McKinnie.
HIGH SCHOOL: Woodbury (N.J.).
JUNIOR COLLEGE: Lackawanna Junior College (Pa.).
COLLEGE: Miami.
TRANSACTIONS/CAREER NOTES: Selected by Minnesota Vikings in first round (seventh pick overall) of 2002 NFL draft.
HONORS: Named offensive tackle on THE SPORTING NEWS college All-America first team (2001). ... Outland Trophy winner (2001).
COLLEGE PLAYING EXPERIENCE: Lackawanna Junior College, 1997 and 1998; Miami, 2000 and 2001. ... Games: 1997 (games played unavailable), 1998 (-), 2000 (11), 2001 (11). Total: 22.

McMICHAEL, RANDY   TE   DOLPHINS

PERSONAL: Born June 28, 1979, in Fort Valley, Ga. ... 6-3/247.
HIGH SCHOOL: Peach County (Fort Valley, Ga.).
COLLEGE: Georgia.
TRANSACTIONS/CAREER NOTES: Selected by Miami Dolphins in fourth round (114th pick overall) of 2002 NFL draft.

Year Team	G	RECEIVING No.	Yds.	Avg.	TD
1999—Georgia	11	34	457	13.4	3
2000—Georgia	11	32	475	14.8	1
2001—Georgia	10	24	281	11.7	1
College totals (3 years)	32	90	1213	13.5	5

METCALF, TERRENCE   OT/G   BEARS

PERSONAL: Born January 28, 1978, in Clarksdale, Miss. ... 6-3/318. ... Full name: Terrence Orlando Metcalf.
HIGH SCHOOL: Clarksdale (Miss.).
COLLEGE: Mississippi.
TRANSACTIONS/CAREER NOTES: Selected by Chicago Bears in third round (93rd pick overall) of 2002 NFL draft.
HONORS: Named guard on THE SPORTING NEWS college All-America second team (1999). ... Named offensive tackle on THE SPORTING NEWS college All-America third team (2001).
COLLEGE PLAYING EXPERIENCE: Mississippi, 1997-2001. ... Games played: 1997 (12), 1998 (2), 1999 (11), 2000 (11), 2001 (11). Total: 47.

MILLER, AHMAD   DT   TEXANS

PERSONAL: Born April 10, 1978, in Bradenton, Fla. ... 6-3/306. ... Full name: Ahmad Rasheed Miller.
HIGH SCHOOL: Bradenton Southeast (Fla.).
COLLEGE: UNLV.
TRANSACTIONS/CAREER NOTES: Selected by Houston Texans in seventh round (261st pick overall) of 2002 NFL draft..

Year Team	G	SACKS
1999—UNLV	11	2.0
2000—UNLV	12	1.0
2001—UNLV	11	2.0
College totals (3 years)	34	5.0

MILONS, FREDDIE — WR — EAGLES

PERSONAL: Born June 27, 1980, in Starkville, Miss. ... 5-11/190.
HIGH SCHOOL: Starkville (Miss.).
COLLEGE: Alabama.
TRANSACTIONS/CAREER NOTES: Selected by Philadelphia Eagles in fifth round (162nd pick overall) of 2002 NFL draft.
COLLEGE NOTES: Attempted four passes with three completions for 81 yards and one touchdown (1999).

		RUSHING				RECEIVING				PUNT RETURNS				KICKOFF RETURNS				TOTALS	
Year Team	G	Att.	Yds.	Avg.	TD	No.	Yds.	Avg.	TD	No.	Yds.	Avg.	TD	No.	Yds.	Avg.	TD	TD	Pts.
1998—Alabama	11	1	15	15.0	0	19	213	11.2	0	0	0	0.0	0	4	141	35.3	0	0	0
1999—Alabama	12	15	178	11.9	1	65	733	11.3	2	29	282	9.7	1	11	237	21.5	0	4	24
2000—Alabama	10	12	39	3.3	0	32	287	9.0	1	6	112	18.7	1	9	165	18.3	0	2	12
2001—Alabama	11	4	10	2.5	0	36	626	17.4	3	8	37	4.6	0	16	374	23.4	0	3	18
College totals (4 years)	44	32	242	7.6	1	152	1859	12.2	6	43	431	10.0	2	40	917	22.9	0	9	54

MITCHELL, MEL — CB — SAINTS

PERSONAL: Born February 2, 1979, in Rockledge, Fla. ... 6-1/220. ... Full name: Melvin Mitchell III.
HIGH SCHOOL: Rockledge (Fla.).
COLLEGE: Western Kentucky.
TRANSACTIONS/CAREER NOTES: Selected by New Orleans Saints in fifth round (150th pick overall) of 2002 NFL draft.

		INTERCEPTIONS				SACKS	KICKOFF RETURNS				TOTALS	
Year Team	G	No.	Yds.	Avg.	TD	No.	No.	Yds.	Avg.	TD	TD	Pts.
1999—Western Kentucky	11	1	0	0.0	0	0.5	0	0	0.0	0	0	0
2000—Western Kentucky	13	3	43	14.3	0	0.0	10	275	27.5	1	1	6
2001—Western Kentucky	12	3	29	9.7	0	0.0	10	295	29.5	1	1	6
College totals (3 years)	36	7	72	10.3	0	0.5	20	570	28.5	2	2	12

MONK, QUINCY — LB — GIANTS

PERSONAL: Born January 30, 1979, in Jacksonville, N.C. ... 6-3/250. ... Full name: Quincy Omar Monk.
HIGH SCHOOL: White Oak (Jacksonville, N.C.).
COLLEGE: North Carolina.
TRANSACTIONS/CAREER NOTES: Selected by New York Giants in seventh round (245th pick overall) of 2002 NFL draft.

		INTERCEPTIONS				SACKS
Year Team	G	No.	Yds.	Avg.	TD	No.
1997—North Carolina				Redshirted.		
1998—North Carolina	11	0	0	0.0	0	0.0
1999—North Carolina	11	0	0	0.0	0	2.0
2000—North Carolina	11	0	0	0.0	0	2.0
2001—North Carolina	11	2	1	0.5	0	0.0
College totals (4 years)	44	2	1	0.5	0	4.0

MONROE, DERRIUS — DE — SAINTS

PERSONAL: Born July 21, 1978, in Tallahassee, Fla. ... 6-4/269. ... Full name: Derrius Reshard Monroe.
HIGH SCHOOL: Godby (Tallahassee, Fla.).
COLLEGE: Virginia Tech.
TRANSACTIONS/CAREER NOTES: Selected by New Orleans Saints in seventh round (224th pick overall) of 2002 NFL draft.

Year Team	G	SACKS
1998—Virginia Tech	11	1.0
1999—Virginia Tech	11	0.0
2000—Virginia Tech		Did not play.
2001—Virginia Tech	10	2.0
College totals (3 years)	32	3.0

MORRIS, MAURICE — RB — SEAHAWKS

PERSONAL: Born December 1, 1979, in Chester, S.C. ... 5-11/208. ... Full name: Maurice Autora Morris.
HIGH SCHOOL: Chester (S.C.).
JUNIOR COLLEGE: Fresno City College.
COLLEGE: Oregon.
TRANSACTIONS/CAREER NOTES: Selected by Seattle Seahawks in second round (54th pick overall) of 2002 NFL draft.

		RUSHING				RECEIVING				TOTALS	
Year Team	G	Att.	Yds.	Avg.	TD	No.	Yds.	Avg.	TD	TD	Pts.
1998—Fresno City College	10	328	2085	6.4	26	0	0	0.0	0	26	156
1999—Fresno City College	10	265	1623	6.1	19	0	0	0.0	0	19	114
2000—Oregon	12	286	1188	4.2	8	23	208	9.0	2	10	60
2001—Oregon	11	180	1049	5.8	9	12	99	8.3	1	10	60
Junior college totals (2 years)	20	593	3708	6.3	45	0	0	0.0	0	45	270
College totals (2 years)	23	466	2237	4.8	17	35	307	8.8	3	20	120

MURPHY, MATT — TE — LIONS

PERSONAL: Born February 23, 1980, in New Haven, Mich. ... 6-5/253.
HIGH SCHOOL: New Haven (Mich.).
COLLEGE: Maryland.
TRANSACTIONS/CAREER NOTES: Selected by Detroit Lions in seventh round (252nd pick overall) of 2002 NFL draft.

		RECEIVING			
Year Team	G	No.	Yds.	Avg.	TD
1998—Maryland	...	0	0	0.0	0
1999—Maryland	...	0	0	0.0	0
2000—Maryland	...	0	0	0.0	0
2001—Maryland	...	15	179	11.9	0
College totals (4 years)	...	15	179	11.9	0

NALL, CRAIG — QB — PACKERS

PERSONAL: Born April 21, 1979, in Alexandria, La. ... 6-3/227. ... Full name: Craig Matthew Nall.
HIGH SCHOOL: Alexandria (La.).
COLLEGE: Louisiana State, then Northwestern State.
TRANSACTIONS/CAREER NOTES: Selected by Green Bay Packers in fifth round (164th pick overall) of 2002 NFL draft.

		PASSING							RUSHING				TOTALS	
Year Team	G	Att.	Cmp.	Pct.	Yds.	TD	Int.	Avg.	Rat.	Att.	Yds.	Avg.	TD	TD	Pts.
1997—Louisiana State					Redshirted.										
1998—Louisiana State	8	57	28	49.1	340	0	2	5.96	92.2	0	0	0.0	0	0	0
1999—Louisiana State	6	20	7	35.0	91	0	2	4.55	53.2	0	0	0.0	0	0	0
2000—Louisiana State	3	2	0	0.0	0	0	0	0.0	0.0	0	0	0.0	0	0	0
2001—Northwestern State	12	250	142	56.8	2022	11	3	8.09	136.9	0	0	0.0	0	0	0
College totals (4 years)	29	329	177	53.8	2453	11	7	7.46	123.2	0	0	0.0	0	0	0

NASH, KEYON — CB — RAIDERS

PERSONAL: Born March 11, 1979, in Colquitt, Ga. ... 6-3/215.
HIGH SCHOOL: Miller County (Ga.).
COLLEGE: Albany State.
TRANSACTIONS/CAREER NOTES: Selected by Oakland Raiders in sixth round (189th pick overall) of 2002 NFL draft.

		INTERCEPTIONS			
Year Team	G	No.	Yds.	Avg.	TD
1998—Albany State		Statistics unavailable.			
1999—Albany State		Statistics unavailable.			
2000—Albany State		Statistics unavailable.			
2001—Albany State	9	2	7	3.5	0
College totals (1 years)	9	2	7	3.5	0

NED, LARRY — RB — RAIDERS

PERSONAL: Born August 23, 1978, in Eunice, La. ... 5-11/215. ... Full name: Larry Lee Ned Jr.
HIGH SCHOOL: Rancho Verde (Calif.).
COLLEGE: San Diego State.
TRANSACTIONS/CAREER NOTES: Selected by Oakland Raiders in sixth round (197th pick overall) of 2002 NFL draft.

		RUSHING				RECEIVING				TOTALS	
Year Team	G	Att.	Yds.	Avg.	TD	No.	Yds.	Avg.	TD	TD	Pts.
1997—San Diego State					Did not play.						
1998—San Diego State	...	153	762	5.0	0	0	0	0.0	0	0	0
1999—San Diego State	...	162	894	5.5	0	13	161	12.4	0	0	0
2000—San Diego State	...	139	357	2.6	6	0	0	0.0	0	6	36
2001—San Diego State	...	311	1612	5.2	0	16	138	8.6	0	15	90
College totals (4 years)	...	765	3625	4.7	6	29	299	10.3	0	21	126

NEWSON, KENDALL — WR — JAGUARS

PERSONAL: Born March 5, 1980, in Decatur, Ga. ... 6-1/195. ... Full name: Kendall Montrae Newson.
HIGH SCHOOL: Columbia (Decatur, Ga.).
COLLEGE: Middle Tennessee.
TRANSACTIONS/CAREER NOTES: Selected by Jacksonville Jaguars in seventh round (222nd pick overall) of 2002 NFL draft.

		RECEIVING			
Year Team	G	No.	Yds.	Avg.	TD
1998—Middle Tennessee State	10	30	415	13.8	4
1999—Middle Tennessee State	11	69	918	13.3	5
2000—Middle Tennessee State	11	74	945	12.8	5
2001—Middle Tennessee State	11	65	796	12.2	7
College totals (4 years)	43	238	3074	12.9	21

O'SULLIVAN, J.T.   QB   SAINTS

PERSONAL: Born August 25, 1979, in Burbank, Calif. ... 6-2/220. ... Full name: John Thomas O'Sullivan.
HIGH SCHOOL: Jesuit (Folsom, Calif.).
COLLEGE: California-Davis.
TRANSACTIONS/CAREER NOTES: Selected by New Orleans Saints in sixth round (186th pick overall) of 2002 NFL draft.

			PASSING						RUSHING			TOTALS	
Year Team	G	Att.	Cmp.	Pct.	Yds.	TD	Int.	Avg.	Rat.	Att.	Yds.	Avg.	TD	TD	Pts.
1999—California-Davis	...	341	208	61.0	3217	26	0	9.43	165.4	0	0	0.0	0	0	0
2000—California-Davis	...	318	204	64.2	3679	38	0	11.57	200.8	70	473	6.8	4	4	24
2001—California-Davis	...	406	255	62.8	3826	32	0	9.42	168.0	92	371	4.0	2	2	12
College totals (3 years)	...	1065	667	62.6	10722	96	0	10.07	176.9	162	844	5.2	6	6	36

OFFORD, WILLIE   S   VIKINGS

PERSONAL: Born December 22, 1978, in Palatka, Fla. ... 6-1/215.
HIGH SCHOOL: Palatka (Fla.).
COLLEGE: South Carolina.
TRANSACTIONS/CAREER NOTES: Selected by Minnesota Vikings in third round (70th pick overall) of 2002 NFL draft.

		INTERCEPTIONS				SACKS
Year Team	G	No.	Yds.	Avg.	TD	No.
1998—South Carolina	10	0	0	0.0	0	0.0
1999—South Carolina	11	0	0	0.0	0	0.0
2000—South Carolina	11	1	2	2.0	0	1.0
2001—South Carolina	12	1	2	2.0	0	1.0
College totals (4 years)	44	2	4	2.0	0	2.0

OVERSTREET, WILL   LB   FALCONS

PERSONAL: Born October 7, 1979, in Jackson, Miss. ... 6-2/259. ... Full name: William Sparkman Overstreet.
HIGH SCHOOL: Jackson (Miss.) Prep.
COLLEGE: Tennessee.
TRANSACTIONS/CAREER NOTES: Selected by Atlanta Falcons in third round (80th pick overall) of 2002 NFL draft.

		INTERCEPTIONS				SACKS
Year Team	G	No.	Yds.	Avg.	TD	No.
1998—Tennessee	12	0	0	0.0	0	2.0
1999—Tennessee	11	0	0	0.0	0	7.5
2000—Tennessee	11	1	0	0.0	0	4.5
2001—Tennessee	10	0	0	0.0	0	5.0
College totals (4 years)	44	1	0	0.0	0	19.0

OWENS, JOHN   TE   LIONS

PERSONAL: Born January 10, 1980, in Washington, D.C. ... 6-3/266. ... Full name: John Wesley Owens.
HIGH SCHOOL: DeMatha (Hyattsville, Md.).
COLLEGE: Notre Dame.
TRANSACTIONS/CAREER NOTES: Selected by Detroit Lions in fifth round (138th pick overall) of 2002 NFL draft.
COLLEGE NOTES: Played defensive end (1999). ... Recorded one sack (1999).

		RECEIVING			
Year Team	G	No.	Yds.	Avg.	TD
1998—Notre Dame	10	0	0	0.0	0
1999—Notre Dame	9	0	0	0.0	0
2000—Notre Dame	11	0	0	0.0	0
2001—Notre Dame	11	6	79	13.2	1
College totals (4 years)	41	6	79	13.2	1

PALEPOI, ANTON   DE   SEAHAWKS

PERSONAL: Born January 19, 1978, in American Samoa. ... 6-3/279. ... Full name: Anton Charles Palepoi.
HIGH SCHOOL: Hunter (Salt Lake City, Utah).
JUNIOR COLLEGE: Dixie College (Utah).
COLLEGE: UNLV.
TRANSACTIONS/CAREER NOTES: Selected by Seattle Seahawks in second round (60th pick overall) of 2002 NFL draft.

Year Team	G	SACKS
1998—Dixie College	Statistics unavailable.	
1999—Dixie College	Statistics unavailable.	
2000—UNLV	12	8.0
2001—UNLV	6	4.5
College totals (2 years)	18	12.5

PATE, WES   QB   RAVENS

PERSONAL: Born March 24, 1979, in Longview, Texas. ... 6-2/228. ... Full name: John Wesley Pate.
HIGH SCHOOL: Arp (Texas).
COLLEGE: Louisiana Tech, then Stephen F. Austin State.
TRANSACTIONS/CAREER NOTES: Selected by Baltimore Ravens in seventh round (236th pick overall) of 2002 NFL draft.

PEARSON, MIKE — OT — JAGUARS

					PASSING						RUSHING			TOTALS	
Year Team	G	Att.	Cmp.	Pct.	Yds.	TD	Int.	Avg.	Rat.	Att.	Yds.	Avg.	TD	TD	Pts.
1997—Louisiana Tech						Redshirted.									
1998—Louisiana Tech	10	26	12	46.2	149	2	1	5.73	112.0	0	0	0.0	0	0	0
1999—Stephen F. Austin State	11	245	117	47.8	1840	17	8	7.51	127.2	0	0	0.0	0	0	0
2000—Stephen F. Austin State	8	236	118	50.0	1592	13	11	6.75	115.5	0	0	0.0	0	0	0
2001—Stephen F. Austin State	10	333	197	59.2	2626	19	8	7.89	139.4	0	0	0.0	0	0	0
College totals (4 years)	39	840	444	52.9	6207	51	28	7.39	128.3	0	0	0.0	0	0	0

PERSONAL: Born August 2, 1980, in Tampa, Fla. ... 6-7/304. ... Full name: Michael Wayne Pearson.
HIGH SCHOOL: Armwood (Seffner, Fla.).
COLLEGE: Florida.
TRANSACTIONS/CAREER NOTES: Selected after junior season by Jacksonville Jaguars in second round (40th pick overall) of 2002 NFL draft.
HONORS: Named offensive tackle on THE SPORTING NEWS college All-America first team (2001).
COLLEGE PLAYING EXPERIENCE: Florida, 1998-2001. ... Games played: 1998 (redshirted), 1999 (10), 2000 (12), 2001 (11). Total: 33.

PEELLE, JUSTIN — TE — CHARGERS

PERSONAL: Born March 15, 1979, in Fresno, Calif. ... 6-4/255. ... Full name: Justin Morris Peelle.
HIGH SCHOOL: Dublin (Calif.).
COLLEGE: Oregon.
TRANSACTIONS/CAREER NOTES: Selected by San Diego Chargers in fourth round (103rd pick overall) of 2002 NFL draft.

			RECEIVING		
Year Team	G	No.	Yds.	Avg.	TD
1998—Oregon	7	0	0	0.0	0
1999—Oregon	11	5	65	13.0	0
2000—Oregon	12	24	388	16.2	5
2001—Oregon	12	34	491	14.4	9
College totals (4 years)	42	63	944	15.0	14

PEPPERS, JULIUS — DE — PANTHERS

PERSONAL: Born January 18, 1980, in Wilson, N.C. ... 6-6/283. ... Full name: Julius Frazier Peppers.
HIGH SCHOOL: Southern Nash (Bailey, N.C.).
COLLEGE: North Carolina.
TRANSACTIONS/CAREER NOTES: Selected after junior season by Carolina Panthers in first round (second pick overall) of 2002 NFL draft.
HONORS: Lombardi Award winner (2001). ... Chuck Bednarik Award winner (2001). ... Named defensive end on THE SPORTING NEWS college All-America first team (2001).

			INTERCEPTIONS			SACKS
Year Team	G	No.	Yds.	Avg.	TD	No.
1999—North Carolina	11	1	0	0.0	0	6.0
2000—North Carolina	11	1	27	27.0	1	15.0
2001—North Carolina	12	3	42	14.0	0	9.5
College totals (3 years)	34	5	69	13.8	1	30.5

PETERS, SCOTT — C/G — EAGLES

PERSONAL: Born November 23, 1978, in Pleasanton, Calif. ... 6-3/300. ... Full name: Scott Thomas Peters.
HIGH SCHOOL: Amador Valley (Pleasanton, Calif.).
COLLEGE: Arizona State.
TRANSACTIONS/CAREER NOTES: Selected by Philadelphia Eagles in fourth round (124th pick overall) of 2002 NFL draft.
COLLEGE PLAYING EXPERIENCE: Arizona State, 1997-2001. ... Games played: 1997 (redshirted), 1998 (11), 1999 (12), 2000 (12), 2001 (11). Total: 46.

PETERSON, ADRIAN — RB — BEARS

PERSONAL: Born July 1, 1979, in Gainesville, Fla. ... 5-10/214.
HIGH SCHOOL: Sante Fe (Alachua, Fla.).
COLLEGE: Georgia Southern.
TRANSACTIONS/CAREER NOTES: Selected by Chicago Bears in sixth round (199th pick overall) of 2002 NFL draft.

			RUSHING				RECEIVING			TOTALS	
Year Team	G	Att.	Yds.	Avg.	TD	No.	Yds.	Avg.	TD	TD	Pts.
1998—Georgia Southern	11	257	1932	7.5	25	5	33	6.6	1	26	156
1999—Georgia Southern	11	248	1807	7.3	28	9	163	18.1	1	29	174
2000—Georgia Southern	9	230	1345	5.8	14	3	16	5.3	0	15	90
2001—Georgia Southern	11	261	1459	5.6	18	4	12	3.0	0	18	108
College totals (4 years)	42	996	6543	6.6	85	21	224	10.7	3	88	528

PHILLIPS, JERMAINE — S — BUCCANEERS

PERSONAL: Born March 27, 1979, in Roswell, Ga. ... 6-1/214.
HIGH SCHOOL: Roswell (Ga.).
COLLEGE: Georgia.
TRANSACTIONS/CAREER NOTES: Selected by Tampa Bay Buccaneers in fifth round (157th pick overall) of 2002 NFL draft.
COLLEGE NOTES: Played wide receiver (1998 and 1999). ... Returned one punt for eight yards (1999).

		INTERCEPTIONS				RECEIVING			TOTALS	
Year Team	G	No.	Yds.	Avg.	TD	No.	Yds.	Avg.	TD	TD	Pts.
1997—Georgia						Redshirted.					
1998—Georgia	11	0	0	0.0	0	0	0	0.0	0	0	0
1999—Georgia	11	0	0	0.0	0	18	235	13.1	1	1	6
2000—Georgia	11	2	0	0.0	0	0	0	0.0	0	0	0
2001—Georgia	11	3	89	29.7	1	0	0	0.0	0	1	6
College totals (4 years)	44	5	89	17.8	1	18	235	13.1	1	2	12

PITTS, CHESTER — G — TEXANS

PERSONAL: Born June 26, 1979, in Inglewood, Calif. ... 6-4/320. ... Full name: Chester Morise Pitts II.
HIGH SCHOOL: California Academy for Math and Science (Los Angeles).
COLLEGE: San Diego State.
TRANSACTIONS/CAREER NOTES: Selected by Houston Texans in second round (50th pick overall) of 2002 NFL draft.
COLLEGE PLAYING EXPERIENCE: San Diego State, 1998-2001. ... Games played: 1998 (0), 1999 (1), 2000 (9), 2001 (11). Total: 21.

POPE, MONSANTO — DT — BRONCOS

PERSONAL: Born January 27, 1978, in Norfolk, Va. ... 6-3/300.
HIGH SCHOOL: Hopewell (Va.).
COLLEGE: Virginia.
TRANSACTIONS/CAREER NOTES: Selected by Denver Broncos in seventh round (231st pick overall) of 2002 NFL draft.

Year Team	G	SACKS
1998—Virginia	11	0.0
1999—Virginia	5	0.0
2000—Virginia	11	2.0
2001—Virginia	12	5.0
College totals (4 years)	39	7.0

PORTIS, CLINTON — RB — BRONCOS

PERSONAL: Born September 1, 1981, in Gainesville, Fla. ... 5-11/204. ... Full name: Clinton Earl Portis.
HIGH SCHOOL: Gainesville (Fla.).
COLLEGE: Miami (Fla.).
TRANSACTIONS/CAREER NOTES: Selected after junior season by Denver Broncos in second round (51st pick overall) of 2002 NFL draft.

		RUSHING				RECEIVING				TOTALS	
Year Team	G	Att.	Yds.	Avg.	TD	No.	Yds.	Avg.	TD	TD	Pts.
1999—Miami (Fla.)	10	143	838	5.9	8	4	44	11.0	2	10	60
2000—Miami (Fla.)	8	77	485	6.3	2	5	103	20.6	0	2	12
2001—Miami (Fla.)	11	220	1200	5.5	10	12	125	10.4	1	11	66
College totals (3 years)	29	440	2523	5.7	20	21	272	13.0	3	23	138

PUCILLO, MIKE — G — BILLS

PERSONAL: Born July 14, 1979, in Cleveland. ... 6-4/316. ... Full name: Michael Pucillo.
HIGH SCHOOL: Brandon (Fla.).
COLLEGE: Auburn.
TRANSACTIONS/CAREER NOTES: Selected by Buffalo Bills in seventh round (215th pick overall) of 2002 NFL draft.
COLLEGE PLAYING EXPERIENCE: Auburn, 1997-2001. ... Games played: 1997 (redshirted), 1998 (5), 1999 (10), 2000 (12), 2001 (11). Total: 38.

PUGH, DAVID — DT — COLTS

PERSONAL: Born July 24, 1979, in Madison Heights, Va. ... 6-2/270. ... Full name: David Winston Pugh Jr.
HIGH SCHOOL: Amerherst County (Va.).
COLLEGE: Virginia Tech.
TRANSACTIONS/CAREER NOTES: Selected by Indianapolis Colts in sixth round (182nd pick overall) of 2002 NFL draft.
HONORS: Named defensive tackle on THE SPORTING NEWS college All-America third team (2001).

		INTERCEPTIONS				SACKS
Year Team	G	No.	Yds.	Avg.	TD	No.
1998—Virginia Tech	11	0	0	0.0	0	1.0
1999—Virginia Tech	11	0	0	0.0	0	4.0
2000—Virginia Tech	11	1	0	0.0	0	5.0
2001—Virginia Tech	10	0	0	0.0	0	3.5
College totals (4 years)	43	1	0	0.0	0	13.5

2002 DRAFT PICKS

PUTZIER, JEB — TE — BRONCOS

PERSONAL: Born January 20, 1979, in Eagle, Idaho. ... 6-4/256.
HIGH SCHOOL: Eagle (Idaho).
COLLEGE: Boise State.
TRANSACTIONS/CAREER NOTES: Selected by Denver Broncos in sixth round (191st pick overall) of 2002 NFL draft.

		RECEIVING			
Year Team	G	No.	Yds.	Avg.	TD
1997—Boise State			Redshirted.		
1998—Boise State	...	10	120	12.0	2
1999—Boise State	...	39	514	13.2	2
2000—Boise State	...	35	592	16.9	3
2001—Boise State	...	44	824	18.7	12
College totals (4 years)	...	128	2050	16.0	19

QUACCIA, ZACK — G — BUCCANEERS

PERSONAL: Born April 20, 1979, in Oakdale, Calif. ... 6-4/309.
HIGH SCHOOL: Oakdale (Calif.).
COLLEGE: Stanford.
TRANSACTIONS/CAREER NOTES: Selected by Tampa Bay Buccaneers in seventh round (255th pick overall) of 2002 NFL draft.
COLLEGE PLAYING EXPERIENCE: Stanford, 1998-2001. ... Games played: 1998 (11), 1999 (11), 2000 (8), 2001 (11). Total: 41.

RAMSEY, PATRICK — QB — REDSKINS

PERSONAL: Born February 14, 1979, in Ruston, La. ... 6-2/219. ... Full name: Patrick Allen Ramsey.
HIGH SCHOOL: Ruston (La.).
COLLEGE: Tulane.
TRANSACTIONS/CAREER NOTES: Selected by Washington Redskins in first round (32nd pick overall) of 2002 NFL draft.

		PASSING								RUSHING				TOTALS	
Year Team	G	Att.	Cmp.	Pct.	Yds.	TD	Int.	Avg.	Rat.	Att.	Yds.	Avg.	TD	TD	Pts.
1998—Tulane	3	5	3	60.0	27	1	0	5.40	171.4	4	-5	-1.3	0	0	0
1999—Tulane	11	513	310	60.4	3410	25	24	6.65	123.0	64	-61	-1.0	0	1	6
2000—Tulane	10	389	229	58.9	2833	24	14	7.28	133.2	39	53	1.4	2	2	12
2001—Tulane	11	448	256	57.1	2935	22	13	6.55	122.6	45	-115	-2.6	1	1	6
College totals (4 years)	35	1355	798	58.9	9205	72	51	6.79	126.0	152	-128	-0.8	3	4	24

RANDLE EL, ANTWAAN — WR — STEELERS

PERSONAL: Born August 17, 1979, in Markham, Ill. ... 5-10/184.
HIGH SCHOOL: Thornton (Riverdale, Ill.).
COLLEGE: Indiana.
TRANSACTIONS/CAREER NOTES: Selected by Pittsburgh Steelers in second round (62nd pick overall) of 2002 NFL draft.
COLLEGE NOTES: Punted one time for 31 yards (1998). ... Punted three times for 117 yards (1999). ... Punted five times for 181 yards (2000). ... Punted eight times for 240 yards and returned 16 punts for 149 yards (2001).

		PASSING							RUSHING				RECEIVING				TOTALS	
Year Team	G	Att.	Cmp.	Pct.	Yds.	TD	Int.	Avg.	Att.	Yds.	Avg.	TD	No.	Yds.	Avg.	TD	TD	Pts.
1998—Indiana	11	273	127	46.5	1745	6	11	6.39	227	873	3.8	10	2	54	27.0	1	11	66
1999—Indiana	11	279	150	53.8	2277	17	7	8.16	224	788	3.5	13	1	6	6.0	0	13	78
2000—Indiana	11	277	133	48.0	1783	10	14	6.44	218	1270	5.8	13	0	0	0.0	0	13	78
2001—Indiana	11	231	118	51.1	1664	9	5	7.20	188	964	5.1	8	4	30	7.5	0	8	48
College totals (4 years)	44	1060	528	49.8	7469	42	37	7.05	857	3895	4.5	44	7	90	12.9	1	45	270

RASHEED, SALEEM — LB — 49ERS

PERSONAL: Born June 15, 1981, in Birmingham, Ala. ... 6-2/229.
HIGH SCHOOL: Shades Valley (Birmingham, Ala.).
COLLEGE: Alabama.
TRANSACTIONS/CAREER NOTES: Selected after junior season by San Francisco in third round (69th pick overall) of 2002 NFL draft.

Year Team	G	SACKS
1999—Alabama	12	3.0
2000—Alabama	11	0.0
2001—Alabama	11	2.0
College totals (3 years)	34	5.0

REED, ED — S — RAVENS

PERSONAL: Born September 11, 1978, in St. Rose, La. ... 5-11/205. ... Full name: Edward Earl Reed.
HIGH SCHOOL: Destrehan (St. Rose, La.).
COLLEGE: Miami (Fla.).
TRANSACTIONS/CAREER NOTES: Selected by Baltimore Ravens in first round (24th pick overall) of 2002 NFL draft.
HONORS: Named free safety on THE SPORTING NEWS college All-America first team (2001).

			INTERCEPTIONS			SACKS	PUNT RETURNS			TOTALS	
Year Team	G	No.	Yds.	Avg.	TD	No.	No.	Yds.	Avg. TD	TD	Pts.
1997—Miami (Fla.)	2	0	0	0.0	0	0.0	0	0	0.0 0	0	0
1998—Miami (Fla.)	11	2	53	26.5	0	2.0	6	40	6.7 0	0	0
1999—Miami (Fla.)	12	2	38	19.0	0	4.0	2	29	14.5 0	0	0
2000—Miami (Fla.)	11	8	92	11.5	2	0.0	0	0	0.0 0	2	12
2001—Miami (Fla.)	11	9	206	22.9	2	0.0	4	54	13.5 0	2	12
College totals (5 years)	47	21	389	18.5	4	6.0	12	123	10.3 0	4	24

REED, JOSH — WR — BILLS

PERSONAL: Born May 1, 1980, in Lafayette, La. ... 5-10/203. ... Full name: Joshua Blake Reed.
HIGH SCHOOL: Rayne (La.).
COLLEGE: Louisiana State.
TRANSACTIONS/CAREER NOTES: Selected after junior season by Buffalo Bills in second round (36th pick overall) of 2002 NFL draft.
HONORS: Named wide receiver on THE SPORTING NEWS college All-America first team (2001). ... Fred Biletnikoff Award winner (2001).

		RUSHING				RECEIVING				PUNT RETURNS				KICKOFF RETURNS				TOTALS	
Year Team	G	Att.	Yds.	Avg.	TD	No.	Yds.	Avg.	TD	No.	Yds.	Avg.	TD	No.	Yds.	Avg.	TD	TD	Pts.
1999—Louisiana State	7	8	58	7.3	1	8	134	16.8	0	0	0	0.0	0	1	21	21.0	0	1	6
2000—Louisiana State	11	1	-2	-2.0	0	65	1127	17.3	10	0	0	0.0	0	0	0	0.0	0	10	60
2001—Louisiana State	12	2	7	3.5	0	94	1740	18.5	7	2	5	2.5	0	5	108	21.6	0	7	42
College totals (3 years)	30	11	63	5.7	1	167	3001	18.0	17	2	5	2.5	0	6	129	21.5	0	18	108

RICHARD, KRIS — CB — SEAHAWKS

PERSONAL: Born October 28, 1978, in Carson, Calif. ... 5-11/186.
HIGH SCHOOL: Serra (Gardena, Calif.).
COLLEGE: Southern California.
TRANSACTIONS/CAREER NOTES: Selected by Seattle Seahawks in third round (85th pick overall) of 2002 NFL draft.
COLLEGE NOTES: Returned kickoff one time for 20 yards (1998).

		INTERCEPTIONS				SACKS	PUNT RETURNS				TOTALS	
Year Team	G	No.	Yds.	Avg.	TD	No.	No.	Yds.	Avg.	TD	TD	Pts.
1998—Southern California	11	0	0	0.0	0	0.0	0	0	0.0	0	0	0
1999—Southern California	12	6	63	10.5	2	0.0	0	0	0.0	0	2	12
2000—Southern California	12	0	0	0.0	0	0.0	13	98	7.5	0	0	0
2001—Southern California	12	2	94	47.0	1	2.0	0	0	0.0	0	2	12
College totals (4 years)	47	8	157	19.6	3	2.0	13	98	7.5	0	4	24

RODRIGUEZ, MAURICE — LB — CHIEFS

PERSONAL: Born August 30, 1978, in Puerto Rico. ... 6-1/237.
HIGH SCHOOL: Redwood (Visalia, Calif.).
COLLEGE: Fresno State.
TRANSACTIONS/CAREER NOTES: Selected by Kansas City Chiefs in seventh round (221st pick overall) of 2002 NFL draft.

Year Team	G	SACKS
1999—Fresno State	9	1.0
2000—Fresno State	10	1.0
2001—Fresno State	13	1.0
College totals (3 years)	32	3.0

ROGERS, NICK — LB — VIKINGS

PERSONAL: Born May 31, 1979, in East Point, Ga. ... 6-2/251. ... Full name: Nicholas Quixote Rogers.
HIGH SCHOOL: St. Pius X (East Point, Ga.).
COLLEGE: Georgia Tech.
TRANSACTIONS/CAREER NOTES: Selected by Minnesota Vikings in sixth round (177th pick overall) of 2002 NFL draft.

		INTERCEPTIONS				SACKS
Year Team	G	No.	Yds.	Avg.	TD	No.
1998—Georgia Tech	5	0	0	0.0	0	0.0
1999—Georgia Tech	9	1	17	17.0	0	1.5
2000—Georgia Tech	11	0	0	0.0	0	9.0
2001—Georgia Tech	12	0	0	0.0	0	6.0
College totals (4 years)	37	1	17	17.0	0	16.5

ROGERS, VICTOR — OT — LIONS

PERSONAL: Born October 10, 1978, in Seattle. ... 6-6/331.
HIGH SCHOOL: Decatur (Federal Way, Wash.).
COLLEGE: Colorado.
TRANSACTIONS/CAREER NOTES: Selected by Detroit Lions in seventh round (259th pick overall) of 2002 NFL draft..
COLLEGE PLAYING EXPERIENCE: Colorado, 1997-2001. ... Games played: 1997 (redshirted), 1998 (7), 1999 (5), 2000 (10), 2001 (12). Total: 34.

ROSS, DEREK — CB — COWBOYS

PERSONAL: Born January 5, 1980, in Rock Hill, S.C. ... 5-10/210.
HIGH SCHOOL: Northwestern (Rock Hill, S.C.).
COLLEGE: Ohio State.
TRANSACTIONS/CAREER NOTES: Selected after junior season by Dallas Cowboys in third round (75th pick overall) of 2002 NFL draft.

			INTERCEPTIONS			SACKS	PUNT RETURNS				TOTALS	
Year Team	G	No.	Yds.	Avg.	TD	No.	No.	Yds.	Avg.	TD	TD	Pts.
1998—Ohio State	12	0	0	0.0	0	0.0	2	39	19.5	0	0	0
1999—Ohio State						Did not play.						
2000—Ohio State	12	2	23	11.5	0	0.0	0	0	0.0	0	0	0
2001—Ohio State	11	7	194	27.7	1	1.0	0	0	0.0	0	1	6
College totals (3 years)	35	9	217	24.1	1	1.0	2	39	19.5	0	1	6

ROYAL, ROBERT — TE — REDSKINS

PERSONAL: Born May 15, 1979, in New Orleans. ... 6-4/253. ... Full name: Robert Shelton Royal Jr.
HIGH SCHOOL: Karr (New Orleans).
COLLEGE: Louisiana State.
TRANSACTIONS/CAREER NOTES: Selected by Washington Redskins in fifth round (160th pick overall) of 2002 NFL draft.

		RECEIVING			
Year Team	G	No.	Yds.	Avg.	TD
1998—Louisiana State	9	0	0	0.0	0
1999—Louisiana State	10	19	143	7.5	1
2000—Louisiana State	11	22	340	15.5	5
2001—Louisiana State	12	18	224	12.4	1
College totals (4 years)	42	59	707	12.0	7

RUMPH, MIKE — CB — 49ERS

PERSONAL: Born November 8, 1979, in Delray Beach, Fla. ... 6-2/205. ... Full name: Michael Jamaine Rumph.
HIGH SCHOOL: Atlantic (Delray Beach, Fla.).
COLLEGE: Miami (Fla.).
TRANSACTIONS/CAREER NOTES: Selected by San Francisco 49ers in first round (27th pick overall) of 2002 NFL draft.

		INTERCEPTIONS			
Year Team	G	No.	Yds.	Avg.	TD
1998—Miami (Fla.)	11	1	0	0.0	0
1999—Miami (Fla.)	11	4	-3	-0.8	0
2000—Miami (Fla.)	11	1	45	45.0	1
2001—Miami (Fla.)	11	0	0	0.0	0
College totals (4 years)	44	6	42	7.0	1

RUSSELL, CLIFF — WR — REDSKINS

PERSONAL: Born February 8, 1979, in N.C. ... 5-11/185. ... Full name: Clifford Russell.
HIGH SCHOOL: Campbell (Ewa Beach, Hawaii).
COLLEGE: Utah.
TRANSACTIONS/CAREER NOTES: Selected by Washington Redskins in third round (87th pick overall) of 2002 NFL draft.

		RUSHING				RECEIVING				TOTALS	
Year Team	G	Att.	Yds.	Avg.	TD	No.	Yds.	Avg.	TD	TD	Pts.
1998—Utah	2	0	0	0.0	0	0	0	0.0	0	0	0
1999—Utah	9	1	6	6.0	0	34	601	17.7	3	3	18
2000—Utah	8	1	5	5.0	0	37	517	14.0	3	3	18
2001—Utah	11	5	26	5.2	0	53	744	14.0	4	4	24
College totals (4 years)	30	7	37	5.3	0	124	1862	15.0	10	10	60

SANDERS, DARNELL — TE — BROWNS

PERSONAL: Born March 16, 1979, in Warrensville Heights, Ohio. ... 6-6/267.
HIGH SCHOOL: Warrensville Heights (Ohio).
COLLEGE: Ohio State.
TRANSACTIONS/CAREER NOTES: Selected after junior season by Cleveland Browns in fourth round (122nd pick overall) of 2002 NFL draft.

		RECEIVING			
Year Team	G	No.	Yds.	Avg.	TD
1998—Ohio State			Redshirted.			
1999—Ohio State	11	1	7	7.0	1
2000—Ohio State	12	23	270	11.7	5
2001—Ohio State	12	18	197	10.9	3
College totals (3 years)	35	42	474	11.3	9

SCHIFINO, JAKE — WR — TITANS

PERSONAL: Born November 15, 1979, in Pittsburgh. ... 6-1/200.
HIGH SCHOOL: Penn Hills (Pa.).

COLLEGE: Akron.
TRANSACTIONS/CAREER NOTES: Selected by Tennessee Titans in fifth round (151st pick overall) of 2002 NFL draft.

Year Team	G	RECEIVING No.	Yds.	Avg.	TD
1998—Akron	9	16	250	15.6	2
1999—Akron	9	37	452	12.2	1
2000—Akron	11	42	778	18.5	4
2001—Akron	11	36	506	14.1	3
College totals (4 years)	40	131	1986	15.2	10

SCHOBEL, MATT TE BENGALS

PERSONAL: Born November 4, 1978, in Columbus, Texas. ... 6-5/263. ... Full name: Matthew Thomas Schobel.
HIGH SCHOOL: Columbus (Texas).
COLLEGE: Texas A&M, then Texas Christian.
TRANSACTIONS/CAREER NOTES: Selected by Cincinnati Bengals in third round (67th pick overall) of 2002 NFL draft. ... Signed by Bengals May 10, 2002.
COLLEGE NOTES: Attempted one pass with one completion for seven yards (1999).

Year Team	G	RECEIVING No.	Yds.	Avg.	TD
1997—Texas A&M		Redshirted.			
1998—Texas Christian		Did not play.			
1999—Texas Christian	10	4	26	6.5	0
2000—Texas Christian	10	4	42	10.5	1
2001—Texas Christian	10	19	310	16.3	5
College totals (3 years)	30	27	378	14.0	6

SCOBEY, JOSH RB CARDINALS

PERSONAL: Born December 11, 1979, in Oklahoma City, Okla. ... 5-11/218.
HIGH SCHOOL: Del City (Oklahoma City, Okla.).
JUNIOR COLLEGE: Northeastern A&M Community College (Okla.).
COLLEGE: Kansas State.
TRANSACTIONS/CAREER NOTES: Selected by Arizona Cardinals in sixth round (185th pick overall) of 2002 NFL draft.

Year Team	G	RUSHING Att.	Yds.	Avg.	TD	RECEIVING No.	Yds.	Avg.	TD	KICKOFF RETURNS No.	Yds.	Avg.	TD	TOTALS TD	Pts.
1998—Northeast Oklahoma A&M							Statistics unavailable.								
1999—Northeast Oklahoma A&M							Statistics unavailable.								
2000—Kansas State	13	169	718	4.2	16	4	29	7.3	0	0	0	0.0	0	16	96
2001—Kansas State	11	240	1263	5.3	15	9	52	5.8	0	4	55	13.8	0	15	90
College totals (2 years)	24	409	1981	4.8	31	13	81	6.2	0	4	55	13.8	0	31	186

SCOTT, GREG DE REDSKINS

PERSONAL: Born October 2, 1979, in Courtland, Va. ... 6-4/268.
HIGH SCHOOL: Southampton (Courtland, Va.).
COLLEGE: Hampton.
TRANSACTIONS/CAREER NOTES: Selected by Washington Redskins in seventh round (234th pick overall) of 2002 NFL draft.

Year Team	G	INTERCEPTIONS No.	Yds.	Avg.	TD	SACKS No.
1998—Hampton		Did not play.				
1999—Hampton	10	1	7	7.0	0	2.0
2000—Hampton	11	0	0	0.0	0	6.5
2001—Hampton	11	0	0	0.0	0	3.0
College totals (3 years)	32	1	7	7.0	0	11.5

SCOTT, TRAVIS G RAMS

PERSONAL: Born August 9, 1979, in Artesia, Calif. ... 6-6/300. ... Full name: Travis Lee Scott.
HIGH SCHOOL: Westwood (Mesa, Ariz.).
JUNIOR COLLEGE: Mesa (Ariz.) Community College.
COLLEGE: Arizona State.
TRANSACTIONS/CAREER NOTES: Selected by St. Louis Rams in fourth round (130th pick overall) of 2002 NFL draft.
COLLEGE PLAYING EXPERIENCE: Mesa (Ariz.) Community College, 1998 and 1999. ... Arizona State, 2000 and 2001. ... Games played: 1998 (games played unavailable), 1999 (-), 2000 (2), 2001 (11). Total: 13.

SHAFFER, KEVIN OT FALCONS

PERSONAL: Born March 2, 1980, in Salisbury, Md. ... 6-5/290.
HIGH SCHOOL: Conestoga (Md.).
COLLEGE: Tulsa.
TRANSACTIONS/CAREER NOTES: Selected by Atlanta Falcons in seventh round (244th pick overall) of 2002 NFL draft.
COLLEGE PLAYING EXPERIENCE: Tulsa, 1998-2001. ... Games played: 1998 (6), 1999 (11), 2000 (12), 2001 (11). Total: 40.

SHAW, JOSH — DT — 49ERS

PERSONAL: Born September 7, 1979, in Fort Lauderdale, Fla. ... 6-2/279.
HIGH SCHOOL: Dillard (Fort Lauderdale, Fla.).
COLLEGE: Michigan State.
TRANSACTIONS/CAREER NOTES: Selected by San Francisco 49ers in fifth round (172nd pick overall) of 2002 NFL draft.

Year — Team	G	SACKS
1998—Michigan State	12	1.0
1999—Michigan State	12	0.0
2000—Michigan State	10	2.0
2001—Michigan State	7	2.0
College totals (4 years)	41	5.0

SHEPPARD, LITO — CB — EAGLES

PERSONAL: Born April 8, 1981, in Jacksonville. ... 5-10/194. ... Full name: Lito Decorian Sheppard.
HIGH SCHOOL: Raines (Jacksonville).
COLLEGE: Florida.
TRANSACTIONS/CAREER NOTES: Selected after junior season by Philadelphia Eagles in first round (26th pick overall) of 2002 NFL draft.
HONORS: Named cornerback on The Sporting News college All-America second team (2000 and 2001).

		INTERCEPTIONS			PUNT RETURNS				KICKOFF RETURNS				TOTALS	
Year — Team	G	No.	Yds.	Avg.	TD	No.	Yds.	Avg.	TD	No.	Yds.	Avg.	TD	TD	Pts.
1999—Florida	11	0	0	0.0	0	1	6	6.0	0	1	3	3.0	0	0	0
2000—Florida	12	6	179	29.8	1	22	307	14.0	2	13	298	22.9	0	3	18
2001—Florida	11	2	7	3.5	0	26	246	9.5	0	7	171	24.4	0	0	0
College totals (3 years)	34	8	186	23.3	1	49	559	11.4	2	21	472	22.5	0	3	18

SHOCKEY, JEREMY — TE — GIANTS

PERSONAL: Born August 18, 1980, in Ada, Okla. ... 6-5/252. ... Full name: Jeremy Charles Shockey.
HIGH SCHOOL: Ada (Okla.).
JUNIOR COLLEGE: Northeastern A&M Community College (Okla.).
COLLEGE: Miami (Fla.).
TRANSACTIONS/CAREER NOTES: Selected after junior season by New York Giants in first round (14th pick overall) of 2002 NFL draft.

		RECEIVING			
Year — Team	G	No.	Yds.	Avg.	TD
1999—Northeast Oklahoma A&M	10	33	484	14.7	7
2000—Miami (Fla.)	10	21	296	14.1	3
2001—Miami (Fla.)	11	61	815	13.4	7
Junior college totals (1 year)	10	33	484	14.7	7
College totals (2 years)	21	82	1111	13.5	10

SIMMONS, KENDALL — G — STEELERS

PERSONAL: Born March 11, 1979, in Ripley, Miss. ... 6-3/313. ... Full name: Henry Alexander Kendall Simmons.
HIGH SCHOOL: Ripley (Miss.).
COLLEGE: Auburn.
TRANSACTIONS/CAREER NOTES: Selected by Pittsburgh Steelers in first round (30th pick overall) of 2002 NFL draft.
COLLEGE PLAYING EXPERIENCE: Auburn, 1997-2001. ... Games played: 1997 (11), 1998 (9), 1999 (3), 2000 (12), 2001 (11). Total: 46.

SIMMONS, SAM — WR — DOLPHINS

PERSONAL: Born November 25, 1979, in Kansas City, Kan. ... 5-9/200. ... Full name: Samuel Leeland Simmons.
HIGH SCHOOL: F.L. Schlagle (Kansas City, Kan.).
COLLEGE: Northwestern.
TRANSACTIONS/CAREER NOTES: Selected by Miami Dolphins in fifth round (170th pick overall) of 2002 NFL draft.

		RUSHING				RECEIVING				PUNT RETURNS				KICKOFF RETURNS				TOTALS	
Year — Team	G	Att.	Yds.	Avg.	TD	No.	Yds.	Avg.	TD	No.	Yds.	Avg.	TD	No.	Yds.	Avg.	TD	TD	Pts.
1998—Northwestern	11	31	124	4.0	1	5	132	26.4	1	0	0	0.0	0	22	607	27.6	0	2	12
1999—Northwestern	7	7	65	9.3	0	12	261	21.8	1	11	169	15.4	1	5	131	26.2	0	2	12
2000—Northwestern	11	11	61	5.5	0	38	498	13.1	5	13	172	13.2	0	9	198	22.0	0	5	30
2001—Northwestern	11	5	74	14.8	0	50	807	16.1	7	15	162	10.8	1	1	1	1.0	0	8	48
College totals (4 years)	40	54	324	6.0	1	105	1698	16.2	14	39	503	12.9	2	37	937	25.3	0	17	102

SIMS, RYAN — DT — CHIEFS

PERSONAL: Born May 4, 1980, in Spartanburg, S.C. ... 6-4/311. ... Full name: Ryan O'Neal Sims.
HIGH SCHOOL: Paul M. Dorman (Spartanburg, S.C.).
COLLEGE: North Carolina.
TRANSACTIONS/CAREER NOTES: Selected by Kansas City Chiefs in first round (sixth pick overall) of 2002 NFL draft.

Year Team	G	SACKS
1998—North Carolina	11	2.0
1999—North Carolina	11	1.0
2000—North Carolina	11	6.0
2001—North Carolina	11	5.0
College totals (4 years)	44	14.0

SLOWIKOWSKI, BOB — TE — COWBOYS

PERSONAL: Born October 30, 1979, in Pittsburgh. ... 6-5/261. ... Full name: Robert Joseph Slowikowski.
HIGH SCHOOL: Central Catholic (Pittsburgh).
COLLEGE: Virginia Tech.
TRANSACTIONS/CAREER NOTES: Selected by Dallas Cowboys in sixth round (211th pick overall) of 2002 NFL draft.

		RECEIVING			
Year Team	G	No.	Yds.	Avg.	TD
1998—Virginia Tech	11	2	40	20.0	0
1999—Virginia Tech	10	3	47	15.7	0
2000—Virginia Tech	11	3	101	33.7	1
2001—Virginia Tech	11	4	98	24.5	0
College totals (4 years)	43	12	286	23.8	1

SMITH, RAONALL — LB — VIKINGS

PERSONAL: Born October 22, 1978, in Mesa, Ariz. ... 6-2/244. ... Full name: Raonall Aarrig Smith.
HIGH SCHOOL: Peninsula (Gig Harbor, Wash.).
COLLEGE: Washington State.
TRANSACTIONS/CAREER NOTES: Selected by Minnesota Vikings in second round (38th pick overall) of 2002 NFL draft.

		INTERCEPTIONS			SACKS
Year Team	G	No.	Yds.	Avg.	TD	No.
1998—Washington State	6	0	0	0.0	0	2.0
1999—Washington State	8	0	0	0.0	0	0.0
2000—Washington State	11	0	0	0.0	0	3.0
2001—Washington State	11	1	54	54.0	1	0.5
College totals (4 years)	36	1	54	54.0	1	5.5

SMITH, STEVE — CB — JAGUARS

PERSONAL: Born June 28, 1979, in Torrance, Calif. ... 6-1/190. ... Full name: Steven Michael Smith.
HIGH SCHOOL: San Pedro (Calif.).
COLLEGE: Oregon.
TRANSACTIONS/CAREER NOTES: Selected by Jacksonville Jaguars in seventh round (246th pick overall) of 2002 NFL draft.

		INTERCEPTIONS			SACKS
Year Team	G	No.	Yds.	Avg.	TD	No.
1998—Oregon	11	1	5	5.0	0	0.0
1999—Oregon	10	3	23	7.7	0	0.0
2000—Oregon	12	2	11	5.5	0	1.0
2001—Oregon	12	8	118	14.8	1	1.0
College totals (4 years)	45	14	157	11.2	1	2.0

STALEY, LUKE — RB — LIONS

PERSONAL: Born September 16, 1980, in Bountiful, Utah. ... 6-1/227. ... Full name: Lucas Staley.
HIGH SCHOOL: Tualatin (Ore.).
COLLEGE: Brigham Young.
TRANSACTIONS/CAREER NOTES: Selected after junior season by Detroit Lions in seventh round (214th pick overall) of 2002 NFL draft.
HONORS: Doak Walker Award winner (2001). ... Named running back on THE SPORTING NEWS college All-America first team (2001).

		RUSHING				RECEIVING				KICKOFF RETURNS				TOTALS	
Year Team	G	Att.	Yds.	Avg.	TD	No.	Yds.	Avg.	TD	No.	Yds.	Avg.	TD	TD	Pts.
1999—Brigham Young	8	92	432	4.7	10	26	339	13.0	3	0	0	0.0	0	13	78
2000—Brigham Young	10	130	479	3.7	7	28	327	11.7	0	0	0	0.0	0	7	42
2001—Brigham Young	11	196	1596	8.1	24	32	334	10.4	4	3	102	34.0	0	28	168
College totals (3 years)	29	418	2507	6.0	41	86	1000	11.6	7	3	102	34.0	0	48	288

STALLWORTH, DONTE' — WR — SAINTS

PERSONAL: Born November 10, 1980, in Sacramento, Calif. ... 6-0/197. ... Full name: Donte' Lamar Stallworth.
HIGH SCHOOL: Grant (Sacramento, Calif.).
COLLEGE: Tennessee.
TRANSACTIONS/CAREER NOTES: Selected after junior season by New Orleans Saints in first round (13th pick overall) of 2002 NFL draft.

		RUSHING				RECEIVING				PUNT RETURNS				TOTALS	
Year Team	G	Att.	Yds.	Avg.	TD	No.	Yds.	Avg.	TD	No.	Yds.	Avg.	TD	TD	Pts.
1999—Tennessee	11	1	6	6.0	0	23	407	17.7	1	1	5	5.0	0	1	6
2000—Tennessee	11	2	13	6.5	0	35	519	14.8	2	1	17	17.0	0	2	12
2001—Tennessee	9	1	11	11.0	0	41	821	20.0	10	6	98	16.3	1	11	66
College totals (3 years)	31	4	30	7.5	0	99	1747	17.6	13	8	120	15.0	1	14	84

STAMPER, JOHN — DE — BUCCANEERS

PERSONAL: Born August 30, 1978, in Andrews, S.C. ... 6-4/265.
HIGH SCHOOL: Andrews (S.C.).
COLLEGE: South Carolina.
TRANSACTIONS/CAREER NOTES: Selected by Tampa Bay Buccaneers in sixth round (193rd pick overall) of 2002 NFL draft.

Year Team	G	SACKS
1998—South Carolina	11	2.0
1999—South Carolina	8	0.0
2000—South Carolina	11	1.0
2001—South Carolina	11	3.0
College totals (4 years)	41	6.0

STEPHENS, TRAVIS — RB — BUCCANEERS

PERSONAL: Born June 26, 1978, in Clarksville, Tenn. ... 5-8/194. ... Full name: Travis Tremaine Stephens.
HIGH SCHOOL: Northeast (Clarksville, Tenn.).
COLLEGE: Tennessee.
TRANSACTIONS/CAREER NOTES: Selected by Tampa Bay Buccaneers in fourth round (118th pick overall) of 2002 NFL draft.
HONORS: Named running back on THE SPORTING NEWS college All-America second team (2001).

		RUSHING				RECEIVING				KICKOFF RETURNS				TOTALS	
Year Team	G	Att.	Yds.	Avg.	TD	No.	Yds.	Avg.	TD	No.	Yds.	Avg.	TD	TD	Pts.
1997—Tennessee	7	9	36	4.0	0	0	0	0.0	0	0	0	0.0	0	0	0
1998—Tennessee	12	107	477	4.5	4	2	3	1.5	0	8	169	21.1	0	4	24
1999—Tennessee								Redshirted.							
2000—Tennessee	11	81	359	4.4	7	6	28	4.7	0	2	56	28.0	0	7	42
2001—Tennessee	12	291	1464	5.0	10	19	169	8.9	1	0	0	0.0	0	11	66
College totals (4 years)	42	488	2336	4.8	21	27	200	7.4	1	10	225	22.5	0	22	132

STEVENS, JERRAMY — TE — SEAHAWKS

PERSONAL: Born November 13, 1979, in Boise, Idaho. ... 6-7/265.
HIGH SCHOOL: River Ridge (Olympia, Wash.).
COLLEGE: Washington.
TRANSACTIONS/CAREER NOTES: Selected after junior season by Seattle Seahawks in first round (28th pick overall) of 2002 NFL draft.

		RECEIVING			
Year Team	G	No.	Yds.	Avg.	TD
1999—Washington	11	21	265	12.6	4
2000—Washington	11	43	600	14.0	3
2001—Washington	5	10	88	8.8	1
College totals (3 years)	27	74	953	12.9	8

STEVENSON, DOMINIQUE — LB — BILLS

PERSONAL: Born December 28, 1977, in Gaffney, S.C. ... 6-0/231. ... Full name: Antone Dominique Stevenson.
HIGH SCHOOL: Gaffney (S.C.).
COLLEGE: Tennessee.
TRANSACTIONS/CAREER NOTES: Selected by Buffalo Bills in seventh round (260th pick overall) of 2002 NFL draft..

		INTERCEPTIONS			SACKS
Year Team	G	No.	Yds.	Avg.	TD	No.
1998—Tennessee	12	0	0	0.0	0	0.0
1999—Tennessee	11	0	0	0.0	0	1.5
2000—Tennessee	10	1	3	3.0	0	4.0
2001—Tennessee	12	1	0	0.0	0	1.0
College totals (4 years)	45	2	3	1.5	0	6.5

TA'AMU, ED — G — VIKINGS

PERSONAL: Born November 8, 1979, in Honolulu, Hawaii. ... 6-1/335.
HIGH SCHOOL: Samoa International (Hawaii).
COLLEGE: Utah.
TRANSACTIONS/CAREER NOTES: Selected by Minnesota Vikings in fourth round (132nd pick overall) of 2002 NFL draft.
COLLEGE NOTES: Played defensive end (1998). ... Played defensive tackle and offensive guard (1999).
COLLEGE PLAYING EXPERIENCE: Utah, 1998-2001. ... Games played: 1998 (3), 1999 (3), 2000 (11), 2001 (9). Total: 26.

TAYLOR, BEN — LB — BROWNS

PERSONAL: Born August 31, 1978, in Bellaire, Ohio. ... 6-2/236. ... Full name: Benjamin Frazier Taylor.
HIGH SCHOOL: Bellaire (Ohio).
COLLEGE: Virginia Tech.
TRANSACTIONS/CAREER NOTES: Selected by Cleveland Browns in fourth round (111th pick overall) of 2002 NFL draft.
HONORS: Named linebacker on THE SPORTING NEWS college All-America third team (2001).
COLLEGE NOTES: Punted three times for 101 yards (2000).

		INTERCEPTIONS				**SACKS**
Year	Team	G	No.	Yds.	Avg.	TD	No.
1998—Virginia Tech		11	0	0	0.0	0	0.0
1999—Virginia Tech		11	0	0	0.0	0	1.0
2000—Virginia Tech		11	2	42	21.0	0	1.5
2001—Virginia Tech		11	1	0	0.0	0	4.5
College totals (4 years)		44	3	42	14.0	0	7.0

TAYLOR, CHESTER RB RAVENS

PERSONAL: Born September 22, 1979, in River Rouge, Mich. ... 5-11/213. ... Full name: Chester Lamar Taylor.
HIGH SCHOOL: River Rouge (Mich.).
COLLEGE: Toledo.
TRANSACTIONS/CAREER NOTES: Selected by Baltimore Ravens in sixth round (207th pick overall) of 2002 NFL draft.

			RUSHING				**RECEIVING**				**TOTALS**	
Year	Team	G	Att.	Yds.	Avg.	TD	No.	Yds.	Avg.	TD	TD	Pts.
1998—Toledo		9	103	583	5.7	5	10	136	13.6	1	6	36
1999—Toledo		11	182	1176	6.5	12	8	47	5.9	0	12	72
2000—Toledo		11	250	1470	5.9	18	17	129	7.6	1	19	114
2001—Toledo		11	268	1492	5.6	20	26	242	9.3	3	23	138
College totals (4 years)		42	803	4721	5.9	55	61	554	9.1	5	60	360

TAYLOR, JOHN DT LIONS

PERSONAL: Born August 29, 1979, in Denver. ... 6-3/260.
HIGH SCHOOL: Manual (Denver).
COLLEGE: Montana State.
TRANSACTIONS/CAREER NOTES: Selected by Detroit Lions in fourth round (134th pick overall) of 2002 NFL draft.

Year	Team	G	SACKS
1997—Montana State		Redshirted.	
1998—Montana State		11	0.0
1999—Montana State		11	8.0
2000—Montana State		11	3.5
2001—Montana State		11	4.5
College totals (4 years)		44	16.0

THOMAS, BRYAN DE JETS

PERSONAL: Born June 7, 1979, in Birmingham, Ala. ... 6-4/266.
HIGH SCHOOL: Minor (Birmingham, Ala.).
COLLEGE: Alabama-Birmingham.
TRANSACTIONS/CAREER NOTES: Selected by New York Jets in first round (22nd pick overall) of 2002 NFL draft.

Year	Team	G	SACKS
1998—Alabama-Birmingham		10	6.0
1999—Alabama-Birmingham		10	5.0
2000—Alabama-Birmingham		11	10.0
2001—Alabama-Birmingham		11	14.0
College totals (4 years)		42	35.0

THOMAS, KEVIN CB BILLS

PERSONAL: Born July 28, 1978, in Phoenix. ... 5-11/180. ... Full name: Marvin Kevin Thomas.
HIGH SCHOOL: Foothill (Calif.).
COLLEGE: UNLV.
TRANSACTIONS/CAREER NOTES: Selected by Buffalo Bills in sixth round (176th pick overall) of 2002 NFL draft.

			INTERCEPTIONS			
Year	Team	G	No.	Yds.	Avg.	TD
1998—UNLV		11	0	0	0.0	0
1999—UNLV		11	5	75	15.0	1
2000—UNLV		13	2	39	19.5	0
2001—UNLV		11	7	213	30.4	3
College totals (4 years)		46	14	327	23.4	4

THOMAS, ROBERT LB RAMS

PERSONAL: Born July 17, 1980, in El Centro, Calif. ... 6-0/229. ... Full name: Robert W. Thomas.
HIGH SCHOOL: Imperial (Calif.).
COLLEGE: UCLA.
TRANSACTIONS/CAREER NOTES: Selected by St. Louis Rams in first round (31st pick overall) of 2002 NFL draft.
HONORS: Named linebacker on THE SPORTING NEWS college All-America first team (2001).

Year	Team	G	SACKS
1998—UCLA		8	0.0
1999—UCLA		8	1.5
2000—UCLA		12	0.0
2001—UCLA		11	6.5
College totals (4 years)		39	8.0

THOMPSON, LAMONT   S   BENGALS

PERSONAL: Born July 30, 1978, in Richmond, Calif. ... 6-1/220. ... Full name: Lamont Darnell Thompson.
HIGH SCHOOL: El Cerrito (Richmond, Calif.).
COLLEGE: Washington State.
TRANSACTIONS/CAREER NOTES: Selected by Cincinnati Bengals in second round (41st pick overall) of 2002 NFL draft.
HONORS: Named free safety on THE SPORTING NEWS college All-America second team (2001).

			INTERCEPTIONS			RECEIVING				PUNT RETURNS				KICKOFF RETURNS				TOTALS	
Year Team	G	No.	Yds.	Avg.	TD	No.	Yds.	Avg.	TD	No.	Yds.	Avg.	TD	No.	Yds.	Avg.	TD	TD	Pts.
1997—Washington State	10	6	39	6.5	0	0	0	0.0	0	0	0	0.0	0	0	0	0.0	0	0	0
1998—Washington State	11	4	44	11.0	0	2	34	17.0	0	16	123	7.7	0	1	14	14.0	0	0	0
1999—Washington State	11	4	43	10.8	0	0	0	0.0	0	0	0	0.0	0	0	0	0.0	0	0	0
2000—Washington State								Redshirted.											
2001—Washington State	12	10	97	9.7	1	0	0	0.0	0	0	0	0.0	0	0	0	0.0	0	1	6
College totals (4 years)	44	24	223	9.3	1	2	34	17.0	0	16	123	7.7	0	1	14	14.0	0	1	6

THORNTON, DAVID   LB   COLTS

PERSONAL: Born November 11, 1978, in Goldsboro, N.C. ... 6-2/236. ... Full name: David Dontay Thornton.
HIGH SCHOOL: Goldsboro (N.C.).
COLLEGE: North Carolina.
TRANSACTIONS/CAREER NOTES: Selected by Indianapolis Colts in fourth round (106th pick overall) of 2002 NFL draft.

			INTERCEPTIONS			SACKS
Year Team	G	No.	Yds.	Avg.	TD	No.
1998—North Carolina				Did not play.		
1999—North Carolina	10	0	0	0.0	0	0.0
2000—North Carolina	11	0	0	0.0	0	0.0
2001—North Carolina	11	1	19	19.0	0	3.0
College totals (3 years)	32	1	19	19.0	0	3.0

TRIPPLETT, LARRY   DT   COLTS

PERSONAL: Born January 18, 1979, in Los Angeles. ... 6-1/305.
HIGH SCHOOL: Westchester (Los Angeles).
COLLEGE: Washington.
TRANSACTIONS/CAREER NOTES: Selected by Indianapolis Colts in second round (42nd pick overall) of 2002 NFL draft.
HONORS: Named defensive tackle on THE SPORTING NEWS college All-America second team (2000). ... Named defensive tackle on THE SPORTING NEWS college All-America third team (2001).

Year Team	G	SACKS
1998—Washington	4	0.0
1999—Washington	11	1.0
2000—Washington	11	6.5
2001—Washington	11	2.0
College totals (4 years)	37	9.5

WALKER, JAVON   WR   PACKERS

PERSONAL: Born October 14, 1978, in Lafayette, La. ... 6-3/210.
HIGH SCHOOL: St. Thomas More (Lafayette, La.).
JUNIOR COLLEGE: Jones Junior College (Miss.).
COLLEGE: Florida State.
TRANSACTIONS/CAREER NOTES: Selected by Green Bay Packers in first round (20th pick overall) of 2002 NFL draft.

			RECEIVING		
Year Team	G	No.	Yds.	Avg.	TD
1998—Jones County Junior College	12	37	735	19.9	8
1999—Jones County Junior College	11	61	906	14.9	7
2000—Florida State	9	20	313	15.7	3
2001—Florida State	11	45	944	21.0	7
Junior college totals (2 years)	23	98	1641	16.7	15
College totals (2 years)	20	65	1257	19.3	10

WALKER, LANGSTON   OT   RAIDERS

PERSONAL: Born September 3, 1979, in Oakland. ... 6-8/344.
HIGH SCHOOL: Bishop O'Dowd (Calif.).
COLLEGE: California.
TRANSACTIONS/CAREER NOTES: Selected by Oakland Raiders in second round (53rd pick overall) of 2002 NFL draft.
COLLEGE PLAYING EXPERIENCE: California, 1997-2001. ... Games played: 1997 (redshirted), 1998 (11), 1999 (11), 2000 (4), 2001 (11). Total: 37.

WALKER, MARQUISE   WR   BUCCANEERS

PERSONAL: Born December 11, 1978, in Syracuse, N.Y. ... 6-2/219.
HIGH SCHOOL: Henninger (Syracuse, N.Y.).
COLLEGE: Michigan.

TRANSACTIONS/CAREER NOTES: Selected by Tampa Bay Buccaneers in third round (86th pick overall) of 2002 NFL draft.
HONORS: Named wide receiver on THE SPORTING NEWS college All-America second team (2001).

			RUSHING				RECEIVING				PUNT RETURNS				TOTALS	
Year	Team	G	Att.	Yds.	Avg.	TD	No.	Yds.	Avg.	TD	No.	Yds.	Avg.	TD	TD	Pts.
1998—Michigan		13	0	0	0.0	0	4	31	7.8	0	0	0	0.0	0	0	0
1999—Michigan		12	2	-14	-7.0	0	37	396	10.7	2	1	23	23.0	0	2	12
2000—Michigan		12	1	-1	-1.0	0	49	699	14.3	4	1	41	41.0	1	5	30
2001—Michigan		12	4	29	7.3	0	86	1143	13.3	11	23	206	9.0	0	11	66
College totals (4 years)		49	7	14	2.0	0	176	2269	12.9	17	25	270	10.8	1	18	108

WALKER, RAMON   CB   TEXANS

PERSONAL: Born November 8, 1979, in Akron, Ohio. ... 6-0/197. ... Full name: Ramon D. Walker.
HIGH SCHOOL: John R. Buchtel (Akron, Ohio).
COLLEGE: Pittsburgh.
TRANSACTIONS/CAREER NOTES: Selected after junior season by Houston Texans in fifth round (153rd pick overall) of 2002 NFL draft.

			INTERCEPTIONS				SACKS
Year	Team	G	No.	Yds.	Avg.	TD	No.
1999—Pittsburgh		11	1	0	0.0	0	1.0
2000—Pittsburgh		7	0	0	0.0	0	0.0
2001—Pittsburgh		11	1	18	18.0	0	1.0
College totals (3 years)		29	2	18	9.0	0	2.0

WALTER, TYSON   OT   COWBOYS

PERSONAL: Born March 17, 1978, in Bainbridge, Ohio. ... 6-4/303.
HIGH SCHOOL: Kenston (Ohio).
COLLEGE: Ohio State.
TRANSACTIONS/CAREER NOTES: Selected by Dallas Cowboys in sixth round (179th pick overall) of 2002 NFL draft.
COLLEGE PLAYING EXPERIENCE: Ohio State, 1996-2001. ... Games played: 1996 (2), 1997 (12), 1998 (12), 1999 (12), 2000 (did not play), 2001 (12). Total: 50.

WANSLEY, TIM   CB   BUCCANEERS

PERSONAL: Born November 11, 1978, in Buford, Ga. ... 5-8/180.
HIGH SCHOOL: Buford (Ga.).
COLLEGE: Georgia.
TRANSACTIONS/CAREER NOTES: Selected by Tampa Bay Buccaneers in seventh round (233rd pick overall) of 2002 NFL draft.

			INTERCEPTIONS				PUNT RETURNS				TOTALS	
Year	Team	G	No.	Yds.	Avg.	TD	No.	Yds.	Avg.	TD	TD	Pts.
1998—Georgia		11	1	0	0.0	0	0	0	0.0	0	0	0
1999—Georgia		11	0	0	0.0	0	3	39	13.0	0	0	0
2000—Georgia		11	6	0	0.0	0	1	0	0.0	0	0	0
2001—Georgia		10	2	0	0.0	0	4	79	19.8	0	0	0
College totals (4 years)		43	9	0	0.0	0	8	118	14.8	0	0	0

WEARY, FRED   G   TEXANS

PERSONAL: Born September 30, 1977, in Montgomery, Ala. ... 6-4/308. ... Full name: Fred Edward Weary Jr..
HIGH SCHOOL: Robert E. Lee (Montgomery, Ala.).
COLLEGE: Tennessee.
TRANSACTIONS/CAREER NOTES: Selected by Houston Texans in third round (66th pick overall) of 2002 NFL draft.
HONORS: Named guard on THE SPORTING NEWS college All-America second team (2001).
COLLEGE PLAYING EXPERIENCE: Tennessee, 1997-2001. ... Games played: 1997 (redshirted), 1998 (10), 1999 (11), 2000 (2), 2001 (12). Total: 35. ... Played offensive and defensive tackle (1998).

WEAVER, ANTHONY   DE   RAVENS

PERSONAL: Born July 28, 1980, in Saratoga Springs, N.Y. ... 6-3/300. ... Full name: Anthony Lee Weaver.
HIGH SCHOOL: Saratoga Springs (N.Y.).
COLLEGE: Notre Dame.
TRANSACTIONS/CAREER NOTES: Selected by Baltimore in second round (52nd pick overall) of 2002 NFL draft.

			INTERCEPTIONS				SACKS
Year	Team	G	No.	Yds.	Avg.	TD	No.
1998—Notre Dame		11	0	0	0.0	0	2.0
1999—Notre Dame		11	0	0	0.0	0	0.0
2000—Notre Dame		11	2	4	2.0	0	8.0
2001—Notre Dame		11	1	0	0.0	0	7.0
College totals (4 years)		44	3	4	1.3	0	17.0

WELLS, JONATHAN — RB — TEXANS

PERSONAL: Born July 21, 1979, in River Ridge, La. ... 6-1/243.
HIGH SCHOOL: John Curtis (River Ridge, La.).
COLLEGE: Ohio State.
TRANSACTIONS/CAREER NOTES: Selected by Houston Texans in fourth round (99th pick overall) of 2002 NFL draft.

			RUSHING				RECEIVING				KICKOFF RETURNS				TOTALS	
Year Team	G	Att.	Yds.	Avg.	TD	No.	Yds.	Avg.	TD	No.	Yds.	Avg.	TD	TD	Pts.
1998—Ohio State	12	41	197	4.8	2	1	11	11.0	0	4	82	20.5	0	2	12
1999—Ohio State	9	51	292	5.7	3	5	17	3.4	0	0	0	0.0	0	3	18
2000—Ohio State	12	136	598	4.4	6	9	88	9.8	0	10	168	16.8	0	6	36
2001—Ohio State	12	251	1331	5.3	16	11	117	10.6	0	1	18	18.0	0	16	96
College totals (4 years)	45	479	2418	5.0	27	26	233	9.0	0	15	268	17.9	0	27	162

WESLEY, DANTE — CB — PANTHERS

PERSONAL: Born April 5, 1979, in Pine Bluff, Ark. ... 6-0/211.
HIGH SCHOOL: Watson Chapel (Pine Bluff, Ark.).
COLLEGE: Arkansas-Pine Bluff.
TRANSACTIONS/CAREER NOTES: Selected by Carolina Panthers in fourth round (100th pick overall) of 2002 NFL draft.

		INTERCEPTIONS			
Year Team	G	No.	Yds.	Avg.	TD
1998—Arkansas-Pine Bluff	11	0	0	0.0	0
1999—Arkansas-Pine Bluff	11	3	57	19.0	0
2000—Arkansas-Pine Bluff	10	0	0	0.0	0
2001—Arkansas-Pine Bluff	11	4	31	7.8	0
College totals (4 years)	43	7	88	12.6	0

WESTBROOK, BRIAN — RB/KR — EAGLES

PERSONAL: Born September 2, 1979, in Washington, D.C. ... 5-8/200.
HIGH SCHOOL: DeMantha (Ft. Washington, Md.).
COLLEGE: Villanova.
TRANSACTIONS/CAREER NOTES: Selected by Philadelphia Eagles in third round (91st pick overall) of 2002 NFL draft.
HONORS: Walter Payton Award winner (2001).

		RUSHING				RECEIVING				PUNT RETURNS				KICKOFF RETURNS				TOTALS	
Year Team	G	Att.	Yds.	Avg.	TD	No.	Yds.	Avg.	TD	No.	Yds.	Avg.	TD	No.	Yds.	Avg.	TD	TD	Pts.
1997—Villanova	13	97	630	6.5	7	12	113	9.4	4	0	0	0.0	0	14	301	21.5	0	11	66
1998—Villanova	11	200	1046	5.2	10	89	1144	12.9	11	15	192	12.8	0	25	644	25.8	1	22	132
1999—Villanova								Did not play.											
2000—Villanova	11	179	1220	6.8	15	59	724	12.3	5	0	0	0.0	0	38	1048	27.6	2	22	132
2001—Villanova	11	249	1603	6.4	22	59	658	11.2	6	8	122	15.3	0	17	440	25.9	1	29	174
College totals (4 years)	46	725	4499	6.2	54	219	2639	12.1	26	23	314	13.7	0	94	2433	25.9	4	84	504

WHITE, GREG — DE — TEXANS

PERSONAL: Born July 25, 1979, in East Orange, N.J. ... 6-3/268.
HIGH SCHOOL: Malcolm X Shabazz (Newark, N.J.).
COLLEGE: Minnesota.
TRANSACTIONS/CAREER NOTES: Selected by Houston Texans in seventh round (229th pick overall) of 2002 NFL draft.

Year Team	G	SACKS
1999—Minnesota	11	1.0
2000—Minnesota	12	6.0
2001—Minnesota	11	5.0
College totals (3 years)	34	12.0

WILLIAMS, BRIAN — CB — VIKINGS

PERSONAL: Born July 2, 1979, in High Point, N.C. ... 5-11/207.
HIGH SCHOOL: Southwest Guilford (N.C.).
COLLEGE: North Carolina State.
TRANSACTIONS/CAREER NOTES: Selected by Minnesota Vikings in fourth round (105th pick overall) of 2002 NFL draft.

		INTERCEPTIONS				SACKS	PUNT RETURNS				TOTALS	
Year Team	G	No.	Yds.	Avg.	TD	No.	No.	Yds.	Avg.	TD	TD	Pts.
1998—North Carolina State	10	0	0	0.0	0	0.0	1	8	8.0	0	0	0
1999—North Carolina State	12	2	11	5.5	0	0.0	1	16	16.0	0	0	0
2000—North Carolina State	11	0	0	0.0	0	1.0	1	5	5.0	0	0	0
2001—North Carolina State	11	3	3	1.0	0	0.0	0	0	0.0	0	0	0
College totals (4 years)	44	5	14	2.8	0	1.0	3	29	9.7	0	0	0

– 476 –

WILLIAMS, CHAD — S — RAVENS

PERSONAL: Born January 22, 1979, in Birmingham, Ala. ... 5-9/207.
HIGH SCHOOL: Wenonah (Birmingham, Ala.).
COLLEGE: Southern Mississippi.
TRANSACTIONS/CAREER NOTES: Selected by Baltimore Ravens in sixth round (209th pick overall) of 2002 NFL draft.

			INTERCEPTIONS			SACKS	PUNT RETURNS				KICKOFF RETURNS				TOTALS	
Year Team	G	No.	Yds.	Avg.	TD	No.	No.	Yds.	Avg.	TD	No.	Yds.	Avg.	TD	TD	Pts.
1998—Southern Mississippi	10	0	0	0.0	0	0.0	0	0	0.0	0	0	0	0.0	0	0	0
1999—Southern Mississippi	11	1	26	26.0	0	0.0	0	0	0.0	0	0	0	0.0	0	0	0
2000—Southern Mississippi	11	0	0	0.0	0	8.0	4	94	23.5	0	0	0	0.0	0	0	0
2001—Southern Mississippi	11	1	11	11.0	0	2.0	10	78	7.8	0	2	24	12.0	0	0	0
College totals (4 years)	43	2	37	18.5	0	10.0	14	172	12.3	0	2	24	12.0	0	0	0

WILLIAMS, MIKE — OT — BILLS

PERSONAL: Born January 11, 1980, in Dallas. ... 6-6/370. ... Full name: Michael D. Williams.
HIGH SCHOOL: The Colony (Texas).
COLLEGE: Texas.
TRANSACTIONS/CAREER NOTES: Selected by Buffalo Bills in first round (fourth pick overall) of 2002 NFL draft.
HONORS: Named offensive tackle on THE SPORTING NEWS college All-America second team (2001).
COLLEGE PLAYING EXPERIENCE: Texas, 1998-2001. ... Games: 1998 (12), 1999 (12), 2000 (11), 2001 (12). Total: 47.

WILLIAMS, ROOSEVELT — CB — BEARS

PERSONAL: Born September 10, 1978, in Jacksonville, Fla. ... 5-11/204.
HIGH SCHOOL: Terry Parker (Jacksonville, Fla.).
COLLEGE: Tuskegee.
TRANSACTIONS/CAREER NOTES: Selected by Chicago Bears in third round (72nd pick overall) of 2002 NFL draft.

		INTERCEPTIONS				KICKOFF RETURNS				TOTALS	
Year Team	G	No.	Yds.	Avg.	TD	No.	Yds.	Avg.	TD	TD	Pts.
1998—Savannah State	11	2	29	14.5	0	20	577	28.9	1	1	6
1999—Savannah State	11	2	11	5.5	0	13	305	23.5	0	0	0
2000—Tuskegee	12	4	26	6.5	0	9	155	17.2	0	0	0
2001—Tuskegee	12	5	13	2.6	0	2	77	38.5	0	0	0
College totals (4 years)	46	13	79	6.1	0	44	1114	25.3	1	1	6

WILLIAMS, ROY — S — COWBOYS

PERSONAL: Born August 14, 1980, in Redwood City, Calif. ... 6-0/219.
HIGH SCHOOL: James Logan (Union City, Calif.).
COLLEGE: Oklahoma.
TRANSACTIONS/CAREER NOTES: Selected after junior season by Dallas Cowboys in first round (ninth pick overall) of 2002 NFL draft.
HONORS: Named strong safety on THE SPORTING NEWS college All-America first team (2001). ... Jim Thorpe Award winner (2001).

		INTERCEPTIONS				SACKS	PUNT RETURNS				TOTALS	
Year Team	G	No.	Yds.	Avg.	TD	No.	No.	Yds.	Avg.	TD	TD	Pts.
1998—Oklahoma	3	0	0	0.0	0	0.0	0	0	0.0	0	0	0
1999—Oklahoma	11	2	22	11.0	0	1.0	1	2	2.0	0	0	0
2000—Oklahoma	12	2	53	26.5	1	4.0	0	0	0.0	0	1	6
2001—Oklahoma	12	5	25	5.0	0	2.0	0	0	0.0	0	1	6
College totals (4 years)	38	9	100	11.1	1	7.0	1	2	2.0	0	2	12

WILLIAMS, TANK — S — TITANS

PERSONAL: Born June 30, 1980, in Bay St. Louis, Miss. ... 6-3/223. ... Full name: Clevan Williams.
HIGH SCHOOL: Bay (Bay St. Louis, Miss.).
COLLEGE: Stanford.
TRANSACTIONS/CAREER NOTES: Selected by Tennesse Titans in second round (45th pick overall) of 2002 NFL draft.

		INTERCEPTIONS				SACKS
Year Team	G	No.	Yds.	Avg.	TD	No.
1998—Stanford	10	0	0	0.0	0	0.0
1999—Stanford	9	1	18	18.0	0	2.0
2000—Stanford	11	3	10	3.3	0	1.0
2001—Stanford	11	5	22	4.4	0	2.0
College totals (4 years)	41	9	50	5.6	0	5.0

WIRE, COY — S — BILLS

PERSONAL: Born November 7, 1978, in Camp Hill, Pa. ... 6-0/209.
COLLEGE: Stanford.
TRANSACTIONS/CAREER NOTES: Selected by Buffalo Bills in third round (97th pick overall) of 2002 NFL draft.

COLLEGE NOTES: Played running back, 1998 and 1999. ... Rushed 85 times for 298 yards and two touchdowns; and caught 15 passes for 83 yards (1998). ... Rushed 88 times for 317 yards and four touchdowns; and caught four passes for 32 yards (1999).

		INTERCEPTIONS			SACKS	KICKOFF RETURNS			TOTALS	
Year Team	G	No.	Yds.	Avg.	TD	No.	No.	Yds.	Avg.	TD	TD	Pts.
1998—Stanford	6	0	0	0.0	0	0.0	10	160	16.0	0	0	0
1999—Stanford	11	0	0	0.0	0	0.0	0	0	0.0	0	0	0
2000—Stanford	11	1	11	11.0	0	8.0	0	0	0.0	0	0	0
2001—Stanford	11	0	0	0.0	0	3.0	0	0	0.0	0	1	6
College totals (4 years)	39	1	11	11.0	0	11.0	10	160	16.0	0	1	6

WISTROM, TRACEY TE BUCCANEERS

PERSONAL: Born August 28, 1978, in Webb City, Mo. ... 6-4/245.
HIGH SCHOOL: Webb City (Mo.).
COLLEGE: Nebraska.
TRANSACTIONS/CAREER NOTES: Selected by Tampa Bay Buccaneers in seventh round (250th pick overall) of 2002 NFL draft.
HONORS: Named tight end on THE SPORTING NEWS college All-America third team (2001).

		RECEIVING			
Year Team	G	No.	Yds.	Avg.	TD
1998—Nebraska	12	2	84	42.0	1
1999—Nebraska	11	16	429	26.8	2
2000—Nebraska	11	19	314	16.5	5
2001—Nebraska	11	21	323	15.4	2
College totals (4 years)	45	58	1150	19.8	10

WITHERSPOON, WILL LB PANTHERS

PERSONAL: Born August 19, 1980, in Panama City, Fla. ... 6-1/231. ... Full name: William Cordell Witherspoon.
HIGH SCHOOL: Rutherford (Panama City, Fla.).
COLLEGE: Georgia.
TRANSACTIONS/CAREER NOTES: Selected by Carolina Panthers in third round (73rd pick overall) of 2002 NFL draft.

Year Team	G	SACKS
1998—Georgia	11	0.0
1999—Georgia	8	0.5
2000—Georgia	11	2.0
2001—Georgia	9	1.0
College totals (4 years)	39	3.5

WOMACK, ANTWOINE RB PATRIOTS

PERSONAL: Born March 20, 1978, in Hampton, Va. ... 5-11/214. ... Full name: Antwoine D. Womack.
HIGH SCHOOL: Phoebus (Hampton, Va.).
COLLEGE: Virginia.
TRANSACTIONS/CAREER NOTES: Selected by New England Patriots in seventh round (237th pick overall) of 2002 NFL draft.

		RUSHING				RECEIVING				KICKOFF RETURNS				TOTALS	
Year Team	G	Att.	Yds.	Avg.	TD	No.	Yds.	Avg.	TD	No.	Yds.	Avg.	TD	TD	Pts.
1997—Virginia	5	44	208	4.7	0	0	0	0.0	0	3	71	23.7	0	0	0
1998—Virginia	11	112	708	6.3	4	2	17	8.5	0	12	236	19.7	0	4	24
1999—Virginia							Did not play.								
2000—Virginia	11	210	1028	4.9	9	8	81	10.1	0	4	97	24.2	0	9	54
2001—Virginia	5	63	263	4.2	0	6	46	7.7	0	0	0	0.0	0	0	0
College totals (4 years)	32	429	2207	5.1	13	16	144	9.0	0	19	404	21.2	0	13	78

WRIGHT, RODNEY WR BILLS

PERSONAL: Born November 18, 1979, in Bakersfield, Calif. ... 5-9/180.
HIGH SCHOOL: Bakersfield (Calif.).
COLLEGE: Fresno State.
TRANSACTIONS/CAREER NOTES: Selected by Buffalo Bills in seventh round (249th pick overall) of 2002 NFL draft.

		RUSHING				RECEIVING				KICKOFF RETURNS				TOTALS	
Year Team	G	Att.	Yds.	Avg.	TD	No.	Yds.	Avg.	TD	No.	Yds.	Avg.	TD	TD	Pts.
1998—Fresno State	4	0	0	0.0	0	6	116	19.3	2	0	0	0.0	0	2	12
1999—Fresno State	11	11	70	6.4	0	74	1062	14.4	7	27	584	21.6	0	7	42
2000—Fresno State	7	6	44	7.3	0	38	466	12.3	2	13	279	21.5	0	2	12
2001—Fresno State	11	23	114	5.0	1	104	1630	15.7	12	0	0	0.0	0	13	78
College totals (4 years)	33	40	228	5.7	1	222	3274	14.7	23	40	863	21.6	0	24	144

YOUNG, CHRIS S BRONCOS

PERSONAL: Born January 23, 1980, in Senoia, Ga. ... 5-11/210. ... Full name: Christopher Lamont Young.
HIGH SCHOOL: East Cowetta (Ga.).
COLLEGE: Georgia Tech.
TRANSACTIONS/CAREER NOTES: Selected by Denver Broncos in seventh round (228th pick overall) of 2002 NFL draft.

			INTERCEPTIONS				SACKS
Year Team	G	No.	Yds.	Avg.	TD		No.
1998—Georgia Tech	10	0	0	0.0	0		0.0
1999—Georgia Tech	11	1	14	14.0	0		1.0
2000—Georgia Tech	11	2	5	2.5	0		2.0
2001—Georgia Tech	12	1	14	14.0	0		2.0
College totals (4 years)	44	4	33	8.3	0		5.0

ZASTUDIL, DAVE   P   RAVENS

PERSONAL: Born October 26, 1978, in Bay Village, Ohio. ... 6-3/225.
HIGH SCHOOL: Bay Village (Ohio).
COLLEGE: Ohio.
TRANSACTIONS/CAREER NOTES: Selected by Baltimore Ravens in fourth round (112th pick overall) of 2002 NFL draft.
HONORS: Named punter on THE SPORTING NEWS college All-America third team (2001).

				PUNTING			
Year Team	G	No.	Yds.	Avg.	Net avg.	In. 20	Blk.
1998—Ohio	...	50	2266	45.3	.0	12	0
1999—Ohio	...	60	2595	43.3	.0	13	0
2000—Ohio	...	47	2084	44.3	.0	19	0
2001—Ohio	...	50	2280	45.6	.0	16	0
College totals (4 years)	...	207	9225	44.6	0.0	60	0

2002 DRAFT PICKS

HEAD COACHES

BELICHICK, BILL — PATRIOTS

PERSONAL: Born April 16, 1952, in Nashville. ... Full name: William Stephen Belichick. ... Son of Steve Belichick, fullback with Detroit Lions (1941); head coach at Hiram (Ohio) College (1946-49); assistant coach, Vanderbilt (1949-53); assistant coach, North Carolina (1953-56); assistant coach, Navy (1956-83); and administrative assistant, Navy (1983-89).
HIGH SCHOOL: Annapolis (Md.) and Phillips Academy (Andover, Mass.).
COLLEGE: Wesleyan University (degree in economics, 1975).

HEAD COACHING RECORD

BACKGROUND: Assistant special teams coach, Baltimore Colts NFL (1975). ... Assistant special teams coach, Detroit Lions NFL (1976 and 1977). ... Assistant special teams coach/assistant to defensive coordinator, Denver Broncos NFL (1978). ... Special teams coach, New York Giants NFL (1979 and 1980). ... Linebackers coach, Giants (1981 and 1982). ... Defensive coordinator/linebackers coach, Giants (1983-1988). ... Defensive coordinator/secondary coach, Giants (1989 and 1990). ... Assistant head coach/secondary coach, New England Patriots NFL (1996). ... Assistant head coach/secondary coach, New York Jets NFL (1997-1999).

		REGULAR SEASON				POST-SEASON	
	W	L	T	Pct.	Finish	W	L
1991—Cleveland NFL	6	10	0	.375	3rd/AFC Central Division	0	0
1992—Cleveland NFL	7	9	0	.438	3rd/AFC Central Division	0	0
1993—Cleveland NFL	7	9	0	.438	3rd/AFC Central Division	0	0
1994—Cleveland NFL	11	5	0	.688	2nd/AFC Central Division	1	1
1995—Cleveland NFL	5	11	0	.313	4th/AFC Central Division	0	0
2000—New England NFL	5	11	0	.313	5th/AFC Eastern Division	0	0
2001—New England NFL	11	5	0	.688	1st/AFC Eastern Division	3	0
Pro totals (7 years)	52	60	0	.464	Pro totals (2 years)	4	1

NOTES:
1994—Defeated New England, 20-13, in first-round playoff game; lost to Pittsburgh, 29-9, in conference playoff game.
2001—Defeated Oakland, 16-13 (OT), in conference playoff game; defeated Pittsburgh, 24-17, in AFC championship game; defeated St. Louis, 20-17, in Super Bowl XXXVI.

BILLICK, BRIAN — RAVENS

PERSONAL: Born February 28, 1954, in Fairborn, Ohio. ... Full name: Brian Harold Billick. ... Played tight end.
HIGH SCHOOL: Redlands (Calif.).
COLLEGE: Air Force, then Brigham Young.
TRANSACTIONS/CAREER NOTES: Selected by San Francisco 49ers in 11th round of 1977 NFL draft. ... Signed by 49ers for 1977 season. ... Released by 49ers (August 30, 1977). ... Signed by Dallas Cowboys (May 1978). ... Released by Cowboys before 1978 season.

HEAD COACHING RECORD

BACKGROUND: Assistant coach, University of Redlands (1977). ... Graduate assistant, Brigham Young (1978). ... Assistant public relations director, San Francisco 49ers NFL (1979 and 1980). ... Assistant coach and recruiting coordinator, San Diego State (1981-1985). ... Offensive coordinator, Utah State (1986-1988). ... Assistant coach, Stanford (1989-1991). ... Tight ends coach, Minnesota Vikings (1992). ... Offensive coordinator, Minnesota Vikings (1993-1998).

		REGULAR SEASON				POST-SEASON	
	W	L	T	Pct.	Finish	W	L
1999—Baltimore NFL	8	8	0	.500	3rd/AFC Central Division	0	0
2000—Baltimore NFL	12	4	0	.750	2nd/AFC Central Division	4	0
2001—Baltimore NFL	10	6	0	.625	2nd/AFC Central Division	1	1
Pro totals (3 years)	30	18	0	.625	Pro totals (2 years)	5	1

NOTES:
2000—Defeated Denver, 21-3, in first-round playoff game; defeated Tennessee, 24-10, in conference playoff game; defeated Oakland, 16-3, in AFC championship game; defeated New York Giants, 34-7, in Super Bowl XXXV.
2001—Defeated Miami, 20-3, in first-round playoff game; lost to Pittsburgh, 27-10, in conference playoff game.

CALLAHAN, BILL — RAIDERS

PERSONAL: Born July 31, 1956, in Chicago.
COLLEGE: Illinois Benedictine.

HEAD COACHING RECORD

BACKGROUND: Head coach, Oak Lawn (Ill.) high school (1978). ... Head coach, De La Salle Institute, Chicago (1979). ... Graduate assistant, University of Illinois (1980). ... Tight ends coach/offensive line coach/quarterbacks coach/special teams coach, University of Illinois (1981-1986). ... Offensive line coach, Northern Arizona (1987 and 1988). ... Offensive coordinator, Southern Illinois University (1989). ... Offensive line coach, University of Wisconsin (1990-1994). ... Offensive line coach, Philadelphia Eagles NFL (1995-1997). ... Offensive coordinator/tight ends coach, Oakland Raiders NFL (1998). ... Offensive coordinator/offensive line coach, Raiders (1999-2001).

CAMPO, DAVE — COWBOYS

PERSONAL: Born July 18, 1947, in New London, Conn. ... Full name: David Cross Campo.
HIGH SCHOOL: Robert E. Fitch (Groton, Conn.).
COLLEGE: Central Connecticut State.

– 480 –

HEAD COACHING RECORD

BACKGROUND: Coach, Central Connecticut State (1971 and 1972). ... Coach, Albany State (1973). ... Coach, Bridgeport (1974). ... Coach, University of Pittsburgh (1975). ... Coach, Washington State (1976). ... Coach, Boise State (1977-1979). ... Coach, Oregon State (1980). ... Coach, Weber State (1981 and 1982). ... Coach, Iowa State (1983). ... Coach, Syracuse (1984-1986). ... Secondary coach, Miami, Fla. (1987 and 1988). ... Secondary coach, Dallas Cowboys NFL (1989-1994). ... Defensive coordinator, Cowboys (1995-1999).

	REGULAR SEASON					POST-SEASON	
	W	L	T	Pct.	Finish	W	L
2000—Dallas NFL	5	11	0	.313	4th/NFC Eastern Division	0	0
2001—Dallas NFL	5	11	0	.313	5th/NFC Eastern Division	0	0
Pro totals (2 years)	10	22	0	.313			

CAPERS, DOM — TEXANS

PERSONAL: Born August 7, 1950, in Cambridge, Ohio. ... Full name: Dominic Capers.
HIGH SCHOOL: Meadowbrook (Byesville, Ohio).
COLLEGE: Mount Union, Ohio (bachelor's degree in psychology and physical education), then Kent (master's degree in administration).

HEAD COACHING RECORD

BACKGROUND: Graduate assistant, Kent State (1972-1974). ... Graduate assistant, Washington (1975). ... Defensive backs coach, Hawaii (1975). ... Defensive coordinator, Hawaii (1976). ... Defensive assistant coach, San Jose State (1977). ... Defensive assistant coach, California (1978 and 1979). ... Defensive backs coach, Tennessee (1980 and 1981). ... Defensive backs coach, Ohio State (1982 and 1983). ... Defensive backs coach, Philadelphia Stars USFL (1984). ... Defensive backs coach, Baltimore Stars USFL (1985). ... Defensive backs coach, New Orleans Saints NFL (1986-1991). ... Defensive coordinator, Pittsburgh Steelers NFL (1992-1994). ... Defensive coordinator, Jacksonville Jaguars NFL (1999 and 2000).
HONORS: Named NFL Coach of the Year by THE SPORTING NEWS (1996).

	REGULAR SEASON					POST-SEASON	
	W	L	T	Pct.	Finish	W	L
1995—Carolina NFL	7	9	0	.438	T3rd/NFC Western Division	0	0
1996—Carolina NFL	12	4	0	.750	T1st/NFC Western Division	1	1
1997—Carolina NFL	7	9	0	.438	T2nd/NFC Western Division	0	0
1998—Carolina NFL	4	12	0	.250	T4th/NFC Western Division	0	0
Pro totals (4 years)	30	34	0	.469	Pro totals (1 year)	1	1

NOTES:
1996—Defeated Dallas, 26-17, in conference playoff game; lost to Green Bay, 30-13, in NFC championship game.

COUGHLIN, TOM — JAGUARS

PERSONAL: Born August 31, 1946, in Waterloo, N.Y. ... Full name: Thomas Richard Coughlin.
HIGH SCHOOL: Waterloo (N.Y.) Central.
COLLEGE: Syracuse (bachelor's degree in education, 1968; master's degree in education, 1969).

HEAD COACHING RECORD

BACKGROUND: Graduate assistant, Syracuse (1969). ... Quarterbacks/offensive backfield coach, Syracuse (1974-1976). ... Offensive coordinator, Syracuse (1977-1980). ... Quarterbacks coach, Boston College (1980-1983). ... Receivers coach, Philadelphia Eagles NFL (1984 and 1985). ... Receivers coach, Green Bay Packers NFL (1986 and 1987). ... Receivers coach, New York Giants NFL (1988-1990).

	REGULAR SEASON					POST-SEASON	
	W	L	T	Pct.	Finish	W	L
1970—Rochester Tech	4	3	0	.571	Eastern College Athletic Conference	0	0
1971—Rochester Tech	5	2	1	.688	Eastern College Athletic Conference	0	0
1972—Rochester Tech	4	5	0	.444	Eastern College Athletic Conference	0	0
1973—Rochester Tech	3	5	1	.389	Eastern College Athletic Conference	0	0
1991—Boston College	4	7	0	.364	7th/Big East Conference	0	1
1992—Boston College	8	2	1	.773	3rd/Big East Conference	1	0
1993—Boston College	8	3	0	.727	3rd/Big East Conference	0	0
1995—Jacksonville NFL	4	12	0	.250	5th/AFC Central Division	2	1
1996—Jacksonville NFL	9	7	0	.563	2nd/AFC Central Division	0	1
1997—Jacksonville NFL	11	5	0	.688	T1st/AFC Central Division	1	1
1998—Jacksonville NFL	11	5	0	.688	1st/AFC Central Division	1	1
1999—Jacksonville NFL	14	2	0	.875	1st/AFC Central Division	0	0
2000—Jacksonville NFL	7	9	0	.438	4th/AFC Central Division	0	0
2001—Jacksonville NFL	6	10	0	.375	5th/AFC Central Division		
College totals (7 years)	36	27	3	.568	College totals (2 years)	1	1
Pro totals (7 years)	62	50	0	.554	Pro totals (4 years)	4	4

NOTES:
1992—Lost to Tennessee, 38-23, in Hall of Fame Bowl.
1993—Defeated Virginia, 31-13, in CarQuest Bowl.
1996—Defeated Buffalo, 30-27, in first-round playoff game; defeated Denver, 30-27, in conference playoff game; lost to New England, 20-6, in AFC championship game.
1997—Lost to Denver, 42-17, in first-round playoff game.
1998—Defeated New England, 25-10, in first-round playoff game; lost to New York Jets, 34-24, in conference playoff game.
1999—Defeated Miami, 62-7, in conference playoff game; lost to Tennessee, 33-14, in AFC championship game.

COWHER, BILL — STEELERS

PERSONAL: Born May 8, 1957, in Pittsburgh. ... Full name: William Laird Cowher. ... Played linebacker.
HIGH SCHOOL: Carlynton (Carnegie, Pa.).
COLLEGE: North Carolina State (bachelor of science degree in education, 1979).
TRANSACTIONS/CAREER NOTES: Signed as non-drafted free agent by Philadelphia Eagles (May 8, 1979). ... Released by Eagles (August 14, 1979). ... Signed by Cleveland Browns (February 27, 1980). ... On injured reserve with knee injury (August 20, 1981-entire season). ... Traded by Browns to Eagles for ninth-round pick (WR Don Jones) in 1984 draft (August 21, 1983). ... On injured reserve with knee injury (September 25, 1984-remainder of season).
PLAYING EXPERIENCE: Cleveland NFL, 1980 and 1982; Philadelphia NFL, 1983 and 1984. ... Games: 1980 (16), 1982 (9), 1983 (16), 1984 (4). Total: 45.
PRO STATISTICS: 1983—Recovered one fumble.

HEAD COACHING RECORD

BACKGROUND: Special teams coach, Cleveland Browns NFL (1985 and 1986). ... Defensive backs coach, Browns (1987 and 1988). ... Defensive coordinator, Kansas City Chiefs NFL (1989-1991).
HONORS: Named NFL Coach of the Year by The Sporting News (1992).

	REGULAR SEASON					POST-SEASON	
	W	L	T	Pct.	Finish	W	L
1992—Pittsburgh NFL	11	5	0	.688	1st/AFC Central Division	0	1
1993—Pittsburgh NFL	9	7	0	.563	2nd/AFC Central Division	0	1
1994—Pittsburgh NFL	12	4	0	.750	1st/AFC Central Division	1	1
1995—Pittsburgh NFL	11	5	0	.688	1st/AFC Central Division	2	1
1996—Pittsburgh NFL	10	6	0	.625	1st/AFC Central Division	1	1
1997—Pittsburgh NFL	11	5	0	.688	T1st/AFC Central Division	1	1
1998—Pittsburgh NFL	7	9	0	.438	3rd/AFC Central Division	0	0
1999—Pittsburgh NFL	6	10	0	.375	4th/AFC Central Division	0	0
2000—Pittsburgh NFL	9	7	0	.563	3rd/AFC Central Division	0	0
2001—Pittsburgh NFL	13	3	0	.813	1st/AFC Central Division	1	1
Pro totals (10 years)	99	61	0	.619	Pro totals (7 years)	6	7

NOTES:
1992—Lost to Buffalo, 24-3, in conference playoff game.
1993—Lost to Kansas City, 27-24 (OT), in first-round playoff game.
1994—Defeated Cleveland, 29-9, in conference playoff game; lost to San Diego, 17-13, in AFC championship game.
1995—Defeated Buffalo, 40-21, in conference playoff game; defeated Indianapolis, 20-16, in AFC championship game; lost to Dallas, 27-17, in Super Bowl XXX.
1996—Defeated Indianapolis, 42-14, in first-round playoff game; lost to New England, 28-3, in conference playoff game.
1997—Defeated New England, 7-6, in conference playoff game; lost to Denver, 24-21, in AFC championship game.
2001—Defeated Baltimore, 27-10, in conference playoff game; lost to New England, 24-17, in AFC championship game.

DAVIS, BUTCH — BROWNS

PERSONAL: Born November 17, 1951, in Tahlequah, Okla. ... Full name: Paul Hilton Davis.
HIGH SCHOOL: Bixby (Okla.).
COLLEGE: Arkansas (degree in biology and life science).

HEAD COACHING RECORD

BACKGROUND: Assistant coach, Fayetteville (Ark.) High School (1973). ... Assistant coach, Pawhuska (Okla.) High School (1974 and 1975). ... Assistant coach, Sand Springs (Okla.) High School (1976 and 1977). ... Head coach, Rogers High School, Tulsa, Okla. (1978). ... Assistant coach, Oklahoma State (1979-1983). ... Assistant coach, University of Miami (1984-1988). ... Assistant coach, Dallas Cowboys NFL (1989-1992). ... Defensive coordinator, Cowboys (1993 and 1994).

	REGULAR SEASON					POST-SEASON	
	W	L	T	Pct.	Finish	W	L
1995—Miami (Fla.)	8	3	0	.727	T1st/Big East Conference	0	0
1996—Miami (Fla.)	9	3	0	.750	T1st/Big East Conference	1	0
1997—Miami (Fla.)	5	6	0	.455	T5th/Big East Conference	0	0
1998—Miami (Fla.)	9	3	0	.750	T2nd/Big East Conference	1	0
1999—Miami (Fla.)	9	4	0	.692	2nd/Big East Conference	1	0
2000—Miami (Fla.)	11	1	0	.917	1st/Big East Conference	1	0
2001—Cleveland NFL	7	9	0	.438	3rd/AFC Central Division	0	0
College totals (6 years)	51	20	0	.718	College totals (4 years)	4	0

NOTES:
1996—Defeated Virginia, 31-21, in CarQuest Bowl.
1998—Defeated North Carolina State, 46-23, in Micron PC Bowl.
1999—Defeated Georgia Tech, 28-13, in Gator Bowl.
2000—Defeated Florida, 37-20, in Sugar Bowl.

DUNGY, TONY — COLTS

PERSONAL: Born October 6, 1955, in Jackson, Mich. ... Full name: Anthony Kevin Dungy. ... Played defensive back and quarterback. ... Name pronounced DUN-gee.
HIGH SCHOOL: Parkside (Jackson, Mich.).
COLLEGE: Minnesota (degree in business administration, 1978).
TRANSACTIONS/CAREER NOTES: Signed as non-drafted free agent by Pittsburgh Steelers (May 1977). ... Traded by Steelers to San Francisco 49ers for 10th-round pick in 1980 draft (August 21, 1979). ... Traded by 49ers with RB Mike Hogan to New York Giants for WR Jimmy Robinson and CB Ray Rhodes (March 27, 1980).

CHAMPIONSHIP GAME EXPERIENCE: Played in AFC championship game (1978 season). ... Played in Super Bowl XIII (1978 season).
PRO STATISTICS: 1977—Attempted eight passes with three completions for 43 yards and two interceptions, rushed three times for eight yards and fumbled once. 1978—Recovered two fumbles for eight yards. 1979—Recovered two fumbles.

			INTERCEPTIONS			
Year Team	G	GS	No.	Yds.	Avg.	TD
1977—Pittsburgh NFL	14	0	3	37	12.3	0
1978—Pittsburgh NFL	16	0	6	95	15.8	0
1979—San Francisco NFL	15	0	0	0	0.0	0
Pro totals (3 years)	45	0	9	132	14.7	0

HEAD COACHING RECORD

BACKGROUND: Defensive backs coach, University of Minnesota (1980). ... Defensive assistant, Pittsburgh Steelers NFL (1981). ... Defensive backs coach, Steelers (1982 and 1983). ... Defensive coordinator, Steelers (1984-1988). ... Defensive backs coach, Kansas City Chiefs NFL (1989-1991). ... Defensive coordinator, Minnesota Vikings NFL (1992-1995).

	REGULAR SEASON					POST-SEASON	
	W	L	T	Pct.	Finish	W	L
1996—Tampa Bay NFL	6	10	0	.375	4th/NFC Central Division	0	0
1997—Tampa Bay NFL	10	6	0	.625	2nd/NFC Central Division	1	1
1998—Tampa Bay NFL	8	8	0	.500	3rd/NFC Central Division	0	0
1999—Tampa Bay NFL	11	5	0	.688	1st/NFC Central Division	1	1
2000—Tampa Bay NFL	10	6	0	.625	2nd/NFC Central Division	0	1
2001—Tampa Bay NFL	9	7	0	.563	3rd/NFC Central Division	0	1
Pro totals (6 years)	54	42	0	.563	Pro totals (4 years)	2	4

NOTES:
1997—Defeated Detroit, 20-10, in first-round playoff game; lost to Green Bay, 21-7, in conference playoff game.
1999—Defeated Washington, 14-13, in conference playoff game; lost to St. Louis, 11-6, in NFC championship game.
2000—Lost to Philadelphia, 21-3, in first-round playoff game.
2001—Lost to Philadelphia, 31-9, in first-round playoff game.

EDWARDS, HERMAN — JETS

PERSONAL: Born April 27, 1954, in Fort Monmouth, N.J. ... Full name: Herman Lee Edwards. ... Played cornerback.
HIGH SCHOOL: Monterey (Calif.).
JUNIOR COLLEGE: Monterey (Calif.) Peninsula College.
COLLEGE: California, then San Diego State (degree in criminal justice).
TRANSACTIONS/CAREER NOTES: Signed as non-drafted free agent by Philadelphia Eagles (May 1977). ... Released by Eagles (September 8, 1986). ... Signed by Los Angeles Rams (September 15, 1986). ... Released by Rams (October 20, 1986). ... Signed by Atlanta Falcons (November 3, 1986). ... Announced retirement (November 24, 1986).
CHAMPIONSHIP GAME EXPERIENCE: Played in NFC championship game (1980 season). ... Played in Super Bowl XV (1980 season).
PRO STATISTICS: 1977—Recovered two fumbles and fumbled once. 1978—Recovered one fumble for 26 yards and a touchdown and fumbled once. 1979—Recovered one fumble. 1981—Recovered one fumble for four yards. 1985—Recovered one fumble for four yards.

			INTERCEPTIONS			
Year Team	G	GS	No.	Yds.	Avg.	TD
1977—Philadelphia NFL	14	0	6	9	1.5	0
1978—Philadelphia NFL	16	0	7	59	8.4	0
1979—Philadelphia NFL	16	0	3	6	2.0	0
1980—Philadelphia NFL	16	0	3	12	4.0	0
1981—Philadelphia NFL	16	0	3	1	0.3	0
1982—Philadelphia NFL	9	0	5	3	0.6	0
1983—Philadelphia NFL	16	0	1	0	0.0	0
1984—Philadelphia NFL	16	0	2	0	0.0	0
1985—Philadelphia NFL	16	0	3	8	2.7	1
1986—Los Angeles Rams NFL	4	0	0	0	0.0	0
—Atlanta NFL	3	0	0	0	0.0	0
Pro totals (10 years)	142	0	33	98	3.0	1

HEAD COACHING RECORD

BACKGROUND: Defensive backs coach, San Jose State (1987-1989). ... Scout, Kansas City Chiefs NFL (1990, 1991 and 1995). ... Defensive backs coach, Chiefs (1992-1994). ... Assistant head coach/defensive back coach, Tampa Bay Buccaneers NFL (1996-2000).

	REGULAR SEASON					POST-SEASON	
	W	L	T	Pct.	Finish	W	L
2001—New York Jets NFL	10	6	0	.625	3rd/AFC Eastern Division	0	1

NOTES:
2001—Lost to Oakland, 38-24, in first-round playoff game.

FASSEL, JIM — GIANTS

PERSONAL: Born August 31, 1949, in Anaheim. ... Full name: James Fassel. ... Played quarterback.
HIGH SCHOOL: Anaheim (Calif.) High.
JUNIOR COLLEGE: Fullerton (Calif.) College.
COLLEGE: Southern California, then Long Beach State (degree in physical education, 1972).
TRANSACTIONS/CAREER NOTES: Selected by Chicago Bears in seventh round of 1972 NFL draft.

HEAD COACHING RECORD

BACKGROUND: Coach, Fullerton College (1973). ... Player/coach, Hawaii Hawaiians WFL (1974). ... Quarterbacks/receivers coach, Utah (1976). ... Offensive coordinator, Weber State (1977 and 1978). ... Offensive coordinator, Stanford (1979-1983). ... Offensive coordinator, New Orleans Breakers USFL (1984). ... Quarterbacks coach, New York Giants NFL (1991). ... Offensive coordinator, Giants (1992) ... Assistant head coach/offensive coordinator, Denver Broncos NFL (1993 and 1994). ... Quarterbacks coach, Oakland Raiders NFL (1995). ... Offensive coordinator/quarterbacks coach, Arizona Cardinals NFL (1996).

HONORS: Named NFL Coach of the Year by The Sporting News (1997).

	REGULAR SEASON					POST-SEASON	
	W	L	T	Pct.	Finish	W	L
1985—Utah	8	4	0	.667	2nd/Western Athletic Conference	0	0
1986—Utah	2	9	0	.182	9th/Western Athletic Conference	0	0
1987—Utah	5	7	0	.417	7th/Western Athletic Conference	0	0
1988—Utah	6	5	0	.545	4th/Western Athletic Conference	0	0
1989—Utah	4	8	0	.333	7th/Western Athletic Conference	0	0
1997—New York Giants NFL	10	5	1	.656	1st/NFC Eastern Division	0	1
1998—New York Giants NFL	8	8	0	.500	3rd/NFC Eastern Division	0	0
1999—New York Giants NFL	7	9	0	.438	3rd/NFC Eastern Division	0	0
2000—New York Giants NFL	12	4	0	.750	1st/NFC Eastern Division	2	1
2001—New York Giants NFL	7	9	0	.438	3rd/NFC Eastern Division	0	0
College totals (5 years)	25	33	0	.431			
Pro totals (5 years)	44	35	1	.556	**Pro totals (2 years)**	2	2

NOTES:
1997—Lost to Minnesota, 23-22, in first-round playoff game.
2000—Defeated Philadelphia, 20-10, in conference playoff game; defeated Minnesota, 41-0, in NFC championship game; lost to Balitmore, 34-7, in Super Bowl XXXV.

FISHER, JEFF — TITANS

PERSONAL: Born February 25, 1958, in Culver City, Calif. ... Full name: Jeffrey Michael Fisher. ... Played safety.
HIGH SCHOOL: Taft (Woodland Hills, Calif.).
COLLEGE: Southern California (degree in public administration, 1981).
TRANSACTIONS/CAREER NOTES: Selected by Chicago Bears in seventh round (177th pick overall) of 1981 NFL draft. ... On injured reserve with broken leg (October 24, 1983-remainder of season). ... On injured reserve with ankle injury entire 1985 season.
CHAMPIONSHIP GAME EXPERIENCE: Played in NFC championship game (1984 season).
PRO STATISTICS: 1981—Recovered one fumble. 1984—Recovered one fumble.

			INTERCEPTIONS				PUNT RETURNS				KICKOFF RETURNS				TOTALS			
Year Team	G	GS	No.	Yds.	Avg.	TD	No.	Yds.	Avg.	TD	No.	Yds.	Avg.	TD	TD	2pt.	Pts.	Fum.
1981—Chicago NFL	16	0	2	3	1.5	0	43	509	11.8	1	7	102	14.6	0	1	0	6	3
1982—Chicago NFL	9	0	3	19	6.3	0	7	53	7.6	0	7	102	14.6	0	0	0	0	2
1983—Chicago NFL	8	0	0	0	0.0	0	13	71	5.5	0	0	0	0.0	0	0	0	0	0
1984—Chicago NFL	16	0	0	0	0.0	0	57	492	8.6	0	0	0	0.0	0	0	0	0	4
1985—Chicago NFL								Did not play.										
Pro totals (4 years)	49	...	5	22	4.4	0	120	1125	9.4	1	14	204	14.6	0	1	0	6	9

HEAD COACHING RECORD

BACKGROUND: Defensive backs coach, Philadelphia Eagles NFL (1986-1988). ... Defensive coordinator, Eagles (1989 and 1990). ... Defensive coordinator, Los Angeles Rams NFL (1991). ... Defensive backs coach, San Francisco 49ers NFL (1992 and 1993). ... Defensive coordinator, Houston Oilers NFL (February 9-November 14, 1994). ... Oilers franchise moved to Tennessee for 1997 season.

	REGULAR SEASON					POST-SEASON	
	W	L	T	Pct.	Finish	W	L
1994—Houston NFL	1	5	0	.167	4th/AFC Central Division	0	0
1995—Houston NFL	7	9	0	.438	T2nd/AFC Central Division	0	0
1996—Houston NFL	8	8	0	.500	T3rd/AFC Central Division	0	0
1997—Tennessee NFL	8	8	0	.500	3rd/AFC Central Division	0	0
1998—Tennessee NFL	8	8	0	.500	2nd/AFC Central Division	0	0
1999—Tennessee NFL	13	3	0	.813	2nd/AFC Central Division	3	1
2000—Tennessee NFL	13	3	0	.813	1st/AFC Central Division	0	1
2001—Tennessee NFL	7	9	0	.438	4th/AFC Central Division	0	0
Pro totals (8 years)	65	53	0	.551	**Pro totals (2 years)**	3	2

NOTES:
1994—Replaced Jack Pardee as head coach (November 14) with 1-9 record and club in fourth place.
1999—Defeated Buffalo, 22-16, in first-round playoff game; defeated Indianapolis, 19-16, in conference playoff game; defeated Jacksonville, 33-14 in AFC championship game; lost to St. Louis, 23-16, in Super Bowl XXXIV.
2000—Lost to Baltimore, 24-10, in conference playoff game.

FOX, JOHN — PANTHERS

PERSONAL: Born February 8, 1955, in Virginia Beach, Va.
HIGH SCHOOL: Castle Park (Chula Vista, Calif.).
JUNIOR COLLEGE: Southwestern Junior College (Calif.).
COLLEGE: San Diego State (physical education).

BACKGROUND: Graduate assistant, San Diego State (1978). ... Assistant coach, U.S. International University, Calif. (1979). ... Secondary coach, Boise State (1980). ... Secondary coach, Long Beach State (1981). ... Secondary coach, University of Utah (1982). ... Secondary coach, University of Kansas (1983). ... Secondary coach, Iowa State (1984). ... Secondary coach, Los Angeles Express USFL (1985). ... Defensive coordinator/secondary coach, University of Pittsburgh (1986-1988). ... Secondary coach, Pittsburgh Steelers NFL (1989-1991). ... Secondary coach, San Diego Chargers NFL (1992-1993). ... Defensive coordinator, Los Angeles Raiders NFL (1994). ... Defensive coordinator, Oakland Raiders NFL (1995). ... Consultant, St. Louis Rams NFL (1996). ... Defensive coordinator, New York Giants NFL (1997-2001).

GRUDEN, JON — BUCCANEERS

PERSONAL: Born August 17, 1963, in Sandusky, Ohio. ... Son of Jim Gruden, scout, San Francisco 49ers; and brother of Jay Gruden, quarterback with Tampa Bay Storm of Arena League (1991-96) and current head coach, Orlando Predators of Arena League.
HIGH SCHOOL: Clay (South Bend, Ind.).
COLLEGE: Dayton, then Tennessee (degree in communications, 1985).

HEAD COACHING RECORD

BACKGROUND: Graduate assistant, Tennessee (1986 and 1987). ... Passing game coordinator, Southeast Missouri State (1988). ... Wide receivers coach, Pacific (1989). ... Assistant coach, San Francisco 49ers NFL (1990) ... Wide receivers coach, University of Pittsburgh (1991). ... Offensive/quality control coach, Green Bay Packers NFL (1992). ... Wide receivers coach, Packers (1993 and 1994). ... Offensive coordinator, Philadelphia Eagles NFL (1995-1997).

	REGULAR SEASON					POST-SEASON	
	W	L	T	Pct.	Finish	W	L
1998—Oakland NFL	8	8	0	.500	T2nd/AFC Western Division	0	0
1999—Oakland NFL	8	8	0	.500	T3rd/AFC Western Division	0	0
2000—Oakland NFL	12	4	0	.750	1st/AFC Western Division	1	1
2001—Oakland NFL	10	6	0	.625	1st/AFC Western Division	1	1
Pro totals (4 years)	38	26	0	.594	Pro totals (2 years)	2	2

NOTES:
2000—Defeated Miami, 27-0, in conference playoff game; lost to Baltimore, 16-3, in AFC championship game.
2001—Defeated New York Jets, 38-24, in first-round playoff game; lost to New England, 16-13 (OT), in conference playoff game.

HASLETT, JIM — SAINTS

PERSONAL: Born December 9, 1957, in Pittsburgh. ... Full name: James Donald Haslett. ... Cousin of Hal Stringert, defensive back with San Diego Chargers (1974-80). ... Played linebacker.
HIGH SCHOOL: Avalon (Pittsburgh).
COLLEGE: Indiana University, Pa. (degree in elementary education).
TRANSACTIONS/CAREER NOTES: Selected by Buffalo Bills in second round (51st pick overall) of 1979 NFL draft. ... On injured reserve with back injury (September 13-November 17, 1983). ... On injured reserve with broken leg (September 1, 1986-entire season). ... Released by Bills (September 7, 1987). ... Signed by New York Jets as replacement player (September 30, 1987). ... On injured reserve with back injury (October 20, 1987-remainder of season).
HONORS: Played in Pro Bowl (1980 and 1981 seasons).
PRO STATISTICS: 1979—Recovered two fumbles. 1980—Recovered one fumble. 1982—Recovered one fumble and caught one pass for four yards. 1984—Recovered three fumbles for ten yards. 1985—Recovered three fumbles and fumbled once. 1987—Recovered one fumble.

				INTERCEPTIONS			
Year Team	G	GS	No.	Yds.	Avg.	TD
1979—Buffalo NFL	16	0	2	15	7.5	0
1980—Buffalo NFL	16	0	2	30	15.0	0
1981—Buffalo NFL	16	0	0	0	0.0	0
1982—Buffalo NFL	6	0	0	0	0.0	0
1983—Buffalo NFL	5	0	0	0	0.0	0
1984—Buffalo NFL	15	0	0	0	0.0	0
1985—Buffalo NFL	16	0	1	40	40.0	0
1986—Buffalo NFL			Did not play.			
1987—New York Jets NFL	3	0	1	9	9.0	0
Pro totals (8 years)	93	0	6	94	15.7	0

HEAD COACHING RECORD

BACKGROUND: Linebackers coach, University of Buffalo (1988). ... Defensive coordinator, University of Buffalo (1989 and 1990). ... Defensive coordinator, Sacramento Surge W.L. (1991 and 1992). ... Linebackers coach, Oakland Raiders NFL (1993 and 1994). ... Linebackers coach, New Orleans Saints NFL (1995). ... Defensive coordinator, Saints (1996). ... Defensive coordinator, Pittsburgh Steelers NFL (1997-1999).

	REGULAR SEASON					POST-SEASON	
	W	L	T	Pct.	Finish	W	L
2000—New Orleans NFL	10	6	0	.625	1st/NFC Western Division	1	1
2001—New Orleans NFL	7	9	0	.438	3rd/NFC Western Division	0	0
Pro totals (2 years)	17	15	0	.531	Pro totals (1 year)	1	1

NOTES:
2000—Defeated St. Louis, 31-28, in first-round playoff game; lost to Minnesota, 34-16, in conference playoff game.

– 485 –

HOLMGREN, MIKE — SEAHAWKS

PERSONAL: Born June 15, 1948, in San Francisco. ... Full name: Michael George Holmgren. ... Played quarterback.
HIGH SCHOOL: Lincoln (San Francisco).
COLLEGE: Southern California (degree in business finance, 1970).
TRANSACTIONS/CAREER NOTES: Selected by St. Louis Cardinals in eighth round of 1970 NFL draft. ... Released by Cardinals (1970).

HEAD COACHING RECORD

BACKGROUND: Assistant coach, Sacred Heart Cathedral Prep School, San Francisco (1972 and 1973). ... Assistant coach, Oak Grove High School, San Jose, Calif. (1975-1980). ... Offensive coordinator/quarterbacks coach, San Francisco State (1981). ... Quarterbacks coach, Brigham Young (1982-1985). ... Quarterbacks coach, San Francisco 49ers NFL (1986-1988). ... Offensive coordinator, 49ers (1989-1991).

	REGULAR SEASON					POST-SEASON	
	W	L	T	Pct.	Finish	W	L
1992—Green Bay NFL	9	7	0	.563	2nd/NFC Central Division	0	0
1993—Green Bay NFL	9	7	0	.563	T2nd/NFC Central Division	1	1
1994—Green Bay NFL	9	7	0	.563	T2nd/NFC Central Division	1	1
1995—Green Bay NFL	11	5	0	.688	1st/NFC Central Division	2	1
1996—Green Bay NFL	13	3	0	.813	1st/NFC Central Division	3	0
1997—Green Bay NFL	13	3	0	.813	1st/NFC Central Division	2	1
1998—Green Bay NFL	11	5	0	.688	2nd/NFC/Central Division	0	1
1999—Seattle NFL	9	7	0	.563	T1st/AFC Western Division	0	1
2000—Seattle NFL	6	10	0	.375	4th/AFC Western Division	0	0
2001—Seattle NFL	9	7	0	.563	2nd/AFC Western Division	0	0
Pro totals (10 years)	99	61	0	.619	Pro totals (7 years)	9	6

NOTES:
1993—Defeated Detroit, 28-24, in first-round playoff game; lost to Dallas 27-17, in conference playoff game.
1994—Defeated Detroit, 16-12, in first-round playoff game; lost to Dallas, 35-9, in conference playoff game.
1995—Defeated Atlanta, 37-20, in first-round playoff game; defeated San Francisco, 27-17, in conference playoff game; lost to Dallas, 38-27, in NFC championship game.
1996—Defeated San Francisco, 35-14, in conference playoff game; defeated Carolina, 30-13, in NFC championship game; defeated New England, 35-21, in Super Bowl XXXI.
1997—Defeated Tampa Bay, 21-7, in conference playoff game; defeated San Francisco, 23-10, in NFC championship game; lost to Denver, 31-24, in Super Bowl XXXII.
1998—Lost to San Francisco, 30-27, in first-round playoff game.
1999—Lost to Miami, 20-17, in first-round playoff game.

JAURON, DICK — BEARS

PERSONAL: Born October 7, 1950, in Swampscott, Mass. ... Full name: Richard Manuel Jauron. ... Played defensive back.
COLLEGE: Yale (degree in history).
TRANSACTIONS/CAREER NOTES: Selected by Detroit Lions in fourth round of 1973 NFL draft. ... Released by Lions (August 23, 1978). ... Signed by Cincinnati Bengals (August 29, 1978). ... On injured reserve with knee injury (November 12, 1980-remainder of season).
HONORS: Played in Pro Bowl (1974 season).

			INTERCEPTIONS				PUNT RETURNS				KICKOFF RETURNS				TOTALS		
Year Team	G	GS	No.	Yds.	Avg.	TD	No.	Yds.	Avg.	TD	No.	Yds.	Avg.	TD	TD	2pt.	Pts.	Fum.
1973—Detroit NFL	14	0	4	208	52.0	1	6	49	8.2	0	17	405	23.8	0	1	0	6	0
1974—Detroit NFL	14	0	1	26	26.0	0	17	286	16.8	0	2	21	10.5	0	0	0	0	0
1975—Detroit NFL	10	0	4	39	9.8	0	6	29	4.8	0	0	0	0.0	0	0	0	0	0
1976—Detroit NFL	6	0	2	0	0.0	0	0	0	0.0	0	0	0	0.0	0	0	0	0	0
1977—Detroit NFL	14	0	3	55	18.3	0	11	41	3.7	0	0	0	0.0	0	0	0	0	0
1978—Cincinnati NFL	16	0	4	52	13.0	1	3	32	10.7	0	0	0	0.0	0	1	0	6	0
1979—Cincinnati NFL	16	0	6	41	6.8	0	1	10	10.0	0	0	0	0.0	0	0	0	0	0
1980—Cincinnati NFL	10	0	1	11	11.0	0	0	0	0.0	0	0	0	0.0	0	0	0	0	0
Pro totals (8 years)	100	...	25	432	17.3	2	44	447	10.2	0	19	426	22.4	0	2	0	12	0

HEAD COACHING RECORD

BACKGROUND: Secondary coach, Buffalo Bills NFL (1985). ... Defensive backs coach, Green Bay Packers NFL (1986-94). ... Defensive coordinator, Jacksonville Jaguars NFL (1995-1998).
HONORS: Named NFL Coach of the Year by THE SPORTING NEWS (2001).

	REGULAR SEASON					POST-SEASON	
	W	L	T	Pct.	Finish	W	L
1999—Chicago NFL	6	10	0	.375	5th/NFC Central Division	0	0
2000—Chicago NFL	5	11	0	.313	5th/NFC Central Division	0	0
2001—Chicago NFL	13	3	0	.813	1st/NFC Central Division	0	1
Pro totals (3 years)	24	24	0	.500	Pro totals (1 year)	0	1

NOTES:
2001—Lost to Philadelphia, 33-19, in conference playoff game.

LeBEAU, DICK — BENGALS

PERSONAL: Born September 9, 1937, in London, Ohio. ... Full name: Charles Richard LeBeau. ... Name pronounced luh-BO. ... Played defensive back.
HIGH SCHOOL: London (Ohio).
COLLEGE: Ohio State (degree in education, 1963).

TRANSACTIONS/CAREER NOTES: Selected by Cleveland Browns in fifth round of NFL draft (1959). ... Released by Browns (1959). ... Signed by Detroit Lions (1959).
HONORS: Played in Pro Bowl (1964-1966 seasons).
PRO STATISTICS: 1960—Returned two kickoffs for 16 yards. 1962—Recovered one fumble for a touchdown.

Year Team	G	GS	No.	Yds.	Avg.	TD
1959—Detroit NFL	6	0	0	0	0.0	0
1960—Detroit NFL	12	0	4	58	14.5	0
1961—Detroit NFL	14	0	3	45	15.0	0
1962—Detroit NFL	14	0	4	67	16.8	†1
1963—Detroit NFL	14	0	5	158	31.6	1
1964—Detroit NFL	14	0	5	45	9.0	0
1965—Detroit NFL	14	0	7	84	12.0	1
1966—Detroit NFL	14	0	4	66	16.5	0
1967—Detroit NFL	14	0	4	29	7.3	0
1968—Detroit NFL	14	0	5	23	4.6	0
1969—Detroit NFL	14	0	6	15	2.5	0
1970—Detroit NFL	14	0	9	96	10.7	0
1971—Detroit NFL	13	0	6	76	12.7	0
1972—Detroit NFL	14	0	0	0	0.0	0
Pro totals (14 years)	185	0	62	762	12.3	3

HEAD COACHING RECORD

BACKGROUND: Special teams coach, Philadelphia Eagles NFL (1973-1975). ... Defensive backs coach, Green Bay Packers NFL (1976-1979). ... Defensive backs coach, Cincinnati Bengals NFL (1980-1983). ... Defensive coordinator, Bengals (1984-1991). ... Assistant coach, Pittsburgh Steelers NFL (1992-1994). ... Defensive coordinator, Steelers (1995 and 1996). ... Assistant head coach/defensive coordinator, Bengals (1997-September 25, 2000).

	REGULAR SEASON					POST-SEASON	
	W	L	T	Pct.	Finish	W	L
2000—Cincinnati NFL	4	9	0	.308	5th/AFC Central Division	0	0
2001—Cincinnati NFL	6	10	0	.375	6th/AFC Central Division	0	0
Pro totals (2 years)	10	19	0	.345			

NOTES:
2000—Replaced Bruce Coslet as head coach (September 25), with 0-3 record and club in sixth place.

MARIUCCI, STEVE — 49ERS

PERSONAL: Born November 4, 1955, in Iron Mountain, Mich. ... Full name: Steven Mariucci. ... Played quarterback.
HIGH SCHOOL: Iron Mountain (Mich.).
COLLEGE: Northern Michigan.
TRANSACTIONS/CAREER NOTES: Signed with Hamilton Tiger-Cats of CFL for 1978 season.

HEAD COACHING RECORD

BACKGROUND: Quarterbacks/running backs coach, Northern Michigan (1978 and 1979). ... Quarterbacks/special teams coordinator, Cal State Fullerton (1980-1982). ... Assistant head coach, Louisville (1983 and 1984). ... Receivers coach, Orlando Renegades USFL (1985). ... Quality control coach, Los Angeles Rams NFL (fall 1985). ... Wide receivers/special teams coach, University of California (1987-1989). ... Offensive coordinator/quarterbacks coach, University of California (1990 and 1991). ... Quarterbacks coach, Green Bay Packers NFL (1992-1995).

	REGULAR SEASON					POST-SEASON	
	W	L	T	Pct.	Finish	W	L
1996—California	6	6	0	.500	T5th/Pacific-10 Conference	0	1
1997—San Francisco NFL	13	3	0	.813	1st/NFC Western Division	1	1
1998—San Francisco NFL	12	4	0	.750	2nd/NFC Western Division	1	1
1999—San Francisco NFL	4	12	0	.250	4th/NFC Western Division	0	0
2000—San Francisco NFL	6	10	0	.375	4th/NFC Western Division	0	0
2001—San Francisco NFL	12	4	0	.750	2nd/NFC Western Division	0	1
College totals (1 year)	6	6	0	.500	College totals (1 year)	0	1
Pro totals (5 years)	47	33	0	.588	Pro totals (3 years)	2	3

NOTES:
1996—Lost to Navy, 42-38, in Aloha Bowl.
1997—Defeated Minnesota, 38-22, in conference playoff game; lost to Green Bay, 23-10, in NFC championship game.
1998—Defeated Green Bay, 30-27, in first-round playoff game; lost to Atlanta, 20-18, in conference playoff game.
2001—Lost to Green Bay, 25-15, in first-round playoff game.

MARTZ, MIKE — RAMS

PERSONAL: Born May 13, 1951, in Sioux Falls, S.D.
HIGH SCHOOL: Madison (San Diego).
JUNIOR COLLEGE: San Diego Mesa Community College.
COLLEGE: UC Santa Barbara, then Fresno State.

HEAD COACHING RECORD

BACKGROUND: Coach, Bullard High School, Fresno, Calif. (1973). ... Coach, San Diego Mesa Community College (1974, 1976 and 1977). ... Coach, San Jose State (1975). ... Coach, Santa Ana College (1978). ... Coach, Fresno State (1979). ... Coach, Pacific University (1980 and 1981). ... Running backs coach, University of Minnesota (1982). ... Quarterbacks/receivers coach, Arizona State (1983, 1986 and 1987). ... Offensive coordinator, Arizona State (1984 and 1988-1991). ... Offensive assistant, Los Angeles Rams NFL (1992 and 1993). ... Quarterbacks coach, Rams (1994). ... Offensive assistant, St. Louis Rams NFL (1995 and 1996). ... Quarterbacks coach, Washington Redskins NFL (1997 and 1998). ... Offensive coordinator, Rams (1999).

— 487 —

	REGULAR SEASON					POST-SEASON	
	W	L	T	Pct.	Finish	W	L
2000—St. Louis NFL	10	6	0	.625	2nd/NFC Western Division	0	1
2001—St. Louis NFL	14	2	0	.875	1st/NFC Western Division	2	1
Pro totals (2 years)	24	8	0	.750	Pro totals (2 years)	2	2

NOTES:
2000—Lost to New Orleans, 31-28, in first-round playoff game.
2001—Defeated Green Bay, 45-17, in conference playoff game; defeated Philadelphia, 29-24, in NFC championship game; lost to New England, 20-17, in Super Bowl XXXVI.

McGINNIS, DAVE — CARDINALS

PERSONAL: Born August 7, 1951, in Independence, Kan.
HIGH SCHOOL: Snyder (Texas).
COLLEGE: Texas Christian (degree in business administration).

HEAD COACHING RECORD
BACKGROUND: Freshman coach, Texas Christian (1973 and 1974). ... Linebackers/secondary coach, University of Missouri (1975-1977). ... Secondary coach, Indiana State (1978-1981). ... Defensive backfield coach, Texas Christian (1982). ... Defensive ends/linebackers coach, Kansas State (1983-1985). ... Linebackers coach, Chicago Bears NFL (1986-1995). ... Defensive coordinator, Arizona Cardinals (1996-October 23, 2000).

	REGULAR SEASON					POST-SEASON	
	W	L	T	Pct.	Finish	W	L
2000—Arizona NFL	1	8	0	.111	5th/NFC Eastern Division	0	0
2001—Arizona NFL	7	9	0	.438	4th/NFC Eastern Division	0	0
Pro totals (2 years)	8	17	0	.320			

NOTES:
2000—Replaced Vince Tobin as head coach (October 23), with 2-5 record and club in fifth place.

MORNHINWEG, MARTY — LIONS

PERSONAL: Born March 29, 1962, in Edmond, Okla.
HIGH SCHOOL: Oak Grove (San Jose, Calif.).
COLLEGE: Montana.

HEAD COACHING RECORD
BACKGROUND: Receivers coach, University of Montana (1985). ... Graduate assistant/quarterbacks coach, University of Texas-El Paso (1986 and 1987). ... Running backs coach, Northern Arizona (1988). ... Offensive coordinator/quarterbacks coach, Southeast Missouri State (1989 and 1990). ... Tight ends coach, University of Missouri (1991). ... Offensive line coach, Missouri (1992 and 1993). ... Offensive coordinator, Northern Arizona (1994). ... Offensive assistant/quality control, Green Bay Packers NFL (1995). ... Quarterbacks coach, Packers (1996). ... Offensive coordinator, San Francisco 49ers NFL (1997-2000).

	REGULAR SEASON					POST-SEASON	
	W	L	T	Pct.	Finish	W	L
2001—Detroit NFL	2	14	0	.125	5th/NFC Central Division	0	0

REEVES, DAN — FALCONS

PERSONAL: Born January 19, 1944, in Rome, Ga. ... Full name: Daniel Edward Reeves. ... Played running back.
HIGH SCHOOL: Americus (Ga.).
COLLEGE: South Carolina.
TRANSACTIONS/CAREER NOTES: Signed as non-drafted free agent by Dallas Cowboys for 1965 season.
CHAMPIONSHIP GAME EXPERIENCE: Played in NFL championship game (1966 and 1967 seasons). ... Played in NFC championship game (1970 and 1971 seasons). ... Played in Super Bowl V (1970 season). ... Member of Super Bowl championship team (1971 season).
HONORS: Named halfback on THE SPORTING NEWS NFL Eastern Conference All-Star team (1966).
PRO STATISTICS: 1965—Returned two kickoffs for 45 yards. 1966—Returned two punts for minus one yard, returned three kickoffs for 56 yards and fumbled six times. 1967—Fumbled seven times. 1969—Fumbled twice. 1970—Fumbled four times. 1971—Fumbled once.

				PASSING						RUSHING				RECEIVING				TOTALS		
Year	Team	G	GS	Att.	Cmp.	Pct.	Yds.	TD	Int.	Avg.	Att.	Yds.	Avg.	TD	No.	Yds.	Avg.	TD	TD	2pt.	Pts.
1965—Dallas NFL	13	0	2	1	50.0	11	0	0	5.50	33	102	3.1	2	9	210	23.3	1	3	0	18
1966—Dallas NFL	14	0	6	3	50.0	48	0	0	8.00	175	757	4.3	8	41	557	13.6	8	16	0	96
1967—Dallas NFL	14	0	7	4	57.1	195	2	1	27.86	173	603	3.5	5	39	490	12.6	6	11	0	66
1968—Dallas NFL	4	0	4	2	50.0	43	0	0	10.75	40	178	4.5	4	7	84	12.0	1	5	0	30
1969—Dallas NFL	13	0	3	1	33.3	35	0	1	11.67	59	173	2.9	4	18	187	10.4	1	5	0	30
1970—Dallas NFL	14	0	3	1	33.3	14	0	1	4.67	35	84	2.4	2	12	140	11.7	0	2	0	12
1971—Dallas NFL	14	0	5	2	40.0	24	0	1	4.80	17	79	4.6	0	3	25	8.3	0	0	0	0
1972—Dallas NFL	14	0	2	0	0.0	0	0	0	0.0	3	14	4.7	0	0	0	0.0	0	0	0	0
Pro totals (8 years)	100	...	32	14	43.8	370	2	4	11.56	535	1990	3.7	25	129	1693	13.1	17	42	0	252

HEAD COACHING RECORD

BACKGROUND: Player/coach, Dallas Cowboys NFL (1970 and 1971). ... Offensive backs coach, Cowboys (1972 and 1974-1976). ... Offensive coordinator, Cowboys (1977-1980).
HONORS: Named NFL Coach of the Year by The Sporting News (1993 and 1998).

	REGULAR SEASON					POST-SEASON	
	W	L	T	Pct.	Finish	W	L
1981—Denver NFL	10	6	0	.625	T1st/AFC Western Division	0	0
1982—Denver NFL	2	7	0	.222	12th/AFC	0	0
1983—Denver NFL	9	7	0	.563	T2nd/AFC Western Division	0	1
1984—Denver NFL	13	3	0	.813	1st/AFC Western Division	0	1
1985—Denver NFL	11	5	0	.688	2nd/AFC Western Division	0	0
1986—Denver NFL	11	5	0	.688	1st/AFC Western Division	2	1
1987—Denver NFL	10	4	1	.700	1st/AFC Western Division	2	1
1988—Denver NFL	8	8	0	.500	2nd/AFC Western Division	0	0
1989—Denver NFL	11	5	0	.688	1st/AFC Western Division	2	1
1990—Denver NFL	5	11	0	.313	5th/AFC Western Division	0	0
1991—Denver NFL	12	4	0	.750	1st/AFC Western Division	1	1
1992—Denver NFL	8	8	0	.500	3rd/AFC Western Division	0	0
1993—New York Giants NFL	11	5	0	.688	2nd/NFC Eastern Division	1	1
1994—New York Giants NFL	9	7	0	.563	2nd/NFC Eastern Division	0	0
1995—New York Giants NFL	5	11	0	.313	4th/NFC Eastern Division	0	0
1996—New York Giants NFL	6	10	0	.375	5th/NFC Eastern Division	0	0
1997—Atlanta NFL	7	9	0	.438	T2nd/NFC Western Division	0	0
1998—Atlanta NFL	14	2	0	.875	1st/NFC Western Division	2	1
1999—Atlanta NFL	5	11	0	.313	3rd/NFC Western Division	0	0
2000—Atlanta NFL	4	12	0	.250	5th/NFC Western Division	0	0
2001—Atlanta NFL	7	9	0	.438	4th/NFC Western Division	0	0
Pro totals (21 years)	**178**	**149**	**1**	**.544**	**Pro totals (8 years)**	**10**	**8**

NOTES:
1983—Lost to Seattle, 31-7, in wild-card playoff game.
1984—Lost to Pittsburgh, 24-17, in conference playoff game.
1986—Defeated New England, 22-17, in conference playoff game; defeated Cleveland, 23-20 (OT), in AFC championship game; lost to New York Giants, 39-20, in Super Bowl XXI.
1987—Defeated Houston, 34-10, in conference playoff game; defeated Cleveland, 38-33, in AFC championship game; lost to Washington, 42-10, in Super Bowl XXII.
1989—Defeated Pittsburgh, 24-23, in conference playoff game; defeated Cleveland, 37-21, in AFC championship game; lost to San Francisco, 55-10, in Super Bowl XXIV.
1991—Defeated Houston, 26-24, in conference playoff game; lost to Buffalo, 10-7, in AFC championship game.
1993—Defeated Minnesota, 17-10, in first-round playoff game; lost to San Francisco, 44-3, in conference playoff game.
1998—Defeated San Francisco, 20-18, in conference playoff game; defeated Minnesota, 30-27, in NFC championship game; lost to Denver, 34-19, in Super Bowl XXXIII.

REID, ANDY — EAGLES

PERSONAL: Born March 19, 1958, in Los Angeles. ... Full name: Andrew Walter Reid.
HIGH SCHOOL: John Marshall (Los Angeles).
COLLEGE: Brigham Young (bachelor's degree in physical education; master's degree in professional leadership, physical education and athletics).

HEAD COACHING RECORD

BACKGROUND: Graduate assistant, Brigham Young University (1982). ... Offensive coordinator, San Francisco State (1983-1985). ... Offensive line coach, Northern Arizona University (1986). ... Offensive line coach, University of Texas-El Paso (1987 and 1988). ... Offensive line coach, University of Missouri (1989-1992). ... Tight ends coach, Green Bay Packers NFL (1993-1996). ... Quarterbacks coach, Packers (1997 and 1998).
HONORS: Named NFL Coach of the Year by The Sporting News (2000).

	REGULAR SEASON					POST-SEASON	
	W	L	T	Pct.	Finish	W	L
1999—Philadelphia NFL	5	11	0	.313	5th/NFC Eastern Division	0	0
2000—Philadelphia NFL	11	5	0	.688	2nd/NFC Eastern Division	1	1
2001—Philadelphia NFL	11	5	0	.688	1st/NFC Eastern Division	2	1
Pro totals (3 years)	**27**	**21**	**0**	**.563**	**Pro totals (2 years)**	**3**	**2**

NOTES:
2000—Defeated Tampa Bay, 21-3, in first-round playoff game; lost to New York Giants, 20-10, in conference playoff game.
2001—Defeated Tampa Bay, 31-9, in first-round playoff game; defeated Chicago, 33-19, in conference playoff game; lost to St. Louis, 29-24, in NFC championship game.

SCHOTTENHEIMER, MARTY — CHARGERS

PERSONAL: Born September 23, 1943, in Canonsburg, Pa. ... Full name: Martin Edward Schottenheimer. ... Played linebacker. ... Brother of Kurt Schottenheimer, defensive coordinator, Detroit Lions; father of Brian Schottenheimer, quarterbacks coach, San Diego Chargers.
HIGH SCHOOL: McDonald (Pa.).
COLLEGE: Pittsburgh (degree in English, 1964).
TRANSACTIONS/CAREER NOTES: Selected by Buffalo Bills in seventh round of 1965 AFL draft. ... Released by Bills (1969). ... Signed by Boston Patriots (1969). ... Patriots franchise renamed New England Patriots for 1971 season. ... Traded by New England Patriots to Pittsburgh Steelers for OT Mike Haggerty and a draft choice (July 10, 1971). ... Released by Steelers (1971).
CHAMPIONSHIP GAME EXPERIENCE: Member of AFL championship team (1965 season). ... Played in AFL championship game (1966 season).
HONORS: Played in AFL All-Star Game (1965 season).
PRO STATISTICS: 1969—Returned one kickoff for 13 yards. 1970—Returned one kickoff for eight yards.

Year Team	G	GS	INTERCEPTIONS No.	Yds.	Avg.	TD
1965—Buffalo AFL	14	...	0	0	0.0	0
1966—Buffalo AFL	14	...	1	20	20.0	0
1967—Buffalo AFL	14	...	3	88	29.3	1
1968—Buffalo AFL	14	...	1	22	22.0	0
1969—Boston AFL	11	...	1	3	3.0	0
1970—Boston NFL	12	...	0	0	0.0	0
AFL totals (5 years)	67	...	6	133	22.2	1
NFL totals (1 year)	12	...	0	0	0.0	0
Pro totals (6 years)	79	...	6	133	22.2	1

HEAD COACHING RECORD

BACKGROUND: Linebackers coach, Portland Storm WFL (1974). ... Linebackers coach, New York Giants NFL (1975 and 1976). ... Defensive coordinator, Giants (1977). ... Linebackers coach, Detroit Lions NFL (1978 and 1979). ... Defensive coordinator, Cleveland Browns NFL (1989-October 22, 1984).

	W	L	T	Pct.	REGULAR SEASON Finish	POST-SEASON W	L
1984—Cleveland NFL	4	4	0	.500	3rd/AFC Central Division	0	0
1985—Cleveland NFL	8	8	0	.500	3rd/AFC Central Division	0	1
1986—Cleveland NFL	12	4	0	.750	1st/AFC Central Division	1	1
1987—Cleveland NFL	10	5	0	.667	1st/AFC Central Division	1	1
1988—Cleveland NFL	10	6	0	.625	T2nd/AFC Central Division	0	1
1989—Kansas City NFL	8	7	1	.531	2nd/AFC Western Division	0	0
1990—Kansas City NFL	11	5	0	.688	2nd/AFC Western Division	0	1
1991—Kansas City NFL	10	6	0	.625	2nd/AFC Western Division	1	1
1992—Kansas City NFL	10	6	0	.625	2nd/AFC Western Division	0	1
1993—Kansas City NFL	11	5	0	.688	1st/AFC Western Division	2	1
1994—Kansas City NFL	9	7	0	.563	T2nd/AFC Western Division	0	1
1995—Kansas City NFL	13	3	0	.813	1st/AFC Western Division	0	1
1996—Kansas City NFL	9	7	0	.563	2nd/AFC Western Division	0	0
1997—Kansas City NFL	13	3	0	.813	1st/AFC Western Division	0	1
1998—Kansas City NFL	7	9	0	.438	4th/AFC Western Division	0	0
2001—Washington NFL	8	8	0	.500	2nd/NFC Eastern Division	0	0
Pro totals (16 years)	153	93	1	.621	Pro totals (11 years)	5	11

NOTES:
1984—Replaced Sam Rutigliano as coach of Cleveland (October 22), with 1-7 record and in third place.
1985—Lost to Miami, 24-21, in conference playoff game.
1986—Defeated Ney York Jets, 23-20 (2 OT), in conference playoff game; lost to Denver, 23-20 (OT), in AFC championship game.
1987—Defeated Indianapolis, 38-21, in conference playoff game; lost to Denver, 38-33, in AFC championship game.
1988—Lost to Houston, 24-23, in wild-card playoff game.
1990—Lost to Miami, 17-16, in conference playoff game.
1991—Defeated Los Angeles Raiders, 10-6, in first-round playoff game; lost to Buffalo, 37-14, in conference playoff game.
1992—Lost to San Diego, 17-0, in first-round playoff game.
1993—Defeated Pittsburgh, 27-24 (OT), in first-round playoff game; defeated Houston, 28-20, in conference playoff game; lost to Buffalo, 30-13, in AFC championship game.
1994—Lost to Miami, 27-17, in first-round playoff game.
1995—Lost to Indianapolis, 10-7, in conference playoff game.
1997—Lost to Denver, 14-10, in conference playoff game.

SHANAHAN, MIKE — BRONCOS

PERSONAL: Born August 24, 1952, in Oak Park, Ill. ... Full name: Michael Edward Shanahan.
HIGH SCHOOL: Franklin Park (East Leyden, Ill.).
COLLEGE: Eastern Illinois (bachelor's degree in physical education, 1974; master's degree in education, 1975).

HEAD COACHING RECORD

BACKGROUND: Graduate assistant, Eastern Illinois (1973 and 1974). ... Running backs/wide receivers coach, Oklahoma (1975 and 1976). ... Backfield coach, Northern Arizona (1977). ... Offensive coordinator, Eastern Illinois (1978). ... Offensive coordinator, University of Minnesota (1979). ... Offensive coordinator, University of Florida (1980-1983). ... Quarterbacks coach, Denver Broncos NFL (1984, 1989 and 1990). ... Offensive coordinator, Broncos (1985-1987 and 1991). ... Offensive coordinator, San Francisco 49ers NFL (1992-1994).

	W	L	T	Pct.	REGULAR SEASON Finish	POST-SEASON W	L
1988—Los Angeles Raiders NFL	7	9	0	.438	3rd/AFC Western Division	0	0
1989—Los Angeles Raiders NFL	1	3	0	.250	—	0	0
1995—Denver NFL	8	8	0	.500	T3rd/AFC Western Division	0	0
1996—Denver NFL	13	3	0	.813	1st/AFC Western Division	0	1
1997—Denver NFL	12	4	0	.750	2nd/AFC Western Conference	4	0
1998—Denver NFL	14	2	0	.875	1st/AFC Western Division	3	0
1999—Denver NFL	6	10	0	.375	5th/AFC Western Division	0	0
2000—Denver NFL	11	5	0	.688	2nd/AFC Western Division	0	1
2001—Denver NFL	8	8	0	.500	3rd/AFC Western Division	0	0
Pro totals (9 years)	80	52	0	.606	Pro totals (4 years)	7	2

NOTES:
1989—Replaced as Raiders coach by Art Shell (October 3) with club tied for fourth place.
1996—Lost to Jacksonville, 30-27, in conference playoff game.
1997—Defeated Jacksonville, 42-17, in first-round playoff game; defeated Kansas City, 14-10, in conference playoff game; defeated Pittsburgh, 24-21, in AFC championship game; defeated Green Bay, 31-24, in Super Bowl XXXII.
1998—Defeated Miami, 38-3, in conference playoff game; defeated New York Jets, 23-10, in AFC championship game; defeated Atlanta, 34-19, in Super Bowl XXXIII.
2000—Lost to Baltimore, 21-3, in first-round playoff game.

SHERMAN, MIKE — PACKERS

PERSONAL: Born December 19, 1954, in Norwood, Mass.
COLLEGE: Central Connecticut State.
BACKGROUND: Head coach, Stamford High School, Stamford, Conn. (1979 and 1980). ... Coach, University of Pittsburgh (1981 and 1982). ... Coach, Tulane (1983 and 1984). ... Offensive coordinator, Holy Cross (1985-1988). ... Offensive line coach, Texas A&M (1989-1993). ... Offensive line coach, UCLA (1994). ... Offensive line coach, Texas A&M (1995-1996). ... Tight ends coach, Green Bay Packers NFL (1997-1998). ... Offensive coordinator/tight ends coach, Seattle Seahawks NFL (1999).

HEAD COACHING RECORD

	REGULAR SEASON					POST-SEASON	
	W	L	T	Pct.	Finish	W	L
2000—Green Bay NFL	9	7	0	.563	3rd/NFC Central Division	0	0
2001—Green Bay NFL	12	4	0	.750	2nd/NFC Central Division	1	1
Pro totals (2 years)	21	11	0	.656	**Pro totals (1 year)**	1	1

NOTES:
2001—Defeated San Francisco, 25-15, in first-round playoff game; lost to St. Louis, 45-17, in conference playoff game.

SPURRIER, STEVE — REDSKINS

PERSONAL: Born April 20, 1945, in Miami Beach. ... Full name: Stephen Orr Spurrier Sr. ... Played quarterback and punter.
HIGH SCHOOL: Science Hill (Johnson City, Tenn.).
COLLEGE: Florida.
TRANSACTIONS/CAREER NOTES: Selected by San Francisco 49ers in first round (third pick overall) of 1967 AFL-NFL draft. ... Traded by 49ers to Tampa Bay Buccaneers for WR Willie McGee, LB Bruce Elia and second-round pick (April 2, 1976).
HONORS: Heisman Trophy winner (1966). ... Named College Football Player of the Year by THE SPORTING NEWS (1966). ... Named quarterback on THE SPORTING NEWS college All-America team (1966).
PRO STATISTICS: 1967—Punted 73 times for 2,745 yards. 1968—Punted 68 times for 2,651 yards. 1969—Punted 12 times for 468 yards. 1970—Punted 75 times for 2,877 yards. 1971—Punted twice for 77 yards. 1972—Recovered two fumbles. 1973—Recovered one fumble.

			PASSING							RUSHING			TOTALS		
Year Team	G	GS	Att.	Cmp.	Pct.	Yds.	TD	Int.	Avg.	Rat.	Att.	Yds.	Avg.	TD	TD	2pt.	Pts.
1967—San Francisco NFL	14	0	50	23	46.0	211	0	7	4.22	18.4	5	18	3.6	0	0	0	0
1968—San Francisco NFL	14	0	0	0	0.0	0	0	0	0.0	...	1	-15	-15.0	0	0	0	0
1969—San Francisco NFL	6	0	146	81	55.5	926	5	11	6.34	54.8	5	49	9.8	0	0	0	0
1970—San Francisco NFL	14	0	4	3	75.0	49	1	0	12.25	155.2	2	-18	-9.0	0	0	0	0
1971—San Francisco NFL	6	0	4	1	25.0	46	0	0	11.50	75.0	1	2	2.0	0	0	0	0
1972—San Francisco NFL	13	0	269	147	54.6	1983	18	16	7.37	75.9	11	51	4.6	0	0	0	0
1973—San Francisco NFL	11	0	157	83	52.9	882	4	7	5.62	59.5	9	32	3.6	2	2	0	12
1974—San Francisco NFL	2	0	3	1	33.3	2	0	0	0.67	42.4	0	0	0.0	0	0	0	0
1975—San Francisco NFL	11	0	207	102	49.3	1151	5	7	5.56	60.3	15	91	6.1	0	0	0	0
1976—Tampa Bay NFL	14	0	311	156	50.2	1628	7	12	5.23	57.1	12	48	4.0	0	0	0	0
Pro totals (10 years)	105	0	1151	597	51.9	6878	40	60	5.98	60.1	61	258	4.2	2	2	0	12

HEAD COACHING RECORD

BACKGROUND: Quarterbacks coach, Florida (1978). ... Quarterbacks coach, Georgia (1979). ... Offensive coordinator and quarterbacks coach, Duke (1980-1982).

	REGULAR SEASON					POST-SEASON	
	W	L	T	Pct.	Finish	W	L
1983—Tampa Bay USFL	11	7	0	.611	3rd/Central Division	0	0
1984—Tampa Bay USFL	14	4	0	.778	2nd/Southern Division	0	1
1985—Tampa Bay USFL	10	8	0	.556	5th/Eastern Conference	0	1
1987—Duke	5	6	0	.455	7th/Atlantic Coast Conference	0	0
1988—Duke	7	3	1	.682	6th/Atlantic Coast Conference	0	0
1989—Duke	8	4	0	.667	1st/Atlantic Coast Conference	0	1
1990—Florida	9	2	0	.818	1st/Southeastern Conference	0	0
1991—Florida	10	2	0	.833	1st/Southeastern Conference	0	1
1992—Florida	9	4	0	.692	1st/Southeastern Conference East Division	1	0
1993—Florida	11	2	0	.846	1st/Southeastern Conference East Division	1	0
1994—Florida	10	2	1	.808	1st/Southeastern Conference East Division	0	1
1995—Florida	12	1	0	.923	1st/Southeastern Conference East Division	0	1
1996—Florida	12	1	0	.923	1st/Southeastern Conference East Division	1	0
1997—Florida	10	2	0	.833	T2nd/Southeastern Conference East Division	1	0
1998—Florida	10	2	0	.833	2nd/Southeastern Conference East Division	1	0
1999—Florida	9	4	0	.692	1st/Southeastern Conference East Division	0	1
2000—Florida	10	3	0	.769	1st/Southeastern Conference East Division	0	1
2001—Florida	10	2	0	.833	2nd/Southeastern Conference East Division	1	0
College totals (15 years)	142	40	2	.777	**College totals (12 years)**	6	6
Pro totals (3 years)	35	19	0	.648	**Pro totals (2 years)**	0	2

NOTES:
1984—Lost to Birmingham, 36-17, in conference playoff.
1985—Lost to Oakland, 48-27, in conference playoff game.
1989—Lost to Texas Tech, 49-21, in All America Bowl.
1991—Lost to Notre Dame, 39-28, in Sugar Bowl.
1992—Defeated North Carolina State, 27-10, in Gator Bowl.
1993—Defeated West Virginia, 41-7, in Sugar Bowl.
1994—Lost to Florida State, 23-17, in Sugar Bowl.
1995—Lost to Nebraska, 62-24, in Fiesta Bowl.
1996—Defeated Florida State, 52-20, in Sugar Bowl.
1997—Defeated Penn State, 21-6, in Citrus Bowl.
1998—Defeated Syracuse, 31-10, in Orange Bowl.
1999—Lost to Michigan State, 37-34, in Citrus Bowl.
2000—Lost to Miami, 37-20, in Sugar Bowl.
2001—Defeated Maryland, 56-23, in Orange Bowl.

TICE, MIKE — VIKINGS

PERSONAL: Born February 2, 1959, in Bayshore, N.Y. ... Full name: Michael Peter Tice. ... Brother of John Tice, tight end, New Orleans Saints (1983-1992).
HIGH SCHOOL: Central Islip (N.Y.).
COLLEGE: Maryland.
TRANSACTIONS/CAREER NOTES: Signed as non-drafted free agent by Seattle Seahawks (April 30, 1981). ... On injured reserve with fractured ankle (October 15-December 7, 1985). ... Granted unconditional free agency (February 1, 1989). ... Signed by Washington Redskins (February 20, 1989). ... Released by Redskins (September 4, 1990). ... Signed by Seahawks (November 28, 1990). ... Granted unconditional free agency (February 1-April 1, 1991). ... Re-signed by Seahawks (July 19, 1991). ... Granted unconditional free agency (February 1, 1992). ... Signed by Minnesota Vikings (March 18, 1992). ... On injured reserve with back injury (September 25-October 21, 1992). ... Granted unconditional free agency (March 1, 1993). ... Re-signed by Vikings (May 4, 1993). ... Released by Vikings (August 30, 1993). ... Re-signed by Vikings (August 31, 1993). ... Granted unconditional free agency (February 17, 1994). ... Re-signed by Vikings (December 7, 1995). ... Granted unconditional free agency (February 16, 1996).
CHAMPIONSHIP GAME EXPERIENCE: Played in AFC championship game (1983 season).
PRO STATISTICS: 1982—Recovered one fumble. 1983—Recovered one fumble. 1986—Recovered one fumble. 1991—Recovered one fumble. 1992—Recovered one fumble for four yards.

				RECEIVING				KICKOFF RETURNS				TOTALS		
Year Team	G	GS	No.	Yds.	Avg.	TD	No.	Yds.	Avg.	TD	TD	2pt.	Pts.	Fum.
1981—Seattle NFL	16	0	5	47	9.4	0	0	0	0.0	0	0	0	0	0
1982—Seattle NFL	9	0	9	46	5.1	0	0	0	0.0	0	0	0	0	0
1983—Seattle NFL	15	0	0	0	0.0	0	2	28	14.0	0	0	0	0	0
1984—Seattle NFL	16	0	8	90	11.3	3	0	0	0.0	0	3	0	18	0
1985—Seattle NFL	9	0	2	13	6.5	0	1	17	17.0	0	0	0	0	0
1986—Seattle NFL	16	0	15	150	10.0	0	1	17	17.0	0	0	0	0	0
1987—Seattle NFL	12	0	14	106	7.6	2	0	0	0.0	0	2	0	12	0
1988—Seattle NFL	16	0	29	244	8.4	0	1	17	17.0	0	0	0	0	1
1989—Washington NFL	16	0	1	2	2.0	0	0	0	0.0	0	0	0	0	0
1990—Seattle NFL	5	0	0	0	0.0	0	0	0	0.0	0	0	0	0	0
1991—Seattle NFL	16	0	10	70	7.0	4	3	46	15.3	0	4	0	24	0
1992—Minnesota NFL	12	9	5	65	13.0	1	0	0	0.0	0	1	0	6	0
1993—Minnesota NFL	16	12	6	39	6.5	1	0	0	0.0	0	1	0	6	1
1995—Minnesota NFL	2	1	3	22	7.3	0	0	0	0.0	0	0	0	0	0
Pro totals (14 years)	176	...	107	894	8.4	11	8	125	15.6	0	11	0	66	2

HEAD COACHING RECORD

BACKGROUND: Tight ends coach, Minnesota Vikings NFL (1996). ... Offensive line coach, Vikings (1997-2000). ... Assistant head coach/offensive line coach, Vikings (2001).

	REGULAR SEASON					POST-SEASON	
	W	L	T	Pct.	Finish	W	L
2001—Minnesota NFL	0	1	0	.000	4th/NFC Central Division	0	0

NOTES:
2001—Replaced Dennis Green as head coach (January 4) with 5-10 record and club in fourth place.

VERMEIL, DICK — CHIEFS

PERSONAL: Born October 30, 1936, in Calistoga, Calif. ... Full name: Richard Albert Vermeil. ... Brother of Al Vermeil, conditioning coach with San Francisco 49ers (1979-82) and brother-in-law of Louie Giammona, running back with Philadelphia Eagles (1978-82).
HIGH SCHOOL: Calistoga (Calif.).
JUNIOR COLLEGE: Napa College (degree in physical education, 1958).
COLLEGE: San Jose State (master's degree in physical education, 1959).

HEAD COACHING RECORD

BACKGROUND: Assistant coach, Del Mar High School, San Jose, Calif. (1959). ... Head coach, Hillsdale High School, San Mateo, Calif. (1960-1962; record: 17-9-1). ... Assistant coach, College of San Mateo (1963). ... Assistant coach, Stanford (1965-1968). ... Assistant coach, Los Angeles Rams NFL (1969 and 1971-1973). ... Assistant coach, UCLA (1970).
HONORS: Named NFL Coach of the Year by THE SPORTING NEWS (1979 and 1999).

	REGULAR SEASON					POST-SEASON	
	W	L	T	Pct.	Finish	W	L
1964—Napa College	8	1	0	.889	2nd/Golden Valley Conference	0	0
1974—UCLA	6	3	2	.636	T3rd/Pacific-8 Conference	0	0
1975—UCLA	8	2	1	.773	T1st/Pacific-8 Conference	1	0
1976—Philadelphia NFL	4	10	0	.286	4th/NFC Eastern Division	0	0
1977—Philadelphia NFL	5	9	0	.357	T4th/NFC Eastern Division	0	0
1978—Philadelphia NFL	9	7	0	.563	2nd/NFC Eastern Division	0	1
1979—Philadelphia NFL	11	5	0	.688	T1st/NFC Eastern Division	1	1
1980—Philadelphia NFL	12	4	0	.750	T1st/NFC Eastern Division	2	1
1981—Philadelphia NFL	10	6	0	.625	2nd/NFC Eastern Division	0	1
1982—Philadelphia NFL	3	6	0	.333	5th/NFC Eastern Division	0	0
1997—St. Louis NFL	5	11	0	.313	5th/NFC Western Division	0	0
1998—St. Louis NFL	4	12	0	.250	T4th/NFC Western Division	0	0
1999—St. Louis NFL	13	3	0	.813	T1st/NFC Western Division	3	0
2001—Kansas City NFL	6	10	0	.375	4th/AFC Western Division	0	0
College totals (3 years)	22	6	3	.758	**College totals (1 year)**	1	0
Pro totals (11 years)	82	83	0	.497	**Pro totals (5 years)**	6	4

NOTES:
1975—Defeated Ohio State, 23-10, in Rose Bowl.
1978—Lost to Atlanta, 14-13, in conference playoff game.
1979—Defeated Chicago, 27-17, in first-round playoff game; lost to Tampa Bay, 24-17, in conference playoff game.
1980—Defeated Minnesota, 31-16, in conference playoff game; defeated Dallas, 20-7, in NFC championship game; lost to Oakland, 27-10, in Super Bowl XV.
1981—Lost to New York Giants, 27-21, in conference playoff game.
1982—Only nine of 16 games were played due to the cancellation of games because of a players strike.
1999—Defeated Minnesota, 49-37, in conference playoff game; defeated Tampa Bay, 11-6, in NFC championship game; defeated Tennessee, 23-16, in Super Bowl XXXIV.

WANNSTEDT, DAVE — DOLPHINS

PERSONAL: Born May 21, 1952, in Pittsburgh. ... Full name: David Raymond Wannstedt.
HIGH SCHOOL: Baldwin (Pittsburgh).
COLLEGE: Pittsburgh (bachelor of science degree in physical education, 1974; master's degree in education, 1975).
TRANSACTIONS/CAREER NOTES: Selected by Green Bay Packers in 15th round (376th pick overall) of 1974 NFL draft. ... On injured reserve with neck injury for entire 1974 season.

HEAD COACHING RECORD

BACKGROUND: Graduate assistant, University of Pittsburgh (1975). ... Defensive line coach, University of Pittsburgh (1976-1978). ... Defensive line coach, Oklahoma State (1979 and 1980). ... Defensive coordinator, Oklahoma State (1981 and 1982). ... Defensive line coach, Southern California (1983-1985). ... Defensive coordinator, Miami, Fla. (1986-1988). ... Defensive coordinator, Dallas Cowboys NFL (1989-1992). ... Assistant head coach, Miami Dolphins NFL (1999).

	REGULAR SEASON					POST-SEASON	
	W	L	T	Pct.	Finish	W	L
1993—Chicago NFL	7	9	0	.438	4th/NFC Central Division	0	0
1994—Chicago NFL	9	7	0	.563	T2nd/NFC Central Division	1	1
1995—Chicago NFL	9	7	0	.563	3rd/NFC Central Division	0	0
1996—Chicago NFL	7	9	0	.438	3rd/NFC Central Division	0	0
1997—Chicago NFL	4	12	0	.250	5th/NFC Central Division	0	0
1998—Chicago NFL	4	12	0	.250	5th/NFC Central Division	0	0
2000—Miami NFL	11	5	0	.688	1st/AFC Eastern Division	1	1
2001—Miami NFL	11	5	0	.688	2nd/AFC Eastern Division	0	1
Pro totals (8 years)	62	66	0	.484	**Pro totals (3 years)**	2	3

NOTES:
1994—Defeated Minnesota, 35-18, in first-round playoff game; lost to San Francisco, 44-15, in conference playoff game.
2000—Defeated Indianapolis, 23-17, in first-round playoff game; lost to Oakland, 27-0, in conference playoff game.
2001—Lost to Baltimore, 20-3, in first-round playoff game.

WILLIAMS, GREGG — BILLS

PERSONAL: Born July 15, 1958, in Excelsior Springs, Mo.
COLLEGE: Northeast Missouri, then Central Missouri (master's degree in education).

HEAD COACHING RECORD

BACKGROUND: Assistant coach, Excelsior Springs (Mo.) High School (1980-1983). ... Head coach, Belton (Mo.) High School (1984-1987). ... Graduate Assistant, University of Houston (1988 and 1989). ... Quality control coach, Houston Oilers NFL (1990-1992). ... Special teams coach, Oilers (1993). ... Linebackers coach, Oilers (1994-1996). ... Defensive coordinator, Tennessee Oilers NFL (1997 and 1998). ... Defensive coordinator, Tennessee Titans NFL (1999 and 2000).

	REGULAR SEASON					POST-SEASON	
	W	L	T	Pct.	Finish	W	L
2001—Buffalo NFL	3	13	0	.188	5th/AFC Eastern Division	0	0

The Sporting News
Book Publishing Group presents

SportingNews SELECTS

PRO FOOTBALL'S GREATEST TEAMS

1999 ST. LOUIS RAMS • 1998 DENVER BRONCOS • 1996 GREEN BAY PACKERS • 1992 DALLAS C
1989 SAN FRANCISCO 49ERS • 1986 NEW YORK GIANTS • 1985 CHICAGO BEARS • 1984 NEW Y
1976 OAKLAND RAIDERS • 1974 PITTSBURGH STEELERS • 1972 MIAMI DOLPHINS • 1971 DALLA
1968 NEW YORK JETS • 1967 GREEN BAY PACKERS • 1966 GREEN BAY PACKE

Regularly $29.95
Yours for only
$19.95!
plus S&H
Save $10.00!

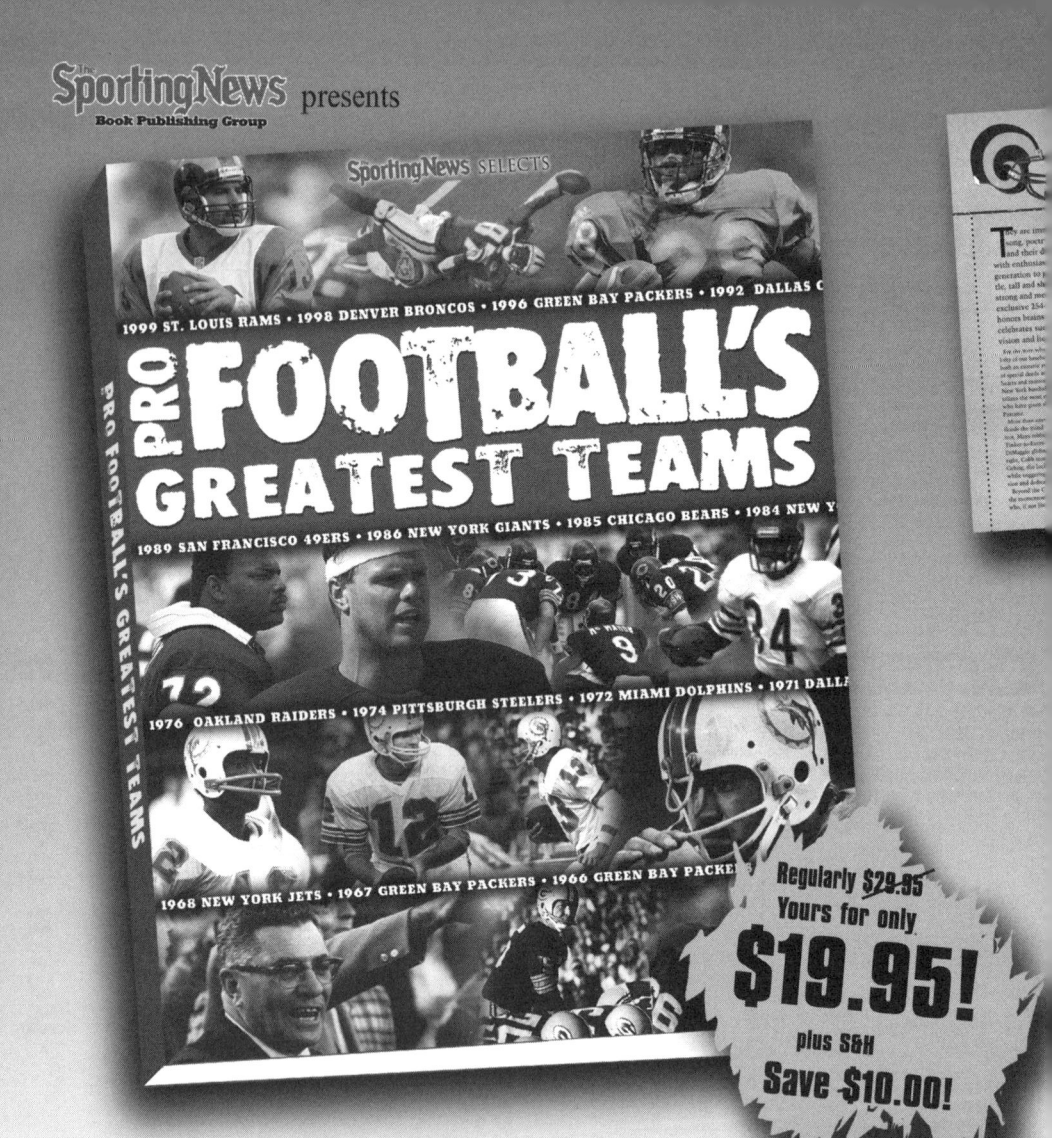

Pro Football's Greatest Teams

What's the greatest NFL team of all-time? Is it the '78 Pittsburgh Steelers? Is it the '62 Green Bay Packers? Is it the San Francisco 49ers' dynasty of the 1980s, or is it the only undefeated and untied team in league history, the '72 Dolphins?

With over 200 historic black and white and full color photographs throughout, Pro Football's Greatest Teams recaptures the greatness of each of those teams, and more, in special chapters that remember those seasons.

Football fans will bask in the memories of Walter Payton and Franco Harris, of Kurt Warner and Bob Griese.

Then we take the next step and dare to name the very best.

More than 200 historic b&w and full-color photos throughout.
" x 11 ¼ • 176 pages.
Hardbound with dust jacket

Available August 2002

Call Toll Free:

1-800-825-8508 Dept. PFR02

Send check or money order to: The Sporting News, Dept. PFR02, P.O. Box 11229, Des Moines IA 50340. Or fax your order to 515-246-7933 Dept. PFR02. Credit card only for phone or fax orders. Shipping and handling: No P.O. Boxes please. Charges: For U.S. orders, $4.95 for the first book, $1.95 for each additional book. For Canadian orders, $6.95 for the first book, $1.95 for each additional book.

Real Sports For the Real Fan

BASKETBALL · BASEBALL · FOOTBALL · HOCKEY · STOCK CAR RACING

- The Teams
- The Stats
- The Strategies
- Trades, Drafts & Deals
- Complete, In-Depth, Up-to-Date Coverage
- Thousands of facts & statistics
- Every Week

SAVE 75%

SPECIAL NEW SUBSCRIBER OFFER

30 issues of The Sporting News for just 99¢ each (75% off the newsstand price).

Canada add $14.50 for subscription postage. Other international rates available on request. The Sporting News is published weekly, with special double issues.

www.sportingnews.com

To Order, Call Toll-Free:
1-800-777-6785
Mention code 5CMA